GW00888674

The Commonwealth Yearbook 2012

Commissioned and researched by Rupert Jones-Parry
with Andrew Robertson

Published for the Commonwealth Secretariat
by Nexus Strategic Partnerships

GW00888674

The Commonwealth Yearbook 2012

Commissioned and researched by Rupert Jones-Parry with Andrew Robertson

First published 2012

ISBN 978-0-9563060-9-8

Nexus

Published by Nexus Strategic Partnerships and available from:

Online:	**www.nexuspartnerships.com**
	www.commonwealth-of-nations.org
Telephone:	+44 (0) 1223 353131
Fax:	+44 (0) 1223 353130
Email:	orders@nexuspartnerships.com
Mail:	Nexus Strategic Partnerships
	St John's Innovation Centre
	Cowley Road
	Cambridge CB4 0WS
	UK

And through good booksellers

For the Commonwealth Secretariat
Marlborough House
Pall Mall
London SW1Y 5HX
UK
www.thecommonwealth.org

Printed at Stephens and George, UK

The flags illustrated are stylised representations and neither the proportions nor the colours are guaranteed true.

Preface

The year 2012 sees not only the Queen (head of the modern Commonwealth) celebrate the 60th anniversary of her accession to the British throne, it is also a time of reflection on the 2011 CHOGM, which took place in Perth, Australia. Heads of Government met there in October to discuss the theme 'Building National Resilience, Building Global Resilience'.

The Communiqué from Perth has been included in this publication, along with a substantial amount of new material focusing on some of the important issues that the Commonwealth is currently addressing. The 'Commonwealth in Action' section of the 2012 Yearbook reviews the work of the Commonwealth and the Commonwealth Secretariat during 2011/12 as well as looking forwards to the future. Additionally, a number of essays from a diverse range of contributors highlight areas of concern to the Commonwealth.

The profiles of member countries and their overseas territories and associated states have been researched and compiled using a broad range of national and international sources. They are also published online and maintained up to date at the websites of the Commonwealth Secretariat and Nexus Strategic Partnerships. The directory of Commonwealth organisations has been compiled and updated from information supplied by the organisations.

This edition also includes comprehensive information on the major Commonwealth awards, highlighting the creative talent of the Commonwealth's youth, and on Commonwealth-related publications.

Data sources

The primary sources of the data in the country profiles, and in the statistical and other tables are international agencies, in particular the World Bank, and UNICEF who kindly provided pre-publication access to The State of the World's Children Report 2012.

Definitions and acronyms

Definitions of principal socio-economic indicators in the country profiles and the statistical tables are given in 'Definitions, acronyms and abbreviations' in the Reference section.

Notations

2010/11 denotes a period of exactly 12 months – usually a fiscal year – that does not coincide with the calendar year.

2010–11 refers to the entire two-year period from the start of 2011 to end 2012.

2010/2011 indicates that the relevant date is either 2010 or 2011.

Commissioned, researched, edited and compiled by Rupert Jones-Parry with Andrew Robertson; country profiles prepared by Richard Green

April 2012

Contents

Editor's Preface 3
Map of the Commonwealth 8

An Essay by Kamalesh Sharma, Commonwealth Secretary-General

Cherishing and celebrating culture 12

Commonwealth Day

Commonwealth Day 16
National Days in 2012 17

Commonwealth Heads of Government Meeting (CHOGM)

Biennial summits 22
Declaration of Commonwealth Principles 23
Harare Declaration 24
Millbrook Programme 26
Perth Declaration on Food Security Principles 27
Summit Statements 28
The Perth Communiqué 31
Agreement by Heads of Government regarding the
EPG Proposals 37
Commonwealth leaders agree to strengthen
Ministerial Action Group (CMAG) 45

Ministerial Meetings in 2011

Health ministers meeting 48
Law ministers meeting 49
Finance ministers meeting 55

What is the Commonwealth?

Introducing the Commonwealth 58
History of the Commonwealth 60
The Commonwealth and its members 64
Member Countries' Heads of State and Government 67
Commonwealth Members 68

Official Commonwealth Organisations

Commonwealth Secretariat 70
Commonwealth Secretariat organisational structure 71
Strategic plan 2008/09 to 2011/12 71
Commonwealth Secretariat websites 73
Senior Commonwealth staff 74
Commonwealth Foundation 75
Commonwealth of Learning 81

Her Majesty Queen Elizabeth II: 60 Years as Head of the Commonwealth

The Queen and the Commonwealth 89
Jubilee Time Capsule: a people's history 94

Commonwealth in Action

Democracy, peace-building and consensus:
the work of the Political Affairs Division 96

Upholding the Rule of Law:
the work of the Legal and Constitutional Affairs Division 101

The work of the Human Rights Unit: participation,
accountability, non-discrimination, empowerment, legality 108

Public Sector Development:
reducing poverty and deepening democracy 116

Economic Development (1): supporting inclusive
and sustainable economic growth in member states 126

Economic Development (2):
resilience building in the face of environmental challenges 133

Managing social transformation:
the Secretariat's Education, Gender and Health teams 140

Empowering young people: the Youth Affairs Division;
Commonwealth Youth Programme (CYP) 151

Sport for Development and Peace 161

After Perth: the way forward?

Delivering the promise of a stronger Commonwealth **168**
　by Julia Gillard, Prime Minister of Australia
　and Commonwealth Chair-in-Office

Perth: a turning point for the Commonwealth? **170**
　by Derek Ingram

Queen and Commonwealth: the Headship at 60 .... **172**
　by Professor Philip Murphy

Picking up the Commonwealth and using it............................ **174**
　by Daisy Cooper

Reform in the Commonwealth **177**
　by Stephen Cutts, Commonwealth Assistant
　Secretary-General

The Commonwealth of Nations: private club or
global force for good?... **179**
　by Senator Hugh D Segal CM

People, power and the new global politics **181**
　by Dr Dhananjayan Sriskandarajah

Engagement with the Commonwealth:
a report on Zimbabwe... **183**
　by Richard Bourne

Commonwealth Awards

RCS Young Commonwealth Competitions **188**
Commonwealth Essay Competition.. **189**
Commonwealth Vision Awards **193**
Commonwealth Photographic Awards **194**
Commonwealth Broadcasting Awards...................................... **196**

Commonwealth Member Countries

Antigua and Barbuda **198**
Australia **202**
Australia: External Territories... **207**
The Bahamas **213**
Bangladesh **217**
Barbados **222**
Belize... **227**
Botswana... **233**
Brunei Darussalam **242**
Cameroon **247**
Canada... **253**
Republic of Cyprus **259**
Dominica **264**
Fiji **268**
The Gambia.. **273**
Ghana **279**
Grenada **296**
Guyana... **300**
India **306**
Jamaica.. **313**
Kenya **321**
Kiribati... **332**
Lesotho.. **336**
Malawi **341**
Malaysia **346**
Maldives **352**
Malta.. **357**
Mauritius **363**
Mozambique **369**
Namibia.. **377**
Nauru **388**
New Zealand **392**
New Zealand: Associated Countries and External Territories **397**
Nigeria.. **403**
Pakistan.. **422**
Papua New Guinea... **429**
Rwanda **437**
St Kitts and Nevis... **445**
St Lucia.. **449**
St Vincent and the Grenadines **453**
Samoa **457**
Seychelles **461**
Sierra Leone... **466**
Singapore **472**
Solomon Islands... **477**
South Africa **485**
Sri Lanka.. **502**
Swaziland **509**
Tonga **514**

Trinidad and Tobago 519
Tuvalu 530
Uganda.. 535
United Kingdom 540
United Kingdom: Overseas Territories 547
United Republic of Tanzania 569
Vanuatu 575
Zambia 581

Reference

Directory of Commonwealth Organisations 596
Membership of international and regional organisations 610
Commonwealth Declarations and Statements 612
Commonwealth Secretariat publications.................................. 624
Commonwealth bibliography 630
Commonwealth Games athletics records................................. 632
Literary prize-winners... 633
Definitions, acronyms and abbreviations.................................. 636

Facts and figures

Key indicators on the Millennium Development
Goals (MDGs) 640

Geography and population... 641
    area and population 642
    young and ageing population 643
    urbanisation and density... 644

Economy.. 645
    national income.. 646
    growth and inflation... 647
    public spending and public debt.. 648
    trade and foreign investment.. 649

Education 650
    overall enrolment and government spending 651
    enrolment 652
    teachers 653

Health... 654
    life and infant mortality 655
    HIV/AIDS 656
    public expenditure 657
    access to qualified health personnel 658

Environment 659
    energy use 660
    CO_2 emissions.. 661
    deforestation 662

Information and communication technology 663
    telephones... 664
    mobile phones 665
    PCs and internet... 666

Small states... 667
    population 668
    economy.. 669
    information and communication technology 670

Acknowledgements 671

Project partners... 672

An Audi. A safe bet.

The new Audi A8L Security.

As the brand's high-tech flagship, the Audi A8L W12 is an armoured car that complies with the highest protection class, VR7/VR9 (in line with BRV 2009). The new Audi A8L Security* combines certified protection and sheer elegance in a single vehicle concept that'll leave more than just your security experts bowled over. A tank made from high-quality steel, reinforced glass and aramid fibres covering the entire passenger cell ensures superb security that has even received the German Proof House's seal of approval. Innovative features such as the patented emergency exit system or the Night Vision assistant also serve to step up your security. Exceptional comfort at the highest level – combined with outstanding driving quality thanks to quattro four-wheel drive, adaptive air suspension and optional electrically adjustable rear seat with fold-out leg rest – definitely makes every journey a safe and exciting experience. So you can rest assured that you have the right companion – at every opportunity. For more detailed information on armoured cars, please send an email to: **Audi-Security@audi.de; www.audi.de/a8lsecurity**

* Fuel consumption in l/100 km: urban 19.9; extra urban 9.8; combined 13.5; CO_2 emissions in g/km: combined 464–228.

Audi
Vorsprung durch Technik

Map of the Commonwealth

1	Antigua and Barbuda	11	Republic of Cyprus	18	India
2	Australia	12	Dominica	19	Jamaica
3	The Bahamas	13	Fiji	20	Kenya
4	Bangladesh		(fully suspended from	21	Kiribati
5	Barbados		the Commonwealth	22	Lesotho
6	Belize		in September 2009)	23	Malawi
7	Botswana	14	The Gambia	24	Malaysia
8	Brunei Darussalam	15	Ghana	25	Maldives
9	Cameroon	16	Grenada	26	Malta
10	Canada	17	Guyana	27	Mauritius

Map source: Commonwealth Secretariat/Maps-in-Minutes™

The designations and the presentation of material on this map, based on UN practice, do not imply the expression of any opinion whatsoever on the part of the Commonwealth Secretariat or the publishers concerning the legal status of any country, territory or area, or of its authorities, or concerning the delimitation of its frontiers or boundaries.

28 Mozambique
29 Namibia
30 Nauru
31 New Zealand
32 Nigeria
33 Pakistan
34 Papua New Guinea
35 Rwanda
36 St Kitts and Nevis
37 St Lucia

38 St Vincent and the Grenadines
39 Samoa
40 Seychelles
41 Sierra Leone
42 Singapore
43 Solomon Islands
44 South Africa
45 Sri Lanka
46 Swaziland

47 Tonga
48 Trinidad and Tobago
49 Tuvalu
50 Uganda
51 United Kingdom
52 United Republic of Tanzania
53 Vanuatu
54 Zambia

MARLIN MARITIME LTD

ABOUT US

Marlin Maritime Limited is a 100% indigenous marine logistics Company with its head office in Port Harcourt, Rivers State Nigeria. The Company was incorporated in August, 2004 but commenced its operations in January, 2006. Marlin has liaison offices both in Lagos and Abuja, Nigeria with over seventy workers.

The Company has two operational jetties, with a warehouse, at Abuloma in Port Harcourt where it leases marine equipment and vessels to multinational and private companies.

Among other services Marlin renders, are goods clearing, haulage of products (mainly petroleum products), import and export, trucking and Floating Production Storage and Off-loading(FPSO).

Marlin's client list includes **Addax Petroleum, Idorama, Daewoo Nigeria Limited, Vandrezzer Energy Services Limited, Mega Star Construction Limited** and **Oil Field Facilitators**.

Our customers' interest is of utmost importance to us and with the aid of our highly skilled and qualified staff, we supply and maintain quality services.

Marlin has grown immensely in the past years and has routinely surpassed expectations.

- Customs licensed agents
- Freight forwarders
- Ship chandlers
- Shipping agents
- Marine Equipment and vessels leasing
- Warehousing
- Rigmove

CONTACT

Port Harcourt Office
12 Worgu Street
Dline
Port Harcourt
Tel: +234 84 46 3545

Abuja Address
No. 5 Agatu Street, next to Petrus Hotel, off Gimbiya Street
Area 11, Garki
Abuja
Tel: +234 80 33 10 2729 • 80 25 29 4999

E-mail: marlin_maritime@yahoo.com
www.marlinmaritime.com

Cherishing and celebrating culture

Commonwealth Secretary-General Kamalesh Sharma

'The unique gift of being able to draw together a group of nations and people so diverse, and yet with a shared sense of belonging and vision, along with a dedication to universal global welfare, is our greatest strength.'

This Commonwealth Yearbook for 2012 must rightly begin by acknowledging with the deepest appreciation and gratitude the leadership, inspiration and enduring service of HM Queen Elizabeth II, Head of the Commonwealth, who celebrates her Diamond Jubilee this year.

Throughout the past 60 years, the Queen has personified and exemplified all that is positive, admirable, and important to the Commonwealth. Her Majesty has been selfless in her consideration and concern for others; active in working to bring together and reinforce the Commonwealth's rich diversity, potential, values and principles; and committed to it in an exemplary way.

The Queen's role has been to symbolise the free association of all those members that join the Commonwealth. Her Majesty has done that and more: by her actions and words the Queen has been the keystone in an ever-expanding Commonwealth arch which had eight members when she assumed the role of Head in 1952 and which today has 54 members spanning the globe and representing one-third of all humanity.

Connecting Cultures

This year our Commonwealth theme is 'Connecting Cultures'. Our aim is to celebrate and cherish the cultures of others that are brought together in a Commonwealth tapestry of diversity, and also to explore how we can use culture to build bridges of understanding, mutual respect and opportunity between us.

Culture gives us an insight into the range of characteristics that make up each individual Commonwealth citizen. We seek to avoid looking at people simplistically or only in terms of their faith, or gender, or through some other single lens. Each of us is far more complex than that. We recognise that all individuals can be seen through a multitude of lenses at the same time: nationality, faith, gender, family status, musical preferences, sporting passion and so on. Our challenge is to find the common points in all this complexity and to build on those first, rather than on the differences.

This Yearbook gives us a snapshot of the scope and practical engagement of our global family. Together we share values, pursue goals and strive for objectives that we have set for ourselves through our shared commitment to the good of one another – and that of future generations.

Kamalesh Sharma, the Commonwealth Secretary-General

Our values include a commitment to the rule of law, human rights, democracy, good governance, development and growth, gender equality, freedom of expression and a vibrant civil society. Our principles embrace inclusiveness, common action, accountability and transparency.

At the last two Commonwealth Heads of Government Meetings, in 2009 and 2011, decisions were taken that raise the standards expected of our members. The 2009 Affirmation of Commonwealth Values and Principles lifted the bar for our member governments by setting out with renewed clarity the commitments by which, of their own free will, leaders have agreed to abide. Then the 2011 CHOGM in Perth, Australia, gave impetus and a sense of urgency to reform and renewal. Now, 2012 will be the year when the expectations of a higher level of commitment to our values and a more dynamic and contemporary Commonwealth are demonstrated – when word becomes deed.

Evolution and reform

As the Commonwealth continues to evolve and reform itself, it works hard to ensure that the voices of our citizens at all levels are taken fully into account. Events around the world during the past year have reminded us of the aspirations and impatience of youth in particular for participation in the processes that shape the societies in which they live and the world in which they will earn their livelihood and pursue their ambitions.

One of the most striking impressions of today's Commonwealth is the high proportion of the population in Commonwealth countries that are in their 20s or below: the future *does* belong to the young. It is their good that our myriad Commonwealth organisations and bodies seek to serve.

Youth empowerment, through encouraging opportunities for youth leadership, engagement and entrepreneurship, is a high priority for the Commonwealth. Where a culture is created that encourages investment in youth enterprise, jobs are generated and economic benefits multiply for the wider community. The very adult financial institutions, and industry and trade bodies, need to become partners in achieving this great goal.

The overarching goal is to lay a strong foundation on which national and global resilience can be built. There can be no better way of doing this than by endowing our youth with the spirit of optimism, skills, self-belief and the spur of personal responsibility.

Our approach is also to draw on a multiplicity of networks and resources, always seeking to make the best use of any means available to advance towards a particular goal. We may rely on ministers, or officials, or any of our numerous Commonwealth professional associations, or civil society at large, or on any combination of these. The new Commonwealth Connects portal (www.commonwealthconnects.org) is providing a platform for modern networking, resource sharing and exchanging best practice.

Yearbooks inevitably focus on the period of 365 days in hand. The Commonwealth, however, has always collectively sought to be forward-looking over a longer timeframe, fitting itself to the changing context of the contemporary world and addressing emerging challenges. Our dynamism comes from striving together with shared ambition for the future.

The global wisdom function of the Commonwealth is needed more than ever in these times of widespread economic stress and uncertainty. As this Yearbook shows, the unique gift of being able to draw together a group of nations and people so diverse, and yet with a shared sense of belonging and vision, along with a dedication to universal global welfare, is our greatest strength.

February 2012

ZAMBIA CONGRESS OF TRADE UNIONS

Representing the Zambia labour movement

The Zambia Congress of Trade Unions (ZCTU) is the largest and oldest labour federation in Zambia, having been established in 1965, a year after Zambia's independence. It represents around 30 affiliate national unions from most of the sectors of the national economy, and has a total membership close to 350 000.

Mission

ZCTU is a democratic membership-based workers representative organisation committed to the promotion and protection of the interests and rights of workers in Zambia. It strives to promote harmonious workplace co-operation and understanding which enhances trust and confidence among the social partners, especially employers, government and other stakeholders.

Vision

ZCTU's vision as a labour federation is to organise and unite all workers in Zambia, both in formal and informal sectors, into a unified, strong and self-sustaining labour movement. It will then be used as a springboard for attaining sustainable socio-economic development, social justice and equity, and good governance in its widest meaning.

The movement regards itself as an indispensable partner in the socio-economic development and governance of Zambia with a co-mission to:

- Contribute to the transformation of Zambia into a proud nation free from poverty, inequality and injustice, in line with the Decent Work Agenda of the International Labour Organisation (ILO).

- Ensure that socio-economic polarisation is not allowed, meaning that pockets of grotesque wealth and affluence are not allowed to exist in the midst of obscene levels of poverty and human misery. Also to fight for the establishment of a poverty datum line which shall be used as an objective basis for determining decent wages for all workers, especially in setting up the minimum wage.

- Ensure that employers and the government respect workers rights as enshrined in ILO Conventions and Recommendations.

Services provided

Education and training, policy analysis, awareness and development, research, representation and negotiations at national, regional, continental and international level, information resource centre and technical and financial assistance to affiliates.

Sources of funding

- Members' subscriptions
- Project, programme and activity support from co-operating partners
- Interest and rentals: estimated annual income: ZK4,900,000,000

Contact: Roy Mwaba, Secretary-General, Maria Kabwe, Director, PO Box 20652, Solidarity House, Oxford Road, Ndola Tel: +260 977 148 640 • +260 955 833 638 • Email: zctu@microlink.zm

Commonwealth Day

The second Monday of March is Commonwealth Day – 12 March in 2012. Commonwealth Day is a day to remember, celebrate and learn about the Commonwealth.

On Commonwealth Day, the Head of the Commonwealth, Queen Elizabeth II, delivers her Commonwealth Day message and leads a multifaith observance at Westminster Abbey in London. This is attended by representatives of Commonwealth countries and children offer the flags of member nations for blessing. Flags also fly in Parliament Square and at Marlborough House in London, where the Commonwealth Secretariat is housed.

The Queen's message is broadcast throughout the Commonwealth, and in many countries augmented by a message from the president or prime minister, or another senior minister. The Commonwealth Secretary-General also issues a statement, which is read on radio or published in many countries.

The multifaith observance held at Westminster Abbey, too, is replicated in the cathedrals, temples, mosques and churches of other member countries. As with the London ceremony, these include readings from the sacred texts of the Commonwealth's major religions of Buddhism, Christianity, Hinduism, Islam, Judaism and others.

Commonwealth Day each year focuses on a different theme. The theme for 2011 was 'Women as Agents of Change', reflecting the theme of the Queen's message.

For 2012, the Commonwealth theme is 'Connecting Cultures'. The association will celebrate the Commonwealth's diversity through this theme, and the Commonwealth Day Observance itself was a vibrant mix of world music, dance and personal testimonies, as the event explored the golden threads that tie together people from every continent, faith and ethnicity. The website www.commonwealththeme.org includes information on the 2012 theme, news, events, projects and competitions.

Young people are central to Commonwealth Day, and the second Monday in March was selected by Commonwealth leaders because it was a day when most schools would be in session. The many activities schools have initiated include mini-Commonwealth Games, simulated Heads of Government Meetings (where students play the roles of different leaders), project studies of the geography, ecology, products or societies of other Commonwealth countries, and celebrations of the cultural and artistic diversity of the Commonwealth through exhibitions, readings, dance and drama. Quizzes to test student knowledge of Commonwealth affairs are popular, as are collections of stamps and product labels.

Commonwealth Day message

The Commonwealth Day message is addressed to the people of the Commonwealth, not to governments, and each year the Queen takes as her theme an issue of importance to the Commonwealth on which she thinks the people can have an impact.

Over the years, she has dealt with the sense of the Commonwealth as a family, human rights, the position of young people and of women, diversity, and working together for the eradication of poverty.

Messages have thus covered a very wide range of important subjects over the years and the themes of recent messages have been as follows:

1994 The Commonwealth Games

1995 Tolerance

1996 Working in Partnership

1997 Communications

1998 Sport

1999 Music

2000 The Communications Challenge

2001 A New Generation

2002 Celebrating Diversity

2003 Partners in Development

2004 Building a Commonwealth of Freedom

2005 Education – Creating Opportunity, Realising Potential

2006 Health and Vitality

2007 Respecting Difference, Promoting Understanding

2008 The Environment – Our Future

2009 *thecommonwealth@60* – serving a new generation

2010 Science, Technology and Society

2011 Women as Agents of Change

2012 Connecting Cultures

UK Prime Minister David Cameron (left) with Kamla Persad-Bissessar, Prime Minister of Trinidad and Tobago, HM The Queen and Secretary-General Kamalesh Sharma at the Commonwealth Day reception at Marlborough House, 14 March 2011 (photographer and copyright: Richard Lewis / © Commonwealth Secretariat)

National Days in 2012

January
26 Australia
26 India
31 Nauru

February
 4 Sri Lanka
 6 New Zealand
 7 Grenada
18 The Gambia
22 St Lucia
23 Brunei Darussalam
23 Guyana

March
 6 Ghana
12 Mauritius
21 Namibia
23 Pakistan
26 Bangladesh

April
27 Sierra Leone
27 South Africa

May
20 Cameroon

June
 1 Samoa
16 United Kingdom (The
    Queen's official birthday*)
18 Seychelles
25 Mozambique

July
 1 Canada
 1 Rwanda
 6 Malawi
 7 Solomon Islands
10 The Bahamas
12 Kiribati
26 Maldives
30 Vanuatu

August
 6 Jamaica
 9 Singapore
31 Malaysia
31 Trinidad and Tobago

September
 6 Swaziland
16 Papua New Guinea
19 St Kitts and Nevis
21 Belize
21 Malta
30 Botswana

October
 1 Cyprus
 1 Nigeria
 1 Tuvalu
 4 Lesotho
 9 Uganda
10 Fiji
24 Zambia
27 St Vincent and the
    Grenadines

November
 1 Antigua and Barbuda
 3 Dominica
 4 Tonga
30 Barbados

December
 9 United Republic of
    Tanzania
12 Kenya

*The first, second or third
Saturday in June*

African Center *for* Economic Transformation

'In Liberia, ACET is making an invaluable contribution in assisting us to strengthen the policy and institutional foundations of our recovery and reform agenda. It is becoming an institution that gives meaning to African ownership of African destiny.'

Ellen Johnson Sirleaf | President of the Republic of Liberia

Going *beyond* growth

Our work is grounded in research and analysis through the lens of economic transformation. And we work to make transformation happen by advocating policies, facilitating the exchange of knowledge and supporting implementation.

What we research

Country case studies
Our country case studies are in-depth analyses of the environment and prospects for transformation in selected countries. For 2012, we examine Botswana, Burkina Faso, Cameroon, Ghana, Ethiopia, Kenya, Mauritius, Mozambique, Nigeria, Rwanda, South Africa, Tanzania, Uganda and Zambia.

Transformation drivers
We delve into what we have identified to be the key drivers of transformation: state capability, business environment, state-business collaboration, infrastructure, employment, education and skills development, foreign direct investment, and export promotion strategies.

Industry studies
Industry studies explore the prospects for introducing new exports and examine opportunities for increasing competitiveness in existing exports or import substitutes.

Special studies
When policy issues emerge that we consider to have a high potential for impact on transformation, we undertake special studies to lend our insights to the public discussion and choices for policy makers. We have conducted such studies on agriculture, economic integration of ECOWAS and China's role in Africa.

The African Center for Economic Transformation (ACET) is an economic policy institute supporting the long-term growth *with* transformation of African economies. Our vision is that by 2025 all African countries will drive their own growth and transformation agendas, led by the private sector and supported by capable states with strong institutions and good policies. As a think-and-do tank, we apply knowledge by directly engaging citizens and decision makers. With a core staff of more than 20 professionals in Accra, we bring an authentic African perspective, augmented by our vast network of leading thinkers throughout the world.

African Transformation Report
The bulk of our research leads to our flagship publication, the *African Transformation Report*, with the inaugural edition to be published in 2012. The Report captures the progress of African countries toward economic transformation, using our new African Transformation Index (ATI). With the ATI, we aim to provide a common quantitative tool for comparing countries on economic transformation.

How we engage

Engaging countries
Through the process of developing the African Transformation Report, ACET is building a unique competence to analyse countries through the lens of transformation. Upon request we put our insights into action by supporting countries develop and implement their transformation strategies, especially in making institutional reforms, identifying their key drivers and leveraging their mineral resources.

Exchanging knowledge
We advance South-South learning by fostering peer networks and brokering the exchange of knowledge between African governments, businesses and academics and their counterparts in countries that have significantly transformed their economies, such as Korea, Malaysia, Singapore, Brazil and India. We also facilitate the sharing of experiences among African countries.

Involving the private sector
Our research generates data and insights into economic sub-sectors with high potential for African countries and we work with business leaders and policy makers to turn those opportunities into reality.

Learn more at www.acetforafrica.org

Queen's Commonwealth Day Message for 2011

Last week, on the 8th of March, we marked the hundredth anniversary of the first International Women's Day. The idea of having a women's day was first proposed against the backdrop of the rapid industrialisation of the early twentieth century. From small beginnings, this idea has grown to become a widely recognised way of celebrating women around the world. While some people use this day to acknowledge the love, admiration and respect for women, others use it to remember the great social and political strides made both by and for women in the last hundred years. There is no right or wrong approach.

In the Commonwealth, every year, 26 million girls are born; and this equates to one new baby girl arriving almost every second of every day. In the time it takes to hold the Commonwealth Observance Service at Westminster Abbey, nearly four thousand girls will have been born in Commonwealth lands. And every one of these births marks the start of a new life, a journey which begins with the hopes of parents, families and communities, and which is continued through the aspirations of those girls themselves.

This year, the Commonwealth celebrates the important role that women already play in every walk of life and in every Commonwealth country – from the richest to the poorest areas, across continents and oceans, from villages to places of international debate, in every culture and faith – recognising that women are 'agents of change' in so many ways: as mothers and sisters, teachers and doctors, artists and craftspeople, smallholders and entrepreneurs, and as leaders of our societies, unleashing the potential of those around them.

And also this year, the Commonwealth reflects on what more could be achieved if women were able to play an even larger role. For example, I am encouraged that last year the Commonwealth launched a global effort to train and support half a million more midwives worldwide.

In all this work the commendable goal is to create a greater opportunity for women as children and adults to pursue their hopes and dreams, to attain their goals, and to make best use of their talents and knowledge.

This year, and on Commonwealth Day especially, as governments continue to search for new ways to tackle these important challenges, let us all give a thought to the practical ways in which we, as individuals or as groups, can provide support to girls and women – so that everyone can have a chance of a fuller and more rewarding life, wherever they happen to be born.

Queen's Commonwealth Day Message for 2012

One of the great benefits of today's technology-based world is the range of opportunities it offers to understand and appreciate how others live: we can see, hear and enter into the experience of people in communities and circumstances far removed from our own.

A remarkable insight we gain from such windows on the world is that, however different outward appearances may be, we share a great deal in common.

Our circumstances and surroundings may vary enormously, for example in the food we eat and the clothes we wear, but we share one humanity, and this draws us all together. The joys of celebration and sympathy of sadness may be expressed differently but they are felt in the same way the world over.

How we express our identities reveals both a rich diversity and many common threads. Through the creative genius of artists – whether they be writers, actors, film-makers, dancers or musicians – we can see both the range of our cultures and the elements of our shared humanity.

'Connecting Cultures', our Commonwealth theme this year, encourages us to consider the special opportunities we have, as members of this unique gathering of nations, to celebrate an extraordinary cultural tapestry that reflects our many individual and collective identities. The Commonwealth treasures and respects this wealth of diversity.

Connecting cultures is more, however, than observing others and the ways in which they express themselves. This year, our Commonwealth focus seeks to explore how we can share and strengthen the bond of Commonwealth citizenship we already enjoy by using our cultural connections to help bring us even closer together, as family and friends across the globe.

To support this theme, a special song has been composed for the Commonwealth, 'Stronger as One'. There are any number of ways in which that single piece of music alone can be played or sung anywhere in the Commonwealth. And by sharing the same music with our own personal interpretations and contributions, the wonderful human attribute of imagination is nourished, and we gain insights of understanding and appreciation of others.

The Commonwealth offers a pathway for this greater understanding and the opportunity to expand upon our shared experiences in a wider world. A world in which paths to mutual respect and common cause may also be explored and which can draw us together, stronger and better than before.

Biennial summits

The Commonwealth Heads of Government Meetings, held every two years since 1971, are the association's ultimate policy-and decision-making forum. The next meeting is scheduled to take place in Sri Lanka in 2013. The last meeting was held in Perth, Australia, in October 2011.

The Commonwealth summits have three broad objectives. First, they allow Commonwealth leaders to review international political and economic developments, to decide, where appropriate, what action the association will take, and then to issue a communiqué stating the Commonwealth position.

Second, leaders examine avenues for Commonwealth co-operation for development, considering both the work done over the previous two years, and agreeing priorities and programmes for the future.

Third, and this is implicit in all the deliberations, leaders see these summits as an opportunity to strengthen the sense of the Commonwealth itself, as an association which has characteristics of friendship, business partnership and stabilising ballast in a world of change and turmoil.

The Commonwealth summits, known as Commonwealth Heads of Government Meetings (or CHOGMs), are held in different Commonwealth countries and organised by the host government and the Commonwealth Secretariat.

Informal discussion

Commonwealth summits have qualities which add up to something unique among gatherings of the leaders of states. There is no other international forum where the leaders of a globally representative range of countries meet regularly for informal dialogue.

The deliberations of the Commonwealth summits are private and, by design, frank and informal. Each summit includes a 'retreat' held away from the conference room and in relaxing surroundings, intended to enhance understanding by allowing leaders to meet as friends. From these retreats have come agreements about Commonwealth action over some difficult issues.

Even in formal session, agreement at Commonwealth summits is reached by consensus, not voting. While the system has on occasion enabled one country or a small group of countries to paralyse action by the vast majority in its favour, it has in the longer term prevented the entrenching of views. Consensus, an older and more instinctive way for groups to reach agreement, has been retained to keep the 'family' together and avoid the development of factions or parties.

These techniques of dialogue developed when the Commonwealth was much smaller. As it has grown to 54 members, and as the extension of multiparty democracy has shortened the average life of national leadership, so that more new faces appear at each summit, the association has worked to retain these traditions.

The Commonwealth now represents, outside of the United Nations, the largest international forum bringing together so many countries from different points on the development spectrum. The association includes a few of the world's richest nations, and many of its poorest; a handful of technologically advanced or rapidly advancing industrial nations, and many of its least developed.

Communiqués and declarations

Though the discussions are private, at the end of each meeting, Commonwealth leaders issue a communiqué recording their decisions. This is launched at a press conference chaired by the Head of Government hosting the meeting, accompanied by the Commonwealth Secretary-General. (The Perth Communiqué from the 2011 CHOGM is reproduced at the end of this section.)

Commonwealth leaders also issue declarations or statements on matters of particular concern (*Declaration of Commonwealth Principles, Harare Declaration, Millbrook Programme* and the declaration emanating from the 2011 CHOGM in Perth are reproduced in this section; others in 'Reference').

History

Today's summits evolved, in stages, out of the Colonial Conferences of the late 19th century and Imperial Conferences of the early 20th century. Here, the British Prime Minister and leaders of the Dominions met to discuss, in particular, constitutional issues, foreign affairs, defence and trade. From 1944 the summits were called Commonwealth Prime Ministers' Meetings, but were still held in the UK, chaired by the UK Prime Minister and organised by the UK Commonwealth Office.

In 1966, at the time of the establishment of the Commonwealth Secretariat, the venue moved to another Commonwealth country for the first time. This was a special meeting in Lagos, Nigeria, called to discuss the constitutional crisis which followed the rebellion of a white minority party in Rhodesia. In 1971, when the first regular summit was held outside the UK – in Singapore – leaders also decided to change the name to Commonwealth Heads of Government Meetings, as there were increasing numbers of republics headed by Presidents rather than Prime Ministers.

Since then, the summits have been held in every region, though not yet in every country. The chronology runs as follows:

Perth, Australia. Host city of the Commonwealth Heads of Government Meeting (CHOGM 2011)

- Singapore 1971
- Ottawa, Canada 1973
- Kingston, Jamaica 1975
- London, UK 1977
- Lusaka, Zambia 1979
- Melbourne, Australia 1981
- New Delhi, India 1983
- Nassau, The Bahamas 1985
- Vancouver, Canada 1987
- Kuala Lumpur, Malaysia 1989
- Harare, Zimbabwe 1991
- Limassol, Cyprus 1993
- Auckland, New Zealand 1995
- Edinburgh, UK 1997
- Durban, South Africa 1999
- Coolum, Australia 2002
- Abuja, Nigeria 2003
- Valletta, Malta 2005
- Kampala, Uganda 2007
- Port of Spain, Trinidad and Tobago 2009
- Perth, Australia 2011

In addition to the special meeting at Lagos in 1966, another special meeting, of a representative group of seven leaders, was held in London in 1986 to discuss further Commonwealth action towards the ending of apartheid in South Africa.

More recently, a mini-summit of eleven Commonwealth leaders was held in London in June 2008, resulting in the Marlborough House Statement on Reform of International Institutions. A Special Heads of Government Meeting was also held in New York in September 2008 to consider and endorse the Marlborough House Statement.

Copies of the communiqués, declarations and statements of recent meetings may be obtained from the Commonwealth Secretariat.

Declaration of Commonwealth Principles

The Commonwealth's structure is based on unwritten traditional procedures, and not on a formal constitution or other code. The Commonwealth does, however, have a series of agreements defining its principles and aims. These are the declarations or statements which have been issued by Commonwealth Heads of Government at various summits. The first – which remains the statement of core beliefs – is the Declaration of Commonwealth Principles, issued at the Commonwealth summit in Singapore in 1971.

The Commonwealth of Nations is a voluntary association of independent sovereign states, each responsible for its own policies, consulting and co-operating in the common interests of their peoples and in the promotion of international understanding and world peace.

Members of the Commonwealth come from territories in the six continents and five oceans, include peoples of different races, languages and religions, and display every stage of economic development from poor developing nations to wealthy industrialised nations. They encompass a rich variety of cultures, traditions and institutions.

Membership of the Commonwealth is compatible with the freedom of member governments to be non-aligned or to belong to any other grouping, association or alliance.

Within this diversity all members of the Commonwealth hold certain principles in common. It is by pursuing these principles that the Commonwealth can continue to influence international society for the benefit of mankind.

We believe that international peace and order are essential to the security and prosperity of mankind; we therefore support the United Nations and seek to strengthen its influence for peace in the world, and its efforts to remove the causes of tension between nations.

We believe in the liberty of the individual, in equal rights for all citizens regardless of race, colour, creed or political belief, and in their inalienable right to participate by means of free and democratic political processes in framing the society in which they live. We therefore strive to promote in each of our countries those representative institutions and guarantees for personal freedom under the law that are our common heritage.

We recognise racial prejudice as a dangerous sickness threatening the healthy development of the human race and racial discrimination as an unmitigated evil of society. Each of us will vigorously combat this evil within our own nation. No country will afford to regimes which practise racial discrimination assistance which in its own judgement directly contributes to the pursuit or consolidation of this evil policy.

We oppose all forms of colonial domination and racial oppression and are committed to the principles of human dignity and equality. We will therefore use all our efforts to foster human equality and dignity everywhere, and to further the principles of self-determination and non-racialism.

We believe that the wide disparities in wealth now existing between different sections of mankind are too great to be tolerated; they also create world tensions; our aim is their progressive removal. We therefore seek to use our efforts to overcome poverty, ignorance and disease, in raising standards of life and achieving a more equitable international society. To this end our aim is to achieve the freest possible flow of international trade on terms fair and equitable to all, taking into account the special requirements of the developing countries, and to encourage the flow of adequate resources, including governmental and private resources, to the developing countries, bearing in mind the importance of doing this in a true spirit of partnership and of establishing for this purpose in the developing countries conditions which are conducive to sustained investment and growth.

We believe that international co-operation is essential to remove the causes of war, promote tolerance, combat injustice, and secure development among the peoples of the world; we are convinced that the Commonwealth is one of the most fruitful associations for these purposes.

In pursuing these principles the members of the Commonwealth believe that they can provide a constructive example of the multinational approach which is vital to peace and progress in the modern world. The association is based on consultation, discussion and co-operation. In rejecting coercion as an instrument of policy they recognise that the security of each member state from external aggression is a matter of concern to all members. It provides many channels for continuing exchanges of knowledge and views on professional, cultural, economic, legal and political issues among member states.

These relationships we intend to foster and extend, for we believe that our multinational association can expand human understanding and understanding among nations, assist in the elimination of discrimination based on differences of race, colour or creed, maintain and strengthen personal liberty, contribute to the enrichment of life for all, and provide a powerful influence for peace among nations.

Singapore, 22 January 1971

Harare Declaration

The Harare Commonwealth Declaration is the association's second general statement of beliefs. It was issued by Commonwealth Heads of Government at their meeting in Zimbabwe in 1991. This declaration, issued 20 years after the Declaration of Commonwealth Principles, reinforces the earlier declaration, updates it where necessary, and defines the core values to take the Commonwealth into the 21st century and beyond. It also outlines a programme of action, placing priority on areas where the Commonwealth is particularly well placed to operate, such as in strengthening democracy, human rights and the rights of women.

The Heads of Government of the countries of the Commonwealth, meeting in Harare, reaffirm their confidence in the Commonwealth as a voluntary association of sovereign independent states, each responsible for its own policies, consulting and co-operating in the interests of their peoples and in the promotion of international understanding and world peace.

Members of the Commonwealth include people of many different races and origins, encompass every state of economic development, and comprise a rich variety of cultures, traditions and institutions.

The special strength of the Commonwealth lies in the combination of the diversity of its members with their shared inheritance in language, culture and the rule of law. The Commonwealth way is to seek consensus through consultation and the sharing of experience. It is uniquely placed to serve as a model and as a catalyst for new forms of friendship and co-operation to all in the spirit of the Charter of the United Nations.

Its members also share a commitment to certain fundamental principles. These were set out in a Declaration of Commonwealth Principles agreed by our predecessors at their Meeting in Singapore in 1971. Those principles have stood the test of time, and we reaffirm our full and continuing commitment to them today. In particular, no less today than 20 years ago:

- we believe that international peace and order, global economic development and the rule of international law are essential to the security and prosperity of mankind

- we believe in the liberty of the individual under the law, in equal rights for all citizens regardless of gender, race, colour, creed or political belief, and in the individual's inalienable right to participate by means of free and democratic political processes in framing the society in which he or she lives

- we recognise racial prejudice and intolerance as a dangerous sickness and a threat to healthy development, and racial discrimination as an unmitigated evil

- we oppose all forms of racial oppression, and we are committed to the principles of human dignity and equality

- we recognise the importance and urgency of economic and social development to satisfy the basic needs and aspirations of the vast majority of the peoples of the world, and seek the progressive removal of the wide disparities in living standards amongst our members.

In Harare, our purpose has been to apply those principles in the contemporary situation as the Commonwealth prepares to face the challenges of the 1990s and beyond.

Internationally, the world is no longer locked in the iron grip of the Cold War. Totalitarianism is giving way to democracy and justice in many parts of the world. Decolonisation is largely complete. Significant changes are at last under way in South Africa. These changes, so desirable and heartening in themselves, present the world and the Commonwealth with new tasks and challenges.

In the last 20 years, several Commonwealth countries have made significant progress in economic and social development. There is increasing recognition that commitment to market principles and openness to international trade and investment can promote economic progress and improve living standards. Many Commonwealth countries are poor and face acute problems, including excessive population growth, crushing poverty, debt burdens and environmental degradation. More than half our member states are particularly vulnerable because of their very small societies.

Only sound and sustainable development can offer these millions the prospect of betterment. Achieving this will require a flow of public and private resources from the developed to the developing world, and domestic and international regimes conducive to the realisation of these goals. Development facilitates the task of tackling a range of problems which affect the whole global community such as environmental degradation, the problems of migration and refugees, the fight against communicable diseases, and drug production and trafficking.

Having reaffirmed the principles to which the Commonwealth is committed, and reviewed the problems and challenges which the world, and the Commonwealth as part of it, face, we pledge the Commonwealth and our countries to work with renewed vigour, concentrating especially in the following areas:

- the protection and promotion of the fundamental political values of the Commonwealth:

  - democracy, democratic processes and institutions which reflect national circumstances, the rule of law and the independence of the judiciary, just and honest government

  - fundamental human rights, including equal rights and opportunities for all citizens regardless of race, colour, creed or political belief

- equality for women, so that they may exercise their full and equal rights

- provision of universal access to education for the population of our countries

- continuing action to bring about the end of apartheid and the establishment of a free, democratic, non-racial and prosperous South Africa

- the promotion of sustainable development and the alleviation of poverty in the countries of the Commonwealth through:

  - a stable international economic framework within which growth can be achieved

  - sound economic management recognising the central role of the market economy

  - effective population policies and programmes

  - sound management of technological change

  - the freest possible flow of multilateral trade on terms fair and equitable to all, taking account of the special requirements of developing countries

  - an adequate flow of resources from the developed to developing countries, and action to alleviate the debt burdens of developing countries most in need

  - the development of human resources, in particular through education, training, health, culture, sport and programmes for strengthening family and community support, paying special attention to the needs of women, youth and children

  - effective and increasing programmes of bilateral and multilateral co-operation aimed at raising living standards

- extending the benefits of development within a framework of respect for human rights

- the protection of the environment through respect for the principles of sustainable development which we enunciated at Langkawi

- action to combat drug trafficking and abuse and communicable diseases

- help for small Commonwealth states in tackling their particular economic and security problems

- support of the United Nations and other international institutions in the world's search for peace, disarmament and effective arms control; and in the promotion of international consensus on major global political, economic and social issues.

To give weight and effectiveness to our commitments we intend to focus and improve Commonwealth co-operation in these areas. This would include strengthening the capacity of the Commonwealth to respond to requests from members for assistance in entrenching the practices of democracy, accountable administration and the rule of law.

We call on all the intergovernmental institutions of the Commonwealth to seize the opportunities presented by these challenges. We pledge ourselves to assist them to develop programmes which harness our shared historical, professional, cultural and linguistic heritage and which complement the work of other international and regional organisations.

We invite the Commonwealth Parliamentary Association and non-governmental Commonwealth organisations to play their full part in promoting these objectives, in a spirit of co-operation and mutual support.

In reaffirming the principles of the Commonwealth and in committing ourselves to pursue them in policy and action in response to the challenges of the 1990s, in areas where we believe that the Commonwealth has a distinctive contribution to offer, we the Heads of Government express our determination to renew and enhance the value and importance of the Commonwealth as an institution which can and should strengthen and enrich the lives not only of its own members and their peoples but also of the wider community of peoples of which they are a part.

Harare, Zimbabwe, 20 October 1991

Millbrook Programme

The Millbrook Commonwealth Action Programme on the Harare Declaration provides an operating structure for the two central declarations: the Declaration of Commonwealth Principles and the Harare Commonwealth Declaration. It also defines the Commonwealth's role in global and national affairs. The Millbrook Programme covers democratic and humane government, co-operation for development, and Commonwealth partnership on agreed positions in international forums. One of its measures was to set up the Commonwealth Ministerial Action Group to address serious and persistent violations of the Harare principles, particularly the overthrow of a democratically elected government.

At Harare in 1991, we pledged to work for the protection and promotion of the fundamental political values of the association, namely democracy, democratic processes and institutions which reflect national circumstances, fundamental human rights, the rule of law and the independence of the judiciary, and just and honest government. We agreed at the same time to work for the promotion of socio-economic development, recognising its high priority for most Commonwealth countries. During our Retreat at Millbrook, we decided to adopt a Commonwealth Action Programme to fulfil more effectively the commitments contained in the Harare Commonwealth Declaration. This Programme is in three parts:

- Advancing Commonwealth Fundamental Political Values

- Promoting Sustainable Development

- Facilitating Consensus-building.

Advancing Commonwealth Fundamental Political Values

1 Measures in Support of Processes and Institutions for the Practice of the Harare Principles

The Secretariat should enhance its capacity to provide advice, training and other forms of technical assistance to governments in promoting the Commonwealth's fundamental political values, including:

- assistance in creating and building the capacity of requisite institutions

- assistance in constitutional and legal matters, including with selecting models and initiating programmes of democratisation

- assistance in the electoral field, including the establishment or strengthening of independent electoral machinery, civic and voter education, the preparation of Codes of Conduct, and assistance with voter registration

- observation of elections, including by-elections or local elections where appropriate, at the request of the member governments concerned

- strengthening the rule of law and promoting the independence of the judiciary through the promotion of exchanges among, and training of, the judiciary

- support for good government, particularly in the area of public service reform, and

- other activities, in collaboration with the Commonwealth Parliamentary Association and other bodies, to strengthen the democratic culture and effective parliamentary practices.

2 Measures in Response to Violations of the Harare Principles

Where a member country is perceived to be clearly in violation of the Harare Commonwealth Declaration, and particularly in the event of an unconstitutional overthrow of a democratically elected government, appropriate steps should be taken to express the collective concern of Commonwealth countries and to encourage the restoration of democracy within a reasonable time-frame. These include:

- immediate public expression by the Secretary-General of the Commonwealth's collective disapproval of any such infringement of the Harare principles

- early contact by the Secretary-General with the *de facto* government, followed by continued good offices and appropriate technical assistance to facilitate an early restoration of democracy

- encouraging bilateral *démarches* by member countries, especially those within the region, both to express disapproval and to support early restoration of democracy

- appointment of an envoy or a group of eminent Commonwealth representatives where, following the Secretary-General's contacts with the authorities concerned, such a mission is deemed beneficial in reinforcing the Commonwealth's good offices role

- stipulation of up to two years as the time-frame for the restoration of democracy where the institutions are not in place to permit the holding of elections within, say, a maximum of six months

- pending restoration of democracy, exclusion of the government concerned from participation at ministerial-level meetings of the Commonwealth, including CHOGMs

- suspension of participation at all Commonwealth meetings and of Commonwealth technical assistance if acceptable progress is not recorded by the government concerned after a period of two years, and

- consideration of appropriate further bilateral and multilateral measures by all member states (e.g. limitation of government-to-government contacts; people-to-people measures; trade restrictions; and, in exceptional cases, suspension from the association), to reinforce the need for change in the event that the government concerned chooses to leave the Commonwealth and/or persists in violating the principles of the Harare Commonwealth Declaration even after two years.

3 Mechanism for Implementation of Measures

We have decided to establish a Commonwealth Ministerial Action Group on the Harare Declaration in order to deal with serious or persistent violations of the principles contained in that declaration. The Group will be convened by the Secretary-General and will comprise the Foreign Ministers of eight countries, supplemented as appropriate by one or two additional ministerial representatives from the region concerned. It will be the Group's task to assess the nature of the infringement and recommend measures for collective Commonwealth action aimed at the speedy restoration of democracy and constitutional rule.

The composition, terms of reference and operation of the Group will be reviewed by us every two years.

Promoting Sustainable Development

We reaffirmed our view that the Commonwealth should continue to be a source of help in promoting development and literacy and in eradicating poverty, particularly as these bear on women and children. With a view to enhancing its capacity in this area, we agreed on the following steps:

- to strengthen the Secretariat's capacity for undertaking developmental work through support for its various Funds and especially by restoring the resources of the CFTC to their 1991/92 level in real terms; and to provide adequate resources to the Commonwealth of Learning and to the Commonwealth Foundation

- to support a greater flow of investment to developing member countries through such schemes as the Commonwealth Private Investment Initiative

- to work for continued progress in assisting countries with unsustainable debt burdens and to promote enhanced multilateral concessional financial flows to developing countries; in particular, to support new and innovative mechanisms for relief on multilateral debt, such as the one proposed by the British Chancellor of the Exchequer at the 1994 Commonwealth Finance Ministers Meeting in Malta, and reiterated subsequently

- to support the Secretariat in facilitating the adoption by more Commonwealth countries of successful self-help schemes, with non-governmental agencies and others acting as catalytic agents, for mobilising the energies of people in alleviating poverty

- to support the efforts of small island developing states to mitigate the effects on their development of environmental change, natural disasters and the changing international trading system, and

- to combat the spread of HIV/AIDS, which threatens large parts of the younger population of many countries, recognising that the effective exploitation of economic opportunities requires a healthy and educated population; and to provide further resources to renew the core funding of the Southern African Network of AIDS Organisations (SANASO), along with increased funding for UNICEF initiatives in Southern Africa.

Facilitating Consensus-building

We were convinced that the Commonwealth, with its global reach and unique experience of consensus-building, was in a position to assist the wider international community in building bridges across traditional international divides of opinion on particular issues. We therefore agreed that there was scope for the association to play a greater role in the search for consensus on global issues, through:

- use of their governments' membership of various regional organisations and attendance at other international gatherings to advance consensual positions agreed within the Commonwealth

- use, where appropriate, of special missions to advance Commonwealth consensual positions and promote wider consensus on issues of major international concern, and

- use of formal and informal Commonwealth consultations in the wings of meetings of international institutions with a view to achieving consensus on major concerns.

Millbrook, Queenstown, New Zealand, 12 November 1995

Perth Declaration on Food Security Principles

At their 2011 summit Heads of Government issued the Perth Declaration on Food Security Principles, listing 12 such principles which they hoped would be implemented by the next CHOGM in 2013. They recognised in particular the humanitarian crisis in the Horn of Africa and to support African agricultural production, they pledged direct action through major investments in agricultural productivity.

Food insecurity is one of the most pressing and difficult global challenges of our time. This is a profound concern for the Commonwealth – half of the world's one billion hungry live in our nations. The global food crises of 2007 and 2008 and the ongoing volatility and uncertainty of world food markets underscore the need for sustained international engagement with the issue. The distressing humanitarian crisis in the Horn of Africa, most particularly in Somalia, and the drought, famine and famine-like situations occurring in other most vulnerable countries in the developing world highlight the difficulties we face.

Population growth will have a major impact on global demand for food. Additional factors, including scarce land and water resources, the diversion of fertile land, the reduction in crop species and use of crops for non-food purposes, urbanisation, distorted markets, and climate change, are intensifying pressures on supply. The world's poor and most vulnerable suffer most from food insecurity.

Commonwealth countries reaffirm the right of everyone to have access to safe, sufficient and nutritious food, consistent with the progressive realisation of the right to adequate food in the context of national food security.

Commonwealth member states affirm the important role that women, youth, farming and fishing communities, civil society, and the private sector play in sustainable development and the need for their effective involvement in driving climate-smart agriculture and the food security agenda.

The Commonwealth is uniquely placed to support global food security efforts through Commonwealth countries' membership in all major global and regional forums that are engaged on this issue. Commonwealth countries therefore commit to use their membership of these forums to advocate the Perth Declaration on Food Security Principles to achieve outcomes that are relevant and meaningful to members. Commonwealth members further commit to use the Perth Declaration principles as a guide to support domestic efforts to build food security.

The Perth Declaration principles reflect our shared approach to addressing the challenge of food insecurity and are focused on meeting the needs of the most vulnerable, particularly women and children.

The Perth Declaration principles on food security call for:

- co-ordinated and timely regional and global emergency relief efforts to deal with immediate crises

- undertaking decisive and timely measures to prevent crises occurring, mitigate their impact when they do and build resilience

- delivering practical measures over the medium-term to make agriculture, including irrigated agriculture, and fisheries more productive and sustainable

- strengthening support to government-led programmes and initiatives based on the spirit of effective partnerships

- development of country-led medium to long-term strategies and programmes to improve food security and ensure alignment of donor support to implementation of country priorities

- scaling up nutritional interventions, including those that target mothers and young children, and incorporating nutrition considerations into broad food security initiatives

- enhancing research and development over the longer term to build a sustainable agricultural sector, including through the promotion and sharing of best agricultural practices, in order to feed and nourish the people of the world

- strengthening fisheries and marine resource management in member states' waters to ensure sustainability of these resources for national and global food security, including through addressing illegal unregulated and unreported fishing

- improving international market access for food producers, including smallholders and women, through trade liberalisation measures such as the elimination of tariff and non-tariff trade barriers and avoidance of restrictions on food exports

- addressing the impediments that are inhibiting economic opportunities for these important producers, including lack of affordable financing, local value-added and adequate infrastructure

- collaboration between international organisations, donor countries, and national governments to address production, storage, waste reduction, elimination of post-harvest losses, transportation and marketing challenges; this collaboration could include more effective ways of meeting infrastructure financing gaps that engage the private sector, and

- improving the institutional framework for global food security efforts, including by supporting reform of the UN Food and Agriculture Organization (FAO).

Commonwealth countries recognise that Africa has the potential not only to achieve food security but to become a significant net food exporter. Leaders commit to supporting efforts and initiatives

such as the Comprehensive Africa Agriculture Development Programme (CAADP), designed to realise the long-term potential of Africa as a food producer and exporter.

To support African agricultural production, Commonwealth countries have committed to direct action through major investments in agricultural productivity.

Commonwealth countries recognise the critical role played by national and international agricultural research in promoting and sharing agricultural technologies for enhanced crop yields, and undertake to deepen their co-operation.

Commonwealth countries also underline their critical role in managing and safeguarding a large proportion of the world's fish stocks.

In advocating the Perth Declaration principles, Commonwealth countries acknowledge the central role played by the United Nations in global food security governance and commit to show leadership in the United Nations by supporting food and nutrition security initiatives.

Committed to using the collective Commonwealth voice to influence global action, Commonwealth members urge the UN Conference on Sustainable Development in Rio de Janeiro in June 2012 to commit to an ambitious programme of action to drive increased investment to boost sustainable global agricultural and fisheries productivity.

The Commonwealth, through its five G20 members, further commits to advocate for strong outcomes on food security at the G20 Cannes Summit, including to increase investment in appropriate agricultural technologies and sustainable productivity, to address market volatility and other market-distorting factors, and for food security, including fisheries, to be accorded a high priority within the forward G20 development agenda.

Recognising the ongoing critical food security needs, the Commonwealth welcomes the substantial contributions made by Canada, the UK and Australia in fulfilment of their L'Aquila Food Security Initiative commitments, and calls on countries that have not yet fulfilled their food security commitments to do so.

Commonwealth countries will continue to prioritise food security and will assess progress towards implementation of these principles on food security at the next Commonwealth Heads of Government Meeting in 2013.

Perth, Australia, 29 October 2011

Summit Statements

The Declaration of Commonwealth Principles, Harare Declaration and Millbrook Programme have provided the basis for Commonwealth action. However, the summit statements of position and action have long been a feature of the Commonwealth association.

In 1944, during the Second World War, Commonwealth Prime Ministers used their summit as the occasion on which to announce commitment to the establishment, after the war, of a 'world organisation' to prevent further conflict. This organisation, the United Nations, has since come into existence, and has always had strong Commonwealth backing. At the Commonwealth summit of

1951, leaders made a pledge to peace, and announced that the achievement of true peace depended on resolving problems of poverty. This was a pioneering statement of commitment to development co-operation and assistance to poor countries. In 1961, Commonwealth prime ministers pledged to work towards total global disarmament. Ten years later, the Declaration of Commonwealth Principles was issued. As can be seen from the statements previously issued, the Declaration of Principles was the codification in six clear points of the ethical standards which were already developing as central to the Commonwealth.

Statements or declarations issued at Heads of Government Meetings from the time of the Singapore declaration are as follows:

Declaration of Commonwealth Principles

Singapore, 1971: The core Commonwealth beliefs, quoted in full above.

Statement on Nuclear Weapon Tests

Ottawa, Canada, 1973: Issued during the intense arms-race phase of the Cold War, this statement affirms the unfailing support of Commonwealth governments for the international Treaty banning nuclear weapon tests in the atmosphere, in outer space and under water. It appeals, furthermore, to the international community for a total ban on nuclear weapon tests in any environment.

Commonwealth Statement on Apartheid in Sport

Gleneagles, Scotland, UK, 1977: This famous statement, which became widely known as the Gleneagles Agreement, or the Commonwealth boycott of apartheid sport, was the first international move in the global campaign to isolate South Africa (then under a white racist government) from world sport. Agreed some six months before a parallel UN boycott, it was powerfully effective, and its success may have led the way to sanctions in cultural and economic areas. All sanctions against South Africa have, of course, been lifted since the end of apartheid.

Lusaka Declaration on Racism and Racial Prejudice

Lusaka, Zambia, 1979: The central Commonwealth statement of its abhorrence of all forms of racism, including in members' own societies, quoted in full in 'Reference'.

Melbourne Declaration

Melbourne, Australia, 1981: This announcement clarifies and extends the Commonwealth commitment to a fair international economic and financial system, and support for struggling poor countries.

Goa Declaration on International Security

Fort Aguada, Goa, India, 1983: Here, Commonwealth leaders denounce the Cold War and the extension of nuclear arsenals, and call for the transferral of resources from weaponry to partnership in development.

New Delhi Statement on Economic Action

New Delhi, India, 1983: This statement outlines a programme of co-operation to strengthen development in poor countries.

Nassau Declaration on World Order

Nassau, The Bahamas, 1985: Here, leaders outline their commitment to international co-operation through the United Nations system.

Commonwealth Accord on Southern Africa

Nassau, The Bahamas, 1985: This provides a detailed programme to increase pressure, through sanctions and other measures, to force an end of apartheid.

Vancouver Declaration on World Trade

Vancouver, Canada, 1987: This adds to the Melbourne Declaration and New Delhi Statement with a strong attack on protectionism in world trade, and calls for strengthening of liberalisation through the GATT system.

Okanagan Statement and Programme of Action on Southern Africa

Okanagan, Canada, 1987: Here, stronger measures than those of the 1985 Accord are announced.

Statement on Fiji

Vancouver, Canada, 1987: This short statement announces the departure of Fiji, which had recently become a republic and so was required to reapply for membership, and whose military government had enacted racist measures unacceptable to the association, from the Commonwealth.

Langkawi Declaration on Environment

Langkawi, Malaysia, 1989: This is the first Commonwealth statement specifically to include environmental protection as a vital factor in development.

Southern Africa: The Way Ahead (The Kuala Lumpur Statement)

Kuala Lumpur, Malaysia, 1989: This brought about further strengthening of the Commonwealth attack on racism in South Africa, while also boosting Commonwealth support for the majority-ruled Southern African countries then subject to military destabilisation by South Africa.

Ottawa Declaration on Women and Structural Adjustment

Harare, Zimbabwe, 1991: This declaration, first prepared and submitted by Ministers responsible for Women's Affairs at their meeting in Ottawa, Canada, in October 1990 and endorsed by Heads of Government meeting in Harare, Zimbabwe, expresses concern at the damage to women and the family by structural adjustment measures affecting peasant agriculture, food prices, health and education, and asks for such measures to be redrawn to avoid damage to the most vulnerable sectors of society.

Harare Commonwealth Declaration

Harare, Zimbabwe, 1991: The Commonwealth's second general statement of beliefs, this declaration, issued 20 years after the Declaration of Commonwealth Principles, reinforces the earlier declaration, updates it where necessary, and defines the core values to take the Commonwealth into the 21st century and beyond. It also outlines a programme of action, placing priority on areas where the Commonwealth is particularly well placed to operate, such as in strengthening democracy, human rights and the rights of women; quoted in full above.

Limassol Statement on the Uruguay Round

Limassol, Cyprus, 1993: This deals with the global trade negotiations under the General Agreement on Tariffs and Trade, and calls for agreements which will genuinely allow the products of poor countries access to world markets and, where necessary, give preference to them.

Millbrook Commonwealth Action Programme on the Harare Declaration

Millbrook, New Zealand, 1995: This provides an operating structure for the two central declarations: the Declaration of Commonwealth Principles and the Harare Commonwealth Declaration. It also defines the Commonwealth's role in global and national affairs. The Millbrook Programme covers democratic and humane government, co-operation for development, and Commonwealth partnership on agreed positions in international forums. One of its measures was to set up the Commonwealth Ministerial Action Group; quoted in full above.

Edinburgh Commonwealth Economic Declaration

Edinburgh, UK, 1997: This recognises that the Commonwealth, with its shared traditions and global reach, is uniquely placed to play a key role in promoting trade and investment, eradicating poverty, and protecting the environment, to the mutual benefit of its members; quoted in full in 'Reference'.

Fancourt Commonwealth Declaration on Globalisation and People-Centred Development

Fancourt, South Africa, 1999: The declaration expresses the concern of Commonwealth leaders at the 1999 summit in South Africa that, while globalisation offers unprecedented opportunities for wealth creation and for the improvement of the human condition, its benefits are not shared equitably; quoted in full in 'Reference'.

Coolum Declaration on the Commonwealth in the 21st Century: Continuity and Renewal

Coolum, Australia, 2002: At the outset of the new century, Commonwealth Heads of Government addressed the role of the association, and renewed their enduring commitment to shared values and principles; quoted in full in 'Reference'.

Aso Rock Commonwealth Declaration on Development and Democracy: Partnership for Peace and Prosperity

Aso Rock, Abuja, Nigeria, 2003: Building on the landmark declarations in Singapore, Harare and Fancourt, Heads of Government committed themselves to strengthen development and democracy, through partnership for peace and prosperity. Heads also issued a separate *Aso Rock Statement on Multilateral Trade*, annexed to this declaration; both quoted in full in 'Reference'.

Valletta Statement on Multilateral Trade

Valletta, Malta, 2005: Commonwealth leaders urged the WTO Ministerial Conference in Hong Kong, 13–18 December 2005, to agree that all forms of export subsidies be eliminated by 2010.

Malta Declaration on Networking the Commonwealth for Development

Valletta, Malta, 2005: This declaration affirms the importance of harnessing new technologies and strengthening networks to bridge the digital divide and accelerate economic development in the Commonwealth; quoted in full in 'Reference'.

Gozo Statement on Vulnerable Small States

Gozo, Malta, 2005: Commonwealth leaders recognised the particular challenges of small states which make up 32 of the members of the association.

Lake Victoria Commonwealth Climate Change Action Plan

Kampala, Uganda, 2007: Building on the 1989 Langkawi Declaration on Environment, this action plan indicates the level of Commonwealth political commitment to the UN process aimed at developing a successor to the Kyoto Protocol.

Munyonyo Statement on Respect and Understanding

Kampala, Uganda, 2007: Heads of Government endorsed the report of the Commonwealth Commission on Respect and Understanding, *Civil Paths to Peace*, and in responding to its recommendations identified priority fields of action.

Kampala Declaration on Transforming Societies to Achieve Political, Economic and Human Development

Kampala, Uganda, 2007: This declaration calls for the inclusiveness of transformation, to involve citizens at every level, and to be as much a democratic transformation as an economic one; quoted in full in 'Reference'.

Port of Spain Climate Change Consensus: The Commonwealth Climate Change Declaration

Port of Spain, Trinidad and Tobago, 2009: Commonwealth leaders in this declaration called for continued implementation of all six elements of the 2007 *Lake Victoria Commonwealth Climate Change Action Plan*, and stressed that a global climate change solution was central to the survival of peoples, the promotion of development and facilitation of a global transition to a low emission development path; quoted in full in 'Reference'.

Trinidad and Tobago Affirmation of Commonwealth Values and Principles

Port of Spain, Trinidad and Tobago, 2009: In the 60th anniversary year of the modern Commonwealth, Heads of Government reiterated their strong and abiding commitment to the association's fundamental values and principles. Heads also agreed that consideration be given to strengthening the role of CMAG; quoted in full in 'Reference'.

The Declaration of Port of Spain: Partnering for a More Equitable and Sustainable Future

Port of Spain, Trinidad and Tobago, 2009: The declaration affirmed the key role of partnerships in forging a more sustainable and equitable future for all people, recognising that to effectively address the unprecedented combination of social, economic and environmental challenges facing the world would require international co-operation, sustained commitment and collective action; quoted in full in 'Reference'.

A Declaration on Young People: 'Investing in Young People'

Port of Spain, Trinidad and Tobago, 2009: In this declaration Heads of Government acknowledge the role and active contributions of young people in promoting development, peace and democracy, and recognise that the future successes of the Commonwealth rest with young people; quoted in full in 'Reference'.

Commonwealth Statement on Action to Combat Non-Communicable Diseases

Port of Spain, Trinidad and Tobago, 2009: Here, concerned that non-communicable diseases account for over half of all deaths worldwide and noting international co-operation is critical in addressing this emerging health crisis, Commonwealth leaders call for a UN summit to be held in 2011 in order to develop strategic responses to these diseases and their repercussions; quoted in full in 'Reference'.

Perth Declaration on Food Security Principles

Perth, Australia, 2011: The declaration reflects the shared approach of Commonwealth Heads of Government to addressing the challenge of food insecurity; quoted in full above.

The Perth Communiqué

Commonwealth Heads of Government met in Perth, Australia, from 28 to 30 October 2011, under the theme 'Building National Resilience, Building Global Resilience'.

Reflecting on the unique nature of the Commonwealth, a voluntary association which brings together 54[1] developing and developed nations from six continents, Heads reaffirmed their commitment to the values and principles of the Commonwealth and agreed to a series of actions to maintain the Commonwealth's relevance, to ensure its effectiveness in responding to contemporary global challenges and to build resilient societies and economies. Given the significant challenges facing the global economy, Heads emphasised the importance of the international community working co-operatively to secure a sustainable global recovery. Heads highlighted the importance of a strong response to these challenges to provide the necessary confidence to global markets.

Heads welcomed the report of the Eminent Persons Group, 'A Commonwealth of the People: Time for Urgent Reform', and thanked members of the Group for their outstanding work. They agreed that the report provided a strong basis to revitalise the Commonwealth and its institutions and ensure its continued relevance to member states and their people – today and in the future.

To this end, Heads agreed to the following.

Reform of the Commonwealth to ensure that it is a more effective institution, responsive to members' needs, and capable of tackling the significant global challenges of the 21st century.

This includes:

* the reform of the Commonwealth Ministerial Action Group (CMAG)

* consideration of the Eminent Persons Group (EPG) recommendations on reform

* strengthening the management and delivery of Commonwealth programmes, including through regular review of their efficiency, effectiveness and results, against measurable indicators

* one member, Fiji, is currently suspended; to this end, focusing delivery of practical assistance to members through greater prioritisation and alignment of programmes to members' priorities on the basis of Commonwealth comparative advantage and, where necessary, retiring programmes that do not meet these criteria, and

* undertaking associated reform of the Commonwealth Secretariat and ensuring the adequacy of resources and their appropriate use to enable it to deliver on its agreed mandates.

To actively promote, uphold, preserve and defend the fundamental values, principles and aspirations of the Commonwealth.

Heads agreed to do this by:

* agreeing to the recommendations of CMAG to strengthen the role of CMAG, in order to enable the Group to deal with the full range of serious or persistent violations of Commonwealth values

* resolving that the composition of CMAG for the next biennium should be as follows: Australia, Bangladesh, Canada, Jamaica, Maldives, Sierra Leone, Tanzania, Trinidad and Tobago, and Vanuatu

* agreeing that there should be a 'Charter of the Commonwealth', as proposed by the Eminent Persons Group, embodying the principles contained in previous declarations, drawn together in a single, consolidated document that is not legally binding

* Heads will agree to a text for the Charter in 2012, following a process of national consultations, consideration by a Task Force of Ministers drawn from all geographical groupings of the Commonwealth, and a full meeting of Foreign Ministers in New York in September

* tasking the Secretary-General and CMAG to further evaluate relevant options relating to the EPG's proposal for a Commissioner for Democracy, the Rule of Law and Human Rights and to report back to Foreign Ministers at their September meeting in New York

* noting that the EPG's recommendations relating to CMAG were consistent with the CMAG reforms adopted by Heads at this meeting

* responding to the remaining EPG recommendations as follows:

    – adopting without reservation 30 recommendations

- adopting, subject to consideration of financial implications, 12 further recommendations

- asking the Task Force of Ministers (mentioned above) to provide more detailed advice on 43 other recommendations to Foreign Ministers at their September meeting in New York, as a basis for further decision by Heads, and

- deeming 11 recommendations inappropriate for adoption

- strengthening the newly established Commonwealth Network of Election Management Bodies as well as election monitoring, and supporting capacity-building for professional election administrators

- urging the interim government of Fiji to restore democracy without further delay, to respect human rights, and to uphold the rule of law, and reaffirming that the Commonwealth should continue to remain engaged with Fiji and support efforts towards that end

- urging members to consider becoming parties to all major international human rights instruments; to implement fully the rights and freedoms set out in the Universal Declaration of Human Rights and the Vienna Declaration and Programme of Action, as well as those human rights treaties to which they are a party; to uphold these rights and freedoms; to share best practice and lessons learned, including from the United Nations Universal Periodic Review process; and to continue to support the work of National Human Rights Institutions, and

- promoting tolerance, respect, understanding and religious freedom which, *inter alia*, are essential to the development of free and democratic societies.

Revitalising the Commonwealth's development priorities to ensure it effectively articulates and meets the development needs of member states today and in the future.

To this end, Heads:

- agreed the Perth Declaration on Food Security Principles

- reflected on the multiple development challenges confronting small states in the global economy as a result of their inherent vulnerabilities, and agreed that this is having an adverse impact on their sustainable development and growth prospects; and in this context:

  - welcomed and endorsed the outcomes of the first Global Biennial Conference of Small States held in 2010

  - endorsed the outcomes of the Commonwealth and Developing Small States meeting, which stressed in relation to Commonwealth and developing small states, Least Developed Countries (LDCs) and Small Island Developing States (SIDS): the importance of taking urgent action on climate change and sustainable development, particularly through the G20, the UN climate change conference in Durban, and Rio+20; the need to work towards legally binding outcomes under the UN Framework Convention on Climate Change (UNFCCC) capable of avoiding dangerous climate change; the need for enhanced action on adaptation and transparent and accessible climate finance to support developing small states; the need for practical outcomes at Rio+20 on the 'blue economy' to ensure the sustainable management of our oceans as the basis for livelihoods, food security and economic

development; and for Commonwealth G20 members to reflect these concerns and perspectives at the upcoming G20 summit

- agreed that vulnerability to climate change is widespread and particularly affects small states; the Commonwealth has an important role to play in advancing the climate change priorities of Commonwealth small and vulnerable states as well as fostering mutual collaboration among Commonwealth countries in order to address such priorities

- agreed to assist small and climate vulnerable states develop their capacity to respond in a timely and effective way to disasters and to build their national disaster response capabilities

- welcomed the establishment of the Commonwealth Office for Small States in Geneva and urged further support for it

- considered the substantive work that the Commonwealth has done on the issue of small states, including on SIDS, and called for this expertise to be shared with other international institutions, such as the UN, which are involved in the implementation of the Mauritius Strategy and the Barbados Programme of Action

- recalled the *Port of Spain Climate Change Consensus* and noted the undisputed threat that climate change poses to the security, prosperity and economic and social development of the people, as well as the impact it has in terms of deepening poverty and affecting the attainment of the Millennium Development Goals (MDGs), and reaffirmed their commitment to work towards a shared vision for long-term co-operative action to achieve the objective of the UNFCCC, addressing mitigation, adaptation, finance, technology development and transfer, and capacity-building in a balanced, integrated and comprehensive manner; in this context:

  - committed to advocate for these actions at the UNFCCC conference in Durban and beyond, for legally binding outcomes

  - committed to work together to build climate resilience and to facilitate the efficient mobilisation of funding for urgent and effective mitigation, adaptation and capacity-building, prioritising the most vulnerable developing countries, including small island developing states; and recognised the importance of markets in maximising global emission reductions at the least possible cost, and the promotion of technology transfer to these countries

  - recognising the existential impact of climate change on coastal and island communities, emphasised the great importance of building national resilience to ameliorate local climate change-induced population displacement, as well as the imperative to reach strong and effective solutions to reduce global emissions and enhance multilateral, regional and bilateral co-operation on adaptation

  - committed to practical action in line with the *Lake Victoria Commonwealth Climate Change Action Plan*, including efforts to facilitate immediate access to climate change finance and technology transfer, especially for mitigation and adaptation

- agreed to focus on practical and ambitious outcomes at the UN Conference on Sustainable Development (Rio+20) in June 2012 to address the challenges facing this and future generations, including with a view to expediting implementation of the outcomes of the Global Conference on Sustainable Development of Small Island Developing States; in this regard:

- committed to advocate urgent action at Rio+20 to assist developing states to build resilience through sustainable development, in particular by taking steps to transition towards green growth trajectories and to strengthen institutional frameworks for achieving this transition; Rio+20 should deliver an outcome which allows progress to be measured in a meaningful way; the value of natural resources should be given due consideration in economic decision-making

- agreed to explore options for sharing best practice on resource management and promote initiatives to provide access to monitoring, research, education and training, and technical and policy expertise

- welcomed the briefing they received on the emerging conclusions of the UN Secretary-General's High-level Panel on Global Sustainability

- recognised the need to preserve the policy space of countries to frame their own national strategies to prioritise according to their national circumstances

- supported and upheld the role and place of local government, in partnership with the private sector, for promoting strategies for localism, sustainable development and economic growth, and supported the implementation of the *Cardiff Consensus for Local Economic Development in the Commonwealth*

- recognised the valuable role clean and renewable energy will play in a sustainable future and the importance of promoting the implementation of green technology

- recognised the importance of energy security through improved efficiency measures and the promotion of clean and affordable energy, including renewable energy

- recognised also the need for sustainable management of oceans for livelihoods, food security and economic development

- emphasised that poverty eradication and the provision of universal access to energy for all remain important priorities and that the green economy is a pathway to achieve these objectives on the basis of the Rio Principles of Sustainable Development

• agreed to promote more effective natural resource management through greater transparency and better governance, and taking account of the values of natural capital in decision-making, build on the Commonwealth's longstanding practical contributions to member governments in this area; to that end:

- agreed to build capacity in and share best practice on resource management, and welcomed members' initiatives to provide access to research, education and training, and technical and policy expertise

- welcomed the Extractive Industries Transparency Initiative principles and encouraged Commonwealth countries to consider supporting or implementing them

- committed to combating the illegal exploitation of natural resources, including through supporting the *Lusaka*

Declaration of the International Conference of the Great Lakes Region

• agreed to promote inclusive education and to accelerate efforts to achieve quality universal primary education, in line with the MDGs and Education For All goals; they further agreed to:

- help children attain basic levels of literacy and numeracy by strengthening international mechanisms and co-operation, including through new technologies

- create opportunities for skills development and quality secondary and higher education

- call for a successful completion of the first replenishment of the Global Partnership for Education in Copenhagen in November 2011

• committed to universal access to healthcare, and services to improve maternal and reproductive health, supporting access to safe, affordable and quality medicines, and support for all Commonwealth people by accelerating the implementation of international conventions and eradicating disease by improving domestic health strategies and immunisation systems; Heads agreed to do this by:

- accelerating action and financial support to eradicate polio including by improving routine immunisation systems

- accelerating implementation of the Political Declaration of the UN High-Level Meeting on the Prevention and Control of Non-Communicable Diseases and the World Health Organization Framework Convention on Tobacco Control

- committing to accelerating action to implement the objectives outlined in the 2011 UN Political Declaration on AIDS

- recognising that malaria is one of the leading causes of death and a major obstacle to the achievement of sustainable development and poverty alleviation, agreeing to work proactively with key stakeholders and partners towards accelerated implementation of strategies to reduce malarial morbidity and mortality in member countries

- addressing malnutrition, measles, acute respiratory infections and diarrhoea as leading causes of death for children under five, as well as prevalent diseases such as tuberculosis and rotavirus, including through proven international mechanisms such as the GAVI Alliance

• committed to maximise the economic and social benefits of migration to improve the resilience and prosperity of Commonwealth members, whilst addressing the challenges posed by irregular migration which undermines legal migration policies; they:

- called for stronger international co-operation to manage migration effectively in countries of origin, transit and destination, in order to bolster migration's positive effects and to enhance safety nets for migrants

- called for co-operation in the fight against irregular migration, including in particular the readmission of own nationals staying irregularly in other states, in accordance with bilateral agreements and international obligations

- in this context, articulated the link between migration and development, affirming the importance of adopting migration strategies that would reduce the cost of migration, and create incentives for diaspora communities to invest their financial resources and expertise in the development of their countries of origin

- noted and encouraged participation in the Global Forum on Migration and Development, which Mauritius will host in 2012

- agreed to work together, provide financial support to, and make the policy and institutional changes needed to accelerate achieving the MDGs; and:

  - directed the Commonwealth Secretariat to assist members in having their priorities reflected at the special event to be organised by the President of the Sixty-Eighth session of the UN General Assembly to take stock of efforts made towards achieving the MDGs

- called for renewed international commitment to the principles of aid effectiveness to achieve the MDGs by 2015, more imperative than ever in the current challenging global economic and financial environment and, in this regard, noted with appreciation the Commonwealth Statement on Accelerating Development with More Effective Aid, and expressed their desire to achieve a successful outcome at the Fourth High-Level Forum in Busan

- welcomed the launch of the Commonwealth Connects portal as a contemporary platform for networking, building partnerships and strengthening the Commonwealth's values and effectiveness, and encouraged its use, and

- reiterated their support for the Commonwealth Connects programme which is encouraging greater effort from member countries to harness the benefits provided by technology, through promoting strategic partnerships, building information and communication technology (ICT) capacity and sharing ICT expertise; encouraged member countries to contribute to the Commonwealth Connects Special Fund; and requested the Secretariat's continued support for the programme.

Working together and with global partners to secure the global economic recovery and ensure a stronger, more sustainable and balanced global economic system that will benefit all Commonwealth countries, by:

- committing to avoid trade protectionism and advocating the importance of an open, transparent and rules-based multilateral trading system as a driver of global growth and to support development, and in this context:

  - congratulated the thirteen Commonwealth countries that have agreed to formal negotiations to create an African Free Trade Area, covering 26 countries from the Cape to Cairo, by 2014

- committing also to support regional economic integration, enhancing market access and building the capacity of LDCs, landlocked developing states, and other small and vulnerable economies, including SIDS, to participate in and benefit from the global trading and economic system and to further encourage pan-Commonwealth trade

- reaffirming their commitment to pursuing development-oriented and ambitious results in the World Trade Organization (WTO) Doha Development Round, but noting with grave concern the

impasse in current negotiations and calling upon WTO members to make substantive progress at the Eighth WTO Ministerial Conference in December 2011 for an early conclusion of the Doha Round, they:

- reaffirmed the role of the WTO in making rules which keep pace with demands generated by global economic shifts, help police protectionist measures, and contribute to a sustainable global economic recovery

- urged the international community to accelerate efforts to enhance market access for LDCs, landlocked developing states and SIDS at the forthcoming WTO Ministerial Conference

- urged support for an anti-protectionist pledge at the forthcoming WTO Ministerial Conference

- considered innovative approaches to drive forward trade liberalisation and to strengthen the multilateral rules-based trading system

- further reaffirmed the importance of sustained and predictable Aid for Trade in strengthening the capacity of developing country members, in particular small and vulnerable economies, to become more competitive and better able to capture opportunities created by more open regional and global markets; to this end, Heads called for continued support for Aid for Trade and improved disbursement procedures at the forthcoming WTO Ministerial Conference

- urging the G20 to take the necessary steps to address current economic instability and to take concrete steps to put open trade, jobs, social protection and economic development at the heart of the recovery; this will provide the necessary confidence to global markets and ensure a more stable global economic environment; in support of this, Commonwealth countries:

  - committed to take all necessary steps to support the global economic recovery

  - supported ongoing high-level political engagement with the G20 chair and, in this context, welcomed the interaction of the Secretaries-General of the Commonwealth and La Francophonie with the Chair of the G20, as initiated in 2010

  - agreed that Commonwealth G20 members would undertake to convey Commonwealth members' perspectives and priority concerns to the G20 Summit in Cannes, France

  - agreed to launch an annual officials-level Commonwealth meeting on the G20 development agenda, building on the Commonwealth's current contributions to the G20 Development Working Group, and

- agreeing to reduce the cost of remittance transfers by removing barriers to remitting and encouraging greater competition in the transfer market, by endorsing the World Bank's General Principles for International Remittance Services

  - in line with this, Commonwealth countries committed to implement practical measures at the national level to reduce the cost of remittances.

Improving gender equality and the empowerment of women in the Commonwealth, by:

- supporting national programmes to this effect, including initiatives to eliminate gender-based violence, intensifying efforts to promote women's decision-making roles at all levels, and continuing to improve advocacy for women's leadership and the empowerment of women as leaders

- implementing international instruments and agreements on women's rights, including the *Convention on the Elimination of All Forms of Discrimination against Women (CEDAW)*, the *Beijing Declaration and Platform for Action*, the Commonwealth's *Plan of Action for Gender Equality 2005–2015*, and the *Joint Statement on Advancing Women's Political Participation*,[2] and UN Security Council Resolutions (UNSCRs) 1325, 1888 and 1889[3]

- applauding the work of the Commonwealth Secretariat in promoting the significance of the 2011 Commonwealth Day Theme 'Women as Agents of Change' and the centrality of gender equality and the empowerment of women to achieving the MDGs

- directing the Commonwealth Secretariat to institutionalise the principles of gender mainstreaming, as enshrined in the Commonwealth Plan of Action; and to provide recommendations to Heads, through the Tenth Commonwealth Women's Affairs Ministers Meeting (WAMM) on steps that need to be taken to mainstream gender equality across all Commonwealth work; and to make real progress on implementation of the Plan of Action

- supporting the call made by Ministers at the Ninth WAMM held in Bridgetown, Barbados in June 2010, for a more effective response from all actors in the global community to the disproportionately negative impact of the current international and national economic crises on women, and

- giving due consideration to the domestic legislation of member countries, the Commonwealth may address the issue of early and forced marriage, and consider actions to support the rights of women and children and to share its best practices to promote the implementation of measures to tackle early and forced marriage.

Providing a greater voice and more effective role for youth in the Commonwealth, who represent over 50 per cent of the Commonwealth population, by:

- directing the Commonwealth Secretariat to undertake an assessment of the Commonwealth's progress on the Plan of Action for Youth Empowerment, to be submitted with recommendations to Heads, through the Commonwealth Youth Ministers Meeting in 2012, on steps that need to be taken to improve youth engagement and empowerment

- enhancing communication with youth, collecting and sharing good practices, and ensuring the voice of youth is represented in Commonwealth actions at the national and international level, and

- recognising the important role of government, the private sector and technical and vocational training institutions in addressing youth unemployment and the vital importance of sport in assisting young people to stay healthy, contribute to society and develop into leaders of their communities.

Maintaining their commitment to a stable and secure national and international environment, as a foundation for sustainable growth and resilience for Commonwealth countries and the broader international community.

Heads committed to improve international security by:

- unequivocally preventing the use of their territories for the support, incitement to violence or commission of terrorist acts, implementing the necessary legal framework for the suppression of terrorist financing, and preventing the raising and use of funds by terrorists, terrorist front organisations, and transnational terrorist organisations

- accelerating efforts to conclude negotiations on a Comprehensive Convention on International Terrorism

- accelerating efforts to combat piracy in a manner consistent with international law and to strengthen maritime security, including through enhancing the capacity of coastal states

- urging the international community to recognise that the menace of piracy in the Indian Ocean cannot be effectively tackled in the absence of political stability and security in Somalia; urging concerted efforts towards strengthening the Transitional Federal Government and other state institutions, including the security sector; encouraging the international community to mobilise additional funding for AMISOM (African Union Mission in Somalia), as appropriate; and encouraging global support in combating piracy and terrorism, including through enhanced maritime security

- encouraging states to continue supporting the Contact Group on Piracy off the Coast of Somalia in its co-ordination of international counter-piracy efforts

- combating proliferation and trafficking of illicit small arms and light weapons

- embracing moderation as an important value to overcome all forms of extremism, as called for in the 'Global Movement of the Moderates'

- encouraging participation in the 2012 Diplomatic Conference to negotiate on the basis of consensus an effective Arms Trade Treaty which is of broad universal acceptance

- improving legislation and capacity in tackling cyber crime and other cyber space security threats, including through the Commonwealth Internet Governance Forum's Cyber Crime Initiative

- affirming support for the Biological and Toxin Weapons Convention and its Seventh Review Conference in December 2011, and

- continuing to tackle the root causes of conflict, including through the promotion of democracy, development and strong legitimate institutions.

Combating people smuggling and human trafficking by clamping down on illicit criminal organisations and bringing the perpetrators of these crimes to justice, while protecting and supporting the victims of trafficking.

Heads committed to:

- fight people-smuggling as part of their broader efforts to maintain border integrity and manage migration, including through enhancing border security and regional co-operation

- put in place the necessary legal and administrative framework to address the challenge of human trafficking; and affirmed their commitment to the principle of solidarity and co-operation between states with regard to the identification, assistance and protection of victims of trafficking, and

- comply with all obligations arising under international law and urged all countries to become parties to and implement the UN Convention against Transnational Organised Crime and the Protocols thereto, in particular the Protocol to Prevent, Suppress and Punish Trafficking in Persons, Especially Women and Children, and the Protocol against the Smuggling of Migrants by Land, Sea and Air.

To promote the future of the Commonwealth through the strong and important voice of its people, by:

- welcoming the contribution made by intergovernmental, associated and other Commonwealth organisations, including the Commonwealth Foundation, Commonwealth of Learning, Commonwealth Parliamentary Association, Commonwealth Business Council, Commonwealth Local Government Forum and the Commonwealth Association for Public Administration and Management

- urging Commonwealth organisations and civil society to enhance Commonwealth networks and partnerships with a view to achieving the fundamental values and aspirations of the Commonwealth

- relaunching the Commonwealth Foundation in 2012, while retaining its fundamental intergovernmental nature and maintaining its accountability to member states, with a revised mandate and Memorandum of Understanding so that it can more effectively deliver the objectives of strengthening and mobilising civil society in support of Commonwealth principles and priorities, and

- welcoming the outcomes of the Commonwealth People's Forum, Business Forum, and Youth Forum.

To reaffirm previous CHOGM Communiqués on Cyprus and express full support for the sovereignty, independence, territorial integrity and unity of the Republic of Cyprus and the efforts of the leaders of the two communities, under the auspices of the UN Secretary-General's Good Offices Mission, to bring about a comprehensive Cyprus settlement, based on the UN Charter and the relevant UNSCRs for a State of Cyprus with a single sovereignty, single international personality and a single citizenship, in a bi-communal, bi-zonal federation with political equality as described in the relevant UNSCRs. Heads called for the implementation of UNSCRs, in particular 365 (1974), 541 (1983), 550 (1984), and 1251 (1999) and reiterated their support for the full respect of the human rights of all Cypriots and for the accounting for all missing persons. To extend their full support and solidarity to the Republic of Cyprus in the exercise of its sovereign rights under international law, including the United Nations Convention on the Law of the Sea, to explore and exploit the natural resources in its Exclusive Economic Zone.

To note recent developments in the ongoing efforts of Belize to seek a just, peaceful and definitive resolution to Guatemala's territorial claims. Heads noted that, due to the electoral campaigns scheduled in both Belize and Guatemala in the coming months, it was envisaged that the earliest date for the referenda required to submit the matter to the International Court of Justice (ICJ) would be in late 2013. Heads expressed a high level of confidence that the dispute could be resolved through the judicial procedure of the ICJ, and urged the support and financial assistance of the international community for this process. Heads further expressed satisfaction with the ongoing Confidence Building Measures supported by the Organization of American States, which had contributed immensely

to stability in the adjacent border areas of Belize and Guatemala. They noted with concern the environmental problems being faced by Belize in its national parks along its adjacent areas with Guatemala due to the increasing encroachments by Guatemalan citizens for illegal logging. Heads reiterated their firm support for the territorial integrity, security and sovereignty of Belize, and mandated the Secretary-General to continue to convene the Commonwealth Ministerial Committee on Belize whenever necessary.

Having received a report on Guyana-Venezuela relations, to express their satisfaction that the relations between the two countries continued to grow and deepen. Heads noted that the Foreign Ministers of Guyana and Venezuela had met recently in Trinidad and Tobago to address the concerns of the Government of Venezuela over Guyana's submission of a claim to an extended continental shelf to the Commission on the Limits of the Continental Shelf. Heads expressed the view that the current climate in the relations between Guyana and Venezuela was conducive to the realisation of the mandate of the UN Good Offices Process. Heads reaffirmed their unequivocal support for the maintenance and safeguarding of Guyana's territorial integrity and sovereignty.

To welcome the interest shown by the Government of South Sudan in joining the Commonwealth, and to request the Commonwealth Secretariat to pursue the established procedures in this regard.

To look forward to the conditions being created for the return of Zimbabwe to the Commonwealth and continue to encourage the parties to implement the Global Political Agreement faithfully and effectively.

To congratulate the Head of the Commonwealth on her Diamond Jubilee in 2012. Heads welcomed proposed Commonwealth initiatives to mark this historic occasion, in particular the establishment of a Queen Elizabeth Diamond Jubilee Trust, which would be funded by private donations and voluntary contributions from governments. This will support charitable projects and organisations across the Commonwealth, focusing on areas such as tackling curable diseases, the promotion of all forms of education and culture and other Commonwealth priorities.

To reappoint Mr Kamalesh Sharma as Commonwealth Secretary-General for a further four-year term commencing April 2012.

Finally, to reaffirm their decisions to meet next in Sri Lanka in 2013 and thereafter in Mauritius in 2015, as well as to welcome the offer by Malaysia to host the 2019 CHOGM.

Perth, Australia, 30 October 2011

Notes

[1] One member, Fiji, is currently suspended.

[2] From the 'Women's Political Participation – Making Gender Equality in Politics a Reality' high-level event during the 66th Session of the UN General Assembly in New York.

[3] UNSCRs 1325, 1888 and 1889 are each titled 'Women and peace and security'.

The full version of 'A Commonwealth of the People: Time for Urgent Reform' (The Report of the Eminent Persons Group to Commonwealth Heads of Government, Perth, October 2011) can be found at **www.thecommonwealth.org/files/241620/FileName/ EminentPersonsGroupReport.pdf**

'A Commonwealth of the People: Time for Urgent Reform':

agreement by Heads of Government regarding the Eminent Persons Group (EPG) proposals, CHOGM 2011

Decisions by Heads of Government regarding the Proposals of the Eminent Persons Group

In welcoming the report of the Eminent Persons Group (EPG), and thanking its members for their outstanding work, Heads of Government:

- Agreed that there should be a 'Charter of the Commonwealth', as proposed by the EPG, embodying the principles contained in previous declarations, drawn together in a single, consolidated document that is not legally binding;

- Tasked the Secretary-General and CMAG to further evaluate relevant options relating to the EPG's proposal for the Commissioner for Democracy, the Rule of Law and Human Rights and to report back to Foreign Ministers at their September 2012 meeting in New York;

- Noted that the EPG's recommendations relating to the Commonwealth Ministerial Action Group (CMAG) were consistent with the CMAG reforms adopted at this Commonwealth Heads of Government Meeting. The EPG's recommendations related to CMAG or the rule of law (2–10) were therefore superseded by the agreement on CMAG's own reform plan.

- Adopted without reservation a further 30 recommendations;

- Adopted, subject to consideration of financial implications, 12 further recommendations;

- Asked a Task Force of Ministers to provide more detailed advice on 43 other recommendations to Foreign Ministers at their September 2012 meeting in New York, as a basis for further decision by Heads; and

- Deemed, for a variety of reasons, 11 of the recommendations inappropriate for adoption.

Against this background, attached is a list of the adopted recommendations, and those which are subject to further consideration and advice.

Agreement by Heads of Government regarding the EPG Proposals

The following 30 proposals were adopted without reservation.

Rec no.	Page no.	Summary of Recommendation
17	52	The **Secretariat should continue actively to explore**, with the International Institute for Democracy and Electoral Assistance and other relevant institutions, **ways in which the Commonwealth could co-operate with them** in training programmes for Commonwealth countries.
18	55	The core values of **the 2009 Affirmation** of Commonwealth Values and Principles (which updates and expands on the earlier **1971 Singapore Declaration** and **1991 Harare Declaration** and the **2003 Commonwealth [Latimer House] Principles** on the Three Branches of Government) **should be deemed to be 'core Commonwealth priorities'** about which the Secretary-General shall speak out publicly as appropriate.
20	63	The **Secretary-General should develop a clear strategy**, marked by identified priorities, **to maximise the Commonwealth's contribution to the achievement of the development goals of its member states.** Such enhanced development work, informed by Commonwealth values and aspirations, by Commonwealth positions, and with guidance from member governments, should include: (i) advocacy and consensus building on pertinent issues as required; (ii) networking between all member governments for co-operation; and (iii) provision of assistance for institutional development.
29	73	The **Secretariat should develop an overall strategy for capacity development in small states** – including, but not limited to, training of personnel – that is appropriate to the needs and constraints of small states.
31	75	**Heads of Government should take a collective interest in the debt challenges facing developing Commonwealth states and small states** in particular. In this context, they should instruct **the Secretariat to continue to advise member countries on how to avoid unsustainable and risky debt** by putting in place adequate legislation and institutional structures for the prudent management of their debts. This should include periodic analysis of the long-term cost and risk of borrowings and the development of appropriate debt management policies to ensure that debt levels remain sustainable at all times.
33	76	**The five Commonwealth members of the G20 should advocate for the Commonwealth's perspectives and policy proposals on debt, and press for discussions on this issue in the G20's policy-making bodies** such as the High-Level Development Working Group. **The Secretary-General should also seek to advance these issues through high level engagement with successive G20 Chairs.**
34	76	**Member states should take advantage of the Secretariat's debt management software** and the Secretary-General should be proactive in informing member states, as appropriate, of the availability and utility of software.

Rec no.	Page no.	Summary of Recommendation
39	86	**The Commonwealth's work in respect of climate change should place a special focus on small island developing states** [Ministers agreed that the focus should be expanded to include climate change-vulnerable developing states], particularly advocacy in the international community to provide them with financing for adaptation and mitigation.
40	86	**All Commonwealth governments should keep the dangers of climate change alive in the international community** through regular statements by Ministers in all the relevant multilateral and international organisations.
41	87	**Heads of Government and Ministers should regularly brief the media** in their own countries and in other capitals to which they travel **on the specific challenges of climate change** with which their countries and the global community are confronted.
44	89	Heads of Government should **endorse the Commonwealth Cultural Festival** proposed to take place in London in 2012 to coincide with the celebration of the Diamond Jubilee of the Head of the Commonwealth.
46	89	**Heads of Government should mandate Ministers responsible for culture and sport to explore adding to their national and regional cultural, sports, and music festivals, a specific Commonwealth dimension** including by inviting the participation of cultural groups from other Commonwealth countries.
47	90	**Heads of Government should welcome the creation of the Commonwealth Youth Orchestra** and express the hope that this venture will become the first of many initiatives that celebrate the variety and excellence of art and culture in all their forms throughout the Commonwealth.
50	94	**The Commonwealth Youth Programme (CYP) should be encouraged to develop a constitution** that will help to form an independent and youth-led Commonwealth Youth Council that becomes the recognised voice of youth in the Commonwealth. This Council could significantly strengthen and widen the current pan-Commonwealth Youth Caucus and represent a wide cross section of youth in the Commonwealth.
54	97	**All Commonwealth organisations should review their governance arrangements**, including employment policies, oversight boards/committees, and work programmes **to ensure that women are included as decision-makers, and also take women's concerns and needs into account** in a manner that would advance their status.
55	97	The Secretariat should be authorised to **strengthen its advocacy of women's issues** and to make greater efforts to highlight the specific needs of women in its work related to the challenges of development, trade and investment, debt and climate change.
57	101	The Secretary-General should **ensure that HIV/AIDS is prominent in the agendas of all relevant Commonwealth meetings** including those of law ministers, health ministers, ministers for women's affairs and youth ministers to determine and prioritise on-going measures that Commonwealth governments could implement at the national level as well as such advocacy and mobilisation efforts that could be undertaken internationally.
66	110	*Duration:* It is not practical for CHOGM to be any longer than its current duration. While we acknowledge the considerable number of demands by those gathering in events at the margins to have access to leaders, **the essence of successful CHOGMs lies in continuing to ensure maximum amount of time possible for Heads of Government to meet privately for frank and full discussion.**
73	116	**Ministers should continue to consider the relative usefulness of stand-alone Commonwealth meetings as against meetings coinciding with larger international conferences.** If meetings are held alongside other international events, **Ministers should commit themselves to attending them fully.** The duration and programme of such sessions should reflect the special Commonwealth dimensions and produce an action-oriented set of initiatives.
74	116	Meetings of Education Ministers and Law Ministers and Attorneys-General **should continue to be stand-alone events.**
82	124	**The Secretariat and the Foundation should continue to explore the alignment and sharing, where appropriate, of corporate functions,** so as to ensure consistency in working practices, as well as to reduce costs and duplication.
87	132	**The Commonwealth Secretariat should co-ordinate its work with associated Commonwealth institutions, at annual meetings convened by the Secretary-General,** to draw on their technical and other expertise so as to avoid utilising expensive external consultants, where possible, and reduce in-house costs. The Secretariat should allocate funds for which these organisations can apply to implement programmes for which they are better suited than the Secretariat.
88	132	**The Commonwealth Business Council should review its governance to make its membership and its work inclusive of businesses in all Commonwealth countries.** It should mount programmes specifically for **investment from developed Commonwealth countries into developing Commonwealth states.** It should also organise seminars and conferences to utilise the knowledge, expertise and venture capital of economically successful developing countries in other developing member states that are lagging behind.

Rec no.	Page no.	Summary of Recommendation
90	132	Commonwealth governments should continue to support the 'Commonwealth Connects' portal as a cornerstone of twenty-first century networking and partnership, and to support expansion of professional 'communities of practice' such as CommonLII.
95	145	Member governments of the Commonwealth should demonstrate a higher public commitment to the Commonwealth, for instance through investment and support for Commonwealth Day events in member states; references to the Commonwealth's values and aspirations in public addresses including in statements to the UN General Assembly and other international and regional bodies; and references to shared Commonwealth bonds during bilateral visits and other engagements.
98	145	The Secretary-General should be encouraged to consult the Commonwealth Media Group (CMG) about an immediate programme of practical co-operation between the Secretariat and CMG to help distribute the Commonwealth's messages to its constituent publics.
102	149	Every effort should be made by the Commonwealth Games Federation (CGF) and the countries that host the Commonwealth Games to enhance the attractiveness of the Games and to preserve their integrity and reputation.
103	149	Heads of Government should request the CGF to include in its mandate the use and presentation of the Games as an instrument for peace and development.
105	149	National sports federations should also be requested to commit themselves to establishing and strengthening linkages between sport, development and peace.
106	149	The Secretariat should be authorised to play a co-ordinating role through policy analysis, training and development, data collection, monitoring and evaluation, to help Commonwealth member states develop 'Sport for Peace and Development' initiatives.

The following 12 proposals were adopted, subject to consideration of financial implications.

Rec no.	Page no.	Summary of Recommendation
21	63	The Secretary-General should reform the Secretariat's structures and systems in order to deliver this enhanced vision of the Commonwealth's contribution to development as well as relevantly strengthening its role as a central knowledge and co-ordination hub (a Network of Networks). The Secretary-General should report to the Executive Committee of the Board of Governors on a regular basis on progress in achieving this reform.
27	73	The Secretary-General should establish High-Level Advocacy Missions to engage in dialogue with the International Monetary Fund (IMF), the World Trade Organization (WTO) and the World Bank to make progress on specified issues such as a review of the criteria used by international financial institutions to determine the economic well-being and entitlements of a country. Such criteria should take account, additionally, of factors such as a country's level of indebtedness; its fiscal capacity to finance development programmes; and the higher costs it pays for trade because of its remoteness.
28	73	The Secretariat's Office in Geneva for small states should be staffed by technically experienced and entrepreneurial officers with knowledge of the WTO and its negotiating bodies, to provide technical assistance to small states in: (a) negotiating their positions within the negotiating bodies of the WTO; (b) all aspects of trade facilitation; and (c) safeguarding their special interests in the development of the proposed Anti-Counterfeiting Trade Agreement (ACTA) which may involve serious dangers for many Commonwealth countries.
30	73	Heads of Government should re-establish annual meetings of the Ministerial Group on Small States with a mandate to give enhanced political focus and guidance on small states' priorities.
32	76	The Secretary-General should establish a mechanism so that progress on the debt issue, including responses from international financial institutions, could be tracked and considered by annual meetings of Ministers of Finance and CHOGMs.
35	76	The Secretary-General should include in the Secretariat's spending plans, for approval by the Board of Governors, the strengthening of its support to member states in their debt management through advocacy, policy advice and technical assistance.
42	87	Commonwealth governments should renew their commitment to the Iwokrama Rainforest programme by mandating the establishment of machinery to provide it with core funding, and to make use of the knowledge and research outcomes gained from its research. The Secretariat should be authorised to set-up a funding mechanism including through seeking partners for the Iwokrama programme from among Commonwealth and non-Commonwealth countries as well as private sector groups and foundations that have an interest in climate change, conservation and sustainable use of forests.

Rec no.	Page no.	Summary of Recommendation
52	95	**All Commonwealth member governments should establish national mechanisms,** such as national youth councils, so that **the views of young people can be taken into account** in all possible aspects of national policy development.
58	101	The Secretary-General should be authorised to **work with UN bodies,** such as UNAIDS, the World Health Organization and UNDP, to **develop joint programmes** with private sector organisations, including the pharmaceutical industry and philanthropic organisations inside and outside the Commonwealth that could have an impact **on preventing and treating HIV/AIDS.**
59	101	The Secretary-General should be authorised to **mount a high-level mission to relevant UN bodies to advocate a review of any criteria that may unfairly disqualify vulnerable developing countries** in the Commonwealth from gaining access to the Global Fund to Fight HIV/AIDS on the basis of their per capita income.
63	107	The Secretary-General should be mandated to **prepare, by 31 March 2012, a draft plan on which the Secretariat's work and its future development would be focused.** The plan should be submitted to the Board of Governors of the Secretariat by May 2012 for its assessment and recommendations, with the aim that the Secretary-General should implement it from 1 January 2013. The next Secretariat strategic plan, currently under consideration, is to be completed by 30 June 2012. This plan should be merged into the process outlined above so that the Secretariat Strategic Plan for the ensuing four years is only finalised after the recommendations of the intergovernmental discussions can be fully taken into account.
94	139	Heads of Government should consider the **expansion of currently available scholarships and fellowships** by the provision of additional opportunities in the form of Jubilee awards available after 2012. Additionally, **the range and types of scholarships should be widened to encourage entrepreneurship, innovation and business studies.**

The following 43 proposals were referred to a Task Force of Ministers for more detailed advice.

Rec no.	Page no.	Summary of Recommendation
11	50	The Commonwealth should broaden its election observation mandate beyond the existing period (which is now ordinarily two weeks prior to the date on which the elections are held). The Secretariat should **provide Commonwealth Democracy Observer Teams that arrive in some strength, optimally two months in advance** of a planned election day (where this is possible), or where the election is called suddenly, as close as possible to the date on which the election is called to meet electoral officials, political parties and civil society to ensure, through promotion and engagement, an open and democratic electoral process leading up to, including, and following, election day.
12	50	**Observer Teams should report publicly at regular intervals** leading up to, during, and after voting day on relevant issues particularly the freedom of political parties, legitimacy and fairness of election financing rules; freedom of the media in reporting on the electoral process; the integrity of electoral lists; and the efforts by all parties to avoid violence and intimidation.
13	51	To ensure that there is sufficient and effective capacity to carry out these observation functions, the Secretariat should: (i) in the lead up to elections identified as potentially problematic, **establish and maintain at least three deployment-ready observer teams** made up of individuals with relevant political and administrative experience, comprised of a regionally representative group and staffed by both the Secretariat and competent electoral officials from Commonwealth countries; and (ii) review on a regular basis the availability of such teams as a ready-to-deploy facility.
14	51	**Where an adverse report is made by a Commonwealth Observer Group** concerning a significant aspect of a general election, **a report should be made by the Secretary-General to CMAG immediately and a joint course of action adopted.** The Secretariat should systematically follow-up the implementation of the recommendations made by the Commonwealth Observer Groups so that observed deficiencies can be rectified well in time for the next electoral cycle, and be provided the necessary resources for this purpose. Member governments, for their part, should demonstrate their commitment and willingness to address deficiencies identified by Commonwealth Observer Groups in timely fashion before an ensuing election.
15	51	The remit of the Commonwealth Democracy Observer Missions should be expanded **to include an assessment** of the adequacy of institutional and operational arrangements **for post-election political transition** and to advise the Secretary-General on actions that may be required to improve such arrangements and to ensure that political transitions respect the results of elections.
16	51	One or more Commonwealth governments, preferably of developing member states, should consider **establishing an Academy for Democracy and Electoral training for governments, elections commissions, and civil society organisations on a fee-for-service basis.** If established, the Academy should work co-operatively with the Network of Commonwealth Electoral Management Bodies established by the Secretariat.

Rec no.	Page no.	Summary of Recommendation
19	55	Aside from the deployment of 'good offices', the **Secretary-General should be explicitly mandated**, when serious or persistent violations appear in his judgement to be either imminent or actually occurring, **to: (i) indicate concern publicly** to the extent appropriate; (ii) **where necessary, refer any matter urgently to CMAG or to the proposed Commissioner** for Democracy, the Rule of Law and Human Rights for advice; **and (iii) take such other action as (the Secretary-General) he considers appropriate**.
22	63	Heads of Government should **authorise an enlarged capacity within the Secretariat to provide technical assistance** through the placement of technical experts in areas where they are needed by developing member states. **Increased financial resources for this enhanced Commonwealth contribution to development** are an inescapable obligation if the declared Commonwealth commitment to development is to be taken seriously.
23	64	**Heads of Government should give direction** and priority at the national level in the implementation of CHOGM mandates **to make available increased resources to the Commonwealth Fund for Technical Co-operation (CFTC)** to provide expert help to carry out the development tasks required by developing member countries and to train national personnel on the job.
24	66	Commonwealth countries should collectively **monitor the ramifications of migration and development** in the international community, and the **Secretariat should foster partnerships with organisations** such as The Ramphal Centre **to undertake studies** that would inform collective Commonwealth decision-making.
25	69	Commonwealth governments should collectively: (i) **accelerate as a matter of urgency UN reforms** and their effective implementation, through lobbying and advocacy in the UN itself, as well as other international fora; **and (ii) further address reforms of the IMF and the World Bank** so that they serve the needs of all members and the broader global community.
26	69	Commonwealth governments should **strengthen their advocacy by involving** in a systemic way **the full gamut of Commonwealth networks**, including civil society and professional associations.
36	80	**A meeting of Commonwealth Trade Ministers, supported by an Expert Group, should be convened to: (i) try to reach a consensus that would inform the current Doha Round** of negotiations at the WTO (if it is still in place by the time Heads of Government see this report), with the objective of trying to bring the Round to a successful conclusion; and (ii) **consider reform of the WTO in the post-Doha Round**, to identify how in the future the shortcomings of the Doha Round process could be avoided and how the needs of capacity-constrained economies could be better advanced within the WTO. If the Round has collapsed, Heads of Government might consider the **establishment of a Commonwealth Expert Group to consider and recommend the possible future of the post-Doha trading system** to bring greater clarity to discussions in the international monetary sphere and to explore how a new effort in international trade and investment might be launched **that includes the perspectives of the G20 countries as well as a range of developing nations, including small states.**
37	86	The Secretary-General's mandate should be renewed to: (i) **explore the potential for partnerships between the Commonwealth, the World Bank and others to provide specific programmes of support to vulnerable economies;** and (ii) **convene an Expert Group to provide a study to advance the Lake Victoria Climate Change Action Plan,** including which programmes are a priority, how they could be structured, and how they could be financed and implemented. Such a study should be started immediately after the CHOGM in Perth and completed as soon as possible thereafter.
38	86	**Additional financial resources should be provided for the study by the Expert Group.** The report of the Expert Group should be widely publicised and made available to all UN bodies, international financial institutions, and regional organisations.
43	87	The Secretariat should **establish a working relationship with organisations concerned with disasters** occurring in Commonwealth countries and should **maintain a roster of professionals upon whom it could call to provide: (i) a rapid response** to a member state that requests the help of experienced personnel after a disaster; and (ii) training and guidance in disaster preparation and mitigation. Additionally, the Secretariat should **develop with governments an automatic standard for the entry of experts and equipment** into affected countries.
45	89	**The Commonwealth Foundation should consult** with the Commonwealth Games Federation and others including the Commonwealth Broadcasting Association (CBA), **on the feasibility of organising a Commonwealth Cultural Festival at the time of every Commonwealth Games.** Such a festival should be broadcast throughout the Commonwealth, and funded by private sponsorship and contributions, commercial activities, and where appropriate, contributions from governments.
48	94	Heads of Government should agree to the **creation of a Commonwealth Youth Corps (CYC)**, organised by the Commonwealth Foundation and managed by a board made up of existing and appropriate Commonwealth organisations experienced in the movement of young people, to provide the opportunity for thousands of Commonwealth young people to learn about each other's cultures and aspirations while contributing to education, mentoring, development, democracy education and sport skills development.

Rec no.	Page no.	Summary of Recommendation
49	94	Consideration should be given to mandating the Secretary-General to explore the **creation of a Commonwealth Youth Development Fund (CYDF)** to which youth across the Commonwealth could apply for funding to deliver innovative, entrepreneurial solutions to youth employment challenges in their communities. Such a Fund could be administered by a consortium of regional development banks with funding sourced from international financial institutions, the private sector and governments.
51	94	The CYP, in association with the Commonwealth Secretariat, should **develop a pan-Commonwealth programme building on the youth enterprise** scheme that currently exists in some Commonwealth countries, through which banks are being encouraged to accept their responsibility to create special facilities for young people.
53	95	The Secretary-General should be authorised to **establish a Youth Implementation Index** for the purpose of measuring actions relating to the implementation of the country's national youth policies.
56	97	At the national level, **all Commonwealth governments should ensure that: (i) the specific needs of women are addressed in all aspects of law, public policy and allocation of public resources; (ii) women are not discriminated against** in law or practice and that remedies for discrimination are provided; **(iii) machinery is established to encourage and promote the active participation of women** at all levels of decision-making; and **(iv) social victimisation,** leading to crimes against women and tolerance of harmful traditional practices and economic disempowerment, **is brought to an end by the force of law and well-targeted administration**. The Secretary-General should monitor and report on these reforms to CHOGMs.
60	102	**Heads of Government should take steps to encourage the repeal of discriminatory laws that impede the effective response of Commonwealth countries to the HIV/AIDS epidemic**, and commit to programmes of education that would help a process of repeal of such laws.
61	102	**Heads of Government should consider the implications of the global laws regarding intellectual property protection (patents) for Commonwealth countries that face the HIV/AIDS epidemic.** They should **ensure protection of the flexibilities provided in the Trade and Intellectual Property Service Agreements (TRIPS)** of the World Trade Organization in the context of new obligations that are imposed, or may be proposed, by bilateral free trade agreements and by the current negotiations of the Anti-Counterfeiting Trade Agreement (ACTA).
62	107	Heads of Government should consider authorising **the Secretary-General to examine the existing work programmes of the Secretariat using the following criteria to recommend to governments, through the Board of Governors, areas that could be retired**: (i) work that enjoys no specific Commonwealth advantage; (ii) work where the size of the Commonwealth Secretariat's resources, compared to those of other organisations involved in the same field, such as the UN, World Bank, regional development banks and major bilateral donors, is too small to make a significant impact; and (iii) work that overall has demonstrated no significant impact. Further, **the operations of the Secretariat should be reviewed by the Secretary-General to improve the integration, cohesion and efficiency of its divisions and their capacity to deliver the mandates set by members**.
64	108	The Secretary-General should be mandated to consult with member governments on the desirability of **establishing a legal personality for the Commonwealth as an intergovernmental organisation,** so that its members may have greater ownership of the organisation, including appropriate rights and responsibilities towards it.
65	108	In agreeing that **remuneration and terms and conditions of service must be competitive with the United Nations family** of organisations and other comparable institutions, Heads of Government should mandate the Secretary-General to **develop a proposal, for consultation with the Board of Governors, to make the necessary changes.**
67	110	*Communiqués:* Communiqués issued by CHOGM have been too lengthy, and sometimes impenetrable to the media and the public. We suggest that **the CHOGM Communiqué should be replaced altogether with a Chair's Summary, determined by the Chair of the particular CHOGM**, with assistance from the Secretariat and following a consultative process with participating Heads of Government. This document should be significantly shorter and should more accurately reflect the subjects actually discussed by the Heads of Government.
68	110	*Mandates to the Secretariat:* **Mandates for the Secretariat**, which arise from meetings of the Committee of the Whole, and which have been accepted by governments prior to CHOGM, **should be tabled for approval by Heads at CHOGM and issued separately from the Chair's Summary** of the actual discussion and decisions made during the meeting.
69	110	*Theme:* Having a CHOGM 'theme' can sometimes help to guide discussions and facilitate submissions from Commonwealth bodies and civil society organisations. However, it can also limit Heads from taking advantage of opportunities themselves to 'set the global agenda' and/or to respond to recent or upcoming events. The CHOGM theme also runs the risk of reflecting the interest of one country rather than the collective concerns of Commonwealth leaders even if there is consultation with all leaders before it is settled. Moreover, each such 'theme' tends to create new mandates and work programmes for the Secretariat where the necessary resources for implementation may not exist. We believe that Heads should discuss contemporary issues, and carve out a Commonwealth position where possible. Therefore, we suggest **the idea of a special theme should be dropped altogether unless truly exceptional circumstances warrant it.**

Rec no.	Page no.	Summary of Recommendation

70   111   *Access and engagement:* We are aware that there are ambiguities in the pre-CHOGM process surrounding civil society engagement. Many of those with whom we consulted suggested that the level and degree of access to Heads for civil society should be enhanced, and that such access should be more democratic, ensuring that all stakeholders are represented. We are conscious of the need to balance access and engagement with the ultimate value of Heads meeting to talk amongst themselves in a very limited time frame. With this in mind, we propose a **strengthened engagement between civil society organisations (CSOs) and Foreign Ministers at a pre-CHOGM meeting in the year in-between CHOGMs** with a report of the engagement presented to Heads for action.

71   111   *Presence of non-Commonwealth leaders:* The attendance at CHOGM 2009 in Trinidad and Tobago of President Sarkozy of France, Prime Minister Rasmussen of Denmark and UN Secretary-General Ban Ki-moon raised the profile of the Commonwealth and CHOGM. This occurred because of the then imminence of the Copenhagen Conference on Climate Change. **However, while we consider it useful for CHOGM to be seen to be having such high-level interface with other global processes, it should be ventured only in exceptional circumstances** where global circumstances clearly warrant it. **It is important that CHOGM focus on Commonwealth matters,** the constructive role that the Commonwealth can play in agreed international issues and specific Commonwealth problems and opportunities.

72   112   *Media:* It is essential that **each CHOGM should have a considered plan that informs the media regularly of the progress of discussions and provides full disclosure to the outcomes of the conferences** and their relevance to the people of the Commonwealth and the wider global community. The structure of the CHOGM needs to be conscious of the requirements of the media in a world of instant communication and a 24-hour news cycle. Therefore, we recommend that **there should be thrice daily media briefings by representative Heads of Government drawn from across the Commonwealth and a final full-length media Conference** attended by the Chair of the Meeting, the Secretary-General and at least two other Heads of Government.

81   124   **The Secretariat and the Foundation should strengthen collaboration** in the interest of promoting shared values, and specific Commonwealth mandates, including those contained in this report.

83   124   **Member governments, facilitated by the Secretariat, should strengthen the current system of accreditation which should have at the centre of its criteria whether or not an organisation, in its everyday activities, is living up to the values of the Commonwealth.** This will ensure that there is recognised and demonstrable value in being accredited to the Commonwealth as well as setting out the associated expectations and responsibilities that apply by virtue of the privilege of that accreditation.

85   131   **Commonwealth governments should create a 'Commonwealth' page on their official websites** including a list and contact details for all Commonwealth accredited organisations, and membership of Commonwealth professional networks and civil society organisations should be promoted through relevant Ministries and national umbrella organisations.

86   131   **The Commonwealth Foundation should be given an explicit mandate to mobilise Commonwealth civil society around global issues.** This would be another expression of the Foundation's existing mandate to be a focal point for drawing together the strands of Secretariat-accredited Commonwealth civil society organisations including non-governmental bodies and professional associations.

89   132   The Secretary-General should refocus the work of the Civil Society Liaison Unit, whose task would be to **develop better linkages and functional co-operation between Commonwealth agencies in the field** so as to unify and integrate their work more effectively with the Secretariat's.

92   139   Heads of Government should **mandate the Secretariat to continue to develop strategic relationships** within the UN system and with: (i) other intergovernmental organisations; (ii) private sector and philanthropic organisations within and outside the Commonwealth; and (iii) development agencies of Commonwealth and non-Commonwealth governments.

93   139   The Secretary-General should be mandated to: (i) proactively **promote the Commonwealth Scholarship and Fellowship Plan** (CSFP); and (ii) **appoint one staff member with special responsibilities to carry out a co-ordinating role** for Commonwealth countries that contribute awards to the CSFP.

99   146   The Secretary-General should be mandated to **invite appropriate organisations throughout the Commonwealth to offer themselves for selection to carry out a full review and overhaul of the Secretariat's information processes** that will result in a more effective, open, and timely communication strategy and the establishment of machinery to implement it.

100   146   The Secretary-General should be authorised **to convert the four Commonwealth Youth Centres into Commonwealth Regional Centres to provide information and research material on the Commonwealth** to media, educational institutions and the general public in addition to its current activities related to youth.

101   147   Heads of Government should authorise the Secretary-General to **create an Expert Group** to report to the next CHOGM **on ways in which entry to Commonwealth countries by Commonwealth citizens on business or holiday might be gradually improved** either across the Commonwealth or through bilateral arrangements between Commonwealth states.

The following 11 proposals were deemed inappropriate for adoption.

Rec no.	Page no.	Summary of Recommendation
75	116	**Ministerial meetings should be made more attractive and interactive by doing away altogether with set statements (where possible), and by encouraging group discussions,** candid exchanges and facilities for discussions, where appropriate, by Ministers without their officials.
76	116	**Each Ministerial meeting should reduce the mandates to a small number of priorities, enabling the Secretariat to pursue a realistic and coherent programme of work,** rather than a number of sometimes marginal small-scale interventions.
77	116	**Ministerial meetings should provide space for unstructured dialogue with representatives of civil society** on matters of particular relevance and urgency, but should also receive, through the Secretariat, written submissions from CSOs for consideration and action.
78	116	**Ministers should meet in-between scheduled meetings,** in exceptional situations, to pursue priority or urgent agenda items.
79	120	**The arrangement of a Chairperson-in-Office (CiO) and a Troika of Heads should be abolished. The pre-existing system should be re-instituted under which the Secretary-General is the Chief Executive Officer of the Commonwealth, unambiguously responsible for gauging consensus from Heads of Government, acting as the organisation's public voice and interlocutor, and accountable to member governments.** However, the Secretary-General should be able to call on Commonwealth Heads of Government, as appropriate and convenient, including the host of the last CHOGM, to perform functions and make statements on behalf of the Commonwealth at the United Nations and at regional and multilateral organisations in which Commonwealth countries are represented.
80	123	The Secretary-General should continue to have primary responsibility for managing the interface between civil society and governments, and the **Commonwealth Foundation should bolster its efforts in grant-making to, and capacity-building of, civil society** based on an early review of productive outcomes.
84	131	To spread the face of the Commonwealth across all regions, **governments should offer incentives for existing and new Commonwealth civil society organisations to locate themselves in their countries.** Such incentives could include start-up grants to cover cost of office space and a small number of staff and/or project funds.
91	134	**Foreign Ministers should hold dedicated and pre-planned meetings with representatives of CSOs and professional organisations in the years between CHOGMs** to agree on recommendations for joint programmes and projects which would be submitted to the next CHOGM for endorsement and implementation.
96	145	**Heads of Government should designate a Minister of State responsible for Commonwealth Affairs.** This would not only accord a higher profile to the Commonwealth, it would also act as a catalyst for promoting knowledge and understanding of the association.
97	145	The Secretary-General should be authorised to **seek, international expertise to help enhance the profile of the Commonwealth.** Should this recommendation be pursued, clear terms of reference should be established, the financial outlay assessed, and a clear client relationship created that would be tied to performance.
104	149	The Commonwealth Secretariat and the CGF should be asked **to build better linkages** between themselves in order to provide more opportunities for young people **around sports for development and peace.** Additionally, the **CGF should be asked to pay the Secretariat a modest royalty for the use of the Commonwealth 'brand'** to help finance sports for peace and development in developing Commonwealth countries.

Commonwealth leaders agree to strengthen Ministerial Action Group (CMAG)

CHOGM News Release, 28 October 2011: Approval in Perth follows recommendation of the Group set up to deal with serious or persistent violations of Commonwealth values and principles.

Leaders meeting in Perth, Australia, for the Commonwealth Heads of Government Meeting (CHOGM) have agreed to a series of reforms to strengthen the role of CMAG in its dealings with serious or persistent violations of Commonwealth political values.

Outcomes from the report, entitled *Strengthening the Role of the Commonwealth Ministerial Action Group* were released 28 October 2011.

It follows two years of deliberations by CMAG, which was mandated in 2009 by Heads of Government in Trinidad and Tobago to consider ways of more effectively addressing the full range of violations.

'CMAG noted the widely shared view that it had hitherto been too reactive, and not sufficiently proactive,' it said.

Core changes include clearer guidelines and timeframes for engagement with agreed indicators as to the types of situations and developments that might be regarded as constituting a serious or persistent violation of Commonwealth values.

Leaders also agreed that the Secretary-General will speak out publicly in expression of collective disapproval of serious or persistent violations and that CMAG will be the custodian of the *2009 Affirmation of Commonwealth Values and Principles*.

Salient points from CMAG's Report to Heads of Government

- CMAG will continue to respond as before to instances where there is an unconstitutional overthrow of an elected government. In these instances CMAG has done well and has drawn upon the measures adopted at Millbrook.

- CMAG has concentrated on identifying how it might be more proactive and constructive, with clearer guidelines and timeframes for engagement when the situation in a country is causing concern.

- The core changes in CMAG's mandate now accepted by Commonwealth leaders include using the following as among the types of situations that might be regarded as constituting a serious or persistent violation of Commonwealth values:

  - the unilateral abrogation of a democratic constitution or serious threats to constitutional rule

  - the suspension or prevention of the lawful functioning of parliament or other key democratic institutions

  - the postponement of national elections without constitutional or other reasonable justification, and

  - the systematic denial of political space, such as through detention of political leaders or restriction of freedom of association, assembly or expression.

The following developments could also be taken into account:

- a national electoral process that is seriously flawed

- the abrogation of the rule of law or undermining of the independence of the judiciary

- the systematic violation of human rights of the population, or of any communities or groups, by the member government concerned, and

- significant restrictions on the media or civil society that prevent them from playing their legitimate role.

- The first call is, as always, on the Secretary-General's Good Offices, which include the ability to offer Commonwealth technical assistance to help deal with the perceived deficiencies. However, in the more serious cases, if an offer of engagement and assistance by the Secretary-General is not accepted within a specified timeframe and the government in question fails to respond appropriately and serious or persistent violations of fundamental political values continue, the Secretary-General may consult with the Chair of CMAG on the way forward. The Secretary-General may permit a longer response period in cases where structural or other considerations in the relevant country in question would so warrant.

- The timeframe for engagement by CMAG itself has also been clarified so that if, following consultation and further attempts at engagement with a member government by the Secretary-General, the response and progress remain inadequate, the Secretary-General will brief CMAG. If, after a further two months from CMAG being briefed on the situation the judgement of the Secretary-General and the Chair of CMAG is that all efforts at engagement have been exhausted without progress, the situation will be brought to the agenda of CMAG, first informally and thereafter formally.

- CMAG will meet twice a year on a regular basis. It shall continue to convene on an ad hoc basis as needed and respond rapidly if an unconstitutional overthrow of government occurs.

- It has been agreed that CMAG will be the custodian of the 2009 *Affirmation of Commonwealth Values and Principles* (which is an update and strengthening of the *Harare Principles*).

- The Secretary-General will speak out publicly in expression of collective disapproval of serious or persistent violations.

Background

The Commonwealth Ministerial Action Group (CMAG) was established by Heads of Government in 1995 as a mechanism to deal with serious or persistent violations of Commonwealth political values.

CMAG's role is to assess the nature of such infringements, and to make use of a series of measures in response to serious or persistent violations that were identified by Commonwealth leaders in 1995 in their *Millbrook Action Programme*.

At CHOGM 2009 in Trinidad and Tobago, '*Heads of Government agreed that consideration be given to strengthening the role of CMAG, in order to enable the Group to deal with the full range of serious or persistent violations of the Harare Principles*'.

In considering that 2009 mandate, CMAG noted the widely shared view that it had hitherto been too reactive, and not sufficiently proactive. Thus, it had dealt decisively with situations where constitutionally elected governments had been overthrown, but had not always been able to address other situations where Commonwealth values and principles were being seriously or persistently violated.

CMAG was conscious of the prevalent perception of the Group as a punitive body and that member governments felt a stigma associated with being placed on its agenda; they believed this made it difficult at times for CMAG to engage with members constructively.

In its 2011 report entitled *Strengthening the Role of the Commonwealth Ministerial Action Group*, CMAG put forward recommendations to Heads of ways in which the work of the Group could be made more effective.

Ministers meetings

Health ministers meeting

Commonwealth Health Ministers met in Geneva, Switzerland, 15 May 2011.

Commonwealth ministers of health held their annual meeting in Geneva, Switzerland, on the eve of the 64th World Health Assembly. The theme of the meeting was 'Non-communicable diseases – a priority for the Commonwealth'. The keynote address was delivered by Professor Jean-Claude Mbanya, President, International Diabetes Federation.

Ministers noted with concern that in 2008, 47 per cent of the estimated 19.5 million deaths in the Commonwealth were due to non-communicable diseases (NCDs). These diseases are mainly cancers, cardio-vascular diseases, chronic respiratory diseases and diabetes. They further noted that these diseases are disproportionately impacting the low and middle income Commonwealth member countries. Ministers discussed their concern at the rise of NCD risk factors, particularly tobacco use, in middle- and low-income countries, being aware that tobacco use alone accounts for one in six of all deaths resulting from NCDs. In this regard, ministers acknowledged the serious threat that NCDs have upon development.

Ministers recognised the opportunity presented by the forthcoming UN High-Level Meeting on the Prevention and Control of NCDs (19–20 September 2011, New York) to secure attention and commitment at the highest levels to address and respond to the NCD crisis. Discussions recalled the experience and outcomes of the UN Summit on HIV (2001), acknowledging that there are lessons to be learned from the HIV experience. These relate to: integration, monitoring and evaluation, partnerships and engagement of civil society.

Ministers considered specific Commonwealth objectives for the UN High-Level Meeting on NCDs to be raised by member countries. In this regard, they:

* acknowledged the severe impact of NCDs on development

* recognised NCD co-morbidities such as mental health, haemoglobinopathies, violence, injuries and oral health, recommending a holistic approach to patient care

* noted the importance of an integrated, multi-sectoral approach to tackling NCDs

* supported the implementation of five priority interventions with time bound targets, where applicable. These were identified as:

  – leadership: maintaining high-level leadership and support at national and international levels

  – prevention: addressing risk factors such as tobacco use, harmful use of alcohol, unhealthy diets and physical inactivity

  – treatment: facilitating access to low-cost essential medicines and technologies and to strengthening health systems for the provision of patient-centred care

  – international co-operation: raising the profile of NCDs on global agendas, increasing funding for NCDs, and promoting synergies between programmes for NCDs and other global priorities

  – developing systems for surveillance, monitoring, evaluation and accountability

* recognised the gender considerations of NCDs – both in terms of susceptibility and impact

* urged NCD responses to prevention, treatment and care to be integrated into the current health structures, policies and implementation strategies.

Ministers also supported the need for:

* more technical support for strengthening country health systems and capacities to assess and respond to the burden of NCDs and their determinants

* sharing of expertise and technical assistance between Commonwealth countries, both North–South and South–South.

Ministers supported the Commonwealth Secretariat's work in this important field of health, and the progress made in implementing activities outlined within the Commonwealth NCD road map which was adopted in May 2010. It was recognised that the Secretariat will continue to work to fully implement all of these activities, including the NCD media strategy and strengthening country capacity for assessing the burden of NCDs and their determinants.

Ministers welcomed the health work plan being pursued by the Secretariat, approved the actions taken and commended the results achieved. They acknowledged that the work plan to achieve the targets defined by the Millennium Development Goals (MDGs) should continue to provide the framework for co-ordinated and integrated action.

Ministers agreed that the themes for the Commonwealth health ministers for the subsequent two years will be:

* May 2012: The linkages between NCDs and communicable diseases
* May 2013: Mental health.

Law ministers meeting

Commonwealth Law Ministers met in Sydney, Australia, 11–14 July 2011.

The meeting, which was attended by law ministers and attorneys-general from 44 countries, was opened by the Commonwealth Secretary-General, Kamalesh Sharma. In surveying the many important and practical matters in the agenda before the meeting, he spoke of access to justice for all citizens as fundamental to the work of law ministers and of the continuing importance of the Latimer House Principles to the Commonwealth as a whole. The meeting elected as its chairperson Robert McClelland MP, Attorney-General of Australia, who shared the chairing of the meeting with Brendan O'Connor MP, Minister of Home Affairs and Justice of Australia.

The meeting had as its theme 'Fostering a just and secure Commonwealth'. It addressed many of the challenging issues currently faced by Commonwealth member states in today's fast-changing social, economic and legal environment. In the discussions, there was an awareness of the special needs of small jurisdictions with limited legal resources. Ministers hoped that their decisions would enhance their already close co-operation and the work of the Commonwealth Secretariat in securing the rule of law to the benefit of all their citizens.

Legal work of the Commonwealth Secretariat

The meeting received a comprehensive report on the legal work undertaken by the Commonwealth Secretariat, and particularly its Legal and Constitutional Affairs Division, since the last law ministers meeting in 2008. Law ministers welcomed Akbar Khan, Director of the Legal and Constitutional Affairs Division since October 2009, who spoke of the highlights of the Secretariat's Rule of Law programme since 2008 and of the current moves to refocus and prioritise the work to be undertaken. Ministers noted that, despite resource constraints, the work of the division continued to be wide-ranging and of high quality. Notwithstanding this, ministers encouraged the efforts to sharpen the focus of the work of the Secretariat. Ministers thought that it might be desirable to identify at each triennial meeting themes around which the work of the Secretariat could be planned and organised.

International judicial development assistance

Ministers recognised that the effective administration of justice required not only an independent judiciary of high competence but also an efficient court system. In many countries, the courts face a number of challenges: chronic delays, the need to reform procedural rules, the introduction of alternative dispute resolution processes and case management systems, and the deployment and effective use of modern technology. There had developed in recent years a valuable but largely unco-ordinated practice of international judicial development assistance. Ministers noted that a number of Commonwealth countries had established judicial training institutes; some of the courses provided by these institutes were already attended by judges from countries which had no equivalent

resources. The Pacific Judicial Development Programme had a number of projects in 14 Pacific island countries designed to enhance the professional competence of judicial officers and the processes and systems they use. Ministers recognised the particular circumstances of small states and their special needs in the design and delivery of programmes.

Ministers resolved:

* to mandate the Commonwealth Secretariat to establish or enable the establishment of an online 'clearing house' which would co-ordinate information as to what judicial development assistance programmes had been provided by Commonwealth countries to other countries, and would receive and assess applications for judicial development assistance and notify them to those member states which might have the capacity to respond to such requests, having regard to regional considerations

* that the Secretariat would develop a framework which Commonwealth countries could adopt with the aim of better co-ordination and targeting of international judicial development assistance, addressing the needs of recipient countries. The framework would ensure that assistance provided was based upon consistent standards of approach, enabled programmes to draw on previous experience, avoided duplication and had a rigorous approach to evaluation.

Climate change and its impact on security and survival

The meeting recalled the Commonwealth Climate Change Action Plan, endorsed by Commonwealth Heads of Government in 2007. Climate change represents a threat to human security, even to the existence of some Commonwealth member states. It threatens the progress of development by reducing access to drinking water and causing desertification, putting agriculture and direct access to means of subsistence at risk.

Ministers resolved:

* that the United Nations Framework Convention on Climate Change (UNFCCC) is the key instrument for addressing climate change and that any initiatives undertaken by the Commonwealth Secretariat should be consistent with and complementary to the UNFCCC and any related instruments

* without prejudice to any eventual outcome, to mandate the Commonwealth Secretariat to conduct a comprehensive assessment of the adequacy of such legal frameworks as are currently applicable to populations displaced due to climate change both within states and between states and access to vital natural resources

* that consideration for the development of new legal architecture with regard to displaced migrant populations and access to vital natural resources arising from climate change may be required after the comprehensive assessment is completed

* that, where appropriate, co-operation between member states with regard to immigration policies may be further developed and the Commonwealth Secretariat may provide such assistance as states may require, and

- that the Commonwealth should offer assistance to small developing states in particular in raising awareness of climate change and its impact, and taking adaptation measures to lessen the inevitable impacts of climate change.

The independence and integrity of magistrates

The meeting received a paper prepared by the Commonwealth Magistrates' and Judges' Association (CMJA) presenting the preliminary results of an examination of the position of magistrates within the Commonwealth, 'magistrate' for this purpose including all judges serving in a court which is not a court of unlimited jurisdiction in civil or criminal matters. The paper recorded concerns that in some Commonwealth jurisdictions the independence of the magistracy was without legislative protection; that appointments were made by processes which were not transparent; that in some countries magistrates' security of tenure was limited; and that adequate resources were not always made available to magistrates' courts. Ministers shared the experiences of their jurisdictions and noted the importance of issues such as those of remuneration and judicial pensions and of the accountability of magistrates.

The meeting agreed to note suggested Guidelines for Ensuring the Independence and Integrity of Magistrates prepared by the CMJA, and ministers resolved to consider taking appropriate steps to strengthen their domestic legal frameworks and other measures for assuring the independence and integrity of their magistracy in compliance with the Commonwealth fundamental values, having due regard to the suggested guidelines.

Conventional weapons and international humanitarian law

The meeting received a paper prepared by the International Committee of the Red Cross (ICRC) on the international weapons related treaties adopted in recent years. These treaties prohibit or restrict the use of certain conventional weapons and seek to deal with the dangerous explosive remnants left after armed conflicts, including those remaining in a number of Commonwealth countries. The Convention on the Prohibition of Anti-Personnel Mines of 1997 and the Protocol to the Conventional Weapons Convention on Explosive Remnants of War 2003 (Protocol V) have now been joined by the Convention on Cluster Munitions adopted in 2008. Negotiations are continuing at an international level on the topic of arms trade in conventional weapons. Ministers were informed of the West African (ECOWAS) initiative on arms trade which has supported its member states on the implementation of rules relating to the trade in conventional weapons and the development of measures and processes for the control of their import and export. Ministers noted that in some jurisdictions, matters relating to conventional weapons did not fall within the province of law ministers.

Ministers resolved:

- to encourage states to actively consider ratification of outstanding weapons related treaties, to incorporate the provisions of these treaties into their domestic law and to report on progress as required by these conventions

- that the Commonwealth Secretariat may be invited, in co-operation with the ICRC, to assist states to ratify the various weapons-related treaties and to put domestic law in place to fulfil their obligations under such treaties, and

- to give legal support to enable their respective countries to participate actively in the 2012 Diplomatic Conference to negotiate a truly effective Arms Trade Treaty (ATT) that complies with international humanitarian law.

Forced or servile marriages

Ministers discussed the issue of forced or servile marriages which constituted a human rights violation that impeded individuals' most basic and fundamental rights. Many forced marriages had a transnational quality and their prevention could require active co-operation between the states concerned.

Ministers resolved:

- to reiterate their support for the Convention on the Elimination of All Forms of Discrimination against Women (CEDAW), and

- to note the useful discussion of measures that member states can take to protect women against forced and servile marriage and agree to consider actions to support the rights of women in such circumstances and to share best practices between member states.

International civil legal co-operation

The meeting recognised that the increasing international mobility of people, assets, goods and services means that more businesses and individuals are involved in international civil and commercial transactions. The secure planning of such transactions would be served by better mechanisms for obtaining reliable and authoritative information about the laws and practices of other legal systems. Where litigation took place, courts would be assisted by closer judicial co-operation with the courts and administrative agencies of other countries, in such matters as the service of process and obtaining evidence abroad.

Ministers judged that there could be value in a Commonwealth scheme that could usefully supplement existing international conventions including those of the Hague Conference. This would be a counterpart to the existing Harare Scheme for Mutual Assistance in Criminal Matters. It would draw on the shared legal traditions of the Commonwealth but would also reflect the development of modern information and communication technology and the agreements made in recent years between some Commonwealth member states.

Ministers resolved to mandate the Secretariat to develop a proposed scheme on international civil legal co-operation for consideration at the next meeting of senior officials.

Cybercrime

A feature of this meeting was a special thematic session on cybercrime introduced by presentations followed by a high-level ministerial panel discussion. The starting point was a recognition that the use of technology in the commission of crime presented significant challenges to government, law enforcement and to individuals and businesses. Much personal information was now available on the internet, creating possibilities for identity theft and other forms of fraud. The rapid pace of technological change continually threatened to outpace efforts at regulation, and many offences had a transnational character to which the traditional territorial approach of the criminal law was ill-suited: the sharing of information between national law enforcement agencies was essential. Many countries have found it necessary to create extra-territorial offences, making certain types of conduct punishable even when committed abroad.

Ministers received a presentation on an example of successful international co-operative work to deal with an internet-based paedophile ring. The meeting heard of legislation, specialist agencies and awareness-raising material developed in Australia, Botswana and Canada, noting that the issues were of equal importance to developing countries. There was a sharing of the experience of many jurisdictions. Ministers noted the existence of a comprehensive international instrument, the Council of Europe's 2001 Convention on Cybercrime, the work which led to the preparation of the Commonwealth draft Model Law on Computer and Computer Related Crime in 2002, and of regional efforts in West Africa.

Ministers resolved:

- to recognise the significant threat cybercrime poses to national security and law enforcement in all countries of the Commonwealth

- that the Commonwealth Secretariat form a multidisciplinary working group of experts to review the practical implications of cybercrime in the Commonwealth and identify the most effective means of international co-operation and enforcement, taking into account, among others, the Council of Europe Convention on Cybercrime, without duplicating the work of other international bodies, and

- that the working group collaborates with other international and regional bodies with a view to identifying best practice, educational material and training programmes for investigators, prosecutors and judicial officers.

Mutual legal assistance in criminal matters: the Harare Scheme

The Harare Scheme relating to Mutual Legal Assistance in Criminal Matters within the Commonwealth has for a quarter of a century provided a constructive and pragmatic approach to mutual co-operation between Commonwealth countries in combating transnational crime. At their meeting in Edinburgh in 2008, ministers asked for a comprehensive review of the scheme in the light of the contemporary upsurge and increased sophistication of transnational criminal activity. The present meeting received the results of this review in the form of a revised and updated scheme including new provisions as to the interception of telecommunications and postal items; covert electronic surveillance; the use of live video links in the course of investigations and judicial procedures; and asset recovery. The revised scheme which, like other rules and guides issued by the Commonwealth law ministers, provides a non-binding arrangement for the widest possible co-operation in criminal matters between Commonwealth countries is to be applied in a flexible manner in compliance with domestic law and international law. It does not preclude police-to-police co-operation.

Ministers resolved:

- to adopt the revised and updated Harare Scheme relating to Mutual Legal Assistance in Criminal Matters within the Commonwealth, and

- to approve the Secretariat's continuing programme of work in this area, which includes:

  - the development of model legislation to assist member countries in implementing the revised Harare Scheme

  - the development and delivery of capacity-building initiatives by 30 June 2013, in particular on the interception of telecommunications and asset recovery, to further enhance international co-operation within the Commonwealth, and

  - the promotion of the Commonwealth Network of Contact Persons and other similar networks.

The Secretariat will report to the next senior officials meeting on progress in developing this body of work.

Strategies to combat corruption

The Commonwealth Heads of Government Meeting gave the Commonwealth Secretariat an anti-corruption mandate in 2005. The majority of Commonwealth member states have become parties to the United Nations Convention against Corruption and the Secretariat, as part of its response to the mandate, prepared a Commonwealth Legislative and Technical Guide to the Convention, which was approved by law ministers in 2008. This guide has been kept under review and the present meeting received an updated guide, which contains up-to-date guidance, not only on legislative issues, but also on global best practice, and provides a comprehensive point of reference for member states still preparing to implement the convention and for those seeking to review and update their legislation and practice.

Ministers resolved:

- to approve the 2010 Updated Commonwealth Legislative and Technical Guide to the United Nations Convention against Corruption and its appendices

- to approve the Secretariat's programme of work in combating corruption including publication and dissemination of the Guide, and

- to approve delivery of a series of criminal justice system regional or country specific training programmes incorporating anti-corruption modules.

Rights and pre-trial procedures: requirements for police and prison authorities

Ministers received a study commissioned by the Secretariat on the minimum human rights standards available to detainees at the pre-trial stage in selected countries of both the civil law and common law traditions. The study, by the British Institute of International and Comparative Law (BIICL), contained recommendations on applicable human rights standards and best practices.

Ministers resolved to take note of the paper which was suitable for publication as a research paper by the BIICL.

Victims of crime

Ministers recalled the Commonwealth Statement of Basic Principles of Justice for Victims of Crimes which they adopted at their meeting in Accra in 2005. One aspect of justice for victims is their protection and support as witnesses throughout an investigation and subsequent proceedings. Witnesses who are not themselves the victims of crime may also need protection and support.

Ministers resolved:

- to approve the *Best Practice Guide for the Protection of Victims/Witnesses in the Criminal Justice Process* (the Guide), and

- to approve a programme of work to be carried out by the Secretariat, including:

  - to disseminate the Guide

  - to develop sensitisation and capacity-building programmes for criminal justice officials

  - to assist member countries with specific training on request, and

  - to facilitate pro-bono mentoring and placements to develop sustainable capacity-building in areas of victim/witness assistance and protection by 30 June 2012.

The Secretariat will report to the next senior officials meeting on progress in developing this body of work.

Overcrowding in correctional facilities

In recent years both law ministers meetings and meetings of law ministers and attorneys-general of small Commonwealth jurisdictions have considered two related issues: that of promoting alternative sentencing; and that of the overcrowding in prisons and the excessive use of pre-trial detention in many countries. At their 2008 meeting, law ministers requested the Commonwealth Secretariat to work with Commonwealth member states to formulate a strategy towards reducing the overall number of prisoners held in detention. Ministers now note that the issue was considered in depth last year at the Twelfth United Nations Congress on Crime Prevention and Criminal Justice. Rather than continuing with a separate Commonwealth study, ministers agreed to make use of the UN material.

Ministers resolved:

- to consider the material set out in Annex A to paper LMM(11)15, and

- to approve the Secretariat's programme of work in combating overcrowding in correctional facilities, including:

  - expansion of the Alternative Sentencing Programme by incorporating the UN's recommendations as topics for analysis and discussion at future regional meetings, and

  - delivery of technical assistance relating to alternative sentencing/prison population reduction to individual member countries, upon request.

This work is to be delivered by 30 June 2013. The Secretariat is to report on progress at the next meeting of senior officials.

Prosecution disclosure obligations

At their meeting in Edinburgh in 2008, law ministers considered prosecution disclosure obligations and mandated the Commonwealth Secretariat to undertake a comparative study of the approach to prosecution disclosure in criminal proceedings in Commonwealth member states, paying attention also to other critical considerations, such as witness protection, defence disclosure and the wider public interest. The Secretariat was to identify international best practices; to develop model legislative provisions and detailed guidance addressing the issue of disclosure, particularly in relation to unused material; and to conduct related training programmes. Ministers received a Model Criminal Disclosure Act and related Model Prosecution Disclosure Guidelines produced in fulfilment of that mandate.

Ministers resolved:

- to approve the model guidelines and model legislative provisions as helpful models for addressing issues relating to prosecution disclosure obligations in member countries

- to encourage member countries to draw on the model disclosure legislation and guidelines to the extent that it assists each member country in addressing these issues, and

- to approve the Secretariat's programme of work in promoting best practice in prosecution and prosecution disclosure, including:

  - the delivery of a series of criminal justice system regional training programmes with web-intensive and mentoring components incorporating modules on prosecution disclosure obligations and related areas

  - assistance to member countries with specific training requests, and

  - the facilitation of pro-bono mentoring and placements to develop sustainable capacity-building in prosecution disclosure and related areas.

The International Criminal Court

The meeting welcomed Judge Sang-Hyun Song, President of the International Criminal Court, and witnessed the signing by the President and the Commonwealth Secretary-General of a Memorandum of Understanding on Co-operation between the Commonwealth Secretariat and the International Criminal Court. The Secretary-General recalled that Commonwealth Heads of Government are committed to end impunity for perpetrators of genocide, crimes against humanity and war crimes and attach importance to building national capacity through the implementation of the Rome Statute of the International Criminal Court. President Song spoke of his pleasure at signing a historic Memorandum of Understanding and of being able to do so in the presence of law ministers from all parts of the world. Both the Commonwealth and the International Criminal Court were of global significance in upholding the rule of law, and the President noted with pleasure that over half the Commonwealth member states had already become parties to the Rome Statute.

The meeting recognised that for a state to become a party was but the first step and that implementing legislation covering a range of matters (which would vary from state to state) was required. In

2004 a Commonwealth Model Law on the implementation of the Rome Statute was adopted. Revision of the Model Law has become appropriate to take account of developments following the Kampala Review Conference held in June 2010 and to reflect the various amendments made to the Rome Statute. Ministers received a revised draft Model Law.

Ministers resolved:

- to approve the revised draft model law for dissemination to Commonwealth member states which are drafting implementing national legislation for the Rome Statute of the International Criminal Court

- to note the contents of the revised Report of the Commonwealth Expert Group on Implementing Legislation for the Rome Statute of the International Criminal Court

- to request the Commonwealth Secretariat to carry out further work with a view to consideration of the inclusion of provisions relating to the crime of aggression within the model law in due course, and

- to request the Commonwealth Secretariat alone or in partnership with other relevant organisations to undertake pan-Commonwealth and regional activities aimed at promoting the revised model law for adoption by member countries, together with the provision of expert technical assistance, as required, in respect of the ratification and implementation of the Rome Statute.

Legislative drafting

At many of their meetings, including that in Edinburgh in 2008, law ministers have examined the difficulties facing their legislative drafting offices. They are acutely aware that the difficulties in the recruitment and retention of drafters remain major impediments to the realisation of policy objectives in many Commonwealth states. External expertise could prove valuable, but effective drafting required a full understanding of the legal context in a particular jurisdiction and of the policies underlying legislative proposals. At their present meeting, ministers addressed practical issues around financial and technical resources.

On financial resources for drafting, ministers resolved:

- to give explicit support to Secretariat initiatives aimed at identifying extra-budgetary resources for drafting (given the resonance of rule of law and governance ideals with donor agencies, and awareness of the challenges of legislative drafting in smaller and developing jurisdictions, it is possible to foresee donor uptake of well-designed proposals underpinned by law ministers' resolutions)

- in order to tap into more substantial resources, donor-focused strategies and overtures by the Secretariat and/or ministries ought to be addressed to the substantial aid programmes of other countries

- the Secretariat should continue to act as a 'clearing house' for proposals and requests for funding outside of the Commonwealth Fund for Technical Co-operation (CFTC) and related pools without necessarily being joined as project partner

- the Secretariat should continue to encourage drafting offices in regions to form networks for sharing ideas and proposals on

funding. The Secretariat may then be in a position to co-ordinate a 'network of networks' whose combined input will be more persuasive to donors seeking maximum breadth and depth in their assistance, and

- recalling that previous law ministers meetings have recognised that recruitment and retention of drafters remain a concern, putting in place measures to retain drafters including through the creation and maintenance of well-structured drafting offices and through the provision of training the trainers courses in order to promote sustainability in the drafting field.

In regard to technical resources, ministers resolved to approve:

- the acquisition and development of software and training materials for the following three components of a legislation management system especially for small jurisdictions:

  - a drafting and paper-oriented (PDF) publishing application that automates many tasks and improves the efficiency, consistency and quality of the product and the working environment

  - an electronic publishing application that permits enacted legislation (including consolidations when available) to be quickly, easily and inexpensively published on the internet, and

  - a conversion application that assists in moving legislation from whatever its current format is to the format used in the drafting and publishing applications

- the development of a model statute to provide for an ongoing electronic consolidation of laws, and training materials for preparing consolidations

- the implementation of the legislation management system as a pilot project in the legislative drafting offices in some selected Commonwealth jurisdictions, and

- the setting up of an advisory group drawn from experts including those in the Commonwealth Association of Legislative Counsel to assist in the development of software.

Modalities for civil society engagement with law ministers

Law ministers at the Edinburgh meeting in 2008 requested work on the modalities for civil society engagement with them in view of the Commonwealth's commitment to the involvement of civil society organisations (CSOs) in key deliberative processes such as ministerial and Heads of Government meetings. It was necessary at the same time to respect the need for confidentiality and protect law ministers from inappropriate and untimely lobbying. A set of proposed modalities was before the present meeting.

Ministers resolved:

- that the growing influence of civil society in Commonwealth processes should be recognised without diminishing the relevance of intergovernmental processes (indeed the relevance of the Commonwealth may be enhanced through constructive engagement with relevant CSOs; but this should not lessen the authority of governments in Commonwealth processes)

- that constructive engagement of civil society can strengthen intergovernmental deliberations by informing them, sensitising them to public opinion and grassroots realities and increasing public understanding of their decisions, and

- that in the circumstances senior officials are tasked to develop proposals to enhance and achieve a more constructive engagement with CSOs for further consideration by ministers within the next 12 months so that the modalities can be agreed by the next meeting of senior officials.

The Commonwealth Secretariat's Rule of Law programme

Ministers recalled their discussion at their meeting in Edinburgh in 2008 on how the Commonwealth Secretariat could refocus and redefine its Rule of Law programme in order to ensure that it remained relevant, co-ordinated and effective in the delivery of assistance to member states. They received the report of an expert group which had met in March 2011 under the chairmanship of Michael Kirby AC CMG of Australia to formulate recommendations.

Ministers resolved:

- to take note of the Report of the Chairman of the Commonwealth Expert Group on the Rule of Law

- to endorse the Outcome Statement included in the Final Report of the Commonwealth Expert Group on the Rule of Law and adopt the recommendations stated at paragraphs 6, 7 and 10 of the Outcome Statement

- to agree to sunsetting by 30 June 2012 of the proposed mandates listed under the column headed 'Recommended for Sunsetting' in the document titled 'Matrix of Current Rule of Law Mandates of Legal and Constitutional Affairs Division – Recommendations for Sunsetting', as amended by the Senior Officials Working Group in their Report

- to agree that in future mandates to the Secretariat should include specification of timeframes and deliverables in each case

- that mandates involving the development of a scheme or model legislation necessarily involve capacity-building to support and facilitate its implementation (it was suggested that these tasks should be completed within a period of 12 to 18 months after the scheme or model legislation is adopted by the ministers)

- future reports by the Secretariat on the programme should include information about the resources applied to each mandate

- that as new mandates are given, the implications for work on existing mandates should be highlighted by the Secretariat, and

- to give continued support to the Latimer House Principles, and encourage Commonwealth Heads of Government to give better effect to them.

International child abduction

The meeting received a presentation by Lord Justice Thorpe, Head of International Family Justice for England and Wales, on extending the 1980 Hague Child Abduction Convention throughout the Commonwealth. He urged accession to the convention and emphasised the need for Commonwealth member states to support the work of the Hague Conference in the field of family law, including its network of specialist judges and the Malta Process which sought to build links between states

with Islamic law and other states. Ministers took note of the presentation.

Reports received

Ministers received and took note of a number of reports. These were reports:

- on the activities of the Human Rights Unit of the Commonwealth Secretariat (which prompted discussion of the desirable focus of the unit's work, of the differing views within the Commonwealth on the death penalty, and of the burden of compliance with some of the reporting obligations of human rights instruments)

- on the activities of the Gender Section of the Secretariat's Social Transformation Programmes Division (ministers stressing the importance of gender equality, in practice and not merely in principle, as a fundamental human right)

- on the activities of the International Institute of Humanitarian Law

- by the International Committee of the Red Cross and the British Red Cross

- on the activities of the Commonwealth Secretariat in the field of maritime boundaries and related Law of the Sea matters, and

- from the Legal and Constitutional Affairs Division's partner organisations: the Commonwealth Association of Law Reform Agencies (CALRAs); the Commonwealth Magistrates' and Judges' Association (CMJA); the Commonwealth Lawyers' Association (CLA); the Commonwealth Legal Education Association (CLEA); and the Commonwealth Association of Legislative Counsel (CALC).

Women as agents of change

Ministers took part in a forum on Women as Agents of Change held in Government House and hosted by the Governor of New South Wales, Professor Marie Bashir AC CVO. Law ministers welcomed the presentation by Catherine Branson QC – President of the Australian Human Rights Commission. The participation of the Commonwealth Deputy Secretary-General was particularly welcomed as underscoring the mainstreaming of this issue in the work of the Secretariat.

Pacific Young Lawyers Forum

In his remarks in opening the meeting, the Commonwealth Secretary-General referred to a parallel event held in association with the law ministers meeting, the Pacific Young Lawyers Forum, which had met on 10 July 2011. The forum provided an opportunity for discussion of the ways in which the Commonwealth could assist young lawyers in Pacific countries with small legal professions. There was emphasis on the importance of supporting young lawyers' careers and providing guidance on professional conduct to address the ethical dilemmas sometimes faced by them in the course of their work. The Commonwealth's commitment to youth development led to support for the promotion of mentoring and continuing legal education as well as pro bono activities in law schools and among lawyers in member states. There was recognition of the key role of young lawyers in providing access to justice to the poor and vulnerable. The forum saw the inauguration of the South Pacific Lawyers Association (SPLA).

Planning of law ministers and senior officials meetings

The meeting considered a suggestion that there should be one or more organising themes for each law ministers meeting which would produce a more focused agenda, while leaving room in the agenda for topical items. It was for further consideration whether the timing and frequency of senior officials meetings should be reviewed, but it was already clear there was a need for such a meeting in 2012 to review current work.

The meeting accepted a generous offer of Botswana to host the next Commonwealth Law Ministers Meeting in 2014.

Finance ministers meeting

Commonwealth Finance Ministers met in Washington DC, USA, 21 September 2011.

Finance ministers and senior officials of the 54 Commonwealth nations met in Washington DC in a meeting hosted by Commonwealth Secretary-General Kamalesh Sharma and chaired by South Africa's Finance Minister, Pravin Gordhan.

Ministers noted that the meeting was taking place in a period of significant global economic and financial uncertainty and substantial international regulatory reform. This environment presented acute challenges for all Commonwealth members, particularly the association's smallest, poorest and most vulnerable members. International macroeconomic and financial policies since the global crisis were not securing broad-based global growth. Ministers noted that in an increasingly interdependent global environment this had resulted in significant adverse consequences for Commonwealth members, with a loss of trade, output and employment, particularly among the poorest, smallest and most vulnerable members of the association. Ministers recognised that while these countries had not contributed to the causes of the crisis, they were experiencing disproportionately both the adverse consequences of the crisis and the inability to secure global recovery.

Ministers urged strengthened and more effective international macroeconomic policy co-ordination to sustain global economic recovery and stability, and noted that achieving this will require building both international and domestic resilience. It was agreed on a number of measures to be taken forward within the Commonwealth and the wider international community, to strengthen resilience.

G20

Ministers discussed the role of the G20 in contributing to accelerating global recovery. They noted that the G20, while representing a systemically important group of countries, did not possess all elements of a solution to global recovery. Many solutions were in fact to be found in other developing countries, and the G20 had a key responsibility to ensure that the voices of

those not in the G20 are continuously heard. The Commonwealth was well placed to reflect the views of these countries, particularly the smallest and most vulnerable. The current uncertain economic environment also offered the opportunity to re-examine approaches to sustainable growth and the G20 Development Working Group was well placed to do this.

Ministers noted the continued potential and effectiveness of the Commonwealth as a forum through which consensus on global policy issues can emerge. They commended recent initiatives to progressively strengthen the Commonwealth–G20 relationship, including the Secretary-General's annual consultations with the G20 presidency and technical contributions to the G20 Development Working Group. Ministers supported the pursuit of a more systematic and effective interaction between Commonwealth members and non-members of the G20 and considered options to further strengthen this collaboration, in order to improve the formulation, development and implementation of global economic policy. They urged the Secretariat to undertake continued work in pursuit of this and welcomed the close co-operation between the Commonwealth and the Organisation Internationale de la Francophonie (OIF) in strengthening relations with the G20.

Ministers welcomed the Commonwealth Secretary-General's forthcoming meeting, together with the Secretary-General of the Francophonie, with the President of the Republic of France in his capacity as 2011 G20 President and Chair of the forthcoming G20 Cannes summit.

Aid effectiveness

Ministers considered how aid can be more effectively delivered within a cohesive system of development finance. They acknowledged that important progress had been achieved in strengthening aid effectiveness in recent years, which has contributed to better development results. At the same time, they pointed to the need for further substantial reform and in this regard recognised the importance of the forthcoming fourth High Level Forum (HLF-4) in Busan, Korea, on aid effectiveness. They also agreed that it is crucial that developed countries meet their aid commitments. The Commonwealth has a unique depth and breadth of experience in aid, with a substantial number of aid recipients and a growing number of aid donors. Ministers agreed that this feature enables the Commonwealth to offer a number of valuable and detailed recommendations to the international community, for improving the effectiveness of aid, and in so doing, accelerating development.

Ministers discussed and endorsed a Commonwealth Statement on Accelerating Development with More Effective Aid. The statement identifies Commonwealth consensus and sets out Commonwealth recommendations on a selected number of aid effectiveness issues, which can contribute to the success of the HLF-4 meeting and to building a more effective international system of aid. Commonwealth recommendations focus on: transparency; increased use of country systems; risk management; climate finance; mutual accountability; non-DAC actors; and the post-Busan architecture.

Ministers commended these recommendations to Commonwealth Heads of Government for their attention at their forthcoming meeting in Perth, Australia. Ministers requested the Commonwealth Secretary-General to promptly convey the

Statement to the Chair of the Working Party on Aid Effectiveness and to other relevant international agencies involved in the preparation of the HLF-4. They agreed that Commonwealth members will press for the achievement of these core recommendations in the run-up to and at HLF-4.

Ministers emphasised the importance of ensuring that all efforts to support development are complementary and have a transformative impact on development outcomes within a more cohesive framework of development finance. They recognised that aid and other forms of development finance have become increasingly complex and more fragmented, pointing to the need for a more cohesive and 'joined-up' approach to development. Ministers encouraged the Secretariat to pursue further examination of how these challenges are impacting effectiveness in Commonwealth developing country members.

Ministers noted that a new approach to effective development partnerships is emerging, characterised by increased South–South co-operation, increased contribution to aid and development finance by emerging markets, and a greater sharing of responsibility by developing countries themselves in promoting their development, including through creating new investment opportunities and identifying new financing instruments for development. Ministers urged that this process continue and recognised that the Commonwealth had an important role to play in this regard.

Innovative finance for development

Ministers shared their experiences in both providing and utilising existing sources of innovative finance for development (IFD). They recognised that securing additional, new and innovative finance for development is crucial for the developing country members of the Commonwealth as they strive to achieve the MDG targets by 2015, secure adequate climate finance for adaptation and mitigation, and address their wide-ranging development challenges including infrastructure development. Ministers also recognised that the current global environment poses significant challenges in securing this outcome. Ministers offered a number of suggestions and recommendations – regarding content, principles for IFD, sharing of knowledge, information and best-practice, as well as on monitoring – for the Commonwealth in its advocacy to the broader international community.

Ministers urged the Secretariat to pursue a programme of work to widen the sharing of experience and knowledge within the Commonwealth, on current and potential future sources of innovative finance for development.

They welcomed a report from the senior officials meeting; endorsed recommendations for further Commonwealth work on aid effectiveness, South–South co-operation and mobilising domestic capital for investment; and agreed that future meetings of the Commonwealth Ministerial Debt Sustainability Forum would take place as required.

New practical Commonwealth initiatives

Ministers welcomed the imminent operationalisation of the 'Commonwealth Connects' internet gateway and recognised the opportunities this portal offers to a variety of actors and communities of practice in member states in transmitting knowledge and creating prospects of partnerships.

Ministers welcomed the initiatives to advance financial inclusion and entrepreneurship amongst women and the burgeoning population of youth in Commonwealth countries.

Ministers noted that this 2011 meeting represented the second in an experimental sequence of three annual meetings to take place at the location of the Annual World Bank/IMF meetings. They welcomed the Commonwealth Secretariat's continued efforts to respond to ministers' calls for a focused and streamlined agenda. Ministers asked the Secretariat to evaluate members' views on progress to date, and to provide a report at their 2012 meeting, setting out recommendations for the location, duration and content of future meetings.

Introducing the Commonwealth

The Commonwealth is an association of sovereign nations that support each other and work together towards international goals. It is also a 'family' of peoples. With their common heritage in language, culture, law, education and democratic traditions, among other things, Commonwealth countries are able to work together in an atmosphere of greater trust and understanding than generally prevails among nations. At the start of 2012, there were 54 member countries in the Commonwealth.

However, the Commonwealth has no formal constitutional structure. It works from understood procedures, traditions and periodic statements of belief or commitment to action. Intergovernmental consultation is its main source of direction, enabling member governments to collaborate to influence world events, and setting up programmes carried out bilaterally or by the Commonwealth Secretariat, the association's main executive agency. The most widely used definition of the Commonwealth is taken from the Declaration of Commonwealth Principles, 1971:

> The Commonwealth is a voluntary association of independent sovereign states ... consulting and co-operating in the common interests of their peoples and in the promotion of international understanding and world peace.

A voluntary association ...

The Commonwealth has no charter and membership is entirely voluntary. And of nations eligible to join, very few chose not to do so. This distinguishing characteristic has been of considerable historic importance: when countries had recently achieved their independence from the UK, it was important for them to stress the change in their relationship, from dependent status to equal partnership. The emphasis on equality has helped the association to play leading roles in decolonisation, combating racism and advancing sustainable development in poor countries.

... of sovereign states ...

Only independent countries are members of the Commonwealth, although member countries' overseas territories and associated states – mainly small island developing countries in the Caribbean and the Pacific – are eligible for assistance and may take part in certain activities. Some of them contribute to the Commonwealth's development funds. The restriction of membership to sovereign states has helped to retain the sense of equal partnership in the forums in which Commonwealth policy and programmes are discussed.

... consulting ...

Commonwealth consultation is a continuous process which takes place at many levels and in many ways. Heads of Government meet regularly. So do ministers responsible for education, environment, finance, foreign affairs, gender affairs, health, law and youth. Other ministers and senior officials meet from time to time. Consultation over particular Commonwealth programmes brings together the heads of leading institutions and policy-making officials. These regular discussions and meetings ensure that Commonwealth policies and programmes represent the views of the members and also give Commonwealth governments an understanding of each other's problems.

... and co-operating ...

The work of the Commonwealth is done through co-operation, at three general levels:

- Commonwealth governments often work together in international forums to advance causes of particular concern to the association.

- They also learn from each other through their regular meetings.

- And, through their Commonwealth Fund for Technical Co-operation (CFTC), they have enabled the skills and training facilities of member countries to be shared across the association.

In parallel with these activities of governments, there is the work of some 100 Commonwealth organisations which promote international co-operation in a particular professional, cultural or welfare area.

... in the common interests of their peoples ...

The Commonwealth is a notable force in the development of universal education, just legal systems, fair and open democracies, good governance and human rights, and all Commonwealth programmes aim ultimately at advancing development, particularly human development.

Commonwealth governments also work together in international forums to support members whose territorial integrity has been challenged or which are vulnerable to the vicissitudes of climate and global economic forces.

28 October 2011: Middar Dance Troupe at the Opening Ceremony of CHOGM 2011 at the Perth Convention and Entertainment Centre in Perth, Australia (© Annaliese McDonough / Commonwealth Secretariat)

... and in the promotion of international understanding and world peace

The Commonwealth includes many of the world's poorest and smallest countries, and its peoples embrace all the world's major racial groups. The Commonwealth is also committed to the solution of problems by negotiation, and to the guidance of policy through principle. It strongly supports the United Nations system and the global moral code contained in the UN declarations. Consequently, the Commonwealth has become a powerful voice in international forums, and has come to be known as:

- a global opponent of racism

- a promoter of democracy and good governance

- an advocate of human rights and gender equality

- a champion of small countries and participation of young people in development, and

- a determined negotiator in working towards global economic systems which give a fairer deal to the poor.

History of the Commonwealth

The Commonwealth has been described as an organism that could evolve, but could not have been constructed from a blueprint. This distinguishes it from the United Nations, built around its charter in the conscious endeavour to establish universally recognised standards for international conduct.

Unlike other international official organisations, the character of the Commonwealth is less markedly that of an alliance or contractual arrangement as of a family. Many Commonwealth presidents and prime ministers, and its Head, Her Majesty Queen Elizabeth II, have drawn attention to this feeling of family. Like a family, the Commonwealth exists because its members feel they have a natural connection of long standing. Its work for development has been possible because the Commonwealth connection was already there.

Members see the connection as natural because they have a shared past, a common language and, despite their differences, an enhanced capacity to trust one another. They have used this link to strengthen each other's development, and to work in partnership to advance global agreement over crucial issues such as trade, debt, gender equality, the environment, the threat of terrorism and the international financial system.

A product of history and foresight

The Commonwealth of today was by no means an inevitable development. It came about through the powerful bonds that developed among leaders and people, notably during the decolonising process and in the early years of the Commonwealth's evolution as an association of sovereign states. The consequences of changes led by Jawaharlal Nehru and Kwame Nkrumah are best known, but there are several such turning points.

Dominion status

In the early nineteenth century, British imperial policy began to soften under pressure for greater self-determination, initially mainly from the British-descended populations of the most advanced colonies. Canada was first to obtain self-government (in the 1840s) and also the first to become a dominion (1867). Dominion status, which allowed self-government and extensive independence in foreign affairs, fundamentally changed the relationship between colony and imperial power. It was perhaps in this spirit that British politician Lord Rosebery, visiting Adelaide in Australia in 1884, called the empire 'a Commonwealth of nations'.

Australia achieved dominion status when its states united as the Commonwealth of Australia in 1901. New Zealand followed in 1907, South Africa in 1910 and the Irish Free State in 1921. The five dominions and India had their own representation in the League of Nations, the forerunner of the UN.

Great Britain and the dominions were characterised in the Balfour Report of 1926 as:

> autonomous communities within the British Empire, equal in status, in no way subordinate one to another in any aspect of their domestic or external affairs, though united by a common allegiance to the Crown, and freely associated as members of the British Commonwealth of Nations.

The Statute of Westminster, passed by the UK parliament in 1931, gave legal recognition to the *de facto* independence of the dominions. The parliaments of Canada, South Africa and the Irish Free State swiftly passed legislation enacting the statute. Australia adopted it in 1942 and New Zealand in 1947. Newfoundland relinquished its dominion status and was incorporated into Canada in 1949.

Republican membership

At the same time, the struggle for self-government was growing in India (then also including Bangladesh and Pakistan). India and Pakistan achieved independence – as dominions and members of the Commonwealth – in 1947, and Sri Lanka followed in 1948.

These events marked a change in direction for the Commonwealth, as these were the first countries where the pressure for independence came from the indigenous populations rather than communities descended mainly from British settlers. This laid the groundwork for the evolution of a multiracial Commonwealth.

Then the Commonwealth faced a constitutional crisis. It was assumed that the association's principal bond would be that all members would have the monarch of the United Kingdom as head of state. India's constituent assembly decided to adopt a republican form of government, yet wished to remain within the Commonwealth. At the Commonwealth Prime Ministers Meeting of 1949, it was agreed that India might remain a member as a republic but accepting the monarch 'as the symbol of the free association of independent member nations and as such Head of the Commonwealth'.

This development opened the way for other countries which adopted republican constitutions (or had a national monarch) to become Commonwealth members. At the start of 2012, 38 of the 54 members did not have Queen Elizabeth II as titular head of state, but all accepted her as Head of the Commonwealth.

Commonwealth Secretary-General Kamalesh Sharma (2nd from right) with former Secretaries-General Don McKinnon (left), Emeka Anyaoku (2nd left) and Sonny Ramphal (right) at thecommonwealth@60 *ceremony, 27 April 2009, Marlborough House, London, UK*

The Queen is also head of state in 16 Commonwealth countries, all of them fully independent. She is head of each of these states individually. Excluding the UK, the countries of which the Queen is sovereign are now formally known as realms (though the term is, in practice, virtually obsolete) and the Queen is represented by a governor-general who carries out the formal offices of head of state.

Head of the Commonwealth

The Queen's role as Head of the Commonwealth carries no formal functions, but has great symbolic significance and has helped to underline the sense of the Commonwealth as a family of nations. The Queen has laid considerable stress on her role as Head of the Commonwealth, and made a great contribution to the association.

However, when the Queen dies or if she abdicates, her heir will not automatically become Head of the Commonwealth. It will be up to the Commonwealth Heads of Government to decide what they want to do about this symbolic role.

This sense of a new Commonwealth was noted by Queen Elizabeth II at her Christmas broadcast from New Zealand in 1953, shortly after her accession to the throne. She said: 'The Commonwealth bears no resemblance to the empires of the past. It is an entirely new conception built on the highest qualities of the spirit of man: friendship, loyalty, and the desire for freedom and peace.'

The Queen's role now includes, by developing tradition, a number of symbolic functions that enhance the sense of family and the

vitality of the Commonwealth connection. She holds discussions with Commonwealth leaders, in national capitals and in London, and during Heads of Government Meetings. She visits the host country during each summit, meeting the leaders in individual audience and at larger formal functions. Her state visits have included most Commonwealth countries – not only those in which she is head of state – meeting the people as well as leaders. She delivers a Commonwealth Day broadcast and is present at other Commonwealth Day events including the multifaith observance at Westminster Abbey and the Commonwealth Secretary-General's reception.

Wind of change

The Gold Coast, in West Africa, became independent as the Republic of Ghana and joined the Commonwealth in 1957, the first majority-ruled African country to join. This marked the start of a new development, what UK Prime Minister Harold Macmillan called 'the wind of change sweeping through Africa'. Over the next two decades, the UK's rule ended in many parts of Africa, Asia, the Caribbean, the Mediterranean and the Pacific. Commonwealth membership expanded rapidly.

Malaya (later incorporated into Malaysia) also achieved independence in 1957, followed by Nigeria and Cyprus (1960), Sierra Leone and Tanzania (1961), Jamaica, Trinidad and Tobago, and Uganda (1962) and so on. The vast majority of countries coming to independence chose to join the Commonwealth. With South Africa's readmission after the elections of 1994, membership

HM Queen Elizabeth II with Commonwealth leaders at the 1962 Commonwealth Prime Ministers' Meeting, 10–19 September, London, UK

rose to 51 countries. Cameroon, independent since 1960, joined in October 1995 and Mozambique, which had long expressed a desire to join the association and had been connected with it throughout the long Southern African struggle for racial equality, was admitted to membership in November 1995. Rwanda joined the Commonwealth in November 2009 as its newest and 54th member.

A few countries did not join. Myanmar (then Burma, independent 1947) chose not to join, and Ireland withdrew in 1949. A number of mainly Middle Eastern countries – former UK dependencies, mandates, protectorates or protected states – elected not to join the Commonwealth on independence. Maldives became independent in 1965 but did not join the association until 1982. Samoa (formerly a UN Trust Territory administered by New Zealand) became independent in 1962, but did not join until 1970.

Three countries left the Commonwealth and then rejoined. Pakistan left in 1972, after other members recognised the new state of Bangladesh (previously part of Pakistan), but was welcomed back into the association in 1989 when the democratically elected government applied to rejoin.

South Africa's membership lapsed in 1961. Having become a republic it was required to make a formal reapplication for membership. The Commonwealth's resistance to the apartheid policies of the government of the time made it clear that this would not be granted and so South Africa withdrew. Following the democratic elections of 1994, South Africa, too, was welcomed back into the association, and rejoined on 1 June 1994.

Fiji ceased to be a member in 1987: following a military coup and the declaration of a republic, Fiji allowed its membership to lapse

when it too received little encouragement from other members to reapply. Ten years later and after embarking on a process of constitutional reform, the country once again became a member in October 1997.

Nigeria, a member of the Commonwealth since independence in 1960 and an active participant in many important initiatives, was suspended from membership in November 1995 when Heads of Government decided it had violated the principles of the 1991 Harare Declaration. The suspension was initially for two years. The Commonwealth Ministerial Action Group (CMAG) monitored developments in Nigeria (and The Gambia and Sierra Leone) from 1995. In mid-1998, with the accession of a new head of state, Nigeria embarked on a transition programme towards a civilian democracy. After completing its electoral timetable in early 1999, its suspension from the Commonwealth was lifted with the swearing in on 29 May 1999 of a democratically elected civilian president.

Three members – Fiji, Pakistan and Zimbabwe – have each in recent years been suspended from the councils of the association, pending restoration of democracy in accordance with the constitution. Fiji's suspension was lifted in December 2001 but then imposed again in December 2006 following overthrow of the democratically elected government by the military. In July 2009, CMAG noted that Fiji's situation had deteriorated strikingly with the purported abrogation of its constitution and further entrenchment of authoritarian rule. The Group also expressed grave concern at the regime's intention to further delay a return to democracy by more than five years. Fiji was fully suspended from the Commonwealth on 1 September 2009. Pakistan's suspension was lifted in May 2004 but reimposed in November 2007 after a meeting of the CMAG in Kampala pending the restoration of democracy and the rule of law. This second suspension of Pakistan from the councils of the Commonwealth was lifted by CMAG at its next meeting in May 2008. After the Commonwealth Heads of Government Statement on Zimbabwe in December 2003, the Government of Zimbabwe withdrew from the Commonwealth.

Expanding Commonwealth role

While the Commonwealth's membership evolved, its functions have evolved in parallel. In 1965, the Commonwealth Secretariat was set up in London, providing the association with its own administrative capacity to service consultation and other forms of co-operation. The Commonwealth Foundation was also established by Commonwealth leaders in 1965 and started operations the following year, initially to link members of the professions, and subsequently also to support non-governmental organisations and promote Commonwealth culture and arts and, latterly, civil society. Then in 1988 the Commonwealth of Learning (COL) was established to encourage development and sharing of open learning and distance education knowledge, resources and technology.

In 1971, the Commonwealth Fund for Technical Co-operation (CFTC) was launched, establishing the Commonwealth as a channel through which member countries could assist each other in their development. From the start, the CFTC was envisaged not as a capital fund but as a mutual scheme for the exchange of skills. Member countries contribute to it, on a voluntary basis, and may draw on its resources, according to need. The CFTC was an early pioneer of technical co-operation among developing countries, since its finance enables experienced specialists from developing countries to offer their skills to other countries, one or two steps behind them in that area of development. In part through its work in technical co-operation, the Commonwealth developed particular skills in assisting countries in such areas as the advancement of women, protection of the environment and participation of young people in development.

The Commonwealth role in international politics grew from the 1960s. The association became one of the major centres of global pressure against racism, particularly in Rhodesia (Zimbabwe), South Africa and Namibia – countries with a Commonwealth connection.

It has also made an important contribution to global debates on international economic issues, notably through its expert group reports on subjects such as the world financial and trading systems, and the debt of developing countries. These reports were prepared by groups of specialists from rich and poor countries in different parts of the world, and represented a consensus between North and South on the way to make progress in these global debates.

Especially since the adoption of the Harare Commonwealth Declaration by Heads of Government in October 1991, and further reinforced with the Trinidad and Tobago Affirmation of November 2009, the Commonwealth has attached considerable importance to the promotion of democracy.

The four main ways in which the Commonwealth Secretariat has helped has been by:

- observing elections

- providing democracy experts on request

- organising workshops, and

- producing publications.

Since 1990 the Commonwealth has observed some 100 elections and demand for the presence of a Commonwealth team to observe an election continues unabated. In 2011, the Commonwealth deployed teams to nine elections: Cameroon, The Gambia, Guyana, Maldives, Nigeria, St Lucia, Seychelles, Uganda and Zambia. The Secretariat has also organised a major series of workshops with attendant publications, for chief election officers, leaders of political parties and civil society. Additionally, since 1995, the Commonwealth has had a self-disciplinary mechanism, through the Millbrook Programme and the Commonwealth Ministerial Action Group, to deal with 'serious or persistent violations' of the principles contained in the Harare Declaration.

The Commonwealth has also embarked on a programme of assisting member countries in economic development through, for example, reform of the public sector, encouragement of the growth of the private sector, and promotion of trade and investment – through the setting up of a Commonwealth Business Council, the Commonwealth Private Investment Initiative, and the Trade and Investment Access Facility.

The Commonwealth and its members

The Commonwealth had 54 member countries as at the start of 2012. Although it is an intergovernmental organisation, with countries as its members, it remains very much an association of people, a 'family' of some 2.2 billion people spanning the globe.

Among the Commonwealth's members are rich and poor countries, large and small, and countries on every continent. The association includes the world's second largest countries in terms of population (India) and territory (Canada), and many of the smallest and most remote, among these Nauru and Tuvalu, two of the world's smallest nations. It includes one of the world's driest and most sparsely populated countries (Namibia), and also Guyana, with some of the world's best-conserved tropical forests.

Several of its members are small and isolated island states; others have the opposite disadvantage of being landlocked. The world's first industrialised country (United Kingdom) is a member; so is one of the pioneer 'Asian tigers' (Singapore), and some of the world's rapidly industrialising countries (Malaysia, Mauritius, Trinidad and Tobago).

Also among the Commonwealth's members are some of the world's poorest countries in terms of per capita GNI (Malawi, Sierra Leone), and some of the most disadvantaged, notably Bangladesh, Kiribati and Maldives with their vulnerability to flooding as sea level rises.

Commonwealth members are also politically diverse: there are 16 parliamentary monarchies headed by Queen Elizabeth II, five other national monarchies (Brunei Darussalam, Lesotho, Malaysia, Swaziland and Tonga) and 33 republics. The association includes the world's first parliamentary democracy (United Kingdom), its largest democracy (India), the first to extend the franchise to women (New Zealand), and countries which have maintained stable and open democracies during periods of political change and upheaval in their region (Barbados, Botswana). There are countries which have returned to multiparty systems after a generation of one-party rule (Kenya, Malawi, United Republic of Tanzania, Zambia) and countries where military government has voluntarily given way to the ballot box (Ghana, Nigeria). In another, South Africa, democratic government peacefully – and with global rejoicing – replaced one of the world's most hated racist systems.

Through all this diversity, Commonwealth countries have a strong feeling of kinship. The historic link is their common use of the English language and the common culture inherited from their colonial past. This has bequeathed to them similar systems of education, government and law, shared cultural traditions and the sense of belonging to a family of nations. All Commonwealth countries accept Queen Elizabeth II as the symbol of their free association and thus Head of the Commonwealth.

The apex of the association's activities is the two-yearly Commonwealth Heads of Government Meeting (CHOGM), where the policy and programmes of the Commonwealth are decided. Most programmes are executed by the Commonwealth Secretariat, based in London and led by a Secretary-General (see the profile of the Commonwealth Secretariat in the section titled 'Official Commonwealth Organisations'). The Commonwealth has no constitution or charter, but members commit themselves to the statements of belief set out by Heads of Government. The basis of these is the Declaration of Commonwealth Principles, agreed at Singapore in 1971 (reproduced in full in the section titled 'CHOGM').

Withdrawals and suspension

Some countries which would have been welcomed into Commonwealth membership – Republic of Ireland, Myanmar and several countries in the Middle East and North-East Africa formerly associated with the United Kingdom as dependencies, mandated territories or protected states – chose not to apply. Samoa, Maldives and Cameroon joined some years after gaining independence.

Three countries left the Commonwealth but have since returned to membership. South Africa withdrew in 1961 when it became clear that its reapplication for membership on becoming a republic would be rejected. After the democratic elections of 1994, South Africa was welcomed back into the association.

Pakistan left in 1972, when other member countries recognised Bangladesh, and returned after the democratic elections of 1989. However, following the overthrow of the democratically elected government in October 1999, the country was suspended from the councils of the Commonwealth pending the restoration of democracy. This suspension was lifted in May 2004, but reimposed in November 2007 after a meeting of the Commonwealth Ministerial Action Group (CMAG) in Kampala pending the restoration of democracy and the rule of law. CMAG met again on 12 May 2008 and agreed that the Government of Pakistan had taken positive steps to fulfil its obligations in accordance with Commonwealth fundamental values and principles; it accordingly decided to restore Pakistan to the councils of the Commonwealth.

Fiji's membership lapsed in 1987, after a military coup imposed a constitution contrary to Commonwealth principles, and returned to membership in October 1997, when it had embarked on constitutional reform. Then following overthrow of the democratically elected government in May 2000, the country was suspended from the councils of the Commonwealth. Suspension was lifted in December 2001 when democracy and the rule of law

Commonwealth Secretary-General Kamalesh Sharma (right) with Indian Vice-President Mohammad Hamid Ansari at CHOGM 2011 (© Annaliese McDonough / Commonwealth Secretariat)

had been restored in accordance with the constitution, but was then imposed again in December 2006 when the democratically elected government was again overthrown by the military. In May 2008 CMAG reiterated that it was essential that elections be held by the deadline of March 2009, as agreed between the Pacific Islands Forum and Fiji's interim government. Elections did not, however, take place and CMAG subsequently deplored the fact that Fiji remained in contravention of Commonwealth values and principles.

At the end of July 2009, CMAG noted that Fiji's situation had deteriorated strikingly with the purported abrogation of its constitution and further entrenchment of authoritarian rule. It also expressed grave concern at the regime's intention to further delay a return to democracy by more than five years. Fiji was fully suspended from the Commonwealth on 1 September 2009 (only the second such case of suspension of a country's membership – Nigeria being the first in 1995). The Commonwealth Secretariat has nonetheless remained engaged with Fiji to support and promote inclusive political dialogue and the return to civilian constitutional democracy.

No country has formally been expelled, but in November 1995, Commonwealth Heads of Government took the then unprecedented step of suspending the membership of one of its members – Nigeria. This suspension was lifted on 29 May 1999 with the swearing in to office of a democratically elected civilian president.

One country, Zimbabwe, which had been a member since independence in April 1980, was suspended from Commonwealth councils in March 2002, following the presidential election, which was marred by a high level of politically motivated violence and during which the conditions did not adequately allow for a free expression of will by the electors. Then in December 2003, following the CHOGM Statement on Zimbabwe, the Government of Zimbabwe withdrew from the Commonwealth.

Membership criteria

All member states, except for Mozambique (which joined in 1995) and now Rwanda (which joined in 2009), have experienced direct or indirect British rule or been linked administratively to another Commonwealth country. At the 1997 summit in Edinburgh, Heads of Government considered the criteria for Commonwealth membership and agreed that in order to become a member of the Commonwealth, an applicant country should, as a rule, have had a constitutional association with an existing Commonwealth member state; that it should comply with Commonwealth values, principles and priorities as set out in the Harare Commonwealth Declaration of 1991; and that it should accept Commonwealth norms and conventions.

At the 2005 summit in Malta, aware of a growing interest in the Commonwealth from many countries, including outstanding applications to join, Heads of Government mandated a Committee on Commonwealth Membership that would prepare a report on the various issues of membership for the next CHOGM in Kampala, Uganda, in 2007. The committee – chaired by P J Patterson, former prime minister of Jamaica – met twice (in December 2006 and May 2007) prior to submitting its report to Commonwealth leaders for their consideration. Heads of Government subsequently set out their agreed 'core criteria' for membership in the Kampala Communiqué (see the box on this page).

The application of the Republic of Rwanda for membership of the Commonwealth was considered by Heads of Government in Port of Spain, Trinidad and Tobago, in November 2009. This was done in accordance with the criteria and procedures agreed at their meeting in Kampala in 2007. At the end of their deliberations, they warmly welcomed Rwanda into the Commonwealth family as its 54th member.

In October 2011 the Republic of South Sudan expressed an interest in joining the Commonwealth. An ongoing informal assessment of the approach is being undertaken followed by consultation with member states; this process could last as long as two years.

Associated states and overseas territories

Commonwealth membership is confined to sovereign countries, but self-governing states linked to member countries and overseas territories of member countries are eligible to take part in many activities and to receive technical assistance. Some of them contribute to Commonwealth funds and programmes. Representatives of such territories do from time to time attend ministerial meetings as part of the delegation of the member government to which they are linked.

The peoples of these states are regarded as part of the Commonwealth family. Their numbers total about 260,000 people. The associated states and overseas territories are as follows.

Australian External Territories: Ashmore and Cartier Islands, Australian Antarctic Territory, Christmas Island, Cocos (Keeling) Islands, Coral Sea Islands Territory, Heard Island and the McDonald Islands, and Norfolk Island.

Self-governing Countries in Free Association with New Zealand: Cook Islands and Niue.

New Zealand External Territories: The Ross Dependency and Tokelau.

UK Overseas Territories: Anguilla, Bermuda, British Antarctic Territory, British Indian Ocean Territory, British Virgin Islands, Cayman Islands, Falkland Islands, Gibraltar, Montserrat, Pitcairn Islands, St Helena and dependencies (Ascension, Tristan da Cunha), South Georgia and the South Sandwich Islands, and Turks and Caicos Islands.

Extract from the 2007 Kampala Communiqué ...

... on the core criteria for Commonwealth membership

Heads of Government reviewed the recommendations of the Committee on Commonwealth Membership and agreed on the following core criteria for Membership:

(a) an applicant country should, as a general rule, have had a historic constitutional association with an existing Commonwealth member, save in exceptional circumstances

(b) in exceptional circumstances, applications should be considered on a case-by-case basis

(c) an applicant country should accept and comply with Commonwealth fundamental values, principles, and priorities as set out in the 1971 Declaration of Commonwealth Principles and contained in other subsequent Declarations

(d) an applicant country must demonstrate commitment to: democracy and democratic processes, including free and fair elections and representative legislatures; the rule of law and independence of the judiciary; good governance, including a well-trained public service and transparent public accounts; and protection of human rights, freedom of expression, and equality of opportunity

(e) an applicant country should accept Commonwealth norms and conventions, such as the use of the English language as the medium of inter-Commonwealth relations, and acknowledge Queen Elizabeth II as the Head of the Commonwealth, and

(f) new members should be encouraged to join the Commonwealth Foundation, and to promote vigorous civil society and business organisations within their countries, and to foster participatory democracy through regular civil society consultations.

Heads of Government also agreed that, where an existing member changes its formal constitutional status, it should not have to reapply for Commonwealth membership provided that it continues to meet all the criteria for membership.

Heads endorsed the other recommendations of the Committee, including a four-step process for considering applications for membership; new members being required to augment the existing budget of the Secretariat; and countries in accumulated arrears being renamed 'Members in Arrears'. They also agreed with the Committee's recommendations on Overseas Territories, Special Guests and strategic partnerships.

Member Country (Capital)	Population ('000) 2010	Status	Head of State/Governor-General	Head of Government
Antigua and Barbuda (St John's)	89	M	G-G: HE Mrs Louise Lake-Tack	PM: The Hon Baldwin Spencer
Australia (Canberra)	22,268	M	G-G: HE Ms Quentin Bryce	PM: The Hon Julia Gillard
The Bahamas (Nassau)	343	M	G-G:HE Sir Arthur Foulkes	PM: The Rt Hon Hubert Alexander Ingraham
Bangladesh (Dhaka)	148,692	R	P: HE Mr Zillur Rahman	PM: The Hon Sheikh Hasina
Barbados (Bridgetown)	273	M	G-G: HE Mr Elliot Belgrave (acting)	PM: The Hon Freundel Stuart
Belize (Belmopan)	312	M	G-G: HE Sir Colville Norbert Young Sr	PM: The Hon Dean Oliver Barrow
Botswana (Gaborone)	2,007	RE	P: HE Lt-Gen Seretse Khama Ian Khama	The President
Brunei Darussalam (Bandar Seri Begawan)	399	M*	HM Paduka Seri Baginda Sultan Haji Hassanal Bolkiah Mu'izzaddin Waddaulah	The Sultan
Cameroon (Yaoundé)	19,599	RE	P: HE Mr Paul Biya	PM: The President
Canada (Ottawa)	34,017	M	G-G: HE The Rt Hon David Johnston	PM: The Rt Hon Stephen Harper
Cyprus (Nicosia)	1,104	RE	P: HE Mr Demetris Christofias	The President
Dominica (Roseau)	68	R	P: HE Dr Nicholas Liverpool	PM: The Hon Roosevelt Skerrit
Fiji (Suva)[1]	861	R	P: HE Ratu Epeli Nailatikau	PM: Commodore Voreqe Bainimarama
The Gambia (Banjul)	1,728	RE	P: HE Sheikh Professor Alhaji Dr Yahya Jammeh	The President
Ghana (Accra)	24,392	RE	P: HE Professor John Evans Atta Mills	The President
Grenada (St George's)	104	M	G-G: HE Sir Carlyle Arnold Glean	PM: The Hon Tillman Thomas
Guyana (Georgetown)	754	RE	P: HE Mr Donald Ramotar	The President
India (New Delhi)	1,224,614	R	P: HE Mrs Pratibha Patil	PM: The Hon Dr Manmohan Singh
Jamaica (Kingston)	2,741	M	G-G: HE The Most Hon Sir Patrick Linton Allen	PM: The Most Hon Portia Simpson Miller
Kenya (Nairobi)	40,513	RE	P: HE Mr Mwai Kibaki	The President
Kiribati (Tarawa)	100	RE	P: HE Mr Anote Tong	The President
Lesotho (Maseru)	2,171	M*	HM King Letsie III	PM: The Rt Hon Bethuel Pakalitha Mosisili
Malawi (Lilongwe)	14,901	RE	P: HE Ms Joyce Hilda Banda	The President
Malaysia (Kuala Lumpur)	28,401	M*	HM Yang di-Pertuan Agong XIV Tuanku Alhaj Abdul Halim Mu'adzam Shah ibni Al-Marhum Sultan Badlishah	PM: The Hon Dato' Sri Mohd Najib bin Tun Haji Abdul Razak
Maldives (Malé)	316	RE	P: HE Dr Mohamed Waheed	The President
Malta (Valletta)	417	R	P: HE Dr George Abela	PM: The Hon Dr Lawrence Gonzi
Mauritius (Port Louis)	1,299	R	P: HE The Rt Hon Sir Anerood Jugnauth	PM: The Hon Dr Navinchandra Ramgoolam
Mozambique (Maputo)	23,391	RE	P: HE Mr Armando Emilio Guebuza	The President
Namibia (Windhoek)	2,283	RE	P: HE Mr Hifikepunye Pohamba	The President
Nauru (Nauru)	10	RE	P: HE Mr Sprent Dabwido	The President
New Zealand (Wellington)	4,368	M	G-G: HE Lt-Gen the Rt Hon Sir Jerry Mateparae	PM: The Hon John Key
Nigeria (Abuja)	158,423	RE	P: HE Dr Goodluck Ebele Jonathan	The President
Pakistan (Islamabad)	173,593	R	P: HE Mr Asif Ali Zardari	PM: The Hon Syed Yousaf Raza Gilani
Papua New Guinea (Port Moresby)	6,858	M	G-G: HE Sir Michael Ogio	PM: The Hon Peter O'Neill
Rwanda (Kigali)	10,624	RE	P: HE Mr Paul Kagame	The President
St Kitts and Nevis (Basseterre)	52	M	G-G: HE Sir Cuthbert Montraville Sebastian	PM: The Hon Dr Denzil Llewellyn Douglas
St Lucia (Castries)	174	M	G-G: HE Dame Pearlette Louisy	PM: The Hon Dr Kenny Anthony
St Vincent and the Grenadines (Kingstown)	109	M	G-G: HE Sir Frederick Ballantyne	PM: The Hon Dr Ralph Everard Gonsalves
Samoa (Apia)	183	R	HH Tuiatua Tupua Tamasese Efi	PM: The Hon Tuilaepa Lupesoliai Sailele Malielegaoi
Seychelles (Victoria)	87	RE	P: HE Mr James Alix Michel	The President
Sierra Leone (Freetown)	5,868	RE	P: HE Mr Ernest Bai Koroma	The President
Singapore (Singapore)	5,086	R	P: HE Dr Tony Tan Keng Yam	PM: The Hon Lee Hsien Loong
Solomon Islands (Honiara)	538	M	G-G: HE Sir Frank Ofagioro Kabui	PM: The Hon Gordon Darcy Lilo
South Africa (Tshwane, formerly Pretoria)	50,133	RE	P: HE Mr Jacob Gedleyihlekisa Zuma	The President
Sri Lanka (Colombo)	20,860	RE	P: HE Mr Mahinda Rajapaksa	The President
Swaziland (Mbabane)	1,186	M*	HM King Mswati III	PM: The Hon Dr Sibusiso Barnabas Dlamini
Tonga (Nuku'alofa)	104	M*	HM King Tupou VI	PM: The Hon Lord Siale'ataonga Tu'ivakano
Trinidad and Tobago (Port of Spain)	1,341	R	P: HE Professor George Maxwell Richards	PM: The Hon Kamla Persad-Bissessar
Tuvalu (Funafuti)	10	M	G-G: HE Sir Iakoba Italeli	PM: The Hon Willy Telavi
Uganda (Kampala)	33,425	RE	P: HE Mr Yoweri Kaguta Museveni	The President

➤

Member Countries' Heads of State and Government

Member Country (Capital)	Population ('000) 2010	Status	Head of State/Governor-General	Head of Government
United Kingdom (London)	62,036	M	HM Queen Elizabeth II	PM: The Rt Hon David Cameron
United Republic of Tanzania (Dodoma)	44,841	RE	P: HE Mr Jakaya Mrisho Kikwete	The President
Vanuatu (Port Vila)	240	R	P: HE Mr Iolu Johnson Abbil	PM: The Hon Sato Kilman
Zambia (Lusaka)	13,089	RE	P: HE Mr Michael Sata	The President
Commonwealth	**2,191,395**			

Abbreviations: G-G Governor-General; HE His/Her Excellency; HH, HM His/Her Highness/Majesty; M Monarchy under HM Queen Elizabeth II; M* National Monarchy; P President; PM Prime Minister; R Republic; RE Republic with Executive President.

¹ *Currently suspended from membership of the Commonwealth*

Commonwealth Members

Member Country	Joined Commonwealth
Antigua and Barbuda	1981
Australia	1931 (Statute of Westminster*)
The Bahamas	1973
Bangladesh	1972
Barbados	1966
Belize	1981
Botswana	1966
Brunei Darussalam	1984
Cameroon	1995 (independent 1960)
Canada	1931 (Statute of Westminster*)
Cyprus	1961 (independent 1960)
Dominica	1978
Fiji	1970 (left in 1987, rejoined in 1997**)
The Gambia	1965
Ghana	1957
Grenada	1974
Guyana	1966
India	1947
Jamaica	1962
Kenya	1963
Kiribati	1979
Lesotho	1966
Malawi	1964
Malaysia	1957
Maldives	1982 (independent 1965)
Malta	1964
Mauritius	1968
Mozambique	1995 (independent 1975)
Namibia	1990
Nauru	1968
New Zealand	1931 (Statute of Westminster*)

Member Country	Joined Commonwealth
Nigeria	1960 (suspended 1995–99)
Pakistan	1947 (left in 1972, rejoined in 1989)
Papua New Guinea	1975
Rwanda	2009 (independent 1962)
St Kitts and Nevis	1983
St Lucia	1979
St Vincent and the Grenadines	1979
Samoa	1970 (independent 1962)
Seychelles	1976
Sierra Leone	1961
Singapore	1965
Solomon Islands	1978
South Africa	1931 (Statute of Westminster*, left in 1961, rejoined in 1994)
Sri Lanka	1948
Swaziland	1968
Tonga	1970
Trinidad and Tobago	1962
Tuvalu	1978
Uganda	1962
United Kingdom	
United Republic of Tanzania	1961
Vanuatu	1980
Zambia	1964

* *The Statute of Westminster of 1931 gave effective independence to the dominions of Australia, Canada, New Zealand and South Africa.*

** *Suspended from the councils of the Commonwealth in December 2006 and subsequently suspended from membership of the Commonwealth in September 2009.*

Commonwealth Secretariat

The Commonwealth Secretariat, established in 1965, is the main intergovernmental agency of the Commonwealth, facilitating consultation and co-operation among member governments and countries. It is responsible to member governments collectively. The programmes with which the Secretariat is currently involved are outlined in this text – the Secretariat's new Strategic Plan will be announced in mid-2012.

Based in London, UK, the Secretariat organises Commonwealth summits, meetings of ministers, consultative meetings and technical discussions; it assists policy development and provides policy advice, and facilitates multilateral communication among the member governments. It also provides technical assistance to help governments in the social and economic development of their countries and in support of the Commonwealth's fundamental political values.

The Secretariat is headed by the Commonwealth Secretary-General who is elected by Heads of Government for no more than two four-year terms. The two Deputy Secretaries-General and one Assistant Secretary-General – who serve for a maximum of two three-year terms – support the Secretary-General in the management and executive direction of the Secretariat. The present Secretary-General is Kamalesh Sharma, from India, who took office on 1 April 2008, succeeding Sir Donald McKinnon of New Zealand (2000–2008). He is currently in his second term, which began in April 2012. The first Secretary-General was Arnold Smith of Canada (1965–1975), followed by Sir Shridath Ramphal of Guyana (1975–1990) and Chief Emeka Anyaoku (1990–2000).

Secretariat headquarters

The Secretariat has its headquarters at Marlborough House, built in 1709 by Sarah Churchill, first Duchess of Marlborough, on the site given to her by Queen Anne. This royal palace was made available to the Commonwealth by Queen Elizabeth II in 1959. Marlborough

Mission statement

We work as a trusted partner for all Commonwealth people as:

- a force for peace, democracy, equality and good governance

- a catalyst for global consensus-building, and

- a source of assistance for sustainable development and poverty eradication.

House also houses the Commonwealth Foundation, and it and nearby Lancaster House have been the venue of many important Commonwealth conferences.

Funds and finances

The Secretariat and its work are funded by three separate budgets or funds – namely, the Commonwealth Secretariat Fund, the Commonwealth Youth Programme (CYP) Fund, and the Commonwealth Fund for Technical Co-operation (CFTC). The Secretariat and CYP budgets are financed by assessed contributions from member governments. The assessed contributions are primarily based on capacity to pay. The CFTC budget is financed by voluntary contributions from member governments. For 2011/12 the Secretariat's budget is UK£15.85 million, the CFTC budget is UK£31.78 million and the CYP budget is UK£2.98 million.

Funding the CFTC

All contributions to the CFTC are voluntary. The top eight contributors (by receipts) over the last six financial years (to 2010/11) are: Australia, Botswana, Brunei Darussalam, Canada, India, New Zealand, Nigeria and the United Kingdom. Some member countries' overseas territories and associated states also contribute. For various special CFTC projects, contributions have been received from non-Commonwealth governments and voluntary organisations.

Governance arrangements

The Commonwealth Secretariat is headed by the Commonwealth Secretary-General. The Secretary-General is elected by Heads of Government for a maximum of two four-year terms. The two Deputy Secretaries-General and one Assistant Secretary-General – each serving for a maximum of two three-year terms – support the Secretary-General in the management and executive direction of the Secretariat. Around two-thirds of the 54 member countries are currently represented among the staff – 285 permanent staff as well as 27 members of staff on temporary and fixed-term contracts – of the Secretariat (as at the end of 2011).

Under the current strategic plan for the period 2008 to 2012, the work undertaken by the Secretariat is implemented through a framework of eight Programmes. Responsibility for Programme implementation rests with specific divisions and units. This framework approach allows the Secretariat to be 'programme driven' but 'division-led', creating the necessary governance mechanisms to fulfil the priorities of the Commonwealth established in the Harare Declaration in 1991.

Following CHOGM 2002, the Secretariat has a Board of Governors and an Executive Committee. The Chair of the Board of Governors,

Organisational Structure 2011

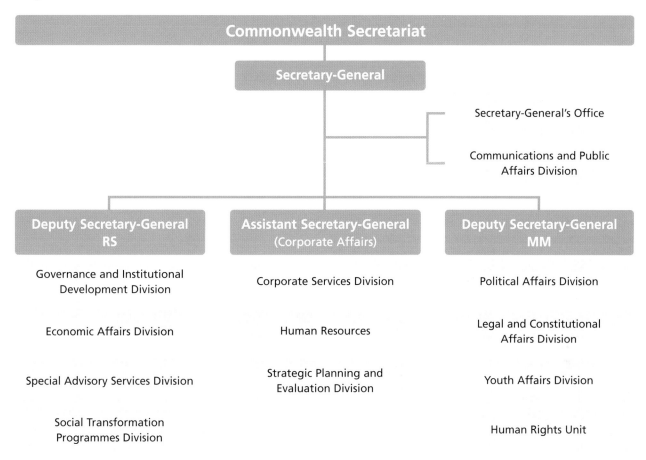

as well as the CHOGM Chair-in-Office, are considered *ex-officio* members of the Committee. All member governments are represented on the Board of Governors, and a 16-member Executive Committee was constituted by the Board in June 2002. These arrangements were intended to further improve efficiency and transparency, as well as to strengthen governments' direction and oversight of the total resources they contribute to Commonwealth activities. The Board of Governors meets annually, and provides strategic direction and reviews the Secretariat's implementation of mandates from Heads of Government as well as approving strategic plans, work programmes and budgets.

The Executive Committee, which is a sub-committee of the Board of Governors, meets every four months, and makes policy recommendations to the Board and oversees budgets and audit functions. The Committee includes the eight largest contributors to the Secretariat's total resources: Australia, Brunei Darussalam, Canada, India, New Zealand, Nigeria, South Africa and the UK. Other member countries are elected to the Executive Committee on a regional basis, to serve two-year terms.

Membership of the Executive Committee 2011 to 2012
The eight largest contributors are:
- United Kingdom
- Canada
- Australia
- India
- New Zealand
- South Africa

- Brunei Darussalam
- Nigeria (Vice-Chair of the Executive Committee).

Regional representatives (final year of two-year term)
The regional representatives are:
- Rwanda
- Bangladesh
- St Lucia (Chair of the Executive Committee)
- Tonga.

Regional representatives (first year of two-year term)
The regional representatives are:
- Zambia
- Maldives
- Guyana
- Papua New Guinea

Ex-Officio
- Sri Lanka (as Chair of the Board of Governors)
- Australia (as CHOGM Chair-in-Office)

Strategic plan 2008/09–2011/12

Executive summary

The Commonwealth Secretariat's Strategic Plan (hereinafter 'the Plan') sets out the overall strategic focus, objectives and expected results of the organisation for the four-year period 2008/09–2011/12. The Plan was approved by the Secretariat's Board of Governors on 15 May 2008, and is the document against which the Board and the Secretariat will measure the progress and impact of its work.

While the Plan reflects the Secretariat's rigorous focus on areas in which it can add value, it also provides, as usual, for some flexibility in programme design and responsiveness in delivery. This flexibility and responsiveness will also give scope to the organisation to respond to new challenges and priorities as they arise, and to maximise its ability to develop innovative solutions. The Plan will be subject to a formal Mid-Term Review.

The Strategic Plan has a stronger focus (than its predecessor) on learning lessons and articulating expected results. While the structure of the last Strategic Plan 2004/05–2007/08 served the organisation well and has thus been largely replicated here, a new section on lessons learned has been included.

The Plan sets out the Secretariat's commitment to adopting a rights-based approach to development, and to mainstreaming gender, youth and human rights concerns throughout all levels of its work: strategic, programmatic, project and operational. These concerns therefore are reflected throughout the Plan.

The Plan sets out eight interlinked Programmes. Each Programme Statement will continue to have a defined objective, and results and indicators. These will reflect the organisation's mainstreaming commitments. The statements will also articulate the Commonwealth's comparative advantage or 'added value' in that Programme.

The Plan reaffirms the Secretariat's focus on the important needs and concerns of small states, and maintains its support for them through activities across the eight Programmes.

The Plan also addresses the important issue of how the Secretariat does its work. It sets out the organisation's ways of working and modes of delivery, and the importance of strategic partnerships, which can enhance impact, extend its reach, and resources, and help realise innovative ideas, is noted. It contains discussions on how the organisation will integrate capacity-building priorities with those of policy analysis and advice, to develop a comprehensive portfolio of assistance.

The Plan has two ongoing and interlinked Goals for the Secretariat reflecting the Commonwealth's emphasis on the promotion of democracy and development.

Goal 1: *To support member countries to prevent or resolve conflicts, strengthen democratic practices and the rule of law, and achieve greater respect for human rights.*

Goal 2: *To support pro-poor policies for economic growth and sustainable development in member countries.*

These two goals establish the framework for the two broad pillars – Democracy and Development – under which the Programme is structured.

Goal 1 (Peace and Democracy) will be achieved through four Programmes:

> *Democracy Pillar – promoting Commonwealth fundamental political values*
> Programme 1 Good Offices for Peace
> Programme 2 Democracy and Consensus-Building
> Programme 3 Rule of Law
> Programme 4 Human Rights

Goal 2 (Pro-Poor Growth and Sustainable Development) will be achieved through four Programmes:

> *Development Pillar – developing national capacity of member countries*
> Programme 5 Public Sector Development
> Programme 6 Economic Development
> Programme 7 Environmentally Sustainable Development
> Programme 8 Human Development

The new, more compact and refocused programme structure reflects, and is designed to support and deliver, the major priorities and mandates guiding the Secretariat's work for the current Plan period, including in particular those deriving from CHOGM.

Each of the eight Programmes has a Programme Statement. Each Statement specifies the Programme objective, results and indicators that guide the form and content of the portfolio and which will be used to measure the performance and progress towards the Plan's Goals.

The Plan establishes for the first time a package of corporate management and business functions that support the Programmes and will ensure the Secretariat operates in an efficient and effective manner.

The Secretariat began the shift to a stronger focus on outcomes and measuring results in the last Strategic Plan (2004/05–2007/08). This Plan (2008/09–2011/12) establishes more firmly the principles and operational framework essential for implementing results-based management.

The Plan outlines the international standards and principles which will inform and guide the design and delivery of the Secretariat's work.

The Plan will be funded by the assessed budget of the Secretariat, the assessed budget of the Commonwealth Youth Programme as well as voluntary contributions to the CYP, and voluntary contributions to the Commonwealth Fund for Technical Co-operation. The revised scale of assessed contributions for the Secretariat, and the new scale of assessed contributions to the CYP, both take effect from the start of the Plan period.

The resources of the CFTC will be used across all eight Programme areas. The Plan treats 'capacity-building and institutional

Divisions and units of the Commonwealth Secretariat

CPAD	Communications and Public Affairs Division		**PAD**	Political Affairs Division
CSD	Corporate Services Division		**SASD**	Special Advisory Services Division
EAD	Economic Affairs Division		**SGO**	Secretary-General's Office
GIDD	Governance and Institutional Development Division		**SPED**	Strategic Planning and Evaluation Division
HR	Human Resources		**STPD**	Social Transformation Programmes Division
HRU	Human Rights Unit		**YAD**	Youth Affairs Division
LCAD	Legal and Constitutional Affairs Division			

Commonwealth Secretariat websites

Commonwealth Secretariat website   **www.thecommonwealth.org**

Short cuts to information about the Secretariat's work

Democracy and Consensus Building	www.thecommonwealth.org/democracy
Economic Development	www.thecommonwealth.org/economics
Education	www.thecommonwealth.org/education
Eminent Persons Group	www.thecommonwealth.org/epg
Environmentally Sustainable Development	www.thecommonwealth.org/environmentallysustainabledevelopment
Gender	www.thecommonwealth.org/gender
Good Offices for Peace	www.thecommonwealth.org/goodofficesforpeace
Governance	www.thecommonwealth.org/governance
Health	www.thecommonwealth.org/health
Human Development	www.thecommonwealth.org/humandevelopment
Human Rights	www.thecommonwealth.org/humanrights
Rule of Law	www.thecommonwealth.org/law
Secretary-General	www.thecommonwealth.org/secretarygeneral
Sport	www.thecommonwealth.org/sport
Youth	www.thecommonwealth.org/cyp
CHOGM	www.thecommonwealth.org/chogm

Other sites

Commonwealth Secretariat Debt Recording and Management System (CS-DRMS)	www.csdrms.org
Commonwealth Connects project site	www.commonwealthconnects.org
Commonwealth Day 2012 theme site	www.commonwealththeme.org
Commonwealth Images	http://images.thecommonwealth.org
Commonwealth (Local Government) Finance Officers Network	http://cfonet.thecommonwealth.org
Commonwealth Secretariat Publications	www.thecommonwealth.org/publications
Commonwealth Secretariat Publications (US site)	www.commonwealthpublications-usa.com
Gender and Trade	www.genderandtrade.org
Young Commonwealth	www.youngcommonwealth.org
Your Commonwealth	www.yourcommonwealth.org

Social media pages

Official Flickr pages	www.flickr.com/photos/comsec
Official Facebook fan page	www.facebook.com/commonwealthsec
Official Twitter page	http://twitter.com/commonwealthsec
Official YouTube channel	www.youtube.com/commonwealthtube

development' as a mode of delivery rather than as a Programme of work (as in the last Plan). The closer integration of the Secretariat's capacity-building activities with its policy formulation and advisory services will improve coherence and sustainability.

CYP resources will be dedicated to meeting the CYP Plan objectives within Programme 8: Human Development. It is assumed that the Secretariat and CYP assessed budgets will increase in line with inflation (zero growth in real terms) and that the CFTC receipts will increase by 6 per cent per annum in real terms for five years, in line with the undertakings of Commonwealth leaders at the 2005 CHOGM.

Programme statements

The Secretariat remains 'at the service of all Commonwealth governments'. The activities of the Secretariat have expanded in response to global changes, international reforms and shifts in the concerns and priorities of members, particularly small and vulnerable economies. However, the primary duties of the Secretariat remain focused on:

- facilitating and promoting consultation and exchanges among member countries

- preparing and disseminating information on issues of concern

- assisting and advancing the development of member countries

- acting as a focal point for specialised Commonwealth institutions

- organising and servicing intergovernmental meetings.

For further information or reference on the eight Programmes and Programme Statements currently in place to meet this mandate, please see the Commonwealth Secretariat website (http://www.thecommonwealth.org/files/182141/FileName/Strategic Plan2008-2012FINAL.pdf). These Programmes will be updated mid-2012 in the new Commonwealth Secretariat Strategic Plan, which will also be available on the Secretariat's website.

Commonwealth Secretariat, London, UK

Commonwealth Secretary-General
Kamalesh Sharma (India)
+44 20 7747 6103

Deputy Secretary-General
Ransford Smith (Jamaica)
+44 20 7747 6118

Deputy Secretary-General
Mmasekgoa Masire-Mwamba (Botswana)
+44 20 7747 6112

Assistant Secretary-General
Stephen Cutts (UK)
+44 20 7747 6354

Director, Communications and Public Affairs (from April 2012)
Richard Uku (Nigeria)
+44 20 7747 6381

Interim Director, Corporate Services
Roderick John Mercer (UK)
+44 20 7747 6140

Director, Economic Affairs
Dr Cyrus Rustomjee (South Africa)
+44 20 7747 6251

Director, Governance and Institutional Development
Max Everest-Phillips (UK)
+44 20 7747 6349

Director, Legal and Constitutional Development
Akbar Khan (UK)
+44 20 7747 6411

Director, Office of the Secretary-General
Simon Gimson (New Zealand)
+44 20 7747 6107

Director, Political Affairs
Amitav Banerji (India)
+44 20 7747 6402

Director, Social Transformation Programmes
Dr Sylvia Anie (Ghana)
+44 20 7747 6460

Director, Special Advisory Services
José Maurel (Mauritius)
+44 20 7747 6301

Director, Strategic Planning and Evaluation
Nabeel Goheer (Pakistan)
+44 20 7747 6236

Director, Youth Affairs
Katherine Ellis (Australia)
+44 20 7747 6463

Head, Human Resources
Monica Oyas (Kenya)
+44 20 7747 6170

Acting Head, Human Rights Unit
Karen McKenzie (South Africa)
+44 20 7747 6121

Commonwealth Foundation, London, UK

Director
Vijay Krishnarayan (Trinidad and Tobago/UK)
+44 20 7747 6570

Commonwealth of Learning, Vancouver, Canada

President and Chief Executive Officer
Sir John Daniel (Canada/UK)
+1 604 775 8200

Vice-President (until 31 May 2012; takes over as President and Chief Executive Officer on 1 June 2012)
Professor Asha Kanwar (India)
+1 604 775 8226

Commonwealth Foundation

Marlborough House, Pall Mall, London SW1Y 5HY, UK

Tel:	+44 20 7930 3783
Fax:	+44 20 7839 8157
Email:	geninfo@commonwealth.int

www.commonwealthfoundation.com

Officers

Chair:	Simone de Comarmond
Director:	Vijay Krishnarayan

The Commonwealth Foundation is an intergovernmental organisation set up almost 50 years ago to make civil society stronger. It works on behalf of the people of the Commonwealth of Nations, a voluntary association today spanning 54 countries, six continents and almost one-third of the world's population.

Established in 1965 and funded principally by Commonwealth governments, the Foundation exists to empower charities, non-governmental organisations, professional associations, trade unions, faith groups and cultural practitioners – the lifeblood of any healthy society. It equips these groups with the tools required to contribute to national and international goals of democracy, good governance, sustainable development and cultural diversity.

The Foundation awards excellence in the arts and helps to influence key policy-makers. It champions, develops and invests in activities that enrich and strengthen society. It acts as a vital resource for Commonwealth people, enabling them to raise their voice, instigate change and fashion a better world.

Grants

The Commonwealth Foundation gives grants to promote dialogue, exchanges and partnerships between Commonwealth peoples. Through its responsive grants and Commonwealth Association grants it aims to give UK£1 million.

In 2011 and again in 2012, the Foundation launched a Special Grants Initiative to promote the Commonwealth theme. In 2012 and in partnership with the United Nations Alliance of Civilizations (UNAOC), the Special Grants Initiative will undertake strategic and innovative projects that will promote 'Connecting Cultures'.

The 'Connecting Cultures' Special Grants Initiative complements the existing Commonwealth Foundation's programmes and grants, and aims to create deeper understanding between different cultures within the Commonwealth.

A sum of UK£100,000 has been made available for the initiative and it is expected that four awards will be made.

Responsive grants

The Foundation's civil society responsive grants are designed to promote international or intercultural exchange, co-operation and sharing of skills, and knowledge and ideas between people from developing Commonwealth countries. Hundreds of non-governmental organisations around the Commonwealth benefit from these grants. They support activities such as short training courses, workshops, conferences, festivals, study visits or voter education activities.

Commonwealth Association annual grants

Around 20 associations accredited to the Commonwealth benefit each year from funding in the form of annual grants. These grants are designed to support those professional membership associations that have limited financial resources.

The Foundation awards annual grants to cover planned activities as well as core costs. Activities that encourage skills transfer and experience sharing between Commonwealth countries are particularly encouraged.

Culture

Commonwealth Writers

Commonwealth Writers sits at the heart of the Commonwealth Foundation's culture programmes. It targets and develops distinctive, emerging voices through online development, on-the-ground activities and two literary prizes: the Commonwealth Book Prize; and the Commonwealth Short Story Prize.

It is a new initiative to inspire, inform and connect fiction writers from all over the world. Members are encouraged to join up to share stories and experiences from their region.

Commonwealth Writers works in partnership with international literary organisations, the wider cultural industries and civil society to help writers develop their craft. With an online writer in residence, interviews with authors and guidance from publishers and industry experts, www.commonwealthwriters.org is also a forum where members can exchange ideas and contribute to debates. The programme will explore what being 'published' means in the twenty-first century. It is particularly interested in how writers can use technology to find a readership in different parts of the world and how they can effectively utilise online publishing networks.

In 2012, Commonwealth Writers will help to shape an equitable and inclusive publishing industry (digital and otherwise) through carrying out research, followed by a debate (streamed online) that brings together key figures from a local, regional and digital publishing industry to debate its future and relevance to our members. It will also be setting up various on-the-ground initiatives to develop and promote writers within their region.

Commonwealth Shorts

The Commonwealth Foundation has embarked on a new project called Commonwealth Shorts. Shorts invites film-makers from across the Commonwealth to submit an idea for a short film about relationships. Individual film-makers or collectives will submit a proposal which explores the theme of love in its broadest sense, whether inter-racial, inter-generational or within and between the sexes. The theme should be relevant to the film-maker and their community.

Commonwealth Connections in 2011

Commonwealth Connections, the artist-in-residence project facilitated by the Commonwealth Foundation, has announced its 2011 winners. The scheme will not run in 2012. The seven winners are as follows.

Ruth Feukoua: installation art, Cameroon

A pioneering artist in her native Cameroon and the first winner from that country, Ruth Feukoua is an installation and performance artist,

Ruth Feukoua, 'Reserved Parking' (2010); installation

whose practice revolves around issues related to the ecology and environment. An activist, whose work is to 'educate consciences', she proposes to undertake a specific project, 'Getting to Green', in Canada. This will merge seeds from Cameroon and Canada in a striking art project promoting nature and the environment.

Olaniyi Rasheed Akindiya (Akirash): installation art, Nigeria

Described as 'one of the most progressive, dedicated and innovative artists of his generation in West Africa' (Carol Padberg, Hartford Arts School, CT, USA), Nigerian-born, Ghana-based Akirash produces mixed media installations bringing disparate objects together in intriguing ways. His work is daring, original and informed by both the world and global contemporary art practices, while remaining true to his West African identity. Akirash's aim on his residency is to work in new media and technology as well as immerse himself in Zulu and Ndebele culture in Southern Africa.

Pradeep Thalawatta: installation art, Sri Lanka

Sri Lankan cutting-edge artist Pradeep Thalawatta marries technical expertise with innovative experimentation to produce sculptural installations, lately incorporating digital video, focusing on issues of social strata and human relationships. A dedicated and committed artist, he is a visiting lecturer at the University of Jaffna and works on community projects with Colombo-based Theerta International Arts Collective amalgamating art, archaeology and heritage management. Thalawatta intends to work on a new urban project in Bangalore, India, with 1 Shanthi Road, an artist-led initiative running an alternative public space in the heart of the city, hosting visiting international artists and exhibitions.

Rodell Warner: photography, Trinidad and Tobago

A photographer and graphic designer who works in Trinidad and Tobago, Rodell Warner's photographs range from images of community-based environmental protection and enhancement programme workers to an exploration between public and private spaces. Filled with energy, creativity and excitement, his photographs provide a specific take on memory and experience.

Often working collaboratively, Warner also creates and executes his own projects, consistently exploring and presenting new conversations about the ways we see ourselves. He plans to travel

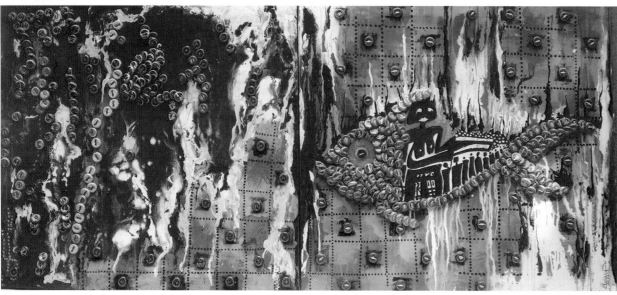

Akirash, 'Across the Sea' (2010); mixed media painting

to South Africa to work alongside the South African photographer Pieter Hugo, as well as engage with the wider artistic community in South Africa.

Emma Wolukau-Wanambwa: installation art, United Kingdom

A graduate from the Slade School of Fine Art in London with an MA in Fine Art, Emma Wolukau-Wanambwa's work is highly original and engaging. Her outstanding grasp of conceptual practice is augmented by technical knowledge. She works with a range of media to explore the stories that we tell ourselves about the world and about one another – looking particularly at representations of the past, and of people, places and events considered 'distant'.

Wolukau-Wanambwa is intending to explore issues of land and land ownership within Uganda and how this is changing, working with artists and film-makers as well as screening artists' films and documentaries and discussions. She wishes to work with moving image and sound, and aims to contribute to development discourse within the UK arts community and beyond.

Meralda Warren: painting, Pitcairn Islands

The first winner from the Pitcairn Islands, Meralda Warren is an innovative and creative artist and teacher. She is leading the rediscovery of the art of tapa-making (which uses the bark of a mulberry tree) on Pitcairn, teaching children and others to carry on

Rodell Warner, 'Closer'

Pradeep Thalawatta, 'City Circle' (2011)

Meralda Warren, Whakatane lino print workshop

Emma Wolukau-Wanambwa, presentation at the Margaret Trowell School of Industrial and Fine Art, Kampala, Uganda, 2011

this tradition, which died out 70 years ago. With the children of Pitcairn she has written a book, *Mi Base side orn Pitcairn* – the first book to be written in Pitkern as well as English.

Working in isolation on Pitcairn, Warren wishes to use the residency to connect with artists and tapa-makers from around the Pacific, based in New Zealand, and to engage with artists who use tapa in their art practice. She hopes this will enrich her ability to pass on knowledge and new techniques to the next generation of Pitcairn Islanders and install pride in their heritage.

Neila-Ann Ebanks: dance, Jamaica

A dancer, choreographer and teacher, Neila-Ann Ebanks works across different forms of dance, including modern, contemporary, jazz and folk. Her strong performance skills are matched with creative thinking and an innovative use of method, style and original conceptualisation, her work being rooted at all times in her

Jamaican ancestry. Improvisation, site-specific and theatre work are all part of her dance experience.

Committed to developing dance in Jamaica during her residency in Canada, Ebanks wishes to explore the use of video, using performing bodies with filmed projections. She will work specifically alongside four diverse Canadian artists in the arena of dance and theatre to enrich and expand the dance scene in Jamaica on her return.

Civil society

Capacity development

Good governance relies on a meaningful dialogue between state and society. The Commonwealth Foundation has a strong track record of delivering high quality and high impact capacity development activities, either by funding and/or delivering training, convening organisations and stakeholders at the governmental, civil society and citizen levels, and by producing materials and resources aimed at strengthening civil society.

Working with national umbrella bodies to increase knowledge and skills of civil society in country, the Foundation supports the development and dissemination of trainings, toolkits and resources to bolster the efforts of local bodies to promote legitimacy, transparency and accountability across the Commonwealth. A key example of this is the work being carried out on production and supporting training on, and dissemination of, six country-specific accountability toolkits representing the range of differing contexts across the Commonwealth. The countries the six toolkits cover are Belize, India, Sierra Leone, Trinidad and Tobago, Uganda, as well as the Pacific region.

Strategic relations

The Commonwealth Foundation's intergovernmental status enables it to influence decisions at policy-making level and provide unparalleled access to members of government at the highest levels.

This access not only allows the Foundation to voice the thoughts, desires and needs of civil society at different venues, but it also provides civil society with important information about the thoughts and direction of the Commonwealth and its member countries.

The civil society programme supports the strengthening of institutional structures of the Commonwealth to allow civil society access to discussions and forums.

The programme works closely with the different Commonwealth bodies and associations, civil society and citizens to shape their messages, and provides, through grant-making and convening, access to the different ministerial and multilateral meetings so that their voices are heard.

In addition, understanding that the Commonwealth is one of many intergovernmental or multilateral organisations, the programme actively works to co-ordinate and influence the work that is undertaken at the regional and international level.

Knowledge generation

The ability to access and utilise up-to-date, well researched and accurate information lies at the core of any organisation's ability to

Neila-Ann Ebanks, 'Stained Soul'; photographer, Tricia Bent

understand what has happened, react to the present and plan for the future.

Within civil society the reality is no different; service delivery organisations need to be able to assess their clients' needs and wants, and be able to develop plans, practices and products accordingly. For advocacy civil society organisations (CSOs), a strong understanding of the past and the present will inform their understanding of the future and what it may hold.

Through strategic priority-setting and grant-making, the civil society programme encourages research to be undertaken, co-ordinates multinational stakeholder involvement, and develops high quality assessments and publications around issues affecting the Commonwealth today – disseminating them widely.

From this research, the Foundation draws direction for its work, policy recommendations and education of national and local partners on current trends and issues to best inform their current work.

Learning exchanges

To fulfil its fullest potential civil society must have leaders who are not only knowledgeable about the issues nationally and internationally and who have the ability to enact change, but who also have the experience to meet and overcome problems as they arise.

This requires that civil society leaders are knowledgeable about the experiences (both positive and negative of all civil society), are equipped with the right tools to deal with new challenges and have the resources to direct change as appropriate.

Through the co-ordination and facilitation of learning exchanges around identified priority areas the Commonwealth Foundation supports the sharing of knowledge and thought leadership for the purpose of creating value and supporting change. The individual

participants are empowered through a suite of workshops, facilitated discussions, and the sharing of expertise and experience of all participating members who contribute ideas and perspectives around thematic issues and areas of common concern and challenge. An example of this is the first Commonwealth Leadership Exchange, which aims to bring together leaders in civil society from across the Commonwealth to drive peer-to-peer learning and make a more effective civil society.

The knowledge, expertise, advice, guidance and case studies provide an invaluable tool that the Foundation captures and publishes, to bolster the work of the wider civil society collective.

Civic education

Worthwhile democratic participation requires a citizenry of informed individuals who understand their rights and responsibilities as members of democratic process, who are able to critique and provide constructive input when needed.

Built on an understanding that civic participation is synonymous with a 'good society', the programme works to enable and develop the capacity of citizens to have responsible and productive participation in political, social, economic and cultural life.

The programme educates, trains and supports activities that build and entrench participatory and democratic principles across the Commonwealth. The programme undertakes extensive research and training on civic education – developing materials and publications to promote practical ways to bring greater citizen participation in national governance.

Friends of the Commonwealth

Friends of the Commonwealth is a group of ordinary people unified by a desire to build a fair, proactive Commonwealth

The Commonwealth People's Forum: driving change for a dynamic Commonwealth

In October 2011 Commonwealth civil society came together in Perth for the Commonwealth People's Forum (CPF) 2011 with a view to influencing Heads of Government at their 21st Commonwealth Heads of Government Meeting (CHOGM 2011). The Commonwealth Foundation has consistently supported these forums that take place in advance of CHOGM in conjunction with partners from civil society, colleagues at the Commonwealth Secretariat, and the host government. Civil society delegates met in Perth with a hope to shape civic engagement and network at the CHOGM 2011.

Each CHOGM bears the imprint of its host as well as the broader context within which it takes place and CPF 2011 was no different in that respect, taking place against a backdrop that included several important elements. The prevailing global economic outlook, the proposed Eminent Persons Group and the outcomes of the Commonwealth Conversation all required Commonwealth organisations to demonstrate their relevance and prove their worth. Perth was indeed the opportunity for the Commonwealth Family to respond to this new context.

The theme of 2011's Forum spoke to the process of reform that the Commonwealth has embarked upon. It challenged the Commonwealth to see itself as more than an association of governments but as a contemporary network of people and their interests. The theme asserted that these groups and organisations are not an accessory for the Commonwealth, but an integral part of its fabric. More than this, the energy, innovation and creativity required for the Commonwealth's renewal can be found in people's organisations delivering locally, influencing nationally or connecting internationally.

The Civil Society Statement produced to influence the CHOGM Communiqué stated that the Commonwealth must confront its own weaknesses. Civil society – authors of the statement – highlighted the disconnect between the Commonwealth's high level goals and ideas agreed at the intergovernmental level and the lack of follow-through at the national level. A positive force for change would be to address this problem and see proper interaction and acceptance of civil society.

For more information and to read the full statement please visit **www.cpf2011.org**

Commonwealth Lecture

The annual Commonwealth Lecture excites intellectual debate around current development challenges faced by the Commonwealth. This keynote address has been delivered by internationally respected experts including Kofi Annan and Mary Robinson. The subject is inspired by the annual Commonwealth theme. The 2011 Commonwealth Lecture, on 'Women as Agents of Change', was delivered by Sonia Gandhi, President, Indian National Congress, and Chairperson, United Progressive Alliance. The 15th Commonwealth Lecture was delivered in March 2012 by multiple prize-winning author Chimamanda Ngozi Adichie, on 'Connecting Cultures'.

community. It aims to develop, by a variety of means, a wider appreciation of the Commonwealth – to increase awareness of the vast opportunities it offers to its citizens so they are understood and utilised. It encourages a Commonwealth-wide network of Friends to share more, learn more and achieve more, and to build support so that more people can benefit with a better quality of life. It encourages young people to participate in community projects.

Friends aims to provide the knowledge, skills and opportunity for disadvantaged people around the Commonwealth to help themselves; it encourages young people to participate in community projects that strengthen livelihoods and give people a voice in determining their own future.

2012 sees the relaunch of Friends to become a dynamic network linking people around the Commonwealth. For more information please see **www.commonwealthfriends.org**

Commonwealth of Learning

1055 West Hastings Street, Suite 1200
Vancouver, British Columbia V6E 2E9, Canada

Tel:	+1 604 775 8200
Fax:	+1 604 775 8210
E-mail:	info@col.org

www.col.org

Officers

Chair:	Burchell Whiteman OJ (Jamaica)
President and Chief Executive Officer:	Sir John Daniel (Canada/UK) until 31 May 2012; Professor Asha Kanwar (India) from 1 June 2012

Foundation

The Commonwealth of Learning (COL) is an intergovernmental organisation established by the Commonwealth Heads of Government in 1988 to encourage the development and sharing of open learning and distance education knowledge, resources and technologies.

COL is hosted in Canada by the Government of Canada. The major voluntary contributors – currently Canada, India, New Zealand, Nigeria, South Africa and the United Kingdom – are each entitled to seats on COL's Board of Governors.

COL works in close association with Commonwealth governments and local institutions and agencies, operating through a wide range of partnerships undertaken in a spirit of equality and participation. It seeks to create mutually beneficial linkages, especially of a South–South character, among Commonwealth countries. Some of COL's key international partners are:

* Caribbean Community Secretariat (CARICOM)

* Commonwealth Association of Polytechnics in Africa (CAPA),

* Commonwealth Secretariat

* Consultative Group on International Agricultural Research (CGIAR)

* Economic Community of West African States (ECOWAS)

* Indira Gandhi National Open University (India)

* National Institute of Open Schooling (India)

* National Assessment and Accreditation Council (India)

* Southern African Development Community (SADC)

* Teacher Education in Sub-Saharan Africa (TESSA)

* UNESCO

* UNICEF

* World Bank

* World Health Organization, and

* World Intellectual Property Organization.

COL's regional agency, the Commonwealth Educational Media Centre for Asia (CEMCA), was established in 1994 to promote co-operation and collaboration in the use of electronic media resources for distance education. CEMCA is particularly active in supporting the expansion of community radio in India and other Commonwealth Asian countries.

COL also supports two regional agencies in Africa: the Regional Training and Research Institute for Distance and Open Learning (RETRIDOL) in Nigeria; and the SADC Centre for Distance Education (SADC-CDE) in Botswana.

COL's work is supported by:

* focal points – individuals nominated by the minister of education in each country to act as COL's primary contact

* honorary advisers – 12 eminent open and distance learning (ODL) professionals from across the Commonwealth, and

* UNESCO-COL chairs – distinguished serving academics who serve in an honorary capacity, complementing the political and administrative role of the focal points and honorary advisers.

In addition, COL sustains links with non-governmental organisations (NGOs) in many countries and has an important relationship with the William and Flora Hewlett Foundation for developing the use of open educational resources (OER).

Mission

COL's mission is to help governments and institutions expand the scope, scale and quality of learning by using new approaches and technologies.

Programmes and initiatives

Through its own resources and its extensive networks, COL provides a wealth of services and collaborative opportunities for policy-makers, institutions and distance education practitioners to encourage the development of, and help enhance, the use of ODL policies, system and applications.

COL's mission focuses on helping Commonwealth member states to use technology as a means of increasing the scope, scale, quality and impact of their education and training systems. The application of technology through ODL techniques has shown its power and value in many countries and for many purposes.

'Learning for Development' is the theme of COL's three-year plan, 2009–2012. It expresses a vision that reaches beyond formal education to embrace areas of learning that are vital for better

Ebonyi State University

You are welcomed to study and do research at Ebonyi State University Abakaliki, Nigeria!

The University was established in 1999 by the Ebonyi State University law No 7, 1999.

EBSU offers academic programmes with a wide range of courses, tailored to suit individual desires and prepare students to achieve their dreams and ambitions. Pure and applied research are also emphasised at both undergraduate and postgraduate levels.

VISION
"To rank among the best citadels of learning in the world with excellence in learning, research and community service."

MISSION
To provide a conducive atmosphere for teaching, learning, research and rapid development in order to transform the hitherto, untapped, abundant unskilled, human resources in Nigeria into skilled manpower.

FACULTIES AND SCHOOLS

Agriculture and Natural Resources Management	Law
Arts and Humanities	Management Sciences
Basic Medical Sciences	Physical Sciences
Biological Sciences	Social Sciences
Clinical Medicine	School of Postgraduate Studies
Education	Pre-Degree School
Health Science and Technology	Directorate of Work and Study

STATISTICS 2010/2011

Academic staff:	752
Non-academic:	1,971
Undergraduate:	21,920
Postgraduates:	2,000

Vice-Chancellor,
Engr. Prof. F. I. IDIKE
(fnse, fniae, pe, OON)

CONTACT

PMB 053 Abakaliki Nigeria
Tel/Fax: +234 (0) 4322 1093
vc@ebsu-edu.net/registrar@ebsu-edu.net

www.ebsu-edu.net

---

health, greater prosperity and a safer environment. Understanding development as the process of increasing the freedoms that people can enjoy, COL pursues this vision operationally within the framework of the Millennium Development Goals (MDGs), the campaign for Education for All and Commonwealth values.

COL's three-year plan, 2009–2012, groups COL's work into two sectors of activity: Education, and Livelihoods and Health. Each sector pursues its aims through five core strategies.

1. Partnerships: fostering sustainable partnerships and networks in support of these aims.

2. Models: refining and sharing models for applying teaching and learning technologies to development challenges.

3. Policies: assisting countries and organisations to develop and implement policies that support technology-mediated learning.

4. Capacity: facilitating training and organisational development to increase the overall ability of partners to deploy learning systems and technologies effectively.

5. Materials: working with partners to co-create learning materials and make them widely available.

Education

The education sector focuses on capacity-building, models and materials development, and supporting quality assurance. There are four education programme initiatives: Open Schooling, teacher education, higher education, and Virtual University for Small States of the Commonwealth.

Open Schooling

There is an urgent need to expand access to quality secondary education. Open schooling is an important initiative to achieve this aim. COL is working with policy-makers, practitioners and managers responsible for secondary education in all regions of the Commonwealth. The key strategy is partnerships with organisations that have similar values and share the vision for open schooling, with a focus on South–South collaboration.

COL is helping to increase access to quality education while increasing student achievement through the expansion of open schooling. COL's Open Schooling initiatives span 40 countries and include the following.

- **Advocacy:** COL works with partners in government, NGOs and education institutions to promote open schooling.

- **Collaboration:** COL led the establishment of the Commonwealth Open Schooling Association (COMOSA), a group of open schooling and distance education practitioners that is working to support the expansion and improvement of open schooling.

- **Development of open schools:** COL has helped to develop policies and proposals for the establishment of open schools in The Bahamas, Belize, Cameroon, the Caribbean, Ghana, Nigeria, Pakistan, Trinidad and Tobago, and the United Republic of Tanzania.

- **Capacity-building:** COL works with partners to train educators, administrators and policy-makers in the development and operation of open schools. Workshops have focused on materials development, instructional design, multimedia content development, radio broadcasting, learner support, e-learning, management of open schools, strategic planning for open schools and quality assurance.

- **'OER for Open Schools':** funded by a grant from the William and Flora Hewlett Foundation, COL worked with educators in six countries – Botswana, Lesotho, Namibia, Seychelles, Trinidad and Tobago, and Zambia – to train teachers in the effective use of technology in classrooms and how to create OER. These master teachers developed 20 new secondary-level courses in print and electronic formats that are freely available as OER.

- **Research:** COL has commissioned research into the provision of secondary level open schooling in India and Namibia, the use of mobile technologies in open schools, the role of gender and information and communication technology (ICT) in open schools, and open schooling as a strategy for 'second-chance' education in the Pacific Islands.

- **Quality assurance:** COL provides training and has developed a Quality Assurance Toolkit for Open Schools.

- **Publications:** COL publishes handbooks, guides and reports about open schooling costs and financing, learner support, administration and course development.

- **Learning materials:** COL assists with the development of quality learning materials for open schools.

Teacher education

Addressing shortfalls in teacher supply and enhancing the quality of teachers and teacher education in the context of Education for All and the MDGs are key areas of concern for developing countries of the Commonwealth. Current and projected numbers of teachers required are huge and cannot be adequately addressed by existing teacher education institutions. COL promotes the use of ODL for teacher development.

COL works in partnership with teacher training institutions, government ministries and development partners in 23 Commonwealth countries. COL's activities in teacher education include:

- advocating the use of ODL in teacher education by supporting policies for professional development

- working with selected teacher education institutions to ensure the design and delivery of quality teacher education programmes

- emphasising the development of pedagogic content knowledge and skills among ODL practitioners

- building capacity in teacher education through training workshops in areas such as learner support, quality assurance and instructional design

- promoting quality through the development of a Quality Assurance Toolkit for Teacher Education

- supporting conventional teacher education institutions to make the transition to dual-mode, and

- facilitating the development and use of OER.

COL has been working in partnership with UNICEF to mainstream Child-Friendly Schools models and approaches into teacher education curricula and enhance the quality of education in schools. More than 600 teacher educators and 150 teacher resource centre managers, head teachers and other education personnel in 10 Commonwealth countries have received Child-Friendly Schools training. Developed to address growing global concerns about the poor quality of schools, teaching and learning at the basic education level, the Child-Friendly Schools approach is based on the concept that quality education involves the total needs of the child; quality goes beyond good teaching methods and learning outcomes in order to include health, safety and adequacy of school facilities.

COL is involved with a number of international partnerships committed to improving teacher education, including Teacher Education in Sub-Saharan Africa. This consortium of 18 organisations, universities and teacher training institutions is collaborating to develop an extensive range of multilingual OER for primary school teachers.

Higher education

Most governments in the Commonwealth aim to enhance access to higher education. This can be achieved through the increased use of quality ODL provision. COL's work in higher education is geared towards ensuring greater access, better systems, more effective and efficient institutional management, and quality teaching and learning.

COL facilitates the expansion of quality higher education and sharing of programmes among institutions through a number of initiatives:

- supporting the training of trainers in both curriculum and instructional design in tertiary institutions

- providing technical assistance to new open universities

- supporting the transition of colleges into universities

- offering scholarship to support the training of academics in and through ODL methods, and

- supporting quality assurance. COL's Review and Improvement Model (COL RIM) offers higher education institutions with the tools to conduct a cost-effective institutional quality audit. This 'do-it-yourself' approach to quality assurance monitoring and evaluation is freely available to higher education institutions.

COL is also building capacity through its Executive MBA/MPA programmes and postgraduate diploma programme in Legislative Drafting, available at partner universities throughout the Commonwealth.

Virtual University for Small States of the Commonwealth

The Virtual University for Small States of the Commonwealth (VUSSC) is a network of 32 small states of the Commonwealth committed to the collaborative development of open content resources for education, capacity-building and the use of ICT to broaden access to education.

VUSSC is led by a management committee of representatives from small states in all regions of the Commonwealth, supported by COL. VUSSC is focusing on creating skills-related post-secondary courses in areas such as tourism, entrepreneurship, professional development, disaster management, and a range of technical and vocational subjects. These non-proprietary, electronically held

Educators from 16 countries developed a Business and Entrepreneurship programme that includes certificate, diploma and degree levels at a Virtual University for Small States of the Commonwealth materials development workshop in Lesotho in March 2011

course materials – developed by small states, for small states – can readily be adapted to the specific context of each country. Small states thus become active contributors to global development and leaders in educational reform through the innovative use of ICT.

COL is building capacity in online materials development among educators in small states of the Commonwealth by hosting intensive training workshops or 'boot camps'. Educators from small states learn computer literacy skills and how to collaboratively develop learning materials. On return to their home countries, workshop participants continue to collaborate on course materials and share their skills with colleagues.

VUSSC's Transnational Qualifications Framework (TQF) is a system of accreditation for VUSSC courses that facilitates the movement of courses and learners among countries. The TQF ensures all OER created for VUSSC can be adapted into recognised courses that students can take for credit through educational institutions in small states.

VUSSC's online learning portal, freely available to all VUSSC participating institutions, offers free online materials and resources for learners and educators. The site features the Moodle Learning Management System, which enables educators to collaborate on the development of online courses.

Livelihoods and Health

The Livelihoods and Health sector aims to improve the income, livelihoods and quality of life of communities through new knowledge and skills gained through ODL. There are four programme initiatives in this sector: skills development, Learning for Farming, Healthy Communities and integrating e-learning.

Skills development

COL supports formal technical and vocational education and training (TVET) institutions and non-formal organisations to use appropriate technology and ODL to improve access to quality skills training. Activities include:

- supporting strategic planning and policy development at institutional and national levels

- building capacity to integrate technology and flexible delivery mechanisms into skills training

- assisting institutions and ministries to define and contextualise effective ODL models of skills development, and

- supporting the development of new learning materials and re-purposing OER.

COL is working in partnership with the Commonwealth Association of Polytechnics in Africa to expand flexible and blended delivery approaches in TVET in Africa. COL and CAPA are spearheading Flexible Skills Development training workshops, policy development and an online Community Learning Network, all aimed at alleviating poverty by increasing access to quality skills development.

COL has commissioned research about expanding flexible approaches to TVET in the Pacific and is working with partners to expand skills development efforts in that region.

Learning for Farming

Lifelong Learning for Farmers (L3 Farmers) demonstrates COL's ability to partner with communities and organisations, and make effective use of ICT to facilitate learning for development. COL's L3 Farmers programme helps people in rural communities to find appropriate technology-based open and distance education to improve their livelihoods.

The programme is a response to a critical need: the wealth of information resulting from agricultural research and development often fails to travel the last mile to the villages of the developing world where it is most needed. While governments face challenges in funding adequate agricultural extension, globalisation is creating increasing competition for poor rural farmers.

L3 Farmers is based on a web of partnerships that brings together farmers, research/educational institutions, ICT providers and banks. In collaboration with partners, resource-poor farming communities use ODL to increase their knowledge and skills to access new information, training and financing that improves their livelihoods through various economic activities. The various stakeholders are active participants in a 'win-win' situation.

L3 Farmers was introduced in four villages in southern India in 2004. In one district, C$2.5 million in assets and income was generated by 2,000 women participating in L3 Farmers. Livelihoods are improving significantly as previously marginalised people create profitable farming enterprises. In recent years, COL has overseen expansion of the programme to Jamaica, Kenya, Mauritius, Papua New Guinea, Sri Lanka and Uganda.

Increasingly, mobile phones are used to disseminate information and knowledge. Farmers access learning through daily audio messages. L3 Farmers is using the Learning through Interactive Voice Education Systems (LIVES) system to reach thousands of farmers in India and Jamaica.

Healthy Communities

The Healthy Communities initiative uses ODL to expand learning opportunities about community health and development in non-formal settings. COL promotes a distinctive community-learning model based on collaboration among community networks, public authorities and media/ICT groups.

COL aims to increase access to appropriate information, knowledge, learning materials and tools to enable better community responses to HIV/AIDS and other health and development challenges, particularly in remote and resource-poor areas. By encouraging participation by community members and other partners, COL facilitates effective learning and enables better responses to development challenges such as maternal and child health, and HIV/AIDS.

COL is working with partners in 19 countries to increase their capacity to create and use ODL materials to improve the health and well-being of their communities. Activities include:

- working with key actors in ICT/media, health, development and education to develop quality content that will be freely available as OER

- using community media for education, training and health promotion

- developing the capacities of 'knowledge info-mediaries' to reach larger numbers of people in the community, and

- building research and evaluation into projects to ensure knowledge is shared and to foster the development of model practices and policies.

Integrating e-learning

Commonwealth countries want to integrate e-learning into their educational systems but often do not know where to start. COL helps countries and institutions to understand e-learning and implement it using technologies that are practical, user-friendly and compatible with available and existing equipment. Activities include:

- increasing digital literacy in institutions and communities

- advocating and building capacity to develop and use OER, and

- providing policy support to governments and institutions.

In 2010, COL worked in partnership with UNESCO to improve understanding of OER by educational decision-makers in order to expand their use. The initiative, 'Taking OER beyond the OER Community', involved four capacity-building workshops, online forums and a concluding policy forum. Two new publications were created: *Guidelines for OER in Higher Education* and *A Basic Guide to Open Educational Resources*, and materials for a one-day workshop introducing institutions to OER are freely available as an OER.

COL is currently leading 'Fostering Governmental Support for Open Educational Resources Internationally', an extension of the UNESCO–COL partnership to spread awareness of the value of open content. Funded by the William and Flora Hewlett Foundation, this initiative involves encouraging governments worldwide to officially recognise the importance of sharing OER.

Cross-cutting themes

The cross-cutting themes of gender, quality and appropriate technology are pervasive throughout COL's three-year plan. COL pursues the goals of gender equality and equity across all initiatives. As access to education and training increases, the quality of what is provided to students is a growing concern. COL assists member states to improve quality assurance, with an emphasis on standards and outputs. ICT is the backbone of ODL. An important

COL is working with partners in Northern Cape Province, South Africa, on an HIV/AIDS community learning programme

part of COL's mandate is to encourage the use of accessible, affordable and effective technologies in support of learning.

E-learning for international organisations

Recognising COL's extensive technical experience and understanding of issues in the developing world, international organisations are increasingly turning to COL for their training needs. COL has developed customised e-learning programmes for the Commonwealth Secretariat, United Nations agencies, the World Bank and many other international agencies. Course subject matter ranges from effective communication and report writing to operational data management and debt management. Each course is tailored to the specific requirements of the contracting organisation so that learners can apply learning to their daily occupations.

COL's eLearning for International Organisations team has trained more than 7,000 learners in more than 130 countries since 2000. These training solutions use ODL to widen access to professional development opportunities, especially for female and junior workers based in field and country offices. This contract work is performed on a fee-for-service basis with full cost recovery.

Women involved in COL's Lifelong Learning for Farmers programme in Kenya celebrate opening personal bank accounts

The Excellence in Distance Education Awards at the Sixth Pan-Commonwealth Forum on Open Learning in Kochi, India, in November 2010

Events and awards

COL hosts a biennial Pan-Commonwealth Forum on Open Learning (PCF) and Excellence in Distance Education Awards programme. PCF7 will be held in Abuja, Nigeria, in November 2013, co-hosted by the Federal Ministry of Education. The National Open University of Nigeria (NOUN) is the lead partner institution. More than 600 people took part in PCF6 in Kochi, India, in November 2010.

Knowledge management

COL continues to build its information and knowledge resources as well as develop mechanisms to effectively disseminate them across the Commonwealth. COL's website, www.col.org, gets over 1,000 unique visits every day, making it one of the most visited sites in the field.

Resources

COL's website offers a wide range of information resources (www.col.org/resources) including several online databases and knowledge retrieval services. The website also offers free access to an extensive collection of publications including studies, reports and research documents.

Connections: COL's newsletter provides news about COL's work and updates about ODL from around the globe. It is published three times annually and is available online at www.col.org/connections.

Blog: COL's online blog (www.col.org/blog) encourages interaction, discussion and knowledge sharing on issues related to learning for development.

Information Resource Centre: COL's online library catalogue (www.col.org/irc) offers access to a wide range of publications, OER and news feeds, as well as extensive search tools.

COL's Resource CD-Rom: This collection of COL's most popular resource publications, news, and software contains over 60 publications including training manuals, start-up guides and research, including all 21 titles in COL's popular Knowledge Series, as well as free and open source software. While most of the contents are also available in print or on www.col.org, the CD-Rom provides a convenient, fast-loading compilation of the open and distance learning resources that COL has produced for public distribution and use. It is updated regularly and available upon request at info@col.org.

Knowledge Finder: COL's online search service (www.col.org/kf) provides access to information related to ODL. Knowledge Finder offers 36 specialised search fields, each catering to the need for finding information in focused areas. If users do not find what they need on COL's web pages, they are directed to narrow sets of information from websites selected by COL specialists.

Governor-General's House of Grenada

'Grenada joins with all other Commonwealth territories to celebrate the Diamond Jubilee of Her Majesty Queen Elizabeth II and offers sincerest congratulations on this great milestone. It is with a very special sense of appreciation and joy that we recall Her Majesty's reign and contribution, as Head of State of the Commonwealth, over the past sixty years. In Grenada, we can look back with a sense of pride to the specific years 1966 and 1985, when Her Majesty would have graced our shores with her presence, in the form of two Royal visits.'

Sir Carlyle Glean, Governor-General of Grenada

'It is with tremendous pleasure that I extend a hearty welcome to all readers, those from within the family of the Commonwealth and those from beyond. I consider it an honour and privilege to share with you, at this time, and to reflect on our beautiful land of Grenada and its role within the Commonwealth.'

Mission

To give logistic and administrative support for the discharge of the constitutional and ceremonial functions of the Head of State and to be the link between the Governor-General and various Government Agencies and External Organisations.

Functions

- Appointment of prime ministers; and on the advice of the prime minister, the appointment of ministers
- Swearing-in of the aforementioned upon taking the Oath of Office
- Opening of Parliament when the Governor-General reads the Throne Speech
- Processing of recommendations for conferring Queen's Honours on deserving citizens
- Receiving ambassadors on presentation of their credentials
- Hosting of royalty and dignitaries at State functions

Superintendent Godfrey Edwards, Aide-de-Camp

The Governor-General's House as a unit consists of two Divisions: Residence and Office. The Residence is now located in Morne Rouge, Grand Anse, and the Office is on the Carenage, St. George's. The Governor General's House consists of four sections. The Office security, household and ground staff are headed by the Personal Assistant to the Governor-General and security is headed by the Aide-de-Camp.

Contact

Office of the Governor-General
Building #5
Financial Complex
Carenage
St. George's

Tel: +1 473 440 6639/440 2401
Fax: +1 473 440 6688
Email: patogg@spiceisle.com

Ms Gertrude Telesford, Personal Assistant to Governor-General

The Queen and the Commonwealth

'The Commonwealth bears no resemblance to the empires of the past. It is an entirely new conception built on the highest qualities of the spirit of man: friendship, loyalty, and the desire for freedom and peace.' This quote from Her Majesty Queen Elizabeth II's Christmas day broadcast of 1953 encapsulates the values and founding principles of the Commonwealth, and highlights the Queen's immense understanding of, and belief in, this international institution to which she has been continually committed since adopting the role of figurehead on 6 February 1952.

Queen Elizabeth II arrives in Perth, Australia, for CHOGM, October 2011; she first attended a CHOGM in 1973 and has since travelled thousands of miles to attend subsequent CHOGMs or be present in the host country at the same time (photograph by Andrew Taylor / CHOGM)

Looking back over her reign, it is clear that the Queen's involvement as Head of the Commonwealth has been vital and inspirational. The Queen's guidance and wisdom have enabled this institution to grow from a small group of nations to an association of 54 independent countries spanning six continents and over 2 billion people. It is her quiet diplomacy, subtle encouragement and unifying presence over the past 60 years that will undoubtedly afford the Queen a legacy in which the next 60 years of the Commonwealth are shaped by an endurance of the principles of democracy, equality and peace that have thus far commanded a central focus. Aside from her father, King George VI, Her Majesty is the only person to fulfil the role of Head of the Commonwealth. Despite the fact that the position of Head of the Commonwealth is not enshrined in the Coronation Oath, the Queen's genuine affection for the countries under her headship and desire for the institution to succeed is demonstrated by her ever-increasing involvement, which has always surpassed her expected duties. The past 60 years have seen the Queen extend her role as figurehead into new areas including symbolic functions such as meeting Commonwealth leaders and opening parliament in a number of member nations.

Through her role as Head of the Commonwealth, the Queen not only promotes unity and increases the profile of the association but also acts as a role model for all kinds of societal actors. While she clearly values her role as Head of the Commonwealth and constitutional monarch she acknowledges that she will perform these roles only as long as the people happily wish her to do so. This is just one of many ways in which she demonstrates and embodies respect for democratic process.

The Queen at Commonwealth Heads of Government Meetings

On a biennial basis, the heads of government from all Commonwealth nations meet to discuss important issues across the Commonwealth at the Commonwealth Heads of Government Meeting (CHOGM). The Queen first attended a CHOGM in 1973, in Ottawa, as part of a royal visit to Canada. Her Majesty has attended, or been present in the host country, for every CHOGM since then, although her formal appearances at the meetings only began in 1997. Speaking at the opening ceremony of CHOGM 2011 in Perth, she said of these meetings that: 'Their importance has always been in precise relationship to their relevance: always being attuned to the issues of the day, and always looking to the future with a sense of vision and practical action to match.' The Queen's attendance at these meetings may be seen to reinforce her unifying role in strengthening co-operation among Commonwealth countries; her sense of commitment is clear and exemplified by considering that, despite the disagreement of then Prime Minister Margaret Thatcher, Her Majesty attended the 1979 CHOGM in

Government of Gibraltar

*Chief Minister of Gibraltar,
Fabian Picardo*

Letter from the Chief Minister of Gibraltar, Fabian Picardo

When I was a teenager, I was lucky enough to be selected – together with three colleagues – to represent my country in London at a Commonwealth Parliamentary Association event for young people. Some twenty odd years later, as Chief Minister of Gibraltar, I instinctively understand the importance of the Commonwealth even for those of us in the Overseas Territories who form a small part of it. The fact is that the Commonwealth remains a point of reference throughout the world and in the nations that make it up.

Her Majesty, Queen Elizabeth II, Queen of Gibraltar, has similarly been an inspiration for her exemplary dutiful service and commitment in the sixty years she has served as Monarch.

In celebrating the Diamond Jubilee, there will be few who do not see Her Majesty as a point of reference also. Indeed, for most of the generations of citizens of the Commonwealth she has been the only Monarch we have known.

In Gibraltar, many still warmly recall her visit of 1954 and those of us who have never seen her in our homeland remain expectant of a new visit as soon as Her Majesty is able to travel to see us.

From 'The Rock', we will be joining in the international celebrations of the Diamond Jubilee with drama festivals, street parties, concerts and – as a highlight – we will be welcoming the Earl and Countess of Wessex to Gibraltar.

I know that the people of Gibraltar are looking forward to the celebrations; in particular because they feel a part of the wider British family and of our affiliation to the Commonwealth of Nations.

This year will also mark the arrival of the Olympic torch in London; in part in the hands of Gibraltarian athletes who will run with the torch after it arrives in the United Kingdom, with a Gibraltarian contestant as part of the GB Rhythmic Gymnastics Team and with a Gibraltarian hockey umpire.

For all of these reasons, we in Gibraltar stake our place amongst the nations of the world that enjoy the benefits that the Commonwealth brings – and which Her Majesty has so effectively nurtured in her sixty years on the throne.

As a modern parliamentary democracy at the cross roads of the Mediterranean and the Atlantic, open for business and an important part of the British military establishment in the defence of Southern Europe, Gibraltar remains the immoveable, steadfast and loyal Rock that has for so long been the stuff of limestone legend.

In modern times, we have diversified our economy away from reliance on the Ministry of Defence to a service-based economy, principally delivering world-class financial services and the premier online gaming jurisdiction on the planet.

That is the success story of the past quarter century of Gibraltar's history – something of which we are all justly proud.

In coming years, we look forward to further expansion within the EU as we enjoy the benefits of membership of the single market, whilst remaining outside the VAT (Common Union) area.

That is the celebration which we invite you to join us in by asking you all to come to Gibraltar, experience the hospitality of our people and enjoy the beauty of our landscape – enjoying the views of Africa from this British southern tip of Europe.

You will not be disappointed!

Contact
Office of the Chief Minister
No.6 Convent Place
Gibraltar

Personal Secretaries and Private Secretaries
Tel: +350 2007 0071
Fax: +350 2007 6396

Media Director
Tel: +350 2005 1088
Fax: +350 2004 6541

Press Officer
Tel: +350 2005 1739
Fax: +350 2004 3057
Email: pressoffice@gibraltar.gov.gi

www.gibraltar.gov.gi

Lusaka, Zambia, regardless of security concerns. This was the Queen's first visit to Zambia and demonstrated her selfless awareness that the then President of Zambia, Kenneth Kaunda, was in need of her support. The subsequent summit was a success, with the Queen utilising her renowned diplomacy to perform a conciliatory role.

The Queen and Commonwealth countries

Beginning with her first official Commonwealth tour, which set off in November 1953, the Queen has paid numerous visits to virtually every country in the Commonwealth. This first tour lasted six months, included 13 countries and saw the Queen and Prince Philip travel by plane, car, rail and sea. Many of the countries visited had never before seen their Queen, and thus the trip provided a timely opportunity not only to promote the image and values of the Commonwealth, but also to reiterate Her Majesty's position as symbolic leader around the world. Since then, the Queen has continued to visit Commonwealth countries across Asia, Africa, the Pacific, the Americas and the Caribbean, and Europe. Often planning her meetings around CHOGMs and the Commonwealth Games, the Queen also manages to find time to greet members of the public and pay her respects to the memories of the many Commonwealth soldiers who lost their lives in World Wars I and II. During these visits, through her warmth and support the Queen has seen her relationships with world leaders grow from strength to strength, with many now looking upon her with feelings of friendship as well as respect. Her Majesty has formed an enduring friendship with former South African president Nelson Mandela, with him referring to her as 'my friend Elizabeth' and she signing off her letters to him with the words 'Your sincere friend, Elizabeth R'. The continuation of such visits and the network of friendships that they cultivate around the Commonwealth are vital in reiterating the association as a family of nations that holds common interests at heart.

The Queen and her realms

The Commonwealth is also home to all 16 of the Commonwealth realms. Following independence from the UK, these former British colonies have chosen to retain constitutional relationships and the tradition of having the Queen as head of state. Aside from the United Kingdom, there are 15 Commonwealth realms in existence today: Antigua and Barbuda, Australia, The Bahamas, Belize, Barbados, Canada, Grenada, Jamaica, New Zealand, Papua New Guinea, St Kitts and Nevis, St Lucia, St Vincent and the Grenadines, Solomon Islands and Tuvalu.

In her capacity as monarch of all Commonwealth realms Queen Elizabeth II has made over 80 visits to these countries. Beginning with her maiden official visit to a Commonwealth realm as Queen of New Zealand in 1953, Her Majesty's visits have stretched the breadth and range of all habitable continents of the world, with her many subsequent official visits including:

- her visits as Queen of Jamaica in 1966, 1975, 1983, 1994, 2002

- her numerous visits as Queen of Canada from her first visit in 1957 to a score of others in every decade of her reign

- her visit to the small South Pacific country of Tuvalu as Queen of Tuvalu in 1982

- her 1985 grand round trip to the Caribbean as Queen in each of the following sovereign countries: Antigua and Barbuda, The Bahamas, Belize, Grenada, St Lucia, and St Vincent and the Grenadines

- her most recent visit as Queen of Australia in 2011, which was preceded by many others to the country.

Historically, many Commonwealth republics that now have presidents as their head of state did, at one point, have the Queen as their monarch following their independence from the UK. This was reflected in the Queen's visits over the decades as Queen of Ceylon (now Sri Lanka), Queen of Sierra Leone, Queen of Trinidad and Tobago, Queen of Malta and as Queen of Mauritius. All these countries are now republics and instead maintain a ceremonial link to the Queen by virtue of their Commonwealth membership.

The Queen cannot always fulfil the role of head of state in each of her realms and thus out of practicality she is represented, constitutionally, by a governor-general in each country. The role of the governor-general is unique to the Commonwealth and involves the carrying out of ceremonial day-to-day duties of head of state on behalf of the Queen. Such duties include the appointment of government ministers, ambassadors, and judges on the advice of a prime minister, and giving Royal Assent to legislation. Governors-general are elected or chosen by the country's parliament, cabinet or prime minister and all formally appointed by the Queen. On the advice of a Commonwealth realm's government, almost all governors-general are knighted by the Queen as an accepted norm and accorded the title 'Dame' when female and 'Sir' when male. Canada and Australia are the exceptions to this.

The Queen and Commonwealth Day

At the 1975 CHOGM in Kingston, Jamaica, then Prime Minister of Canada Pierre Trudeau suggested that a 'simultaneously observed Commonwealth Day would focus attention upon the association and its contribution to a harmonious global environment'. Thus, Commonwealth Day was born with the second Monday of March each year now dedicated to a day that acknowledges achievements of the Commonwealth over the past year and reminds its members, and the world, of the principles of democracy, equality and peace that lie at its core. The day is marked by a multifaith observance at Westminster Abbey and a themed message from the Queen in which she expresses her own heartfelt sentiments, rather than taking suggestions from her advisers. In the knowledge that her message is broadcast in all countries and territories of the Commonwealth, Commonwealth Day provides an opportunity for the Queen to demonstrate her commitment and cement her unifying role. Over the years, Commonwealth Day themes incorporated into the Queen's message have included 'Talking to One Another', 'Music', 'Building a Commonwealth of Freedom', 'Health and Vitality' and, most recently, 'Connecting Cultures'.

The Queen's involvement in Commonwealth organisations

From her work with Commonwealth organisations such as the Commonwealth Secretariat in organising important events, and her central participation in the Commonwealth Heads of Government Meetings, Queen Elizabeth II plays an essential role in preserving the fabric of unity of the Commonwealth. Her continued commitment to such unity across all founding principles of the Commonwealth is further demonstrated through her involvement in various Commonwealth organisations performing altruistic efforts and fraternal undertakings throughout the 54 nations of this inspiring institution. These organisations include Commonwealth affiliated bodies founded by Royal Charter, for some of which the Queen and members of the Royal Family are patrons or presidents: the Royal Agricultural Society of the Commonwealth (RASC); Royal Commonwealth Ex-Services League (RCEL); the Commonwealth War Graves Commission; the Royal Commonwealth Society (RCS); Royal Over-Seas League; and Sightsavers (The Royal Commonwealth Society for the Blind). The involvement of the Queen and the Royal Family in such bodies helps to raise awareness of, and provide solutions to, the day-to-day challenges faced by Commonwealth citizens in matters such as advancement of agriculture in the poor rural communities in Africa and Asia, respect, inclusion and healthcare for people with disabilities and promotion of creative talent throughout the Commonwealth, regardless of background. In ensuring the preservation of the annual tradition of Commonwealth Day the Queen also works closely with the Council of Commonwealth Societies (CCS). The CCS is an eclectic coalition of over a dozen organisations involved in many fields of Commonwealth society such as education (Association of Commonwealth Universities), media (Commonwealth Broadcasting Association), telecommunications (Commonwealth Telecommunications Organisation), civil society capacity-building (Commonwealth Foundation) and governance (Commonwealth Local Government Forum and Commonwealth Parliamentary Association).

The Queen and the Commonwealth Games

The Queen is a great advocate for the role of sport in society and has been a consistent supporter of the Commonwealth Games which, in testimony to the values of the Commonwealth, have often been termed 'the friendly games'. First held in London in 1911 under the name the 'Inter-Empire Sports Meeting', these world-class games are now held once every four years and hosted by different countries across the Commonwealth. Despite having grown in terms of both the number of participating countries and the number of events, the Commonwealth Games have always tried to maintain their ethos of being 'merrier and less stern' than the Olympic Games. Over the years there have been both sporting highlights and social controversies; the 1958 Games in Cardiff, Wales, saw the breaking of 10 world records but was also the year of public outcry against the South African team choice, which prioritised race ahead of ability. It was also in 1958 that the tradition of the Queen's baton relay began; starting at Buckingham Palace, the Queen handed the baton over to a team of relay runners who then carried it to Cardiff. Once it arrived at the location of the Games, the Queen's message stored within the baton was received and read aloud by the Duke of Edinburgh. The tradition has continued and evolved, with the baton now travelling vast distances; in 2006 it took just over a year to reach the destination in Melbourne after having visited all Commonwealth nations and territories participating in the Games.

The Queen and the Commonwealth armed forces

Queen Elizabeth II holds honorary positions in armed forces of the Commonwealth. In addition to the UK, where she is the Head of the Armed Forces, the Queen and members of the Royal Family hold titular ranks as heads of various regiments in Commonwealth countries such as Australia, Canada, New Zealand, Papua New Guinea and the UK territory of Bermuda. Members of British Regiments born in Commonwealth countries have distinguished themselves in battle. In 2005 Lance Corporal Johnson Gideon Beharry, born and raised in Grenada, became the first living person in over 30 years to be awarded the Victoria Cross, the highest military decoration for valour in the British and Commonwealth armed forces. The Queen pays tribute by laying wreaths at various war memorials during her official visits to Commonwealth countries, as well as at the Cenotaph in London's Whitehall each Remembrance Day. The Queen is Patron to over 100 armed services charities and organisations including the Air Force Association of Canada, the Partially Blinded Soldiers' Association of Australia and the Royal Malta Artillery Association.

The future of the Commonwealth

By heeding Her Majesty's words on Christmas Day 1953 the Commonwealth will continue to bind member nations together in a spirit of friendship and peace.

Jubilee Time Capsule:
a people's history

Certain moments in the human experience transcend national borders and cultural differences. Since its launch on Commonwealth Day 2011, the Jubilee Time Capsule has allowed Commonwealth citizens to submit memories that speak to what is truly universal.

Entries to the Jubilee Time Capsule (JTC) recount world events, births, deaths and marriages with the same sense of significance, wonder and sentiment, revealing both a common humanity and heritage across our association of nations. The variety in subject and format of JTC content is fast proving the originality of the project, which will commemorate HM Queen Elizabeth II's Diamond Jubilee in 2012.

The JTC presents a novel way to review the last 60 years. And, as an online archive that tells the people's history of the Commonwealth through modern technology, it is a far cry from the dusty history books we were brought up with at school.

The innovation behind the project is also its attraction, as entries have steadily grown since March 2011 and contributors have recollected personal and national stories through a range of video, photos, artwork, music and writing.

Themes and trends

With so many submissions being made, it is possible to see a few trends emerging. One such trend is the number of pieces that have a cross-generational element to them. Illustrating this is an entry by South African student Lara Clauss, who tells the story of her mother's act of defiance in taking down the *slegs blankes* ('whites only') sign above the door to the nurses' changing room at the hospital where she worked in 1992.

Another recurring theme is evident in the popularity of submissions about the royal family. The JTC has received entries about many royal weddings, memories of meeting Her Majesty The Queen and even photos of the royal party watching lions at Nairobi National Park in Kenya in 1952.

Given the popularity of royal-related entries, the capsule also contains an interview with the Very Reverend Dr John Hall, Dean of Westminster, who gives his account of the most recent royal wedding. He speaks of the event as being an intimate ceremony despite the estimated 2.2 billion people who watched it on televisions or listened on radios across the world. He also recalls greeting Catherine at the Great West Door of the Abbey, and explains how the wedding is a sign of hope for the future.

A third noticeable JTC trend is the rise of the Super School. Since the project's inception, it was hoped the JTC would forge and strengthen links between schools across the Commonwealth – and it has. Participating schools will be rewarded with special prizes for the best entries and have been encouraged to learn from each other as they make their submissions. The JTC will also be incorporated into lessons through a selection of teaching resources that have been made available online.

St Katherine's School in Johannesburg blazed an early trail for the Super Schools. The wide-ranging themes and creativity in the presentation of the entries are truly representative of the spirit of the project. One student tells the story of her father's last night in his family home before he was conscripted to the South African army. Another contribution explains how a sewing box and thimble have been passed down from generation to generation. Another is a pictorial representation of 14 June 2009, the day the Confederations Cup started in South Africa.

From the big moments to the small, the entries received demonstrate what an exciting and important project the JTC is. A colourful and vibrant history of the last six decades has begun to emerge and grow leading up to the 2012 Diamond Jubilee celebrations.

The response to the JTC has been very positive and is responsible for building a unique Commonwealth history. The strength of the ambitious project – much like that of the Commonwealth – lies in its creativity and diversity. The JTC is certain to become an outstanding legacy.

For more details of submissions visit www.jubileetime capsule.org. The JTC blog is at www.jubileetimecapsule. org/discover/news); Twitter is on @JTC_2012; and a Facebook page is at www.facebook.com/ JubileeTimeCapsule

Democracy, peace-building and consensus:

the work of the Political Affairs Division

'Although the cases are comparatively few, flawed political transitions are destabilising. They trigger political violence, undermine peace, intensify individual and group insecurity, and can cause humanitarian crisis. Apart from the adverse effects on the countries concerned, flawed political transitions affect neighbouring countries through, for example, the flight of refugees.'

– Commonwealth Eminent Persons Group, 2011

As long ago as in 1992, the Commonwealth brokered an agreement whereby the then military government in Lesotho allowed the exiled King of Lesotho back into the country, triggering a chain of events that eventually led to Lesotho becoming a multiparty democracy. In 1994, the efforts of a Commonwealth Special Envoy led to the development of a formula that allowed Bangladesh to establish a caretaker government 90 days before each election.

In 2002 on the island of Zanzibar in the United Republic of Tanzania, the Commonwealth helped bring about a 'Mwafaka', or agreement, between the main political parties, which helped to restore stability in the wake of disputed and violent elections. And between 2002 and 2006, the Commonwealth promoted dialogue between President, opposition and civil society in Guyana. A Media Monitoring Unit was set up for the 2006 election, and major media outlets pledged not to report any statements that incited racial hatred. This contributed to the most peaceful election in 40 years.

In 2012, the Commonwealth is engaged with other multilateral players ahead of Kenya's upcoming elections. At the time of going to press, it has also sent a political and human rights fact-finding mission to Maldives immediately following tensions in the country. The Commonwealth Secretariat is also committed to the International Criminal Court (ICC), the first permanent treaty-based court of its kind, established (Rome Statute, 1998) to prosecute perpetrators of crimes against humanity, war crimes and genocide. The majority of Commonwealth countries are signatories, but small states in particular may be in need of technical assistance to undertake the ratification process.

A trusted partner

These are examples of the Commonwealth Secretariat's functions of upholding democracy and helping to prevent and resolve situations that could endanger national stability or deteriorate into violence. When playing a mediator or facilitator role, the Commonwealth's key principle is that it must enjoy the trust of all protagonists as an impartial and objective arbiter that has no 'agenda' of its own.

Amitav Banerji, Director of the Secretariat's Political Affairs Division, explains: 'Unlike the United Nations, or the North Atlantic Treaty Organization, the Commonwealth does not engage in "peace-keeping" or "peace-enforcement"; it has no security responsibilities, no Security Council, and no battalions of soldiers to maintain peace – although peacekeepers from Commonwealth countries contribute hugely to UN peacekeeping. On the other hand, "peace-making" and "peace-building" are important Commonwealth priorities. Virtually everything the Commonwealth does contributes to these goals.

'The most notable achievement of the Perth CHOGM was an enhanced role for the Commonwealth Ministerial Action Group, the nine-member ministerial body that leaders set up in 1995 to address serious or persistent violations of Commonwealth values. At the recommendation of CMAG itself, the Group was empowered to become more proactive and pre-emptive, using newly defined triggers for engagement, but acting in a constructive way. The Secretary-General and CMAG have also been tasked to further evaluate relevant options in regard to the Eminent Persons Group recommendation for a Commonwealth Commissioner for Democracy, the Rule of Law and Human Rights – and to report to the Commonwealth Foreign Affairs Ministers Meeting in New York in September 2012.'

The Commonwealth has ongoing Political Affairs engagements in Cameroon, The Gambia (on judiciary and penal reforms), Lesotho, Swaziland, Guyana, Fiji (currently suspended from the Commonwealth – to support domestic initiatives aimed at returning Fiji to full democracy), Tonga and elsewhere. The Secretariat works closely with the African Union, the Caribbean Community (CARICOM), European Union, Pacific Islands Forum and the UN as well as sub-regional organisations and, where warranted, other member and non-member governments. National non-governmental partners are mainly the civil society groups including human rights institutions (for example, the Human Rights Commission for Cameroon) and national NGOs.

Election observation

As well as helping to strengthen the democratic process through its findings and recommendations, Commonwealth teams can also offer a degree of confidence to the public and political stakeholders alike … The quality of a country's election is, to a large extent, dependent upon the quality of its election management body. They can make the crucial difference. Our aim is to ensure they are a force for good, upholders of the highest electoral standards.

Mark Stevens, Head of Democracy Section, Commonwealth Secretariat

In 2009 Heads of Government reaffirmed their belief in the inalienable right of the individual to participate by means of free and democratic political processes in shaping the society in which they live. The observation of elections remains one of the Commonwealth's most visible activities in terms of its programmes to support the strengthening of democratic institutions and processes in member countries. Since 1990 the Commonwealth has observed some 100 elections and demand for the presence of a Commonwealth team to observe an election continues unabated. In 2011, the Commonwealth deployed teams to nine elections: in Cameroon, The Gambia, Guyana, Maldives, Nigeria, St Lucia, Seychelles, Uganda and Zambia.

Elections can sometimes be tense and fraught affairs and while the presence of international observers can, in worst case scenarios, help to shine a light on shortcomings and identify lapses in the procedures, in other instances such a presence can help to increase confidence in the outcome and also to reassure those present to trust in the process.

Commonwealth teams of observers bring together a wide variety of expertise, under the leadership of a senior political figure – often a former head of state. This enables the team to look at a broad range of issues affecting the process, including the political dynamic, media coverage, human rights context, legal framework, gender considerations and of course technical aspects of the administration of the election. The Commonwealth Observer Group for the 20 September 2011 General Elections in Zambia brought together such a team under the leadership of General Yakubu Gowon, former Head of State of Nigeria.

The Zambian elections ended up being a closely contested poll, which in the end resulted in victory for the main opposition party. Thus, for the second time in its history Zambia experienced a change of power from one elected party to another. Commonwealth observers, together with other international observers, were able to help all stakeholders trust in the process being managed by the Electoral Commission of Zambia (ECZ).

As the election entered the crucial calculation of the results there were some tensions. During this period, the Chair of the Commonwealth team urged 'all Zambians to continue to exercise patience and to allow the ECZ to conclude its work creditably'. In the event the people did wait and the handover of power was orderly, as the new president was sworn in the day after the announcement of results by the Chair of the Electoral Commission. Ultimately, the election, while experiencing some shortcomings, was a testimony to that Commission's administrative skills. The second exchange of power through the ballot box also marks the deepening democratic culture in the country.

Commonwealth Electoral Network

The initiative to create the Commonwealth Electoral Network (CEN) as a tool to provide increased support and assistance to election management bodies (EMBs) across the Commonwealth was endorsed by Heads of Government at the 2009 CHOGM. The network was officially launched at a pan-Commonwealth conference of election officials in Accra, Ghana, in May 2010. At the outset it was agreed that such a Network could be a force for good, harnessing existing electoral skills across the Commonwealth to offer peer-to-peer support to EMBs and promoting good practices in all aspects of the electoral process.

Since its inception in May 2010, CEN has established a web forum, as part of the Commonwealth's new web portal Commonwealth

Election day in Zambia on 20 September 2011 (photographer: Liesl Harewood)

Connects; held three working groups to advance the thinking on best electoral practices; established contact points in each member country's election management body to facilitate communication across the network; and established a working plan to take CEN forward into 2012 and beyond. The three Working Groups have respectively looked at voter education, voter registration and the results process. The aim is to take the findings of these groups and use them as a format for promoting good electoral practice, both through CEN's online output as well as through its assistance programmes.

Says Mark Stevens, '2012 will be the year in which the Network takes off. CEN's Steering Committee has identified a number of exciting initiatives that will ensure it starts to offer tangible programmes of support to members. These include: a survey to identify priority needs among member EMBs; a capacity-building programme for young election administrators; continuation of the series of working groups, with one on independence of EMBs to be held in Jamaica; and a second pan-Commonwealth conference of EMBs, to be held in Canada in June.'

The International Criminal Court (ICC): Secretary-General's remarks at Commonwealth Law Ministers Meeting

Excellencies, ladies and gentlemen,

We are honoured by your presence to witness the signing of this Memorandum of Understanding formalising the strategic partnership between the Commonwealth Secretariat and the International Criminal Court. We have worked together since the Court was set up in 2002 and the presence of Presiding Judge Song with us here today, and throughout our Commonwealth Law Ministers' Meeting, is testimony to the nature of our relationship. The establishment of the International Criminal Court under the Rome Statute of 1998 was a landmark in the development of international criminal law and towards achieving justice for victims. It signalled a new coming together, internationally, to confront the worst crimes known to mankind, crimes against humanity, war crimes, genocide and aggression.

One hundred and sixteen states are now party to the Rome Statute and the number of ratifications rises steadily. The Court has rapidly established itself as a component in the architecture of international justice and set the stage for a new era of accountability; it promises to make a significant contribution to maintaining global peace and security. At the Commonwealth Heads of Government Meeting held in Coolum in 2002, our member states were urged to ratify and implement the Rome Statute. It is therefore pleasing to be back in Australia to conclude this agreement in the context of the Commonwealth Law Ministers Meeting. Over half of the Commonwealth's 54 member states have ratified the Rome Statute.

I express my appreciation to those who have negotiated the terms of this Memorandum of Understanding, and brought us to this culmination. The Memorandum provides the context within which the Commonwealth Secretariat will provide support for those of our member states that are party to the Rome Statute. We are able to share valuable experience and expertise in assisting with the process of integrating the Statute into domestic law, and have developed a model law for that purpose.

Above all, the conclusion of this Memorandum of Understanding demonstrates our deep-rooted commitment to the rule of law. It is a fundamental Commonwealth value within the new humanism we espouse. In concrete terms, this means providing mutual support in upholding human rights, in providing access to justice for victims and in fighting impunity.

Sydney, Australia, 13 July 2011

Election snapshots: 2011

Canada: Canadians went to the polls for the fourth time in seven years on 2 May, delivering a decisive victory to Stephen Harper's Conservative Party and a crushing defeat for the once dominant Liberals. The Conservatives, having won the two previous elections but only with enough seats to form minority governments, secured an elusive majority – winning 167 of the 308 electoral districts. For the first time ever, the Liberal Party was pushed into third place, overtaken by the left-leaning New Democratic Party (NDP), which took 105 seats, well above its previous record of 43. The NDP also decimated the vote of the separatist Bloc Québécois, which managed to retain only four of the 47 seats it had previously held. Green Party leader Elizabeth May became the Greens' first and only elected Member of Parliament. The elections were triggered by a vote of no confidence in late March.

New Zealand: In the wake of New Zealand's success on home soil in the Rugby World Cup, the general elections on 27 November brought a narrow victory for the incumbent National Party and its leader, John Key. The party's share of the vote was 48 per cent, taking 60 seats in the 120-seat parliament. The Labour Party performed poorly, retaining only 34 seats. The third party by size is the Greens, with 13 seats, followed by Winston Peters' New Zealand Front, which won 8 seats. The National Party prefers to work primarily with the right-wing United Front and the ACT Party (each has only one seat) in the hope that they will support it through the next round of economic reforms, including curbs on spending and the sale of shares in state-owned energy companies.

Nigeria: The elections held at all levels of government in Nigeria during April were widely judged to be the fairest ever conducted in the country, despite the fact that there was widespread rioting in the aftermath, with the loss of an estimated 800 lives. In the presidential ballot, Goodluck Jonathan took approximately 59 per cent of the votes cast, against 32 per cent for his nearest rival, Muhammadu Buhari. Jonathan, representing the People's Democratic Party (PDP), won by very large margins in southern and Middle Belt states while Buhari, standing for the Congress for Progressive Change (CPC), won the majority of votes in northern states. The National Assembly polls also gave the PDP a clear lead, with the Action Congress of Nigeria (ACN) taking second place, significantly ahead of the CPC. At the state level, however, the 36 governorships were distributed primarily between the PDP (with 24 states across the country), the ACN (in the south-west) and the All Nigeria People's Party (in the north-east and Zamfara state), with the CPC winning only in Nassarawa state. The performance of the Independent National Electoral Commission, headed by Attahiru Jega, who was appointed last year to provide new leadership, was widely praised.

Seychelles: James Michel secured a third term as President ensuring that his People's Party's 34-year rule will continue for another five years. His nearest rival, Anglican priest Wavel Ramkalawan, won 41.43 per cent of the vote compared to Michel's 55.46 per cent. Voting took place over three days (19–21 May) to give residents on the outlying islands an opportunity to participate. Just over 80 per cent of Seychelles' 69,000 registered voters cast their ballot, with turnout in some districts exceeding 90 per cent.

Singapore: In elections on 7 May, the ruling People's Action Party (PAP) recorded its lowest result since separation from Malaysia in 1965, securing only 60.1 per cent of the vote, down from 66.6 per cent in 2006 and 75.3 per cent in 2001. The prevalence of Group Representation Constituencies (GRCs), requiring seats to be contested by slates of four to six candidates, has, in the past, made it difficult for smaller parties to field representatives in more than half of these seats. This year the opposition was co-ordinated and managed to run in all but one of the multi-member constituencies, gaining its first-ever GRC slate victory in Aljunied.

Uganda: Uganda's long-serving President, Yoweri Museveni, extended his quarter-century period in office for a further five years. In elections on 18 February, Museveni polled 68 per cent of the vote, up from 59 per cent in 2006 but down from the 75 per cent support he enjoyed in 1996. His nearest rival, veteran opposition leader Kizza Besigye – Museveni's former physician – mustered only 26 per cent. There was a large turnout in the north

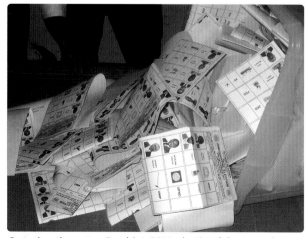

Counting the votes: Zambia's 2011 election (photographer: Liesl Harewood)

of the country where, for the first time, people were able to go to the polls without fear of attack from the rebel Lord's Resistance Army.

Zambia: After ten years of campaigning at the head of his Patriotic Front party, veteran politician Michael Sata finally won the presidency, replacing the incumbent Rupiah Banda of the Movement for Multiparty Democracy, in historic elections on 20 September. Sata had promised a new constitution and rapid action on several fronts, including a redistribution of Zambia's mining wealth and an end to corruption. He took 43 per cent of the vote, against 36 per cent for Banda, and his party was especially successful across the Copperbelt.

Adapted from Global *Magazine*

The 2011 Zambian elections: a view from Guyana

by Liesl Harewood

I was introduced to the idea of Election Observation Missions through Juliette Maughan. She had participated in several missions across Latin America and I longed to break into this field. As fate would have it, the Commonwealth sent out a request for a youth representative for the elections in Tanzania in 2010. I was unsuccessful in that application but a few weeks later was invited to participate in the Commonwealth Sub-Committee on Youth, Human Rights and Democracy as a member.

I clearly remember the moment when I opened the email inviting me to participate in Zambia as the Youth Representative on the mission. I immediately called Juliette and began excited discussion with her and Thandeka Percival, another member of the Committee who was the youth representative on the mission to Nigeria earlier that year. It was reassuring to hear their experiences and obtain pointers about practicalities – like getting sleep when you can.

The many meetings prior to deployment provided me with the opportunity to invite some youth representatives including Dennis Ngosa, the Commonwealth Youth Programme representative from Zambia, as well as members of youth focused non-governmental organisations. Since there were 1.2 million new registered voters and 54 per cent of them were between the ages of 18 and 35 years old, it was critical that the youth perspective be considered throughout all our observations and I felt the enormity of my task at hand.

After the first few days in Lusaka, it was time to be deployed and I was sent to one of the furthest corners of the country – a 10-hour drive north to Mansa, renowned for its friendliness and fish. My partner in the field and I spent our first evening making calls to the other observers in the area and strategising over dinner for our first full day ahead. We charted our path so that we could become familiar with the area, and get a greater understanding of how many stations we would be able to cover by car on election day.

When it came, I woke up with tingles. Prior to this moment, election day meant putting an 'X' on the ballot. Now I was here to observe the politics *behind* the politics. Having done it, I have a greater appreciation for what goes into an election, I am grappling with my understanding of governance and democracy and above

all, I want to see more youth rocking the vote in all countries. It is more than a privilege it is our right to vote and this is something I cannot emphasise enough.

I thought this was just a one-off experience, but I was proven wrong. Two months later in November I was an observer with a local NGO in Guyana, and ran into Commonwealth staff and observers on my own soil. By December, another election observation group was inviting me to participate in a mission to Jamaica. With three missions under my belt I feel like I can now consider myself an 'election observer'. No matter where this journey takes me, it is the Commonwealth that got me started – and you never forget the first time.

The 2011 Zambian elections: a view from New Zealand

by Sarah Fradgley

My Kenyan colleague, Kennedy Nyaundi, and I left Lusaka early on the morning of 18 September 2011 to travel 860 kilometres to Kasama, Northern Province, for election day. We travelled through the Lusaka suburbs full of stunning lilac jacaranda trees, on to Kabwe in Central Province, before turning on to the long Great North Road in the direction of Tanzania. In the small towns along the way, we passed Electoral Commission of Zambia billboards encouraging participation in the elections. For the rest of the journey, there was just a vast, empty and beautiful landscape.

Our 12-member Commonwealth Observer Group and excellent Secretariat team felt like a microcosm of the Commonwealth family of nations in partnership, in action. Observers had come from all continents and oceans of the Commonwealth. We heard about election preparations from the Chair of the Electoral Commission, Justice Irene Mambilima, immediately after her return from the airport to witness the unloading of ballots from South Africa. Over subsequent days, we met with the Movement for Multiparty Democracy and the Patriotic Front, as well as other political parties; and we had discussions with the Zambia National Women's Lobby, Young Women in Action, Transparency International, the Zambia Chapter of the Media Institute for Southern Africa, as well as the Commonwealth high commissioners to Lusaka. Secretariat staff gave first-class briefings on the political and electoral history of Zambia and our reporting duties during deployment to the provinces, and we became proud owners of multi-pocketed Commonwealth fishing jackets.

Prior to election day, the main issues raised were worries about election materials not reaching the most remote of areas; domestic observers perhaps not being able to be present at each of the streams and polling stations across the Province; and, as a result of the sometimes irresponsible campaigning and reporting, concern about what might happen after polling. From about 0300 hours on 20 September, long, good-natured queues started to form across Zambia. At 0545, in the presence of party agents, domestic and international observers, the empty ballot boxes were shown to everyone and the boxes were closed with numbered seals. At 0600 polling stations opened. Thereafter, men and women, old and young – young in particular for there were more than one million new voters on the voters' register for these elections – began to vote.

Afterwards, the long road home to Lusaka was punctuated by news of results, and concern for a colleague whose car had been attacked (thankfully he and his driver were fine) as he was leaving Kitwe. In between receiving the latest election-related updates, delicious chicken and 'nshima' were once again essential, as were the anecdotes of our driver, who'd seen the Berlin Wall fall [in 1989] and driven for Rupiah Banda decades earlier. Following a team debrief, we spent our remaining few days agreeing the final report.

It was an absolute privilege to take part – to represent the Commonwealth, to meet such great colleagues, and to be present in a fascinating country at such an important time in its history.

Upholding the Rule of Law:

the work of the Legal and Constitutional Affairs Division

'Some scholars regarded the repressive nature of the state as one of the factors that enhanced its developmental capacity. But what is of central importance is the state's ability to use its autonomy to consult, negotiate, and elicit consensus and co-operation from its social partners.'

– Omano Edigheji (quoted in *Commonwealth Good Governance 2011/12* by Duncan Green, Oxfam GB)

How does the state – or indeed anyone – consult, negotiate and elicit consensus and co-operation? The rule of law is a precursor to the successful promotion of development and democracy. Respect for, and adherence to it is recognised by Commonwealth governments as a fundamental Commonwealth value.

Where democracy is incomplete, the rule of law can provide a measure of 'good governance'. But for a well-functioning democracy, the rule of law is an absolute requirement. This is because it underpins the building blocks of free and fair electoral systems, respect for human rights, and a vibrant and participative civil society. In post-conflict societies, rebuilding and reconciliation often begin with the restoration of the rule of law to enable the fragile political process to begin.

Shared heritage

One of the Commonwealth's unique advantages is the commonality in the legal systems of its member countries occasioned by a shared history of the common law. The similarities provide a basis for exchanging best practices from one jurisdiction to another based on shared Commonwealth principles. This also promotes legal harmonisation, and makes legal co-operation easier and perhaps more cost-effective between its members. Further the Commonwealth is privileged to exercise a high-level convening power – the Commonwealth is the only global organisation that convenes meetings of law ministers. The triennial meetings of Commonwealth law ministers provide the Commonwealth Secretariat with excellent opportunities to facilitate exchanges of good practice and peer-learning among Commonwealth members, and to focus on the particular needs of small jurisdictions.

Commonwealth Schemes on criminal law are reciprocal arrangements between Commonwealth countries to co-operate within the parameters of their national laws. Assistance can be given in criminal matters, extradition, the return of material cultural heritage and in allowing those convicted in foreign countries to serve their sentences in their home country. Where two or more countries have common peculiarities, the Secretariat can help them to develop a legal framework to cater for their specific needs.

Assistance can also be given to member countries to negotiate similar arrangements with non-Commonwealth countries – helping member countries to engage with the rest of the world.

The Commonwealth's rule of law programmes support, promote and strengthen the rule of law and the administration of justice that underpins strong democratic and accountable governance. The Secretariat therefore works with Commonwealth countries to develop legal, judicial and constitutional reform and strengthen both legal and regulatory frameworks. The Secretariat provides assistance to member countries with the implementation of national programmes to give effect to international obligations. This includes the promotion of international co-operation, judicial reforms and the administration of justice, penal reforms, training of legislative drafters and the implementation of the various United Nations conventions and resolutions relating to issues such as the Rome Statute, terrorism, money laundering, corruption, and combating serious organised transnational crime.

Meeting in July 2011 (Sydney, Australia), Commonwealth law ministers recognised that the increasing international mobility of people, assets, goods and services means that more businesses and individuals are involved in international civil and commercial transactions. The secure planning of such transactions would be served by better mechanisms for obtaining reliable information about other legal systems and for strengthening judicial co-operation – and ministers requested the Commonwealth Secretariat to develop international civil legal co-operation mechanisms for the benefit of member states. The mechanisms would assist in matters such as the service of process and obtaining evidence abroad.

Development benefits

This is just one illustration of the need for 'legal certainty' in today's world. Legal certainty means that investors, particularly foreign investors, can feel safe and confident to enter the market and can assume risk that forms the basis of a market economy development. Lack of investment will slow economic growth and deny government the revenue to invest in education and social safety nets that are critical for sustainable development. But an environment premised on a strong respect for the rule of law will promote legal certainty and social trust, and in turn, promote and foster economic and human development.

Since the onset of globalisation and establishment of the UN's poverty-reduction targets, the Millennium Development Goals (MDGs) and World Trade Organization (WTO) agreements, the Commonwealth Secretariat has been helping countries to develop many legal frameworks to help them become credible trading partners, fulfil their international legal obligations and chart a course for domestic society and businesses. When international conventions are adopted, countries are expected to ratify and implement them so they become part of their national laws. Some of the important international instruments the Secretariat is working on include the UN Convention against Corruption (UNCAC) designed to address the challenges faced by many countries in implementing strategies for achieving transparent and accountable governance. Another is the International Criminal Court (ICC) Statute, which deals with the crimes of genocide, crimes against humanity and war crimes.

Other focus areas include the abuse of intellectual property rights (IPR) through the production and distribution of counterfeit and pirate goods, which has attained such magnitude that the global market is estimated at US$200 billion by the Organisation for Economic Co-operation and Development (OECD). The Rule of Law Programme has enabled the Secretariat to assist countries in developing stronger enforcement mechanisms, which (among others) has seen IP offences criminalised.

Fake goods are produced with substandard and sometimes dangerous materials that represent a danger to public health and safety; and because they are sold cheaply, they kill the market for bona fide goods, whose production ultimately ceases. Fake and pirate goods are also smuggled into countries, depriving governments of much needed revenue and sometimes funding organised crime. The Federal Government of Nigeria, for example, is to strengthen its agencies in the fight against the influx of substandard goods. Minister of Trade and Investment, Dr Olusegun Aganga made the declaration in December 2011 at an event of the Standards Organisation of Nigeria – a Commonwealth Secretariat partner in developing Small and Medium Enterprise.

Small states and LCAD strategy

In delivering its work under the Rule of Law Programme, the Legal and Constitutional Affairs Division (LCAD) works with a variety of sectors, lawyers, judges, registrars, policy-makers, investigators, prosecutors, the police and other law enforcement officials, academics, officials of international and regional organisations, and representatives of civil society. There is a strong reflection of issues such as gender, youth, human rights, environment and health in the Rule of Law Programme which brings a multi-faceted and robust approach to the Secretariat's work.

The Rule of Law Programme gives special attention to the legal issues relating to small states. Legal reform tailored to the needs of small states is therefore an important part of the portfolio which takes into consideration their special needs. In 2011, the Commonwealth Law Ministers Meeting (CLMM) involved a parallel Pacific Young Lawyers Forum. The Forum provided an opportunity for discussion of the ways in which the Commonwealth could assist young lawyers in Pacific countries with small legal professions. The Commonwealth's commitment to youth development led to support for the promotion of mentoring and continuing legal education as well as pro bono activities in law schools and among lawyers in member states. There was recognition of the key role of young lawyers in providing access to justice to the poor and vulnerable. The Forum saw the inauguration of the South Pacific Lawyers Association.

LCAD organises meetings every two years for law ministers and attorneys-general of small Commonwealth jurisdictions (LMSCJ). The meeting is immediately preceded by the meeting of senior

officials of law ministries (SOLM), thus making it convenient and cost-effective for officials from small states to attend both meetings if they so wish. The LMSCJ provides an important platform to determine matters of mutual interest and to develop a common legal policy based on their shared circumstances. Another platform is provided through the triennial CLMM itself. CLMM 2011 discussed the threat to human security, and to the very existence of some small states, posed by climate change. Ministers also noted that climate change has implications for migration and the level of international policy co-operation needed.

Some LCAD initiatives fall within the primary responsibility of other, 'non-legal' ministries such as those responsible for women and gender. Given the entrenched gender biases and discrimination in the context of culture and the law, the Commonwealth Plan of Action for Gender Equality 2005–2015 calls for advancing women's rights in the administration of justice, customary practices and the law. Working with the Gender Section, LCAD assists in integrating gender in justice systems in the Commonwealth. This indicates the interdependence of the development issues in member countries and the need to co-ordinate, avoid compartmentalisation of the issues, and develop a comprehensive solution to achieving development as embodied by the MDGs.

Listening to regional and professional networks

Collaboration with other international, regional and national partners in the implementation of rule of law projects in the Commonwealth is essential. These partner organisations include the Commonwealth Magistrates' and Judges' Association, the Commonwealth Lawyers Association, the International Criminal Court, the Commonwealth Legal Education Association, the Commonwealth Association for Legislative Counsel, the International Bar Association, the UN and the British Red Cross Society.

In May 2011, the Legal and Constitutional Affairs Division's Criminal Law Section co-ordinated a regional forum for South Asian judges on economic and financial crime. Judges from Bangladesh, Maldives, Pakistan and Sri Lanka participated along with judges from Australia, Malaysia, Singapore and the United Kingdom. The overall purpose of the forum was to enhance the capacity of judiciaries from Commonwealth South Asian countries in the adjudication of economic and financial crimes and, in particular, transnational crimes such as money laundering and the financing of terrorism.

CLMM 2011 received a paper prepared by the Commonwealth Magistrates' and Judges' Association (CMJA), presenting the preliminary results of an examination of the position of magistrates within the Commonwealth. The paper recorded concerns that in some Commonwealth jurisdictions the independence of the magistracy was without legislative protection; that appointments were made by processes which were not transparent; that in some countries, magistrates' security of tenure was limited; and that adequate resources were not always made available to magistrates' courts. Law ministers resolved to consider taking appropriate steps to strengthen their domestic legal frameworks and other measures for assuring the independence and integrity of their magistracy in compliance with the Commonwealth fundamental values.

Legal dissemination

The *Commonwealth Law Bulletin* (CLB) is a quarterly flagship publication of the Commonwealth Secretariat and plays an important role in legal dissemination. In 2011, the *Bulletin* continued to provide its steadily increasing readership with topical articles and information on key legal developments from around the Commonwealth. Around 5,000 institutions have access to the CLB, either as paying subscribers, through sales packages, via the EBSCO database (an electronic journals service), or through a small number of subscriptions paid for by the Secretariat.

March 2011 saw the publication of an issue featuring articles on such varied topics as child labour in India, the death penalty in Ghana and a review of the role of the Commonwealth by Eminent Persons Group (EPG) member Michael Kirby. June's issue featured a look at building regulations in Nigeria and a paper on the impact of the Human Rights Act in the UK, among others. As part of an ongoing commitment to collaborate increasingly with partner organisations, September's CLB was a 'special issue' on legislative drafting, published in collaboration with the Sir William Dale Centre for Legislative Studies, Institute of Advanced Legal Studies, University of London.

The Secretariat has also continued to disseminate materials from training programmes, workshops and meetings run across the Commonwealth. In this respect, the *Handbook of Best Practices for Registrars of Final/Appellate, Regional and International Courts and Tribunals* (due to be published April 2012) will provide examples of good practice in the workings of the courts, helping registrars to benefit from the challenges faced by other courts and tribunals throughout the Commonwealth and worldwide.

> The Commonwealth Law Ministers Meeting will next be held in Botswana in 2014.

Training prosecutors and police in East Africa

In 2011, the Commonwealth Secretariat implemented a prosecution and police training programme for the East Africa region through its Criminal Law Section. This training programme was originally piloted in the Asia-Pacific region, in 2009, and focuses on key aspects of criminal law and enhancing international co-operation in the prevention and combating of transnational organised crime.

The extension of this programme to the East Africa region was realised through the involvement of six key member countries (Kenya, Mauritius, Rwanda, Seychelles, Uganda and the United Republic of Tanzania).

Initially, the participants worked through a four-week web based component, assisted by experts and comparing their individual experiences and case studies on various subjects. The first two modules focused on foundational skills including case preparation, co-ordination and liaison between relevant criminal justice agencies, disclosure, victim and witness assistance and protection, and bail/sentencing. The last two modules focused on international co-operation, in particular, mutual legal assistance and extradition. Discussion forums which enabled the participants to work together

with each other and the relevant experts on relevant issues were also included.

In the week of on-site intensive training held in June 2011, in Sydney, Australia, the subject matter of the above modules was expanded, real case-studies were presented and the participants along with regional experts and Secretariat staff members analysed regional specific issues to do with international co-operation and mutual legal assistance. In addition, officers from the New South Wales police force and the Australian Federal Police, as well as barristers from various Commonwealth jurisdictions, held presentations on countering terrorism, anti-money laundering, victim/witness protection and prosecution disclosure. The participants were also taken to the New South Wales police academy and both the district and local courts in Sydney to witness firsthand some of the skills covered in the lectures.

The training was followed up with national mentoring programmes for prosecutors and investigators in Nairobi, Kenya (February 2012) for Kenya, Rwanda, Tanzania and Uganda; in Port Louis, Mauritius (February 2012) for Mauritius and Seychelles; and Arusha, Tanzania (May 2012) for Tanzania and Uganda.

> The Harare Scheme relating to Mutual Legal Assistance in Criminal Matters within the Commonwealth has, for a quarter of a century, provided a constructive and pragmatic approach to mutual co-operation between Commonwealth countries in combating transnational crime. The Commonwealth Secretariat is developing model legislation to assist member countries in implementing revisions. By June 2013 it will have delivered capacity-building initiatives on the interception of telecommunications and asset recovery.

Judicial development assistance

I am pleased that the Commonwealth is able to support the judges of Papua New Guinea in ensuring they conduct their important roles in accordance with fundamental Commonwealth values, notably the Commonwealth [Latimer House] Principles on the Three Branches of Government.

Commonwealth Secretary-General Kamalesh Sharma, 2012

The 2011 CLMM recognised that the effective administration of justice required not only an independent judiciary of high competence, but also an efficient court system. In many countries, the courts face a number of challenges: chronic delays, the need to reform procedural rules, the introduction of alternative dispute resolution processes and case management systems, and the deployment and effective use of modern technology. The most serious consequence of the backlog of criminal cases is the detention of people awaiting trial. Where there is a backlog of civil and commercial cases, this discourages commerce in a country. Litigation is an ordinary component of business and inefficiencies can be very costly for investors.

The Commonwealth is ready to assist all member countries wishing to strengthen their administration of justice and the cost of the assistance is borne by the Secretariat. A recent seminar for Papua New Guinea judges (February 2012) tackled judicial independence and ethics. It was conducted in collaboration with the Papua New

Export industries: international commercial law is key

Guinea Centre for Judicial Excellence, the National and Supreme Court of Papua New Guinea, and the Commonwealth Magistrates' and Judges' Association. The seminar was part of ongoing co-operation between the Commonwealth and the Papua New Guinea judiciary, under way since 2010.

Two new Commonwealth judges were appointed to Swaziland in October 2011. The Commonwealth is ready to assist all member countries wishing to strengthen their administration of justice and the cost of the assistance is borne by the Secretariat. Often the role of a Commonwealth-funded judge is to clear a backlog of cases.

- A judge at the Court of Appeal of The Gambia is spending 2011–12 clearing a backlog of over 80 appeal cases.

- A judge assigned to the High Court of Lesotho heard over 150 commercial cases and advised the Chief Justice on new rules for the commercial court, while a court administration expert introduced new case management software. For the first time, this is producing accurate figures on the number of applications lodged, the court caseload and the case disposal rate.

- A legal expert assigned to the Magistrates Commission of Namibia provided training to 32 of its 33 offices across the country.

- A judge assigned to the High Court of Solomon Islands has reduced the backlog of cases by 25 per cent.

Rwanda: a new legal system under construction

I certainly found the seminar useful; it will add value to the work that I do. It has given me confidence, skills and knowledge to apply when assessing damages in civil matters.

Justice Julian Ndinda, Rwanda

Rwanda has recently joined the Commonwealth and is moving from a civil law system to a mix of civil and common law. The Rwandan Judiciary requested Secretariat assistance in evaluation of evidence; sentencing; use of technology in courts; and training of judges on (common law) assessment of damages in civil cases. The damages assessment seminar (December 2011) involved 30 judges drawn from the Commercial Court and the Supreme Court in Kigali.

Speaking at the seminar, Deputy Chief Justice Sam Rugege noted that as Rwanda's legal system was 'under construction' it was important that judges are fully equipped with common law norms that will help in strengthening the delivery of justice. 'Because presently there is not much guidance in the application of the law regarding assessment of damages, the seminar was a right step in the right direction,' he said.

Jarvis Matiya, Head of the Secretariat's Justice Section, explains: 'The participating judges were also able to relate the common law system to their own local circumstances, and how it could apply in Rwanda. They looked at how the common law jurisprudence has developed on the subject matter, and learned from other jurisdictions' experience in the adoption and application of the common law in assessing damages and taxing costs.' Matiya has pledged ongoing support.

In order to make the impact of the seminar more sustainable, the Deputy Chief Justice requested that there should be a special training session for trainers during the second seminar to take place in 2012. The aim is to have judges who could train others on the subject matter as an ongoing activity.

A model integrity law for small states

In November 2011 nine Commonwealth Pacific islands countries and associated states took part in consultations on a draft model law to ensure public officials act ethically. It was the second regional seminar of its kind.

The draft Integrity in Public Life Act, which will become a model for all Commonwealth small jurisdictions, includes a code of conduct for public officials and guidelines on conflict of interest. It was reviewed by representatives of law ministries and attorneys-general from Kiribati, Nauru, Papua New Guinea, Samoa, Solomon Islands, Tonga, Vanuatu, Cook Islands, Niue and Marshall Islands (a non-Commonwealth country) at a consultation in Auckland, New Zealand.

Provisions in the draft include the creation of an Integrity Commission to investigate breaches of the code of conduct and to publish guidelines on conflict of interest, to avoid any perception that public officials have an interest in decisions that they may take. Mark Guthrie, Legal Adviser in the Justice Section of the Legal and

Constitutional Affairs Division at the Commonwealth Secretariat, said the process is unique as it allows small countries to have a say in what will become a model for use by all Commonwealth small jurisdictions.

The model law was mandated at the 2007 Meeting of Law Ministers and Attorneys-General of Small Commonwealth Jurisdictions and a first draft was put together as a result of recommendations made at a 2010 Caribbean regional seminar in Montego Bay, Jamaica.

'The Auckland seminar provided us with valuable material to revise and supplement the draft. The next step will be for our experts to produce a second draft,' said Guthrie. 'The model law is not intended to rival or displace other models or options available. It will be for each small jurisdiction considering enacting a law on Integrity in Public Life to consider its provisions and to adapt them according to their particular needs.'

A third round of regional consultation will be held in Africa in 2012 before the final draft is presented to law ministers of small Commonwealth jurisdictions at their next meeting.

Legislative drafting: the language of law

Lawyers like me can only benefit from courses like this. When the Law Reform Commission where I work chooses to have its own drafting team then my colleagues and I will be ready to let this training come into good use.

David Osei Asare, Ghana

Legal drafting is a technical skill, conducted far from the limelight, whose fine detail and great impact on society is not widely known or appreciated. According to the *Commonwealth Law Bulletin*, this profession requires the cultivation of detachment. Yet its purpose, strength and values lie in its efforts to hold its audience to the ideas behind the policy decisions. Laws are made out of words; in this field even one poorly constructed sentence can turn good policy into bad law – the rights and liberties of people may be put at risk and the policy may not be given effect. Unnecessary controversy and litigation, and perverse effects on the operation of public and private interests, are likely to be the result.

Construction law: public safety and environmental responsibility (photographer and copyright: Michael N de la Hay / © Commonwealth Secretariat)

Commonwealth law ministers are acutely aware that difficulties in the recruitment and retention of drafters remain major impediments to the realisation of policy objectives in many member states. The demand for Commonwealth assistance to provide drafters for member countries is therefore as high as ever – especially given current reforms taking place in most countries.

Segametsi Mothibatsela, former Acting Deputy Attorney-General of Botswana, is one of the Commonwealth's leading experts. She has recently assisted law-makers in Belize and Dominica, and in 2011 undertook a Commonwealth-funded assignment with the Caribbean Community (CARICOM) in Guyana. The aim is to have as many drafters as possible so member states can address their social, economic and political challenges. Says Mothibatsela, 'I believe this project has had a positive impact and that the people I train will become agents of change as well.' In 2011 there were five other CFTC (Commonwealth Fund for Technical Co-operation) legal drafters on assignment in Swaziland, Kenya and Tonga.

The Commonwealth Secretariat, in conjunction with the Ghana Law School, organises an annual 16-week course for legislative drafters from Africa.

The Secretariat collaborated with the Commonwealth Association of Legislative Drafters to organise a regional meeting for legislative drafters from across the Asia region in Colombo, Sri Lanka, in September 2011. The conference discussed drafting in small jurisdictions; legislative responses to transnational crime; statutory interpretation; legislating for development; ICT resourcing; and adaption of laws in Pakistan.

The law/human rights interface

Human rights are about the rights of people. Proclaimed in 1948 by the UN General Assembly in the Universal Declaration of Human Rights, they have been elaborated by two International Covenants adopted in 1966: the International Covenant on Civil and Political Rights and the International Covenant on Economic, Social and Cultural Rights. As core values we regard them as inseparable ... we are equally concerned about the wretchedness of the weak under despotic regimes as we are about the degradation of the poor under inequitable national and international structures.

Commonwealth Eminent Persons Group, 2011

CLMM 2011 discussed the issue of forced or servile marriages which constituted a human rights violation that impeded individuals' most basic and fundamental rights. Many forced marriages had a transnational quality and their prevention could require active co-operation between the states concerned. Ministers reiterated their support for the Convention on the Elimination of All Forms of Discrimination against Women (CEDAW).

The Meeting also received a presentation by Lord Justice Thorpe, Head of International Family Justice for England and Wales, on extending the 1980 Hague Child Abduction Convention throughout the Commonwealth. He urged accession to the Convention and emphasised the need for Commonwealth member states to support the work of the Hague Conference in the field of family law, including its network of specialist judges and the Malta Process which sought to build links between states with Islamic law and other states.

In recent years both Commonwealth Law Ministers Meetings and Meetings of Law Ministers and Attorneys-General of Small Commonwealth Jurisdictions have considered two related issues: that of promoting alternative sentencing and that of the overcrowding in prisons and the excessive use of pre-trial detention in many countries. These were considered in depth in 2010 at the Twelfth United Nations Congress on Crime Prevention and Criminal Justice. Up to June 2013, the Secretariat is delivering technical assistance on reducing overcrowding, upon request of member countries.

CLMM Essay Competition for Law Students and Young Lawyers

Question: What practical steps could the Australian Government and pro bono providers take to ensure that the legal assistance provided by Australian agencies and pro bono providers is sustainable in recipient countries within the Pacific region?

From the winning entry by Adam Arnold, University of New South Wales, Australia

… Before making recommendations, it is necessary to briefly explore the notion of sustainability. In the context of legal assistance, activities will be sustainable if they lead to results in legal institutions and practices which endure after assistance is phased out. The Office of Development Effectiveness notes that there are several possible criteria for sustainability in the law and justice sector. These include adequate personnel, financial resources, appropriate considerations of the host culture, management structures and ownership of reforms. Accordingly, this note makes recommendations across most of these areas.

First, Australia should provide additional opportunities for Pacific Islanders to engage in legal studies in Australia. This will provide a

Children are rights-bearers

sustainable 'career pipeline' for qualified law and justice professionals to influence processes in their own countries, which is far more effective than external development providers could be. In the view of one Australian legal advisor in the Solomon Islands, 'substantial change' in the law and justice sector is impossible unless human resources are developed 'dramatically and consistently'.

The ongoing AusAID evaluation into Australia's assistance in the law and justice sector concurs that this sustainability is a particular issue in Pacific Island states, and warns against the danger of capacity substitution by Australian staff instead of promoting growth in the local resourcing of the sector. This article notes with great enthusiasm the introduction of the Pacific Legal Twinning Program in 2010. The programme, where legal officers undertake a three month placement in legal policy divisions within the Attorney General's Department, is a critical first step in building capacity in the law and justice sector in Pacific states. The present author urges the Department to support additional staff beyond the two-person programme which was conducted in 2010.

In order to build capacity in the legal sector, particularly among students and new graduates, the 2007 Parliamentary Inquiry into Australia's Aid Program in the Pacific recommended the establishment of a reverse Australian Youth Ambassadors Scheme for youth from Pacific Island states (The Pacific Island Youth Ambassador Scheme – 'PIYA'). This programme would place participants in host organisations, including human rights bodies, and some government agencies. The PIYA proposal is consistent with the Framework's goal of 'building and embedding institutional linkages that will enable more sustainable access to, and sharing of, technical expertise and resources over the longer term'.

In its response to the Parliamentary report, the Government noted that existing programmes, such as the Australian Leadership Awards Fellowship Scheme, provided capacity for people from the Asia-Pacific region to study and work in Australian organisations. However, the Asia-Pacific region is far broader than the Pacific states and thus is not focused on the particular needs of Pacific states. The government also stated that in its response that it would consider the feasibility of a PIYA-style scheme during a review of its international volunteering programmes. That review was concluded in 2009 and there was no reference to or discussion of the Committee's proposal for PIYA or another similar initiative.

Recommendation 1: Implement the Pacific Island Youth Ambassador Scheme in line with the Committee's recommendation. Consider as part of the programme a quota for law and justice related applicants to study and work within Australian legal and justice institutions and organisations.

Second, Australian provision of legal assistance should take its guiding principle to be the ownership of the initiative by the host state. Where possible, Australia should seek to encourage 'local leadership and decision-making roles'. Australian instrumentalities and pro bono providers should engage in the discourse of facilitation instead of rule-making. It should be noted that instances of Australian-directed activities are not intended to bring about ill will, but that is their effect. For example, in the law and justice sector development within the Regional Assistance Mission to the Solomon Islands ('RAMSI'), some commentators have noticed the continuation of a 'donor-recipient mentality rather than being a true partnership' and an Australia which 'needs to be more cognisant of Melanesian values'.

There is also concern regarding the fact that Australian advisors in the Solomon Islands are required to report their progress to an Australian bureaucracy rather than the Solomon Islands Government. This example, and the broader discussion above, demonstrate the need for the government of the recipient nation to take ownership of the initiatives, with Australian expertise being used to facilitate change, not to oversee or direct it. …

Recommendation 2: Ideally, ownership and accountability for development initiatives should lie with the host nation. Australian instrumentalities should reinforce the desire for countries to gain ownership of reforms and initiatives. At the same time, Australia should be aware that despite best intentions, there is often a lack of sufficient capacity to take ownership. In these circumstances, Australia should exercise an administrative role and engage with partner states on any matter relating to broader strategic reforms.

The Australian Government should ensure that its instrumentalities and pro bono providers stipulate this in any development proposals and constantly reinforce it through regular dialogue with national governments. This proposal is consistent with the *Framework*'s emphasis on 'working in partnership' with Pacific states.

Finally, Australian government and pro bono assistance should work where possible to reform existing community based justice systems. This is particularly the case in the Pacific region and the dominance of this informal justice sector in many Pacific states. In Papua New Guinea and the Solomon Islands, it is estimated that eighty per cent of the population rely on traditional justice systems rather than formal justice systems. However, these institutions must be reformed; some are known to deliver a brand of justice which is inimical to the rights of women and children and inconsistent with existing international human rights protections and obligations.

Recommendation 3: The Australian Government and pro bono providers should, where possible, develop and update existing community based justice systems. These systems carry with them a significant history and substantial community backing. However, as a baseline requirement, these systems must reflect contemporary understandings of human rights, particular in the area of gender equality and youth. Simultaneously, efforts should be directed to enhancing the efficiency (cost and time) of involvement in the developing formal justice sector.

The work of the Human Rights Unit:

participation, accountability, non-discrimination, empowerment, legality

'The Government of Mauritius feels privileged to have been able to share its experience of the [human rights review] process with Swaziland, a country in the region with which it has much in common. We strongly believe that small countries can assist each other in reinforcing capacity and are grateful to the Commonwealth for facilitating the process … I was greeted from day one as a neighbour.'

– Aruna Narain, Assistant Solicitor- General, Mauritius

CHOGM declarations and communiqués – including the 1991 Harare Declaration and the 2007 Kampala Communiqué – have consistently reaffirmed the commitment of the Commonwealth to the advancement of fundamental human rights as a core political value of the association. Through its Human Rights Unit (HRU), the Secretariat continues to develop promotional and assistance programmes to support Commonwealth members' stated human rights commitments. It has been pleasing to see that many member states have found the HRU technical assistance of value and that they continue to request it.

As human rights become increasingly embedded in the fabric of everyday life, so do the expectations placed on any value-based organisation – governmental, non-governmental or intergovernmental. The Commonwealth Secretariat is committed to progressively mainstreaming human rights into its programme of work as a whole. The unit regularly advises the Secretary-General and Secretariat staff on human rights issues arising from current Secretariat work or developments across the Commonwealth, including on rights-based approaches to HIV/AIDS treatment, trafficking of persons, including women, and other gender issues; and promotes human rights awareness among young people. Training is also regularly provided to election observer missions.

The Commonwealth continues to liaise with the United Nations human rights mechanisms, as well as regional forums, to ensure efficient and complementary programme activity. Through a Memorandum of Understanding with the UN High Commissioner for Human Rights (UNHCHR), the Secretariat works with a number of UN regional offices – for example, to ensure that counter-terrorism measures are compliant with basic human rights standards. Other partners include the Asia Pacific Forum of NHRIs, Interights and Pacific Regional Rights Resource Team.

Monitoring progress

[A] *contemporary Commonwealth challenge to be addressed is in the area of sexual orientation. Our shared commitment, reaffirmed at CHOGM 2009, is to have 'rights for all without discrimination on any grounds' and opposition to stigmatisation and victimisation. But progress has been uneven towards ensuring that domestic legislation reflects our belief that vilification and targeting on grounds of sexual orientation is at odds with the fundamental values of the Commonwealth.*

Secretary–General Kamalesh Sharma at Commonwealth Law Ministers Meeting 2011

The Universal Periodic Review (UPR, established in 2006) looks at the human rights records of all 192 UN member states once every four years – the only review mechanism of its kind. The UPR is a co-operative, state-driven process, under the auspices of the Human Rights Council, which provides the opportunity for each state to declare what actions they have taken to improve the human rights situations in their countries and to fulfil their human rights obligations. The Secretariat seized the moment in beginning its work on UPR in March 2008. With the pivotal support of the UK Foreign and Commonwealth Office (FCO), it has been able to place the UPR at the heart of its human rights work.

As of 2012, almost every Commonwealth state has been involved. For the mechanism to have impact, it does indeed depend on the active, informed and positive involvement of all stakeholders. Adopting a tripartite formula, seminars have brought together government officials, national mechanisms such as national human rights institutions (NHRIs)/ombudsman offices and civil society organisations, as well as staff from UNHCHR – the key stakeholders in the UPR process. The seminars have allowed Commonwealth countries the opportunity to share best practices and ask questions in the run-up to preparation of national reports. The HRU has also consistently attended reviews of the resultant reports (in Geneva, Switzerland). At the sessions, the HRU team engages with member states' representatives, providing information, support and offers of further technical co-operation. For example, in May 2011, the team observed the review of Seychelles, Solomon Islands, Sierra Leone, Singapore, Samoa, St Vincent and the Grenadines, and Papua New Guinea.

Having gone through the process in 2010, Mauritius was able to assist Swaziland when it came up for its first review (presented in Geneva in October 2011). HRU's Karen McKenzie explains: 'Swaziland is a small state with limited financial and human resources and capacity to fulfil country reporting obligations. When we started the workshop, it was clear the UPR was a process unknown to the participants; on the second day, they felt the process had been demystified for them – the work done during group exercises clearly indicated their new-found confidence in engaging with the knowledge and material.'

Sicelo Dlamini, Principal Secretary of Swaziland's Ministry of Justice, agrees: 'The workshop helped clarify the process. All the stakeholders who attended were very appreciative of the assistance provided. We are more confident about it now.'

In response to member states' requests, HRU commenced a programme in early 2011 that focuses on the implementation phase of UPR. Regional follow-up seminars aim to focus on the time between the first and second UPR cycles – four and a half years when states are expected to take forward UPR recommendations.

Ratifications of rights instruments

I congratulate all governments of the Commonwealth for ratifying the Convention on the Rights of the Child. The Convention is not a list of aspirations; it is a list of rights. Our duties to our children cover their political, economic and social and cultural rights. Despite significant achievements made, children around the world are still victims of discrimination, violence, abuse and exploitation … A renewed commitment is an obligation of every individual, every family, every state. It is an obligation of every single adult citizen.

Dr Graça Machel, international advocate for women's and children's rights, member of the Commonwealth Eminent Persons Group and former Chairperson, Commonwealth Foundation

In order to provide a normative framework for the national promotion and protection of rights, the Secretariat continues to encourage and assist member countries, particularly small states, with the process of ratifying the major human rights conventions, with drafting and implementing legislation to give them effect in national law, and with reporting obligations arising from them. The coverage of these conventions is ever growing. For example, in 2011 Nauru ratified the Convention on the Elimination of All Forms of Discrimination against Women, and Zambia ratified the International Convention for the Protection of All Persons from Enforced Disappearance.

The first new human rights instrument of the 21st century is the Convention on the Rights of Persons with Disabilities (CRPD, 2006). All Commonwealth countries have signed the UNCRPD. That means they recognise that disability results from the interaction between persons with impairments (long-term physical, mental, intellectual or sensory impairments) and the barriers that hinder their full and effective participation in society on an equal basis. So, for example, the UNCRPD says disabled children should have an education on an equal footing, with necessary means to reach their full potential. And yet today, only 2–3 per cent of disabled children worldwide are in school at all.

The rights model of disability is no small challenge for governments to implement, given the many decades in which (people with) disabilities have been medicalised. Belize, Cyprus and Pakistan are among the countries that ratified the Convention in 2011. As of November that year, 27 member countries had done so.

National Human Rights Institutions

HRU warmly congratulates Nigeria and Sierra Leone's National Human Rights Institutions on their being awarded 'A' status by the UN International Coordinating Committee of NHRIs.

The Commonwealth 'Best Practice' Guidelines on the Establishment of NHRIs are an example of jointly developed best practice standards that are being used in project work, including by the UN,

to strengthen the institutional capacity of human rights commissions, and other bodies, to protect individuals and groups. The Secretariat also continues to work with governments to strengthen the capacity of existing NHRIs to operate confidently, competently and independently, based on these guidelines. The Secretariat provides advice both in countries where an NHRI is proposed and where the NHRI is in a nascent stage, requiring support. This kind of support was provided to the interim government of Bangladesh, leading to the establishment of a human rights commission there in 2010.

Meetings of NHRIs took place in London in May 2011, and again before the 2011 CHOGM. Australia, as CHOGM host, assumed chair of the Commonwealth Forum of National Human Rights Institutions (CFNHRI) until 2013. In March 2011, the HRU together with the Office of the High Commissioner for Human Rights (OHCHR) co-hosted a regional workshop for Ombudsman Offices in the English-speaking Caribbean countries, in Trinidad and Tobago. The overall objective of the regional workshop was to contribute to the dialogue on human rights in the region.

Human rights education

Business and human rights is not an ephemeral issue to be considered at some future date. It is and must remain at the core of our concerns today.

Professor John Ruggie, UN Special Representative on business and human rights, 2009

Lack of awareness about basic rights protections is a major barrier to realising ideals of human equality and dignity. Human rights awareness and education is therefore of great importance to the Commonwealth, especially for business, teachers, police and other government officials, distance learners, women and young people.

Debates about the impact of business, particularly as conducted by transnational corporations, are not new. Long before the first large-scale anti-globalisation demonstrations at meetings of the World Trade Organization in Seattle, USA, in 1999 and the World Economic Forum in Melbourne, Australia, in 2000, questions had been raised about the effects of international trade and the internationalisation of production on vulnerable communities and people in developing countries. Many recognise the positive influence of international trade on the lives of consumers and producers alike – the right to food, to a livelihood, to an adequate standard of living can all be bolstered by the integration of an economy into international trade and business.

But the negative effect on human rights, direct or indirect, remains a reality, with severe consequences for individuals, families and communities around the world. The main focus in relation to the practices of multinational companies operating in developing countries has been on labour and environmental standards, and the impact of their activities on the local community. Less attention has been paid to the complex supply chains in which the large businesses are several steps removed from the producers and the workers, and their families and communities. Yet the decisions taken by these businesses can have profound effects across borders, on the lives of people living thousands of kilometres away who depend on trade for their livelihoods

The Secretariat continues to publish and disseminate widely best practice guidelines on a range of rights issues. Through the

ZUFIAW
The Zambia Union of Financial Institutions and Allied Workers

Equal rights, equal opportunities, progress for all!

ZUFIAW is the union of choice for workers in the finance, banking, building societies, pension funds, insurance and all financial related institutions in Zambia. Established in 1970 as the Zambia Union of Bank Officials (ZUBO), ZUFIAW has a membership of 4,000 drawn from 28 institutions. ZUFIAW is affiliated to the Federation of Free Trade Unions of Zambia (FFTUZ) and UNI Global Union.

President Cephas Mukuka addressing the press

ZUFIAW members in action

ZUFIAW has a strong **commitment to gender equality**. At its last Congress in 2006, the Union scored a first by achieving 70 per cent women's representation – a record in the labour movement locally and regionally.

With their motto **'Workers' First'** ZUFIAW is advancing the interests of workers at every decision-making level, and building partnerships with civil society and the community. In 2002, ZUFIAW spearheaded a **'Save Our Parastatals'** campaign which ensured that Zambians retained ownership of the national commercial bank, ZANACO, that was privatised. This has saved thousands of jobs and maintained banking services in rural areas.

In 2003, ZUFIAW co-ordinated a protest action and petitioned the government on **'Child Sexual Abuse and Defilement'** an action that led to the stiffening of legislation on child sex offenders and defilement. And again in 2003, the union won the **Best Labour Management Partnership Award** for their successful partnership on HIV/AIDS with the National Pension Scheme (NAPSA). In the same year, ZUFIAW was the only trade union appointed to sit on the Constitutional Review Commission.

Global competition has brought about a downward pressure on workers' rights. ZUFIAW has risen to this challenge by organising workers and empowering them with a voice at the workplace. As ZUFIAW we have continued to put **'workers first'** because development is about people!

First Woman General Secretary of ZUFIAW, Mrs Joyce Nonde Simukoko

Contact
Zambian Union of Financial Institutions and Allied Workers
1st Floor, Luangwa House
Cairo Road
P O Box 31174
Lusaka

Tel: + 260 212 22 2105
Fax: + 260 212 23 1364
Email: zufiaw@microlink.zm

www.zufiaw.org.zm

publication of human rights information such as the *Human Rights Update* newsletter, the Secretariat acquaints countries with human rights developments in the Commonwealth and the wider world, and helps in developing policies in line with international human rights standards. In collaboration with Interights, a UK-based international human rights non-governmental organisation, the *Commonwealth Human Rights Law Digest*, which compiles human rights cases from across the Commonwealth, is published on a bi-annual basis.

Human rights training for police

Once you start to take short cuts with the law, once you start to put the law to one side, you open the floodgates … Torture is not, in any way, an effective means of getting information. And even if it were, it ought to be outlawed. It is no way for any civilised nation to behave and I say that as someone who has experienced both physical and mental torture.

Terry Waite CBE, Commonwealth Lecture 2009
(Waite, a former hostage negotiator, was himself kidnapped and held captive from 1987 to 1991)

A human rights-based approach to policing for communities begins with knowledge and awareness on the part of police officers as to the limits of lawful police authority and conduct. This means attention to human rights during police officers' initial, continuation and refresher training. The Commonwealth Secretariat has trained officers from 45 police forces. In 2012 it is being followed up with training for prison staff.

Both legal and normative (attitudes and values) issues, as well as practical aspects, are covered in the training. For Ernest Quatre, Seychelles Police Commissioner, the Commonwealth programme is useful because 'a sound knowledge of human rights is crucial in the application of the law. It precludes the outcome of controversy and enables the police force to retain its dignity and credibility in the face of the public whom it serves and protects.'

Another player in police reform, the Commonwealth Human Rights Initiative (CHRI), stresses that accountability to not just government, but also a wider network of agencies and organisations, working on behalf of the interests of the people, is critical to 'democratic policing'. Says CHRI Director Maja Daruwala, 'Police forces are the trusted protectors not only of life and security of property, but also

Police protect not just life and property, but also civil liberties

of civil liberties which have been won for the people. In some countries, while the situation is not perfect, they have had the time, uninterrupted by conflict, to improve their policing.' But, in many cases, forces are governed by frameworks that have not been updated for many years and 'if there is lack of reform then both police and public suffer'.

Human rights are also about simple human contact. According to one young respondent in Honiara, Solomon Islands, 'Our police officers do their patrol in vehicles, not on foot. The police should come to our community to give awareness talks, and work closely with youths, chiefs and other community leaders both in rural and urban areas. If they could do this, I believe there would be fewer problems in our country' (Regional Assistance Mission to Solomon Islands, 2009).

Education and employment for persons with disabilities

Integration is about putting someone into an environment where they are expected to fit into it. Inclusion is about making changes to ensure that everyone can be included, rather than expecting the person to change.

Zara Todd, Commonwealth Young Disabled People's Forum/Alliance for Inclusive Education (2012)

That disabled people do not enjoy equal access to their human rights has been internationally acknowledged since the mid-1980s. The majority of persons with disabilities live in poverty. For this 10 per cent of the population – 20 per cent of the poorest – society itself tends to be excluding, discriminatory, at best condescending, and ultimately disabling.

In January 2012 participants from 14 Commonwealth countries explored best practice for implementation of the UNCRPD. Commonwealth Secretary-General Kamalesh Sharma said the exclusion of persons with disabilities from school or work militates against the Commonwealth's deeply held conviction that equal opportunity is what contributes to the progress and well-being of communities.

The Convention is unique in being both a development and a human rights instrument. It is legally binding. Its purpose is 'to promote, protect and ensure the full and equal enjoyment of all human rights and fundamental freedoms by all persons with disabilities, and to promote respect for their inherent dignity.' Disabled people 'shall have effective enjoyment of the universal right to life', on an equal basis with others. Disabled people must be recognised as persons before the law, and enjoy legal capacity. They must be able to own and inherit property, and have access to credit. They must have effective access to justice, on an equal basis with others.

Participants at the roundtable included representatives from UNICEF, the International Labour Organization (ILO), International Paralympics Committee, Commonwealth Disabled People's Forum, Commonwealth Young Disabled People's Forum, Commonwealth Advisory Body on Sport, Cricket for Change, practitioners from governments, national human rights protection mechanisms and civil society organisations. The meeting's resolutions will be carried forward at forums such as the Conference of Commonwealth Education Ministers in Mauritius in August 2012, the UN

Disabled people should have effective enjoyment of the universal right to life on an equal basis with others (photograph © Commonwealth Photographic Awards)

Conference on Sustainable Development in Brazil in June 2012, and the UN General Assembly's high-level meeting on disability and development in September 2013.

- Girls with disabilities are almost 10 per cent less likely to finish primary school than their male classmates according to a World Health survey.

- A 2011 video about the UN Convention, made by disabled school students, can be accessed from www.whizz-kidz.org.uk.

Gender and disability: a campaigner's view

Abia Akram from Pakistan began her education at an education centre for persons with disabilities before attending a mainstream school. But it was at her new school that the 'special' dispensations her teachers afforded her because of her disability caused Akram to realise that teachers and students needed greater training on working with children with disabilities.

As she explains, 'If I did not complete my assignments they would say, "It's okay, we can manage." At the time I was not a wheelchair user but they would discourage you from using one if you needed it, as they believed they could cope with getting you to your classes. They would use the word "special" for persons with disabilities. But persons with disabilities are not "special". They are human beings and need to be treated equally. Children with disabilities who need to use a wheelchair should be allowed to use it as it gives them their independence to make their own way.'

Akram has been working to help women with disabilities to raise their voices by inviting them to peer-counselling - meetings where they can share their own experiences with others – to empower them, to consolidate and expand peer support groups, and to sensitise people to the positive aspects of integrating women with disabilities into society. In some cases the meetings were also the first opportunity that women with disabilities had to leave their homes.

The young campaigner continues: 'In the first place a woman in a developing country will already face a lot of challenges because of her gender. For women with disabilities they can face double, even

triple the discrimination than men with disabilities are confronted with. For some there are no employment opportunities, they are not allowed to go out and contribute to society, to marry, to have families. They are hidden away and some families even spend huge amounts of money trying to "cure" the disability.

'Persons with disabilities need to be included in the decision-making process of these organisations and at the local decision-making level, so they can give their input as equals and as events unfold, rather than at the final stages. After the earthquake in Pakistan in 2011 Handicap International, who I was working for at the time, reviewed all the proposals for funding coming in from organisations seeking to help. Persons with disabilities were not included in any of the proposals and we went back to the organisations to ask them to review their programmes from a disability perspective.'

Abia Akram attended the Commonwealth Secretariat Expert Roundtable on Inclusive Education and Sustainable Employment for Persons with Disabilities in the Commonwealth to give her views as a youth representative. She is currently studying for her master's in International Development and Gender.

- Participation is recognised in the Disabilities Convention as a right and obligation, an important principle for identifying specific needs, and for empowering the individual. Specific reference is given to disabled people's participation in organisations that speak on their behalf.

Agricultural trade and human rights

International agricultural trade presents unique challenges to the field of business and human rights. Businesses in importing countries make decisions that weaken producers' incentive to meet human rights standards; yet these businesses remain far removed from the human rights consequences of the decisions. Too often these issues are viewed separately, which puts suppliers in the difficult position of being required to protect and respect the human rights of workers while facing constraints imposed by buyers. There appears to be a strong appetite in the Commonwealth to address the supply chain as a whole.

Commonwealth Secretariat Discussion Paper, 2011

The trade in agricultural products touches a large portion of the world's population, be it as consumers or workers and their dependants. It remains the largest sector of employment in most developing countries and employs one-third of the world's workforce, according to the ILO. Even more people rely on agriculture as family dependants, as traders in the local market, or as transport and shipment workers or packers. However, agricultural production is a vulnerable sector with high cost and price fluctuations. Sometimes, there is a need to export even though the market price is below the cost of production.

Agricultural supply chains are international, long and complicated. As with any market the behaviour of the buyers – the businesses that source their products through imports – can have profound effects on people living thousands of kilometres away who depend on agriculture for their livelihoods. In the agricultural sector, this situation is more intense due to the relatively small number of

Under pressure: the rights of agricultural workers

buyers (when compared to the large number of suppliers, farmers and potential consumers) who control the food retail market – particularly in Europe. It could be said that suppliers in Commonwealth countries are the epitome of price-takers; they must accept the price terms or lose access to important markets.

In a 2010 Commonwealth Symposium, producers highlighted the following key human rights fields negatively impacted by the ripple effect of market imbalance: labour rights in general, including temporary and casual labour; rights to adequate standard of living (living wage); rights to safe and healthy working conditions; rights to health (particularly in relation to pesticides); women's rights; and migrant workers' rights.

In June 2011 the UN unanimously endorsed a 'three pillar' framework for states and enterprises to ensure that business activities do not harm human rights:

Pillar 1: the state's duty in international law to protect citizens from abuses by third parties, including business

Pillar 2: the corporate responsibility to respect human rights

Pillar 3: greater access by victims to effective remedy, both judicial and non-judicial.

> Already five companies are running pilot projects based on the Special Representative of the Secretary-General's guidance for company-based grievance mechanisms. One example is Tesco, the UK supermarket, which is supporting a grievance mechanism pilot in its South African fresh fruit supply chain.

Forced and servile marriage

Early and forced marriage discriminates against girls and takes away their opportunities to access education, often excluding them from paid work and meaningful participation in the development of their communities. Affecting millions of girls in every region of the Commonwealth, it often represents a truly brutal transition from childhood to adulthood.

Ashley Johnson, Royal Commonwealth Society

The Commonwealth Law Ministers Meeting 2011 recognised forced and servile marriages as 'a human rights violation that impeded individuals' most basic and fundamental rights' and called for concerted Commonwealth action to end the practice.

Ending early and forced marriage is a prerequisite to the successful delivery of a number of Millennium Development Goals (MDGs), especially those dealing with infant and maternal health, universal primary education, gender equality and empowerment, and eradicating poverty. Of the 20 countries in the world where early and forced marriage is most prevalent, 12 are in the Commonwealth.

In 2012, the Family Planning Association of Pakistan stated that child marriage is a major cause of high maternal mortality. Girls who marry before the age of 18 are more likely to experience domestic violence than their peers who marry late. Child brides often show signs symptomatic of child sexual abuse and post-traumatic stress. Such symptoms include feeling of hopelessness, helplessness and severe depression. Child brides are at a heightened risk of sexual and physical abuse, reproductive health complications, HIV/AIDS infection and other adverse physiological and social outcomes. Girls aged 10–14 are five times more likely to die in childbirth than women aged 15–19, they said (www.dawn.com).

Current non-governmental campaigns against the practice include 'Girls Not Brides' (the Clinton Global Imitative, The Elders, the Ford Foundation, the Nike Foundation and the NoVo Foundation) and at the Commonwealth level, 'Ending Forced Marriage, Empowering Girls' (Commonwealth Foundation, Plan International).

In September 2011 Desmond Tutu, Chairman of The Elders, told the UK *Guardian* newspaper: 'A lot of the responsibility lays with men, and I want to make a call – especially to my fellow men – and say we can make a huge difference if you say no to child marriage … Ultimately, this has to be a partnership of both sexes.'

The responsibility to protect

Since 2005, the international community has taken on a specific responsibility to protect populations. The agreement adopted restricted the responsibility to the four most heinous offences: genocide, war crimes, crimes against humanity and ethnic cleansing. This commitment grew out of earlier attempts to lay the foundation for a general doctrine to protect human life, although the specific aspirations of the International Commission on Intervention and State Sovereignty – reporting in the aftermath of the failure to prevent genocide in Rwanda in 1994 and Srebrenica in 1995 – were left untested in the years following 9/11 and the launch of the war on terror.

If there is one clear message that emerged from the new understanding of the Responsibility to Protect (R2P), it is the recognition of international human rights standards as the immediate foundation of this principle. Viewed from the standpoint of the four crimes, the lineage of R2P is thus clearly associated with a broader and more significant trend by which international instruments on human rights, international humanitarian law and refugee law had made sovereignty conditional and contingent upon the respect of fundamental human rights throughout the world. Between 2007 and 2011, under the leadership of UN Secretary-General Ban Ki-moon and his two Special Advisers, Francis Deng and Edward C Luck, R2P was debated and discussed in the UN General Assembly. In particular,

Ahmed Zakari & Co.
(CHARTERED ACCOUNTANTS)

Ahmed Zakari & Co. *(Chartered Accountants)* is a dynamic and multi-disciplinary professional firm of chartered accountants, tax practitioners and business advisory and insolvency practitioners.

Our ambition is to 'be the number one indigenous multi-disciplinary professional services firm in Nigeria'.

Our aim is to *'Create Value for Clients'* and to achieve this we habitually play an active and constructive part in our relationships with clients, guiding and assisting them to a degree that is unusual in our profession. This requires an in-depth understanding of every client's situation, whilst relating it to overall objectives and priorities.

We operate from offices in Kano, Lagos and Abuja offering a wide range of high quality services, many of which are unusual for a firm of our size including:

- Accountancy & Financial Reporting
- Audit & Assurance
- Business Consulting & Financial Advisory
- Corporate Finance
- Forensic Accounting & Litigation Support
- Insolvency & Business Recovery
- Islamic Finance Advisory
- Taxation
- Training

If you would like to have more information about our firm, please contact **Tajudeen A. Oni FCA** – Partner, Business Development, on +234(0)818 507 3911 | +234 1 743 1279 | +234 1 743 1280 or email at t.oni@ahmedzakari.com

Further information about the firm and our services are available on our website at **www.ahmedzakari.com**

two constructive and forward-looking debates – one formal in 2009 and one informal in 2010 – helped broaden the understanding of R2P and the consensus behind the emerging norm.

Some have argued that it was not until the advent of R2P that the international community accepted, for the first time, the 'collective responsibility' to act should a state fail to protect its population from these crimes. However, the reality is that human rights activists had long been calling on the international community to uphold human rights and to hold governments to account.

If in its first iteration, R2P was expected to prompt states and international organisations to undertake efforts to 'protect and assist war victims', it was by no means ready to relinquish the aspiration of impartiality that has long accompanied efforts at conflict prevention. Since 2005, R2P has been charged with the explicit and clear task of preventing and halting mass human rights violations.

It would be difficult to understand the unanimous condemnation of the international community to ongoing and threatened atrocities in Libya in the absence of the dialogues in the General Assembly. These positive and vigorous debates provided a key background to the decisions taken by the Security Council on both Ivory Coast and Libya. Indeed, in the spring of 2011, the UN Security Council adopted a number of resolutions that evoked or explicitly referred to R2P. Although from a legal standpoint neither Security Council Resolution 1973 on Libya nor Resolution 1975 on Ivory Coast have altered the standing prohibition on the use of force outside self-defence and Security Council-authorised enforcement action, some observers have considered these as landmark resolutions, signalling the readiness of the Council to take action in the face of mass atrocities.

Monica Serrano, Executive Director of the Global Centre for the Responsibility to Protect between 2008 and 2011; adapted from Global Magazine (Fourth Quarter 2011)

Public Sector Development:

reducing poverty and deepening democracy

'Just and honest Government – that is, effective public institutions, clear-sighted and ethical political leadership, and capable and fair public administration – is of critical importance. This is because it is fair and effective public administration that makes the state legitimate in the eyes of its citizens. The Commonwealth's shared tradition of public administration is therefore an enormously valuable asset.'

– Commonwealth Secretary-General Kamalesh Sharma

The work of the Governance and Institutional Development Division (GIDD)

The Commonwealth Secretariat's work is structured around delivering on these two main aims of our membership: the promotion of effective democratic institutions, and the implementation of sustainable development, including achievement of the Millennium Development Goals (MDGs). The Commonwealth believes that democracy and development are intricately interrelated.

Twenty years ago, in 1991, the Harare Declaration called for the promotion of the fundamental political values and principles of the Commonwealth, including 'just and honest government', and so committed the Commonwealth 'to respond to requests from members for assistance in entrenching the practices of democracy, *accountable administration* and the rule of law'. This commitment to 'just and honest government' as a fundamental political value was re-endorsed in 1995 by the Millbrook Commonwealth Action Programme on the Harare Declaration, which called for 'support for good government, particularly in the area of public service reform', and by the Latimer House Principles of 1998 endorsed at the Malta Commonwealth Heads of Government Meeting (CHOGM) in 2005.

The 2009 CHOGM modernised 'just and honest government' into the broader concept of 'good governance' (defined as rule of law, transparency, accountability and tackling corruption), but in so doing perhaps lost, for an intergovernmental organisation, the focus and power of the original wording. The whole governance agenda – how a country manages the use of power and authority – is a basic requirement for development, and improving the quality of public administration is a critical component of this broader picture.

The academic literature, although deeply divided about the relationship between democracy and development, recognises that creating and sustaining an effective bureaucracy is essential for

both. A capable public administration helps democratic political culture to endure and consolidate, by managing inequalities and containing distributional conflicts in a way that allows politics to develop democratic maturity. Democracy and development may pull in opposite directions in developing countries, requiring an effective state to manage the resulting tensions. Democratisation may create checks and balances mechanisms and diffuse power, while development may require strengthening state capacity through greater autonomy and centralisation of authority. That different political regimes are capable of implementing similar policies suggests that it is not just the nature of the political institutions or leadership but also the nature of public administration and the political-administrative interface that needs much greater attention.

For nearly two decades, the Commonwealth Secretariat has quietly been working on this, building democratic developmental states by forging positive relations between the political and administrative arms of the public sector at the highest levels at the centre of government. Its innovative approach has been to provide a platform that brings together cabinet ministers and top civil servants to help them work better together as they support the Executive to deliver on the government's policy-making agenda.

Research suggests that impartial and effective public administration builds trust between the state and its citizenry and also in markets. By preventing arbitrariness and bias, and by institutionalising respect for contracts and transparency, a fair and effective public administration is therefore crucial for economic growth, political stability and for the legitimacy of the state. The primary state-building challenge of taxation neatly illustrates this, as it is difficult to raise taxes without the tax authority being perceived as fair, effective and efficient, and its enforcement as a legitimate exercise of state power in the eyes of its citizens and the private sector.

Economic growth requires not 'secure' property rights but public administration widely accepted as fair. Impartial and competent public administration is, therefore, essential for both development and democracy. To help countries help themselves in this, GIDD needs to capitalise on the unique political relationships and influence of the Commonwealth which it believes are its comparative advantages. It believes these to include the following.

- Trusted partnership with membership as the Commonwealth has no vested personal or organisational interests. It is important to note that development work is paid for by a mutual fund that all recipients contribute to, so there is more genuine country 'ownership'.

- Convening power as other agencies may not be so trusted.

- Ability to foster communities of practice and South–South learning, by making the most effective use of networks for brokering exchange of ideas and practice between member countries.

EFFECTIVE PUBLIC AUTHORITY

Three core dimensions of the state: what is it that 'builds the state'?

Functional authority: The extent to which the regime projects its power over all the territory – and uses it for the public good

- Secure borders
- Absence of significant organised political violence
- No civil war
- No ungoverned spaces
- Limited communal or ethnic violence and strife
- Low levels of criminality
- No serious 'organised' crime
- Effective systems of dispute resolution
- A disciplined security force
- Effective police service

Institutional capacity: The extent to which the regime gets things done

- Effective and respected institutions generally – whether 'modern' or traditional
- Government 'promises' carry credibility
- Prevalence of the rule of law
- Basic services delivered: education, health, water, transport
- Reasonable public infrastructure
- Functioning banking system
- Reasonable fiscal and policy environment for entrepreneurship

Domestic political legitimacy: The extent to which citizens feel that their system of government is somehow appropriate and the ruling regime has the right to rule

- A broadly agreed 'political settlement'
- Freedom of opposition to oppose
- Relatively free media
- Citizens enjoy a modicum of civil and political liberties
- Trade unions can form and agitate
- No exclusion of significant minorities from power and the political process
- Reasonably 'free and fair' elections
- Freedom to compete for public office
- Respect for political and legal institutions
- Tolerance of dissent
- Civil society has voice and organising ability

* A view from Graham Teskey (Senior Adviser, World Bank), writing in Commonwealth Good Governance 2011/2012

- Helping small and vulnerable member states that are neglected by others.

- Rapid response in a manner that large aid agencies – both bilateral donors and the international financial institutions – often cannot provide.

- Seed-funding good ideas, which can then be taken up by major funders.

As the Commonwealth Secretariat moves towards its next strategic plan, it is increasingly focusing efforts on the following.

- Tackling political sensitivities that donors and other development agencies cannot address, prioritising activities where there is comparative advantage, notably tackling politically sensitive 'state-building at the centre of government' reforms.

- Responding promptly and professionally to its membership's concerns and to CHOGM mandates.

- Nurturing networks (especially advancing South–South learning of 'good fit' – rather than 'best practice') that are effective in promoting reform.

- Championing the unique problems of improving governance in the smaller poorer, more vulnerable countries of the Commonwealth, including small island and landlocked states.

Why Public Service Commissions matter

Public Service Commissions (PSCs) are often a crucial component in attempts to reform the public sector, especially in the developing world. This is because, in principle at least, PSCs have a critical role to play in providing strategic direction in terms of human resources management and civil service policy and regulation, as well as in ensuring and maintaining the integrity of the public service. One crucial function is to guarantee effective and transparent recruitment and promotion processes that will lead to competent staff selection and retention in the public service. PSCs are also intended to provide overall guidance for staff discipline functions and policy for ministries, departments and agencies (MDAs) on human resources management to ensure consistency throughout the public service.

However, in practice, PSCs may not always be able to perform their key functions effectively. They are often politicised because, among other things, human resources and the civil service are a key source of patronage and clientelism.[1] This is especially true of fragile states that are attempting to recover from conflict. As these states attempt to build more effective and responsive institutions, they also need to maintain a precarious balance between contending groups and forces seeking privileged access to state resources (OECD, 2011). The case of Sierra Leone's PSC (see the text titled

'Supporting Sierra Leone's Public Service Commission') is a powerful illustration of the challenging and political nature of public sector reform in fragile states. As recently as 2008, the PSC in Sierra Leone was a very weak institution, unable to carry out its key functions and responsibilities and unsure of its role in leading/supporting efforts to reform the public sector as articulated in the country's Poverty Reduction Strategy Paper (PRSP II).

South–South co-operation

It is extremely important for countries to share experiences and learn from each other. That is why we have agreed to work with the Commonwealth Secretariat in our diplomatic training of Foreign Service officials from across Asia at the Malaysian Institute of Diplomacy and Foreign Relations. The training will present diplomats with the necessary skills to deal with any manner of situations they are confronted with.

Hidah Misran, Federal Government Administrative Centre, Malaysia

Due to member states' similar governance systems, the Commonwealth is ideally placed in arranging South–South co-operation with them. Over 70 per cent of Commonwealth expertise is provided on a South–South basis. The goal is to improve the political conditions and economic growth upon which poverty reduction and the Millennium Development Goals depend (95 per cent of worst economic performances in the last 40 years have been in non-democratic regimes).

The Commonwealth has been deepening democracy by supporting Parliamentary learning from successful systems, processes and procedures – for example, linking the Sri Lankan Parliament with the Lok Sabha Secretariat in India (see the text titled 'Capacity and accountability'). Good governance is also about the private sector and relations with it. The Commonwealth Public Procurement Network links regulators and tender boards in 17 countries, strengthening leadership and systems through peer review. In 2011 insurance regulators from Kenya, Malawi, Rwanda, United Republic of Tanzania and Zambia were hosted by the Ugandan Insurance Commission to discuss corporate governance principles and accountability.

On economic prospects, one of Africa's most respected economists, K Y Amoako, reminds us that sustained high growth creates opportunities that would not otherwise exist, but is insufficient on its own to produce an economic transformation. Economic transformation – growth plus structural change – depends on how well the opportunities provided by renewed growth are used to build skills and technological capabilities, leading to widely shared improvements in productivity and to the conquest of new markets.[2]

The policy requirements of making the current growth spurt sustainable by turning it into a genuine economic transformation are considerable. The Asian experience in the period since most Commonwealth African countries gained their independence clearly indicates a number of preconditions for the achievement of broad-based growth and structural change.[3] As Amoako puts it, they include:

- a national vision imparting a shared sense of purpose
- government policies facilitating industrial upgrading
- robust strategic planning
- effective mass and elite education

- public investment in rural infrastructure and external aid targeted at such investments, and
- public-private partnership across a range of activities.

By 2011 the Commonwealth had advised over 30 governments about the issue of Public Private Partnerships (PPPs), and assisted in creating or strengthening PPP units in five countries. In 2011, the Commonwealth partnered with the Malaysian Public Private Partnership Unit (3PU) to train policy-makers and 450 business leaders in managing the process. Malaysia has offered to host a Commonwealth PPP Centre of Excellence to act as a repository of PPP knowledge and experiences for the benefit of member countries.

3PU's Director-General, Dr Ali Hamsa, said: 'We will be happy to share our experiences with other Commonwealth countries through South–South co-operation. PPP – within the right legal, social, economic and political frameworks – could open the path to greater investment.' Pauline Matthias of the Sri Lanka Board of Investment agrees: 'Dialogue with other Commonwealth countries enables you to learn from case studies, both successes and failures, and to gain input from fresh resource persons. It sparks a lot of ideas.'

Notes

[1] O'Neil, T (2007), quoted in Jones-Parry, R (ed.) *Commonwealth Good Governance*, 2011/12

[2] Amoako, K Y (2011) quoted in Jones-Parry, R (ed.) *Commonwealth Good Governance*, 2011/12

[3] Booth, D (2011), writing in *Commonwealth Good Governance*, 2011/12

Supporting Sierra Leone's Public Service Commission (PSC): how the Commonwealth Secretariat has made a difference

What has made Commonwealth support so meaningful and effective? Part of the explanation has to do with the ability of the Secretariat to work closely with an organisation largely neglected by other donors. This intervention helps to highlight the Secretariat's capacity to focus on areas that may appear small or marginal – but are in fact essential. Now that the PSC has begun to show some of its potential and that it has a roadmap for reform, other donors have become more interested, and international support has been more forthcoming through UNDP, the EU and others.

Oluwatoyin Job, Adviser (West Africa), GIDD

Sierra Leone's PSC approached the Commonwealth Secretariat for support. The Commission requested assistance from the Commonwealth Fund for Technical Co-operation (CFTC) in helping it to assume its constitutional mandate more effectively. Between September 2009 and March 2010, a Management Function Review (MFR) was carried out, aiming to:

- assist the PSC to redefine its role in light of the ongoing challenges of public sector reforms in a post-conflict setting

- assess the legislative implications of the new functions of the PSC, and its capacity to work under the proposed Multi-Donor Funded Public Sector Reform Programme, and

- analyse human resource and other management issues.

Photographer and copyright: Victoria Holdsworth / © Commonwealth Secretariat

The Government of Sri Lanka actively sought donor support to strengthen the capacity and effectiveness of its parliament and upgrade the knowledge and skills of its parliamentary officials. However, several different donors were not in a position to provide such assistance. For many, larger, donors, the level of support being sought in monetary terms was relatively small compared to the kinds of programmes they usually fund. In addition, despite its importance, parliamentary support remains a relatively rare area of international donor engagement. The reasons include:

- a lack of clarity about exactly how to engage with a complex body and whether the entry point for support should be the speaker, parliamentary committee chair and/or other parties

- perceptions that parliamentary assistance is 'too political'

- the low regard in which the public may hold parliaments and political parties in countries where support is needed

- a lack of capacity on the donor side to understand and adequately support parliaments, and

- the fact that support to parliaments is a long-term process that may take some time to show results when donors are under pressure to demonstrate quick value for money and return on investments.*

The Commonwealth Secretariat has partnered with the Bureau of Parliamentary Studies and Training (BPST) and the lower parliamentary assembly – the Lok Sabha Secretariat – in India to support the training of a small group of Sri Lankan parliamentarians who were identified, selected and nominated by both the ruling party and the opposition. The annual programme is attended by senior and middle-management-level officials from diverse political and constitutional systems, including political parties, who undergo a period of intensive study and practical training. Through short-term attachments with branches and services of the two Houses of the Indian Parliament, participants obtain hands-on experience of how these agencies work.

* Power, G (2008); Hudson, A (2007), both quoted in Jones-Parry, R (ed.) Commonwealth Good Governance, 2011/12

The cost of the consultancy, getting stakeholder inputs through a seminar, and printing and disseminating the study, was approximately UK£10,000 (in addition, of course, to staff inputs in terms of designing the terms of reference, reviewing and providing inputs for the different drafts of the final report). However, as confirmed by follow-up visits (March 2011), the catalytic effect of the MFR has been much wider and more significant. Among other things, the Review has led to the publication of a report that has been widely circulated and discussed among a wide range of relevant stakeholders, including donors and government representatives.

The report's conclusions and recommendations have been endorsed as a viable basis to reform the PSC going forward. The President of Sierra Leone, Dr Ernest Bai Koroma, has been solidly behind the report's findings. He launched the MFR himself, thereby signalling that its implementation is a key national priority. Today, the PSC is beginning to turn into an empowered institution with leadership and vision – a situation that seemed unimaginable a few years ago. The CFTC will continue to be there to support the human capacity development of the PSC and to co-ordinate donor support as may be required in the years to come.

Capacity and accountability: the Parliamentary Internship Programme in Sri Lanka

This pairing of India and Sri Lanka makes a lot of sense given their geographical proximity and similar colonial legacy. One of the advantages of this approach is that the Indian parliamentary system is more accessible and historically and culturally more relevant to Sri Lanka than a Western model.

Mohammad Jasimuddin, Adviser (Asia), GIDD

Supporting public service reform, Kenya

Changes in the Constitution have been very positive, both psychologically and substantively. Infrastructure is a key driver but an additional driver, going forward, in my view, will be the improved governance in the country … it will encourage foreign investment. I think an environment with more transparency, greater accountability, a greater focus towards improving the business environment and incentives. Not to mention the fact that we are reforming the judiciary.

Mugo Kibati, Director-General of Kenya's 2030 Delivery Secretariat

In Africa, effective public service is central to achieving poverty reduction. In turn, management development institutes (MDIs) are central to up-skilling the public service and re-engineering its business processes. Investing in MDIs is an efficient way of influencing whole systems and reducing dependency on outside expertise. According to Dr Margaret Kobia, Director of the Kenya Institute of Administration (KIA), this has not always been understood. 'African MDIs were certainly neglected in the decade after 1990. Policy reform and research was scaled down in favour of income generation activities, consequently the knowledge base deteriorated.'

For Kobia, support from the Commonwealth has been critical. The journey began in 2005 when she made study visits to counterpart organisations like the UK School of Government. Since 2007 technical assistance has been provided in performance management, negotiation, talent management, Public-Private Partnerships and Business Process Re-engineering.

'I would say the Commonwealth Secretariat's "personality" as an organisation is straightforwardness and a good understanding of needs. I would like to thank them for making a difference. By working on a direct, institution to institution basis, we have now moved to a position of also hosting other African countries' training.'

International trainings have led to better appreciation and demand for KIA's work within Kenya.

And compared with hotels in Nairobi, the venue comes in at around half the cost. By looking at real-life case studies and sharing perspectives on what African public services are struggling with today, there is 'global convergence of ideas'.

Source: Global *Magazine Country Report: Kenya (First Quarter 2011)*

Leadership excellence: a view from CAPAM

(Commonwealth Association for Public Administration and Management)

Over a million public servants across the Commonwealth occupy positions of leadership and are in need of support and development to strengthen their capacity to lead. The Chinese philosopher Lao Tzu wrote that 'a leader is best when people barely know he exists. When his work is done, they will say: we did it ourselves.' This sentiment was echoed centuries later by Dwight D Eisenhower, who said 'Leadership is the art of getting someone else to do something you want done because he wants to do it.' There is no doubt that effective leaders have the aptitude to motivate their fellow workers to achieve the intended results.

Public service organisations have to satisfy multiple 'bottom lines'. For example, governments are expected to: stimulate economic growth while reducing the impact of industries on the environment; improve social services while reducing government expenditures; and respond to the views of the majority without undermining the rights of minority groups. With these competing objectives, it is easy to be trapped in endless cycles of consultations and studies. The ensuing 'paralysis through analysis' will generate a frenzy of activity while achieving no meaningful results.

Furthermore, the provision of government services is often the largest 'business activity' in many countries. Government is frequently the largest employer, with offices that span across the country from urban centres to remote locations. It is also responsible for administering the largest budget and is accountable for the efficient collection of taxes and prudent allocation of this

revenue. Within this complex environment, the performance of any organisation is inextricably linked with the quality of its leaders. Strong, effective and ethical leaders are needed to set priorities, clarify objectives, investigate opportunities and threats, formulate strategies, amass resources, consolidate support, galvanise commitments, implement strategies, assess results and refine strategies for better outcomes.

Since 2008, CAPAM has undertaken extensive consultations, deliberations and research to understand the need for, and the challenges of, leadership development across the Commonwealth. This work culminated in a two-day symposium in May 2011, in Nairobi, Kenya. It was organised in partnership with the Commonwealth Secretariat and brought together a guiding coalition of stakeholders agreed on the Commonwealth Leadership for Development Initiative to strengthen the leadership capacity of Commonwealth nations.

Unlike academic achievements where degrees and titles are conferred at the end of much study, the cultivation and refinement of leadership is a lifelong endeavour. CAPAM's mission is to provide opportunities for this sharing and learning. Leadership excellence is the essential catalyst in our collective quest to achieve results for citizens.

Adapted from an article by David Waung and David Menyah in Commonwealth Good Governance 2011–2012

Implementing the Zambia National Anti-Corruption Policy

The question is, are national anti-corruption agencies able to achieve their objectives on their own, or do we need to bring on board other institutions concerned with governance? From our interaction with the Commonwealth since 2009, that looks the correct emphasis. Yes we had an anti-corruption policy, but the work has generated valuable ways to actually implement it. The Commonwealth has really added value here by bringing ideas from other jurisdictions.

Kayobo Ng'andu, Zambia Anti-Corruption Commission

In March 2009 President Rupiah B Banda launched the National Anti-Corruption Policy (NACP), the first policy of its kind in Zambia. At a legal level, the NACP seeks to harmonise, review and revise conflicting laws and regulations with a view to strengthening anti-corruption laws. At a political level, a national steering committee, chaired by the Cabinet secretary, has been set up to implement and operationalise the policy. In response to a request from the Anti-Corruption Commission, the Commonwealth Secretariat has been playing a significant role.

A governance adviser proved instrumental in brokering a memorandum of understanding (MOU) to establish the terms and conditions under which the different sub-committees and institutions should work together to implement the policy. The Secretariat also sponsored a series of capacity-building workshops to equip committee members with the skills they need to perform their anti-corruption functions more effectively. As a result of the work of integrity committees, organisational processes and procedures have been streamlined to remove opportunities for corrupt practices. Trained integrity committee members have made a number of advances, as listed.

- The Zambia Revenue Authority has introduced a 'taxpayer's charter' as a measure to reduce corruption and to improve revenue mobilisation.

- The Kitwe City Council has streamlined its land administration and plot allocation processes and made them more transparent.

- The Ndola City Council has prosecuted offending officers for engaging in fraudulent plot allocations that were unearthed by members of the integrity committee.

- Konkola Copper Mines has been able to shed its associations with corruption through the work of the integrity committee in scrutinising the awarding of contracts, identifying conflicts of interest, and ensuring transparent staff recruitment processes.

Taking the concept of country autonomy and ownership to heart, the Commonwealth Secretariat has not sought to impose prescriptions and blueprints from the outside, but rather to broker internal processes of reform. In this respect, it has been at the cutting edge of development efforts.

Corruption control in small states

Small states are under increasing pressure to improve their governance to attract investment, increase competitiveness and effectively deliver public goods and services to their citizens. Cultural context of these countries is important, and the potential of traditional integrity systems should be explored. South to South forms of policy transfer can be helpful, for example, learning from successful and culturally sensitive anti-corruption interventions implemented in similar countries. Regional networks and organisations should not be overlooked as they can help overcome some of the capacity challenges that anti-corruption institutions face in individual countries.

Dr Roger Koranteng, Commonwealth Secretariat

Small states are diverse in terms of the extent of corruption risks and their respective level of governance, and law enforcement capacity. However, in most of these countries, anti-corruption efforts are hampered by both geography and social factors. Often the most relevant level of decision-making is the village, with limited citizen's involvement in broader political process. The low electoral ratio of parliamentary representatives to citizens makes it more likely for elected officials to know many of their constituents. This can be a plus, but can also facilitate the development of corrupt networks and personalisation of decision-making. People tend to consider themselves citizens of their tribe or island rather than of larger and dispersed units, and may only engage in national political processes to a limited extent.

Yet, at the same time, government is generally the largest employer of labour and the most important agency for identifying political issues and seeking their resolution. The government of a small state is likely to supply not only administrative and public services, but also elements of the productive and commercial life of the country including ownership/involvement in production enterprises as well as transport and financial services. As in all countries, corruption ranges from small payments made to speed up bureaucratic processes and the delivery of public services, through to concerns of administrative abuses. It is common practice in many countries to offer gift and favours to voters during the election campaigns and this is not always perceived as strictly

Tuvalu Speaker of Parliament Kamuta Latasi (second from right) with GIDD team and Commonwealth Deputy Secretary-General Ransford Smith (centre), 2011

corrupt behaviour, thereby providing a challenging slippery slope towards more systematic vote-buying.

The cross-border nature of crime makes prevention and eradication of corruption a responsibility of all states and calls for co-operation between and among states. Non-state actors such as churches and NGOs should also be engaged as important targets and drivers of anti-corruption efforts. Modest goals and objectives, clearer implementation arrangements, stronger monitoring, and concrete prioritisation of issues, can all make inroads.

Local heroes: a view from the Commonwealth Local Government Forum (CLGF)

Our lives are lived locally, our governments are experienced locally. For most people, local government is their first and perhaps only contact with the authorities in their country.

Commonwealth Secretary-General Kamalesh Sharma

Democratic local government – run justly and honestly – provides the best opportunity for local people to play a role in decision-making that affects their quality of life, including many of the basic services such as health, water, sanitation, housing and education. Many national governments are acknowledging this and are moving towards a more decentralised and localised approach to development to ensure that services and development are provided where and when they are needed. These are exactly the areas in which the Commonwealth Local Government Forum needs to ensure progress if it is to meet the Millennium Development Goals (MDGs) and improve the quality of life for the two billion citizens of the Commonwealth.

CLGF has a small secretariat based in London, and offices in Southern Africa, India and the Pacific. As the local government arm of the Commonwealth, CLGF is recognised as a Designated Associated Organisation, with direct accreditation to the Commonwealth Heads of Government Meeting (CHOGM). CLGF has taken the lead in encouraging and developing democracy and good governance at the local level, working closely with the Commonwealth Secretariat and with key international partners, such as the United Nations Development Programme (UNDP), UN-Habitat and national governments.

CLGF actively promotes and advocates for democratic, elected local government throughout the Commonwealth, and works to improve local government structures and services, particularly in countries where local democracy is under threat or where local government and elected structures are just beginning to emerge. CLGF has been present at and has assessed the outcomes of local elections in these countries in partnership with the Commonwealth Secretariat, the most recent being in Maldives, which held its first democratic local elections in February 2011.

CLGF believes that sharing experience, skills and ideas nationally and internationally is of great benefit to those working in local government, and the Commonwealth offers a vast array of experience, expertise and good practice in decentralisation and local government. Learning from the past experiences of others, from innovations in policy and service delivery, and from models of good practice is vital if local governments are to meet the global challenges and the needs of their citizens. Local economic development (LED) was the focus of discussions at the 2011 Commonwealth Local Government Conference in Cardiff, UK (see also the text titled 'Commonwealth Youth Exchange Council: a strategic *partner*' in the article titled 'Empowering young people'). The next major conference will be in Kampala, Uganda, in 2013, and will focus on how democracy and development at the local level can help transform communities.

Adapted from an article by Carl Wright, Secretary-General, CLGF, in Commonwealth Good Governance 2011–2012

Preventing and combating corruption: the UN Public Service Awards 2011

This new anti-corruption category is an exciting development in recognising excellence in public service. Through United Nations Public Service Day 2011 and the awards ceremony, the Electoral Commission South Africa was deservedly recognised at the global level. We look forward to further entrants and winners from Commonwealth member countries in the years to come.

Haiyan Qian, Director, Division for Public Administration and Development Management

As stated in the United Nations Convention against Corruption (2004), corruption hurts the poor disproportionately by diverting funds intended for development, undermining a government's ability to provide basic services, feeding inequality and injustice, and discouraging foreign aid and investment. Corruption is a key element in economic underperformance and a major obstacle to poverty alleviation and development.

The United Nations Public Service Awards (UNPSA) is the most prestigious international recognition of excellence in public service and rewards the creative achievements and contributions of public service institutions that lead to more effective and responsive public administrations worldwide. The UNPSA are awarded annually on 23 June, which was designated by the General Assembly as the United Nations Public Service Day to 'celebrate the value and virtue of service to the community'.

In 2011, the new UNPSA category 'Preventing and Combating Corruption in Public Service' was established by the Department of Economic and Social Affairs, through its Division for Public Administration and Development Management (DPADM/UNDESA), in partnership with the United Nations Office on Drugs and Crime (UNODC) to recognise efforts across the globe to promote integrity in government and combat corruption. The three initiatives that follow were awarded as first place winners.

For more information on these and other projects, see www.unpan.org/unpsa

Initiative 1: Transparent Town, Town Hall of Martin, Slovakia

Martin, a district town of approximately 60,000 inhabitants located in northern Slovakia (Eastern Europe), launched the Transparent Town project in 2008. The project was undertaken in collaboration with the local branch of Transparency International Slovensko (TIS).

The initiative provides tools for citizens to monitor their municipality maximising the level of transparency with the municipality employees, as well as its elected officials, and minimising the room for corrupt behaviour in municipal administration. Prior to the project, not only was internal auditing carried out by administrators themselves, but the participation of the public or civil society organisations in the decision-making process was missing. Lack of public confidence was reinforced when, after a change in the municipality's top administrative representatives, a number of cases of embezzlement of public funds were documented. The main question the new leaders of the town of Martin were confronted with was how to fight corruption and regain public trust in the local administration.

Initiative 2: 'Electoral Result Slip Scanning Project', Electoral Commission of South Africa

The Electoral Commission (IEC) is a permanent body created by the Constitution of the Republic of South Africa to promote and safeguard representative democracy in South Africa. Although publicly funded and accountable to parliament, the Commission is independent of government. Its immediate task is the impartial management of free and fair elections at all levels of government. One of the Commission's strategic objectives is to 'deliver well-run elections which produce results that are credible'.

During the 2009 national and provincial elections, the Commission marked a crucial step towards electoral transparency when it introduced the project of scanning the result slips of all voting stations. Political parties and electoral staff could view the scanned result slip images and compare the signed copies to the results captured on the results system at all levels. Originally designed for national and provincial elections, the process has been extended to all elections nationwide and voter registration forms as well. As testified by representatives of political parties and the media, South African election results are transparent, verifiable and free from manipulation.

Initiative 3: 'Transparent Migrant and Business Friendly Recruitment System', Human Resources Development Service of the Republic of Korea

In 2004, the Government of the Republic of Korea adopted a migration-friendly policy called the Employment Permit System (EPS) in order to increase transparency and prevent corruption in the management of its migrants and supply the domestic market with the labour shortage with which it has been confronted.

The initiative aims to tackle the following economic paradox. On the one hand, unemployment is one of the major issues affecting young people, especially from developing countries; on the other hand, industrialised countries face serious labour shortage either due to a rapidly ageing population or the urgent need for substantial economic growth. Migration from developing to industrialised countries, far from filling this obvious labour gap, has been generating additional tremendous challenges such as harassment of illegal migrants or involuntary repatriation in the worst case.

The first attempt to manage inland migration dates back to the 1990s when the government adopted the Industrial Training System legalising the importation of foreign workers with industrial trainee status and conferring the right of importation to the companies that had branches and factories abroad. The Republic of Korea, however, could not break the deadlock as the Industrial Training System led to improper employment of workers as trainees, unstable status of trainees, recruitment irregularities, masses of undocumented migrant workers, and violation of human and labour rights.

A system was developed to select migrant workers through an objective criterion to build a job-seeker pool of qualified migrant workers from countries that signed an agreement with the Government of the Republic of Korea. The system relies on an active participation of both the host and foreign governments in the migration's application process. Upon selection of migrant workers by their future employers, they are granted the right to travel to and work within the Republic of Korea, enjoying the same rights as Korean workers. Not only has the system eliminated inappropriate costly services of private brokers and facilitated legal cross-border migration, but also, and more importantly, it has provided migrants with ideal labour conditions and full social inclusion through a package of pre- and post-employment services.

Lessons learned

The success of EPS in better managing cross-border labour migration and preventing corruption depends on the political commitment as well as the ability of the Government of the Republic of Korea to find a solution to domestic labour shortage in its neighbouring countries' demography. In comparison with the Industrial Training System, EPS proves to be a significant enhancement by extending a migrant worker's stay from three to five years as well as by introducing language and skill tests to counter applicants' mismatching.

EPS is a non-profit programme set up and monitored by non-profit public organisations. Putting the recruitment process in the hands of governments significantly reduced travel costs for migrant workers.

A tool for e-governance: Commonwealth Connects

Today I am a very proud government technologist. This is no easy feat: 54 countries spread out around the world, various stages of economic and democratic development … on one single cloud! This is a true representation of a citizen services centre, Commonwealth Connects will help you connect to other governments, businesses, youth, social groups; all is being made possible now via the mobile device enabled, cloud based e-government programme.

Alex Benay (Open Text) on the launch of Commonwealth Connects, October 2011

Commonwealth Connects is an advanced internet gateway for strengthening political, social and cultural ties across the Commonwealth and supporting new kinds of partnership among people, organisations and governments. It is a visionary initiative that will allow individual citizens to take their interaction and membership of the Commonwealth 'family' to the next level.

The Commonwealth is a global community that has grown far beyond just intergovernmental co-operation. Outreach, networking and information are its life-blood. The Commonwealth Media Development Fund has trained 5,000 journalists over the last ten years. Some 30,000 copies of official Commonwealth publications are distributed every year, and countries as diverse as Cyprus and Grenada have developed Commonwealth depository libraries. Turning to the web, WikiEducator, launched by the Commonwealth of Learning in 2006, gets about 10 million hits a month.

Richard Simpson (formerly with GIDD) commented: 'There is an impressive volume of Commonwealth information products and services – the Connects platform is looking to index over 150 of these. But there's a need for greater visibility, coherence and co-ordination. The way to do this is to get beyond institution-based information, to themed information that responds to citizens' values and interests. And more than information – *spaces* where people can freely associate. For example, election observers or youth leaders concerned with human rights can make a lot of headway through forums and social networking online. That is the essence of the Commonwealth – a community of communities.'

A major technology provider is a Canadian-based company, Open Text, which has recently provided secure social networking for the G20. But the success of the platform will ultimately depend on content driven by a whole range of Commonwealth partners – from the Commonwealth Foundation and Secretariat to businesses, professional groups, NGOs and places of learning.

Says Kamalesh Sharma, Commonwealth Secretary-General: 'There is a whole range of important applications for Commonwealth Connects, including helping youth groups or government officials from across the Commonwealth collaborate; playing a role in election monitoring; or helping to fuel economic growth through digital business.'

WORLD TRADE CENTER®
AFRICA INITIATIVE

Julius Steyn, *President* World Trade Center Africa Initiative and **Theo Poggenpoel,** *Vice President Africa Relations* World Trade Center Africa Initiative

Unlocking Africa's
POTENTIAL

THESE WORLD TRADE CENTERS FUNCTION AS AN INTEGRATED PAN AFRICAN NETWORK OF CENTERS OF EXCELLENCE WITH A COMMON GOAL – TO DEVELOP TRADE WITH AFRICA.

THE PURPOSE OF A WORLD TRADE CENTER IS TO MEET THE LOCAL AND INTERNATIONAL BUSINESS NEEDS OF THE REGION IT SERVES.
It supports business and government agencies involved in trade development, stimulating the economy of the respective region of location. It is the focal point for local and foreign trade in a city or region and gives companies of all sizes a platform to gain access to international markets.

A few visionary individuals supported by various governments and private sector companies across Africa and Europe have embarked on creating successful operating World Trade Centers across Africa. These World Trade Centers function as an integrated Pan African Network of centers of excellence with a common goal – to develop trade with Africa.

The World Trade Center Africa Initiative, as it is known, currently consists of 13 World Trade Centers and its sponsors are embarking on growing the number across sub-Saharan Africa. The current countries that are benefiting from the World Trade Center Africa Initiative are; South Africa (WTC Cape Town and Johannesburg), Botswana (WTC Gaborone), Burundi (Bujumbura), DRC (WTC Kinshasa), Kenya (WTC Nairobi), Mozambique (WTC Maputo), Namibia (WTC Windhoek), Rwanda (WTC Kigali), Tanzania (WTC Dar Es Salaam), Uganda (WTC Kampala), Zambia (WTC Lusaka) and Zimbabwe (WTC Harare).

With the hub of the World Trade Center Africa Initiative in Cape Town, South Africa, our vision is to increase Intra-Africa and Inter-Africa Trade and thereby accelerating regional economic integration, reducing poverty on the continent, creating wealth for its inhabitants, and stimulating peace and security amongst its people.

World Trade Center Africa Initiative forms sophisticated links between businesses across Africa that serve a diverse range of economic sectors. These sectors include: mining, energy, construction, agriculture, tourism, finance, communication, logistics, health and technology. It aims to support the Small Medium Enterprises of Africa, which is the primary economic driver to develop jobs and stimulate a consumer driven economy. These enterprises typically suffer from a lack of access to growth capital, a lack of understanding of and access to international markets and frequently experience large corporate and foreign company exploitation.

These are amongst the primary elements that The World Trade Center Africa Initiative seeks to address, thus helping the local companies to sell more of their products and services abroad. This enables them to grow their businesses in the region of a World Trade Center presence and to employ more human resources in these regions. It achieves this objective by engaging with more than 300 other World Trade Centers globally and thereby developing new markets for its clients.

World Trade Center Africa Initiative has as its vision:

To increase Intra-Africa and Inter-Africa Trade and thereby accelerating regional economic integration, reducing poverty on the continent, creating wealth for its inhabitants, and stimulating peace and security amongst its people

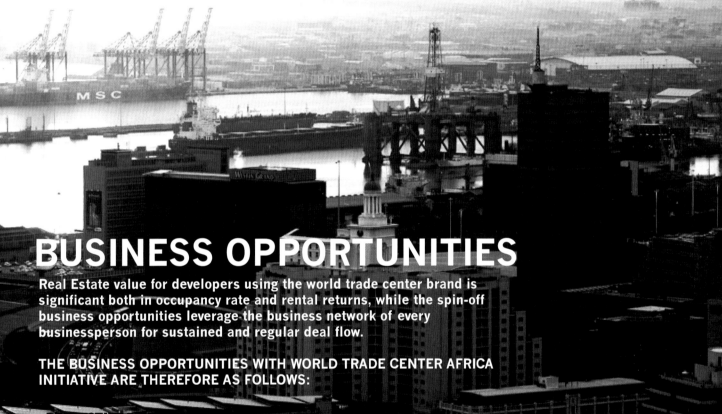

BUSINESS OPPORTUNITIES

Real Estate value for developers using the world trade center brand is significant both in occupancy rate and rental returns, while the spin-off business opportunities leverage the business network of every businessperson for sustained and regular deal flow.

THE BUSINESS OPPORTUNITIES WITH WORLD TRADE CENTER AFRICA INITIATIVE ARE THEREFORE AS FOLLOWS:

- REAL ESTATE DEVELOPMENT
- COMMODITY TRADING
- TRADE FINANCE
- EXPORT AND IMPORT
- STRATEGIC PARTNERSHIPS

SERVICES

Services offered by World Trade Center Africa Initiative:

- Trade Promotion
- Transactional Trade Services and Trade Education
- Import Export Management
- Financial and Risk Management solutions pertaining to Importing & Exporting
- Exclusive business services including: executive travel, personalised & individualised executive global introductions, reciprocal office facilities in more than 300 cities, fast track access to all World Trade Center services and multiple first mover opportunities
- Trade Facilitation

WORLD TRADE CENTER®
AFRICA INITIATIVE

HEAD OFFICE
World Trade Center Cape Town
Crystal Towers
Century City Cape Town
South Africa

T. +27 87 944 4072
F. +27 21 552 9602
info@wtc.co.za

www.wtc.co.za

Economic Development (1):

supporting inclusive and sustainable economic growth in member states

'There can never be sustainable development for small states if we don't participate fully and meaningfully in trade. We need to master the skills and concepts of trade policy issues … No other international institution has today matched the Commonwealth in doing advocacy and technical assistance to small states. We hugely value our membership of the Commonwealth.'

– Dr Timothy Harris, Minister of International Trade, Industry and Commerce, St Kitts and Nevis

Supporting social and economic development is one of the Commonwealth Secretariat's twin strategic objectives, and promoting higher living standards for the people of the Commonwealth has been a constant in its work since its establishment. In discharging this role, the Agreed Memorandum on the Commonwealth Secretariat, which first set out the purposes of the Secretariat in 1965, identified two broad areas of activity in the economic sphere: the first was the provision of analysis and 'factual information' to the membership on areas of interest; the second was to conduct development projects.

Equally relevant – and a guiding principle of all Secretariat activity – is the emphasis placed in the Agreed Memorandum on adding value to the international system and not duplicating activities that are undertaken by others. Although the line between 'analysis' and 'development project' is easier to define in theory than in practice, the emphasis in the Economic Affairs Division's (EAD) work (see later) is on the part of the Secretariat's remit that deals with the understanding and shaping of developments in the global economy for the benefit of the membership. In this work, it undertakes three interrelated functions:

St Kitts and Nevis, Caribbean

- providing analysis and interpretation of the global economy for the benefit of the Commonwealth countries
- putting across the case for the membership need in international settings, and
- supporting members in achieving their domestic and international economic objectives.

The other division responsible for Secretariat work in this area is the Special Advisory Services Division (SASD), which focuses its assistance in the following areas: debt management, economic and legal services relating to the management of natural resources and maritime boundaries, enterprise and agriculture, and trade.

Meeting the needs of small states

The new Maldives Mission in the Commonwealth facility represents a win-win for the Maldives: a larger and better equipped office for less cost; and a chance to work more closely with our fellow Small Island States at the UN. The Foreign Ministry has worked closely with the Commonwealth on this project for four years, lobbying other Commonwealth States, especially donors, at various Head of State and Ministerial meetings. Today therefore represents an important achievement for the Maldives Government and for the Commonwealth.

Maldives' Ambassador in Geneva, Iruthisham Adam, May 2011

Both EAD and SASD place particular emphasis on the needs of its 32 member countries defined as 'small states' – those with populations of up to 1.5 million, or sharing similar structural characteristics. The latter include Botswana, The Gambia, Jamaica, Lesotho, Namibia and Papua New Guinea. Small states thus comprise more than half of the total membership.

The Secretariat has been at the forefront of getting the particular needs of small states recognised in the international system and their voices heard. In 2011 the Commonwealth opened a purpose-built diplomatic facility in Geneva to house Small Island State (SIS) delegations to the United Nations. The aim of the facility is to provide a cost-efficient option for small states to maintain a presence in Geneva, the seat of many UN bodies, as well as to encourage closer co-operation between SISs, which make up around one-third of the total UN membership. Maldives was the first state to move into the new facility, and has since been followed by Seychelles, Solomon Islands, the Pacific Islands Forum, Samoa and The Bahamas.

As noted by the Commonwealth Eminent Persons Group (EPG) in 2011: 'Small states can benefit from an efficient and well designed rules-based international system. It is obvious from the manner in which they conducted themselves in the Doha Round of global trade negotiations at the WTO [World Trade Organization], and their response to rule-making bodies in the UN system, that small states are willing to meet the standards set by the international community. However, it is equally clear that they require flexibilities in the application of global rules precisely because their small size, lack of capacity and severe vulnerability to external economic shocks and natural disasters make them different from, and less resilient than, larger states.'

The Secretariat assists small states through two main channels. First, it assists these countries to shape the international environment. These countries face a paradox. No group is more exposed to the impacts of global events on their economies, but no group is less able to shape those global events.

A Small States Forum, which grew out of Secretariat work in this area and is now organised with the World Bank, meets annually to monitor the responsiveness of the international system to small states' needs and to provide a mechanism of mutual lesson-sharing and support.

Second, the Secretariat is working with stakeholders to make information about particular needs more easily available through resources like the online database of development indicators. By assembling all the economic information on small states, this ensures that hard-pressed policy-makers have easy access to the data they need. Ground-breaking analysis taken forward by the Secretariat and the World Bank is the basis for advocacy and practical policy support.

More recently, there has been a particular focus on supporting countries in the development of plans for strengthening the resilience of their vulnerable economies. A key part of this work has been the development of resilience indicators working closely with the University of Malta.

Trade and debt: working for an open and fair economy

Commonwealth countries are, on average, more integrated with the global economy through trade than other countries. A commitment to an effective and open trading system is one of the uniting economic characteristics of the group – but the smallest and most vulnerable members of the Commonwealth are especially trade dependent. This has been a priority area for the Secretariat for many years, but its importance has again been highlighted by the recent economic crisis. For most developing Commonwealth countries, it has been the dramatic reversal of trade flows that has been the principal channel through which their economies have been affected by the crisis. This has reinforced the need for Commonwealth work for a stable and fair global trading system.

Many parts of the Secretariat are involved in different aspects of supporting members who realise the potential of trade in driving national prosperity. Within EAD, for example, there are a number of overlapping and mutually reinforcing areas of activity, united by the overall objective of achieving a trading system that supports prosperity for all. With this goal in mind, capacity-constrained member countries are assisted through analysis directly relevant to international negotiations and the provision of training. The year 2009 saw analysis of a range of topics of particular importance in the ongoing negotiations including the liberalisation of trade in services and non-agricultural markets.

As progress towards conclusion of the Doha Development Round of multilateral trade negotiations has been slow, the Secretariat has supported members in the understanding and negotiation of regional trading agreements. Many members have a direct interest in the negotiation of Economic Partnership Agreements (EPAs) with the European Union. The Secretariat has been engaged in ensuring that information flows across the Commonwealth so that members in different regions can learn from each other and enhance the benefits for their people as a result. Additionally, the value of the Commonwealth in supporting members has been seen in the past year with the convening of a meeting at the request of the European Commission, under the auspices of the Commonwealth, to exchange ministerial views about the impact of the EPA process.

The second area is the analysis of the changing global trading system. The global economy is altering at a bewildering speed and with it the opportunities for trade are also changing. The Secretariat's analysis of these trends is provided to help policy-makers in member states identify the opportunities that will in turn allow economic growth to flourish. This includes understanding the impact of the changing composition of global income provided by emerging market countries on trading opportunities and the analysis of how the benefits of trade can be maximised for Africa. This high quality technical work supports members in creating the trade that supports the livelihoods of many in the Commonwealth.

The Secretariat's programme of assistance in debt management, spearheaded by SASD, is as relevant today as it was at its inception in the 1980s. A key component in the integrated programme of assistance in debt management is its highly regarded debt recording and management system (CS-DRMS). Installed in 60 Commonwealth and non-Commonwealth countries, the software provides a state-of-the-art facility to record, manage and analyse all categories of debt whether external or domestic, public or private.

Through SASD, the Secretariat also provides advisory services in legal and institutional matters (for example, the setting up of debt management offices) as well as training in various aspects of debt recording and management (including the undertaking of debt sustainability analysis and the formulation of debt management strategies). It is currently developing a suite of e-learning courses in debt management with the assistance of the Commonwealth of Learning. The Secretariat is increasingly focusing its efforts on providing the necessary tools and building member countries' capacity to undertake debt sustainability analysis so as to enable them to put in place sound debt management policies and strategies.

Ocean governance

Ocean management is complex and the outcome of policies can sometimes have unintended consequences:

* incentives and investments that lead to resource degradation and social decline

* fisheries incentives that support unsustainable fishing operations and agricultural policies which provide investment into land-based operations that increase erosion into the coastal waters and increased flows of pollutants and nutrient-enriching chemicals.

Some values like the financial worth of sectors such as oil, gas, fisheries and tourism are easier to realise than indirect values to

Fish farming, Uganda (photographer and copyright: Victoria Holdsworth / © Commonwealth Secretariat)

communities from a sustainable supply of food, social values via recreation and tradition, and aesthetic values from landscape appreciation, which are more difficult to quantify.

As Commonwealth Heads of Government recognised in their 2011 Perth Communiqué, it is paramount that practical solutions are found and progressed towards a more integrated use of ocean resources and a greener economy based in the oceans. We are already seeing the emergence of new approaches to ocean governance in regions such as the South Pacific and the region of

the Organisation of Eastern Caribbean States. There can be no one-fits-all model as governance arrangements need to be closely tailored to the specific structures and interest groups of each country and region. However, emerging experiences provide valuable lessons to build on.

Real issues of social, economic and environmental dimensions are at stake and if change does not occur from the status quo then Commonwealth states highly dependent on the ocean for wealth and jobs will suffer first, but ultimately all members will feel the effect in time through global markets.

Maritime boundaries and the Law of the Sea

The delimitation of our maritime borders, apart from clarifying and affirming the sovereignty of our states, creates the conditions for better use of our resources at sea … We shall adopt and apply the principle of peaceful and friendly solutions to these differences, always in the spirit of good neighbourliness.

President of Mozambique Armando Guebuza, commenting on an agreement signed with Tanzania and Comoros (December 2011)

Only seven out of 54 Commonwealth countries are landlocked – and of these fully six (Botswana, Lesotho, Malawi, Swaziland, Uganda and Zambia) have direct interests at stake through the UN

Convention on the Law of the Sea, which 47 Commonwealth countries have signed. Hailed as a constitution for the oceans, the Convention has been shaped in key ways by Commonwealth states and can be traced to proposals by Malta to the UN General Assembly in 1967. The treaty regulates all aspects of the use of ocean space including rights of navigation – both civil and naval – the exploitation of living and non-living marine resources, the protection of the marine environment, and the conduct of marine scientific research.

The Commonwealth is the only international organisation in the world today that provides fully funded legal and technical assistance to governments concerning the delimitation of maritime boundaries. Assisting countries in their continental shelf submissions to the United Nations is another major focus. In 2011, with Commonwealth assistance, Bangladesh became the 55th country to lodge a submission for such additional territory. (In January 2012 Guyana announced its intention to do likewise.) Wider issues of sovereignty within environmental governance are addressed by a pocket guide developed by the Commonwealth and Stakeholder Forum, published in 2011.

[Some] *80 per cent of respondents valued the work done by the Commonwealth Secretariat as efficient in terms of resolving maritime boundary issues; 100 per cent of respondents would seek or accept help from the Commonwealth Secretariat on future ocean management related issues. The Maritime Boundary programme has proven very worthwhile for member countries.*

Evaluation by Jonathan McCue (Atkins Ltd) and Martin Pratt (International Boundaries Research Unit, Durham University), 2010

> Nauru has become the first Pacific Island country to sponsor deep-sea mining exploration. The International Seabed Authority has granted a Nauru-registered company (Nauru Ocean Resources Incorporation) a licence to scope equatorial waters for nodules of copper, manganese, cobalt and nickel. The company's vice-president, Robert Heydon, says work will begin in the second half of this year. Robotic devices will carry out the work, which will occur at depths of up to five kilometres.
>
> *Source: Radio New Zealand International, February 2012*

Enterprise, agriculture and export competitiveness

The vast majority of Commonwealth citizens work in micro and small enterprises (including self-employment). This includes a high proportion of youth and many of the Commonwealth's 45 million international migrants. It is increasingly recognised that small businesses include not only survival strategies but also stable, dynamic and growing enterprises.

The Enterprise and Agriculture Section of SASD aims to promote viable and competitive micro, small and medium enterprises (MSMEs) that contribute to equitable economic growth and poverty reduction in member countries. Emphasis is on MSMEs in the agricultural, fisheries, light manufacturing and services sectors. Key areas of support include strategy and policy formation for sustainable development of MSMEs as well as capacity-building to

enhance their competitive advantage (including the use of information technologies). In view of the focus on food and food security on the world agenda, and the pressing and continuing need to end hunger and feed more people globally, more emphasis is being placed on support activities that contribute to improved agricultural productivity and food security.

Commonwealth businesswomen meet the competition

The Commonwealth-India Small Business Competitiveness Development programme has directly reached over 700 entrepreneurs and policy-makers since 2004, 50 per cent of them women, and affected many more. Held in Chandigarh in 2011, the 11th programme in the series attracted more than 85 entrepreneurs and business leaders from 35 Commonwealth countries.

Says Srinivasan Sridhar, Chairman and Managing Director of the Central Bank of India, 'This project is a tremendous opportunity for small businessmen and women to network and hear about the problems and opportunities other companies come up against. Participants are exposed to field visits and a galaxy of expert speakers who have a vast experience.' The Commonwealth-India programme is a collaboration between the Commonwealth Secretariat and the Central Bank of India, Corporation Bank and Export-Import Bank of India. The Central Bank of India assisted St Lucia with capacity-building of its Development Bank and is also providing gratis assistance to develop a framework for small business financing in Jamaica.

Strengthening business advisory services in Ghana

Our interaction with the Commonwealth has been very helpful because it was practical. While they know business, many of our clients have next to no education or are illiterate – that means you have to tailor the training accordingly at their level and in their own languages. They learn best when really involved, for example through learning games and role-plays. Within days we saw them make real progress. Now they understand that business plans are for guiding their business, not just for loan applications.

Anna Armo-Himbson, National Board for Small Scale Industries, Ghana

In February 2012 the Commonwealth Secretariat provided a four-week training of trainers on new product development and market access for SMEs in Accra. In collaboration with the National Board for Small Scale Industries (NBSSI), the course combined theoretical training and practical fieldwork to build the capacity of the trainees to serve as SME advisers. In 2011, similar trainings (20 in all) took place for all of Ghana's ten regions.

Small and micro businesses, usually owned by women, make up the vast majority of enterprises in Ghana – over two-thirds of workers and farmers are self-employed sole traders, and 85 per cent of manufacturers employ fewer than ten people. This structure puts severe constraints on the growth prospects of the economy and the survival rate of businesses. Lukman Abdul-Rahim, NBSSI Executive Director, said lack of technical and managerial skills, finance, marketing opportunities and poor quality and design

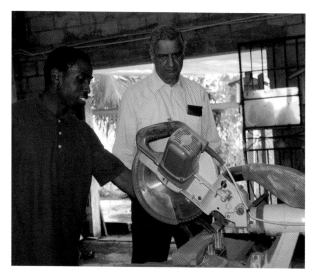

Secretary-General Kamalesh Sharma visiting a small enterprise, St Lucia (photographer and copyright: Julius Mucunguzi / © Commonwealth Secretariat)

of products were some of the problems facing the sector. He lauded the collaboration with the Commonwealth Secretariat in building the capacity of Business Advisers of the Board.

Nana Tweneboah Boateng, Executive Director of EMPRETEC Ghana Foundation, reiterated the need for governmental interventions to support the private sector for accelerated growth and development. Boateng, who is the Sanaahene of Anyinam, called for attitudinal change among SME operators, entrepreneurs and business community, saying 'collectively let's change Ghana'.

Stretching some 7,000 kilometres along the West African coastline, a submarine fibre-optic cable emerges off the coast of Nigeria to help bridge the digital divide in the continent. In Ghana, the cable has lowered wholesale prices by up to 80 per cent – a boon to small and medium enterprise. Dubbed Main One Cable, the system links West Africa with Europe, bringing ultra-fast broadband in the region. It runs from Seixal in Portugal through Accra to Lagos in Nigeria and branches out in Morocco, Canary Islands, Senegal, and Ivory Coast. The US$240 million raised for the project was all African financing (*Joy Online*/CNN, January 2012).

Energy and extractive industries

Abundant natural resources offer no guarantee of prosperity for the countries that possess such wealth. Good resource governance cannot depend solely on an active civil society, well-meaning politicians or enlightened companies. Rather, it requires the collaboration and innovations of all three.

Revenue Watch Institute

Many Commonwealth countries are endowed with natural resources such as minerals, oil and gas. More than 15 are endowed with significant petroleum and mineral reserves and are major producers of certain precious metals such as platinum, gold and chromium. Commonwealth member countries also contribute some 10 per cent of the world's crude oil and 17 per cent of

natural gas production. For those countries, the Secretariat, through SASD, provides a programme to maximise the benefits countries can derive. Its work in this area assists member countries to establish legal, fiscal and commercial regimes to govern mining as well as oil and gas activities. The objective is to help countries secure foreign investment while maximising the economic and social benefits accruing from these activities.

In response to requests from member governments, it has recently started working in a number of new areas such as deep-sea mining, coal-bed methane, uranium mining, as well as power generation and distribution. It considers the relationship between energy, natural resources and the environment as a crucial one. The scope of its interventions continues to expand, and now comprises an integrated approach covering issues from revenue management, procurement, and health and safety, as well as environmental aspects such as climate change considerations and site closure and rehabilitation.

- The Commonwealth Secretariat is assisting Guyana's Geology and Mines Commission on strategies to further develop the country's extractive industries. Focus will be placed on how Guyana can improve the entire mining sector with new emphasis on the potential oil and gas sectors. The ministry is also engaging in discussions with the Extractive Industries Transparency Initiative to further enhance the integrity and transparency of the sector.

- Rwanda is to invest about US$1 billion in geothermal energy development. The cost will involve power plant construction, drilling of more wells, infrastructure, drilling materials and services. Well drilling will soon begin on the slopes of Mount Karisimbi, Kinigi and Gisenyi. By 2017, the Rwandan Government expects to be producing at least 300 MW from geothermal energy and this has the potential to provide half the energy the country will require by 2020 (*The New Times Rwanda*, February 2012).

Pakistan's mining and minerals policy

For me personally, and for the Commonwealth, what has been great about this assignment is the involvement of private sector stakeholders in the review of the Mineral Policy. It has been most useful incorporating and reconciling the expectations of the Miners Association, especially with regard to small-scale mining. This is not often done, and should be.

Dr Ekpen Omonbude, Commonwealth Secretariat

Recent discoveries have provided strong evidence of significant mineral deposits in Pakistan. The country has a large base for industrial minerals, and growing interest from international mining companies carries significant potential for rapid development of the sector. One of the major projects, Reko Diq Copper, could go a long way to enhancing the country's economic position. The feasibility study carried out by the Tethyan Copper Company (TCC) puts the initial investment for Reko Diq at around US$3.3 billion, with anticipated export revenue at US$1 billion per annum. The project would produce 250,000 tons of copper and 200,000 ounces of gold.

The Commonwealth is providing technical assistance to the Government of Pakistan with respect to mining sector policy and regulatory issues. This involves reviewing and making recommendations concerning Pakistan's revised National Mineral Policy, Mineral Concession Rules, and the drafting of a Model Mineral Agreement. The secondary aim of this assignment has been to provide capacity-building assistance to the ministry in terms of reviewing the government's mineral concession rules, as well as advisory input in the negotiation of mineral agreements.

Informal artisanal mining provides rural employment and non-farm income in Pakistan. However, it is usually performed beyond the purview of government oversight using methods that are hazardous to workers, who are usually among the poorest rural labourers, and can cause substantial environmental damage (USAID). In March 2011, 43 miners in Balochistan were killed by a series of methane explosions. After the accident, the national newspaper *The Express Tribune* reported that over 60,000 miners working in 1,200 mines in Pakistan do not have adequate safety conditions.

In January 2012 Pakistan granted India 'most favoured nation' status in a significant boost to bilateral ties. The Indian Government welcomed the news, as did business leaders on both sides of the border.

Debt and harmful litigation

The debt problem faced by many small states has grown during the recent global economic and financial crisis, largely because of their traditional trading relationships with countries in which the crisis began and mushroomed. Debt in such small states was already high before the crisis because of a variety of factors. Among these factors are rebuilding costs after natural disasters and the necessity to borrow on commercial terms since many of them have been 'graduated' by international financial institutions from borrowing on concessional terms.

Commonwealth Eminent Persons Group, 2011

'Vulture funds' are private financial institutions aimed at buying sovereign debt at a low price and pursuing governments through the courts for the full value plus interest. The Commonwealth has hosted a series of workshops on the issue for Heavily Indebted Poor Country (HIPC) governments. Following a seminar in United Republic of Tanzania (June 2009), 22 countries benefited from debt relief, ten of them Commonwealth members: Cameroon, Ghana, Guyana, Malawi, Mozambique, Rwanda, Sierra Leone, Tanzania, Uganda and Zambia. The Legal Clinic designed to help member countries in litigation with creditors has subsequently expanded into capacity-building on legal issues arising in sovereign debt matters. The UK's Debt Relief (Developing Countries) Act, which restricts the actions of vulture funds in the UK, was passed in April 2010. Its effect was made permanent by a decision taken in March 2011.

Claims by vulture funds in recent years amount to some US$2.3 billion. The US$1 billion already collected by the funds is equivalent to more than double the International Committee of the Red Cross's entire budget for Africa in 2011, or the amount of money raised by Save the Children in 2010. Nutan Pitamber of the

Commonwealth Lawyers Association points out that for HIPCs, such litigation has the potential to remove sovereignty from elected government. 'Providing these governments with economic protection is of vital importance to maintain stability and the rule of law.'

A 2010 Evaluation by Sanga Sangarabalan, Ed Humphrey and Anne Thomson of Oxford Policy Management found that the debt management programme 'is highly regarded by its client countries and has clearly achieved a lasting impact in improving debt management in the Commonwealth. The programme scores highly for relevance, effectiveness, efficiency and sustainability. The forward looking component of the evaluation is particularly relevant as the external environment for the debt management programme has evolved.'

Inclusive finance

Increases in employment and personal incomes were not accompanied by an increase in personal savings but rather, by sharp increases in private consumption and rising consumer debt. At the same time, the buoyancy of the economy gave rise to the creation of more complex financial products and services. In too many cases, consumers' decisions about these were made on the basis of insufficient knowledge.

Elizabeth Austin, Central Bank of Trinidad and Tobago

National prosperity depends on accessing the necessary finance for investment whether from domestic or external sources. The factors that support high levels of investment are complex, but the Commonwealth Secretariat works to make a contribution to facilitating these needed flows of finance. To directly support investment flows, the Secretariat is supporting countries in the development of a template for foreign investment under Economic Partnership Agreements. It has also worked with partners in the private sector to help the creation of a vehicle to deliver US$400 million of investment in Africa. At the other end of the scale, projects are undertaken to support investment in small and medium-sized enterprises. In the past year, youth unemployment has been high on the agenda (see the article titled 'Empowering young people').

This work involves close collaboration between public and private sector partners. Another aspect of realising higher levels of investment is the existence of strong financial systems in member countries with the ability to channel sufficiently high levels of saving into effective investment. Equally, the recent global financial crisis has put a new emphasis on the need for effectively designed and consistently implemented regulation in the financial sector.

Credit unions are a popular vehicle of financial inclusion in the Caribbean, Canada (with 11 million members), Australia and elsewhere. Because the regulatory regime is slightly different for credit unions, there is a need to mediate the interests of civil society, central banks and concerned global bodies such as the International Monetary Fund. For example, in The Bahamas credit union membership has grown 29 per cent over the last five years, and growth in funds has outstripped that in conventional banks. The country's Central Bank has obtained, via the Commonwealth Secretariat, the services of a specialist consultant to oversee transition of credit unions to Central Bank regulation.

Credit unions from nine Pacific countries met in Port Moresby, Papua New Guinea, in September 2011. Discussion and training took place on issues of women's leadership, setting interest rates, governance, and managing risk. The congress was a joint effort of global, regional and national networks. Through the Credit Union Foundation Australia (CUFA), the Commonwealth Foundation supported delegates from outlying parts of Papua New Guinea to attend. With offices in Solomon Islands, Timor Leste, Cambodia and Fiji, CUFA's staff are mostly aged under 35 and half of its directors are women (*Commonwealth People*, March 2012).

Community banking: a view from Jamaica

Teneica Barnaby (MA Communications, UWI Mona)

I am an educator at secondary level, with ten years' classroom experience and five years at senior level. I have worked with the Jamaican Financial Services Commission and others to research and deliver Financial Literacy to high school students. While talking with persons in Clarendon (Jamaica) my eyes were opened to the cultural practices in the rural communities.

Partner banking is at the heart of the excellent fiscal management and educational practices that exist in Jamaica. The partner system has a group of persons that agree to deposit a sum of money either daily, weekly or bi-weekly, and make a withdrawal at a pre-determined time. The system helps to carry on the culture of saving that was passed on from one generation to the next. Even school-age children are a part of class partners.

Clarendonians created the system to meet the needs of the members of their community. Persons joined the partner because it is convenient and provides funds for education, housing and entrepreneurship. The money is mostly used to purchase school and household supplies, pay tuition and invest in business ventures (such as small shops and transportation services). The banker or leader is in charge of collecting and distributing the money. In most instances the banker is a female who is known to be a positive role-model in the communities. This individual maintains a close relationship with the persons in the community. She is the centre of the fiscal management of the local economy. The persons in the partner place a high level of trust and reliance on the banker, as he or she decides what financial needs are most important and gives emergency withdrawals.

Most persons indicated that they joined the partner because they knew the banker and that she got them involved in the partner. This strong leadership makes the home partner very successful in getting community members to be financially prudent. Many young persons are involved in the partner because it allows them to get funds to purchase school supplies, and furniture. Being involved in the partner is also a way for them to demonstrate that they are responsible.

Clarendonians think that the home partner makes their communities self-sufficient. The partner gives persons the opportunity to be self-employed as well as employ other members of their community. The business operators in the rural communities lamented that the process to secure a loan (from a financial institution) and the repayment procedures are burdensome. But, unlike these institutions, the home partner is designed to allow persons to withdraw a significant sum of money in a short time.

With thanks also to Roderick Sanatan, CARIMAC Department (a Commonwealth partner in financial literacy training)

Economic Development (2):

resilience building in the face of environmental challenges

'Commonwealth member states are beginning to emerge at very different speeds from the fuel and food crises of 2008 and the recession caused by the global financial crisis. Along with this recovery, the call for more holistic, sustainable, resilient forms of development is growing – to avoid damaging lurches from boom to bust and from one crisis to another.'

– Janet Strachan, Economic Affairs Division, Commonwealth Secretariat

The Commonwealth Secretariat gathers and shares practical policy approaches to building resilient and sustainable economies, especially in small states and vulnerable states which are prone to natural disasters and fluctuations in global markets. Recent areas of focus have been the profiling of economic resilience at the national level, nurturing climate-adapted development and support for the visioning and implementation of a Green Economy, with the delivery of climate financing to support these efforts.

Economic resilience building

Economic resilience building is a process through which small states can identify and adopt policies to cope with their inherent vulnerabilities. In terms of economic resilience, the rule of law and effective property rights, and macroeconomic stability and market efficiency, are central requirements. But other aspects of governance are important as well. Social development in terms of education and health support a resilient (productive, flexible, adaptive) workforce. It also indicates the extent to which relations within a society are properly developed, enabling an effective functioning of the economic apparatus without the hindrance of civil unrest and enabling collaborative dialogue and approaches towards the undertaking of challenging corrective measures in the face of adverse shocks. The environment is an important source of vulnerability by giving rise to shocks of an adverse nature, principally by rapid events such as earthquakes and floods, but also longer-term challenges to resilience such as climate change and the loss of biodiversity.

Good environmental management provides support for the productive base of economies and the social well-being of societies. The Secretariat has worked with experts on an economic resilience index and framework, piloted in Vanuatu, Seychelles and St Lucia, to identify areas in which small states are most vulnerable and pinpoint gaps in the resilience framework that can be addressed. The resulting resilience building tool has been further developed and implemented by the United Nations Economic and Social Commission for Asia and the Pacific, and will shortly be implemented in small states across the Atlantic and Indian Ocean through a partnership with the Indian Ocean Commission. The Secretariat's work on resilience building is supported by a substantial policy research and publications programme and high-level consultations among member states to identify and explore new and emerging development challenges for small states. These efforts also inform the Secretariat's advocacy role on the concerns of small states in international processes.

Visioning a green economy

June 2012 sees the twentieth anniversary of the UN Conference on Environment and Development – the Earth Summit – which took place in Rio de Janeiro, Brazil. That landmark conference agreed the climate change and biodiversity conventions, and led to practical policy tools to consolidate the definition of sustainable development set out in the 1987 report *Our Common Future* as '*development that meets the needs of the present without compromising the ability of future generations to meet their own needs*'. While sustainable development provides a robust framework to achieve more resilient and environmentally sound development, countries are still experiencing a lack of progress on the Millennium Development Goals (MDGs) and global environmental indicators.

One challenge is that sustainable development, which is centred on rights-based approaches, equity and law-based rule making, is running in parallel with an approach to economic development that is based on first-mover advantage; competition and the use of common environmental resources and services for free as though there are no ecological limits. These two spheres need to be brought closer together through shared objectives if sustainable development is to become a reality. The UN Conference on Sustainable Development (Rio+20), which takes place in June 2012, provides an opportunity to initiate this process through its themes of a green economy in the context of poverty eradication and sustainable development, and the International Framework for Sustainable Development. In reality gaps exist in the current process.

While the two Rio+20 themes are interdependent, they have been progressing largely along parallel tracks with little discussion in the context of the Rio+20 summit of the type of system that is required to deliver a green economy in the context of poverty eradication and sustainable development. In considering ways to promote transformation to a green economy, policy-makers have a significant opportunity to put in place new governance and institutional

Ministry of Forestry, Solomon Islands

Policy goal:
'The harvesting of forest resources at a sustainable rate with fair returns to landowners and the government and the replanting and care for the environment including promoting of all protected areas and to ensure Solomon Islands receives fair returns on the export of round logs that reflect true international market value.'

The Ministry of Forestry is responsible for the overall management of the forest resources of Solomon Islands.

It is also responsible for the drafting, enacting and implementing of forestry legislation and policy. The MoF supports family-based reforestation initiatives and encourages sustainable forestry activities, establishment of plantations, and domestic processing of timber.

Further to the efforts to sustainably manage the country's forests, the government introduced a Code of Practice for Timber Harvesting (CPTH), specifically designed to improve and minimise the negative effects of large-scale logging. The code incorporates best practices within the forest industry and promotes high environmental standards.

Conservation of forest biodiversity

The Forest Resources and Timber Utilisation Act, which guides the Ministry, provides for the conservation of forests and the improved management of forest resources, control of timber harvesting, encouragement and facilitation of sustainable forestry activities, establishment of plantations, and domestic processing of timber.

The sector's main players are the logging industry, international and national NGOs, and communities working in partnerships to conserve and manage the forest and its resources sustainably. Most of the forest resources are under the custody of the local communities who own them. The national government issues timber rights after agreements are made between logging companies and landowners. Landowners are also encouraged to have a holistic and

Monarcha richardsii, endemic to Solomon Islands

Solomon Islands dragonfly

integrative approach to developing their land, forest and water resources, and be mindful of the need to protect and conserve biodiversity.

The Ministry is working towards implementing a major forest conservation programme focusing on some of the unique forest ecosystems.

Monitoring climate change and land use

The Solomon Islands will soon be able to better monitor climate change and land use through the country's own remote sensing mapping and Geographic Information System capability to map forest cover, agriculture, pasture, mangroves, plantations, coral reefs and water bodies and biodiversity.

This is a joint initiative between the Solomon Islands government with support from UNDP's Project Strengthening Environment Management and Reducing the Impact of Climate Change, and the SOPAC Division of the South Pacific Community was presented recently at the Solomon Islands National Vegetation and GIS Technical Workshop.

Contact: Mr Jeffery Wickham, Permanent Secretary, Ministry of Forestry, P.O. Box G24, Honiara, Solomon Islands
Tel: +677 2 8611 • Email: zepi.wickham36@gmail.com

frameworks at the national level for more holistic forms of development that are broadly owned beyond the environmental community and into the mainstream economy. Commonwealth countries are among those playing a leading role in this endeavour.

Commonwealth finance ministers, recognising the key leadership role that their departments have in transforming the economy, have considered priority first steps in the development of the green economy, highlighting the need for effective concessional financing mechanisms to support capital investments for adaptation – such as sea defences – as well as investments in renewable energy, including solar and hydropower, which would increase the competiveness of small economies, reduce the cost of power to poor communities, and address severe imbalances in export/import earnings, driven by the cost of imported fuel. For some countries, the importance of agro-forestry and forest carbon industries is critical. Similarly, Commonwealth environment ministers have examined practical approaches to building a green economy, ranging from the development of national strategies, as is happening in Barbados, Botswana and Guyana, to step-by-step changes to build resilience, reduce waste and enhance the natural capital base for the economy.

The Commonwealth Secretariat is delivering training to officials from a range of government departments in small states on the international framework for sustainable development through an innovative online course being delivered residentially and through the Commonwealth of Learning. The complex interrelationship between trade, climate change and development in smaller developing countries has also helped to provide new insights on the impact of climate change on the trade competitiveness and economic development prospects of least developed countries, small and vulnerable economies and small states. Studies have also been conducted to identify impact pathways of climate change through key growth sectors of interest to Commonwealth small states, including the fisheries, agriculture and tourism sectors.

The challenge is to build investment in holistic development in a challenging world economy, continued uncertainty and rapid change. A strategic ability to respond to change and take advantage of new opportunities is required. The Commonwealth is supporting analysis of the institutional and governance requirements for a green economy for the oceans and in other areas (see 'Ocean governance' in the article titled 'Economic Development (1)'), and will shortly work to build the capacity of planning and finance ministries to drive forward practical transition pathways to a green economy through integrated investments across and between different sectors.

Climate financing: negotiating the 'spaghetti bowl'

Although there is some US$2 billion of climate finance available to developing countries, only around $400 million has been disbursed according to a study by the Overseas Development Institute. Low level of disbursement and absorption indicates capacity challenges when dealing with a complex array of funding streams.
Mechanisms are needed to attract climate financing to the neediest countries in an effective manner. This means paying great attention to the many lessons learned from recipient countries' decades of experience with development.

Commonwealth Deputy Secretary-General Ransford Smith, 2011

Responsible tourism balances heritage, environment and development

In Trinidad and Tobago in 2009, Heads of Government announced the Port of Spain Climate Change Consensus (POSCCC) – an expression of Commonwealth priorities on climate change in the context of the Copenhagen climate change summit in 2009. The process was described by some leaders as one of the most positive discussions on international climate change that had taken place that year. Elements of the POSCCC related to the need for fast-start financing later evolved to find expression in the outcomes from the climate summits in Copenhagen and Cancun.

As a result of the POSCCC, the Commonwealth Secretariat has explored blockages in the flow of climate financing to the Commonwealth's poorest and most vulnerable members, and practical options for supporting improved and more rapid disbursement to highly vulnerable and capacity constrained member states. The process has drawn on an innovative mix of officials from Commonwealth ministries of planning and finance, foreign affairs and environment, together with development partners, regional organisations and experts on climate finance. A complex range of issues has emerged from the consultations – from the level of financing available and difficulties in accessing existing sources, to an imbalance between mitigation and adaptation financing, and the challenge of connecting to a highly fragmented funding landscape.

As discussed at the consultations, each of the 30 funds in play has a different set of rules, regulations, terms and conditions that countries have to fulfil before they are granted access. Julius Mucunguzi, the Secretariat's assistant spokesperson for Africa, points out, 'The rules apply to the process for application, accountability, monitoring and evaluation ... The limited number of officials in ministries in these poor countries spend huge amounts of their time and energy filling complex forms – and putting together plans, what in the technical language are called National Adaptation Plans of Action, or NAPAs.'

According to Janet Strachan of the Secretariat's Economic Affairs Division: 'There is a clear potential to have Commonwealth member countries help each other more to facilitate a step-change in climate financing on the ground. Areas of focus in the future will include the transfer of knowledge, experience and targeted, applied expertise; mutual support in the strengthening of national capacities and institutions; Commonwealth work with regional organisations to help build support mechanisms at the regional level, including perhaps the establishment of a stream of projects ready for funding; and sharing of ideas on effective design of mechanisms to suit highly capacity constrained countries.'

Commonwealth Consultative Group on Environment (CCGE)

The CCGE is the principal forum for debate on environmental issues of concern to member states. It enables ministers and senior officials to share experiences in the context of current international processes on environment and sustainable development, convening annually in conjunction with the United Nations Environment Programme (UNEP) Governing Council or the UN Commission on Sustainable Development. The strength of the CCGE is that it provides an opportunity for ministers to meet outside of the formal negotiations and beyond their usual economic or regional groupings. Recent debates (for example, at the February 2012 meeting in Nairobi, Kenya) have focused on forest carbon finance, international environmental governance, ocean governance, and priorities for the Rio+20 conference.

In conclusion, the Commonwealth Secretariat continues to support consensus-building and policy development issues. This work is based on its strengths in the areas of advocacy, policy support and technical co-operation, especially in areas related to climate change, the emerging agenda on rapidly developing Commonwealth cities, and international governance concerns. It continues to focus on achieving a deeper integration of the three pillars of sustainable development – the social, economic and environmental – and to mainstream both gender perspectives and human rights in its approach.

Profiling vulnerability and resilience in St Lucia

Our stewardship of the earth and our sharing of its bounty concerns not so much what we inherit from our ancestors, as what we borrow from our children, and all generations.

Commonwealth Secretary-General Kamalesh Sharma speaking at the Natural Resources Forum, London, 2011

Economic vulnerability is defined as the exposure of an economy to harmful external economic shocks that are outside the economy's control, typically resulting from high degrees of economic openness and dependence on a narrow range of exports. Economic resilience refers to policy-induced ability of an economy to withstand and rebound from the negative effects of such shocks. St Lucia's sustainable development challenges are similar to those faced by other small island developing states (SIDS). In addition, economic growth over the past ten years has been negatively affected by loss of preferential treatment in its banana exports. Issues such as deforestation* and coastal zone management now call for attention.

Building a country profile of economic vulnerability and resilience requires an array of quantitative and qualitative information. Information used by the Commonwealth Secretariat was compiled through:

- available statistical sources from St Lucia sources, the International Monetary Fund and the World Bank

- presentations delivered during a two-day country consultation conference organised for the purposes of compiling this report, and

- a key stakeholder survey undertaken by means of a detailed questionnaire on the four aspects of economic resilience, namely macroeconomic stability, market efficiency, governance and social and environmental concerns.

A two-day consultation conference yielded a significant amount of qualitative information regarding the sources of vulnerability and resilience of St Lucia. A key stakeholder survey gathered further qualitative information.

Disaster management and civil protection management systems have improved in recent years, but further progress is called for in this crucial area, especially in the development of appropriate insurance schemes and early warning systems. Environmental governance institutions are also relatively underdeveloped and can be expected to become a necessity in future with the further development of construction, real estate and tourism activity.

* Worldwide, the highest rates of unsustainable forest depletion occur in India, Pakistan and Bangladesh (and the non-Commonwealth country, Ethiopia). Almost half of the world total occurs in India, where the annual timber depletion exceeds that of the next 25 territories combined, although this is also true of India's population size. For territories where data is available, India's forest depletion per capita is ranked 19th (Dorling, Newman and Barford, 2010, The Atlas of the Real World, Thames and Hudson).

Aligning climate finance with sustainable development at national level

The provision of international climate finance in support of actions in developing countries does not take place in a vacuum. International relations between developed and developing countries are longstanding and complex; major flows of finance have been associated with official development assistance for several decades, building up a rich experience of lesson learning of what works and what does not.

Paper for Commonwealth High Level Meeting on Climate Finance, 2011

One of the major lessons of aid effectiveness is the recognition that national ownership over the development process is paramount. National governments, together with civil society and the private sector, have to decide the priorities of national investments. One-off project interventions supported by external finance that are not embedded within some national priority setting process are unlikely to succeed. In fact, by working outside of national systems some development projects have tended to undermine national systems, or at least not taken advantage of the opportunity to improve them.

An important consideration in the move away from unco-ordinated project interventions is the opportunity created to move finance at scale. Larger investments can be justified if they are seen to be supporting a national programme. However, this raises the need for national planning to become more effective. National planning is an area of the public administration that has frequently been seriously weakened by years of project support going straight to sectoral ministries and their subordinate departments and agencies.

There is now a need, more than ever before, to work across government, involving ministries of finance and economic planning, and ensuring that spending goes through the national budget and is subject to the full rigours of national accountability. This is the lesson of 'mainstreaming' that has been learned (if not always acted upon) in numerous sectors: from gender, to HIV and AIDS, to youth development and employment.

At the national scale, where experience is more limited, multi-donor trust funds are also being established. Within the Commonwealth, Bangladesh is playing a leadership role. These funds should soon begin to offer additional lessons on how to manage diverse sources of funding, ensure predictable flows of resources and secure co-ordination between funders and within-country sector based institutions.

A 2011 Commonwealth Secretariat publication, *Integrating Sustainable Development into National Frameworks: Policy Approaches for Key Sectors in Small States* is available as a paperback and e-book. By Constance Vigilance and Janet Strachan, the handbook brings policy-making for sustainable development into the mainstream of decision-making at all levels of governance and in all sectors.

Water management

In addition to the environmental impact, damage by untreated wastewater to the marine environment can result in severe social and economic consequences for people in the region.

Jamaica's Minister of Water, Environment, Land and Climate Change, Robert Pickersgill (Kingston, February 2012) at the launch of the Global Environment Facility/Caribbean Regional Fund for Wastewater Management (GEF/CReW) project

As much as 85 per cent of wastewater entering the Caribbean Sea is untreated – yet this is the region in the world more dependent on tourism for jobs and income. Citing statistics from the Pan American Health Organization (PAHO), Robert Pickersgill said that in 2001, 51.5 per cent of households in the Caribbean region lacked sewer connections of any kind, and only 17 per cent were connected to acceptable connections and treatment systems.

Within Caribbean countries, less than 2 per cent of urban sewage is treated before disposal, and unfortunately the figure is even lower for rural communities, he stated.

Among the positive developments, Pickersgill said, are the establishment of the protocol concerning pollution from land-based sources and activities (LBS Protocol) and the convention for the protection and development of the marine environment of the wider Caribbean region (Cartagena Convention), and gave the assurance that Jamaica will become a signatory to the LBS Protocol, which was ratified in 2010, in short order. The four-year GEF/CReW initiative will receive support from the Inter-American Development Bank and UNEP, which will serve as co-implementers.

The Project Co-ordination Group, based in Jamaica, will be supported by Pilot Executing Agencies in four Caribbean countries: the National Water Commission in Jamaica; the Ministry of Finance in Belize; the Ministry of Housing and Water in Guyana; the Tobago House of Assembly in Trinidad and Tobago; and by the Secretariat of the Cartagena Convention based in Kingston, Jamaica (*Caribbean News Now!*, February 2012).

- The Commonwealth Secretariat's ongoing assistance in the area of public-private partnerships has learned from Singapore's approach to this issue. High-purity treated used water has become a major source of water for the city-state; the government has even decided not to use the term 'waste water' any longer. Ulu Pandan NEWater Plant, awarded to Keppel Seghers under a 20-year Design-Build-Own-Operate contract, provides 15 per cent of Singapore's water needs: 32 million gallons a day.

- The UN 'World Water Development Report' has warned that renewable water resources in Pakistan are decreasing towards a dangerous level that could go as low as 550 cubic metres per person by the end of 2025.

Global water resources are stressed by depletion and pollution (photographer and copyright: Noel-Mackson Wasamunu / © Commonwealth Secretariat)

Responsible tourism

Biodiversity conservation is an area where the gap between environmental ethics and environmental practice is arguably the widest … At the bottom of every policy and political statement on the subject, there lies implicit a normative position about the relationship between nature and human beings, as well as the diverse social, political, and moral communities to which individuals belong.

Niraja Gopal Jayal writing in *Moral and Political Reasoning in Environmental Practice*

What is the role of government in making tourism more sustainable? Why should communities living near a game reserve not hunt for food? Or why should they keep the forests as animal habitat rather than clearing them for arable farmland? These were among the many issues raised during a panel discussion organised by the Commonwealth Secretariat at the World Travel Market (London, November 2011), as it marked World Responsible Tourism Day.

The business case for sustainable practices in tourism management has to be actively put forward. Commonwealth Deputy Secretary-General Ransford Smith, who chaired the session, noted that the objectives of sustainable development endorsed at the World Summit on Sustainable Development in Johannesburg, South Africa, in 2002 also applied to tourism. The basic principle in sustainable practice is that in our attempt to use resources today, we should do so in a manner that does not jeopardise the needs of the future generation. 'We need to attain a balance between economic, environment, social and cultural goals,' said Mr Smith.

U V Jose, the Director of Kerala Institute of Tourism and Travel Studies in India, demonstrated an initiative that his institution undertook to create community ownership of tourism activities in specific locations across the state. He said that a key outcome of the initiative was promotion of procurement of fruits and vegetables by hotels and resorts from local communities, which benefited the local community by UK£60,000 between 2010 and 2011.

* Light, A and De-Shalit, A (eds). MIT Press, 2003. That year the world's population made 665 million international tourist trips – Dorling, Newman and Barford (2010) The Atlas of the Real World. The country travelling the most, ahead of Europe, was Antigua and Barbuda – where residents left their islands on average 3.66 times.

Food security

As our countries continue to tackle, head-on, the issue of food security, I congratulate you for adopting the Perth Declaration on Food Security Principles; and for the collective agreement on strong and united advocacy on behalf of the Commonwealth membership at the global level, including upcoming meetings of the G20, Durban Climate Change, and Rio+20.

St Kitts and Nevis Prime Minister Dr Denzil Douglas, addressing the closing session of CHOGM 2011

In 2012, one of the Commonwealth countries most affected by food shortages is Cameroon. The north of the country is in the Sahel region (in common with Senegal, southern Mauritania, Mali, Burkina Faso, southern Algeria, Niger, northern Nigeria, Chad, Sudan, South Sudan, and Eritrea), where 10 million people are facing starvation (UN, February 2012). Harvests plummeted 25 per cent in the region compared to 2010. In response, the government is boosting tree-planting projects in an effort to improve rainfall in the region and reduce desertification. Unsurprisingly, given relatively poor infrastructure and high levels of poverty, central Africa has the highest per capita usage of traditional fuels (including wood) worldwide.*

Cameroon's director-general of customs, Minette Libom Li Likeng, has said: 'The sharp drop in agricultural production and consequently trade in 2011 in the northern regions of Cameroon and its neighbouring countries has been attributed partly to a prolonged dry season caused by aggravated global warming' (Reuters, February 2012). Rice consumption in Cameroon has more than doubled since the end of the 1990s, but domestic production failed to keep pace even before the effects of the recent drought. According to the Cameroon Ministry of Agriculture, a drop of 80,000 tonnes in rice production in 2010 led to the importing of 120 billion CFA francs (US$240 million) worth of rice.

- One of the cash crops that climbed the production ladder in the 1960s and 70s was coffee, but despite good performance on the international market, disease and climate change have brought exports in 2011/2012 marketing season down to 26,300 metric tonnes from 48,000 metric tonnes in 2010 (all Africa.com/*Cameroon Tribune*, January 2012).

- In January 2012 US Kosmos Energy signed an agreement with Cameroon's state oil company SNH allowing it to explore in the country's offshore Fako block. Kosmos will invest 9 billion CFA francs to explore within the 1,289-square-kilometre block, which sits near Cameroon's productive Rio del Rey and Kribi-Campo basins, for six years. Cameroon is one of Africa's oldest oil producers but has seen output slump to around 65,000 barrels per day from 185,000 barrels per day at its peak in 1985 (Thomson Reuters).

* The USA, despite its high consumption of fossil fuels and generation of nuclear power, still consumes, per person, more traditional fuels than many parts of Central and South America; 2.5 times more than India; and four times more than China. Dorling, Newman and Barford (2010) The Atlas of the Real World. Thames and Hudson.

Fish in figures

In its most recent report, the Food and Agriculture Organization (FAO) put 'total capture fisheries production' at around 80 million tonnes in 2008. Although this figure has been stable for the past decade, the proportion of marine fish stocks estimated to be under-exploited has declined from 40 per cent in the mid-1970s to 15 per cent in 2008.

As global fishing activity has intensified over recent decades, the numbers of over-exploited, depleted and recovering stocks have exceeded their maximum sustainable yield. Although some stocks can experience a temporary rise in abundance, they do so because of release from predation and competition. Once the stocks in abundance are over-fished, the next species down will be prey to excessive exploitation – a process known as 'fishing down the web'. Such trends and statistics point to the conclusion that fish stocks are in serious jeopardy.

The issue of depletion is often cited as the most significant change in marine biomass, but it is also important to consider other causes of change. Some projections conclude that climate-induced redistribution of stocks will mean a 40 per cent drop in maximum catch potential in the Tropics and a 30–70 per cent increase in high latitude regions such as Alaska and Greenland. The changes to water temperature and ocean currents mean that fisheries are likely to shift towards the High North and deeper water. Some argue that fish harvested from deeper water may assist in the management of stocks by exploiting under-utilised species, but studies show that many deep-water species are less resilient to over-fishing – which should make them new candidates for conservation instead of targets for exploitation.

The process of translating such negative trends into corrective management policies is slow, and compromises often have to be made to the original intentions. As yet it is only Regional Fisheries Management Organisations (RFMOs) that have the authority to govern the High Seas – and 67 per cent of the fish stocks under RFMO jurisdiction are already depleted or over-fished.

A recent study evaluating the FAO's 1995 voluntary Code for Responsible Fishing showed that compliance, by the 53 parties to the code, is at best weak.

Illegal, unreported and unregulated fishing is one of the biggest challenges to the sustainable management of marine ecosystems and it is estimated to cause losses valued between US$10 and US$23.5 billion each year, as well as leading to environmental degradation and undermining food supply. These activities seriously hamper the ability of the fisheries sector to meet economic, social and environmental objectives. With 37 per cent of the global fish harvest entering international trade, there is a powerful opportunity for trade-based initiatives to counter such activities by banning unregulated products. But this needs to be developed into a regime that is uniform and consistent throughout the RFMOs, without it being used as a tool to make unnecessary restrictions on trade.

Source: Homera Cheema, co-ordinator for the Commonwealth Fisheries Programme 2008–2010, adapted from Global *Magazine (Third Quarter 2011)*

Photographer and copyright: Kevin Nellies / © Commonwealth Secretariat

Supporting the Climate Change Centre, Belize

What we have to recommend is whether to re-examine our building laws – do we need more resilient structures? Do utility lines need to be above or beneath ground? If we have floods, how do we deal with them? Does it mean building more structures, more sluices, more pump stations, or does it just mean changing the way we conduct certain activities? ... We have a single major goal. We hope to show the policy-makers the cost of inaction.

Dr Mark Bynoe, a Commonwealth expert working at the Caribbean Community Climate Change Centre, Belize

In 2011, the Commonwealth Secretariat continued to provide technical assistance to the Climate Change Centre. Mark Bynoe, an environmental and resource economist, completed a review of climate change preparedness in the region – also with funding from the Australian Agency for International Development (AusAID). This was presented to the UN Economic Commission for Latin America and the Caribbean as it prepared for the COP-17 negotiations in Durban, South Africa, in late 2011.

Around half of the 18 countries involved have now made budget allocations specific to climate change and extreme events. Working with the University of the West Indies, the University of Suriname, the University of Guyana and the University of Belize, the Centre is also building capacity in economic assessment of climate change and climate adaptation options. This is being delivered via a master's level online programme. Cost-benefit analysis of adaptation projects in St Lucia, St Vincent and the Grenadines, and Dominica have been drafted.

Bynoe has been instrumental in the Caribbean's Climate Change Programme with the European Union, and agreements between the Centre, the Caribbean Development Bank and the UK Department for International Development. He has also provided comments on the draft CARICOM Regional Food and Nutritional Security Plan and developed a Resilience Framework implementation plan that was agreed by Heads of Government in February 2012.

Says Max Everest-Phillips, Director of Governance and Institutional Development at the Commonwealth Secretariat, 'One of the immediate aspects of climate change is an increase in the frequency and magnitude of disasters such as floods, droughts and cyclones. The impacts of these on small states have already been estimated at 10–15 per cent of their GDP.'

Managing social transformation:

the Secretariat's Education, Gender and Health teams

In 16 Commonwealth countries, people cannot expect to live more than 60 years. In 17 countries, children receive fewer than 6 years of education. And in only 10 of the 54 countries of the Commonwealth are more than one-quarter of members of parliament women.[1]

A healthy, educated workforce, free from discrimination, is essential to economic growth, peace and security, and the fulfilment of individual and national potential. Without accelerated progress in education, gender and health, the development aspirations of Commonwealth countries will not be met.

The continuing global economic crisis means that governments, communities and individuals must seek innovative ways to finance their development efforts. With aid budgets being reduced, and investors still wary of risks, the focus has been on ensuring that funding results in maximum value for money. But even when development programmes are maximally effective and efficient, there still might not be enough to go round to ensure that social safety nets and the provision of basic services such as education and health are protected and sustained.

The Commonwealth Secretariat's Social Transformation Programmes Division (STPD) assists governments to maximise the impact and reach of the resources they spend on development. By integrating education, gender and health, STPD is able to develop policies that take a holistic approach to development. This helps to create efficiencies.

Like many development actors, the Secretariat through STPD aims to help countries achieve the Millennium Development Goals (MDGs) and Education for All (EFA) goals. It focuses on key areas that target the most vulnerable, but that might not currently attract the same global attention as other issues. Work currently being undertaken, for example, looks at the role and status of refugee teachers in education in emergencies. Such teachers are frequently overlooked when governments are planning education delivery, and yet they could contribute much to increasing access to high quality education for children. The work will support governments in countries where forced migrant teachers are living to maximise these teachers' potential.

Another area is women's unpaid work in the HIV care economy. Unpaid carers are often missing from policy and programmes on treatment and care, yet the protection of carers' rights is a fundamental prerequisite to an effective response to HIV. STPD is leading on advocacy work on this issue and has set out a clear agenda for action. An outcome of the research on HIV unpaid care is the work on social protection in the context of public debt, rural subsistence and the care economy. The outputs in this area include

an information paper sharing good practices on gender and social protection among Commonwealth countries, a recently concluded round table on social protection, and the planned international panel at the AWID (Association for Women's Rights in Development) Forum. The planned research study on social protection is also underway.

Quality education for all

The Commonwealth is committed to the achievement of universal primary education. Many Commonwealth countries have made enormous gains in education access and quality, and are on track to reach the internationally agreed goals – the MDGs and EFA – by 2015. But enormous challenges remain. Globally, over 67 million primary school-age children are out of school. Of these, 42 per cent are in Commonwealth countries. And of these 28,337,300 children, 56 per cent are girls.[2] In 16 Commonwealth countries, more than one-quarter of the population cannot read or write.

The theme of the 18th Conference of Commonwealth Education Ministers, to be held in Mauritius in August 2012, is 'Education in the Commonwealth: bridging the gap as we accelerate towards achieving the internationally agreed goals'. The closer we get to universal primary education, the harder it is to achieve it and sustain. By definition it is the most difficult to reach children who remain out of school. This means the very poorest, those in conflict situations, those with special learning needs or disabilities, or those from highly marginalised groups. But even as the Commonwealth gets more children into school, the pressures on education systems increase. This endangers the quality of education that children have a right to.

What are 'the gaps'? They are the gap between countries and communities with high access rates and those with low; the gap between access and quality; the gap between what a child can rightfully expect and what a country is currently able to deliver; and, increasingly, the technology gap – the digital divide.

Through its Education Section, STPD works with governments and partners to develop appropriate tools to help countries bridge these gaps. Key areas of focus are professional standards, multi-grade teaching, gender-responsive schools, inclusive education, disability, skills development, technical and vocational education and training, migrant teachers, education in emergencies, and education for economically and environmentally sustainable development – particularly relevant to small states.

A robust professional standards framework helps to ensure consistency between pre-service teacher training, education in the classroom, performance management of teachers, the inspection of schools and teachers' continuing professional development. The Education Section has supported the development of professional standards for teachers and school leaders in the Caribbean, and

Children at Mbai Primary School, Siaya, Kenya (photographer and copyright: Rebecca Nduku / © Commonwealth Secretariat)

will be supporting the establishment of national teaching councils in the region to ensure they are implemented effectively. In line with the Commonwealth's commitment to sharing, the learning from this experience will inform the Section's approach as it works with member countries on similar standards for the African and Pacific regions.

Gender equality and women as agents of change

Gender equality must become a lived reality. Today, between 15 and 76 per cent of women are targeted for physical and/or sexual violence in their lifetime. Globally, while 125 countries now outlaw domestic violence, 603 million women live in countries where it is still not considered a crime. And, every 90 seconds, a woman dies in pregnancy or due to childbirth-related complications – despite us having the knowledge and resources to make childbirth safe. With the recent economic downturn, women's economic position has further deteriorated ... Available evidence suggests that greater diversity and inclusiveness in decision-making leads to better outcomes, and that women's needs and priorities get better reflected in these decisions.

Michelle Bachelet, Under-Secretary-General and Executive Director of UN Women

Source: Interview with Global *Magazine (Fourth Quarter 2011)*

Gender equality means all of us having equal rights, responsibilities, benefits and opportunities – regardless of whether we are born male or female. The way to achieve gender equality is always to look at the possible implications for women and men, whatever the action, policy or project we have in mind ('Gender mainstreaming'). Through STPD's Gender Section, the Secretariat ensures that gender equality is supported by all Secretariat programmes and becomes a legitimate and integral part of the structure, systems, laws and culture of Commonwealth governments. Mainstreaming is a strategy for making women's as well as men's issues a part of what we plan, what we do and how we measure results, 'so that women and men benefit equally and inequality is not perpetuated' (United Nations Department of Economic and Social Affairs – UNDESA).

Recognising that gender equality is intertwined with social, economic and political challenges created by conflict, globalisation, poverty and HIV/AIDS, the Secretariat has been working to help countries implement international legal instruments and harmonise national laws with international standards. The Secretariat supports the implementation of UN Security Council Resolution 1325, which calls for respect of women's rights, support and full participation in peace negotiations.

Cutting-edge research and gender analysis have been conducted to highlight gender dimensions in the implementation of trade liberalisation policies. When policy-makers are not aware of existing gender biases and inequalities and how these affect women's access to resources and credit, trade policies and export promotion schemes may have counterproductive outcomes. Gender inequalities (e.g. in education or consumption) often dampen productivity and hinder trade. They can make it harder to build capacity in the current workforce and the future one.

The proposed 'target of no less than 30 per cent of women in decision-making in the political, public and private sectors by 2005'

(5th Commonwealth Women's Affairs Ministers Meeting report, 1996) is attracting increasing support from member countries. More concerted efforts by Commonwealth governments are required to enhance women's representation in both public and private sectors to the agreed minimum of 30 per cent.

Health systems: technology and management

Through STPD's Health Section, the Secretariat addresses priority health concerns and works to strengthen health systems in member countries through technical assistance for policies and programmes. They help to support vital advocacy work, increasing access to universal healthcare and utilising technology, helping to ensure that national issues are reflected in global policy-making.

The sustainable adoption and implementation of e-health is a strategic and innovative means for the Commonwealth's developing countries to provide additional impetus to existing health initiatives and to enable developing countries to begin to catch up on e-health. The Secretariat sees e-health as a combination of information and communication technology (ICT) and organisational change. The development and use of ICT in health systems is lagging behind other sectors in many countries' economies. This is particularly so in many Commonwealth member states, with African countries behind further, according to the World Health Organization (WHO). E-health creates a focus on ICT as a resource that provides new and better information, and organisational change that contributes to using the information to realise benefits for patients, carers, communities, health workers and healthcare provider organisations by strengthening healthcare systems.

Transforming consumption and lifestyles

Governments have a responsibility to modify the environment – so you smoke less and drink less. Regulation, taxation, and legislation represent the major instruments the state can use.

Sir George Alleyne, Director Emeritus, Pan American Health Organization, 2011

A major priority is assisting governments to respond to the challenges of non-communicable diseases (NCDs). Like obesity, NCDs are not contagious; rather, they are caused by a person's lifestyle, genetics or environment. Cardiovascular diseases, cancers, chronic respiratory diseases and diabetes are the world's four biggest killers, causing 60 per cent of all deaths and with 80 per cent of these in low and middle-income countries. The risk factors include tobacco, alcohol, poor diet and lack of exercise. Interventions in these cultural and economic (consumption and production) areas are not always well integrated in mainstream systems of healthcare.

The impact of NCDs in countries such as Canada, India, Nigeria and Pakistan can be counted in billions of US dollars. NCDs rank alongside energy prices and the state of the Chinese economy in terms of their economic importance. In at least ten Pacific countries excessive consumption of low quality, fatty or processed food has resulted in obesity rates of 50–90 per cent (WHO, 2011), with epidemics of associated diabetes.

It was the Commonwealth Heads of Government Meeting in 2009 that called for a high-level UN summit on NCDs, held in September

HIV/AIDS awareness-raising, India (photographer and copyright: Ramanathan Iyer / © Commonwealth Secretariat)

2011 in New York. This was a 'seminal moment' according to Mark Lodge, Director of the International Network for Cancer Treatment and Research UK. 'I'm so proud of the Commonwealth that as an organisation it is so committed to working at the highest level to drive the issue of NCDs forward.'

The focus of the Commonwealth Health Ministers Meeting in Geneva, May 2012, is on the connections between NCDs and communicable (infectious) diseases.

Combating AIDS, tuberculosis and malaria

We are finally seeing the fruits of our labours: deaths from all three diseases are falling and new science has shown that the AIDS epidemic can be halted – as well as millions of lives saved – in just a few years, but this will require new determination by African leaders and donor governments to finish the job.

Lord Paul Boateng

In the past 30 years, there have been many positive achievements in the fight against the HIV/AIDS epidemic, but we still have a long way to go towards realising universal access to prevention, treatment, care and support. The new UNAIDS Strategy 2011–2015, *Getting to Zero*, and the outcomes of the High Level Meeting on AIDS in June 2011 both underscore the critical importance of highly focused and well co-ordinated responses, in the context of an urgent need for sustained attention to the prevention, treatment and care needs of children and young people, in and out of the school setting.[3] Further, AIDS is one of several epidemics affecting Commonwealth countries.

According to research published in February 2012, malaria kills 1.2 million people a year – nearly twice the previous estimate.[4] The study also found that 42 per cent of deaths were in older children and adults, overturning long-held assumptions that malaria chiefly threatens the under-fives. Also in February, WHO figures showed the highest levels yet of drug-resistant tuberculosis (TB). TB kills around 2 million people a year worldwide because of poverty and poor housing, and is the leading cause of death (25%) among people living with HIV.

These developments have compounded alarm about the financial state of the Global Fund to Fights AIDS, Tuberculosis and Malaria. Recent figures show that funding for HIV and AIDS was down 10 per cent in 2010. Two-thirds of all those in the world with HIV and AIDS are Commonwealth citizens. In Africa the growth of democracy, urbanisation and decentralisation have made local government a key player (see extract below).

Political engagement and capacity at the local level are critical in order to translate national policy into local action that benefits those most in need. This kind of political engagement seldom happens spontaneously. Sensitisation, not only of mayors and municipal leaders, but also of civil servants – including city managers – needs to happen for HIV and AIDS to become institutionalised within the service delivery agenda and financial systems of local authorities.

Alliance of Mayors' Initiative for Community Action on AIDS at Local Level (AMICAALL), a strategic partner of the Commonwealth Secretariat

In all these areas, STPD works closely with governments, development partners, civil society and other stakeholders to address emerging challenges, and build member countries' capacity to meet the education, gender and health targets of the MDGs.

Notes

1 United Nations Development Programme Human Development Index, 2011.

2 UNESCO Institute for Statistics database, 2010.

3 UNESCO, 2011.

4 See www.thelancet.com/journals/lancet.

HIV: access to prevention and treatment in East/Southern Africa

Universal access is a metaphor for social justice, for fundamental human rights, and for global solidarity … An annual investment of US$22 billion is needed by 2015 to avert 12 million HIV infections and 7.4 million deaths.

UNAIDS East and Southern Africa Regional Support Team

The 2011 UN Political Declaration on HIV/AIDS set a number of targets, as follows.

- To substantially reduce AIDS-related maternal deaths.

- By 2015, reduce sexual transmission of HIV by 50 per cent.

- By 2015, reduce transmission of HIV among people who inject drugs by 50 per cent.

- By 2015, eliminate mother-to-child transmission of HIV.

- By 2015, work towards 15 million people living with HIV receiving antiretroviral treatment.

- By 2015, reduce tuberculosis deaths in people living with HIV by 50 per cent.

- By 2015, reach an overall target of annual global expenditure on HIV and AIDS, based on current estimates, of between US$22 billion and US$24 billion in low- and middle-income countries.

How member countries operationalise these priorities was the focus of a 2011 consultation held by the Commonwealth Secretariat in partnership with the Southern African Development Community (SADC) and hosted by Botswana's Ministry of Health.

Health adviser at the Secretariat, Dr Mbololwa Mbikusita-Lewanika said: 'In responding to the epidemic, the Secretariat encourages a multi-sectoral and rights-based approach, which puts some of the most vulnerable groups, such as women and young people, at the centre of the agenda. The Commonwealth recognises the linkages between development and health: poverty, gender inequality, human resource constraints, democracy and governance.'

She added that assisting countries in responding effectively to the UN recommendations was of critical importance, as many countries most affected by the HIV epidemic are Commonwealth member states, and that about two-thirds of those living with HIV are in the Commonwealth.

The consultation brought together ministry of health officials, national AIDS programme directors, managers and co-ordinators from Botswana, Kenya, Lesotho, Malawi, Swaziland, Uganda, United Republic of Tanzania, and Zambia.

Research and case studies presented included one on unpaid HIV care work. Commissioned by the Secretariat, the study highlighted the need for:

- increased financial and technical support for people living with HIV at household-level

- cross-cutting activities and multi-level prevention and intervention programmes to reduce stigma and discrimination, and

- ensuring that the dignity and human rights of people living with HIV are upheld.

Education, gender and climate change

The influence of gender in education is multi-faceted. Addressing a frequently overlooked area, the Secretariat has explored the implications of the feminisation of the teaching profession with its innovative work titled *Women and the Teaching Profession: Exploring the Feminisation Debate*. This will inform gender-sensitive teacher management policies. Keeping up the commitment to providing practical guidance of real world use, the Secretariat has published *Implementing Inclusive Education: A Commonwealth Guide to Implementing Article 24 of the UN Convention on the Rights of People with Disabilities* (Second Edition). Additionally, its field report titled *Education of Children with Albinism in Malawi* draws attention to the particular challenges – and draws inspiration from the solutions – presented by a condition that affects many throughout the world.

Climate change is now at the top of the agenda for Commonwealth countries. Yet many countries have struggled to find a place for education for sustainable development (ESD) in their policies, curricula and classroom practice. A far-reaching study on innovative ESD practices in small island developing states will provide policy-makers and practitioners with real-life examples of projects that work, together with an analysis of why they work, helping their replication. This will complement the Secretariat's *Education in Small States: Policies and Priorities*, and provide the basis for Secretariat technical assistance to countries wanting to adopt a whole-sector approach to ESD.

Education and gender are generally on the margins of vulnerability analyses. Implications for education in such contexts include how education can help communities to reduce their vulnerability to major environmental challenges, and how disaster preparedness can be incorporated into educational planning and cross-sectoral skills training for personnel working in all sectors of society. Meanwhile, after Structural Adjustment Programmes and associated national budgets, municipal budgets and trade agreements, climate financing is emerging as a new arena of gender analysis and gender-responsive budgeting (as the extract below explains).

The Cancun Agreements acknowledge that gender equality and the effective participation of women are important for all aspects of climate change, but especially for adaptation. Gender-responsive climate financing instruments and funding allocations are needed. This is a matter of using scarce public funding in an equitable, efficient and effective way. It also acknowledges that climate finance decisions are not made within a normative vacuum, but must be guided by acknowledging women's rights as unalienable human rights. Currently, gender considerations are not addressed systematically in existing climate funds.

Liane Schalatek and Smita Nakhooda, Overseas Development Institute, 2011

Migration of health and education professionals

The Commonwealth now hosts 45 million international migrants. World Bank research shows that the highest per capita rates of 'brain drain' are not from sub-Saharan Africa, Asia or Latin America, but from small states ... While the largest number of foreign-born doctors working in the industrialised nations of the Organisation for Economic Co-operation and Development are from India, among the ten countries with the highest expatriation rates are six Commonwealth small states: Antigua and Barbuda, Grenada, Guyana, Dominica, Trinidad and Tobago, and St Vincent and the Grenadines.

The Commonwealth Eminent Persons Group, 2011

Through the Commonwealth Code of Practice for the International Recruitment of Health Workers, the Secretariat works with health ministries to help with health workforce migration, organising workshops to raise awareness about the code and promote its implementation. Training curricula developed with support from the Secretariat at educational institutions in East, Central and Southern Africa and the UK have helped to boost the number of professionals from Malawi to Seychelles trained in midwifery and women's health.

Similarly, the Commonwealth Teacher Recruitment Protocol recognises that inequalities and differences exist within and across Commonwealth countries. The protocol been adopted by all member countries and some non-members too. The Secretariat will use the findings of its study on refugee teachers to provide technical assistance to governments coping with rapid influxes of forced migrants, a scenario that is predicted to increase in scale and frequency in coming years. Often in an emergency, teachers leave the education system, and children in refugee camps are taught by volunteers from the community. This can have a negative impact on quality and access. The Secretariat will assist countries to incorporate planning for emergencies into their policies, making it easier for teachers to stay in the profession.

The protocols are an example of the Secretariat leading the way in setting standards for the ethical recruitment of professionals across borders, and are becoming evermore relevant as migration as a whole is set to rise. If migration continues to grow at the same pace as over the last 20 years, some analysts predict there could be 405 million international migrants by 2050 (source: International Organization for Migration). South-to-South migration is important, as are professionals who are forced to migrate because of conflict, natural disasters, environmental stress or other non-voluntary reasons. According to the United Nations High Commissioner for Refugees (UNHCR), the number of refugees reached a 15-year high in 2010, with over half of them being children under 18 in need of education.

Says Jonathan Penson (STPD, Education Section), 'Well-managed teacher migration can contribute both to increased access to education for at-risk children (such as refugees) and the quality of education children receive, even in difficult circumstances. It is critically important to provide frameworks that protect teachers, especially when cross-border migration is involuntary as teachers are then at their most vulnerable. It is also important to acknowledge that, if formally recognised and properly supported, these same teachers can present an important resource for host countries to educate children.'

Women in political leadership: global targets

To change a woman is to change a nation. The Commonwealth is a pacesetter in gender equality work; many of our initiatives would not have been possible without Commonwealth technical and financial assistance. The Commonwealth Plan of Action for Gender Equality 2005–2015 has been a guiding framework for us; we have been promoting it throughout our country and crucially, educating the men.

Kejetue Agatha, Co-ordinator of Human Rights Focus, Cameroon

The under-representation of women in leadership roles and political participation still persists, with particular weakness in the Pacific Island member countries where women represent an average of less than 4 per cent of all elected representatives, and less than 9 per cent in the West Africa region. Some of the barriers to women's political participation are linked to:

* persistent gender stereotypes

* patriarchy

- the lack of enabling political environment, and

- inadequate funding to support female candidates.

Recognising the under-representation of women in leadership positions and decision-making, the Secretariat, in partnership with the Office of the Prime Minister of Trinidad and Tobago, convened the Caribbean Regional Colloquium for Women Leaders as Agents of Change held under the aegis of the Prime Minister of Trinidad and Tobago, Kamla Persad-Bissessar, in Port of Spain from 28 to 30 June 2011, the first to be convened by a prime minister during her term as Commonwealth Chair-in-Office.

Recommendations made by the women leaders were outlined in the Port of Spain Consensus on Transformational Leadership for Gender Equality. Similar regional colloquiums will be convened in Africa, Europe and the Pacific in Ghana and Australia in 2012.

UN General Assembly and Commonwealth Heads of Government Meeting

Increasing women's effective leadership is critical for the achievement of democratic and developmental goals. Of the 20 women world leaders, only four are from Commonwealth countries. Prime Minister Persad-Bissessar called for 'greater efforts to promote women's participation in politics' at a side event to the 66th UN General Assembly (UNGA) Session in New York on 19 September 2011 titled: 'Women's Political Participation: Making Gender Equality in Politics a Reality'. Dignitaries included Commonwealth Secretary-General Kamalesh Sharma, US Secretary of State Hillary Clinton, the Executive Director of UN Women, Michelle Bachelet, and five female presidents and Heads of Government. The side event saw the signing of a Joint Statement on women's political participation, to be negotiated by the UN Security Council. The programme will follow up on the adoption of the resolution at the 67th UN General Assembly in New York in September 2012.

At the 2011 Commonwealth Heads of Government Meeting in Perth, Australia, a woman leader handed over to another woman leader as Chair-in-Office. The Commonwealth theme for 2011, 'Women as Agents of Change', was particularly significant, and a special side event was held in the margins of CHOGM titled 'Women Empowered to Lead' (hosted by the Australian Government), which was well attended by Heads of Government, ministers and senior officials of the Commonwealth Secretariat. Australia plans to champion the call for Commonwealth nations to sign the UNGA Joint Statement prior to its negotiation for possible adoption by the UN Security Council.

Women in business leadership

Gender inequality coupled with trade liberalisation processes can mean that women producers and exporters may struggle to secure the financial and other resources they need to develop their businesses properly and compete on an international scale. The Secretariat, in recognising this problem, continues to make interventions to bring about a change of perceptions, policies and practices, helping to empower each generation to achieve more.

Nine women entrepreneurs from Africa and the Caribbean were selected from over 60 applicants to market their products at

A teacher and her secondary-level pupils, Kenya

Europe's largest buyers fair, the Spring Fair International, 5 to 9 February 2012, in Birmingham, UK, through sponsorship from the Commonwealth Secretariat. The project aims to raise the capacity of businesswomen to access global markets. The women successfully secured orders from some of Europe's largest traders.

Kenyan businesswoman Jennifer Mulli penned an agreement to export crafts from her business 'Katchy Kollections' to the UK and believes she will now be able to double production within two years. 'It was an amazing opportunity for me. I was able to meet people who are interested in working with my company right from the design stage up to production,' she said.

Haitian-born Marie Roberte Laurent, who sells beauty products from the Caribbean island of Grenada, signed a deal to produce a line of chocolate soaps, body lotions and gels for a UK- and Israel-based retailer.

The businesswomen now hope to use the knowledge they gained to help other women entrepreneurs in the Commonwealth break into the global market.

Women leaders in education

On World Teachers' Day (5 October 2011) *Women and the Teaching Profession: Exploring the Feminisation Debate*, a new Commonwealth-UNESCO book, was launched by Dr Sylvia Anie, Director of STPD and Qian Tang, UNESCO's Assistant Director-General for Education in Paris. The book discusses the gender imbalance in the teaching profession and its impact on learning and on women's empowerment.

While most of the research in this area has focused on developed countries, where the majority of teachers have been women for many years, this study explores the teacher feminisation debate in developing countries. The book draws on the experiences of Dominica, Lesotho, Samoa, Sri Lanka and India.

Speaking at the launch, Anie said: 'Research on trends in the teaching profession indicates that women have increased their presence in nearly all levels of teaching, most notably at the primary and university levels.' She explained that despite this increase, many women continue to experience inequity relating to remuneration, career progression and lack of promotion to managerial positions.

'At the other end of the spectrum, it is argued that in some countries, boys have been negatively impacted by an overabundance of female teachers who cannot provide the role models they need.'

Gender, culture and the law

Traditional cultural mindsets of women as 'left-handed, half-a-glass, thinking backwards' form a powerful barrier to women's reclamation of the law for themselves … in fighting laws and fighting for laws, one is, in fact, being called upon to fight minds. Mindsets, customs and the unquestioning acceptance of debilitating traditions can present the biggest barriers to the progress of legal and judicial systems in Africa. Yet, traditional rites and roles can be revisited, reclaimed and harnessed to work in women's favour.

Professor Irene Odotei, Anthropologist, Ghana, at the Commonwealth West Africa Colloquium on Gender, Culture and the Law

Traditional or religious laws and practices – and culture – often have greater significance and value for people in their daily lives than the formal laws of a country. Identity, values and behaviour are formed at household and community level, often being shaped by elders, traditional leaders or religious institutions.

That's why the Commonwealth held five regional meetings on Gender, Culture and the Law, each of them making concrete proposals for law reform and access to justice. The meetings are backed up by work with the legal system, particularly the judiciary, local chiefs, widows' rights campaigners and other interested groups. In Cameroon, the host for West Africa, land ownership and inheritance was discussed at a key dialogue with human rights groups and traditional leaders (both male and female).

The Secretariat is currently engaged in developing a handbook on land rights in four African jurisdictions (Cameroon, Kenya, Nigeria and Sierra Leone) targeting rural women, lay magistrates, traditional authority and advocacy groups. Similarly, a review of land legislation in four Pacific jurisdictions has been commissioned. Judge Florence Awasom (Cameroon) said the Commonwealth handbook on women's land rights would influence and assist traditional rulers in Cameroon: 'Essentially, traditional authority is informed by traditional practices, some of which may be repugnant to women's rights, the very practices we are trying to eradicate. The handbook will go a long way to keep them up to date with women's statutory rights. It will also help educate women about protecting these rights, for example the need to register customary lands.'

> In her 2011 Commonwealth Lecture on 'Women as Agents of Change', Sonia Gandhi pointed out that solidarity is difficult because women's concerns are divided 'by class, by community, by caste, by culture'. But culture and law are not immovable. Indian women's movements have progressed by 'banding together on issues like dowry and violence, household labour, discriminatory customs, property rights and wages. These campaigns resulted in the enactment of radical new laws.'

Artisans market, Nairobi, Kenya (photographer and copyright: Rebecca Nduku / © Commonwealth Secretariat)

E-health

There is no question that the prosperity of a nation is vitally dependent on the health of its citizens. To that end, it is equally important that a country's medical care facilities and equipment are at the highest standard that is reasonably attainable.

Prime Minister Hubert Ingraham of The Bahamas

The Commonwealth Health Ministers Meeting (CHMM) 2008 mandated the Secretariat to provide support to the e-health initiatives of member countries with developing economies to:

• identify regional priorities and challenges

• foster strategic partnerships, and

• reach a consensus on e-health projects in selected countries.

The Secretariat has completed high-level dialogues on e-health for East Africa, South Asia and West Africa. The events brought together senior leaders from ministries for health and ICT, partners from regional organisations including CISCO, Microsoft and the DHI, part of the MDG 8 initiative. The dialogues provided a setting to exchange ideas and information, and enable countries to reassess their e-health opportunities, needs, constraints and their next steps.

The Secretariat has also provided direct support to Kenya, Maldives and Uganda in the development of their e-health policies.

In e-health and m-health strategy, the Secretariat has given training support to Botswana, Lesotho, Malawi, Mozambique, Namibia, Swaziland and Zambia. The workshop provided technical assistance in the drafting and completion of e-health policies and strategies, as well as identifying issues and challenges critical to moving the process forward. A publication, *Developing an E-Health Strategy: A Commonwealth Workbook of Mythologies, Content and Models*, is available and has been circulated among member countries.

The case of The Bahamas

When it comes to infrastructure, not all parts of The Bahamas are equal, and nowhere is this more striking than in the health sector. There are 29 inhabited islands scattered between some 700 isles and 2,500 cays that stretch across nearly 260,000 square kilometres of ocean bed. The demands of each populated area stretch government resources to the maximum, particularly on those remote settlements, far removed from the seats of power in Nassau, the capital, situated on New Providence island.

But when it comes to medical technology, The Bahamas goes the extra mile. The government is aggressively promoting a public-private partnership to connect the archipelago with a 'health bridge'. In January 2011, it launched a virtual skin clinic in Abaco, a chain of islands 170 kilometres north-east of Nassau. A

dermatologist stationed on New Providence runs a surgery in Abaco using advanced digital communication technology – video-conferencing for patient consultations backed up by high-quality digital photographs or video taken by nursing assistants in the remote clinic. He sees his local patients from 9 am to mid-day, and those in Abaco from 2 pm onwards.

In the first month of the programme the clinic treated 42 patients who would have otherwise have had to incur significant costs to travel to Nassau for treatment. Of that cohort, three patients needed further testing in the capital, and one patient tested positive for cancer. The government is almost ready to roll out the programme in Andros and Long Island, two other major population centres. Additionally, plans are already in place to replicate the skin clinic model with paediatric clinics.

'We have X-ray facilities in many of the Family Islands that have been there in excess of eight years, sometimes up to ten years, and they have never been used. They are still in the box. That is because the X-rays we purchased were using analogue technology, and they required a technician and radiologist. We are converting those analogue machines to digital, so you only need a technician on the island,' said Hubert Minnis, Minister of Health.

There will never be a sufficient number of dermatologists, radiologists, paediatricians or other medical specialists to staff each and every island of The Bahamas. The scale of the archipelago is simply too vast. The public health system is, however, sufficiently

Eleuthra, The Bahamas (© Edward Yelland)

staffed to support a structure that requires technician-level workers in outlying clinics with radiologists stationed in the main hospitals. The use of telemedicine is, therefore, an important strategy for providing quality healthcare for all Bahamians and visitors across the islands.

From an article by Noelle Nicolls in Global *Magazine (Third Quarter 2011)*

Maternal and child health

Millennium Development Goals 4 and 5 remain top agendas … a lot remains to be done towards reducing maternal and child mortality rates in East, Central and Southern Africa. A scaling up of the training of midwifery tutors to enable expectant mothers to give birth safely will add fresh impetus towards the achievement of these goals.

Kenya Vice-President Kalonzo Musyoka

The Commonwealth Secretariat is committed to high-level advocacy in pursuit of MDGs 4 and 5, led by Secretary-General Kamalesh Sharma – who was involved in drafting the goals ahead of the UN Millennium Summit. The Commonwealth is currently assisting Kenya, Lesotho, Malawi, Mauritius, Seychelles, Swaziland, Tanzania, Uganda and Zambia, to build capacity of midwives in order to address maternal mortality.

In December 2011 a forum on the issue was convened in partnership with the East, Central and Southern Africa Health Community (ECSA-HC). It brought together midwifery lecturers and policy-makers from ten countries. At the meeting the Vice-President of Kenya noted that women in Sub-Saharan Africa faced a 1 in 300 risk of death during childbirth, while in developed nations it stood at 1 in 4,300. 'This number in regard to our region is unacceptable and reason enough for urgent intervention.' ECSA-HC has been a Secretariat partner since 1974 and has played a pioneering role in raising standards.

According to the World Health Organization, in 2010 two-thirds of all maternal deaths occurred in 13 countries, seven of which are Commonwealth members: Bangladesh, India, Kenya, Nigeria, Pakistan, Tanzania and Uganda. Member countries are striving to improve women's health but are faced by competing priorities, low budgets and the migration of skilled health workers. Grenada is among the three countries with the lowest maternal mortality ratio in the world, followed by Japan and Mauritius. There are zero deaths per 100,000 live births in the country. To achieve these levels of success, midwives need to be trained beyond nursing skills to include record-keeping, communication skills, monitoring and evaluation systems, and networking.

Gender and child rights interact

Health at birth and in early childhood is strongly linked to women's economic empowerment. Renée Giovarelli, Executive Director of the Landesa Center for Women's Land Rights, says this is a useful lesson in tackling India's malnutrition crisis. 'A study in Nepal found that children are less likely to be underweight if their mothers own land. Another, in Nicaragua and Honduras, presented at the World Bank, found that families spend more on food when the woman of the house owns land. And a study in Ghana found that families allocate a larger proportion of their

household budget to food when the woman owns a larger share of the household's farmland. Across India, national and some state governments are recognising this and are working to put a powerful asset – land – into the hands of women' (*The Guardian*, January 2012).

Preparing young women and men for social transformation

Commonwealth countries represent great diversity and thus offer exciting opportunities for increased knowledge-sharing. A quality education should aim to change the way we think, behave, look at the world, interact with nature, and address key societal and environmental problems such as climate change and poverty reduction.

Qian Tang, Assistant Director-General for Education, UNESCO

Experience has shown that most conflicts since the late 20th century, and especially in the Commonwealth, are not *between* states but *within* them. They can stem from divisions that are political, ethnic, linguistic and cultural, religious or economic. According to Professor Amartya Sen, Chair of the 2007 Commonwealth Commission on Respect and Understanding, violence is not only – perhaps not even primarily – a military challenge: 'It is fostered in our divisive world through capturing people's minds and loyalties, and through exploiting the allegiance of those who are wholly or partly persuaded.' It follows that peace-building is in part an exercise in coping with far-reaching social change, and that some interventions must themselves be transformative in nature.

The 2007 *Civil Paths to Peace* report gave education a central role in promoting a 'respect and understanding' agenda and responding to these challenges. *Citizenship Education in Commonwealth Countries* assesses the role that education – and citizenship education in particular – can play in developing respect and understanding. Citizenship education aims to develop learners' capacities to participate in the political sphere, and to understand and defend their own rights and the rights of others.

The importance of opening alternative pathways to achievement and employment for youth is increasingly being recognised. The Commonwealth Secretariat is undertaking research into technical and vocational education and training. This will draw attention to recent innovations, policy gaps and emerging international initiatives. The review will result in member countries recognising the importance of technical skills and how vocational education is a necessary part of the education structure in today's global economy. It will support the development of policies, programmes and good practices that will result in member countries' increased capacity to deliver relevant and effective alternative pathways for young people.

In post-conflict situations, former combatants largely consist of young people in their prime. As a workforce, they can contribute enormously to reconstruction challenges. As society and institutions are rebuilt, there are valuable opportunities to re-examine gender inequalities – which tend to reach an extreme during conflict, and may be some of the underlying causes. Emerging from situations of armed conflict, women may seek full citizenship, social justice and empowerment based on respect for their human dignity and human rights.

Sex workers receiving HIV information and protection

HIV/AIDS and education

The goals of EFA (Education for All) cannot be achieved where there is a high prevalence of debilitating illness and related stigma and discrimination. In highly affected countries, the HIV epidemic is eroding the capacity of the education sector, causing shortages of teachers and education staff, increasing the vulnerability of children and learners, and adding new difficulties for planning. Over the past decades, much has been learned about HIV and AIDS, about the drivers of the epidemic, about the role and importance of education, and about the actions that need to be taken by the education sector.

There is ample evidence that education in itself – even in the absence of HIV-specific interventions – offers an important measure of protection against HIV, simply because good quality education can provide a safe and protective environment. Education also creates a circle of support within the community, which can have a sustained impact on reducing vulnerability and behaviours that cause, increase or perpetuate risk. The Global Campaign for Education (GCE) has estimated that universal primary education (UPE) would prevent 700,000 new HIV infections each year (GCE, 2004). The ability of girls and young women to protect themselves from HIV is frequently compromised by a combination of biological factors, lack of access to HIV information, services and commodities, and disempowering, often exploitative, social, cultural and economic conditions. Education offers important protection from HIV infection to girls and young women by building young women's self-esteem and capacity to act on HIV-prevention messages, improving their economic prospects, influencing the power balance in relationships, and affecting their social and sexual networks.

Well-planned and implemented life skills or sex and HIV education interventions, even when provided for only short periods, have been found to: increase knowledge; develop skills (such as self-efficacy to refuse sex and obtain male and female condoms) and positive attitudes required to change risk behaviours (such as values about sex and pressuring someone to have sex); and reduce sexual risk behaviours among the sexually active. HIV and AIDS education can reduce the risk of HIV by delaying the age of the first sexual encounter, increasing male and female condom use, reducing the number of sexual partners among the already sexually active, promoting the early treatment of sexually transmitted infections (STIs), facilitating access to confidential and voluntary counselling and testing (VCT), and reducing other behaviours that increase risk, such as drug use and particularly injecting drugs.

A review of HIV and AIDS interventions in schools in Africa has confirmed the potential of education to bring about an improvement in attitudes towards people living with HIV. The review found attitudinal changes in all programmes where they were measured, with school children showing greater acceptance of people living with HIV or AIDS regardless of the programme form, duration, content or target population.

Source: UNESCO Section of Education and HIV and AIDS, adapted from Commonwealth Education Partnerships 2011–2012

Health education in the community: radio and mobiles for interactive learning

The same rationale that underpins the arguments for open and distance learning (ODL) – that the appropriate use of educational technology allows for greater scale and quality of learning while keeping provision costs low – also applies to learning in non-formal and development contexts. Learning needs about health issues, such as maternal and child health, HIV/AIDS and non-communicable illnesses like diabetes and hypertension, are big and growing bigger all the time. These needs are particularly acute in remote and resource-poor areas, and among women. ODL models help us to rethink processes – not only can they change how education is delivered but also how it is designed, ideally facilitating a greater focus on learning and the learner.

The Commonwealth of Learning (COL) has been working to develop a collaborative and participatory model of community ODL that uses a blended approach, combining low-cost broadcast media with face-to-face networking at district level. Working with national and regional partners, community learning programmes have been developed in Belize and Jamaica; Cameroon, Kenya, Malawi, South Africa and Tanzania; Bangladesh; and Papua New Guinea and Solomon Islands.

At the community or district level, it is rare that any one group will have the knowledge, skills or resources to realise quality health- or development-oriented educational programming on their own. Collaborative approaches that bring groups together into win-win partnerships, however challenging, are a proven strategy. A participatory approach to educational programming starts with decision-making by the target community about the priority subjects for learning programmes and continues through the design, implementation and evaluation. In contrast to a one-way transfer of expert messages to ignorant learners, a participatory approach demands an open-ended process in which dialogue between and among citizens and learners, and experts and authorities, informs both the form and content of the programming.

Community learning programmes about health issues like HIV/AIDS and maternal health place a high priority on educational content that reflects lived experience of the issues at hand and reinforces key

Community radio for women's health (© Commonwealth of Learning)

learning messages through real stories. The involvement of experts is also critical – both for accuracy of information and for the credibility of the programmes overall; however, expert information alone is not enough. Ideally, programming should integrate both expert information and lived experiences that illustrate the benefits and consequences of particular practices and behaviours.

Although conventional mass media, particularly radio, remain the most accessible learning technologies on offer in many developing areas of the Commonwealth, mobile telephony has great promise. Mobile phones can make important contributions to each of the three key pillars of ODL –learning materials, learner support and logistics. Radio is a one-way technology: you cannot know who is actually listening, how listeners are using the programme or whether or not they are learning anything at all. There is no feedback, no interaction. Broadcasting is also a 'push' technology: listeners have to tune in at a certain time to hear it. Mobiles additionally face limitations as a learning technology: they remain costly to use, and they are generally conducive only to individual use and for accessing content in very small bits and pieces. And yet, together, mobile phones and media are proving to be a winning combination.

Adapted from Ian Pringle (Commonwealth of Learning) in Commonwealth Education Partnerships 2011–2012.

Social transformation and language policy: the case of Rwanda

The Government of Rwanda places a high premium on the development of human capital with the necessary knowledge and skills as a vehicle for socio-economic development. Within this context, Rwanda follows a trilingual education policy so as to have regional and international advantages associated with trade, foreign relations, employment and education, and in line with the constitution which stipulates that Kinyarwanda, French and English are official languages.

Rwanda Teacher Service Commission

With Rwanda's membership of the East African Community (EAC) and accession to the Commonwealth, and having developed new international partnerships, the use of English has become more prominent and the need for literacy in English greater. Additionally, the Rwandan Government has made science, technology and ICT priority areas in education, and views English as the gateway to the global knowledge economy. The sector-wide shift to English-medium education is thus a bold and ambitious plan to help meet goals in education curricula with other EAC member states and promoting science, technology and ICT in education so as to further stimulate economic development and support poverty reduction. It also affords access to a wide range of competitively priced teaching and learning materials in English.

The Rwanda English in Action Programme

As the main planned intervention to facilitate the transition to English medium in basic education, the Rwanda English in Action Programme (REAP) sets out to address the English language learning needs of more than 50,000 school teachers. Given the high costs of providing residential training to such large numbers, MINEDUC's (Rwanda's Ministry of Education's) preferred option is a sector-based approach to training, supported by self-directed study and school-based mentoring. A standardised English language assessment tool for measuring teacher proficiency at various levels makes up the final element of REAP and helps ensure all teachers can perform in English to the level required.

Seven pillars of REAP

The activities of REAP will centre on the following seven pillars of Language in Education (LED) development.

- Development of reading and writing skills in Kinyarwanda.

- Promotion of academic literacy skills in English.

- Teaching language for use/communication (vs. teaching about the language).

- Language-supportive subject teaching.

- School-based mentoring of less experienced teachers.

- Teacher Resource Centres in Teacher Training Colleges.

- Enriched language and literacy resources in schools and classrooms.

Empowering young people:

the Youth Affairs Division; Commonwealth Youth Programme (CYP)

'They are tomorrow's leaders, parents, professionals and workers and today's assets. Properly supported and given the right opportunities, girls and boys, young women and young men can play a significant part in lifting themselves, their families and communities out of poverty. Too often, however, youth are considered only or mainly as a problem to be contained; a threat to peace and security.'

– Sarah Maguire (Consultant, UK Department for International Development)

The Commonwealth defines 'youth' as persons of 15-29 years. This is helpful in capturing many of those who have finished schooling, are sexually active or facing livelihood transitions. Many Commonwealth cultures construct 'youth' as something that lasts well into one's 20s – particularly if economic realities exclude young

adults from work, home ownership or marriage. At the same time, 'adult' care/working responsibilities often begin well before the age of 15. Identifying youth is not about artificial and potentially divisive classification of different age cohorts. On the contrary, it is part of making sure that none of the population, young or old, is excluded from development and nation-building.

The high and peaking proportion of 15–24 year olds in many Commonwealth populations is referred to as the 'youth bulge'. For example, in Uganda the median age is 15 and roughly half of 15–24 year-old women have given birth at least once. The duration of the youth bulge is a limited window in which to develop a larger and younger workforce who can drive economic development and play a significant role in the social development of their communities and society.[1]

For the Commonwealth Secretariat's Youth Affairs Division and Commonwealth Youth Programme (CYP) Regional Centres, the framework for seizing this opportunity is the Commonwealth Plan of Action for Youth Empowerment (PAYE). In its current phase (2007 to 2015), the PAYE articulates the role of youth development within broader Millennium Development Goals (MDGs), as outlined over.

Commonwealth Youth Forum: emerging leaders (photographer and copyright: Della Batchelor / © Commonwealth Secretariat)

- Today's livelihoods programmes must take account of adolescent-headed households, out-of-school youth. Youth work expertise is needed to help resolve resource conflict issues, build consensus between the generations and promote skills transfer (Poverty Eradication). The MDG of 'Developing a global partnership for development' sets out a number of macro objectives that would improve young people's access to sustainable livelihoods. It also makes specific reference to young people: 'In co-operation with the developing countries, develop decent and productive work for youth.'

- Although youth workers usually educate in the non-formal setting, they play a role in encouraging out-of-school youth to go back to education, and also in making sure the parent community understands the value of education (Access to Education).

- A 'youth-worked' community is one in which young women have a voice. Raising young women's expectations and building their self-esteem is at the heart of informal education (Gender Equality). 'Youth-worked' health services are ones that are approachable and non-judgemental towards young mothers, with information campaigns that connect with youth cultures (Maternal and Child Health).

- As agencies look to peer-education as part of combating HIV/AIDS and encouraging healthy lifestyles, the ability to communicate with young people becomes a life-saving issue. Self-esteem issues are central to young people's negotiating and sustaining behaviour change (Combating HIV and AIDS, Malaria and other diseases).

- Youth workers have a role to play in mitigating unsustainable urbanisation: by helping young people towards a more realistic understanding of life in today's cities, and by building recreation and livelihoods in rural areas. Youth workers are also vital to conservation and public health efforts (Ensuring Environmental Sustainability).

Consultation: the life-blood of the Commonwealth

The touchstone of the Plan of Action, and of professional youth work in the Commonwealth, is participation of young people in the decisions that affect their lives. The participation rights of 15–18 year-olds, in accordance with age and maturity, are set out in the Convention on the Rights of the Child (1989). The participation rights of 18–29 year-olds are shared with all adults, although youth structures also make the case for specific needs and challenges faced by this age group.

Realising these rights is a challenge. One cannot simply start with the development language of 'participation' and look for equivalents in other languages. Instead we should look at actual practices by and with young people, and try to understand them in their social and cultural settings. For some young people, participation may open up opportunities and choices. For others it is about survival. While paternalism and authoritarianism can be a barrier to participation, deference to adults and responsibilities to community can also be interpreted as expressions of solidarity and interdependence between generations.[2]

The eighth Commonwealth Youth Ministers Meeting (November 2012, Papua New Guinea) will see the first sitting of a reformulated Commonwealth Youth Council (CYC) and ratify its draft constitution. For some years, selected young leaders have had a place at the table with Commonwealth youth ministers.

Like all social dialogue, youth participation is not a panacea and cannot be approached as a substitute for justice. It needs to be *part* of strategies for social integration which put the creation of employment, the reduction of unemployment and the promotion of appropriately and adequately remunerated employment at the centre of strategies and policies.[3] National youth development is often the sole responsibility of the government ministry or department where the youth portfolio lies, whereas youth issues should be mainstreamed across various sectors and line ministries.

A Commonwealth of the (young) people

Each generation of youth faces different challenges, and so when working with, and planning for youth, it is important to ask – which? However, there are some generalisations we can make.

- Young people share some characteristics with both children and adults. As with all age groups they require assiduous recognition and provision of their rights. They *may* require care and protection; they always need 'support, autonomy, the provision of opportunities, responsibilities, training in marketable skills and empowerment as they emerge to become fully fledged adults in society' (Peace Child International).

- Segregation, silencing and (gendered) disadvantage of young people have been features of most societies, traditional and modern.

- In their life history, young people go through multiple transitions – physical, emotional, cognitive and social. Without appropriate investment in young people, these transitions carry risks.[4]

In poorer communities, youth often operate at the margins of society, excluded from the mainstream aspects of life – that is, 'youth' itself is a marginalised category. Exclusion is a process whereby individuals (or groups) are 'systematically disadvantaged because they are discriminated against on the basis of their ethnicity, race, religion, sexual orientation, caste, descent, gender, disability, HIV status, immigrant status or where they live' (DFID, 2005).

Exclusion has multiple dimensions.

- **Economic exclusion:** unemployment, underemployment, lack of livelihood, ownership of assets.

- **Political exclusion:** lack of political participation, voice and decision-making power.

- **Social exclusion:** access to services (education, health, water, sanitation and housing).

- **Cultural status:** lack of recognition of group's cultural practices, discrimination, loss of status/respect, humiliation/honour, lack of identity.[5]

Varieties of exclusion overlap and interact. It is not enough just to look at one possible category of exclusion in isolation. However, gender is a major factor. Today, 75 million girls are denied the opportunity to go to school. As Staunton and Goulds (2011) have said, that's not right – it's against the gender, equality and human rights principles of the Commonwealth (see text titled 'Growing up in the Commonwealth'). It's also not smart – if our fragile global economy is to fully recover, it needs girls to make their economic contribution. However, the fact that time is spent in the classroom does not guarantee that young people progress educationally or socially. Conflict, family breakdown, domestic violence, crime and anti-social behaviour are all highly gendered phenomena having an impact. Confronting them requires close attention to the resources and role models available to young women and men.

Enterprise and employment

Knowing the costs of inaction, many governments around the world do prioritise the issue of youth employment and attempt to develop reactive policies and programmes. But are such stopgap policies and their levels of implementation effective? There is no change in the 28 per cent share of young people who do work but remain trapped earning US$1.25 a day … Dealing with trade, debt and other macro policy areas can ensure sustainable economic development that young people can drive and benefit from. Growth alone is not enough. Self-employment through isolated enterprise programmes is not enough.

Sara Elder (International Labour Organization), speaker at the Commonwealth Secretariat's 'Investing in Youth' conference, 2011

Work is central to young adults' well-being. As well as providing income, work can lead to broader social and economic advancement, strengthening individuals, their families and communities. Such progress, however, assumes that work is decent. The economic crisis is reflected in the largest ever cohort of unemployed young people. Between 2007 and 2008, it increased twice as fast as non-youth unemployment and 20 times the average over the previous decade.

In Zambia, the International Labour Organization (ILO) country office is a training partner for the Commonwealth. Workshops are targeted at development practitioners, enterprise mentors and trainers who are engaged in youth work. The Zambia regional office of the Commonwealth Youth Programme has also provided a technical adviser to the Youth Enterprise Fund in Swaziland. Consultations on youth employment have been held in Africa, Asia, the Caribbean and the Pacific.

The year 2011 also saw the launch of new Commonwealth support for budding small and medium enterprises (SMEs) in India. A collaboration with non-governmental organisations, the Central Bank of India, Corporation Bank and the Export-Import (Exim) Bank, the training programme began in Punjab. It is being extended to Uttar Pradesh, Himachal Pradesh, Kerala, Karnataka, Rajasthan and West Bengal. These projects draw on previous experience with the Commonwealth Youth Credit Initiative, which has proven self-sustaining in India. Namibia recently adopted the model, which combines micro-credit with training and coaching.

Reform and renewal

The CYP, which is 40 years old next year (2013), is supported by a dedicated Commonwealth fund (UK£3 million per annum), administered by the Youth Affairs Division. The division completed a nine-month internal review in 2009, and found a number of gains directly attributable to the work of the Secretariat in areas including the following.

- National Youth Councils (establishment, training and access to policy forums).

- Professionalisation of Youth Work, including through the Commonwealth Diploma in Youth Development Work – a strong network of 27 partner universities in 46 countries.

- Participation of youth leaders in election observation.

- Progressively mainstreaming human rights into programme work; implementing programme work based on the Report of the Commonwealth Commission on Respect and Understanding (*Civil Paths to Peace*).

The review involved CYP staff from Africa, Asia, the Caribbean and the Pacific; Secretariat divisions and units (Human Rights Unit, Political Affairs Division and others); and external partners including UNAIDS, UNICEF, UNDESA, and the United Nations Alliance of Civilizations (UNAOC). It continued with an independent review of the Commonwealth Youth Credit Initiative commissioned by the Governance and Institutional Development Division (GIDD), and in 2011 discussions with a civil society reference group.

In 2011–2012 the Commonwealth Secretariat reviewed youth structures to see how they can be made more representative – including those which are given a Commonwealth platform, or are long-term partners in programme work, such as national youth councils. As with other 'mainstreaming' fields, the purpose of assessing the implications for youth (of legislation, policies or programmes) is to ensure that inequality is not perpetuated (ECOSOC Agreed Conclusions 1997/2).

Following the 2011 CHOGM and Eminent Persons Group (EPG) review (which featured strongly in the Perth Commonwealth Youth Forum), the Youth Affairs Division's programme direction includes the following.

- Improved communications[6] and research capacity, and more opportunities for young people (both elected and unaffiliated) to contribute to policy debates online.[7] More consistent marketing and messaging, to better distinguish specific sub-groups (still within the 15–29 age range).

- A widening of focus from youth enterprise to youth employment, and from micro-credit to inclusive finance (including youth financial literacy).

- Greater collaboration with other Sport for Development and Peace (SDP) networks and culture-based interventions. Greater attention to non-communicable diseases.

- Updating of HIV and AIDS work from de-stigmatisation projects, planned in full partnership with people living with HIV and AIDS and their advocacy organisations.

- Renewed focus on partnerships for regional and national capacity, rather than small-scale pilot projects (see the 'Policy Issues' table). Workable monitoring and evaluation of youth interventions is a priority.

- Greater collaboration with formal education structures, including higher education. In many Commonwealth countries, student unions provide positive examples of independent, self-organised and democratic youth bodies. It has been proposed (2011) to link them together through a Commonwealth Student Association.

Notes

[1] UNFPA 2005, NORAD 2005, DANIDA 2007, DFID 2007, World Bank 2007, UN 2007 and Africa Commission 2009.

[2] Manfred Liebel and Iven Saadi in Barry Percy-Smith and Nigel Thomas (2010), *A Handbook of Children and Young People's Participation*.

[3] World Summit for Social Development, Copenhagen, 1995. Quoted at Commonwealth Youth Ministers Meeting 2008 in Colombo, Sri Lanka.

[4] Sarah Huxley et al (2010), *Youth Participation in Development*. Published by DFID/CSO Youth Working Group (members include Commonwealth Youth Exchange Council and Restless Development).

[5] Stewart (2008), Kabeer (2006), McLean and Fraser (2009), quoted in Huxley et al (2010) *Youth Participation in Development*.

[6] A Change Communications plan and re-brand will be complete by December 2012.

[7] The Your Commonwealth website went live in January 2011.

From the eighth Commonwealth Youth Forum Communiqué (Perth, Australia, 2011)

The Commonwealth and its member states are expected to promote peace. Youth believe that the Commonwealth has the responsibility to act quickly and appropriately in the best interests of its citizens. This should be in accordance with the Commonwealth's guiding principles that relate to democracy, development, diversity, peace and human rights.

Health is a fundamental right, imperative in accessing other human rights, and achieving economic development. Youth are concerned about the lack of progress in addressing health inequities, and believe that outcomes for vulnerable groups must be prioritised in a culturally appropriate manner. We call on the Commonwealth to increase investment in health, including health systems strengthening and addressing the social determinants of health.

Commonwealth member states should strengthen their commitment to investing in youth through a transparent mechanism, ensuring

Table 1	Multilateral donor recommendations on youth affairs	
Policy issue	Recommendations	Agency
Governance, voice and accountability	Political will and capacity at national level is critical. Youth ministries in many Commonwealth countries have engaged peak youth organisations in formulating National Youth Policies; in order to effect change and achieve accountability to young people, these policies need to be multi-sectoral and use a mainstreaming approach to engage the main actors (Heads of State, large ministries such as Finance, Planning, etc.)	CYP, World Bank
	Intensive advocacy by young people and youth practitioners is required in order to change perceptions and win commitment to the idea of young people as assets to national development.	CYP
	Build intergenerational partnerships (both within organisations and at community level) to improve receptiveness to youth voices.	UNFPA, UNICEF
Post-conflict transitions and livelihoods	Emphasise continuing education beyond primary level, vocational skills and enterprise education for decent work.	Africa Commission, UN, YEN
	Engage young people in social dialogue and rights education for long-term conflict prevention (Commonwealth 'Respect and Understanding' agenda).	CYP, UNAOC, UNICEF, UNDESA
Sexual reproductive health and rights	Engage young PLWHA (people living with HIV/AIDS) in decision-making throughout project cycles.	IPPF, UNAIDS, UNFPA
	Acknowledge the bigger social picture including intergenerational factors of HIV transmission (transactional sex with older adults, etc.)	UNAIDS
Social exclusion	Address gender within any youth strategy – assessing issues where different genders are excluded and the need to adjust programmes to address this.	NORAD, UNFPA, UN
	Invest in 'protective factors' throughout adolescence. Use a research-based approach to goal-setting, monitoring and evaluation in youth programming.	UNICEF, CYP, UN
	Explain young people's position as both inheritors and drivers of cultural and economic change; multiple identities; globalisation.	UN, UNDP, UNAOC
	Engage young people in poverty assessments and poverty strategy consultations; integrate with youth policy and macroeconomic policy.	UNFPA, World Bank, CYP

access to information and communication technology, education and funding for skills and enterprise development.

Youth call on the Commonwealth member states to urgently prioritise environmental challenges, including climate change, and work together to evaluate, establish and implement policy frameworks and improve budgetary allocations to address these challenges.

We request that within one year of the culmination of each Commonwealth Youth Forum a right of reply regarding the progress and input on each recommendation is provided by Commonwealth Heads of Government to the Commonwealth community. We will take responsibility for ensuring that recommendations from the Commonwealth Youth Forum are followed up by the Commonwealth and member states and inform peers of progress made in regard to the recommendations emanating from the Commonwealth Youth Forum.

Core recommendation

That the Commonwealth Heads of Government support the establishment of an independent youth-led governing body to oversee the administration of a youth development fund.

In addition to our above core recommendation, the supporting recommendations should be pursued in a formal partnership between the Commonwealth Heads of Government and the youth of the Commonwealth with the intent of driving progress and building momentum. Our core recommendation initiative reflects a desire for young people to be active participants in the call to action, which can be achieved through initiating the above-mentioned governing body, as well as addressing and implementing the supporting recommendations. This partnership is an acknowledgment of the shared responsibility between the Commonwealth Heads of Government, its member states and the Commonwealth youth.

Commonwealth Youth Forum 2011, Perth, Australia:

a participant's view by John Loughton, Chair, Commonwealth Youth Exchange Council (CYEC) Youth Action Group and former Chair, Scottish Youth Parliament

'In October last year I touched down in Perth, Western Australia, as the UK Planning Group member for the Commonwealth Youth Forum. It was the eighth summit of its kind, and is a formally recognised parallel event to CHOGM. The forum exists to act as the flagship Commonwealth platform to give young leaders and campaigners from all member countries an opportunity to debate issues important to youth and form radical solutions to many of the world's most pressing problems. It is also an opportunity to have a direct dialogue with Heads of State.

'As our societies grow younger and youth make up 60 per cent of the Commonwealth, countries must do more to promote the values of the Commonwealth and highlight how young people can be drivers for progressive change. That's exactly what I wanted to do. I am not a blind romantic to the Commonwealth, nor was I blinded by the pageantry and importance of CHOGM for the sake of it, rather I see the Commonwealth and CHOGM as a practical vehicle for progressive change – where we can place emphasis on political equality, voluntary association and the common thread being that of values, not only military or financial interests.

'Commonwealth Youth Forum is a powerful and unique platform because it is run by young people, for young people. We had effective plans for progress and were able to engage politicians at the highest rank. It is so important this continues and young people are seen as part of the solution, not part of the problem. CYF8 was also an amazing opportunity to share our vibrant cultures with one another. From me donning my tartan kilt to the Pacific Islanders showing us the Haka, it was clear that we are all proud of our local heritage, as well as our Commonwealth identity. We were very much all different, all equal.

'At our opening ceremony, we were joined by Australian Prime Minister Julia Gillard, the Commonwealth Secretary-General, and a whole host of ministers, diplomats and media from across the globe. I was particularly touched when during Prime Minister Gillard's speech she chose to single out my story as an example of excellence and overcoming adversity to fight for a better and fairer society. This generated a lot of press interest, and I found myself being interviewed by local and international media. I was keen to highlight and demand action on human rights, gender equality, gay rights and Commonwealth reform.

'The core recommendation from CYF8 was the establishment of an independent youth led governing body to oversee the administration of a youth development fund. This was seen as youth's opportunity to work in *partnership* with Governments to act together to address the needs of all the Commonwealth people. There was also light shone on the devastating impact that the economy is having on young people, with a real demand for more to be done to generate jobs and opportunities. It is fundamental to stimulate economic activity among our young people now if we are to have a sustainable global economy.

'It also became clear to me, however, that the Commonwealth has to quickly change course. The Commonwealth has reached a point in its history where it must ask itself the big questions. What is it for? Who does it service? Where is it relevant? What difference can it make? And how effectively is it upholding its own values day to day? The way the Commonwealth itself sought to answer these questions was through the EPG. Made up of a host of accomplished, powerful and wise individuals, the package of EPG recommendations published in 2011 was a radical roadmap to get the Commonwealth on course for the future. It called for a charter of values, a Commissioner on Human Rights and a host of progressive new ideas that would throw open the doors of the Commonwealth and give it real political teeth. Young people were disappointed that the publication of this report had been delayed and very concerned that many of its recommendations might be blocked or kicked into the long grass. However, it was finally published and some of the ideas were approved. I can't help feel however that the people of the Commonwealth roared and the governments whimpered.

'I got to air my views when I was elected to attend the formal CHOGM Youth Dialogue breakfast with 15 Heads of State. I said at the meeting, we must give voice to the voiceless and engage the disengaged. This is our duty whether we are youth leaders or political Heads of State.'

Source: With thanks to CYEC and the Royal Over-Seas League

The impact of armed conflict on young people

It is time ... to engage more actively on human rights advocacy aimed at ending what the UN Secretary-General has described as 'our collective failure' to protect those lives destroyed by sexual violence. We already have the roadmap to guide our actions. Security Council Resolution 1820 was a historic response to the heinous reality of sexual violence. The challenge is to turn that resolution into practical action – to close the gap between words and action. That challenge starts at the national level [and] support for the development of justice systems that are based on the rule of law, and are accessible to women.

Mary Robinson, UN High Commissioner for Human Rights (1997–2002) and Co-Chair of the Civil Society Advisory Group to the UN on Women, Peace and Security

Over the decade to 2008, 35 countries experienced armed conflict, of which 30 were low-income and lower middle-income countries. The average duration of violent conflict episodes in low-income countries was 12 years. Only 79 per cent of young people are literate in conflict-affected poor countries, compared with 93 per cent in other poor countries. State and non-state parties involved in armed conflicts are increasingly targeting civilians and civilian infrastructure. Schools and school children are widely viewed by combatants as legitimate targets, in clear violation of international law. Over 43 million people are reported to have been displaced mostly by armed conflict, though the actual number is probably far higher. Refugees and internally displaced people face major barriers to education.

Armed conflict is diverting public funds from education into military spending. Military spending is also diverting aid resources. It would take just six days of military spending by rich countries to close the US$16 billion Education for All external financing gap. Education accounts for just 2 per cent of humanitarian aid. And no sector has a smaller share of humanitarian appeals funded: just 38 per cent of aid requests for education are met, which is around half the average for all sectors.

Source: UNESCO's Education for All *2011 Report*

Mary Robinson, Co-Chair of the Civil Society Advisory Group to the UN on Women, Peace and Security

What is 'meaningful' participation?: findings of the London Symposium (May 2011)

- It mobilises other young people.
- It focuses on the quality of youth input.
- Processes are transparent.
- It is fully inclusive and accessible to all.
- It includes spaces for youth to lead processes.
- It is visible and recognised by other stakeholders.
- It is carried out with young people who have legitimacy.
- The roles of young people involved are clearly defined.
- It builds the capacity of young people to participate.
- Social responsibility: implementation and monitoring of actions is included.
- It is not just young people going to forums but leaders going to youth spaces.
- National contexts are taken into account, as is local implementation of international decisions.
- Learning and good practice is disseminated.
- It is connected to policy and to everyday realities that have an impact.
- It needs others to let go of some power. It changes power dynamics in the long term.

The London Symposium on Meaningful Participation by Young People in International Decision-making (May 2011) was organised by the CYEC and funded by the British Council and Open Society Foundations. Participating organisations included the Commonwealth Secretariat, Commonwealth Youth Caucus, Council of Europe, World Association of Girl Guides and Girl Scouts, British Youth Council, UN Youth, Peace Child International, Young Feminist Fund, UN-HABITAT, Taking IT Global, DFID-CSO Youth Working Group and IPPF. The meeting had a youth steering group including Chad Blackman (a former Commonwealth Caribbean representative, also involved with the Secretariat's Investing In Youth initiative). The meeting also heard from Devon Rachae, former senator of Grenada and CARICOM Youth Ambassador.

Nominations for the 2012 Commonwealth Youth Awards (for excellence in development work) are open until 31 July.

Kamalesh Sharma, Commonwealth Secretary-General (photographer and copyright: Joseph Jones / © Commonwealth Secretariat)

Youth Employment: the condition and position

The first ever Commonwealth Conference on Investing in Youth Employment was a milestone in our commitment to unleash the full potential of the Commonwealth's young people. It brought together more than 100 global experts and practitioners in the field of youth enterprise from 65 countries. Together we were able to review current trends and developing practice around the world. Specific commitments were made on new programmes to promote youth employment and enterprise. These will open up opportunities for young people to take a pivotal role as nation-builders and agents of economic growth. There is also a significant social dividend in terms of community cohesion, inclusion and resilience.

The Commonwealth Secretariat is committed to building strategic partnerships for youth empowerment with the World Bank, International Labour Organization, civil society organisations and others to improve economic opportunities for young people. As well as through direct access to policy-makers and governments in 54 countries, the Commonwealth has a growing part to play in developing partnerships with the private sector, particularly the banks and other institutions that can provide start-up loans and investment capital. The financial services sector also has an important role in providing mentoring to help young people in making them more employable and successful as entrepreneurs and professionals.

Kamalesh Sharma, Commonwealth Secretary-General, 2011

Support for youth entrepreneurship not only helps bring opportunities for self-employment, it helps create other new jobs

and assets for the society at large. The launch in 2010 of the Youth Enterprise Financing Programme in India, a joint programme of the Central Bank of India and the Commonwealth Secretariat, is an example of such collaboration.

Says Dr Cyrus Rustomjee, Director of the Economic Affairs Division, 'Active labour market interventions like this are necessary – especially in the aftermath of the global economic recession. In addition, changes need to be made to a whole package of macro policies including international trade, increasing debt challenges of small and vulnerable economies, climate change, institutional development and the effectiveness of aid. Only long-term structural interventions will ensure sustainable economic development of youth.'

Over 90 per cent of entrepreneurs in developing countries report that they have taken to self-employment because of lack of opportunities in the formal sector – their inability to find a paid job.

ILO/MasterCard research on school-to-work transitions

School-to-work transition indicators are designed to measure the ease or difficulty with which young people are able to access decent work: for example, the progression of a young person from the end of schooling to the first 'career' job or 'regular' job with decent work characteristics. The stage 'in transition' comprises youth who are unemployed, or employed and planning to change jobs or return to education – for example, people in a non-career job; those employed but exposed to decent work deficits (measured in terms of job satisfaction and type of contract); and those currently inactive or not in school, but seeking work. The 'transited' stage includes young people actively employed in a career job and wanting to stay there.

Prior school-to-work transition surveys (see www.ilo.org/youth) have shown they can provide a solid basis for the formulation of youth employment policies and programmes. For instance, the survey in Kyrgyzstan served to integrate youth employment policy interventions in the country's National Employment Programme. In Egypt, Kosovo, Indonesia, Mongolia and Sri Lanka, the findings of the survey were used for the design of national action plans on youth employment and for assigning priority to youth employment in national policy-making. A recent synthesis survey of eight countries has shown the following.

- More than two-thirds of unemployed youth in Egypt and Nepal would consider emigrating for employment purposes. The shares in the other countries – Azerbaijan, China, Islamic Republic of Iran and Mongolia – averaged around 40 per cent.

- Those with higher education are not guaranteed an easier transition from school to work. Egyptian youth with higher education remained in transition 33 months after graduation.

- The expected relationship between hours of work and earnings is an upward sloping curve. However, only in Azerbaijan and Egypt was the relationship positive, while in the other countries there were no obvious relationships. Assuming the findings are accurate, no matter how long youth worked, their total earnings at the end of the month did not change considerably. This probably indicates low-productivity work, taken up as the only option to earning some income.

Adapted from Sara Elder, Senior Research Specialist at the ILO's Work4Youth Programme, in Commonwealth Education Partnerships 2011–2012

More reflections from Investing In Youth (London, 2011)

Financial products, services and education are some of the basic building blocks that lay the foundation for sustainable and vibrant youth-led enterprises. Without access to financial products and services, young people are restricted in saving their incomes in safe instruments, receive credit to start small businesses, or invest in any assets. Financial education can complement life skills, entrepreneurial education and might also open up opportunities for mentorship.

Henry Charles, Director of the Youth Affairs Division 2010–2011, comments:

On the one hand the efficient harnessing of the creative abilities and productive capacities of young people can serve to significantly transform the global development landscape and indeed the sustainability and quality of life within communities. While on the flipside the failure to effectively harness young people's productive capacity contributes immensely to a pervasive and extremely volatile socio-political environment. Decent work opportunities for young people are therefore a matter of exceeding urgency.

Srinivasan Sridhar, Chairman and Managing Director of Central Bank of India, comments:

Youth enterprises require support because [in addition to employment creation] *they contain in them the germ of large enterprises; they incorporate local dimensions of entrepreneurship through the pooling of local resources and talent; they tend to be more innovative, bring new ideas to the table, respond more swiftly to demands.*

Dr A Otuoma Paul Nyongesa, Minister of Youth Affairs and Sports, Government of Kenya, comments:

The formal economy is not creating jobs to match the demands of an expanding demography of young working people. There has been economic growth but this does not automatically lead to job creation. It is necessary to undertake innovative job initiatives now. Young people peg their hopes on governments to offer them a future but, is it the job of governments alone?

Herman Mulder, formerly Head of Group Risk Management, ABN Amro Bank, comments:

[Government should] *seek partners, remove obstacles, use their convening power to sit with businesses and civil society organisations, re-visit the value chains of companies and bank policies. Encourage young people to help young people so that they build a shared future – engage young employees in corporations or governments as mentors to youth at the bottom of the pyramid.*

Growing up in the Commonwealth: the life chances of girls

The half a billion girls in the Commonwealth are not our problem – they are our opportunity, if we give them a chance. Given that

chance, given equal opportunities, they can change their lives, and their children's lives, for generations to come.

Plan International

Education goes beyond what happens in school. Girls need time and space to build skills for life, to learn about planning their families, running their finances and becoming computer literate. Too many young women get pregnant too early and drop out of school. After giving birth, it is very hard for them to get back into education and to learn the skills they will need to support their families.

But it can happen. At 15, Gloria (Uganda) became pregnant, was taken out of school and married. However, last year, aged 18, she got a place on a life skills course run by the local vocational training college and was given a small sum to pay for her expenses. At a weekly lesson she learned crucial skills – from how to space her children to managing her finances and starting up a business. Gloria saved her expenses money to buy seeds and asked her father-in-law for the use of a field for one season. With the proceeds of the crop she paid rent on a small hair salon and now employs two hairdressers.

It does not take a lot to invest in young women like Gloria. But it does take more than money. It means being aware of the particular needs and challenges that girls face. Earlier this year, Plan International teamed up with the Royal Commonwealth Society to find out where is the best country in the Commonwealth to be a girl. We measured eight indicators – survival, education, early pregnancy, access to scholarships, women in politics, success in sports, the pay gap and life expectancy. There was little negative correlation between poverty and gender equality. Rwanda, Mozambique and Malawi all scored very highly on our gender equality criteria, and of the six poorest countries in the Commonwealth, only Sierra Leone, still recovering from years of civil war, remains on the bottom.

It is estimated that girls need at least three years of post-primary education in order to emerge into the world as successful economic participants so, despite its limitations, we chose for the education indicator to look at years in school. Girls in Pakistan spend the least number of years in school, under six, followed by Nigeria at seven. In both cases, girls lag well behind their brothers, though in Bangladesh, girls stay in school a little longer than boys. In India, Tanzania and Mozambique, girls also trail behind boys in terms of years spent in school. Investing in girls is the right thing to do. But it also makes economic sense, simply by educating girls you can raise your country's gross domestic product.

However, gender disparity exists everywhere, even among the top ranked countries. In New Zealand, which by our criteria was the best place to be born a girl, women still earn only 72 per cent of the male average and there are twice as many men as women in parliament.

Source: Adapted from an article by Marie Staunton (CEO, Plan UK) and Sharon Goulds in Commonwealth Education Partnerships 2011–2012

Mobilink and UNESCO: empowering Pakistani girls

With more than 98 million mobile phone users in Pakistan versus a 60 million illiterate population, the mobile phone holds endless potential if placed in the right hands. A leading cause for extremely low female literacy in Pakistan is either because the educational facility is far or the family does not want the girl to go outside the house. There are however, two flip sides to this socio-cultural barrier: the female, while being confined to the home space in Pakistan, is inadvertently the centre of knowledge and learning for her offspring, most of whom don't make it past primary school; and she has relatively more time available to participate actively in mLearning programmes.

Bilal Munir Sheikh, Vice-President of Marketing, Mobilink

Pakistani mobile operator Mobilink, a subsidiary of Orascom, has sought to demonstrate the power of mobile phones to improve literacy rates for adolescent girls in rural areas of Pakistan where reading materials are often scarce. In 2009, Mobilink partnered with UNESCO and a local non-governmental organisation (NGO), Bunyad, on a pilot project in a rural area of southern Punjab province involving 250 females aged 15–24 who had recently completed a basic literacy programme. This has now been scaled up.

Each of the girls was provided with a low-cost mobile phone and prepaid connection. Teachers were trained by Bunyad to teach students how to read and write using mobile phones. The company set up a system for the NGO to send out SMS messages in an effort to maintain and improve participants' literacy, which often lapses because of inadequate access to interesting reading material.

Crucially, low-cost phones were selected that can send and receive messages in Urdu, the local language, rather than in English. The girls received up to six messages a day on a variety of topics, including religion, health and nutrition, and were expected to practise reading and writing down the messages and responding to their teachers via SMS. Monthly assessments of participants' learning gains were conducted to assess impact. Programme organisers encountered considerable resistance on the part of parents and community leaders to the idea of allowing girls to have mobile phones, largely due to the conservative social norms of the area. This resistance began to soften, however, once people began to see the nature of the messages the girls were receiving and the benefits the programme conferred.

The programme showed striking early gains in literacy, with the share of girls receiving the lowest exam scores dropping nearly 80 per cent. Participants and their families are even taking advantage of other features of the phones, including the calculator.

Source: GSM Association/Commonwealth Education Partnerships 2011–2012. The GSMA represents the interests of mobile operators worldwide. Within the GSMA, the Development Fund works in Mobile Learning and five other areas: Mobile Money for the Unbanked, Green Power for Mobile, Mobile Agriculture, mWomen and Mobile Health

Commonwealth Youth Exchange Council: a strategic *partner*

At Commonwealth Youth Fora young people have consistently asked to be seen and treated as partners in democracy and development; they have contributions to make as agents of peace-building, of climate change awareness and as drivers of social and economic enterprise.

Vic Craggs, Chief Executive, CYEC (www.cyec.org.uk)

The CYEC is a youth development and education charity working alongside young people to support them as active global citizens through sharing lives, exchanging ideas and working together. Young people are a crucial catalyst for nation building and for developing a stronger 21st-century Commonwealth. CYEC promotes youth exchanges and programmes for young adults that enable them to share and compare views, learn about the reality of each other's lives and build Commonwealth links and awareness. Interchange gives young people an opportunity to educate each other because they understand best the problems that they and their contemporaries face and how best to solve them.

Alongside youth exchanges CYEC supports a number of youth-led development activities and networks and is particularly proud of its role in helping to found the Commonwealth Youth Forum, held at the time of CHOGM.

- In May 2011 CYEC organised the London Symposium on Meaningful Participation by Young People in International Decision-making. Funded by the British Council and Open Society Foundations, the forum brought together 85 people from 45 countries. Youth participation may be a '100 million dollar industry' but despite the investment there are countless examples of charters, declarations and recommendations drafted in advance or without youth input – or written by young people then ignored. Much greater tracking, monitoring and evaluation of commitments is needed.

- Also in 2011, CYEC managed the Young Professionals Forum of the Commonwealth Local Government Forum in Cardiff, Wales, whose theme was Local Economic Development (LED). LED is still at an incipient stage in many developing countries, having emerged 30–40 years ago in developed country localities failing to benefit from supply-side strategies.

- Following the eighth Commonwealth Youth Forum in Perth, a range of new ideas, partnerships and projects were formed. One of these was an exciting new Young Leaders Exchange between the UK and Sri Lanka, which takes place throughout 2012. The lead partner in Sri Lanka is the Sri Lanka Federation of Youth Clubs with financial and visa support from National Youth Services Council of Sri Lanka. On the UK side, CYEC is working with an NGO, dare2lead. Young people will be openly recruited based on equal opportunity, as well as respecting ability and past commitment to Commonwealth values and community action.

Open University Malaysia: partner in Commonwealth youth development training

Open University Malaysia (OUM) was established on 10 August 2000 as Malaysia's seventh private university and was the first to operate via open and distance learning (ODL). It is owned by a consortium of the country's 11 public universities. Built on the philosophy that education should be democratised, OUM has focused on creating an affordable and accessible pathway to higher education, while placing importance on flexible entry requirements, a learner-friendly academic system and a blended pedagogy that combines different modes of learning. Each of these components is designed to fulfil the diverse needs of its learners and is backed by a state-of-the-art information and communication technology (ICT) infrastructure. OUM has enrolled over 100,000 learners, with more than 36,000 having successfully graduated as at June 2011.

Passing the one-decade mark gives OUM the opportunity to reflect upon its growth. Looking back, the university has certainly come a long way. At just over ten years old, OUM is still relatively young, especially when compared to other Commonwealth Diploma partners, such as Open University United Kingdom (established 1969), Allama Iqbal Open University (established 1974) and Indira Gandhi National Open University (established 1985). Having said that, OUM is proud of its progress and anticipates more milestones in the future.

The pinnacle of its achievements is having created access for thousands of people to obtain higher education – most of whom would not have had the same opportunity had ODL not emerged in Malaysia. For working adults, who make up the majority of OUM's learners, the motives for pursuing higher or continued education are usually associated with personal development and career advancement. Moreover, in today's globalised economy, the knowledge capital of a country's labour force is considered vital for national growth. Without continuous betterment of the people's education, a country will certainly find it difficult to compete on the global stage. Thus, providing the means for these working adults to partake in education has great implications for both lifelong learning and national economic development.

By focusing heavily on ICT, OUM has opened the door to higher education, giving working adults the chance to continue learning and to upgrade their skills and knowledge, thus improving not only themselves, but also their families, professions and, ultimately, their country.

In 2011 OUM signed an agreement with Perbadanan Hal Ehwal Bekas Angkatan Tentera (PERHEBAT), an organisation that manages various training and education needs for former members of the country's armed forces. The arrangement for prison inmates is also a unique example. For lifelong learning to be truly democratised (and to truly realise a 'University for All'), educational opportunities must reach every individual, regardless of age, creed, gender or socio-economic status.

Text by Professor Emeritus Anuwar Ali, President/Vice-Chancellor, Open University Malaysia; former Director of Higher Education at the Ministry of Education (1995–98); and Chairman of the Malaysian Examination Council (2001–03)

The Diploma in Youth Development Work is part of wider efforts to professionalise youth work through associations, codes of ethics and integration with competency standards of public service commissions. These issues are the subject of a June 2012 conference in Johannesburg, South Africa.

Sport for Development and Peace

'We prize the bonds and shared values of sport in the Commonwealth … At the grassroots level, we see sport as a means to develop individuals, communities, and even nations.'

– Commonwealth Eminent Persons Group (2011)

Commonwealth countries are at the forefront of efforts to utilise sport as a tool to promote development and support peace-building efforts. The increased profile and credibility of this field, commonly referred to as Sport for Development and Peace (SDP), has not only seen an expansion in programmes and agencies undertaking this type of work but also critical reflection on how sport can best support development and peace objectives.

Over the past two decades the recognition of the role sport can play in development and peace-building efforts has increased significantly. The United Nations General Assembly's Resolution 65/4 endorses sport as a means to promote education, health, development and peace. In turn the UN Office on Sport for Development and Peace was established to provide an entry point to the UN system on these issues, bringing together what can be separate worlds.

Equally, Commonwealth leaders have long endorsed the role sport can play in achieving the Commonwealth's goals of Democracy and Development, in particular highlighting the potential of sport to engage and promote the development of youth. The Eminent Persons Group (EPG) rightly points out that sport can instil 'teamwork, aspiration, effort, social cohesion, gender equality, and healthy competition', and that these can in turn serve other Commonwealth values. At the 2011 Commonwealth Heads of Government Meeting (CHOGM) the Commonwealth Secretariat was authorised to play a co-ordinating role in this area. Heads' endorsement builds on the requests made by Commonwealth sports ministers, who have consistently highlighted the need for the Commonwealth to stay at the forefront of the SDP field.

November 2011: Gold Coast (Australia) learns that it will host the Commonwealth Games in 2018. The next Commonwealth Games will be held in Glasgow in 2014; the next Commonwealth Youth Games will be in Samoa in 2015, followed by St Lucia in 2017 (photograph © Commonwealth Games Federation)

Defining pillars

In response, an SDP unit has been established within the Youth Affairs Division of the Secretariat, supported by Sports Advisers. Thus far the Advisers have been seconded from the governments of India and the United Kingdom. The work of the Secretariat is supported by the Commonwealth Advisory Body on Sport (CABOS), who provide advice to the Secretariat and Commonwealth governments on sport policy, particularly with respect to SDP.

Two pillars define SDP:

- a focus on grassroots and community-based initiatives, and

- recognition that the human and social development aims are paramount: they supersede the development of sport for its own sake, or identification of future elite performers.

These pillars focus definitions of SDP to highlight the deliberate and intentional use of sport, physical activity and play to attain specific development and peace objectives (CABOS, 2010). Emphasising the distinction between SDP and the development of sport, leading academic and Chair of CABOS Professor Bruce Kidd explains that sport for development seeks out those not already involved, and is unconcerned about whether participants ever become involved in organised training and competition.

Good practice

Examples of effective SDP programmes across the Commonwealth are plentiful and in many countries innovative non-governmental organisations (NGOs) have played a leading role. In Kenya the youth-led Mathare Youth Sport Association consistently receives international plaudits for its programmes using sport as a tool to engage young people living in the Mathare slum in Nairobi. Sport is at the core of an approach that encompasses health education, education support and programmes encouraging community service.

In India, the Magic Bus India Foundation uses sport-based programmes to empower youth in the slums of Delhi and Mumbai in areas of gender equality, education, health, leadership and livelihood. Its work has been recognised and supported by the Indian Government and other international stakeholders. The Government of India's Panchayat Yuva Krida Aur Khel Abhiyan (PYKKA) initiative, one of the largest SDP programmes in the world, is aimed at providing infrastructure and capacity at the village level. Co-ordination with policies focused on the school curriculum, rural development and social inclusion has maximised the programme's reach and impact.

Cricket for Change, based in the United Kingdom, has received wide recognition for its work, which uses cricket as a vehicle to engage at-risk youth in some of Britain's most deprived areas and provide opportunities for people with disability. The Trinidad and Tobago Alliance for Sport and Physical Education has a similar focus and, in expanding its work across the Caribbean, is seen as a sector leader by the international SDP community. In the Pacific, UNAIDS is partnering with the Oceania National Olympic Committees using sports as a mobilisation tool to deliver sexual health education. UNICEF, the Office of the UN High Commissioner for Refugees and UN-Habitat have established strategic frameworks that include sport-based interventions.

Sport in the community, Papua New Guinea

More recently the sport community has taken a more significant role in the interplay between sport and development. Led most prominently by the International Olympic Committee, sport federations, organisations and clubs today are more active in promoting sports' contribution to development goals. The International Table Tennis Federation, International Volleyball Federation and International Federation of Netball Associations, alongside their regional and national members, are among a number of sport organisations that have led SDP programmes in Commonwealth countries.

A 'panacea' for development?

The examples above are recognised and effective SDP initiatives. However, the field encompasses a large and ever-expanding number of stakeholders and, as in any area, the expertise and approach of stakeholders varies. At times the case for SDP is overstated, almost as if participation in sport can *solve* complex development and peace-building issues (particularly with regard to young people). But the development community is well aware that no single intervention type can be a short cut to development and peace. Although it is rules-based, recreational and photogenic, sport cannot produce well-being and stability overnight or in isolation. Effective and credible SDP approaches recognise and articulate the limits of what it can do.

Sport can be either an effective addition or an alternative approach to other interventions, and vice versa. For example, in Mathare, teams are awarded points for community service as well as for on-field results. In every case, SDP must be aware of the cultural and economic context. As put by International Olympic Committee President Jacques Rogge, 'It is not a question of whether sport contributes to the betterment of society; we are all in agreement that it does. The real question is how to make it contribute in more impactful ways.'[1]

Policy and regulatory frameworks

Many challenges could be addressed by more developed SDP policies and regulatory frameworks. At the 5th Commonwealth Sports Ministers Meeting held in Delhi in 2010, ministers affirmed the importance of SDP, but acknowledged that few of the necessary policies have been drafted or implemented to provide a scalable framework for it. As a result, the benefits of sport participation are enjoyed by only a small population of children and youth across the Commonwealth.

An analysis of the stakeholders involved in the SDP field may shed light on the underlying cause of this dynamic. The SDP International Working Group highlights that a broad cross-section of stakeholders contributes to the field. The working group outlines government, local and international NGOs, the sport community, multilateral institutions, business and academia's involvement in the field. Many of these stakeholders are from a sports background, be they sporting federations, sport ministries or corporate bodies with an interest in sport. But, even within the broadening profile of SDP, a significant number of stakeholders in the field remain isolated from broad development policy and networks. If sport is a 'universal language', co-ordination with other development disciplines is nevertheless key.

Fresh ground: cross-sector approaches

As the Secretary-General told a CABOS meeting in Delhi in 2010, the Commonwealth Secretariat is focused on breaking fresh ground. In government and policy domains, SDP is most often designated as the responsibility of the ministry, institutions and agencies overseeing sport and physical activity. Across many Commonwealth countries national sport policy includes the key pillars of achieving international success and recognition through sport and broadening participation in sport and physical activity.

Elite sport, the first of these pillars, tends to dominate public and media attention and is, more often than not, the criteria by which the effectiveness of the national sport mechanism is judged.

Malaysian children playing volleyball (© Commonwealth Photographic Awards)

However, elite sport is highly resource-intensive and beyond messaging, perhaps the area of the sporting landscape with least relevance to SDP. The second pillar, mass participation in sport, is however highly significant in maximising sport's contribution to development goals.

In framing new cross-sector approaches to SDP the articulation of objectives is key. For example, if increasing physical activity levels forms part of a national strategy to combat non-communicable diseases (NCDs), then the health stakeholders clearly have an important role to play in the design, implementation and resourcing of initiatives. Platforms for physical activities that go beyond sport also have to be in the mix – from cycle and pedestrian commuting (requiring green spaces, road and street safety, sanitation), to active living initiatives encompassing dance, cultural activities and other areas. Some of these – for example, dance and drama, or search and rescue – will have their own specialist perspectives on physical training, teamwork and well-being. Similarly, if increasing the provision of sport programmes in a particular region is part of a strategy to re-engage disenfranchised groups in formal learning or to promote dialogue between conflicting groups, then broader spheres should be engaged including police, education and community mobilisation organisations.

Australia's Active After School programme, aimed at tackling growing obesity levels in the country, is a good example of cross-sector collaboration – in this case, between sport and education stakeholders. The partnership has enhanced preventative health capacity for 3,176 schools and Out of School Hours Care Services around the country.[2]

Working with member governments to achieve shared goals in democracy and development, the Commonwealth Secretariat engages with a broad cross-section of ministries, government departments and non-government stakeholders, and boasts professionals with a breadth of expertise and experience. In playing a co-ordinating role across member countries and championing mainstreaming, the Secretariat is uniquely positioned to support cross-sector approaches – to gender equality, to youth empowerment, to respect and understanding, and more. These are all areas where, through SDP policy and practice, the Commonwealth can break fresh ground.

Notes

[1] 2nd International Forum on Sport, Peace and Development. UN/IOC, May 2011.

[2] See www.ausport.gov.au/participating/aasc.

Sport for Development and Peace: seven Commonwealth Asian countries share practice – and principles

I urge that SDP be integrated into national and international agendas and become an integral part of development ... If you want to be a part of group, then you must comply with certain basic principles: healthy environment and empowered people.

Beng Choo Low, International Olympic Committee Member and Vice-Chair of the Commonwealth Advisory Body on Sport (CABOS)

There is renewed interest in the cause of SDP in Commonwealth Asia, with line ministries, youth and other civil society representatives developing common agendas. In response to requests from Commonwealth sports ministers, policy dialogue and recommendations have been facilitated by Sports Advisers and CYP Asia staff of the Commonwealth Secretariat. Opened by Beng Choo Low, the consultations and workshops were held in October 2011 in Delhi.

- **Bangladesh:** 'The most popular sport is cricket, followed by football and kabaddi, the national sport. According to National Sports Policy, we have festivals based on traditional and indigenous sports. During Bengali New Year and in different Bengali months, different sports activities are organised – not only cricket, football and kabaddi but also local games.'

- **Malaysia:** 'National Sport Policy is a *sport for all policy*, which includes High Performance Sport and Sport for All. The National Fitness Programme in Malaysia consists of physical and mental development, healthy lifestyle and mass involvement. The Malaysian government also gives importance to minority sport catering to specific needs. Malaysia, being a multi-racial, multi-cultural and multi-faceted country, believes communities that play together stay together.'

- **Singapore:** 'Singapore has been ranked second in the Ultimate Sports Cities Awards. But parents generally focus on their young people's academic development, rather than a culture of sport. Every youth should be given the opportunity to grow and develop in sports, have positive experiences and not be left out or left behind.'

- **Magic Bus India Foundation:** 'Peace-building starts taking place when children from different caste, gender start coming from different areas to play together. The initial four or five months are just consumed in building rapport with the children. Encouraging a girl child to come and play is significant in itself, especially in a setting where one caste does not even see the other caste.'

- **Sri Lanka:** 'National Sports Policy sees every citizen as a sportsman, acknowledging that sport has the potential to be a unifying force and build stronger, healthier and happier communities.'

For Sri Lankan cricket legend Muttiah 'Murali' Muralitharan, 'Sport doesn't have any religion or any caste or anything, it's all one common thing, winning and losing, and participating, and that makes people happier, makes spectators happier, so that makes us more united than anything else' (Commonwealth Conversation, Royal Commonwealth Society).

Next Steps: 'Global Partnerships in Sport for Development'

Relations within the field are evolving from a linear donor–recipient model to a more collaborative partnership based on equality, mutual respect and shared benefits. There is positive growth. However, we are still challenged by inability to access resources; the prevalence of gender-based violence; specific skills shortages; and gaps in co-ordination at the international level.

Next Steps conference participants

The Next Steps 'Global Partnerships' meeting in 2011, the fourth of its kind, was hosted by the Trinidad and Tobago Alliance for Sport and Physical Education (TTASPE), convening delegates from 26 countries and 58 organisations active in Sport for Development and Peace (SDP). The key recommendations arising included the following.

- That governments, national governing bodies, NGOs and community-based organisations be encouraged to address gender-based violence in broader society, and specifically to adopt guideline standards within the field of SDP.

- To commission an independent review of SDP's effectiveness (on personal and social issues), and develop materials for lobbying, advocacy and sharing of effective practices.

- To create regional working 'hubs' and monitor regional, age and gender representation in all related structures as part of addressing inequities.

According to TTASPE's Mark Mungal, 'Delegates emphasised that to realise international frameworks – for example, those of the Commonwealth Secretariat and CABOS – they need to partner with practitioners and academics. Sports for life skills, education and development has been around for little over a century in many parts of the world, and our understanding of the potential is still evolving. Recent high-level support from Ban Ki-moon (UN Secretary-General) and others is hugely encouraging.'

The conference received significant support from the Australian Sports Commission via its Australian Sports Outreach Programme. The Commonwealth Games Association of Canada and UK Sport also provided support.

Sport for Development and Peace: the potential of large-scale events

Debbie Lye, International Director, UK Sport; Chair, UN International Working Group on SDP

Sport, through the Commonwealth Games and Commonwealth Youth Games, is arguably the most visible face of the modern Commonwealth. Yet the significant contribution that sport makes to the broad goals of social and youth development in many countries is less acknowledged ... We believe that the potential for the Games to contribute to peace and development should be developed as a central purpose.

Commonwealth Eminent Persons Group, 2011

When London bid to the Singapore International Olympic Committee Convention in July 2005 to host the 2012 Olympic and Paralympic Games, Lord Sebastian Coe promised that, if successful, they would use the opportunity to 'reach young people all around the world and connect them to the inspirational power of the games so they are inspired to choose sport'.

International Inspiration

The vision of International Inspiration is to 'enrich the lives of 12 million children and young people in 20 countries through the power of high quality physical education, sport and play'. Twelve are Commonwealth members – Bangladesh, Ghana, India, Malaysia, Mozambique, Nigeria, Pakistan, South Africa, Tanzania, Trinidad and Tobago, Uganda and Zambia. (The total is 16 when including the involvement of Northern Ireland, Scotland, England and Wales.)

International Inspiration is an ambitious seven-year initiative (2007–2014) delivered for the London 2012 Organising Committee (LOCOG) by a partnership of UK Sport, the British Council and UNICEF working collaboratively with government and sport sector partners in each country on programmes designed to help meet specific sporting and wider developmental needs of children and young people. The unity of the whole project derives from the single shared vision to which each country programme contributes, and a common set of outcomes and indicators.

A fundamental principle is sustainability, and to that end political engagement is prioritised so that initiatives demonstrated, piloted and developed through International Inspiration become embedded in national policy, practice and strategy. Notable Commonwealth examples are:

- the inclusion of the right to physical education in the 2010 Right to Education Act in India

- the adoption of the first ever nationwide school sports policy in South Africa

- development of a Community Sport Strategy in Uganda

- the development of specialist resources for the inclusion of children with disabilities in Malaysia in conjunction with the National Paralympics Committee

- Youth Sport Leadership training rolled out to every school in Manikgonj province, Bangladesh.

With 2014 approaching, International Inspiration achievements have exceeded expectations: 12.9 million children and young people have already participated, 116,000 practitioners have been trained and developed new skills and knowledge, 728 policy-makers have been engaged in their country programmes and 35 policy/strategic developments can be attributed to International Inspiration. In addition, 488 schools have been linked together through 244 International Inspiration school partnerships between the UK and schools overseas. An additional set of development indicators is being monitored by the UK's Department for International Development (DFID), which has committed significant funding to International Inspiration.

Legacies of the future

Is it realistic in uncertain economic times to expect sporting event candidate cities and nations to incorporate development legacies such as International Inspiration into their hosting plans? Part of the answer lies in how host nations wish to be perceived. Mega sporting events are about much more than sport. They provide a platform for a country to showcase itself and its values to the world. One of the most appealing aspects of International Inspiration is its altruism. A host nation is asking not, 'What can staging a global sporting event do for us?' but considering 'How can we use this opportunity to connect with young people around the world?'

Emerging and developed economies alike care about national prestige and it is telling that all four cities bidding to host the 2016 Olympic and Paralympic Games included international legacy proposals, although there is no obligation in the International Olympic Committee (IOC) host city contract to do so. The victor, Rio de Janeiro, has since developed its own legacy plan in consultation with the International Inspiration partners. There is every reason to believe that the 2020 Olympic candidate cities will each make a similar commitment when they present their bids to the IOC next year (2013).

Such initiatives are not restricted to the Olympic movement. FIFA committed significant investment to the development of football in Africa linked to South Africa's hosting of the 2010 World Cup, and similar projects are thriving in Brazil in the run-up to FIFA 2014. London's successful bid for the 2017 World Athletics Championships in November 2011 included a specific proposal for UK Sport and UK Athletics to work with the International Association of Athletics Federations (IAAF) to develop the sport of athletics in schools and communities and build a cadre of young sports leaders in developing countries. Other sports federations that generate 'mega events' – cricket, rugby union, rugby league – are also considering how their World Cup events can create wider legacies. There is manifestly a growing recognition that sporting events provide high profile and nationally salient platforms for policy-makers to try new approaches to human and social development challenges through sports-based programming.

From Delhi to Glasgow

The Delhi Commonwealth Games Sports Ministers Meeting profiled the rapidly growing momentum of sport for development in India and the Commonwealth Games Federation's support, alongside UK Sport, for the International Netball Federation's work in Southern Africa.

The Commonwealth Games Federation of Scotland vigorously advocated the power of sport for development during its 2014 Commonwealth Games bid campaign, hosting jointly with the City of Glasgow the first Sport for Development Commonwealth Conference in 2006 and subsequently twice more, in 2008 and 2010. A fourth conference in 2013 will set the tone for Scotland's Commonwealth Games as an event committed to showcasing and sharing learning about how individuals and groups in schools and communities across the Commonwealth can confront and tackle health, social and educational challenges through sports-based programming.

The Glasgow Commonwealth Conferences have advanced understanding around the necessary conditions for the successful use of sport for development programming, including the need to combine high quality sporting activity with a clearly articulated programme theory that sets out the desired human or social change and beliefs about how this will be achieved with specific target groups.

Inclusive Education and the right to play

The participation of excluded children and youth is the only way to mainstream disability in the development agenda and ensure reductions in inequalities. It is also the only way to increase community understanding and foster greater social cohesion which is sustainable in the long run. Sport for development and peace (SDP) is an important tool for inclusion.

Stacey Cram, Right To Play

In Ethiopia, Right To Play has established strong partnerships with 11 disability-specific schools and institutions, and more than 1,000 children living with a disability currently participate in weekly sport and play sessions. As a result Right To Play Ethiopia was recognised by UNICEF as the best international NGO for its efforts in raising the profile of people living with disabilities. Speaking after a meeting at the Commonwealth Secretariat in 2012, Right To Play encouraged Commonwealth members to continue recognising and promoting not only the rights of persons with disabilities but also the crucial role of sport in addressing international development goals.

As of 2012, all Commonwealth member countries had signed the UN Convention on the Rights of Persons with Disabilities, and half (27) had ratified it. According to the Convention, people with disabilities have the right to develop their personality, talents and creativity, as well as their mental and physical abilities, to their fullest potential. Children with disabilities must also have equal access with other children to participation in play, leisure and sport, including within the school system.

Disability activist Gordon Cardona (National Commission Persons with Disability, Malta) writes that being included in mainstream education was positive: 'While there are many things that I learned from my non-disabled peers at school and beyond, I hope that I also contributed to their experience and indirectly helped them enrich their lives ... On one occasion, an older boy hit me full in the face with a football that was aimed at the goalpost, giving me mild concussion! I only remember this because I ended up getting a good scolding from my teacher for being in the wrong place at the wrong time' (*Commonwealth Education Partnerships 2011–2012*).

Young children wearing T-shirts displaying 'Right To Play' (photographer and copyright: Victoria Holdsworth / © Commonwealth Secretariat)

Julius Hamya, a director of the Uganda National Association of the Blind (UNAB), remembers: 'I studied at Butalejja Integrated Primary School, where I freely interacted with the sighted students. I also participated in extra-curricular activities such as football, bicycle riding and athletics using guides. But I had to deal with a lack of special needs teachers, outdated technology, lack of Braille paper, and segregation by some students who thought that visual impairment was a curse. In secondary school sighted students would assist me with transcribing material – but would then get jealous when I came out with the top grades. I eventually went on to Makerere University' (from a Commonwealth Foundation grant story in *The Commonwealth: Making a Difference*, 2011).

The Duke of Edinburgh's Award International Association

The award is nothing without adventure, literally stretching those boundaries, conceptually, mentally and physically of what we can do as individuals and together. This sense of venturing out into a wider world, the discovery of new experiences and the sharing of them across all the boundaries of race and religion and class and creed, that's the mountain that we've all got to climb.

Lord Paul Boateng, International Award Association (IAA) Trustee

The International Award for young people is a self-development programme offered to 14–25 year-olds in 135 countries worldwide. The award involves physical recreation and expeditions alongside skills-building and community service. In 2012 there are some 65,000 participants in Commonwealth member countries.

In Solomon Islands, Sierra Leone, Angola, Brazil and elsewhere there is a strong peace-building component. In partnership with SOS Children's Village International, the award has been introduced in Rwanda and Burundi. Building on the award's philosophy of non-discrimination, these two nations are hoping to use the programme to strive for unity without discrimination on the basis of a person's tribe. Meanwhile a new initiative of IAA's Africa Office (Project Murembo) focuses on young girls in marginalised areas in Arusha (Tanzania), Gulu (Uganda) and Turkana (Kenya).

I have grown up in a humble neighbourhood in Nairobi where we face enormous challenges trying to make a living. Drugs, violent crimes and HIV/AIDS are a common occurrence in my neighbourhood ... The award has made the difference for me to make the right choices amid all these difficulties.

Olunga Otieno, Kenya (IAA Youth Representative 2008–2011)

The International Award collaborates with the Commonwealth at a number of levels. In Zambia, the President's Youth Award is led by the Commonwealth Youth Programme together with the National Youth Development Council, and delivered through 20 schools and youth organisations. In 2011, delegates at a major leadership training event in Kenya (International Gold Event) went on to participate at the Commonwealth Youth Forum in Perth, Australia.

Peter Anum, President of the Gold Award Holders' Association of Ghana, was also a facilitator at the 2011 Commonwealth Local Government Young Professionals Forum, which took place in Cardiff, UK. Following these experiences he says, 'I am more convinced than ever that the award is the most powerful tool for nation-building.'

Delivering the promise of a stronger Commonwealth

Julia Gillard, Prime Minister of Australia and Commonwealth Chair-in-Office

The first twelve months following the Perth meeting of Commonwealth Heads of Government provide an excellent opportunity to deliver on the great promise of our association.

As current Commonwealth Chair-in-Office I am delighted to contribute to the 2012 edition of *The Commonwealth Yearbook*. It is now nearly six months since the 2011 Commonwealth Heads of Government Meeting (CHOGM) was held in Perth, Australia, and this presents a good moment to reflect on what was achieved at that meeting, to take stock of what is still to be done, and to cast our eyes forward to a vision of how our unique association might look in the years to come.

This vision is a promising one. By the end of 2012, the Commonwealth will have, for the first time in its history, the text of a charter. It will have a targeted approach to development, allowing the organisation to deliver better results for the people of the Commonwealth. It will also have new and improved mechanisms to support our fundamental values, including through early and active engagement with members. These practical changes will help create a Commonwealth equipped to meet the needs of its members and to fulfil the aspirations of its peoples, both in the security of their democratic freedoms and in their economic and social development.

Building resilience

CHOGM 2011 was a milestone meeting for the Commonwealth. Building on the foundation laid down at CHOGM 2009 in Port of Spain, leaders committed to practical reforms to make our association more modern, efficient and focused on the challenges of the 21st century.

First, we strengthened the Commonwealth's institutions so that we can more readily put our values into action. We agreed to reform the Commonwealth Ministerial Action Group (CMAG), as the custodian of these values. CMAG has played a vital role since its inception in 1995 and, thanks to the reforms agreed in Perth, it will continue to play a vital role into the future. We have equipped CMAG with the mandate necessary to build positive relationships with members and boost proactive diplomacy when Commonwealth political values are under strain.

CHOGM 2011 also welcomed the landmark report of the Commonwealth Eminent Persons Group (EPG). Leaders demonstrated their commitment to act on this report in Perth, giving full consideration to the EPG's 106 recommendations. Together, we agreed to adopt 30 recommendations without reservation, plus a historic decision to develop our first Commonwealth charter. Together, we agreed to consider further

the majority of the remaining recommendations in 2012, which will be a key part of our work this year.

Second, we made decisions for strong economic and development action that will make a difference to the countries and peoples of the Commonwealth, particularly small and developing states. Australia put action on the challenges of small and developing states front and centre at CHOGM 2011. I am proud that we also hosted a dedicated small and developing states meeting in Perth in recognition of the major challenges that affect these states, especially climate change and sustainability. This work will continue in 2012, including through the second Commonwealth biennial global small states meeting in May, and beyond.

Third, we made decisions to enhance the collective voice of the Commonwealth on key global issues. One particularly important challenge that was addressed in Perth was food security. The *Perth Declaration on Food Security Principles* is a concrete statement of the Commonwealth's commitment to addressing food insecurity and to meeting the needs of the world's most vulnerable, particularly women and children. The Perth Declaration's vision is being brought to life through new partnerships. Australia, Canada, New Zealand and the United Kingdom announced at CHOGM 2011 an agreement to bolster co-operation on food security and nutrition in Africa, including in support of African-led initiatives to lift agricultural productivity, improve nutrition and alleviate the impacts of food crises. I was also proud to announce a new Australian International Centre for Food Security, which will increase access to, and sharing of, research and development and technical expertise. Partnerships such as these will help build economically resilient communities better able to meet future adversity.

In addition to our efforts on food security, Commonwealth leaders called for urgent action on climate change and agreed to advocate for legally binding outcomes on emissions reductions, enhanced action on adaptation, and transparent and accessible climate finance. We also agreed to establish an annual officials-level Commonwealth meeting on the G20 development agenda.

I was also delighted to join with the leaders of Canada, Nigeria, Pakistan and the United Kingdom, and with Bill Gates, to demonstrate our renewed commitment and financial support to eradicate polio, a crippling disease that remains endemic in four countries worldwide. Three of these four countries are Commonwealth members and CHOGM 2011 saw a commitment of both political will and over US$100 million in new funding for global eradication efforts. There is no doubt that progress is happening in this fight – in January this year India celebrated twelve months without a new case of polio.

These outcomes highlight that, while the Perth meeting will be remembered for our efforts to achieve progress on much-needed reform of Commonwealth institutions, it also reminded us how

Commonwealth countries, working together, can have a positive impact on the lives of our people.

The road ahead in 2012

We are rightly proud of what was achieved at CHOGM 2011 to help build the resilience of the countries in our Commonwealth association. The Perth summit achieved many substantial outcomes at a time when reform and renewal of the Commonwealth has never been more important. Our efforts this year will be equally significant as we carry forward our momentum and commitment to deliver the substance of decisions taken in Perth.

This year will see us agree text for a Commonwealth charter – the first in our history. The Commonwealth is remarkable not only because of its diversity as an association but because its membership is united by a set of shared values that continue to stand the test of time. These values are the result of over 60 years of collaboration and development, and have been articulated at Singapore, Harare, Millbrook, Coolum, and Port of Spain. Adopting a Commonwealth charter will bring these values and aspirations together in one place, making them more relevant and accessible to the people of the Commonwealth.

As a record of the values and principles that unite us, a charter will belong as much to the people of Commonwealth as it does to member countries. Members have undertaken national consultations on a charter and conveyed the results of these consultations to the Commonwealth Secretariat. The text of the new charter will be considered by a special ministerial taskforce in June and by Commonwealth foreign ministers in September, before being submitted to Heads of Government.

Our ability to uphold Commonwealth values will be strengthened by other work we do this year to carry forward outcomes from CHOGM 2011. CMAG will meet in April 2012 in London and work on implementing its new and strengthened mandate so that it can build positive relationships with members through timely and proactive engagement.

We also have the chance to support and complement CMAG reform by establishing, for the first time, a Commonwealth position dedicated to providing information and advice on serious or persistent violations of our fundamental values. In its report to leaders at CHOGM 2011, the EPG recommended the creation of a Commonwealth commissioner for democracy, the rule of law and human rights. Leaders decided in Perth that the Commonwealth Secretary-General and CMAG should evaluate options for such a role and how it might work in practice. These options will be considered by Commonwealth foreign ministers in September 2012.

The Commonwealth can be proud of the efforts its institutions undertake, often out of the spotlight, to work with members to help build enduring institutions that underpin democracy and good governance. A new Commonwealth role to support CMAG and the 'good offices' interventions of the Secretary-General can help us, as an association based on values, better support and promote these values.

Much work will also be done this year on the 43 other EPG recommendations that leaders in Perth identified as deserving further consideration, as well as 12 more recommendations which leaders agreed to adopt subject to a consideration of financial implications.

Our efforts in 2012 will also focus on delivering outcomes from CHOGM 2011 that improve the economic and social development of members. In Perth, we heard that continued global economic uncertainty and weak global growth are affecting members of the Commonwealth in different ways and to varying degrees. We agreed to revitalise the Commonwealth's development priorities to ensure they articulate and meet the needs of member states both today and in the future.

The Commonwealth Foundation is also revitalising its activities. We will see the Foundation relaunched in 2012, with a revised mandate so that it can more effectively deliver the objectives of strengthening and mobilising civil society in support of Commonwealth principles and priorities. Particularly pleasing is the focus on youth, who represent more than half of the population of Commonwealth countries. In 2012 the Commonwealth Secretariat will assess progress on our Plan of Action for Youth Empowerment and recommendations will be made to Heads of Government on steps we can take to improve our work in this area.

Many challenges affecting Commonwealth members demand global responses. The Commonwealth's diversity means that we are well-placed as an association to contribute to global action. We will continue to use our memberships in international forums in 2012 to renew efforts to drive global action on challenges that impact on the lives of the Commonwealth's peoples.

We can do more in this respect and we are taking practical action to do so. This year we will launch a new annual officials-level Commonwealth meeting on the G20 development agenda. This meeting will ensure the concerns and perspectives of Commonwealth members, particularly small and vulnerable states, are represented at the G20, including at this year's summit in Mexico in June. This summit will be followed by the Rio+20 Sustainable Development Conference in Brazil, where we will take forward our commitment from Perth to press for practical outcomes on the 'blue' economy. Our efforts in international forums will continue beyond 2012 as we maintain our commitment to promote the future of the Commonwealth through the voice of its people.

Delivering the promise of reform

2012 is proving already to be a busy year for the Commonwealth. We should be energised and encouraged by what we stand to gain in implementing the outcomes of CHOGM 2011. We stand to deliver an association that is, in some very clear ways, certain about its place in world affairs, better able to communicate and support its values, and focused on how it can best serve the needs of its members.

I look forward to continuing work with Commonwealth partners in my time as Chair-in-Office as we take steps to realise the great promise of our association. I am confident that together, we can deliver a Commonwealth that remains relevant to future generations, has a framework for modern and effective operations, and continues to make a positive contribution to the peace and prosperity of its peoples.

THE HON JULIA GILLARD MP is the 27th prime minister of Australia. She was first sworn into office on 24 June 2010, and is the country's first female prime minister. Following the hosting of CHOGM 2011 in Perth, Australia, Prime Minister Gillard holds the position of Chair-in-Office of the Commonwealth until 2013.

Perth: a turning point for the Commonwealth?

Derek Ingram

Whenever the Commonwealth is discussed these days one question crops up sooner or later: is it any longer relevant?

How, people argue, can an organisation of states that has its origins in an empire dating back five centuries possibly be of practical value to the world in 2012? My answer is that it is still proving that it can be, and the simple – some may argue simplistic – explanation is the flexibility of structure that has enabled it to be designed and redesigned to meet the needs as the years have moved along. For example, until after the Second World War the British monarch was head of state of all Commonwealth countries. Then newly independent India wanted to become a republic but remain in the Commonwealth. In 1949 Heads of Government met and agreed the simple four-paragraph London Declaration under which King George VI would henceforth become known as Head of the Commonwealth. After that, as decolonisation proceeded, more countries became republics on achieving independence until today of the 54 member countries of the Commonwealth 33 are republics. More are likely to become so in the years to come.

Again, when in the 1960s it became obvious that Whitehall could longer go on organising the Commonwealth's affairs, an independent secretariat under a secretary-general was created – an idea that had first been mooted half a century earlier.

Then, as a number of member states drifted from democracy and a few suffered coups and fell under military rule, the Commonwealth Ministerial Action Group (CMAG) of foreign ministers was created in 1995 – a self-disciplinary body with power to suspend or even expel a country from the association. Until that time no international body, including the United Nations, had such a mechanism.

This was a great step forward, but over the years it became apparent that CMAG was not proving effective enough for the Commonwealth to cope with undemocratic situations in some places such as Pakistan, Fiji and The Gambia, so by the time Heads of Government met in Trinidad and Tobago in 2009, public questioning as to the Commonwealth's relevance was still an increasingly serious and nagging matter.

The Royal Commonwealth Society now carried out an important exercise on the internet which it called the Commonwealth Conversation. The public worldwide were invited to voice their frank opinions on many aspects of the Commonwealth. The response was great. Views were hugely varied. After publication of the report on the Conversation was published on the eve of the 2009 Commonwealth Heads of Government Meeting (CHOGM), one local newspaper in Port of Spain carried a banner headline on its front page flatly declaring that the Commonwealth was

irrelevant. In fact, the findings were not nearly as simple as that. They showed that the real problem was widespread ignorance of the work carried on by both the official Commonwealth and the extensive civil society network.

Concern about talk of an irrelevant Commonwealth led the Trinidad summit to set up the so-called Eminent Persons Group (EPG) – ten people from as many countries chaired by Malaysian former prime minister Tun Abdullah Ahmad Badawi. Its task was to suggest reforms that would create a better framework of co-ordination and collaboration for the Commonwealth. It was also, importantly, to enhance the public profile of the association.

The EPG report, *A Commonwealth of the People: Time for Urgent Reform*, is arguably the best statement produced in recent times to point a way ahead for the Commonwealth. However, it was given a rough ride on publication and its recommendations less than well handled by Heads at the Perth (Australia) CHOGM.

The EPG had originally planned that its findings should be published at least two months before CHOGM so that Heads and their officials as well as the public and the media would have plenty of time to consider their response and the implications of the proposals. The group submitted its report to the Secretary-General on 11 August 2011 asking for it to be released before Heads met on 28 October. They wanted to generate some public debate before the CHOGM opened.

Instead the text was not made public until the Heads convened. Widespread leaks in the weeks before led to some confusion. One result was that only 31 of the EPG's recommendations in their 204-page report were adopted without reservation and 12 more subject to the costs involved. Another 43 were passed on to foreign ministers to consider and 11 were rejected. It was not exactly a ringing endorsement of the report.

Nevertheless, the 2011 CHOGM may be seen in the years to come as having opened a new and positive chapter in the history of the Commonwealth. This is not just because the EPG report and its message may grow in importance in the next few years. A second reason is because the leaders in Perth also had before them an important report from CMAG on how it planned to tighten up its act.

CMAG

CMAG is one of the most advanced components of the Commonwealth machinery. Through it member countries subject themselves to democratic self-discipline at the highest level. Over the years several have been suspended from the Commonwealth (from its councils or membership) – most notably Pakistan, Fiji and Nigeria – but several others have also not conformed to the Millbrook Programme of 1995, which laid down the rules about serious or persistent violations of the democratic principles governments accepted as part of their commitment to the Commonwealth.

The alternative route prescribed by Millbrook – so-called quiet diplomacy by the Secretary-General or his envoys – has proved slow and produced too few results. Governments are inevitably sensitive about what they see as intrusions into their country's internal affairs and for many years calls for the strengthening of the powers of CMAG went unheeded, but when it became clear that the Commonwealth was seriously in danger of ignoring its basic principles CMAG was asked before Perth to recommend ways in which it could toughen up its act. This it did in a report to the Perth CHOGM, which Heads accepted. They also agreed with suggestions in the EPG report that the Secretary-General should feel free to be more outspoken in public.

This report was soon put to the test and a change in approach quickly became evident when President Mohamed Nasheed of Maldives suddenly left office in early 2012. The President resigned on 7 February in dubious circumstances. A team from the Commonwealth Secretariat – whose presence had been previously requested by the Chief Justice and Government of Maldives and which had arrived in the country on 6 February to explore how the Commonwealth could respond to the country's urgent priorities, including strengthening the judiciary and the separation of powers – was immediately involved in getting at the facts. The Secretary-General pointed out that under CMAG's strengthened mandate it was now expected to become involved in a more proactive and positive manner that would include political values, constitutional rule, more democracy, human rights and the rule of law.

Days later CMAG, chaired by the Trinidad and Tobago Foreign Minister, Surujrattan Rambachan, held an extraordinary meeting by teleconference, which was briefed by Nasheed and Maldives' Foreign Minister Mohamed Naseer on the events leading up to what had been described in the immediate aftermath as a coup.

Subsequently, Commonwealth Secretary-General Kamalesh Sharma announced the Commonwealth ministerial mission to Maldives to be led by Rambachan. This delegation also included Amitav Banerji, director of political affairs at the Secretariat. They talked to Mohamed Waheed, who had been sworn in as president following Nasheed's resignation, Nasheed himself, the speaker of parliament (the Majlis), the chief justice, political parties, independent institutions, military and police personnel and civil society.

CMAG met in London on 22 February to discuss the mission's report and called for elections to be held before the end of the year. Under the new remit from Perth, action had been swifter and broader than before and set a pattern for a more proactive Commonwealth.

Looking ahead

Looking ahead, the Commonwealth may face anxious days in the lead-up to the 2013 CHOGM, which is scheduled to take place in Sri Lanka – a venue some member countries have been uneasy about in the light of UN reports about the human rights violations that occurred in the aftermath of the civil war. Canadian Prime Minister Stephen Harper said he, for one, would not attend if no progress had been made by Sri Lanka in the areas of post-conflict accountability and meaningful reconciliation.

Later, in a tough speech to the Royal Commonwealth Society in London, Harper's Foreign Minister John Baird said Canada would continue to press countries in the Commonwealth to live up to their international obligations and uphold the basic contract any government should have with its people. Mauritius had been lined up for 2013 if Sri Lanka had to opt out as host.

Canada's firm line on Sri Lanka marked a strong return by Ottawa after several years to a more active role in Commonwealth affairs. One of Harper's moves was to appoint Senator Hugh Segal, who had played a prominent role as a member of the EPG, as Canada's Special Envoy for Commonwealth Renewal – a new post that emphasised Canada's renewed support for the Commonwealth.

Baird spoke out in favour of a Commonwealth Commissioner for Human Rights, Democracy and the Rule of Law – an important recommendation from the EPG that had not been accepted by several governments in Perth but that was up for further discussion. Baird also pledged support for minority groups, such as homosexuals, whose relationships are criminalised in 41 Commonwealth countries, adding that Commonwealth countries 'must be accountable for their actions and their inactions'.

In a year that marked the 60th anniversary of Queen Elizabeth II's reign speculation was bound to arise in the media and elsewhere about the future of the Headship of the Commonwealth. In a remarkable way the Queen had created a role unique in history for which the London Declaration of 1949 had laid down no guidelines. Over the decades she has met a huge number of presidents and prime ministers from across the world – more in history, it can safely be said, than any other single person who has ever held high office. Her performance has been another example of the Commonwealth's flexibility that has ensured not just its survival but also its growth and pointed to new ways to adapt to global change.

As the EPG report had pointed out, the Commonwealth's membership makes up more than 25 per cent of the UN membership, nearly 40 per cent of the World Trade Organization, more than 35 per cent of the Organization of American States, just under 40 per cent of the African Union, 60 per cent of the South Asian Association for Regional Cooperation, around 90 per cent of the Caribbean Community and the Pacific Islands Forum, and over one-fifth of the Organisation of Islamic Cooperation.

As the global balance of power moves east these figures seem to make the Commonwealth more and more relevant.

DEREK INGRAM is a journalist, author, and co-founder (with Patrick Keatley) of the Commonwealth Journalists Association. Formerly a deputy editor of the London *Daily Mail*, he is commonly regarded as the foremost writer on the Commonwealth.

Queen and Commonwealth: the Headship at 60

Professor Philip Murphy

I should like to thank the Commonwealth Eminent Persons Group for their work, and I look forward to hearing the outcome of discussion of their recommendations. And I wish Heads of Government well in agreeing further reforms that respond boldly to the aspirations of today and that keep the Commonwealth fresh and fit for tomorrow. In these deliberations we should not forget that this is an association not only of governments but also of peoples. That is what makes it so relevant in this age of global information and communication.

HM Queen Elizabeth II at the Commonwealth Heads of Government Meeting 2011, Perth, Australia

What is so fascinating about the history of the modern monarchy is the relationship between the personal and the political. As the Queen's reign reaches its 60th year, it becomes ever more difficult to distinguish between the characteristics of constitutional monarchy in the UK and the other Commonwealth Realms, and the character given to those institutions by the Queen herself. In the case of her role as Head of the Commonwealth, making that distinction is virtually impossible. It would be rather like discussing the role of the Secretary-General of the United Nations if Dag Hammarskjöld, who in 1953 became only the second incumbent, were still in office. Furthermore, the formal duties of the UN Secretary-General are fairly well defined. This is not true of the Head of the Commonwealth.

Beginnings

The Queen assumed the title less than three years after it had been enunciated in the London Declaration of April 1949. The Declaration spoke of India's 'acceptance of the King as the symbol of the free association of its independent member nations and as such Head of the Commonwealth'. In so far as any thought was given to that matter, it was recognised that the title could not be hereditary, since there was no body capable of passing a law of succession for the Commonwealth as a whole. At the same time, perhaps paradoxically, it seems to have been assumed by the parties to the Declaration that the Headship would pass in due course to King George VI's successor. In the event, the role of India was crucial. In September 1951, some months before George VI's death, when Commonwealth high commissioners were consulted on the procedures that would be followed on his passing, the Indian representative, Krishna Menon, appears to have been pressed on whether he would feel able to sign the Accession Proclamation, given India's status as a republic. He suggested that if the phrase 'Head of the Commonwealth' was inserted into the proclamation, it would be possible for him to do so.[1] On King George VI's death, India's Prime Minister, Jawaharlal Nehru, wrote

to Queen Elizabeth II welcoming her as the 'new Head of the Commonwealth'. This gap between the probable intentions of the architects of the London Declaration and the formal status of the headship presents an obvious problem for anyone charged with planning for the next succession, particularly given the profound changes that have taken place in the nature and composition of the Commonwealth since 1949.

The other anomaly of the London Declaration is that it was designed to meet the concerns of the South African Prime Minister, D F Malan, that the Commonwealth itself should not appear to have any formal constitutional identity. The King was therefore only to be regarded as head of the Commonwealth by virtue of being a *symbol* of the free association of its member states. And it was explicitly stated that the King did not discharge any constitutional function by virtue of the Headship.[2] The role did not even have any ceremonial functions attached to it. Indeed, when the Queen addressed the UN in 1957, the South African government strongly objected to the idea that she should do so in her capacity as head of the Commonwealth. As the Queen's private secretary noted in November 1959, 'The idea of "The Head of the Commonwealth" is quite a fragile flower of which the life can be endangered just as easily by too much watering as by too little.'

A long-term commitment

Nevertheless, during the subsequent decades, the Queen's extraordinary commitment to the Commonwealth has given substance to the headship and has led to it being associated with certain public functions. In the course of her overseas tours she has managed to visit all but one of the 54 countries that currently make up the Commonwealth. It has been a particular point of principle for the Queen to be present at Commonwealth Heads of Government Meetings (CHOGMs), even when, in the case of the Lusaka gathering in 1979, fears were expressed about her safety. Since Edinburgh in 1997, the Queen has had a formal role in CHOGMs, delivering an address to the opening ceremony. She has, of course, maintained the tradition of producing Christmas and Commonwealth Day messages, something she does without ministerial advice. She attended the first Commonwealth Day Multi-Faith Observance in St Martin-in-the-Fields in 1966. Since its move to Westminster Abbey in 1972, she has signalled her support for the service by attending it whenever possible, despite occasional rumblings of discontent from the evangelical wing of the Church of England.

She and other members of the Royal Family have also played an important ceremonial role in the Commonwealth Games. The Duke of Edinburgh, who was patron of the Games from 1955 to 1990, opened most of the early Games of the Queen's reign; but the Queen herself opened the Commonwealth Games for the first time in 1978, and made a point of attending all the Games from 1970 to 2006.

Since the Kampala CHOGM in 2007, every country wishing to join the Commonwealth has been required explicitly to acknowledge Queen Elizabeth II as head of the association (something that was previously only an unspoken implication of membership).

There was a vivid reminder at the 2011 CHOGM in Perth of the close interest the Queen takes in the activities of the Commonwealth. Her speech at the opening ceremony contained a discreet but unmistakable invitation to Heads of Government to embrace Commonwealth reform and renewal. There were also reminders at Perth of the Queen's other major role: as sovereign of 16 Commonwealth Realms. Her visit to the city came at the end of a highly successful tour of Australia. On the fringes of CHOGM, UK Prime Minister David Cameron and Australian Prime Minister Julia Gillard convened a meeting of representatives of all the Realms to discuss changes to the laws of succession. This secured agreement in principle to two important changes: an end both to the male primogeniture rule for all descendants of the Prince of Wales, and to the rule that anyone marrying a Catholic would be barred from succession to the throne.

Complexities

The agreement reached in Perth points to the complex constitutional issues raised by the Commonwealth Realms. By the time the Queen ascended to the throne in 1952, there was a broad (although not yet universal) acceptance of the doctrine of the divisibility of the Crown: that she reigned over a series of quite separate Realms. It was certainly accepted that she was as much Queen of Canada or Tuvalu as she was of the United Kingdom. Yet in practice, the Queen plays a quite different role in the UK from the one she plays in the other Commonwealth Realms. She is, within the strictly limited sense of a constitutional monarch, an active participant in the British political system. She has access to a wide range of highly confidential UK government papers, and has regular meetings with the British prime minister, whom she is able to question on matters of particular concern. In certain circumstances – for example, following an inconclusive general election in which no party leader was able to command a working majority in Parliament – the Palace might play a role in the consultations leading to the construction of a new government.

In the case of the other Realms, the Queen does not have the same direct involvement. Her powers are exercised by a governor-general, usually a local figure nominated by the government of the country concerned. Although governors-general often provide the Palace with valuable information, they are under no obligation to consult London before making key decisions. As supporters of the current arrangements often point out, the system operates in ways very similar to some republics with non-executive presidents. It offers the Realms what in some cases can be an extremely valuable element of stability without restricting their autonomy.

Nevertheless, it is quite understandable that the phenomenon of a sovereign resident overseas remains controversial in many of the Realms. In January 2012, the new prime minister of Jamaica, Portia

Simpson Miller, who had recently won a landslide election victory, announced her intention to introduce a package of constitutional reforms that would lead to the country becoming a republic. The issue of the monarchy had become conflated with that of another residual constitutional link to the UK – the right of appeal to the Judicial Committee of the Privy Council. Supporters of the use of the death penalty had expressed resentment at what they saw as interference from London. Simpson Miller has vowed to end the right of appeal, making the Caribbean Court of Justice the highest authority in criminal matters. Although she has the necessary two-thirds majority to change the constitution, the republican issue will also have to be put to a referendum – a process that may delay any changes. Throughout the Queen's reign, Buckingham Palace has consistently made clear that any move towards a republic by a Commonwealth Realm is entirely a matter for the country concerned. The Queen's only concern is that change should take place by constitutional means.

Anyone familiar with the fortunes of the Crown in the various Commonwealth Realms over the last few decades will be aware that they can fluctuate quite rapidly, often in response to purely local factors. One could set alongside the case of Jamaica other examples which tend to suggest that support for the monarchy is enjoying something of a renaissance, and the Queen's position as Head of the Commonwealth arguably commands more general support across the Commonwealth in 2012 than it has for some decades. Like her role in the Commonwealth Realms, this is in many ways a personal accolade. Yet it is also perhaps true that the Headship has grown in substance in relationship to the Commonwealth itself. When in 2010 the Queen once again spoke at the UN, the fact that she did so in her capacity as Head of the Commonwealth did not attract controversy. There was a general recognition that the Commonwealth has a collective point of view, based on shared values, which the Queen was entitled to articulate as the symbol of the free association of its member states.

Notes

[1] Extract from *The Accession Proclamation*, Commonwealth Relations No. 21, The UK National Archives (hereafter TNA), DO 161/334.

[2] Minutes of Prime Ministers' Meeting, PMM (49) 4th meeting, 27 April 1949, TNA CAB 133/89.

PROFESSOR PHILIP MURPHY is Director of the Institute of Commonwealth Studies at the University of London. He was previously Professor of British and Commonwealth History at the University of Reading, UK, and has published extensively on decolonisation (particularly in Africa), intelligence liaison and the development of the modern Commonwealth. Professor Murphy is joint editor of the *Journal of Imperial & Commonwealth History*, and his book on the monarchy and the post-war Commonwealth is forthcoming from Oxford University Press.

Picking up the Commonwealth and using it

Daisy Cooper

The first Secretary-General, Arnold Smith, used to say: 'The Commonwealth is a tool to be picked up and used when the moment is right and the issue is appropriate.' But is that currently what's happening?

Less than 20 years ago, Commonwealth leaders understood how to use the Commonwealth. They regularly convened small 'Commonwealth Action Groups' of Heads of Government or high-ranking cabinet ministers to help solve country or global political challenges. Today they barely engage with the Commonwealth at any time other than the biennial Commonwealth Heads of Government Meetings (CHOGMs). The year 2012 will bring its own political challenges and with these come opportunities: opportunities for Commonwealth leaders to once again put themselves at the service of the international community under the auspices of the Commonwealth.

The 63-year history of the association in its modern form is littered with examples where individual Heads of Government, or a small group of them, have put the Commonwealth to work. The most famous example is the role that Commonwealth leaders played in helping to fight apartheid in South Africa. By 1985, the apartheid regime there was increasingly engulfed in crisis. All Commonwealth leaders except the UK's Margaret Thatcher supported sanctions against South Africa. At the 1985 CHOGM, a small group of Commonwealth Heads of Government, convened by Secretary-General Sir Shridath (Sonny) Ramphal, was able to debate with Thatcher and grind out an agreement.

In the Nassau Accord, leaders agreed to 'establish a small group of eminent persons to encourage through all practicable ways the evolution of that necessary process of political dialogue'. Eleven days later, back in London, Thatcher wrote confidentially to President P W Botha of South Africa. While she reported that the debate on South Africa was 'highly unpleasant', she urged Botha to receive the Eminent Persons Group (EPG) and allow it to make contact with various communities. The EPG itself included two former Heads of Government, and two former foreign ministers. Its final report quickly became a best seller.

More significant still was the political impact of the report. The political journalist Anthony Sampson called it 'a document that will change history'. At a special Commonwealth summit in 1986, six of seven Commonwealth leaders (Thatcher standing aside) agreed to a package of eleven sanctions, subsequently agreed by all Commonwealth leaders. Following this, and within a few days, the United States Senate voted by a large majority for a package of sanctions and the European Community to agree on further sanctions. The imposition of sanctions by the Nordic countries and

Japan followed.[1] This is a prime example of how Heads of Government, through the Commonwealth and with the support and direction of the Secretary-General, helped the people of a country deliver a historic transition from apartheid to democracy.

Range of initiatives

There were other Heads of Government initiatives too. For example, the 1983 New Delhi Commonwealth summit coincided with a new crisis in the Cyprus situation: the previous week the Turkish Cypriot authorities had carried out their long-standing threat to proclaim the independence of the island's northern sector which had been under their de facto control since Turkey had invaded in 1974. According to the 1985 Commonwealth Yearbook, 'Within three days, the [United Nations] Security Council had adopted Resolution 541 denouncing the Turkish Cypriot action as legally invalid and calling both for its non-recognition by other states and for its immediate withdrawal. In New Delhi Heads of Government unreservedly endorsed the Security Council's stand, and set up a Commonwealth Action Group to assist in securing compliance with Resolution 541. Comprising five countries, together with the Secretary-General, the group met at Heads of Government level immediately after the Delhi Summit and agreed to try, through quiet diplomacy both at the UN and in the relevant capitals, to assist the UN Secretary-General's good offices mission to help bring about a just solution for Cyprus.'[2]

At a later date, the Commonwealth Secretary-General invited all Heads of Government to consider supportive action on an individual basis, including approaches to the Government of Turkey. While, on this occasion, the Commonwealth's efforts did not bring about much significant change, it is still another example of how leaders have sought to use the Commonwealth to help solve political challenges.

Another successful example of leaders using the Commonwealth occurred at the 1993 CHOGM in Cyprus. There, leaders issued the Limassol Statement on the Uruguay Round of trade talks warning that: 'The time that remains for successful conclusion of the Round is now very short. Only 55 days remain and we are therefore despatching a Ministerial mission to selected capitals to call upon key participants and to urge them to negotiate positively and flexibly to reach final agreement.' High-ranking cabinet ministers and representatives from four Commonwealth countries, supported by the Commonwealth Deputy Secretary-General, conducted an eight-day mission to Geneva, Brussels, Paris, Bonn, Washington, Tokyo and London. They impressed on key governments and other officials the urgent need for the Uruguay Round of talks to be successfully concluded by 15 December. As a result, the talks did conclude, and with the signing of a 'historical deal'.[3]

Over the years, Commonwealth leaders have sought to solve problems around border disputes, invasions, deadlocks in multilateral negotiations, and supporting global efforts against a despotic apartheid regime. They have done so by:

- using small groups of leaders and high-ranking cabinet ministers

- appointing an active Secretary-General who convenes groups of leaders

- holding special summits, and

- issuing action-oriented communiqués.

In essence, Heads of Government and high-ranking ministers have historically taken action on international issues and have used the Commonwealth as a vehicle through which to do so.

Lost opportunities

Since 2000, Commonwealth commentators have bemoaned a number of lost opportunities for similar initiatives. For example, 2005 was an important year for international development commitments: in July, the G8 made unprecedented funding pledges to fight climate change and help African development (arising from the Commission for Africa) and in September, the UN held an 'MDG+5' global summit. The November CHOGM could have added an important voice to the debate, with its strong contingent of both African and small developing states, but instead focused on the theme of the 'digital divide'. The 2007 report of the Commonwealth Commission on Respect and Understanding, Civil Paths to Peace, was intellectually ground-breaking (for its proposals for practical action based on the idea of multiple identities) at a time when the UN was talking about a clash of civilisations (namely Christianity and Islam, and 'the West and the rest') – yet Commonwealth leaders and institutions failed to champion the report's ideas. In 2008, Commonwealth leaders were seized with reform of international institutions in the wake of the global economic crisis; a group of 11 Commonwealth leaders met in London in June, and a special summit was called in September. However, the initiative was effectively stillborn for lack of political will: having highlighted the importance of 'reform efforts being inclusive, so that all states irrespective of size and strength have the opportunity to participate and contribute to global discussions on the issue', leaders did no more than ask the Commonwealth Secretary-General to take forward their reform agenda, rather than take forward a political consensus themselves.[4]

At the 2009 CHOGM, leaders agreed the Port of Spain Climate Change Consensus calling for an internationally legally binding agreement and a Launch Fund, just weeks before the UN Climate Change conference in Copenhagen. The attendance of President Nicolas Sarkozy of France, Prime Minister Lars Løkke Rasmussen of Denmark and UN Secretary-General Ban Ki-moon further raised the profile of the agreement. However, following the agreement, Commonwealth leaders failed to establish any sort of group to advance the consensus in key capitals around the world (unlike the ministerial mission to close the Uruguay trade round negotiations some 16 years before); indeed, the Commonwealth Secretary-General didn't even attend the Copenhagen summit! Two years later it happened again. The 2011 Perth CHOGM took place just one month before the UN Climate Change conference in Durban – this time, Heads of Government didn't even release a standalone statement on climate change.

That leaders can use the Commonwealth to advance international negotiations has always been understood. Indeed, it is central to the Commonwealth's current reform agenda. In 2011, an Eminent Persons Group (EPG) was established to develop options for reform to reinvigorate the Commonwealth association. Five of their recommendations[5] call on Commonwealth leaders to act themselves, and two of these call specifically for 'high-level' missions such as the ones described earlier. Moreover, speaking at a meeting of the Round Table in Perth at the time of the 2011 CHOGM, in a speech titled 'A Courageous Commonwealth', former Prime Minister of Australia (and member of the 1986 EPG to South Africa) Malcolm Fraser warned:

> If the Commonwealth is to show vision and leadership for the future it will be because significant leaders of the Commonwealth believe in it and inspire it.

> Government leaders need to be prepared to drive it and make it a significant part of their foreign policy and of their international cooperation. The Commonwealth is much more than a CHOGM every couple of years.

> The Secretary-General and his team, and the Heads of Government or the Heads of State themselves, all need to believe in the institution and its capacity to contribute greatly to a better world.[6]

2012: an opportunity for revival?

The global political challenges of 2012 cannot be underestimated:

- there is an ongoing economic crisis

- the 2008–2012 Kyoto Protocol, which sets binding targets to reduce greenhouse gas emissions, expires, and

- the Doha Trade Round faces collapse after 11 years of fruitless talks.

In Cyprus, the scheduled UN meetings of leaders in the divided country end in January 2012, and Sri Lanka – which stands accused of war crimes – will embark on reconciliation efforts after nearly 30 years of a civil war ahead of hosting the 2013 CHOGM. South Sudan, which has expressed interest in joining the Commonwealth, is facing deepening dispute over oil revenue sharing, cross-border conflict and a looming famine; as some Commonwealth members are encouraging a formal application, others are asking whether it can remain a viable state. Any and all of these situations could benefit from the constructive engagement of a group of Commonwealth Heads of Government.

Conclusion

The 2011 Perth CHOGM promised to deliver a 'renewed Commonwealth', yet it achieved very little. In June 2012, many Commonwealth leaders will gather in London, UK, to celebrate Queen Elizabeth II's Diamond Jubilee, marking 60 years of her reign of 16 Commonwealth countries, and 60 years as Head of the Commonwealth. There is an opportunity for the Commonwealth to convene a Special Summit. There is no need for it to overshadow the Jubilee; rather, it would demonstrate the Commonwealth's political relevance. David Cameron, Julia Gillard, Manmohan Singh, Goodluck Jonathan, Kamla Persad-Bissessar or any other leader must be prepared to take the first step, and the Secretary-General must encourage them too.

The Commonwealth's role as a political vehicle was understood from the outset and will be central to its future. Looking forward, the Commonwealth will only ever be as effective as its leaders want it to be. The first Secretary-General, Arnold Smith, used to say: 'The Commonwealth is a tool to be picked up and used when the moment is right and the issue is appropriate.' In 2012, Heads of Government must pick up the Commonwealth and use it.

Notes

[1] This summary is based on the text of a background paper prepared for the 'Negotiating with apartheid: the mission of the Commonwealth Eminent Persons Group 1986' Witness Seminar, Institute of Commonwealth Studies, University of London, 13 June 2011, by Stuart Mole, Senior Research Fellow, Institute of Commonwealth Studies.

[2] *Commonwealth Yearbook* 1985, pages 7–8.

[3] Chief Emeka Anyaoku, quote in 'Commonwealth Secretary-General on how to ensure all countries will benefit from Uruguay Round', Commonwealth News Release 93/57, 16 December 1993.

[4] See www.thecommonwealth.org/news/34580/34581/183739/250908reforminstitutions.htm.

[5] 'A Commonwealth of the People: Time for Urgent Reform', the Report of the Commonwealth Eminent Persons Group to Commonwealth Heads of Government. Recommendations 27, 33, 36, 41, and 59. Available www.thecommonwealth.org/files/241620/FileName/EminentPersonsGroupReport.pdf.

[6] Available www.moot.org.uk/pdf/Talk-2011-Fraser-CHOGM-courageous-Commonwealth.pdf.

DAISY COOPER joined the Commonwealth Advisory Bureau as Director in January 2011. Prior to this, she was the Senior Strategic Planning Officer at the Commonwealth Secretariat, spearheading major change management processes. Additionally, she is a director and editorial advisory board member of *The Round Table* (the Commonwealth Journal of International Affairs).

Reform in the Commonwealth

Stephen Cutts, Commonwealth Assistant Secretary-General

A former Deputy Secretary-General in the Organisation for Economic Co-operation and Development (OECD), where I used to work, was very fond of quoting Yogi Berra, a famous exponent of that most un-Commonwealth of sports, baseball. One of his quirky sayings was: 'The future ain't what it used to be.' Perhaps that is a good place to start in an article about Commonwealth reform – what needs to change in terms of what we do, how we do it and who does it.

About 18 months ago, I was asked to address the newly formed Eminent Persons Group (EPG). I used the opportunity to set out a bold vision of what my senior management colleagues think the Commonwealth could and should be: a powerful association underpinned by a family of intergovernmental organisations that are valued and used by members to take forward international issues within our remit. In an increasingly crowded field of international actors, the Commonwealth needs to be an association with a voice, and a reputation for quality and impact. I think a similar vision for the Commonwealth is central to the thrust of the EPG's final report.

While it was clear that some proposals from the EPG were going to be highly contentious (especially the creation of the post of Commissioner for Democracy, the Rule of Law and Human Rights), many of us approached the Perth CHOGM in October 2011 anticipating broad agreement to the bulk of the EPG recommendations. With hindsight, perhaps we should have recognised that dealing with such a large number of often fundamental proposals would take more time. Hence, we shouldn't be surprised that most of the more significant proposals have been referred for further consideration, whether fundamentally or in the detail. However, this delay does not necessarily mean that anything has been lost as a result of this process – indeed, provided we prepare the meetings properly, an opportunity for more careful analysis of some of these proposals may well improve the final product.

What we do

On what we do, much has been said and written about whether the Commonwealth should speak out more clearly and decisively in defence of its values, or whether this would impede the work it does behind the scenes, assisting countries experiencing difficulties. The Commonwealth Ministerial Action Group (CMAG) reforms and the debate about the Commissioner for Democracy, the Rule of Law and Human Rights, and the debate about the role of the Secretary-General in this regard have received extensive exposure. Suffice it to say that, in light of the CMAG reforms agreed by CHOGM, and even before the proposals concerning the Commissioner are determined, stakeholders will be watching intently to see what impact Perth has made.

The problem around what we do, however, goes far deeper – it concerns the Commonwealth's current broad scope of activity. While the Secretariat is the largest intergovernmental arm of the Commonwealth, it is still very small for an intergovernmental organisation (IGO), comprising 300 people and a total budget of less than £50 million per annum. For an IGO, it is tiny. Yet, with not many more than 100 professional and diplomatic staff working in programmatic posts, we try to cover a *huge* array of areas.

The goal set by the Heads of Government for the Secretary-General is to develop a more focused programme, so that we work only in areas where the Commonwealth has a clear comparative advantage by virtue of its diverse membership, shared legal and political systems and values and track record of success. We simply don't have the resources to do otherwise. Heads have asked the Secretary-General to retire work where necessary to create more focus in our new Strategic Plan. This process needs to result in us doing fewer things ourselves, but with demonstrably greater impact. In developing strategic partnerships and using Commonwealth networks work doesn't necessarily have to be abandoned; the aim should be to ensure that the needs of members are met even where the Commonwealth Secretariat isn't the primary actor.

Given the current broad range of activity, it is perhaps unsurprising that we have struggled to deliver on the results-based management (RBM) requirement that we report on the results and impact of our work. We have been trying to do too many things, responding to too many demands across too many areas, to spend the time needed to plan our projects carefully in a way that we can show they are delivering results, a process that should involve identifying the right indicators, monitoring and reporting on progress and then learning lessons for the future.

Focusing on impact – or RBM – isn't a difficult concept. It simply means that whatever we do as an organisation should be driven by the difference we are trying to make, and be monitored and assessed accordingly. In today's world, our claims about how much benefit the Commonwealth brings as a 'great global good', or saying 'we produce great bang for the buck' is simply no longer sufficient by itself – we need evidence. The Commonwealth is primarily funded with taxpayers' money – much of it coming from some of the least developed countries on this planet. If we cannot show impact, we have no business using taxpayers' money for that activity. And the fear is that if we don't make that call now moving forward, our funders will make that decision for us by steadily withdrawing their funding. We have the technical elements in place: a project planning and management information system, ARTEMIS, was rolled out in 2011, and we have in place a transparent, robust and impartial system for evaluating our work. Finally, we have also recruited an RBM expert to a substantive post who is actively advising the Secretariat on improving the design of its projects for results and working towards standardising the processes related to monitoring and evaluation. But as noted earlier, we need to be more focused to demonstrate the impact of our work.

So, in which direction should we move? Yogi Berra is also quoted as saying: 'When you come to a fork in the road, take it!' The process for determining the right 'road' to take is starting, with consultations internally, and between the Secretary-General and high commissioners.

How we do it

The next challenge is around the 'how' we work. The Department for International Development (DFID), the UK's aid agency, broadly criticised the Secretariat in its Multilateral Aid Review just over a year ago for two reasons – the very broad work programme (as discussed earlier) and our apparent inability to demonstrate real impact save in a handful of areas, but also our weaknesses in our corporate governance systems. On the latter point, I am pleased that we have made remarkable advances in the past year, and that these have been acknowledged by management, our Audit Committee and our members. In this regard, I am pleased that we can report a number of significant achievements:

- implementation of a top-down planning and budgeting process which aligns resources with priorities and has, over the past three years, facilitated significant budget reallocations

- implementation of International Public Sector Accounting Standards (IPSAS), which is the gold standard for international organisations

- finalisation of a new procurement policy

- agreement to a strategic risk register and risk management policy

- development of an anti-fraud policy

- consistent and fair application of human resource policies, and now a new staff handbook, reflecting best practice in our sector

- changes to our pay and benefits to bring our system more into line with international norms and to provide a modest improvement in our competitiveness for international talent (although more needs to be done – see the text that follows)

- a thorough review of our internal control framework, resulting in weaknesses being addressed and new financial regulations being developed, as well as improvements in our provision of financial information

- recruitment of a 'Big 4' company (KPMG) as our internal audit partner

- the selection of another 'Big 4' firm (Deloitte) as our external auditor which has required additional testing and reassurances to ensure robustness of our financial statements (and the qualification placed on the Secretariat's accounts a couple of years ago has not been repeated).

This may not be the most salivating list of achievements for a *Commonwealth Yearbook*, but robust internal governance is vital for ensuring that our members have the confidence to continue investing in the institution, knowing their contributions are being used efficiently, effectively and are delivering value for money.

More needs to be done, but the progress is impressive, as the Secretary-General proudly noted to Heads in Perth. However, the 'how' has a different dimension. The extent to which the Secretariat can be a meaningful provider of direct assistance in areas where there are other agencies doing the same, only with a more focused mandate and vastly more resources, is being questioned. A greater focus on advocacy and consensus-building, and using the Commonwealth's political convening power to overcome entrenched deadlocks on major development issues, might be a better use of some of our resources in future. We need to be able to generate positive news stories about the impact we are having through our substantive work.

Who does it

Finally, the challenge of 'who' does our work. The Commonwealth Secretariat is the primary intergovernmental organisation of the Commonwealth, and is looked to by leaders to deliver their mandates. As a knowledge organisation, it needs to be staffed with a high quality professional workforce to deliver a new Commonwealth that has strengthened networks, heightened profile and is delivering greater impact. Yet, the remuneration package offered is woefully short of that made available by other intergovernmental organisations, including the UN which is usually considered the poorest paying of these bodies. We need to improve our internal policies and incentives for staff, but until we can recruit and retain the excellence we need by offering a competitive package, a major structural barrier to improved performance will remain.

The EPG recommendations address all of these points, and more. Hence, going back to the theme of this article – the future of the Commonwealth – I would argue that 2012 is a vital year, during which we must seize the reform momentum of the EPG and the new Strategic Plan, to reshape the position of the Commonwealth, and its institutions, and refocus their efforts to where they can and should be making a positive difference. The procedure for taking forward reform, through senior officials, a ministerial task force, foreign ministers and finally Heads, has been mapped out, together with an ambitious timetable. But this is a process that must deliver.

A final piece of advice from Yogi Berra: 'Always go to other people's funerals, otherwise they won't come to yours.' At the end of 2012, we should be looking at a revitalised association, unarguably fit for purpose for the 21st century, with any serious talk about the growing irrelevance of the Commonwealth, or its imminent demise or slow death, consigned to the past.

STEVE CUTTS is Commonwealth Assistant Secretary-General for Corporate Affairs with oversight responsibilities for the Commonwealth Secretariat's Corporate Services Division, its Strategic Planning and Evaluation Division, and Human Resources.

The Commonwealth of Nations: private club or global force for good?

Senator Hugh D Segal CM

The challenge faced by the Perth Commonwealth Heads of Government Meeting (CHOGM) was clear: how to embrace reforms vital to the Commonwealth's meaningful survival within the context of a decision-averse consensual deliberative structure – always the challenge when reform is necessary. And how to do so in a way that advanced the Commonwealth's role in the world as a force for good, rather than a drifting talk shop with little connection to, or impact upon, the realities faced by its 2.2 billion inhabitants.

The Eminent Persons Group (EPG) report commissioned by these same Heads of Government at Port of Spain in 2009 became the focal point of this challenge. The EPG recommendations were premised upon the simple notion that an activist-engaged Commonwealth, on development, human rights, poverty reduction, technical assistance, democracy and rule of law is a preventative voluntary association that mitigates against intolerance, discrimination and violence – something the world desperately and still needs.

I would be less than frank were I to say that all went swimmingly at Perth. By Saturday, 29 October 2011, mid-day, Heads had dealt with exactly two of our 106 recommendations – accepting one on the Charter with public consultation input to follow and assigning the recommendation on a Commissioner for Rule of Law, Democracy and Human Rights to a joint Commonwealth Secretariat and Commonwealth Ministerial Action Group (CMAG) consideration this spring (2012). This was consistent with where foreign ministers had been on Wednesday and Thursday. Four things transpired on the Friday and Saturday that advanced the cause of a relevant and engaged Commonwealth.

The Chair, Prime Minister Gillard, was frustrated in her desire to publish the EPG report upon assuming the Chair from the Prime Minister of Trinidad and Tobago, who had recommended, as Chair-in-Office, to delay its release until CHOGM so it could be considered more intensely before it was released. When various countries would not let the new Chair-in-Office publish the report, the media uproar became a self-generating force creating its own pressures.

For the 31 recommendations that were approved, and the 12 approved in principle and sent for costing, we have one person to thank. Queen Elizabeth II, the Head of the Commonwealth, formally opened the Perth CHOGM, after two days of foreign ministers meeting. Her words, always judicious and clear were precise:

I should like to thank the Commonwealth Eminent Persons' Group for their work, and I look forward to hearing the outcome of discussion of their recommendations. And I wish Heads of Government well in agreeing further reforms that respond boldly to the aspirations of today and that keep the Commonwealth fresh and fit for tomorrow. In these deliberations we should not forget that this is an association not only of governments but also of peoples. That is what makes it so relevant in this age of global information and communication.

Her Majesty did, as she always does, raise the tone, remind everyone about what matters and, above all, symbolise and personify the level of service to others and to a greater good and cause that must motivate all governments and international associations such as the Commonwealth. Her words were not lost on the media or on the delegates.

The third catalyst was the unwavering leadership of Commonwealth pillars like Canada's Prime Minister, Stephen Harper, Prime Minister Cameron of the UK, and strong and engaged leaders and ministers from places like Malta, Ghana, Jamaica, Cyprus, Mauritius, Malaysia, New Zealand and others. As well, the unanimous approval of new and more robust terms of engagement for the CMAG, proposed by the outgoing membership under the sentinel leadership of Ghana's foreign minister, was a shining ray of light at Perth, the benefits of which are already being seen in the engaged and focused CMAG involvement after the recent precipitous change of government in Maldives.

Mid-day Saturday, just before lunch, the EPG held a full media conference under the firm hand of Sir Ronald Sanders of Guyana, who is a journalist and former diplomat himself. Our Chairman, former Malaysian Prime Minister Badawi, former Australian High Court Justice Michael Kirby, Sir Malcolm Rifkind MP, a former UK Foreign Secretary, Samuel Kavuma, a young and dynamic Commonwealth Youth Forum leader from Uganda, Emmanuel Akwetey, CEO of the Ghana Centre for the Study of Democracy, and your humble servant held forth. We attacked the non-release of our report, the lack of action to that moment on 104 of our 106 recommendations, the 'private club' feel of the meeting so far, the fact that, as Her Majesty had said, this was a Commonwealth of the people, not a private club for the Secretary-General and Commonwealth leaders.

After the EPG lunched with the Heads at their retreat, they got down to business on the EPG recommendations and put their foreign ministers back to work as well. In the end, they accepted 31 recommendations outright. These include: enhancing the Secretary-General's mandate and role so that the Secretary-General can and will speak out publicly regarding the Commonwealth's core priorities as set out in the 2009 Affirmation; that the

Secretary-General develop a clear strategy relating to networking between member governments and the capacity-building of small states; providing advice and support to small states in avoiding unsustainable debt; having Commonwealth G20 members advocate for the Commonwealth perspective; work further on climate change; assist with the development of a constitution for the Commonwealth Youth Programme; confronting the challenges and strengthening Commonwealth advocacy relating to the needs of women and their issues; ensuring that the issue of HIV/AIDS is prominent on the agendas of all relevant Commonwealth meetings; considering the sharing of corporate functions between the Commonwealth Secretariat and Commonwealth Foundation; putting in place a plan for the Secretariat to co-ordinate work with other Commonwealth institutions to draw on expertise from within rather than using expensive external consultants; reviewing the governance of the Commonwealth Business Council to make its membership inclusive; recommending that the Secretary-General consult the Commonwealth Media Group regarding a programme to help better distribute the Commonwealth's message to its constituents; and preserving the integrity of the Commonwealth Games and using the Games as an instrument for peace and development.

Recommendations that were tentatively accepted but submitted for review of possible cost implications include: the reform of the Secretariat's structures and systems; the establishment of High-Level Advocacy Missions to engage in dialogue with the International Monetary Fund, World Trade Organization and World Bank; the competent staffing of the Secretariat's Office in Geneva for small states; the establishment of a mechanism for tracking the responses of international financial institutions for consideration at finance ministers and CHOGM meetings; the renewing of Commonwealth governments' commitment to the Iwokrama Rainforest programme by providing core funding; the maintenance of a roster of professionals who could be called on when disasters occur in Commonwealth countries; the establishment of national youth councils for their input in national policy development; the Secretary-General's co-operation and work with United Nations bodies such as UNAIDS, the WHO and UNDP to develop joint programmes in the prevention and treatment of HIV/AIDS; the authorisation of the Secretary-General to mount high-level missions to UN bodies to advocate a review of any criteria that may disqualify vulnerable countries from accessing the Global Fund to Fight HIV/AIDS based on their per capita income; and the preparation by the Secretary-General of a draft plan relating to the Secretariat's work and its future, making the Secretariat more productive and significant.

The recommendations that were rejected outright include providing space at foreign ministers meetings for dialogue with representatives of civil society on matters of relevance or urgency;

recommending that ministers meet outside of scheduled meetings on high-priority or urgent items; abolishing the arrangement of Chair-in-Office and Troika, and return to the pre-existing system; designating by Heads a Minister of State responsible for Commonwealth Affairs; and requesting that the Commonwealth Games Federation pay the Secretariat a modest royalty for the use of the Commonwealth 'brand' to assist the Secretariat finance sports for peace and development.

Others were approved in principle, contingent on costing by the Secretariat in co-operation with the Commonwealth Board of Governors; and others have been approved pending more information.

Half a loaf? Yes, but it was a nutritious high fibre and protein loaf to begin with, so some digestion time is not unrealistic. Some matters, like the Charter, will be dispersed for consultation and review this spring (Canada has already had Senate Foreign Affairs Committee hearings on the draft charter).

We must shine a light on the full value-for-money proposition of the Secretariat in London. This is not about waste – there are some great people who work very hard there. It is about being fit for purpose, which requires change. We are either on the cusp of a great transformative modernisation of a Commonwealth of the People, or the high grass will preserve a private club at Marlborough House that faces extinction and irrelevance.

We can have a Commonwealth of principle and values, enduring as a force for good and arguing for more education, less poverty, and more development and democracy, all of which are mutually reinforcing; a Commonwealth where forced marriage, negative discrimination and intolerance against minorities, linguistic, ethnic, gay or otherwise is discouraged and diminished; a Commonwealth where the rule of law, democracy and human rights is the surging trend.

Inaction, silence and complacency are not the right instruments here. Continuing pressure for change is the right answer.

SENATOR HUGH D SEGAL CM is Canada's Special Envoy For Commonwealth Renewal and was a member of the Commonwealth Eminent Persons Group. Senator Segal was appointed to the Canadian Senate in 2005 and has served as Chair of the Senate Foreign Affairs Committee. He served as Chief of Staff to the Prime Minister of Canada, Associate Cabinet Secretary (Ontario) for Federal-Provincial Affairs and Policies and Priorities, and Legislative Assistant to the Leader of the Opposition (Ottawa). He was President of the independent Institute for Research on Public Policy.

People, power and the new global politics

Dr Dhananjayan Sriskandarajah

In Tunisia early in 2011 a fruit vendor set himself on fire in an act of desperation and defiance so singularly tragic, it was hard to foresee the many dramatic consequences that would follow. But follow they did.

With no ballot box to trust, people in Tunisia, Egypt, Libya, Syria, Yemen and Bahrain turned to the streets. They demanded a voice and insisted on being heard. The year 2011 would become the year of insurrection, the year of the protester. Demonstrations spanned the globe, from London to Swaziland, and Oaxaca to Wall Street. Technology provided information and momentum, but it wasn't Twitter or Facebook at the heart of these protests, it was people. People tired of the imperiousness of their leaders, fed up with the fecklessness of international institutions in dealing with them.

In a year of significant global transformation, the power and primacy of people could not be more visible. Across the world – and in many Commonwealth countries – individuals at once occupied the political space they craved and seized the moral authority they deserved.

Globalisation and technology have only increased that individual influence. But well before the advent of social media, the Commonwealth recognised the potential and power of civil society as international actors, the defenders of hope at the heart of the Commonwealth.

Of course, some Commonwealth members are not themselves paragons of democracy, but the institution was built on shared principles and values that aspire for all its 2.2 billion citizens a democratic voice.

The events of this past year have served to reinforce the knowledge that global governance has new paramount actors. It is 'civil society' – individuals, groups, professional associations and non-governmental organisations – that increasingly demonstrates the energy, innovation and influence in the Commonwealth and across the world.

The foundation of Commonwealth civil society

The Commonwealth project was – and remains – an unprecedented experiment in international co-operation, not just between political actors, but also with civil society.

When the Secretariat, our Commonwealth version of an administrative civil service, was officially established at Marlborough House in 1965, the Commonwealth Foundation was created at the same time, designed to foster links between Commonwealth citizens and strengthen the association's burgeoning people-to-people networks.

By creating this novel kind of institution, Heads of Government displayed an early recognition of the civic. It was a very progressive act at the time – predating buzzwords like 'NGOs' and 'civil society' – appreciating the importance of non-governmental actors to the success of the Commonwealth.

Indeed, some Commonwealth civil society and professional organisations are older than the institution itself: the Commonwealth Parliamentary Association held its centenary in 2011; the Association of Commonwealth Universities will mark its in 2013.

Friends: mobilising the Commonwealth network

In Australian Prime Minister Julia Gillard's speech at the opening ceremony of the 2011 Commonwealth People's Forum she said: 'When people call for change and ask where it will come from, we already know. It will come from us.'

Gillard acknowledged the potential for great action and influence in the crowd who had gathered that day. And to adapt to the changing power dynamics she implicitly referenced, the Royal Commonwealth Society (RCS) has reimagined its international network, partnering with Friends of the Commonwealth to form an online community of information and action.

Sir Colin Shepherd, Chair of Friends of the Commonwealth, said: 'Friends won't be just a one-way channel used to transmit Commonwealth news; rather as a network it will enable the active involvement of members in Commonwealth affairs and

projects. Together we can realise the potential of Friends of the Commonwealth, ensuring that "Friends" is a modern, flexible tool with scope to influence and deliver.'

Peter Kellner, Chair of the RCS, sees the creation of Friends as the moment 'civil society grew teeth' and likened the network to 'a virtual Tahrir Square'.

The internet age has created a world of competing narratives, but Friends hopes to become the coherent voice for a passionate but disorganised Commonwealth civil society – becoming an accessible, accurate and active network of people who want to make a significant impact on international and national affairs, linking Commonwealth people to each other, and linking the Commonwealth to the world.

The Commonwealth Foundation now has a budget of approximately £3.4 million, with voluntary membership maintained by 47 of the 54 Commonwealth countries. £1 million is dispersed in grants each year to Commonwealth accredited bodies and wider civil society. These grants are not always large, but they can be catalytic.

The centrality of a strong and robust civil society is necessary to buttress good governance across the Commonwealth. And in order to ensure that tradition continues, the Foundation will relaunch in 2012, after a critical renewal process that will strengthen it and allow it to support organisations across the Commonwealth, adding the civic flavour so vital for contemporary global politics.

Perth 2011 and the People's Charter

That civic flavour has been an important ingredient at official Commonwealth meetings for years. Since 1991, civil society has assembled in the shadows of Commonwealth Heads of Government Meetings (CHOGMs) in various iterations of what we now call the Commonwealth People's Forum (CPF).

Another innovation of the Commonwealth, the CPF is a major consultative opportunity for an ever-widening network of civil society organisations. And while the forum itself provides a valuable arena for delegates to debate issues of international importance, perhaps the most compelling symbol of contemporary co-operation between Commonwealth governments and civil society comes during the foreign ministers' engagement session.

The informality and amity nurtured among leaders at their biennial retreats – a CHOGM tradition since 1973 – could also be seen in Perth at the round table between Commonwealth foreign ministers and civil society representatives. Just as member states, irrespective of size and power, are considered equal in the Commonwealth arena, so too are civil society and foreign ministers at their dialogue session.

Perhaps it was that very feeling of equality that allowed each group to speak so frankly with the other that afternoon in October 2011.

Civil society members implored action on a host of key development issues, from indigenous rights and the rights of people with disabilities, to progress on HIV/AIDS, reform of international financial architecture and the rights and safety of lesbian, gay, bisexual, transgender and intersex (LGBTI) communities across the Commonwealth.

When foreign ministers were given the opportunity to speak, the variety of topics discussed rivalled that of their colleagues across the table. Comments were made – and tensions revealed – about transparency and accountability in civil society, the controversial Eminent Persons Group (EPG) recommendation for a Commissioner for Democracy, Human Rights and the Rule of Law and the decision to delay the release of the EPG's report.

While there may not have been universal agreement on development approaches or priorities around the table, one item that garnered swift consensus was the drafting of a Commonwealth Charter.

We know the best democracies in the world are achieved through partnerships between government, civil society and business. And at a CHOGM where some of the most potent recommendations for reform would eventually be deemed 'inappropriate for adoption', the Charter represented an important opportunity for the Commonwealth to return to its founding principles and rearticulate its values and aspirations in the modern world.

From the Singapore and Harare Declarations to the Latimer House Principles, there are countless documents and declarations outlining the values and principles of the Commonwealth; but over time, this has led to confusion about what the Commonwealth actually stands for. Dubbed the 'People's Charter' by some, the Commonwealth Charter – drafted by the EPG and set to go through public consultations in 2012 – may very well become a new Commonwealth contract between governments and civil society.

The Charter is a rare opportunity – a democratic exercise – meant to capture the public imagination and allow civil society to demonstrate what they believe to be the true meaning of Commonwealth membership today.

Indeed, in Her Majesty's remarks to leaders in Perth, the Queen as Head of the Commonwealth reminded the audience that 'this is an association not only of governments but also of peoples'. The Charter could do a great deal to clarify the association's purpose and reclaim some of its legitimacy and relevance among Commonwealth citizens.

Conclusion

This group of 54 nations is fundamentally different from other intergovernmental organisations. Instead of being bound by regional proximity, treaties or accords, the Commonwealth is joined by a shared commitment to democracy and development. Beyond the ties of history, language and institutions, this family of nations endures through the pursuit of common goals and aspirations. And it is the Commonwealth's expansive network of civil society organisations and professional bodies that reinforce and strengthen its intergovernmental framework.

This past year was an especially poignant – and incredibly violent – example of the power of the civic, the restless hope that democracy inspires and the ability of individuals to transform world affairs.

In the Commonwealth, civil society organisations have grown in force and number over the last century, but even in this voluntary association, real democracy is not guaranteed. We must take every opportunity to deepen democratic values across the Commonwealth and make the political process more inclusive and meaningful for all of our citizens.

In a world of increasing complexity, of global instability and widespread unrest, true strength lies beyond classic state–state relationships. In the Commonwealth, civil society has claimed not only enormous power, but has also come to embody the enormous potential of the entire institution.

If the Commonwealth hopes to survive in a crowded marketplace of international actors, it is civil society that can translate its values from words on a page into policy and action. It is time for civil society to once more revisit the Commonwealth's initial promise, and summon the courage to uphold it.

DR DHANANJAYAN (DANNY) SRISKANDARAJAH has been Director of the Royal Commonwealth Society (RCS) since January 2009. He spent 2011 on secondment as Interim Director of the Commonwealth Foundation. Prior to joining the RCS, he was a researcher and commentator on migration and economic development.

Engagement with the Commonwealth: a report on Zimbabwe

Richard Bourne

The Commonwealth was crucial in the achievement of a recognised independence for Zimbabwe in 1980. But the ZANU–PF government of Robert Mugabe left the Commonwealth in 2003 for much the same reason that the white minority government of South Africa left in 1961 – that it could no longer abide its principles for democracy, the rule of law and fundamental human rights. Now, nearly a decade later, other questions arise. Can the Commonwealth play any part in Zimbabwe's recovery? And when might a Zimbabwe government wish to rejoin?

It is sobering to be reminded of the efforts that the Commonwealth, and neighbouring states – particularly Zambia and Tanzania – made to support Zimbabwean nationalists in the run-up to the independence elections of 1980. Lusaka was bombed by the white Rhodesian air force and 25 Commonwealth countries provided some 6,000 awards to black Zimbabweans to help them prepare for nationhood. Although not formally part of the Lancaster House talks in late 1979, it was Sonny Ramphal (the Commonwealth Secretary-General) and the then Frontline States which kept on track the difficult negotiations to end a brutal civil war.

After Lancaster House it was Commonwealth troops from several countries who managed camps for the guerrillas during the run-up to the elections, and 63 observers who certified that Robert Mugabe's ZANU (Zimbabwe African National Union) party had won. After Mugabe became prime minister it was not just traditional donor countries that assisted in reconstruction. Nigeria helped to create a national news agency and Pakistan helped to rebuild an air force.

The contrast with what has happened since Zimbabwe's departure in 2003 is enormous. For six years the country was ignored in Heads' biennial meetings. Initially, the Commonwealth Foundation (the intergovernmental body tasked to assist civil society links) was prohibited by its governors from making Zimbabwe-related grants. Changes have only been made gingerly since. Following a meeting in Kampala in Uganda organised by the Royal Commonwealth Society in 2007, addressed by Morgan Tsvangirai who was then leader of the opposition MDC (Movement for Democratic Change) but is now prime minister, attitudes began to alter.

In 2009, following a catastrophic nadir for Zimbabwe the year before, Commonwealth leaders applauded the 'Global Political Agreement' which ushered in an inclusive government combining ZANU–PF (Patriotic Front) and the two factions of the MDC. They said much the same at CHOGM, Perth, in 2011. But in reality they were deferring to a slow-moving conciliation process facilitated by President Jacob Zuma of South Africa on behalf of the Southern African Development Community (SADC). Meanwhile the Commonwealth Foundation aided a committee of Commonwealth bodies in London, which managed to bring five young Zimbabwean professionals for study tours in the UK and South Africa. A sixth was unable to come, arrested on false charges for attending a discussion in Harare of the Arab Spring.

Meanwhile Zimbabwe itself is making only a slow recovery in its economy, and its politics are still log-jammed. Following the land invasions, which began imposingly in 2000, the first decade of the twenty-first century saw:

- hyperinflation and a final collapse of the Zimbabwe dollar

- three-quarters of the population, at worst, dependent on food aid

- around one-quarter to one-third of citizens moving abroad

- a life expectancy decrease from around 60 years to 34–45 years

- severe disruption of education, health and basic services such as power, water and rubbish collection, and

- security of individuals threatened by political intimidation, torture and ruthless government campaigns such as Marambatsvina ('clearing out the rubbish'), which destroyed up to 700,000 homes, affecting 2.4 million people, in 2005.

The compromise 'unity government', which was set up in February 2009 after the disastrous second presidential round the previous year, has stabilised the economy and social services but remains dysfunctional. ZANU–PF has retained the security ministries and control of the recently discovered diamond fields at Marange. Threats of 'indigenisation' have discouraged foreign investors and only a minority of Zimbabweans have paid employment. More newspapers have been allowed on to the streets, but ZANU has retained control of broadcasting.

Impact and developments

All of this has impacted on a number of Commonwealth countries, especially South Africa, which is home to the largest number of Zimbabwean exiles. In 2005 the government tried to expel 150,000 Zimbabweans, and xenophobia has been a factor in township riots. Zimbabweans, often better educated than black South Africans, have been working at all levels, from farm labourer to chief executive officer positions in large firms. The UK has been returning asylum seekers since the coalition government took power in 2010.

There were two major developments in 2011 that are likely to affect Zimbabwe's future. The first was the 'Arab Spring' and, more particularly, the demise of Muammar Gaddafi (a notable friend to and investor in the Mugabe regime) and the overthrow of Laurent Gbagbo of Côte d'Ivoire (who had tried to resist an election defeat). There is no doubt that the SADC has, in consequence, toughened its stance on the need for fair elections in Zimbabwe. President Zuma has taken the lead in engaging with the internal parties on developing a roadmap for elections following a referendum on a new constitution. Although Zuma has his own problems there is a new steely realism in the approach of SADC, and an appreciation that the claims deriving from liberation will not necessarily appease a younger, jobless generation, intolerant of corruption and alert to world events through the internet.

For just as the December 2010 congress of ZANU–PF called for elections the following year, so too did the December 2011 congress. Yet the slow progress of constitution-making, hampered by disorganisation and ZANU violent actions, means that it is quite likely that there will be further delays before there can be a referendum. That, and a cleaned-up electoral register and impartial election commission, will have to be put in place before there can be an election whose result will be accepted by SADC and the world. And if Mugabe (who was 88 years old in February 2012) were no longer to be around, who would be the ZANU candidate to run against Tsvangirai?

Repealing repression?

by Tabani Moyo, Media Institute of Southern Africa (MISA) Zimbabwe Chapter

A civil society view on media freedoms in Zimbabwe.

Since the enactment of the Broadcasting Services Act (BSA), which formed the Broadcasting Authority of Zimbabwe (BAZ) as an administrative arm in 2001, no private players have been licensed to operate independent radio and television stations. On 24 November 2011, the BAZ announced Zimpapers Talk Radio and AB Communications as Zimbabwe's first ever licensed free-to-air independent national commercial radio stations since independence in 1980. This is irrespective of the calls from the media stakeholders in Zimbabwe calling for the dissolution of the illegally constituted BAZ.

It is common knowledge that the current BAZ board which proceeded to issue the two licences in question was not procedurally constituted as required in terms of the law as its members were unilaterally appointed by the Ministry of Media, Information and Publicity on 30 September 2009.

In terms of the BSA as amended in 2007, the President is vested with the powers to appoint the BAZ members after consultation with the minister and the parliamentary Standing Rules and Orders Committee. The other three are appointed by the President from a list of six nominees submitted to the President by the same committee.

Neighbouring media 'thriving'

The restrictive nature of the BSA contrasts with the diversity of public, commercial and free-to-air television and radio stations in neighbouring Commonwealth countries. South Africa leads on all fronts with several thriving community, commercial and public radio stations. The Mozambique broadcasting sector is one of the most vibrant and pluralistic in the region, registering remarkable growth in community radio. Church and faith-based organisations have come to dominate radio broadcasting in Malawi and Zambia. Namibia has many community and commercial radio stations.

And Zimbabweans are well aware of this: due to inadequate transmission sites and obsolete equipment, only 30 per cent of the country receives radio and television coverage from the state broadcaster; the other 70 per cent relies on foreign stations.

The African Charter on Broadcasting states that 'the legal framework for broadcasting should include a clear statement of the principles underpinning broadcast regulation, including promoting respect for freedom of expression, diversity, and the free flow of information and ideas'. Further, that the right to communicate includes 'access to telephones, email, internet and other communication systems, including through the promotion of community-controlled information technology centres'.

Yet the Global Political Agreement signed by the three political forces of Zimbabwe's inclusive government states that the registration and re-registration of new and closed media players respectively will be done under the BSA and the Access to Information and Protection of Privacy Act (AIPPA). But how can these two pieces of repressive legislation possibly be the basis of reform or transformation? Previous to the AIPPA and the intimidation it instigated, any publisher who wanted to start his or her newspaper would simply notify and register with the General Post Office of Zimbabwe and proceed as planned with the publication. This should be the spirit that governs meaningful media reforms.

- The Media Institute of Southern Africa (www.misa.org) is a non-governmental organisation with members in 11 of the Southern African Development Community (SADC) countries. In 2010 Tabani Moyo attended the Commonwealth Broadcasting Association (CBA) Conference in Johannesburg, South Africa, and visited a number of Commonwealth, parliamentary and media players in the UK. He also spoke on 'The Role of Media in Zimbabwe's Transition' at the Royal Commonwealth Society.

- In February 2012 the Commonwealth Journalists Association (CJA) held its triennial meeting in Malta with a focus on journalism and democracy in the new media age. The programme also explored the future of the Commonwealth and was addressed by Commonwealth Assistant Secretary-General Steve Cutts. Senator Hugh Segal made his first official speech as Canada's newly appointed Special Envoy for Commonwealth Renewal.

- At Malta the CJA elected Rita Payne, former BBC Asia editor, as international president. Payne said: 'I am honoured to have been elected International President of the CJA at the end of its conference at which delegates unanimously called for the repeal of repressive media laws in Commonwealth countries.' She takes over from Hassan Shahriar of CJA Bangladesh.

Source: Adapted from Commonwealth People *(January 2011) by kind permission of the Commonwealth Foundation.*

The other major development of 2011 was the murder of Solomon Mujuru who, under his *nom de guerre* Rex Nhongo, made good after 1980 and was a key faction leader in ZANU. His wife, Joice Mujuru, is one of the vice-presidents. General Mujuru was burned alive in his farmhouse in August 2011, allegedly after having a row with Mugabe in which he told his president it was time to go. More substantively there had been continuing speculation that the Mujuru faction was ready to do a deal with Tsvangirai and the MDC, to outwit the securocrat faction led by Emmerson Mnangagwa. For just as all Zimbabweans recognise that Mugabe is not immortal – and he had at least eight medical visits to Singapore in 2011, probably for pancreatic cancer treatment – so it is widely accepted that, in a fair election, the larger MDC formation, led by Tsvangirai, would win a comfortable majority. Nonetheless, in order to get the chance to rule as president, Tsvangirai must square the opposition of the army, police and Central Intelligence Organisation.

Thus, 2011 showed that Africans are less willing to put up with despots and hinted at the conflicts that could break out on Mugabe's decease.

The Commonwealth's position

Where does this leave the Commonwealth? Should it continue to defer in its political stance to President Zuma? Is the small fellowship programme supported by the Commonwealth Foundation and the UK's Commonwealth Scholarship and Fellowship Plan really the best that civil society can do? What do Zimbabweans themselves want of the Commonwealth – if anything? Is a Commonwealth Secretary-General, encouraged to be more proactive by the Eminent Persons Group and leaders at the Perth summit, ready to engage?

There is little doubt that many Zimbabweans would like Commonwealth involvement. The presence of Zimbabwean civil society and youth representatives at the relevant forums at the Perth CHOGM demonstrated as much. A post-Mugabe government may well apply to rejoin in due course, but this is less likely if there is a feeling that the Commonwealth abandoned Zimbabwe in its time of crisis. It could be that 2012 will be the year in which it is possible and necessary for the Commonwealth to do more. Ten years after a Commonwealth group last observed a Zimbabwean election it might be good if SADC invited Commonwealth observers to join them in assessing a constitutional referendum, likely in mid-2012. In a new dispensation the Commonwealth could actively encourage a reduction in the anti-ZANU sanctions, anathematised by Mugabe, to match genuine progress on democracy, the rule of law and human rights. Assistance in reforming the police and military, and help for the struggling Human Rights and Anti-Corruption Commissions would be naturals for the Commonwealth.

But what about civil society? The real opportunity lies not with the small London-based Commonwealth bodies. It is civil society in South Africa, Zambia, Mozambique and Botswana that deserves support in mounting a structured programme to help put Zimbabwe back on its feet. This is where the Commonwealth Foundation, which has just undergone a change of management, could make a real contribution. For the Commonwealth bodies in London have other avenues. In particular the Foreign Affairs Committee of the UK House of Commons is examining the future of the Commonwealth in 2012, and the UK Department for International Development (DFID), which has been critical of Commonwealth Secretariat development work, has rising budgets. Commonwealth bodies can advocate with Members of Parliament in London and partner Zimbabwean NGOs in programmes supported by DFID.

In conclusion, therefore, there is much that the Commonwealth and citizens of Commonwealth countries can do to help Zimbabwe now, even before it rejoins the association. We can be confident that at some point in the future, after Mugabe's departure from the scene, Zimbabwe will be a member state again, but by more active engagement the Commonwealth family could do more to facilitate that return.

RICHARD BOURNE, author of *Catastrophe: What Went Wrong in Zimbabwe?*, is a Senior Research Fellow at the Institute of Commonwealth Studies, London University.

Nigerian Civil Aviation Authority (NCAA)

Dr Harold O. Demuren D.Sc. (MIT), Director General and CEO

RESPONSIBILITIES

- Regulation of safety of aircraft operations, air navigation and aerodrome operations
- Monitoring of aircraft operating environment for safety and security
- Regulating of methods of entry and conduct of air transport business
- Advising the Ministry on policy formulation on aviation related matters
- Balancing the economic interest of operators, users of aviation services as well as the general public and the nation as a whole
- Setting of Aviation Training Standards and approval of Training Institutions
- Facilitating take off and operation of E-Ticketing and Billing Settlement Plan (BSP)

BRIEF

Nigerian Civil Aviation Authority is the regulatory body for aviation in Nigeria. It became autonomous with the passing into law of the Civil Aviation Act 2006 by the National Assembly and assent of the President of the Federal Republic of Nigeria. The Act not only empowers the Authority to regulate Aviation Safety without political interference, but also to carry out oversight functions of Airports, Airspace, Meteorological Services, etc as well as economic regulations of the industry.

A recent challenge to the Nigerian aviation industry has been to achieve the highly desired Category One status from the U.S. Federal Aviation Administration (FAA), which permits national carriers to operate direct flights to and from the United States. The process normally takes five years but the NCAA diligently worked to achieve the required status in under four years and in August 2010, Nigeria attained FAA IASA Category One status. Dr Demuren, Director General and CEO of the NCAA, congratulated all and said he was proud that Nigeria did not cut corners and that the main challenge going forward is to maintain its Category One status.

A noteworthy development in Nigeria's burgeoning aviation industry is the proliferation of domestic carriers. Improved access to funds has intensified competition between aviation carriers within Nigeria, while simultaneously encouraging increased standards of service, reliability and choice — all tremendous benefits to domestic and international passengers alike.

Contact

Nigerian Civil Aviation Authority
Aviation House
Murtala Mohammed Airport
Ikeja Lagos
Nigeria

Tel: +234 1 472 1521/ 279 0421
Fax: +234 1 279 0421
Email: info@ncaa.gov.ng

www.ncaa.gov.ng

RCS Young Commonwealth Competitions

The Royal Commonwealth Society (RCS) has been running international creative competitions for well over a century. With a rich history of nurturing the talents of young Commonwealth citizens, the RCS was delighted to celebrate the work of its 2011 competition winners at the Commonwealth Heads of Government Meeting (CHOGM) in Perth, Australia.

Since 2010, the Commonwealth Essay Competition (the world's oldest and largest schools' writing contest), Commonwealth Vision Awards, and Commonwealth Photographic Awards, have been run as one prestigious awards scheme. In 2011, more than 6,500 young people from across the world entered the competitions.

Over 2,000 essays, short films and photographs were selected for awards, with the winners coming from every corner of the Commonwealth – including Australia, Bangladesh, Barbados, Canada, Ghana, Mauritius, Singapore and Uganda (to name just a few).

For 2011, all competitions took the Commonwealth theme 'Women as Agents of Change'. Entrants were encouraged to reflect on both the opportunities and barriers faced by women around the world, as well as the many roles women play in their homes, communities and countries.

The winners of these competitions are often those picking up a camera or putting pen to paper for the first time. What the RCS looks for is a creative spark or a unique idea.

Many of this year's entries dealt with hard-hitting topics such as female circumcision, child labour, bullying of transgender youth and female political participation.

Looking towards 2012

The 2012 Young Commonwealth Competitions are themed around 'Connecting Cultures', and all entries will relate to a single day in the last 60 years since Queen Elizabeth II came to the throne on 6 February 1952. To celebrate this very special occasion, and for one year only, all entries into the Young Commonwealth Competitions will become part of the world's biggest history project, the Commonwealth Jubilee Time Capsule. Those who take part in the competitions will have their entries join 22,000 others – one for each day that the Queen has been Head of the Commonwealth – in the capsule.

The objectives of the competitions are to:

- promote literacy, expression and creativity among young people by celebrating excellence, imagination and talent

- develop young people's skills in writing, photography, film-making and musical composition as they enter the competitions

- promote a sense of international understanding among young people through their participation in a global competition that engages with issues of mutual interest

- give young people from diverse backgrounds a platform to express their views about the world and their dreams for the future

- stimulate and provoke thought about the issues addressed in the competitions by disseminating the results to a worldwide audience

- demonstrate, through the interaction of young people from across the globe, the continued relevance and importance of the Commonwealth to younger generations, and

- raise awareness of the Commonwealth and its values, principles and activities.

The following pages (189 to 195) take a look at some of the 2011 RCS competitions, their winners and their entries. There is also a more detailed look at the Commonwealth Jubilee Time Capsule on page 94.

For detailed information about the 2011 competitions (and their winners and runners-up), visit the RCS website at www.thercs.org/youth/418

For a further outline of the Royal Commonwealth Society Young Commonwealth Competitions, contact Catherine Clark, Head of Programme Development, on Catherine.Clark@thercs.org or +44 20 7766 9204.

Commonwealth Essay Competition

Every year, the Commonwealth Essay Competition inspires thousands of young writers from all over the world. Organised by the Royal Commonwealth Society, this international youth writing contest has been running for more than 100 years and is a highly regarded and popular international education project.

As the world's oldest global writing prize for young people, this extraordinary project gives young people a voice by promoting literacy, academic excellence, story telling, reflection, awareness and creativity. Writing is a universal mode of expression: no matter what their scholastic or social background, young people all over the world have access to pens and paper or a computer.

The Essay Competition for 2011 saw the top senior prize going to Deep Vaze (aged 16) of India. The Senior Runner-Up was Michelle Lee YY (14), of Singapore. Iman Agha (12), of Pakistan, was the Junior Prize Winner. The Junior Runner-Up was Afrah Juhi (10), of Singapore.

You can read all of these essays on the following pages. Alternatively, you will find them on www.thercs.org/youth/412

'Discuss the statistic that 51% of the world are women but only 8% of countries have an elected female leader'

by Deep Vaze

Are fifty-one percent of the world women?

The statistic is disputed. As Nobel-winning economist Amartya Sen shows in his essay 'More than 100 million Women are Missing', the global gender imbalance is significant, and perhaps growing – especially in developing countries. Sen argues that it may be unwise to derive a global ratio by 'generalizing from the contemporary situation in Europe and North America, where the ratio of women to men is typically around 1.05 or 1.06, or higher. In South Asia, West Asia, and China, the ratio of women to men can be as low as 0.94 or even lower.'

In much of the developing world, societal ignorance and neglect – poverty's terrible by-products – conspire against girls, often from the moment they are born. In agrarian societies, the monetary value of male children appears self-evident: boys can earn their keep working the land, provide for their parents in old age, and eventually inherit the family land. By contrast, girls are often viewed as a drain on the family purse, expensive to marry off in communities where dowries are still accepted, and precluded by patriarchal custom from inheriting their father's land.

Thus, it is not uncommon amongst poor families in many parts of the world for the men and boys to be fed first, or for boys to be favoured over their sisters when scarce family funds are allocated for school fees or even medical expenses. Consequently, in South-east Asia and sub-Saharan Africa more than anywhere else in the world, girls die prematurely due to malnourishment at a disproportionately high rate. Of course, this applies only to families who have chosen to raise a girl in the first place. Despite legislation to stamp out female infanticide and gender-based abortion, illicit markets continue to cater to desperate parents who believe they are too poor to raise a daughter. It is, appallingly, still no exaggeration to say that at the poorest levels in developing countries, girls are often second class citizens in their own families.

With such a start in life and such bleak prospects, is it any wonder that few women make it to the top job in government in developing countries? In a society where women are fewer in numbers and discriminated against from birth when they seek access to nutrition, health care, education and a fair inheritance, should we really be surprised that so few women have realised their political aspirations?

Those that have tend to have been cocooned from the systematic subordination that many of their countrywomen face. India's Indira Gandhi, Pakistan's Benazir Bhutto and Sri Lanka's Chandrika Kumaratunga were all daughters of charismatic prime ministers. In Bangladesh, power has consistently been lobbed back and forth between two women: Sheikh Hasina, the daughter of Bangladesh's founding father, Sheikh Mujibur Rahman, and Khaleda Zia, the widow of assassinated president and former army chief Ziaur Rahman. The achievements of these women in being elected to the highest political offices in four of the world's most populous countries are arguably less representative of the possibilities open to most Indian, Pakistani, Sri Lankan and Bangladeshi women than of the enduring power and privilege of political dynasties in the Indian subcontinent.

How can this state of affairs be corrected? While most developing countries are pursuing vigorous economic development and headline growth rates, it is worth remembering that economic development is not a panacea for all of the hardships that women face. While growth does tend to bring higher literacy rates and reduced malnutrition, it does not automatically result in dramatically more representative government.

Even in developed countries, the correlation between educational attainment and public leadership has not been apparent. In the United Kingdom, for instance, over 50% of women hold a university degree compared with only around 40% of men, yet this has not translated into political power – Margaret Thatcher stands out as a lone female prime minister. In America where higher education figures are similar to those in the UK, less than 3% of Fortune 500 companies have a woman CEO.

Why? Growth and globalisation have created immense economic opportunities for well-educated women – but they have also brought with them increasing demands on time, which women, still often the primary care-givers in families, can ill afford. Consider, for example, the modern financial sector. With the ability to make deals instantly across time-zones, money, as the phrase has it, truly never sleeps. Those who trade in and analyse international markets, therefore, increasingly adopt an 'always on call' lifestyle. Such lives are very difficult for parents with young children to sustain, and societal mores often expect a woman to sacrifice her career for her family.

Even in other sectors, a globalised workforce necessitates the adoption of globalised working times: waking up at dawn in Hong Kong to join a transnational conference call with Head Office in California is now considered an unremarkable requirement of professionals from diverse fields. Working for a multinational corporation often requires global flexibility: moving with the job and uprooting the family. Even large companies often fail to accommodate the needs of working parents – by providing an onsite crèche, for example, or allowing staff to adopt flexible working hours – while small businesses often simply cannot afford to do so. With so many highly qualified women dropping out of the workforce mid-career to raise families, few remain to attain the highest offices in both corporate and political spheres. The case of America's 'First Family' is telling. Michelle Obama, a graduate of Princeton and Harvard, was at one time senior to her husband at the law firm where they met; after they started a family, it was Barack's career that accelerated.

How, then, can we get more women to prepare for and attain positions of public leadership? It is important to remember that there are no quick fixes. The reasons for male dominance in high office are deep-rooted. Religious and military power have long gone hand-in-hand with political might. The traditional primacy of war in national life has naturally favoured men aspiring to high political office. And those seeking to exclude women from public office have also often used selective – and self-serving – interpretations of religious texts and traditions to bolster their cause.

Governments of both developed and developing countries must work to widen the pool of capable and qualified candidates for leadership roles throughout society. Only when women regularly attain the top jobs running schools and hospitals, local governments and charities, media and the arts, and banks and corporations will there be significant numbers of women qualifying to lead their countries.

The spread of democracy should give rise to qualified candidates, whatever their background, aspiring to high office. But the nature and practice of democracy is as important as the mere fact of it. Mandatory voting for all people of voting age may be one major step that most countries could take towards 'true' democracy. Voting rates amongst women are markedly lower than rates amongst men; hence, if women *had* to vote then we could expect greater success for female candidates. Implementing firm ceilings on the value of political campaign contributions, too, should

reduce the considerable advantage that men – who hold a disproportionate share of national wealth – have in running for office.

In the developing world, legislation that promotes gender equality is often already in place. It is the enforcement of these policies – the difficulty of changing long-standing practices – that is problematic. It is one thing to pass a bill banning gender discrimination, but quite another to make sure a poor mother feeds her son and daughter equally, to make sure boys and girls receive the same vaccines and the same education, to make sure young women feel safe enough to move to cities to pursue a career, and to make sure that assets are passed down to all of a couple's heirs, not only to the male ones.

Similarly, governments in developed countries should not simply congratulate themselves on the high educational attainment of their women. Corporate culture may need a governmental nudge to recognise the needs of working mothers – and the dangers of losing them. Fathers increasingly play a more active role in raising their children than in previous generations – this is a trend that is to be encouraged, not only for the benefits to the children but for the alleviation of pressure on mothers who work outside the home or aspire to do so. It is vital that children of both genders be taught their equal responsibilities – and opportunities – in both the home and in public life.

Truly substantive change at the highest levels of government begins not in Downing Street and the White House, Rashtrapati Bhavan and the Kremlin. It begins at more fundamental levels: through systemic changes in the way we run our families, our civic institutions and our corporations. Only when men and women feel equally able and qualified to aspire to their nation's supreme office can that nation harness the full potential of all its people.

'Girl power! OR, Boy power!'

by Michelle Lee YY

They came for him one hot afternoon as he was walking home from school. Hands slammed into his back, and as he turned around, someone twisted his arm sharply behind his back and laughed as he cried out. The sun was behind their faces and shining into his eyes, so he could recognize the group only by their uniforms; students from his school. He tried to wrench his arm free, struggling desperately, but they wouldn't let go. Instead, they moved in to surround him, tightening their circle. Someone punched him hard, across his face, and through the pain, he suddenly realized how much they hated him. And more fearfully, he wondered how much they would hurt him. He turned, searching desperately for a break in their circle, a way to escape, but he was surrounded all around by face after anonymous face. With a last futile struggle, he tried to break free and run. He stumbled. Then the mob surged, and struck at the boy at its center, and surged and struck again.

They kicked him, and this time he fell, lost in the tangle of arms all reaching to grab, to twist, to hurt. He screamed. It was a high-pitched torrent of raw sound that he didn't know could come from inside him, and they slapped him to make him shut up, till he was silent and still. Above him, someone was laughing raucously. Another kick in the ribs, and he groaned and rolled away. With shattered glasses, he strained to hear what was going on – he heard the sound of metal, and he flinched away in fear, silently begging that it wasn't a knife, they could hurt him as much as they wanted with their bare hands but with a knife they could cut, they could kill. They held him down so he couldn't turn his head. Next to his head, he heard blades closing, and with a sickening ache he realized they were cutting his hair. It was far too long, pushing the school's rules to the limit; his father hated it. He said it looked like a girl's. The scissors snipped, and snipped again, and he felt his shorn head lighten.

Finally, they let him go, and he lay there, wondering what they would do next. Someone cleared their throat slowly. Then he felt saliva, wet and slightly warm, hitting his face and running down the curve of his cheek. They walked away without speaking.

Lying there, he wished that he were dead.

Then he heard the sound of footsteps, running towards him, and felt a hand on his shoulder. 'Are you okay?' It was his best friend's voice, and he nodded dully. 'I heard you screaming. Do you need me to call an ambulance?' He shook his head, and stumbled to his feet. 'I'm fine. They didn't hurt me that badly.'

She helped him up, frowning at the obvious lie, and they walked along slowly in silence. He held his glasses against his face with one hand, squinting through the intact lens against the sunlight's glare. With every step he took, he could feel his legs trembling.

She spoke unexpectedly, almost brusquely. 'Is this about what happened on Wednesday? When we were allowed to come in normal clothes?' He stared at her, taken by surprise; he knew that they'd have to talk about what happened, but he had never expected the anger in her voice.

He didn't know where he had gotten the courage to wear a skirt that day, or even why he did it. The impulse had risen out of some deep, dark part of him he hadn't noticed before. One morning, he had squinted into the foggy mirror and noticed that he could pass as a girl. His hair was long enough, at least. And tentatively, he had realized he liked this distorted reflection, a reflection that somehow went beyond the surface to strike at his core.

When the day came, he had brought spare clothes, to change out. As soon as he stepped into the school, the whispers had started. He changed into his spare clothes before the first lesson started, face burning with shame. When he went back to class, someone had thrown his bag out of the window, spilling its contents onto the field below. He ate his lunch alone that day, for the first time.

'I don't even understand why you want to pretend that you're a girl! It's not like you'll ever really be one, anyway. You're on the rugby team and everything, you're really popular. And you didn't even fight back.'

He choked the words around his swollen tongue, feeling confused. 'I only joined rugby because I didn't want to let my dad down. He wants me to take after him, but I don't. Not at all.'

She looked at him angrily. 'Aren't you just letting him down more now? At least he expects something of you. If I were you, I'd have fought them. What are you going to tell him?' He tried to think of a way to explain his injuries, but he couldn't think of any.

Instead, he examined his best friend in the harsh afternoon sunlight. For the first time, he realized how much she had changed over the past few years. When had she changed from just being his friend, coming over to play video games in her baseball cap and jeans, to the way she was now? She was taller now, and neater,

standing up straight and taking small steps as she walked. She had given up her advanced mathematics classes for cheerleading, stopped playing D&D with him to go shopping after school. He looked at her, and realized painfully that she had become a stranger.

*   *   *

Monday came, and he went back to school for the last time. His father had taken a day off work to drive him there, saying that he didn't want him to get beaten up again. When his father said that, he didn't look him in the eye. They hadn't spoken about what had happened, but he could hear the disappointment in his father's voice. When was the last time his father had been unconditionally proud of him? He couldn't answer that. Without the distraction of school, his days blended into each other like cotton wool, his insides numb as he waited for each next day to arrive. When he thought about the future, he never got very far. All he could feel was anxiety, the feeling of having nowhere left to go.

Going back to school, he walked through the corridors feeling isolated. There were stares and whispers, but no open taunts. The crowds parted as he walked through them. He had somehow become untouchable, invisible, someone who wasn't part of them. When he closed his locker after collecting his books, hearing how final the click sounded, he saw his best friend walking past his classroom. Her normally messy hair had been pulled back into a sleek ponytail. She said something, and the girl next to her laughed. As he walked out of the classroom, he raised his hand to wave tentatively. She glanced at him, and then with a deliberate movement, turned back to her friends.

When he got back to the car, his father took one look at his face and frowned, turning the keys sharply in the ignition. The engine started with a roar.

'Boys don't cry.'

*   *   *

33.2% of transgendered youth have attempted suicide. 55% of transgendered youth report being physically attacked. 90% reported feeling unsafe at school due to their gender expression, and 74% have been sexually harassed. In a survey of 403 transgender people, 78% reported having been verbally harassed and 48% reported having been victims of assault, including assault with a weapon, sexual assault or rape.

Instead of writing about Girl Power or Boy Power in the traditional sense, I chose to write this essay about those who do not conform to the gender roles that are expected of them by society. By dividing power and ability into two categories, 'girl' power and 'boy' power, not only are we enforcing stereotypes by defining the limits of what one can do by gender, we are also ignoring youth who do not conform to these categories. By writing about characters like these, I tried to both represent the gender roles related to the concepts of Girl Power and Boy Power, and also represent what happens to people who go against what society expects of them. With the recent brutal beating of a transgender woman in a Baltimore McDonald's, resulting in her having an epileptic seizure while onlookers videotaped her and laughed, the issue of transphobic violence is even more relevant.

I hope that in the future, this outdated concept of different genders having different abilities will be abolished, and people will no longer discriminate against transgender youth.

'My Woman of the Year 2011'

by Iman Agha

Glamour and fame, I had thought, were the two main criteria for a Woman of the Year award. This concept was instilled and strengthened in my mind by the international magazines lying around my house. However, this idea was shattered this February when I saw a photograph of a hijab-wearing, baby-clutching, fist-clenching, Egyptian woman at Cairo's Tahrir Square, protesting against their President Hosni Mubarik.

Who was she? What was she shouting? What was the baby's name? These thoughts and many more raced through my mind. I knew not the answer to these questions, but I knew what she wanted … freedom! Freedom to express herself and claim her rights, which had probably been denied to her.

Flashback four years ago, driving along a road in Islamabad with my mother, we came across a roadblock where police had stopped a group of women lawyers protesting against the government of President Musharraf. My mother told me that they were protesting for their rights and freedom. Though feeling a bit scared, I still knew then that they were courageous women, who had ventured out of their homes and offices and that moment was etched in my memory.

With the Tahrir women, I felt there was a strong connection to what I had seen and magically felt transported to Tahrir square and could almost hear the shouts and the chants (though I think it must have something to do with the video on BBC!). This time I didn't feel scared, but proud of what women across the world were doing and achieving. They could be out on the streets and show the world what they wanted. I know this was not possible just a few years ago, in many Muslim countries.

I would like to nominate the Tahrir woman as the Woman of the Year 2011. She is not someone I know personally, neither is she famous. But it's a connection that I feel personally, that is important to me. She may not be pretty or tall, but she *stands* tall as she has a strong character and willpower. She stands up for what she believes in. She has a voice.

My woman of the year has a strong faith. She will not give up easily, but instead she will show the world that she can express her feelings just like a man. I strongly believe in the rights of women and my woman of the year, I am sure, must feel the same way.

She doesn't have to be famous, rich, or live in a mansion. She can be poor, live in a mud house and be from a country I've never even heard of. I should just be able to know how she feels. Connect with her. Relate to her.

Look at what this woman, along with others at the Tahrir square, has achieved. She is part of the great revolution in Egypt. She has made her voice be heard amongst those of a million others and has forced Hosni Mubarak to resign, changed the constitution allowing for greater democratic freedom, long awaited in Muslim societies. This is no tiny feat.

She is that kind of person, the kind who can show the world that 'Hey, I'm here to be counted amongst the living, make my voice heard and chart a different course for my nation and my children.' She believes in herself. She doesn't whine about how bad her life is, rather go out and make a difference. She will be remembered as a woman who made a difference.

For these reasons, that inspiring woman with a scarf around her head, and a good heart, pure soul, and a spirit that can never be dampened, is my woman of the year 2011.

'How grandma saved the day'

by Afrah Juhi

'Again, it's a girl!', he gritted his teeth as his huge fist pummelled onto the chest of the weak woman whose uplifted saree was still drenched with the blood of the newborn. She parted a weak gasp, and closed her eyes forever. The beating took her miserable life away.

With a last look of utter revulsion at the newborn, he started preparing the primitive poison, cactus milk, which would be its first and last sip. Just then, a loud shriek rung out in the dilapidated hut. Grandma had a heart-attack!

That was the day when I was born and my mum died in a savage beating. It was also the day my grandma saved me and it was not to be for the last time.

Born in absolute poverty in god-forsaken rural village, a newborn girl is a never-ending curse to the family. Upbringing is an irretrievable expense and a huge penalty, called dowry, is demanded in marriage. So, it's much easier to kill an unwelcomed female infant and hope for the next proverbial son who can promise prosperity.

As for me, I grew up with the unenviable stigma of 'swallowing' up mum's life at birth. My fate was sealed to the hot stoves of the kitchen. Yet, grandma's loving sight and grace never left me. Her quiet ways and toothless grin always delighted me. It was much later in my life that I realized that my grandma selflessly paid the price, losing all her teeth and speech to my dad's savagely furious punch, for deceiving him with a fake heart attack.

Years rolled by. Yet, my ill-fate continued to haunt me. New prosperity has set in the village. Children have become valuable resources for impoverished families, especially the disabled and disfigured. Almost every day, one could see touts eyeing a child's worth. Their treacherous eyes would silently assess a perfect child, mutilate, maim, and re-appraise its increased value as a street beggar in a faraway city.

Soon, one set his eyes on me. He came over and my father eagerly welcomed him. Within the almost inaudible whispers, a huge price was struck. My heart immediately sank. With pleading eyes, I silently appealed to my grandma. Tears rolled down her cheeks, as her slightly gaped mouth revealed that she has no more teeth to lose.

Just then, grandma collapsed. My heart skipped an eager beat, as I concealed my excitement, shrieked at the top of my voice, 'Grandma has an heart attack!!'

My father came racing over. He took a closer look at the crumpled figure on the floor, snarled and gave it a hard kick. I could almost hear her rib-cage cracking. Grandma did not move. He pulled her up by her shrivelled hair. Her face was pale but calm. He let her drop, her face smashing into the raw mud floor. He shook his head begrudgingly at the tout, who immediately left cursing the ill-omen.

Then, the reality struck me. My heart burst with sudden overwhelming grief. My dearest grandma had died, to save me for another day. Uncontrollable flood of tears rolled down my cheeks as meagre hopes of a better life drained away. There is no one else to save me tomorrow.

Commonwealth Vision Awards

The Commonwealth Vision Awards, organised jointly by the Royal Commonwealth Society and the Commonwealth Broadcasting Association, promote excellence in film-making. The year 2011 marked the tenth year of these awards, open to professional and aspiring film-makers from across the Commonwealth.

Entrants were asked to create a short film responding to the Commonwealth theme 'Women as Agents of Change', and many chose to explore the opportunities and barriers women face today as well as the many roles they play in their families, communities and countries.

Interestingly, the subject matter of all three winning films – which were also screened at the Commonwealth Festival in Perth – focused on education: both the importance of educating women and the impact women can have through teaching.

Chair of the judges, former BBC World News anchor Keshini Navaratnam, explained why the panel was so impressed with 'Love Never Fails' by 16-year-old Wai Lun Suen: 'This inspirational film was rich in mood and atmosphere due to the combination of filming and music with a lovely story, which conveyed vividly the importance of women in educating and shaping the world through the tale of a young boy helped by his mother.'

Wai Lun hopes the film proves 'women can make a huge change, even if it is one that does not affect many'.

Winners

The top Senior Gold Award (18–30 years) for 2011 went to 23-year-old Pratik Jain from India for 'Meena', a film just 1 minute 16 seconds long. Silver was awarded to Anthony Abuah, 26, of Nigeria/Rwanda. Bronze was awarded to both Faustina Appiah, 25, of Ghana, and Tianyu Han, 19, of Singapore. In the Junior category (under 18), Himanil Gole, 16, of India/Mauritius and Wai Lun Suen, 16, of Singapore were both awarded Gold. Silver was awarded to Raiya Jessa, 13, of Canada; and Bronze to Low Gin Wee, Leonard Pang and Wu Nien Ting, of Singapore.

Comment on Pratik Jain's film

The judges were impressed by the powerful messaging that came through this highly evocative, short film which promoted the importance of education for women as agents of change. Its apparent simplicity is a testament to the talent of the film-maker. The judges were struck by both the skill and confidence that were embodied in this entry.

To view all of the shortlisted entries for the Young Commonwealth Competitions, visit www.thercs.org/youth/420

Commonwealth Photographic Awards

Capturing the Commonwealth on film

The only photographic prize of its kind reaching every country in the Commonwealth, the Photographic Awards competition has been running since the 1990s and has drawn together hundreds of young photojournalists and photographers each year. The standard of entry for this competition, which is organised by the Royal Commonwealth Society, is unfailingly exceptional.

This aspiring photographic prize celebrates the ways in which young people from all backgrounds across the Commonwealth, from different races, creeds, cultures and ways of life, see themselves and others. The 2011 winning senior photograph, taken by Amit Madheshiya, demonstrates this perfectly. Sister Mabel walks for hours each week into the thick Attapady jungle in Kerala, India, to visit children from the remote Irula tribe, many of whom do not attend school. In his photo, the Sister is telling the young girls a wonderful story about a girl's first day at school. 'In an instant,' says judging Chair Michael Hallett, 'Amit has recorded an entire narrative appropriate to this year's theme.'

The RCS competition encourages young people to explore themes of international importance in a creative way. Their images, sent in 2011 from 46 Commonwealth countries, often display the diversity and remarkable similarities of human experience in the modern Commonwealth.

Entries were submitted on digital, analogue, disposable and even mobile phone cameras. Caitlin Montie Greer, judge and Artist in Residence for a women's refuge, called the competition an 'incredibly inclusive way to encourage young people to express themselves'. 2011's youngest participant was just 11 years old. The judging panel also included Tate Curator and Associated Director at The Drawing Room, Katharine Stout, photojournalist Peter Hayes, and Belgian photographer and artist Thierry Bal.

Winners

Award winners include: Senior (18–30) Gold winner Amit Madheshiya, 29, of India; Senior Silver winner Rehnuma Tasnim Sheefa, 18, from Bangladesh; Senior Bronze winners Martin Iversen, 21, of Australia and Diana Lewis, 24, of Barbados; Junior (under 18) Gold winner Siddharth Murali, 16, of India/Oman; Junior Silver winner Nishtha Garg, 17, from India; and Junior Bronze winners Ann Hui Ching, 14, of Malaysia and Shintaro Tay, 15, of Singapore. The judges selected 14 additional entries to feature in a special exhibition commissioned by Commonwealth Festival Perth.

Amit Madheshiya of India won Senior Gold for his portrait of Sister Mabel

Rehnuma Tasnim Sheefa of Bangladesh won Senior Silver with this touching portrait

© Royal Commonwealth Society – Rehnuma Tasnim Sheefa

The 2011 photographic award winners can all be seen on www.thercs.org/youth/371

Diana Lewis of Barbados won Senior Bronze with this affectionate photograph

Martin Iversen of Australia won Senior Bronze with this powerful image

Commonwealth Broadcasting Awards

The Commonwealth Broadcasting Awards 2011 award winners have been noted as being the 'epitome of all that is good about Public Service Broadcasting' …

Excellence in media production across the Commonwealth was celebrated in the winning entries of the 2011 Commonwealth Broadcasting Awards. Engaging and high quality programme content is acknowledged as the key driver for digital transition, which the Commonwealth Broadcasting Association (CBA) is committed to supporting. The CBA (www.cba.org.uk) would like to thank all Award sponsors for making this celebration of excellence possible, with thanks also to the many judges who took time from their busy schedules to select these winners.

Amnesty International Award for Human Rights Programme
Assignment – Guinea on the Brink, BBC World Service (UK)

Judges' comments
This is a very powerful programme, radio documentary at its best. Guinea on the Brink makes an important contribution to the fight for human rights because it brings this issue to the attention of millions around the world.

CBA-IBC Award for Innovative Engineering
EPG Innovation Project, SABC (South Africa), and MCR Project, Televisao Independente de Mocambique (Mozambique)

Judges' comments
Both these entries showed initiative and judges felt that they were equally important to their respective stations, despite the very different sizes and strengths of the two organisations. The SABC project made excellent use of well-documented tools and TIM Engineers made pragmatic use of available resources.

One World Media Award for Best Programme produced in a Developing Country
Maternal Mortality, Radio Kisima FM (Kenya)

Judges' comments
This was a highly creative, innovative programme, with excellent use of available resources. Maternal Mortality is engaging, informative listening. This is 3D radio!

Thomson Foundation Journalist of the Year Award
Samuel Agyemang, Reporter/Anchor, Metro TV (Ghana)

Judges' comments
We were hugely impressed by Samuel's determination to get to the heart of the story – in difficult and challenging circumstances. His reporting had evident impact, brought clear results, and showed courage and a social conscience. We want to commend him on his investigative skill and encourage him to persevere in setting the highest standards of journalism.

UNESCO Award for Science Reporting and Programming
Honeybee Blues, SBS (Australia)

Judges' comments
Honeybee Blues is the epitome of all that is good about Public Service Broadcasting: it entertained, informed and educated. The Bee's story was a story in and of itself and also was used as a vehicle to explore wider environmental issues.

CBA Roll of Honour
Patrick Cozier, Secretary-General, Caribbean Broadcasting Union (CBU; Barbados)

A smiling but surprised Patrick Cozier accepted the award to the applause of colleagues from all over the Caribbean at an evening reception during the 'CBA: Live in Kingston' event. Cozier has been Secretary-General of the CBU since 1996, which functions in both an advocacy and representational role. In giving the award, the CBA's Project Manager, Adam Weatherhead, stated: 'One of our strongest and most effective partners has been the CBU with Patrick at its head.'

The CBA Roll of Honour is given to members who have served their organisations, the CBA and the principles of Public Service Broadcasting. Criteria include an outstanding record of achievement and a close association with the CBA.

Patrick Cozier (left) receives his CBA Roll of Honour from Adam Weatherhead

Antigua and Barbuda

KEY FACTS

Joined Commonwealth:	1981
Population:	89,000 (2010)
GDP p.c. growth:	1.7% p.a. 1990–2010
UN HDI 2011:	world ranking 60
Official language:	English
Time:	GMT minus 4hr
Currency:	Eastern Caribbean dollar (EC$)

Geography

Area:	443 sq km
Coastline:	153km
Capital:	St John's

Antigua and Barbuda, at the north of the Leeward Islands in the Eastern Caribbean, is composed of three islands: Antigua, Barbuda (40km north of Antigua) and Redonda (40km south-west of Antigua). Antigua comprises six parishes: St George, St John, St Mary, St Paul, St Peter and St Philip.

Area: Antigua 280 sq km; Barbuda 161 sq km; Redonda 1.6 sq km

Topography: With about 365 beaches on Antigua, further beaches of pink and white sand on Barbuda, coves that were once volcanic craters, and luxuriant palms, the country was an early proponent of sea-and-sun tourism. Antigua is generally composed of low-lying coral and limestone, although Boggy Peak among the volcanic rocks to the west rises to 402m. It has an indented coastline and a good harbour at English Harbour Town. There are a few springs; drought can be a problem. Barbuda is flat with a large lagoon on its west side. Redonda is a tiny rocky island, and is uninhabited.

Climate: Tropical and drier than most of the West Indies. The hot season, when most rain falls, is May to November. Hurricane Luis, the first hurricane in many decades, struck in mid-1995, causing particular damage to Barbuda where it flooded 75% of the island, including the main town of Codrington.

Environment: The most significant environmental issue is limited natural freshwater resources which is aggravated by clearing of trees to increase crop production, causing rainfall to run off quickly.

Did you know...

Sir Vivian Richards, born in St John's in 1952, was Wisden Leading Cricketer in the World in 1976, 1978 and 1980.

Jamaica Kincaid, born Elaine Potter Richardson in St John's in 1949, has been heralded as the 'most important West Indian woman writing today'.

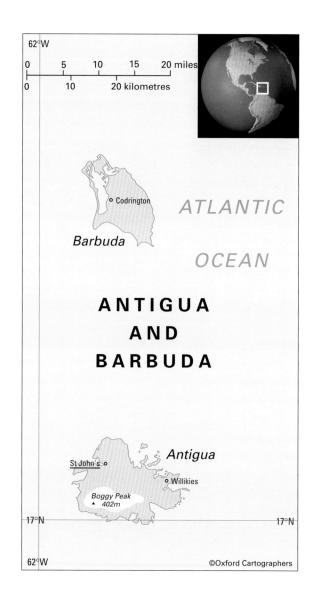

©Oxford Cartographers

Vegetation: Little remains of Antigua's natural vegetation, as the island was formerly cleared for sugar planting. Unlike other islands in the Leeward group, it has little forest; mangoes, guavas, coconuts and bananas grow in the south-west. Barbuda is well wooded in the north-east, providing a haven for wildlife. Forest covers 22% of Antigua and Barbuda's land area and there was no significant loss of forest cover during 1990–2010.

Wildlife: More than 150 species of birds have been recorded. Barbuda is a game reserve with a variety of wildlife: deer, wild pigs, duck, guinea-fowl, and a large colony of frigatebirds in the mangrove lagoon. Redonda has become a haven for species such as the burrowing owl, which have been driven out of the other, inhabited, islands.

Main towns: St John's (capital, pop. 22,200 in 2010), All Saints (4,800), Liberta (3,100), Potters Village (3,100), Bolans (2,100) and English Harbour on Antigua; and Codrington on Barbuda.

Transport: There is a good road network of about 1,170km, 33% paved. St John's deep water harbour is a regional centre for cargo and passengers and the country's main port. VC Bird International Airport is 8km north-east of St John's; and an airstrip at Codrington, Barbuda, is suitable for light aircraft.

Society

KEY FACTS 2010

Population per sq km:	201
Life expectancy:	75 years (est.)
Net primary enrolment:	90%

Population: 89,000 (2010); some 2,000 on Barbuda; 30% lives in urban areas; growth 1.8% p.a. 1990–2010; birth rate 16 per 1,000 people (est. 26 in 1970); life expectancy 75 years (est. 67 in 1970). 91% of the population is of African descent (2001 census).

Language: English; an English-based Creole is also spoken.

Religion: Mainly Christians (Anglicans 26%, Seventh Day Adventists 12%, Pentecostals 11%, Moravians 11%, Roman Catholics 10%, 2001 census).

Health: Public spending on health was 4% of GDP in 2009. The country has a general hospital (220 beds), a private clinic, seven health centres and 17 associated clinics. Government finances visits by specialists in diabetics, heart disease, hypertension and glaucoma. A new hospital was built in the late 1990s. Infant mortality was 7 per 1,000 live births in 2010.

Education: Public spending on education was 2.7% of GDP in 2009. There are 11 years of compulsory education starting at age five. Primary school comprises seven years and secondary five. Some 97% of pupils complete primary school (2007). The school year starts in September. The government administers the majority of the schools.

Antigua State College in St John's provides technical and teacher education, GCE A-Level and first-year University of the West Indies courses. Antigua and Barbuda is a partner in the regional University of the West Indies, which has its main campuses in Barbados, Jamaica, and Trinidad and Tobago. The female–male ratio for gross enrolment in tertiary education is 2.21:1 (2009).

Media: *Antigua Sun* and *Daily Observer* are dailies; *The Worker's Voice* (Antigua Labour Party) is published twice weekly, and *The Sunday Scoop* weekly (from September 2004).

Antigua and Barbuda Broadcasting Service provides public radio and TV services. Observer Radio was the country's first independent radio station, launched in 2001. Crusader Radio is owned by the United Progressive Party. Cable television is widely available.

Some 97% of households have TV sets (2008). There are 207 personal computers (2006) and 800 internet users (2010) per 1,000 people.

Communications: Country code 1 268; internet domain '.ag'. Mobile phone coverage is good.

There are 409 main telephone lines and 1,894 mobile phone subscriptions per 1,000 people (2010).

Public holidays: New Year's Day, Labour Day (early May), CARICOM Day (early July), Carnival (Monday and Tuesday in early August), Independence Day (1 November), National Heroes' Day (9 December), Christmas Day and Boxing Day.

Religious and other festivals whose dates vary from year to year include Good Friday, Easter Monday and Whit Monday.

Economy

KEY FACTS 2010

GNI:	US$1.2bn
GNI p.c.:	US$13,170
GDP growth:	1.2% p.a. 2006–10
Inflation:	2.3% p.a. 2006–10

After three decades of prosperity as a tourist centre, foreign debt, dependence on a single industry and relatively low growth in the early 1990s led to recession, despite attempts in the 1980s to diversify. An economic reform programme was agreed in 1994. But in 1995 Hurricane Luis severely damaged tourism at the same time as expenditure was increased to finance the recovery, and the economy contracted by 5%.

Real Growth in GDP

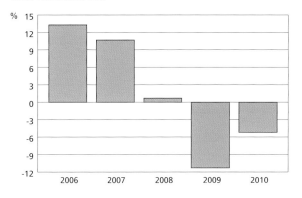

Inflation

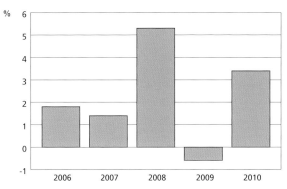

GDP by Sector (2010)

■	Agriculture	3%
□	Industry	26%
▨	Services	71%

The government introduced a tougher economic programme in 1996. This aimed to reduce debt and stimulate the private sector, including offshore financial activities, by cutting public expenditure, improving tax collection, undertaking privatisations and encouraging tourism and manufacturing of electronic components and household appliances for export; and clothes, food and beverages, furniture, paint and paper for the domestic market. Manufacturing production grew by at least 4% p.a. during 2001–08.

The economy responded and there followed a period of good growth until 2000, when it slowed, due mainly to a fall in tourism. Growth recovered in 2003 and was vigorous until 2008 due mainly to increased construction activity in both public and private sectors. The economy remained vulnerable to natural disasters, shocks to tourist activity and volatile international oil prices, and from 2008 the global economic downturn and consequent sharp decline in tourism pushed the economy sharply into recession, shrinking by 11.3% in 2009 and 5.2% in 2010, before returning to weak growth in 2011.

Constitution

Status:	Monarchy under Queen Elizabeth II
Legislature:	Parliament
Independence:	1 November 1981

Agreed at independence in 1981. The country is a constitutional monarchy which recognises Queen Elizabeth II as head of state. She is represented by a governor-general appointed on the advice of the prime minister. Government is by parliamentary democracy with a bicameral legislature.

There is a directly elected lower House of Representatives of 17 members for a term of not more than five years (plus speaker and attorney-general) and an upper Senate of 17 members appointed by the governor-general, one at his/her own discretion, 11 on the prime minister's recommendation (including one inhabitant of Barbuda), four on that of the leader of the opposition, one on the recommendation of the Barbuda Council. The latter is responsible for local government on Barbuda, and consists of nine directly elected members. The constitution guarantees individual rights and freedoms.

Politics

Last elections:	March 2009
Next elections:	2014
Head of state:	Queen Elizabeth II, represented by governor-general, Louise Lake-Tack (2007–)
Head of government:	Prime Minister Baldwin Spencer
Ruling party:	United Progressive Party

The Antigua Labour Party (ALP) led by Lester Bird won its sixth consecutive general election in March 1999 (in the presence of a Commonwealth observer group), gaining 12 of the 17 seats with 53% of the votes cast. The United Progressive Party (UPP) took four seats, with 44% of the votes, and the Barbuda People's Movement (BPM) one seat.

Vere Bird Sr, who led the country to independence in 1981, and was prime minister until he retired from active politics before the 1994 general election, died in June 1999 at the age of 89.

At the request of the prime minister, a two-person Commonwealth expert group visited the country in July 2000, to consult the people and review the 'operations of the arrangements' between Antigua and Barbuda as established at a constitutional conference at Lancaster House, London, in 1980. In November 2000, at St John's, Commonwealth Secretary-General Don McKinnon presented the group's report and recommendations to the government, saying that implementation of these recommendations would bring an end to long-standing discord between the islands of Antigua and Barbuda.

In April 2003 the Electoral Office of Jamaica was engaged to compile a new voters' list and collect photos and fingerprints to be used on identity cards, in preparation for the next general election. This work and the election itself in March 2004 were observed by a Commonwealth expert team. The UPP won the contest with 55% of the votes and 12 seats, and Baldwin Spencer became prime minister, ending a 28-year run of power for the ALP and the Bird family.

In March 2009, the UPP, led by Spencer, was returned to power with a reduced majority, winning nine of the 17 seats and 51% of the votes. The ALP took seven seats (47%), and the BPM one (1%). During the election campaign, the UPP had promised to sell off shares of state-owned corporations to the public, while the main opposition ALP had said that it would introduce tax cuts. Turnout was 80%.

International relations

Antigua and Barbuda is a member of the African, Caribbean and Pacific Group of States, Association of Caribbean States, Caribbean Community, Non-Aligned Movement, Organisation of Eastern Caribbean States, Organization of American States, United Nations and World Trade Organization.

Traveller information

Local laws and conventions: Local people are conservative and visitors must not wear beachwear in towns or villages.

It is illegal for anyone, including children, to wear camouflage clothing. All drug offences carry severe penalties.

Handshaking is the usual form of greeting among the islanders. Dress is informal and a lightweight suit is customary for business meetings. Business cards are expected from foreign business people. A large number of hotels offer conference facilities. Office hours are Mon–Fri 0800–1200 and 1300–1630.

Immigration and Customs: Passports must be valid for six months from the date of arrival and visas are required by some nationals. Visitors should check with their local Antigua and Barbuda high commission or embassy for visa requirements.

Visitors staying longer than 24 hours must pay an airport departure tax. Visitors should make a copy of their passport photo page and relevant visa stamp, and keep their passport safe at all times.

A yellow fever vaccination certificate is required by those travelling from an infected area.

Travel within the country: Driving is on the left and visitors must purchase a local driving licence before hiring a car; these can be bought from the car hire company on production of a national driving licence. The national speed limits are 65kph on highways and 32kph in built-up areas. Most roads are well maintained, although care should be taken as stray cattle, goats and dogs may wander onto the roads; pedestrians also walk on the roads because there are no pavements.

There are local bus networks but services are infrequent. Taxis are widely available and have standardised rates. Additionally, many taxi drivers will agree to take visitors on sightseeing trips.

Local boats are available for excursions, and visitors can take the Barbuda Express ferry to and from St John's five days a week; journey time is 90 minutes. Carib Aviation has daily flights to Barbuda and journey time is around 20 minutes.

Travel health: Visitors are advised to take out comprehensive health insurance, which includes medical evacuation by air. Dengue fever is endemic and is spread by day-biting mosquitoes; visitors will need to take insect repellent and suitable clothing to avoid being bitten.

Tuberculosis and Hepatitis B vaccinations are sometimes recommended. All current vaccination requirements should be checked before travel.

If taking prescription drugs, visitors should ensure they are kept in their original containers, clearly labelled to avoid any misunderstandings.

Mains water is normally chlorinated and bottled water is advised for the first few weeks of stay. Milk is pasteurised.

Money: Pounds sterling and US dollars can be exchanged at hotels and in the larger shops. American Express, Diners Club, Mastercard and Visa are widely accepted. ATMs are available in the major resorts and there are international banks in St John's. Travellers cheques can be exchanged at international banks, hotels and the larger stores. Visitors are advised to take travellers cheques in US dollars to avoid additional charges. Banking hours are Mon–Thur 0800–1500, Fri 0800–1300 and 1500–1700; some banks open until mid-day on Saturday.

There were 234,000 tourist arrivals in 2009.

Further information

Government of Antigua and Barbuda: www.ab.gov.ag

Eastern Caribbean Central Bank: www.eccb-centralbank.org

Commonwealth Secretariat: www.thecommonwealth.org

Commonwealth of Nations: www.commonwealth-of-nations.org/Antigua_and_Barbuda

History

The first inhabitants were the Siboney, who can be dated back to 2400 BC. Arawaks settled subsequently, around the 1st century AD. The Caribs arrived later, but abandoned Antigua around the 16th century, due to the shortage of fresh water. Christopher Columbus sighted the larger island in 1493, and named it after a church in Seville, Santa Maria de la Antigua. After unsuccessful attempts at colonisation by the Spaniards and French, Antigua was colonised by Sir Thomas Warner in 1632 and formally became a British colony in 1667. Britain annexed Barbuda in 1628; in 1680 Charles II granted the island to the Codrington family, who held it until 1860, in which year it was annexed to Antigua.

Sugar succeeded tobacco as the chief crop and led to the importation of enslaved Africans to work on the highly profitable estates. After the abolition of the slave trade (1807), the Codringtons established a big 'slave-farm' on Barbuda, where children were bred to supply the region's unpaid labour force, until slaves were emancipated in 1834. As the only Caribbean island under British rule to possess a good harbour, Antigua was the dockyard for the British West Indies, used by the Royal Navy from 1725 until 1854.

Demand for self-determination developed in parallel with a concern to create political and economic linkages with other small Caribbean countries. The labour movement became the main focus of political development, and gathered strength during the economically troubled mid-years of the 20th century. Vere C Bird formed the country's first trade union in 1939, and later became leader of the Antigua Labour Party (ALP).

The first elections under universal adult suffrage took place in 1951, and were won by the ALP. The country joined the West Indies Federation at formation in 1958; this arrangement replaced the earlier Leeward Islands federal grouping of which Antigua and Barbuda had been part. The West Indies Federation collapsed in 1962 – too late to revive the old Leeward Islands federation, since most of the eligible Eastern Caribbean countries were in the process of moving towards independence.

Under the West Indies Act 1967, Antigua became an associated state with internal self-government, the UK retaining control of foreign affairs and defence. Vere Bird Sr became the first premier, but the ALP was ousted at the next elections in 1971 by the Progressive Labour Movement (PLM), led by George Walters. Both parties had their roots in the labour movement; the main difference at that time was that the PLM was campaigning for early independence, while the ALP wanted stronger economic foundations to be developed first.

The ALP returned to power at the 1976 elections. Following the ALP's victory, Bird led the country to full independence on 1 November 1981. Antigua and Barbuda joined the Organisation of Eastern Caribbean States at its formation in 1981.

The ALP remained in power during the 1980s, its position enhanced by divisions within the opposition. However, by the late 1980s divisions also appeared in the ALP, precipitated by allegations of financial misdealing in 1986, and of armaments sales in 1990, both involving senior government ministers. These matters led to ongoing parliamentary controversy.

In April 1992 three opposition parties merged to form the United Progressive Party (UPP). In September 1993, on the retirement of Vere Bird, his son Lester Bird became prime minister. In March 1994 the ALP won its fifth consecutive election victory, securing 11 of the 17 seats in the House; the UPP led by Baldwin Spencer took five and the Barbuda People's Movement one.

Australia

KEY FACTS

Joined Commonwealth:	1931 (Statute of Westminster)
Population:	22,268,000 (2010)
GDP p.c. growth:	2.3% p.a. 1990–2010
UN HDI 2011:	world ranking 2
Official language:	English
Time:	GMT plus 8–11hr
Currency:	Australian dollar (A$)

Geography

Area:	7,682,395 sq km
Coastline:	25,800km
Capital:	Canberra

The Commonwealth of Australia is a Federation with six states – New South Wales (state capital Sydney), Victoria (Melbourne), Queensland (Brisbane), South Australia (Adelaide), Western Australia (Perth) and Tasmania (Hobart) – and two territories, Northern Territory (capital Darwin) and the Australian Capital Territory, where the federal capital, Canberra, is situated. Australia also has external territories (described in the profiles following this one). These have small populations or are uninhabited and, apart from the vast Australian Antarctic Territory, are small islands.

The term 'Australia' is derived from *Terra Australis*, the name given to a southern landmass whose existence geographers deduced before it was discovered. Papua New Guinea (to the north) and New Zealand (to the east) are Australia's closest neighbours. To the south lie the Southern Ocean and Antarctica.

Time: There are three time zones: western (GMT plus 8hr, and no change in summer); central (GMT plus 9.5hr, no change in summer in Northern Territory, and GMT plus 10.5hr October–March in South Australia); and north-east/south-east (GMT plus 10hr, and in

all eastern states except Queensland, GMT plus 11hr October–March).

Area: 7,682,395 sq km including the State of Tasmania and some smaller island territories.

Topography: Australia is the largest link in the chain running between South-East Asia and the South Pacific. Much of central Australia is desert. The main mountain chain, the Great Dividing Range, runs down the east coast, rising to Australia's highest point at Mt Kosciusko (2,230m). Consequently, many of the rivers draining to the east are short; those flowing to the west, of which the Murray–Darling river system is the most considerable, tend to flow only after heavy rains and end in lakes which are often dry with a salt-bed.

Climate: The Tropic of Capricorn almost bisects the continent, running just north of Alice Springs, Australia's central settlement. The subtropical areas north of this line have summer rainfall and dry winters. South of the Tropic, the rest of the continent and Tasmania are temperate. Continental considerations affect this basic pattern, most coastal areas having some rainfall, whereas a large tract of central Australia has less than 300mm p.a. Drought and consequent bushfires are a serious problem.

This pattern of rainfall will be dramatically affected by occasional La Niña events which occur in the central and eastern Pacific Ocean causing the sea to cool and increasing the probability that strong cool onshore winds will bring heavy rains to the eastern regions of Australia, as occurred from November 2010, when there were devastating floods first in Queensland, then in Victoria.

Environment: The most significant environmental issues are soil erosion and desertification; loss of the natural habitat of many

Did you know...

Australia was a founder member of the Commonwealth in 1931 when its independence was recognised under the Statute of Westminster.

It is one of 28 island nations in the association; the mainland of Australia is the largest island in the world.

Of the many internationally acclaimed Australian writers, eleven have won overall Commonwealth Writers' Prizes, eight for Best Book and three for Best First Book.

Australia is one of the world's largest exporters of wine; only Italy, France and Spain exported more in 2007.

unique animal and plant species due to increases in agricultural and industrial production; and damage to the Great Barrier Reef, the largest coral reef in the world, due to increased shipping and tourism.

Vegetation: A wide range, from the tropical jungle of Queensland to the sparse flowers of the desert, with many unique species which evolved in the continent's long geological isolation. Over 500 species of eucalyptus and over 600 species of acacia (wattle). The main fertile areas are in the south and east in New South Wales and Victoria – arable land comprises 6% of the total land area, while the north-east has tropical forest and bush – forest covers 19% of the country.

Wildlife: Many indigenous animal species are unique to the continent. The most distinctive are the marsupials, of which there are 120 species from the kangaroo to the tiny desert mouse, and the monotremes, the rare order of mammals which lay eggs, such as the duck-billed platypus and the echidna. There are also several species of flightless birds – the emu, second only to the African ostrich in size, and the cassowary.

Main towns: Canberra (capital, Australian Capital Territory, pop. 334,300 in 2010), Sydney (New South Wales, 3.75m), Melbourne (Victoria, 3.55m), Brisbane (Queensland, 1.83m), Perth (Western Australia, 1.32m), Adelaide (South Australia, 1.06m), Gold Coast–Tweed Heads (Queensland, 504,800), Newcastle (New South Wales, 295,600), Hobart (Tasmania, 228,700) and Darwin (Northern Territory, 63,800).

Transport: There are 815,070km of roads, 40% paved; Australian road design is known for the long, straight roads in rural areas. Some roads may be impassable after heavy rain.

Rail services link main towns across the country and the total system extends to 9,660km. The 4,000km Indian–Pacific from Sydney to Perth takes three days. The 3,000km north–south line, linking Adelaide in the south with Alice Springs in the centre and Darwin in the north was completed in 2003.

The country has 25,800km of coastline and many deep-water harbours.

International airports are at Sydney, Adelaide, Melbourne, Perth, Darwin, Brisbane, Hobart, Townsville and Cairns.

Society

KEY FACTS 2010

Population per sq km:	3
Life expectancy:	82 years
Net primary enrolment:	97%

Population: 22,268,000 (2010); density is one of the lowest in the world; 89% lives in urban areas and 58% in urban agglomerations of more than 1 million people; growth 1.3% p.a. 1990–2010; birth rate 14 per 1,000 people (20 in 1970); life expectancy 82 years (71 in 1970); life expectancy in the Aboriginal population about 62 years.

People of Asian origin comprise 8.7% of the population, and Aboriginal or Torres Strait Island peoples 2.5%. 70% of the population were born in Australia (2006 census).

Language: English, the official language, is spoken at home by 78.5% of the population. The largest other home languages are Italian, Greek, Cantonese, Arabic and Mandarin (2006 census).

Religion: Mainly Christians (Roman Catholics 26%, Anglicans 19%), small minorities of Buddhists, Muslims, Hindus and Jews (2006 census).

Health: Public spending on health was 6% of GDP in 2009. Health facilities are a responsibility of the states, although the federal government administers the Medicare insurance scheme, introduced in 1984. Infant mortality was 4 per 1,000 live births in 2010 (20 in 1960).

Education: Public spending on education was 4.4% of GDP in 2008. Responsibility for education lies with the states and education systems vary. There are 11 years of compulsory education starting at age five. The school year starts in January.

There are 39 universities with some one million students enrolled (2011). The female–male ratio for gross enrolment in tertiary education is 1.32:1 (2009). There is virtually no illiteracy among people aged 15–24.

Media: Newspapers have a high circulation rate throughout the country. National dailies are *The Australian* and *Australian Financial Review*. Regional newspapers include *The Advertiser* (Adelaide), *The Age* (Melbourne), *The Courier-Mail* (Brisbane), *The Daily Telegraph* (Sydney), *Herald-Sun* (Melbourne), *The Sydney Morning Herald* and *The West Australian* (Perth).

The Australian Broadcasting Corporation (ABC) operates national and regional public radio and TV stations. The Special Broadcasting Service is the other principal public broadcaster, running radio and TV networks that broadcast in many languages. Pay TV networks are widely used, and digital TV is available via satellite and cable.

Some 99% of households have TV sets (2007). There are 776 personal computers (2008) and 760 internet users (2010) per 1,000 people.

Communications: Country code 61; internet domain '.au'. Payphones are red, green, gold or blue. Only local calls can be made from red phones; green, gold and blue phones also have international direct dialling. Mobile phone coverage is good in the more populous areas.

There are 389 main telephone lines and 1,010 mobile phone subscriptions per 1,000 people (2010).

Public holidays: New Year's Day, Australia Day (26 January), ANZAC Day (25 April), Queen's Official Birthday (Monday in June, not all states), Labour Day (early October in most states, otherwise in March), Christmas Day and Boxing Day. States have additional public holidays.

Religious and other festivals whose dates vary from year to year include Good Friday and Easter Monday.

Economy

KEY FACTS 2009

GNI:	US$957.5bn
GNI p.c.:	US$43,770
GDP growth:	2.9% p.a. 2005–09
Inflation:	3.0% p.a. 2006–10

Australia has a high degree of prosperity, based on its wealth of natural resources, policies of redistribution and welfare, and stable democratic society. Significant minerals include aluminium, coal, copper, diamonds, gold, iron, nickel, oil and gas, silver, tin,

Real Growth in GDP

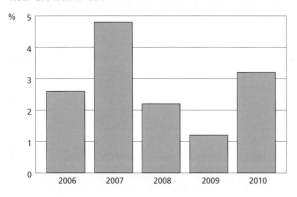

Inflation

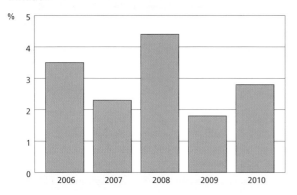

GDP by Sector (2010)

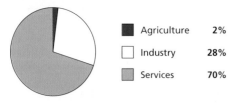

■ Agriculture	2%
□ Industry	28%
▨ Services	70%

titanium, uranium and zinc. Proven reserves of oil were estimated in January 2011 to be 4.1 billion barrels, and of gas, 2.9 trillion cubic metres. The economy relied mainly on agriculture and mining until manufacturing boomed after the Second World War. Service industries have since led growth, rising from about 60% of GDP in the 1960s to about 70% in the 2000s.

However, the economy remained vulnerable to variations in agricultural output and fluctuations in world commodity prices. There is a high level of foreign investment resulting in a serious current account deficit as interest and dividends leave the country; domestic investment is relatively low.

From the 1980s major economic reforms were introduced, including liberalisation of trade and foreign investment, deregulation of financial system and markets, privatisation of public enterprises and government services, and decentralisation of wage settlements.

During the 2000s the economy grew well, with average GDP growth of 3.4% p.a. in 2003–07. It continued to grow at 3.7% in 2008, benefiting from strong world commodity prices. It then slowed in the last quarter of 2008 due to the global economic

downturn and consequent fall in commodity prices. With slower growth of 1.3% in 2009, unemployment rose again, after reaching its lowest level since the 1970s in early 2008 (4.0%), but the economy recovered in 2010, growing by 2.6% in 2010 and about 2% in 2011.

Constitution

Status:	Monarchy under Queen Elizabeth II
Legislature:	Parliament of Australia

Under the Australian constitution, the legislative power of the Commonwealth of Australia is vested in the Parliament of the Commonwealth, which consists of the monarch, the Senate (the upper house) and the House of Representatives (the lower house). Queen Elizabeth II is represented by a governor-general who holds the office for a five-year term. The Senate comprises 76 senators, 12 from each of the six states, and two from each of the two territories. Senators are directly elected for six years; half the Senate retires every three years. The House of Representatives comprises 150 members directly elected; elections – using the preferential voting system – for both houses are held simultaneously at a maximum of three-year intervals. There is compulsory universal suffrage for all Australians over the age of 18. All amendments to the constitution must be passed by absolute majority in both houses. There must then be a referendum in every state.

Areas of authority of the federal government are defined in the constitution as defence, foreign policy, immigration, customs and excise, and the post office. Other powers (justice, education, health and internal transport) are the responsibility of the state governments. During the Second World War, a temporary arrangement was made whereby the federal government would collect taxes and refund the states using an agreed formula. This arrangement has become permanent, leaving the states financially dependent on the federal government.

Each of the states also has its own government, with a governor representing the Queen. Five states have bicameral legislatures, and Queensland has a single chamber. The federal government is responsible for administration of the Australian Federal Territory and, since 1978, Northern Territory has had a degree of self-government.

Politics

Last elections:	August 2010
Next elections:	2013
Head of state:	Queen Elizabeth II, represented by governor-general, Quentin Bryce (2008–)
Head of government:	Prime Minister Julia Gillard
Ruling party:	Labor Party

Prime Minister John Howard's Liberal–National coalition was comfortably returned for a third consecutive term in November 2001, winning 81 seats (Liberal Party 68, National Party 13) to Labor Party's 65. In an election dominated by the issue of Asian immigration, the government's firm action in August 2001 of denying a shipload of Afghan asylum-seekers entry into the country seemed to have proved decisive.

The October 2004 election which had been thought too close to predict was again won comfortably by the Liberal–National coalition and Howard was returned to government, winning 85 seats (Liberal Party 73, National Party 12) while the Labor Party took 57.

Kevin Rudd became the Labor Party leader in December 2006.

In the fiercely fought contest, in November 2007, the Labor Party took 84 seats, the Liberal–National coalition 64 and independent candidates two; Rudd became prime minister and immediately signalled a significant shift in domestic and foreign policy by ratifying the Kyoto Protocol on climate change.

In September 2008, Quentin Bryce was sworn in as Australia's 25th governor-general; she is the first woman to hold the post.

In June 2010, after a dramatic fall in the popularity of Prime Minister Rudd, Deputy Prime Minister Julia Gillard successfully challenged Rudd for the Labor Party leadership and became prime minister, the first woman to hold the post.

In the early general election in August 2010 neither Labor (winning 72 out of 150 seats in the lower house) nor the Liberal–National

History

Fifty million years ago the Australian continent broke away from the great southern landmass of Gondwanaland, which comprised South America, Africa, India, Australia and Antarctica. Apart from a period during the last Ice Age when the sea level was 100m lower than it is today, Australia existed in isolation. This resulted in the evolution of vegetation and wildlife which is substantially unique.

It was thought that the Aboriginal population may have lived in Australia for 50,000 years. However, recent evidence from the Kimberley region of Western Australia suggests much older human habitation. When European explorers arrived, the Aboriginal peoples lived by hunting and gathering and using stone tools. Estimates of the historical size of the population range up to 750,000 people. Aboriginal society, though technologically undeveloped, had complex cultural and religious forms, and some 500 languages, in 31 basic groups. There was a rich oral tradition of songs and stories, and many different styles of rock art.

The first known Europeans to land were Dutch. In 1606, William Jansz landed on the west coast of Cape York Peninsula, and thereafter various landings were made. The Dutch named this land New Holland, but showed no interest in further exploration.

In April 1770, Captain James Cook in HMS *Endeavour* with the botanist Sir Joseph Banks landed in Botany Bay (in what is now New South Wales) and claimed the east coast for the English Crown. Having just lost the American colonies, England needed new penal colonies, and the first shipload of Australian settlers were convicts, arriving with Governor Arthur Phillip in 1788. They moved to Port Jackson (now part of Sydney Harbour) on 26 January, now Australia Day. However, even before transportation to New South Wales was abolished in 1840, free settlers were arriving in increasing numbers. Further exploration, often dangerous, revealed that the land known as New Holland and the English colony were one and the same large island.

In 1831, Western Australia became the second colony, followed by South Australia in 1836, Victoria in 1851, Tasmania in 1856, and Queensland in 1859. The Northern Territory was, for some time, part of South Australia and later the responsibility of the federal government, achieving self-government in 1978.

The settler population in early years lived mostly in coastal areas, deploying large tracts of land for sheep and cattle. The annexation of land was often accompanied by brutal treatment of the Aboriginal population, who were forced into the interior. Gold was first discovered in Victoria in the 1850s and prompted Australia's gold rush with a consequent opening up of the interior

and more displacement of the Aboriginals. Wheat farming developed, and the country rapidly became a leading exporter. With the invention of refrigeration, export trade in mutton and dairy products began. An extensive railway system was built. Between 1860 and 1890, immigrants, and capital, mostly from Britain, contributed to a long economic boom. In 1891, the country had a population of 3 million, and was exporting wool, mutton, dairy products and wheat.

The colonies, all of which had Westminster-style representative institutions by 1890, became one nation on 1 January 1901. The Commonwealth of Australia, with a federal structure, was established. By the time of the First World War, Australian politics emphasised social policy, industrial development, and protectionism to cushion local industries and maintain full employment. The development of the steel industry after 1915 and advances in mining assisted development, so that by 1939, industry was responsible for 40% of GDP. Sophisticated industries such as car manufacture developed in the 1950s. By the latter 1980s, Australians enjoyed one of the world's highest living standards.

Australia's political party system traditionally consisted of the Liberal Party, National Party (originally known as the Country Party) and Labor Party (ALP). The Liberal and National parties were frequently in coalition. A new party, the Australian Democrats, was formed in the 1970s as a breakaway group from the Liberal–National coalition. The Liberal–National coalition was in office from 1949 until 1972, and again from 1975 to 1983, under Malcolm Fraser. The Labor Party, under Bob Hawke and then Paul Keating, was in office from 1983 to 1996, when the Liberal–National coalition led by John Howard returned to power. Howard's conservative coalition's majority was reduced in an early general election in October 1998, in the face of a strong showing by the Labor Party now led by Kim Beazley.

In February 1998, the Constitutional Convention voted by 89 votes to 52 for Australia to become a republic by 2001, and by 73 votes to 57 to replace the British monarch with a president. It was agreed that there would be a referendum on the issue.

Despite evidence from opinion polls that most Australians were in favour of a republic, in the referendum of November 1999 – when asked if they supported 'an act to alter the constitution to establish the Commonwealth of Australia as a republic, with the Queen and governor-general being replaced by a president appointed by a two-thirds majority of the members of the Commonwealth Parliament' – almost 55% registered a 'No' vote. The result was widely attributed to widespread dissatisfaction about the right of parliamentarians to choose a president.

coalition led by Tony Abbott (73 seats) was able to secure a parliamentary majority. The remaining seats were won by the Green Party (one) and independents (four). After several weeks of negotiations with these members, Gillard was successful in winning the support of the Green Party member and three of the independents, giving the Labor party a narrow overall majority. In her new cabinet Kevin Rudd was appointed to the foreign affairs portfolio.

International relations

Australia is a member of Asia–Pacific Economic Cooperation, Indian Ocean Rim Association for Regional Cooperation, Organisation for Economic Co-operation and Development, Pacific Community, Pacific Islands Forum, United Nations and World Trade Organization.

Traveller information

Local laws and conventions: Smoking is not allowed in most restaurants. There is a strict drugs policy in Australia and penalties for the trafficking or possession of drugs are severe. Prosecution can lead to a lengthy jail sentence and non-Australian nationals are usually deported at the end of their sentence.

Visitors to Australia can expect a largely informal atmosphere. Handshaking is the customary greeting and casual clothing is worn everywhere except in the most exclusive restaurants, social gatherings and important business meetings.

Suits are usually worn when conducting business in Sydney and Melbourne, while in Brisbane, shirts, ties and shorts may be acceptable. Appointments for meetings are customary and punctuality is important. Business transactions may be conducted over drinks. The best months for business travel are March to November. Office hours are Mon–Fri 0900–1700.

Immigration and customs: Visas are required by everyone except New Zealanders, and passports must be valid for six months from the date of entry.

A yellow fever vaccination certificate is required by all those arriving from infected countries.

Visitors must declare all food, plant material and animal products on arrival in Australia to ensure they are free of pests and diseases; any items that pose pest and disease risks will be destroyed.

There are very strict regulations against the import of non-prescribed drugs, weapons, firearms, wildlife, domestic animals and foodstuffs, plants or parts of plants, animal products, and other potential sources of disease and pestilence (such as vaccines or viruses).

Travel within the country: Driving is on the left, and car hire is available at all major airports and hotels for those aged over 21. Visitors may drive on a national licence for a maximum of three months, although an international driving permit is needed by all those whose official language is not English.

In most states the maximum speed limit on freeways is 100kph and ranges from 50–80kph in suburban districts. Drink-driving is illegal and the wearing of seatbelts is mandatory. If driving in the outback, visitors should be aware that summer rains can turn roads into dirt tracks and make driving conditions hazardous. Distances between the main cities can be considerable, and drivers should ensure they seek up-to-date information on road and weather conditions before setting out.

Urban transport services are good and there are suburban rail networks in the state capitals; Melbourne and Adelaide also have a tram system. Taxis are widely available and are metered.

There are good cross-country coach services, although flying is the most common way of travelling between cities. Domestic flights are easily booked and many airlines operate special deals at greatly reduced prices.

Rail travel is slow and expensive. There is a twice-weekly train service that travels from Sydney to Perth and takes three days. Another service links Adelaide with Perth and runs weekly in each direction; journey time is two nights. Reservations are essential on all long-distance train services.

Travel health: Health care facilities are high and hospitals well equipped. British nationals may receive free treatment for emergencies, as there is a reciprocal health agreement with the UK. All visitors are advised to take out comprehensive health insurance.

Occasional outbreaks of dengue fever and Ross River fever have been known to occur in rural parts of northern Australia and visitors should take adequate precautions to prevent mosquito bites.

For bathers, corals, jellyfish and fresh water crocodiles may prove a hazard and visitors must not swim in unguarded remote locations.

Money: Exchange facilities can be found at all airports and international-class hotels. Major credit cards are accepted, although there may be restrictions in small towns and outback areas. Travellers cheques are easily changed and should be in a major currency to avoid additional charges. Banking hours are Mon–Thur 0930–1600, Fri 0930–1700.

There were 5,885,000 tourist arrivals in 2010.

Further information

Australian, State, Territory and Local Governments: www.gov.au

Parliament of Australia: www.aph.gov.au

Reserve Bank of Australia: www.rba.gov.au

Commonwealth Secretariat: www.thecommonwealth.org

Commonwealth of Nations: www.commonwealth-of-nations.org/Australia

Australia: External Territories

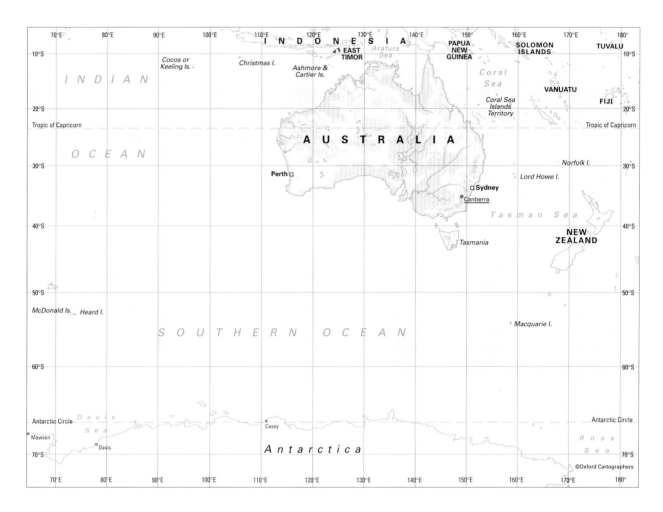

The External Territories of Australia are: Australian Antarctic Territory; Ashmore and Cartier Islands, Christmas Island, Cocos (Keeling) Islands, Heard Island and the McDonald Islands (Indian Ocean); Coral Sea Islands Territory, Norfolk Island (Pacific Ocean).

Australian Antarctic Territory (AAT)

Geography

The AAT consists of all islands and territories south of latitude 60°S and between longitudes 45° and 160° east except for the French sector of Terre Adélie, which comprises the islands and territories south of 60°S latitude and between longitudes 136° and 142° east. The AAT is the single largest sector of the continent and covers much of east Antarctica.

Time: GMT plus 4.5–10hr, depending on longitude

Area: 5,800,000 sq km

Topography: The icy landscapes of Antarctica, offering sweeping distant views, are of outstanding scenic beauty. The continent is the highest landmass in the world, thanks to its high ice cover, averaging over 2,000m. A broad mountain ridge (the Transantarctic Mountains) stretches into the AAT; the terrain is also high in Enderby Land and around the ice-packed bay of the Amery Ice Shelf, with Mt Menzies rising to 3,355m. The land area is fringed by a wide belt of ice up to hundreds of kilometres wide. Around the coast, icebergs continually 'calve' (break off) the glaciers into the sea. Over 95% of the continent is permanently covered in ice.

Climate: Antarctic, with severe wind chill increasing the harshness of the climate. On the central plateau, temperatures drop to minus 80°C. Local ('katabatic') winds of incredible ferocity develop on the plateau and sweep towards the coast. Around the French sector of Terre Adélie, full gales blow for 200 days a year. Precipitation is surprisingly light, with annual snowfall at 60mm of water equivalent on the central plateau and 1.5m on the coastal belt. Within the Antarctic Circle, there are days of complete darkness during the Antarctic winter and conversely of midnight sun during the summer.

Vegetation: Plant life is primitive and sparse, but lichens and mosses can survive where the harsh climate permits it.

Wildlife: Plankton and krill (shrimp-like creatures) abound in the rich Antarctic waters, supporting the marine food chain. The glaciers add nutrient minerals as they melt, diluting the saltiness of the sea and enabling marine life to thrive. Various species of penguins are found: Adélie and emperor penguins are especially resilient to the cold. Female emperor penguins settle their egg on the feet of the male parent because nesting on the ice is impossible. Other birdlife includes the Antarctic petrel and the South Polar skua, which breed exclusively on the continent. Whales, porpoises and seals visit Antarctic waters; the fur seal breeds furthest south. Huskies, imported to haul sledges and latterly for companionship, are now banned as a non-indigenous species.

Society

Population: There are three stations (Mawson, Davis and Casey), plus various summer bases and temporary field camps. There is a temporary population of scientists, ranging from about 70 in winter to 200 in summer.

Economy

There is no economic activity, and mining is not permitted. All activity relating to mineral resources, other than strictly for scientific research, is also prohibited. Additionally, Australian nationals are prohibited from mining elsewhere in Antarctica. Environmental protection is a priority. Scientific activities are concerned with global climate change and with studies of the Antarctic ecosystem. These studies include land and marine biology, cosmic-ray physics, upper atmosphere physics, meteorology, earth sciences and glaciology. Regular flights between Hobart, Australia, and the Territory were introduced in the summer of 2007/08, following completion in December 2007 of a new runway at the Wilkins Aerodrome, situated 75km from Casey.

History

Sealing vessels from a number of countries, notably Britain but also including Australia, visited the Antarctic waters during the 19th century. From the early 20th century serious exploration took off, and Douglas Mawson reached the magnetic South Pole in 1909. Various territorial claims were later made and the AAT was transferred to Australian authority in 1933 by the British Government through an imperial order in council. The Australian Antarctic Territory Acceptance Act was passed in the same year, and in 1936 the governor-general put the order into force by proclamation. Mawson Station (named after the explorer) was set up in February 1954 by the Australian National Antarctic Research Expeditions. Davis Station (named after Mawson's second-in-command, Captain John King Davis) was set up in 1957; Casey Station (named after a former governor-general of Australia, Lord Casey) in 1969. An earlier station, Wilkes, was made inoperable by snow and ice inundation, and closed.

Administration

The Territory is administered by the Australian Antarctic Division on behalf of the minister for the environment and heritage. Australia is a party to the Antarctic Treaty. A Protocol on Environmental Protection was added to the Antarctic Treaty in 1991, making Antarctica a natural reserve, devoted to peace and science.

Ashmore and Cartier Islands

The Ashmore and Cartier Islands lie on the outer edge of the Australian continental shelf in the Indian Ocean, midway between north-western Australia and Timor and some 850km to 790km west of Darwin. The Ashmores consist of three islands: Middle, East and West Islands.

Geography

Area: Ashmore Islands: 93 hectares (0.93 sq km); Cartier Islands: 0.4 hectares (0.004 sq km).

Topography: The islands are small and low-lying, rising to a maximum of 2.5m above sea level. They are formed of coral and sand, and are surrounded by shoals and reefs.

Vegetation: Grass and scrub.

Wildlife: The Ashmore Reef islands abound in birdlife. Béche-de-mer (sea cucumber) is abundant; so are turtles at certain times of the year.

Society

Population: There are no permanent residents.

Economy

Indonesian fishermen are permitted to fish in some of the territory's waters. During the fishing season (March–November) Australian observers, stationed on a vessel at Ashmore Reef, monitor activities. The Jabiru and Challis oilfields lie within the adjacent area of the territory. In 1983 Ashmore Reef was made a national nature reserve. It is visited regularly by officers of the National Parks and Wildlife Service.

History

The Ashmores became a British possession in 1878; Cartier Island in 1909. The islands were put under Australian authority in July 1931, by an imperial order in council, and accepted by Australia in 1933 under the Ashmore and Cartier Islands Acceptance Act, which was amended in 1938 to make them part of the Northern Territory. In July 1978, when the Northern Territory was given self-government, the Ashmores and Cartier came under the administration of the Government of the Commonwealth of Australia.

Administration

Administration is the responsibility of the Department of Transport and Regional Services, at Canberra.

Christmas Island

Geography

Christmas Island lies in the Indian Ocean, south of Java and 2,600km north-west of Perth.

Area: approx. 135 sq km

Topography: The island consists of a central plateau rising to 250m in the east and 150m in the west, with several high points 360m above sea level. Much of the coast consists of 10–20m-high sheer cliffs, with a few small sandy beaches. The main anchorage is at Flying Fish Cove. The ground is porous but there is ample fresh water from springs.

Climate: Tropical. South-easterly winds from May to December; the wet season is from December to April when the north-west monsoon blows. Average rainfall is about 2,000mm p.a., and humidity averages 80–90%.

Vegetation: Tropical rainforest covers much of the island; some 60% of forest is in the National Park. There are 16 endemic plant species.

Wildlife: Most of the animal species are endemic. The Abbott's booby and Christmas Island frigatebird are endangered.

Main settlement: Flying Fish Cove

Transport/Communications: There are 140km of roads, of which 30km are paved. A ship operates between Singapore, Perth, Christmas Island and Cocos (Keeling) Islands, and an air service from Perth to Christmas Island and Cocos (Keeling) Islands, with extra flights to allow students to come home for holidays. The international dialling code is 61.

Society

Population: 2,000 (2010); population density 15 per sq km; mostly of Chinese descent (70% in 2001), with European and Malay minorities. There is no indigenous population.

Language: English is the official language; Mandarin, Cantonese and Malay are most commonly spoken at home.

Religion: Buddhists 30%, Muslims, Christians (2006).

Health: Christmas Island has a modern hospital with a fully equipped operating theatre.

Education: Free and compulsory from age six to 15. The Christmas Island District High School follows the Western Australia curriculum. It caters for children from kindergarten to secondary school level. After Year 10, students attend schools on the mainland.

Media: *The Islander* is a fortnightly newsletter published by the Shire of Christmas Island.

Radio VLU2, a community station, broadcasts in English, Malay and Mandarin. Mainland Australian radio and TV stations are received via satellite.

Economy

Mining and exporting some 600,000 tonnes p.a. of phosphate to South-East Asia and the Australian mainland is the main and stable economic activity. The mining company is 40%-owned by Christmas Islanders. It pays royalties, based on exports, to the Commonwealth of Australia, and these are used for rehabilitation of the mined areas. Environmental controls are in force, and rainforest clearing is prohibited.

The island also offers specialist diving and fishing holidays and eco-tourism.

History

Britain annexed Christmas Island (then uninhabited) in 1888. A 99-year lease was taken out in 1891 by John Murray and George Ross, who transferred it to the Christmas Island Phosphate Company in 1897. In 1900 Christmas Island was incorporated into the Straits Settlements and became subject to the laws of Singapore. It was occupied by the Japanese army from March 1942 until August 1945. In 1947 the Straits Settlements ceased to exist, and Singapore, together with Cocos (Keeling) Islands and Christmas Island, became the Colony of Singapore. From 1 January to 30 September 1958, Christmas Island was a British Crown colony. Subsequently, it became an Australian territory, administered initially by the minister for external territories.

Under the Migration Act of 1981, Christmas Island residents were entitled to become residents and citizens of Australia. In 1984 the benefits of Australian social security, enfranchisement, health and education were extended to them; and progressively from 1985 to 1989, they became liable for income and other taxes. A proposal to secede from Australia was rejected in an unofficial referendum held in 1994.

Administration

Christmas Island is an Australian territory, the administration of which is the responsibility of the Department of Infrastructure, Transport, Regional Development and Local Government at Canberra. An administrator is appointed by the Governor-General of Australia. Local government services are provided by the Shire of Christmas Island, which is responsible to a council of nine elected representatives.

Cocos (Keeling) Islands

Geography

The territory lies in the Indian Ocean, 2,768km north-west of Perth. It consists of two atolls made up of 27 small coral islands. Only two of them – West and Home – are inhabited. The largest island, West Island, is about 16km by 0.5km in area. North Keeling Island lies 24km north of the main lagoon.

Area: 14 sq km

Topography: The islands are flat and low-lying. The northern part of the main atoll, which surrounds a lagoon, has anchorage, but navigation is difficult.

Climate: Generally equable (temperatures 22–32°C), with south-east trade winds for much of the year and occasional violent storms. Rainfall is high, averaging 2,000mm a year.

Vegetation: The main atoll has extensive vegetation and coconut palms.

Wildlife: Birdlife is abundant, with both sea birds (terns, gannets and petrels) and land birds which have reached the islands from Indonesia.

Transport/Communications: A ship sails from Singapore and Perth, Australia, every few weeks. The airport is on West Island and there are regular flights from Perth. The international dialling code is 61.

Society

Population: 600 (2010); population density 43 per sq km; comprising mainly of people of Australian (largely on West Island) and Malayan (Home Island) descent.

Language: English and Cocos Malay.

Religion: Muslims 75% (2006 census).

Education: Free and compulsory from age six to 15. There is one primary school from kindergarten to Year 6 and one secondary from Years 7 to 12.

Media: Mainland Australian TV and radio programmes are relayed to the islands.

Economy

There is local fishing and domestic cultivation of vegetables, bananas and pawpaws, but the islands are not self-sufficient in food.

Tropical reef fish are exported, and the islands offer specialist diving and fishing holidays and eco-tourism.

History

The islands were all uninhabited in 1609 when Captain William Keeling (East India Company) visited them. In 1826 John Clunies-Ross (joined a year later by Alexander Hare) started to set up various small settlements on the main atoll and established the copra industry, bringing in Chinese, Malay and African workers. Annexed by Britain in 1857, the islands were placed under the Governors of Ceylon in 1878; in 1886 they became part of the Straits Settlements. Later they were part of the Colony of Singapore. In 1955 they were transferred to Australian sovereignty; in April 1984 the inhabitants voted by referendum (observed by UN observers) for integration with Australia, and became Australian citizens. In 1978 the government bought the greater part of the land owned by the Clunies-Ross family under a grant in perpetuity made in 1886; the rest of the family's property, which was on Home Island, was bought in 1993.

Administration

The territory is managed by an administrator (appointed by Australia's governor-general), who is responsible to the minister for infrastructure, transport, regional development and local government. The Cocos (Keeling) Islands Shire Council is responsible for local government. The territory is part of the Northern Territory electoral district; like all Australian citizens, the residents vote in parliamentary elections.

Coral Sea Islands Territory (CSIT)

The CSIT lies east of Queensland. It consists of all the islands between the Great Barrier Reef and longitude 156°E, between latitudes 12° and 24°S.

Geography

Land and sea area: About 780,000 sq km.

Topography: The islands are small, formed mostly of coral and sand. No permanent supply of fresh water on any of them.

Climate: Tropical; occasional cyclones.

Vegetation: Grass and shrubs grow on some of the islands.

Wildlife: Lihou Reef and Coringa-Herald are national nature reserves for the protection of wildlife. *Dermochelys coriacea*, the world's largest and most endangered species of sea-turtle, nests in the territory, as well as five other species of sea-turtle. There are more than 24 species of birds, many of which are protected under agreements with Japan and China. Herbaria and museums in Australia contain many specimens of CSIT flora and fauna.

Society

Uninhabited, except for a meteorological station with a small staff on Willis Island.

Economy

There is no economic activity. There are automatic weather stations on Cato Island, Flinders Reef, Frederick Reef, Holmes Reef, Lihou Reef, Creal Reef, Marion Reef and Gannet Cay, relaying data to the mainland. Navigational aids are located on many of the islands and reefs.

History

Until 1921, when the meteorological station was set up on Willis Island, the CSIT was totally uninhabited. Navigation in the territory is extremely difficult, and there were frequent shipwrecks during the 19th century. Many of the islands and reefs are named after ships wrecked on them. Since 1859, expeditions of botanists and zoologists have visited the territory.

Administration

Under the Coral Sea Islands Act of 1969, the Coral Sea Islands are an Australian territory administered by the minister for infrastructure, transport, regional development and local government. The governor-general of Australia can make ordinances relating to peace, order and the good government of the territory.

Heard Island and the McDonald Islands

Heard Island (about 43km by 20km) is the biggest of a group of islands in the South Indian Ocean about 4,100km south-west of Fremantle. The McDonald Islands are 43km west of Heard Island.

Geography

Topography: Heard Island is dominated by the only active volcano on Australian territory, the 2,745m-high Big Ben. The McDonald Islands are small, steep and rocky.

Climate: Sub-Antarctic.

Vegetation: Heard Island is regarded as one of the last Antarctic habitats remaining free of introduced organisms, and is of considerable scientific interest. Vegetation is sparse, but cushion plants, tussock grass, mosses and lichens can survive.

Wildlife: Visited by elephant seals, leopard seals and penguins. Petrels, albatrosses and skuas breed on Heard Island.

Society

No permanent inhabitants. Occasional visits by scientists for research.

Economy

There is no economic activity. Zoological and geological expeditions are made to Heard Island from time to time. In 1985, research was conducted into the coastal zone's maritime resources and there have been a small number of expeditions since then. In 1991, international research on global warming was undertaken at Heard Island, which has direct paths to the world's five principal oceans.

History

Heard Island was first sighted in 1833 and named in 1855 after an American captain. After 1855 the island's elephant seals and penguins were exploited for their oil. The territory was transferred by the UK to Australian control in 1947. Between 1947 and 1955, a research station was maintained on Heard Island, to conduct various scientific and meteorological investigations. The station was closed after 1954, when Mawson station was established on the Antarctic mainland.

The McDonald Islands were first visited in 1971 by an Australian National Antarctic Research Expedition. In December 1997 the territory was inscribed on the World Heritage List.

Administration

The islands are administered by the Australian Antarctic Division on behalf of the minister for the environment and heritage. The Environment Protection and Management Ordinance (January 1988) set up a framework for sustained conservation. A management plan under the ordinance came into force in 1996.

Norfolk Island

Geography

Norfolk Island lies in the South Pacific, about 1,676km east of Sydney. The territory includes the uninhabited islands of Phillip and Nepean (7km and 1km south of the main island).

Area: 34.5 sq km

Topography: Norfolk Island is steep and rocky, with sheer cliffs rising out of the sea; access is impossible, except at Kingston on the south side and at Cascade in the north.

Climate: Subtropical, with sea-breezes; equable. Average rainfall: 1,350mm a year.

Vegetation: Most of the island has been cleared for crops or pasture, but a national park was established in 1985–86 to protect the remaining native forest. Phillip Island forms part of the national park. The Norfolk Island pine remains a notable feature. There is a wide variety of native and introduced plants.

Wildlife: There is abundant birdlife, geckos, bats and turtles. The Norfolk green parrot, guavabird and boobook are unique to the territory.

Main town: Kingston

Transport/Communications: There is about 80km of road, 53km sealed. There are ship services from Australia and New Zealand every few weeks, and regular air services from Brisbane and Sydney in Australia and Auckland, New Zealand. The international dialling code is 672.

Society

Population: 1,860 (2010); population density 54 per sq km; consists of islanders (that is, Pitcairn/Bounty descendants) and mainlanders (originally from Australia, New Zealand and the UK). The right of residence on Norfolk Island is strictly controlled.

Language: English and Norfuk, a Creole which – like Pitkern (the language of the Pitcairn Islanders) – is based on 18th century English and Tahitian.

Religion: Mainly Christians (Anglicans 32%, 2006 census).

Education: Free and compulsory between age six and 15. There is a school – Norfolk Island Central School – under the authority of the New South Wales Education Department, taking pupils from kindergarten to Higher School Certificate level (year 12). In 1997 there were 318 pupils. Some bursaries are available, and there are some scholarships for vocational training outside the island. Greenwich University, a private distance-learning enterprise, opened in Norfolk Island in 1999.

Media: There are two weeklies: the independent *Norfolk Islander* and the official *Norfolk Island Government Gazette*.

The administration runs a local radio service (VL2NI – Norfolk Island Radio) and the television service is privately owned (TVN). Television programmes are relayed via the AUSSAT satellite.

Economy

Norfolk Island is a self-governing territory and exercises control over most of its economic activities and developments. The main economic activity is tourism. The territory offers the attractions of remoteness, conservation sites and the poignant remains of the old penal settlement. There are some 30–35,000 visitors each year. External revenue is also gained through philatelic sales. No income tax is payable on income earned within the island.

There is agriculture for domestic consumption. The soil is fertile and there is also some commercial cultivation of plants and flowers. A programme to increase planting of Norfolk Island pine and to introduce eucalyptus trees has been established. Seed and seedlings of the Norfolk Island pine are exported. There is also fishing for local consumption. Fish are plentiful, but so far efforts to establish a commercial industry have been hampered by the lack of a sheltered harbour. There is the potential for exploitable offshore hydrocarbon deposits.

History

The island was uninhabited in 1774, when Captain James Cook visited it and was impressed by the commercial potential of the native pines for ship's masts. In the periods 1788 to 1814, and 1825 to 1855, the island was a penal settlement of notable severity. In 1855 the penal settlement was closed and the following year 194 people living on Pitcairn Island, which had become overpopulated, accepted an invitation from Queen Victoria to transfer to Norfolk Island. However, two small parties returned to Pitcairn. These Pitcairn Islanders were descended from the mutineers from *The Bounty* who had sailed from Tahiti to Pitcairn Island in 1790 together with their Tahitian wives.

Administration

Initially, Norfolk Island was a separate settlement but became a dependency of New South Wales in 1897 and was finally transferred to Australian administration in 1913.

There is an administrator, appointed by the governor-general of Australia and responsible to the minister for infrastructure, transport, regional development and local government. A legislative assembly with nine members elected for three years, established in 1979, has internal self-governing powers. An executive council is made up of members of the assembly who have ministerial-type responsibility. Proposed laws passed by the assembly go to the administrator for consent (or otherwise).

The Bahamas

KEY FACTS

Joined Commonwealth:	1973
Population:	343,000 (2010)
GDP p.c. growth:	1.0% p.a. 1990–2010
UN HDI 2011:	world ranking 53
Official language:	English
Time:	GMT minus 5hr
Currency:	Bahamian dollar (B$)

Geography

Area:	13,939 sq km
Coastline:	3,540km
Capital:	Nassau

The Commonwealth of The Bahamas is a coral archipelago of around 700 islands and more than 2,000 rocks and cays in the West Atlantic south-east of the coast of Florida, USA, and north-east of Cuba. It straddles the Tropic of Cancer and stretches 970km.

Topography: About 30 islands are inhabited, the most important of which are New Providence, in the middle of the group, where the capital Nassau is situated, and Grand Bahama, the northernmost, with the city of Freeport. The other islands are known collectively as the Family Islands or Out Islands. The islands lie on a submarine shelf which rises steeply from deep waters in the east; to the west lie the shallow waters of the Great Bahama Bank. The islands, built of coralline limestone to an undersea depth of about 1,500m, are low-lying. The highest, Cat Island, rises to 62m at Mount Alvernia; Grand Bahama barely reaches 12m. The limestone rock of the islands is permeable and there are no streams. The water supply is taken from wells or collected from rainwater.

Climate: The climate is cooler than other countries in the Caribbean region but still pleasantly mild in winter. Winter temperatures average 21°C, summer temperatures 30°C. Most of the rain (averaging 1,100mm p.a.) falls in May–June and September–October and there are frequent thunderstorms in summer. The Bahamas islands are subject to hurricanes during June–November.

Did you know...

Robert Antoni, born in The Bahamas in 1958, was winner of the Commonwealth Writers' Prize Best First Book award with his novel, *Divina Trace*, in 1992.

The country is a coral archipelago of about 700 islands and more than 2,000 cays and rocks.

Environment: The most significant environmental issues are coral reef decay and solid waste disposal.

Vegetation: The soil is thin, and generally infertile, but cultivation has produced exotic flowers (as well as subtropical fruit and vegetables) on the more developed islands. Some islands have large areas of pine forests. Forest covers 51% of the land area and there was no significant loss of forest cover during 1990–2010.

Wildlife: Animal life is restricted to small species, such as agouti, frogs, iguana, and bats. The Inagua National Park on Great Inagua Island is the home of more than 50,000 flamingos, the largest flock in the world and The Bahamas' national bird.

Main towns: Nassau (capital, pop. 241,200 in 2010) on New Providence; Freeport (44,300), West End (13,100) and High Rock (3,900) on Grand Bahama; Cooper's Town (9,300) and Marsh Harbour (5,800) on Abaco; Freetown (4,300) and Spanish Wells (1,800) on Eleuthera; Andros Town (2,300) on Andros; and Clarence Town (1,700) on Long Island.

Transport: The total road system extends to some 2,700km, about 60% of it paved. There are almost 1,000km of roads on New Providence (some of which are privately owned), 209km of roads on Eleuthera, 156km on Grand Bahama, and more than 885km on the Out Islands.

Main ports are Nassau (New Providence), Freeport (Grand Bahama) and Matthew Town (Inagua). The Out Islands are served by a mail boat that leaves Nassau several times a week.

The principal airports are Lynden Pindling International (16km west of the city) and Freeport International (5km from the city), and some 50 airports or airstrips in all.

Society

KEY FACTS 2010

Population per sq km:	25
Life expectancy:	75 years
Net primary enrolment:	92%

Population: 343,000 (2010); 67% lives in New Providence, 84% in urban areas; growth 1.5% p.a. 1990–2010; birth rate 15 per 1,000 people (31 in 1970); life expectancy 75 years (66 in 1970).

Bahamians are largely of African (85%), Afro-European and European origin, as the indigenous Arawaks were wiped out.

Language: English is the official and first language; a French-based Creole is spoken by Haitian immigrants.

Religion: Mainly Christians (Baptists 35%, Anglicans 15%, Roman Catholics 14%, Pentecostals 8%, Church of God, Methodists; 2000 census).

Health: Public spending on health was 3% of GDP in 2009. New Providence has the Princess Margaret Hospital, mental hospital and rehabilitation unit, geriatric hospital, private hospital, with an emergency facility, and private clinic which undertakes plastic surgery. Grand Bahama has a general hospital and the Out Islands cottage hospitals. In addition there are medical centres and clinics, and a flying doctor and dentist service covers the islands. Infant mortality was 14 per 1,000 live births in 2010 (51 in 1960). In 2009, 3.1% of people aged 15–49 were HIV positive.

Education: There are 12 years of compulsory education starting at age five. Primary school comprises six years and secondary six. Some 91% of pupils complete primary school (2007). The school year starts in September.

The College of The Bahamas, the country's leading higher education institution, provides a diverse curriculum with courses leading to bachelor's degree level. The Eugene Dupuch Law School opened in September 1998, as a part of the University of the West Indies. It offers the same curriculum as the Norman Manley Law School in Jamaica and the Hugh Wooding Law School in Trinidad and Tobago. Students are eligible for places at the University of the West Indies, which also has an extra-mural department in Nassau and main campuses in Barbados, Jamaica, and Trinidad and Tobago. Other government-assisted higher technical and professional schools and private colleges provide clerical, secretarial, accounting and computer training.

Media: Daily newspapers are *The Bahama Journal*, *Freeport News*, *The Nassau Guardian* and *The Tribune*; *The Punch* is published twice weekly, and there are several weeklies.

The Broadcasting Corporation of The Bahamas provides public radio and TV services, comprising one TV channel and several radio stations; there are several private radio stations. Cable TV is widely available.

There are 123 personal computers (2005) and 430 internet users (2010) per 1,000 people.

Communications: Country code 1 242; internet domain '.bs'. Coin- and card-operated phone booths on all the islands; phonecards can be purchased at shops and post offices. Mobile phone coverage is mainly good; it is patchy in some of the more remote islands.

There are 377 main telephone lines and 1,249 mobile phone subscriptions per 1,000 people (2010).

Public holidays: New Year's Day, Labour Day (first Friday in June), Independence Day (10 July), Emancipation Day (first Monday in August), National Heroes' Day (12 October), Christmas Day and Boxing Day.

Religious and other festivals whose dates vary from year to year include Good Friday, Easter Monday and Whit Monday.

Economy

KEY FACTS 2010

GDP:	US$7.5bn
GDP p.c.:	US$21,984
GDP growth:	–1.5% p.a. 2006–10
Inflation:	2.6% p.a. 2006–10

The Bahamas is among the wealthiest countries in the Caribbean region. With independence in 1973, the country freed itself from the UK's exchange-control legislation and set up an offshore banking and investment industry; it is now a significant financial centre and ship registry, among the largest in the world in terms of gross tonnage registered. Since 1717 there has been virtually no tax on individuals or companies. Government revenue is raised through a range of excise duties and fees.

Real Growth in GDP

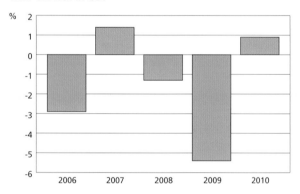

Inflation

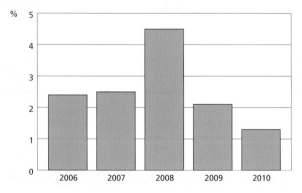

GDP by Sector (2010)

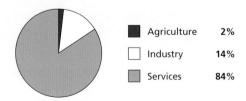

■	Agriculture	2%
□	Industry	14%
■	Services	84%

Though agricultural and forestry production and commercial fishing expanded from the 1990s, and the country is an exporter of fruit and vegetables as well as seafood, it nevertheless imports most of its foodstuffs and consumer goods, and is strongly influenced by the economic climate in the USA, not least because the majority of its tourist visitors are from that country.

From the early 1990s, facing severe recession, the government introduced an economic reform programme which emphasised fiscal responsibility, privatisation of government-owned hotels, investment promotion, infrastructure development and diversification of the economy. From the mid-1990s, as the USA came out of recession, this resulted in a long period of good growth with modest inflation.

The economy stalled in 2001–02, reflecting the downturn in the USA and consequent fall in tourism. Good growth and modest inflation resumed from 2003, until the world economic downturn caused a sharp fall in tourism and offshore financial services (accounting together for more than half of GDP in 2007) and the economy moved sharply into recession, shrinking by more than 4% in 2009, and recovering in 2010–11.

Constitution

Status:	Monarchy under Queen Elizabeth II
Legislature:	Parliament
Independence:	10 July 1973

The Bahamas is a constitutional monarchy recognising Queen Elizabeth II as head of state. She is represented by a governor-general chosen on the advice of the cabinet. The country is a parliamentary democracy with a bicameral legislature. The Senate has 16 members, nine appointed on the advice of the prime minister, four on the advice of the opposition leader, and three after joint discussions. The House of Assembly (presently of 41 elected members, 40 before the 2007 elections and 49 before the 1997 elections) is directly elected on a district basis for a term not exceeding five years; elections are on the basis of universal adult suffrage.

A commission meets at intervals of not less than five years to review the constituency boundaries. The constitution allows for three distinct types of legislation: the 'specially entrenched' provisions relating to parliament itself and the judicial system require a three-quarters majority in both houses and a popular referendum; 'entrenched' provisions require a two-thirds majority in both houses; and other legislation a simple majority vote.

Politics

Last elections:	May 2007
Next elections:	2012
Head of state:	Queen Elizabeth II, represented by governor-general, Sir Arthur Foulkes (2010–)
Head of government:	Prime Minister Hubert Alexander Ingraham
Ruling party:	Free National Movement

The March 1997 elections were won by the Free National Movement (FNM), led by Hubert Ingraham, securing 34 seats, the remaining seats being taken by the Progressive Liberal Party (PLP).

After the elections Sir Lynden Pindling, who had led the PLP for 32 years, stood down and was replaced by Perry Christie.

In May 2002, the PLP won a landslide victory, taking 29 seats and Christie became prime minister. The FNM took seven and independents four.

Tommy Turnquest, who had succeeded Ingraham as FNM leader before the elections, lost his seat, but was subsequently appointed to the Senate.

Three years after stepping down as leader of the FNM, Hubert Ingraham returned to head the party in November 2005, subsequently leading it to victory in the general elections of May 2007 – FNM taking 23 seats and PLP 18. The turnout was 91% of registered electors.

On the retirement of Arthur Dion Hanna in April 2010 Sir Arthur Foulkes succeeded him as governor-general.

International relations

The Bahamas is a member of the African, Caribbean and Pacific Group of States, Association of Caribbean States, Caribbean Community (though not the CARICOM Single Market and Economy), Non-Aligned Movement, Organization of American States and United Nations.

Traveller information

Local laws and conventions: The Christian Church has a strong influence on local life and islanders place much emphasis on traditional values. Visitors should dress modestly in towns; beachwear must never be worn outside beach areas.

Visitors must always seek permission before taking photographs of locals or their property.

Penalties for possession or trafficking of drugs are severe and can lead to a heavy prison sentence.

Handshaking is the usual form of greeting for both men and women.

The exchange of business cards is customary when conducting business. Conference facilities are good, with some venues seating up to 2,000 people. Office hours are Mon–Fri 0900–1700.

Immigration and customs: Some nationals will require a visa to enter the country and current visa requirements must be checked well before travel. Passports must be valid for six months from the intended length of stay. It is recommended that visitors carry a copy of their passport and travel documents, and keep the originals in a safe place.

Lone parents coming into the country will need documentary evidence to show parental responsibility for accompanying children.

A yellow fever vaccination certificate will be required by all those arriving from infected countries.

Firearms and fireworks, plants, flowers and fruit are all prohibited imports.

Travel within the country: Traffic drives on the left and car hire is available on the larger islands to drivers aged 25 or over. A national driving licence can be used for the first three months of stay. The wearing of seat belts is mandatory.

Air-conditioned ferries run daily from Nassau to North Eleuthera and Harbour Island, and there is a twice-weekly service to Governor's Harbour in South Eleuthera. The mail boats that deliver mail and provisions between the islands will also carry passengers, who share facilities with the crew.

Domestic flights are available and are operated by Bahamasair; a number of charter services also run inter-island flights.

Minibuses (*Jitneys*) operate in Freeport and Nassau, and are an inexpensive way of travelling around. Paradise Island is served by a bus service which stops at every hotel. Taxis are the main form of transport on the smaller islands, where there is no public transport. Most taxis are metered and rates are government-controlled.

Travel health: Medical facilities are good but expensive. Emergency health care is limited, however, and visitors should have comprehensive health insurance that includes air evacuation.

Tuberculosis and Hepatitis B vaccinations are sometimes recommended, and visitors should check the most up-to-date inoculation requirements well before travel.

Although there have been no reported cases in The Bahamas, dengue fever is endemic to Latin America and the Caribbean, and visitors may wish to take insect repellent to protect against mosquito bites.

Tap water is safe to drink; bottled water is widely available. Milk is pasteurised.

Money: American Express, Diners Club, Mastercard and Visa are widely accepted, and there are ATMs on the major islands and at the airport. Travellers cheques should be taken in US dollars to avoid additional exchange rate charges. Banking hours are Mon–Thur 0930–1600 and Fri 0930–1700.

There were 1,368,000 tourist arrivals in 2010.

Further information

Government of The Bahamas: www.bahamas.gov.bs

Central Bank of The Bahamas: www.centralbankbahamas.com

Commonwealth Secretariat: www.thecommonwealth.org

Commonwealth of Nations: www.commonwealth-of-nations.org/Bahamas%60_The

History

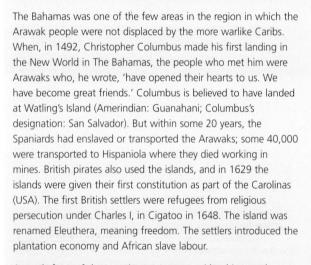

The Bahamas was one of the few areas in the region in which the Arawak people were not displaced by the more warlike Caribs. When, in 1492, Christopher Columbus made his first landing in the New World in The Bahamas, the people who met him were Arawaks who, he wrote, 'have opened their hearts to us. We have become great friends.' Columbus is believed to have landed at Watling's Island (Amerindian: Guanahani; Columbus's designation: San Salvador). But within some 20 years, the Spaniards had enslaved or transported the Arawaks; some 40,000 were transported to Hispaniola where they died working in mines. British pirates also used the islands, and in 1629 the islands were given their first constitution as part of the Carolinas (USA). The first British settlers were refugees from religious persecution under Charles I, in Cigatoo in 1648. The island was renamed Eleuthera, meaning freedom. The settlers introduced the plantation economy and African slave labour.

An early form of democratic government, with a bicameral parliament and elected lower house, developed but was abolished in 1717, when the Crown resumed government. Although the other colonial powers did not formally dispute possession, the settlers were at times harassed by the French and Spanish as well as by pirates. Fortunes fluctuated. The population soared in the late 18th century with the arrival from America of Loyalist families and their slaves after the American Revolution. In 1783–84 the population was 4,058; by 1789, it was more than 11,000, with the white settlers forming a significant minority. The abolition of slavery in 1834 caused major economic changes as the islands had been used as a centre of slave-trading.

In 1861–65 the islands enjoyed prosperity as a depot for ships running the blockade against the Confederate States during the American Civil War. Decline followed, however, compounded by a severe hurricane in 1866.

Prosperity returned in the 20th century, when the islands became an entrepot for the American bootlegging trade during prohibition. More conventional industries also developed, supplying sisal, conch shells for cameo brooch-making, pineapples and sponges. The sponge industry reached a peak in 1901 during generally lean years but collapsed in 1939 as a result of fungal diseases. In the early 1950s the islands again prospered; the success of tourism, and later offshore banking, produced phenomenal growth. In 1953, the Progressive Liberal Party (PLP) was founded to represent black interests in a system till then still dominated by whites.

In 1964, a new constitution set up a ministerial system of government, and the legislature was reformed to represent majority interests. After the subsequent general election in 1967, the United Bahamian Party (the so-called 'Bay Street Boys') was forced into opposition for the first time in the assembly's history. Lynden Pindling, leader of the PLP, formed a government with the support of the Labour Party. The PLP won the next two general elections outright, and Pindling led The Bahamas to independence under a new constitution on 10 July 1973.

Pindling and the PLP continued in power until 1992, when they were ousted by the Free National Movement (FNM), led by Hubert Ingraham, a former PLP minister, the FNM winning 32 seats to the PLP's 17. Subsequent investigations gave the FNM another seat, taking their total to 33.

Bangladesh

KEY FACTS

Joined Commonwealth:	1972
Population:	148,692,000 (2010)
GDP p.c. growth:	3.5% p.a. 1990–2010
UN HDI 2011:	world ranking 146
Official language:	Bangla
Time:	GMT plus 6hr
Currency:	taka (Tk)

Geography

Area:	143,998 sq km
Coastline:	580km
Capital:	Dhaka

The People's Republic of Bangladesh is a fertile and densely populated delta country in southern Asia bordered by the Bay of Bengal, India and Myanmar (formerly Burma).

Topography: Apart from hills to the south-east, most of Bangladesh is a flat alluvial plain crossed by navigable waterways – the Ganges (Padma), Brahmaputra (Jamuna) and Meghna river systems – flowing into the Bay of Bengal. About 14% of the country is normally under water. Flooding is frequent and can be disastrous.

Climate: Tropical monsoon-type. Hot and humid April to October, with the monsoon running June to September. Cool and dry, November to March. The country is vulnerable to cyclones, which can be devastating. The cyclone of April 1991 killed 138,000 people. In November 2007, Cyclone Sidr hit the southern coastal strip of Bangladesh, also killing and making homeless thousands of people.

Environment: The most significant issues are severe overpopulation, high risk of flooding in large area of country, soil degradation and erosion, ground water contaminated by naturally occurring arsenic, and poisoning of fish by use of commercial pesticides.

Did you know...

Muhammad Yunus, Founder of the Grameen Bank in Bangladesh, delivered the 6th Annual Commonwealth Lecture, on 'Halving Poverty by 2015', in 2003; he was awarded the Nobel Peace Prize in 2006, jointly with the Bank.

Two Bangladeshi-born writers have won the Commonwealth Writers' Prize Best First Book award: Adib Khan (1995) and Tahmima Anam (2008).

Bangladesh hosts a national chapter of the Commonwealth Human Ecology Council.

Vegetation: Intensely cultivated; paddy fields dominate the delta; palms, bamboo, mango, the plains. Water hyacinth is a serious menace to waterways. Forest on the south-eastern hills; forest covers 11% of the land area, having declined at 0.2% p.a. 1990–2010. Soil is mostly very rich, supporting intensive cropping, with up to three crops p.a. in many places; arable land comprises 58% of the total land area.

Wildlife: The country has a varied wildlife population, although 18 species became extinct during the 20th century and around 70 are endangered or threatened. Mammal species include 26 types of bat, the famous Bengal tiger (now virtually confined to the Sundarbans and numbering a few hundred) and the Gangetic dolphin, and reptile species include turtles, river tortoise, crocodile, gavial, python, krait and cobra. There are several 'protected' areas for wildlife.

Main towns: Dhaka (capital, pop. 10.86m in 2010), Chittagong (3.87m), Narayanganj (1.49m), Khulna (1.44m), Rajshahi (808,400),

Tungi (437,400), Sylhet (410,200), Mymensingh (395,100), Narsingdi (361,600), Comilla (344,800), Rangpur (330,000), Barisal (270,900), Jessore (260,800), Bogra (260,200), Dinajpur (182,700), Pabna (182,600), Nawabganj (177,800) and Brahman Baria (157,900).

Transport: There are 239,230km of roads, 9.5% paved; these roads are vulnerable to damage by storms or floods, and have many bridges. The 4.8km Jamuna multipurpose bridge was inaugurated in 1998, linking the east and the west of the country by road and railway.

A rail network of some 2,840km links the main towns. The Dhaka–Chittagong line has frequent daily services. Rail is broad gauge in the west, narrow gauge in the east, with ferry links across rivers.

Bangladesh has 5–8,000km of navigable waterway, depending on extent of flooding, and a well-developed water transport network, carrying more than 30% of domestic freight. The main ports are Chittagong and Mongla, Chittagong dealing with the bulk of foreign trade. Shahjalal (formerly Zia) International Airport is 19km north of Dhaka.

Society

KEY FACTS 2010

Population per sq km:	1,033
Life expectancy:	69 years
Net primary enrolment:	89%

Population: 148,692,000 (2010); density among world's highest; 28% lives in urban areas and 14% in urban agglomerations of more than 1 million people; growth 1.7% p.a. 1990–2010; birth rate 20 per 1,000 people (47 in 1970), controlled by vigorous family planning schemes; life expectancy 69 years (44 in 1970).

Language: Bangla (Bengali) is the official language. English is widely spoken, especially in government and commerce.

Religion: Muslims 90%, Hindus 10%, a few Buddhists and Christians (2004); Islam is the state religion.

Health: Public spending on health was 1% of GDP in 2009. Public-sector medical facilities remain scarce, though there are clinics run by a major NGO, BRAC. To provide safe drinking water, between the 1970s and the mid-1990s some 5 million wells were drilled, and in 2009 the UN estimated that 80% of the population was using an improved drinking water source and 53% had access to adequate sanitation facilities. However, from 1996 naturally occurring arsenic was detected in the ground water (supplying over 1 million tube wells), putting nearly 50% of the population at risk. By the 2000s there was an epidemic of health problems caused by arsenic poisoning.

Bangladesh has maintained a high level of immunisation coverage against diseases such as diphtheria, whooping cough, tetanus and measles. Infant mortality was 38 per 1,000 live births in 2010 (149 in 1960).

Education: Public spending on education was 2.4% of GDP in 2008. There are five years of compulsory education and eight years of free education, starting at age six. Almost all primary schools are government-managed. Secondary schools (11–16, comprising a first cycle of three years and a second cycle of two years) and higher secondary colleges (17–18) are mostly private, often

government-subsidised. There are more than 17 million students in primary school and more than 8 million at secondary level. Some 67% of pupils complete primary school (2008). The school year starts in January.

A parallel system of education – madrassa education – offers Islamic instruction from primary level up to postgraduate level.

The main universities are at Dhaka, Rajshahi, Chittagong, Jahangirnagar and Mymensingh (agriculture). There are also several private universities in Dhaka, including North–South University and Independent University. The Bangladesh Open University provides distance learning for a wide range of students at secondary and tertiary levels. The female–male ratio for gross enrolment in tertiary education is 0.56:1 (2009). Literacy among people aged 15–24 is 76% (2009).

Media: Bangladesh has a lively and thriving press, with very many newspapers and weeklies in circulation. Leading English-language newspapers are *The Bangladesh Observer* (since 1949), *The Daily Star*, *New Age*, *The New Nation*, *The Dhaka Courier* (weekly), and *The Independent*. Dailies in Bengali include *Ittefaq*, *Prothom Alo* and *Jugantor*.

Television is Bangladesh's most popular medium, especially in the cities. The country's sole terrestrial TV channel, Bangladesh Television, is a public service. Satellite and cable television are popular in urban areas. Betar-Radio Bangladesh is the national public radio service, and Radio Metrowave is a commercial music and news station for younger audiences.

Some 48% of households have TV sets (2006). There are 23 personal computers (2006) and 37 internet users (2010) per 1,000 people.

Communications: Country code 880; internet domain '.bd'. Mobile phone coverage is good in urban areas but patchy elsewhere. Internet connections exist in main towns.

There are 6 main telephone lines and 462 mobile phone subscriptions per 1,000 people (2010).

Public holidays: Shaheed Day (International Mother Language Day, 21 February), Independence Day (26 March), Labour Day (1 May), Bank Holiday (early July), National Mourning Day (15 August), National Revolution Day (7 November), Victory Day (16 December) and New Year's Eve. The weekend comprises Friday/Saturday.

Religious and other festivals whose dates vary from year to year include Prophet's Birthday, Bangla Naba Barsha (Bengali New Year, around 14 April), Buddha Purnima (April/May), Shab-e-Bharat (Ascension of the Prophet), Eid al-Fitr (End of Ramadan, three days), Durga Puja (Dashami, October), Shab-e-Qadr (Evening of Destiny), Eid al-Adha (Feast of the Sacrifice, three days) and Islamic New Year.

Economy

KEY FACTS 2010

GNI:	US$104.7bn
GNI p.c.:	US$700
GDP growth:	6.2% p.a. 2006–10
Inflation:	7.7% p.a. 2006–10

The country has a high population density, limited natural resources and an agricultural economy vulnerable to floods and cyclones, but it nevertheless achieved economic growth averaging around 4%

Real Growth in GDP

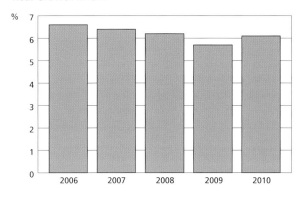

Inflation

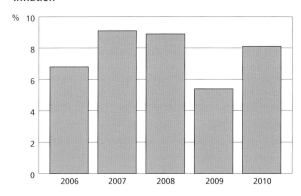

GDP by Sector (2010)

Agriculture	**19%**
Industry	**28%**
Services	**53%**

p.a. from the 1970s. It does also have huge reserves of natural gas (estimated at 400 billion cubic metres in January 2011) and some coal.

Economic policy has long aimed at the alleviation of poverty through increasing food production and expanding education, while developing an industrial and technological base, but severe floods have often frustrated development plans.

From the mid-1990s, successive governments were committed to free-market policies, privatisation of state-owned enterprises, attracting overseas investment and banking reform. More than 60 state-owned enterprises, in areas as diverse as manufacturing, agriculture, transport and communications, were identified for divestment, but progress was slow due to strong popular opposition. These policies led to an improvement in economic performance, even in 1998 when the country was devastated by the floods that covered nearly two-thirds of the land area.

From 2000 the economy grew strongly, with growth rates of over 6% p.a. in 2006–11 driven by strong exports and investment. In 2008–09, despite the world economic downturn, the economy remained buoyant with continuing growth in clothing exports and

remittances from Bangladeshis living abroad. Keeping inflation under control, however, proved more challenging.

Constitution

Status:	Republic
Legislature:	Jatiya Sangsad
Independence:	1971

Bangladesh is a republic with a non-executive president. Under the Twelfth Constitutional Amendment (1991) there is a parliamentary system. The unicameral parliament (Jatiya Sangsad) comprises 300 directly elected members from geographical constituencies for five-year terms, plus 50 seats reserved for women nominated by political parties – based on their share of the elected seats – and then voted on by sitting lawmakers. The allocation of seats reserved for women was provided by the Fourteenth Constitutional Amendment (2004). One parliamentary candidate can stand in up to three constituencies. If a candidate wins in more than one constituency a by-election or by-elections are called. Parliament may sit no longer than five years. Constitutional amendments require a two-thirds majority of parliament.

Executive power is with the prime minister, who heads a council of ministers (the cabinet), and whose advice is necessary for all presidential acts. The head of state is the president who is elected by the national parliament for a five-year term. The presidency is a largely ceremonial role, although the president appoints members of the cabinet and the judiciary and has the power to dissolve parliament.

The Thirteenth Constitutional Amendment (1996) requires a non-partisan caretaker administration to oversee the election process.

In November 2007 the caretaker government declared the independence of the judiciary from the executive, following a directive issued by the Supreme Court in December 1999 – in accordance with Article 22 of the Constitution of Bangladesh. Previous elected governments of the Bangladesh Nationalist Party and Awami League had effectively filibustered implementing the directive.

Politics

Last elections:	December 2008
Next elections:	2014
Head of state:	President Zillur Rahman (2009–)
Head of government:	Prime Minister Sheikh Hasina
Ruling party:	alliance led by the Awami League

Following a very violent campaign, in October 2001, the four-party alliance led by the Bangladesh Nationalist Party (BNP) won a surprise landslide victory, taking a total of 214 of the directly elective seats; the Awami League took 62 and the Islamic National Unity Front, which included a faction of the Jatiya Party led by Hossain Ershad, 14.

Although international observers declared the general election to be largely free and fair and both the head of the caretaker government and the chief election commissioner rejected the Awami League's allegation of massive vote-rigging, Sheikh Hasina called for the elections to be run again, threatening mass protests and a parliamentary boycott, which had characterised opposition politics during previous administrations. The Awami League subsequently returned to parliament and assumed its role as opposition.

The political temperature remained very high in 2003. In June 2003 the Awami League began a boycott of parliament, which

From its earliest pre-history Bangladesh has been subject to waves of migration and the incursions of regional – and later European – powers. An Indo-Aryan population, Hindu in belief, arrived between 3,000 and 4,000 years ago and the evidence suggests a flourishing, sophisticated civilisation.

The Moghul dynasty, conquering the territory in the 16th century, spread Islam widely through the country. The following successions of arrivals were the Portuguese, Armenians, French and British, who established military and trade outposts. In 1757 a British force defeated the local army of Nawab Siraj-ud-Dwola and set in train 190 years of British rule.

In 1947 East Bengal and Sylhet (then part of Assam) came to independence out of the UK's Indian Empire, as the eastern part of the Muslim state of Pakistan. From the start, East Pakistan was beset by problems. In particular, it resented the dominance of its richer and more powerful though less populous partner, West Pakistan, from which it was geographically separated by about 1,600km of Indian territory. Political control, language and economic policy were among the large areas of disagreement. In 1949 the Awami League was established in East Pakistan to campaign for autonomy.

Protests and violent demonstrations followed the declaration, in 1952, that Urdu was to be Pakistan's official language. Bengali was finally accepted as the joint official language two years later. By the mid-1960s, continued under-representation in the government administration and armed forces and a much less than fair share of Pakistan's development expenditure gave rise to the belief by many in East Pakistan that the only remedy was greater autonomy and thus more control over its own resources and development priorities and politics.

In 1970, Sheikh Mujibur Rahman, leader of the Awami League, won an electoral majority in Pakistan's general election on a platform demanding greater autonomy for East Pakistan. At the same time Zulfikar Ali Bhutto gained a majority in the West. Despite Mujib's victory, he was prevented by the Pakistan authorities from becoming prime minister of the combined state.

The Awami League then issued its own plans for a new constitution for an independent state, as a result of which the Pakistani army took control and Mujib was arrested in March 1971 after a fierce crackdown. This precipitated civil war, with an estimated 9.5 million refugees fleeing to India as a result, and led to military intervention by India on the side of the *Mukti Bahini* (Bengali 'freedom fighters') at the beginning of December. Two weeks later, Pakistan forces surrendered and the separate state of Bangladesh emerged. Sheikh Mujib returned from captivity in Pakistan in January 1972 and became prime minister.

Instability in the new state was compounded by floods, famine, the assassination of Sheikh Mujib in August 1975 – shortly after he became president – and a succession of military coups, with martial law and frequent states of emergency. After a coup in 1975, Major-General Ziaur Rahman (Zia) assumed the leadership and in 1978 he became president. The 1979 general election brought his Bangladesh Nationalist Party (BNP) to government. The country then enjoyed a period of economic and political stability. But in 1981 President Zia was murdered in an attempted coup.

In 1982 the then army chief, Lt-General Hossain Ershad, assumed power after another coup and became president in 1983. In May 1986 elections were held in violent conditions and boycotted by the BNP under Zia's widow, Begum Khaleda Zia. Ershad's Jatiya Party (JP) won and the Awami League, led by Sheikh Hasina, the daughter of Sheikh Mujib, boycotted parliament. Ershad won presidential elections in October 1986, and he lifted martial law and reinstated the constitution.

The following year was marked by riots and strikes, a state of emergency, thousands of arrests, and house-arrest for Begum Zia and Sheikh Hasina. A general election of March 1988, boycotted by the opposition, returned the JP with 238 seats, and the state of emergency was lifted. Then ensued devastating floods covering up to 75% of the country and making tens of millions homeless.

In December 1990, following mass demonstrations, President Hossain Ershad resigned and was put under house arrest. During 1991 he was convicted of illegal possession of firearms and other offences and sentenced to 20 years' imprisonment. In the February 1991 elections the BNP won 138 of the 300 directly elective seats and Begum Khaleda Zia was confirmed as the country's first woman prime minister. The main opposition was the Awami League and its allies, with 95 seats. A national referendum then endorsed a return to parliamentary democracy with a non-executive president. In 1991 a cyclone devastated the south-east coast, killing an estimated 250,000 people.

Political tensions mounted and opposition demands for a fresh general election increased from late 1993 into 1994, culminating in the resignation of all the opposition members from the Jatiya Sangsad in December. In 1995, following further strikes and violent protests staged by the opposition, the Jatiya Sangsad was dissolved at the request of the prime minister, pending the holding of a general election in 1996. The Awami League, Jatiya Party and Jamaat-e-Islami boycotted the poll and the BNP took the majority of votes cast. The opposition parties renewed their campaign and paralysed the country causing severe damage to the economy. In March 1996, the government agreed to the appointment of a neutral caretaker government to oversee the holding of fresh elections. Begum Zia resigned and the Jatiya Sangsad was dissolved.

In the parliamentary elections that followed in June 1996, the Awami League won 146 seats, the BNP 116, Jatiya Party 32 and Jamaat-e-Islami three. An informal alliance with the Jatiya Party allowed the Awami League to gain control of the majority of seats in parliament and Sheikh Hasina became prime minister, with Begum Zia's BNP now the main opposition which soon began a new campaign of strikes and street protests and a series of long parliamentary boycotts. In 1997 Ershad was released from prison and in March 1998 the Jatiya Party left the ruling coalition. The Awami League, which as a result of a number of by-elections now had an absolute majority, continued on its own. In 1998 the country was again devastated by floods which covered nearly two-thirds of the land area.

continued until June 2004. During 2004 the opposition called 21 general strikes as part of a campaign to oust the government.

In October 2006, a general election was called for January 2007 and President Iajuddin Ahmed formed a caretaker government. In early January 2007, it was confirmed that the Awami League and other smaller opposition parties were to boycott the election on the belief that the interim government and election commission were biased. Following national transport blockades raised by Awami League supporters who wanted the election postponed and ensuing riots, a state of emergency was imposed and President Ahmed postponed the election, stood down as chief adviser of the interim government and was succeeded by Dr Fakhruddin Ahmed, former central bank governor. The Election Commission then established a road map for electoral reform, including preparation of a new voters' list with photographs.

The election – held in December 2008 with Commonwealth observers present – was won by the alliance led by the Awami League, which itself took 230 seats; its ally the Jatiya Party 27. The BNP won 29 seats and its allies three. The turnout of the electorate was estimated at 70%. Awami League leader Sheikh Hasina was sworn in as prime minister in January 2009. On 11 February, Zillur Rahman was elected unopposed to replace Iajuddin Ahmed as non-executive president.

In late February 2009, the new government faced its first crisis when a section of the paramilitary Bangladesh Rifles (BDR) mutinied, ostensibly over pay and conditions. Officials reported 74 deaths – mostly BDR officers – and more than 1,000 soldiers were arrested and interrogated. Six special military courts were established in November 2009 to try BDR personnel accused of mutiny, while others charged with murder, looting and other serious offences were put to trial in civilian courts. On 23 January 2011 the BDR was officially renamed Border Guard of Bangladesh in accordance with the 'Border Guard Bangladesh Bill 2010' passed by the parliament on 8 December 2010.

In late 2010 the government established a tribunal to prosecute those accused of committing war crimes during Bangladesh's war of independence in 1971.

International relations

Bangladesh is a member of the Indian Ocean Rim Association for Regional Cooperation, Non-Aligned Movement, Organisation of Islamic Cooperation, South Asian Association for Regional Cooperation, United Nations and World Trade Organization.

Traveller information

Local laws and conventions: Local laws reflect the country's Muslim beliefs and should be respected at all times, especially during the holy month of Ramadan or when visiting religious sites.

During Ramadan, when Muslims fast between sunrise and sunset, visitors should avoid eating, drinking or smoking in public, as it is likely to cause offence. Women travellers should wear trousers or long skirts and should dress modestly at all times.

There are severe penalties for possession and trafficking of illegal drugs and some drug-related offences are punishable by death.

It is not acceptable to photograph local people or their property without first seeking their permission.

Dress is usually informal for men, though modesty must be maintained by both sexes.

For business meetings, exchange of business cards is customary. The best time to visit on business is October to March. Office hours are Sun–Thur 0900–1700.

Immigration and customs: Passports must be valid for three months from the intended date of departure. Visa requirements vary and should be checked well in advance of travel. Visitors are advised to carry photocopies of their passport and travel documents, and to keep the originals in a safe place.

A yellow fever vaccination certificate is required by all those arriving from infected areas.

Travel within the country: Traffic drives on the left and car hire is available with an international driving permit.

The rail network is slow and old, though upgrading is currently taking place. The main train line is between Dhaka and Chittagong, and there are a number of daily services.

Domestic flights are also available and connect Dhaka with most of the other main towns. A ferry operates from Dhaka to Khulna four times a week.

There are inexpensive bus services which connect most of the towns and villages. In urban areas buses are generally overcrowded, but cycle-rickshaws are widely available. Taxis are the best and safest means of travelling short distances.

Travel health: Medical facilities are poor outside the capital and visitors are advised to take out comprehensive health insurance that includes medical evacuation.

Humidity and pollution in downtown Dhaka, especially at certain times of the year, can cause breathing problems. There is a risk of malaria in the Chittagong Hill Tracts, and dengue fever is prevalent; visitors must take adequate precautions to protect themselves at all times, and pack insect repellent and suitable clothing to discourage mosquito bites. Tuberculosis and Hepatitis B and E are also present.

Drinking water must be boiled or sterilised.

Money: Hotel bills must be paid in a major convertible currency or with travellers cheques. Money can be changed in banks but many local shops offer better exchange rates. Credit cards are not generally accepted outside the capital. ATMs are only available in the major cities. Travellers cheques can be cashed at banks and airports. Banking hours are Sun–Wed 0900–1500 and Thur 0900–1300. Some banks may open on a Saturday.

There were 289,000 tourist arrivals in 2007.

Further information

National Web Portal of Bangladesh: www.bangladesh.gov.bd

National Parliament of Bangladesh: www.parliament.gov.bd

Bangladesh Bank: www.bangladesh-bank.org

Commonwealth Secretariat: www.thecommonwealth.org

Commonwealth of Nations: www.commonwealth-of-nations.org/Bangladesh

Barbados

KEY FACTS

Joined Commonwealth:	1966
Population:	273,000 (2010)
GDP p.c. growth:	0.8% p.a. 1990–2010
UN HDI 2011:	world ranking 47
Official language:	English
Time:	GMT minus 4hr
Currency:	Barbados dollar (Bds$)

Geography

Area:	431 sq km
Coastline:	97km
Capital:	Bridgetown

Barbados, the most easterly of the Caribbean islands, lies south of St Lucia, east of St Vincent and the Grenadines, and north of Trinidad and Tobago.

Topography: Barbados is a comparatively flat island, rising in a series of terraced tablelands to Mount Hillaby at 336m. The north-east (Scotland area) is broken, eroded and rocky. The rest of the island is coral limestone crossed with deep river-bed gullies which fill with water during heavy rain. There are no permanent rivers. On the east coast, much of the shoreline is rocky, pounded by a strong surf; elsewhere, natural coral reefs surround turquoise seas and beaches of white sand.

Climate: Mild subtropical. In the December–June dry season cooling north-east trade winds blow steadily; the wet season is humid and hotter, but the climate is generally pleasant even then, thanks to sea-breezes. The island is on the southern edge of the West Indian hurricane zone.

Environment: The most significant environmental issues are pollution of coastal waters from waste disposal by ships; soil erosion; and the threatened contamination of the underground water supply by illegal disposal of solid waste.

Vegetation: Vestiges of indigenous forest cover 19% of the land area and there was no significant loss of forest cover during

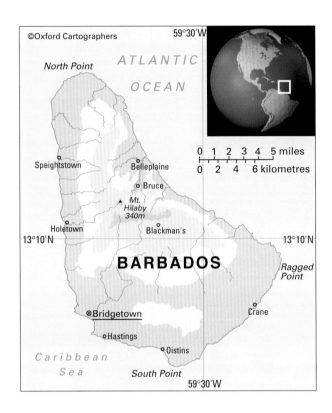

1990–2010. Sugar cane and food crops predominate in rural areas. There is a rich diversity of tropical flowers and flowering trees.

Wildlife: Natural wildlife has largely been displaced by sugar cane but the Barbados Wildlife Reserve was established in 1985 in the Scotland district, its 1.6 hectares of mature mahogany trees being the home of the Barbados green monkey and the red-footed Barbados tortoise.

Main towns: Bridgetown (capital and only seaport, pop. 94,200 in 2010), Speightstown (2,400), Bathsheba (1,600), Holetown (1,500) and Oistins (1,500); extensive spread of hotels and apartments along the coast.

Transport: A good road network of 1,600km (virtually all paved) covers the entire island, with a trans-insular highway from Bridgetown to the east coast.

Bridgetown is a deep-water port with a cruiseship terminal and yacht harbour.

Grantley Adams International Airport is 13km east of Bridgetown.

Society

KEY FACTS 2010

Population per sq km:	633
Life expectancy:	77 years

Did you know...

Sir Garfield Sobers, born in Bridgetown in July 1936, was the Wisden Leading Cricketer in the World in 1958, 1960, 1962, 1964, 1965, 1966, 1968 and 1970, achieving 8,032 runs and 235 wickets in 93 Test matches.

Austin Ardinel Chesterfield Clarke, born in St James, Barbados, in July 1934, won the 2003 Commonwealth Writers' Prize with his tenth published novel, *The Polished Hoe*.

Population: 273,000 (2010); 44% lives in urban areas; growth 0.3% p.a. 1990–2010; birth rate 11 per 1,000 people (22 in 1970); life expectancy 77 years (69 in 1970).

The population is 93% of African descent, 3% of European descent, and the rest of Asian or mixed descent (2000 census).

Language: English is the official and first language. An English-based Creole is also widely spoken.

Religion: Mainly Christians (Anglicans 28%, Pentecostals 19%, Methodists 5%, Roman Catholics 4%), with small Hindu, Muslim and Jewish communities.

Health: Public spending on health was 4% of GDP in 2009. Barbados has a national health service and the general health profile and life expectancy of a developed country; the entire population uses an improved drinking water source and adequate sanitation facilities (2009). Infant mortality was 17 per 1,000 live births in 2010 (74 in 1960). In 2009, 1.4% of people aged 15–49 were HIV positive.

Education: Public spending on education was 6.7% of GDP in 2009. There are 12 years of compulsory education starting at age five. Primary school comprises seven years and secondary six. Computers are widely available to schools. Some 94% of pupils complete primary school (2007). The school year starts in September.

The University of the West Indies has a campus at Cave Hill, Barbados, as well as in Jamaica, and Trinidad and Tobago. A UNESCO Chair in Educational Technologies was established in 1999 at the Barbados campus of the University of the West Indies. Other tertiary institutions include the Barbados Community College, with its Hospitality Institute, Samuel Jackson Prescod Polytechnic, and Erdiston College (offering teacher education). There is virtually no illiteracy among people aged 15–24.

Media: Newspapers are privately owned and include *The Barbados Advocate/Sunday Advocate* and *The Nation*, and *Broad Street Journal* (business weekly).

CBC Radio, CBC TV (the only terrestrial television channel) and MCTV (a multichannel pay-TV service) are operated by the public Caribbean Broadcasting Corporation. There are several private commercial and faith radio stations.

There are 158 personal computers (2005) and 702 internet users (2010) per 1,000 people.

Communications: Country code 1 246; internet domain '.bb'. Mobile phone coverage is good on the island.

History

Prehistoric Barbados is believed to have been inhabited by cave-dwellers of the Siboney culture, from Florida. At an unknown later time, Arawaks arrived from South America. These latter were agriculturists, and excellent weavers and potters. They survived invasions and raids by the warlike Caribs (also from South America), which took place before the 1490s. By the early 1500s, Spanish and Portuguese sailors had sighted the island. It was invaded in 1518 by Spanish colonists from Hispaniola. No Spanish settlement was made, as there appeared to be no mineral resources, but the island acquired a Spanish name – *Barbados* (or 'bearded'), apparently a reference to local fig trees. By 1536 the island was deserted, either because the slavers had depopulated it or because the remaining inhabitants had fled.

In 1625 it was formally claimed for King James I of England. In 1627 English immigrants settled there and King Charles I granted a Barbados patent to Lord Carlisle; after 1660, this patent was surrendered to the Crown and a 4.5% duty on exports levied, which, bitterly resented, was levied until 1838. Between 1627 and 1640, the island was settled by British colonists, who brought with them indentured labour from Britain and some enslaved Africans, to produce tobacco, cotton and indigo. The introduction of sugar in the 1650s had led to the development of large plantations, and by 1685 the population was around 50,000, consisting mainly of African slaves.

By the end of the 18th century, Barbados had 745 plantations worked by more than 80,000 African and African-descended slaves. Harsh working conditions led to slave revolts in 1702 and 1816. Slavery was abolished throughout the British Empire in 1833–34.

Barbados had a house of assembly since 1639 but, due to the property qualifications for the franchise, this was dominated by plantation owners until the franchise began to be widened in 1944. Universal adult suffrage followed in 1951, a full ministerial system in 1954, and cabinet government in 1958.

The Barbados Labour Party (BLP), which developed out of the trade unions, was set up under the leadership of Grantley Adams, and began working for economic improvement and the extension of political rights. The BLP, led first by Adams, and after 1958 by Dr Hugh Cummins, gained a majority in the House of Assembly between 1944 and 1961. In 1955 a split in the BLP led to the formation of the Democratic Labour Party (DLP), led by Errol Barrow, who won the 1962 elections.

Thus, by 1957, Barbados had virtual self-government under a democratic system, a status formally recognised in 1961. Barbados had been a member of the Federation of the West Indies, set up in 1958. When the Federation was dissolved in 1962, the Barbados Government announced its intention to seek independence separately. Arrangements were agreed at a constitutional conference in London, and Barbados became an independent sovereign state within the Commonwealth on 30 November 1966.

The DLP was in power from 1966 to 1976, and the BLP from 1976 to 1986, led by Tom Adams, Sir Grantley Adams's son. In 1986 the DLP, still led by Errol Barrow, won a decisive election victory, maintaining its majority in the 1991 elections. This was despite a breakaway movement by DLP dissidents who formed a new National Democratic Party (NDP) but failed to win any seats in the 1991 elections. Erskine Sandiford became prime minister in June 1987 after the death of Barrow. Sandiford and the DLP were ousted in September 1994 by the BLP led by Owen Arthur. The BLP won 19 seats (48.3% of the vote), the DLP eight and NDP one.

THE BARBADOS OLYMPIC ASSOCIATION, INC.

Building a vibrant Olympic movement

Vision

The Barbados Olympic Association will be recognized as the premier organization in the Caribbean promoting the overall development of sporting excellence.

Mission

The Barbados Olympic Association shall work with our National Federations (NFs) and other stakeholders to bring a professional and business emphasis to the culture of sport in Barbados.

About the BOA

The goals:

- enhance sport performance at all levels
- provide support for the NFs
- demonstrate national leadership in sport
- represent sport as a collective voice
- model good governance
- increase awareness of the Olympic Movement
- ensure proper infrastructure development
- work with several stakeholders to ensure that essential sport programming is widely available at all levels throughout Barbados

Contact

Mr Steve Stoute, President
Olympic Centre, Garfield Sobers
Sports Complex
Wildey
St. Michael
Barbados
BB15094

Tel: +1 246 429 1998
Email: info@olympic.org.bb

There are 503 main telephone lines and 1,281 mobile phone subscriptions per 1,000 people (2010).

Public holidays: New Year's Day, Errol Barrow Day (21 January), National Heroes' Day (28 April), Labour Day (early May), Emancipation Day (1 August), Kadooment Day (early August), Independence Day (30 November), Christmas Day and Boxing Day.

Religious and other festivals whose dates vary from year to year include Good Friday, Easter Monday and Whit Monday.

Economy

KEY FACTS 2010

GDP:	US$4.1bn
GDP p.c.:	US$15,034
GDP growth:	−0.4% p.a. 2005–09
Inflation:	5.8% p.a. 2006–10

Barbados has an exceptionally high 'quality of life' rating for a developing country. The economy, formerly a sugar monoculture, was developed over three decades to achieve a balance of growth and social development, and diversified into three main sectors:

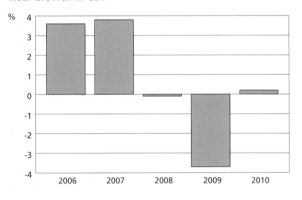

Real Growth in GDP

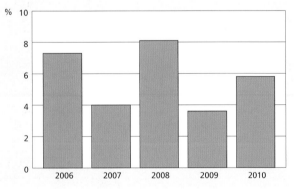

Inflation

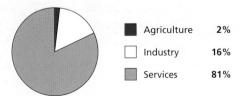

GDP by Sector (2010)

Agriculture	2%
Industry	16%
Services	81%

services, light industry and sugar. An offshore financial services sector, launched in 1985, has become the country's second biggest source of foreign exchange after tourism.

Despite its economic success, Barbados experienced little growth in the 1980s and a recession in the early 1990s, when sugar and tourism earnings slumped. It had to call on the IMF for economic adjustment support and the government introduced economic austerity measures. By 1993 the economy was recovering and from 1994 it continued to grow well throughout the 1990s and during 2000, driven by tourism and construction. Action against drug-trafficking since the 1990s has made security and defence a significant item of expenditure.

As a small and open economy Barbados lacks scope for further diversification and remains vulnerable to economic downturn in its trade partners. After 2000 the economy went into recession due to the downturn in the USA and Europe and resulting falls in tourist numbers. It picked up in 2003 and grew steadily until 2008 when the world economic downturn again caused a sharp fall in tourism and pushed the economy into reverse. After a sharp recession in 2009 (GDP declining by 5.3%), the economy grew slowly in 2010–11.

Constitution

Status:	Monarchy under Queen Elizabeth II
Legislature:	Parliament
Independence:	30 November 1966

Barbados is a parliamentary democracy and constitutional monarchy, recognising Queen Elizabeth II as head of state. She is represented by a governor-general appointed on the recommendation of the prime minister. There is a bicameral legislature and party system, based on universal adult suffrage.

The Senate has 21 members appointed by the governor-general, 12 on the advice of the prime minister, two on that of the leader of the opposition, and the remaining seven at the governor-general's discretion.

The House of Assembly has 30 directly elected members. Leaders of each house (president and deputy president of the Senate and speaker and deputy speaker of the assembly) are elected by the members of the respective houses.

The governor-general appoints as prime minister the parliamentarian who commands – in the governor-general's opinion – the largest support within the House of Assembly, and the prime minister heads the cabinet. Other ministers are appointed from either house by the governor-general as advised by the prime minister. The governor-general appoints the leader of the opposition – the MP who, in his/her judgement, leads the party commanding the support of the largest number of MPs in opposition to the government. The normal life of parliament is five years.

The constitution may be amended by act of parliament passed by both houses, except for entrenched clauses which require two-thirds majorities in both houses. These clauses relate to citizenship, rights and freedoms, the governor-generalship, composition of parliament and its sessions, prorogation and dissolution, general elections, senatorial appointments, executive authority, judicature, civil service and finance.

Politics

Last elections:	January 2008
Next elections:	2013
Head of state:	Queen Elizabeth II, represented by acting governor-general, Elliot Belgrave (November 2011–)
Head of government:	Prime Minister Freundel Stuart
Ruling party:	Democratic Labour Party

Sir Henry Forde's Constitutional Commission's much-delayed report was published in December 1998. Its main proposals were to introduce more checks and balances on the government, to create the institutional structures to ensure politicians behave with greater probity, and to replace the British monarch as the head of state by a ceremonial president.

In the general election of January 1999, the Barbados Labour Party (BLP) had a strong endorsement of their management of the economy and a mandate for their proposals for constitutional change. They gained 26 seats, with 65% of the votes, while the Democratic Labour Party (DLP) took only two. Owen Arthur began his second term of office as prime minister.

During 1999 and 2000 the new government pressed on with the proposed changes to the constitution, adding further issues to the agenda for public debate, for example limiting the number of terms a prime minister may serve, equal rights for women, and the independence of the judiciary. However, the debate proceeded slowly.

In 2001, David Thompson, DLP leader in the 1994 and 1999 general elections, was succeeded by Clyde Mascoll.

Arthur and the BLP were once again given a strong endorsement in the May 2003 elections, though with 23 seats to the DLP's seven, not as strong as in 1999. The BLP still had the two-thirds majority needed to enact constitutional amendments, although constitutional issues, such as replacing the British monarch as the head of state by a ceremonial president, had not been prominent in the election campaign. But in 2005 the UK Privy Council was replaced as the final court of appeal by the Trinidad and Tobago-based Caribbean Court of Justice.

Thompson returned to head the DLP in 2006 following the defection of Mascoll to the BLP. The DLP went on to win the general election in January 2008 ending the BLP's 13 years in government; the DLP taking 20 of the 30 contested seats and BLP 10. Thompson was sworn in as prime minister.

Prime Minister David Thompson died on 23 October 2010. He was succeeded by Deputy PM and Attorney-General Freundel Stuart.

International relations

Barbados is a member of the African, Caribbean and Pacific Group of States, Association of Caribbean States, Caribbean Community, Non-Aligned Movement, Organization of American States, United Nations and World Trade Organization.

Traveller information

Local laws and conventions: There are severe penalties for all those caught possessing or dealing in illegal drugs.

The wearing of camouflage or military clothing, even by children, is illegal.

Business in Barbados

The Small Business Association (SBA) is Barbados' non-profit representative body for micro, small and medium enterprises (MSMEs).

The Association, which was formed in 1982, has as its aim the creation of an enabling environment for MSMEs through the provision of training and education, the facilitation of trade and marketing opportunities, business development services and advocacy.

The SBA's membership is represented by a diverse group of businesses. Many of these are currently involved in cross-border trade and are capable of providing a range of goods and services for the international market.

To create synergies with international networks, the membership is clustered into several economic sectors such as tourism-related services, professional services, information and communications technology, manufacturing, wholesale/retail, the creative industries, construction and agriculture.

The SBA also provides support for foreign businesses and intermediary organisations seeking local trading partners. This is done through the provision of market intelligence, the facilitation of matchmaking forums, training, export promotion assistance and technical support.

Contact

Head Office	Eastern Office
#1 Pelican Industrial Park,	**Six Roads**
Bridgetown, BB11144	**St. Philip**
Barbados	**Barbados**
Tel: **+1 246 228 0162**	Tel: **+1 246 271 1129**
Fax: **+1 246 228 0613**	Fax: **+1 246 271 1128**
Email: **theoffice@sba.org.bb**	Email: **easternoffice@sba.org.bb**

www.sba.org.bb

Building Networks;
Creating Wealth

Casual dress is widely accepted, though visitors must cover up their swimwear when away from beach areas. Handshaking is the usual form of greeting.

Many of the larger hotels have excellent conference facilities, equipped to handle international conferences and trade shows. Office hours are Mon–Fri 0800–1600.

Immigration and customs: Passports must be valid for the intended length of stay. Visa requirements differ for each country and should be checked well in advance of travel.

A yellow fever vaccination certificate will be requested from those arriving from infected countries.

Travel within the country: Traffic drives on the left and car hire is available with a local driving permit. These can be purchased from car hire firms, the Ministry of Transport, or local police stations on production of a national driving licence.

The national speed limits are 40kph, 60kph and 80kph. The road network is good on most of the island.

An efficient, frequent and inexpensive bus service connects all major points on the island.

Taxis are widely available in Bridgetown as well as elsewhere on the island. Fares are government controlled but it is advisable to check the price of the journey before stepping into a taxi. Visitors can pay with US dollars as well as with local currency.

Mini-vans operate in much the same way as buses and are a fast and efficient means of getting around. There are no fixed schedules, but they can be flagged down anywhere on the island.

Travel health: Barbados has very good medical facilities. The country has a reciprocal health agreement with the UK, which allows British citizens access to free hospital treatment. Comprehensive medical insurance is advised for all other nationals.

Hepatitis B is present on Barbados and vaccination is sometimes advised. There is a low risk of dengue fever.

Those with asthma and hay fever may find that their symptoms are exacerbated during the sugar cane harvesting period.

Money: Local currency is the Barbados dollar. Commercial banks provide the best exchange rates and ATMs are available all over the island. The major credit cards are accepted in most resort areas, and travellers cheques can be cashed at any bank or at most of the larger hotels. Visitors are advised to take travellers cheques in US dollars or pounds sterling to avoid additional exchange charges. Banking hours are Mon–Thur 0800–1500 and Fri 0800–1700.

There were 532,000 tourist arrivals in 2010.

Further information

Barbados Integrated Government Portal: www.gov.bb

Parliament: www.barbadosparliament.com

Central Bank of Barbados: www.centralbank.org.bb

Commonwealth Secretariat: www.thecommonwealth.org

Commonwealth of Nations: www.commonwealth-of-nations.org/Barbados

Belize

Joined Commonwealth:	1981
Population:	312,000 (2010)
GDP p.c. growth:	1.9% p.a. 1990–2010
UN HDI 2011:	world ranking 93
Official language:	English
Time:	GMT minus 6hr
Currency:	Belizean dollar (Bz$)

Geography

Area:	22,965 sq km
Coastline:	386km
Capital:	Belmopan

Belize forms part of the Commonwealth Caribbean, and is located in central America, bordering Mexico to the north and Guatemala to the west and south.

Topography: The long east coast is mostly flat with lagoons and mangrove swamps. For 16–32km out to sea the water is only about 5m deep and a barrier reef (second in size only to Australia's) stretches nearly 297km, with many tiny islands known as cays or cayes inside. Three smaller reefs lie further out. Inland, the terrain rises with Victoria Peak (1,122m), the country's highest point, in the Cockscomb range to the east, and the heavily forested Maya Mountains to the south-west. Continuing north, the Western (Cayo) District is also hilly, with the Mountain Pine Ridge. The northern districts have wide areas of tableland. There are 17 principal rivers, navigable at best only by vessels of shallow draught.

Climate: The climate is subtropical, moderated by trade winds. The average temperature from November to January is 24°C and from May to September 27°C; inland there is a greater range. There are two dry seasons: March–May and August–September (the Maugre season). Annual rainfall ranges from 1,290mm in the north to 4,450mm in the south. The country is susceptible to hurricanes; Hurricane Iris in October 2001 – the fourth in three years – was the

©Oxford Cartographers

Did you know...

Of 13 Commonwealth member countries in the Americas, only Belize, Canada and Guyana lie on the mainland, three of the most sparsely populated in the association; all the others are islands or archipelagos.

The country's current prime minister, Dean Barrow, is the first of African descent.

The mayor of Belize City, Zenaida Moya, is Chair of the Commonwealth Local Government Forum.

worst for 40 years. Several years later in August 2007 another hurricane, Hurricane Dean, hit Belize affecting the livelihoods of up to 2,500 families in the northern parts of the country.

Environment: The most significant environmental issues are deforestation; water pollution from sewage, industrial effluents and agricultural run-off; and solid waste disposal.

Vegetation: Forest covers 61% of the land area and includes rainforest with mahoganies, cayune palms, and many orchids. Higher in the mountains, pine forest and cedar predominate. Arable land comprises 3% of the land area.

Wildlife: There is a strong emphasis on conservation. By 1992, 18 national parks and reserves had been established, including the world's only jaguar reserve. Other native species include ocelots, pumas, baboons, howler monkeys, toucans and many species of parrot.

Main towns: Belmopan (capital, pop. 21,800 in 2010), Belize City (former capital and commercial centre, 68,300), San Ignacio (20,800), Orange Walk (16,900), San Pedro (14,200), Dangriga (12,800), Benque Viejo (9,800), Corozal (9,700) and Punta Gorda (5,600).

Transport: There is a road network of some 2,870km, 17% paved, with 1,420km of all-weather roads. The four main highways are: Northern Highway (Belize City to Chetumal on the Mexican border); Western Highway (Belize City via Belmopan to the

Guatemalan border); Hummingbird Highway (Belmopan to Dangriga); and Southern Highway (Dangriga to Punta Gorda).

Belize City is the main port; the international airport, Philip S W Goldson, lies 16km north-west of Belize City.

Society

KEY FACTS 2010

Population per sq km:	14
Life expectancy:	76 years
Net primary enrolment:	100%

Population: 312,000 (2010); 52% lives in urban areas; growth 2.5% p.a. 1990–2010; birth rate 25 per 1,000 people (40 in 1970); life expectancy 76 years (66 in 1970).

Belizeans descend from Mayans, Caribs, and the many groups who came as loggers, settlers, refugees, slaves and imported labour: English, Spanish, Africans and East Indians.

According to the 2000 census, the population comprises 49% Mestizos (Maya–Spanish), 25% Creoles (Afro-European), 11% Mayans and 6% Garifuna (Afro-Carib). There is a small Mennonite farming community who speak a dialect of German, and a fast-growing Chinese community.

Language: English is the official language, but Spanish is spoken by more than half the population, and English-based Creole is widely understood. Other languages are Maya, Garifuna and Ketchi. Most Belizeans are bilingual and many trilingual.

Religion: Mainly Christians (Roman Catholics 50%, Pentecostals 7%, Anglicans 5%, Seventh Day Adventists 5%, Mennonites, Methodists); small minorities of Baha'i, Muslims and Jews (2000 census).

Health: Public spending on health was 4% of GDP in 2009. There are government hospitals in Belize City, Belmopan and other main towns, and health-care centres and mobile clinics in rural areas. Malaria requires constant surveillance. The National Primary Healthcare Centre organises preventive programmes. 99% of the population uses an improved drinking water source and 90% adequate sanitation facilities (2009). Infant mortality was 14 per 1,000 live births in 2010 (74 in 1960). In 2009, 2.3% of people aged 15–49 were HIV positive.

Education: Public spending on education was 6.1% of GDP in 2009. There are ten years of compulsory education starting at age five. Primary school, which is free of charge, comprises eight years and secondary four. Some 95% of pupils complete primary school (2008). The school year starts in September.

The University of Belize opened in 1986. Belize also shares in the regional University of the West Indies, which has its main campuses in Barbados, Jamaica, and Trinidad and Tobago. Galen University at San Ignacio is a private university partnered with the University of Indianapolis in the USA. The female–male ratio for gross enrolment in tertiary education is 1.85:1 (2009).

Media: Weekly newspapers include *Amandala*, *The Belize Times* (People's United Party), *The Guardian* (United Democratic Party), *The San Pedro Sun* and *The Reporter*.

Radio stations and TV channels are all privately owned; one radio station is broadcast in Spanish, one is affiliated to the United Democratic Party, another to the People's United Party.

There are 153 personal computers (2007) and 140 internet users (2010) per 1,000 people.

Communications: Country code 501; internet domain '.bz'. Mobile phone coverage is good in most areas, especially on the coast and along the main routes to Mexico and Guatemala.

There are 97 main telephone lines and 623 mobile phone subscriptions per 1,000 people (2010).

Public holidays: New Year's Day, Baron Bliss Day (9 March), Labour Day (1 May), Commonwealth Day (24 May), St George's Caye Day (10 September), Independence Day (21 September), Pan-American Day (12 October), Garifuna Settlement Day (19 November), Christmas Day and Boxing Day.

Religious and other festivals whose dates vary from year to year include Carnival (week before Lent), Good Friday and Easter Monday.

Economy

KEY FACTS 2010

GNI:	US$1.3bn
GNI p.c.:	US$3,810
GDP growth:	2.5% p.a. 2006–10
Inflation:	2.5% p.a. 2006–10

Belize's economy is predominantly agricultural, and it is vulnerable to volatility in world commodity markets. Efforts have been made to diversify from traditional export products such as sugar and timber into bananas, citrus concentrates, seafood and fish products. Forestry has been revitalised and tourism expanded to become a significant foreign currency earner. Since 1990, an

Real Growth in GDP

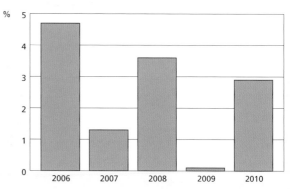

Inflation

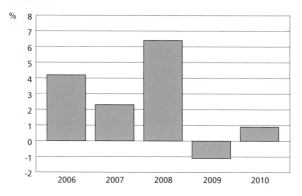

GDP by Sector (2010)

■ Agriculture	12%
□ Industry	21%
▨ Services	67%

export-processing zone has been developed near Belize City International Airport, mainly for clothing production. And, mainly for domestic consumption, a free zone has been established at Corozal on the coast near the Mexican border.

Though Belize had not had a formal relationship with the IMF, it implemented its own structural adjustment programme, with expenditure controls, a public-sector wage freeze and job cuts, and some privatisation, aimed at restoring a fiscal surplus.

History

The earliest known inhabitants were the Mayans, whose extensive civilisation (AD 250–900) reached its peak in about the 8th century, spreading northward throughout Yucatan. The Mayans cultivated most of the arable land in the country and built cities and ceremonial centres out of limestone. By the time the Spanish arrived, in the early 16th century, the numbers of Mayans had declined, and many of the remainder were sent to Guatemala or died of introduced diseases.

The Spanish then moved north to Mexico, and British pirates (who had lost their occupation when Britain and Spain made peace in 1670) moved in to cut logwood for export to Europe. In time, the settlers expanded inland to cut mahogany and cedar, and African slaves were brought over from Jamaica. Attempts by the Spanish to dislodge the Baymen (as the woodcutters were called) failed, but the settlers asked England for help.

In 1765 Admiral Sir William Burnaby arrived with a fleet from Jamaica and, without recourse to violence, established a constitution known as Burnaby's Code and the Public Meeting, a law-making body. Friction continued, however, until 1798, when the Spanish were defeated at the battle of St George's Caye.

In 1847, Mayans in neighbouring Mexico rebelled against Spanish rule and refugees (Mayans, Mestizos and dissident Spaniards) made their way into Belize, a migration which set up new tensions. In an attempt to resolve the situation, the settlement, at its own request, became a British colony (supervised by the governor of Jamaica) in 1862 and the country took the name British Honduras. It became a Crown colony in 1870. In 1884, it was detached from Jamaica and given its own governor. Burnaby's Code and the Public Meeting were abolished in 1840 and 1853 respectively and replaced by a nominated legislative council.

Economic recession followed. Mahogany prices slumped in the 1870s and sugar (introduced by the immigrants from Mexico) slumped in the 1880s. An upturn in the early 20th century was short-lived and poverty continued between the world wars.

In 1935, the principle of voting was reintroduced, with elections for five of the 12 seats on the legislative council, although with a very limited franchise (1,000 out of the population of 50,000). The number of elected members increased under a new constitution in 1954, when the council changed its name to legislative assembly and extended the franchise to universal adult suffrage. By now the movement for independence was under way; it had gained momentum in 1949 when the British Honduras dollar was devalued. This became a rallying point with the cry: 'Give us back our dollar. Give us independence.'

In 1954 the first general election was won by the People's United Party (PUP), headed by George Price (the PUP won all subsequent elections until 1984). In 1964, the country became self-governing with a bicameral legislature. In 1971, the seat of government was moved from Belize City to the new inland site of Belmopan. In 1961 Hurricane Hattie left Belize City in ruins. The country's name was changed from British Honduras to Belize in 1973.

Independence was delayed by the claim to the whole of its territory by neighbouring Guatemala and in 1975 and 1977 British troops and aircraft were used to protect Belize from the threat of invasion. The UN passed several resolutions asserting Belize's right to its sovereignty and territorial integrity. By the late 1970s, although the claim was unresolved, constitutional talks on independence were successful, and the UK agreed to provide a defence guarantee, notably by patrolling the border with Guatemala.

After 20 years in power, George Price and the PUP lost the 1984 elections to the United Democratic Party (UDP) led by Manuel Esquivel; returned to government in 1989; and were ousted again in 1993 by UDP in coalition with the National Alliance for Belizean Rights, a new party which was formed after five members left the UDP in 1992 following disagreements over the negotiations with Guatemala.

Relations with Guatemala

From 1986 relations between the two countries improved and in 1991 Guatemala recognised Belizean sovereignty, Belize joined the Organization of American States (OAS) and diplomatic relations between Belize and Guatemala were established.

In January 1994 responsibility for defence was transferred to the Belize Defence Force and later that year the UK withdrew most of its 1,500-strong garrison. In March 1994, however, Guatemala renounced its earlier agreements and formally reaffirmed its claim to the territory of Belize. A tense period ensued during which Belize continued to receive strong support from the Caribbean Community and the Commonwealth.

It was thus not until February 1997 that an ambassador was sent to Guatemala City, opening the way for a diplomatic resolution of the dispute. The two countries embarked, through the good offices of the OAS, on a peace process leading, in September 2005, to agreement on a framework for negotiations to resolve the dispute and confidence-building measures. Included in this agreement was a mechanism, should the parties fail to reach agreement in negotiations, to allow recourse to an international judicial body.

There was a short pause in the vigorous economic growth of the early 2000s when, in 2001, the fourth hurricane to strike Belize in three years caused heavy damage to tourist facilities and rice production in the southern part of the country. Another short pause ensued in 2007, when the economy felt the impact of Hurricane Dean on agricultural output and tourism. The recovery of 2008 was then summarily reversed by the world economic downturn and consequent fall in tourism, and the economy stalled in 2009, picking up briskly in 2010–11.

Constitution

Status:	Monarchy under Queen Elizabeth II
Legislature:	National Assembly
Independence:	21 September 1981

Belize is a parliamentary democracy and constitutional monarchy which recognises Queen Elizabeth II as head of state, represented by a governor-general. The governor-general, appointed on the advice of the prime minister, must be of Belizean nationality. The legislature, the National Assembly, is bicameral, composed of the Senate and House of Representatives.

The Senate has 12 members (plus the president of the senate): six are appointed on the advice of the prime minister, three on the advice of the leader of the opposition, and one each by the churches, business community and trade unions.

The House of Representatives comprises 31 members, directly elected at intervals of no longer than five years on the basis of universal adult suffrage (plus the speaker). The prime minister and cabinet have executive power.

There are six administrative districts. With the exception of Belize City, they are administered by a locally elected town board of seven members. The island resort of San Pedro on Ambergris Caye was granted township status in 1984. Belize City is administered by a city council of nine elected members. There are also village councils.

Politics

Last elections:	March 2012
Next elections:	2017
Head of state:	Queen Elizabeth II, represented by governor-general, Sir Colville Norbert Young Sr (1993–)
Head of government:	Prime Minister Dean Oliver Barrow
Ruling party:	United Democratic Party

In the general election of August 1998 the opposition People's United Party (PUP) won 26 of the 29 seats in the House of Representatives and Said Musa became prime minister. The ruling United Democratic Party (UDP) took three seats and Esquivel handed over the party leadership to Dean Barrow.

For the first time since independence, the ruling party was returned to power in the March 2003 general election. The PUP took 22 seats to the UDP's seven, and Said Musa resumed as prime minister.

In January 2005, the government increased tax rates on commodities and property and riots broke out. Civil unrest continued until April with trade unions and government opponents demanding Musa's resignation. This and allegations of corruption in the PUP government proved decisive in the subsequent elections.

The February 2008 general election resulted in a landslide victory for the opposition UDP, which won 25 seats to the ruling PUP's six. UDP leader Barrow became the country's first prime minister of African descent.

The general election in March 2012 was again won by Barrow and the UDP with 17 seats, the PUP taking 14.

International relations

Belize is a member of the African, Caribbean and Pacific Group of States, Association of Caribbean States, Caribbean Community, Non-Aligned Movement, Organization of American States, United Nations and World Trade Organization.

Belize is strengthening its links with its Central American neighbours through its membership of the Sistema de la Integración Centroamericana.

Traveller information

Local laws and conventions: Possession of drugs is considered a serious crime in Belize and can lead to a fine and or even imprisonment.

Dress is casual, although beachwear must not be worn in towns.

Appointments for business meetings are customary and business cards are often exchanged. Office hours are Mon–Fri 0800–1200 and 1300–1700.

Immigration and customs: Passports must be valid for six months beyond the intended length of stay. When entering the country, visitors must prove they have sufficient funds for their stay as well as a return or onward ticket. All visa requirements must be checked well in advance of travel.

A yellow fever vaccination certificate is required by all those arriving from infected areas.

Prohibited imports include Pre-Columbian articles, marine products, unprocessed coral, and turtle shells.

Travel within the country: Traffic drives on the right and visitors can hire cars with a national driving licence for the first three months of stay. Car hire is available in larger towns and at the international airport. All-weather highways link the main towns and most of the roads are in good condition. Visitors should be aware, however, that the Manatee Highway running from the Western Highway to Dangriga is prone to severe flooding after torrential rain.

National speed limits are 40kph in built-up areas and 90kph on the highways.

The country's main domestic airline is Maya Island Air, which operates scheduled flights from Belize City to most of the main towns and cayes (islands). Boat services connect Belize City to Ambergris Caye, Caye Chapel and Caye Caulker.

Bus services are frequent and inexpensive, and link most of the towns and villages. Many of the vehicles are ex-school buses imported from the USA.

Travel health: There are government-run hospitals in all the main towns. Visitors are advised to take out comprehensive medical insurance.

Dengue fever is present in Belize, and visitors will need to protect themselves from mosquito bites with insect repellent and suitable clothing. Tuberculosis and Hepatitis B also occur, and vaccinations are sometimes required. All those planning to travel to Belize should check the most up-to-date inoculation requirements.

Tap water is usually safe to drink, though it is advisable to check before drinking; bottled water should be used if there is any doubt. Milk is unpasteurised and should be boiled before use.

Money: Local currency is the Belize dollar, although most businesses accept US dollars. ATMs accept some foreign cards but should not be relied on for cash. Visa and Mastercard are widely accepted. Travellers cheques can be exchanged at most banks, many hotels and some travel agencies. Banking hours are Mon–Thur 0800–1300 and Fri 0800–1630.

There were 232,000 tourist arrivals in 2009.

Further information

Government of Belize: www.belize.gov.bz

National Assembly: www.belize.gov.bz

Central Bank of Belize: www.centralbank.org.bz

Commonwealth Secretariat: www.thecommonwealth.org

Commonwealth of Nations: www.commonwealth-of-nations.org/Belize

Botswana Couriers

We deliver, whatever wherever   www.botscouriers.co.bw

Botswana Couriers is the premier courier and logistics company in Botswana. Since its inception in 2001, a 100% wholly owned subsidiary of the Botswana Post Group, Botswana Couriers has grown to become a prominent player within the logistics industry.

Botswana Couriers offers courier, freight and logistics services to individuals and businesses in all segments of the industry. We also have a diverse portfolio of service offerings, specially designed to suit the specific needs of our customers.

SAME DAY DELIVERIES are frequently used by clients where contracts, paperwork and documents all need to be processed within a limited timeframe. Same day deliveries are offered between major centres in Botswana and Johannesburg.

OVERNIGHT DOMESTIC AND INTERNATIONAL COURIER: you can rely on our overnight delivery services to ensure the timely delivery of goods. These daily services are provided between Gaborone and major centres in Botswana, as well as between Johannesburg (including the surrounding region) and Gaborone.

MESSENGER SERVICES offer customised mail pick-up and delivery services within town. Dedicated couriers are responsible for the day-to-day runnings of mail services for specific organisations. Proof of delivery documents are produced for accurate recording.

For *TENDER AND EMBASSY COLLECTIONS* we offer a convenient post-paid solution. All collections and submissions are made with prior written notice. For non-account holders, upfront payment will be required for the collection or submission to be made.

Our growth strategy is now focused on *WAREHOUSING AND DISTRIBUTION,* making us the first and only courier company in Botswana to offer such distinguished services. These are available to both our local and international clientele.

BOTSWANA COURIERS ONLINE

Our website allows customers to track and trace their parcels from origin to destination. Collection bookings can be done online through a detailed booking form. Once submitted, a response is sent directly to the customer's email address bearing a collection reference number as confirmation.

CONTACT

Mr L Medupe, Managing Director
Botswana Couriers House
Plot 89, Tshukudu Road
Gaborone International Commerce Park

Tel: +267 393 0629
Fax: +267 393 0630
Email: customerservices@botscouriers.co.bw
sales@botscouriers.co.bw
www.botscouriers.co.bw

Botswana

KEY FACTS

Joined Commonwealth:	1966
Population:	2,007,000 (2010)
GDP p.c. growth:	3.5% p.a. 1990–2010
UN HDI 2011:	world ranking 118
Official languages:	Setswana, English
Time:	GMT plus 2hr
Currency:	pula (P)

Geography

Area:	582,000 sq km
Coastline:	none
Capital:	Gaborone

The Republic of Botswana is a large, roughly circular, landlocked plateau in the centre of Southern Africa, bordered by South Africa, Namibia, Zambia and Zimbabwe.

Topography: The average elevation of the country is 1,000m. To the south-east are hills, the highest being 1,491m Otse Mountain near Lobatse. In the north-west are the Tsodilo Hills, famous for rock-paintings. Also in the north-west, the Okavango river flows into an enormous inland delta, home of a great variety of wildlife. To the north-east is the salt desert of the Makgadikgadi Pans. However, about 85% of the country consists of the tableland of the Kalahari desert, a vast sandveld.

Climate: Botswana lies across the Tropic of Capricorn. The climate ranges from semi-arid through subtropical to temperate. Eastern Botswana is temperate, with enough rainfall to support arable farming, but rainfall decreases and temperature range increases westwards and southwards. Summer (October to April) is the rainy season and is very hot. Rainfall varies from 650mm per annum in the east to 230mm in the south-west. May to October is usually dry. In winter the nights can be cold and sometimes frosty,

Did you know...

Novelist and human rights campaigner Unity Dow was appointed a High Court judge in 1998, the first woman to hold the post.

Scholarships for postgraduate study are awarded by Botswana to citizens of other Commonwealth countries under the Commonwealth Scholarship and Fellowship Plan.

Botswana was the largest producer of gem-quality diamonds in the world in 2011, a position it has held since it displaced Australia in 1999.

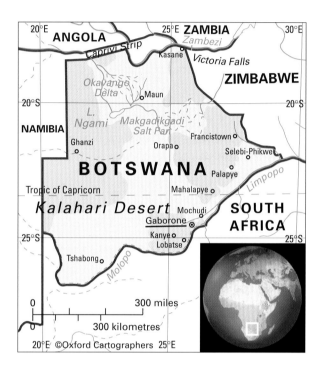

especially in the desert. Mean maximum temperature at Gaborone is 32.5°C. From August, annual seasonal winds cross the Kalahari from the west, raising dust and sandstorms.

Environment: The most significant environmental issues are overgrazing, desertification and limited resources of fresh water.

Vegetation: Mostly dry savannah with grasslands and thornbush to semi-desert and some true desert. Acacia, bloodwood and Rhodesian teak trees in the forest in the north-west. Forest covers 20% of the land area, having declined at 0.9% p.a. 1990–2010. Arable land comprises 0.7% of the total land area.

Wildlife: Wildlife is protected in the three national parks and five game reserves, extending to 105,000 sq km or 18.5% of the total land area. The Okavango Delta supports a world-famous variety of water-birds and attracts thousands of animals in the dry season. The Chobe National Park, also in the north, has more than 50,000 elephants. The Gemsbok National Park abuts South Africa's Kalahari Gemsbok NP, which together make one of the world's biggest wilderness regions. The country has recorded 164 species of mammals, six of which are threatened with extinction.

Main towns: Gaborone (capital, pop. 237,000 in 2010), Francistown (98,000), Molepolole (74,500), Mogoditshane (59,900), Selebi–Phikwe (58,100), Maun (57,600), Serowe (53,600), Mahalapye (50,200), Kanye (49,300), Mochudi (48,000), Palapye (36,300), Lobatse (31,900), Tlokweng (31,700), Thamaga (24,000), Bobonong (23,300) and Ramotswa (21,700). Most of Botswana's main settlements are in the south-east of the country.

BOTSWANA SECTORS OF EDUCATORS TRADE UNION

Teacher Pillar of the Nation

VISION

BOSETU exists to ensure that teachers' rights and welfare are realised and protected.

MISSION

BOSETU is an educators' union in Botswana that represents the interests of educators, and enhances the importance of the teaching profession through advocacy and collaboration.

CORE VALUES

- Caring: we will treat our employees and our members with compassion.

- Collaborative: we will work together as employees and members to achieve our common goal.

- Consultative: this is at the heart of what we do – we will create solutions that our members want, not what we think they want, by getting to understand their needs.

- Creative: we will innovate, improvise and work tirelessly to find a solution to challenges.

- Professionalism: we will strive to always do our work with passion, interest, diligence, competence and commitment.

CONTACT

Mr Tobokani Nicholas Rari
Secretary General
Plot 871/2/3/4 Babereki House,
African Mall, Gaborone,
Botswana

Tel: +267 393 7472/3
Email: nicholasrari@yahoo.com

Shandukani Hlhabano, President

Board members

Justin C. Hunyepa

BOSETU SPECIAL CONGRESS

Transport: There are 25,800km of roads, 33% paved. The north–south highway links South Africa with Zambia. The Trans-Kalahari highway, completed in 1998, links Botswana to Walvis Bay on the Namibian coast, shortening the route between Johannesburg and the Namibian capital, Windhoek, and opening up the hitherto inaccessible western regions of the country.

The 888-km railway line runs north–south along the eastern side of the country from Plumtree in Zimbabwe to the border with South Africa. Exports from Zimbabwe and elsewhere in Southern Africa use this line to reach the South African ports of Durban and Richards Bay. Local railway lines service Botswana's mining industries.

Air services operate to several regional destinations plus regular domestic flights between Gaborone and Francistown, Maun, Selebi-Phikwe, Ghanzi, Pont Drift and Kasane.

Society

KEY FACTS 2010

Population per sq km:	3
Life expectancy:	53 years
Net primary enrolment:	87%

Population: 2,007,000 (2010); 61% lives in urban areas; growth 1.9% p.a. 1990–2010, with rapid growth in urban areas; birth rate 24 per 1,000 people (46 in 1970); life expectancy 53 years, down from a peak of 63 years in the early 1990s, as a result of AIDS (52 in 1970).

Around 80% of the people are of Setswana-speaking origin and most of the rest of Kalanga-speaking origin. Bushmen (i.e. San or Basarwa), Herero, Mbukushu, Yei and Mazezuru, whites and others constitute the balance.

Language: Setswana is the national language; English is an official language.

Religion: Most people are Christians (72% in 2001 census) or hold traditional beliefs. Traditional religions incorporate some Christian practices.

Health: Public spending on health was 8% of GDP in 2009. There are some 30 hospitals and more than 500 clinics and health centres. Malaria is endemic in northern Botswana. 95% of the population uses an improved drinking water source and 60% have access to adequate sanitation facilities (2009). Infant mortality was 36 per 1,000 live births in 2010 (118 in 1960). In 2009, 24.8% of people aged 15–49 were HIV positive. Full AIDS control and prevention programmes are now in place.

Education: Public spending on education was 7.8% of GDP in 2009. There are 12 years of school starting at age seven, comprising seven years of primary and five of secondary. The private sector provides about one-third of secondary places. Some 87% of pupils complete primary school (2005). The school year starts in January. The Brigades movement, now established throughout the Commonwealth, was founded in Serowe by Patrick van Rensburg to provide vocational training in skilled trades for early school-leavers.

There are about 30 vocational and technical training centres, four teacher-training colleges, two colleges of education and one university, the University of Botswana. A second public university, the Botswana International University of Science and Technology, is under construction at Palapye. The Institute of Development Management accepts students from throughout the region. Other tertiary institutions include Botswana College of Agriculture, Botswana Institute of Administration and Commerce, and Botswana College of Distance and Open Learning. Literacy among people aged 15–24 is 95% (2009).

Media: The government-owned *Daily News* is published in English and Setswana, and *Mmegi* is an independent daily. There are several privately owned weeklies including *The Botswana Gazette* (Wednesday, since 1985), *Botswana Guardian* (weekend) and *The Midweek Sun*.

Botswana's media has a long tradition of lively public debate. Press circulation is limited to urban areas and radio is the main source of information for most people. Radio Botswana is the public service, broadcasting in Setswana and English. Public service TV, Botswana Television, was launched in 2000. There are a number of privately owned radio and TV stations.

Some 9% of households have TV sets (2006). There are 63 personal computers (2008) and 60 internet users (2010) per 1,000 people.

Communications: Country code 267; internet domain '.bw'. There are very few public phone boxes. Mobile phone coverage is generally confined to the most populous areas. Gaborone and Maun have a number of internet cafes. There are post offices in all towns and the larger villages.

There are 69 main telephone lines and 1,178 mobile phone subscriptions per 1,000 people (2010).

Public holidays: New Year (two days), Labour Day (early May), Sir Seretse Khama Day (1 July), President's Day (Monday and Tuesday in July), Botswana Day (30 September), Christmas Day and Boxing Day.

Religious festivals whose dates vary from year to year include Good Friday, Easter Monday and Ascension Day.

Economy

KEY FACTS 2010

GNI:	US$13.6bn
GNI p.c.:	US$6,790
GDP growth:	2.9% p.a. 2006–10
Inflation:	9.2% p.a. 2006–10

Real Growth in GDP

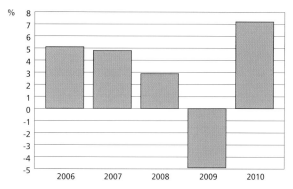

Train • Develop • Grow
Tshimologo Business Services (Pty) Ltd

History

Since its founding in 2000, Tshimologo Business Services (Pty) Ltd has evolved to offer renowned professional services by providing the most effective and efficient growth fostering solutions that give companies a reason to exist.

The Company's philosophy is to provide the most professional services and meeting clients' exclusive requirements. We believe that needs are different and ever changing therefore the one-size-fits-all approach is indeed history.

Background

Founded by Ms Neo Tina Masu, TBS is proudly a hundred per cent female and Motswana-owned company that focuses on business solutions: business or company registration, maintenance of statutory records, licensing, permits, procurement registration, training and personal and business development. The workforce comprises young and experienced staff from different fields of study.

TBS is a locally recognised company and has international clients and affiliates. We are registered members and accredited to non-governmental organisations, government, parastatals and the private sector.

The international market, now more than ever, presents a unique set of challenges and opportunities for all business and investors. TBS proactively guides businesses to rise to challenges and meet the demands of today's economy. Trends in globalisation, shorter response times and increased business complexity have brought the importance of risk to the forefront, placing an additional burden on the already busy finance agenda.

Services

- Accounting and auditing
- Company secretaries
- Finance and on- and offshore investment
- Personal and business development
- Taxation
- Training

Vision

To be the leader in the provision of personal and business development services locally and internationally.

Mission

To offer service excellence to public and private enterprises resulting in personal and business growth.

Value proportion

TBS aims to redefine business by adding time-to–time value and performance, development of best-proven practices and reduced risk, increased productivity and profitability which in turn will transform a business into a market leader. TBS is a one-stop for immaculate business solutions.

We have the missing piece to the puzzle.

Tel: +267 393 0757
Fax: +267 395 6965
Email: info@tshimologo.co.bw
        www.tshimologo.co.bw

Inflation

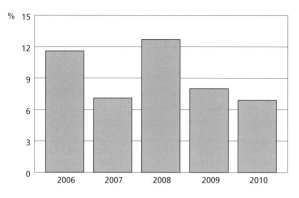

GDP by Sector (2010)

■ Agriculture	2%
□ Industry	45%
▨ Services	52%

Botswana has benefited from a stable social structure and a wealth of natural mineral resources; it has an unbroken record of parliamentary democracy and one of Africa's highest sustained records of economic growth since independence. However, the economy is dependent on mining and agriculture, and has had to cope with the vagaries of the diamond market and frequent droughts. During 1999–2003, only the year 2000 was free of drought. It is also strongly influenced by economic trends in South Africa, the economic giant of the region.

Minerals have provided the financial base for welfare projects and the development of manufacturing. Since the 1990s the government has encouraged foreign investment in export-oriented industries, especially in manufacturing, and notably car assembly (which started in 1994, boosted exports for the rest of the decade and then ceased production in 2000 when the South African investor company went into liquidation); textiles; and diamond jewellery (the first jewellery factory was established with Indian investment in 2010).

The economy generally grew well in the 2000s: by 5.1% in 2006 and 4.8% in 2007. But during 2008 (2.9%), in the face of the global downturn, world demand for diamonds and eco-tourism slumped, and the Botswana economy moved sharply into recession, shrinking by 4.9% in 2009, but recovering strongly in 2010–11, with rises in world commodity prices, recording growth of 7.2% in 2010 and about 7% in 2011.

Mining

Mining started near Orapa in 1967 only a year after independence. The country is among the world's largest producers of diamonds. Minerals – notably diamonds, copper and nickel – generate most of the government's revenue.

Constitution

Status:	Republic with executive president
Legislature:	Parliament
Independence:	30 September 1966

Under the 1965 constitution, Botswana is a republic with an executive president chosen by the National Assembly for the concurrent five-year term. After the 2004 general election, the Assembly had 57 members directly elected by universal adult suffrage plus the president, speaker, attorney-general and four members nominated by the president. The 35-member Ntlo ya Dikgosi (formerly known as the House of Chiefs) advises on tribal matters; 30 of the members are elected by senior tribal authorities and five members appointed by the president.

The Botswana Democratic Party has ruled that the party leadership is only to be held by any one person for two full terms.

Substantive constitutional amendments require a two-thirds majority of the Assembly and major amendments, a national referendum. Constitutional amendments approved in April 1997 retained the system by which the president is elected by parliament but allowed the vice-president automatically to succeed in the event of the president's death or resignation during his term of office. It also reduced the voting age from 21 to 18.

Local elections for the nine district councils, two city councils and four town councils are held – also on a party basis – simultaneously with general elections.

Politics

Last elections:	October 2009
Next elections:	2014
Head of state:	President Lt-Gen Seretse Khama Ian Khama
Head of government:	the president
Ruling party:	Botswana Democratic Party

The October 1999 general election was won by the Botswana Democratic Party (BDP), led by Festus Mogae, taking 33 seats, with 57% of the votes, while the Botswana National Front (BNF) held six seats, with 26% of the votes. There was an increase in the numbers of female and younger parliamentarians.

In October 2004 the BDP won with 44 of the 57 seats in the enlarged Assembly and 52% of the votes and Mogae was returned for a second term as president. The BNF took 12 seats and 26% of the votes, and Botswana Congress Party (BCP), one seat and 17%.

On Festus Mogae's retirement in April 2008, Ian Khama (the son of former President Sir Seretse Khama) became the country's fourth president. In October 2009, he led the BDP to victory in the general election, taking 45 seats and 53% of the votes. The BNF took six seats (22%), the BCP four (19%), the Botswana Alliance Movement one (2%) and independents one. Khama was shortly afterwards sworn in again as president.

International relations

Botswana is a member of the African, Caribbean and Pacific Group of States, African Union, Non-Aligned Movement, Southern African Customs Union, Southern African Development Community, United Nations and World Trade Organization.

Improve your business performance

Ban Ki-moon, UN Secretary-General and Joseph Pheto, Managing Director of Jorisma

Contact

Mr Joseph Pheto
Managing Director
Plot 50667, Block A
Medical Mews, Fairgrounds
Private Bag BR31
Gaborone
Botswana

Tel: +267 393 0521
Fax: +267 393 0519
Email: info@jorisma.co.bw

Jorisma offers successful planning, organisation and management of world-class conferences and summits. Jorisma achieves through its focus on quality and excellence, passion and integrity, experience and knowledge, detailed planning and effective costing. Jorisma has extensive experience of attending and organising conferences and summits in more than 20 countries spanning four continents.

Jorisma offers training in Effective Leadership, Entrepreneurship, Change Management and human achievement technologies such as Emotional Intelligence and Neuro-Linguistic Programming. Jorisma complies with the requirements of Botswana Training Authority (BOTA) with regard to training services. Jorisma also offers business consultancy around training field areas.

Jorisma subscribes to the Project Management Body of Knowledge (PMBOK) and through its team or in collaboration with its partner companies, offers project management services for projects of all sizes from initiation to completion.

JORISMA'S PHILOSOPHY

MISSION

To provide delightful and satisfactory customer experience in all our services – conferencing, events management, training, project management and business consultancy.

VISION

To be the benchmark service provider in our industries and beyond.

VALUES

- Passion
- Integrity
- Innovation
- Excellence
- Contribution

Why Jorisma?

- **Events and Conferences:** Jorisma specialises in the organisation and management of national and international conferences and summits addressing business, NGO or governmental needs.

- **Life Skills:** Jorisma offers the latest human achievement technologies including Emotional Intelligence (EI) and Neuro-Linguistic Programming(NLP).

  NLP is also offered on a one-on-one or group consultancy basis.

- **Management/Leadership:** Jorisma offers high quality training in effective leadership and change management.

- **Entrepreneurship:** Jorisma offers high quality training in various aspects of entrepreneurship start-ups, business plan development, business management, marketing and innovation.

- **Project Management:** Jorisma through its experienced project managers provides project management services in medium and large projects for government and business companies.

- **Business Consultancy:** Jorisma provides business consultancy services in the training field areas but also including innovation.

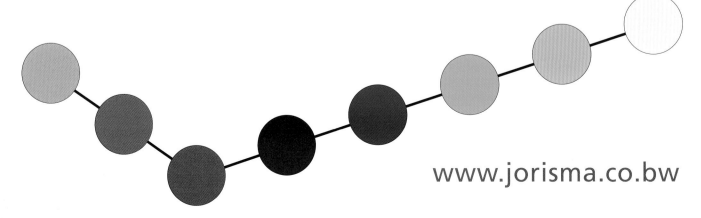

www.jorisma.co.bw

Botswana hosts the headquarters of the Southern African Development Community in Gaborone.

Traveller information

Local laws and conventions: Photography of airports, official residences and defence establishments is prohibited. It is good practice to seek permission before photographing local people. Drug-taking and smuggling is an offence, and punishments can be severe.

Most people in Botswana follow traditional life patterns.

Casual clothing is acceptable but not worn for meetings. Office hours are Apr–Oct: Mon–Fri 0800–1700; Oct–Apr: Mon–Fri 0730–1630.

Immigration and customs: Passports are required by all and must be valid for at least six months after the intended departure date. Visitors must also have outgoing travel documents and sufficient funds to finance their stay.

Visas are not required for most Commonwealth and EU countries, nor for the USA. For those wishing to stay longer than three months, applications must be made to the Chief Immigration Officer prior to arrival.

Visitors are advised to have some sort of identification on them at all times. A yellow fever vaccination certificate is required by all those travelling from an infected area.

History

The earliest inhabitants of Botswana were San or Basarwa (Bushmen) who have been in the area an estimated 30,000 years. Their nomadic hunter-gatherer lifestyle has left few traces except rock paintings (there are some 3,500 paintings at 350 sites in the Tsodilo Hills). More technologically advanced and powerful pastoral and agricultural Bantu groups moved in from the north-west and east around the first and 2nd century AD. The first Setswana-speaking group, the Bakgalagadi, arrived sometime in the 14th century. While there was plenty of land, the different peoples coexisted peacefully but in the early 19th century, Mzilikazi (a captain of Zulu chief Shaka) broke away and led a Zulu force northwards. The local people were scattered and forced into more arid lands.

The upheavals of the region were greatly exacerbated when, from around 1836, the Boer Trekkers, escaping British rule, began to arrive and displace other groups. In the 1840s British missionaries David Livingstone and Robert Moffat established stations among the Bakwena; Moffat translated the Bible into Setswana.

In 1872 Khama III became chief of Bamangwato, one of the tribes of the Batswana group. A capable general and administrator, he secured immunity from Matabele raids and increased order and stability. To avoid Boer rule, particularly after the discovery of gold at Tati, Khama asked for British protection; this was given in 1885. The terms were that Khama retained control of administration, law and justice, while Britain was responsible for security.

The territory south of the Molopo river was annexed to the Cape Colony in 1895 while the rest remained under British protection as Bechuanaland. A capital was chosen at Mafikeng, a town settled almost exclusively by Tswana-speaking tribes. At Mafikeng, which was actually in South Africa, outside the Protectorate, the now global boy scout movement was started by Lord Baden-Powell. Bechuanaland successfully resisted pressure to grant mining concessions to the British South Africa Company and also (in 1909) successfully resisted becoming part of South Africa.

Over the next half-century, the country languished: it became a provider of cheap labour for South Africa's mines, education and welfare were neglected, and the administration came entirely into colonial hands.

In 1923 Khama III died; his son and successor, Sekgoma, died after being in power only two years. Three-year-old Seretse

Khama then inherited the leadership, with his uncle, Tshekedi Khama, as Regent.

Seretse Khama's accession in 1950 changed the tone of Bechuanaland politics. While studying law in London, he married a white English woman. This was rated as a serious breach of tribal custom in Botswana, and also in racially segregated South Africa and Rhodesia. Seretse Khama was forced to stand down as chief of the Ngwato. The UK yielded to pressure and held him in exile until 1956. On his return to Bechuanaland, Seretse Khama campaigned for change and in the 1960s founded the Botswana Democratic Party (BDP). Its policy sought a non-racial and democratic but traditional society in which chiefs and traditional courts still had a role.

In 1960 a representative legislative council was set up; there was now a formal negotiating mechanism and independence was achieved in a series of peaceful moves. Central authority was strengthened, the position of the chiefs and African courts defined. The seat of government was transferred from Mafikeng to Gaborone. In the pre-independence elections of 1965, the BDP won 28 of the 31 elective seats. The country achieved independence as a republic on 30 September 1966 with Seretse Khama as president.

Seretse Khama led the country from 1965 until his death in 1980, when he was succeeded by Dr Quett Masire, formerly vice-president, who was knighted as Sir Ketumile Masire in 1991.

Although the BDP had easily won every election since multiparty democracy was established in 1965, in the general election of 1994 the main opposition party, the Botswana National Front (BNF), won 13 seats (37% of the vote) as against the BDP's 27 seats (54%), with the smaller parties failing to win any seats.

In November 1997 at the age of 73, President Masire announced he would retire in March 1998. On 1 April 1998 Festus Mogae, who had served as vice-president since 1992, was sworn in as president. He also became leader of the BDP. The only new member of Mogae's first cabinet was Ian Khama (son of former President Sir Seretse Khama), who retired as commander of the Botswana Defence Force to take up the key post of minister of presidential affairs and public administration and was appointed vice-president in July 1998.

InnoLead is a 100% citizen-owned organisation offering Management Services incorporating the Project Management Services of X-Pert ® Group Botswana. InnoLead Consulting was born out of a desire by a team of Batswana citizen-consulting professionals to create a consulting firm that has a deep understanding of the challenges faced by organisations in Botswana.

Our consulting focuses on 'customer requirements' and delivers innovative solutions based on best practices. The founders of Innolead Consulting founded X-pert Group Botswana in 2002, whose core purpose has been to improve the Project Management capability in Botswana through the 'Managing by Project' (MBP™) methodology they pioneered.

InnoLead Consulting provides professional consultancy in Corporate Strategy, Process Improvement, IT consulting and Performance Management. X-Pert Group Project Management Services are provided under the umbrella of InnoLead, and under license through X-Pert Group International. The services offered are vested in proven capability, led by citizen professionals with a depth of experience in Managing Change and Project Management. We have ready access to regional and global expertise if required for delivery of large scale projects.

Vision
When customers have a choice, they will consistently choose Innolead for innovative consulting solutions

Core purpose
To provide innovative management advisory services through an inspired team of leading consultants

InnoLead and X-Pert has matured into an organisation that has a reputation of being a leader in the field of Project Management and have a track record in the Batswana market. We pride ourselves in giving you:

Management Consulting
- Strategy and Innovation
- Performance Management and Balanced Scorecard
- Talent Management
- Change Management
- Leadership Development
- Team Building
- Executive Coaching
- Records Management

Project Management Consulting
- Projects Staffing/ Resourcing
- Project Management Office design and implementation
- Project Administration and Support
- Project Management Training (through Xpert Group)
- End-to-End Project Management

InnoLead through X-pert is registered with a number of international professional bodies such as the Project Management Institute and the Association of Project Management.

Mr Oabona Kgengwenyane, Managing Director

Contact us
Unit 2, Plot 140, Kgale Terrace, GIFP Gaborone, Botswana

Tel: +267 390 9102
Fax: +267 318 0565
Email: innolead@innolead.co.bw

www.innolead.co.bw

People Focused Consulting

A permit is needed for the importation of firearms and ammunition, boats and aquatic equipment. All animal souvenirs or 'trophies' are subject to National Trophy Law, which strictly regulates the sale, possession or export of animals or their durable parts. Travellers carrying such items will need to present a government permit or receipt from a licensed store on departure.

Travel within the country: Traffic drives on the left and car hire is available in the larger cities. An international driving permit is recommended. The speed limit is 60kph in urban areas and 120kph in rural areas. Particular care must be taken if driving after dark (wildlife and stray livestock) and during the rainy season. In rural areas, there are long distances between petrol stations, and reserve fuel and water and emergency supplies are recommended on longer journeys.

Flying is an efficient way to travel around the country and chartered flights are available.

A bus service links Gaborone, Francistown and Maun. Taxis are found in most major towns, but visitors must agree on the tariff before getting into a taxi. Botswana Railway (BR) runs a daily service between Francistown, Gaborone and Lobatse.

Travel health: The public health system is good. All main towns have chemists, and pharmaceutical supplies are readily available. Comprehensive health insurance is essential, however, and should include cover for evacuation to South Africa for serious medical treatment. Visitors will need protection against malaria, especially in northern Botswana, together with insect repellent and suitable clothing to prevent mosquito bites. Hepatitis A, tetanus and typhoid vaccinations are recommended. There is a risk of rabies, and to prevent bilharzia visitors should only swim in well-chlorinated pools. Tick bite fever can be a problem and regular checks must be taken after rural walks.

Tap water is considered safe, but outside of cities visitors should observe routine precautions and drink either boiled or bottled water. Milk is pasteurised.

Money: Local currency is the pula (1 pula = 100 thebe). American Express, Diners Club, Mastercard and Visa are widely accepted. ATMs are available in larger cities and towns, and travellers cheques should be in pounds sterling or US dollars to avoid extra exchange rate charges. Banking hours are Mon–Fri 0800–1700 and Sat 0815–1045.

There were 1,553,000 tourist arrivals in 2009.

Further information

Government of Botswana: www.gov.bw

Parliament: www.parliament.gov.bw

Bank of Botswana: www.bankofbotswana.bw

Commonwealth Secretariat: www.thecommonwealth.org

Commonwealth of Nations: www.commonwealth-of-nations.org/Botswana

BOTSWANA INSTITUTE FOR DEVELOPMENT POLICY ANALYSIS

Research and Policy Analysis

Capacity Building in Policy Analysis

Consultancy on the Economy

Monitoring Botswana Economy

Public Education

Vision

The Botswana Institute for Development Policy Analysis will be a globally competitive policy research institute.

Mission

To be a centre of excellence that provides policy research, analysis, advice and capacity building.

The Botswana Institute for Development Policy Analysis (BIDPA) was established by the Government of Botswana as an independent trust, and started operations as a non-governmental policy research institute or 'think tank' in 1995. The Institute was established due to the need to effectively link and harmonise economic policy analysis functions with national development efforts.

BIDPA's areas of focus are: Welfare and Poverty; Macroeconomic Forecasting and Planning; Microeconomic Policy; International Economics; and Public Sector Reforms

www.bidpa.bw

Contact
Programme Co-ordinator,
134 International Finance Park, Tshwene Drive, Kgale Hill, Private Bag BR-29, Gaborone, Botswana

Tel: +267 397 1750 • Fax: +267 397 1748
Email: enquiries@bidpa.bw

Brunei Darussalam

KEY FACTS

Joined Commonwealth:	1984
Population:	399,000 (2010)
GDP p.c. growth:	–0.4% p.a. 1990–2010
UN HDI 2011:	world ranking 33
Official language:	Malay
Time:	GMT plus 8hr
Currency:	Brunei dollar (Br$)

Geography

Area:	5,765 sq km
Coastline:	161km
Capital:	Bandar Seri Begawan

Brunei Darussalam (*Brunei* – 'Abode of Peace') is a small state in South-East Asia on the north-west coast of the island of Borneo, in the Indonesian Archipelago. Its 161km coastline faces the South China Sea. On the land side, it is enclosed by the Malaysian state of Sarawak, which divides it in two. The districts of Brunei–Muara, Tutong and Belait make up the larger, western part of the country; Temburong district the east.

Topography: The coastal plain is intersected by rivers descending from the hilly hinterland. To the east are mountains, the highest point being Bukit Pagon at 1,812m. Most towns and villages are beside estuaries.

Climate: Tropical, with high humidity and heavy rainfall. There is no distinct wet season; the wettest months are January and November. Much of the rain falls in sudden thundery showers.

Environment: The most significant environmental issue is seasonal smoke/haze resulting from forest fires in Indonesia.

Vegetation: Mangrove swamps lie along the coast, and forest covers 72% of the land area, a large part of this being primary forest, dense in places and of great genetic diversity. There are 15 forest reserves, covering about 40% of the total land area. The government plans to increase the area of the forest reserves. Around 15% of the land area is cultivated.

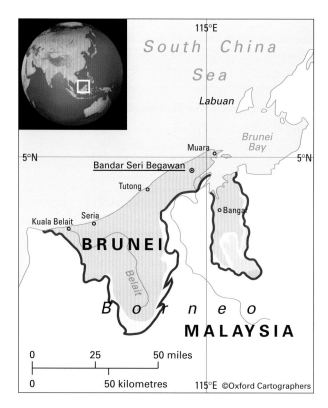

©Oxford Cartographers

Wildlife: Most of the mammals are small and nocturnal, including tree shrews, moon rats and mouse deer. There are numerous bird species, especially hornbills.

Main towns: Bandar Seri Begawan (capital, pop. 76,200 in 2009, comprising Kampong Ayer 42,500), Kuala Belait (28,400), Seria (28,300), Tutong (21,500), Muara and Bangar.

Transport: The country has 3,650km of roads, 77% paved. The main deep-water port is at Muara, with a dedicated container terminal. The Brunei, Belait and Tutong rivers provide an important means of transport. Passenger vessels and water-taxis run between the shallow draught port at Bandar Seri Begawan, Temburong district, and the Malaysian port of Limbang. Brunei International Airport is 6km north-east of the capital.

Society

KEY FACTS 2010

Population per sq km:	69
Life expectancy:	78 years
Net primary enrolment:	97%

Population: 399,000 (2010); 76% lives in urban areas, concentrated along the coast; growth 2.3% p.a. 1990–2010; birth rate 19 per 1,000 people (36 in 1970); life expectancy 78 years (67 in 1970).

Did you know...

Brunei Darussalam is a monarchy.

Scholarships for doctoral study are awarded by Brunei Darussalam to citizens of other Commonwealth countries under the Commonwealth Scholarship and Fellowship Plan.

Malays comprise some two-thirds of the population, and Chinese (about 11%), Europeans, Indians and other races the balance.

Language: Official language is Malay; English is widely spoken. Other languages include Chinese (various dialects), Tamil, Iban and Dusun.

Religion: Official religion is Islam; minorities of Buddhists, Christians, Confucians and Taoists. The national ideology, *Melayu Islam Beraja* (MIB, Malay Muslim monarchy) fuses Islamic values and Brunei Malay culture.

Health: Public spending on health was 3% of GDP in 2009. There are ten hospitals, health clinics, travelling clinics and a flying doctor service. Infant mortality was 6 per 1,000 live births in 2010 (63 in 1960). Malaria has been completely eradicated.

Education: Public spending on education was 2.0% of GDP in 2010. A new education system is being introduced during 2009–11, referred to as 21st Century National Education System or SPN21, which will be broad-based and provide multiple pathways enabling students with different skills and abilities to survive in a fast-changing world. Under this system, there are six years of primary school, starting at age 6 and leading to Primary School Assessment or Penilaian Sekolah Rendah, and, depending on academic ability, either four or five years of secondary school, leading to the Brunei–Cambridge GCE O level exams. Those aiming for higher education will then study for the Brunei–Cambridge GCE A level exams; others will move into vocational education. Some 97% of pupils complete primary school (2008). The school year starts in January. The primary curriculum puts the emphasis on literacy and numeracy, including information and communication technology skills.

The University of Brunei Darussalam (UBD) provides courses taught in Malay and English. On the establishment of the UBD in Bandar Seri Begawan in 1985, local pursuit of degree courses became possible. The government, nevertheless, continued to award scholarships to qualified Brunei citizens to undertake courses of study not yet available at UBD and many Bruneians continue their studies in other Commonwealth countries or other countries such as the USA. Other institutions at tertiary level include the Jefri Bolkiah College of Engineering at Kuala Belait, and the Sultan Sharif Ali Islamic University and Institut Teknologi Brunei at Gadong, Bandar Seri Begawan. The female–male ratio for gross enrolment in tertiary education is 1.76:1 (2009). There is virtually no illiteracy among people aged 15–24.

Media: *Borneo Bulletin* is an English-language daily newspaper. *Media Permata* is published daily in Malay, and *BruDirect* is an online news service.

Radio Television Brunei provides radio and television services, broadcasting in Malay, English, Mandarin Chinese and Gurkhali. Foreign TV stations are available via a cable network.

There are 89 personal computers (2005) and 500 internet users (2010) per 1,000 people.

Communications: Country code 673; internet domain '.bn'. Coin- and card-operated public telephones are available throughout the country. There is good mobile phone coverage in and around the main towns, particularly in the north-west.

There are 200 main telephone lines and 1,091 mobile phone subscriptions per 1,000 people (2010).

Public holidays: New Year's Day, Chinese New Year, National Day (23 February), Royal Brunei Armed Forces Day (31 May), Sultan's Birthday (15 July) and Christmas Day.

History

The pre-Islamic history of Brunei is unclear, but archaeological evidence shows the country to have been trading with the Asian mainland as early as AD 518. Islam became predominant during the 14th century and the Brunei Sultanate rose to prominence in the 15th and 16th centuries, when it controlled coastal areas of North-West Borneo, parts of Kalimantan and the Philippines. The Dutch, Portuguese and Spanish began arriving after the 16th century. Brunei lost outlying possessions to the Spanish and the Dutch and its power gradually declined as the British and Dutch colonial empires expanded.

In the 19th century the Sultan of Brunei sought British support in defending the coast against Dayak pirates, and ennobled James Brooke, a British adventurer, as Rajah of Sarawak in 1839. The British proceeded to annex the island of Labuan in 1846. North Borneo became a British protected state in 1888 and Brunei voluntarily accepted the status of a British protected state under the Sultan, with Britain having charge of its foreign relations. The loss of Limbang district to Sarawak in 1890 split Brunei into two and remains an obstacle to good relations with Malaysia to this day.

In 1906 a treaty was signed between Britain and Brunei making Brunei a full protectorate. The treaty assured the succession of the ruling dynasty, with the arrangement that a British resident would advise the Sultan on all matters except those concerning local customs and religion.

In 1929 large resources of oil were discovered in Seria; these and subsequent discoveries made Brunei a wealthy country. In 1959 a written constitution was introduced, giving Brunei internal self-rule and allowing for a legislative council. The residency agreement of 1906 was revoked, transferring the resident's power to the Sultan and appointed officials below him.

During 1962 there were sporadic and unsuccessful attempts at rebellion, instigated by the North Borneo Liberation Army. These were put down with the help of British Gurkha units flown in from Singapore and the Sultan declared a state of emergency. This has been renewed every two years since.

In the 1960s, Brunei considered merging with the Federation of Malaysia, which at the time included the provinces of the Malaysian peninsula, Sabah, Sarawak and Singapore. The idea was opposed by the Brunei People's Party, which at that time held 16 seats in the 33-member legislative council, and which proposed instead the creation of a state comprising Northern Borneo, Sarawak and Sabah. The Sultan finally decided against joining the Federation.

In 1971, under an agreement with the UK, Brunei ceased to be a British protected state. The constitution was amended to give the Sultan full control over all internal matters, the UK retaining responsibility for defence and foreign affairs. Brunei became a fully independent sovereign state on 1 January 1984.

Religious festivals whose dates vary from year to year include Prophet's Birthday, Isra Mikraj (Ascension of the Prophet), First Day of Ramadan, Nuzul al-Quraan (Anniversary of the Revelation of the Quran), Hari Raya Aidil Fitri (Eid al-Fitr/end of Ramadan), Hari Raya Aidil Adha (Eid al-Adha/Feast of the Sacrifice) and Hijriah (Islamic New Year).

Economy

KEY FACTS 2009

GDP:	US$10.7bn
GDP p.c.:	US$26,750
GDP growth:	0.2% p.a. 2005–09
Inflation:	0.9% p.a. 2006–10

Due to its extensive resources of oil and gas and small population, Brunei is among the world's richer countries. The oil and gas sector dominates the economy and generates the bulk of export earnings and government revenues. Brunei is vulnerable to fluctuations in world prices: the slump in oil prices was largely responsible for negative growth in the 1980s.

The economy and social infrastructure have been developed through a series of national development programmes. During the 1990s, the emphasis was on social services and public utilities. This continued into the 2000s, together with diversification of manufacturing, and encouragement of private investment, including foreign investment. Major projects include a gas pipeline, a power plant, upgrade of the international airport, development at the port of Muara, and an industrial park with a methanol plant which began production and exports in mid-2010.

As the regional economic crisis of 1997–98 receded, the government announced plans to encourage fuller private-sector participation in public enterprises, to promote foreign investment – including, for the first time, allowing foreigners to own land in Brunei – and for the country to become a regional trade and services centre.

The economy benefited from high global energy prices in the early 2000s, with little inflation. It then stalled in 2004 and 2005, picking up in 2006 with growth of 4.4%, only to slow again in 2007 (0.2%). In the strongly adverse climate of the world economic downturn, the economy shrank in 2008 (–1.9%) and 2009 (–1.8%) before returning to growth in 2010 (2.6%) and 2011 (2.0%).

Oil and gas

The oil and gas sector contributes about 62% to GDP (2010) and the bulk of exports. The country produced about 150,000 barrels of oil a day in the second quarter of 2009. Estimates of oil and gas reserves are rising with new offshore discoveries. Proven reserves of oil were estimated in January 2011 to be 1.1 billion barrels, and of gas, 300 billion cubic metres.

Constitution

Status:	National Monarchy
Legislature:	Legislative Council
Independence:	1 January 1984

Under the 1959 constitution, the Sultan is the head of state with full executive authority and is assisted and advised by five councils – the Religious Council, the Privy Council, the Council of Cabinet Ministers, the Legislative Council and the Council of Succession.

The Legislative Council was suspended in 1984, since when the Sultan has ruled through emergency decree. He has sole power to amend the provisions of existing laws. There are no elections; the last election was held in 1962. The national ideology, *Melayu Islam Beraja* (MIB), invokes Islam and Brunei's history in support of the Sultan's absolute power, as well as the paramountcy of the Malays in Brunei.

In September 2004 a Legislative Council was revived and 21 members appointed, with no immediate timetable for election of the proposed 15 directly elected members. In September 2005 the Sultan dissolved the existing Legislative Council and appointed 29 new members.

Politics

Next elections:	no elections
Head of state:	Paduka Seri Baginda Sultan Haji Hassanal Bolkiah Mu'izzaddin Waddaulah
Head of government:	the Sultan

Real Growth in GDP

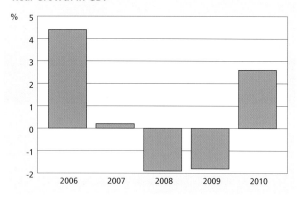

Inflation

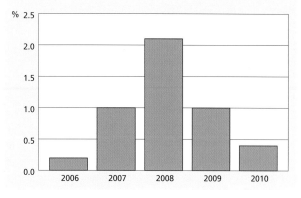

GDP by Sector (2010)

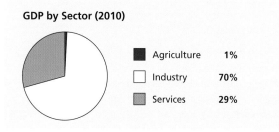

Agriculture	1%
Industry	70%
Services	29%

The Parti Kebangsaan Demokratik Brunei (PKDB) or Brunei National Democratic Party, with a membership of about 3,000, mostly Malay businessmen and professionals, was formed in 1985. It called for free elections and an end to emergency rule. The party was de-registered in 1988, after failing to conform to the requirements of the law. The only legal and registered political party at present is the Parti Pembangunan (National Development Party).

The present Sultan, head of state and government and concurrently prime minister, defence minister and finance minister is Sultan Hassanal Bolkiah. Official policy is to encourage economic growth while preserving cultural and religious values.

International relations

Brunei Darussalam is a member of Asia–Pacific Economic Cooperation, Association of Southeast Asian Nations, Non-Aligned Movement, Organisation of Islamic Cooperation, United Nations and World Trade Organization.

Traveller information

Local laws and conventions: The legal system in Brunei is partly based on Sharia law and can, occasionally, apply to non-Muslim visitors. Women should ensure that their head, knees and arms are covered at all times.

There are severe penalties for all drug offences in Brunei, including, in some cases, the death penalty.

The sale of alcohol in Brunei is prohibited and during Ramadan restaurants close during the day.

Malays make up the majority of the country's population, though there are also Chinese Bruneians who have their own social and business etiquettes.

A light handshake is the traditional form of greeting among Muslim men.

Food may only be touched with the right hand and is never given or received with the left. It is regarded as discourteous to eat or drink in public places when Muslims are fasting during Ramadan.

Dress is generally informal except for special occasions. Suits are the norm for business meetings and appointments must be made. Business cards are customary among Chinese Bruneians. Although Malay is the official language, English is used in business circles. The best time to visit on business is outside the monsoon season (between November and December). Office hours are Mon–Thur 0800–1700 and Sat 0800–1200. (Business hours may be interrupted during Ramadan or the Chinese New Year.)

Immigration and customs: Visas are required by most nationals and visitors should contact their local consulate to check current visa requirements. Passports must be valid for six months from the date of departure and a return ticket is required. Visitors are advised to carry photocopies of their passport and travel documents, and to keep the originals in a safe place. Non-Muslims over 17 years of age may import duty free goods, but must declare them to Customs on arrival.

Lone parents coming into the country will need documentary evidence to show parental responsibility for accompanying children.

A yellow fever vaccination certificate will be required by all those arriving from infected countries.

Travel within the country: Traffic drives on the left, and car hire is available at the airport and from major hotels for those with an international driving permit. The best roads are found in the Brunei-Muara district.

There is a good national bus service linking the main towns, and local buses are well maintained and efficient.

Taxis are widely available in Bandar Seri Begawan and can be found near the major hotels. Fares are usually metered, but travellers should ensure they agree a price if no meter is visible.

There is a water taxi service to Kampong Ayer, where boats are the most common means of getting around Brunei's 'water village'. Fares are negotiated before travel.

Travel health: Brunei's health care facilities are good. Should complications arise, medical evacuation to Singapore may be necessary and visitors should ensure they have comprehensive health insurance that covers this.

Air quality periodically reaches hazardous levels because of smoke haze and this may affect some travellers.

Dengue fever is endemic to Brunei, and visitors will need insect repellent and suitable clothing to discourage mosquito bites. All current vaccination requirements must be checked well before travel.

Water for drinking, brushing teeth and making ice should first have been boiled or sterilised. Milk is unpasteurised.

Money: Credit cards are accepted at most major establishments. Travellers cheques can be cashed at banks or major hotels. Singapore dollars may also be used in Brunei and are of the same value as the Brunei dollar. Most other major currencies are convertible at banks, hotels or official moneychangers.

There were 226,000 tourist arrivals in 2008.

Further information

Prime Minister's Office of Brunei Darussalam: www.jpm.gov.bn

Commonwealth Secretariat: www.thecommonwealth.org

Commonwealth of Nations: www.commonwealth-of-nations.org/Brunei_Darussalam

Cameroon Customs Administration
A capable and efficient administration at the service of an emerging Cameroon

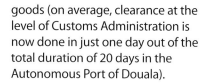

Mrs Minette Libom Li Likeng, Director General of Cameroon Customs

The volume of revenue collected over the past five years has placed the Customs Administration second in terms of overall contribution to the State budget.

This achievement is certainly the result of the successful implementation of a management strategy that focuses on transparency, oversight and accountability.

Major challenges

➢ Provide economic and international trade stakeholders with simplified and clear procedures.

➢ Promote a sustainable and balanced development through the implementation of a simplified fiscal policy that includes incentives adapted to the specificities of each production sub-sector.

➢ Protect citizens, consumers and legitimate trade by providing increased security for traded products or those circulating within the country.

Key reforms

1. The introduction of the Automated Customs System, or as it is better known in French Système Douanier Automatisé (SYDONIA++), which was created in January 2007. This system automates as many of the customs procedures as possible and has resulted in increased transparency and objectivity and streamlined procedures.

2. Efficiency and performance are controlled through the performance indicators outlined by SYDONIA++. This is carried out through the assessment of performance contracts signed between the administration and customs inspectors in the relevant services, and performance contracts with business operators in some 20 private sector enterprises. This initiative has helped reduce corruption and other bad practices in the sector. It has also led to a reduction in the number of days needed to clear goods (on average, clearance at the level of Customs Administration is now done in just one day out of the total duration of 20 days in the Autonomous Port of Douala).

3. The Customs-Enterprises Forum: a forum where the Customs Administration and business enterprises consult each other and exchange views on measures that will enable the Customs General Directorate to strike a balance between streamlining and the facilitation of customs clearing operations and mobilisation of revenue for the state in a win-win partnership.

4. Securement of merchandise in transit through the geo-location of bonded goods passing through the country using the system known as NEXUS+. This has led to a sharp drop in transit delays which, today, oscillate between 2.13 days and 5 to 6 days at the borders with the Central African Republic or Chad, as opposed to the 100 days as was the case in 2007.

5. The setting up of the Ethics and Governance Promotion Committee which helps the Director General of Customs to enforce the principles of ethics and good governance. This committee has a hotline, 8044, through which any person can reach it to ask for assistance if faced with any deviant behaviour.

6. The drawing up and publication of a user's guide Guide de l'Usager to help users and facilitate customs clearing transactions.

Contact

General Directorate of Customs
P.O. Box 33035 Yaoundé-Cameroon
Tel/Fax: +237 22 20 2546
Hotline: 8044

Cameroon

KEY FACTS

Joined Commonwealth:	1995
Population:	19,599,000 (2010)
GDP p.c. growth:	0.6% p.a. 1990–2010
UN HDI 2011:	world ranking 150
Official languages:	French, English
Time:	GMT plus 1hr
Currency:	CFA franc (CFAfr)

Geography

Area:	475,442 sq km
Coastline:	402km
Capital:	Yaoundé (constitutional); Douala (economic)

Cameroon is called Cameroun in French, Kamerun in German, Camarões in Portuguese, and Cameroon in English. The country's name derives from *camarões*, meaning 'shrimps', so called by the 15th-century Portuguese explorer Fernando Po who named the River Wouri *Rio dos Camarões* ('shrimp river'), after the many shrimps. Cameroon in central Africa is bounded clockwise (from the west) by the Gulf of Guinea, Nigeria, Chad, Central African Republic, Congo, Gabon and Equatorial Guinea. The country comprises ten provinces: Adamaoua, Centre, Coastal, East, Far North, North, North-West, South, South-West and West.

Topography: The physical geography is varied, with forests, mountains, large waterfalls and deserts, falling into four regions. At the border of the northern Sahel region lies Lake Chad and the Chad basin; further south the land forms a sloping plain, rising to the Mandara Mountains. The central region extends from the Benue (Bénoué) river to the Sanaga river, with a plateau in the north. This region includes the Adamaoua plateau which separates the agricultural south from the pastoral north. In the west, the land is mountainous, with a double chain of volcanic peaks, rising to a height of 4,095m at Mt Cameroon. This is the highest and wettest peak in western Africa. The fourth region, to the south, extends

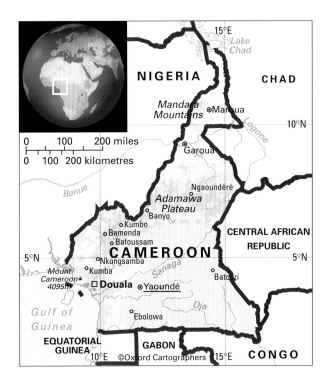

from the Sanaga river to the southern border, comprising a coastal plain and forested plateau. There is a complicated system of drainage. Several rivers flow westwards: the Benue river which rises in the Mandara Mountains and later joins the River Niger, and the Sanaga and Nyong rivers which flow into the Gulf of Guinea. The Dja and Sangha drain into the Congo Basin. The Logone and Chari rivers flow north into Lake Chad.

Climate: In the northern Sahel region, there is a long dry season from October to April, with temperatures varying from cool to very hot. Further south, on the Adamaoua plateau, there are sharp drops in temperature at night. In the south the climate is hot and humid, with two rainy seasons, in September/October and from March to June.

Environment: The most significant issues are overgrazing, desertification, deforestation, poaching, and overfishing.

Vegetation: There is tropical rainforest (including ebony and mahogany) in the hot humid south, with mangroves along the coast and river mouths. The southern coastal plain and south-east plateau also contain the cocoa and banana farms and the rubber and oil palm plantations. The central region has mixed deciduous and evergreen forest. Above the forest zone are drier woodlands, with taller grasses and mountain bamboos. High in the interior and on Mt Cameroon the grasses are shorter. Further north there is savannah bushland, with trees becoming sparse towards the Chad basin. Forest covers 42% of the land area, having declined at 1.0%

Did you know...

Celebrated writers originating from Cameroon include Ferdinand Oyono, who was born in Ebolowa, South Province, in 1929; and Mongo Beti, born in Akométan, Central Province, in 1932 and died in 2001.

Three Cameroon nationals have excelled in international football: Samuel Eto'o was African Footballer of the Year in 2003, 2004, 2005 and 2010; Patrick Mboma in 2000; and Roger Milla in 1976 and 1990.

p.a. 1990–2010. Arable land comprises 13% and permanent cropland 2.6% of the total land area.

Wildlife: The Waza National Park in the north, originally created for the protection of giraffe and antelope, also abounds in monkeys — screaming red and green monkeys and mandrills — and lions and leopards. There are gorillas in the great tracts of hardwood rainforest in the south and east.

Main towns: Yaoundé (capital, in Centre Province, pop. 1.81m in 2010), Douala (principal port, in Coastal Province, 2.13m), Garoua (North Province, 573,700), Bamenda (North-West, 546,400), Maroua (Far North, 436,700), Bafoussam (West, 383,200), Ngaoundéré (Adamaoua, 314,100), Bertoua (East, 297,200), Loum (Coastal, 249,100), Kumbo (North-West, 222,600), Edéa (Coastal, 209,600), Mbouda (West, 188,200), Kumba (South-West, 180,000), Foumban (West, 171,600), Dschang (West, 149,300), Nkongsamba (Coastal, 131,100), Ebolowa (South, 129,600), Kousséri (contiguous with Ndjamena in Chad, Far North, 95,100) and Buéa (South-West, 59,700).

Transport: There are 51,350km of roads, 8% paved. The rail network runs 977km north–south from Ngaoundéré to Yaoundé, with connections between Douala and Yaoundé, and from Douala to Nkongsamba and Kumba.

Douala is the principal port, Kribi handles mainly wood exports, Garoua on the Benue river is navigable only during the wet season and Limbo-Tiko is a minor port, severely silted up.

International airports are at Douala (10km south-east of the city), Yaoundé (25km from city) and Garoua.

Society

KEY FACTS 2010

Population per sq km:	41
Life expectancy:	51 years
Net primary enrolment:	92%

Population: 19,599,000 (2010); 58% in urban areas and 20% in urban agglomerations of more than 1 million people; growth 2.4% p.a. 1990–2010; birth rate 36 per 1,000 people (45 in 1970); life expectancy 51 years (44 in 1970).

The population is ethnically diverse. In the north, the people are mostly Hausa, Fulbé (Fulani), Sudanese and Choa Arab. In the west, the Bamiléké are the biggest ethnic group, followed by Tiker and Bamoun. South of the River Sanaga, there are Bantu groups: Fang, Ewondo, Boulou, Eton, Bassa, Bakoko, Douala. Some pygmies (including Baka) live in the south-eastern forested country.

Language: French and English are both official languages; French is spoken by about 80% of the population, English by about 20%. There are about 240 indigenous languages including 24 major language groups.

Religion: Christians about 50%, Muslims 20% and a substantial minority holding traditional beliefs.

Health: Public spending on health was 2% of GDP in 2009. There are three referral hospitals, some 70 general hospitals, some 50 private hospitals, plus a wide network of public and private health centres – some of which are for the treatment of leprosy. 74% of the population uses an improved drinking water source and 47% have adequate sanitation facilities (2009). Infant mortality was 84 per 1,000 live births in 2010 (151 in 1960). In 2009, 5.3% of people aged 15–49 were HIV positive.

Education: Public spending on education was 3.5% of GDP in 2010. There are six years of compulsory education starting at age six. Primary school comprises six or seven years and secondary seven, with a first cycle of four or five years. School attendance is lower in the Far North province, where the population is partly nomadic. Some 69% of pupils complete primary school (2008). The school year starts in September. Many secondary schools are bilingual, with instruction in both French and English. Faith schools play an important role in the education system and are partly subsidised by the government.

There are public universities at Yaoundé, Dschang, Ngaoundéré, Douala and Buéa. The most prominent is the University of Yaoundé, established in 1962, which now comprises two separate universities on several campuses (University of Yaoundé I and University of Yaoundé II). The École Normale Supérieure of University of Yaoundé I is the leading school for teacher education. Many private institutions offer tertiary education. The female–male ratio for gross enrolment in tertiary education is 0.79:1 (2009). Literacy among people aged 15–24 is 83% (2007).

Media: *Cameroon Tribune* (daily in French and English editions) is the official newspaper. *Le Messager* is the leading independent daily in French, published in Douala since 1979. Other independent papers include *Mutations*, *La Nouvelle Expression* and *The Post* (twice weekly, in English).

CRTV operates the national radio and TV networks. After broadcasting was liberalised in 2000, dozens of private radio stations and several private TV channels were launched.

Some 31% of households have TV sets (2007). There are 11 personal computers (2005) and 40 internet users (2010) per 1,000 people.

Communications: Country code 237; internet domain '.cm'. There are telephone booths in all towns. Mobile phone coverage is patchy but more extensive in the south.

There are 28 main telephone lines and 441 mobile phone subscriptions per 1,000 people (2010).

Public holidays: New Year's Day, Youth Day (11 February), Labour Day (1 May), National Day (20 May), Sheep Festival (21 May), Assumption (15 August), Unification Day (1 October) and Christmas Day.

Religious festivals whose dates vary from year to year include Prophet's Birthday, Good Friday, Easter Monday, Ascension Day, Ascension of the Prophet, Eid al-Fitr (End of Ramadan), Eid al-Adha (Feast of the Sacrifice) and Islamic New Year.

Economy

KEY FACTS 2010

GNI:	US$23.2bn
GNI p.c.:	US$1,180
GDP growth:	2.8% p.a. 2006–10
Inflation:	3.1% p.a. 2006–10

Cameroon developed rapidly from 1978 thanks to its oil wealth, agricultural diversity and well developed agro-industries. However, after the mid-1980s, the economy declined and debt rose. From the late 1980s, the World Bank and IMF supported a series of

Real Growth in GDP

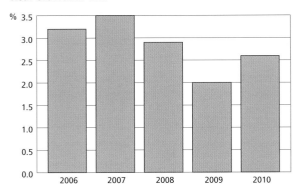

Inflation

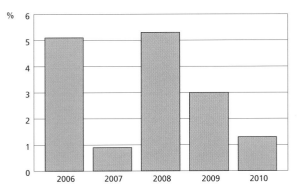

GDP by Sector (2010)

■ Agriculture	25%
□ Industry	32%
▨ Services	43%

economic reform programmes, which included cuts in public expenditure (public-sector wages were reduced by 70% in 1993), structural adjustment, privatisation of the many publicly owned enterprises, and rescheduling external debt.

In the run-up to privatisation, some 70 state-owned enterprises were closed down and others restructured, with a loss of about 20,000 jobs. Then from the late 1990s the state-owned rail company Régifercam (having been streamlined by halving its staff), CAMSUCO (sugar), SOCAPALM (palm oil), BICEC (the last remaining state-owned bank) and SONEL (electricity) were privatised; SNEC (water) was restructured as a public–private partnership; and Cameroon Airlines was liquidated (2006).

From the mid-1990s, growth was sustained at 4–5% p.a. in a climate of relatively low inflation, as a result of the prudent monetary policies of the regional central bank. From 2003 the Cameroon economy grew more slowly, growth averaging 3.3% p.a. 2003–07. It then slowed again in response to the global economic downturn in 2008 (2.9%), 2009 (2.0%) and 2010 (2.6%), before recovering in 2011 (about 4%).

Cameroon reached the IMF/World Bank Heavily Indebted Poor Countries Initiative completion point in 2006, qualifying for present value debt-relief of US$1.3 billion.

Oil and gas

Oil production began in 1978 but fell steadily from its peak of 186,000 barrels a day in 1985 to about 64,000 barrels a day in 2010, although government has made exploitation of marginal oilfields more viable and new small fields have boosted production. Crude oil is, nevertheless, the largest foreign-currency earner and accounted for 50% of export earnings in 2007.

Oil is found in the Rio del Rey basin, close to the Nigerian border, natural gas at Rio del Rey and in the basin extending to the south of Douala. Further oil exploration has been initiated in the north, close to the Chad border, and in the west around Mamfé, close to the Nigerian border. Prospects for large offshore finds of oil and gas were dramatically improved in 2006 when Nigeria agreed that the Bakassi peninsula would be ceded to Cameroon.

Constitution

Status:	Republic with executive president
Legislature:	National Assembly
Independence:	1 January 1960

Under the constitution adopted in 1996 Cameroon is a unitary republic with an executive president – elected every seven years – who appoints the prime minister and council of ministers. The president also appoints the provincial governors, the judges and government delegates in main towns. In April 2008, Cameroon's parliament approved a constitutional amendment allowing the president to serve for more than two terms. Presidential elections must then be conducted not less than 20 days or more than 120 days following the vacancy.

The National Assembly has 180 members, directly elected every five years by universal adult suffrage, and has three sessions a year, in March, June and November. There was also provision in the constitution for an upper house, the Senate, with 30% of its members nominated by the president and 70% directly elected every five years, as well as a Constitutional Council and elected regional assemblies. The Senate, the Constitutional Council and regional assemblies, provided for under the constitution, were in 2012 yet to be established.

Politics

Last elections:	July 2007 (legislative), October 2011 (presidential)
Next elections:	2012 (legislative), 2018 (presidential)
Head of state:	President Paul Biya
Head of government:	the president
Ruling party:	Cameroon People's Democratic Movement

In the June 2002 general election, the third since the introduction of multi-party politics in 1990, the ruling Cameroon People's Democratic Movement (CPDM) gained 133 seats, substantially extending its parliamentary majority, while the Social Democratic Front (SDF) took 21 (mainly in the English-speaking North-West), the Union for Democracy and Change (UDC) five and Union of the

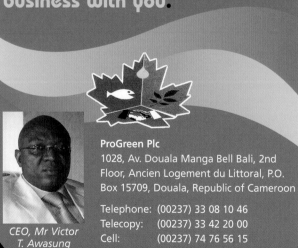
Populations of Cameroon three. Elections in nine constituencies with 17 Assembly seats were annulled by the Supreme Court and re-run in September 2002, when 16 were won by the CPDM.

Incumbent President Paul Biya won a landslide victory in the October 2004 presidential election receiving 75% of the votes.

The elections in July 2007 extended the ruling CPDM's majority in the National Assembly. On announcement of the results, 103 petitions for annulment were filed with the Supreme Court. A re-run ordered by the Court for 17 of the 180 seats in September 2007 resulted in reducing the CPDM's holding to 153 seats; while SDF took 16, the National Union for Democracy and Progress six, UDC four and Progressive Movement one.

In early 2008 the National Assembly approved a constitutional amendment removing presidential term limits which opened the way for President Biya to seek re-election. Biya won the presidential election in October 2011 increasing his share of the vote to 78%. His main rival in a field of more than 20 candidates was John Fru Ndi (SDF) who secured 10.7% of the vote. Turnout was 66% and the election was observed by a Commonwealth expert team.

International relations

Cameroon is a member of the African, Caribbean and Pacific Group of States, African Union, Non-Aligned Movement, Organisation internationale de la Francophonie, Organisation of Islamic Cooperation, United Nations and World Trade Organization.

Traveller information

Local laws and conventions: Photographing military establishments and official buildings, in particular the airports, is strictly forbidden. If photographing local residents or their property, visitors should exercise discretion and should always ask permission.

Drug use and possession are prohibited. Penalties for all drug offences are severe and usually lead to a prison sentence.

Visitors should carry identification documents on them at all times; failure to produce them may lead to detention.

Islamic traditions must be respected in the north and visitors must never enter a Muslim prayer circle of rocks. In rural areas, tact should be shown for the traditional beliefs.

Clothing varies between cities and rural areas and a conservative style of dress is best adopted. Long sleeves and some form of head cover are advisable when entering religious buildings.

Handshaking is the usual form of greeting in Cameroon. Business is conducted primarily in English and French. Office hours are Mon–Fri 0730–1700.

Immigration and customs: Passports must be valid for a minimum of six months and visas are required by most nationals. Visas (tourist and business) are valid for up to six months. All visitors must present a return or onward ticket when entering the country.

Pornographic materials may not be brought into the country and licences are required for sporting guns.

A yellow fever vaccination certificate must be presented by all travellers arriving from infected areas.

Archaeological evidence suggests that the region may have been the first homeland of the Bantu peoples, who developed methods of working iron and an advanced agriculture. After around 200 BC, the Bantu peoples spread east and south, to become the dominant ethnic group of sub-Saharan Africa.

European exploration began in the 15th century with the Portuguese who established sugar plantations and gained control of the slave trade around the coast in the following century. Dutch slave traders subsequently gained the ascendancy. Slavery ravaged West African societies until the middle of the 19th century, when Britain's abolition of the slave trade (in 1807) and the activities of the anti-slavers became effective. In northern Cameroon, during the 19th century, nomadic Fulani arrived and settled.

Germany (a late entrant into the European scramble for colonial possessions in Africa) claimed Cameroon as a German Protectorate in 1884; it remained so until 1916, when Britain, France and Belgium took it by military force in a combined operation. The German administration built the railways between Douala and Eséka and between Douala and Nkongsamba in the west; and German farmers settled in the areas that are now North-West and South-West provinces.

After the First World War, the country was divided into two zones. The western zone (comprising two separate areas, later known as the Northern and Southern Cameroons) was administered by Britain under a League of Nations mandate. The rest of the country (comprising four-fifths of the total) was administered by France, directly from Paris. During the French administration, the port at Douala was built, the coffee and cocoa industries increased and extensive road-building was undertaken. In the British area, there was local participation in government, and both Northern and Southern Cameroons were joined to parts of Nigeria for administrative purposes. After 1945, the UK and France continued to administer the country as UN Trust Territories.

During this period, political parties emerged, the largest being the Union of the Populations of Cameroon (UPC) led by Ruben Um Nyobe. The UPC, which demanded that French and British Cameroons should be united into one independent country, was banned in the mid-1950s, leading to a rebellion in which thousands of people were killed, including Um Nyobe in 1958. Nonetheless, the country proceeded to partial self-government in 1957 and full independence on 1 January 1960.

After a UN plebiscite in 1961, Northern Cameroons chose union with Nigeria, as part of the Northern Region. Southern Cameroons joined the Republic in October 1961. The country became a federal republic in the same year, with both components retaining their local parliaments. In 1972 the federation was dissolved and the country became a unitary republic (the United Republic of Cameroon), the name changing once again to the Republic of Cameroon in 1984.

Following independence, the country was ruled first by President Ahmadou Ahidjo (from 1960 to 1982) and then by President Paul Biya, who took office as president in 1982. A one-party regime was established in 1966 through the merger of the two governing parties and several opposition groups. In 1968 the ruling party was reconstituted as the Union national

camerounaise (UNC) and was renamed once again the Rassemblement démocratique du peuple camerounais (Cameroon People's Democratic Movement – RDPC or CPDM) in 1985.

Cameroon has never had a successful military coup. A plot by military officers was uncovered in 1979. A further planned coup was discovered in 1983 and in February 1984 the former President Ahmadou Ahidjo (then in exile where he subsequently died) was tried *in absentia* and found guilty, along with two of his military advisers. Two months later, the Republican Guard attempted a coup. This was foiled by the army, but 500–1,000 people were killed in the fighting; the Republican Guard was then disbanded.

Political protest against the one-party system was widespread up to 1992, through a campaign of civil disobedience known as *villes mortes* or 'ghost towns', when towns were virtually closed down to prompt reform. Multiple political parties became legal in 1990 and legislative elections were held in March 1992. They were contested by 48 political parties but boycotted by the Social Democratic Front (SDF). The ruling CPDM took 88 seats, the opposing parties a total of 92 seats. The CPDM formed a coalition with the Movement for the Defence of the Republic, which had six seats, thus securing a majority of eight.

At presidential elections in October 1992 Paul Biya was re-elected with 40% of the votes (in 1988 he had stood unopposed, winning 98% of the vote). Of the eight candidates, his nearest rival was John Fru Ndi of the SDF, who gained 36%.

In 1995, with the approval of all other member countries, Cameroon joined the Commonwealth.

Before the May 1997 general election there was an outbreak of violence in the North-West province, which was attributed to the Anglophone separatist movement. A curfew was enforced and public meetings banned. In the election, with Commonwealth observers present, CPDM took 109 of the 180 Assembly seats, the SDF 43, the National Union for Democracy and Progress 13, and the Union for Democracy and Change five.

In the run-up to the presidential election, the leading opposition parties, the SDF, the National Union for Democracy, and Progress and the Union for Democracy and Change, were urging reform of the presidential electoral system, and introduction of a two-tier process. The three parties boycotted the election and advised their supporters not to vote. The Commonwealth therefore declined to send an observer mission. In October 1997 President Paul Biya was re-elected for a seven-year term, defeating the six other candidates in a landslide victory, receiving more than 92% of the votes cast.

Relations with Nigeria

The International Court of Justice ruled in 2002 that the long disputed and fought-over border areas of Nigeria should be ceded to Cameroon. These areas include the Bakassi peninsula in the south which is believed to contain very large offshore reserves of oil and gas. In a UN-brokered agreement in June 2006, the two countries agreed on a phased transfer of the peninsula. Nigerian troops withdrew in August 2006 and Nigeria formally ceded the border areas to Cameroon in August 2008.

Travel within the country: Traffic drives on the right. An international driving permit is required to drive in Cameroon and must be carried at all times. Car hire is available in Douala, Yaoundé and Limbé. Roads are paved between the main cities.

The most efficient and reliable means of travelling between the cities is by taking an internal flight. Unitair has daily flights between Douala and Yaoundé and operates less regular flights to other major towns.

Train services, run by CAMRAIL (Cameroon Railways), are generally good – if relatively slow.

There is a modern coach service between Yaoundé and Douala, and there are local services that serve the more rural areas.

Taxis are a cheap and fast means of travelling around the cities and are widely available. All fares must be agreed on before travel, as taxis are not metered.

Travel health: Travellers are advised to have full medical insurance.

Visitors will need protection against malaria, together with insect repellent and suitable clothing to prevent mosquito bites. Dysentery, dengue fever, typhoid, tetanus, diphtheria and Hepatitis A also occur, and visitors should exercise caution and protect themselves at all times. Paddling or swimming in fresh water should be avoided as there is a risk of catching bilharzia. In the northern areas, meningococcal meningitis and cholera are an additional risk during the dry season.

Outside of the main hotels, all water should be boiled or sterilised before use. Only powdered or tinned milk is recommended.

Money: Local currency is the CFA franc. Visitors should note that only currency issued by the Banque des États de l'Afrique Centrale is valid; it is not valid if issued by the Banque des États de l'Afrique de l'Ouest. Cash in a hard currency is preferred to travellers cheques. ATMs are rare, and debit and credit cards cannot be used in banks to obtain cash. Limited numbers of hotels and airline offices will accept major credit cards. Banking hours are Mon–Fri 0730–1530.

There were 185,000 tourist arrivals in 2007.

Further information

Republic of Cameroon Prime Minister's Office: www.spm.gov.cm

National Assembly: www.assemblenationale.cm

Bank of Central African States: www.beac.int

Commonwealth Secretariat: www.thecommonwealth.org

Commonwealth of Nations: www.commonwealth-of-nations.org/Cameroon

Canada

KEY FACTS

Joined Commonwealth:	1931 (Statute of Westminster)
Population:	34,017,000 (2010)
GDP p.c. growth:	1.9% p.a. 1990–2010
UN HDI 2011:	world ranking 6
Official languages:	English, French
Time:	GMT minus 8–3hr
Currency:	Canadian dollar (C$)

Geography

Area:	9,976,000 sq km
Coastline:	202,100km
Capital:	Ottawa

The second largest country in the world, Canada comprises the northern half of the North American continent, bordering with the USA to the south and north-west (Alaska). It is bounded by three oceans: the Pacific to the west; the Arctic to the north; and the Atlantic to the east. Indented shores and numerous islands (some very large) give it the longest coastline of any country at 202,100km. Cape Columbia on Ellesmere Island is 768km from the North Pole.

Canada is a federation of ten provinces and three territories. The provinces (and provincial capitals) are: Alberta (Edmonton), British Columbia (Victoria), Manitoba (Winnipeg), New Brunswick (Fredericton), Newfoundland and Labrador (St John's), Nova Scotia (Halifax), Ontario (Toronto), Prince Edward Island (Charlottetown), Québec (Québec), Saskatchewan (Regina); and the territories (and capitals): Northwest Territories (Yellowknife), Nunavut (Iqaluit) and Yukon (Whitehorse). Nunavut was formed in April 1999 – from the eastern and central parts of the Northwest Territories – as a semi-autonomous region for the Inuit people.

Did you know...

Canada was a founder member of the Commonwealth in 1931 when its independence was recognised under the Statute of Westminster, and Arnold Smith of Canada was the first Commonwealth Secretary-General (1965–75).

Three Canadians have won the Commonwealth Writers' Prize: Mordecai Richler, in 1990; Rohinton Mistry (born in Bombay, India), in 1992 and 1996; and Lawrence Hill, in 2008.

The Commonwealth Association for Public Administration and Management has its HQ in Ottawa, the Commonwealth of Learning in Vancouver and the Commonwealth Journalists Association in Toronto.

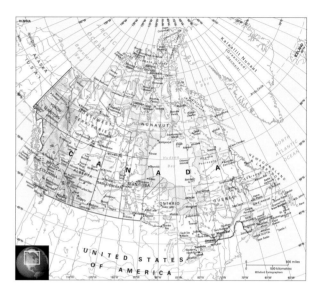

Time: Canada spans six time zones, ranging from Pacific Standard Time (GMT minus 8hr) to Newfoundland Standard Time (GMT minus 4hr). In most areas of the country, one hour is added for Daylight Saving Time from the first Sunday in April to the last Sunday in October.

Topography: There are six physical regions. The largest is the Precambrian (or Canadian) Shield, the dominant geological feature of the country. It consists of ancient, very hard rocks to the north of the St Lawrence river, occupying nearly half of Canada's total area and including plateau-like highlands with thousands of lakes and rivers. Almost a quarter of the world's fresh water is concentrated here.

The second region is the Appalachian mountains to the east, which cover Newfoundland, Nova Scotia, New Brunswick, Prince Edward Island and part of Québec. The mountains have been eroded by glaciers, wind and water over 300 million years; their highest elevation, in Gaspe's Shickshock Mountains, is under 1,300m.

The third region is the Great Lakes–St Lawrence Lowlands in the south-east, stretching from Québec City to Lake Huron. It is the country's most productive agricultural area.

The fertile Interior Plains or prairies, the fourth region, are a vast expanse of land and sky, rising gently from Manitoba to Alberta and spreading northward through the Mackenzie river valley to the Arctic Ocean.

The Western Cordillera, the fifth region, is a rocky spine of mountains along the Pacific coastline. The Cordillera stretches from South America to Alaska, and the Canadian portion includes many peaks over 3,000m, the highest being in the Rocky Mountains.

The Arctic region, finally, consists of hundreds of islands, covering an area of 2,800km by 1,800km and reaching to Canada's northern tip.

Climate: In the High Arctic, temperatures rise above freezing for only a few weeks in July/August. The boreal forest area is snow-bound for more than half the year and precipitation is light, except along the Labrador coast.

The eastern Atlantic region has changeable winter temperatures and heavy snowfall. Fog is common, especially in Newfoundland and Labrador. July/August temperatures are 16–18°C. Winter also brings heavy snowfalls to the Great Lakes–St Lawrence region; but summer temperatures average almost 20°C, with heat waves.

The prairies have cold winters and hot summers, with rapid air flow bringing dramatic weather changes. Annual average precipitation in southern Saskatchewan is less than 350mm, compared with 1,110mm in Vancouver, to the west.

The coast of British Columbia has the most temperate climate in Canada.

Environment: The most significant environmental issues are damage to forests and lakes by acid rain, and contamination of oceans by waste and run-off from agriculture, industry and mining.

Vegetation: The Appalachian region is heavily wooded, with mixed sugar maple and spruce. Similar forests flourish in the Great Lakes–St Lawrence Lowlands, and white pine, spruce and fir thrive in the south of the Precambrian Shield. The far north of the Shield and the Arctic are too cold for trees, but mosses, lichens, short grasses and dwarf shrubs burst into life and quickly fade in a six-week summer.

A desert-like sweep of short grasses in the southernmost parts of Alberta and Saskatchewan is succeeded further north by fertile grasslands, where millions of ponds provide breeding grounds for half of North America's ducks, geese, swans and pelicans, and for mosquitoes. British Columbia is heavily forested, containing some huge trees including some 1,000 year-old Douglas firs.

Purple loosestrife (*Lythrum salicaria*), thought to have arrived from Europe in the 1890s, is causing havoc to wildlife in marshes, ponds and stream banks. Arable land comprises 5% of the total land area and forest 34%, there having been no significant loss of forest cover during 1990–2010.

Wildlife: Canada has 34 national parks, including the Rocky Mountains NP. In the tundra of the far north are found seals, polar bears, the gigantic musk-ox and caribou. In the extensive stretches of forest are moose, brown, black and grizzly bears, and the beaver, one of Canada's national symbols. The grasslands were once home to enormous herds of bison but extensive hunting means these are now only to be found in wildlife reserves.

Main towns: Ottawa (capital, Ontario, pop. 879,400 in 2010), Toronto (Ontario, 5.05m), Montréal (Québec, 3.43m), Vancouver (British Columbia, 2.04m), Calgary (Alberta, 1.08m), Edmonton (Alberta, 928,800), Québec (676,900), Hamilton (Ontario, 668,000), Winnipeg (Manitoba, 649,200), Halifax (Nova Scotia, 287,100), Saskatoon (Saskatchewan, 205,700), Regina (Saskatchewan, 178,800), St John's (Newfoundland and Labrador, 153,800), Fredericton (New Brunswick, 57,800) and Charlottetown (Prince Edward Island, 39,700).

Transport: The country has 1,409,000km of roads (40% paved), including an extensive network of expressways. The 7,821km Trans-Canada Highway is the longest national highway in the world.

East–west routes predominate on both the privately owned freight railway systems. The total system extends over 57,220km. Toronto and Montréal have underground urban railway systems, called the Subway and Metro respectively.

The St Lawrence Seaway, opened in 1959, provides a water transport system from the Atlantic Ocean to the head of the Great Lakes. It has a system of locks to lift vessels 170m between Montréal and Lake Superior. Of the many international ports, the busiest is Vancouver. Remote areas are accessible only by air. There are well over 1,000 airports, more than 800 with paved runways.

Society

KEY FACTS 2010

Population per sq km:	3
Life expectancy:	81 years
Net primary enrolment:	99%

Population: 34,017,000 (2010); 81% lives in urban areas and 44% in urban agglomerations of more than 1 million people; growth 1.0% p.a. 1990–2010; birth rate 11 per 1,000 people (17 in 1970); life expectancy 81 years (73 in 1970). Population density is among the lowest in the world, but large areas are climatically hostile, and 85% of Canadians live within 350km of the US border.

The 2001 census found that about 48% of the population were of British or Irish origin, 16% of French origin, 9% German, 4.3% Italian, 3.7% Chinese, 3.6% Ukrainian, and 3.4% Native American. More than 200,000 immigrants arrive each year from more than 150 countries. The provinces with the largest populations are Ontario (11,410,000; 38% of the total), Québec (7,237,000; 24%) and British Columbia (3,908,000; 13%).

Language: Official languages are English and French; English is the mother-tongue of 57% and French 22% (2006 census). In the prairies, the most common non-official mother tongue is German; in central Canada, Italian; in British Columbia, Chinese; in the Northwest Territories and Nunavut, Inuktitut; in the Yukon, the Athapaskan languages of the Dene family; and in the Atlantic region, Micmac. Canada's aboriginal people speak some 50 languages belonging to 11 distinct linguistic families.

Religion: 84% of people adhere to a religion: Christians 74% (Roman Catholics 43%, Protestants 23%, Eastern Orthodox 1.6%); Muslims 2%; Jews 1.1%; Hindus 1%; Buddhists 1%; and Sikhs 0.9%.

Health: Public spending on health was 7% of GDP in 2009. Health insurance, provided by the provinces with federal government financial support, covers all the population. The leading causes of death are circulatory system diseases, cancer, respiratory diseases and accidents. Serious health problems include AIDS. Smoking has declined dramatically, from over half of men to a minority. Infant mortality was 5 per 1,000 live births in 2010 (28 in 1960).

Education: Public spending on education was 4.8% of GDP in 2008. Education policy varies with province but the period of compulsory education generally starts at age six. Most primary and secondary schooling is publicly funded. The school year starts in September.

Post-secondary education expanded rapidly during the 1980s and 1990s; women have shown the faster increase, and now outnumber men. The Association of Universities and Colleges of Canada represents 95 Canadian public and private not-for-profit universities and university-degree level colleges (2011). There is virtually no illiteracy among people aged 15–24. There are more than 1,000 public libraries, containing more than 70 million volumes.

Media: Leading daily newspapers include *The Globe and Mail* (Toronto, but distributed nationally), *National Post*, *La Presse* (Montréal, in French), *Toronto Star* and *Vancouver Sun*. *Maclean's* is a weekly news magazine.

The Canadian Broadcasting Corporation (CBC) provides national, public radio and TV services in English and French, and in the indigenous languages of the northern provinces; also an external service, Radio Canada International. Siétié Radio-Canada is the national, public radio and TV provider in French. Numerous private radio and TV stations are licensed to broadcast.

Some 99% of households have TV sets (2009). There are 944 personal computers (2006) and 816 internet users (2010) per 1,000 people.

Communications: Country code 1; internet domain '.ca'. Mobile phone coverage is good. Most areas have good internet connections, and there are internet cafes in most towns; post offices in all towns.

There are 500 main telephone lines and 707 mobile phone subscriptions per 1,000 people (2010).

Public holidays: New Year's Day, Victoria Day (Monday on or preceding 24 May), Canada Day (1 July), Civic or Provincial Holiday (first Monday in August, except Québec which has its National Day on 24 June), Labour Day (first Monday in September), Thanksgiving (second Monday in October), Remembrance Day (11 November), Christmas Day and Boxing Day. Most provinces have additional public holidays.

Religious and other festivals whose dates vary from year to year include Good Friday and Easter Monday.

Economy

KEY FACTS 2010

GNI:	US$1,475.9bn
GNI p.c.:	US$43,270
GDP growth:	1.2% p.a. 2006–10
Inflation:	1.7% p.a. 2006–10

Canada is among the largest economies in the world (ranking tenth in 2010, in terms of GNI). Until the early 20th century Canada had a predominantly agricultural economy. Even after the Second World War, a quarter of the workforce was still engaged in agriculture. Today, it is highly industrialised with one of the world's highest per capita income rates. Ontario is the centre of economic activity and the province with the largest manufacturing base and agricultural sector. Toronto in Ontario is the leading financial and services centre. The country is exceptionally well endowed with natural resources: minerals, petroleum and natural gas, forests, extensive coastal waters for fishing, and rivers and falls for hydroelectric power.

Real Growth in GDP

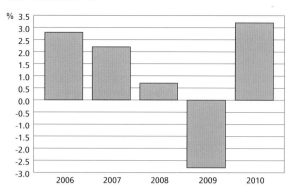

Inflation

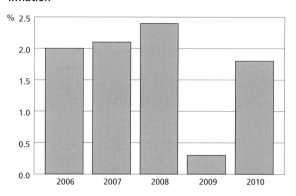

GDP by Sector (2010)

■	Agriculture	**2%**
□	Industry	**29%**
▨	Services	**69%**

Canada is among the world's leading exporters of potash, uranium, nickel, zinc and asbestos and a major producer of aluminium, cadmium, cobalt, copper, gold and, in the 2000s, diamonds. There are large reserves of nickel, copper and cobalt, as well as oil and gas – proven reserves of oil were estimated in January 2011 to be 32.1 billion barrels, and of gas, 1.7 trillion cubic metres.

Economic links with its giant neighbour were cemented by the Free Trade Agreement of 1989. This was subsequently enlarged to include Mexico under the North American Free Trade Agreement (NAFTA).

Both federal and provincial governments have undertaken privatisation in order to reduce their fiscal deficits. Air Canada was privatised in the late 1980s and rail networks Canadian Pacific and Canadian National Railway followed by the mid-1990s. There are limits to the level of foreign ownership permitted in areas such as broadcasting, telecommunications, transportation and uranium mining.

The country has one of the world's most open economies. It enjoyed strong growth from the mid-1990s, mainly in exports and the services sector, and growth in manufacturing output averaged around 3% p.a. during the decade.

Good economic growth continued into the 2000s, until 2008 when investment and exports collapsed in the world economic downturn and the economy went sharply into recession. Despite the government's taking strong measures to stimulate the economy, recession persisted into 2009, with an overall decline of 2.8% in that year, recovering in 2010 (3.2%) and 2011 (2.3%). The unemployment rate which had fallen below 6% in 2007 – its lowest level for over three decades – averaged 8.3% in 2009, 8.0% in 2010 and 7.5% in 2011.

Constitution

Status:	Monarchy under Queen Elizabeth II
Legislature:	Parliament of Canada

Canada is a constitutional monarchy, with Queen Elizabeth II (Queen of Canada) as head of state, represented by a governor-general appointed on the recommendation of the prime minister. The British North America Act of 1867 set up a machinery of government that has remained basically unchanged; however, the constitution is contained in the Constitution Act of 1982, which includes the Charter of Rights and Freedoms as well as procedures for amending the constitution.

Government is federal, with ten provincial governments and three northern territories. The provinces have jurisdiction for provincial constitutional amendments; direct taxation and debt raising for provincial purposes; provincial prisons; education; health care; municipal government; (nearly all) provincially incorporated companies; local works; property and civil rights; provincial justice, civil law and procedure; and enforcement of provincial laws. They also hold sway in most labour and social security matters.

Territories do not have the status of provinces and are controlled and administered by the federal government, although elected territorial councils have increasing jurisdiction in local matters.

The federal parliament is bicameral. The House of Commons has 308 members directly elected in general elections which, if not called earlier, must be held on the third Monday in October in the fourth calendar year following the last election. The Senate has 105 members appointed on a regional basis by the prime minister,

History

North America has been inhabited for more than 25,000 years by Amerindian and Inuit peoples who migrated from Asia, crossing the Bering Strait. By 1600 the indigenous population of present-day Canada may have been around 250,000. These native inhabitants, living in bands and larger tribes where climatic conditions were not too hostile, developed sophisticated cultures. Populations thrived in the east and on the prairies, with the Algonquian- and Iroquoian-speaking peoples constituting the largest linguistic groups. A rich culture also developed in the west and along the Pacific coast.

The first Europeans to arrive, in about AD 1000, were Vikings under Leif Ericson, who founded short-lived settlements in Newfoundland and Labrador. The next wave of Europeans arrived in search of an imagined north-west passage to Asia, which they found blocked by the Canadian landmass. The abundance of fish off Newfoundland attracted French, Spanish, Portuguese and English fishermen from the 16th century onwards. Settlements developed as bases for the fish and fur trades. English settlements developed in Newfoundland and the Atlantic seaboard. The English Hudson's Bay Company, founded in 1670, claimed trading rights over Rupert's Land, the area whose rivers drained into Hudson Bay. Samuel de Champlain founded the colony of New France or Québec in 1608.

In 1663 Québec became a French royal province, with a governor entrusted with the general policy of the colony, the direction of its military affairs and its relations with the Indian tribes. The Roman Catholic Church, as a result of its Jesuit missions, became a powerful force. The population of the British settlements was largely Protestant, laying the basis for the religious and cultural diversity of Canada today.

Fish and fur trade rivalry between France and England was reinforced by wars in Europe. In 1713, France surrendered all claims to Rupert's Land, Nova Scotia and French settlements in Newfoundland. In 1763, France lost the rest of Canada apart from two small islands, St Pierre and Miquelon.

From 1763 until the 1775 American War of Independence, the whole of North America to the east of the Mississippi was held by Britain, the various colonies having a population of nearly 2 million. In 1774 the Québec Act, passed by the British Parliament, secured for the French colonists the right to retain their language, religion and civil law. As a result of the American Revolution, about 35,000 Loyalists moved north to remain under British rule.

In 1791 the country was divided between the English-speaking and French-speaking regions: Upper Canada (now Ontario); and Lower Canada (now Québec). The USA relinquished claims to Vancouver Island in 1846. British North American colonies were swelled by immigration from Europe from the 1830s to the 1850s.

The British North America Act of 1867 brought together four British colonies: Upper and Lower Canada, New Brunswick and Nova Scotia in one federal Dominion under the name of Canada. Rupert's Land and the Northwestern Territory joined the federation as the province of Manitoba and the Northwest Territories in 1870. The colony of British Columbia joined in 1871 and Prince Edward Island in 1873. The Treaty of Washington in 1871 ended American hopes of Canada becoming part of the USA.

In the 20th century the confederation continued to grow: Alberta and Saskatchewan were created as new provinces in 1905, Norway abandoned claims to the Sverdrup islands in 1931 and Newfoundland joined in 1949. In the late 19th century the population of the country was still small: 3.7 million (1871 census), three-quarters of whom were rural. An important factor in unifying the country was the building of the transcontinental railway, completed, after various setbacks, in the 1880s.

After the First World War, Canada sought an end to colonial status. The Balfour formula of 1926, endorsed by the Statute of Westminster in 1931, recognised Canada as a sovereign country having complete independence within the Commonwealth.

in consultation with the cabinet. The leader of the party with the most seats in the House of Commons becomes prime minister and appoints a cabinet which has executive power at the federal level.

General amendments to the constitution require the consent of the federal parliament and of seven provinces representing at least 50% of the population.

Politics

Last elections:	May 2011
Next elections:	2015
Head of state:	Queen Elizabeth II, represented by governor-general, David Johnston (2010–)
Head of government:	Prime Minister Stephen Harper
Ruling party:	Conservative Party

In a surprise early general election in November 2000, the Liberal Party gained a decisive 173 seats, including 100 of 103 seats in the largest province of Ontario and 37 of 73 in Québec and increasing their majority by 18. Jean Chrétien continued as prime minister. The opposition Canadian Alliance increased its share of the popular vote – largely at the expense of the Progressive Conservative Party (PCP) – but failed to challenge the Liberal Party in the east of the country.

In December 2003, Chrétien retired and was succeeded by former finance minister Paul Martin, and an early general election followed in June 2004, in which the ruling Liberal Party, taking 135 seats, was ahead of the Conservatives (99 seats, the Conservative Party was formed by a merger of PCP and Canadian Alliance), but did not achieve an overall majority in the House of Commons and depended on the support of the smaller parties.

Only 17 months into its new term, in December 2005 opposition parties challenged the government on the payment by the previous Liberal government in the late 1990s of large sums of public money to advertising agencies, and, for the first time ever, carried a vote of no confidence in the government. Martin then had to call a new general election for January 2006. In this election, on a platform of tax cuts and measures to combat corruption, the

➤ From 1968 to 1984, Canadian politics was dominated by Pierre Trudeau, leader of the Liberal Party and four times prime minister. During his administrations, social welfare was increased, immigration liberalised and multiculturalism promoted. After his retirement in 1984, his party was eventually ousted by the Progressive Conservative Party (PCP) under Brian Mulroney, who promoted more stringent social policies, some privatisation and free trade.

Brian Mulroney was succeeded in 1993 by Kim Campbell, Canada's first woman prime minister. Campbell and the Conservatives were crushingly defeated in the October 1993 elections, winning only two seats. The Liberal Party, led by Jean Chrétien, won 177 seats. Recently established parties, the Reform Party (52 seats) and Bloc Québécois (54), did well in the election.

In an early general election in June 1997, Chrétien and the Liberal Party retained power with a reduced majority, winning 155 seats. The Reform Party took 60 seats, Bloc Québécois 44. The PCP recovered to 20 seats and the New Democratic Party also won 20, up from nine in 1993. The elections exposed the increasing regionalisation of Canadian politics, with 101 of the Liberal seats being won in Ontario and the remainder in a few large cities. The Reform Party's seats were almost exclusively in the west of the country.

The Canadian Alliance became the official opposition in the federal House of Commons in March 2000 when the Reform Party joined it.

Québec

The Parti Québécois (PQ) was founded in 1968, with a separatist programme. It came to power in Québec in 1976 and a referendum on Québec sovereignty was held in 1980 in which 60% of Québec voters rejected secession. However, Québec did not approve the new Federal Constitution of 1982, and the issue remained unresolved.

A way forward was apparently found by the Meech Lake accord in 1987. Its main points were the recognition of Québec as a 'distinct society' and new provincial powers. However, Manitoba and Newfoundland failed to ratify the accord before the 1990 deadline and New Brunswick then halted its own ratification process. Many Québécois were antagonised by what they interpreted as a rejection of their interests, culture and language. Extensive public consultations on constitutional reform followed, culminating in the Charlottetown accord of 28 August 1992. Among other things, this accord recognised Québec as a distinct society and also recognised aboriginal rights to self-government within Canada. However, the Charlottetown Accord proposals were rejected in a national referendum in October 1992.

Despite the clear practical difficulties of secession, the PQ, winning the provincial elections of 1994, held a referendum on the separatist option on 30 October 1995. The result was a narrow defeat for the secessionists: a majority of less than 1% voted to remain within the federation of Canada.

In August 1998 the Supreme Court unanimously ruled that under both federal and international law Québec only had the right to secede with the agreement of both federal and seven of the ten provincial legislatures. However, it did stipulate that should a clear majority of the people of Québec vote to secede, then the federal and provincial governments should enter into negotiations with it in good faith.

In Québec's provincial elections in November 1998, the vote was evenly divided between the PQ and the Liberals, although the PQ was returned with 75 of the 125 seats – but only 43% of the votes cast. With voters divided, it seemed unlikely that the PQ would risk another referendum in the near future.

During 2000, the federal parliament passed legislation giving it the right to approve questions to be posed in future referendums on secession by individual provinces.

Conservative Party won 124 seats, the Liberal Party 103, Bloc Québécois 51 and the New Democratic Party (NDP) 29. Conservative Party leader Stephen Harper became prime minister but, short of an outright majority, he was only able to introduce new legislation with support from members of other parties.

In a bid to strengthen his minority government, Harper called an election in October 2008. In the contest when turnout was 59%, his Conservatives won 143 seats with 37.6% of votes. Their gain was largely at the expense of the Liberals who took 77 seats; while Bloc Québécois was also down at 49 seats, NDP won 37 and independents 2. Harper was returned as prime minister, once again in a minority government.

At an early general election, held in May 2011 after the government lost a parliamentary vote of no confidence on 25 March 2011, the ruling Conservatives secured a majority in the House of Commons with 167 of the 308 seats (39.6% of votes). The NDP (102 seats and 30.6%) overtook both the Liberal Party (34 seats and 18.9%) and Bloc Québécois (4 seats and 6.1%); the remaining seat was won by the Green Party (3.9%). The new legislature included 76 women, more than ever before.

International relations

Canada is a member of Asia–Pacific Economic Cooperation, North Atlantic Treaty Organization, Organisation for Economic Co-operation and Development, Organisation internationale de la Francophonie, Organization of American States, United Nations and World Trade Organization.

With the USA and Mexico, Canada is a member of the North America Free Trade Association.

Traveller information

Local laws and conventions: Most restaurants and bars are non-smoking.

Penalties for trafficking or possessing illegal drugs are severe. The Quat plant is also illegal, and those found in possession of it may face a prison sentence.

Handshaking is the usual form of greeting in Canada. Dress is usually informal and practical.

Business appointments must be made and punctuality is important. The exchange of business cards is customary. Many of the larger cities have excellent conference facilities. Office hours are Mon–Fri 0900–1700.

Immigration and customs: Passports must be valid for at least one day beyond the intended length of stay. Some nationals may need a visa to enter the country and visa requirements should be checked with the local embassy.

For cameras, radios, computers and other electrical items, visitors may be asked to pay a deposit on entering; this will be refunded when the visitor provides proof of export.

It is prohibited to import firearms, explosives, endangered species of animals and plants, animal products, and some food products. The import of turtle shells and articles from Haiti made of animal skins are prohibited. Visitors may be interrogated by an examining official if it is believed they are not in good health or are not planning to return to their original country of origin.

Lone parents should carry documentary evidence of parental responsibility for all accompanying children. Sometimes a letter of consent is required of the parent who is not travelling.

Travel within the country: Traffic drives on the right, and car hire is available from all airports and in major towns to all those aged 21 and over. Visitors may use their national driving licence if staying for less than three months.

Speed limits are 100kph on motorways, 80kph on rural highways and 50kph in urban areas. The wearing of seatbelts is compulsory, as is the use of car seats for children. Road networks cover vast areas of the country and roads are good. Visitors must be vigilant in rural areas, as wild moose and deer are prone to roaming on country roads.

Coaches are the cheapest way of travelling around the country and each region has an efficient network of coach services.

There are a number of domestic airlines that serve the main cities as well as the more remote regions.

National and regional rail services operate throughout the country, and there is a fast intercity service between Québec, Montréal, Halifax, Toronto, Windsor and Ottawa. Rail services that run directly from Toronto to Vancouver operate three times a week and journey time is three days. The Rocky Mountaineer train service connects the main towns in the Rockies and is a seasonal service aimed at showing visitors the breathtaking scenery.

Travel health: Canada has excellent health facilities, although it is recommended that visitors carry first-aid kits if travelling to the more remote parts of the country. Comprehensive medical insurance is recommended, as hospital treatment is expensive. There is a slight risk of contracting rabies if bitten by an animal and vaccination before travel is advisable.

Money: Local currency is the Canadian dollar. Travellers cheques are widely accepted and should be in Canadian dollars to avoid paying additional exchange rate charges. ATMs are widely available and major credit cards can be used in most places. Banking hours are 0930–1600 (or 1700).

There were 16,095,000 tourist arrivals in 2010.

Further information

Government of Canada: canada.gc.ca

Parliament of Canada: www.parl.gc.ca

Bank of Canada: www.bankofcanada.ca

Commonwealth Secretariat: www.thecommonwealth.org

Commonwealth of Nations: www.commonwealth-of-nations.org/Canada

Republic of Cyprus

In 1974 Turkish troops invaded and occupied the northern 36% of the Republic of Cyprus. This area was later declared independent. The secession has not been recognised internationally, except by Turkey. The UN and Commonwealth have for many years protested about the occupation and tried to resolve the problem by negotiation.

Due to this division of the Republic of Cyprus, aggregated information is not always available. Economic and social data given here generally cover the government-controlled areas only, although legally and constitutionally the Republic of Cyprus includes the occupied north.

KEY FACTS

Joined Commonwealth:	1961
Population:	1,104,000 (2010)
GDP p.c. growth:	2.1% p.a. 1990–2010
UN HDI 2011:	world ranking 31
Official languages:	Greek, Turkish
Time:	GMT plus 2–3hr
Currency:	euro (€)

Geography

Area:	9,251 sq km
Coastline:	648km
Capital:	Nicosia

Cyprus is an oval-shaped island with 'pan-handle' north-east peninsula in the eastern Mediterranean. Its closest mainland neighbours are Turkey (to the north) and Syria and Lebanon (to the east).

Time: GMT plus 2hr winter, GMT plus 3hr summer

Topography: The Troodos Mountains, in the central and western part of the island, rise to 1,951m at Mt Olympus. The Troodos, of infertile igneous rock, are characterised by steep slopes, narrow valleys and precipices. The Kyrenia Mountains (also known as the Pentadaktylos range), along the north coast, rise to 1,024m and are mainly limestone. Passes and valleys allow access to the north

Did you know...

It is one of only three Commonwealth member countries located in Europe, all of which are island states and members of the European Union.

Cyprus has one of the lowest infant mortality rates in the Commonwealth: 997 infants survive every 1,000 births.

coast. The fertile Messaoria Plain lies between them. About half of its 186,000 hectares is irrigated. Most water sources are in the south – all major rivers originate in the Troodos and flow east, south or west. Many rivers dry up in the summer. There are sandy beaches on the south of the island and some rugged rocky coastline in the north.

Climate: Mediterranean type. Hot dry summers (June to September) and mild wet winters (November to March).

Environment: The most significant environmental issues are limited water resources – due to lack of rain in the summer and pollution of the island's largest aquifer by sea water; water pollution by sewage and industrial wastes; coastal degradation; and loss of wildlife habitats due to urbanisation.

Vegetation: Mediterranean scrub, succulents and pine woods, adapted to the dry summers, with 1,800 species and subspecies of flowering plants. The mountains are forested and less than 20% of the land is arable and permanently cropped, about 20% of which is irrigated. The occupied north is generally more thickly vegetated and fertile.

Wildlife: The only large wild animal is the agrino, a species of wild sheep, which is now protected. Snakes, once so abundant as to give the island its old name *Ophiussa* ('abode of snakes'), are now comparatively rare.

Main towns: Nicosia (Lefkosia, capital, pop. 217,600 in 2010, with a further 54,000 in the occupied north), Limassol (172,100), Larnaca (53,500), Paphos (43,600). In the occupied north, other main towns are Famagusta (36,700), Kyrenia (31,000), Morphou and Lefka.

Transport: There is a good road network in the Republic, extending to 12,280km (65% paved), with motorways between Nicosia, Limassol, Paphos and the Famagusta area; comprising 2.2% of the total network. Cyprus has no railway.

Major ports are at Larnaca and Limassol.

Nicosia airport was closed in 1974. There are international airports 5km south of Larnaca, and 15km east of Paphos.

Society

KEY FACTS 2010

Population per sq km:	119
Life expectancy:	79 years
Net primary enrolment:	99%

Population: 1,104,000 (2010); 70% lives in urban areas; growth 1.8% p.a. 1990–2010; birth rate 12 per 1,000 people (19 in 1970); life expectancy 79 years (71 in 1970).

The population comprises Greek Cypriots (approximately 80%) and Turkish Cypriots, and small populations of Armenians, Maronites and 'Latins' (the term used in Cyprus for Roman Catholics of European origin). The population of the occupied north was estimated at 257,000 in 2005, and included around 160,000 Turkish illegal settlers.

Language: Official languages are Greek and Turkish. English is widely spoken; German and French spoken in tourist centres.

Religion: Most Greek Cypriots belong to the autocephalous Cypriot Orthodox Church; most Turkish Cypriots are Sunni Muslims. There are small religious groups of Maronites, Armenians, Roman Catholics and Anglicans.

Health: Public spending on health was 2% of GDP in 2009. In the Republic, medical care is free for government employees, displaced persons and low-income families, including in all about 65% of the population. The government has proposed a national health insurance scheme. A new general hospital was built in Nicosia in the latter 1990s. Infant mortality was 3 per 1,000 live births in 2010 (30 in 1960).

The Government of Cyprus offers free treatment in government hospitals to all Turkish Cypriots residing in the occupied north.

Education: Public spending on education was 7.4% of GDP in 2008. There are nine years of compulsory education starting at age five. Primary school comprises six years and secondary six, with two cycles of three years. There are many private schools. Some 95% of pupils complete primary school (2007). The school year starts in September.

Greek Cypriots have one of the world's highest proportions of graduates. The University of Cyprus is a bilingual (Greek and Turkish) university which opened in 1992. The other public universities are Cyprus University of Technology (2007) and Open University of Cyprus (2002). Private universities include European University Cyprus (2007), which developed out of Cyprus College (1961); Frederick University (2007), which developed out of the Frederick Institute of Technology (1965); Neapolis University, Paphos (2010); and University of Nicosia (2007), which developed out of Intercollege (1980). Other public tertiary institutions include Cyprus Forestry College (1951); Higher Hotel Institute of Cyprus (1966); Higher Technical Institute (1968); Mediterranean Institute of Management (1976, postgraduate); and Nursing School. The

female–male ratio for gross enrolment in tertiary education is 0.87:1 (2009). There is virtually no illiteracy among people aged 15–24.

Media: There are several daily papers, most in Greek but the *Cyprus Mail* is in English. Of the several bi-weekly, weekly and fortnightly papers, two (*Cyprus Weekly* and *Cyprus Financial Mirror*) are in English.

The public radio and TV provider is the Cyprus Broadcasting Corporation, broadcasting in Greek, English and Turkish. Private radio and TV stations compete with the public networks. The switch from analogue to digital TV was completed in July 2011.

There are 383 personal computers (2006) and 530 internet users (2010) per 1,000 people.

Communications: Country code 357; internet domain '.cy'. Mobile phone coverage is good.

There are 374 main telephone lines and 937 mobile phone subscriptions per 1,000 people (2010).

Public holidays: New Year's Day, Epiphany (6 January), Greek Independence Day (25 March), EOKA Day (1 April), Labour Day (1 May), Assumption (15 August), Independence Day (1 October), Ochi Day (28 October), Christmas Day and St Stephen's Day (26 December). Fixed-date holidays falling on a Saturday or Sunday are not moved.

Religious and other festivals whose dates vary from year to year include Green Monday (start of Lent, 50 days before Greek Orthodox Easter), Good Friday (Greek Orthodox), Easter Monday (Greek Orthodox) and Kataklysmos (Pentecost, 50 days after Greek Orthodox Easter).

Economy

(In this section, unless otherwise stated, figures do not include the occupied north.)

KEY FACTS 2010

GNI:	US$23.7bn
GNI p.c.:	US$29,430
GDP growth:	2.4% p.a. 2006–10
Inflation:	2.4% p.a. 2006–10

Despite occupation of the north and the consequent forced movement of population and loss of resources, the economy of the Republic has grown steadily with relatively low inflation, particularly in the tourism and offshore financial services sectors, while the agriculture sector and exports of citrus fruits and potatoes became relatively less important. Oil and gas exploration was under way in 2011 and large offshore finds of natural gas were announced in December 2011, amounting to an estimated 140–230 billion cubic metres.

From the latter 1990s, the government introduced economic reforms with a view to joining the EU. The economy continued to grow strongly, until it slowed in the tougher international climate after 2000, picking up again from 2004, the year in which the Republic of Cyprus joined the EU, and continuing at about 4% until 2008, when the impact of the world economic downturn on tourism and trade caused growth to stall in the latter part of that year and go into reverse in 2009 (–1.7%), before returning to weak positive growth in 2010–11. Cyprus adopted the euro currency at the beginning of 2008 replacing the Cyprus pound.

Real Growth in GDP

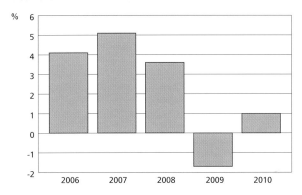

Inflation

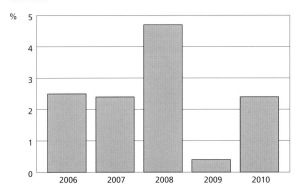

GDP by Sector (2010)

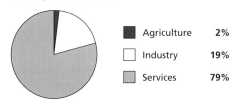

Agriculture	2%
Industry	19%
Services	79%

In the occupied north, the economy has suffered from a number of factors including inflation and the weakness of the Turkish currency.

Constitution

Status:	Republic with executive president
Legislature:	House of Representatives
Independence:	16 August 1960

The Republic of Cyprus is a democracy with a directly elected executive president, serving a five-year term. The 1960 constitution has provisions to ensure a balance of power between the Greek and Turkish Cypriot communities. The legislature, the House of Representatives, was to be elected by universal suffrage with 35 Greek and 15 Turkish seats and a term of no longer than five years. Under the amendment of 1985, the legislature was to comprise 80 seats (56 Greek, 24 Turkish). In 1996 a system of proportional representation was introduced. The seats reserved for Turkish Cypriots have been unoccupied since 1963.

The executive was to comprise a Greek president, a Turkish vice-president and a council of ministers, with seven Greek and three Turkish members. Ministers may not be members of parliament. The president is to be elected by absolute majority. If this is not achieved, a second election between the two top candidates is to be held. All Cypriots must declare themselves either to be Cypriot Greeks or Cypriot Turks (the Armenian, Maronite and Latin communities declared themselves Greek for this purpose).

The ratio of Greek to Turk in the army must be 6:4, and 7:3 in the police, judiciary and civil service. Nicosia, Paphos, Larnaca, Limassol and Famagusta each have separate Greek and Turkish municipal authorities. Equal status was granted to the Greek and Turkish languages.

Politics

Last elections:	May 2011 (parliamentary), February 2008 (presidential)
Next elections:	2016 (parliamentary), 2013 (presidential)
Head of state:	President Demetris Christofias
Head of government:	the president
Ruling party:	AKEL

In the parliamentary elections in May 2001, AKEL took an increased share of 34.7% of votes but the ruling coalition of Democratic Rally (34.0%) and United Democrats (2.6%) narrowly won the contest. Centre-right DIKO (14.8%) and social democratic KISOS (called EDEK until 1999 and again from 2006 – 6.5%) both received slightly fewer votes than in 1997. For the first time 18–21 year-olds were entitled to vote and, since voting is compulsory, there was a high turnout (some 92%) of the 468,000 registered voters.

DIKO leader, Tassos Papadopoulos, won the presidential election in February 2003, with the support of AKEL and EDEK, receiving 52% of the votes, defeating incumbent President Glafkos Clerides (39%).

The parliamentary elections in May 2006 were won by the governing coalition of AKEL, with 18 seats and 31% of the votes, DIKO (11 seats and 18% of the votes) and EDEK (KISOS) with five seats and 9% of the votes. Democratic Rally gained 18 seats and 30% of the votes.

In the lead-up to the presidential election of 2008, the ruling coalition of DIKO, AKEL and EDEK was unable to reach a consensus on a common candidate and so Papadopoulos was to run for re-election with the support only of DIKO and EDEK. Communist party AKEL left the coalition and chose its general secretary and House of Representatives president, Demetris Christofias, as its candidate. Ioannis Kasoulidis of Democratic Rally was the other major candidate.

In the election in February 2008 – with turnout of around 90% – the three candidates each received about one-third of the votes (Kasoulidis 33.5%; Christofias 33.3%; Papadopoulos 31.8%). No candidate having more than 50% of the votes, Christofias and Kasoulidis went into a second round and the incumbent Papadopoulos was eliminated from the contest. Christofias defeated Kasoulidis by 53.4% to 46.6%. Christofias immediately invited DIKO and EDEK members to join his cabinet. DIKO leader Tassos Papadopoulos died in December 2008.

Formal UN-supported negotiations between the Government, led by President Christofias, and the Turkish Cypriots, led by Mehmet

Ali Talat, began in September 2008. In June 2009, at the 32nd meeting, the economic agenda was concluded and discussions on territorial issues began. The first round of negotiations was concluded with the 40th meeting in August 2009. A second round of talks, covering economic matters, power-sharing, property rights and the EU was conducted from September 2009 to January 2010. A new round of talks got under way in May 2010, continuing through 2011 into 2012, the Turkish Cypriots now led by Dervis Eroglu.

In the May 2011 parliamentary elections, Democratic Rally secured 20 of the 56 seats contested (34.3% of the vote); AKEL took 19 (32.7%), DIKO nine (15.8%), EDEK five (8.9%), the European Party two (3.9%) and the Green Party one (2.2%), with turnout of 79%. AKEL and DIKO formed a coalition government. The coalition collapsed in August 2011 following policy disagreements, leaving AKEL in a minority government.

International relations

Cyprus is a member of the Council of Europe, European Union, Organisation internationale de la Francophonie, Organization for Security and Co-operation in Europe, United Nations and World Trade Organization.

Traveller information

Local laws and conventions: The Republic of Cyprus has a strict policy of zero tolerance towards drugs. Those caught in possession of any type of narcotic will face a fine or prison sentence. Photography is forbidden near military camps or installations.

Respect should be shown for religious beliefs and traditional values. It is customary to shake hands and other normal courtesies should be observed.

Cypriot dress is generally casual, although businessmen should wear a suit and tie and businesswomen should dress smartly but conservatively. A brief but firm handshake is the accepted custom at the start and end of a meeting.

Avoid arranging meetings for August or around the times of national holidays. Office hours are Mon–Fri 0900–1730.

Immigration and customs: Agricultural products and propagating stock such as natural fruit, flowers and seeds are not allowed to be imported into Cyprus without the approval of the relevant authorities. The importation of a number of other articles such as uncooked meat, fish and dairy products, animals, fire arms and explosives, pirated or counterfeit goods, and obscene publications is also prohibited or restricted.

History

The civilisation of Cyprus, recorded through archaeological finds, myths and later written history, can be traced through 9,000 years. The island, perfectly placed as a strategic base for the great civilisations of the Near-Eastern ancient world, has been much fought over. It was subject to the empires of Assyria, Egypt, Persia, Macedonia and Rome in the BC period. Its population has been predominantly ethnically Greek since then. After the collapse of the Roman Empire in the 4th century, it was ruled by Byzantium, the Franks, the Venetians and the Ottoman Turks. It was during the Ottoman period that the ancestors of the Turkish Cypriots settled on the island. Through these rich and varied influences, Cyprus acquired a great archaeological legacy.

In 1878, Britain concluded an alliance with the Sultan on Cyprus, and gained effective control. When Turkey sided with Germany in the First World War, Britain annexed the island. In 1925, Cyprus became a Crown colony.

From the 1930s, Greek Cypriots campaigned for enosis (union with Greece), a movement that came to be led in the 1950s by Archbishop Makarios. The UK proposed instead (in 1948, 1954 and 1955) various forms of internal self-government, all of which were deemed unacceptable by the Greek Cypriot Ethnarchy Council. In 1955, the National Organisation of Cypriot Fighters (EOKA) began armed resistance against the UK. Turkey helped the Turkish Cypriot leaders establish the Cyprus Is Turkish Party and the Turkish Resistance Organisation, and the fighting became intercommunal.

In 1960, the UK negotiated an independence agreement with Greece and Turkey, under which the three powers guaranteed to protect the integrity of Cyprus, which was to be allowed neither to unite with any other country nor to be partitioned. Cyprus,

which had not taken part in these negotiations, became independent as the Republic of Cyprus.

Intercommunal fighting broke out again a few years after independence, leading to some 500 deaths and more than 1,000 casualties. British troops imposed order and a plan centred on a ceasefire line known as the Green Line. In 1964, the UN Peacekeeping Force (UNFICYP) succeeded the British troops. A UN force remains in the same position today. However, hostilities continued, with the Greek and Turkish military becoming involved, and very nearly led to war between the two countries. Archbishop Makarios began negotiations towards a settlement.

But in 1974, a military coup in Cyprus overthrew Makarios and installed a fervently nationalist government, led by Nikos Sampson, favouring enosis. Turkey invaded twice, taking control of the northern 36% of the country. Greece, in confusion after its own military coup against President Makarios, was unable to intervene. About 180,000 Greek Cypriots fled from their homes in the north, and came south as refugees; 45,000 Turkish Cypriots were similarly uprooted.

Intercommunal talks under UN auspices began in 1975. In November 1983, the Turkish Cypriot assembly in the north, under the leadership of Rauf Denktash, voted for independence and in 1985 approved a new constitution. Independence has subsequently been recognised solely by Turkey, but condemned by the UN Security Council and other international organisations.

The 1988 presidential election in the Republic brought to power George Vassiliou, on a platform of conciliation. He was not the first leader openly to seek compromise: Makarios had accepted the concept of federation in 1977, and concluded the first high-level agreement with Denktash; and President Spyros Kyprianou ➤

Travel within the country: The Green Line separates the occupied north from the government-controlled areas. The Green Line Regulation provides for the crossing of the people and goods into the government-controlled areas.

Driving is on the left-hand side of the road. Travellers are permitted to take their hired car through the checkpoints, but are strongly advised to check the insurance implications with their car hire company.

Heavy fines are imposed on those driving without a seatbelt or riding a motorbike without a helmet. There are also fines for those caught driving while using a mobile phone or under the influence of alcohol.

Daily bus services connect all towns and villages. There is a limited service on Sundays and public holidays. Taxis run 24 hours a day between all the main towns. Fares are regulated by the government and all taxis have meters.

Travel health: Free or reduced-cost health care is available to European residents on production of a valid European Health Insurance Card (EHIC) – although an EHIC is not valid in the occupied north. Non-European residents must make special arrangements for health care before travel although accident and emergency care is available free of charge regardless of nationality.

Milk is pasteurised and tap water generally safe to drink.

Money: All major credit cards are accepted at most places. Visitors wishing to obtain non-Cypriot currency at Cypriot banks for business purposes are advised that this is only possible by prior arrangement.

New legislation on controls of cash entering or leaving the European Union has been imposed and any person carrying €10,000 euros or more must declare it.

There were 2,173,000 tourist arrivals in 2010.

Further information

Republic of Cyprus Government Web Portal: www.cyprus.gov.cy

House of Representatives: www.parliament.cy

Central Bank of Cyprus: www.centralbank.gov.cy

Commonwealth Secretariat: www.thecommonwealth.org

Commonwealth of Nations: www.commonwealth-of-nations.org/Cyprus

➤ had signed the second high-level agreement with Denktash in 1979 and accepted the notion of bizonality proposing the demilitarisation of the island. But Vassiliou was prepared to go further. In 1993, he went to the elections stating his willingness to accept, as a basis for further negotiations, a UN proposal for a federal republic. However, he lost the election by a narrow margin to Glafkos Clerides, who took a more cautious view of the UN plan.

Parliamentary elections in the Republic held in May 1996 – the first to be held since the adoption of proportional representation – returned the Democratic Rally–Liberal Party coalition (supporting President Glafkos Clerides) with a majority of one seat.

There was optimism that real negotiations might be about to begin when in July 1997, Clerides and Denktash met for the first time in three years at a UN-sponsored meeting in New York. Subsequent meetings were held in Nicosia and Glion (Switzerland) over the next six weeks. However, tension was mounting with successive military exercises on the island by Greece and Turkey, and when it became clear that the EU negotiations would proceed without reference to the occupied north if a settlement had not been reached in the meantime, and also that Turkey was not at this period invited to join the EU, Denktash left the talks and the process was stalled.

The first round of the presidential elections in February 1998 was inconclusive. President Clerides narrowly won the second-round contest with George Iacovou with 51% of the votes. Clerides then formed a broadly based coalition administration, to prepare for further negotiations with the Turkish Cypriots and the accession talks with the EU.

Talks with the Turkish Cypriots continued during 1999 and 2000, but progress remained stalled because the parties were unable to agree on future constitutional arrangements. While the Greek Cypriots, with the support of the international community, were seeking a return to a bi-communal independent federation with a central government, the Turkish Cypriots were insisting on a confederation of two equal states.

Accession negotiations with the EU began in November 1998 and the accession treaty on formal entry of Cyprus and nine other candidate countries in May 2004 was signed in April 2003.

Talks between Greek and Turkish Cypriots continued during 2001–02 and, from January 2002, these were UN-mediated talks between Clerides and Denktash, ending in March 2003 when the two leaders were unable to agree on putting the UN's settlement proposals to referendums in their communities, though both sides agreed to continue negotiations.

Referendums on the UN reunification plan were held simultaneously in the two communities in April 2004. Greek Cypriots were overwhelmingly against the plan and Turkish Cypriots strongly for it. Among the reasons for the plan's rejection by Greek Cypriots were that it would give them only limited rights to return to and recover their original homes, and that it would allow tens of thousands of Turkish settlers to stay and Turkey to maintain a garrison. Turkey would also maintain its status of guarantor power, with the right of unilateral military intervention.

The Republic of Cyprus became a member of the European Union in May 2004. The application of the acquis is suspended in those areas of the Republic of Cyprus in which the Government of the Republic of Cyprus does not exercise effective control.

Dominica

KEY FACTS

Joined Commonwealth:	1978
Population:	68,000 (2010)
GDP p.c. growth:	1.7% p.a. 1990–2010
UN HDI 2011:	world ranking 81
Official language:	English
Time:	GMT minus 4hr
Currency:	Eastern Caribbean dollar (EC$)

Geography

Area:	750 sq km
Coastline:	148km
Capital:	Roseau

The Commonwealth of Dominica is one of the Windward Islands in the Eastern Caribbean, lying between Guadeloupe to the north and Martinique to the south.

Topography: A volcanic island 46km in length, Dominica has a central mountain ridge running from Cape Melville in the north to the cliffs in the south. Morne Diablotin rises to 1,447m. There are numerous mountain streams and rivers, none of them navigable. The scenery is outstandingly beautiful, with waterfalls and luxuriantly wooded mountains. Most beaches are of black volcanic sand, with some of golden sand.

Climate: The climate is subtropical and hot, but cooled by sea breezes, with a rainy season in June–October, when hurricanes may occur. Rainfall is heavy, especially in mountain areas.

Environment: The most significant environmental issues are shortage of drinking water; deforestation; soil erosion; pollution of the coastal zone by chemicals used in farming and factories, and untreated sewage.

Vegetation: Dominica is known as the nature island of the Caribbean. Dense forest and woodland cover 60% of the land

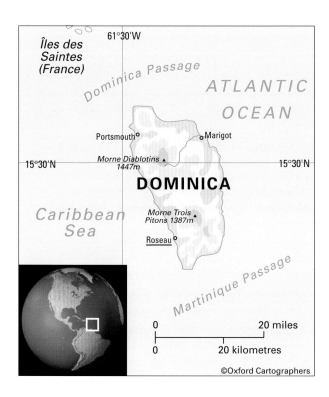

©Oxford Cartographers

area, with subtropical vegetation and orchids in the valleys. Tree ferns are indigenous to the island. Arable and cropped land extends to some 23% of the total land area. The island has a fertile volcanic soil.

Wildlife: The forests have a wide range of bird species (some of them rare and endangered), including the brilliant Dominica parrot, or Sisserou, which is depicted on the national flag, various species of doves and the mountain whistler. There are three distinct vegetation and habitat zones determined by rainfall and elevation at defined levels around the mountains. The country has two marine reserves and several hectares of forest reserve.

Main towns: Roseau (capital, pop. 13,400 in 2010), Canefield (3,400), Portsmouth (3,300), Marigot (2,700), Salisbury (2,600), Atkinson (2,200), Berekua (2,000), St Joseph (1,900), Castle Bruce (1,900), Wesley (1,600) and Mahaut (1,200).

Transport: There are 780km of roads, 50% paved. Round-island network was completed in the late 1980s, despite the technical difficulties presented by Dominica's mountainous terrain and friable volcanic rock.

Banana boats and tourist cruiseships call at Roseau, at the deep-water harbour in Woodbridge Bay, and in Prince Rupert's Bay, Portsmouth.

The airports at Melville Hall, 64km north-east of Roseau, and Canefield, 5km north of Roseau, can accommodate only turbo-

Did you know...

Dominica was the first state in the Americas to have a female prime minister. Dame Eugenia Charles served from 1980 to 1995.

At his appointment in 2004 the current prime minister, Roosevelt Skerrit, was the youngest head of government in the world, aged 31.

Dominica is the only country in the Commonwealth to have recorded an overall decrease in population since 1990.

prop passenger aircraft. Tourists flying into Dominica must therefore generally come via the nearby island of Antigua.

Society

KEY FACTS 2010

Population per sq km:	91
Life expectancy:	76 years (est.)
Net primary enrolment:	98%

Population: 68,000 (2010); 67% lives in urban areas; growth –0.2% p.a. 1990–2010, negative due mainly to the emigration of young people; birth rate 16 per 1,000 people (est. 26 in 1970); life expectancy 76 years (est.)

The population is mostly of African and mixed African/European descent, with European, Syrian and Carib (2.9% in 2001 census) minorities. There is a Carib reserve on part of the east of the island, referred to as the Carib Territory.

Language: The official language is English; a French-based Creole is spoken by most of the population.

Religion: Mainly Christians (Roman Catholics 61%, Seventh Day Adventists 6%, Pentecostals 6%, Baptists 4%, Methodists 4%; 2001 census).

Health: Public spending on health was 4% of GDP in 2009. The health system operates through local clinics, larger health centres, a polyclinic in Roseau, and the national referral hospital, the Princess Margaret Hospital. There is a smaller hospital at Portsmouth, and cottage hospitals at Marigot and Grand Bay. Infant mortality was 11 per 1,000 live births in 2010.

Education: Public spending on education was 4.5% of GDP in 2010. There are ten years of compulsory education starting at age five. Primary school comprises seven years and secondary five. Some 89% of pupils complete primary school (2007). The school year starts in September.

Further education is provided at a teacher-training college, a nursing school and at the regional University of the West Indies, which has a branch in Dominica and main campuses in Barbados, Jamaica, and Trinidad and Tobago. The Dominica State College, a publicly funded institution, offers programmes leading to GCE Advanced Level and associate degrees; it also operates four faculties and has a continuing studies division. The female–male ratio for gross enrolment in tertiary education is 3.22:1 (2008).

Media: *The Chronicle* (founded in 1909), *The Tropical Star* and *The Sun* are all weekly.

The Dominica Broadcasting Corporation provides a public radio service, competing with several commercial or faith stations. There is no national TV service on the island but a private cable network covers part of the country.

There are 475 internet users per 1,000 people (2010).

Communications: Country code 1 767; internet domain '.dm'. The main post office is in Roseau.

There are 229 main telephone lines and 1,558 mobile phone subscriptions per 1,000 people (2010).

Public holidays: New Year's Day, May Day (first Monday in May), August Monday (first Monday in August), Independence Day (3

November), Community Service Day (4 November), Christmas Day and Boxing Day.

Religious festivals whose dates vary from year to year include Carnival (two days in February/March), Good Friday, Easter Monday and Whit Monday.

Economy

KEY FACTS 2010

GNI:	US$458m
GNI p.c.:	US$6,760
GDP growth:	3.2% p.a. 2006–10
Inflation:	3.1% p.a. 2006–10

Dominica's economy is vulnerable. Much of the island is mountainous and less than 25% of the country is under cultivation. Its location exposes it to tropical storms and hurricanes, which have caused severe damage to the crops making up the country's economic base, and particularly bananas. There were three severe hurricanes in the 1980s, and in 1995 Hurricanes Luis

Real Growth in GDP

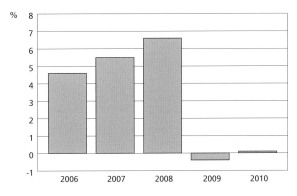

Inflation

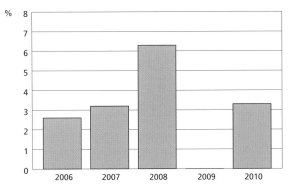

GDP by Sector (2010)

■ Agriculture	**13%**
□ Industry	**15%**
■ Services	**72%**

and Marilyn caused severe damage. The country is also vulnerable in its dependence on banana exports to the EU.

Since the 1980s, successive governments have therefore introduced measures to diversify the economy, encouraging a shift from traditional crops (such as sugar, coffee and cocoa) to new crops (such as citrus, melons, pineapples and mangoes), and developing export-oriented small industries (notably garments and electronics assembly), taking advantage of such preferences as the Caribbean Basin Initiative (CBI), which allows access to the US market.

They have also encouraged development of tourism and especially eco-tourism. The key to expansion of tourism was in the 1990s seen as the construction of a new airport with a runway long enough for long-haul jets from North America and Europe but it proved impossible to secure financial backing for the project.

Between 1991 and 1997, Dominica received about US$15 million in investment and acquired some 750 new citizens – mainly non-resident Taiwanese – under its 'economic citizenship programme' which allowed people to become citizens in return for a substantial investment in Dominica. In the latter 1990s, 200–300 Russians were granted economic citizenship.

The government also encouraged development of an offshore financial-services sector, including company and bank registration and internet gambling.

From the mid-1990s, there was a period of modest economic growth, but by 1999 the economy had stalled, moving into recession in 2000, and shrank by some 9% in 2001–03. The IMF agreed to financial support tied to tax increases and cuts in public expenditure and good growth resumed in 2004–05, driven by tourism, recovery in banana production and a booming construction sector. This growth continued through 2007, when Hurricane Dean caused widespread devastation, and into 2008, when the impact of the global recession was keenly felt, causing the economy to shrink by 0.4% in 2009, recovering only very weakly in 2010–11.

Constitution

Status:	Republic
Legislature:	House of Assembly
Independence:	3 November 1978

Dominica is a republic with a non-executive presidency and parliamentary democracy. It has a unicameral House of Assembly with 30 members plus the speaker and attorney-general. 21 members are directly elected and nine senators appointed by the president, five on the advice of the prime minister, four on the advice of the leader of the opposition. Elections are held at least every five years, with universal suffrage for adults.

The president is nominated by the prime minister and leader of the opposition and elected by the House of Assembly for not more than two terms of five years. He or she appoints the prime minister, who consults the president in appointing other ministers. The

History

Throughout its history the fertile island of Dominica has attracted settlers and colonisers and has been the subject of the military, and often bloody, squabbles of European powers. At the time of Columbus's visit on a Sunday (*dies dominica*) in November 1493, the island was a stronghold of the Caribs from South America who were driving out the Arawaks. In 1627 the English took theoretical possession without settling, but by 1632 the island had become a *de facto* French colony; it remained so until 1759 when the English captured it. In 1660 the English and French agreed to leave the Caribs in undisturbed possession, but in fact French settlers went on arriving, bringing enslaved Africans with them. Dominica changed hands between the two European powers, passing back to France (1778) and again to England (1783). The French attempted to invade in 1795 and 1805 before eventually withdrawing, leaving Britain in possession.

In 1833 the island was linked to Antigua and the other Leeward Islands under a governor-general at Antigua, but subsequently became part of the Federation of the Leeward Islands Colony (1871–1939) before becoming a unit of the Windward Islands group (1940–60). Dominica joined the West Indies Federation at its foundation in 1958 and remained a member until differences among larger members led to its dissolution in 1962.

Within Dominica, the formation of the Dominica Labour Party (DLP) from the People's National Movement and other groups in the early 1960s spurred local demand for greater autonomy in internal affairs. Edward LeBlanc became chief minister in 1961. Under his leadership, in 1967 Dominica became one of the West Indies Associated States, with full internal self-government, while the UK remained responsible for foreign policy and defence. At

LeBlanc's retirement in 1974, Patrick John succeeded as DLP leader and premier. After winning a large majority at the 1975 elections, John pursued the course agreed by the Associated States to seek independence separately.

On 3 November 1978, Dominica achieved independence as a republic within the Commonwealth, and took the name of Commonwealth of Dominica. John became its first prime minister, and Frederick Degazon the non-executive president.

In 1979 the DLP government collapsed and Oliver Seraphine of the Committee for National Salvation (CNS) was invited to form an interim government and prepare the way for elections within six months. The elections in July 1980 were won by the Dominica Freedom Party (DFP) led by Eugenia Charles (who became the first woman prime minister in the region), winning 17 of the 21 seats. Patrick John, who had led the country to independence, and Seraphine lost their seats.

There were two coup attempts early in the 1980s allegedly organised by factions of the Defence Force sympathetic to the John regime. In 1985, John was himself convicted of involvement in one such attempt, and sentenced to 12 years imprisonment; the following year the former commander of the Defence Force was hanged for murdering a police officer during a coup attempt.

Eugenia Charles led the DFP to victory in the 1990 general election, but, in June 1995, shortly after her retirement from politics, the DFP lost its majority. The United Workers Party (UWP) emerged as election victor with 11 seats; the DFP and the DLP each won five. Edison James, leader of the UWP, was invited by the president to form a government.

president may dismiss the prime minister in the event of a no-confidence vote in the House of Assembly. Individual rights are guaranteed under the constitution.

Roseau (the capital) and the Carib Territory have a measure of self-government. The Caribs elect their chief.

Politics

Last elections:	December 2009
Next elections:	2014
Head of state:	President Dr Nicholas Liverpool (2003–)
Head of government:	Prime Minister Roosevelt Skerrit
Ruling party:	Dominica Labour Party

The economy continued to dominate the political agenda. The government's top priority in the run-up to the 2000 elections had been to secure financial backing for its new airport project – the key to expansion of the tourism industry, which was set to become crucial as, inevitably, the international banana market became more competitive.

In the January 2000 general election, the Dominica Labour Party (DLP – ten seats) narrowly defeated the United Workers Party (UWP) (nine seats). The DLP formed a coalition with the Dominica Freedom Party (DFP – two seats) and Roosevelt (Rosie) Douglas became prime minister. Following his sudden death in October 2000, he was succeeded by communications and works minister Pierre Charles.

In October 2003 Dr Nicholas Liverpool was elected president by the House of Assembly for a five-year term. In January 2004 Charles died suddenly and Roosevelt Skerrit was sworn in as prime minister.

In the general election in May 2005, the DLP took 12 seats, the UWP eight and independents one. DFP failed to win any seats and was unable to continue as coalition partner with DLP in government.

In December 2009, in an election that was called early, the DLP won 18 seats – with 61.2% of the vote – and the UWP the balance of three (34.9%). In early January 2010 Skerrit announced his new cabinet, in which he was finance and foreign affairs minister.

International relations

Dominica is a member of the African, Caribbean and Pacific Group of States, Association of Caribbean States, Caribbean Community, Non-Aligned Movement, Organisation internationale de la Francophonie, Organisation of Eastern Caribbean States, Organization of American States, United Nations and World Trade Organization.

Traveller information

Local laws and conventions: The Roman Catholic Church is one of the biggest social influences on the islanders.

Visitors should always ask before taking photographs of local people.

Drug offences carry severe penalties. Visitors must take care to pack their own luggage and not to carry anything through customs for a third party.

It is illegal for anyone, including children, to wear camouflage clothing. Avoid all camouflage patterns, even on bags.

Business dress is smart and the etiquette is formal. Casual dress is the norm for visitors, with evening clothes conservative but informal.

Business hours are Mon 0800–1300 and 1400–1700, Tues–Fri 0800–1300 and 1400–1600.

Immigration and customs: Passports need to be valid for at least six months and a return air ticket is required for entry into the country. Visas requirements should be checked before travel. Visitors are advised to make a copy of the photopage of their passport and entry stamp.

A yellow fever vaccination certificate is required from travellers coming from an infected country.

Plants, varnishes, chemicals and firearms are prohibited imports.

Travel within the country: Driving is on the left. An international driving permit is recommended to drive on the island. A valid foreign driving licence can be used to obtain a temporary visitor's permit for drivers between the ages of 25 and 65. Most roads are well maintained but are narrow, steep and winding. The speed limit is 32kph in towns and villages. Driving at night can be hazardous. Pedestrians walk on the road.

Bus services connect all towns and villages; taxis are efficient and reliable. Taxi rates are set by law and drivers do not expect to be tipped.

Travel health: Comprehensive travel insurance is recommended, including the cost of an air ambulance. Treatment must be paid for in advance. There are four main hospitals across the island as well as a few private clinics.

Visitors should take repellent and suitable loose-fitting clothing to prevent insect bites. Dengue fever outbreaks can occur and these are spread by day-biting mosquitoes.

Water is generally safe to drink but bottled water is advised, especially outside the main towns.

Money: American Express, Mastercard (limited) and Visa are accepted at hotels, restaurants, shops and ATMs located around the island. Foreign currencies can be exchanged at banks and bureaux de change. Banking hours are Mon–Thur 0800–1500, Fri 0800–1700.

There were 85,000 tourist arrivals in 2009.

Further information

Government of the Commonwealth of Dominica: www.dominica.gov.dm

House of Assembly: www.dominica.gov.dm/cms/index.php?q=node/13

Eastern Caribbean Central Bank: www.eccb-centralbank.org

Commonwealth Secretariat: www.thecommonwealth.org

Commonwealth of Nations: www.commonwealth-of-nations.org/Dominica

Fiji

Following the decisions taken by the Commonwealth Ministerial Action Group on 31 July 2009, Fiji was suspended from membership of the Commonwealth on 1 September 2009

KEY FACTS

Joined Commonwealth:	1970 (rejoined in 1997 after ten-year lapse)
Population:	861,000 (2010)
GDP p.c. growth:	1.2% p.a. 1990–2010
UN HDI 2011:	world ranking 100
Official language:	English
Time:	GMT plus 12
Currency:	Fiji dollar (F$)

Geography

Area:	18,333 sq km
Coastline:	1,130km
Capital:	Suva

The Republic of Fiji lies 1,850km north of Auckland, New Zealand, and 2,800km north-east of Sydney, Australia. It consists of about 300 islands (100 inhabited) and 540 islets, spread over 3 million sq km. It is surrounded by the island groups of (clockwise from north) Tuvalu, Wallis and Futuna, Tonga, New Caledonia, Vanuatu and Solomon Islands. The largest islands are Viti Levu ('Great Fiji'), Vanua Levu, Taveuni and Kadavu.

Area: Total land area is 18,333 sq km: Viti Levu 10,429 sq km; Vanua Levu 5,556 sq km.

Topography: Much of Fiji is volcanic in origin, with the larger islands featuring heavily populated coastal plains and uninhabited mountainous interiors. Many of the smaller islands have coral reefs. The highest point is Mt Tomanivi on Viti Levu (1,323m). The main rivers are the Sigatoka, Rewa and Ba on Viti Levu and the Dreketi on Vanua Levu; their deltas contain most of the country's arable land.

Did you know...

The Commonwealth Local Government Forum has its Pacific regional office in Suva, where it works to promote and strengthen democratic local government and encourage the exchange of good practice in the Pacific region.

The country is an archipelago of about 300 islands (100 inhabited) and 540 islets, spread over 3 million sq km, and has some 1,130km of coastline.

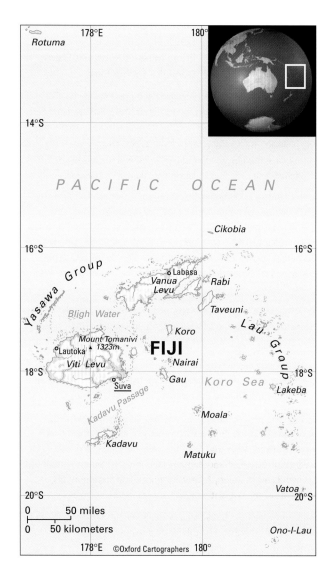

Climate: The climate is tropical and oceanic. South-east trade winds prevail; day temperatures range from 20 to 29°C and humidity is high. The rainy season is November to March throughout the country, though there is rain during June–September. On average, the country is affected by a hurricane every other year, for example Cyclone Ami in January 2003.

Environment: The most significant environmental issues are deforestation and soil erosion.

Vegetation: The distribution of the rainfall is the determining factor in the country's vegetation. Dense forests and coastal mangrove swamps are found in the east and grasslands, with coconut palms on the coasts, in the west. Forest covers 56% of the land area. Indigenous sandalwood resources were exhausted in the 19th century.

Wildlife: Fiji is home to six species of bat, including four fruit bats (flying-foxes), and the Polynesian rat. All other mammals have been introduced, mainly during the 19th and 20th centuries. There are more than 100 species of birds and several snakes and lizards, including the recently discovered crested iguana. Fiji's waters contain turtles, sharks, eels and prawns.

Main towns: Suva (capital, pop. 194,900 in 2010, comprising Nasinu 88,600 and Lami 20,600), Nausori (55,500), Lautoka (55,200), Nadi (47,000) and Ba (16,200) on Viti Levu; and Labasa (28,400) on Vanua Levu.

Transport: 3,440km of roads, 49% paved. The network is vulnerable to flooding and hurricane damage. A coastal road encircles Viti Levu, linked by smaller roads to the villages of the interior.

Lautoka, in the north-west of Viti Levu, is the main port; others are Suva, Levuka and Savusavu. Ferry services operate between the larger islands.

The main international airport is in western Viti Levu, at Nadi. Nausori, near Suva, is the hub for inter-island flights, and receives some international services. Most islands have airports or landing strips.

Society

KEY FACTS 2010

Population per sq km:	47
Life expectancy:	69 years
Net primary enrolment:	92%

Population: 861,000 (2010); 52% lives in urban areas; growth 0.8% p.a. 1990–2010; birth rate 22 per 1,000 people (34 in 1970); life expectancy 69 years (60 in 1970).

More than 50% of the people are ethnic Fijians, who are of mixed Melanesian–Polynesian origin, and most of the rest are of Indian origin. There are small populations of Europeans, Banabans, Tuvaluans and Chinese.

Language: The official language is English, but Fijian, of which there are more than 300 dialects, is widely spoken. A single dialect, Bauan, is used in the media. Hindi is the main language of the Indian population, although it is now distinct from that spoken in mainland India. English, Fijian and Hindi are all taught in schools and most of the population is at least bilingual.

Religion: Christians 65% (Methodists 35%, Roman Catholics 9%, Assembly of God 6%, Seventh Day Adventists 4%), Hindus 28%, Muslims 6%, small number of Sikhs (2007 census).

Health: Public spending on health was 3% of GDP in 2009. There is a comprehensive system providing universal health and dental services for nominal fees. There are 25 hospitals. The country is free of malaria. Infant mortality was 15 per 1,000 live births in 2010 (71 in 1960).

Education: Public spending on education was 4.6% of GDP in 2009. There are eight years of compulsory education starting at age six. Primary school comprises eight years and secondary three. Some 91% of pupils complete primary school (2007). The school year starts in January.

The main campuses of the regional University of the South Pacific (founded 1968) and the National University of Fiji are located in Suva. The University of the South Pacific has further campuses in Fiji, at Labasa and Lautoka. The National University was formed by the merger of seven tertiary institutions: the College of Advanced Education; College of Agriculture (Koronivia campus); Institute of

Technology (Samabula campus, Suva); Lautoka Teachers College (Lautoka campus); School of Medicine (Suva); School of Nursing (Suva); and Training and Productivity Authority, and has many campuses across the country. The School of Medicine and School of Nursing merged with the National University in 2010 to become the College of Medicine, Nursing and Health Sciences.

Media: Daily English-language newspapers are *Fiji Times* (founded 1869), *Fiji Sun* and *Daily Post* (1989), and there are a number of Fijian and Hindi weeklies.

Radio is a major source of information for most people, particularly on the outer islands. The Fiji Broadcasting Corporation provides national Fijian and Hindi services and there are a number of private radio stations. Fiji TV provides a national free-to-air channel and a pay-TV channel.

There are 60 personal computers (2005) and 148 internet users (2010) per 1,000 people.

Communications: Country code 679; internet domain '.fj'. Mobile phone coverage in the outer islands is patchy. There are internet cafes in Suva, Nadi, Lautoka and most resorts.

There are 151 main telephone lines and 811 mobile phone subscriptions per 1,000 people (2010).

Public holidays: New Year's Day, National Youth Day (Friday in March), Ratu Sir Lala Sukuna Day (late May), Queen's Official Birthday (Monday in June), Fiji Day (Monday around 10 October), Christmas Day and Boxing Day.

Religious and other festivals whose dates vary from year to year include Prophet's Birthday, Good Friday, Easter Monday and Diwali (October/November).

Economy

KEY FACTS 2010

GNI:	US$3.1bn
GNI p.c.:	US$3,630
GDP growth:	0.2% p.a. 2006–10
Inflation:	4.8% p.a. 2006–10

The Fijian economy is largely agricultural, and the main cash crop and export is sugar cane. Tourism is the largest foreign-exchange earner and clothing exports grew rapidly from the late 1980s. Other significant activities are gold-mining, fishing and timber production.

More than 80% of land is owned by ethnic Fijians, mainly by the local clans, or *mataqali*, and ownership by outsiders was prohibited from the late 19th century. Indo-Fijians were able to farm sugar cane under land lease arrangements. However, from the late 1990s, as leases came up for renewal, many landlords would only offer short leases at higher rents and many Indo-Fijian farmers have had to return the farms they have worked for many years to the owners.

Both sugar and tourism are vulnerable to the climate; hurricanes are relatively frequent and droughts can also cause problems, for example severe drought in 1997–98 was followed by cyclones and extensive flooding, and the islands were again devastated by Cyclone Ami in January 2003. Moreover tourists can be deterred by political instability.

Thus, economic growth has been uneven, with strong growth in years such as 1999 when the harvest is good and negative growth in years such as 2000 when the government was overthrown, some hotels were closed and tourist numbers fell sharply.

Real Growth in GDP

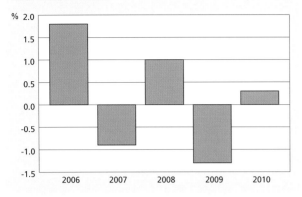

Inflation

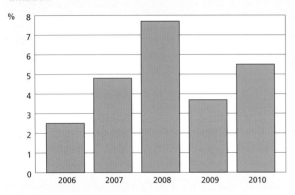

GDP by Sector (2010)

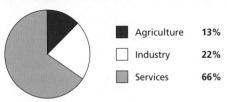

■ Agriculture	13%
□ Industry	22%
▨ Services	66%

After 2000, however, there were four years of good growth (5.3% in 2004), before a decline in clothing exports (due to ending of US market quotas at end 2004) caused much slower growth in 2005. There was a recovery in 2006, but following the coup of December 2006 tourist numbers fell by 70% and the economy shrank by 0.9% in 2007, stagnating in 2008–10, in the face of the global recession.

Constitution

Status:	Republic
Legislature:	Parliament
Independence:	10 October 1970

Fiji's constitution has always reflected the multiracial nature of its society. It provides for a parliamentary democracy with a bicameral parliament comprising an elected House of Representatives and appointed Senate. Some seats in the House of Representatives are reserved for ethnic Fijians, some for Indo-Fijians and some for other ethnic groups. Following the 1987 coups, Fiji became a republic, with a president appointed by the Great Council of Chiefs (Bose Levu Vakaturaga, a body comprising the heads of the ethnic Fijian clans), for a five-year term as head of state. The president appoints as prime minister the member of the House of Representatives who

commands the support of the majority, normally the leader of the largest party or coalition. The prime minister then forms a government which has executive authority. Constitutional amendments require a 75% majority in both houses.

Under the 1997 constitution, the number of seats in the House of Representatives was increased to 71, 25 of which were opened to all ethnic groups (elected by universal suffrage), while the remainder were to be elected by separate communal electoral rolls in the following proportions: ethnic Fijians 23; Indo-Fijians 19; other ethnic groups three; and Rotuman Islanders one. The Senate has 32 members, 14 appointed by the Great Council of Chiefs, nine by the prime minister, eight by the leader of the opposition and one by the Council of Rotuma. The prime ministership, but not the presidency, was opened to all Fijians. In addition, the first-past-the-post electoral system was replaced by an alternative preference system and voting became mandatory. Parties taking more than 10% of the votes in a general election have the right to a number of cabinet posts in proportion to the numbers of votes received.

Politics

Last elections:	May 2006
Next elections:	date uncertain
Head of state:	President Ratu Epeli Nailatikau*
Head of government:	Interim Prime Minister Commodore Voreqe Bainimarama*

In October 2000, President Ratu Josefa Iloilo appointed a constitutional review commission to recommend a new constitutional arrangement for Fiji. In December 2000, Commonwealth Secretary-General Don McKinnon appointed Justice Pius N Langa, Deputy President of the Constitutional Court of South Africa, as his special envoy to help accelerate the restoration of democracy and promote national unity.

A general election was held under the new constitution from 25 August to 5 September 2001 when 26 political parties participated (ten more than in 1999). In a poll that was judged by international including Commonwealth observers to reflect the will of the people, Soqosoqo Duavata ni Lewenivanua (SDL) took 32 seats, pushing the Fiji Labour Party (FLP – 27 seats) into second place, followed by Matanitu Vanua (six). SDL leader and head of the interim government Laisenia Qarase was sworn in as prime minister. Following the country's return to democratic government, the suspension from Commonwealth councils (which had been in force since June 2000) was lifted in December 2001.

A row soon erupted, however, when Qarase failed to appoint any FLP members to his cabinet or the Senate. An impasse continued, with Qarase only prepared to appoint ministers he felt he could work with, and FLP leader Mahendra Chaudhry insisting on his constitutional rights. In February 2002 the High Court ruled Qarase had failed to comply with the constitution when he appointed his cabinet and in July 2003 the Supreme Court upheld this judgment. But the impasse endured, with the two parties unable to agree on a list of cabinet appointments, the key issues being the number of FLP members (14 or 17) and whether Chaudhry himself should be included.

The May 2006 general election was won by SDL with 36 seats, while FLP took 31 seats and the United People's Party (UPP) two. Commonwealth observers present reported that the result reflected the wishes of the people. Qarase continued as prime minister and, in accordance with the constitution, appointed a cabinet in which

Archaeological evidence suggests that Fiji has been inhabited, initially by Melanesian peoples, for more than 3,500 years. The first known contact with Europeans occurred in 1643, when the islands of Vanua Levu and Taveuni were explored by Abel Tasman. British explorers including Captains James Cook and William Bligh passed through in the late 18th century. By this time, the population was mixed, with Melanesians occupying the eastern areas and Polynesians the islands' interiors, organised into a complex hierarchical society.

The first American ships arrived in the 19th century, bringing adventurers attracted by the resources of sandalwood (which were exhausted within ten years) and subsequently traders and Christian missionaries. Later, Europeans began establishing cotton plantations but came into conflict with the Fijians over land, political power and the use of imported labour. The increasing availability of guns caused inter-tribal conflicts to escalate but by the mid-19th century, a single clan dominated, led first by Nauvilou and subsequently by his son Cakobau, and based on the small island of Bau to the south-east of Viti Levu. The Bauan dialect of Fijian consequently became the predominant Fijian language, and an important factor in unifying the clans. Cakobau converted to Methodist Christianity in 1854; in 1874, following British concerns over the interests of the settlers, Cakobau agreed that Fiji should become a Crown colony. In 1881, Rotuma Island in northern Fiji, inhabited by Polynesian people, was added to the territory.

The first governor, Sir Arthur Gordon, collaborated with the local chiefs to protect the traditional ways of life. He forbade the sale of land to non-Fijians, levied taxes in kind and retained the existing political structures. He also encouraged the growth of the sugar industry, and its use of Indian labour. From the 1920s, Indians began to call for more commercial and political influence and, by 1943, despite the restrictions on land ownership, they were in the majority.

The country progressed towards independence through the 1960s, largely in response to international and British pressure, while internally there were divisions over the appropriate forms of government able to provide democracy while protecting the rights of the ethnic Fijians. The resulting constitution offered universal suffrage, with guarantees for Fijian land rights, and the Fijian chiefs, through their dominance of the Senate, had in effect a veto on constitutional change. Fiji became independent on 10 October 1970.

Until 1987, the government was formed by the Alliance Party led by Ratu (Chief) Sir Kamisese Mara which followed policies of moderate multiracialism. The largest Indo-Fijian party, the National Federation Party (NFP), formed the main opposition for most of the period and calls from Indo-Fijians for greater political and property rights increased.

Elections in April 1987 resulted in victory for a coalition consisting of the NFP and the Fiji Labour Party (FLP), led by Dr Timoci Bavadra and supported by both ethnic Fijian and Indo-Fijian trades unions. Bavadra, an ethnic Fijian, became prime minister, but there were Indo-Fijian majorities in both the House of

Representatives and the cabinet. In May 1987 the government was overthrown in a coup led by Lieutenant-Colonel Sitiveni Rabuka, who called for the ethnic Fijian dominance of all future governments.

The May 1987 coup was followed by a period of racial unrest, during which the Great Council of Chiefs attempted to introduce constitutional reforms. Mediated by the governor-general, Ratu Sir Penaia Ganilau, negotiations between Mara and Bavadra resulted in the formation of an interim government of unity.

However, Rabuka led a second coup in September 1987 and in October he declared Fiji a republic. Having become a republic, it was then required to reapply for membership of the Commonwealth and, at their summit in Vancouver in October 1987, Commonwealth Heads of Government decided to allow its membership to lapse, primarily on the grounds that Fiji had adopted a form of government at variance with the democratically expressed wish of the people and so with Commonwealth principles. In December 1987 Rabuka appointed a new civilian government with Mara as prime minister and Ganilau as president.

Between 1988 and 1990, a new constitution was drawn up and approved by the Great Council of Chiefs, but the National Federation Party–Fiji Labour Party coalition announced it would boycott any elections held under its provisions. The constitution was also the subject of international criticism, especially from the Commonwealth led by India, Australia and New Zealand.

Fiji resumed its membership of the Commonwealth in October 1997. Its new 1997 constitution came into force in July 1998. At elections in May 1999 the incumbent Fijian Political Party (SVT, with only eight of the 71 seats in the lower house) and the NFP (no seats) were ousted by a coalition led by the FLP (37 seats) that included the Fijian Association Party (ten), the Party of National Unity (four) and the recently formed Christian Democratic Alliance (three). The turnout was high at these elections where voting was compulsory.

Following his victory, FLP leader Mahendra Chaudhry became the first Indo-Fijian prime minister and, despite his party's overall majority in the House of Representatives, he formed a cabinet representing all four of the coalition partners. His priorities were to defuse ethnic tensions and restore economic growth after the sharp contractions of 1997–99. Soon after the elections, Rabuka resigned from the leadership of the SVT.

In May 2000, armed ethnic Fijians, led by George Speight, overthrew the government, occupying the parliament building and taking about 40 hostages – including the prime minister. There then ensued continuous negotiations between the army and the rebels until the deadlock was finally broken in July, when the hostages were released, a new civilian president and 'emergency' government were appointed and backed by the military. In June the country was suspended from the councils of the Commonwealth pending the restoration of democracy. In July Speight and some of his supporters were arrested and charged with treason.

nine posts were filled by FLP. FLP leader Chaudhry declined a position for himself.

In December 2006 the army took control of government dismissing the prime minister and president; and head of the army Commodore Voreqe Bainimarama assumed the presidency. This coup was immediately condemned by the international community and at a meeting of the Commonwealth Ministerial Action Group (CMAG) on 8 December Fiji's military regime was suspended from the councils of the Commonwealth pending restoration of democracy and the rule of law in the country. In January 2007 Bainimarama reinstated the president and became interim prime minister.

Fiji's Court of Appeal ruled in April 2009 that the military coup, which ousted the elected government in 2006, and the interim government that followed it were illegal. The ruling requested that the president appoint an interim prime minister and call a general election. In response, President Iloilo announced that he had abrogated the constitution and dismissed all the judges. He appointed himself as head of government and subsequently reinstated Bainimarama as prime minister.

In July 2009 Bainimarama announced the retirement of Iloilo from the presidency; Vice-President Ratu Epeli Nailatikau assumed the role of acting president and in November 2009 was confirmed as president.

Following Fiji's suspension from the councils of the Commonwealth in December 2006, sustained efforts were made by the Commonwealth to engage the interim government to promote a return to constitutional democracy and to encourage a national dialogue aimed at tackling the underlying issues that led to military coups. On 1 September 2009, having failed to satisfy CMAG that it was committed to a timetable for restoring democracy, Fiji was fully suspended from the Commonwealth. In announcing this, Commonwealth Secretary-General Kamalesh Sharma said that the Commonwealth remained open to engaging with the interim government towards the restoration of constitutional democracy.

At their biennial meeting in Perth, Australia, in October 2011, Commonwealth Heads of Government urged the interim government of Fiji to restore democracy without further delay, to respect human rights and to uphold the rule of law, and reaffirmed that the Commonwealth should continue to remain engaged with Fiji and support efforts towards that end.

* Following the decisions taken by the Commonwealth Ministerial Action Group on 31 July 2009, Fiji was fully suspended from membership of the Commonwealth on 1 September 2009.*

International relations

Fiji is a member of the African, Caribbean and Pacific Group of States, Pacific Community, United Nations and World Trade Organization.

Fiji was suspended from participation in the Pacific Islands Forum in May 2009, pending the country's return to constitutional democracy through free and fair elections.

Traveller information

Local laws and conventions: Fiji has a strict drugs policy and possession of marijuana carries a mandatory prison sentence.

Since the military coup of December 2006 visitors have been advised to exercise extra caution.

For business meetings, lightweight suits are customary. Businesswomen should dress modestly and cover their shoulders. Office hours are Mon–Fri 0830–1700.

Immigration and customs: Visa requirements are essential for some nationals and should be checked before entering the country. Business travellers are only allowed to stay for 14 days. All passports must be valid for six months on arrival. There is an airport departure tax.

A yellow fever certificate is required from those who have travelled from an infected area.

No meat or dairy products may be brought into Fiji from Europe because of foot and mouth disease, and the import of vegetables and seeds requires a special permit.

Travel within the country: Driving is on the left. The minimum age for car hire is 21 and seatbelts must be worn in the front seats. A valid national or international driving permit is required and third party insurance is compulsory. The national speed limit is 80kph. Livestock may wander freely on to the roads. Driving from Suva to Nadi takes approximately three hours.

Buses are efficient and cheap, and there are frequent services around the islands.

Taxis and minibuses bearing a yellow registration plate comply with Land Transport Authority regulations. The cost of a taxi ride should always be checked before starting out on a journey.

Air Fiji and Pacific Sun operate air shuttle services around the islands. Ferries run by Patterson Brothers, Beachcomber and Consort Shipping serve the larger islands.

Travel health: Health care in Fiji meets most of the World Health Organization goals and is generally good, although full medical insurance is advised. There is a private hospital in Suva.

Typhoid, leptospirosis and dengue fever can occur in Fiji, and visitors must ensure they take insect repellent and suitable clothing to avoid mosquito bites. Vaccinations for Hepatitis A, tetanus and typhoid are recommended but up-to-date inoculation requirements should be checked well before departure.

Tap water is safe to drink in the main towns and resorts but visitors must ensure that it has been boiled or sterilised when visiting rural areas.

Money: Currency exchange is available at the airport and in most hotels as well as in banks on Viti Levu. Most hotels and restaurants accept credit cards but not all ATMs accept all cards. Resorts accept cards but there are limited facilities for obtaining cash. Those travelling to the islands should take sufficient cash with them. Banking hours are Mon–Fri 0800–1700.

There were 632,000 tourist arrivals in 2010.

Further information

Fiji Government: www.fiji.gov.fj

Parliament: www.parliament.gov.fj

Reserve Bank of Fiji: www.reservebank.gov.fj

Commonwealth Secretariat: www.thecommonwealth.org

Commonwealth of Nations: www.commonwealth-of-nations.org/Fiji

The Gambia

Joined Commonwealth:	1965
Population:	1,728,000 (2010)
GDP p.c. growth:	0.1% p.a. 1990–2010
UN HDI 2011:	world ranking 168
Official language:	English
Time:	GMT
Currency:	dalasi (D)

Geography

Area:	11,295 sq km
Coastline:	80km
Capital:	Banjul

The Republic of The Gambia is the smallest country in West Africa. Apart from a stretch of coastline along the Atlantic Ocean, it is entirely surrounded by Senegal.

Topography: The Gambia consists of a long narrow ribbon of land on either side of the River Gambia, one of the major African waterways. At the estuary, the northern and southern boundaries are 45km apart, but the belt of land narrows to about 20km inland. The terrain is generally flat and low-lying; the island capital Banjul (formerly Bathurst) is situated only one metre above sea level. Away from the coast the country rises to a low plateau with flat-topped hills in a few places. From Georgetown to the eastern boundary the area is enclosed by rocky hills. The coast has sand cliffs and 50km of unspoilt silver-sand beaches.

Climate: The climate is tropical with distinct dry and rainy seasons. The dry season at the coast, coinciding with the cooler weather, runs from mid-November to mid-May; the hot rainy season is June to October. The weather is hot and humid inland, with mid-day temperatures up to 38°C in March–June. The harmattan blows from the Sahara in January–March, bringing dust and haze.

Environment: The most significant environmental issues are deforestation, desertification, and the prevalence of water-borne diseases. Erosion of the coastal sand cliffs, caused both by the sea and by sand mining for the construction industry, is a dangerous possibility.

Did you know...

A Gambian citizen, Abdoulie Janneh, was the Regional Director for Africa of the United Nations Development Programme 2000–05, and in 2005 became Executive Secretary of the UN Economic Commission for Africa.

The country hosts a national chapter of the Commonwealth Human Ecology Council.

Vegetation: There are mangrove swamps along the river and its creeks. Tropical forest and bamboo grow on the red ironstone banks of the lower river. Away from the river there is savannah; mahogany, rosewood, oil palm and rubber cover large areas. Forest covers 48% of the land area, having increased at 0.4% p.a. 1990–2010. Arable land comprises 40% of the total land area.

Wildlife: The Gambian wildlife is rich and impressive, including hippos, small game and many small mammals. Concern for wildlife led to the Banjul Declaration of 1977 which aims to conserve and protect as wide a spectrum as possible of the remaining fauna and flora. The Gambia also has an exotic and varied birdlife and the country is becoming an increasingly popular paradise for bird-watchers. There are more than 280 different species, including the rare Egyptian plover. With the River Gambia a dominant feature of the country, fish are plentiful.

Main towns: Banjul (capital, pop. 32,900 in 2010), Serekunda (391,100), Brikama (94,800), Bakau (64,500), Lamin (34,900), Nema Kunku (32,200), Farafenni (28,900), Brufut (28,300), Gunjur (25,200), Basse Santa-Su (17,500) and Sukuta (17,100).

Transport: There are 3,740km of roads, 19% paved. Roads in and around Banjul are mostly bituminised; unsealed roads can be impassable in the rainy season. There is no railway.

The River Gambia extends, east–west, the entire length of the country, providing a vital communications link for cargo and passengers. The river is navigable by ocean-going vessels up to Kuntaur (240km upstream) and by shallow draught vessels up to Basse Santa Su (418km). Exports (mostly groundnuts) are carried down the river to Banjul. The principal port is at Banjul, serving the international and river trade.

Banjul International Airport is situated at Yundum, 29km south-west of the city.

Society

KEY FACTS 2010

Population per sq km:	153
Life expectancy:	58 years
Net primary enrolment:	76%

Population: 1,728,000 (2010); 58% lives in urban areas; growth 2.9% p.a. 1990–2010; birth rate 38 per 1,000 people (49 in 1970); life expectancy 58 years (36 in 1970).

Mandinka people constitute 42% of total population, followed (in descending order of population) by Fula (18%), Wolof (16%), Jola (10%) and Sarahuli (9%, 2003 census). There is also a community of Akus (Creoles), descended mainly from Africans freed from slavery in the early 19th century.

Language: English is the official language. Local languages are Mandinka (widely spoken in the provinces), Fula, Wolof (widely spoken in Banjul), Jola and Sarahuli.

Religion: Muslims about 90%, the rest mostly Christians. Traditional animist religions are often practised alongside both of these religions.

Health: Public spending on health was 3% of GDP in 2009. The country relies partially on expatriate doctors: when Chinese doctors working in the country were recalled in 1995, Cuban doctors replaced them. There are hospitals at Banjul, Bansang and a new one at Farafenni opened in 1998. In addition there are health centres and dispensaries. Traditional healers and midwives are well established in rural areas. There is a leprosy control programme. 92% of the population uses an improved drinking water source and 67% have adequate sanitation facilities (2009). Infant mortality was 57 per 1,000 live births in 2010 (207 in 1960). In 2009, 2.0% of people aged 15–49 were HIV positive.

Education: Public spending on education was 5.0% of GDP in 2010. There are nine years of primary education – comprising cycles of six and three years – and five years of secondary – three and two years. Some 61% of pupils complete primary school (2009). The school year starts in September.

Technical and vocational training are provided at Gambia Technical Training Institute, which opened in 1983, and higher education at University of The Gambia. Literacy among people aged 15–24 is 66% (2009).

Media: Newspapers are in English and include *Daily Observer*, *Foroyaa*, *The Independent* and *The Point* (daily).

The national radio station, Radio Gambia, broadcasts in English and Gambian languages. Gambia Television is the public television station. Privately-owned radio stations and satellite TV compete with the public services.

Some 12% of households have TV sets (2006). There are 35 personal computers (2007) and 92 internet users (2010) per 1,000 people.

Communications: Country code 220; internet domain '.gm'. Mobile phone coverage is patchy in the rural areas. Main towns have internet cafes and post offices.

There are 28 main telephone lines and 855 mobile phone subscriptions per 1,000 people (2010).

Public holidays: New Year's Day, Independence Day (18 February), Labour Day (1 May), Revolution Day (22 July). Assumption (15 August) and Christmas Day.

Religious and other festivals whose dates vary from year to year include Prophet's Birthday, Good Friday, Easter Monday, Koriteh (End of Ramadan), Tabaski (Feast of the Sacrifice) and Al-Hijra (Islamic New Year).

Economy

KEY FACTS 2010

GNI:	US$770m
GNI p.c.:	US$450
GDP growth:	4.6% p.a. 2006–10
Inflation:	4.3% p.a. 2006–10

The Gambia, with its command of an important river system, has considerable potential in trade – depending on development of the hinterland. It is an economically disadvantaged country, hampered by its small size, lack of mineral or other natural resources, and rudimentary infrastructure. The economy rests on agriculture (especially on groundnut production) and tourism, though there is a

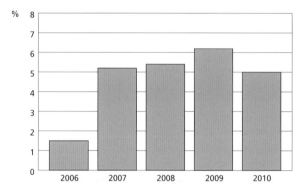

Real Growth in GDP

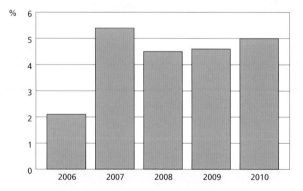

Inflation

GDP by Sector (2010)

■	Agriculture	**32%**
□	Industry	**11%**
▥	Services	**57%**

small-scale processing industry. The largest trading activity by far has been the re-export of imported goods to neighbouring countries (Guinea, Guinea–Bissau, Liberia, Mali, Mauritania and Senegal).

Agricultural production suffered during the droughts of the last two decades, although The Gambia is less vulnerable than its Sahel neighbours. Tourism, the most important source of foreign exchange revenue, flagged in the wake of an abortive coup in 1981 and again after the successful coup of 1994. However,

tourism revenue recovered in 1996, and by 1998 the number of tourist arrivals had overtaken pre-coup levels.

Foreign aid has been vital in developing the infrastructure. From 1985, policy was focused on economic reforms backed by the IMF, leading to a long period of sustained growth with relatively low inflation. The reforms were continued after the 1994 coup, including some privatisation. In 2000, South African electricity company Eskom purchased a 50% stake in electricity and water utility NAWEC.

History

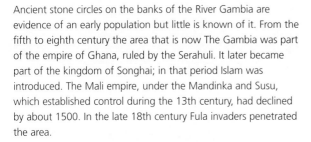

Ancient stone circles on the banks of the River Gambia are evidence of an early population but little is known of it. From the fifth to eighth century the area that is now The Gambia was part of the empire of Ghana, ruled by the Serahuli. It later became part of the kingdom of Songhai; in that period Islam was introduced. The Mali empire, under the Mandinka and Susu, which established control during the 13th century, had declined by about 1500. In the late 18th century Fula invaders penetrated the area.

Europeans started to explore and settle the coast and river area from the 15th century. In 1455 and 1456, Portuguese-sponsored expeditions began exploring the river; the attractions were rumours of gold (in fact gold was shipped down the River Gambia from the interior) and the opportunities for slaving, with local business co-operation. From the 17th century up to and even after the trade became illegal in 1807 the river was a focus for the European slave-trade.

During the 17th century various English and French adventurers and semi-official expeditions came and went, on the trail of gold and slaves. There were Portuguese communities living on the river banks until the mid-18th century, and much intermarriage with local people. From the 18th century the French and the British struggled for control of the region. Between 1765 and 1783 The Gambia and Senegal were combined into the province of Senegambia, under French administration. The British settlement of James Island was recognised by the Treaty of Versailles in 1783.

In the early 19th century Britain established a military post on Banjul island (then called Bathurst) in order to suppress the slave traffic on the River Gambia carried on by American and Spanish vessels. In 1823, MacCarthy Island (270km up-river) became a settlement for liberated slaves. In 1888, alarmed by French influence in Senegal, Britain seized the river and the land on both sides of it; thus The Gambia became a separate country, the downstream part of the country being a colony and the upstream part a protectorate, and a Gambian legislature was established. Previously, the much smaller territory had been administered from Sierra Leone. A legislative council gradually became more representative as progress towards independence was made.

During the 1950s political parties emerged. In 1960, in elections held under a new constitution, the People's Progressive Party established itself. After further constitutional changes, the country became internally self-governing in 1963 and achieved independence on 18 February 1965, with Queen Elizabeth II, represented by a governor-general, as head of state.

In 1970, following a referendum, a republican constitution was introduced. The 1970 constitution enshrined the strong

traditional structures by giving a voice in the legislature to the chiefs.

The Gambia's location, enclosed by Senegal, has suggested the benefits of some form of union between the countries. The Senegambian Confederation, established in 1982 after Senegalese troops had intervened to help deal with an attempted coup, was a loose arrangement bringing benefits to both countries. The Confederation was dissolved in 1989, however, after Gambian resistance to closer union, but in May 1991 the two countries signed a treaty of friendship and co-operation.

After re-election on five occasions (the country retaining multiparty democracy under his 29-year leadership), President Dawda Jawara was deposed in a bloodless coup by junior army officers in July 1994. Captain Yahya Jammeh then set up the Armed Forces Provisional Ruling Council, which pledged a return to democratic civilian government.

An 11-member constitutional commission, chaired by a Ghanaian judge and including British, American and Malawian lawyers, prepared a draft new constitution in 1995. A national referendum on the draft constitution was held in August 1996, and the ban on political activity lifted in the same month (although ex-President Jawara and the leaders of the three main opposition parties were barred). The presidential election was held in September 1996, and won by Jammeh, with 55% of the votes. Three days after this election, the Commonwealth Ministerial Action Group (CMAG) raised serious doubts about the credibility of the poll.

In January 1997, parliamentary elections were contested by Jammeh's party, the Alliance for Patriotic Reorientation and Construction (APRC), the United Democratic Party (UDP) led by Ousainou Darboe, the People's Democratic Organisation for Independence and Socialism (PDOIS), the National Reconciliation Party (NRP) and five independents. The APRC – the only party able to contest every seat – won with a more than two-thirds majority – securing 33 seats. The UDP – which had agreed to take part on condition political detainees were released and the army and security forces did not interfere in the electoral process – won seven; the NRP two; and the PDOIS one. CMAG concluded that these were conducted in a freer atmosphere than the presidential election in September 1996.

The National Assembly was inaugurated in January 1997, and adopted the new constitution. Political prisoners, including ministers of the Jawara government and UDP supporters arrested before the elections, were released in February and charges dropped. In April 1997, the restoration of a civilian government was completed when the four remaining regional military governors were replaced by civilians.

The country's stock of external debt fell from 110% to 50% of GDP after completion of the IMF/World Bank Heavily Indebted Poor Countries and Multilateral Debt Relief Initiatives at the end of 2007. Growth was sustained at more than 5% p.a. 2008–10, despite the extremely adverse economic climate due to the global recession.

The good growth of the 1990s continued into the 2000s and was interrupted only by a dip into recession in 2002; it averaged over 5% p.a. 2003–11, despite the global economic downturn of 2008–09. This impressive growth was sustained by the construction, tourism and telecommunications sectors, and a steady flow of foreign investment.

Constitution

Status:	Republic with executive president
Legislature:	National Assembly
Independence:	18 February 1965

The 1997 constitution provides for a unitary republican democracy, with the president, vice-president and secretaries of state responsible to parliament. The unicameral parliament, the National Assembly, has a five-year term. Five members are nominated by the president, 48 directly elected under universal suffrage. The president is also elected by direct universal suffrage for a five-year term, and there is no limit on the number of terms he may serve. Executive power resides in the president, vice-president and cabinet, both of whom are appointed by the president. The voting age is 18; there is an ombudsman. The constitution provides for an independent judiciary and allows for declaration of a state of emergency, and for special courts to try cases of corruption. A two-thirds majority in parliament is required to change the constitution.

Politics

Last elections:	November 2011 (presidential), January 2007 (parliamentary)
Next elections:	2016 (presidential), 2012 (parliamentary)
Head of state:	President Sheikh Professor Alhaji Dr Yahya Jammeh
Head of government:	the president
Ruling party:	Alliance for Patriotic Reorientation and Construction

In the presidential election in October 2001, the second since restoration of multiparty democracy, Yahya Jammeh won a second term with 53% of the votes, Ousainou Darboe of the United Democratic Party (UDP) came second with 33% and Hamat Bah of the National Reconciliation Party (NRP) third with 8%. Commonwealth observers were present at the election.

This was followed in January 2002 by parliamentary elections when Jammeh's Alliance for Patriotic Reorientation and Construction (APRC) gained virtually all seats in the National Assembly. The elections were boycotted by the UDP – claiming that the electoral roll had been manipulated – and the APRC was unopposed in 33 of the 48 seats. Because of the UDP boycott, the Commonwealth decided not to observe the elections.

Jammeh was returned for a third term with 67% of the votes in the presidential election of September 2006, which was again attended by Commonwealth observers. Darboe (UDP) received

27% of the votes and Halifa Sallah (National Alliance for Democracy and Development) 6%.

In the parliamentary elections that followed in January 2007 the APRC won 42 seats and the UDP four, and the turnout was 42%.

In the presidential election in November 2011 Jammeh won with 72% of the votes; Darboe (UDP) received 17% and Hamat Bah (United Front coalition) 11%. A Commonwealth expert team concluded that, while the elections were peaceful and technically sound, democratic reforms were needed.

International relations

The Gambia is a member of the African, Caribbean and Pacific Group of States, African Union, Economic Community of West African States, Non-Aligned Movement, Organisation of Islamic Cooperation, United Nations and World Trade Organization.

Traveller information

Local laws and conventions: The Gambia is a predominantly Muslim country, and local customs and sensitivities should be respected at all times – especially outside the tourist areas and during the month of Ramadan.

Strong action is taken against anyone importing, exporting or in possession of drugs, and visitors must not accept any packages without inspecting the contents.

Photography of military and official installations is prohibited.

Visitors to the country must have some form of identification on them at all times.

Gambians greet each other by shaking hands. It is customary not to touch food with the left hand.

Casual wear should be confined to the beach. Businessmen should wear jackets and ties, and businesswomen should ensure they dress modestly with shoulders covered and skirts (not trousers) below the knee. Business cards are appreciated. Business hours are Mon–Thur 0800–1600, Fri 0800–1230.

Immigration and customs: Those planning to travel to the country should check entry requirements. Passports must be valid for three months from the date of entry. Single parents travelling with children should carry documentation showing parental responsibility.

Travel within the country: Driving is on the right-hand side. Greater Banjul has a few local and international car hire firms, and an international driving permit will be accepted for up to three months. The best roads are found around Banjul; elsewhere, there is an ongoing programme of road-building and repair but driving outside Greater Banjul can be difficult.

Care must be taken when approaching security checkpoints, as they are not always well lit.

Bush taxis travel between towns and villages, and fares are fixed. Tourist taxis are green and licensed; local taxis are yellow and can be hailed in the street. Fares should be agreed before travelling.

There are many crossing points on the River Gambia either by boat or vehicle and passenger ferries. Tour operators run adventure and fishing trips on converted pirogues.

Travel health: Travellers are advised to have comprehensive medical insurance.

Malaria and water-borne diseases are widespread throughout November, and visitors will need to take insect repellent and loose-fitting clothing to prevent insect bites. Sunscreen and diarrhoea medicine should also be packed, as they may not be easily obtainable locally. Bilharzia is present, so swimming in fresh stagnant water must be avoided. Current vaccination recommendations for The Gambia should be checked before travelling.

It is safe to drink mains water in urban and resort areas, but in all other regions water for drinking, brushing teeth or making ice must be boiled. Powdered and tinned milk is recommended.

Travellers who need prescription medicines should bring them in a sealed container, clearly labelled to avoid misunderstandings.

Money: The Gambia is a cash economy and very few places accept credit cards. There are ATMs in Senegambia, a major tourist area, which accept Visa but not Mastercard. Travellers cheques or cash can be changed at bureaux de change. Banking hours are Mon–Thur 0800–1330, Fri 0800–1100 and Sat 0800–1300.

There were 91,000 tourist arrivals in 2010.

Further information

Republic of The Gambia State House Online: www.statehouse.gm

National Assembly: www.thegambianationalassembly.gm

Central Bank of The Gambia: www.cbg.gm

Commonwealth Secretariat: www.thecommonwealth.org

Commonwealth of Nations: www.commonwealth-of-nations.org/Gambia%60_The

National Sports Authority, Ghana

Propelling Ghana to high international recognition

Mission statement

The National Sports Authority exists to develop, organise promote and manage competitive and social sports with the view to promoting health, fitness, recreation, national cohesion and professionalism that ensures sustainable wealth creation, vigorous infrastructure development and proactive management which leads to sports excellence and international recognition.

We foster teamwork and pursue the highest standard of excellence, honesty, fairplay, innovation and productivity in our service delivery.

Our human resources, being our most treasured assets, operates in a congenial working environment and are continually developed and motivated to instil loyalty, devotion and commitment to win the respect of our stakeholders.

Objectives

1. To promote and encourage the organisation and development of, and mass participation in, amateur and professional sports in Ghana
2. To co-ordinate and integrate all efforts to raise the standards of performance in amateur and professional sports throughout Ghana

Functions of NSA

1. Organise and assist the participation of Ghanaian sportsmen and sportswomen in amateur and professional sports at district, regional, national and international levels
2. Be responsible for taking insurance cover for all sportsmen, sportswomen and sports officials chosen to represent Ghana
3. Provide financial assistance to any team or person for the purpose of enabling that team or person to represent Ghana in international competitions
4. Encourage Ghanaians to participate in sporting activities in or outside Ghana
5. Provide sports instructors to any person, team or organisation
6. Provide and maintain sports centres and facilities for use by all sportsmen and sportswomen
7. Maintain all playing fields and stadia provided by the body known as the National Playing Fields Board
8. Promote the establishment of both amateur and professional associations of sports at districts, regional and national levels
9. Provide financial assistance to all such sporting associations as appear to the National Council to be deserving of such assistance
10. Provide the Regional Sports Councils with such financial and other assistance to encourage and develop sports effectively in their respective regions
11. Undertake and encourage research in to all sports relating matters
12. Provide funding for the holding of special sports festivals

Honourable Minister Clement Kofi Humado, Minister of Youth and Sport

Contact

Mr Wolanyo Agra
Director General
National Sports Authority
P.O.Box 1272
Accra Sports Stadium
Osu-Accra

Tel: +233 302 66 2281
info@sportscouncil.com.gh

Let's Commemorate
Let's live
Let's grow
Let's unite

Ghana

KEY FACTS

Joined Commonwealth:	1957
Population:	24,392,000 (2010)
GDP p.c. growth:	2.4% p.a. 1990–2010
UN HDI 2011:	world ranking 135
Official language:	English
Time:	GMT
Currency:	cedi (¢)

Geography

Area:	238,537 sq km
Coastline:	539km
Capital:	Accra

The Republic of Ghana, formerly the Gold Coast, is a West African country lying on the Gulf of Guinea. It is surrounded (clockwise, from the west) by Côte d'Ivoire, Burkina Faso, Togo. Ghana has ten regions: Greater Accra, Ashanti, Brong Ahafo, Central, Eastern, Northern, Upper East, Upper West, Volta and Western. After Greater Accra, Ashanti is the most populated region; Upper West, the least.

Topography: The Black Volta, Red Volta and White Volta rivers merge into one river Volta, which has been dammed at Akosombo to form Lake Volta (approximately 8,482 sq km). There are hills to the north (averaging 500m), but the country is generally flat. The central forest area is broken up into ridges and valleys. There are lagoons on the coast, and many sandy beaches with coconut trees.

Climate: Tropical; warm and fairly dry in northern areas, hot and humid on the coastal belt. Temperatures usually range between 21°C and 32°C. Annual rainfall varies from 700mm to 2,150mm. In 2007, large parts of West Africa were the subject of severe flooding. Ghana was the worst hit with more than 300,000 of its people made homeless.

Did you know...

Kofi Annan, former Secretary-General of the United Nations, delivered the 3rd Annual Commonwealth Lecture, on 'Africa Wants to Trade its Way out of Poverty', in 2000.

Four Ghanaians have been regional winners in the Commonwealth Writers' Prize: Ama Ata Aidoo (1992), Lawrence Darmani (1992), Lucy Safo (1994) and Benjamin Kwakye (1999 and 2006).

Abédi Pelé, born in Accra, Ghana, in 1964, was voted African Footballer of the Year in 1991, 1992 and 1993.

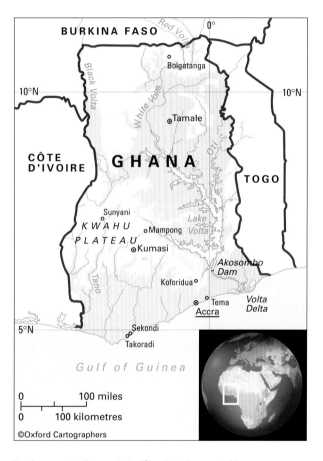

Environment: The most significant environmental issues are deforestation, overgrazing, soil erosion; drought in the north; poaching and habitat destruction threatening wildlife populations; and water pollution and inadequate supplies of drinking water.

Vegetation: Grass occurs on much of the central plain, dense rainforest in the south and west; woodland and dry savannah to the north. Forest covers 22% of the land area, having declined at 2.0% p.a. 1990–2010. Arable land comprises 19% and permanent cropland 11% of the total land area.

Wildlife: Ghana is rich in animal life and had in 2003 protected areas comprising 5.6% of the total land area. The Mole National Park comprises some 736 sq km in the western part of the northern region of Damonoyo and has many species including elephants, hippos, eagles, kites and hornbills. The Digya National Park on the shores of Lake Volta has hippos, water buck, crocodiles and manatees. There are 222 species of mammals, 14 of which are endangered, and 206 species of birds, eight endangered.

Main towns: Accra (capital, pop. 2.45m in 2010), Kumasi (Ashanti, 1.93m), Tamale (Northern, 466,700), Ashiaman (Greater Accra, 289,100), Takoradi (Western, 273,900), Cape Coast

Ministry of Employment and

Employment opportunities for Ghana

The Ministry of Employment and Social Welfare exists to promote sustainable employment opportunities, management and vocational skills development, training and re-training, harmonious industrial relations, safe and group formation and social integration of vulnerable, excluded and the disadvantaged for the development and growth of the economy.

MANDATE

The Ministry's mandate is to facilitate the development of human resources, create an environment conducive to investment promotion, harmonious labour relations as well as a safe and healthy working environment. The Ministry is also responsible for the social integration of people with disabilities (PWDs), the vulnerable, the extremely poor and excluded into the mainstream of society to enable them to contribute towards national development and growth.

VISION

The vision of the Ministry is to become a well resourced, efficient as well as effective Ministry committed to human resources development, creating a sustainable environment for gainful employment and the social well being of all Ghanaians.

OBJECTIVES

The key objectives of the Ministry are:
- To promote and sustain an enabling environment for accelerated growth and employment.
- To improve upon capacity development, skills training and retraining.
- To integrate the vulnerable, excluded, persons with disability and the disadvantaged into the mainstream of development.
- To increase access of young persons to skills development and empower them for productive employment.
- To promote youth employment for sustained growth.
- To facilitate the provision of games recreational facilities in deprived communities.

A feasibility study has been completed on the viability of training the youth in bamboo/rattan craft at Anyinam, Offinso, Akrokerri, Wassa Saa and Assin Jakai

FUNCTIONS

- Vocational Skills Training and Development
- Labour Market Relations
- Co-operative Development
- Occupational Safety and Health
- Productivity Improvement
- Social Welfare and NGO registration and co-ordination

Social Welfare, Ghana

The new Minister for Employment and Social Welfare, Moses Asaga, aims to create further employment opportunities for the people of Ghana.

The Honourable Minister
Mr Moses Asaga

DEPARTMENTS AND AGENCIES

Departments
- Labour Department
- Department of Social Welfare
- Department of Co-operatives
- Department of Factories (DFI)

Agencies
- Management Development and Productivity Institute (MDPI)
- National Vocational Training Institute (NVTI)
- Integrated Community Centres for Employment Skills (ICCES)
- Opportunity Industrialization Centres Ghana (OICG)
- Ghana Co-operative College

COMMISSIONS, COUNCILS AND COMMITTEE

Commissions
- National Fair Wages and Salaries Commission
- Labour Commission

Councils
- Persons with disability Council

Committee
- National Tripartite Committee

HUMAN RESOUCE DEVELOPMENT

The Ministry provides employable skills and management development training through its institutions, namely: Management Development and Productivity Institute, Vocational Training Institute, Integrated Community Centres for Employable Skills, Opportunity Industrialisation Centres of Ghana and the Department of Social Welfare's training and rehabilitation centres.

ACHIEVEMENTS

Recognising the high youth unemployment problem, the Ministry is expanding all its vocational/technical and skills training institutions to maximise their intake. Arrangements have been made to open all social welfare training institutions as well as rehabilitation centres for the disabled to the public.

The vocational training curricula have been reviewed to increase their relevance to the current labour market. Entrepreneurship and co-operative programmes have been added, and graduates are exposed to micro-financing to encourage youth to enter into self-employment.

To ensure quality standards and relevance in skills training, a collaborative committee made up of NVTI, ICCES, OIC and Ghana National Association of Private Vocational and Technical Institutions (GNAVTI) has been established to co-ordinate the training programmes.

The Government of Ghana, through the Ministry of Employment and Social Welfare, and in collaboration with its stakeholders and development partners created the National Ageing Policy and the Implementation Action Plan in July 2010. It is expected that the implementation of the National Ageing Policy will provide the platform for enhanced co-ordination, the designing of new projects and programmes as well as policy deepening of related legislation, policies and programmes for improved living conditions of the elderly in Ghana.

CONTACT

Ms Nancy Lucy Dzah
Chief Director
P.O. Box 1627 State House
Accra, Ghana

Tel: +233 302 68 4532
Fax: +233 302 66 3615
Email: nancylucydzah@yahoo.com

Ghana Mineworkers' Union of TUC

To protect and advance the socio-economic and political interests of members

The Ghana Mineworkers' Union (GMWU) of GTUC is a strong, democratic and independent trade union organisation affiliated locally to the Ghana Trades Union Congress (GTUC) and internationally to the International Federation of Chemical, Energy, Mines and General Workers' Unions (ICEM) based in Geneva, Switzerland. It was founded on 7 June 1944 at Abosso near Tarkwa.

GMWU's core functions include Collective Bargaining, Advocacy, Research and Planning, Training and Education, and Organising. Current membership strength of the Union stands at 17,200, representing about 90 per cent of senior and junior workers in the mining sector in Ghana.

The Union has strong internal democratic structures that govern its operations and is headed by an elected General Secretary, assisted by two elected officers and a team of competent and technical advisers.

Besides its core responsibility of ensuring that its members and their families have better living conditions, the Union also engages in policy dialogue with other stakeholders in the mining industry to ensure that mining serves the interests of the communities, country and the mining companies.

Currently, the Union is engaged in a national campaign that affects the mining economy of Ghana:
- A well-structured, sustainable development agenda by the mining industry.
- A well-regulated, corporate social responsibility arrangement.
- Effective utilisation of mining royalties and receipts for infrastructural development in mining communities.
- Introduction of special windfall taxes on mining companies and other extractive industries.
- The ratification of ILO Convention 176 which deals with safety and health in the mines.
- Critical skills shortage and skills flight in the mining industry.
- Huge income inequalities to bridge the pay inequities in the mining industry.

The Union is exploring the possibility of establishing the Golden Pride Savings and Loans Company to cultivate the habit of saving among mineworkers and also to offer them loans at a reduced interest rate. GWMU is a major shareholder in Labour Enterprise Trust (LET), established by the Ghana Trades Union Congress. The Union is also a shareholder in Bayport Financial Services.

GWMU has lined up a number of future initiatives, notably the establishment of community information technology centres in the two major mining communities at Obuasi and Tarkwa, to build and increase capacities and ICT skills of members and their families through links with overseas colleges and universities. Another future initiative is Community Entrepreneurial Skills Development to provide an alternative livelihood to support family members and in particularly their spouses.

Contact

Ghana Mineworkers' Union of TUC
Office of the General Secretary
Hall of Trade Unions, off Barnes and Liberia Roads, Tudu
P.O. Box 701, Accra
Tel/Fax: +233 302 66 5563
Email: admin@gmwu.org
gmwu_gtuc@yahoo.co.uk

(Central, 182,900), Teshie (Greater Accra, 182,100), Tema (Greater Accra, 178,800), Obuasi (Ashanti, 173,100), Sekondi (Western, 156,200), Madina (Greater Accra, 140,800), Koforidua (Eastern, 111,700), Wa (Upper West, 96,500), Techiman (Brong Ahafo, 91,400), Nungua (Greater Accra, 89,100), Tema New Town (Greater Accra, 87,400), Ho (Volta, 83,700), Sunyani (Brong Ahafo, 83,600), Bawku (Upper East, 66,200) and Bolgatanga (Upper East, 63,500).

Transport: There are 57,610km of roads, 15% paved, and a 953-km railway network, connecting Accra, Kumasi and Takoradi, originally built mainly to link mining centres to the ports but also provides passenger services.

Main ports are at Tema, near Accra, and Takoradi, and the main international airport is at Accra (Kotoka), 10km to the north of the city; other airports are at Takoradi, Kumasi, Sunyani and Tamale.

Society

KEY FACTS 2010

Population per sq km:	102
Life expectancy:	64 years
Net primary enrolment:	76%

Population: 24,392,000 (2010); 51% lives in urban areas and 17% in urban agglomerations of more than 1 million people; growth 2.5% p.a. 1990–2010; birth rate 32 per 1,000 people (47 in 1970); life expectancy 64 years (49 in 1970).

The population is predominantly of African groups: Akan (45% in 2000 census), Mole–Dagbani (15%), Ewe (12%), Ga-Adangbe (7%), Guan (4%), Gurma (4%), Grusi (3%). There are very small minorities of other races.

Language: The official language is English. The principal indigenous language group is Akan, of which Twi and Fanti are the most commonly used forms. Ga is spoken in the Accra region, Ewe in Volta, and the Mole–Dagbani language group in northern Ghana.

Religion: Christians 69% in 2000 census, Muslims 16%, and traditional animist religions are often practised alongside both of these religions.

Health: Public spending on health was 3% of GDP in 2009. Public hospital and other medical care is provided at nominal rates. As well as public hospitals and clinics, some are private and some operated by religious missions. 82% of the population uses an improved drinking water source and 13% have adequate sanitation facilities (2009). Infant mortality was 50 per 1,000 live births in 2010 (126 in 1960). AIDS, malaria and tuberculosis pose serious problems, and there have been cases of yellow fever, bilharzia and intestinal worms in rural areas. In 2009, 1.8% of people aged 15–49 were HIV positive.

Education: Public spending on education was 5.7% of GDP in 2010. There are eight years of compulsory education starting at age six. Primary school comprises six years and secondary six, with two cycles each of three years. Some 73% of pupils complete primary school (2008). The school year starts in September. For those proceeding to tertiary education, the nine years of basic education are followed by three years of senior secondary school.

GHANA NATIONAL ASSOCIATION OF TEACHERS
WE LIVE TO TEACH

GNAT Heights on Independence Avenue, Accra (Product of the Teachers' Fund Operations)

GNAT Headquarters – Teachers Hall, Accra

GNAT's mission is to unify all teachers in pre-tertiary educational institutions and strive for better conditions of service, job security as well as to enhance their professional status.

GNAT, a leading internationally recognised Teachers' Organisation, is the mouthpiece of teachers in pre-tertiary educational institutions and offices in Ghana. It originated in 1931 as the Gold Coast Teachers Union (GCTU). Its headquarters, Teachers Hall, is in Accra, Ghana.

Aims of GNAT
1. **Trade union**
- Protecting individual rights
- Providing job security
- Negotiating better terms and conditions of service for members

2. **Economic and welfare**
- Teachers' fund loans, housing, cars, small businesses
- Credit schemes

- Legal aid for members involved in employment related cases
- Payment of retirement/death benefit
- Subsidised housing for members in regional capitals

3. **Educational and professional development**
- In-service training programmes through professional associate programmes with other affiliates of Education International (EI)
- Courses for deferred and referred teachers
- Promotion courses for aspiring principal superintendents and assistant directors
- Facilitation of subject associations
- Special science education programme for female teachers in primary schools

Mr Samuel Doe Alobuia, AG. President   **Mrs Irene Duncan-Adanusa, General Secretary**

Contact
NATIONAL SECRETARIAT
P.O. BOX 209
ACCRA, GHANA
Tel: +233 30 222 1515 • 30 222 1576
Fax: +233 30 222 6286
Email: info@ghanateachers.org

Ministry of Finance and Economic Planning

The Government of Ghana and the International Fund for Agricultural Development (IFAD) signed a US$31.5 million grant facility agreement to co-finance the up scaling of the first and second phases of the Rural Enterprise Project. Finance Minister, Dr Kwabena Duffuor, initialed for Ghana while associate Vice-President of IFAD, Mr Kevin Cleaver, initialed for IFAD

Nine members of the Board of Directors of the African Development Bank Group (AfDB) visited Ghana to consult with the authorities and to review AfDB-funded programmes in the country. The mission held discussions with Ministers, the Director General of National Development Planning Commission, development partners, representatives of the private sector, civil society and project managers of AFDB-funded projects in Ghana. The visit culminated in a meeting with Vice-President John Dramani Mahama

While in Ghana on a 5-day familiarisation visit, Executive Directors of the World Bank Group met with H.E. President John Atta Mills, the Finance Minister, the Governor of the Bank of Ghana, key government officials, private sector and civil society groups to discuss various economic and developmental issues centred on energy, agriculture, urban management and poverty reduction

Mandate

The Ministry of Finance and Economic Planning (MoFEP) is established under Section 11 of the Civil Service Law 1993 (PNDCL 327).

The Ministry's broad function includes the formulation and implementation of sound economic and financial policies of the government as well as the management of the national economy.

Vision

MoFEP envisages to become a highly professional institution dedicated to providing quality financial management, improving accountability and ensuring good economic governance.

Mission

The Ministry of Finance and Economic Planning exists to ensure macroeconomic stability for the promotion of sustainable economic growth and development of Ghana through:

- Formulation and implementation of sound financial, fiscal and monetary policies

- Efficient mobilisation, allocation and management of financial resources

- Establishment and dissemination of performance-oriented guidelines and accurate user-friendly financial management information systems

- Creation of an enabling environment for investment

The Ministry's mission is achieved by committing to service excellence, transparency, probity and accountability in the management of financial resources.

MoFEP's role in the Ghana Shared Growth and Development Agenda (GSGDA)

In 2010, government launched a medium-term development framework, the Ghana Shared Growth and Development Agenda (GSGDA), to guide policy from 2010 to 2013. The GSGDA thematic areas through which government intends to transform the economy and reduce poverty are as follows:

i. Macroeconomic stability

ii. Private sector competitiveness

iii. Agricultural modernisation and natural resource management

iv. Oil and Gas development

v. Infrastructure and human settlement development

vi. Human development, employment and productivity

vii. Transparent and accountable governance

The Ministry's aim of ensuring economic growth with stability for the promotion of sustainable development is geared towards the attainment of the thematic area (i) and it seeks to promote the achievement of the rest of the thematic areas.

To achieve the above aim, the Ministry has as its goal the efficient and effective management of the economy towards the attainment of upper middle income status and poverty reduction.

Presenting the 2012 Budget Statement and Economic Policy in Parliament

Korean delegation led by former Deputy Prime Minister and Minister of Strategy and Finance Mr Oh-Kyu, paid a courtesy call to Hon. Fifi Kwetey

The Hon. Minister of Finance and Economic Planning, Dr Kwabena Duffuor

Deputy Ministers:
Hon. Fifi Fiavi Kwetey
Hon. Seth E. Terkper

Hon. Seth Terkper addressing journalists from the Institute of Financial and Economic Journalists (IFEJ) on the 2012 budget

Health screening organised by the Ministry to improve staff welfare and effectiveness

Highlights of Economic Achievements in 2011

The Ghanaian economy is underpinned by strong macroeconomic fundamentals which are expected to continue in the medium to long term. The prudent management of the economy in recent times has catapulted the economy into a lower middle income status. The recent oil discovery and favourable commodity prices, particularly for Ghana's major export commodities such as gold and cocoa, have supported the strong performance of the economy.

The following are some of the important achievements in 2011:

- GDP growth rose from 4.1 per cent in 2009 to 7.7 per cent in 2010 and further to 13.6 per cent in 2011 (on provisional basis). The high growth rate for 2011 is partly driven by oil production which started in the last month of 2010. Even without oil, the economy grew by 8.0 per cent in 2011.

- Inflation, which was 18.1 per cent at the end of 2008, has been reduced to 8.58 per cent in December 2011. Single digit inflation has been sustained since June 2010 for the longest period in our history.

- The gross international reserves of US$5.4 billion which was recorded in December 2011 exceeds three months of import cover of goods and services.

- Fiscal deficit was reduced from 8.5 per cent of GDP in 2008 to 4.3 per cent of GDP in 2011.

- Foreign Direct investment (FDI) as a percentage of GDP rose from 4.28 per cent in 2008 to 6.44 per cent in 2009 and further to 8.07 per cent in 2010.

- Ghana has been able to maintain its sovereign ratings at B and B+, and, transfer and convertibility (T&C) assessment remains at B+ with a stable outlook.

Departments and agencies under the Ministry

- Controller and Accountant-General's Department
- Ghana Cocoa Board
- Ghana Revenue Authority
- Institute of Accountancy Training
- National Lotteries Authority
- Public Procurement Authority
- Securities and Exchange Commission

Divisions within the Ministry

- Budget
- Economic Research and Forecasting
- External Economic Relations
- Debt Management
- Financial Sector
- General Administration
- Legal Affairs
- Public Investment
- Real Sector

Postal Address: P.O. Box MB40, Ministries, Accra – Ghana
Physical Address: 28th February Road, Accra
Tel: +233 (0)302 68 6101-99/ 68 6137-99
Fax: +233 (0)302 66 5132/ 66 3854
Email: chiefdirector@mofep.gov.gh • minister@mofep.gov.gh

Homefoods Processing and Cannery Ltd

Award-winning recipe for success

It is our aim that we constantly meet our goals and aspirations in serving our customers by providing the highest quality products on the market whilst contributing to sustainable development to the wider community.

Homefoods has come a long way since its official registration in 1995, several awards later - inter alia the silver award for crude palm oil at the 18th National Awards for Export Achievement in Ghana and the New Millennium Golden Award for Quality and Business Prestige in Geneva, Switzerland - the Company has increasingly shown productive quality values, leading high customer satisfaction into specific regions of the world.

The driving force behind Homefoods is, Ms Felicia Twumasi who believes in maintaining mutually beneficial long-standing business relationships ensuring that customers get the best service and products on the market.

Homefoods Processing and Cannery Limited (HFPCL) is a food processing and agro-foods export company. Its distribution network includes the United Kingdom, Switzerland, Italy, North America, The Gambia and South Africa.

CORPORATE AND SOCIAL RESPONSIBILITY

HFPCL is committed to the empowerment of women and the adoption of orphans and street children, offering financial support to orphanages and supporting children in their education.

The Company ensures that all purchases of its agro-products for export such as Gari and Red Palm Oil are from women co-operative associations. This is in line with the government's poverty alleviation programme, to improve the livelihood of a great number of women in the country's rural regions and districts.

VISION

The Homefoods ® vision is to continue to build a quality food chain, fusing flavours and spices from around the world to meet your every culinary desire. We here at Homefoods aim to focus attention and creativity on basic food ingredients and services to as many people and homes as possible; food products they absolutely need and want.

PRODUCTS

'FEEL GOOD' RANGE

- Extra fruity jams and jellies and savoury jams and jellies for the adventurous food lover
- HFPCL holds the sole distributorship and manufacturing rights in Ghana of Snack-a-Juice, an internationally well-known brand.
- Homefoods Vegetable Oil is a high quality cooking palm oil containing a rich natural source of beta carotene (provitamin A).
- Homefoods Palm Oil Shortening is derived from palm oil and is the Caterer's Choice, colourless, odourless and economical.

GOURMET RANGE

- Rooibos spreads in various flavours; and gourmet spices are a tailored blend of spices and herbs
- 'All Natural Honey' is produced in the Cape Coast area of Ghana, well known for the production of high quality honey

ETHNIC RANGE

- Palm Oil, the flagship product, is increasingly becoming a first choice for many consumers.
- Gari, made from fresh cassava, is a versatile food, with a high intuitive value.
- Tropisoup is a natural palmnut pulp juice ready for use in the preparation of palmnut soup.

CONTACT

Ms Felicia Twumasi, CEO
P.O. Box KA 16519, Airport, Accra, Ghana
Tel: +233 21 30 3914 • Fax/Tel: +233 21 31 8119
E-mail: info@homefoodsghana.com

www.homefoodsghana.com

There are six public universities: University of Ghana (Legon, Accra, established 1948); Kwame Nkrumah University of Science and Technology (Kumasi, 1952); University of Cape Coast (1962); University for Development Studies (main campus at Tamale, 1992); University of Education (Winneba, 2004); and University of Mines and Technology (Tarkwa, 2004). Other major tertiary institutions include the Ghana Institute of Management and Public Administration (Achimota, Accra), which was established in 1961. There are also many teacher-training colleges, polytechnics and specialised tertiary institutions; and many private universities. The female–male ratio for gross enrolment in tertiary education is 0.62:1 (2009). Literacy among people aged 15–24 is 80% (2009).

Media: *Daily Graphic* and *Ghanaian Times* (both state-owned), *The Ghanaian Chronicle* and *Daily Guide* are daily newspapers. *Ghana Palaver*, *The Independent*, *The Mail* (bi-weekly), *The Mirror* and *Sunday Herald* are weeklies.

Ghana Broadcasting Corporation is the public TV and radio provider, broadcasting in Ghanaian languages and English; many private radio stations and TV channels are also available, particularly in the urban areas.

Some 39% of households have TV sets (2007). There are 11 personal computers (2008) and 96 internet users (2010) per 1,000 people.

Communications: Country code 233; internet domain '.gh'. Mobile phone coverage is good around main towns but patchy elsewhere. Internet connections exist in most towns and speeds are increasing.

There are 11 main telephone lines and 715 mobile phone subscriptions per 1,000 people (2010).

Public holidays: New Year's Day, Independence Day (6 March), Workers' Day (1 May), Africa Day (25 May), Republic Day (1 July), Farmers' Day (first Friday in December), Christmas Day and Boxing Day.

Religious and other festivals whose dates vary from year to year include Good Friday, Easter Monday, Eid al-Fitr (End of Ramadan) and Eid al-Adha (Feast of the Sacrifice).

Economy

KEY FACTS 2010

GNI:	US$30.1bn
GNI p.c.:	US$1,230
GDP growth:	6.5% p.a. 2006–10
Inflation:	13.6% p.a. 2006–10

GDP by Sector (2010)

■	Agriculture	30%
□	Industry	19%
▨	Services	51%

Ministry of Health, Ghana

Accelerating efforts to attain the health-related Millennium Development Goals

Ghana, like many other developing countries, is not likely to attain the health-related MDGs (4, 5 and 6) by 2015 unless extra effort is made to scale up priority health interventions to all parts of the country. For instance, Maternal Mortality Ratio in Ghana was 740/100,000 live births in 1990 and came down to 360/100,000 live births in 2008. The challenge is to bring it down to the MDG target of 185/100,000 live births in 2015. Through the concerted effort of the Ministry of Health and development partners, an MDG Acceleration Framework (MAF) has been implemented to assist Ghana in attaining the MDGs.

The social health insurance scheme introduced by Government in 2005 has improved financial access to healthcare for about half the population.

Government has taken advantage of the favourable investment climate in Ghana to construct new hospitals and polyclinics in remote and underserved districts. This will improve physical access to healthcare, and in particular, access to comprehensive emergency obstetric care will be enhanced.

Pre-hospital emergency services will be strengthened when the Government's plan to expand the National Ambulance Service to every district is fully implemented by December 2012.

To improve on the production of the requisite human resources, existing health training institutions have been expanded to increase their intake whilst new schools have been opened in other areas. The private sector has been supported to get involved in the training of health professionals such as nurses and midwives. Besides the increased production of health manpower, the Ministry of Health has also embarked on a leadership development training programme for all levels of healthcare delivery and will also be putting in place a structured in-service training programme to fill-in knowledge and skills gaps in the health workforce, as well as address attitudinal challenges.

Hon. Alban S. K. Bagbin (MP), Minister of Health

Ministry of Energy for a better Ghana

The Ministry of Energy is responsible for formulating, monitoring and evaluating policies, programmes and projects in Ghana's energy sector. It also implements the National Electrification Scheme which seeks to extend the reach of electricity to all communities.

Hon. Minister Dr Joe Oteng-Adjei Oteng

Energy for Everyone

Objectives

- Secure long term fuel supplies for thermal power plants;
- Reduce technical and commercial losses in power supply through employing information from the Energy Commission;
- Increase access to modern forms of energy and infrastructure to meet growing demands and ensure reliability;
- Improve the overall management, regulatory environment and operation of the energy sector;
- Minimise the environmental impact of energy supply and consumption through increased production and use of renewable energy;
- Ensure productive and cost efficient delivery and use of energy;
- Promote and encourage private sector participation in the energy sector; and
- Diversify the national energy mix by promoting renewable energy resources, nuclear and coal.

The Energy Sector Vision

Several goals have been identified in order to meet the vision of ensuring universal access to energy services and export by 2020:

- Infrastructure development for the production and supply of adequate energy services for national and export requirements;
- Development of requisite infrastructure to ensure universal access to energy is efficient and reliable; and
- Ensuring that energy is produced, transported and supplied in an efficient manner that has no adverse health, safety or environmental impacts.

Key players in the Energy sector

Power sector The Power Directorate supports the Ministry through its responsibility for effective utilisation of the country's resources in providing power required for socio-economic development. The programmes and projects of the Power Directorate are aimed at achieving the government's overall developmental agenda for the Energy Sector.

Electricity generation is undertaken by the state-owned **Volta River Authority** (VRA), which operates the Akosombo Hydro Power Station, Kpong Hydro Power Station and the Takoradi Thermal Power Plant (TAPCO) at Aboadze.

The **National Interconnected Transmission System** for electricity is owned and operated by the state-owned **Ghana Grid Company**. Electricity is distributed by the state-owned **Electricity Company of Ghana** and the **Northern Electricity Department**, a subsidiary of VRA. The **Energy Commission** and the independent **Public Utilities and Regulatory Commission** regulate the electricity supply industry.

Hon. Dr Kofi Buah, Deputy Minister

Petroleum sector The Petroleum Directorate is the technical arm of the Ministry that deals with all issues related to oil and gas.

Renewable Energy Sector Resources in Ghana include wood fuel, hydro, solar, wind, biofuels, waste-to-energy and animal traction.

Achievements

- Completion and Commission of Prestea-Obuasi 161 KV Transmission Line.

- Completion of 2nd Bulk Supply Station for Accra for both Transmission (VRA) and Distribution (ECG) segments to meet growing demand and improve system reliability.

- Completion and Commissioning of Tema Oil Refinery Residual fuel catalytic cracker project which allows recovery of refined products from previously wasted residual fuel oil.

- Created self-sufficiency and export capacity in LPG and kerosene.

- Implementation of National Street Lighting Project to enhance living conditions, improve security and support Ghana's tourism attraction drive.

- Advancement towards deregulation of the petroleum downstream sector.

- Single Buoy Mooring allows discharge of crude and refined products by bigger vessels of up to 150,000DWT within 36 hours at reduced freight charges.

- Completion of Buipe Balgatanga Petroleum Products Pipeline Project which will make gasoline, gas oil and kerosene readily available in the northern part of the country in the most cost-effective manner.

- Phase 1 of the Rural Kerosene Distribution Improvement Programme saw 700 kerosene surface tanks distributed throughout the country's 110 districts.

- Electrification of 160 rural Junior High Schools, across ten regions, with solar PV systems. This included the provision of TV sets to enable access to the President's Special Initiative on Distance Learning Programme.

The Ministry of Energy thanks all stakeholders in the energy sector for its continued efforts to ensure that the vision of energy for all is realised. We welcome enquiries from the international community, and local partners.

Contact

Ministry of Energy
P. O. Box T40, Stadium Post Office, Accra, Ghana
Tel: +233 302 66 7152-3 • 68 3961-4
Fax: +233 302 66 8262
Email: moen@energymin.gov.gh
www.energycom.gov.gh

MANET°
Properties. Redefined.

Manet Group

The Manet Group is a fusion of four independent subsidiaries whose core businesses lie in the areas of real estate development, hospitality and civil engineering projects: Manet Housing Limited, Manet Hotels Limited, Manet Construction Limited and Manet Towers Limited.

The Manet Group began in 1994 with the first of these companies, Manet Housing Limited.

Manet Housing Limited has successfully built and delivered nearly 2000 homes in large, serene communities in Accra and Tema. It has grown to become one of the largest real estate developers in Ghana and has won many coveted awards in the process.

The vision of the Manet Group expanded, driven by successes achieved in the residential real estate business and the construction boom in Ghana in the mid 90s. Manet Construction Limited was established as a civil engineering company specialising in the construction of urban roads, motor carriages and related infrastructure around the nation's capital, Accra. Manet Construction Limited also takes credit for the construction of the Teshie bypass and the construction of the twin towers at Airport City for Manet Tower Limited.

Manet Towers is the most recent addition to the Manet Group, founded primarily to professionally manage the Manet Towers project at Airport City in Accra. This subsidiary has ventured boldly into the area of commercial real estate and transformed the skyline of Accra with a set of imposing twin office accommodation in the most expensive and prestigious real estate enclave in Ghana today. At Airport City, the twin tower buildings, known as the Manet Towers, provide prime office accommodation to satisfy the needs of both local and international business interests. It offers an ultra modern, secure, accessible and convenient business location, with expansive parking for up to 230 cars. It is the most preferred office location in the nation's capital.

Contact
Tel: +233 302 77 3800
Email: info@manet.com

www.manet.com

Real Growth in GDP

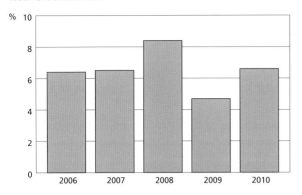

Inflation

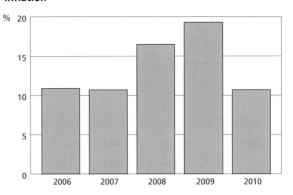

Ghana's formerly strong economy was badly affected by a series of military coups and failed development plans. A highly protected economy and substantial state investment created a large manufacturing sector which by the 1980s was becoming a heavy burden on national resources. While the economy depended heavily on the export of two commodities, gold and cocoa, it would remain vulnerable to fluctuations in world commodity prices and to poor harvests.

The economic situation began to improve with government austerity programmes in the late 1980s, but the early 1990s presented new difficulties including a decline in the international price of cocoa. Donors pledged substantial aid from 1993, in support of IMF-backed economic recovery and reform programmes, which aimed to diversify exports, control public expenditure and privatise a number of state-owned enterprises.

History

According to oral traditions, the ancestors of the Akan people, today the largest ethnic group, entered the country from the north and spread southwards between AD 1200 and 1600. The Fanti State of Denkyira was at that period already established on the coast. By 1400 the Akan had established their Bono and Buida kingdoms in the forested central region.

Their highly developed culture was centred on the city-state, surrounded by vassal villages, and rule by a court where the queen mother was often a more powerful figure than the king who, being sacred, was hidden from the people and consequently often politically isolated. The Akan traded gold and kola nuts for salt and cloth, in the west and north, and were also involved in the slave trade. In the 15th century, the Ashanti people waged war against the Denkyira Kingdom and by 1700 had gained control of the slave trade. They developed a powerful army and a centralised state, ruled by the Asantehene (king of the Ashanti nation).

Portuguese traders, arriving after 1450 in search of gold and ivory, named the country Gold Coast; appropriately since, by the end of the 16th century, it produced 10% of the world's gold.

From the middle of the 16th century other Europeans began arriving; in the mid-18th century there were Dutch, Danish and British settlements. The British became involved in internal conflicts when they backed the Fanti against the Ashanti who were extending their power into the coastal areas. There were four wars in the 19th century.

The Bond of 1844, entered into by Britain and the Fanti chiefs, endorsed British control of small pockets of settlement; six years later Britain set up a legislative council to govern these areas. The

British took over abandoned Danish settlements in 1850 and the Dutch settlements in 1871. By Orders in Council (1901) Britain declared the southern territory a colony by settlement, the northern territory a protectorate and Ashanti a colony by conquest. In 1922 a part of the adjoining German territory of Togoland was placed under British administration by a League of Nations Mandate and after the Second World War it became a UN Trust Territory. The principle of elections was introduced under the 1925 constitution.

During the first half of the 20th century, there was growing national pressure for self-determination, and the UK gradually surrendered control. The 1946 constitution required the legislative council to have an African majority. Following civic disturbances in 1948, the UK agreed that a committee consisting entirely of Africans should examine the structure of the country's government.

In 1949, Kwame Nkrumah set up the Convention People's Party (CPP) to campaign for independence. Elections took place in 1951, and the following year Nkrumah became the country's first premier. The 1954 constitution provided for a legislative assembly of 104 directly elected members, and an all-African Cabinet; the UK kept responsibility for foreign affairs and defence. The CPP campaigned for full independence. The general election of 1956 returned the CPP with a big majority.

Modern-day Ghana was formed when the British-administered part of Togoland voted to join the Gold Coast in an independent state, in a UN-supervised plebiscite in May 1956. Ghana achieved independence within the Commonwealth on 6 March 1957.

In 1960 Ghana became a republic, with Nkrumah as president, ➤

GHANA FREE ZONES BOARD
Searching for a location conducive to investment?
GHANA, your Preferred Investment Destination

WHY LOCATE IN GHANA?

- A stable political environment within the west African sub-region
- Abundant, adaptable and easily trainable labour force
- A competitive daily minimum wage rate
- No restrictions on the issuance of work and residence permits to free zone investors and employees
- Excellent sea and air connections with Europe and the USA
- Strategic and central location within west Africa providing access to a market of 250 million people

PRIORITY SECTORS

- Agro-food Processing
- Textile/Apparel Manufacturing
- Garment Accessories
- Information and Communication Technology (data processing, call centres and software development)
- Light industry/assembling plants
- Petrochemical sector

INCENTIVES

- 100% exemption from payment of duties and levies
- 100% exemption from payment of income tax on profits for 10 years
- 100% ownership of shares by any investor
- Up to 30% of annual production of goods and services can be sold on the local market
- Unlimited expatriate quota
- Free Zone investments are guaranteed against nationalisation and expropriation
- There are no conditions or restrictions on repatriation of dividends or net profit; payments for foreign loan servicing; payments of fees and charges for technology transfer agreements; and remittance of proceeds from sale of any interest in a free zone investment.

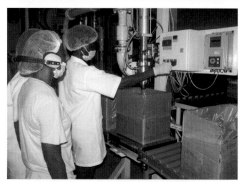

Ghana: Gateway to West Africa

For further information please contact

The Executive Secretary
Ghana Free Zones Board
P.O. Box M626, Accra, Ghana

Tel: +233 302 780535 • 785037
         +233 242 174534
Fax: +233 302 78 0536 • 78 0537
E-mail: info@gfzb.gov.gh

www.gfzb.gov.gh

From the mid-1990s, there followed a period of vigorous economic growth, only dipping below 4% p.a. in 2000, when cocoa prices were weak and oil costs rising. This growth continued in 2008–11 in the teeth of the global economic downturn. Keeping inflation under control, however, proved more challenging.

Ghana has benefited from the G8 debt-relief programme launched at the Gleneagles Summit in Scotland, UK, in July 2005.

Mining

Gold and diamonds are the main mineral exports. There are large reserves of bauxite and manganese. Ghana's aluminium smelter was closed in 2007. The government assumed ownership of the operating company, Valco, in 2010 and announced plans to rehabilitate it and establish a domestic aluminium industry.

Oil and gas

Significant discoveries of offshore oil were announced in 2007. Oil production began in December 2010 at a rate of 55,000 barrels a day and was at some 80,000 barrels a day by the latter part of 2011. As new wells come on stream, production was expected to rise rapidly.

Constitution

Status:	Republic with executive president
Legislature:	Parliament
Independence:	6 March 1957

A new constitution, based on the US model, was approved by national referendum in April 1992. Ghana is a unitary republic with an executive presidency and a multiparty political system. The national legislature is the unicameral Parliament, whose 230 members are elected by universal adult suffrage every four years.

The president, who is head of state and commander-in-chief of the armed forces, is elected by universal suffrage for a maximum of two four-year terms. If no presidential candidate receives more than 50% of votes, a new election between the two leading candidates must take place within 21 days.

The president appoints a vice-president and nominates a council of ministers, subject to approval by the parliament. The constitution also provides for two advisory bodies to the president: a 25-member council of state, composed mainly of regional representatives and presidential nominees, and a 20-member national security council, chaired by the vice-president.

➤ and in 1964 a one-party state, the CPP being the sole authorised party. However, less than a year later, Nkrumah was removed by military coup, the first of four coups.

The army and police set up a National Liberation Council, which dissolved the legislative assembly and suspended the constitution while a new one was drafted. Political activity was permitted again in 1969; a general election followed in August. It returned the Progress Party; its leader Dr Kofi Busia became prime minister, with the National Alliance of Liberals as the opposition.

In 1972, another military coup led by Colonel Ignatius Acheampong overthrew Busia's government and set up a National Redemption Council. In 1978 Acheampong was replaced by General Frederick Akuffo, who promised civilian rule by the middle of the following year.

Two weeks before the elections were to be held in June 1979, a military coup led by junior officers ousted the government. Flt-Lt Jerry J Rawlings and the Armed Forces Revolutionary Council declared that they had assumed power, in order that an honest election could take place. Elections were held as scheduled; they returned the People's National Party, whose leader Dr Hilla Limann took office as president in September 1979.

Another coup, in 1981, put Rawlings back in power. He suspended the constitution and banned political parties. From December 1981 until November 1992 Ghana was ruled by a Provisional National Defence Council (PNDC).

In May 1991 the PNDC government set up a 260-member consultative assembly to oversee the restoration of multiparty democracy. A committee of constitutional experts was appointed to draft a new constitution for submission to this assembly. In

April 1992 the draft constitution was overwhelmingly approved in a referendum; political associations were unbanned; and six opposition movements were granted legal recognition. The National Democratic Congress (NDC) was formed to contest the elections on behalf of the PNDC.

The November 1992 presidential election (witnessed by Commonwealth observers, and considered 'overall free and fair') returned Jerry Rawlings (with 58.3% of the vote). The parliamentary elections of December 1992 returned the NDC with 189 of 200 seats in the new Parliament. The NDC united with the National Convention Party (NCP) and the Every Ghanaian Living Everywhere Party to form the Progressive Alliance. In January 1993 Rawlings was sworn in as president, and the Fourth Republic was inaugurated. In May 1995, the NCP left the coalition.

In the December 1996 elections, President Rawlings was re-elected with 58% of the votes. Turnout was 75%. His party, the NDC, won 133 seats. The opposition alliance of the New Patriotic Party and the People's Convention Party won 66 seats, just reaching the level at which they could successfully oppose constitutional changes (which need a two-thirds majority). The elections were seen as a step towards full multiparty democracy; the opposition had boycotted the 1992 parliamentary elections, but accepted defeat the second time round. Ghana thus acquired a significant legislative opposition for the first time in 15 years.

After Rawlings was chosen as 'life chairman' of the party in December 1998, the NDC suffered a serious split in its ranks with the formation by some of its founding members of the National Reform Party, which was registered in July 1999.

UNION OF
INDUSTRY,
COMMERCE AND
FINANCE WORKERS

OF GTUC

Our members are at the centre of all policy and activities

About us

The Union of Industry, Commerce and Finance Workers (UNICOF) of the Trades Union Congress Ghana (TUC) is the 17th affiliate of TUC and was registered in October 2003.

Mission

To organise, educate and develop the capabilities of workers in the associated sectors towards attaining improved productivity, work conditions and job security.

Vision

To be one of Africa's best managed unions capable of meeting the emerging needs and aspirations of its members.

Membership base

The Union currently has over 11,000 members throughout Ghana.

Strategic plan

The Union has in place a five-year strategic plan (2010-2014), whose strategic objectives include:

- To organise and mobilise female members of the UNICOF fraternity.
- To create a conscious and educated membership to meet new challenges on the job.
- To ensure productive harnessing of human and financial resources.
- Effective cohesion between internal and external stakeholders.

Contact
Mr Francis Davoh
General Secretary
House number 18,
South Liberia Link
Adabraka, Accra, Ghana

Tel: +233 302 22 0254/22 0261/24 6151
Fax: +233 302 22 0305
Email: unicofdavoh@yahoo.com • unicofinfo@unicof.org

www.unicof.org

Ten regional ministers, one for each region, are each assisted by a regional co-ordinating council. There are 138 administrative districts, each having a district assembly, headed by a district chief executive. Regional colleges, which comprise representatives selected by the district assemblies and by regional houses of chiefs, elect a number of representatives to the council of state.

Politics

Last elections:	December 2008 (presidential and legislative)
Next elections:	2012/2013 (presidential and legislative)
Head of state:	President Professor John Evans Atta Mills
Head of government:	the president
Ruling party:	National Democratic Congress

After 19 years at the helm, President Jerry Rawlings was barred by the constitution from seeking another term of office in the December 2000 presidential election. For the first time in Ghana's history there was a democratic transfer of power, after National Democratic Congress (NDC) candidate Vice-President John Atta Mills was defeated in the second round of the presidential contest by New Patriotic Party (NPP) leader, John Kufuor. The NPP also won the parliamentary elections held on the same day in December 2000 as the first round of the presidential election.

Kufuor won the December 2004 presidential election gaining an outright majority in the first round with 53.4% of the votes. His main rival, Atta Mills of the NDC, received 43.7% and the turnout was 83%. In parliamentary elections on the same day the NPP took 128 seats, the NDC 94, People's National Convention (PNC) four and Convention People's Party (CPP) three. Kufuor promised to make reducing poverty his priority in his second term.

The parliamentary and presidential elections in December 2008 were very close. The NDC won the general election but just fell short of an overall majority; the NDC took 114 seats, NPP 107, PNC two, CPP one and independents four. In the second round of the presidential election, NDC's Atta Mills narrowly beat NPP's Nana Addo Dankwa Akufo-Addo (50.2%:49.8%), reversing the first-round result of Akufo-Addo 49.1% and Atta Mills 47.9%. Commonwealth observers were present.

International relations

Ghana is a member of the African, Caribbean and Pacific Group of States, African Union, Economic Community of West African States, Non-Aligned Movement, Organisation internationale de la Francophonie, United Nations and World Trade Organization.

Traveller information

Local laws and conventions: Ghana has a mixture of Christian, Muslim and traditional beliefs which have a strong influence on Ghanaian daily life.

A conservative and deeply religious country, respect must be shown for traditional values. Wearing immodest clothing in public will cause offence and disrespect and the wearing of camouflage or military clothing by civilians is banned. Ghanaians prefer to be asked before they are photographed.

Drugs are a growing concern and the authorities are determined to control the problem. Penalties for drug offences are severe.

Ghanaians should always be addressed by their formal titles unless they specifically request otherwise. Handshaking is the usual form of greeting. In Ghana, as in much of West Africa, it is customary not to touch food with the left hand.

Dress is conservative and respectful. Appointments for business meetings are customary and punctuality is important. The best time to visit on business is September to April. Office hours are Mon–Fri 0800–1200 and 1300–1700.

Immigration and customs: Passports need to be valid for at least six months at the time of applying for a visa. Visitors are advised to copy the photopage of their passport and the entry stamp and to keep their passports with them at all times.

A yellow fever vaccination certificate will be required by visitors arriving from an affected country.

Lone parents must carry documentation showing that they have parental responsibility for the child in their care.

Animals, firearms, ammunition and explosives are prohibited imports.

Duty must be paid on gifts. The export of non-exempt handicrafts and antiques requires a certificate from the Museums and Monuments Board available from the main craft centre or National Museum.

Travel within the country: Traffic drives on the right. An international driving permit is required to drive in Ghana. Driving licences should be carried at all times. Car hire is available.

The speed limit is 80kph, seatbelts are compulsory and drink-driving is illegal. Grass or leaves strewn across the road indicates an accident or hazard ahead. The use of Tro-tros (small private buses) is common.

There are domestic flights between Accra, Kumasi and Tamale. The rail network does a 965km loop by the coast connecting Accra, Takoradi and Kumasi. There are bus and taxi services in Accra and taxis in the main towns.

Travel health: Comprehensive medical insurance is recommended for visitors. Serious medical conditions may require evacuation.

Visitors will need protection against malaria together with repellent and suitable clothing to discourage bites. Bilharzia, Hepatitis E, B and C, dengue fever, tuberculosis and meningitis are also present.

Water should be boiled or bought in sealed bottles. Powdered or tinned milk is recommended.

Money: Credit cards are accepted at many hotels and guesthouses (although Mastercard is not widely accepted). ATMs in Accra and Kumasi will accept most cards. Travellers cheques can be changed in large hotels, banks and bureaux. Banking hours: Mon–Thur 0800–1400, Fri 0800–1500.

There were 803,000 tourist arrivals in 2009.

Further information

Ghana Government: www.ghana.gov.gh

Parliament: www.parliament.gh

Bank of Ghana: www.bog.gov.gh

Commonwealth Secretariat: www.thecommonwealth.org

Commonwealth of Nations: www.commonwealth-of-nations.org/Ghana

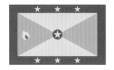

Grenada

KEY FACTS

Joined Commonwealth:	1974
Population:	104,000 (2010)
GDP p.c. growth:	2.9% p.a. 1990–2010
UN HDI 2011:	world ranking 67
Official language:	English
Time:	GMT minus 4hr
Currency:	Eastern Caribbean dollar (EC$)

Geography

Area:	344.5 sq km
Coastline:	121km
Capital:	St George's

Grenada consists of the island of Grenada, the most southerly of the Windwards in the Eastern Caribbean, and some of the southern Grenadine islands, the largest of which is Carriacou (33 sq km). Its Caribbean neighbours include St Vincent and the Grenadines (which includes the more northern Grenadines) and Trinidad and Tobago.

Topography: Mountains, chiefly of volcanic origin, form a backbone stretching the 33km length of the island and rise to 840m at Mount St Catherine. The terrain slopes down to the coast on the east and south-east. The island is watered by its many streams and springs, and a small lake, Grand Etang, occupies an old crater at 530m.

Climate: The tropical climate is especially pleasant in the dry season (February to May) when the trade winds prevail. The rainy season runs from June to December, when hurricanes may occur and in some years – for example, Hurricane Ivan in 2004 – cause extensive damage. The temperature and rainfall vary with altitude, with much heavier rainfall in the mountains.

Vegetation: The natural vegetation is tropical rainforest (about 75% of surviving natural forest is state-owned) and brushwood. Species include the gommier, bois canot and blue mahoe. There are also mangrove swamps and stunted woods. Forest covers 50%

Did you know...

Grenada is an archipelago comprising the island of Grenada – the most southerly of the Windward Islands in the Eastern Caribbean – and some of the Southern Grenadines.

Grenada is the world's second largest producer of nutmeg after Indonesia; a symbol of a clove of nutmeg is on the national flag.

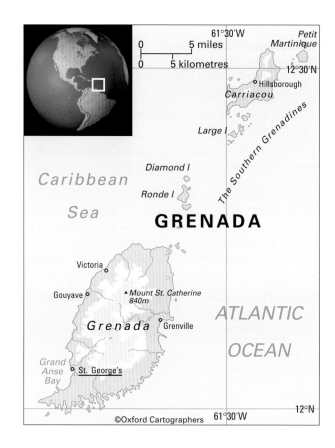

©Oxford Cartographers

of the land area and there was no significant loss of forest cover during 1990–2010.

Wildlife: Mainly smaller species, such as the mona monkey, agouti, armadillo and mongoose. There is a large variety of birds; the Grenada dove and hookbilled kite (an endangered species) are unique to the island.

Main towns: St George's (capital, pop. 5,200 in 2010), Gouyave (3,000), Grenville (2,400), Victoria (2,300), St David's and Sauteurs on Grenada; and Hillsborough (800) on Carriacou.

Transport: There are 1,127km of roads, 61% paved. In the mountainous terrain roads are often narrow and winding.

St George's is a deep-water port. Anchorage and facilities for yachts are offered at St George's (at the Lagoon), Prickly Bay on the south-east coast and Secret Harbour, south of St George's. The port for the Grenadine island of Carriacou is at Hillsborough and ferry services run between Grenada and other islands.

Point Salines International Airport is 11km south of St George's in the south-west of Grenada and there is a small airport at Lauriston on Carriacou.

Society

KEY FACTS 2010

Population per sq km:	301
Life expectancy:	76 years
Net primary enrolment:	98%

Population: 104,000 (2010); 39% lives in urban areas; growth 0.4% p.a. 1990–2010, depressed over this period by emigration; birth rate 19 per 1,000 people (28 in 1970); life expectancy 76 years (64 in 1970).

Most of the population is of African (82% in 1991 census) or mixed African/European descent (13%). The remainder is made up of small European and Asian groups.

Language: English is spoken by almost everyone. A French-based Creole is also spoken.

Religion: Mainly Christians (Roman Catholics 45%, Anglicans 14%, Seventh Day Adventists, Methodists).

Health: Public spending on health was 4% of GDP in 2009. There are three hospitals: General Hospital (St George's), Princess Alice Hospital (St Andrew's) and Princess Royal Hospital (Carriacou). There are homes for handicapped children and geriatric patients. Health centres and district medical stations undertake maternity and child welfare work under the charge of a nurse/midwife. Government hospitals and clinics provide free medical and dental treatment. There is a piped-water supply to all the towns and to many of the villages. Infant mortality was 9 per 1,000 live births in 2010.

Education: There are 12 years of compulsory education starting at age five. Primary school comprises seven years and secondary five. The school year starts in September.

Tertiary education centres on the T A Marryshow Community College, which hosts an open campus of the regional University of the West Indies. T A Marryshow Community College was established in 1988 when Grenada National College merged with several other tertiary institutions including Grenada Teachers College; Grenada Technical and Vocational Institute; and Institute for Further Education. The University of the West Indies has its main campuses in Barbados, Jamaica, and Trinidad and Tobago. St George's University – founded in 1977 – is an offshore American university specialising in medicine. The female–male ratio for gross enrolment in tertiary education is 1.36:1 (2009).

Media: There are no daily newspapers, but *The Grenada Guardian*, *The Grenada Informer*, *The Grenada Times* and *The Grenadian Voice* are weeklies; all in English.

A public–private partnership, the Grenada Broadcasting Network, provides radio and television stations. MTV is privately owned and there are several privately-owned radio stations.

There are 335 internet users per 1,000 people (2010).

Communications: Country code 1 473; internet domain '.gd'. Coin- and card-operated payphones are widely available. There are internet cafes in St George's. The main post office is in St George's.

There are 272 main telephone lines and 1,167 mobile phone subscriptions per 1,000 people (2010).

Public holidays: New Year's Day, Independence Day (7 February), Labour Day (1 May), Emancipation Day (first Monday in August),

Carnival (second Monday and Tuesday in August), Thanksgiving Day (25 October), Christmas Day and Boxing Day.

Religious festivals whose dates vary from year to year include Good Friday, Easter Monday, Whit Monday and Corpus Christi.

Economy

KEY FACTS 2010

GNI:	US$724m
GNI p.c.:	US$6,930
GDP growth:	–0.9% p.a. 2006–10
Inflation:	3.8% p.a. 2006–10

The economy of Grenada (the 'spice island') is based on agriculture, notably nutmeg and mace, and tourism. Consequently it has an outward-looking and open economy, and enjoyed strong growth during the 1990s, even though the world market for spices was sluggish during most of the decade and tourism became increasingly competitive. Grenada is nonetheless vulnerable, its economy being so small, and high public expenditure has brought fiscal difficulties.

Real Growth in GDP

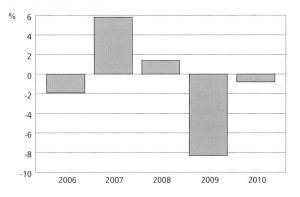

Inflation

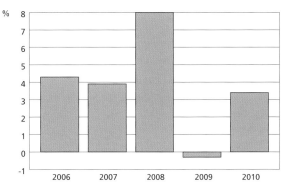

GDP by Sector (2010)

■	Agriculture	**5%**
□	Industry	**14%**
▨	Services	**81%**

An IMF-backed economic adjustment programme was put in place in the 1990s, with fiscal reform, privatisation and staff reductions in the public sector to reduce the deficit, and improve the debt position. The government has encouraged development of industry to broaden the country's economic base, but Grenada's small scale and high costs hinder progress.

A small offshore sector was established in the 1990s including internet gaming companies, but it failed to flourish in the 2000s. A US university, St George's University, with 800 mainly North American students, also brings in substantial foreign exchange.

After three years of strong growth, the economy stalled in 2001, reflecting the US economic downturn and fall in tourism, only picking up again in 2003. In September 2004 Grenada was devastated by Hurricane Ivan and the economy stalled again. Growth of more than 10% in 2005 was followed by shrinkage of 1.9% in 2006, resuming positive in 2007. However, from 2008 the global recession caused a sharp fall in tourism and the economy plunged into recession in 2009–10, recovering weakly in 2011.

Constitution

Status:	Monarchy under Queen Elizabeth II
Legislature:	Parliament
Independence:	7 February 1974

Grenada is a constitutional monarchy with Queen Elizabeth II as head of state. She is represented by a governor-general. A parliamentary democracy, Grenada has a bicameral legislature. The House of Representatives has 15 members elected by universal suffrage for a five-year term, and the Senate 13 members appointed for a five-year term by the governor-general in consultation with the prime minister and the leader of the opposition. The prime minister appoints the cabinet.

Politics

Last elections:	July 2008
Next elections:	2013
Head of state:	Queen Elizabeth II, represented by governor-general, Sir Carlyle Arnold Glean (2008–)
Head of government:	Prime Minister Tillman Thomas
Ruling party:	National Democratic Congress

In the general election in January 1999 – called early after a defection left the New National Party (NNP) government without a parliamentary majority – the NNP won a landslide victory, receiving 62% of the votes and Dr Keith Mitchell continued as prime minister. It was not only the first time a party had taken all 15 seats, but also the first time for any party to have won two successive elections.

In another early election in November 2003 Mitchell and NNP were returned for a third term. NNP won eight seats, with 48% of the votes, and the National Democratic Congress (NDC) seven, with 46%, following a recount in two constituencies where the margin was very small.

In the July 2008 election, Mitchell failed in a bid to secure an unprecedented fourth consecutive term. In a relatively peaceful election, monitored by a strong contingent from the Organization of American States, where the main issues were concerned with management of the economy, NDC took 11 of the 15 House of

Representatives seats and 51% of votes; NNP won four seats and 48% of votes. Tillman Thomas – NDC leader since 2000 – became prime minister.

International relations

Grenada is a member of the African, Caribbean and Pacific Group of States, Association of Caribbean States, Caribbean Community, Non-Aligned Movement, Organisation of Eastern Caribbean States, Organization of American States, United Nations and World Trade Organization.

Traveller information

Local laws and conventions: British, French and African cultures combine in the local culture of Grenada, and the Roman Catholic Church has a strong influence on the way of life.

Dress is casual but beachwear must be confined to the beach and not worn in town. It is an offence for anyone, including children, to dress in camouflage clothing.

There are very severe penalties for all drug offences. Visitors must ensure they pack their own luggage and do not carry anything for a third party.

All business correspondence is in English and dress should be formal for business appointments. There are a number of hotels that offer meeting facilities. Office hours are Mon–Thur 0800–1500, Fri 0800–1700. Government offices are generally closed from 1200–1300.

Immigration and customs: Visas are not required for citizens of the EU, USA and Australia for visits of up to three months. Entry requirements should be checked.

Passports need to be valid for six months from the date of departure from Grenada. Visitors are advised to copy the photopage and the entry stamp from their passport and to keep their passport with them at all times or in a hotel safe. There is a departure tax.

A yellow fever vaccination certificate is required by all travellers who have come from infected areas.

Narcotics, arms and ammunition, fruit, vegetables, meat and soil are prohibited imports. Licensed firearms must be declared and a local licence obtained from the police.

Travel within the country: Driving is on the left and visitors will need to purchase a local driving permit (around EC$30 for three months) after presentation of a full driving licence. Drivers must be over the age of 25. Four-wheel drive vehicles can be hired and are recommended given the terrain. Many roads are steep with hairpin bends.

Minibuses are a relatively cheap and fast means of travel. Standard fares do exist but it is best to confirm the price with the driver. Taxis are available from the airport and most hotels and are the most efficient means of transport. Buses are inexpensive but slow.

There are regular flights from Grenada to Carriacou and Petite Martinique.

Water taxis operate from St George's and there are daily ferry services to the other islands.

Travel health: It is recommended that visitors have comprehensive travel insurance that includes an air ambulance, as serious medical conditions may require evacuation. Dengue fever is endemic to Latin America so visitors will need insect repellent and loose-fitting clothing to discourage mosquito bites.

Immunisation against Hepatitis B should be considered and rabies is present. Current advice on the latest immunisation requirements should be checked before travel.

Mains water is generally safe and bottled water is widely available. Milk is pasteurised.

Money: Barclays Bank, Grenada Bank of Commerce, Grenada National Bank, National Commercial Bank and Scotia Bank are all present in Grenada. American Express, Diners Club, Mastercard and Visa and other major cards are accepted by most shops, car hire companies and hotels. ATMs are available. Banking hours are Mon–Thur 0800–1500, Fri 0800–1700.

There were 113,000 tourist arrivals in 2009.

Further information

Grenada Government: www.gov.gd

Parliament: www.gov.gd/departments/parliament

Eastern Caribbean Central Bank: www.eccb-centralbank.org

Commonwealth Secretariat: www.thecommonwealth.org

Commonwealth of Nations: www.commonwealth-of-nations.org/Grenada

History

Before the 14th century, Grenada was settled by Caribs, who displaced the earlier population of Arawaks. Christopher Columbus visited the island in 1498 and named it 'Concepcion' (later being named by the Spaniards after their own city, Granada). European settlement was slow to follow, due to the fierce resistance of the warlike Caribs, although Britain and France in particular competed for control. A company of London merchants tried and failed to form a settlement in 1605. The French launched more concerted attacks until, by 1674, they had subdued the Caribs and gained control of the island. By 1753, Grenada was a flourishing French possession, with 100 sugar mills and 12,000 enslaved Africans working the industry. The Caribs had been exterminated.

Britain took over from France in 1763 under the Treaty of Paris and again (having meanwhile lost control) in 1783 under the Treaty of Versailles. Britain introduced the cultivation of cacao, cotton and nutmeg; by the time of the emancipation of slaves (1833), the slave population had reached 24,000.

National political consciousness developed through the labour movement, with the formation of the Grenada Manual and Mental Workers Union. In the new environment, a union organiser, Eric Matthew Gairy, formed the first political party, the pro-union, pro-independence Grenada United Labour Party (GULP). In 1951, GULP won the elections and Gairy became leader of the assembly. The Grenada National Party (GNP), led by Herbert Blaize held power between 1957–61 and 1962–67.

Grenada joined the Federation of the West Indies in 1958. When that was dissolved in 1962, it evolved first into an associated state with full internal self-government (1967), and then towards independence, the core of the GULP platform.

Independence was achieved in 1974; Grenada became a constitutional monarchy, with Gairy as prime minister, and Queen Elizabeth II as head of state, represented by a governor-general. Strikes during the independence preparations, which almost prevented the transition, were suppressed by, it was claimed,

'Mongoose Gangs' operating in the manner of Haiti's 'Tonton-Macoutes'.

In 1979, while absent in the USA, Gairy was deposed in a coup by opposition leader Maurice Bishop, who took the New Jewel Movement (NJM) into power as the People's Revolutionary Government. The new government created state farms and industries, and forged links with the socialist world. With Cuba's assistance, it began construction of the modern international airport at Point Salines.

In October 1983, after a military coup in which Bishop, two other ministers, two union leaders and 13 bystanders were killed, Bishop's deputy, Bernard Coard, took control and set up a Revolutionary Military Council. At the request of OECS, in late 1983, the USA then invaded Grenada, supported by a token force of 300 police from Antigua and Barbuda, Barbados, Dominica, Jamaica, St Lucia, and St Vincent and the Grenadines. The governor-general, Sir Paul Scoon, took control of an interim administration, (almost fully) reinstated the 1974 constitution and organised elections for a new government.

The New National Party (NNP), a four-party merger led by Herbert Blaize and supported by the neighbouring islands, easily defeated Gairy's GULP at the December 1984 general election, and Blaize became prime minister.

In the elections in 1990 no single party gained an overall majority and another merger, the National Democratic Congress (NDC), formed the government under Nicholas Brathwaite.

The 1995 elections, contested by seven parties, were narrowly won by the NNP, now led by Dr Keith Mitchell, who became prime minister. The NNP gained eight seats, the NDC, now led by George Brizan, five and GULP, two.

Two no-confidence motions following the elections were unsuccessful. However, in May 1997, five opposition parties, including the NDC, GULP and the Democratic Labour Party formed an alliance to provide a common front against the NNP, leaving the government with a majority of one.

Guyana

KEY FACTS

Joined Commonwealth:	1966
Population:	754,000 (2010)
GDP p.c. growth:	2.5% p.a. 1990–2010
UN HDI 2011:	world ranking 117
Official language:	English
Time:	GMT minus 4hr
Currency:	Guyana dollar (G$)

Geography

Area:	214,970 sq km
Coastline:	459km
Capital:	Georgetown

The Co-operative Republic of Guyana lies in the north-east of South America, north of the equator. It is bordered by Suriname, Brazil and Venezuela and, to the north and east, extends to the North Atlantic Ocean. The country comprises ten regions.

Topography: Guyana has three distinct geographical zones. It has a narrow coastal belt, seldom more than 25km wide and much of it 1–1.5m below sea level, where sugar and rice are grown and 90% of the people live. In the far interior are high savannah uplands; between these, thick, hilly tropical forest covers most of the land area. In the forest zone are found most of the country's resources of bauxite, diamonds, gold, manganese and other minerals. Guyana's massive rivers include the Demerara, Berbice, Essequibo and Corentyne; rapids, bars and other obstacles make navigation difficult. The Kaieteur Falls on the Potaro river have a 222m drop – five times the height of Niagara. The Amerindian

name 'Guiana' (part of the country's former name) means 'Land of Many Waters'.

Climate: Guyana has a warm tropical climate with high rainfall and humidity. The rainy seasons are November–January and May–July with an average rainfall of 2,350mm p.a. in the coastal region. Inland rainfall averages 1,520mm p.a. North-east trade winds moderate coastal temperatures.

Environment: The most significant environmental issues are water pollution by sewage, and agricultural and industrial chemicals; and deforestation.

Vegetation: Guyana's tropical forest, covering 77% of the land area, is among the most ecologically valuable and best preserved in the world. The environment is an issue of great political importance in Guyana. There is concern about climate change and sea-level rise, because the low-lying littoral plain relies on a system of dams, walls and drainage canals to prevent flooding from the sea or the huge rivers. Forest resources are also important; the country has taken a lead in advancing forestry conservation and sustainable development and there was no significant loss of forest cover during 1990–2010.

Did you know...

Sir Shridath Ramphal of Guyana was Commonwealth Secretary-General 1975–90.

Guyanese writers have won the overall Best First Book award of the Commonwealth Writers' Prize in 1991 (Pauline Melville) and in 2006 (Mark McWatt).

The Government of Guyana, at the 1989 CHOGM, offered to set aside about 360,000 hectares of pristine rainforest for research to demonstrate methods for conservation and sustainable use of forest resources and biodiversity: as a result, the Commonwealth's flagship Iwokrama Rainforest Programme was launched the following year.

The Commonwealth Youth Programme Caribbean Centre is based in Georgetown.

Under the Iwokrama Rainforest Programme, some 371,000ha, much of it virgin forest, have been set aside for preservation and scientific study of its ecology and for sustainable development of the parts inhabited by Amerindian tribes or migrant mining communities. The programme was launched by the Guyana Government and the Commonwealth Secretariat.

Wildlife: The tapir is the largest land mammal; cats include the jaguar and ocelot. Monkeys and deer are the most numerous species, and the caiman is the largest freshwater animal. The giant anaconda or water boa is also found in the rivers. The wealth of plant, animal and micro-organism species includes many so far unrecorded, whose properties are unknown to science.

Main towns: Georgetown (capital, pop. 141,300 in 2010), Linden (30,700), New Amsterdam (15,700), Anna Regina (13,800), Corriverton (10,600), Bartica (8,500), Rosignol, Skeldon and Vreed en Hoop. Georgetown is famous for its Dutch-inspired wooden architecture, street layout and drainage canals.

Transport: Surface travel in the interior of the country is hindered by dense forest, rapids on the rivers, and the generally undeveloped character of the interior. Thus, apart from in the coastal belt and on one inland route, most journeys are by air.

There are all-weather roads along the eastern part of the coast and some all-weather roads inland, including one across the country to the border with Brazil, and about 7% of the total network of 7,970km is paved. There is no passenger rail service, although mining companies have private goods lines.

There are some 1,600km of navigable river, 1,000km of which are in areas of some economic activity. Passenger and cargo vessels travel up the Demerara, Essequibo and Berbice rivers, and also along the coast between the rivers. Apart from the Demerara, which has a road bridge, the other major rivers have to be crossed by ferries, which can take some hours for the wider rivers. At the Corentyne river ferry services link Guyana with Suriname.

Georgetown is the main port, and the international airport is CBJ International Airport, at Timehri, 40km from Georgetown; larger towns and many mining companies have airports or landing strips.

Society

KEY FACTS 2010

Population per sq km:	4
Life expectancy:	70 years
Net primary enrolment:	99%

Population: 754,000 (2010); distribution is very uneven, with high concentration of people along the coastal strip and many inland areas virtually uninhabited; 29% lives in urban areas; growth 0.2% p.a. 1990–2010, depressed over this period by emigration; birth rate 18 per 1,000 people (38 in 1970); life expectancy 70 years (60 in 1970).

The ethnic origins of the people are: 44% Indian (resident mostly in agricultural areas); 30% African (mostly in towns); 17% of mixed descent; 9% Amerindian (mainly in the west and south, or on reserves; data from 2002 census).

Language: English is the official language, Guyana being the only English-speaking country in South America. An English-based Creole is widely used; Hindi, Urdu and Amerindian languages are also spoken.

Religion: Christians about 57% (Pentecostals 17%, Roman Catholics 8%, Anglicans 7%, Seventh Day Adventists 5%), Hindus 28%, Muslims 7% (2002 census).

Health: Public spending on health was 7% of GDP in 2009. The Public Hospital at Georgetown is the national referral hospital; there are some 30 hospitals and many health centres throughout the country, with both public and private care available, the former usually free. 94% of the population uses an improved drinking water source and 81% have adequate sanitation facilities (2009). Infant mortality was 25 per 1,000 live births in 2010 (100 in 1960). In 2009, 1.2% of people aged 15–49 were HIV positive.

Education: Public spending on education was 3.7% of GDP in 2010. There are 11 years of compulsory education starting at age five. Primary school comprises six years and secondary seven, with cycles of five and two years. Some 83% of pupils complete primary school (2008). The school year starts in September.

Tertiary institutions include University of Guyana, which has law and medical schools, and campuses at Turkeyen, Georgetown, and Tain, Rose Hall; Cyril Potter College of Education (for teachers), based at the Turkeyen campus of the University, with branches at Linden, New Amsterdam and Rose Hall; Guyana College of Agriculture; and Commonwealth Youth Programme Caribbean Centre at Georgetown (which trains youth workers from Commonwealth countries in the region). The University of Guyana also provides adult education programmes. The female–male ratio for gross enrolment in tertiary education is 0.96:1 (2009).

Media: The state-owned *Guyana Chronicle/Sunday Chronicle* and privately owned *Stabroek News* and *Kaieteur News* are dailies. *The Catholic Standard* is weekly, and *Mirror* twice weekly.

The National Communications Network provides public radio and TV services.

There are 38 personal computers (2005) and 299 internet users (2010) per 1,000 people.

Communications: Country code 592; internet domain '.gy'. Internet connections are slow but improving, and there are internet cafes in Georgetown. There are post offices in the urban areas.

There are 199 main telephone lines and 736 mobile phone subscriptions per 1,000 people (2010).

Public holidays: New Year's Day, Republic Day (Mashramani, 23 February), Labour Day (1 May), Arrival Day (5 May), Independence Day (26 May), CARICOM Day (first Monday in July), Emancipation Day (first Monday in August), Christmas Day and Boxing Day. The Republic Day celebrations continue for about a week, though only one day is a public holiday.

Religious and other festivals whose dates vary from year to year include Prophet's Birthday, Phagwah (Holi, March), Good Friday, Easter Monday, Deepavali (Diwali, October/November) and Eid al-Adha (Feast of the Sacrifice).

Economy

KEY FACTS 2010

GNI:	US$2.2bn
GNI p.c.:	US$2,870
GDP growth:	4.2% p.a. 2006–10
Inflation:	6.3% p.a. 2006–10

Real Growth in GDP

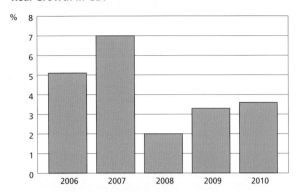

Inflation

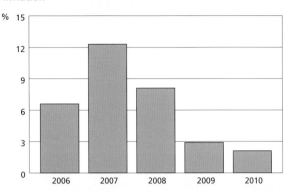

The economy is based on agriculture and mining, notably of gold and bauxite; the main cash crops are sugar and rice. After near collapse in 1982, it was resuscitated by strict implementation of IMF-backed economic reforms. By the mid-1990s, these reforms had had success in stabilising the currency, controlling inflation and increasing output and trade, and the economy was growing at an annual rate of more than 6% in 1996 and 1997. Inflation peaked at 83% in 1991, following substantial devaluations of the Guyana dollar, but was in single figures from the mid-1990s, though it

GDP by Sector (2010)

■ Agriculture	**17%**
□ Industry	**34%**
■ Services	**48%**

History

The original Guiana was inhabited by semi-nomadic Amerindian tribes who lived by hunting and fishing – notably Arawaks and Caribs. It was divided by European powers into Spanish Guiana (Venezuela), Portuguese Guiana (Brazil), French Guiana, Dutch Guiana (Suriname) and British Guiana (Guyana). Colonial competition for territory began with the Spanish sighting in 1499. Probably temporary Spanish or Portuguese settlements were followed by Dutch settlement, first unsuccessfully at Pomeroon, and then (in 1627) under the protection of the Dutch West India Company on the Berbice river. Despite yielding from time to time to British, French and Portuguese invasions, the Dutch kept control until 1814, when the colonies of Essequibo, Demerara and Berbice were ceded to Britain. The Europeans imported African slaves to develop their plantations, first of tobacco and later sugar, and to labour on constructing the coastal drainage system and the elegant city of Georgetown. Some slaves escaped to the forest; these so-called 'bush-blacks' eked out a living by panning for gold, hunting and subsistence agriculture.

The British administration merged the three colonies into British Guiana in 1831, but retained the Dutch administrative, legislative and legal system, whereby the country was directed by a governor, advised by councils of plantation owners. After the abolition of slavery, Indian and smaller numbers of Portuguese, Chinese and Javanese indentured labourers were brought in to work the estates.

In 1928 a legislative council, with members appointed by the British Government, was established, but members were elected after extensions of the franchise in 1943 and 1945. The country was by this period among the most advanced of the British colonial territories in the region, and became the headquarters of

several regional educational and political institutions. CARICOM still has its headquarters in Georgetown.

In 1953, a constitution with a bicameral legislature and ministerial system, based on elections under universal adult suffrage, was introduced. There was a general election, won by the People's Progressive Party (PPP), led by Dr Cheddi Jagan. The PPP had a large East Indian following, whereas the People's National Congress (PNC), a breakaway party formed in 1957, had its roots among Guyanese of African origin. Shortly after the 1953 elections, the UK suspended the constitution, decided to 'mark time' in the advance towards self-government, and administered the country with a government composed largely of nominated members.

When, in 1957, the UK did introduce elected members, the legislature voted for more representative government. The UK called a constitutional conference which was held in 1960 and provided for a new constitution with full internal self-government. In the elections held in August 1961 under this constitution, the PPP again gained the majority. The UK held further constitutional conferences in 1962 and 1963, to settle terms for independence, but ethnic divisions prevented the leaders of Guyana's three political parties from being able to reach consensus among themselves on the terms of a constitution; they then asked the UK to settle the matter.

The UK selected a form of proportional representation which was aimed at preventing domination by any single ethnic group. (It was also argued that, at this period of the 'Cuba crisis' with near-war between the USA and USSR, the UK was under pressure to avoid allowing a socialist government to come to power in Guyana.) Despite renewed disturbances, elections were held

➤

remained relatively high until the late 2000s. Privatisation had led to new investment and creation of new jobs.

The reforms included extensive privatisation of state-owned operations, some of which – for example, the Sugar Corporation and Guyana Airways Corporation – are now under private management and/or ownership.

But the combination of drought, falling commodity prices and political uncertainty in 1998, caused growth to stall. The economy then grew very little during 1998–2005. From 2006 there were signs that the economic policies supported by the international financial institutions were beginning to bear fruit, until late 2008 when collapsing world demand caused the economy to moderate in 2008–10, before returning to good growth in 2010–11.

Constitution

Status:	Republic with executive president
Legislature:	Parliament
Independence:	26 May 1966

Guyana is a republic, divided into administrative regions, with an executive president and parliamentary legislature. The 1980 constitution, amended in 2001, provides for an executive presidency and a unicameral legislature, the National Assembly,

with 65 members directly elected by proportional representation: 40 at a national level and 25 at a regional level. The normal life of parliament is five years.

The leader of the majority party in the Assembly is president for the duration of the Assembly. The president appoints the prime minister and cabinet (which may include those from outside the Assembly), which is responsible to parliament.

Politics

Last elections:	November 2011
Next elections:	2016
Head of state:	President Donald Ramotar
Head of government:	the president
Ruling party:	People's Progressive Party–Civic coalition

In the general election of March 2001, the first to be held under a new electoral system, the ruling People's Progressive Party (PPP)–Civic coalition won 34 seats (53% of the vote). Bharrat Jagdeo retained the presidency and Desmond Hoyte of the People's National Congress Reform (PNCR, 27 seats and 42%) continued to lead the opposition. Voter turnout was nearly 90%. Although the election result was seen by international observers to reflect the will of the people, in the weeks following the elections opposition

➤ under the PR system, and brought to power a coalition of the PNC led by Forbes Burnham and The United Force (TUF).

The new government finalised independence arrangements at a further constitutional conference, which was boycotted by the PPP. Guyana became independent and joined the Commonwealth in May 1966, and became a republic four years later.

The PNC led by Burnham was returned in 1968 elections and remained in power until 1992 (despite repeated electoral disputes). During the 1970s, 80% of the economy was nationalised. These were years of considerable unrest and increasing economic difficulty, as debt rose and world prices for the major exports fell. The PPP, led by Dr Cheddi Jagan, remained in opposition. Executive presidency was introduced in 1980. In 1985 Burnham died and was replaced by Desmond Hoyte.

The elections due in 1990 were postponed twice, in part because the Commonwealth observer team invited by President Hoyte's administration reported irregularities in the voters' rolls and proposed that certain preparatory arrangements should be done again. When the elections were held, in October 1992, the PPP–Civic coalition, led by Jagan, won 53.5% of the votes, giving it 28 seats; the PNC won 23, the TUF and the Working People's Alliance (WPA) one each. The Commonwealth observers described the elections as 'a historic democratic process' which expressed the people's genuine will. Jagan was sworn in as president.

In March 1997 Jagan suffered a heart attack and died. Samuel Hinds, prime minister in Jagan's PPP–Civic government, became president and Janet Jagan, Jagan's US-born widow, was appointed prime minister and vice-president. Mrs Jagan was one of the four founders of the PPP, and had served in two previous

cabinets. In the December 1997 elections the PPP–Civic coalition claimed a decisive victory with 56% of the officially counted votes. Mrs Jagan became Guyana's first woman president and appointed Hinds prime minister.

However, the opposition PNC refused to accept the declared results. Increasingly violent demonstrations followed and were only ended when, in January 1998, CARICOM brokered an agreement between the PPP–Civic and PNC. Under the Herdmanston Accord, CARICOM would undertake an audit of the election results, to be conducted by a team selected by the then CARICOM chair, Dr Keith Mitchell, the prime minister of Grenada. A broad-based Constitutional Reform Commission would be established, to report to the National Assembly within 18 months. And there would be new elections within 18 months after presentation of the report.

The CARICOM audit team reported that although the management of the count left much to be desired 'the results of their recount varied only marginally from that of the final results declared by the Chief Elections Officer'. But the PNC remained dissatisfied and violent demonstrations broke out again. A settlement was finally reached at the CARICOM summit in St Lucia in July 1998, under which the PNC agreed to take their seats in the National Assembly.

President Janet Jagan resigned after suffering a mild heart attack in August 1999 and was succeeded by Finance Minister Bharrat Jagdeo.

The Constitutional Reform Commission's proposals were enacted in 2000. These included establishment of a permanent elections commission and new national identity cards.

EXEMPLARY DEVELOPMENT OF THE GUYANA ELECTIONS COMMISSION (GECOM)

National Elections in Guyana had previously often been accompanied by a degree of turbulence, resulting in burning, looting and the loss of lives.

After the Elections of 2001, a more permanent Elections Commission was brought into being. The establishment of Rules of Procedure governing every facet of GECOM's undertakings together with the implementation of comprehensive Development Plans ensured the much needed stability. A functional menu of measures was introduced to counter any element which had the potential of social and electoral disruption, while recognizing demands of contesting political parties to not only assuage their discontent, but enhance the credibility and transparency of elections.

In addition, the final success was achieved, not lastly, through the bringing together of all contesting political parties to publicly sign, endorse and adhere to a Code of Conduct for Political Parties (CoCPP). (Please note that GECOM is prepared to share the text of the Code of Conduct for Political Parties with all Election Management Bodies in the Commonwealth.) This was a collaborative and co-operative effort which included key stakeholders.

'The Commonwealth Observer Group found that overall, the elections were credible and many of the benchmarks for democratic elections were met. The Group commended the preparedness of the Guyana Elections Commission, notably in terms of the significant improvement in the integrity of the voters' register.'

Extract from the *Final Report* of the Commonwealth Observer Group

Guyana Elections Commission Chairman, Dr R.S. Surujbally

www.gecom.org.gy

supporters continued to mount violent demonstrations expressing doubts about the accuracy of the poll.

These only began to be allayed when in April 2001 Jagdeo and Hoyte initiated a dialogue among parliamentarians and civil society on constitutional and electoral reform. However, this dialogue broke down in March 2002 over differences between PPP–Civic and PNCR on implementation of what had been agreed. The deadlock continued until late August 2002 when, at the government's request, the Commonwealth Secretary-General appointed a special envoy, former Governor-General of New Zealand Sir Paul Reeves, to facilitate resumption of the dialogue between the opposing parties. During 2003 constructive dialogue proceeded between Jagdeo and the new opposition leader, Robert Corbin, political tension eased, and opposition members returned to parliament. During 2004, the constructive dialogue process wavered and the opposition's parliamentary boycott was resumed for some time, before they returned to parliament on the basis of 'selective engagement'.

In relatively peaceful elections in August 2006, President Jagdeo and the PPP–Civic coalition were returned to power, with 36 seats and 54.6% of the votes, while the PNCR–One Guyana coalition took 22 seats and 34.0% of the votes and the newly constituted Alliance for Change – which enjoys support from East Indians and Afro-Guyanese – five seats and 8.1% of the votes. Commonwealth observers present reported that the results reflected the wishes of the people.

Former Prime Minister and President Janet Jagan died in March 2009.

In the 2011 elections PPP–Civic, led by Donald Ramotar, won 32 seats, receiving 48.6% of the vote, one seat short of a parliamentary majority. The new coalition led by PNCR, A Partnership for National Unity, took 26 seats (40%) and the Alliance for Change 7 seats (10.3%). Ramotar was sworn in as president. The Commonwealth observer team present found the elections to be well managed and generally peaceful.

International relations

Guyana is a member of the African, Caribbean and Pacific Group of States, Association of Caribbean States, Caribbean Community, Non-Aligned Movement, Organisation of Islamic Cooperation, Organization of American States, United Nations and World Trade Organization.

Guyana hosts the headquarters of the Caribbean Community in Georgetown.

Traveller information

Local laws and conventions: There are heavy fines and prison sentences for those caught possessing drugs. The minimum sentence is three years. Visitors should ensure they pack their own luggage and must never carry packages through customs for a third party.

Social customs are flexible enough to include everyone, largely because of the multiracial background of the country.

Appointments for business meetings must be made and punctuality is important. Business cards are appreciated. Office hours are Mon–Fri 0800–1200 and 1300–1630.

Immigration and customs: Citizens from the EU, USA, Australia and Canada do not need a visa. Passports must be valid for at least six months on arrival into the country. Visitors are advised to make a copy of the photopage of their passport, which they should have on them at all times.

Visitors are only permitted to stay for up to 30 days but extensions can be arranged from the Ministry of Home Affairs in Georgetown.

A yellow fever vaccination certificate is required from all those travelling from infected areas.

Departure tax must be paid in cash.

Travel within the country: Traffic drives on the left. An international driving permit is recommended to drive in Guyana, although local driving permits are available for one month from the Licence and Revenue Office in Georgetown on presentation of a valid driving licence. Car hire is available in Georgetown. Seatbelts must be worn at all times. The best roads are found on the eastern coastal strip.

Guyana has regular bus services and the minibus terminal can be found at Georgetown's Stabroek Market.

Taxis are the safest means of travelling around towns, especially at night. Most fares are standard but over longer distances a fare should be agreed before travel.

Air travel is the only reliable means of getting around the interior. Ogle aerodrome on the east coast and CBJ International in Timehri are used by several local airlines.

Guyana has extensive waterways and steamers connect with the interior; there is also a coast-hopping service from Georgetown. Use only the scheduled services to cross the Corentyne river between Guyana and Suriname.

Travel health: Comprehensive travel and health insurance is recommended. Visitors should seek medical advice before travelling and ensure that all appropriate vaccinations are up to date.

Dengue fever is endemic to Latin America, and visitors will need insect repellent and appropriate protective clothing to prevent mosquito bites. Visitors will also need anti-malaria tablets and should exercise the same preventative measures as for dengue fever. The latest advice on immunisations should be checked before departure.

All prescription drugs must be kept in their original packaging, clearly marked to avoid confusion.

Mains water is chlorinated, bottled water is widely available.

Money: Credit/debit cards are not widely accepted and it is worth considering bringing a mixture of US dollars and US travellers cheques. Foreign credit cards cannot be used in ATMs. Banking hours are Mon–Fri 0800–1230 and Fri 1500–1700.

There were 141,000 tourist arrivals in 2009.

Further information

Office of the President, Republic of Guyana: www.op.gov.gy

Parliament: www.parliament.gov.gy

Bank of Guyana: www.bankofguyana.org.gy

Commonwealth Secretariat: www.thecommonwealth.org

Commonwealth of Nations: www.commonwealth-of-nations.org/Guyana

India

KEY FACTS

Joined Commonwealth:	1947
Population:	1,224,614,000 (2010)
GDP p.c. growth:	4.9% p.a. 1990–2010
UN HDI 2011:	world ranking 134
Official languages:	Hindi, English
Time:	GMT plus 5.5hr
Currency:	rupee (Rs)

Geography

Area:	3,287,263 sq km
Coastline:	7,520km
Capital:	New Delhi

The Republic of India, which lies across the Tropic of Cancer, comprises most of the Indian subcontinent. It also includes the Andaman and Nicobar Islands in the Bay of Bengal and the Lakshadweep Islands in the Arabian Sea. Its neighbours are Pakistan, Afghanistan and China to the north, then Nepal, Bhutan, Bangladesh and Myanmar (formerly Burma). In the south, the Palk Strait separates it from Sri Lanka. India is a federal republic with 29 states (including the Delhi National Capital Territory), and six union territories.

Topography: India has great topographical variety, with four distinct regions. The northern region rises into the Himalayas, forming a mountainous wall 160km to 320km deep, the mountains losing height to the east. The second region is the plain of the River Ganges and its tributaries, a huge stretch of flat alluvium flowing into the Bay of Bengal in a broad delta. This is

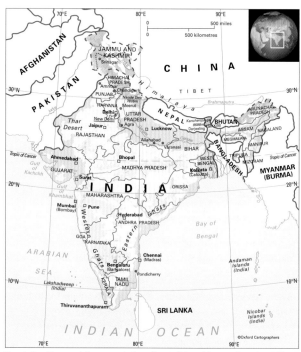

The designations and the presentation of material on this map, based on UN practice, do not imply the expression of any opinion whatsoever on the part of the Commonwealth Secretariat or the publishers concerning the legal status of any country, territory or area, or of its authorities, or concerning the delimitation of its frontiers or boundaries. There is no intention to define the status of Jammu and/or Kashmir, which has not yet been agreed on by the parties.

one of the most fertile and densely populated regions of India. The third region is the Thar Desert, which stretches into Pakistan. The fourth region is the Deccan tableland bordered by ranges of hills, the Western and Eastern Ghats and Nilgiri Hills in the south, and their coastal belts.

The country has many large rivers, the most important of which are the Ganges, Jamuna, Brahmaputra, a stretch of the Indus, Godavari, Krishna, Mahanadi, Narmada and Cauvery. All these rivers are navigable in parts.

Climate: The climate is hot with regional variations. Rajasthan and large parts of the north-west are dry (under 750mm annual rainfall) and the Thar Desert (in fact a semi-desert) receives around 300mm. 80% of rain falls between June and September, the season of the monsoon. April to June is generally hot, dry and dusty.

Environment: The most significant environmental issues are that finite natural resources support a very large and growing population; deforestation, soil erosion and desertification; air pollution with industrial effluents and vehicle emissions; and water pollution with raw sewage and run-off of agricultural pesticides.

Did you know...

Kamalesh Sharma of India became Commonwealth Secretary-General in 2008; and Professor Asha Kanwar was appointed President and Chief Executive Officer of the Commonwealth of Learning in 2012.

Twelve Indians have been regional winners in the Commonwealth Writers' Prize, and three have gone on to take the overall Best Book or Best First Book awards.

The Commonwealth Human Rights Initiative established its HQ in New Delhi in 1993; and the country is also host to the Commonwealth Youth Programme Asia Centre in Chandigarh.

Scholarships for postgraduate study are awarded by India to citizens of other Commonwealth countries under the Commonwealth Scholarship and Fellowship Plan.

History

The Indian subcontinent is one of the cradles of civilisation. An Indus Valley culture of pre-Aryan people flourished from about 3000 BC. This population comprised Dravidian tribes who appear to have migrated from the west, ousting and assimilating aboriginal inhabitants. The Indus Valley civilisation developed writing, art, temples, cities, irrigation and commerce. It was wiped out around 2500 BC by invaders who entered the subcontinent through the mountain passes of the north-west frontier.

Indo-European conquerors (with iron weapons, war chariots and armour) had control of much of the subcontinent by 1500 BC. They settled and established the tightly stratified Vedic civilisation. Much information about this civilisation, which was advanced in various arts and sciences, is derived from the Vedas, a collection of sacred writings. Sixteen autonomous states were established, with the kingdom of Magadha in the Ganges river valley (territory of present-day Bihar) rising to prominence in the 6th century BC. During the reign of King Bimbisara (c. 543–491 BC) Prince Siddhartha and Vardhamana Jnatiputra or Nataputta Mahavira (founders of Buddhism and Jainism) preached in Magadha.

Invasions subsequently came from Persia and Greece, including that of Alexander the Great of Macedon in 326 BC. Through this turmoil, Magadha strengthened its position as the centre of an expanding empire. The Maurya dynasty was founded in 321 BC. At the zenith of the Maurya period under Ashoka (272–232 BC), the empire took in the entire subcontinent, and stretched from Afghanistan to Bengal. Ashoka gave India many of its enduring cultural characteristics, including his emblem, and philosophy. Ashoka spread the teachings of Prince Siddhartha (Buddhism) across India.

This empire in turn fragmented under waves of invasion between about AD 100–300, though, when the Guptas seized power and reunified Magadha in AD 319–606, Indian art, culture and philosophy had another renaissance and Hinduism gained strength again. This power centre was, in its turn, broken up in the Hun invasion, bringing confusion to northern India.

Muslim conquerors began entering the north from around the seventh century; this phase of history had its apogee in the Moghul dynasty of 1526 to 1738. One of the great legacies of Moghul India is aesthetic: it gave to Indian culture new arts in poetry, architecture, garden design and notably some of the world's greatest palace and funerary buildings, of which the Taj Mahal is only one masterpiece. However, the Moghul dynasty also had negative effects, especially for the south, where the trading empires, established for centuries and historically involved in sea trade with such partners as Egypt and the Roman Empire, were destroyed.

With the decline of the Moghul Empire into separate feudal and often feuding states, new invaders, Portuguese, Dutch, French and British, entered the Indian Ocean. In 1690 the British East India Company set itself up at Calcutta to trade in clothes, tea and spices. The company had its own private army, with which it ousted the French from Madras in 1748. French plans for control of the subcontinent were finally ended by decisive British victories in 1756–63. One by one, the company then conquered the Indian states until it had control of virtually the whole subcontinent by 1820. Those states which remained unconquered entered into alliance with Britain.

Sporadic resistance to the rule of the East India Company culminated in a major uprising in 1857, known to the British as the Indian Mutiny. After its suppression, the British Crown took direct control. The high colonial period followed, when the Indian railway system was constructed, a nationwide education system established, and the world's then largest administrative system developed. There was also, however, substantial disruption: India's handloom textile industry was destroyed by competition from British mills and peasant farming hit by reorganisation in favour of cash crops. India's importance to Britain was as more than a source of raw materials and a market for British manufactured goods. India underpinned Britain's imperial influence and strength, the 'Jewel in the Crown' of the British Empire.

However, the independence movement not only brought an end to British rule, but also set the pattern for resistance to colonialism everywhere. The Indian National Congress was set up in 1885; Mohandas (Mahatma) Gandhi became its leader after 1918 and set it on its course of non-violent non-co-operation with the foreign rulers. Gandhi's methods of mass mobilisation greatly impressed the Congress radical wing and a young activist, Jawaharlal Nehru. There was, however, bloodshed at Amritsar, Punjab, in 1919 when British troops killed more than 400 protesters.

The memory of the Amritsar massacre became a rallying cry for the independence movement. Congress launched its 'non-co-operation' campaign: colonial institutions, elections, administrative bodies, schools and British products were boycotted. Campaign participants were instructed to accept passively the legal consequences. With Gandhi's campaign against the state monopoly on salt, the movement spread nationwide. Around 27,000 Indian nationalists were imprisoned and the British administrative system was partially paralysed. The colonial authorities were politely, but insistently, invited to 'go home'. As a result of its much weakened position at the end of the Second World War, the UK accepted the inevitable and began the process of transferring power. India became independent in August 1947.

At independence the subcontinent was divided, at the insistence of Muslim leaders, into the independent Islamic state of Pakistan and the independent secular state of India. Some 12 million refugees were transferred across the borders, as Sikhs and Hindus moved from Pakistan into India and Muslims migrated to Pakistan. An estimated 4 million people migrated in September ➤

1947 alone, amid much violence, including military action in disputed areas and the murder of the Mahatma himself, in 1948, by a Hindu extremist. Nehru's Congress won the general election (India's first general election with universal adult suffrage) of 1952; he remained prime minister until his death in 1964 when he was succeeded by Lal Bahadur Shastri.

During this period the modern nation of India was founded. Nehru had to address four main areas: the constitution, reorganisation of states, development of India as an industrial nation, and settling disputes with neighbours. The main problems with the constitution were the remnants of the princely states, all eventually brought into the Union (although the dispute between Pakistan and India over Kashmir continued into the 2000s), and the redrawing of state boundaries in accordance with linguistic criteria.

Nehru's distrust of world powers and exploitation led his pursuit of a self-sufficient industrial socialist state. He also aimed to resolve religious conflict through a secular state, and to abolish the caste system. Internationally, Nehru set India on its course of non-alignment and was one of the founders of the Non-Aligned Movement. Foreign policy, however, was dogged with problems, chief among these being the ongoing crises with Pakistan (and to some extent Bangladesh) over boundaries, which led to three wars in 1947, 1965 and 1971, and dispute with China over Tibet in 1962, culminating in armed conflict. In time, India developed a large and well-equipped army, and was the first Third World country to develop a nuclear-weapons capability (1974) and equip its army through indigenous production as well as through imports.

Following Lal Bahadur Shastri's death in 1966, Nehru's daughter, Indira Gandhi, became prime minister; she won the 1967 general election, but lost in 1977. Between 1977 and 1980 a Janata coalition – led by Morarji Desai, a former member of the Congress party – and then a Lok Dal coalition ruled the country. Heading her new Congress (I) party, Indira Gandhi returned to power in the 1980 elections.

In 1984, when there was unrest in several states, Sikh nationalists demanding autonomy occupied several places of worship; federal troops stormed the Golden Temple at Amritsar. On 31 October 1984 Indira Gandhi was assassinated in New Delhi by two Sikh members of her personal bodyguard. Rajiv Gandhi, her son, was at once sworn in as prime minister. He called elections in December at which Congress (I) won 49% of the votes and 403 seats.

After the November 1989 general election, although Congress (I) remained the single biggest party in the Lok Sabha, it was unable to command an overall majority and V P Singh, leader of the new Janata Dal party and head of the National Front Coalition, became prime minister. The Janata Dal party (a merger of the old Janata and Lok Dal parties) aimed to be the party of the poor and lower castes.

In 1991, when the Bharatiya Janata Party (BJP) withdrew its support, Janata Dal split and the Lok Sabha was dissolved in March 1991, to prepare for a general election. While campaigning, Rajiv Gandhi was assassinated by a member of an extremist faction supporting the Tamil guerrillas in Sri Lanka. In the elections Congress (I) party took 227 seats and its new leader Narasimha Rao formed a minority government, the BJP winning 119 seats and Janata Dal 55.

The Rao administration introduced economic reforms and turned the economy around, but failed to win an overall majority in the 1996 elections. The BJP and its allies won 194 seats, Congress (I) 136 and a loose alliance of left-wing parties 179 seats, with the remainder won by minor parties and independents. The BJP formed a minority government under Atal Bihari Vajpayee, but this proved too fragile to last and the country was then governed by a coalition of 13, and later 15 parties, with Deve Gowda and then I K Gujral as prime minister, with the support of Congress (I) which was wracked by defections and splits following its election defeat. By late 1997 the coalition had lost its majority and an early general election was called.

But in the February/March 1998 general election again no party emerged with a clear majority. Of the total of 545 seats, BJP took 181, Congress (I) 141 and Communist Party of India (Marxist) 32. But after the negotiations that followed the election the BJP-led coalition had the support of some 265 members, and Vajpayee of the BJP was able to form a coalition government comprising some 40 parties and independent members and finally commanding a majority in an early vote of confidence of 274:261 votes.

Relations with Pakistan

The year 2002 saw higher levels of tension between India and Pakistan over Kashmir, especially in May 2002 when India mobilised a vast army along the Line of Control and the two countries were on the brink of war. Tension eased considerably in October 2002 when India reduced its number of troops along the Line of Control; diplomatic relations were restored in August 2003 and a ceasefire along the Line of Control was agreed and took effect from 26 November 2003.

Peace talks between India and Pakistan began in 2004, marking a historic advance in relations between the two countries. The talks led to the restoration of communication links and a range of confidence-building measures, including co-ordinated relief efforts in the aftermath of the October 2005 earthquake.

A series of co-ordinated terrorist attacks in Mumbai during three days in November 2008 resulted in at least 170 dead and several hundred injured. The principal targets were two luxury hotels. The Indian authorities released a dossier of evidence asserting that the ten gunmen were Pakistan-based. This dossier was subsequently presented to the Government of Pakistan for it to take appropriate action.

Vegetation: Forests in the western Himalayan region range from conifers and broad-leaved trees in the temperate zone to silver fir, silver birch and junipers at the highest level of the alpine zone. The temperate zone of the eastern Himalayan region has forests of oaks, laurels, maples and rhododendrons, among other species. Vegetation of the Assam region in the east is luxuriant with evergreen forests, occasional thick clumps of bamboo and tall grasses. The Gangetic plain is largely under cultivation. The Deccan tableland supports vegetation from scrub to mixed deciduous forests. The Malabar region is rich in forest vegetation. The Andaman and Nicobar Islands have evergreen, mangrove, beach and diluvial forests. Much of the country's flora originated 3 million years ago and are unique to the subcontinent. Forest covers 23% of the land area, having increased at 0.3% p.a. 1990–2010. Arable land comprises 53% of the total land area and permanent cropland 4%.

Wildlife: Among the indigenous mammals are elephants, bisons, pandas, Himalayan wild sheep, deer, antelopes and tapirs. Large cats include lions, tigers, panthers, cheetahs and leopards. The tiger is the Indian national animal, protected since 1973. The tiger population, down to 1,827 in 1972, was in the mid-1990s back to 3,750. Crocodiles and gharials (a crocodile unique to India) are bred in a project begun in 1974 to save them from extinction. Birdlife is abundant and includes pheasants, mynahs, parakeets and hornbills. The spectacular Indian peacock is the national bird. Reptiles include cobras, saltwater snakes and pythons. Endangered wildlife is protected under legislation and there are 83 national parks and 447 wildlife sanctuaries, covering nearly 5.2% of the country.

Main towns: New Delhi/Delhi (capital, pop. 12.57m in 2010), Mumbai (formerly Bombay, in Maharashtra State, 13.83m), Bengaluru (formerly Bangalore, in Karnataka, 5.44m), Kolkata (formerly Calcutta, in West Bengal, 5.14m), Chennai (formerly Madras, in Tamil Nadu, 4.62m), Hyderabad (Andhra Pradesh, 4.07m), Ahmadabad (Gujarat, 3.96m), Pune (Maharashtra, 3.45m), Surat (Gujarat, 3.34m), Kanpur (Uttar Pradesh, 3.22m), Jaipur (Rajasthan, 3.21m), Lucknow (Uttar Pradesh, 2.75m), Nagpur (Maharashtra, 2.45m), Patna (Bihar, 1.88m), Indore (Madhya Pradesh, 1.85m), Bhopal (Madhya Pradesh, 1.79m), Ludhiana (Punjab, 1.74m), Faridabad (Haryana, 1.52m) and Srinagar (Jammu and Kashmir, 1.08m).

Transport: There are 3,316,450km of roads, 47% paved. The number of vehicles and the demand for roads is growing very rapidly.

India has Asia's biggest, and the world's fourth biggest, railway system, with 63,330km of track. The cities are connected by express trains, and there are local trains between most parts of the country.

The chief western port is Mumbai, and the chief eastern ports are Kolkata–Haldia and Chennai. The country has 7,520km of coastline and coastal shipping of freight within India plays an important role. There are about 19,000km of navigable inland waterways, though only 4,600km is navigable by large vessels.

There are international airports at Mumbai, Kolkata, Delhi, Chennai and Ahmadabad, and a total of about 250 airports with paved runways.

Society

KEY FACTS 2010

Population per sq km:	373
Life expectancy:	65 years
Net primary enrolment:	97%

Population: 1,224,614,000 (2010); world's second-largest, after China; 30% lives in urban areas and 13% in urban agglomerations of more than 1 million people; some 56% of all Commonwealth people, and 18% of all people, lives in India; growth 1.7% p.a. 1990–2010; birth rate 22 per 1,000 people (38 in 1970); life expectancy 65 years (29 in 1947 and 49 in 1970). By the late 1990s, 48% of married women were using contraceptive methods.

The population of India is extremely diverse, comprising almost entirely peoples who have migrated from other parts of the world over previous millennia. Dravidian peoples, who came to India from the Mediterranean region some 5,000 years ago, now constitute about 25% of the population and live predominantly in the southern states of India. Indo-Aryans, who account for more than 70% of the population, came from Northern Europe 3,500–4,000 years ago. Later migrations included peoples from Central Asia and China.

Language: The main official languages are Hindi (spoken by 30% of the population), and English (as laid down in the Constitution and Official Languages Act of 1963), but there are also 17 official regional languages, and many other languages. Language has been a major constitutional issue; the states have now been demarcated according to the main language of their populations. Other widely used languages include Urdu (spoken by most Muslims) and (in the north) Bengali, Marathi, Gujarati, Oriya, Punjabi; (in the south) Telugu, Tamil, Kannada, Malayalam.

Religion: Hindus 80.5%, Muslims 13.4%, Christians 2.3%, Sikhs 1.9%, Buddhists, Jains (2001 census).

Health: Public spending on health was 1% of GDP in 2009. Primary health care is provided in rural areas by more than 20,000 centres, backed by sub-centres, community health centres and dispensaries. Western medicine predominates, although Ayurvedic medicine is also practised. The Ayurvedic tradition also gave rise to homeopathy (some 365,000 practitioners). 88% of the population uses an improved drinking water source and 31% have adequate sanitation facilities (2009). Infant mortality was 48 per 1,000 live births in 2010 (146 in 1960). National health programmes have been established to combat malaria, filaria, sexually transmitted diseases (including AIDS), leprosy and tuberculosis. Family welfare centres give advice and education on family planning. In 2009, 0.3% of people aged 15–49 were HIV positive.

Education: There are nine years of compulsory education starting at age six. Some 69% of pupils complete primary school (2006). The school year starts in April.

There are more than 200 universities, 9,000 colleges and 1,000 polytechnics, including some 150 medical colleges. There are schemes to reserve places for scheduled (lowest) castes and scheduled tribes in certain colleges and universities, and special boarding schools for talented children with priority given to those from rural areas. The female–male ratio for gross enrolment in tertiary education is 0.70:1 (2007). Literacy among people aged 15–24 is 81% (2006).

Media: The leading English-language dailies are *The Asian Age* (New Delhi), *Deccan Herald* (Bengaluru), *The Hindu* (Chennai), *Hindustan Times* (New Delhi), *The Indian Express* (New Delhi), *The Pioneer* (New Delhi), *The Statesman* (Kolkata) and *The Times of India* (Mumbai), and *India Today* and *Outlook* are weekly news magazines. There are thousands of daily newspapers published in some 90 languages.

From 1992 private TV channels have been permitted and from 2000, private radio stations. Doordarshan provides a broad range of public TV services. The national, public All India Radio is the only radio network authorised to broadcast news; it also operates an external service, in 17 Indian and ten foreign languages.

Some 53% of households have TV sets (2006). There are 32 personal computers (2007) and 75 internet users (2010) per 1,000 people.

Communications: Country code 91; internet domain '.in'. Mobile phone coverage is good in the main towns. Public phone booths are widely available. Internet cafes are located throughout the country, many with wireless facilities.

There are 29 main telephone lines and 614 mobile phone subscriptions per 1,000 people (2010).

Public holidays: The following are universally observed: Republic Day (26 January), Independence Day (15 August) and Mahatma Gandhi's Birthday (2 October).

Religious and other festivals, of which the observance varies between regions and religions, are: Prophet's Birthday, Mahavir Jayanti (March/April), Good Friday, Buddha Purnima (April/May), Eid al-Fitr (End of Ramadan), Dussehra (October/November), Diwali (October/November), Guru Nanak's Birthday (November), Eid al-Adha (Feast of the Sacrifice), Muharram (Islamic New Year) and Christmas Day (25 December). Those without specific dates vary from year to year.

Economy

KEY FACTS 2010

GNI:	US$1,553.9bn
GNI p.c.:	US$1,330
GDP growth:	8.4% p.a. 2006–10
Inflation:	8.7% p.a. 2006–10

India is among the largest economies in the world (ranking ninth in 2010, in terms of GNI, and ascending rapidly). India's economic policy has traditionally focused on poverty reduction. From the 1950s to the 1980s, there was a drive towards large-scale industrialisation through government investment in public-sector enterprises, notably in heavy industry, aimed at providing employment and increasing self-reliance, with an emphasis on import substitution. The outcome was that India is now one of the world's largest industrial economies, with deliberately labour-intensive systems. It also has large reserves of oil and gas; proven reserves of oil were estimated in January 2011 to be 9.0 billion barrels, and of gas, 1.5 trillion cubic metres.

However, few improvements reached the rural areas where more than 70% of the population lives and depends on agriculture. A balance of payments crisis in 1991 led to policy reform with the emphasis on liberalisation, decentralisation and private-sector investment, increasing opportunities for small- and medium-scale enterprises to strengthen markets and create employment at the grassroots.

During the 1990s the government made some progress with deregulation of trade and industry and privatisation of both infrastructure (including power generation, ports, roads and airlines) and the many inefficient state enterprises, and generally maintained macroeconomic discipline of containing inflation and current-account deficits. At the same time new industries, and especially software, grew rapidly.

However, the government proceeded more slowly with liberalising the financial sector and reforming labour law. In the 2000s progress was stalled due to lack of support for the economic reforms in the governing National Democratic Alliance, especially for labour market reform and further privatisation. In May 2004, the new Indian National Congress-led government announced that there would be no more privatisations of profitable state enterprises and others would be decided case by case.

After the first period of adjustment in the early 1990s, the economy began to enjoy strong export-led growth. India was relatively little affected by the Asian financial crisis of the late 1990s. The economy has expanded rapidly during the 2000s; during 2006–10 growth averaged 8.4% p.a. The country was relatively unaffected by the global economic downturn of

Real Growth in GDP

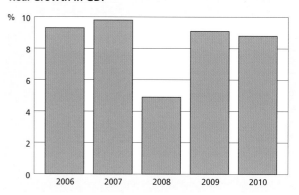

Inflation

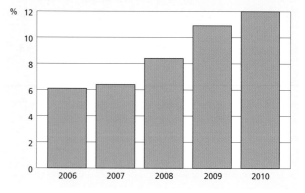

GDP by Sector (2010)

Agriculture	19%
Industry	26%
Services	55%

2008–09; growth dipped in 2008 to 4.9%, but surged to 9.1% in 2009, 8.8% in 2010 and about 7% in 2011.

Constitution

Status:	Republic
Legislature:	Parliament
Independence:	15 August 1947

India is a federal republic with 29 states (including the Delhi National Capital Territory), and six union territories. It has a parliamentary democracy which operates under the constitution of 1950. There is a bicameral federal parliament: the Rajya Sabha or council of states (upper house) and the Lok Sabha or house of the people (lower house).

The Lok Sabha has 545 members, 543 representing the states and union territories – 79 seats are reserved for scheduled castes and 40 for scheduled tribes – and two additional seats reserved for the Anglo-Indian community. Members are elected, on a first-past-the-post system in single-member constituencies, every five years or less, based on universal suffrage.

The Rajya Sabha has 245 members, 12 of which are presidential appointments and 233 are elected indirectly by the assemblies of the states and union territories for a six-year term, with one-third retiring every two years. Legislation may be introduced in either house, but the Lok Sabha has final say in financial matters.

The prime minister is elected by the members of the Lok Sabha and appoints and heads the Council of Ministers. The president is elected for five years by an electoral college consisting of members of the federal parliament and state assemblies.

Each state has its own legislature (usually unicameral), governor (appointed by the president for five years) and a ministerial council headed by a chief minister. There has been a trend towards devolution of union and state power to local government. The 1950 constitution established the division of power between the national and state legislatures.

Responsibility for enacting laws is set out in three lists: the Union List (for legislation by national parliament), the State List and the Concurrent List (either national or state legislatures). State legislatures make their own laws on such matters as education, health, taxation, public order, lands and forests. Constitutional amendments must be passed by both houses and ratified by at least half the state legislatures.

On proclamation of a state of emergency by the president, the federal government may assume temporary executive and financial control of a state and the president may rule it in place of the governor. The president appoints an administrator to govern the union territories. The 1950 constitution set out a number of individual freedoms and abolished discrimination on the basis of caste.

Politics

Last elections:	April/May 2009
Next elections:	2014
Head of state:	President Pratibha Patil (2007–)
Head of government:	Prime Minister Dr Manmohan Singh
Ruling party:	United Progressive Alliance coalition led by Indian National Congress

After a year in which the Bharatiya Janata Party (BJP)-led coalition government faced continuing difficulty in keeping the coalition together, the final results of the early September/October 1999 elections gave the National Democratic Alliance (NDA) – a new 24-party national alliance led by the BJP – a solid majority with 298 seats, though BJP's own total of 182 seats had hardly increased. However, Congress (I) and its allies took only 136 seats. The 1999 elections were the first since 1984 when a pre-election alliance managed to secure a clear majority in parliament.

In an early election, the first using electronic voting machines, held over four days in April/May 2004, the coalition – the United Progressive Alliance (UPA) – led by Indian National Congress (INC) emerged, with 217 seats, ahead of the ruling NDA (185 seats). However, INC leader, Sonia Gandhi, decided not to accept the prime ministership and Dr Manmohan Singh, a former finance minister who had overseen the economic reform programme in the early 1990s, was chosen by INC to form the new government. The Communist Party of India (Marxist), with 43 seats, joined INC to provide the necessary majority in taking the new agenda forward.

The July 2007 presidential election was won by Pratibha Patil of the INC, who was the nominee of UPA and first woman to become president. She defeated the BJP's candidate, Bhairon Singh Shekhawat, in the electoral college vote to choose a successor to Dr Abdul Kalam.

In July 2008, when a key UPA coalition partner, the Communist Party of India (Marxist) – CPI(M), would not support the government's proposed nuclear deal with the USA, the government narrowly survived a vote of confidence (275:256 votes, 11 abstentions), largely due to the support of a non-coalition member, the Samajwadi Party.

In the general election of April/May 2009 the Congress Party-led UPA prevailed, extending its share to 261 of the 545 seats (INC with 206), obviating the need for the complex coalition negotiations that had followed recent elections. Its main rival, the NDA, took 159 seats (BJP with 116); the Third Front coalition – now including the CPI(M) – 78. Prime Minister Manmohan Singh returned to head the government for a second term.

International relations

India is a member of the Indian Ocean Rim Association for Regional Cooperation, Non-Aligned Movement, South Asian Association for Regional Cooperation, United Nations and World Trade Organization.

Traveller information

Local laws and conventions: Traditions and rituals in India have become an integral part of everyday life and should be respected by all visitors. Visitors are advised to observe and respect local dress sense. All visitors should remove footwear before entering places of religious worship.

Penalties for drug offences are severe: there is a minimum sentence of six months for possession of small amounts for personal consumption only, and a ten-year sentence for larger amounts.

There are strict religious and social customs, and visitors must show great respect when visiting a person's home. Indian women prefer not to shake hands. Most people remove footwear before entering houses.

English is widely used in business. Businessmen and women should dress formally for meetings or social functions. The best months for business visits are October to March. Office hours are Mon–Fri 0930–1700, Sat 0930–1300.

Immigration and customs: Business and tourist visas are usually required and are valid for six months. Passports need to be valid for at least six months on arrival into the country. Visitors are advised to make a copy of the photopage of their passport, Indian visa and any entry stamps, and keep their passport safe at all times. A yellow fever certificate is required from anyone travelling from an infected country.

Lone parents travelling with a child/children should carry documentation showing that they have the right to do so.

Prohibited imports include livestock and pig meat products, live plants, dangerous drugs, gold coins and silver bullion.

Travel within the country: Driving is on the left. An international driving permit is required to hire a car.

Buses connect all parts of the country and are often the only means of travelling to mountainous areas. Urban buses are usually crowded.

Taxis and auto rickshaws are available in larger towns and cities, and fares are charged by the kilometre. Chauffeur-driven tourist cars can be found in major centres and cost slightly more than taxis.

The Indian railway system is extensive, and there are six classes of travel. Super-fast trains connect the major cities and luxury tourist trains are available for sightseeing trips.

India Airlines is the state domestic airline and connects more than 70 cities. Outward flights should be reconfirmed, especially between December and April when all flights become very full.

Ferries operate from Kolkata and Chennai, and there is a catamaran service from Mumbai to Goa.

Travel health: Visitors should take out comprehensive medical insurance. Private medical care is available in the major cities but is expensive. Many endemic diseases require that adequate care be taken with water and food hygiene. Water used for brushing teeth or making ice should be boiled.

Dengue fever outbreaks occur and visitors will need to take repellent and appropriate clothing to protect themselves against insect bites. Vaccination for Hepatitis B is sometimes advised, together with Japanese encephalitis and tuberculosis.

All visitors over the age of 18 wishing to stay for longer than one year must take an AIDS test.

Valid certificates of inoculation and vaccination will be required for all those travelling on to countries that impose health restrictions on arrivals from India.

Prescription drugs should be in their original containers, clearly marked to avoid confusion.

Money: Currency can be exchanged at banks and airports and at authorised changers. It is illegal to use unauthorised moneychangers. US dollars and pounds sterling are the easiest currencies to change. American Express, Diners Card, Mastercard and Visa are accepted throughout India. Travellers cheques in dollars or sterling are the most easily changed, although some banks refuse certain brands. Banking hours are Mon–Fri 1000–1400, Sat 1000–1200.

There were 5,584,000 tourist arrivals in 2010.

Further information

National Portal of India: india.gov.in

Lok Sabha (House of the People): loksabha.nic.in

Rajya Sabha (Council of States): rajyasabha.nic.in

Reserve Bank of India: www.rbi.org.in

Commonwealth Secretariat: www.thecommonwealth.org

Commonwealth of Nations: www.commonwealth-of-nations.org/India

Jamaica

KEY FACTS

Joined Commonwealth:	1962
Population:	2,741,000 (2010)
GDP p.c. growth:	0.7% p.a. 1990–2010
UN HDI 2011:	world ranking 79
Official language:	English
Time:	GMT minus 5hr
Currency:	Jamaican dollar (J$)

Geography

Area:	10,991 sq km
Coastline:	1,020km
Capital:	Kingston

Jamaica, whose name comes from the Arawak *Xaymaca*, meaning 'Land of Wood and Water', lies south of Cuba and west of Haiti.

Area: The third largest island in the Caribbean, Jamaica has a land area of 10,991 sq km.

Topography: Jamaica is the ridge of a submerged mountain range. The land rises to 2,256m at Blue Mountain Peak. The coastline is indented, with many good natural bays. Fine sandy beaches occur on the north and west coasts. Small fast-flowing rivers, prone to flash flooding, run in forested gullies.

Climate: Tropical at the coast (22–34°C), with fresh sea breezes; markedly cooler in the mountains. Rainfall ranges from 1,500mm p.a. in Kingston to 3,850mm p.a. in Port Antonio. Jamaica lies in the hurricane zone.

Environment: The most significant environmental issues are deforestation; pollution of coastal waters by industrial waste,

Did you know...

Patricia Francis of Jamaica was in 2010 appointed to the Commonwealth Eminent Persons Group, which presented its recommendations for reform in the Commonwealth to Commonwealth leaders at CHOGM in Australia in October 2011.

Jamaicans hold four Commonwealth Games records and three world records.

Four Jamaican women have won Commonwealth Writers' Prizes: Olive Senior in 1987 (Best Book); Erna Brodber in 1989; Alecia McKenzie in 1993; and Vanessa Spence in 1994.

The Commonwealth Library Association has its secretariat at the Mona, Kingston, campus of the University of the West Indies.

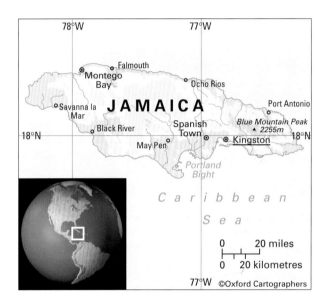

©Oxford Cartographers

sewage and oil spills; damage to coral reefs; and air pollution in Kingston due to vehicle emissions.

Vegetation: Jamaica's luxuriant tropical and, at higher altitude, subtropical vegetation is probably the richest in the region. There are more than 3,000 flowering species, including 194 orchid-species, several cactus-species, of which seven are unique to Jamaica, and 12 native palm-species. Forest covers 31% of the total land area, having declined at 0.1% p.a. 1990–2010. Arable land comprises 11% and permanent cropland 10% of the total land area.

Wildlife: Fauna include 30 bat species. There is also a rich variety of birdlife (of some 75 species recorded, ten were threatened with extinction in 2008), turtles, non-poisonous snakes, lizards, crocodiles, 14 kinds of butterfly unique to Jamaica, and many moths and fireflies. Manatees live in the coastal waters. There are about 500 species of landshell, many of which are unique to Jamaica.

Main towns: Kingston (capital, pop. 577,800 in 2010), Spanish Town (162,400), Portmore (106,000), Montego Bay (79,800), Mandeville (48,300), May Pen (45,700), Old Harbour (28,700), Linstead (22,800), Savanna-la-Mar (19,400), Half Way Tree (18,100), St Ann's Bay (14,900), Port Antonio (14,300), Bog Walk (14,200), Ewarton (14,100), Constant Spring (12,500), Morant Bay (11,100), Hayes (9,800) and Ocho Rios (9,600).

Transport: There are 22,060km of roads, 73% paved. There is no railway.

Main ports are Kingston, with dedicated wharves for bulk cargoes of petroleum, flour, cement, gypsum and lumber, and Montego Bay in the north-west; and the international airports are Norman

Jamaica Celebrates 50 *years... in 2012*

Urban Development Corporation
Making Development Happen Since 1968

The Urban Development Corporation is a proud product of an independent Jamaica and has played its part over the last 44 years as the government's leading urban and rural development agency. Over the decades, the Corporation has been at the forefront of development planning and implementation in virtually every sector of the country. The result has been modern towns and communities, state of the art schools, sporting facilities, cutting edge educational facilities and world class convention and recreational venues. Here are some milestones recorded by the UDC:

Development of Townships

The Corporation transformed the sleepy town of Ocho Rios, St. Ann into a bustling tourist mecca with a myriad of shopping plazas, dotted with numerous attractions including the Ocho Rios Bay Beach and Turtle River Park

Aerial view of Ocho Rios

Sports

The Corporation also delivered this facility in record time for the IFNA Netball World Championships in 2002 in Kingston, Jamaica's capital city.

National Indoor Sports Centre

Education

Green Pond High School, St. James was developed under the North Western Schools Programme in September 2005. The programme saw 17 schools being developed providing over 16, 0000 new spaces for students in the parishes of Westmoreland, Hanover, St James and Trelawny.

Tourism

The Montego Bay Convention Centre, one of the finest in the Caribbean opened its doors to the world in 2011. The facility can host large, medium and small events and exhibitions while catering to a wide variety of cuisine needs through its international onsite caterer Savant. The centre is being managed by SMG International based in the United States of America and was developed through bilateral cooperation with the People's Republic of China and the Government of Jamaica.

External view of the convention centre

Entertainment piece by the Chinese Benevolent Association at the handing over ceremony in April, 2011

Attractions

Green Grotto Caves and Attractions, St. Ann is a rich heritage site owned and operated by the UDC. This Green Globe 21 gold certified facility has a fascinating history that boasts smugglers, slaves and sugar from the 18th C era.

Dunn's River Falls and Park

Dubbed as the Caribbean's Leading Tourist Excursion by the World Travel Awards, Dunn's River remains among the greatest wonders of the world and pulls thousands of visitors each day to its enchanting waters. A thrilling walk up the 600 ft. falls will invigorate and renew brave adventurers.

Reach Falls

A hidden gem in the lush tropical paradise of Jamaica's eastern parish of Portland, Reach Falls remains largely virgin territory and boasts a 45 minute tour up the river revealing quaint facts about Jamaica's fauna and flora.

Two Sisters Caves

Tucked away treasure on the south eastern shores of Jamaica lies the Two Sisters Caves, in St. Catherine. An old world charm pervades this facility which features a 700 years old petroglyph created by the Tainos Indians, its first inhabitants who used it as a religious shrine.

Fireworks on the Waterfront

UDC ushered in the 50th year with its signature Fireworks on the Waterfront. Attracting massive crowds up to 150,000 strong on an annual basis, this event complements the Corporation's thrust to redevelop the Kingston Waterfront, reverse urban decay and breathe a fresh socio-cultural vibrancy in that section of the capital city.

URBAN DEVELOPMENT CORPORATION

12 Ocean Boulevard, Kingston Mall, Jamaica W.I.
Telephone: (876) 922-8310-4. Telefax: (876) 922-9326
Email: info@udcja.com Website: www.udcja.com

For more information on the work of the Urban Development Corporation, please visit them on Facebook, Twitter and Youtube

Jamaica Olympic Association (JOA)

OUR PERFORMANCES ARE DEDICATED TO YOU ALL

When Jamaica's delegation emerges from the tunnel and enters the Olympic Stadium in London, the reception from those fortunate enough to be there will be one fitting for the home country – and after all, it will be like coming home for the Jamaican athletes. It was in London 64 years ago, that Jamaica - in its first appearance at the Olympic Games - demonstrated to the world that track and field athletics was serious business back home. Building on those early successes of 1948, this small country will once again remind all, inside and outside the stadium, that our athletes are worth going miles to see.

Jamaica is expected to participate in the disciplines of Track and Field Athletics, Swimming, Tae kwon do, Boxing, Equestrian and possibly Badminton. Our athletes are expected to dominate the short sprints in the male category and be very competitive in a similar area with our female athletes. Presently, male athletes from Jamaica hold the world records in the 100m, 200m and the 4x100 Relay events and our female athletes are also the defending champions in the women's 100m and 200m events.

Jamaicans at home and in London are expecting our athletes to defend those titles successfully come August 2012 in London. Do not feel too disappointed if you are unable to secure a ticket to be inside the athletics stadium, the television coverage will be very good.

Let us all, here in Jamaica, in London and elsewhere in the world wish our athletes the very best as we cheer them on, from their entry in the stadium to the moment the national flag is draped around them - after every victory.

CONTACT

Jamaica Olympic Association

9 Cunningham Avenue, Kingston 6, Jamaica

Tel: +1 876 927 3017-8   **Fax:** +1 876 946 0588   **www.jamolympic.org**

Manley International, 17km south-east of Kingston, and Montego Bay International, 3km north of the city.

Society

KEY FACTS 2010

Population per sq km:	249
Life expectancy:	73 years
Net primary enrolment:	81%

Population: 2,741,000 (2010); 52% lives in urban areas; growth 0.7% p.a. 1990–2010 but emigration (principally to the UK, Canada and the USA) has been significant for two generations; birth rate 18 per 1,000 people (35 in 1970); life expectancy 73 years (68 in 1970).

The population is predominantly of African descent (91% in 2001 census), with European-, East Indian- and Chinese-descended minorities, and some people of mixed descent (6%).

Language: English; an English-based Creole is widely spoken.

Religion: Mainly Christians (Church of God 24%, Seventh Day Adventists 11%, Pentecostals 10%, Baptists 7%, Anglicans 4%, Roman Catholics 3%), and there is also a significant Rastafarian community (2001 census).

Health: Public spending on health was 3% of GDP in 2009. There are more than 20 hospitals, mostly public, and many health centres. Hospital services and government medical care are subsidised, patients paying modest fees related to their income. Around 9% of the population has private health insurance. 94% of the population uses an improved drinking water source and 83% in urban areas have adequate sanitation facilities (2009). Infant mortality was 20 per 1,000 live births in 2010 (56 in 1960). In 2009, 1.7% of people aged 15–49 were HIV positive.

Education: Public spending on education was 6.0% of GDP in 2009. There are six years of compulsory education starting at age six. Primary school comprises six years and secondary seven, with cycles of three and four years. The school year starts in September.

The regional University of the West Indies (UWI, established in 1946) has its principal campus at Mona, near Kingston, and other main campuses in Barbados, and Trinidad and Tobago. The Norman Manley Law School (1973) is located on the Mona campus of UWI. Some 50 other tertiary institutions registered with the University Council of Jamaica in 2011 include Management Institute for National Development; University of Technology; College of Agriculture, Science and Education; Edna Manley College of the Visual and Performing Arts; G C Foster College of Physical Education and Sports; Knox Community College; and Northern Caribbean University (owned by the Seventh Day Adventists, located in Mandeville, a university since 1999). The female–male ratio for gross enrolment in tertiary education is 2.22:1 (2008). Literacy among people aged 15–24 is 95% (2009).

Media: National dailies are *The Gleaner*, *Jamaica Observer* and *Daily Star* (evenings), and all have weekend editions. *Sunday Herald* is a weekly.

After the Jamaica Broadcasting Corporation was privatised in 1997, many – mostly commercial – radio and TV broadcasters entered the field.

Some 88% of households have TV sets (2009). There are 67 personal computers (2005) and 261 internet users (2010) per 1,000 people.

Communications: Country code 1 876; internet domain '.jm'. There are internet cafes and kiosks in Kingston; elsewhere internet access is available at libraries and hotels.

There are 96 main telephone lines and 1,161 mobile phone subscriptions per 1,000 people (2010).

Public holidays: New Year's Day, Labour Day (23 May), Emancipation Day (1 August), Independence Day (6 August), National Heroes' Day (third Monday in October), Christmas Day and Boxing Day.

Religious and other festivals whose dates vary from year to year include Ash Wednesday, Good Friday and Easter Monday.

Economy

KEY FACTS 2010

GNI:	US$13.0bn
GNI p.c.:	US$4,800
GDP growth:	0.0% p.a. 2006–10
Inflation:	12.3% p.a. 2006–10

Jamaica has a relatively large and diversified economy. It grew strongly in the early years of independence, but then stagnated in the 1980s, burdened with persistent large fiscal and external deficits, due to heavy falls in the price of bauxite (bauxite and alumina make up the bulk of exports by value), fluctuations in the prices of agricultural commodities (sugar being the largest export after alumina and bauxite), and economic policies which left the country with high inflation, a fast devaluating currency, growing external debt and a large public sector containing many loss-making industries. Jamaica signed a series of agreements with the IMF, continuing into the 1990s and 2000s.

Substantial efforts have been made to attract investors through a range of tax, customs and other incentives, developing its equity markets, and encouraging joint ventures and privatisation, notably of hotels. The free-trade zones at Kingston, Montego Bay and Spanish Town allow duty-free importation, tax-free profits and free repatriation of export earnings. The USA, China (Hong Kong) and Taiwan have provided most investment in these zones. Tourism and manufacturing are important industries. Investment and remittances from Jamaicans abroad make a significant contribution to GNI.

The financial sector was troubled from late 1994, with many banks and insurance companies suffering heavy losses and liquidity problems. The government set up the Financial Sector Adjustment Company (Finsac) in January 1997 to assist these banks and companies, providing funds in return for equity, and acquired substantial holdings in banks and insurance companies and related companies, bringing government expenditure on financial-sector rescues to more than US$2.8bn by 2001, exacerbating the economic problems and saddling the country with a large external debt. From 2001, once it had restored these banks and companies to financial health, Finsac divested them.

Despite the reforms, for successive governments it proved very difficult to break out of the cycle of deficits, currency devaluations, very high inflation and falling living standards. Even in the latter 1990s, after reductions in the public sector and when inflation was in single figures, the economy continued to shrink or stagnate.

Three years of recession were followed in the 2000s by modest but steady growth, dipping in 2004 when, in September, the island

TAX ADMINISTRATION
JAMAICA

PURPOSE

Tax Administration Jamaica (TAJ) is a government department, established under the Revenue Administration (Amendment) Act 2011, and has responsibility for administering the domestic tax laws. The organisation is mandated to assess and collect domestic taxes, promote voluntary compliance and enforce the tax laws.

STRUCTURE

TAJ is headed by a Commissioner General who is supported by three Deputy Commissioners General with responsibility for Management Services, Operations and Legal Support and a staff of about 2,500.

VISION

A World-Class Tax Administration.

MISSION

Through excellent service by our highly skilled staff, we will foster voluntary compliance, contribute to a competitive business environment and facilitate economic growth and development.

CORE VALUES

Professionalism
Accountability
Customer-centric
Transparency
Team Work

CONTACT:-
Viralee Bailey-Latibeaudiere
Commissioner General
Tax Administration Jamaica
Head Office, PCJ Building (4th floor)
36 Trafalgar Road, Kingston 10
Tel: +1 876 906-2478 Fax: +1 876 754-9593
Email: viralee.latibeaudiere@taj.gov.jm

Customer Care Centre: 1-888-TAX-HELP
Email: communications@taj.gov.jm
Website: www.jamaicatax.gov.jm
Facebook: www.facebook.com/jamaicatax
Twitter: @jamaicatax

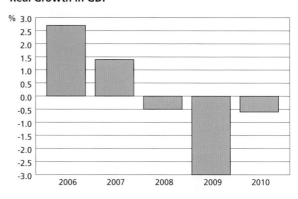

Real Growth in GDP

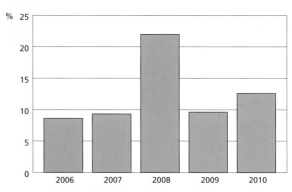

Inflation

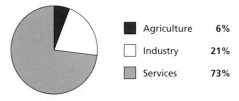

GDP by Sector (2010)

■ Agriculture	6%
□ Industry	21%
▨ Services	73%

was devastated by Hurricane Ivan. Hurricane Dean in August 2007 and heavy rains caused widespread damage to agriculture and disruption in mining activities. Then, as the world moved into recession in 2008, the Jamaican economy itself moved swiftly into reverse, shrinking by 3.0% in 2009. With external debt rising and the economy contracting, in 2009 Jamaica once again sought the support of the IMF, agreeing a standby loan package in February 2010. There was then a modest recovery in 2011.

Constitution

Status:	Monarchy under Queen Elizabeth II
Legislature:	Parliament
Independence:	6 August 1962

Jamaica is a constitutional monarchy with Queen Elizabeth II as head of state. She is represented by a governor-general appointed on the recommendation of the prime minister. The country is a parliamentary democracy with a bicameral legislature and party system, based on universal adult suffrage.

The 21 senators are appointed by the governor-general, 13 of them on the advice of the prime minister, and eight on the advice of the leader of the opposition. The House of Representatives has

63 directly elected members. The governor-general appoints the prime minister (the MP best able to lead the majority of the House) and leader of the opposition. The cabinet (prime minister and at least 11 ministers) has executive responsibility. Elections are held at intervals not exceeding five years.

The constitution may be amended by a simple majority of both houses except for the entrenched provisions (that can be amended only by two-thirds majority of both houses) and specially entrenched clauses (as above, plus ratification through referendum).

Politics

Last elections:	December 2011
Next elections:	2016
Head of state:	Queen Elizabeth II, represented by governor-general, Dr Patrick Allen (2009–)
Head of government:	Prime Minister Portia Simpson Miller
Ruling party:	People's National Party

After a violent campaign, the general election in October 2002 was largely free of violence. In a closer-fought contest than in 1997, the People's National Party (PNP) won an unprecedented fourth successive victory with 34 seats and 52% of the votes and P J Patterson was returned as prime minister. The Jamaica Labour Party (JLP) took the remaining 26 seats.

Following his return to the JLP in 2002 (he had left the JLP in 1995 to found and lead the National Democratic Movement), in 2005 Bruce Golding succeeded the party's veteran leader Edward Seaga as party leader; Seaga had been leader in government and opposition for 31 years.

Professor Kenneth Hall succeeded Sir Howard Felix Cooke as governor-general in February 2006 and Portia Simpson Miller succeeded Patterson as prime minister when he retired after 14 consecutive years in office in March 2006.

In the September 2007 general election, the opposition JLP, led by Golding, won a narrow victory with 33 seats and 50.1% of votes, while PNP took 27 seats and 49.8%. There was a 60% turnout.

Dr Patrick Allen succeeded Sir Kenneth Hall as governor-general on his retirement in February 2009.

On 25 September 2011 Bruce Golding announced his retirement as JLP leader and prime minister. In early October 2011 the JLP chose education minister Andrew Holness as its new leader and Holness was sworn in as prime minister on 23 October. At 39 he was the country's youngest ever prime minister.

The PNP won the early general election of December 2011, securing 42 of the 63 elective seats (increased from 60 since the 2007 election) and 53.0% of the vote; the JLP took the balance of 21 seats and 46.3%. Only some 53% of the registered voters cast their vote. PNP leader Portia Simpson Miller was sworn in as prime minister for a second time.

International relations

Jamaica is a member of the African, Caribbean and Pacific Group of States, Association of Caribbean States, Caribbean Community, Non-Aligned Movement, Organization of American States, United Nations and World Trade Organization.

Jamaica hosts the headquarters of the International Seabed Authority, the autonomous international organisation established in 1994 under the United Nations Convention on the Law of the Sea.

Traveller information

Local laws and conventions: As the birthplace of musician Bob Marley, reggae is at the heart of the island's music, which visitors will hear playing everywhere.

There are harsh penalties for drug offences, including those involving ganja, or marijuana. Smoking ganja is illegal. Possession of even small quantities of illegal drugs can lead to imprisonment. Visitors must ensure they pack their own luggage and never carry packages through customs for a third party.

Handshaking is the usual form of greeting. Business culture is respectful and polite. Punctuality is important and business cards are expected. If bringing in goods other than non-commercial samples, business travellers must clear this with the office of the Trade Administrator before entering the country. Business hours are Mon–Fri 0830–1700.

Immigration and customs: Passports need to be valid for at least six months from the date of arrival. Citizens of the EU, USA, Australia and Canada do not currently require visas to enter the country.

Lone parents should carry documentation showing parental responsibility for any accompanying children.

A yellow fever certificate will be required from all those arriving from infected countries.

Prohibited imports include indecent or obscene material such as prints, paintings, films, lithographs, books, cards or written communications. Publications relating to divination, magic or mysticism are also banned.

Travel within the country: Driving is on the left-hand side. Car hire is available for those aged over 25 at the airport and in all the major towns. Seatbelts are compulsory and motorcyclists must wear helmets.

Visitors are advised to use Jamaican Tourist Board (JTB) taxis and minibuses for getting around, sightseeing and airport transfers. JTB drivers have photo ID and display a blue sticker on their front windscreen. Most taxis have meters but for longer journeys it is best to agree a price before starting out. There is a reliable bus service connecting Kingston and Montego Bay. Outside the main towns and resorts bus services are variable.

Air Jamaica Express runs flights between resort areas. Water taxis, yachts and short cruises are offered by numerous tourist operators.

The railway only carries cargo.

Travel health: Medical treatment can be expensive and comprehensive travel insurance that includes medical evacuation is advised.

Visitors will need protection against dengue fever and should have insect repellent and suitable clothing to discourage mosquito bites. Hepatitis A, diphtheria and tetanus are also present, and vaccine requirements should be checked well before departure.

Mains water is safe in tourist areas and bottled water is widely available.

Money: Local laws require all transactions to be made in Jamaican dollars. Currency can be exchanged at airports, hotels and bureaux. It is important to keep all receipts, as black market exchange is illegal. American Express, Diners Club, Mastercard and Visa are widely accepted, and most Jamaican ATMs accept international bank cards. Many resort areas have 24-hour ATMs. Banking hours are Mon–Thur 0900–1400, Fri 0900–1200 and 1400–1700.

There were 1,922,000 tourist arrivals in 2010.

Further information

Government of Jamaica: www.jamaica.gov.jm

Parliament: www.japarliament.gov.jm

Bank of Jamaica: www.boj.org.jm

Commonwealth Secretariat: www.thecommonwealth.org

Commonwealth of Nations: www.commonwealth-of-nations.org/Jamaica

History

Little is known about the island's early history, except that there are many traces of Arawak habitation, and that Arawaks, agriculturists who made good-quality textiles and pottery, were living there when Christopher Columbus landed on 14 May 1494, on his second American voyage of exploration. He named the island Santiago (Saint-James). However, the name was never adopted and it kept its Arawak name *Xaymaca*, of which 'Jamaica' is a corruption. Lacking gold, Jamaica was used mainly as a staging post in the scramble for the wealth of the Americas.

The Spanish arrival was a disaster to the indigenous peoples, great numbers of whom were sent to Spain as slaves, others used as slaves on site, and many killed by the invaders, despite the efforts of Spanish Christian missionaries to prevent these outrages. There were no Arawaks left on the island by 1665, but there were enslaved Africans replacing them.

In 1645 the British captured Jamaica from the Spaniards, whose former slaves refused to surrender, took to the mountains and repelled all attempts to subjugate them. These people came to be known as Maroons (from the Spanish *cimarron*, meaning 'wild', a word applied to escaped slaves). Between 1660 and 1670 pirates used Jamaica as a place of resort.

In 1670 Spain formally ceded the island to Britain. Two years later the Royal Africa Company, a slave-trading enterprise, was formed. The company used Jamaica as its chief market, and the island became a centre of slave trading in the West Indies. Nonetheless, the battles of the Maroons to retain their freedom succeeded when, in 1740, the British authorities recognised their rights to freedom and ownership of property.

Settlers, using slave labour, developed sugar, cocoa, indigo and later coffee estates. The island was very prosperous by the time of the Napoleonic wars (1792–1814), exporting sugar and coffee; but after the wars sugar prices dropped, and the slave trade was abolished in 1807. After the emancipation of slaves in 1834, the plantations were worked by indentured Indian and Chinese labourers. Sugar prices fell again in 1846. Jamaica's worsening economic situation caused widespread suffering and discontent. In October 1865, a political protest at Morant Bay organised by G W Gordon developed into an uprising during which the local magistrate and 18 other Europeans were killed. The governor, E J Eyre, declared martial law and launched a punitive campaign of ruthless severity, with several executions without trial, including the hanging of Gordon, who had not instigated any violence. The reaction in Britain was astonished outrage. Eyre was removed from office and Jamaica placed under Crown colony rule (1866). The banana industry was established in the second half of the 19th century, on big estates and smallholdings. In the early 20th century, Jamaicans worked on banana plantations in Central America and Cuba, and in the construction of the Panama Canal.

Jamaica's first colonial constitution gave considerable power to settlers. The governor's council included senior figures such as the bishop and chief justice, but the representative assembly was controlled by white settlers. After the imposition of direct Crown colony rule in 1866, settlers lost their power and the governor was advised only by the mainly nominated privy council. With amendments, this constitution was retained until 1944.

In 1938, the People's National Party (PNP), led by Norman Manley, was formed to campaign for independence. The Jamaica Labour Party (JLP), led by Sir Alexander Bustamante, was founded in 1943.

In 1944, an executive council, with half its members elected by universal adult franchise, was established. In 1953, ministers from the council took over most portfolios, and Bustamante became chief minister. Manley followed, in 1955. When Jamaica joined the Federation of the West Indies in 1958, it had full internal self-government with a legislative council (senate) and legislative assembly (holding real power).

On independence in 1962 Bustamante was prime minister. With bauxite in demand, tourism flourishing and a revival in bananas, Jamaica's economy boomed.

In 1972, the PNP, led by Norman Manley's son, Michael, won the elections, and remained in office until 1980, when the JLP under Edward Seaga came to power. The PNP, again under the leadership of Michael Manley, won the elections of 1989.

Due to ill health, Prime Minister Michael Manley retired in March 1992 and was succeeded by P J Patterson, who led the PNP to another victory at elections in March 1993. The PNP won 52 seats, the JLP eight.

Jamaican politics was preoccupied with economic and security issues during the 1990s and this resulted in a high incidence of strikes, with all parties favouring economic liberalisation. In late 1995 the JLP split, leading to the creation of a third party, the National Democratic Movement, headed by Bruce Golding, former chairman of the JLP.

Patterson and the PNP were returned in the general election in December 1997. The poll had been relatively peaceful and the international team of observers led by former US President Jimmy Carter judged it free and fair. With 56% of the votes the PNP took 50 of the 60 seats in the lower house, while the JLP received 39% of the votes and took ten seats.

Kenya

KEY FACTS

Joined Commonwealth:	1963
Population:	40,513,000 (2010)
GDP p.c. growth:	0.3% p.a. 1990–2010
UN HDI 2011:	world ranking 143
Official languages:	Kiswahili, English
Time:	GMT plus 3hr
Currency:	Kenyan shilling (KSh)

Geography

Area:	582,646 sq km
Coastline:	536km
Capital:	Nairobi

Kenya lies astride the equator, extending from the Indian Ocean in the east to Uganda in the west and from the United Republic of Tanzania in the south to Ethiopia and Sudan in the north. On the east and north-east it borders Somalia. The country is divided into eight provinces (Central, Coast, Eastern, Nairobi, North-Eastern, Nyanza, Rift Valley, Western).

Area: 582,646 sq km including 13,400 sq km of inland waters.

Topography: There are four main regions. The north-east plain is arid. The south-east region is fertile along the Tana river, in the coastal strip and in the Taita Hills, which rise to 2,100m. The north-west is generally low-lying and arid but includes Lake Turkana, 260km long, and many mountains, including Nyiru (2,800m). The south-west quarter, a plateau rising to 3,000m, includes some of Africa's highest mountains: Mount Kenya (5,200m), Mount Elgon (4,320m) and the Aberdare Range (4,000m). The Great Rift Valley runs across the plateau from north to south, 50–65km wide and 600–1,000m deep. West of the Rift the plateau falls to Lake Victoria and eastward the rivers Tana and Athi (or Galana downstream) flow into the Indian Ocean.

Climate: The coastal areas are tropical, with monsoon winds. The lowlands are hot and mainly dry. The highlands are much cooler

©Oxford Cartographers

Did you know...

The father of US President Barack Obama was a Kenyan national.

Kenyan athletes hold eight Commonwealth Games records and nineteen world records.

Kenya hosts the UN Human Settlements Programme (UN-Habitat), the UN Environment Programme (UNEP) and a national chapter of the Commonwealth Human Ecology Council.

and have four seasons. Nairobi, 1,700m above sea level, has a mean temperature that ranges from a minimum of 13°C to a maximum of 25°C; Mombasa, on the coast, from a minimum of 23°C to a maximum of 29°C. Rainfall varies from a mean annual 150mm at Lodwar in the north-west to 1,470mm at Kisumu, near Lake Victoria in the west. Northern parts of the country were hit by severe floods in the latter part of 2007.

Environment: The most significant issues are water pollution from urban and industrial wastes; degradation of water quality from increased use of pesticides and fertilisers; water hyacinth infestation in Lake Victoria; deforestation; soil erosion; desertification; and poaching.

Vegetation: Thornbush and grassland are characteristic of much of the country. Varied forest covers about 13,000 sq km of the south-west quarter, at 2–3,500m above sea level. Forest covers 6% of the land area, having declined at 0.3% p.a. 1990–2010. Arable land comprises 9% and permanent cropland 1% of the total land area.

Wildlife: Kenya's wildlife is probably the most famous in the world. Wild mammals include lions, leopards, cheetahs, zebras, antelopes, gazelles, elephants, rhinoceroses, hippopotami, baboons and many kinds of monkeys. There are 359 recorded species of mammals, of which 51 are endangered. Reptiles include crocodiles and more than 100 species of snake. There is a rich variety of

"Fuelling the economy, stimulating the future"

Kenya Pipeline Company is at the forefront of petroleum distribution in Eastern and Central Africa. Petroleum and its related products and services are as integral to the progress and development of the region as blood is to the human body. At KPC, we earnestly seek to reflect that view in the way we discharge our solemn responsibility to the people of Kenya as we aim to be a globally predominant petroleum products handling and related services provider.

www.kpc.co.ke

native birdlife and the country is visited by migrant birds which breed in Europe. There are 344 species of birds, 24 of which are endangered. Wildlife is protected in reserves extending to 45,500 sq km, or some 8% of the total land area.

Main towns: Nairobi (capital, pop. 3.25m in 2010), Mombasa (Coast, 917,800), Nakuru (Rift Valley, 275,300), Eldoret (Rift Valley, 251,900), Kisumu (Nyanza, 230,600), Ruiru (Central, 167,100), Thika (Central, 106,000), Malindi (Coast, 82,200), Kitale (Rift Valley, 81,300), Bungoma (Western, 76,700), Kakamega (Western, 71,300), Garissa (North-Eastern, 63,900), Kilifi (Coast, 63,900), Mumias (Western, 57,900), Meru (Eastern, 51,600), Nyeri (Central, 49,400), Wajir (North-Eastern, 41,400), Lamu (Coast, 32,400) and Marsabit (Eastern, 16,700).

Transport: 63,270km of roads, 14% paved, and around 1,920km of railway. The main railway line runs between Mombasa and Nairobi, and branch lines connect with Taveta on the Tanzanian border in the south and Kisumu on Lake Victoria in the west.

Mombasa is the chief port for Kenya and an important regional port, handling freight for and from Uganda, Rwanda, Burundi and the Democratic Republic of Congo, including a substantial volume of food aid. Ferries ply the coast between Mombasa, Malindi and Lamu.

Jomo Kenyatta International Airport is 13km south-east of Nairobi. Moi International is 13km west of Mombasa.

Society

KEY FACTS 2010

Population per sq km:	70
Life expectancy:	57 years
Net primary enrolment:	83%

Population: 40,513,000 (2010), 22% lives in urban areas and 9% in urban agglomerations of more than 1 million people; growth 2.7% p.a. 1990–2010; birth rate 38 per 1,000 people (51 in 1970); life expectancy 57 years (52 in 1970 and 60 in 1990).

The ethnic composition of the population is estimated as: Kikuyu 22%, Luhya 14%, Luo 13%, Kalenjin 12%, Kamba 11%, Kisii 6% and Meru 6%. There are Masai, Arab, Asian and European minorities.

Language: Kiswahili and English are official languages. Each of the ethnic groups has its own language.

Religion: Christians 78% (mainly Protestants and Roman Catholics), Muslims 10%, and most of the rest hold traditional beliefs.

Health: Public spending on health was 1% of GDP in 2009. 59% of the population uses an improved drinking water source and 31% in urban areas use adequate sanitation facilities (2009). Infant mortality was 55 per 1,000 live births in 2010 (122 in 1960). Malaria is the main endemic health problem, and AIDS is a severe problem. In 2009, 6.3% of people aged 15–49 were HIV positive.

Education: Public spending on education was 6.9% of GDP in 2010. There are eight years of compulsory education starting at age six. Primary school comprises eight years and secondary four. The school year starts in January.

Among the many higher education institutions are University of Nairobi; Kenyatta University; Moi University (in Eldoret since 1984);

Egerton University, the principal agricultural university with its main campus at Njoro, Nakuru (established as a university in 1987); Jomo Kenyatta University of Agriculture and Technology (in Juja since 1994); and a growing number of private universities. The female–male ratio for gross enrolment in tertiary education is 0.70:1 (2009). Literacy among people aged 15–24 is 93% (2009).

Media: English-language daily newspapers include *Daily Nation* and *The Standard* (established 1902). *Taifa Leo* is published daily in Kiswahili. Weeklies include *The EastAfrican* (for an international audience). Newspapers from Uganda and United Republic of Tanzania are widely circulated in the country.

Radio is the main source of news and information for most Kenyans. The Kenya Broadcasting Corporation provides public radio services in English, Kiswahili and 15 other Kenyan languages, and public TV services in English and Kiswahili. Many private radio stations and TV channels compete with the public services, particularly in the urban areas, and private radio stations increasingly provide national services, and broadcast in other national languages as well as Kiswahili.

Some 32% of households have TV sets (2007). There are 14 personal computers (2005) and 259 internet users (2010) per 1,000 people.

Communications: Country code 254, followed by 20 for Nairobi and 41 for Mombasa; internet domain '.ke'. Public phones work with coins or phonecards (card booths are blue, coin-operated booths are red). There are internet cafes and post offices in most towns.

There are 9 main telephone lines and 616 mobile phone subscriptions per 1,000 people (2010).

Public holidays: New Year's Day, Labour Day (1 May), Madaraka Day (1 June), Moi Day (10 October), Kenyatta Day (20 October), Jamhuri Day (Independence Day, 12 December), Christmas Day and Boxing Day.

Religious and other festivals whose dates vary from year to year include Good Friday, Easter Monday and Eid al-Fitr (End of Ramadan, three days).

Economy

KEY FACTS 2010

GNI:	US$31.8bn
GNI p.c.:	US$790
GDP growth:	4.5% p.a. 2006–10
Inflation:	12.5% p.a. 2006–10

Kenya is the most developed of the original three countries of the East African Community (Kenya, Uganda and United Republic of Tanzania). It was formerly one of Africa's strongest economies, with average annual growth of 5% in the late 1980s, based on agriculture (notably tea and coffee production and horticulture) and tourism. Poor harvests and political uncertainty slowed growth in the early 1990s; a foreign exchange crisis resulting from the withholding of aid by donors between December 1991 and November 1993 brought low growth and high inflation (46% in 1993). The country has been afflicted by recurring droughts during two decades.

However, after 1993 the government took steps to liberalise the economy, removing import licensing, price and foreign-exchange

Pamoja Women Development Programme

'Helping women to grow, changing lives...'

Pamoja Women Development Programme (PAWDEP) is a non-profit micro-finance organisation dedicated to fighting poverty among rural, semi-urban and urban women.

PAWDEP is geared towards supporting women, especially the poor and disadvantaged, in gaining access to local banking services for investment in commercial agriculture, fishing projects and small businesses countrywide.

Mission

To promote sustainable economic growth and autonomy among women by identifying, designing and developing strategies that can be used by women to establish and run profitable income-generating activities.

Vision

To enable poor rural and urban women in Kenya to achieve new levels of personal and economic success through innovative enterprise development.

Our loan products include:

- *Nuru*: loans to solidarity women groups
- *Haraka*: an emergency loan for women groups with unforeseen business circumstances
- *Endeleza Akina Mama*: individual self-secured loan
- *Jaza*: individual self-secured loans for business or development
- *Pesa Plus*: an individual emergency loan to deal with unforeseen business circumstances
- *Angaza*: individual self-secured loans and flexible business development loans

Other services offered include:

- Business advice and training
- Value-adding strategies for agricultural products
- Business start-ups, e.g. mushroom cultivation and apiculture

PAWDEP works with the Jomo Kenyatta University of Agriculture and Technology in the application of modern farming techniques, and the International Centre for Insect and Plant Ecology on the transfer of modern apicultural technology to bee farms run by women. Other projects include mushroom cultivation and training on value-addition of agricultural commodities. PAWDEP also works in partnership with the government-sponsored development fund for women.

As of 2008, 50,000 women hold KSh 350 million shillings in loans from PAWDEP. PAWDEP's group loans have registered a 98.8 per cent repayment rate, and their individual loans have registered a 110 per cent repayment rate. PAWDEP employs 86 people at seven branches located in Gatundu, Githunguri, Kirinyaga, Limuru, Nakuru, Nyahururu, Thika and the Head Office in Kiambu.

Contact

Julius Chege, CEO
Head Office, Kikinga House, Biashara Street, Kiambu
P.O. Box 2472 – 00100 Nairobi

Tel: +254 66 202 2205 • 20 238 3881 • 20 204 5049
Fax: +254 66 224 55
Email: customercare@pawdep.org • info@pawdep.org
www.pawdep.org

Real Growth in GDP

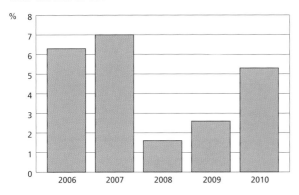

Inflation

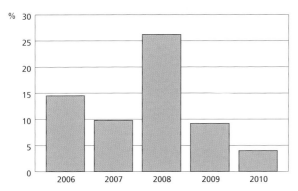

GDP by Sector (2010)

■ Agriculture	25%
□ Industry	20%
▨ Services	55%

controls, and reducing the public sector by privatisation of state enterprises and cutting the civil service. This resulted in a period of lower inflation and positive growth in real GDP – based on tea, coffee and horticulture production, tourism and a growing manufacturing sector. There were good harvests in the mid-1990s, but very heavy unseasonal rains in 1997–98 severely damaged the harvest and transport infrastructure and caused growth to stall. This was followed by drought in 1999–2000.

The relationship with the IMF and other international agencies was turbulent during the 1990s and early 2000s. In August 2000, IMF support – suspended since 1997 – was resumed when it agreed a three-year poverty reduction and growth loan, conditional on all senior officials, including the president, declaring their assets each year. Relations with aid donors were strained during 2001–02, and some disbursements were delayed; relations only improved after the change of government in December 2002. The new government committed itself to structural adjustment, including privatisation of Kenya Commercial Bank, Telkom Kenya and Kenya Railways; it enacted anti-corruption legislation; and concluded a poverty reduction and growth facility with the IMF. Commitments

of support by other multilateral and bilateral donors and a new round of debt-rescheduling then followed.

The 2000s opened with very slow growth, but the economy had recovered by the mid-2000s, when it grew by at least 5% p.a. Then, feeling the impact of both drought and global recession, it slowed sharply (1.6% in 2008), recovering in 2009 (2.6%) and becoming vigorous in 2010 (5.3%) and 2011 (about 4%).

Constitution

Status:	Republic with executive president
Legislature:	Parliament
Independence:	12 December 1963

The constitution in force until August 2010 had been amended many times since the republic was formed in December 1964. It provided for the unicameral National Assembly consisting of 210 members directly elected every five years and 12 non-constituency members appointed by the president, plus the speaker and attorney-general. The multiparty system was introduced in December 1991.

The president – directly elected and limited to two five-year terms – is head of state, head of the cabinet and commander-in-chief of the armed forces, and appoints the vice-president and cabinet. However, under the internationally-brokered power-sharing agreement, a grand coalition government, comprising president and the new post of prime minister, was established in March 2008.

A commission was set up in 2000 to draw up a new constitution, which – following a constitutional court ruling in March 2004 – would be subject to a national referendum. Draft constitutions were discussed at a series of constitutional conferences. The new constitution that was approved by the National Assembly in April 2010, endorsed by the electorate in the national referendum on 4 August 2010 and promulgated on 27 August provides for reduction of the president's power; abolition of the post of prime minister (after the next election); an expanded National Assembly (to 350 seats); creation of a senate; significant devolution of power to new county authorities (to be overseen by the senate); recognition of faith courts; a bill of rights; and creation of a supreme court, a new anti-corruption agency, and an independent land commission to promote land reform. Enabling legislation was to be approved by parliament and these new provisions implemented in a timetable spanning up to five years, most provisions to come into force after the election which was scheduled for the latter half of 2012. The implementation process is being overseen by two new bodies, the Commission for the Implementation of the Constitution and the Commission on Revenue Allocation.

Politics

Last elections:	December 2007 (presidential and legislative)
Next elections:	2012/2013 (presidential and legislative)
Head of state:	President Mwai Kibaki
Head of government:	the president
Ruling party:	grand coalition of Orange Democratic Movement and Party of National Unity

CO-OPERATIVE
BANK OF KENYA
We are you

Co-operative Bank of Kenya is a public limited liability company incorporated in Kenya under the Company's Act and licensed under the Banking Act Cap 486. The Bank was started in 1965 by the Co-operative Movement in Kenya and began operations in 1968 offering affordable financial services to the co-operatives.

In 1994, the Bank diversified its services and is now running a Universal Banking Model providing products and services in retail banking, corporate and trade finance, foreign exchange, electronic banking, co-operatives, asset finance, mortgage, custodial services and shares as well as registrar services. The Bank has three subsidiaries offering a wide range of products and services as outlined below:

- **Co-op Trust Investment Services Limited** provides fund management services to co-operatives, individuals and companies including trust funds; and prepares wills.

- **Co-op Consultancy Services Limited** serves co-operatives to enhance their capacity in operations, strategic planning, performance management and development of operating manuals and procedures.

- **Kingdom Securities Limited** provides stock brokerage services to individuals, limited liability firms and co-operatives.

Recently, the Bank increased its shareholding in **Co-operative Insurance Company Limited** aiming at offering Bancassurance products for motor vehicles, fire and theft, domestic packages, personal accident cover and group life assurance.

Vision

'To be the leading and dominant Kenyan Bank with a strong countrywide presence playing a central role in the co-operative movement and providing relevant and innovative financial services to our customers for optimum benefit of all our stakeholders.'

Mission

'To offer value-added financial services to our chosen market segments with special emphasis on the co-operative movement through a highly effective network of service points, excellent customer service and a highly motivated team of qualified personnel.'

The Bank has enhanced Agri-business products including the introduction of sector-specific products, notably the Amiran Farmer's Kit, *Nafaka* (Grain) Loan Product, *Maziwa* (Milk) Plus and *Vuna Kilimo* (Harvest) products.

In 2010, the Bank launched Commodity Financing whose repayment relies on liquidation of flow of commodities through tailor-made credit enhancement structures.

As of August 2011, the Bank has a network of 89 branches and plans to increase this by more than 30 branches over the next two years. The Bank has continued to increase its ATM network to be accessible in over 410 ATM service points including 35 Auto Banking Centres with deposit-taking capabilities, availing customers of 24-hours banking services.

From 2010 M-Banking customer numbers significantly increased to an active client base of 465,000 customers.

The Bank has taken advantage of improved regulation when the Central Bank of Kenya came up with clear guidelines on Agent Banking and the target is to increase the number of agents to over 2,000 by the end of 2011.

The Bank plans to extend its success in the Co-operative movement in Kenya to other countries in the East African Region starting with Southern Sudan and expand to the entire Eastern African region

Contact

Head Office
Co-operative Bank House
Haile Selassie Avenue
P.O. Box 48231 – 00100
Nairobi
Kenya

Tel: +254 20 327 6000

Fax: +254 20 21 9831

Web: www.co-opbank.co.ke

Email: info@co-opbank.co.ke

*Mr Gideon Muriuki,
Group Managing Director
and CEO*

At his third attempt, in a relatively peaceful contest, Mwai Kibaki, the candidate of the National Rainbow Coalition (NARC), comfortably won the presidential election in December 2002, with 62.2% of the votes, while Uhuru Kenyatta (the son of Kenya's first president), standing for the Kenya African National Union (KANU), received 31.3%. The National Rainbow Coalition gained a substantial majority in the parliamentary elections, winning 125 seats; KANU took 64 and FORD–People 14 (Forum for the Restoration of Democracy). The Commonwealth observer group present commended the Electoral Commission, said that the elections 'represented a major improvement on previous such exercises' and described the electoral process as credible.

In a referendum in November 2005 a proposed new constitution was decisively rejected. Opposition to this constitution was led by a new grouping, the 'Orange team', comprising Uhuru Kenyatta's KANU and the Liberal Democratic Party (LDP), a party with members in Kibaki's cabinet. Kibaki then dismissed his cabinet. When in December he formed a new cabinet he excluded opponents of the new constitution (mainly LDP members) and included members of minority parties to shore up support for his government.

In 2007, when elections were due, the Orange Democratic Movement (ODM) led by Raila Odinga and Orange Democratic Movement-Kenya (ODM–K) led by Kalonzo Musyoka emerged as the main opponents to Mwai Kibaki and his newly formed coalition, the Party of National Unity (PNU). The PNU included KANU which had earlier left the Orange team, FORD–Kenya, NARC–Kenya (an offshoot of NARC) and several smaller parties. Tensions were high in the pre-election period, with outbreaks of violence.

Following a relatively peaceful polling day on 27 December 2007, the Orange team decisively won the parliamentary elections; ODM took 99 seats and its partner NARC three. The ruling PNU took 43 seats and its coalition partners 35 seats. Of the remaining constituencies declared, ODM–K won in 16 and independents in 11. A re-run was ordered in the three undeclared constituencies.

Unofficial results of the presidential election indicated Raila Odinga led Kibaki by at least 200,000 votes and the absence of any official declaration provoked widespread unrest in the country. When on 30 December 2007 the Electoral Commission published results, Kibaki was ahead with 4,584,721 votes, then Odinga with 4,352,993 and Musyoka with 879,903. Commonwealth observers noted that the elections were 'the most competitive in the country's history' but raised doubts on the handling of the final stages of the presidential election, particularly the delay in announcing the results.

Protests about the presidential election results erupted and intensified in a period that became one of the most violent since independence and hundreds of people were killed. Some of the violence assumed an ethnic dimension with the Kikuyu perceived as pro-Kibaki and the Luo as Odinga supporters. The opposing leaders eventually agreed to work together in a power-sharing coalition government with Kibaki as president and Odinga as prime minister. The agreement was brokered by a group of eminent persons led by former UN Secretary-General Kofi Annan. In March 2008 the National Assembly enacted a law to formalise the deal. Odinga subsequently became prime minister in a grand coalition government.

If parliament falls behind in the legislative timetable set by the new constitution (promulgated on 27 August 2010; see *Constitution* above), the constitution provides for the holding of fresh elections earlier than March 2013 (the deadline set by a High Court ruling in January 2012), and the new parliament's first priority would then be to see through outstanding constitutional legislation.

International relations

Kenya is a member of the African, Caribbean and Pacific Group of States, African Union, Common Market for Eastern and Southern Africa, East African Community, Indian Ocean Rim Association for Regional Cooperation, Non-Aligned Movement, United Nations and World Trade Organization.

Kenya was a member, with Uganda and United Republic of Tanzania, of the East African Community, which from 1967 had a common market and many shared services, but collapsed in 1977. The three countries again embarked on developing regional co-operation in 1993, bringing about progressive harmonisation of standards and policies across a wide range of activities and launching a new East African Community in January 2001 and East African Customs Union in January 2005. The Community was enlarged in July 2007 when Burundi and Rwanda became members.

Kenya is also a member of the Intergovernmental Authority on Development, which was established in 1986 by the six countries in the Horn of Africa to combat drought and desertification and promote food security in the region.

Kenya hosts the headquarters of the United Nations Environment Programme in Nairobi.

Traveller information

Local laws and conventions: The population is diverse with more than 40 different tribes and languages and cultures. Visitors must be aware of local sensitivities and dress conservatively, especially in Mombasa town. Local customs must be respected at all times but especially during the holy month of Ramadan or when visiting religious sites. Alcohol is only available on the coast in tourist areas.

Smoking is banned in public places in Nairobi, Nakuru and Mombasa. Infringement will result in arrest, prosecution and a fine of KSh2,000 or six months' imprisonment.

The Kenyan authorities have a strict drugs policy, and the use and trafficking of Class A drugs carries heavy fines and jail sentences.

Working without a permit is punishable by fines, deportation or imprisonment. Visitors must not take pictures of official buildings, including embassies.

Casual lightweight clothes are acceptable for most occasions. Suits are customary for business meetings, which are generally by appointment only.

Main urban centres have conference facilities. Business hours are Mon–Fri 0800–1300 and 1400–1700.

Immigration and customs: A visa is required to enter Kenya and passports must be valid for three months from the date of entry. Airport departure tax is usually included in the price of the airline ticket.

Ministry of Gender, Children and Social Development, Kenya

The Ministry of Gender, Children and Social Development (MGC&SD) is dedicated to achieving full participation of all Kenyans in Social Services in the development process to enhance their socio-economic welfare. Established through Presidential Circular No. 1 of May 2008, the Ministry's mission is to promote, co-ordinate, monitor and evaluate gender equality, women's empowerment, social development, care and protection of children and other vulnerable groups as an integral part of national development.

Our vision

A society where women, men and children enjoy equal rights, opportunities and high quality of life.

The Ministry of Gender, Children and Social Development comprises two departments: **Children's Services** and **Gender and Social Development**.

The Department of Children's Services is responsible for monitoring and providing for parental responsibility, fostering, adoption, custody, maintenance, guardianship, care and protection of children.

Five Divisions of the Department of Children's Services

- Field Services Division: Responsible for child protection services and combating sexual abuse and trafficking.

- Cash Transfer to Orphans and the Vulnerable: Dispenses and monitors government support for poor households.

- Alternative Family Care: Provides adoption services, foster care and guardianship and maintains a registered list of adoption societies in Kenya.

- Statutory Institutions and CCI Services: Responsible for running statutory institutions and regulating over 830 Charitable Children's Institutions (CCI) active in the country.

- Finance and Administrative Division: Co-ordinates the various divisions of the department.

Vision of the Department of Children's Services

A society where children become responsible citizens through fulfilment of their prescribed rights and welfare.

The Department of Gender and Social Development was established in 2006 to promote gender equality, women's empowerment and sustainable socio-economic development through gender mainstreaming in the development process, capacity building, social protection, community participation and public-private partnerships.

Policies Developed by the Department of Gender and Social Development

- National Policy on Older Persons and Ageing

- National Policy on Social Protection

- National Policy on Female Genital Mutilation

- National Policy on Community Development

Vision of the Department of Gender and Social Development

Attainment of gender equality and full participation of men and women, boys and girls in social development.

Contact

Ministry of Gender, Children and Social Development
NSSF Building, Block A,
Eastern Wing, 6th Floor
P.O. Box 16936-00100 Nairobi

Tel: +254 20 272 7980

Fax: +254 20 273 4417

Email: information@gender.go.ke

www.gender.go.ke

Hon. Minister
Dr Naomi Shaban,
EGH, MP

Visitors are advised to leave their passport in the hotel safe and to take with them a copy of the photopage of their passport and visa for ID purposes. It is recommended that all return flights are confirmed.

Prohibited imports include seeds, live animals, plants, ammunition and imitation firearms. Export of gold, diamonds, wildlife skins and game trophies not obtained from the Kenyan government is forbidden.

A yellow fever vaccination certificate will be required for all those arriving from infected countries.

Lone parents should carry documentation showing parental responsibility for an accompanying child.

Travel within the country: Traffic drives on the left. A national driving licence is valid in Kenya, as long as it is in English. Cars should only be hired from recommended car-hire companies. All major roads are paved and there are petrol stations on most highways. Speed limits are 120kph outside urban areas and 60kph in towns.

There are long-distance bus services that connect the towns and cities, and short-distance minibuses (*matatu*). The three-wheeled rickshaw or *tuk tuk* is becoming popular. In Kisumu, cycle rickshaws and bicycle taxis are popular – known locally as *boda-bodas*.

Newer taxis are usually white with a yellow band.

The main train line between Nairobi and Mombasa has a fast and reliable service. The journey takes 13 hours, and first- and second-class sleeping compartments can be booked in advance.

Kenya Airways operates scheduled domestic flights.

Local *dhows* run between Mombasa, Malindi and Lamu but they are not permitted for foreigners. However, visitors may take a short sightseeing *dhow* from Mombasa.

Travel health: Visitors will need to take out comprehensive health insurance which will cover medical repatriation. Serious medical conditions may result in evacuation.

Visitors must exercise caution when travelling outside urban areas, as diphtheria, Hepatitis A, malaria, rabies, tetanus, typhoid and

History

Archaeological evidence suggests that Kenya may be the birthplace of the human race, as 3.25 million years ago the Rift Valley was the home of *Homo habilis*, from whom *Homo sapiens* descended.

Little is known of the early history of Kenya's interior, except that peoples from all over the African continent settled here. Arab merchants established trading posts on the coast during the seventh century. The Portuguese took control of coastal trading from the early 16th century, but by 1720 they had been driven out by the Arabs. For the following century, the coastal region was ruled mainly by the Arabian Omani.

Around 1750 the Masai, a people of nomadic cattle-herders whose young men formed a military elite (*el morani*), began entering Kenya from the north and spreading out southwards, raiding and rustling. At the end of the 1850s there were Masai by the coast near Mombasa. During the 1860s, the Masai drove back Europeans attempting to penetrate the interior of the country. Two outbreaks of cattle-disease in the 1880s, an outbreak of smallpox in 1889–90 and internecine fighting between supporters of two rival chiefs weakened the Masai considerably by the 1890s.

The British were invited to the coastal region during the 1820s by the Omani Mazrui Dynasty, to help it with a local power struggle. By the middle of the century, Britain and Germany were competing for control of the coast and its hinterland. A British protectorate was declared in 1895 over what is now Kenya and Uganda and, following a survey made by Lord Delamere, European and European-descended settlement took place until the start of the 1914–18 war.

A railway was constructed 1895–1901, linking the port of Mombasa with Kisumu on Lake Victoria. Many Asians arrived during this period, in particular to work on the construction of the railway. Nairobi became the headquarters of the British administration.

A legislative council for whites was formed in 1907 (first election 1919). Local native councils were introduced in 1925. White settlers moved increasingly into the fertile lands, displacing African peoples, including the Masai and the Kikuyu. By the 1940s, the Highlands were monopolised by whites.

In 1944, the Kikuyu-dominated Kenya African Union (KAU) was established, part of the first African nationalist movement in East Africa. The KAU demanded access to the Highlands. Jomo Kenyatta, who had spent much of the 1930s and 1940s campaigning in Europe for territorial, economic and political rights for Africans, became president of the KAU in 1947. The KAU came into increasing conflict with the European settlers. A guerrilla war for independence and land resettlement was waged 1952–56 by the nationalist Land Freedom Army, the so-called 'Mau Mau'.

A state of emergency was declared 1952–60, during which more than 80,000 people were detained. During the fighting, large numbers of people were killed, sometimes in fights with settlers, sometimes in internecine fights. The KAU was banned in 1953 and Kenyatta was imprisoned. However, wider African representation followed and in 1957, African members were elected to the legislative council. A transitional constitution, introduced in 1960, allowed for political parties and gave Africans a majority on the legislative council.

The Kenya African National Union (KANU) was then formed. Its leaders, while Kenyatta was in prison (1953–61), were Tom Mboya (a Luo trade unionist), Oginga Odinga (a distinguished Luo) and James Gichuru. Other African politicians formed the Kenya African Democratic Union, led by Ronald Ngala and Daniel arap Moi. Released in August 1961, Kenyatta formed an all-party African government and accepted the KANU presidency. Elections were held in May 1963, as a result of which KANU took power at independence in December 1963.

Kenya became a republic in December 1964, with Kenyatta its first president. In 1966 Odinga resigned from the vice-presidency ➤

CENTUM
tangible wealth

Centum Investment Company Limited is a public limited company listed on the Nairobi Stock Exchange and Uganda Securities Exchange. Through Centum investors can access a portfolio of quality diversified investments. Our services include investing equity capital in companies for favourable investment returns and managing these investment portfolios.

Our vision is to be Africa's foremost investment channel.

Our mission is to create real, tangible wealth by providing the channel through which investors access and build extraordinary enterprises in Africa.

We are the leading listed investment company in East Africa with ongoing initiatives to expand across the African continent. We will be seeking to cross list our shares on the Dar-es-Salaam Stock Exchange and the Rwanda Stock Exchange by the close of the 2011-2012 financial year.

Divisions
The **Private Equity** business line accounts for over 50% of assets under our management. In this division, we invest both in controlling stakes and in significant minority stakes in unquoted companies in Africa including household names such as General Motors East Africa, Aon Kenya, UAP Holdings and Coca Cola Bottling.

The **Quoted Private Equity** business line manages investments in select publicly traded companies. We employ our expertise in private equity to select, invest and create value in illiquid companies across African stock exchanges.

The **Real Estate and Infrastructure** business line, our newest division, is focused on developing world-class branded destinations in Africa. Our aim is to lead the way in developing new, fully serviced neighbourhoods with improved living standards.

Investment strategy
As an active investor, we work alongside our clients to realise strategic and operational improvements that drive sustainable growth without diluting their vision. We emphasise on prudent diversification by sector, geography and security type, to reduce investment risks and to enhance returns.

Centum remains committed to high professional and ethical standards with a passion for excellence and integrity. Whether you are an investor, co-investor or an investee company, we are a supportive, experienced partner aiming to make our customers feel secure, confident and part of a bigger agenda.

Our values
· We promise to deliver
· We have unity of purpose
· We are partners
· We invest responsibly

Centum Investment Company Limited CEO, James Mworia (right), has been named the Africa Young Business Leader of the Year 2011 at the just-concluded inaugural All Africa Business Leader Awards ceremony at Sandton Sun in Johannesburg, South Africa

Contact
Mr James Mworia, CEO, Centum Investment Co. Ltd, Tel: +254 20 31 6303
www.centum.co.ke

yellow fever are all present. They should take insect repellent and suitable clothing to prevent insect bites. Current vaccination requirements for Kenya must be adhered to before travel.

Bottled water is recommended.

Money: ATMs are widely available in Nairobi and the main towns. Credit cards and travellers cheques are accepted. Currency can be exchanged at major banks, bureaux de change and airports. The easiest to change are euros, US dollars and pounds sterling. Banking hours are Mon–Fri 0900–1500 and Sat 0900–1100. The bank at Nairobi airport is open 24 hours.

There were more than 2 million tourist arrivals in 2007 and 1.1 million in 2008.

➤ to form the Kenya People's Union (KPU). Throughout the 1960s, radical elements within KANU challenged the moderates, who were led by Mboya (assassinated 1969 in unclear circumstances) and Moi (who with the entire membership of the Kenya African Democratic Union had earlier joined KANU). Following a dispute, the KPU was banned and Odinga detained. Kenyatta was elected unopposed to a third presidential term in September 1974. He died in 1978, aged 82. The presidency passed to Moi.

There were numerous constitutional amendments under Moi's presidency. In 1982, KANU became the sole legal political party. In 1986, control of the civil service was transferred to the president's office, and the president was given power to dismiss High Court judges and the auditor-general. Also in 1986 the secret ballot for parliamentary elections was replaced by public queue-voting.

Moi was returned to power in the 1988 elections. Ethnic tensions increased in some rural areas. Aid was frozen from 1991, as a result of the dissatisfaction among donors over human rights and economic conditions. The government then began to reform the political system. The secret ballot had been brought back in 1990, the tenure of office of judges and the auditor-general was restored in 1992, a multiparty system was introduced and the government called elections for December 1992.

Several new opposition parties to KANU emerged for the first multiparty elections in December 1992. They included the Forum for the Restoration of Democracy (FORD–Kenya), led by Oginga Odinga until his death in 1994, the Democratic Party led by Mwai Kibaki, and FORD–Asili led by Kenneth Matiba. A Commonwealth observer group at the elections concluded that they were flawed, but sufficiently free and fair for the results to be acceptable as the democratic will. KANU led by Daniel arap Moi won, against a divided opposition. In 1993 aid began slowly to flow again.

Despite the reforms of the early 1990s, the constitution remained the focus of political discontent, the opposition arguing that

centralisation of power weakens the multiparty system. Some prominent figures within KANU were calling for the restoration of *majimbo* features of the independence constitution, to strengthen the rights of ethnic minorities. In September 1997 the National Assembly approved electoral reforms, including abolition of the anti-sedition laws that the government had used to suppress the opposition, granting equal broadcasting time to all political parties and presidential candidates, and giving the opposition representation on the Electoral Commission.

In the December 1997 presidential election, Moi was re-elected with 40% of the votes, Kibaki of the Democratic Party received 31%, Raila Odinga of the National Development Party (NDP) 11%, Michael Kijana Wamalwa of FORD-Kenya 8% and Charity Kaluki Ngilu of the Social Democratic Party 8%. In the simultaneous National Assembly elections, KANU took 109 of the 210 seats, the Democratic Party 39, NDP 21, FORD-Kenya 17, and Social Democratic Party 14.

In November 1999, a further constitutional amendment was enacted to reduce the powers of the president to control the National Assembly, powers that were originally introduced by Kenyatta.

In June 2001, Moi forged the country's first governing coalition when he appointed to the cabinet two members of the opposition NDP – including Raila Odinga, son of Oginga Odinga, the country's first vice-president and a presidential candidate in 1992, and in March 2002 the NDP was merged with KANU. However, Odinga then left KANU and formed the Liberal Democratic Party and in October 2002 joined with Kibaki in the National Rainbow Coalition (NARC). In late 2001, Uhuru Kenyatta, the son of Kenya's first president, was nominated as an MP and appointed minister, emerging in 2002 as KANU's presidential candidate, replacing Moi, who by the end of the year would have been president for 24 years and who was bound by the constitution to stand down.

Kiribati

KEY FACTS

Joined Commonwealth:	1979
Population:	100,000 (2010)
GDP p.c. growth:	1.2% p.a. 1990–2010
UN HDI 2011:	world ranking 122
Official language:	English
Time:	GMT plus 12–14hr
Currency:	Australian dollar

Geography

Area:	811 sq km
Coastline:	1,140km
Capital:	Tarawa

Kiribati (pronounced 'Kirabas') spreads across the central Pacific, intersected by the equator and formerly the International Date Line, with most other Commonwealth Pacific island countries lying to its south. Its 33 islands are scattered across 5.2 million sq km of ocean. There are three groups of islands: 17 Gilbert Islands (including Banaba), eight Line Islands and eight Phoenix Islands. The north/south extent is 2,050km. Kiritimati (formerly Christmas Island) is the world's biggest coral atoll (388 sq km). Kiritimati in the east is about 3,780km from Banaba (formerly Ocean Island) in the west.

Time: GMT plus 12hr except for Kanton Island and Enderbury Islands (GMT plus 13hr – on the same day) and Kiritimati (GMT plus 14hr).

Area: Total land area 811 sq km.

Topography: Kiribati is composed of coral atolls on a submerged volcanic chain, nowhere rising higher than 2m above sea level, except for Banaba, a coral outcrop, which rises to 80m. Most islands have coastal lagoons. Some lagoons are large (up to 80km long), and bounded to the east by narrow strips of land. There are no hills or streams. The UN's 1989 report on the 'greenhouse effect' listed Kiribati as an endangered country in the event of a rise in sea level during the 21st century.

In February 2005, 2.8m waves breached sea walls, devastating some villages, destroying farmland and contaminating freshwater wells.

Did you know...

Former president Sir Ieremia Tabai was in 2010 appointed to the Commonwealth Eminent Persons Group, which presented its recommendations for reform in the Commonwealth to Commonwealth leaders at CHOGM in Australia in October 2011.

The country comprises 33 islands scattered across 5.2 million sq km of the central Pacific Ocean, and has some 1,140km of coastline.

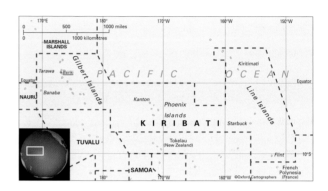

Climate: Varies from maritime equatorial (central islands) to tropical in the north and south. There is little temperature variation: from an average 29°C in the southern Gilberts to 27°C in the Line Islands, dropping by less than 1°C in the coolest months. Humidity is constant at 70–90%. North-west trade winds blow between March and October. From November to April, there are occasional heavy rains, and strong to gale force winds, though Kiribati is outside the cyclone belt. Rainfall patterns vary considerably from year to year; drought is a constant danger.

In 1997, Kiritimati was devastated by El Niño, which, according to scientists studying the island, brought heavy rainfall, a half-metre rise in sea level and extensive flooding. Some 40% of the coral was killed and the 14 million bird population, reputed to be the world's richest, deserted the island.

Environment: The most significant environmental issues are limited natural freshwater resources, and heavy pollution of the south Tarawa lagoon, due to population growth around the lagoon and traditional practices such as lagoon latrines and open-pit dumping.

Vegetation: Poor soil (composed of coral sand and rock fragments) limits vegetation-types and agricultural potential. Coconuts cover most islands, except Banaba and some islands in the Phoenix and Line groups. Forest covers 15% of the land area and there was no significant loss of forest cover during 1990–2010.

Wildlife: Many varieties of sea birds visit the islands, including terns, shearwaters and skuas.

Main towns: The main centre and capital is Tarawa, comprising Bairiki (Tarawa South, pop. 47,900 in 2010), Bonriki (Tarawa South, 4,000) and Buariki (Tarawa North, 3,300). Government offices are in Tarawa South at Betio, Bairiki and Bikenibeu. Other populated areas include Taburao (on the island of Abaiang, 4,300), Temaraia (on Nonouti, 3,000), Butaritari island (2,700) and Utiroa (on Tabiteuea, 2,500).

Transport: There are some 670km of all-weather roads in urban Tarawa and Kiritimati. Causeways and bridges link north and south Tarawa, plus several other islands. Bairiki and Bikenibeu in south Tarawa are connected by causeways. Betio, the port area 3km west of Bairiki, is connected to Bairiki by a causeway. There are about 3,000 vehicles, nearly 75% of them motor cycles.

The principal port is at Betio Islet, Tarawa. International airports are at Bonriki on Tarawa and at Kiritimati, and all inhabited islands have airports. Air Kiribati, the national airline, operates scheduled services to nearly all the country's outer islands, linking them with Tarawa.

Society

KEY FACTS 2010

Population per sq km:	123
Life expectancy:	64 years (est.)

Population: 100,000 (2010); the Phoenix Islands and central and southern Line Islands are mostly uninhabited; 44% lives in urban areas; growth 1.6% p.a. 1990–2010; birth rate 23 per 1,000 people (est.; 41 in 1970); life expectancy 64 years (est.; 49 in 1970).

The government's resettlement programme, which began in 1989, aimed to transfer almost 5,000 people from the densely populated western atolls to the Line and Phoenix Islands. Five of the Phoenix Islands were designated for residential development in 1995, especially for people from the overcrowded island of South Tarawa.

The people are mostly of Micronesian origin (98.8% in 2000 census). There are also Polynesian and European-descended minorities.

Language: I-Kiribati is the national language, English the official language, but not much used outside the capital.

Religion: Mainly Christians (Roman Catholics 55%, Protestants 36%, Mormons, Seventh Day Adventists; 2005 census). There is a small Baha'i minority.

Health: Public spending on health was 10% of GDP in 2009. Infant mortality was 39 per 1,000 live births in 2010. Tuberculosis is a serious public health problem; there are regular outbreaks of dengue fever and occasional cases of leprosy and typhoid. The first AIDS case was reported in Tarawa in 1991.

Education: There are nine years of compulsory education starting at age six, comprising six years of primary school and at least three of secondary. The school year starts in January.

The Institute of Technology offers courses in technical and vocational subjects. The Marine Training Centre runs 18-month courses in deck, engine-room and catering work on merchant-shipping lines; it trains about 200 students each year. There is a training college for primary teachers, and an extra-mural centre of the University of the South Pacific at Tarawa. Kiribati is a partner in the regional University of the South Pacific, which has its main campus in Suva, Fiji, and a campus in Tarawa, Kiribati, with some 3,000 students, enrolled for a wide range of courses using the university's distance-learning facilities.

Media: *Te Uekera* is a weekly newspaper mainly in I-Kiribati, but with main news items also in English. *Kiribati Newstar* is an independent weekly. The Roman Catholic and Protestant churches publish newsletters. Radio Kiribati provides a public service. There is no national television service.

There are 90 internet users per 1,000 people (2010).

Communications: Country code 686; internet domain '.ki'. Radio telephone is used to call the outer islands. Internet connection is available on some of the islands. The main post office is in Bairiki, with branches in Betio, Bikenibeu and the outer islands, including Kiritimati.

There are 41 main telephone lines and 101 mobile phone subscriptions per 1,000 people (2010).

Public holidays: New Year's Day, Women's Day (8 March), Health Day (18 April), Independence (usually several days around 12 July), Youth Day (7 August), Human Rights Day (11 December), Christmas Day and Boxing Day. The Independence celebrations continue for three days.

Religious festivals whose dates vary from year to year include Good Friday and Easter Monday.

Economy

KEY FACTS 2010

GNI:	US$200m
GNI p.c.:	US$2,010
GDP growth:	0.5% p.a. 2006–10
Inflation:	4.8% p.a. 2006–10

Phosphate mining on Banaba by the British Phosphate Commission accounted for 80% of exports and 50% of government revenue until the mines were exhausted in 1979, the year of independence. The loss of the phosphate industry caused a huge drop in GDP; no other product or sector has yet been able to make up the lost revenue. The best prospects for diversification of the economy lie in marine resources. The country's exclusive economic zone of some 3.55 million sq km is among the largest in the world in relation to its land area. After fishing licences, the next largest source of income is remittances from seamen employed on foreign – mainly German – ships.

A vital source of revenue is the Revenue Equalisation Reserve Fund, built up from past phosphate taxation surpluses. It was worth A$571 million by 2009.

Real Growth in GDP

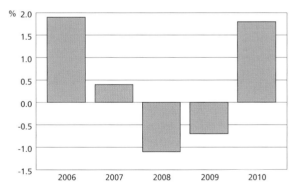

Inflation

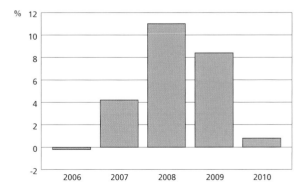

GDP by Sector (2010)

■ Agriculture	26%
☐ Industry	9%
■ Services	65%

There were some years when the economy was buoyant in the 1990s, growing 5% in 1998 and 9.5% in 1999, with modest levels of inflation, but in the 2000s growth was generally slower, when sustainable development became a key objective. This low-lying country faces numerous development challenges, not least that 32 of 33 islands rise no higher than 2m above sea level. The economy stalled in 2005 (0.3%) and 2007 (0.4%); was in recession in 2008 (–1.1%) and 2009 (–0.7%), when many countries were caught in the world economic downturn; and recovered in 2010 (1.8%).

Constitution

Status:	Republic with executive president
Legislature:	Maneaba ni Maungatabu (Parliament)
Independence:	12 July 1979

Under the independence constitution of 1979, Kiribati became a sovereign and democratic republic with a unicameral legislature, the Maneaba ni Maungatabu. The president (*Beretitenti*, pronounced 'Beresitence') is both head of state and head of government, and is elected nationally, from nominations (from among its own members) made by the Maneaba ni Maungatabu. The cabinet consists of the president, the vice-president (*Kauoman-*

History

The present inhabitants are descended mainly from Samoans who migrated to Kiribati at some time between the 11th and 14th centuries. Traces of later contact with other Pacific Islanders and a Chinese influence remain in the population and culture. Social structure was diverse, chiefs ruling in the northern islands and councils of elders having authority in the south.

The islands were sighted by 16th-century Spanish seamen, but settlement was not attempted, and Europeans did not arrive in any numbers until after 1765. Between the late 18th century and 1870 the waters of Kiribati were used by European sperm-whaling ships; deserters from the ships sometimes settled on the islands. Trade in coconut oil began about 1860, followed by trade in copra. By the second half of the 19th century about 9,000 Kiribati people were working overseas, thanks to energetic labour recruitment.

Christian missionaries first arrived in the northern Gilberts in 1857. In 1870 Samoan clergy, sponsored by the London Missionary Society, arrived at Arorae, Tamara, Onotoa and Beru. In 1888 Roman Catholic missionaries arrived in the Gilberts, which are today predominantly Roman Catholic.

In 1892 a British protectorate was proclaimed at Abemama by Captain Davis of HMS *Royalist* on behalf of Queen Victoria. The headquarters were established at Tarawa, district magistrates were assigned to the islands and a code of law was drawn up. Phosphate-rich Banaba (Ocean Island) was annexed by Britain in 1900. In 1915, the Gilbert and Ellice Islands were annexed by a British order in council which came into effect on 12 January 1916.

The Japanese army occupied the Gilbert Islands (1942–43) until driven out by the US army in some of the Pacific War's fiercest fighting. In 1957 three hydrogen bombs were detonated in the vicinity of Kiritimati, as part of the UK's atmospheric testing programme.

In 1975 the Ellice Islands seceded to form the separate territory of Tuvalu. Internal self-government was given to the Gilbert Islands, renamed Kiribati, on 1 January 1977. At a conference in 1978 it was agreed that Kiribati, with other islands appended to the territory by the colonial authorities, should become fully independent as a republic. On Independence Day, 12 July 1979, Kiribati became the 41st member of the Commonwealth.

Ieremia Tabai became the first president of Kiribati in July 1979. He was re-elected in April 1982, but the following December his government was defeated in a vote of no confidence. Re-elected president in February 1983, he went on to win the election of May 1987. Prevented by the constitution from standing for a further term, he was succeeded after the 1991 general election by his former vice-president, Teatao Teannaki.

There were no political parties before September 1985, and candidates continued to stand for election as independent individuals, though loosely structured parties – for example, Teatao Teannaki's National Progressive Party, Teburoro Tito's Maneaban Te Mauri, and Boutokaan Te Koaua – emerged thereafter.

In May 1994, President Teannaki's government lost a vote of no confidence. A general election held in July 1994 brought 18 new members into parliament. The majority of the 39 seats were won by an opposition grouping and in the presidential election that followed in September 1994 Teburoro Tito was elected from a list of four nominations.

In March 1998, among the main recommendations of the first review of the constitution since independence in 1979 was that foreign husbands of I-Kiribati women should have the same automatic rights to Kiribati citizenship as foreign wives of I-Kiribati men.

On 23 and 30 September 1998, elections were held for the House of Assembly. In the first round of voting the government won six seats, and the opposition eight seats. In the second round, the government won a further 14 seats (making 20 in all) and the opposition nine seats (17 in all); the remaining two seats were won by independents. In November 1998, President Tito was re-elected. He defeated opposition members Amberoti Nikora and Harry Tong.

Banaba

Phosphate mining has made Banaba almost uninhabitable. The inhabitants were moved to the Fijian island of Rabi in the mid-1940s; in 1970 they became citizens of Fiji, but kept the ownership of land on Banaba. In 1981, after ten years of discussion and litigation over phosphate royalties and environmental damage caused by open-cast mining, they accepted A$14.58 million compensation from the British Government. The Banabans have special rights of residence and representation in Kiribati.

ni-Maungatabu), the attorney-general (who is the government's principal legal adviser) and up to eight other ministers. These ministers are appointed by the president from the members of the Maneaba ni Maungatabu.

The Assembly has 44 members elected for four years by universal adult suffrage, plus one *ex officio* member (the attorney-general) and one nominated member from the Banaban community in Rabi, Fiji, who have a right to enter and live on Banaba, and have their own Banaba Island Council.

Individual rights and freedoms are guaranteed under the constitution. In the event of dissolution of the House of Assembly on a vote of no confidence, the constitution provides for an interim council of state, composed of the chief justice, the speaker and the chairman of the Public Service Commission.

Politics

Last elections:	October 2011 (legislative), January 2012 (presidential)
Next elections:	2015/2016 (legislative and presidential)
Head of state:	President Anote Tong
Head of government:	the president
Ruling party:	Boutokaan Te Koaua

In the 2002 parliamentary elections, held on 29 November and 6 December, 17 Boutokaan Te Koaua (BTK) candidates were successful while President Teburoro Tito's Maneaban Te Mauri (MTM) won only 16 seats, and seven seats were taken by independents. Teburoro Tito then narrowly won the presidential poll in February 2003, defeating his principal rival, Taberannang Timeon, by some 550 votes.

Less than a month into his third (and necessarily final) term, President Tito lost a no-confidence vote and fresh elections were called. In the parliamentary elections in May 2003, MTM took 24 of the 40 elected seats and the BTK 16, the independents having joined parties. However, in the close presidential poll, in July 2003, Anote Tong of the BTK defeated the MTM's candidate, his younger brother Harry Tong, and formed a new government.

Parliamentary elections were held on 22 and 30 August 2007. Independent candidates won in 19 of the 44 seats available in the two-round contest. BTK was the leading political party taking 18 seats, and MTM seven.

In the October 2007 presidential elections, Anote Tong – with 15,500 votes and 65% of votes – was well ahead of his principal opponent, Nabuti Mwemwenikarawa (33%).

Following the election of a new parliament in October/November 2011 – when President Tong's BTK won 15 seats, the Karikirakean Tei-Kiribati (KTK) ten, and the Maurin Kiribati Party (MKP) three; and 30 of the 44 members were re-elected – the new Assembly nominated three candidates to contest the presidential elections.

The presidential elections, held in January 2012, were won by the incumbent, Anote Tong of the BTK (42%), defeating Tetaua Taitai of the KTK (35%) and opposition leader Rimeta Beniamina of the MKP (23%).

International relations

Kiribati is a member of the African, Caribbean and Pacific Group of States, Pacific Community, Pacific Islands Forum and United Nations.

Traveller information

Local laws and conventions: The people of Kiribati live by Christian values, which have a strong influence on traditional life.

Possession of, or trafficking in, narcotics is a serious offence and can result in heavy prison sentences.

In Kiribati, it is customary, and more polite, to address people by their first name.

Office hours are Mon–Fri 0800–1230 and 1330–1615.

Immigration and customs: Most nationals require a visa and a return ticket to visit Kiribati.

A yellow fever vaccination certificate will be required by those arriving from infected countries.

There is a strict quarantine regime for the import of food, plants, animal and fish products.

Visitors going on to Australia and New Zealand must be aware that there are strict import regulations relating to straw products and seashells. A phytosanitary certificate will be required on products bought in Kiribati.

Travel within the country: Traffic drives on the left. Car hire is available on Tarawa and Christmas Island only, and an international driving permit is required. Minibuses run frequently; taxis operate on Tarawa only.

Air Kiribati operates an internal scheduled service to the outer islands from Tarawa.

There are several passenger ferries between the smaller islands, and boats can be hired locally.

The lagoon in South Tarawa is not safe for swimming because of pollution. Elsewhere, visitors should beware of rip tides.

Travel health: Medical facilities at Tarawa are modest, and visitors are advised to take out comprehensive travel and medical insurance to cover the cost of medical evacuation by air.

Inoculation against diphtheria, Hepatitis A, tetanus and sometimes typhoid are recommended. Dengue fever is prevalent, so visitors should bring insect repellent and cover up with suitable clothing to prevent insect bites.

Prescription medicines should be in their original containers, clearly labelled to avoid confusion.

Only bottled or boiled water should be used for drinking, cleaning teeth and making ice.

Money: Currency can be exchanged at the Bank of Kiribati or at local hotels. Credit cards can be used, although Mastercard and Visa have limited acceptance. There are ATMs at the Bank of Kiribati/ANZ in Betio, Bairiki and Bikenibeu. Travellers cheques in Australian dollars are the most acceptable. Banking hours are Mon–Fri 0930–1500.

There were 3,000 tourist arrivals in 2009.

Further information

Parliament: www.parliament.gov.ki

Commonwealth Secretariat: www.thecommonwealth.org

Commonwealth of Nations: www.commonwealth-of-nations.org/Kiribati

Lesotho

KEY FACTS

Joined Commonwealth:	1966
Population:	2,171,000 (2010)
GDP p.c. growth:	2.2% p.a. 1990–2010
UN HDI 2011:	world ranking 160
Official languages:	Sesotho, English
Time:	GMT plus 2hr
Currency:	loti, plural maloti (M)

Geography

Area:	30,355 sq km
Coastline:	none
Capital:	Maseru

The Kingdom of Lesotho is a small landlocked country entirely surrounded by South Africa. It is known as the 'Mountain Kingdom', the whole country being over 1,000m in altitude. The country is divided into ten districts, each named after the principal town: Berea, Butha Buthe, Leribe, Mafeteng, Maseru, Mohale's Hoek, Mokhotlong, Qacha's Nek, Quthing and Thaba-Tseka.

Topography: Lesotho has two main mountain ranges – the Drakensberg and the Maloti ranges – both running north–south from the northern high plateau. The highest mountain in southern Africa is Thabana–Ntlenyana (3,842m) in eastern Lesotho. The land descends to the west to an arable belt, known as the lowlands, where the capital is situated and two-thirds of the population live. The country is well-watered in a generally dry region, the Orange river and its tributary the Caledon both rising in Lesotho.

Climate: The climate is temperate with well-marked seasons. The rainy season (receiving 85% of total precipitation) is October to April, when there are frequent violent thunderstorms. Rainfall

Did you know...

Lesotho is a monarchy.

The Government of Lesotho spends more on education than any other country in the Commonwealth, relative to GDP.

The country's lowest point of 1,400m above sea level is the highest lowest point of any country in the world. It has relatively very little forest, covering only 1% of the land area.

Through the Lesotho Highlands Water Project, Lesotho exports water to South Africa, which completely surrounds it.

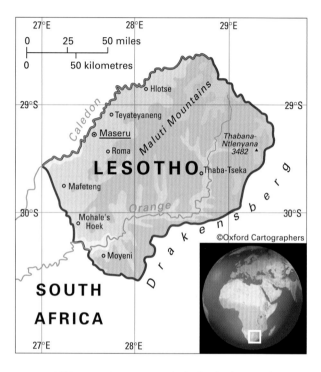

averages 746mm p.a. Temperatures in the lowlands range from 32.2°C to –6.7°C; the range is much greater in the mountains. From May to September, snow falls in the highlands with heavy frosts occurring in the lowlands.

Environment: The most significant issue is overgrazing, resulting in severe soil erosion and desertification.

Vegetation: Mainly grassland and bushveld, with forest in ravines and on the windward slopes of mountains. Forest covers 1% of the land area and arable land comprises 11%. Forest cover increased at 0.5% p.a. 1990–2010.

Wildlife: The Drakensberg Mountains are the last stronghold in southern Africa of the huge bearded vulture, the lammergeier. Large mammals have largely been eradicated by stock farming, and indigenous ground-living species are now restricted to small antelope, hares and the mountain-dwelling rock-rabbit (dassie).

Main towns: Maseru (capital, pop. 253,900 in 2010), Hlotse (45,300), Mafeteng (40,900), Teyateyaneng (27,100), Maputsoa (23,100), Mohale's Hoek (22,400), Qacha's Nek (17,100), Quthing (6,400), Mokhotlong (6,100) and Butha Buthe (5,900).

Transport: There are 5,940km of roads, 18% paved. South African Railways runs a short freight line into Lesotho, terminating at the Maseru industrial estate. The international airport, Moshoeshoe I Airport, lies 20km south of Maseru; there are 31 airstrips around the country for domestic flights.

Society

KEY FACTS 2010

Population per sq km:	72
Life expectancy:	48 years
Net primary enrolment:	73%

Population: 2,171,000 (2010); 27% lives in urban areas; growth 1.4% p.a. 1990–2010; birth rate 28 per 1,000 people (43 in 1970); life expectancy 48 years (49 in 1970 and 59 in 1990).

The people are mostly Basotho, with a few thousand expatriate Europeans and several hundred Asians.

Language: Sesotho and English are official languages; Zulu and Xhosa are also spoken.

Religion: Mainly Christians (Roman Catholics 56%, and Lesotho Evangelicals and Anglicans 24%); the rest hold traditional beliefs, which often coexist with Christianity.

Health: Public spending on health was 6% of GDP in 2009. 85% of the population uses an improved drinking water source and 29% have adequate sanitation facilities (2009). Infant mortality was 65 per 1,000 live births in 2010 (137 in 1960). Lesotho is vulnerable to AIDS and other sexually transmitted diseases; a high proportion of young men work in other countries with serious AIDS problems. In 2009, 23.6% of people aged 15–49 were HIV positive.

Education: Public spending on education was 13.1% of GDP in 2008. There are seven years of compulsory education starting at age six. Primary school comprises seven years and secondary five, with cycles of three and two years. Some 52% of pupils complete primary school (2008). The school year starts in March.

Higher education institutions include National University of Lesotho; Lesotho Institute of Public Administration and Management; Lesotho College of Education; Lerotholi Polytechnic; and Lesotho Agricultural College. Literacy among people aged 15–24 is 92% (2009).

Media: There are several independent weekly newspapers, including *Mopheme/The Survivor* (Sesotho/English), *The Mirror* and *Public Eye* (English), and *Makatolle*, *MoAfrica* and *Mohlanka* in Sesotho. The government newspaper is *Lentsoe la Basotho* in Sesotho.

Radio is the most important source of information. Public broadcasters Radio Lesotho and Lesotho Television provide national services. There are several private commercial and faith radio stations. South African radio and TV are received in Lesotho.

Some 13% of households have TV sets (2006). There are 3 personal computers (2005) and 39 internet users (2010) per 1,000 people.

Communications: Country code 266; internet domain '.ls'. Mobile phone coverage is confined to the main towns.

There are internet cafes in Maseru. Post office branches can be found in all the main cities.

There are 18 main telephone lines and 455 mobile phone subscriptions per 1,000 people (2010).

Public holidays: New Year's Day, Moshoeshoe's Day (11 March), Workers' Day (1 May), Africa/Heroes' Day (25 May), King's Birthday (17 July), Independence Day (4 October), Christmas Day and Boxing Day.

Religious and other festivals whose dates vary from year to year include Good Friday, Easter Monday and Ascension Day.

Economy

KEY FACTS 2010

GNI:	US$2.2bn
GNI p.c.:	US$1,040
GDP growth:	4.0% p.a. 2006–10
Inflation:	7.1% p.a. 2006–10

The economy of this landlocked and mountainous country is inseparably linked with that of its much bigger and more developed neighbour, South Africa. A large number of Basotho work in South Africa – around 100,000 in the mid-1990s, falling to 40,500 in 2010 – and most of the government's income comes from Southern African Customs Union import tariffs. Economic swings in South Africa are the biggest single influence on Lesotho's economy. Moreover, the country has one of the world's highest HIV infection rates.

Measures to diversify the economy have included encouragement of manufacturing, particularly of clothing, textiles, leather goods and footwear, and of tourism, including establishment of a ski resort in the Drakensberg. Manufacturing output grew by some 10% p.a. during the 1980s and by more than 7% p.a. in the 1990s; it surged in the early 2000s but declined during the rest of the decade. The manufacturing sector's contribution to GDP fell from 22% in 2006 to 16% in 2010. With the support of the IMF, economic policy has focused on investment in education, developing the private sector and more effective revenue collection.

Real Growth in GDP

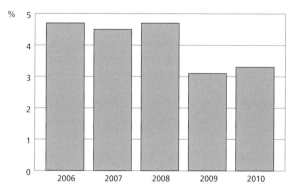

Inflation

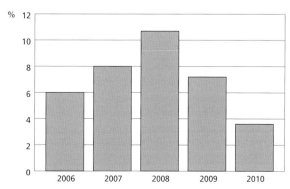

GDP by Sector (2010)

■ Agriculture	8%
□ Industry	34%
▨ Services	58%

The strong growth of the 1990s was interrupted by the outbreak of political unrest in late 1998. There was large-scale damage to property and loss of an estimated 4,000 jobs. The economy was plunged into recession and contracted by nearly 5% in 1998, compounded by rising unemployment due to the return of migrant mine workers. It only recovered in 2000, with a resumption of good growth in 2001 and this was sustained through the 2000s, until it slowed slightly in response to the global economic downturn in 2009–10, picking up again in 2011 (with growth of about 4%).

From 2005 exporters of textiles and clothing faced stronger competition in the US market from Asian producers, as their quotas were raised. But in 2006 measures under the US African Growth and Opportunity Act underpinned a recovery in the clothing industry and diamond production rose.

Energy

The Highlands Water Development Project, undertaken jointly with South Africa and begun in 1986, has made the country self-sufficient in electricity and is providing income by supplying South Africa with water. The project comprises a series of dams and tunnels which will take water from the Orange river and tributaries in the Maloti mountains northwards to the Vaal industrial basin in South Africa. The first phase included construction of a 185-metre dam at Katse – the highest in Africa – and was completed in 1996. The whole scheme is projected to be completed by 2020 and has already provided substantial spin-off benefits of improvements in infrastructure and employment.

Constitution

Status:	National Monarchy
Legislature:	Parliament
Independence:	4 October 1966

Lesotho is a constitutional monarchy. The present constitution came into force in 1993, shortly after the return to multiparty democracy, and was amended in 2001 to introduce an element of proportional representation. The monarch is head of state, the succession being ratified by the College of Chiefs. The prime minister is head of government and appoints a cabinet.

The legislature has two chambers: the National Assembly which is elected for a five-year term, with 80 seats elected on a first-past-the-post basis, and 40 by means of proportional representation; and the non-elected Senate with 33 members, comprising 11 nominated by the monarch on the advice of the prime minister and the 22 principal chiefs of Lesotho.

Politics

Last elections:	February 2007
Next elections:	2012
Head of state:	King Letsie III (1990–95; 1996–)
Head of government:	Prime Minister Bethuel Pakalitha Mosisili
Ruling party:	Lesotho Congress for Democracy

In the first elections following the introduction of an element of proportional representation, in May 2002, the Lesotho Congress for Democracy (LCD) took 77 seats and 55% of the votes, the Basotho National Party (BNP) 21 and 21%, and eight other parties each gained seats. Bethuel Pakalitha Mosisili was again sworn in as prime minister. The Commonwealth observer group present for the elections said that the conditions existed for a free expression of the will of the voters.

In October 2006, Tom Thabane resigned as a minister in the LCD government to form a new political party, the All Basotho Convention (ABC). Sixteen LCD MPs and one independent defected with him, making the ABC the third largest party in the National Assembly with 18 members.

In the February 2007 general election, which was observed by a Commonwealth expert team, Mosisili and the ruling LCD were returned to power, winning 61 seats. The National Independent Party took 21 seats and ABC 17, mainly in urban areas.

After the 2007 elections a political impasse arose following a dispute on the allocation of seats in parliament. Subsequent mediation efforts at resolving the dispute were led by a SADC Special Envoy, Sir Ketumile Masire, and the Christian Council of Lesotho.

International relations

Lesotho is a member of the African, Caribbean and Pacific Group of States, African Union, Non-Aligned Movement, Southern African Customs Union, Southern African Development Community, United Nations and World Trade Organization.

Traveller information

Local laws and conventions: Religion plays an important part in daily life and visitors should respect local laws; wearing immodest dress will cause offence.

Possession of drugs is illegal and penalties for drug offences are severe.

Taking photographs of police stations, government offices, the airport or banks is prohibited.

If visiting rural villages it is polite to inform the head chief. Normal social courtesies are appreciated. Dress should be practical and casual but respectful and modest.

Businessmen should wear a lightweight suit, shirt and tie, and businesswomen should dress conservatively and modestly. The usual business formalities apply. Office hours are Mon–Fri 0800–1245 and 1400–1630, Sat 0800–1300.

Lesotho was settled by the Sotho people sometime in the 16th century, mingling peacefully with the earlier Khoisan whose history can be traced in rock-art in various sites in the mountains. The Basotho were welded into a nation relatively recently by one outstanding leader. Around 1820, Moshoeshoe I, a minor chief of the Bakwena, gathered a following among the tribes who had retreated to the north-western borders of present-day Lesotho to protect themselves against Zulu and Matabele raids. Despite his limited military power, Moshoeshoe's diplomatic skills allowed the kingdom he created to long outlive those of his much stronger rivals. After successful resistance from his stronghold at Thaba Bosiu near Maseru in 1824, Moshoeshoe became chief of the local Basotho and other tribal groups, his following then numbering some 40,000. He was also successful at establishing good relationships with missionaries, especially French Catholics, whom he encouraged to establish missions and schools, and to advise him on negotiations with Europeans.

A new threat then emerged: the emigrant Boers set out on their Great Trek in 1834, in search of new territory. Moshoeshoe sought the protection of the British Crown – an alternative he preferred to annexation by the Boers, then establishing their Republic of the Orange Free State. In 1868 Basutoland (as the country was then called) was granted British protection. The frontiers, substantially unchanged today, were laid down in 1869.

Moshoeshoe died in 1870 and disputes over the succession divided the country. From 1870, migrant Basotho workers had begun working in the Kimberly diamond fields of the Cape. In 1871 Basutoland was annexed to the Cape Colony but, in 1884, it was removed from Cape control and came under direct British rule. It resisted incorporation into the proposed Union of South Africa in 1910; division along racial lines was already entrenched and Basutoland preferred to remain a British colony. The Basutoland Council was then set up as an advisory body and included 99 nominated members, around half of whom subsequently became elected members.

In 1960, a legislature, the Basutoland National Council, was formed and five years later a new constitution came into operation. Moshoeshoe II, Paramount Chief from 1960, became king. The legislature, until then unicameral, became bicameral.

Elections were held in 1965, in which the Basotho National Party (BNP) led by Chief Leabua Jonathan, narrowly defeated the Basutoland Congress Party (BCP). Lesotho became independent on 4 October 1966 with Chief Jonathan as prime minister, and joined the Commonwealth.

Relations between the King and the country's first prime minister soon became strained, and in 1970, Chief Jonathan annulled the country's second elections and suspended the constitution. He exiled the King (later allowing him to return but not to become involved in politics) and repressed opposition; but he was himself overthrown in a military coup in 1986, led by Major-General Justin Lekhanya. Lekhanya then reinstated the King, who was to govern on the advice of a military council; but in 1990 Lekhanya had half the military council arrested and nine ministers dismissed. The King was sent into exile and, *in absentia*, deposed in favour of his son, Letsie III, who was sworn in as monarch in November 1990.

Following the coup of 1986, the Lekhanya government remained in power for five years, but never achieved stability. Lekhanya was himself overthrown in a bloodless coup by his second-in-command, Elias Phitsoane Ramaema, in 1991. Ramaema repealed the ban on political activity, introduced a new constitution (effectively restoring the old one), and scheduled elections. At the elections, in March 1993, with Commonwealth and other international observers present, the BCP, led by Dr Ntsu Mokhehle, won all 65 seats in the new National Assembly leaving Jonathan's BNP without representation in the house.

King Letsie III then abdicated in favour of his father, King Moshoeshoe II, who had returned from London following a reconciliation process assisted by the Commonwealth Secretary-General. He was reinstated as monarch in January 1995. But almost exactly one year later, King Moshoeshoe was killed in a car accident. King Letsie III was sworn in for the second time by the College of Chiefs on 7 February 1996.

The BCP lost its majority and joined the opposition in mid-1997 when many of its members including Prime Minister Mokhehle defected to the newly established Lesotho Congress for Democracy (LCD). In the general election in May 1998 the LCD won 79 of the 80 National Assembly seats with just over 60% of the votes. The BNP took one seat with 24% of the votes. Following the elections the LCD chose Bethuel Pakalitha Mosisili, the party leader, to succeed 79-year-old Ntsu Mokhehle as prime minister.

However, the opposition parties refused to accept the election results, alleging that there had been gross irregularities. An increasingly vigorous campaign of protest reached a peak in August 1998. Stay-away strikes were organised and crowds first gathered at and then camped in front of the Royal Palace in Maseru. Following the intervention of the then South African Deputy President Thabo Mbeki, a team of Botswanan, South African and Zimbabwean experts under the auspices of the Southern African Development Community (SADC) and chaired by a South African judge, Pius Langa, was sent to Lesotho to investigate the allegations.

After conducting hearings in Maseru and a re-count of the votes, the Langa Commission delivered an inconclusive report, which failed to settle the dispute. Further talks between the governing and opposition parties were attempted. But before progress could be made, parts of the Lesotho Defence Forces (LDF) mutinied and, with the security situation in Lesotho deteriorating, the LCD government called on SADC for assistance.

On 22 September 1998 a South African-led SADC force entered Lesotho in response to the government's appeal. After several days of fighting between the SADC force and elements in the LDF, resulting in at least 80 deaths and large-scale looting in Maseru, the situation was eventually stabilised.

The South African military contingent was reduced in size in December 1998 and completely withdrawn in May 1999. In December 1998, an inter-party committee was established to oversee preparations for new elections within 18 months. However, it then took a long time for agreement to be reached between the political parties on the number of proportional representation seats and the arrangements for voter registration, and the elections were delayed. When finally approved by parliament, the legislation allowed for 80 seats on a first-past-the-post basis and further 40 seats by means of proportional representation.

Immigration and customs: Visitors from South Africa, Zimbabwe, Denmark, Sweden, Norway, Finland, Ireland, the UK, Germany, France, Italy, Switzerland, The Netherlands, Canada, Israel and Japan can enter the country for up to 30 days without a visa. Other nationals should check with their Lesotho consulate for visa requirements. Those who overstay their visa may be held in detention.

Passports should be valid for at least six months following departure and must have spare pages for affixing visas.

Lone parents travelling with children should carry documentary evidence of parental responsibility.

A yellow fever certificate will be required from all those travelling from infected areas even if they do not leave the airport.

Those planning on travelling through South Africa should check South African regulations.

Travel within the country: Traffic drives on the left. Car hire is available in Maseru with an international driving permit. Paved roads connect the main towns but outside these areas the road network is underdeveloped and the terrain often difficult. Animals roaming on the road are a hazard, especially at night.

A good bus network connects the major towns but can be slow. Minibuses are quicker but can only be used for shorter distances. All buses are non-smoking.

There is no passenger rail service in Lesotho.

Travel health: Visitors will need comprehensive travel insurance that includes medical evacuation.

Vaccination requirements should be checked well in advance of travel (visit www.nathnac.org/travel/index.htm): diphtheria, Hepatitis A, tetanus and typhoid are generally required.

Tap water is considered safe to drink in the towns but in rural areas bottled water is advised. Milk is pasteurised.

Money: There are few ATMs in Lesotho that accept international cards. Credit cards are not widely accepted. Visitors should take travellers cheques or South African rand, which circulates as an official currency along with the maloti. Banking hours are Mon–Tues and Thur–Fri 0830–1530, Wed 0830–1300 and Sat 0830–1100.

There were 285,000 tourist arrivals in 2008.

Further information

Lesotho Government Portal: www.gov.ls

Central Bank of Lesotho: www.centralbank.org.ls

Commonwealth Secretariat: www.thecommonwealth.org

Commonwealth of Nations: www.commonwealth-of-nations.org/Lesotho

Malawi

Joined Commonwealth:	1964
Population:	14,901,000 (2010)
GDP p.c. growth:	1.0% p.a. 1990–2010
UN HDI 2011:	world ranking 171
Official language:	English
Time:	GMT plus 2hr
Currency:	Malawi kwacha (MK)

Geography

Area:	118,484 sq km
Coastline:	none
Capital:	Lilongwe

Malawi is a long, narrow south-east African country shaped by the dramatic Rift Valley, with Lake Malawi a dominant feature. It is bordered by Mozambique to the east, south and south-west, by Zambia to the north and north-west, and by the United Republic of Tanzania to the north and north-east. There are three regions: the northern (capital Mzuzu), the central (capital Lilongwe) and the southern (capital Blantyre).

Topography: Malawi's deep Rift Valley trench is on average 80km wide. Lake Malawi occupies two-thirds of the Rift Valley floor. It feeds the Shire river, which flows south to join the Zambezi. Plateaux rise west of the trench. The northern region is mountainous, with the open Nyika Plateau, escarpments, valleys and the forested slopes of Viphya Plateau. The central region, the main agricultural area, is a plateau over 1,000m high. The southern region is low-lying apart from the 2,100m high Zomba Plateau and the 3,002m Mulanje Massif, the highest mountain in south-central Africa.

Climate: The tropical climate is tempered by altitude and cooler on the high plateaux. There are three seasons: a cool, dry season from mid-April to August; a warm, dry season from September to November; and a rainy season (receiving 90% of precipitation) from December to April. Most of the country is well watered, receiving 800–2,500mm of rain, with some areas in the high plateaux receiving 3,500mm p.a.

Did you know...

Malawi is one of seven landlocked Commonwealth countries, all of which are in Africa, though it does have a border with Lake Malawi of more than 750km.

Malawi has the lowest per capita income in the Commonwealth, but its economy has grown at more than 7% a year over 2006–10.

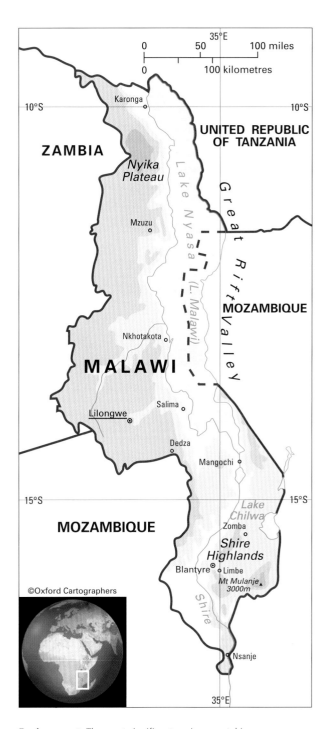

©Oxford Cartographers

Environment: The most significant environmental issues are deforestation; soil degradation; and water pollution by agricultural run-off, sewage and industrial wastes.

Vegetation: The varied climate encourages a range of vegetation. Zomba Plateau, the country's oldest forest reserve, has Mulanje

cedar, cypress and Mexican pine. There is dense tropical rainforest on the lower ranges of the Mulanje Massif; higher up grow ericas, helichrysum, giant blue lobelias, species of iris, staghorn lily and (unique to Malawi) Whyte's sunflower. Forest covers 34% of the land area, having declined at 0.9% p.a. 1990–2010. Arable land comprises 38% and permanent cropland 1% of the total land area.

Wildlife: Animals include leopard, hyena, jackal, hyrax, porcupine, red duiker, bushbuck, reedbuck, klipspringer, baboon, mongoose, vervet monkey, serval, civet, genet, tree frog. More than 219 bird species have been recorded, including the white-tailed crested fly catcher, fiscal shrike and wailing cisticola, and 11 species are thought to be endangered (2002). Birds of prey include the augur buzzard, the eagle owl and the long-crested eagle.

Main towns: Lilongwe (capital, pop. 723,600 in 2010), Blantyre (commercial centre, 694,500), Mzuzu (138,300), Zomba (seat of parliament, 91,900), Kasungu (46,600), Karonga (44,000), Mangochi (42,300), Salima (28,800), Nkhotakota (25,900), Liwonde (25,100), Balaka (23,900), Mzimba (22,400), Dedza (21,200), Nsanje (20,300), Rumphi (18,200) and Mchinji (17,800).

Transport: There are 15,450km of roads (45% paved) and 797km of railway. Rehabilitation of the war-damaged railway line to the Mozambican port of Nacala was completed in 1997. Plans were announced in 1999 for private-sector management of Malawi Railways, leading to eventual privatisation.

Lilongwe International Airport handles the bulk of domestic and international traffic; the second international airport is Blantyre Chileka.

Society

KEY FACTS 2010

Population per sq km:	126
Life expectancy:	54 years
Net primary enrolment:	91%

Population: 14,901,000 (2010); Malawi is one of the most densely populated countries in Africa but with only 20% living in towns, one of the least urbanised; growth 2.3% p.a. 1990–2010; birth rate 44 per 1,000 people (56 in 1970); life expectancy 54 years (41 in 1970).

The largest ethnic group is the Chewa, whose ancestors came from the Congo; the other main groups are Nyanja, Lomwe, Yao and Tumbuka.

Language: Chichewa is the national language and widely spoken. English is the official language. Chinyanja, Chiyao and Chitumbuka (in the north) are major languages.

Religion: Mainly Christians (Protestants 55%, Roman Catholics 20%); Muslims 20%.

Health: Public spending on health was 4% of GDP in 2009. 80% of the population uses an improved drinking water source and 56% have adequate sanitation facilities (2009).

Malaria, dysentery, bilharzia, measles, tuberculosis and hepatitis are common. There has been a successful campaign against leprosy. Infant mortality was 58 per 1,000 live births in 2010 (205 in 1960).

Since the 1990s, the incidence of HIV/AIDS has been among the highest in the world and AIDS treatment continues to make very heavy demands on health resources. In 2009, 11.0% of people aged 15–49 were HIV positive.

Education: Public spending on education was 4.6% of GDP in 2010. There are eight years of compulsory education starting at age six. Primary school comprises eight years and secondary four, with two cycles each of two years. Some 42% of pupils complete primary school (2008). The school year starts in January.

The University of Malawi comprises Chancellor College (located in Zomba); College of Medicine (Blantyre); Bunda College of Agriculture (Lilongwe); and Malawi Polytechnic (Blantyre). Mzuzu University (opened in 1999) and University of Livingstonia (2003, with campuses in Livingstonia and Ekwendeni) are located in the Northern Region. Literacy among people aged 15–24 is 87% (2009).

Media: *The Daily Times* and *The Nation/Weekend Nation* are dailies; *Malawi News* is weekly, and *Boma Lathu* monthly in Chichewa.

Radio is the principal source of information for most Malawians. The public broadcaster, the Malawi Broadcasting Corporation, provides a national radio service and there are several private commercial and faith radio stations. The government launched Television Malawi in 1999, initially reaching the main population centres.

Some 5% of households have TV sets (2006). There are 2 personal computers (2005) and 23 internet users (2010) per 1,000 people.

Communications: Country code 265; internet domain '.mw'. Mobile phone coverage is good in urban areas. Internet connection is available in main towns and there are some internet cafes.

There are 11 main telephone lines and 204 mobile phone subscriptions per 1,000 people (2010).

Public holidays: New Year's Day, John Chilembwe Day (15 January), Martyrs' Day (3 March), Labour Day (1 May), Kamuzu Day (14 June), Republic Day (6 July), Mothers' Day (October), Christmas Day and Boxing Day.

Religious festivals whose dates vary from year to year include Good Friday, Easter Monday and Eid al-Fitr/end of Ramadan.

Economy

KEY FACTS 2010

GNI:	US$4.9bn
GNI p.c.:	US$330
GDP growth:	7.4% p.a. 2006–10
Inflation:	9.3% p.a. 2006–10

At independence in 1964, Malawi was one of the poorest and least developed countries in the world. It was further disadvantaged when civil war in Mozambique strangled its export trade for over a decade, and when afflicted with long periods of drought, for example between 1991 and 1994, and in 2002. Yet it achieved substantial growth from the 1960s, based on agricultural exports, and especially tobacco.

However, the country's dependence on agricultural commodities has meant that there have been periods of slow or negative growth, when commodity prices have been depressed or international demand subdued, or in periods of drought. At these times foreign debt grew far quicker than GDP and exports, and debt servicing became a heavy burden.

Real Growth in GDP

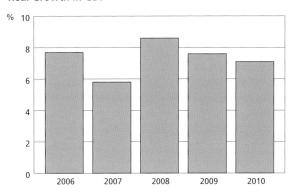

Inflation

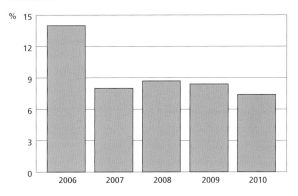

GDP by Sector (2010)

■ Agriculture	**30%**
□ Industry	**17%**
▨ Services	**54%**

After one such period in the early 1990s, the government embarked on economic reforms, including stronger fiscal discipline, public spending cuts, greater accountability and a programme of privatisation, and was supported by a series of World Bank structural adjustment loans and IMF stabilisation programmes. In the 2000s, there was investment in some light manufacturing and especially in the production of clothing and textiles for export to the USA.

These reforms led to a gradual recovery, with better agricultural performance, higher commodity prices (notably for tea) and increased export earnings. However, during 2000, with a poor maize harvest, weaker tobacco prices and the growing burden on the economy of the loss of skilled workers and health care costs of HIV/AIDS, growth slowed and then in 2001 the economy shrank by more than 4%. It recovered in 2002 in a climate of persisting drought and generally maintained good rates of growth, becoming strong during 2006–11, and largely unaffected by the world economic downturn of 2008–09.

In 2006, the country qualified for debt relief under the IMF/World Bank Heavily Indebted Poor Countries Initiative.

Constitution

Status:	Republic with executive president
Legislature:	Parliament
Independence:	6 July 1964

The present constitution was approved by the National Assembly in May 1994 and promulgated in May 1995. It provides for a multiparty democracy on the US model. It curtails the former sweeping and absolute powers of the president, contains a bill of human rights (although it retains the death penalty) and protects the independence of the judiciary.

The head of state is an executive president, who is elected every five years for a maximum of two terms by direct universal suffrage. The president is also head of the cabinet, whose maximum size is 24 members. Legislative authority is vested in the unicameral National Assembly, whose 193 members are directly elected for a five-year term by universal adult suffrage.

The Senate was scheduled to follow the local elections that were eventually held in November 2000, but in January 2001 the National Assembly approved a constitutional amendment that removed the provision for a senate.

History

Malawi was once called *Maravi*, or 'reflected light' – perhaps a reference to sunlight glittering on Lake Malawi. Archaeological excavations have revealed evidence of early settlements around Lake Malawi, dating back to the late Stone and Iron Ages.

The area is mentioned in early Arab writings and in Portuguese writings of the 17th and 18th centuries. The pre-colonial Maravi Empire was a loosely organised society covering an expanse of territory well beyond present-day Malawi and encompassed first the Chewa and later the Tumbuka ethnic groups. The Yao from the north and the Ngoni made successful invasions during the 19th century. The Yao became involved in the commercial slave trade, acting as agents for the coastal Arabs. David Livingstone visited Lake Malawi (then called Lake Nyasa) in 1859 and was followed in succeeding decades by British missionaries, traders and planters. This was an unsettled period, with widespread slave raiding.

In 1891, Britain declared the country the British Protectorate of Nyasaland. In 1953 the UK federated Nyasaland with Northern and Southern Rhodesia (now Zambia and Zimbabwe). The Federation was vigorously opposed and, in 1958, Dr Hastings Kamuzu Banda returned home from Ghana, at the invitation of the Nyasaland African Congress, to lead the fight against it. The government declared a state of emergency in 1959 and arrested Banda and other members of Congress. Following his release in 1960, a series of constitutional conferences was held, as were elections. Internal self-government was achieved in 1963, the Federation was dissolved and Malawi attained independence and joined the Commonwealth on 6 July 1964, with Banda as prime minister.

In 1966 Malawi became a republic, with Banda as president. A new constitution gave the president, who was also commander-in-chief of the armed forces, widespread powers. He held a number of ministerial portfolios, including External Affairs, Agriculture, Justice and Works. Malawi became a one-party state, with Malawi Congress Party (MCP) as the sole party.

The following decade saw widespread political unrest, much of it arising from splits and rivalries. Pressure for democratic reform intensified at the end of the 1980s. The one-party government held out for a period: thousands of arrests were made in the first half of 1992, among those arrested was trade union leader and multiparty democracy campaigner Chakufwa Chihana. Strikes, student demonstrations and political riots were suppressed by police, in the course of which at least 38 people died.

Western donors supported the campaign for multiparty democracy by suspending non-humanitarian aid to Malawi in May 1992. The reformers joined forces in a Public Affairs Committee (PAC) – an umbrella body of religious and political groups calling for change. The Alliance for Democracy (AFORD), chaired by Chihana, and the United Democratic Front (UDF), chaired by Bakili Muluzi, were formed in September 1992 and joined the PAC. The government then established the president's Committee for Dialogue and agreed to hold an internationally supervised national referendum on the one-party system.

Over 78% of the adult population voted in the referendum on 14 June 1993, and 63% supported a multiparty system. The constitution was accordingly amended. Banda also announced an amnesty for all Malawians imprisoned or exiled for political activities. Laws passed by the National Assembly in November 1993 committed Malawi to human rights including freedom of expression. The Constitution (Amendment) Act introduced a bill of rights, the title of life president (which had been assumed by Banda in 1971) was dropped from the constitution and a number of restrictive laws were repealed.

Presidential and parliamentary elections were held in May 1994. Bakili Muluzi won the presidential election, obtaining about one-third more votes than his nearest rival, Dr Hastings Kamuzu Banda. His party, the UDF, obtained the largest number of seats in the parliamentary elections, but not an overall majority. In September 1994, Muluzi appointed ministers from AFORD and other smaller parties, giving the new government a working majority.

In the elections of June 1999 Muluzi won the presidency with 52% of votes cast while Gwanda Chakuamba – the candidate of an alliance of the MCP and AFORD – secured 45%. In the National Assembly, the UDF won 93 seats, the MCP 66 and AFORD 29, a result that gave the opposition alliance a parliamentary majority. However, by August 1999, with the support of four independents, Muluzi gained control of parliament and his position was subsequently strengthened by a succession of by-election victories.

Following a poor harvest in 2000/01, a combination of severe floods and drought devastated food crops in 2001 and by 2002 the country faced food shortages. Meanwhile, its strategic grain reserve of some 167,000 tonnes had been sold off, and by mid-2002 more than 500,000 people were estimated by the World Food Programme to be in need of food aid, increasing to a peak of 3.6 million people in February 2003, after which the new harvest brought recovery to most parts of the country.

Politics

Last elections:	May 2009 (presidential and parliamentary)
Next elections:	2014 (presidential and parliamentary)
Head of state:	President Joyce Hilda Banda
Head of government:	the president
Ruling party:	Democratic Progressive Party

Speculation that President Bakili Muluzi would decide to stand for a third term at the 2004 election, requiring an amendment to the constitution, ended in July 2002, after a narrow majority of parliamentarians had voted against such an amendment. Then in April 2003 Dr Bingu wa Mutharika was confirmed as the presidential candidate of the ruling United Democratic Front (UDF). Muluzi appointed four Alliance for Democracy (AFORD) members as cabinet ministers and AFORD agreed to support the UDF candidate at the next election.

In a close contest in May 2004, Mutharika (UDF) won the presidential election with 35.9%, John Tembo of the Malawi Congress Party (MCP) coming second with 27.1% and Gwanda Chakuamba (Mgwirizano Coalition) third with 25.7%. In the simultaneous parliamentary elections MCP took 60 seats, UDF 49, Mgwirizano Coalition 16 and UDF's ally AFORD six. Though both the ruling UDF coalition and the MCP claimed to have won presidential and parliamentary elections, Mutharika was sworn in as president and formed a government while the opposition mounted violent protests. In the succeeding weeks the president secured the support of first Chakuamba and then the National Democratic Alliance. However, in February 2005, with the support of majority of his cabinet, Chakuamba and a number of MPs, he left the UDF to form a new party, the Democratic Progressive Party (DPP).

In the presidential election in May 2009, Mutharika received 66% of votes, a substantially higher share than in 2004. His main challenger, MCP leader Tembo, took 31%. In the parliamentary elections, the ruling DPP won 114 seats, the MCP 26, the UDF 17 and independents 32. Before the elections former president Muluzi made a further attempt to run for the presidency. The electoral commission ruled that he was not eligible because he had already served two terms, the maximum allowed by the constitution. Muluzi appealed this decision in the High Court, which upheld the electoral commission's ruling. He later made an appeal to the Constitutional Court, which also upheld the ruling.

President Mutharika died suddenly in early April 2012 aged 78. Vice-President Joyce Banda was then sworn in as president.

International relations

Malawi is a member of the African, Caribbean and Pacific Group of States, African Union, Common Market for Eastern and Southern Africa, Non-Aligned Movement, Southern African Development Community, United Nations and World Trade Organization.

Traveller information

Local laws and conventions: Drug taking and smuggling (including the purchase of cannabis) are illegal and penalties can be severe. Buying uncut precious stones is also illegal.

Handshaking is the usual form of greeting. Modest dress should be worn, especially by women who must ensure that their legs and shoulders are covered.

Business meeting appointments should always be made and the use of business cards is customary. Business is conducted in English. Kwacha International Conference Centre in Blantyre is Malawi's only dedicated conference centre, with seating for up to 500 people. The best months for business are May to July and September to November. Business hours are Mon–Fri 0730–1700.

Immigration and customs: Visas are not required for British, Australian, Canadian and US citizens. Passports must be valid for six months from the date of entry. Visitors will need to ensure they have a return air ticket.

A yellow fever vaccination certificate will be required by visitors arriving from infected areas.

It is recommended that visitors copy the photopage of their passport and keep their passports and documents in the hotel safe.

Travel within the country: Traffic drives on the left. Car hire is increasing and chauffeur-driven cars are available. Visitors may drive in Malawi on an international driving permit for up to one year. The wearing of seatbelts is compulsory. Drink-driving is illegal.

Air Malawi provides regular links between Blantyre, Lilongwe, Mzuzu, Makokola and Liwonde.

There is a national rail service run by Central East African Railways which runs between the main towns.

Malawi has a good bus network between the major towns and luxury coaches connect Blantyre to Lilongwe and Mzuzu. Taxis are in short supply and need to be booked.

Travel health: Visitors must ensure they have comprehensive medical insurance, as facilities outside urban areas are limited and for serious medical treatment medical evacuation may be necessary. Visitors will need protection against malaria, together with insect repellent and suitable clothing to discourage bites; bilharzia and rabies are also present.

All prescription medicine should be packaged in their original containers, clearly marked to avoid confusion. It is advisable to bring a sealed, personal emergency medical pack, including syringes.

All water used for drinking, brushing teeth and making ice should be boiled. Bottled water is available. Powdered or tinned milk is advised.

Money: Credit cards are not widely accepted in Malawi. Travellers cheques are recommended. Money can be changed at airports, banks or bureaux de change. US dollars, pounds sterling, euros and South African rand are the easiest to change. There are very few ATM machines even in tourist areas. Banking hours are Mon–Fri 0800–1400.

There were 742,000 tourist arrivals in 2008.

Further information

Government of Malawi: www.malawi.gov.mw

Parliament: www.parliament.gov.mw

Reserve Bank of Malawi: www.rbm.mw

Commonwealth Secretariat: www.thecommonwealth.org

Commonwealth of Nations: www.commonwealth-of-nations.org/Malawi

Malaysia

KEY FACTS

Joined Commonwealth:	1957
Population:	28,401,000 (2010)
GDP p.c. growth:	3.2% p.a. 1990–2010
UN HDI 2011:	world ranking 61
Official language:	Malay
Time:	GMT plus 8hr
Currency:	ringgit or Malaysian dollar (M$)

Geography

Area:	329,758 sq km
Coastline:	4,680km
Capital:	Kuala Lumpur

Lying north of the equator in central South-East Asia, above Singapore and south of Thailand, Peninsular Malaysia is separated by about 540km of the South China Sea from the Malaysian states of Sabah and Sarawak, which share the island of Borneo with Indonesia and Brunei Darussalam. Malaysian islands include Labuan, Penang and the Langkawi Islands.

The Federation of Malaysia has 13 states: Sabah, Sarawak and the 11 states of Peninsular Malaysia. These are: the nine sultanates of Johor, Kedah, Kelantan, Negeri Sembilan, Pahang, Perak, Perlis, Selangor and Terengganu, plus Melaka and Penang. The Federation includes the Federal Territory of Kuala Lumpur and the island of Labuan.

Topography: Peninsular Malaysia has a mountainous spine (highest peak Gunong Tahan, 2,156m) with low plains on either side. In the west, mangrove swamps and mudflats at the coast give way to cultivated plains. Sandy beaches lie along the east coast. The main rivers are the Perak and the Pahang. Sabah's mountains include Mount Kinabalu (4,094m), the highest peak in South-East

Asia. Sarawak's highest mountain is Murud (2,385m), its main river the Rejang.

Climate: Tropical, with heavy annual rainfall and high humidity. The daily temperature throughout Malaysia varies from 21–32°C. In Kuala Lumpur, April and May are the hottest months, December the coldest and April the wettest.

Environment: The most significant environmental issues are deforestation; air pollution by industrial and motor emissions; water pollution by raw sewage; and smoke or haze from Indonesian forest fires.

Vegetation: Intensive logging and replanting operations are gradually changing the forest's form. Most cleared areas are in the north-east and west of Peninsular Malaysia. Huge tracts of Sabah's forests were felled in the 1970s and 1980s; the government is trying to curb logging. Forest covers 62% of the land area, having declined at 0.4% p.a. 1990–2010. Arable land comprises 5% and permanent cropland 18% of the total land area.

Wildlife: East Malaysia has one of the largest and most varied bird populations in the world, including many species of parrots, hornbills and broadbills. The endangered orang-utan, the proboscis monkey and massive wild ox, the seladang or Malayan gaur, also occur.

Main towns/conurbations: Kuala Lumpur (capital, pop. 1.48m in 2010), Subang Jaya (Selangor, contiguous with Kuala Lumpur, 1.55m), Kelang (Selangor, 1.11m), Johor Baharu (Johor, 916,400), Ampang Jaya (Selangor, 804,900), Ipoh (Perak, 704,600), Shah Alam (Selangor, 671,300), Kuching (Sarawak, 658,500), Petaling Jaya (Selangor, 638,500), Kota Kinabalu (Sabah, 604,100), Batu Sembilan Cheras (Selangor, 601,500), Sandakan (Sabah, 501,200), Kajang–Sungai Chua (Selangor, 448,200), Seremban (Negeri Sembilan, 439,300), Kuantan (Pahang, 422,000), Tawau (Sabah, 381,700), Kuala Terengganu (Terengganu, 286,300), Miri (280,500), Kota Baharu (Kelantan, 272,600), Bukit Mertajam (Penang, 228,000), Alor Setar (Kedah, 212,600), Taiping (Perak, 212,600), Melaka (Melaka, 201,400) and George Town (Penang, 157,700).

Transport: There are 93,110km of roads, 80% paved. A good network in Peninsular Malaysia including a motorway from north to south. Toll motorways (such as parts of the North–South Expressway) have been built by private groups.

There is a railway network of 1,665km operated by Malaysian Railway, in Peninsular Malaysia, linking with Singapore in the south and Thailand to the north. Express trains are modern. Sabah has a coastal line; Sarawak has no railway.

Kuala Lumpur's light railway system commenced operations in the late 1990s. It combines underground and raised track and covers the entire city, connecting city centre with airports and suburbs.

Ferry services run between ports on the peninsula and link the peninsula with Sabah and Sarawak. River transport is well developed in the east and the only form of transport in remote areas.

The new Kuala Lumpur International Airport at Sepang, 55km to the south of Kuala Lumpur, was completed in 1998, in time for the Commonwealth Games. Other international airports are at Penang (16km south of George Town), Kota Kinabalu (Sabah), and Kuching (Sarawak).

Society

KEY FACTS 2010

Population per sq km:	86
Life expectancy:	74 years
Net primary enrolment:	94%

Population: 28,401,000 (2010); 80% lives in Peninsular Malaysia, 72% in urban areas and 9% in urban agglomerations of more than 1 million people; growth 2.2% p.a. 1990–2010; birth rate 20 per 1,000 people (37 in 1970); life expectancy 74 years (61 in 1970).

The society is multiracial with an estimated 53% Malays, 25% Chinese, 11% indigenous peoples and 10% Indians. In Sarawak, the main indigenous peoples – collectively known in that state as the Dayaks – are the Iban, Bidayuh and Orang Ulu; and in Sabah, the Kadazan Dusan, Bajau, Melanaus and Murut. Other ethnic groups in Malaysia include Europeans and Eurasians.

Language: The national language is Malay (Bahasa Malaysia), but English is widely spoken. Other languages include various Chinese dialects, Tamil and indigenous languages such as Iban and Kadazan.

Religion: Muslims 60%, Buddhists 19%, Christians 9% and Hindus 6% (2000 census). Islam is the official religion; freedom of worship is guaranteed under the constitution.

Health: Public spending on health was 2% of GDP in 2009. 100% of the population uses an improved drinking water source and 96% have access to adequate sanitation facilities (2009). Infant mortality was 5 per 1,000 live births in 2010 (73 in 1960).

Education: Public spending on education was 4.1% of GDP in 2008. There are 11 years of compulsory education starting at age six. Primary school comprises six years and secondary seven, with cycles of three and four years. Some 96% of pupils complete primary school (2006). The school year starts in January and comprises two terms.

The sector comprises 20 public and many private universities; 28 polytechnics; and some 50 community colleges, located throughout the country. The longest-established universities are

University of Malaya in Kuala Lumpur (1905) and Universiti Teknologi Malaysia in Skudai, Johor (1904 as the Technical School, becoming a university in 1972). Open and distance education is provided by the Open University Malaysia which was established as a private university by a consortium of 11 public universities in 2000. The female–male ratio for gross enrolment in tertiary education is 1.30:1 (2008). Literacy among people aged 15–24 is 99% (2009).

Media: All newspapers in Malaysia must renew their publication licences annually. English-language dailies include *New Straits Times*, *The Star*, *The Sun*, *Malay Mail* and *Business Times*. *Malaysiakini* is an online news service.

Public broadcaster Radio Television Malaysia operates two television channels and many radio stations, in Malay, Tamil, Chinese and/or English. There are several commercial TV networks and a number of private radio stations.

Some 95% of households have TV sets (2006). There are 232 personal computers (2006) and 563 internet users (2010) per 1,000 people.

Communications: Country code 60; internet domain '.my'. Public phones are widely available. Mobile coverage is generally good. There are internet cafes in most towns, and many hotels have high-speed internet access.

There are 161 main telephone lines and 1,192 mobile phone subscriptions per 1,000 people (2010).

Public holidays: New Year's Day, Labour Day (1 May), King's Birthday (first Saturday in June), National Day (31 August), Christmas Day, and some local state holidays. Flower festivals are held in most states during a week in mid-July. For most states the weekend comprises a half-day on Saturday plus Sunday, but in Kelantan, Perlis and Terengganu half-day Thursday plus Friday.

Religious and other festivals whose dates vary from year to year include Chinese New Year, Prophet's Birthday, Wesak Day (Buddha Purnima, April/May), Hari Raya Puasa (Eid al-Fitr/end of Ramadan), Deepavali (Diwali, October/November, except Labuan and Sarawak), Hari Raya Haji (Eid al-Adha/Feast of the Sacrifice) and Hari Raya Tussa (Islamic New Year).

Economy

KEY FACTS 2010

GNI:	US$220.4bn
GNI p.c.:	US$7,760
GDP growth:	4.5% p.a. 2006–10
Inflation:	2.7% p.a. 2006–10

Malaysia is rich in natural resources and its traditional economic strength lay in commodities. It is still an important source of tin and rubber, produces more than half the world's palm oil and is a net exporter of oil and gas. Proven reserves of oil were estimated in January 2011 to be 5.8 billion barrels, and of gas, 2.4 trillion cubic metres.

During the 1980s and 1990s, however, the character of the economy changed radically as it developed into a predominantly manufacturing country focusing on export-oriented electronic and electrical equipment (manufacturing contributed 26% of GDP in 2010) but also cars, and a wide range of goods for the domestic market. Manufacturing output grew by more than 9% p.a. during the two decades 1980–2000 and 3.4% p.a. 2000–10. Latterly, the services sector, too, has been growing rapidly.

The long-term economic plan is to transform the manufacturing sector from the assembly of imported components to the design and production of original products, with the objective of attaining industrialised-country status by 2020. Priority areas are advanced materials, automated manufacturing, biotechnology, microelectronics/IT, and energy technology.

After a brief recession in the mid-1980s, growth was very strong until 1997, when the collapse of some South-East Asian financial markets caught Malaysia in their fall, interrupting its rapid growth

and throwing the economy into recession, shrinking by 7.4% in 1998. Demand for exports collapsed, especially demand in Japan for semiconductors; several large development projects were postponed; many companies experienced difficulties; and unemployment rose. During 1998 the government took measures to stimulate growth and the economy began to grow again in the second quarter of 1999, becoming very strong in 2000, led by manufacturing.

Exports – particularly of electrical and electronic goods – soared and there was a sharp increase in interest in foreign investment. However, in 2001 the economy again stalled, as demand for the country's exports slowed, picking up again, with rising international

History

Peninsular Malaysia

In prehistoric times, the region was inhabited by aboriginal people. In the 2nd century BC settlers arrived from south China. Around the beginning of the 1st century AD, Indian traders began settling in Kedah and along the west coast of the peninsula. Hinduism and Buddhism were introduced during this early period; the Indian kingdom of Kunan was founded in the 1st century AD and Buddhist states developed to the east. The Javanese controlled the peninsula around 1330–50. The port of Malacca was founded in the 15th century; its rulers converted to Islam and traded with Muslim merchants, and Islam replaced Buddhism across present-day Malaysia.

The Sultanate of Malacca was seized by the Portuguese in 1511 but, a century later, they were driven out by the Dutch in alliance with the Sultan of Johor. The peninsula then became a Malay kingdom ruled by Johor. In 1786 the Sultan of Kedah granted the island of Penang to the British East India Company for use as a trading post; less than a decade later, the British took Malacca from the Dutch. In 1819 the British also acquired Singapore. Penang, Malacca and Singapore were ruled directly by Britain as the Straits Settlements.

By a series of treaties between 1873 and 1930, the British colonial administrators took control of the foreign affairs of the nine Malay sultanates on the peninsula. In 1896 the Federated Malay Sates (Selangor, Negeri Sembilan, Perak and Pahang) came into existence, with Kuala Lumpur as the capital. The sultanates of northern Borneo – Brunei, Sabah and Sarawak – also became British protectorates.

Immigrants from southern China and southern India came to work in tin mines and on the plantations, facilitating the peninsula's transition from a trading outpost to a commodity producer. The British introduced rubber farming towards the end of the 19th century.

Reaction to colonial rule began in the early 20th century. In 1915, Indian sepoys rebelled and came close to taking control of Singapore. In 1931, the Malayan Communist Party (MCP) was established. It had links with developing communism in China and drew most of its support from the Chinese community. By 1937–38, anti-colonial nationalism began among the Malay community, with the formation of the Union of Young Malays.

The Japanese occupied the country from 1941–45. Resistance, mainly from the Chinese, was led by MCP guerrillas. British rule

was reintroduced after the war, but met active resistance from the MCP. Malay nationalists also campaigned for independence. The United Malays' National Organisation (UMNO, the principal Malay party) was formed in 1946.

The Federation of Malaya, comprising 11 peninsular states, was established in 1948. A communist-led insurrection in that year was suppressed by the UK (although guerrilla warfare continued in the north of the peninsula and Borneo and the last insurgents only surrendered in 1989).

A delayed general election took place in 1955. This was won by the Alliance Party, formed out of UMNO, the Malayan Chinese Association and the Malayan Indian Congress.

Sabah

Formerly North Borneo, Sabah may have been inhabited since 7000 BC. From the 7th century, the region traded in pottery with China. In the early 15th century the state was ruled mainly by the Sultan of Brunei. In 1847, Britain persuaded the Sultan of Brunei to cede Labuan Island. In 1882 the British North Borneo Chartered Company was established and began administering territory ceded by the Sultan of Brunei and the Sultan of Sulu. In 1888 the territory was made a British Protectorate, still administered by the Company, which also administered Labuan until 1905, when it was joined to the Straits Settlements. From 1942 until 1945 the territory was occupied by the Japanese army. In July 1946 it became the Crown colony of North Borneo.

Sarawak

Archaeological evidence suggests that Sarawak was inhabited from about 5000 BC. From the 15th century, it was ruled by the Sultan of Brunei who, in 1839, ennobled James Brooke, a British adventurer, as Rajah of Sarawak, a reward for his help in calming a rebellion in Brunei. Brooke waged a vigorous campaign against piracy. Sarawak was gradually enlarged with additional grants of land from the Sultan, and the River Lawas area bought from the North Borneo Chartered Company in 1905. Sarawak prospered under Rajah Sir Charles Vyner Brooke (reigned 1917–46), who attempted to set up an elected government in 1941, but the territory was occupied by the Japanese army in the following year. During the Japanese occupation, sickness and malnutrition spread throughout Sarawak. The Rajah, resuming control in 1946, decided that in the interests of Sarawak, he should make a gift of it to the UK Crown. Sarawak became a UK colony in July 1946. ➤

oil and commodity prices, in 2002. Strong growth of more than 5% p.a. continued during 2003–07; then, with the world economic downturn and fall in global demand of 2008–09, the economy slowed in 2008; it contracted by 1.6% in 2009, but then recovered strongly in 2010 (7.2%), continuing buoyant in 2011–12.

Constitution

Status:	National Monarchy
Legislature:	Parliament of Malaysia
Independence:	31 August 1957

Malaysia is a parliamentary democracy with a federal constitutional monarch, the Yang di-Pertuan Agong, as head of state. This monarch is chosen for a five-year term from among their own number by the nine hereditary rulers of Peninsular Malaysia. These rulers also elect a Timbalan (deputy) di-Pertuan Agong. The nine hereditary states are Perlis (ruled by the Raja), Negeri Sembilan (ruled by the Yang di-Pertuan Besar) and Kedah, Perak, Johor, Selangor, Pahang, Terengganu and Kelantan (ruled by Sultans). The head of state in the four states that do not have hereditary rulers – Melaka, Pulau Pinang, Sabah and Sarawak – is the Yang di-Pertuan Negeri, or governor, and is appointed by the Yang di-Pertuan Agong for a four-year term.

➤ The Federation of Malaysia

Early in 1956, the governments of the Federation of Malaya and the UK and the Heads of the Malay States agreed that the Federation should achieve independence by the end of August 1957 if possible. On 31 August 1957 the Federation of Malaya became an independent nation and joined the Commonwealth. Penang and Malacca became states of the Federation. Tengku (prince) Abdul Rahman, leader of the independence movement, became prime minister.

The Malaysia Agreement, under which North Borneo, Sarawak and Singapore (but not Brunei) would become states in the new Federation of Malaysia, was signed in 1963 by the UK, Malaya, North Borneo, Sarawak and Singapore. The Federation of Malaysia came into being on 16 September 1963. In 1965, by mutual agreement, Singapore left the Federation and became an independent state.

In the 1969 elections, the Alliance Party lost many seats to the Pan-Malaysian Islamic Party, Gerakan Rakyat Malaysia and the Chinese-based Democratic Action Party. Amid violent ethnic clashes, the government suspended parliament and the national operations council ruled by decree for two years. On the resignation of Tengku Abdul Rahman in 1970, Tun Abdul Razak became prime minister.

Although Malays formed over half the population, in 1970 they accounted for about 1% of national income. A 'new economic policy' introduced positive discrimination – in education, civil service, armed services and business – designed to increase the share of the Malay and other bumiputera (sons of the soil) groups to 30% of national income within twenty years. After the parliamentary system was restored, the National Front (Barisan Nasional) – a multiethnic alliance led by UMNO – won over two-thirds of seats at all elections of the 1970s, 1980s and 1990s (and this continued into the 2000s). In 1981 Dr Mahathir Mohamad became prime minister.

Malays have dominated the political system since independence, and support in the Malay-dominated rural areas is crucial for political success at the national level. However, to command a parliamentary majority and in the interests of national stability, UMNO has formed coalitions with parties representing other racial groups. Intercommunal relations, particularly between the Malays and the Chinese, have preoccupied governments since independence.

At elections in April 1995, the National Front was returned with a substantially increased majority, winning 162 seats, comprising UMNO (89 seats), Malaysian Chinese Association (30), Sarawak National Front (27), Malaysian Indian Congress (seven) and Gerakan Rakyat Malaysia (seven). The opposition included the Democratic Action Party (DAP, nine), Parti Bersatu Sabah (PBS, eight), the Pan-Malaysian Islamic Party (PAS, seven) and Semangat '46 (six).

In August 1998 Prime Minister Mahathir Mohamad sacked his deputy prime minister and finance minister, Anwar Ibrahim, who was subsequently arrested under the detention-without-trial Internal Security Act for holding a political protest gathering without a police permit. He was also charged on several counts of sexual misconduct and abuse of power, charges he denied and said stemmed from a conspiracy to remove him. Anwar was found guilty of corruption in April 1999 and sentenced to six years in prison. In August 2000, he was found guilty of sodomy and sentenced to a further nine years' imprisonment.

In June 1999, opposition parties led by Anwar's wife Wan Azizah Ismail and her new National Justice Party (Parti Keadilan Nasional) formed the Alternative Front (including the PAS, the DAP and Malaysian People's Party), calling for political liberalisation and an end to repressive laws. However, when the elections were held in November 1999, the ruling National Front coalition won 148 seats; the combined opposition parties took 42 seats, with the PBS securing three seats. PAS won control of the oil-rich state of Terengganu and easily retained its hold on Kelantan and, for the first time, assumed leadership of the opposition in parliament. Wan Azizah won the seat of her husband's former constituency in Penang.

The Alternative Front was, however, divided over the PAS's plan to establish an Islamic state should the Alternative Front win the next elections due by January 2005. Divisions deepened when the party announced it would introduce Islamic law in Terengganu, and subsequently, in July 2002, lost ground to UMNO in by-elections in Kedah State.

In September 2004 Anwar's conviction for sodomy was quashed by the Federal Court and he was released from prison. Then his appeal against his conviction for corruption was rejected, confirming his exclusion from parliament until 2008.

Real Growth in GDP

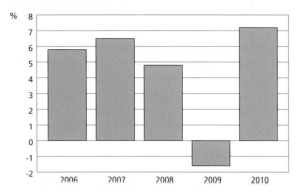

Inflation

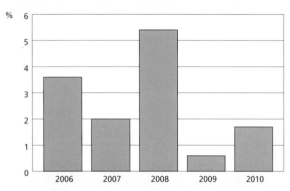

GDP by Sector (2010)

■ Agriculture	10%
□ Industry	44%
▦ Services	46%

The federal parliament consists of two houses. The upper house, Dewan Negara (council of the nation or Senate), has 70 members, of whom 44 are appointed by the Yang di-Pertuan Agong and 26 are elected by the state legislatures (two each). The lower house, Dewan Rakyat (council of the people, more usually called House of Representatives), has 222 members who are directly elected by universal suffrage. The maximum life of the House of Representatives is five years; members of the Senate hold office for six years. The Yang di-Pertuan Agong appoints the prime minister and, on the prime minister's advice, the cabinet.

Bills must be passed by both houses and assented to by the Yang di-Pertuan Agong. A bill may originate in either house, with the exception of a money bill, which may not be introduced in the Senate. The Senate has the power to hold up for one year a bill which is not a money bill and which has been passed by the Dewan Rakyat. Each house regulates its own procedure and has control over its own proceedings, the validity of which may not be questioned in any court. A two-thirds majority of both houses is required before the constitution can be changed.

The federal parliament controls external affairs, defence, internal security, civil and criminal law, citizenship, finance, commerce and industry, shipping, education, health and labour. The central government may also make laws to promote uniformity of the laws of two or more states and it may legislate on any subject at the request of a state legislative assembly.

Each of the 13 states has its own constitution which must be compatible with the federal constitution. Each state has an executive council, which deals with non-federal matters under a Menteri Besar (chief minister), answerable to elected state assemblies.

Politics

Last elections:	March 2008
Next elections:	2013
Head of state:	Yang di-Pertuan Agong XIV Tuanku Alhaj Abdul Halim Mu'adzam Shah ibni Al-Marhum Sultan Badlishah (2011–)
Head of government:	Prime Minister Dato' Sri Mohd Najib bin Tun Haji Abdul Razak
Ruling party:	National Front (Barisan Nasional)

In his closing speech to the United Malays' National Organisation (UMNO) annual congress in June 2002, 76-year-old Prime Minister Dr Mahathir Mohamad announced his retirement, but subsequently agreed to continue as prime minister until October 2003, when his deputy, Abdullah Ahmad Badawi, duly succeeded him as UMNO leader and prime minister.

In an early general election in March 2004, the ruling UMNO-led National Front coalition received a strong mandate to proceed with reforms proposed by the new prime minister, including action against corruption. It took 198 seats in the federal parliament, regaining Terengganu and conceding only one state, Kelantan, by a small margin to the Pan-Malaysian Islamic Party (PAS). The combined opposition parties won 21 seats, with Democratic Action Party (DAP, 12) ahead of PAS (seven).

The Sultan of Terengganu, Tuanku Mizan Zainal Abidin, became Yang di-Pertuan Agong in December 2006.

In the March 2008 elections, the ruling National Front faced a united opposition at both national and state levels. Although it won in 7 of the 12 states contested and took 140 of 222 seats – and 50.3% of votes – in the federal parliament, it was National Front's worst performance since 1969 and the first time the coalition had failed to attain the two-thirds parliamentary majority required to enact constitutional changes. Opposition parties took 82 seats (46.8% of votes). Abdullah was returned as prime minister. In April 2008 three opposition parties that had worked together in the election, DAP, PAS and the People's Justice Party, formed a coalition, Pakatan Rakyat.

His ban from politics having expired (imposed in April 1999 following his conviction for corruption), former deputy prime minister Anwar Ibrahim was elected to parliament in a by-election in August 2008 and became leader of Pakatan Rakyat.

In April 2009 Abdullah stood down as prime minister and UMNO leader. His deputy, Najib Razak (the son of the second prime minister of Malaysia, Abdul Razak), who had been chosen to lead UMNO at the party's general assembly, was sworn in as prime minister.

The Sultan of Kedah, Tuanku Abdul Halim Mu'adzam Shah, who had previously reigned 1970–75, was chosen as Yang di-Pertuan Agong in December 2011.

International relations

Malaysia is a member of Asia–Pacific Economic Cooperation, Association of Southeast Asian Nations, Indian Ocean Rim Association for Regional Cooperation, Non-Aligned Movement, Organisation of Islamic Cooperation, United Nations and World Trade Organization.

Traveller information

Local laws and conventions: Visitors must respect local conventions and religious beliefs at all times, especially during the holy month of Ramadan. Muslim visitors to the country should be aware that they may be subject to Sharia law.

Taking photographs at places of worship is usually allowed but permission should always be obtained.

There are severe penalties for all drug offences in Malaysia and trafficking incurs a mandatory death penalty. Visitors may be asked to take a urine test on arrival if suspected of having used drugs before their visit.

When shaking hands in Malaysia, visitors should adopt a relaxed wrist and gentle touch. Food must only be touched with the right hand.

Most Malaysians dress informally but are not over-casual, and visitors are advised to adopt a modest dress, particularly in rural areas or in places of worship. Shoes must be removed before entering a house, mosque or temple.

Businessmen should wear suits and businesswomen clothes appropriate to local sensibilities. Appointments are customary and punctuality is important. The use of business cards is expected. Business hours are Mon–Fri 0900–1700.

Immigration and customs: Visas are not usually required by British, Australian, Canadian and US citizens for short visits but are needed for all those planning to stay longer than three months. Passports must be valid for six months. It is advisable to store passports in a hotel safe and to keep a copy of the passport photopage and entry stamp as ID.

Before entering the country, care should be taken to read the list of what can be brought into Malaysia without incurring import duty.

Single parents travelling with children should carry documentary evidence of parental responsibility. A yellow fever vaccination certificate will be required from all those travelling from infected areas.

Travel within the country: Traffic drives on the left. Car hire is available through international and domestic companies. An international driving permit is required. There is a speed limit of 110kph on expressways, 90kph on main roads and 60kph in built-up areas.

The wearing of seatbelts is mandatory and driving under the influence of alcohol carries heavy penalties.

Malaysia Airlines links many commercial airports on Peninsular Malaysia, and the budget airline Air Asia has routes across Sabah and Sarawak.

Coastal ferries sail between Penang and Butterworth and there are scheduled passenger services between Port Kelang, Kuantan, Sarawak and Sabah. River boats are often the most efficient way of getting around the eastern part of the country and can be the means of accessing the more remote regions.

The KTM Komuter train connects suburban or adjoining districts with Kuala Lumpur. There is a west coast line and rail services to Penang and Padang Besar. Sabah has the North Borneo Railway.

Public transport in Kuala Lumpur includes buses, taxis, minibuses and pedicabs (trishaws). Trishaw fares must be negotiated before travel. Taxi drivers do not expect tips. There is also a Light Rail Transit (LRT) that links the city to the adjoining Klang Valley District.

Travel health: The cost of treatment in private hospitals is high and visitors are recommended to take out comprehensive travel and medical insurance.

Malaysia can experience problems with air quality because of smoke haze and this may affect some travellers to the country.

Tuberculosis and Hepatitis A are common, and Japanese encephalitis can occur. Malarial cover is required in certain areas and outbreaks of dengue fever are also known to occur, so visitors should take insect repellent and suitable loose-fitting clothing to protect themselves against insect bites. Visitors should check current vaccination requirements well before departure (visit www.nathnac.org/travel/index.htm).

Water needs to be sterilised or boiled before use. Milk is unpasteurised.

Money: Pounds sterling and US dollars are the easiest currencies to change and all commercial banks change money. Hotels are only licensed to accept notes or travellers cheques. Travellers cheques are best exchanged if in US dollars or pounds sterling. Changing money outside tourist centres may be difficult. For most states, banking hours are Mon–Fri 0915–1630, Sat 0930–1130. (For Kedah, Kelantan and Terengganu, banking hours are Sat–Wed 0930–1600, Thur 0930–1130.)

There were 24,577,000 tourist arrivals in 2010.

Further information

Government of Malaysia: www.malaysia.gov.my

Parliament of Malaysia: www.parlimen.gov.my

Bank Negara Malaysia: www.bnm.gov.my

Commonwealth Secretariat: www.thecommonwealth.org

Commonwealth of Nations: www.commonwealth-of-nations.org/Malaysia

Maldives

KEY FACTS

Joined Commonwealth:	1982
Population:	316,000 (2010)
GDP p.c. growth:	4.9% p.a. 1990–2010
UN HDI 2011:	world ranking 109
Official language:	Dhivehi
Time:	GMT plus 5hr
Currency:	Maldivian rufiyaa (MRf)

Geography

Area:	298 sq km
Coastline:	644km
Capital:	Malé

The Republic of Maldives lies in the Indian Ocean, some 670km west-south-west of Sri Lanka. The 1,190 coral islands, 200 of which are inhabited, occur on a double chain of 26 coral atolls. The archipelago is 823km long and 130km at its widest.

The islands are divided into 20 administrative units, called atolls (although they do not necessarily correspond to geographical atolls). Each is known by a letter in the Maldivian alphabet in addition to its geographical name. Huvadhu Atoll, for example, is divided into two administrative units: Gaaf Alif and Gaaf Dhaal.

Area: While the land area is only an estimated 298 sq km, the country's total area of land and sea is some 90,000 sq km.

Topography: Huvadhu Atoll to the south is the largest true atoll formation in the world and has a lagoon of 2,240 sq km. Most of the islands are very small and rise no higher than 2m above sea level. The islands are surrounded by coral reefs but some, especially those furthest from the windward reefs, are liable to erosion. Some islands are additionally protected by breakwaters. The capital, Malé, is only 1.8 sq km. There is a land reclamation project on Malé Atoll. Distinctive features of Maldives are its white beaches and crystal clear lagoons. There are no hills, mountains or rivers.

Did you know...

Maldives is an archipelago in the Indian Ocean, comprising 1,190 coral islands (200 inhabited), on a double chain of 26 coral atolls; none of the islands rise higher than 2m above sea level.

Following the devastating tsunami of December 2004, the Commonwealth Secretariat arranged for deployment of 24 medical volunteers to serve in the islands for periods of up to 15 months.

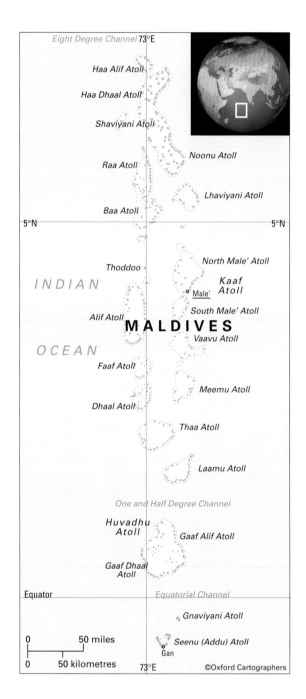

One of the most violent earthquakes ever recorded occurred on 26 December 2004 in the Indian Ocean west of Sumatra and generated a tsunami that devastated the islands, causing about 100 deaths.

Climate: Maldives has a hot tropical climate. The rainy south-west monsoon season is from April to October; the north-east monsoon from December to March. Average annual rainfall is 1,654mm. The temperature ranges between 25°C and 30°C, but generally stays around the average 27°C. Gales occur during the monsoon. In May 1991, abnormal tidal waters caused great damage through the archipelago.

Environment: The most significant issues are: depletion of freshwater aquifers threatening water supplies; global warming and sea level rise; and coral reef bleaching.

Vegetation: There is dense growth of coconut palms, breadfruit, screwpines and lesser vegetation on many islands although the soil lacks nutrients. Forest covers 3% of the land area and there was no significant loss of forest cover during 1990–2010.

Wildlife: Coral reefs support an abundance of marine life. There are over 200 species of coral and over 1,000 species of fish, from the tiny fire goby to the harmless plankton-eating whale shark which can reach 12m in length. On land there are breeding colonies of frigatebirds and noddies, which local fishermen follow to find schools of tuna.

Main towns: Malé (capital, on Malé Atoll, pop. 123,400 in 2010) is the only sizeable town; other settlements are Hithadhu (Siin, 9,500), Foammulah (Ghaviyani, 7,700), Kulhudhuffushi (Haa Dhaal, 7,300), Ugufaaru (Raa, 4,500), Thinadhu (Gaaf Dhaal, 4,200) and Naifaru (Lhaviyani, 3,700), where the administrative units are in the brackets.

Transport: Few of the islands take longer than 30 minutes to cross on foot. Motor scooters are the favoured method of mechanical transport on Malé. There are a total of 88km of paved road.

There are boat and seaplane services between islands during daylight hours. Boat services include traditional small (motor-powered) boats called *dhonis* and speed boats. With the increase in tourism, glass-bottomed boats for viewing coral reef and marine life, and vessels for fishing trips, diving and other water sports transport, have become common.

Malé International Airport is on the island of Hulhule, 2km from the capital; there is a frequent boat service linking airport and capital. The national airline operates regular services to airstrips in the outer atolls. Seaplanes and helicopters are also used to transfer tourists to resorts.

Society

KEY FACTS 2010

Population per sq km:	1,060
Life expectancy:	77 years
Net primary enrolment:	96%

Population: 316,000 (2010); 40% lives in urban areas, mostly in Malé, which was in the mid-1990s doubled in area by land reclamation; growth 1.8% p.a. 1990–2010; birth rate 17 per 1,000 people (40 in 1970); life expectancy 77 years (50 in 1970).

Language: The national language is Dhivehi, which has been most strongly influenced by Sinhala and Arabic. English is widely spoken.

Religion: Predominantly Sunni Muslims; Islam is the state religion.

Health: Public spending on health was 5% of GDP in 2009. 91% of the population uses an improved drinking water source and

98% have access to adequate sanitation facilities (2009). Infant mortality was 14 per 1,000 live births in 2010 (180 in 1960). Malaria has been practically eradicated and diarrhoeal diseases have been considerably reduced.

Education: Public spending on education was 11.5% of GDP in 2009. There are 12 years of school starting at age six, comprising five years of primary, and seven of secondary, in cycles of five and two years. All administrative atolls have government primary schools and an education centre providing education for all age groups. Most of the many private schools receive state subsidies and are run by the community. The school year starts in January.

There are three streams of Maldivian education: traditional religious schools (makhtabs and madrassas), which teach the Qur'an, basic arithmetic, and the ability to read and write Dhivehi; modern Dhivehi-language primary schools; and modern English-language schools, which follow the British system of education.

Maldives College of Higher Education (with its main campus in Malé) provides post-secondary education leading to diplomas and bachelor's degrees. There is an Institute for Islamic Studies, also in Malé, and pre-university education is provided at the Science Education Centre in Malé. A state scholarship scheme funds tertiary education abroad. Vocational training is available in health sciences, teaching, and hotel and catering skills. Literacy among people aged 15–24 is 99% (2006).

Media: The leading Dhivehi dailies are *Aafathis*, *Haveeru* and *Miadhu*, which post daily online news bulletins in English. Some sections of the print versions of *Haveeru* and *Miadhu* are in English.

Voice of Maldives radio and Television Maldives provide public services. The first private radio station was launched in 2007. There is a growing number of private radio and TV providers.

Some 91% of households have TV sets (2009). There are 202 personal computers (2006) and 283 internet users (2010) per 1,000 people.

Communications: Country code 960; internet domain '.mv'. There are public phones and post offices on most of the islands. Mobile phone coverage and internet access is good.

There are 152 main telephone lines and 1,565 mobile phone subscriptions per 1,000 people (2010).

Public holidays: New Year's Day, National Day (26 February), The Day Maldives Embraced Islam (29 March), Independence Day (26 July, usually celebrated over two days), Victory Day (3 November) and Republic Day (11 November).

The opening day of the Citizens' Majlis (announced by the Majlis each year) is also a public holiday and the weekend is Friday–Saturday.

Religious festivals whose dates vary from year to year include Prophet's Birthday, First Day of Ramadan, Eid al-Fitr (End of Ramadan, three days), Hajj Day, Eid al-Adha (Feast of the Sacrifice, three days) and Islamic New Year.

Economy

KEY FACTS 2010

GNI:	US$1.8bn
GNI p.c.:	US$5,750
GDP growth:	9.4% p.a. 2006–10
Inflation:	6.3% p.a. 2006–10

Providing high-quality service to taxpayers

Maldives Inland Revenue Authority (MIRA), established under the Tax Administration Act in 2010, is an independent and separate legal entity directly accountable to parliament.

Currently MIRA administers and collects two major taxes: Business Profit Tax and Goods and Services Tax, implemented in July and October 2011, respectively. Tourism Goods and Services Tax, implemented in January 2011 has been replaced by the Goods and Services Tax. MIRA is also responsible for collecting a major portion of the State's revenue in the form of fees, rents, royalties and other taxes.

Our vision

To be recognised as a leading professional organisation engaged in collection of revenue in an effective and efficient manner and providing high-quality service to taxpayers.

Our mission

To establish a highly committed and competent organisation, delivering effective and fair administration of the tax laws, promoting voluntary compliance and providing quality services to taxpayers.

Mr Yazeed Mohamed,
Commissioner General of Taxation

Mr Hassan Zareer,
Deputy Commissioner General of Taxation

www.mira.gov.mv

MALDIVES
INLAND REVENUE
AUTHORITY

Maldives Inland Revenue Authority
T-Building, Ameenee Magu, Malé, 20379

Tel: +960 332 2261 • Fax: +960 331 6577
Email: info@mira.gov.mv

Real Growth in GDP

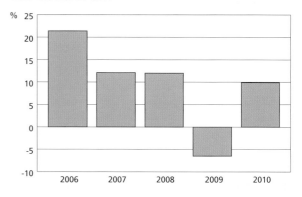

Inflation

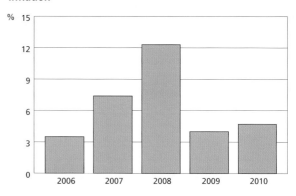

GDP by Sector (2010)

■ Agriculture	5%
□ Industry	12%
■ Services	83%

Maldives is disadvantaged by its small size, the thin scattering of human settlement across atolls spread over hundreds of kilometres of ocean, its distance from centres of economic activity, and the poverty of its coralline soils.

The country has benefited from the support of wealthy Muslim countries, but its steady progress is attributed mainly to its social and economic stability. Since the late 1980s, economic policies combine a liberal economic and investment regime – focused on tourism, fishing (notably skipjack tuna), and a growing manufacturing sector (especially clothing) – with well-directed social expenditure on education, health and providing essential social infrastructure to the outer islands.

The country does, however, face longer-term constraints through erosion of the friable coral rock of which the islands are built, caused by construction and population pressure. Climate change resulting in rising sea level and greater climatic instability also gives cause for concern as the country is very low-lying.

Nonetheless, it has achieved high and steady rates of growth with low inflation over a relatively long period, based mainly on tourism.

GDP grew by 7.8% p.a. 1989–99. In the 2000s, initially growth slowed in response to the international climate, but picked up again in 2002, becoming strong in 2002–04. However, economic infrastructure throughout the country was then devastated by the massive tsunami in late December 2004 and the economy shrank by 4.6% in 2005. Post-tsunami rebuilding and a rebound in tourism spurred a remarkable recovery with GDP growth of 21.4% in 2006, 12.1% in 2007 and 12.0% in 2008. But the impact of the world economic downturn on long-haul tourism caused the economy to contract sharply in 2009 (–6.5%), before bouncing back in 2010 (9.9%).

Constitution

Status:	Republic with executive president
Legislature:	People's Majlis

The 2008 constitution provides for an executive president and a legislature, the People's Majlis, both elected directly every five years by universal suffrage. A president can serve for a maximum of two terms of office. The Majlis comprises two elected members from each of the 20 administrative atolls and Malé. Where the residents registered in an administrative atoll exceed 5,000, one additional member is provided for each group of 5,000 in excess of the first 5,000. All elections are run on a multiparty platform. The constitution provides for an independent judiciary where judicial power is vested in the courts with the Supreme Court as the court of last resort.

Basic rights and freedoms, including freedom of the media, of assembly and of association, are guaranteed as fundamental rights. Freedom of expression is guaranteed so long as such expression is not contrary to any tenet of Islam.

Separate independent commissions and offices are mandated to defend judicial independence; conduct elections; prevent and combat corruption; promote human rights; and ensure an effective and efficient civil service.

Politics

Last elections:	October 2008 (presidential), May 2009 (parliamentary)
Next elections:	2013 (presidential), 2014 (parliamentary)
Head of state:	President Dr Mohamed Waheed Hassan Manik
Head of government:	the president
Ruling party:	National Unity Government

President Maumoon Abdul Gayoom was elected for a sixth term by the Majlis and was confirmed in his sixth term as president at the referendum in October 2003 receiving 90% of the votes. In June 2004, Gayoom announced proposals for wide-ranging constitutional reforms including a multiparty system and a directly elected president.

The general election in January 2005, observed by a Commonwealth expert team, was to be the last before political

History

Archaeological finds reveal that the islands were inhabited as early as 1500 BC. The first settlers arrived around 500 BC and are thought to have been Aryans. In the pre-Islamic period (before AD 1153), according to the accounts of Persian and Arab travellers, the Maldives was ruled by women. After that date, only four queens ruled, the last one in the early 16th century.

Contact with Arab travellers paved the way for the Maldives to adopt the religion of Islam, which gradually replaced Buddhism. In 1153–54, King Dovemi Kalaminja officially accepted Islam.

Although the Maldives voluntarily accepted a period of British protection, the country has been an independent state throughout its known history, except for a very brief period (15 years) of Portuguese occupation in the 16th century and an even briefer three months and 20 days of Mopla (south Indian) rule in the mid-18th century. The Maldivian militia (controlled by the Sultan) defended the country and its independence against incursions by stronger powers. Since the country's conversion to Islam, its history can be traced through a number of dynasties, ruled by 93 Sultans and Sultanas, whose laws were only acknowledged when exercised for the benefit of the people. Otherwise, the ruler, who was advised by councillors, could be dethroned.

The period of the British protectorate began in 1887. The Sultan remained head of state. There was no British governor or representative and Britain did not interfere in the country's internal affairs, confining its interest to foreign affairs and defence. The Maldivian sultanate became elective after 1932.

The country briefly became a republic in 1953–54, but was again a sultanate at the time it terminated the arrangement with the

UK in 1965. Following a public referendum in April 1968, the sultanate was abolished and the Maldives was again declared a republic. Ibrahim Nasir, who had been prime minister since 1954, then became president.

The recent history of Maldives has been characterised by stability, growth and gradual adjustment to a modern economy. The only interruption to this steady progress was an attempted coup in late 1988, involving an attempted invasion. This was quickly put down with the aid of Indian troops. In the early 1990s, President Maumoon Abdul Gayoom devolved some presidential powers, introduced other reforms and established an anti-corruption board.

In the presidential election in October 1993 Gayoom, who had been president since 1978, was re-elected. He won 28 of the 48 votes in the Majlis and went on to win 93% of the popular vote in the subsequent referendum.

The country is isolated and low-lying and much concerned about the threat of rising sea level. It was as a result of an initiative by Gayoom that the Commonwealth first started to focus on the impact of climate change on low-lying countries.

Gayoom was re-elected for a fifth term in the presidential election in October 1998. From a field of six candidates he was unanimously elected by the Majlis and was then endorsed by 90% of the popular vote in the referendum that followed. The 40 elective seats of the Majlis were contested in the general election in November 1999 by individual candidates (there being no political parties in Maldives at the time).

parties were allowed in June 2005. The main parties to emerge were Dhivehi Raiyyithunge Party (DRP), led by the president, Maldivian Democratic Party (MDP), Adalath (Justice) Party, and Islamic Democratic Party. In March 2006 the government published its 'Roadmap for the Reform Agenda', which provided for the first multiparty elections to be held in 2008.

In a constitutional referendum in August 2007, turnout was 77% and 62% of votes were cast for a presidential system as proposed by Gayoom's DRP rather than a 'Westminster' parliamentary system advocated by the opposition MDP. The new constitution, which reduced presidential powers while strengthening the Majlis and the judiciary, was ratified in August 2008.

The first multiparty presidential elections were held in October 2008 and turnout was 86%. Gayoom received 40.3% of votes, Mohamed Nasheed (MDP) 24.9%, Hassan Saeed (independent) 16.7% and Qasim Ibrahim (Republican Party) 15.2%. Nasheed defeated Gayoom in the run-off in late October 2008 receiving 54.2% of the votes cast – turnout was 87% – and Nasheed was sworn in as president on 11 November 2008. On 22 November, Ibrahim Nasir whom Gayoom had succeeded as president in 1978 died.

The first multiparty parliamentary elections followed in May 2009. It was a close contest in which the DRP won the most seats (28 seats and 37% of votes); the president's MDP took 25 (33%), independents 13 (17%) and the People's Alliance seven (9%). The first multiparty local elections were held on 5 February 2011.

Commonwealth observers were present at the 2008 presidential, the 2009 parliamentary and the 2011 local elections.

On 7 February 2012, in circumstances that remain unclear, President Nasheed tendered his resignation. His vice-president, Dr Mohamed Waheed, was sworn in as president. Former President Nasheed asserted that his resignation was tendered under duress from the military. The Commonwealth Ministerial Action Group (CMAG) sent a ministerial mission to Maldives 18–20 February 2012. At an extraordinary meeting on 22 February, CMAG put Maldives on its agenda and Maldives' membership of CMAG in abeyance. In March 2012 Commonwealth Secretary-General Kamalesh Sharma appointed Sir Donald McKinnon, former Commonwealth Secretary-General, as his Special Envoy to Maldives.

International relations

Maldives is a member of the Non-Aligned Movement, Organisation of Islamic Cooperation, South Asian Association for Regional Cooperation, United Nations and World Trade Organization.

Traveller information

Local laws and conventions: Violation of local laws can lead to imprisonment. Visitors will need to respect local customs and sensitivities at all times, especially during the month of Ramadan or when visiting religious sites.

Penalties for all drug offences are severe.

Dress is informal but modest and the wearing of beachwear must be restricted to resort islands only. Handshaking is the most common form of greeting. English is normally used for business and in the commercial sector. Most business is conducted in the morning, by appointment made well in advance. Office hours are Sun–Thur 0730–1430. Friday and Saturday are official rest days.

Immigration and customs: Tourist visas for up to 30 days are available on arrival provided visitors have a valid passport, hold an onward ticket and have enough funds to cover their stay.

All those travelling from infected areas require a yellow fever vaccination certificate.

It is an offence to import explosives, weapons, firearms, ammunition, pornography, material deemed contrary to Islam, including 'idols' for worship, bibles, pork, pork products and alcohol. The export of tortoiseshell and coral is strictly forbidden.

Travel within the country: Traffic drives on the left. A valid international driving permit is required for driving in Maldives. Car hire is available in Malé, though most islands take only around half an hour to cross on foot.

Domestic airline Island Aviation Services runs flights between the major islands, and a number of companies operate seaplane and helicopter services. The main form of local transport is the *dhoni*, a traditional motor-powered boat; larger boats, called *vedis*, are used for longer trips to outer atolls. Visitors should note that many services cease before sunset.

Malé and some other islands offer taxi services. Maldivian taxis have a fixed fee whatever the distance.

Tourism is strictly regulated, and independent travel is discouraged because it is seen as disruptive to traditional island communities. Those wishing to visit the islands outside the tourist zone will need an Inter Atoll Travel Permit, and the Ministry of Atolls Administration will only issue them to those whose visit is sponsored by a resident of the island concerned.

Travel health: Visitors should ensure they have comprehensive health insurance that includes air evacuation. Medical facilities are limited and although most islands are within easy reach of a general physician, many are far from the hospital on Malé. Dengue fever can occur on the islands, and visitors are advised to take a supply of insect repellent and cover up with suitable clothing to avoid being bitten by mosquitoes. Protection should also be taken against both sunburn and dehydration.

Water in tourist areas is generally safe to drink, but if there is any doubt, water should be boiled before use.

Money: Local currency is the rufiyaa (1 rufiyaa = 100 laarees). Island resorts can be costly and visitors should bring sufficient funds for their visit. There are no cash machines, and travellers cheques are not widely accepted. Major credit cards can be used at most resorts, and US dollars can be exchanged at airports, banks and hotels. Banking hours are Sun–Thur 0730–1430.

There were 792,000 tourist arrivals in 2010.

Further information

The President's Office, Republic of Maldives: www.presidencymaldives.gov.mv

People's Majlis: www.majlis.gov.mv

Maldives Monetary Authority: www.mma.gov.mv

Commonwealth Secretariat: www.thecommonwealth.org

Commonwealth of Nations: www.commonwealth-of-nations.org/Maldives

Malta

KEY FACTS

Joined Commonwealth:	1964
Population:	417,000 (2010)
GDP p.c. growth:	2.6% p.a. 1990–2010
UN HDI 2011:	world ranking 36
Official languages:	Maltese, English
Time:	GMT plus 1–2hr
Currency:	euro (€)

Geography

Area:	316 sq km
Coastline:	253km
Capital:	Valletta

The Republic of Malta comprises an archipelago of six islands and islets in the middle of the Mediterranean Sea, 93km south of Sicily and 290km from the coast of North Africa. Malta, Gozo and Comino are inhabited; the other islands are Cominotto, Filfla and St Paul's Island.

Time: GMT plus 1hr. The clock is advanced by one hour from the last Sunday in March to the last Sunday in October.

Area: 316 sq km including Comino (3 sq km) and Gozo (67 sq km).

Topography: Low hills and terraced fields occur on the three main islands. There are no rivers, streams or lakes on Malta Island, which has an indented coast on the eastern side with several good natural harbours. Gozo has cliffs and flat-topped hills. Water is obtained from natural ground water resources and desalination. The latter now accounts for 65% of water production and has relieved the shortage of fresh water.

Climate: Mediterranean type: hot and dry in July–September, with cooling sea-breezes. Winters are mild and wet, with warm westerly winds.

Environment: There are very limited natural freshwater resources, and increasing reliance on desalination.

Did you know...

The Commonwealth Network of Information Technology for Development (COMNET-IT) has its secretariat in Valletta. COMNET-IT has championed the development of the Commonwealth Action Programme for the Digital Divide.

Malta is one of only three Commonwealth member countries in Europe, all of which are island states and members of the European Union.

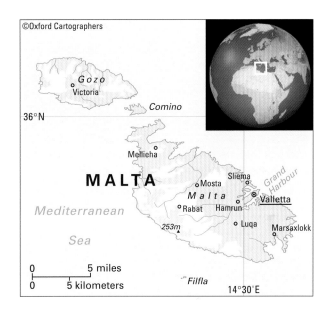

©Oxford Cartographers

Vegetation: The islands have been short of water and the soil is not deep. Mediterranean scrub is the natural vegetation. Approximately 12,000 hectares (less than 5% of which is irrigated) are under cultivation.

Wildlife: There are small mammals, such as hedgehogs, the least weasel and shrews; resident birds include Sardinian warblers, Manx and Cory's shearwaters and the blue rock thrush.

Main towns: Valletta (capital, pop. 6,700 in 2010, greater Valletta includes Birkirkara, Qormi, Zabbar, San Gwann, Sliema, Marsascala, Fgura, Zejtun and Hamrun), Birkirkara (20,700), Mosta (19,300), San Pawl il-Bahar (17,400), Qormi (15,600), Zabbar (14,500), Naxxar (12,900), San Gwann (12,800), Sliema (12,500), Marsascala (12,000), Zebbug (11,400), Fgura (11,200), Zejtun (11,100), Rabat (10,500), Hamrun (8,500) and Victoria (on Gozo, also known as Rabat, 6,200).

Transport: There are 2,254km of roads, 88% paved. There is no railway.

Valletta Grand Harbour is the most important of several harbours. A busy free port has been established at Marsaxlokk in the south-east.

The international airport, Gudja International, is 6km south of Valletta. Helicopter services fly between Malta Island and Gozo.

Society

KEY FACTS 2010

Population per sq km:	1,320
Life expectancy:	79 years
Net primary enrolment:	91%

Population: 417,000 (2010); some 30,000 people on Gozo and Comino; population density among the world's highest; 95% lives in urban areas; growth 0.6% p.a. 1990–2010; birth rate 9 per 1,000 people (17 in 1970); life expectancy 79 years (70 in 1970).

There are no significant ethnic minorities.

Language: Official languages are Maltese and English. Italian is widely spoken.

Religion: Virtually all Christians (Roman Catholics).

Health: Public spending on health was 6% of GDP in 2009. Infant mortality was 5 per 1,000 live births in 2010 (37 in 1960). Summer dust, and sand carried on the wind from North Africa, sometimes cause respiratory problems.

Education: Public spending on education was 5.9% of GDP in 2008. There are 11 years of compulsory education starting at age five. Primary school comprises six years and secondary seven. The numerous church schools are subsidised by the government. The school year starts in September.

Courses at the University of Malta (founded 1592 as the Jesuits' College) include architecture, arts, diplomatic studies, education, engineering, law, medicine, sciences and theology. G F Abela Junior College (University of Malta) was established at Msida (greater Valletta), in 1995. Malta College of Arts, Science and Technology offers a very wide range of vocational and professional education and training, with its main campus at Paola (greater Valletta). The International Maritime Law Institute is based in Malta. The female–male ratio for gross enrolment in tertiary education is 1.44:1 (2008). Literacy among people aged 15–24 is 98% (2005).

Media: There are daily and weekly newspapers in English, including *The Malta Independent*, *The Malta Independent on Sunday*, *The Times*, *The Sunday Times*, *The Malta Business Weekly* and *Malta Today*, and daily and weekly papers in Maltese. The principal newspapers in Maltese have political affiliations, for example *In-Nazzjon* (daily) and *Il-Mument* (weekly) with the Nationalist Party, and *L-Orizzont* (daily) and *It-Torca* (weekly) with the General Workers' Union.

Television Malta is a public channel, which began broadcasting in 1962, and Radio Malta has provided public radio since the mid-1930s. Other TV channels and radio stations are owned by the political parties, the Roman Catholic Church or commercial broadcasters. Net TV is owned by the Nationalist Party and Super One TV by the Malta Labour Party. Cable TV was introduced in 1992 and many households have satellite receivers. Virtually all households have at least one TV set. Digital radio broadcasting was launched in 2008. It is also possible to receive the broadcasts of Italian radio and TV in Malta.

Some 99% of households have TV sets (2009). There are 630 internet users per 1,000 people (2010).

Communications: Country code 356; internet domain '.mt'. Mobile phone coverage is good. Public telephone booths are widely available. Internet connection is fast and reliable. Internet cafes can be found in the main towns. There are post offices in every community.

There are 596 main telephone lines and 1,093 mobile phone subscriptions per 1,000 people (2010).

Public holidays: New Year's Day, St Paul's Shipwreck (10 February), St Joseph's Day (19 March), Freedom Day (31 March), Workers' Day (1 May), Commemoration of 1919 Sette Guigno Riot (7 June), St Peter and St Paul (Harvest Festival, 29 June), Assumption (15 August), Our Lady of Victories (8 September), Independence Day (21 September), Immaculate Conception (8 December), Republic Day (13 December) and Christmas Day.

Religious and other festivals whose dates vary from year to year include Good Friday.

Carnival (not an official holiday) is held Saturday–Tuesday before Ash Wednesday.

Economy

KEY FACTS 2010

GNI:	US$8.0bn
GNI p.c.:	US$19,270
GDP growth:	2.3% p.a. 2006–10
Inflation:	2.4% p.a. 2006–10

Real Growth in GDP

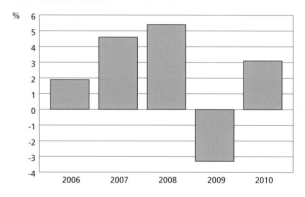

Inflation

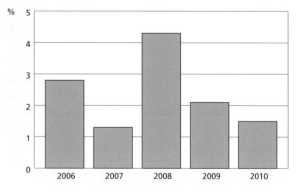

GDP by Sector (2010)

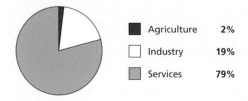

■	Agriculture	2%
□	Industry	19%
▣	Services	79%

Malta has a small domestic market, produces only about 20% of the food it needs, and has no raw materials, a limited supply of fresh water and no energy resources other than solar energy. Its only resources are its ports and its educated and skilled people. Development has been based on shipbuilding and repairing, manufacturing for export, tourism, and, more recently, free port activities and financial and business services.

In 1979 the UK military base (a major employer and generator of government revenue) closed; consequently the 1980s global recession leading to a worldwide collapse of shipbuilding hit Malta particularly hard, and there were numerous factory closures.

During the 1990s, the public sector was reduced and state enterprises privatised. Expansion of tourism and liberalisation of investment, international trade, fiscal policy and the financial

History

Malta (*Melita*, or 'Honey Island', in Latin) was colonised from Carthage during the 6th century BC. Through its long history, it has been subject to complex influences, as shown by its language: the Maltese language descends from Punic, with an Arabic element.

According to tradition, Hannibal was born in Malta (247 BC). From 216 BC the country was under Roman (Byzantine from AD 395) administration until captured by the Arabs in AD 870. In 1070 it became a Sicilian possession. By 1530 it belonged to the Holy Roman Emperor, who gave it to the Knights of St John of Jerusalem, with a mandate to defend Tripoli against Turkish invasion. Building began on Valletta and its fortifications in 1565 after an unsuccessful Turkish siege. Sixteenth-century Malta was prosperous as a trading centre but by the early 18th century the island's fortunes had declined.

The French army under Bonaparte captured it in June 1798, and used it as a base to invade Egypt, but the garrison was expelled by the British navy in 1800 and the island came under British administration. A move to return it to the Knights of St John (1802) provoked a petition from the inhabitants for British protection, and Malta became British under the Treaty of Paris (1814). Malta prospered as a free port, used by British shipping to the Adriatic and the Near East. In 1827 it became the base of the British Mediterranean Fleet. A packet service was established in 1832. After the Suez Canal was opened (1869) the volume of shipping increased. By 1905 the Naval Dockyard, together with British defence services, was the basis of the economy. Blockaded and attacked from the air during the Second World War, Malta was awarded the George Cross in 1942 by King George VI.

Demand for independence (though not representation) came relatively late to Malta, which had benefited from the UK naval presence on the island. In the mid-1950s Dom Mintoff's Labour Party, then in government, inclined towards integration with the UK. This was confirmed by a referendum in 1956. In March 1962 Malta became internally self-governing.

However, by the early 1960s, with nationalism and anti-colonialism sweeping the world, coupled with the decline of the UK navy, the mood had changed. The Labour Party, as well as Dr Borg Olivier's Nationalist Party (PN), campaigned for independence, which was achieved in September 1964.

At independence, Malta entered a turbulent period. The dockyard was nationalised in 1968. Malta became a republic at the end of 1974 and in 1979 the UK military base was closed, which shook the economy, and traditional Maltese faith in UK protection.

Domestically, the country was polarised between the generally socialist Malta Labour Party (MLP) and the pro-western and economically liberal PN. Under the long and forceful leadership of Mintoff, the MLP government made Malta a strong adherent of the Non-Aligned Movement and strengthened cultural and trade links with Malta's North African neighbours, notably oil-rich Libya.

Political conflict was exacerbated by anomalies in the electoral system, which allowed the MLP to retain power after the 1981 parliamentary elections, although the PN had more votes. After strikes and civil unrest, in 1987 Mintoff's successor Dr Karmenu Mifsud Bonnici reformed the electoral system, and the May 1987 elections were won by the PN, under Dr Edward Fenech-Adami, who reversed many of Mintoff's centralist policies.

The PN led by Fenech-Adami strengthened its majority at the general election in 1992, securing 34 of 65 seats, and 51.8% of the votes. A third party, the Democratic Alternative, with strong policies on environmental protection, emerged, but the basic two-party pattern remained fairly intact. After this second defeat under the electoral system he had introduced, Bonnici resigned as leader of the MLP and was replaced by Dr Alfred Sant, who pledged to modernise Labour's policies.

After the EU Council of Ministers decided in 1995 to accept Malta as a candidate to join the European Union, the PN government set about preparing the country for accession – introducing VAT and removing some import tariffs. However, VAT was unpopular, and the changes as a whole controversial, so the next parliamentary elections, scheduled for 1997, were brought forward to October 1996 to settle the issue of EU membership and its required economic disciplines. The elections resulted in a narrow win for the MLP – 50.7% to the PN's 47.8% – with a voter turnout of 98% of the registered voters. On taking office as prime minister, Sant immediately withdrew Malta's application to join the EU and pulled out of NATO's Partnership for Peace plan.

During 1998, the MLP had a majority of one vote in the House of Representatives and on two occasions when former Labour Prime Minister Dom Mintoff had voted with the Nationalist opposition (to defeat a development project affecting his own constituency), it had not been able to command a majority.

The general election scheduled for 2001 was brought forward to September 1998, when the PN, still led by Fenech-Adami, won 35 of the 65 parliamentary seats and 51.8% of the votes, giving the party an endorsement for its planned application for EU membership. The PN government immediately reactivated its application to join the EU and resumed its preparations for accession, and in December 1999 Malta was formally invited to enter into negotiations on accession. Malta became a member of the EU in May 2004.

services sector led to steady growth, averaging nearly 5% p.a. over the decade.

The long period of good, steady growth came to an end in 2001, as export demand fell and the economy stalled during 2001–04. After four years of stagnation growth resumed, rising to 4.6% in 2007 and 5.4% in 2008. But the rapidly worsening international economic conditions and global fall in demand caused growth to collapse in 2009 (–3.3%), recovering in 2010–11.

Malta joined the European Union in May 2004 and adopted the euro currency in January 2008, replacing the Maltese lira.

Constitution

Status:	Republic
Legislature:	Parliament
Independence:	21 September 1964

Under the 1964 constitution – amended in 1974 and 1987 – Malta is a democratic republic with a unicameral House of Representatives of at least 65 members. The country has proportional representation using the single transferable vote system. A party which obtains a majority of votes but minority of seats is allocated additional seats to give it an overall majority of one. The House may not sit for longer than five years.

The president is the head of state and is elected for a five-year period of office by the House of Representatives. The incumbent has executive authority but must act on the cabinet's advice and the position is therefore largely ceremonial. The prime minister and leader of the opposition are both appointed by the president. The cabinet is appointed by the president on the advice of the prime minister. All appointees must be members of parliament.

Under the constitution, Roman Catholic Christianity is the state religion and must be taught in state schools.

Politics

Last elections:	March 2008 (parliamentary), April 2009 (presidential)
Next elections:	2013 (parliamentary), 2014 (presidential)
Head of state:	President Dr George Abela (2009–)
Head of government:	Prime Minister Dr Lawrence Gonzi
Ruling party:	Nationalist Party

Although the referendum in 2003 on EU membership gave the Nationalist Party (PN) government a mandate to proceed with ratifying the treaty for accession to the EU in May 2004, the opposition continued to insist that it would take Malta out of the Union if it won the election in 2004, and so the government called an early election, which in April 2003 decisively closed the debate. The PN won the hard-fought contest with 35 of the 65 seats and 51.8% of the votes, a decisive result in a country where the two main parties normally each enjoy the support of about half the electorate. Following the election, the Malta Labour Party (MLP) decided to end its opposition to EU membership, thus ending a long and intense period when political activity was focused on one issue.

In March 2004, soon after Dr Edward Fenech-Adami's 70th birthday, Dr Lawrence Gonzi succeeded him as prime minister and in April 2004 Fenech-Adami was elected to the presidency.

The PN was returned to power in the March 2008 parliamentary elections, winning 35 seats (49.3% of votes) while MLP secured the balance of 34 seats (48.8%). Turnout was 93%.

In April 2009, at the end of President Fenech-Adami's five-year term, Dr George Abela was unanimously elected president by parliament.

International relations

Malta is a member of the Council of Europe, European Union, Organization for Security and Co-operation in Europe, United Nations and World Trade Organization.

Traveller information

Local laws and conventions: Visitors to Malta should note the importance of the Roman Catholic Church (more than 90% of Maltese are Roman Catholics) and that modesty in dress is expected, particularly the covering of the shoulders and legs. Beachwear is for beaches only.

Smoking is prohibited on public transport, in some public buildings and in all cinemas.

Penalties for drug possession and trafficking are strict and can lead to heavy fines and imprisonment.

Shaking hands is the usual greeting.

Business dress should be smart and modest for both men and women. Appointments for business meetings are customary and punctuality is expected; business cards should be presented. Many of Malta's luxury hotels have state-of-the-art conference facilities. Business hours are Mon–Fri 0800–1230 and 1330–1700.

Immigration and customs: All European Union nationals and residents of the Commonwealth do not require visas to enter the country as a tourist for up to three months. EU nationals are only required to produce evidence of their nationality and identity. Other nationals need a passport valid for three months after departure.

A yellow fever vaccination certificate is required from travellers arriving from an infected area.

New regulations controlling the amount of cash leaving or entering the EU have been in force since June 2007. Anyone leaving or entering Malta will have to declare if they are carrying more than €10,000.

Travel within the country: Traffic drives on the left. There are several car-hire companies and visitors are required to have an international driving permit. The speed limit is 80kph on highways and 50kph in residential areas.

A helicopter service connects Malta and Gozo; there is also a ferry service which takes around 15 minutes. Additionally, visitors can take a passenger ferry to Comino, although this service only operates between March and November.

Taxis are white and visitors are advised to agree a price before travelling. There are good bus services in Valletta and Victoria (Gozo).

Travel health: EU citizens will need a European Health Insurance Card (EHIC), which will entitle them to emergency treatment. Other nationals should ensure they have comprehensive medical insurance.

Mains water is normally chlorinated. Visitors are advised to drink bottled water for the first few weeks of stay. Milk is pasteurised.

Money: Money can be changed at banks, bureaux de change, some hotels, and larger shops and restaurants. Automated foreign exchange machines are available at various locations on the islands and some exchange bureaux are often open 24 hours. American Express, Diners Club, Mastercard and Visa are widely accepted, and there are ATMs on the islands. Travellers cheques can be exchanged in the normal authorised institutions. Banking hours are Mon–Fri 0830–1230, Sat 0830–1130.

There were 1,332,000 tourist arrivals in 2010.

Further information

Government of Malta: www.gov.mt

Parliament: www.parliament.gov.mt

Central Bank of Malta: www.centralbankmalta.org

Commonwealth Secretariat: www.thecommonwealth.org

Commonwealth of Nations: www.commonwealth-of-nations.org/Malta

Connecting
Africa

and the
WORLD

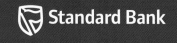

Mauritius

Joined Commonwealth: 1968

Population:	1,299,000 (2010)
GDP p.c. growth:	3.5% p.a. 1990–2010
UN HDI 2011:	world ranking 77
Official language:	English
Time:	GMT plus 4hr
Currency:	Mauritian rupee (MRs)

Geography

Area:	2,040 sq km
Coastline:	177km
Capital:	Port Louis

The Republic of Mauritius, an island country in the Indian Ocean, lies east of Madagascar and the south-east African coast. Its nearest neighbour is the French island of Réunion. The Constitution of Mauritius provides that Mauritius includes the islands of Mauritius, Rodrigues, Agalega, Tromelin, Cargados Carajos and the Chagos Archipelago, including Diego Garcia and any other island comprised in the State of Mauritius. Mauritius has always maintained that it has sovereignty over the Chagos Archipelago but has not been able so far to exercise its sovereignty.

Area: Island of Mauritius 1,864 sq km; Rodrigues 104 sq km; total area, including other islands 2,040 sq km.

Topography: The island of Mauritius is almost entirely surrounded by coral reefs, with lagoons and coral-sand beaches. Mountains, with rocky peaks, rise abruptly from the broad fertile plains; within lies the central plateau. The rivers flow fast through deep ravines, with frequent waterfalls. They are not navigable, but fill eight reservoirs. The longest is the 34km Grand River South-East. There are two natural lakes, Grand Bassin and Bassin Blanc, both craters of extinct volcanoes.

Climate: The climate is maritime subtropical, with south-east trade winds blowing for much of the year. Summer, the rainy season, is from November to April, winter from June to September. Rainfall ranges from 80mm in October to 310mm in February. Heavy rains fall mainly from late December to the beginning of April. Cyclones, occurring in the summer, occasionally do severe damage.

Did you know...

Jean-Marie Gustave Le Clézio, a Frenchman whose parents originated from Mauritius, was awarded the Nobel Prize in Literature in 2008.

Mauritius has one of the highest life expectancies in Africa (73 years).

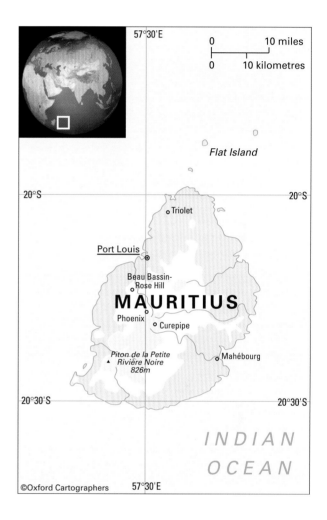

Environment: The most significant issues are water pollution, and degradation of coral reefs.

Vegetation: The mountain foothills are densely vegetated, many planted with sugar cane and tea. Some 4,600 hectares of forest land have been set aside as nature reserves. Remains of the original ebony forests, felled by the early settlers, have survived here. The uplands have been extensively replanted with conifers and eucalyptus. Trees include coastal casuarina trees (called filaos), the Indian almond tree (badamier), ficus (multipliant), flametree (flamboyant), African tulip, bauhinia and jacaranda. Mangroves grow along the east and south-east coasts. Many indigenous trees and tree orchids have vanished, but over 10,000 plant-species remain, of which more than 150 are indigenous to Mauritius and 40 to Rodrigues. Forest covers 17% of the land area, having declined at 0.5% p.a. 1990–2010.

Arable land comprises 43% and permanent cropland 2% of the total land area.

Wildlife: Mauritius was the home of the dodo, an extinct species of flightless large turkey. Conservation systems are now well enforced, but only nine of a known 25 species of indigenous birds remain, including the Mauritius kestrel and the pink pigeon. The Rodrigues fruit bat or golden bat was in danger of becoming extinct until recently; the Mauritius fruit bat is more common. Javanese deer, introduced by the Dutch for food, are found mainly in the uplands and the ravines, and protected by hunting restrictions. There are 12 species of lizards, four of non-poisonous snakes and 2,000 of insects and butterflies. Three of the butterflies – the citrus, ficus and sailor – are unique to the islands. Marine fauna is very rich.

Main towns: Port Louis (capital, pop. 156,700 in 2010), Beau Bassin–Rose Hill (111,000), Vacoas–Phoenix (106,900), Curepipe (84,300), Quatre Bornes (81,100), Triolet (23,800), Goodlands (21,300), Central Flacq (18,100), Bel Air (18,000), Mahébourg (17,300), St Pierre (16,500), Le Hochet (15,500) and Grand Baie (11,700).

Transport: There are 2,020km of roads, 100% paved, including at least 30km of motorways and 940km of main roads. There is no railway.

Port Louis is the main harbour and only commercial port. Facilities include a container terminal and terminals for the bulk handling of sugar, oil, wheat and cement.

Sir Seewoosagur Ramgoolam International Airport at Plaisance is in the south-east of the island, some 50km from Port Louis. There is an airstrip at Plaine Corail on Rodrigues receiving a daily service from Mauritius.

Society

KEY FACTS 2010

Population per sq km:	637
Life expectancy:	73 years
Net primary enrolment:	94%

Population: 1,299,000 (2010); 42% lives in urban areas; growth 1.0% p.a. 1990–2010; birth rate 13 per 1,000 people (28 in 1970); life expectancy 73 years (62 in 1970).

About 68% of the population is of Indian descent, 27% Creole, and the remainder largely of Chinese or French descent.

Language: The official language is English; French-based Creole is the mother tongue of many Mauritians and the most widely spoken language. Other languages include Bhojpuri 12% and French 3% (2000 census).

Religion: Hindus 48%, Christians 32% (Roman Catholics 24%), Muslims 17% (2000 census).

Health: Public spending on health was 2% of GDP in 2009. Overall, the health profile is similar to that of developed countries. Health care in the public sector is free to all Mauritians. As well as some 13 hospitals, there are area and community health centres. 99% of the population uses an improved drinking water source and 91% have access to adequate sanitation facilities (2009). Infant mortality was 13 per 1,000 live births in 2010 (67 in 1960). Malaria was substantially eradicated in the 1950s. A national AIDS prevention and control programme has been running since 1987. In 2009, 1.0% of people aged 15–49 were HIV positive.

Education: Public spending on education was 3.1% of GDP in 2009. There are seven years of compulsory education starting at age five. Primary school comprises six years and secondary seven, with cycles of three and four years. Some 96% of pupils complete primary school (2008). The school year starts in January. Education is free at the primary and secondary levels, partly subsidised at the pre-primary level and heavily subsidised at the tertiary level.

Tertiary education centres on the University of Mauritius, which comprises faculties of Agriculture; Engineering; Law; Management; Science (including the Department of Medicine); and Social Studies and Humanities. Other institutions include University of Technology (operational from September 2001); Mauritius Institute of Education (training teachers); Mahatma Gandhi Institute (courses in Asian culture); Mauritius College of the Air (distance education for adults and primary and secondary students); and Sir Seewoosagur Ramgoolam Medical College (established at Belle Rive in 1999, offers degrees in medicine and dentistry). The female–male ratio for gross enrolment in tertiary education is 1.25:1 (2008). Literacy among people aged 15–24 is 97% (2009).

Media: Daily newspapers and periodicals reflect the country's wide cultural mix and are published in French, English, Hindi, Urdu and Chinese. The leading dailies are *L'Express*, *Le Matinal* and *Le Mauricien* (afternoon), and *Mauritius Times* is a weekly.

The Mauritius Broadcasting Corporation provides public TV and radio and is funded by advertising and licence fees. There are several private TV channels and radio stations.

Some 96% of households have TV sets (2008). There are 174 personal computers (2006) and 283 internet users (2010) per 1,000 people.

Communications: Country code 230; internet domain '.mu'. There are some public telephones. Mobile phone coverage is good. Internet cafes can be found in the main towns. There is a good postal service.

There are 298 main telephone lines and 917 mobile phone subscriptions per 1,000 people (2010).

Public holidays: New Year (two days), Abolition of Slavery (1 February), National Day (12 March), Labour Day (1 May), All Saints' Day (1 November), Arrival of the Indentured Labourers (2 November) and Christmas Day.

Religious and other festivals whose dates vary from year to year include Chinese New Year, Thaipoosam Cavadee (January/February), Maha Shivaratri (February/March), Ougadi (March/April), Ganesh Chathurthi (August/September), Eid al-Fitr (End of Ramadan, three days) and Diwali (October/November).

Economy

KEY FACTS 2010

GNI:	US$9.9bn
GNI p.c.:	US$7,750
GDP growth:	4.5% p.a. 2006–10
Inflation:	6.5% p.a. 2006–10

Mauritius has a very good record of growth. Despite the country's isolation from major world markets, it is among the most successful of small developing countries in diversifying its economy out of dependence on one agricultural commodity (sugar) into manufacturing, tourism, horticulture and, latterly, financial services and ICT. Manufacturing, especially of clothing and textiles (centred

Real Growth in GDP

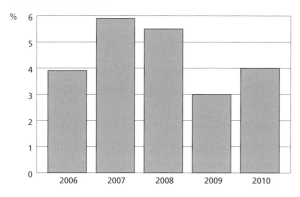

Inflation

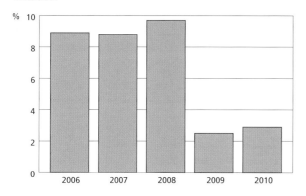

GDP by Sector (2010)

Agriculture	4%
Industry	28%
Services	69%

on the early established export processing zones, or EPZs), and tourism have developed rapidly, providing jobs and income. Manufacturing output grew by more than 10% p.a. during 1980–90 and more than 5% p.a. 1990–2000, but it grew very little at all in the following decade.

By the late 1990s the textile industry was facing stiffer competition from new low-cost producers as well as the erosion of preferential tariff agreements. The government embarked on a programme of privatisation, financial market liberalisation and development of offshore activities, with the aim of turning the island into an international financial and business services centre. By 2005 financial and business services contributed 20% of GDP.

Sugar continued to contribute significantly to export earnings and the economy remained vulnerable to fluctuations in world commodity prices and bad weather. It is difficult to reduce imports in lean years since both the manufacturing and tourism industries are import-intensive.

With relatively high levels of foreign investment, the economy grew steadily during the 2000s – by 3.9% in 2006, 5.9% in 2007 and 5.5% in 2008. Despite the world economic downturn and fall in

world demand in 2008–09, growth was sustained in 2009 (3.0%), 2010 (4.0%) and 2011 (about 4%).

Constitution

Status:	Republic
Legislature:	National Assembly
Independence:	12 March 1968

The independence constitution established a multiparty democracy, and the country became a republic in 1992. The presidency is non-executive; political power lies with the prime minister and the cabinet. The president is appointed for a five-year term by the National Assembly on a motion made by the prime minister and supported by the vote of the majority of all the members of the Assembly. The single-chamber National Assembly comprises up to 70 members, 62 of whom are elected (60 from 20 three-member constituencies on the island of Mauritius plus two from the single constituency of Rodrigues). Up to eight additional seats are allocated to 'best losers', to ensure representation of a variety of ethnic groups.

The constitution provides for the appointment of president, vice-president, speaker, deputy speaker, prime minister, deputy prime minister, a cabinet of ministers, and up to ten parliamentary secretaries. Provision is further made for an attorney-general, a secretary to the cabinet, a commissioner of police, a director of public prosecutions and a leader of the opposition.

General elections take place every five years, based on universal adult suffrage for citizens over the age of 18. The constitution establishes the separation of powers between the legislature, the executive and the judiciary. It guarantees the protection of the fundamental rights and freedoms of the individual: freedom of conscience, freedom of association, movement and opinion, freedom of expression, freedom of creed and religious belief, and the right to private property.

Politics

Last elections:	May 2010
Next elections:	2015
Head of state:	President Sir Anerood Jugnauth (2003–)
Head of government:	Prime Minister Dr Navinchandra Ramgoolam
Ruling party:	Alliance of the Future

The elections in September 2000 were won by an alliance of the two main opposition parties, the Mouvement Socialiste Mauricien (MSM) and the Mouvement Militant Mauricien (MMM), taking 54 seats while the Labour Party won only six, and alliance leader Sir Anerood Jugnauth formed a new government, with MMM leader Paul Bérenger as his deputy until September 2003 when, by agreement, Bérenger became prime minister and caretaker president Karl Offmann made way for Jugnauth to become president.

In the July 2005 general election, the opposition Social Alliance (with 38 seats) defeated the governing alliance (22 seats) and Labour Party leader Dr Navinchandra Ramgoolam became prime minister. Turnout was over 80%.

The general election in May 2010 was won by Ramgoolam's newly formed Alliance of the Future, with 41 of the 62 National Assembly seats, while the opposition Alliance of the Heart – led by Paul Bérenger – won 18.

International relations

Mauritius is a member of the African, Caribbean and Pacific Group of States, African Union, Common Market for Eastern and Southern Africa, Indian Ocean Rim Association for Regional Cooperation, Non-Aligned Movement, Organisation internationale de la Francophonie, Southern African Development Community, United Nations and World Trade Organization.

Mauritius hosts the headquarters of the Indian Ocean Rim Association for Regional Cooperation.

Traveller information

Local laws and conventions: Dress should be modest when visiting religious shrines and footwear removed before entering temples and mosques.

Drug smuggling is a serious offence with severe penalties. The importation of 12 grams of cannabis can lead to a one-year sentence. Cigarette papers are illegal.

Handshaking is the usual form of greeting. Dress is normally informal.

Suits are usually worn in business circles. Mauritius has a newly built conference centre with a capacity of 2,500. Office hours are Mon–Fri 0900–1600.

History

Mauritius was uninhabited until 1598, and had much unique wildlife and plant life. There were Dutch settlers from 1638 until 1710. The French took formal possession in 1715 and sent settlers from 1721; the French East India Company governed the island, called Île de France, from about 1767. Slaves were brought in from Madagascar, Mozambique and other parts of Africa.

The island was captured by the British in 1810, during the Anglo–French war, and renamed Mauritius. Together with its dependencies, including Seychelles and Rodrigues, the island was formally ceded to Britain under the Treaty of Paris (1814). At the time slavery was abolished, in 1834, there were 68,616 registered slaves in the country. After abolition, indentured labourers were recruited, mainly from India, to work in the expanding sugar industry. More than 200,000 Indian labourers arrived between 1840 and 1870. They were later joined by a small number of Chinese traders. The population swelled from 100,000 in 1835 to 371,000 by the end of the century.

From 1810 until they were separated in 1903, Mauritius and Seychelles were administered as a single British colony by a governor and British officials.

The independence movement had its roots in the labour movement which, in the late 1940s, campaigned for the transfer of political power to Mauritians. In 1947 the franchise was extended to every literate adult. A measure of democratic self-government followed, with a general election in 1948 and the first legislative council. Universal adult suffrage was introduced in 1959.

Negotiations for political autonomy in the 1960s were led by Seewoosagur Ramgoolam. Elections were held in 1967, which were won by a pro-independence alliance of Ramgoolam's Labour Party and two smaller groups, the Independent Forward Bloc and the Muslim Action Committee. A new constitution granting internal self-government was then introduced. Mauritius became an independent state and joined the Commonwealth on 12 March 1968.

Alarmed by the growing strength of the socialist Mouvement Militant Mauricien (MMM), led by Paul Bérenger, and union strikes, the government of Ramgoolam refused to allow the general election due in 1972. A state of emergency was declared and MMM and union leaders imprisoned.

In the 1976 general election, Labour retained power by forming an alliance with the Parti Mauricien Social Démocrate (PMSD). But in 1982 the MMM, in alliance with Labour breakaway group the Parti Socialiste Mauricien (PSM), won all the elected seats in the National Assembly. In government, the MMM was less radical than it had been in the early 1970s, but the MMM/PSM alliance broke up within a year. Aneerood Jugnauth, prime minister and MMM president, then broke away from the MMM to form a new party, the Mouvement Socialiste Mauricien (MSM), which formed an alliance with Labour and the PMSD. The new alliance won the elections of 1983, leaving the old MMM in opposition. The Organisation du Peuple Rodriguais again won the two Rodrigues seats and joined the new government.

In 1984, Jugnauth dismissed a number of ministers, most of them members of the Labour Party, and the coalition government split. Those Labour MPs who continued to support the government formed the Rassemblement des Travaillistes Mauriciens (RTM). In an early general election called in June 1987, the MSM/PMSD/RTM coalition unexpectedly won a comfortable majority. The PMSD left the alliance in 1988, and the MMM came into the alliance in its place.

The alliance of MSM and MMM were returned to power in 1991; it held firm until 1993 when MMM leader Paul Bérenger was dismissed from the cabinet and took part of the MMM with him to form an alliance with the Labour Party. Meanwhile, the constitution was amended to make Mauritius a republic on 12 March 1992.

The Labour Party–MMM alliance won a sweeping victory at elections held in December 1995, leaving the country with only a token parliamentary opposition. Labour Party leader Navinchandra Ramgoolam became prime minister and Bérenger deputy prime minister and minister of foreign affairs. The government introduced privatisation policies, despite strong opposition from the MMM and unions. Bérenger and other MMM members resigned from the coalition to rejoin the opposition in June 1997.

Immigration and customs: A three-month visa will be issued on arrival to those in possession of a passport valid for at least six months and a return ticket. Visa requirements are subject to change and should be checked well before travel. Foreigners are sometimes asked for ID so it is advisable for all visitors to keep a copy of the photopage of their passport and their visa on them at all times.

Scheduled drugs like narcotics and strong painkillers need authorisation before import.

Prohibited imports include sugar cane, and related parts thereof, soil micro-organisms and invertebrates. Vegetables, fruits, flowers and seeds must all be declared. Firearms require a permit. All imported animal products require a permit and a health certificate.

A yellow fever certificate is required from anyone travelling from infected countries and those travelling from a malarial area may be asked to take a blood test.

Lone parents travelling with children need documentation showing parental responsibility.

Travel within the country: Traffic drives on the left. There are a number of car-hire firms and drivers must be over 23 years of age. A national driving licence is sufficient and visitors should keep their driving licences on them at all times. There is a good road network around the country. There is an 80kph speed limit on the motorway and 50kph in built-up areas. The wearing of seatbelts is mandatory.

Air Mauritius operates daily flights from Plaisance Airport to Rodrigues and there are also helicopter transfers. Coralin sails from Port Louis to Rodrigues once a week.

There are good and efficient bus services and taxis are available at reasonable rates; all taxis are regulated and metered.

Travel health: Medical care standards are high and there are several private clinics. Foreign visitors have to pay at state-run clinics and hospitals so should ensure they have comprehensive health insurance. Hepatitis A and tetanus are the only required vaccinations at present but inoculations can change at short notice and should be checked before travel.

Chikungunya, a viral infection spread by mosquitoes, can be a problem from October to May and dengue fever also occurs. Visitors should exercise adequate precautions to avoid being bitten and should take insect repellent and suitable loose-fitting clothing.

Water for drinking or cleaning teeth must be boiled, though bottled water is widely available.

Prescription medicines should be kept in their original containers and be clearly labelled to avoid confusion.

Money: Banks and bureaux de change tend to give a better rate on travellers cheques than cash. Mastercard and Visa are the most widely accepted and there are ATMs all over the country. Banking hours are Mon–Thur 0915–1515, Fri 0915–1530 and Sat 0915–1115. (Some banks also open to coincide with airport arrivals and departures.)

There were 871,000 tourist arrivals in 2009.

Further information

Mauritius Government: www.gov.mu

National Assembly: mauritiusassembly.gov.mu

Bank of Mauritius: bom.intnet.mu

Commonwealth Secretariat: www.thecommonwealth.org

Commonwealth of Nations: www.commonwealth-of-nations.org/Mauritius

Attorney General's Office, Republic of Mozambique

Continuing the fight against corruption

As chief law officer, the Attorney General has a special responsibility to be the guardian of the rule of law which protects individuals and society as a whole, and safeguards personal liberties.

The Attorney General's Office is the highest authority of the public ministries, directed by the Attorney General, who is appointed by the President for a period of five years.

Right: Attorney General Augusto Paulino, appointed by the President in 2007

Vision

The Attorney General's Office, the superior organ of the prosecution, is an institution of the justice system committed to the democratic rule of law and constitutional guarantees. It is independent, effective in combating crime and ensures the protection of legitimate rights and interests of citizens and legal entities.

Mission

The Attorney General's Office, as a responsible institution, holds the public prosecution, heads the investigation of criminal offenses, represents public interest and social control, guarantees the protection of minors, citizens and legal entities in general, including respect for human rights.

Strategic priorities

To accomplish its constitutional and legal mission effectively, the Attorney General's Office approved its Strategic Plan for the period 2012-2016 based on eight strategic priorities:

- Institutional development
- Control of legality
- State representation and protection of minors
  1. *Ensure vulnerable groups, such as minors, absent parties and legally incompetent persons are defended and represented in court.*
  2. *Promote the defence and representation of the State and State institutions in litigation before foreign courts.*
- Protection and support for victims, witnesses and other participating individuals
- Legal information and civic education
- Human rights protection
- International co-operation
- Transgender issues

Functions

- Ensure the observance of legality under the Constitution and other laws
- Oversee the enforcement of laws and other legal bodies, and the legal power of the state
- Carry out inspections and investigations for law enforcement
- Issue legal opinions in the event of mandatory consultation prescribed by law or upon request of the Council of Ministers
- Collaborate with agencies to maintain security, public order and tranquility in the prevention and fight against crime
- Participate in actions leading to the development of legal consciousness of citizens, employees and agents of the state
- Combat corruption
- Monitor conformity with the law and fulfillment of the principles of law
- Represent and defend, before the courts, the assets and interests of the State

Contact

Attorney General's Office
Vladimir Lenin Avenue No. 121
Maputo
Mozambique

Tel: +258 21 30 4303/4 • +258 82 316 1920
Fax: +258 21 30 4297
Email: pgr@pgr.gov.mz
www.pgr.gov.mz

Mozambique

KEY FACTS

Joined Commonwealth:	1995
Population:	23,391,000 (2010)
GDP p.c. growth:	4.3% p.a. 1990–2010
UN HDI 2011:	world ranking 184
Official language:	Portuguese
Time:	GMT plus 2hr
Currency:	Mozambique metical (MT)

Geography

Area:	799,380 sq km
Coastline:	2,470km
Capital:	Maputo

Mozambique is in south-east Africa and borders (anti-clockwise, from north) the United Republic of Tanzania, Malawi, Zambia, Zimbabwe, South Africa, Swaziland, and the Indian Ocean. The country is divided into eleven provinces (from south to north): Maputo, Maputo city, Gaza, Inhambane, Manica, Sofala, Zambézia, Tete, Nampula, Niassa, and Cabo Delgado.

Topography: Mozambique occupies the eastern fringe of the great southern African escarpment. The mountains of the interior fall to a broad plateau, which descends to coastal hills and plain. Rivers generally run west to east. The coastal beaches are fringed by lagoons, coral reefs and strings of islands. The extensive low plateau covers nearly half the land area. The Zambezi is the largest of 25 main rivers.

Climate: Tropical and subtropical. Inland is cooler than the coast and rainfall higher as the land rises. The hottest and wettest season is October to March. From April to September the coast has warm, mainly dry weather, tempered by sea breezes. The country is vulnerable to cyclones.

Environment: The most significant environmental issues are desertification, pollution of surface and coastal waters, and persistent migration of people from the hinterland to urban and coastal areas.

Did you know...

Graça Machel is a former Chairperson of the Commonwealth Foundation.

Maria Lurdes Mutola, born in Maputo, took the Commonwealth Games Women's 800 Metres record at the Manchester Games in 2002.

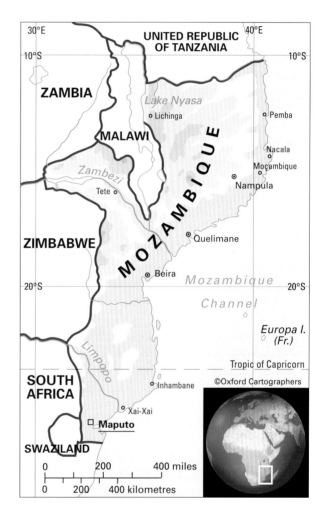

Vegetation: The plateau is savannah – dry and open bushveld and wide stretches of grassland. There are patches of forest in the western and northern highlands. Dense subtropical bush characterises the coastal plain. Forest covers 50% of the land area, having declined at 0.5% p.a. 1990–2010. Arable land comprises 6% and permanent cropland 0.4% of the total land area.

Wildlife: Mozambique has four national parks. Gorongosa, the biggest, extends to 3,770 sq km. There are also many forest and game reserves harbouring zebra, water buffalo, giraffe, lions, elephants and rhinos, and many varieties of tropical water birds such as flamingos, cranes, storks and pelicans. 179 species of mammals have been recorded, 14 of which are endangered (2002).

Main towns: Maputo (capital, pop. 1.13m in 2010), Matola (greater Maputo, 757,800), Nampula (Nampula province, 534,800), Beira (Sofala, 440,400), Chimoio (Manica, 259,200), Nacala

Empresa Moçambicana de Seguros

EMOSE was the first post-independence national insurance company established in Mozambique, formed from the merging of three former insurance companies, Nauticus, Lusitana and Tranquilidade.

EMOSE began operations in 1977, making it the single biggest insurance company in the Republic of Mozambique, with a total capital of MT150,000,000.00. EMOSE has since transformed from a public enterprise into a fully limited company.

Mission

The EMOSE mission is to protect and create wealth for people and organisations, and to ensure the quality of its partners and employees.

Vision

EMOSE wants to lead the market as a source of renovation, business integration and solid growth and to become the preferred insurance company in Mozambique due to the excellence of its services.

It is the only national insurer located in all provincial capitals and select district capitals which creates added value in providing assistance and customer service, especially in cases of accidents. For over 30 years, EMOSE has operated in the domestic insurance market with a broad portfolio of more than 200,000 insurance policies, offering more than 35 products equivalent in quality to those sold in international markets, allowing EMOSE to respond swiftly and expertly to the needs of its clients.

Since its creation, EMOSE has had the privilege of participating in several technical projects, which culminated in the effective insurance of several large engineering initiatives, including dam construction, electrification projects, road rehabilitation of National Highway no. 1, the construction of the Beira Oil Terminal and rehabilitation of 225 km of the Limpopo railway line. EMOSE also insures a vast fleet of ships and planes.

EMOSE maintains positive relations with all national market brokers, and is pleased to have a good relationship with Mozambique's first reinsurer, MOZRE, and various international reinsurance companies such as Munich Re (Germany, South Africa and Mauritius), Swiss Re (Switzerland and South Africa), Tan-Re, Africa Re, East Africa, and ZEP Re.

César Bento Madivádua, CEO

Isaías Diogo Chembeze, Financial Manager

Dra. Matilde de Campos, Commercial and Marketing Manager

Contact

Dra. Matilde de Campos
Commercial & Marketing Manager
Eng. Isaias Chembeze
Financial Manager
Av. 25 de Setembro, No. 1383
Caixa Postal 696 ou 1165
Maputo
Mozambique

Tel: +258 213 2 2095/9 • 213 2 4086 •
+258 82 982 4740
Fax: +258 213 2 6026
E-mail: comercial@emose.co.mz •
matilde.pinhal@emose.co.mz

www.emose.co.mz

(Nampula, 221,400), Quelimane (Zambézia, 204,700), Tete (Tete, 170,000), Lichinga (Niassa, 162,100), Pemba (Cabo Delgado, 160,500), Garue (Zambézia, 129,000), Gurué (Zambézia, 122,300), Xai-Xai (Gaza, 119,700), Maxixe (Inhambane, 107,900), Cuamba (Niassa, 102,500), Angoche (Nampula, 86,400), Dondo (Sofala, 79,700), Montepuez (Cabo Delgado, 79,000), Mocuba (Zambézia, 71,200) and Inhambane (Inhambane, 66,500).

Transport: There are 30,400km of roads, 19% paved. The road network links with all neighbouring countries except Tanzania in the north. There is a new toll road from Maputo to Witbank in the industrial heartland of South Africa.

The railway network extends to 3,116km.

Beyond domestic needs, Beira, Maputo and Nacala are important ports for Malawi, Swaziland, Zambia and Zimbabwe.

International airports are Maputo International, 3km north-west of the city, and Beira, 13km from the city.

Society

KEY FACTS 2010

Population per sq km:	29
Life expectancy:	50 years
Net primary enrolment:	91%

Population: 23,391,000 (2010); 38% lives in urban areas and 7% in urban agglomerations of more than 1 million people; growth 2.7% p.a. 1990–2010; birth rate 38 per 1,000 people (48 in 1970); life expectancy 50 years (39 in 1970 and 43 in 1990).

Ethnic groups include Makua–Lomwe in the north, Makonde in the far north, Thonga in the southern lowlands, Chopi and Thonga in the Inhambane coastal province, and Shona mainly in the central Manica and Sofala provinces.

Language: Portuguese (official) and three main African groups: Tsonga, Sena–Nyanja, Makua–Lomwe. English is widely spoken.

History

From the 10th century or earlier, Arabs and Indians traded with populations in the Mozambique area. Portuguese traders took prominence from the 15th century onwards, vying with Arabs and Swahili people along the coast in the commodity and slave trades. In time, Portuguese settlers came, establishing large estates. However, Portuguese control was fiercely resisted and by 1885, when the colonial powers met for the Berlin Conference to formalise colonial boundaries, Portugal only controlled coastal strongholds and a few scattered inland areas. After a series of military campaigns to subdue the African population, Portugal auctioned off land concessions. The Mozambique Company, the Niassa Company and the Zambezi Company, representing largely non-Portuguese (especially British) capital, established plantations in north and central Mozambique, using forced local labour. Many Mozambicans from the south found employment in South Africa's expanding mining industry.

In 1951 Portugal declared Mozambique to be its overseas province and by 1970 some 200,000 Portuguese settlers – mainly peasant and working class people – had been brought to the country by the Portuguese government.

Nationalist groups began to form in the 1960s; three banned groups merged to form Frelimo (Frente de Libertação de Moçambique), which led a war of attrition to win independence. Frelimo's first president, Dr Eduardo Mondlane, was assassinated by the Portuguese in 1969. After the 1974 revolution in Portugal, the new government soon started negotiations with the liberation movements in the overseas provinces on self-determination. Mozambique became independent on 25 June 1975. Some 90% of the Portuguese settlers left the country, creating a skills vacuum.

Frelimo, under Samora Machel, the country's first president, came to power with strong socialist ideals and the aim of rapid development; initially it made considerable improvements in health and education. However, authority was rigidly centralised

and some policies were heavy-handed – in particular, the forced creation of communal rural villages.

Civil war broke out in the late 1970s between the government and Renamo (Resistência Nacional Moçambicana). Renamo was first supported by the white regime in Rhodesia (now Zimbabwe) and later by South Africa. Commanding widespread support from the disaffected, Renamo was especially active in central provinces such as Sofala, Manica and Zambézia, and later on in the south. Through sabotage, Renamo managed to destroy much of the country's economic and social infrastructure: roads and railways, schools and health centres, houses, shops and factories. Millions of Mozambicans fled as refugees into neighbouring countries, or became *deslocados* (the internally displaced people). More than 1 million people were killed. Machel was killed in a mysterious air crash in 1986 and was succeeded as president by Joaquim Chissano, the former foreign minister.

The new constitution adopted in 1990 introduced into the country a multiparty democratic system and a free-market economy, thus paving the way for the peace process. Negotiations mediated by the Italian Roman Catholic community of Sant'Egidio culminated in a peace agreement in October 1992; a UN peacekeeping force arrived in July 1993, and demobilisation of troops began in mid-March 1994. In the multiparty elections of October 1994 President Chissano was re-elected with 53% of the votes, his main rival, Renamo leader Afonso Dhlakama, securing 34%. In the parliamentary elections Frelimo won 129 seats (44% of the votes), Renamo 112 seats (38%) and the Democratic Union nine seats (5%).

Mozambique, which had long been interested in Commonwealth membership, became the Commonwealth's 53rd member (and the first not to have once been associated with the British Empire) with the agreement of all the other members, at the Commonwealth Heads of Government Meeting in New Zealand in November 1995.

Religion: Christians 30% (mainly Roman Catholics), Muslims 20% (mainly in the north), most of the rest holding traditional beliefs, which incorporate some Christian practices.

Health: Public spending on health was 4% of GDP in 2009. The national health service lost its monopoly of health care in 1992. 47% of the population uses an improved drinking water source and 17% have adequate sanitation facilities (2009). Infant mortality was 92 per 1,000 live births in 2010 (180 in 1960). Malaria and AIDS are serious problems. In 2009, 11.5% of people aged 15–49 were HIV positive – and there are regular outbreaks of cholera.

Education: There are seven years of compulsory education starting at age six. Primary school comprises cycles of five and two years and secondary two cycles each of three years. Some 35% of pupils complete primary school (2009). The school year starts in January.

Tertiary education is provided at Eduardo Mondlane University (in Maputo); Universidade Pedagógica (Maputo, and branches in Beira and Nampula); Higher Institute for International Relations (Maputo); and Universidade Lúrio (established in 2006, with campuses at Nampula, Pemba and Niassa, in the three most northerly provinces). Private tertiary institutions include Higher Polytechnic and University Institute (1996, Maputo, and a branch in Quelimane); Catholic University (1997, Beira); and Higher Institute for Science and Technology of Mozambique (1997, Maputo). Literacy among people aged 15–24 is 71% (2009).

Media: The daily newspapers are *Notícias* (largest and oldest and partly government-owned) and *Diário de Moçambique* (independent), both in Portuguese. *Demos*, *Domingo*, *Fim de Semana*, *Savana* and *Zambeze* are published weekly in Portuguese.

Television is a very popular medium in urban areas, radio in the rural areas. Televisão de Moçambique, the public TV service, is the sole national network, and Radio Moçambique is the public radio provider operating national and provincial services in Portuguese, English and indigenous languages. There are several private TV channels and radio stations.

Some 9% of households have TV sets (2006). There are 14 personal computers (2005) and 42 internet users (2010) per 1,000 people.

Communications: Country code 258; internet domain '.mz'. Main towns are connected by satellite phones. Mobile phone coverage is generally good in urban areas. There are internet cafes in Maputo. Postal services are available in main centres.

There are 4 main telephone lines and 309 mobile phone subscriptions per 1,000 people (2010).

Public holidays: New Year's Day, Heroes' Day (3 February), Women's Day (7 April), Workers' Day (1 May), Independence Day (25 June), Lusaka Peace Agreement Day (7 September), Armed Forces Day (25 September), Peace and National Reconciliation Day (4 October), Maputo City Day (Maputo only, 10 November), Family/Christmas Day (25 December).

Chimoio City Professional School
A Profession, A Challenge

Location
Chimoio, the capital city of Manica Province, is an important commercial centre for the trade of agricultural products which come in from the fertile surrounding areas. Chimoio City Professional School is about 5 km outside the city.

Courses
- 1997: First students enrolled and initial courses offered were Carpentry and Joinery Mechanics
- 1999: Construction courses offered
- 2006: Agricultural Horticulture courses offered

Agriculture
- Two plots of land for cultivation
- 50 hectares for tomato plantation projects
- 70 hectares for livestock projects
- A farm is connected to the school to maintain food for the community

On-going projects
- An industrial centre to process agricultural products is under construction

Potential projects
The School can add to its capacity-building role with the addition of funds and infrastructure for these projects:
- Expansion of woodworking shops
- Construction of an agricultural workshop and training ground for agriculture
- Installation of a hatchery business

The Minister of Education gave Chimoio City Professional School vocational school status in May 2011, in light of the professional training the School offers.

Contact
Manuel Joaquim Jardim
General Director
Escola Profissional da Cidade de Chimoio
Rua de Matshinho
KM5 Chimoio
Mozambique

Director Eng. Manuel Joaquim Jardim

Tel: +258 239 1 0033/34
Fax: +258 239 1 0034
Email: manojjardim@gmail.com

Economy

KEY FACTS 2010

GNI:	US$10.3bn
GNI p.c.:	US$440
GDP growth:	7.3% p.a. 2006–10
Inflation:	9.5% p.a. 2006–10

The government first embarked on economic reforms in the late 1980s, aiming to undercut the unofficial economy, give real value to the currency and remove administrative hindrances to productive enterprises. Subsidies to state enterprises in deficit were progressively reduced. Food subsidies in urban areas were removed in 1988. After 1989, the government focused on reducing poverty, improving living standards and strengthening the country's institutions. An ambitious privatisation programme was implemented from the mid-1990s and efficiency in the former state enterprises rose dramatically. Fishing is an important activity and prawns are a major export. Aluminium exports grew rapidly after the Mozal smelter came on stream in 2000. Large reserves of natural gas and coal have been found, and gas and coal are set to be important exports, driving strong growth in the 2010s. Other

Real Growth in GDP

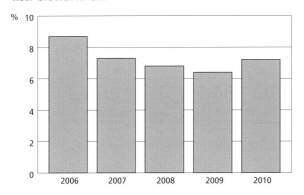

Inflation

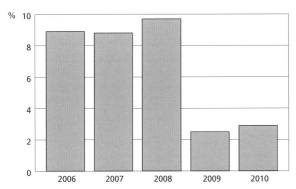

GDP by Sector (2010)

■	Agriculture	4%
□	Industry	28%
▨	Services	69%

Gateway to the Far East

Matola is the second largest city and the biggest industrial area in Mozambique due to its rapid expansion. The City has had its own elected municipal government since 1998.

According to the Mayor of Matola, Arão Nhancale, the municipal area has 500 businesses from several sectors, namely agri-industry, metal-mechanics, construction materials, the food and drinks industry, and chemicals and paints. The industrial sector is dominated by large-scale projects, whose contribution to GDP is a reflection of new investments in Matola and the regeneration of industry.

Highlights

- **Matola Port** has significant regional potential and is handling growing volumes of trade from South Africa, Botswana, Swaziland and Zimbabwe. It is southern Africa's nearest port to the rapidly developing mega-markets of Asia and is the closest deep water port to Johannesburg, Mpumalanga and Limpopo.

- **Matola Coal Terminal (TCM)** has a capacity of 6 million tons per annum. When phase 4 is complete it will expand the capacity to 26 million tons. The project underway should make it possible for ships with a 250,000 ton capacity to moor at the terminal.

- **Matola Gas Company (MGC):** Applying the benefits of natural gas for the social upliftment of the community is a priority for MGC, who recently built and donated the first community kitchen in Matola. This facility was aimed at improving the living conditions of the local people ensuring that the poorer communities have access to and share in the benefits of Mozambique's own energy source. Several industrial investors, notably the Mozal aluminium smelter and the Cimentos de Moçambique cement factory have realised the benefits of natural gas.

The Lord Mayor of Matola Mr Arão Nhancale

Contact

The Lord Mayor of Matola
Mr Arão Nhancale
Matola City Council
Avenida do Municipio No. 44
Matola
Mozambique

Tel: +258 2 481 0006
Email: anhahaia@yahoo.com.br

significant exports include electricity (from the Cahora Bassa dam on the Zambezi river), tobacco and cotton fibre.

Mozambique's economy has since 1994 been recovering after almost two decades of war and underdevelopment. The government's reconstruction and reform programme has been supported by the international financial institutions and from donors. Growth from the mid-1990s was very strong and new confidence in the economy began to attract investment. This growth started from a very low base: the country is among the world's poorest and is heavily dependent on aid, compounded in February 2000 by the disastrous floods, when 650,000 people were made homeless, huge areas of farmland and 30,000 cattle lost, and roads and bridges destroyed, and again in early 2001 – though damage was less severe.

Until 1987 the metical was maintained at an artificially high level and a black market rate of 50 times the official rate developed. Between 1987 and mid-1994 the currency depreciated by 14,000%. Then from the mid-1990s, with continuing strong growth, the metical remained reasonably stable and inflation was brought under control, until it climbed over 10% again in the early 2000s, and monetary policy had to be tightened to stabilise the currency.

The strong growth of the 1990s was interrupted briefly in 2000, due to the devastation caused by the extensive floods, and then resumed at 13% in 2001. The Mozambican economy has been increasingly resilient to external shocks. A booming construction sector and continued growth in agricultural production have helped sustain strong economic growth which averaged nearly 8% p.a. during 2002–07, and continued at 6.8% in 2008, 6.4% in 2009 and 7.2% p.a. in 2010–11, in spite of the world economic downturn.

Constitution

Status:	Republic with executive president
Legislature:	Assembléia da República
Independence:	25 June 1975

A new constitution was adopted in November 1990, replacing the independence constitution. Separating executive, legislative and judiciary powers, it enshrined the principles of political pluralism and election by secret ballot of a government based on majority rule. The president is head of state and government and is directly elected every five years for a maximum of two terms. He or she appoints the prime minister and council of ministers. The national legislature is the 250-member Assembléia da República, members of which are also elected by direct, universal adult suffrage every five years.

The 1990 constitution abolished the death penalty, affirmed the right to strike and protected freedom of movement. It also avows the right to live in a 'balanced environment' and establishes the framework for a liberal market economy and the private ownership of land.

Under the constitution that was adopted in November 2004 and came into force in January 2005, the Constitutional Council was established to ensure strict observance of the constitution, including the electoral acts; also established was the Council of State – comprising the prime minister, and representatives of the opposition and civil society – to advise the president on specific matters. The ombudsman ensures protection of citizens' rights in the public realm. The new constitution emphasises that its interpretation should always be consistent with the Universal Declaration of Human Rights.

Politics

Last elections:	October 2009 (legislative and presidential)
Next elections:	2014
Head of state:	President Armando Emilio Guebuza
Head of government:	the president
Ruling party:	Frelimo

President Joaquim Chissano and his party, Frelimo (Frente de Libertaçâo de Moçambique), won the presidential and parliamentary elections in December 1999. Chissano secured 52.3% of the popular vote and Afonso Dhlakama – leader of Renamo (Resistência Nacional Moçambicana) and the candidate for 11 opposition parties – received 47.7%. In the parliamentary elections Frelimo took 133 seats (48.5%) and Renamo 117 (38.8%).

Chissano announced in mid-2001 that he would not stand for a third term in the election due in 2004 and in June 2002 Frelimo selected Armando Guebuza as its new leader and presidential candidate.

In the December 2004 elections Guebuza – with 63.7% of the votes – and Frelimo – with 160 seats – defeated Dhlakama (31.7%) and Renamo (90 seats). Renamo immediately alleged electoral fraud and threatened to boycott parliament. Commonwealth observers and experts, who attended the elections, expressed concern at the low turnout (estimated at 36%); they further concluded that conditions did exist for the free expression of the will of the people but that some degree of fraud had taken place which could conceivably have been sufficient to affect the results.

In October 2009 Guebuza and Frelimo were returned to power. In the presidential contest Guebuza received 75% of votes, Renamo leader Dhlakama 16% and Daviz Simango of the Democratic Movement of Mozambique (MDM) 9%; the turnout was 45%. In the parliamentary elections Frelimo won 191 seats (with 75% of votes), Renamo 51 seats (18%) and MDM 8 (4%). Commonwealth observers, who were once again present, found that the election had generally been well conducted, though there were concerns about lack of transparency in the work of the National Elections Commission.

International relations

Mozambique is a member of the African, Caribbean and Pacific Group of States, African Union, Indian Ocean Rim Association for Regional Cooperation, Non-Aligned Movement, Organisation of Islamic Cooperation, Southern African Development Community, United Nations and World Trade Organization.

Traveller information

Local laws and conventions: It is a legal requirement to carry identity documents or notarised copies of documents at all times and to present them if stopped at a police checkpoint.

Severe punishments are imposed for smuggling and drug taking, which is illegal.

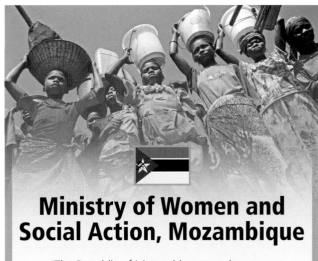

Ministry of Women and Social Action, Mozambique

'The Republic of Mozambique attaches great importance to the issues of gender equality and advancement of women.'
Hon. Minister Iolanda Cintura

The Ministry of Women and Social Action (Ministerio da Mulher e Acção Social (MMAS)) is the state governing body that directs the implementation of policies relating to the emancipation and development of women and social action within the country.

Mission

The Ministry of Women and Social Action promotes the emancipation and advancement of women in the political, economic, social and cultural development of the country. It encourages family stability, enhancing women's role in the protection of its members and helps to shape the citizens of the future. It also provides assistance for population groups which lack social, psychological, material and moral support, especially women, children, the elderly and disabled, and all other social groups in vulnerable positions.

The MMAS promotes and co-ordinates the activities of governmental and non-governmental organisations working in the areas of women, gender and social protection.

Hon. Minister Iolanda Maria Pedro Campos Cintura Seuane

Contact

MMAS
No. 86, Rua da Tchamba
Maputo
Mozambique
Tel: +258 21 35 0300

Mrs Ivete Ferrao Alane
Permanent Secretary
Email: ivete.alane@mmas.gov.mz

Mr Sansao Buque, Press Advisor
Email: sansao.buque@mmas.gov.mz

Mr Graciano Langa,
Deputy Director of Planning and Co-operation
Email: graciano.langa@mmas.gov.mz

www.mmas.gov.mz

It is illegal to photograph airports, government offices, military establishments, residences and the police or officials without permission from the Ministry of Information.

For business meetings prior appointments are recommended. January is best avoided for business trips, as it is the main holiday month. Business is usually conducted in Portuguese, but translation facilities are available in Maputo. Office hours are Mon–Thur 0730–1230 and 1400–1730, Fri 0730–1230 and 1400–1700.

Immigration and customs: Passports must be valid for six months and those planning to travel on to South Africa should ensure they have two pages free in their passport.

Visas are required by all and should be obtained before visiting the country. Tourist visas bought at the border are not accepted. Heavy fines are imposed on those overstaying their visa.

The land-crossing with South Africa – the Lebombo/Ressano Garcia border – can be very busy during holiday periods.

It is prohibited to import or export the local currency, and foreign exchange must be through commercial banks. The import of firearms requires a permit.

A yellow fever vaccination certificate is required by those arriving from an infected area.

Travel within the country: Traffic drives on the left. An international driving permit is recommended and car hire is available in Maputo and Beira (payment must be in a hard currency). Visitors must keep their licences on them at all times. Tarred roads connect Maputo with Beira, and Beira with Tete. Fuel is only available in major towns and all vehicles should be stocked with emergency supplies. Speed limits are usually 40–50kph in towns and 120kph on the open road.

Regular bus services cover most of the country. In more rural areas, converted passenger trucks, known as *chapas*, are also available. Domestic flights link Maputo with Beira, Nampula, Pemba, Quelimane, Vilanculos and Tete. Flights must be booked well in advance. An air taxi service is also available.

There are three unconnected rail networks, and services are infrequent.

Travel health: It is recommended to take out adequate health insurance that will cover transport and treatment in South Africa.

Polio, tetanus, typhoid, cholera and Hepatitis A vaccinations are recommended. In addition, malaria is endemic and presents a serious health risk, and prophylaxis is strongly advised. Visitors should also bring insect repellent and suitable clothing to protect themselves against mosquito bites. Bilharzia is present.

Drinking bottled water is advised.

Money: Credit cards are becoming progressively more accepted in Maputo and some of the larger cities, though it is advisable that visitors check with their bank before using their credit card in Mozambique. Money can be obtained from some ATMs using Visa credit or debit cards. US dollars and South African rand should also be taken, as they are widely accepted; travellers cheques are difficult and expensive to exchange. Banking hours are Mon–Fri 0730–1530.

There were 771,000 tourist arrivals in 2007.

Further information

Government of Mozambique: www.portaldogoverno.gov.mz

Banco de Moçambique (central bank): www.bancomoc.mz

Commonwealth Secretariat: www.thecommonwealth.org

Commonwealth of Nations: www.commonwealth-of-nations.org/Mozambique

Namibia

KEY FACTS

Joined Commonwealth:	1990
Population:	2,283,000 (2010)
GDP p.c. growth:	2.1% p.a. 1990–2010
UN HDI 2011:	world ranking 120
Official language:	English
Time:	GMT plus 1–2hr
Currency:	Namibia dollar (N$)

Geography

Area:	824,269 sq km
Coastline:	1,570km
Capital:	Windhoek

Namibia in south-west Africa is one of the driest and most sparsely populated countries on Earth. It is bounded by the South Atlantic Ocean on the west, Angola to the north, Botswana to the east and South Africa to the south. The Caprivi Strip, a narrow extension of land in the extreme north-east, connects it to Zambia. Namibia comprises 13 regions (from south to north): Karas, Hardap, Khomas, Erongo, Omaheke, Otjozondjupa, Kunene, Oshikoto, Okavango, Omusati, Oshana, Caprivi and Ohangwena.

Time: GMT plus 1hr. The clock is advanced by one hour from the first Sunday in September to the first Sunday in April.

Area: 824,269 sq km (including Walvis Bay 1,124 sq km).

Topography: The country has three broad zones: the Namib Desert to the west; the Kalahari Desert to the east; and the Central Plateau. The plateau, made up of mountains, rocky outcrops, sand-filled valleys and undulating upland plains, covers over 50% of the land area. It includes Windhoek, the capital, and slopes eastward to the Kalahari Basin and northward to the Etosha Pan, the largest of Namibia's saline lakes. The Skeleton Coast, from Swakopmund

Did you know...

Frank Fredericks, born in Windhoek in October 1967, took the Commonwealth Games Men's 200 Metres record at the 1994 Games in Victoria, Canada.

With population density of less than 3 per sq km, Namibia is the most sparsely populated country in the Commonwealth and in Africa.

Namibia is one of the world's major producers of uranium; it was fourth largest in 2010.

The country has some 1,570km of coastline.

to the northern border, is a waterless stretch of high sand dunes pounded by a high surf, much celebrated in tales of the sea. The Kaokoveld Mountains run parallel, covering 66,000 sq km. Shifting sand dunes of the Namib Desert spread inland for 80–130km, covering 15% of the land area.

Climate: Arid, semi-arid and sub-humid. Prolonged periods of drought are characteristic. There is little precipitation apart from rare thunderstorms in the arid zone of the Namib Desert coast, with rainfall rising to 600mm or more in the sub-humid north-eastern border with Angola and the Caprivi Strip. Rain falls in summer (October to April). The cold Benguela current gives the Namib Desert thick coastal fog.

Environment: The most significant environmental issues are the scarcity of natural freshwater resources and desertification.

Vegetation: Much of the terrain is grassland, or plains dotted with scrub. Namibia supports at least 345 different grasses and 2,400 types of flowering plant. Characteristic native plants are acacias, balsam trees, omwandi trees, fig and date palms, makalani palms, mopane (shrubs or trees), monkey-bread trees, marula trees, yellow-blossomed omuparara trees, violet-blossomed apple-leaf trees and shrubs such as the raisin-bush, coffee bush and camphor bush. Aloes, mesembryanthemums and other succulents flower on the Southern Namib dunes after rainfall. White-flowering ana trees flourish in dry river beds. Forest covers 9% of the land area, having declined at 0.9% p.a. 1990–2010. Arable land comprises 1% of the total land area.

Ministry of Safety and Security,

The Ministry of Safety and Security (MSS) was established in March 2005, bringing together the Namibian Police Force and the Namibian Correctional Service, which constitute its two components. The Police Force and Prison Service were established upon the country's independence in 1990.

MISSION

To maintain law and order and rehabilitation of offenders, in partnership with our stakeholders towards ensuring Safety and Security within Namibia.

VISION

To be a leading Institution towards a safe and secure Namibia.

CORE VALUES

Team work	Spirit of togetherness with cohesion towards achievement of the organisation
Integrity	Spirit of togetherness with cohesion towards the achievement of the organisation's goals
Fairness	Incorruptible and free from undue influence and dishonesty
Transparency	Execution of mandate without prejudice
Commitment	Clear written procedures and directives
Accountability	Conscious and answerable for our actions
Loyalty	Being patriotic and duty-bound to the Namibian nation and the government

LEADERSHIP

- The Minister, supported by a Deputy Minister, is the political head of the Ministry of Safety and Security and represents the Ministry in both the Cabinet and the National Assembly

- The Permanent Secretary is the accounting officer and administrative head of the Ministry who reports to the Minister and to the Prime Minister who is the Chief Administrator of the whole public service.

- The Namibian Police Force and the Namibian Correctional Service are headed by the Inspector General of the Namibian Police Force and the Commissioner General of Namibian Correctional Service, respectively. They report directly to the Minister on issues pertaining to the operations of police and correctional services.

OPERATIONAL PLATFORM

The business operation of the Ministry of Safety and Security is mainly guided by the following strategic instruments: the Namibian Constitution, Police Act, 1990, Prisons Act, 1998 (Act 17 of 1998), Vision 2030, the National Development Plans and the Election Manifesto of the SWAPO Party, Millennium Development Goals and the Decentralisation Policy.

Vision 2030 identifies domestic and regional peace security as 'Indispensable conditions for our country's socio-economic development. It also identifies the creation and maintenance of an "atmosphere of peace and security to provide citizens with hope for a better quality of life for all"'.

In ensuring peace and security, the Ministry of Safety and Security will align its mission, strategies and programmes with Cabinet decisions, priorities, directives and its mission to both the goal and the strategy of Vision 2030.

Namibia

Ensuring the internal security, maintenance of law and order, provision of safe custody, rehabilitation, and safe integration for offenders.

NAMIBIAN POLICE FORCE

The provision of safety and security in Namibia vests in the Namibian Police Force, a task which the Force wishes and commits itself to carry out diligently to the satisfaction of the nation.

MANDATE

- Preservation of the internal security of Namibia;
- Maintenance of law and order;
- Investigation of any offence or alleged offence;
- Prevention of crime; and
- Protection of life and property.

These functions are discharged in partnership with all other stakeholders and role players in the maintenance of internal security.

The fundamental functions of policing is to protect and serve all people in Namibia by reducing all kinds of crime, in partnership with the community and other law enforcement agencies.

NAMIBIAN CORRECTIONAL SERVICE

The Namibian Correctional Service was under the Prisons Act, 1998 (Act No. 17 of 1998), prescribing powers, duties and procedures.

MANDATE

- Provide safe custody of offenders;
- Provide care to offenders
- Rehabilitate offenders
- Ensure successful re-integration of offenders into the community as law-abiding citizens

Hon. Minister:	**Nangolo Mbumba**
Deputy Minister:	**Erastus Uutoni**
Inspector-General of Nampol:	**S.H. Ndeitunga**
Commissioner-General, Namibian Correctional Service:	**E. Shikongo**
Permanent Secretary:	**Samuel Goagoseb**

Contact
Mr Samuel Goagoseb
Permanent Secretary
Tel: +264 61 284 6205
Email: sgoagoseb@mpcs.gov.na

www.mpcs.gov.na

Ministry of Defence, Namibia

Introduction

The Ministry of Defence (MOD) is one of the 24 Ministries of the Government of the Republic of Namibia. The MOD was established soon after Independence in 1990 as the department of state responsible for the organisation and administration of the Namibian Defence Force (NDF).

The MOD's main responsibilities include formulating and implementing defence policy for the government, providing a central operational and administrative headquarters for the National Defence Force, overseeing the effective administration, financial management and accountability of the NDF, equipment procurement and ensuring an environment conducive to the welfare of MOD staff. The MOD is tasked with delivering professional services, advice and administrative support to the NDF and ensure that the Namibian people enjoy 'peace and security' in line with the provisions of the Constitution, as stipulated in Articles 118-120 and as elaborated in the Defence Act, 2002.

Vision

The vision of the MOD is to be a reliable and committed national defence organisation with capacity and capability to defend Namibia's interest and render effective peacetime support.

Mission

The MOD mission is to operate a cost-effective, professional and highly mobile national defence system that will safeguard Namibia's territory, inhabitants and national interests and contribute to nation development and world peace.

Core values

Patriotism and Dedication, Respect for the Rule of Law, Integrity, Transparency and Accountability, Professionalism, Teamwork and Co-operation.

Contact

Ministry of Defence
Private Bag 13307
WINDHOEK/NAMIBIA

Hon. Maj. Gen. (Rtd) Charles DNP Namoloh,
(Ho-Chi-Minh), MP
Minister of Defence
Tel: +264 61 204 9111
Fax: +264 61 23 2518
Email: cnamoloh@mod.gov.na

Mr Petrus Shivute
Permanent Secretary
Tel: +264 61 204 2055
Fax: +264 61 22 0523
Email: pshivute@mod.gov.na

Lt Gen. Epaphras Denga Ndaitwah
Chief of Defence Force
Tel: +264 61 204 2087
Fax: +264 61 25 8215
Email: ndaitwah2@yahoo.com

Hon. Maj. Gen. (Rtd) Charles DNP Namoloh, (Ho-Chi-Minh), MP, Minister of Defence

Hon. Lempy Lucas, MP, Deputy Minister of Defence

Mr Petrus Shivute, Permanent Secretary of Defence

Lt Gen. Epaphras Denga Ndaitwah, Chief of Defence Force

Col (Rtd) Clement Muhamubi Mwaala, Deputy Permanent Secretary of Defence

Mr Abraham Iilonga, Under Secretary of Defence

www.mod.gov.na

Wildlife: Namibia's wildlife is famous, particularly the exceptional range of bird species found in the wetlands. There are 201 recorded species of birds (2002), with 11 thought to be endangered. The pans in game parks provide drinking water for most of the typical African wild mammal species. The Etosha National Park, the country's most famous reserve and one of the largest in the world, contains lions, leopards, elephants, rhino and zebras. The government has a strong conservation policy, but game poaching in the reserves is diminishing stocks of many species. The Namibian seas are naturally rich in fish, and in seabirds which prey on fish.

Main towns: Windhoek (capital, Khomas region, pop. 315,900 in 2010), Rundu (Kavango, 81,500), Walvis Bay (Erongo, 67,200), Oshakati (Oshana, 39,700), Swakopmund (Erongo, 34,300), Grootfontein (Otjozondjupa, 29,000), Katima Mulilo (Caprivi, 27,900), Okahandja (Otjozondjupa, 25,300), Otjiwarongo (Otjozondjupa, 23,000), Rehoboth (Hardap, 20,900), Gobabis (Omaheke, 19,900), Usakos (Erongo, 18,700), Lüderitz (Karas, 18,300), Keetmanshoop (Karas, 15,400) and Tsumeb (Oshikoto, 10,800).

Transport: There are 42,240km of roads, 13% paved. Two long-haul road projects were completed in the late 1990s: the Trans-Caprivi Highway and the Trans-Kalahari Highway through Botswana to South Africa. These arteries enable Namibia to provide landlocked central African countries with an outlet to the sea as well as greatly reducing the journey to Johannesburg.

The 2,400km railway network was established under German colonial rule and much-needed upgrading was carried out from the mid-1990s. Walvis Bay, the only deep-water port, which incorporates an export processing zone, is the main outlet for exports. Use of Lüderitz, Namibia's second port, has increased, due to a rise in fishing activities.

Air transport is important because of Namibia's size. There are more than 350 aerodromes and airstrips, with licensed airports in the main towns and mining centres, including the international airport some 40km from Windhoek.

Society

KEY FACTS 2010

Population per sq km:	3
Life expectancy:	62 years
Net primary enrolment:	90%

Population: 2,283,000 (2010); density is extremely low overall and 38% lives in urban areas; growth 2.4% p.a. 1990–2010; birth rate 26 per 1,000 people (43 in 1970); life expectancy 62 years (53 in 1970 and 62 in 1990).

The Ovambo and Kavango together constitute about 60% of the total population. Other groups are the Herero, Damara, Nama and the Caprivians. The San (Bushmen), who are among the world's oldest surviving hunter-gatherers, have lived in this territory for more than 11,000 years. The Basters, who settled in Rehoboth in 1870, stem from marriages between white farmers and Khoi mothers in the Cape. The 'Cape Coloureds', immigrants from South Africa, tend to live in the urban areas. Of the white group of approximately 90,000, about 50% are of South African and 25% of German ancestry, about 20% are Boer 'sudwesters' (longer-established migrants), with a small minority of UK ancestry.

Language: English, Oshiwambo, Herero, Nama, Afrikaans and German. The official language is English, first or second language to only about 20%. Oshiwambo is spoken throughout most of the north. The Caprivians speak Lozi as their main language. Afrikaans is widely spoken and is the traditional language of the Cape Coloureds and Baster communities.

Religion: Christians 80–90% (predominantly Lutherans), the rest holding traditional beliefs.

Health: Public spending on health was 4% of GDP in 2009. 92% of the population uses an improved drinking water source and 33% have access to adequate sanitation facilities (2009). Tuberculosis and malaria are widespread in the north. Infant mortality was 29 per 1,000 live births in 2010 (129 in 1960). AIDS is a serious problem. In 2009, 13.1% of people aged 15–49 were HIV positive.

Education: Public spending on education was 8.1% of GDP in 2010. There are ten years of compulsory education starting at age six. Primary school comprises seven years and secondary five. In 1993 English replaced Afrikaans as the main language of instruction. The Namibian Constitution provides free education until the age of 16 or completion of primary education. Some 83% of pupils complete primary school (2008). The school year starts in January.

Tertiary education is at the University of Namibia, established in 1993, with its main campus in Windhoek and nine other campuses across the country. The university offers courses in agriculture and natural resources; economics and management sciences; education; engineering and information technology; and law. There is also a polytechnic as well as a technical college and four national teacher-training colleges. Namibian College of Open Learning provides open and distance learning. The female–male ratio for gross enrolment in tertiary education is 1.32:1 (2008). Literacy among people aged 15–24 is 93% (2009). There are extensive adult literacy programmes.

Media: Daily newspapers include *The Namibian* (in English and Oshiwambo), *Namibia Economist*, *New Era* (government-owned), *Die Republikein* (in Afrikaans) and *Allgemeine Zeitung* (in German). *Windhoek Observer* is published weekly.

The Namibian Broadcasting Corporation provides public TV and radio services; several private and international TV channels are available via cable or satellite, and there are many private radio stations broadcasting in the country.

Some 37% of households have TV sets (2007). There are 239 personal computers (2007) and 65 internet users (2010) per 1,000 people.

Communications: Country code 264; internet domain '.na'. Mobile phone coverage is good in the towns but patchy in rural areas. Internet connection is available in main towns; there are internet cafes in Walvis Bay, Swakopmund and Windhoek; and a good postal service.

There are 67 main telephone lines and 672 mobile phone subscriptions per 1,000 people (2010).

Public holidays: New Year's Day, Independence Day (21 March), Workers' Day (1 May), Cassinga Day (4 May), Africa Day (25 May), Heroes' Day (26 August), Human Rights Day (10 December), Christmas Day and Family Day (26 December). Cassinga Day

Namibian Directorate of Civil Aviation (NDCA)

The Directorate of Civil Aviation is a regulatory body in the Ministry of Works and Transport consisting of three Divisions, namely Division Aviation, Administration and Navigation, Division Flight Safety and Security and Division Meteorological Services.

The goal of the Directorate of Civil Aviation is to assure a safe, secure and efficient civil aviation system which contributes to Namibia's national economy by fostering the planning and development of air transport so as to secure the safe and orderly growth of civil aviation, development of airways, aerodromes and air navigation facilities, and to meet the needs of the public for safe, secure, efficient and economical air transport.

To the left is His Excellency the President of Namibia Hifikepunye Pohamba and the Minister of Works and Transport, Honourable Erkki Nghimtina at the official opening of the Air Traffic Control Centre at Eros Airport

Facilitating Air Transportation through Airport Development

The Namibia Airports Company (NAC) is a State Owned Enterprise that provides airport infrastructure, facilities and services for domestic and international airlines, passengers, clients and customers. The NAC owns and manages eight airports, namely Hosea Kutako International Airport, Eros, Walvis Bay, Lüderitz, Keetmanshoop, Ondangwa, Rundu and Katima Mulilo Airports. The NAC contributes and learns from the industry through its membership to the Airports Council International, the International Air Cargo Association, Namibia Chamber of Commerce and the Namibian Tourism Board.

The NAC has successfully undertaken several strategic infrastructure and commercial development projects with the aim of improving its overall service delivery. The adoption of contemporary airport planning and management approaches and practices has ensured good and healthy profitable ratios and returns. These good returns have been achieved while maintaining a delicate balance between efficiency of service delivery, affordability of the airport facilities, and services by airport users.

www.airports.com.na

Carrying the spirit of Namibia

Air Namibia (Pty) Limited is a proprietary limited company with the Government of Namibia as its sole shareholder. It is among the seven African carriers operating successful airlines and a certified member of International Air Transport Association. As a national carrier, Air Namibia has a common operational goal, namely to continue operating successfully and achieving consistent commercial success by making a positive contribution to the economic development of Namibia.

Air Namibia was the first airline to achieve the IATA Barcode ticketing system in Africa. As of May 2012, Air Namibia will have destinations into most capital cities of the SADC region. Not only are we technologically attuned to international standards, we also continue to offer excellent customer service. This is evident through our continuous award-winning records for Best Regional Airline Award on no less than six occasions.

www.airnamibia.com.na

Aviation Safety and Security
Ensuring high levels of precision, safety and security

History was made in December 2011 when the country's new air traffic control centre at Eros Airport became operational as a surveillance control centre for the Namibian Flight Information Region (FIR) above FL145 using state-of-the-art equipment. To manage the transfer from procedural control to surveillance control, the DCA is assisted by six controllers from Sweden, recruited by the ICAO.

Last year's launch of surveillance control in Namibian airspace above FL145 is only the first step. Further steps on the way forward include:

- Launch of surveillance operations in Windhoek TMA is expected in the third quarter of this year.
- Surveillance operations will be launched in Walvis Bay TMA.

Contact

Ms A. Simana Paulo, Acting Director of Civil Aviation
Tel: +264 61 70 2212/13/14   **Email:** director@dca.com.na
www.dca.com.na

remembers those killed in 1978 when the South African Defence Force attacked a SWAPO refugee camp at Cassinga in southern Angola. Africa Day commemorates the founding of the Organization of African Unity in 1963 (now African Union). Heroes' Day commemorates the start of SWAPO's armed struggle against South African rule and those killed in the struggle. Human Rights Day remembers those killed in 1959 when residents of a black township near Windhoek resisted forcible removal to the present-day Katutura.

Religious holidays whose dates vary from year to year include Good Friday, Easter Monday and Ascension Day.

Economy

KEY FACTS 2010

GNI:	US$10.3bn
GNI p.c.:	US$4,500
GDP growth:	4.1% p.a. 2006–10
Inflation:	7.1% p.a. 2006–10

Real Growth in GDP

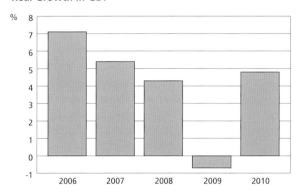

Inflation

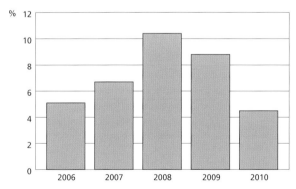

GDP by Sector (2010)

■ Agriculture	10%
□ Industry	33%
▨ Services	57%

Namibia's economy is driven by mining and fish processing. Since independence in 1990, exports of diamonds, uranium, zinc and fish products have grown strongly. Most people in rural areas of this vast country, however, remain largely unaffected by these activities. Government policy is to raise per capita income, to develop the private sector, and to encourage diversification into manufacturing activities, such as clothing and textiles, and eco-tourism. It is also committed to restraining growth in public spending and controlling inflation.

Having fallen short of the national development plan target of 5% p.a. in the latter 1990s and early 2000s – due to environmental factors such as drought and the finite stocks of fish – growth picked up from 2002 on account of increased diamond production, the opening of a new zinc mine and refinery, and increased textiles output. It averaged 5.7% p.a. during 2004–08. But in the face of the world economic downturn and consequent falls in demand for Namibia's minerals, the economy stalled in the latter part of 2008, stagnating in 2009 (–0.7%), but recovering in 2010 (4.8%) and 2011 (about 4%).

Mining

The sector is the largest source of export earnings. Namibia has great mineral wealth, including diamonds, uranium, copper, zinc, gold, silver, phosphate and oil. Zinc production rose rapidly from the mid-1990s. Onshore reserves of diamonds are becoming depleted, but offshore output has risen quickly, helped by new mining technology. The large Husab uranium mine is due to start production in 2014. Large offshore phosphate deposits have been discovered near Walvis Bay. Recent reports suggest good prospects of significant discoveries of offshore oil.

Constitution

Status:	Republic with executive president
Legislature:	Parliament
Independence:	21 March 1990

The constitution provides for a multiparty democracy in a unitary republic. The president is head of state and government and commander-in-chief of the defence force. Elected by direct universal adult suffrage at intervals of not more than five years, he or she must receive more than 50% of the votes cast. The president appoints the government, the armed forces chief of staff and members of a Public Service Commission, but the National Assembly may revoke any appointment. He or she can only serve two successive directly elected five-year terms. The president may dissolve the National Assembly, and may also proclaim a state of national emergency and rule by decree, subject to the approval of the National Assembly.

Legislative power is vested in a National Assembly of 72 elected members, and up to six nominated but non-voting members, all members serving for a maximum of five years. The National Assembly can remove the president from office by passing an impeachment motion with a two-thirds majority. The prime minister is leader of government business in parliament.

An upper house, the National Council, is provided for in the constitution and was formally convened in February 1993. It consists of two members from each of the 13 regions, elected by regional councils and serving for a term of six years. The National

City of Windhoek

City of many faces

It is 22 years since Namibia joined the Commonwealth and nine years after the City of Windhoek joined the Commonwealth Local Government Forum. Today, we renew our commitment to the shared values of mutual respect and equality of our cities as we uphold the fundamental principles of democracy.

Alderwoman Elaine Trepper,
Mayor of the City of Windhoek

Contact
Office of the Mayor
International Relations Office

Tel: +264 61 290 2285
Fax: +264 61 290 2091
E-mail: cei@windhoekcc.org.na
www.cityofwindhoek.org.na

As the capital city of Namibia, the City has drawn a wide spectrum of nationalities that contribute immensely to its multicultural identity. Windhoek is a haven for tourism, conferencing and an ideal investment destination.

Infrastructure development
Windhoek is not only situated in the centre of the country, where it balances Namibia's political and economic leadership, but its position provides an economic impetus to neighbouring countries. The City is linked by well-paved roads to all national parks and tourist attraction sites. The City also offers world-class public security and safety through its local City Police and well-managed traffic flow. Additionally, the City of Windhoek has earned an image of 'the cleanest City in Africa' through its effective waste management and some of the best architecture a city can offer.

Tourism
Many restaurants respond to the City's cultural diversity by offering tourists a wide range of traditional and international cuisine. There are social venues, including bars, which offer a wide selection of international wines and liquor.

Investment
Given the political stability, the City of Windhoek has become an important destination for commercial investments. Its well-organised labour market and investor-friendly laws enable investors to do business. Complimenting Namibia's political stability is the City's good reputation and capability to render essential services to investors and its inhabitants in an efficient manner. The City of Windhoek is a modern and technologically advanced city – ideal for investment.

Conferencing
The City of Windhoek has hosted both regional and international conferences of up to 3000 delegates, notably the Miss Universe Beauty Pageant of 1998 and the Africities Summit 2000. The advanced technology in the City also enables it to use video conferencing to targeted audiences. There are modern broadcasting facilities that are complimented by international print media.

Windhoek lives up to the expectations of many visitors. The warmth of its people, well maintained infrastructure and multicultural vibrancy define it as a city that observes the ideals of tolerance, peace and tranquillity.

A Warm Welcome!

Council has limited powers to review legislation passed by the National Assembly and can block bills.

The constitution includes 25 entrenched clauses regarding fundamental human rights and freedoms. There is no death sentence nor detention without trial and the practice and ideology of apartheid is expressly forbidden. Private property rights are guaranteed. Amendments to the constitution can only be made by two-thirds majorities of both houses.

Politics

Last elections:	November 2009 (presidential and legislative)
Next elections:	2014
Head of state:	President Hifikepunye Pohamba
Head of government:	the president
Ruling party:	SWAPO

History

The San (Bushmen), who are among the world's oldest surviving hunter-gatherers, have lived in this territory for over 11,000 years.

In the 19th century, taking advantage of tribal conflicts, Europeans acquired land from chiefs in return for weapons. The British authorities in the Cape annexed the Penguin Islands in 1866 and Walvis Bay in 1878, in response to a request for protection from missionaries. Germany declared a protectorate in 1884 over a 20km-wide belt of land from Lüderitz to the Orange river, and then gained control of the interior. The inhabitants were relegated to 'native reserves' from 1898 and a 1905 German decree expropriated all Herero land and prohibited Herero people from keeping cattle. This led to the Great Resistance War, 1904–08, during which a large proportion of the Herero and Nama population was massacred by the German military. Pass laws were introduced in 1907, as was the institutionalisation of migrant contract labour. Diamond and copper mining began in 1908–09.

During the First World War, German South-West Africa was occupied by South Africa; after the war South Africa extended its control to the northern Namibian communities, helped by the Portuguese rulers of Angola. The Allied Powers refused to allow South Africa to annex the country, renamed South-West Africa (SWA). Instead, South Africa became the designated power under a League of Nations mandate.

Following the founding of the UN in 1945, South Africa refused to convert its mandate into a UN trusteeship. In 1949, 1955 and 1956, disputes between South Africa and the UN over SWA were taken to the International Court of Justice.

A series of petitions to the UN from black leaders in SWA sought to end South African rule. The first black nationalist movement, the South-West Africa National Union (SWANU), was set up in 1959 with the support of the Herero Chiefs Council. In 1960 the South-West Africa People's Organisation (SWAPO) was founded, Ovambo migrant workers forming the base of its membership. SWAPO launched a guerrilla campaign inside Namibia, first clashing with South African police in August 1966. In October 1966, the UN terminated South Africa's mandate and called for it to withdraw from the country, formally named Namibia in 1968. The International Court of Justice ruled in 1971 that South Africa's administration was illegal.

In 1977 a UN contact group comprising the five Western members of the Security Council – the UK, France, the US, Canada and West Germany – began to negotiate plans for Namibia's independence directly with South Africa and SWAPO. In 1978 South Africa announced its acceptance of the contact group's settlement proposal. However, in May that year, South African forces attacked SWAPO's refugee transit camp at Cassinga in southern Angola, leaving 600 dead.

Independence discussions continued for ten years, in the course of which South Africa made several further attacks on SWAPO bases in Angola. In 1981 South Africa demanded that Cuban troops (which were in Angola assisting the Angolan government in a civil war against UNITA rebels) should withdraw from Angola, and made this a condition of its agreement to the UN plan.

At the same time, South Africa began to ease its grip on Namibia, allowing a 'transitional government of national unity' (a coalition of six parties) control over internal affairs from June 1985.

In December 1988, two agreements were signed: one between South Africa, Angola and Cuba, creating the conditions for implementation of the UN plan, the second between Angola and Cuba, setting out a timetable for withdrawal of Cuban troops. A formal ceasefire came into effect in April 1989; this was followed by clashes in northern Namibia between SWAPO and South African forces, resulting in the deaths of some 300 SWAPO fighters.

Nonetheless, progress towards independence continued through 1989. The interim government was dissolved and by September 43,000 exiled Namibians had returned home. Many SWAPO members had been in exile for 27 years. Namibia achieved independence on 21 March 1990 and became the Commonwealth's 50th member.

In 1977 South Africa had annexed Walvis Bay, Namibia's only deep-water port, together with a surrounding 1,124 sq km enclave and the 12 offshore Penguin Islands. Walvis Bay remained a subject of dispute until March 1994, when it and the islands were returned to Namibia.

Independent state

UN-supervised elections were held in November 1989. Ten political parties stood, including SWAPO, which gained 57% of the votes and 41 of 72 seats in the Constituent Assembly. In February 1990 Dr Sam Nujoma was elected by the Constituent Assembly to be the first president of an independent Namibia. Nujoma (76% of the popular vote in the first presidential election) and SWAPO (73% in the National Assembly elections) were returned to power in the December 1994 elections.

In late November 1998, parliament passed a constitutional amendment to allow Nujoma to serve more than two terms. Namibia's High Commissioner to the UK, Ben Ulenga, resigned in protest against both the amendment and Namibia's military involvement in the Democratic Republic of Congo. Ulenga later formed a new political grouping which was registered as the Congress of Democrats.

Sustaining local farmers

Ndeya Manufacturing Services began with Ms Ottilie Haufiku's vision of producing preservative-free peanut butter made from ground nuts grown by local farmers. Having inspired the Development Bank of Namibia's Innovation Fund with this vision, the company received N$50 000 in start-up capital. Ms Haufiku used this money to move the operations of Ndeya Manufacturing closer to her groundnut suppliers, and now employs four full-time employees and directly supports

local community groundnut harvesters through production of 'Mr Peanut'. Following the success of her business within Namibia, Ms Haufiku is now looking to expand into the Angolan market.

As a vibrant upcoming entrepreneur, Ms Haufiku was recently invited to attend the International Visitor Leadership Programme on African Women's Entrepreneurship, held in the United States. As the sole representative from Namibia, Ms Haufiku found this to be a great opportunity to network her peanut butter business and promote Namibia as a stable investment environment. The conference inspired Ms Haufiku to develop better packaging for her product, and to expand her manufacturing business to exporting Namibian fish in the coming year.

Having met inspiring entrepreneurs, such as the US Secretary of State Ms Hilary Clinton, Ms Haufiku is convinced of the value of professional mentoring.

Contact

Ms Ottilie Haufiku
CEO
PO Box 20440
Windhoek
Namibia

Tel: +264 65 24 0943
Email: ndeyagrace@yahoo.com

Ndeya Manufacturing Services is supported by the Innovative Grant Mechanism (IGM) of the Ministry of Environment and Tourism. If you would like to learn more about the IGM or Ndeya Manufacturing Services please contact the CPP office on +264 61 284 2730 or email us esiebritz@cppnam.net. You can also connect with us on Facebook (www.facebook.com/CPP.ISLM)

The elections in November/December 1999 produced a clear win for both the South-West Africa People's Organisation (SWAPO) and President Sam Nujoma. Nujoma secured close to 75% of the votes cast in the presidential poll, while Ben Ulenga of the recently formed Congress of Democrats (CoD) took 11% and the Democratic Turnhalle Alliance (DTA) candidate Kautuuture Kaura 10%. In the parliamentary contest, SWAPO won 55 seats (76% of the votes), the CoD seven (10%) and the DTA seven (9.5%).

In 2001 Nujoma announced he would not seek a fourth term of office and, at its 2004 congress, Hifikepunye Pohamba was chosen as the SWAPO candidate for the presidential election in November 2004.

The November 2004 presidential and legislative elections were won in landslide victories by Pohamba (76.4% of votes) and SWAPO (55 of 72 seats and 75% of the votes). Ulenga (CoD) received 7.3% of the votes in the presidential election and Kaura (DTA) 5.1%, while the CoD won five seats and DTA four.

Pohamba and SWAPO were again returned to government in November 2009 in another landslide. In the presidential poll Pohamba received 76.4% of votes and his main challenger, Hidipo Hamutenya of the Rally for Democracy and Progress (RDP), 11.1%. In the legislative elections SWAPO won 54 seats (and 75.3% of votes) and the RDP 8 seats (11.3%).

International relations

Namibia is a member of the African, Caribbean and Pacific Group of States, African Union, Non-Aligned Movement, Southern African Customs Union, Southern African Development Community, United Nations and World Trade Organization.

Namibia hosts the secretariat of the Southern African Customs Union; the SADC Tribunal; and the SADC Parliamentary Forum.

Traveller information

Local laws and conventions: Drug taking and smuggling is illegal, and penalties for all drug offences are severe. Visitors must not photograph military sites or government buildings and should always seek permission before photographing local people or their property.

Diamonds and other protected resources should be purchased from licensed shops. Those convicted of illegal dealings in diamonds may face large fines or prison sentences. The purchase and export of other protected resources, such as elephant ivory, may be subject to restrictions.

Handguns are strictly prohibited in Namibia.

Visitors should dress conservatively. If visiting rural settlements, travellers should always follow the advice of a local guide.

Lightweight suits are the norm for business meetings. Prior appointments are always necessary. The best times for visiting on business are February to May and September to November. Office hours are Mon–Fri 0800–1700.

Immigration and customs: Passports must be valid for six months after the intended departure date, and visas are required by all except those from Australasia, North America, most of Europe, and some African and Asian countries. Return tickets are essential.

Visitors are advised to make a copy of the relevant pages of their passport and keep it on them at all times for ID purposes.

A yellow fever vaccination certificate will be required by all those arriving from infected countries.

Hunting rifles need a permit, issued by customs when entering the country.

Travel within the country: Traffic drives on the left, and car hire is available at the international airport, in Windhoek and in Walvis Bay. An international driving permit is required.

The speed limit is 60–80kph in urban areas, 80–90kph on gravel roads and 120kph on tar roads.

Flying is the most efficient way to travel the country. Eros Airport (Windhoek) is linked to all major towns via Air Namibia. Chartered flights are also available.

A luxury bus service connects all major cities from North Namibia to South Africa. Travel within Windhoek is limited and it is advisable to use a taxi service.

Rail services are generally slow and most trains run overnight. There are two dedicated luxury train services – one connecting with Upington in South Africa, and the other a weekly connection between Windhoek and Swakopmund that crosses the Namib Desert.

Travel health: Comprehensive health insurance is recommended and all current vaccination requirements should be checked well before travel. Polio vaccinations need to be up to date.

Malaria is endemic in northern Namibia. Visitors will need protection against malaria, and should take insect repellent and suitable loose-fitting clothing to discourage mosquito bites. There is a risk of rabies; bilharzia is present. Cholera cases occur in rural northern Namibia.

Tap water is normally chlorinated. Bottled water is available and is advised for the first few weeks of the stay. Mains water in rural areas should be boiled or sterilised before use.

Money: American Express, Diners Club, Mastercard, Visa and Cirrus cards can be used at most businesses and at some cash machines, though some may not be accepted at petrol stations. Taking travellers cheques in South African rand or US dollars will avoid extra exchange rate charges. The South African rand may also be used as currency. Banking hours are Mon–Fri 0900–1530 and Sat 0900–1100.

There were 929,000 tourist arrivals in 2007.

Further information

Parliament: www.parliament.gov.na

Bank of Namibia: www.bon.com.na

Commonwealth Secretariat: www.thecommonwealth.org

Commonwealth of Nations: www.commonwealth-of-nations.org/Namibia

Nauru

KEY FACTS

Joined Commonwealth:	1968
Population:	10,000 (2010)
Official language:	English
Time:	GMT plus 12hr
Currency:	Australian dollar

Geography

Area:	21.3 sq km
Coastline:	30km

Nauru is a small oval-shaped island in the western Pacific Ocean.

Topography: Phosphate mining in the central plateau has left a barren terrain of jagged coral pinnacles, up to 15m high. A century of mining has stripped four-fifths of the land area. The island is surrounded by a coral reef, exposed at low tide and dotted with pinnacles. The island has a fertile coastal strip 150–300m wide. Coral cliffs surround the central plateau. The highest point of the plateau is 65m above sea level.

Climate: The climate is tropical, with sea breezes. North-east trade winds blow from March to October. Day temperatures range from 24 to 34°C; average humidity is 80%. Rainfall is erratic and often heavy; average annual rainfall is 2,060mm. The monsoon season is November to February. With the destruction of the forested areas on the plateau land to enable phosphate mining, climate changes have been noted with extensive dry periods. If global warming causes sea level to rise, the habitable low-lying land areas will be at risk from tidal surges and flooding.

Environment: The most significant environmental issues are devastation of some 90% of the island by intensive phosphate mining during most of the 20th century, and dependence on an ageing desalination plant and collection of limited rainwater for water supply.

Vegetation: The only presently fertile areas are the narrow coastal belt, where there are coconut palms, pandanus trees and indigenous

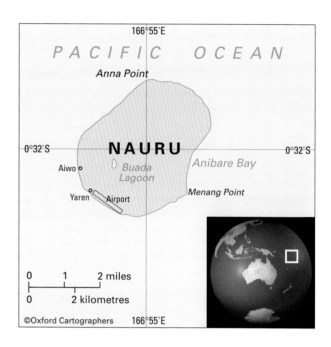

hardwoods such as the tomano, and the land surrounding Buada lagoon, where bananas, pineapples and some vegetables are grown. Some secondary vegetation grows over the coral pinnacles.

Wildlife: Many indigenous birds have disappeared or become rare, owing to destruction of their habitat, notably the noddy, or black tern. Frigatebirds have traditionally been caught and tamed.

Main towns: Yaren (pop. 4,800 in 2010), Aiwo, Denigomodu, Uaboe, Anabar, Ijuw and Meneng. Nauru has no capital; government offices are in Yaren district.

Transport: A sealed road 19km long circles the island. Other roads run inland to Buada District and the phosphate areas. A 5km railway serves the phosphate workings and carries the phosphate to the dryers preparatory to loading on ships.

The airport is in the south-west of the island. The national airline, Our Airline, offers services to Guam, Fiji, and Brisbane and Melbourne in Australia.

Society

KEY FACTS 2010

Population per sq km:	476
Life expectancy:	65 years (est.)

Population: 10,000 (2010); 100% lives in urban areas; growth 0.6% p.a. 1990–2010; birth rate 28 per 1,000 people (est.); life expectancy 65 years (est.)

The indigenous people of Nauru are Micronesians. Increased population since the 1960s has put extreme pressure on the coastal

Did you know...

Before he embarked on his political career, former President Marcus Stephen won weightlifting medals at the Commonwealth Games in 1990 (1 gold, 2 silver), 1994 (3 gold), 1998 (3 gold) and 2002 (3 silver), as well as at the 1999 World Championships (1 silver).

With populations of about 10,000, Nauru and Tuvalu are the smallest Commonwealth member countries. They are also two of the world's smallest democracies.

Nauru was admitted as the 187th member state of the United Nations in September 1999.

fringe surrounding the island, which is currently the only space available for housing.

Language: Nauruan and English are spoken, but English, the official language, is the usual written language.

Religion: Mainly Christians (predominantly Protestants).

Health: There is a high incidence of diabetes, cancer and heart disease. There is no malaria. Medical and dental treatment is free for all Nauruans and for government employees and their families. There are two hospitals, one for Nauruans and one provided by the Nauru Phosphate Corporation which is mainly for employees of the corporation. A pure water supply is provided by the Nauru Phosphate Corporation's desalination plant. Infant mortality was 32 per 1,000 live births in 2010.

Education: There are 11 years of compulsory education starting at age six. The school year starts in January.

History

By the time of the first recorded European sighting of Nauru (by Captain John Fearn in 1798), the Nauruans were a distinct people with their own language and culture. They had little contact with Europeans until whaling ships, traders and beachcombers began to visit regularly in the 1830s.

The introduction of firearms and alcohol destroyed the social balance of the 12 clans living on the island and led to a ten-year internal war, which reduced the population to around 900 by 1888: in 1843 there had been 1,400 people on Nauru. Peace was only restored when Germany took action to remove firearms from the island.

The island was allocated to Germany under the 1886 Anglo-German Convention. Phosphate was discovered a decade later and the Pacific Phosphate Company started to exploit the reserves in 1906, by agreement with Germany. The island was captured by Australian forces in 1914 and administered by Britain. In 1920 the League of Nations gave Britain, Australia and New Zealand a Trustee Mandate over the territory. In reality the island was administered by Australia. The three governments bought out the Pacific Phosphate Company and established the British Phosphate Commissioners, who took over the rights to phosphate mining.

Nauru was damaged by German naval gunfire and later by Allied bombing in the Second World War. During Japanese occupation (1942–45), 1,200 Nauruans were deported to work as labourers to Truk (now Chuuk), Micronesia, where 463 died as a result of starvation or bombing. The survivors were returned to Nauru in January 1946.

After the war, the island became a UN Trust Territory, administered by Australia in a similar partnership to the previous League of Nations mandate, and it remained a trust territory until independence in 1968. Anticipating the exhaustion of the phosphate reserves, a plan by the partner governments to resettle the Nauruans on Curtis Island, off the north coast of Queensland, Australia, was put forward in 1964. However, the islanders decided against resettlement. Legislative and executive councils were established in 1966, giving the islanders a considerable measure of self-government.

In 1967, the Nauruans contracted to purchase the assets of the British Phosphate Commissioners and in June 1970 control passed to the Nauru Phosphate Corporation.

Nauru became independent as a republic in 1968. Following a constitutional convention in 1967–68, a new constitution protecting fundamental freedoms and establishing a parliamentary democracy was adopted. Sir Hammer DeRoburt became president and went on to dominate parliament during the next 20 years, leading the government for most of the period. In the absence of a formal party system, there have been many periods when governments have been sustained by a single vote.

In August 1989 DeRoburt was ousted in a vote of no confidence. Kenas Aroi succeeded him but was himself succeeded by Bernard Dowiyogo after he suffered a severe stroke in November 1989. Dowiyogo went on to win the next presidential election, but in the November 1995 election was narrowly defeated by Lagumot Harris (nine votes to eight). In November 1996, there was an early general election which, due to a number of votes of no confidence, was followed by three changes of president in as many months.

Kinza Clodumar was elected president in a further general election in February 1997. He was defeated in a no-confidence vote in June 1998 when Dowiyogo again took over the leadership. In April 1999 Dowiyogo was himself defeated in a vote of no confidence and René Harris was chosen by parliament to succeed him. Following the general election in April 2000, the 18 newly elected members re-elected Harris as president. When he resigned a week later, Dowiyogo was chosen for the sixth time. In March 2001, when Dowiyogo was in Australia undergoing medical treatment, he was narrowly defeated in a no-confidence vote; Harris was then chosen to succeed him. Having superseded René Harris in January 2003 following a no-confidence vote, Bernard Dowiyogo died in March while on a visit to the USA, and an election was held in May 2003

In August 2001, the government agreed with the Australian Government – for an initial A$30 million – to accommodate some 1,000 mainly Afghan boat people while their eligibility for asylum in Australia was assessed. In October 2005 the Australian Government decided to bring 25 of the remaining 27 asylum-seekers to Australia. Only one asylum seeker remained on the island in mid-2006, but 7 Burmese asylum seekers were transferred to Nauru for assessment in September 2006 and 82 Sri Lankan refugees in March 2007. Then in late 2007 the new Australian Labor government indicated the camp would be closed.

On 27 February 2010, a popular referendum rejected a package of proposed changes to Nauru's constitution, following a constitutional reform process which had been under way for several years. Among other things, the changes had been intended to stabilise government and establish a popularly-elected presidency.

For higher education, students need to go overseas, mainly to Australia and New Zealand, and scholarships are available for this. Nauru is a partner in the regional University of the South Pacific, which has a centre in Nauru and its main campus in Suva, Fiji.

Media: There is no daily newspaper. *The Bulletin* is published weekly in Nauruan and English by the government, and *Central Star News* and *The Nauru Chronicle* fortnightly.

The Nauru Broadcasting Service provides public radio and TV services. Radio Nauru broadcasts in English and Nauruan and includes material from Radio Australia and the BBC, and Nauru Television includes programmes from Australia and New Zealand.

There are 60 internet users per 1,000 people (2010).

Communications: Country code 674; internet domain '.nr'. There is no mobile phone coverage in Nauru; only satellite mobiles can be used. Internet access is available on the island and there is an internet cafe in Aiwo district; and one post office on the island.

There are 605 mobile phone subscriptions per 1,000 people (2010).

Public holidays: New Year's Day, Independence Day (31 January), Constitution Day (17 May), Angam Day (26 October), Christmas Day and Boxing Day. The word *Angam* means 'homecoming' and Angam Day commemorates the various times in history when the size of the Nauruan population has returned to 1,500, which is thought to be the minimum number necessary for survival.

Religious and other festivals whose dates vary from year to year include Good Friday and Easter Monday.

Economy

KEY FACTS 2010

GDP:	US$28m
GDP p.c.:	US$2,802
GDP growth:	–4.8% p.a. 2006–10
Inflation:	2.4% p.a. 2006–10

Nauru's economy is based on phosphate mining, and phosphate revenues have given the country a relatively high per capita income (though little economic data is published). Phosphate reserves are not, however, expected to last beyond the mid-2010s, and the government has been exploring other sources of income (for example, fishing, tourism and offshore financial services). There is very limited potential for agriculture and the country is dependent on imports for basic necessities such as food, consumer and capital goods. Very few Nauruans work, or are permanently resident, abroad.

Real Growth in GDP

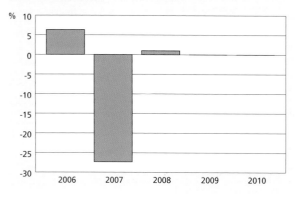

Inflation

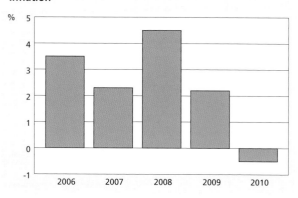

GDP by Sector (2010)

■ Agriculture	6%
□ Industry	36%
▨ Services	58%

Surpluses from the phosphate industry have been invested abroad by the Nauru Phosphate Royalties Trust to provide income as the phosphate runs out. The management of these funds has for years been one of the major issues on the island.

The Nauru Agency Corporation was established to encourage foreign investment in international financial services; it assists with the registration of holding and trading companies and in obtaining banking, trust and insurance licences.

In January 1999 Nauru signed its first loan agreement with the Asian Development Bank, under which the government was to diversify the economy to prepare for the exhaustion of phosphate reserves and to embark on a programme of economic reforms, including a sharp reduction in public sector expenditure and rises in taxes and duties.

From 2001, when its camp for processing asylum-seekers was established, Australia made substantial contributions to government revenues and there was for several years a boost for the catering sector. In 2007 revenues generated by the processing camp amounted to around a fifth of the country's GDP. Following its decision to close the camp during 2008, the incoming Labor administration in Australia committed itself to maintaining its aid programme, which was worth about US$26.2 million in 2011/12.

GDP fell by about a third over 2005–07 owing to a fall in public expenditure and suspension in phosphate mining following storm damage to the island's port facilities. The recovery that was under way with the resumption of phosphate mining in mid-2006 was stopped in its tracks by the world economic downturn and consequent collapse of demand for phosphate in 2008–09.

Constitution

Status:	Republic with executive president
Legislature:	Parliament
Independence:	31 January 1968

The constitution of the Republic of Nauru came into force in January 1968. It provides for a unicameral Parliament, whose 18 members are elected by universal adult suffrage in multi-seat constituencies. Voting is compulsory for all Nauruans over the age of 20. It is mandatory for a parliamentary general election to be held not less than once every three years.

The president is the head of state and head of government and is elected by the parliament from among its members. Executive authority is vested in the cabinet, which consists of the president and four or five members of the parliament chosen by the president. The cabinet is collectively responsible to parliament. The parliament also elects a speaker and a deputy speaker.

The 18 members of parliament represent eight constituencies. The number of representatives for each constituency is determined on the basis of population numbers.

The constitution protects fundamental rights and freedoms. There is a treasury fund from which monies may be taken by appropriation acts. A public service is provided for and the chief secretary is the public service commissioner. Special mention is made in the constitution of the allocation of profits and royalties from the sale of phosphate.

Politics

Last elections:	June 2010
Next elections:	2013
Head of state:	President Sprent Dabwido
Head of government:	the president
Ruling party:	no party system

By 2003 the country faced a severe financial crisis. The government was unable to pay salaries and was under pressure from OECD countries to regulate offshore banking and stop money-laundering. Following elections in May 2003 – the first after formation of Nauru First party – the three presidential candidates were each supported by six members and there were no candidates for the post of speaker, and it was three weeks before the Nauru First members gave their support to Ludwig Scotty. However, he retained the confidence of the MPs only until August 2003, when parliament chose former president René Harris to be president.

In September 2004 Scotty was again elected to the presidency and an early general election was held in October 2004, observed by a joint Pacific Islands Forum/Commonwealth observer mission. The new parliament then elected Scotty unopposed as president.

In the general election in August 2007, President Scotty's supporters took 14 seats and MPs subsequently re-elected him. His opponent Marcus Stephen was supported by three members. However, Scotty's third term lasted only four months; he was deposed in a vote of no confidence in December 2007 and Marcus Stephen was chosen by parliament to be president.

Following his election Stephen had the support of only 9 of 18 MPs. The government was paralysed, Stephen declared a state of emergency and dissolved parliament. At the ensuing elections in April 2008 the president's supporters achieved a working majority, winning 12 of the 18 parliamentary seats; Stephen was re-elected president and the deadlock ended.

An early general election in April 2010, occasioned by the defection of three members, returned exactly the same members, and parliament continued to be deadlocked. Negotiations and another election in June 2010 failed to secure a resolution. The deadlock finally ended in November 2010 when parliament re-elected Stephen as president, defeating Milton Dube 11–6.

President Stephen stepped down in November 2011 amid allegations of corruption in a phosphate deal. In two parliamentary votes in November – both won by 9 votes to 8 – Freddie Pitcher defeated Milton Dube only to be ousted by Sprent Dabwido less than a week later.

International relations

Nauru is a member of the African, Caribbean and Pacific Group of States, Pacific Community, Pacific Islands Forum and United Nations.

Traveller information

Local laws and conventions: Many Nauruans belong to the Nauruan Protestant Church, but there is also a significant Roman Catholic minority. Society is matrilineal. All drug offences carry heavy penalties.

Dress is casual and formal wear is needed only for very special occasions. Smart businesswear is expected for meetings, and the best time to visit on business is May to October. The Menen hotel in Meneng district has conference facilities for up to 200 people. Business hours are Mon–Fri 0800–1200 and 1330–1630.

Immigration and customs: Passports must be valid for at least six months beyond the length of intended stay in Nauru and all travellers require a visa. Visitors are advised to make a copy of the relevant pages of their passport to avoid any complications if lost or stolen. Airport departure tax is in Australian dollars and must be paid in cash.

It is prohibited to import explosives, firearms, pornography, drugs and pornographic films and literature.

A yellow fever vaccination certificate is required from visitors arriving from an infected country.

Travel within the country: Traffic drives on the left. Cars can be hired with a national driving licence. The speed limit is 50kph. Most of the island can be accessed on foot. Nauru has a free public bus service and taxis are available. There is no passenger rail service on the island. Our Airline is the national airline and connects the island with Australia and other Pacific and Asian countries.

Travel health: Comprehensive medical insurance that includes medical evacuation is recommended. The country is subject to periodic outbreaks of typhoid, and vaccinations against tuberculosis and Hepatitis B are recommended for visitors planning to stay for six months or longer. All visitors should check current vaccination requirements well before their departure date. Tap water is safe to drink, though bottled water is widely available.

Money: The Australian dollar is legal tender in Nauru. The only place to change money is the Bank of Nauru in Aiwo district. Visitors are advised to bring Australian dollars in cash. Credit cards are not usually accepted and there are no ATMs.

Further information

Goverment of the Republic of Nauru: www.naurugov.nr

Parliament: www.naurugov.nr/parliament

Commonwealth Secretariat: www.thecommonwealth.org

Commonwealth of Nations: www.commonwealth-of-nations.org/Nauru

New Zealand

Joined Commonwealth:	1931 (Statute of Westminster)
Population:	4,368,000 (2010)
GDP p.c. growth:	1.9% p.a. 1990–2010
UN HDI 2011:	world ranking 5
Official languages:	English, Maori
Time:	GMT plus 12–13hr
Currency:	New Zealand dollar (NZ$)

Geography

Area:	270,500 sq km
Coastline:	15,130km
Capital:	Wellington

New Zealand's Maori name is *Aotearoa*, meaning 'Land of the Long White Cloud'. A well-watered and fertile mountainous island country in the South Pacific, New Zealand consists of two large islands (North Island and South Island), Stewart Island and a number of offshore islands. It is somewhat isolated, being about 1,600km east of Australia, the nearest land mass. Other neighbouring countries are Vanuatu and Tonga.

Time: GMT plus 12hr. The clock is advanced by one hour from the first Sunday in October to the third Sunday in March.

Topography: New Zealand being in the 'Pacific ring of fire', volcanic activity has shaped the landscape. Earthquakes, mostly shallow, are common, and volcanic eruptions occur in the North Island and offshore to the Kermadec Islands. 75% of the country is higher than 200m above sea level. Around one-tenth of the North Island

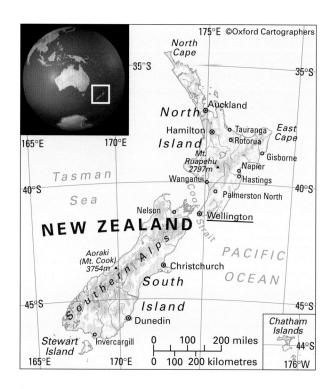

Did you know...

New Zealand was a founder member of the Commonwealth in 1931 when its independence was recognised under the Statute of Westminster.

Sir Don McKinnon of New Zealand was Commonwealth Secretary-General 2000–08.

Five New Zealanders have won overall Commonwealth Writers' Prizes: Witi Ihimaera in 1987 (Best First Book); Janet Frame in 1989; John Cranna in 1990 (Best First Book); Lloyd Jones in 2007; and Craig Cliff in 2011 (Best First Book).

Scholarships for postgraduate study are awarded by New Zealand to citizens of other Commonwealth countries under the Commonwealth Scholarship and Fellowship Plan.

(113,729 sq km) is mountainous. Its Rotorua area, a much-visited tourist attraction, has boiling mud pools and geysers. The South Island (150,437 sq km) is very mountainous; the Southern Alps extend almost its entire length; they have many outlying ranges to the north and south-west; there are at least 223 peaks over 2,300m above sea level and 360 glaciers. There are numerous lakes, mostly at high altitude, and many rivers, mostly fast-flowing and difficult to navigate, which are important sources of hydroelectricity (which provides more than 90% of the country's power). Stewart Island, named after Captain Stewart, who first charted the island in 1809, and (further out) the Auckland Islands lie south of the South Island. The Chatham and Pitt Islands are 850km east of Christchurch. In addition, the Kermadec Islands were annexed in 1887 and the Ross Dependency in Antarctica was acquired in 1923. The country has a long coastline (15,130km) in relation to its area.

Climate: Temperate marine climate influenced by the surrounding ocean, the prevailing westerly winds, and the mountainous nature of the islands. The weather tends to be changeable. Winds can be very strong, sometimes damaging buildings and trees. Rain, sometimes very heavy, occurs throughout the year. Cold southerly winds bring snow in winter, sometimes in spring. At Wellington, yearly average rainfall is 1,270 mm (143mm in July, and averaging 87mm from November to February); average January temperature is 13–20°C, and July temperature 6–11°C. Most of the country experiences at least 2,000 hours of sunshine annually. In recent years, weather patterns have been affected by La Nina and El Niño;

some unusually high temperatures have been recorded; and drought and unusually heavy rainfall have occurred.

Environment: The most significant environmental issues are deforestation and soil erosion and the impact on native flora and fauna of species introduced from other countries.

Vegetation: Forest cover includes species of conifer, kauri (North Island only) and beech – forest covers 31% of the land area, having increased at 0.3% p.a. 1990–2010. A great range of flora, depending on latitude and altitude, from subtropical rainforest to alpine, with 25% of plants growing above the tree-line. Many species are unique to New Zealand. Arable land comprises 2% of the total land area.

History

The Polynesian ancestors of the present Maori, skilled navigators of canoes fitted with sails and outriggers, arrived in New Zealand around the 10th century from Hawaiki (Eastern Polynesia). The Maori population may have been over 100,000 at the time the first Europeans arrived. The Dutchman Abel Tasman sighted New Zealand in 1642 in his search for the southern continent, i.e. Antarctica, but was driven off by Maori on his one attempt to land. He named the South Island Nieuw Zeeland after the Dutch province.

James Cook, on a search for the southern continent combined with general scientific and navigational observation, sighted the North Island in 1769. He circumnavigated both islands and charted the shores. He visited the country twice more, in 1773–74 and in 1777. His encounters with Maori were usually peaceful, though occasional skirmishes resulted in one Maori and ten European deaths. Jean de Surville (France) arrived in the country in the mid-1770s; his relations with the Maori, bad from the beginning, ended in the deaths of 25 of his men and the subsequent massacre of over 200 Maori. Cook's good reports attracted sealers and traders, some from the new community in Sydney (established in 1788 as Port Jackson, a penal settlement), and whalers came from America, Britain and France.

With extensive European arrival, the Maori suffered severely from influenza, dysentery and diphtheria, to which they had no resistance. In 1814 the Maori were taken under the protection of the British monarch, but this protection was not always effective in practice. In 1828 the jurisdiction of the courts of New South Wales was extended to New Zealand whose population of European and European-descended settlers was estimated at 2,000 by 1839. Pressure from settlers, traders and missionaries led to intervention by Britain. On 14 January 1840 the Governor of New South Wales proclaimed British sovereignty over New Zealand and appointed a governor. Under the Treaty of Waitangi (6 February 1840) the Maori received the full rights and privileges of British subjects, and 46 Maori chiefs ceded sovereignty to Queen Victoria, in exchange for retaining ownership of their natural resources. The treaty has been widely interpreted and is now applied in all aspects of New Zealand public life, notably in organisation and employment practice.

When New Zealand became a British territory in 1840, it was divided into two provinces. Twelve years later the number of provinces was increased to six (and later increased still further) and a general assembly established, consisting of the governor, a nominated Legislative Council (an upper house) and an elected House of Representatives (a lower house). This bicameral system lasted until 1950. Maori-occupied land was governed according to Maori custom.

Immigration from Britain increased in the mid-19th century, and by 1858 settlers outnumbered Maori. A census of Maori, in

1857–58, put their numbers at about 56,000. Pressure to acquire land from reluctant Maori led to land wars from 1860 to 1872, which resulted in general but not absolute European domination. Sheep farming was expanded in the late 1840s. Wool overtook timber and flax as export commodities and in 1882 the first ship carrying refrigerated meat sailed for England. There was gold mining on the South Island during the 1860s; this attracted considerable European immigration but ended in a slump.

During the 1890s a series of laws turned New Zealand into what was probably the most socially advanced state in the world. New Zealand women were the first in the world to be enfranchised, obtaining the vote in 1893. Men had been enfranchised in 1890, the year of the country's first general election. From 1936 the country developed into a pioneering welfare state.

In 1907, New Zealand became a Dominion – in effect an acknowledgement of its independence, which was formally recognised by the Statute of Westminster in 1931. In 1947 the last restrictions on the right of its parliament to amend its constitution were removed.

Maori membership of the House of Representatives was increased on six occasions. A Ministry of Maori Development was established in 1992, replacing the Ministry of Maori Affairs. The purpose of the Ministry of Maori Development is to assist in developing an environment of opportunity and choice for Maori, consistent with the Treaty of Waitangi.

At the general election in November 1993, the National Party won 50 seats, the Labour Party 45 seats. The National Party, not having an overall majority following defections and realignments, agreed in February 1996 on a coalition with the United New Zealand Party, which had seven MPs.

The first general election under the mixed member proportional representation system was held in October 1996. It gave 53 seats to a grouping consisting of: the National Party (44 seats) and its allies the Association of Consumers and Taxpayers of New Zealand (eight) and United New Zealand (one). The Labour Party won 37 seats, New Zealand First 17 and the Alliance Party 13. Although 34 parties contested the elections, only five received more than 5% of the votes and so earned the right to party seats. As no single party had an overall majority in the 120-member house, New Zealand First held the balance of power. Only when that party decided to support the National Party was party leader Jim Bolger able to form a government.

In November 1997 Bolger announced his resignation as prime minister, when it became clear that Transport Minister Jenny Shipley had enough support among National Party MPs to force his resignation from the job he had held continuously since 1990. He took on a foreign affairs role outside the cabinet until he became US ambassador in April 1998.

Wildlife: Fauna are often also unique because of geographical isolation, and include such flightless birds as the kiwi, kakapo and weka, and a great diversity of seabirds, as well as 400 kinds of marine fish and many sea-mammals including 32 whale-species. The introduction of land-mammals (unknown before the arrival of humans, save for three species of bat) by successive settlers, Polynesian and European, has seriously damaged the habitat of many species, including the flightless birds – of which the moa, adzebill and flightless goose have become extinct – and reduced the forest area.

Main towns: Wellington (capital, pop. 188,600 in 2010; greater Wellington includes Lower Hutt, Porirua and Upper Hutt), Auckland (421,900; greater Auckland includes Manukau, North Shore and Waitakere), Manukau (greater Auckland, 410,200), Christchurch (South Island, 377,400), North Shore (greater Auckland, 269,500), Waitakere (greater Auckland, 206,300), Hamilton (166,700), Napier–Hastings (120,700), Tauranga (119,900), Dunedin (South Island, 112,100), Lower Hutt (greater Wellington, 97,700), Palmerston North (77,600), Rotorua (54,100), Whangarei (50,600), New Plymouth (49,700), Porirua (greater Wellington, 48,900), Invercargill (South Island, 46,200) and Nelson (South Island, 43,800).

Transport: There are 93,580km of roads, 66% paved. The railway network, privatised in 1993, extends over 3,900km, with many scenic routes.

There are 13 major commercial ports, including those in Whangarei (shipping oil products), Tauranga (timber and newsprint) and Bluff (alumina and aluminium) as well as container ports in Auckland, Wellington, Lyttleton (near Christchurch) and Dunedin.

There are international airports in Auckland (23km to the south of the city), Christchurch (10km north-west), Wellington (8km south-east), Hamilton and Dunedin.

Society

KEY FACTS 2010

Population per sq km:	16
Life expectancy:	81 years
Net primary enrolment:	99%

Population: 4,368,000 (2010); 86% lives in urban areas and 32% in urban agglomerations of more than 1 million people; growth 1.3% p.a. 1990–2010; birth rate 15 per 1,000 people (22 in 1970); life expectancy 81 years (71 in 1970).

The 2006 census recorded 2,609,592 people of European origin (65%); 565,329 people of Polynesian (Maori) descent (14%); 265,974 Pacific Island Polynesians (6.6%), mostly from Samoa (131,103), Cook Islands (56,895) and Tonga (50,478); some 139,728 Chinese (3.5%); and 97,443 Indians (2.4%). About 75% of the population lives in North Island, of which the average population density is 24 per sq km (South Island: 6 per sq km).

Language: English and Maori are the official languages and many information documents are also translated into Polynesian.

Religion: 70% of people adhere to a religion: Christians 56% (Anglicans 14%, Roman Catholics 13%, Presbyterians/Congregational/Reformed 10%, Methodists 3%); Hindus 1.6%; and Buddhists 1.3% (2006 census).

Health: Public spending on health was 8% of GDP in 2009. Treatment in public hospitals is free for everyone. Infant mortality was 5 per 1,000 live births in 2010 (22 in 1960).

Education: Public spending on education was 6.4% of GDP in 2009. There are 12 years of compulsory education starting at age five. The school year starts in January.

There are many colleges of education across the country, and the University of Waikato has its own School of Education. There are eight government-funded universities (Auckland, Auckland University of Technology, Waikato, Massey, Victoria at Wellington, Canterbury, Lincoln and Otago) and 20 institutes of technology and polytechnics. The Maori Education Trust awards scholarships and grants to promote Maori education. The female–male ratio for gross enrolment in tertiary education is 1.45:1 (2009). There is virtually no illiteracy among people aged 15–24.

Media: Largest dailies include *The New Zealand Herald* (Auckland, the main national newspaper), *The Dominion Post* (Wellington) and *The Press* (Christchurch). Many other daily papers – mostly evening editions – are published locally and regionally. The principal Sunday papers are *Sunday Star Times* and *Sunday News*.

Broadcasting was deregulated in 1988. Television New Zealand operates two public channels and further digital channels, and Maori Television promotes Maori language and culture. TV3, Prime TV and Sky TV are private channels.

Radio New Zealand provides three public stations and an external service, RNZI. Ruia Mai is a Maori-owned radio station broadcasting in Maori, and Niu FM provides a public service for the Pacific Islander communities. There are several private radio stations.

Some 97% of households have TV sets (2009). There are 530 personal computers (2006) and 830 internet users (2010) per 1,000 people.

Communications: Country code 64; internet domain '.nz'. Public phones are generally phonecard- or credit card-operated. Mobile phone coverage is good. Internet access and internet cafes are widely available.

There are 428 main telephone lines and 1,149 mobile phone subscriptions per 1,000 people (2010).

Public holidays: New Year (two days), Waitangi Day (anniversary of the 1840 treaty, 6 February), ANZAC Day (25 April), Queen's Official Birthday (first Monday in June), Labour Day (fourth Monday in October), Christmas Day and Boxing Day. The anniversaries of the former provinces of New Zealand are observed locally as holidays.

Religious and other festivals whose dates vary from year to year include Good Friday and Easter Monday.

Economy

KEY FACTS 2009

GDP:	US$126.7bn
GDP p.c.:	US$29,695
GDP growth:	1.0% p.a. 2005–09
Inflation:	2.9% p.a. 2006–10

From the 1950s, the country has diversified both its economy and its export markets, reducing its dependence on sheep and butter. Diversification has taken it into new agricultural products (kiwi fruit, apples, timber and wine), and seen significant growth in fishing, tourism, manufacturing and services.

In 1984, after a period when the economy stalled, inflation was high and the currency devalued, the country embarked on a policy

Real Growth in GDP

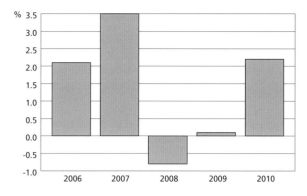

Inflation

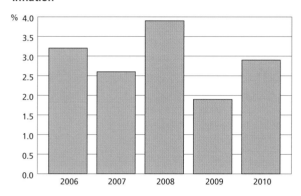

GDP by Sector (2010)

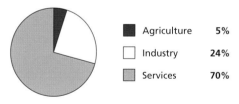

■ Agriculture	**5%**
□ Industry	**24%**
▨ Services	**70%**

of liberalisation, deregulation and privatisation. In 1989, control of inflation was passed to the Reserve Bank: the subsequent austerity measures brought inflation to below 2% by the end of 1991, and tight fiscal policy was maintained. Economic policy has been to protect the core of social spending while reducing government expenditure through privatisations and cost-cutting. New Zealand is a proponent of regional free trade, including the entire Pacific Rim.

The economy grew steadily during the 1990s until 1998. By mid-1998 the impact of the Asian financial crisis had become very serious, causing a sharp fall in trade with Asia and the government announced emergency spending cuts. However, in 1999 there was a return to confident growth.

The early 2000s saw the start of a strategy to reduce the gap between rich and poor, which had opened up since the introduction of free-market policies in the mid-1980s. Measures included increases in spending on health, education and public housing, focused on the Maori and Pacific Islander communities. Economic growth was steady at around 4% p.a. 2002–04 but slowed to 1.9% p.a. during 2004–08. As demand for New Zealand's exports collapsed in the global recession in 2008, the economy moved sharply into recession, resulting in a contraction

for the year of 1.5%. However, after exports picked up during 2009, the economy began to grow again (about 2% in 2010 and 1.5% in 2011).

Constitution

Status:	Monarchy under Queen Elizabeth II
Legislature:	Parliament

New Zealand is a constitutional monarchy and parliamentary democracy, with Queen Elizabeth II titular head of state, represented in the country by the governor-general.

There is a unicameral House of Representatives, directly elected on a three-year term, with universal suffrage for everyone over 18. The number of MPs rose from 99 to 120 in 1996, under the new electoral system when the country moved to a form of proportional representation known as MMP (mixed member proportional). Voters have an electorate vote and a party vote. The former is used to select the local MP (since the 2001 census, when the number and shape of constituencies were last determined, 69 are elected on first-past-the-post basis, including seven representing Maori constituencies), while the latter is used to select a party and determine the total number of seats for each party in parliament. All parties polling more than 5% of this vote (or with at least one electorate seat) are entitled to further seats based on the proportion of the party votes cast. Normally 51 members are party MPs but this number can be increased (increasing the total number of seats in parliament for the term) when a party wins more electorate seats than it is entitled to according to the party vote. This happened for the first time in September 2005, when there was a single Maori Party 'overhang' MP.

The prime minister is appointed by the governor-general on the basis of party strength in the House of Representatives and the prime minister appoints a cabinet.

The MMP system is designed to prevent domination by a majority group and to give voice to minorities, under-represented in Westminster (first-past-the-post) systems. It is also intended to encourage voting on the basis of policies rather than a party bloc. In the first election under MMP, the proportion of women MPs rose by half to about one-third of the total and the Maori community obtained representation to match its 13% share in the population.

Politics

Last elections:	November 2011
Next elections:	2014
Head of state:	Queen Elizabeth II, represented by governor-general, Lt-Gen Sir Jerry Mateparae (2011–)
Head of government:	Prime Minister John Key
Ruling party:	National Party

In the general election of November 1999 the Labour Party, led by Helen Clark, won 49 seats and its coalition partner Alliance ten. The National Party, led by Jenny Shipley, took 39 seats and its ally, the Association of Consumers and Taxpayers of New Zealand (ACT New Zealand), nine. With the support of the Green Party (seven seats), Labour was able to command a majority in the 120-member House of Representatives and Helen Clark became prime minister.

In the July 2002 general election, Labour (52 seats) and its coalition partner – Progressive Coalition Party (two) – were unable to command a parliamentary majority without the support of smaller parties. These now included United Future (eight) and the Greens (nine). The National Party secured 27 seats and ACT New Zealand nine, while its former coalition partner, New Zealand First, strengthened its position to 13.

The September 2005 general election was very close, but when all the votes were counted, the ruling Labour–Progressive coalition (Labour 50 seats, Progressive one) was returned for a third successive term and Helen Clark continued as prime minister, still able to command a majority in parliament only with support from New Zealand First (seven) and United Future Party (three). The National Party won 48 seats on a platform of tax cuts, cuts in state aid to Maori communities and closer ties with the USA.

The National Party – under the leadership of John Key – won the November 2008 election with 59 seats and 45.5% of votes, and like previous governments would only be able to command a majority in the House with support from minority parties. Turnout was 79% and Labour took 43 seats (33.8% of votes), Green Party eight, ACT New Zealand five, the Maori Party five, Jim Anderton's Progressive one, United Future one and New Zealand First none.

In the November 2011 election the National Party increased its share of votes to 47.3%, though with 59 seats still short of an absolute majority in parliament. Labour took 34 seats (27.5%), the Green Party 14 (11.1%), New Zealand First eight (6.6%) and the Maori Party three. ACT New Zealand, Mana and United Future each won one seat. With the support of ACT and United Future, John Key was sworn in as prime minister for a second time. In December 2011 the National Party formed a coalition government with ACT New Zealand, United Future and the Maori Party.

International relations

New Zealand is a member of Asia–Pacific Economic Cooperation, Organisation for Economic Co-operation and Development, Pacific Community, Pacific Islands Forum, United Nations and World Trade Organization.

Traveller information

Local laws and conventions: Smoking is banned on public transport and in public buildings as well as in pubs or restaurants.

Penalties for possession and use of even small amounts of drugs are severe and may lead to prison sentences.

Should a visitor be invited to a formal Maori occasion, the *hongi* (pressing of noses) is common. Casual dress is widely acceptable.

Business approach is fairly conservative in New Zealand. Businesswear is generally conservative and suits are usually worn. Appointments are necessary and punctuality is appreciated. Business cards are normally exchanged. It can be difficult to schedule meetings in December and January since these are the prime months for summer vacations. The best months for business visits are February to April and October to November. Office hours are Mon–Fri 0900–1700.

Immigration and customs: Passports must be valid for at least three months beyond the period of intended stay.

New Zealand has strict bio-security regulations and it is illegal to import most foodstuffs; there are strict penalties imposed on those who break these rules. Care must also be taken if importing wood products, golf clubs, shoes and items made from animal skin.

Travel within the country: Traffic drives on the left. Car hire is available from airports and most major cities and towns and an international driving permit is recommended. The minimum age for driving a hired car is 21. Speed limits are 100kph on open roads and 50kph in built-up areas. Main roads are paved, but some country roads are not. Motor insurance is not a legal requirement in New Zealand, as it has removed the legal right of victims to sue a third party in the event of an accident. Therefore private accident insurance is strongly recommended. Drivers and passengers are legally required to wear seatbelts at all times.

New Zealand has a modern and efficient transport network. Regional bus services serve most parts of the country. Taxis are available throughout, and are metered.

Toll New Zealand runs New Zealand's passenger train service and there are three scenic long-distance routes run by Tranz Scenic. All train services are one-class travel only. Commuter trains serve Auckland and Wellington.

Air New Zealand Link serves most of the smaller airports throughout the islands. The North and South Islands are also linked by regular ferry services.

Travel health: Comprehensive medical insurance is recommended. Medical facilities, both public and private, are of a high standard and many hotels have a doctor on call.

Adventure activities are very popular in New Zealand and visitors should ensure that their travel insurance adequately covers them for these.

Mains water is considered safe to drink. Milk is pasteurised.

Money: The local currency is the New Zealand dollar. Credit cards are widely accepted. Travellers cheques should be taken in pounds sterling, US dollars or Australian dollars in order to avoid additional exchange rate charges.

There were 2,525,000 tourist arrivals in 2010.

Further information

New Zealand Government: newzealand.govt.nz

Parliament: www.parliament.nz

Reserve Bank of New Zealand: www.rbnz.govt.nz

Commonwealth Secretariat: www.thecommonwealth.org

Commonwealth of Nations: www.commonwealth-of-nations.org/New_Zealand

New Zealand: Associated Countries and External Territories

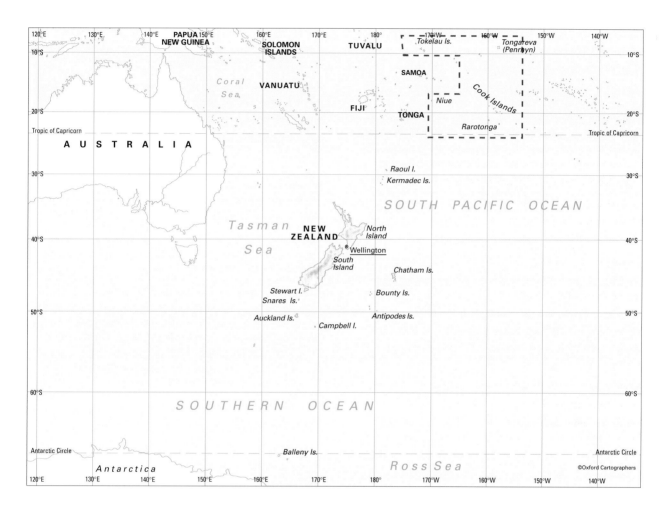

Cook Islands and Niue have full self-government in free association with New Zealand. Tokelau and the Ross Dependency in the Antarctic are New Zealand External Territories administered directly by New Zealand.

Cook Islands

Status: Self-governing in free association with New Zealand.

Geography

The Cook Islands archipelago lies in the South Pacific, with the largest island, Rarotonga, 3,013km north-east of Auckland, New Zealand. There are 15 islands (Rarotonga, Mangaia, Atiu, Mauke, Mitiaro, Aitutaki, Penrhyn, Suwarrow, Manihiki, Rakahanga, Pukapuka, Nassau, Manuae, Takutea, Palmerston), of which 13 are inhabited. The islands, which form two groups, extend over 2 million sq km of ocean.

Area: 237 sq km (Rarotonga 65 sq km)

Main town: Avarua (capital; pop. 13,300 in 2010) on Rarotonga.

Topography: The southern group of islands, which accounts for about 90% of the total land area, is of mainly volcanic formation. The northern group consists of low-lying coral atolls, except for Nassau, a sandy cay. The highest island is Rarotonga, rising to 653m at Te Manga, and surrounded by a coral reef. Most of the larger islands have lagoons surrounded by fertile soil backed by hills. Valuable metals, including significant amounts of manganese nodules, have been discovered on the sea bed and cover almost one-third of the Cook Islands' exclusive economic zone (EEZ).

Climate: April to November: mild and equable (20–26°C). December to March: wet and humid (22–28°C). Average rainfall on Rarotonga: 2,030mm p.a.

Vegetation: Lush tropical on Rarotonga and the fertile southern group of islands. Vegetation on the coral atolls is sparse; mainly pandanus and coconuts. Forest covers 67% of the land area (2010).

Wildlife: There is a bird-nesting sanctuary on Suwarrow. Varied marine life, including coral-reef dwelling species.

Transport/Communications: A 33km surfaced coastal road encircles Rarotonga, while roads in the outer islands are not surfaced.

There are two deep-water ports: one in Rarotonga in the southern group and the other in Penrhyn in the northern group. Cargo for all outer islands is carried between ship and shore through passages in the reef in barges or lighters.

The international airport is 3km west of Avarua on Rarotonga. Air Rarotonga operates internal flights; Air New Zealand, scheduled services to regional destinations such as Tahiti, Auckland, Suva and Honolulu.

The international dialling code is 682. There are 356 main telephone lines, 385 mobile phone subscriptions and 357 internet users per 1,000 people (2010).

Society

Population: 23,600 (2010); population density 100 per sq km; more than half lives on Rarotonga and some 75% in urban areas; growth 0.7% p.a. 1990–2010.

The indigenous people are Cook Islands Maori. There are 56,895 Cook Islanders living in New Zealand, more than 70% of whom were born there (2006 New Zealand census). Virtually all land is owned by Cook Islands Maori under a land-tenure system, which

precludes its sale or mortgage except under very constrained circumstances. Land may be leased for up to 60 years, again under constrained circumstances.

Language: Maori (official), English

Religion: Mainly Christians (Cook Islands Congregationalists).

Health: Most health services are free, but new user charges are being implemented. There is a central hospital on Rarotonga, plus seven island cottage hospitals, and outpatient clinics, health centres and maternity/child clinics. The outer islands are mainly serviced by nurses. There is no malaria, but lifestyle diseases such as hypertension, diabetes and gout are increasing. Infant mortality was 8 per 1,000 live births in 2010.

Education: There are 11 years of compulsory education starting at age five. Net enrolment ratio for primary is 98%. The school year starts in January.

Tertiary education is provided by a teachers' college, nursing school, tourism training school, trade training centre and University of the South Pacific extension centre. Overseas scholarships are available for university-level studies. Cook Islands is a partner in the regional University of the South Pacific, which has its main campus in Suva, Fiji. Adult literacy is about 95%.

Media: *Cook Islands News* (daily, in English and Maori), *Cook Islands Herald* (weekly) and *Cook Islands Independent* (weekly). There are private providers of radio and TV.

Public holidays: New Year's Day, ANZAC Day (25 April), Queen's Official Birthday (first Monday in June), Rarotonga Gospel Day (25 July, only in Rarotonga), Constitution Day (early August), National Gospel Day (26 October), Christmas Day and Boxing Day. The Constitution Day celebrations begin on the last Friday in July and continue for up to two weeks. Most islands celebrate their own Gospel Day, as well as the National Gospel Day.

Religious festivals whose dates vary from year to year include Good Friday and Easter Monday.

Economy

The Cook Islands economy is based on agriculture (especially copra and citrus), fishing and tourism. The copra industry has declined. Clam and pearl oyster farming have been developed. Offshore banking was established in 1982. Tourism, largely in Rarotonga, accounts for around 65% of GDP. There were 99,000 tourist arrivals in 2009/10, mostly from New Zealand; the numbers holding up well despite the global downturn in 2008–09.

Despite the economy's relative diversity, in the 1990s there was a heavy reliance on imports, a large civil service (almost 20% of the population) and many young people emigrated – largely to New Zealand – though remittances from expatriates make a significant contribution. After the mid-1990s, when growth was very slow, the government embarked on economic reforms including a reduction of civil service jobs from 3,350 in 1996 to 1,340 in 1998 and of ministries from 52 to 22.

There was a surge of growth in 2000 (13.9%) and 2001 (4.9%), before the downturn in long-haul tourism after 11 September 2001 and the reduction in air services in the Pacific region caused growth to moderate.

History

The islands were colonised by Polynesians during the 7th and 8th centuries. James Cook – the islands take his name – sighted them in 1773 and in 1789 Rarotonga was visited by the mutineers from *The Bounty* during their bid for freedom. In 1888 the islands were made a British protectorate and administered by a British resident. In 1891 an elective federal parliament was set up, but in 1901 it was abolished, following a petition by prominent Cook Islanders, and the country was annexed by New Zealand.

In 1957 a legislative assembly was set up, consisting of 14 members elected by universal adult suffrage. In 1962 the Assembly debated the question of the country's political future and chose self-government in free association with New Zealand. United Nations observers attended the general election of April 1965, at New Zealand's request. Albert Henry became the country's first premier, after his Cook Islands Party won 14 of the 22 seats.

Since Cook Islands became self-governing, power has alternated between the Cook Islands Party (CIP) and the Democratic Party, later becoming the Democratic Alliance Party. In the general election in June 1999, the coalition of the CIP and recently established New Alliance Party (NAP), led by Norman George, gained a majority and Sir Geoffrey Henry, the CIP leader, was confirmed as prime minister for another five-year term. The CIP won 11 seats, the NAP four – one by one vote – and the Democratic Alliance Party (DAP) ten seats. A period of political instability followed the elections when first Joe Williams of CIP became prime minister, and then, in November 1999, Terepai Maoate of DAP, who formed a government in coalition with George's NAP.

In February 2002 a vote of no confidence brought Dr Robert Woonton to office, forming a four-way coalition of DAP, NAP, CIP and independents. In January 2003, following reunification of the Democratic Party and a merger with NAP, Woonton formed a new government with a two-thirds majority in the legislature, and the CIP left the government and became the opposition.

Constitution

Under the 1965 constitution, Cook Islands is a sovereign state with Queen Elizabeth II as head of state and a unicameral legislature, which has exhaustive and (since 1981) exclusive legislative powers (including constitutional reform); the New Zealand House of Representatives cannot legislate under any circumstances in respect of the Cook Islands. The parliament has 24 members elected by universal adult suffrage; elections are held at intervals of not more than five years.

The cabinet consists of the prime minister and between six and eight ministers of the prime minister's choice. The House of Ariki consists of hereditary chiefs representing their respective islands who are elected annually. The House concerns itself largely with advising government on issues relating to land use and traditional customs. Local government consists of island councils, district councils (*vaka*) and village committees. Cook Islands residents are also New Zealand citizens.

Under a constitutional relationship, New Zealand may exercise, if requested by Cook Islands, certain responsibilities for its defence. Cook Islands has full constitutional capacity to conduct its own external affairs and to enter directly into international arrangements engaging its international responsibility.

Politics

Last elections: November 2010

Next elections: 2015

Head of state: Queen Elizabeth II, represented by the Queen's Representative

Head of government: Prime Minister Henry Puna

Ruling party: Cook Islands Party

The general election in September 2004 was a very close contest with a turnout of over 80%. The Democratic Party took 47% of the votes and won 13 seats to the Cook Islands Party's (CIP) 44% and ten seats. Several of the results including Prime Minister Robert Woonton's own narrow majority were challenged. After a recount he had the same number of parliamentary supporters as his CIP opponent and then declined to stand in the by-election that was called for February 2005 and was unable to continue in office. In the ensuing parliamentary vote, Jim Marurai of the recently formed Demo Tumu party was elected prime minister.

When in July 2006 the CIP won a by-election and the government no longer had a majority in parliament, an early general election was called in September 2006. The ruling Demo Tumu won 14 seats and CIP eight. One seat was tied and CIP won the consequent by-election in November 2006.

The CIP won 16 seats in the November 2010 election and Demo Tumu the remaining eight. CIP leader Henry Puna was sworn in as prime minister shortly afterwards.

Niue

Status: Self-governing in free association with New Zealand.

Geography

Niue is a coral island in the South Pacific, stretching 19km from north to south, lying 480km east of Tonga and 930km west of the Cook Islands.

Area: 259 sq km

Main town: Alofi (capital; pop. 560 in 2010); there are 14 villages. The government may not sell the freehold to land, but may grant 60-year leases.

Topography: Niue is a raised coral outcrop rising to a height of 65m, and full of caves and fissures. The coast is steep and jagged; a coral reef surrounds the island. There are no rivers, but good-quality water from wells is plentiful. The soil is fertile, but not abundant and endangered by over-cropping and by bulldozing and burning to clear the land. Since 1983, cover crops have been allowed to grow along with the crops, to keep the soil moist.

Climate: Tropical, with cooling south-east trade winds and occasional storms. The rainy season is from December to March.

Environment: There is increasing attention to conservationist practices to counter loss of soil fertility from traditional slash and burn agriculture.

Vegetation: Bush and forest. Forest covers 73% of the land area (2010).

Transport/Communications: There are some 120km of paved roads.

Only small ships are able to berth at Alofi, Niue's port, so goods and passengers are transferred to and from larger ships in smaller vessels.

The international dialling code is 683. There are 681 main telephone lines per 1,000 people (2010).

Society

Population: 1,500 (2010); population density 6 per sq km; some 38% lives in urban areas; growth –2.3% p.a. 1990–2010.

The people are largely of Polynesian descent (originally from Samoa and Tonga). There are 22,476 Niueans living in New Zealand (2006 New Zealand census). The government is attempting to stem depopulation and encourage Niueans to return home.

Language: Niuean and English are official languages; Niuean is the national language.

Religion: Mainly Christians (Ekalesia Niue 61%, Latter-day Saints 9%, Roman Catholics 7%).

Health: A new hospital, Niue Foou, opened in 2006 following the devastation of Niue's then only hospital, Lord Liverpool Hospital, by Cyclone Heta in January 2004. Tropical diseases are not generally prevalent, though there have been occasional outbreaks of dengue fever. Infant mortality was 19 per 1,000 live births in 2010.

Education: There are 12 years of compulsory education starting at age five. The pupil–teacher ratio for both primary and secondary is 8:1 (2005). The school year starts in January.

Education beyond Form 6 is largely provided in New Zealand, Australia and Fiji. Niue is a partner in the regional University of the South Pacific, which has its main campus in Suva, Fiji. There is an extension centre of the university in Niue. Adult literacy is virtually 100%.

Media: *Niue Star* is published weekly. Niue Broadcasting Corporation provides radio and TV services.

Public holidays: New Year's Day, Takai Commission Holiday (2 January), Waitangi Day (anniversary of the 1840 treaty, 6 February), ANZAC Day (25 April), Queen's Official Birthday (first Monday in June), Constitution Day (two days in October), Peniamina Day (anniversary of the landing of the first missionaries, October), Christmas Day and Boxing Day.

Religious and other festivals whose dates vary from year to year include Good Friday and Easter Monday.

Economy

With its tiny economic base, declining population and limited potential for exports (mainly vegetables, honey and vanilla), Niue is dependent on aid from New Zealand, which gradually declined during the 1990s. Despite attempts to diversify the economy (for example, into offshore finance) it remains fragile and self-sufficiency is not likely. There were some 4,750 tourist arrivals in 2008.

History

Samoans and Tongans are thought to have been Niue's first inhabitants. The island was visited by Captain James Cook in 1774; he named it 'Savage Island' after the warlike reputation of the people. The London Missionary Society began administering the island in 1846. It became a British protectorate in 1900, and the following year it was annexed to New Zealand as a dependency. Emigration began with the recruitment of Niueans to work in the phosphate mines of the region.

In 1974 Niue became self-governing in free association with New Zealand. Robert Rex was Niue's first premier. He remained in post, with three-yearly general elections, from 1974 until his death in 1992. He was succeeded by Young Vivian, who lost power to Frank Lui in the elections of March 1993. Lui lost his seat in the general election in March 1999 and was succeeded by Sani Lakatani of the Niue People's Party (formed in 1987), which gained a majority in the 20-seat assembly.

After ten years of discussions with the USA, a treaty fixing the sea boundary between Niue and American Samoa was signed in May 1997.

Constitution

Under the 1974 constitution, Niue is self-governing in free association with New Zealand, which is still responsible for defence and the conduct of foreign affairs. Its people are citizens of New Zealand and UK subjects. The legislative assembly has 20 members (one for each village and six elected every three years on a common roll) with universal adult suffrage. Government is headed by the premier, elected by the assembly. The cabinet consists of the premier and three members of the assembly. The New Zealand High Commissioner conducts transactions between the Niue and New Zealand governments. There are 14 village councils whose members are elected and serve for three years.

Politics

Last elections: May 2011

Next elections: 2014

Head of state: Queen Elizabeth II, represented by the governor-general of New Zealand

Head of government: Premier Toke Talagi

Until 1987 – when the Niue People's Party (NPP) was formed – politics was conducted on an individual and not a party basis. In the general election in April 2002 there was close to 100% voter turnout and all 20 assembly members were returned, eight of the village representatives unopposed. The NPP won six seats and formed a government with the support of independent members. Young Vivian of the NPP became premier. In 2003 the NPP was dissolved.

In the April 2005 election Vivian was elected unopposed, and was subsequently confirmed as premier when he received the endorsement of 17 of the 20 assembly members.

In the Niue Assembly vote following the general election in June 2008, Toke Talagi defeated incumbent premier Young Vivian by 14 votes to 5 and became premier for the first time.

Following the May 2011 general election Talagi was re-elected premier with the support of 12 of the 20 assembly members.

The Ross Dependency

Status: New Zealand external territory, directly administered by New Zealand.

Geography

The Ross Dependency in the Antarctic comprises all the islands and territories south of 60°S latitude between 160°E and 150°W longitude.

Area: Estimated at 413,540 sq km and permanent shelf ice of 336,770 sq km.

Topography: Antarctica is a vast plateau continent, covered in ice, its landscape made up of glaciers, mountain ranges and deep crevasses. The Transantarctic Mountains extend across the continent, dividing the eastern and western ice sheets. The volcanic Mt Erebus rises to 3,794m. The deep embayment of the Ross Ice Shelf forms part of the western ice sheet; here, at 30–60m, the ice is 200–300 years old and samples show the increase in atmospheric pollution at the start of the industrial revolution in Europe. Flat-topped tabular icebergs, peculiar to the Antarctic (Arctic bergs are jagged), break off the ice cliffs and drift north. Bergs are 30–45m high (four or five times deeper below the surface) and up to 100–115km (even 145km) long. As they move north, the bergs calve (that is, fracture), emitting a continuous sound like frying fat as they melt. In fine weather, the air is very clear, allowing distant vistas of great sharpness.

Climate: The Antarctic latitudes are far colder than their Arctic equivalents. The Antarctic climate is bitter, windy and inhospitable (average temperature at the Pole is –50°C). Fierce winds blowing outwards from the central plateau scour the icy surfaces; blizzards can rage for weeks. During white-outs, shadows and horizon vanish as the light from the overcast sky bounces off the snow. Snowfall is light near the South Pole, heavier at the coastal margins. Within the Antarctic circle, winter days are very short, with corresponding days of midnight polar sun in summer.

Wildlife: The Antarctic landmass is barren: it is treeless and virtually plantless, with only lichens and mosses able to survive. However, the Antarctic waters are rich in plankton and shrimp-like krill which attract larger marine life. There are 18 species of penguins, of which only the emperor and Adélie penguins are truly Antarctic, spending their entire lives on the coast or close to its shores. Other birds include skuas and petrels. There are six species of seals in Antarctic waters; the Ross seal (nicknamed the 'singing seal' for its gentle cooing noise) inhabits the perennial pack ice and gives birth on the ice. The fur seal (once hunted almost to extinction and now protected) has small ears and is closer to the sea-lion. Various species of whales visit the region.

Society

Population: There are no permanent inhabitants, but the Scott Base on Ross Island is staffed all the year round and there are two seasonal bases.

Economy

There is no economic activity and the continent is protected under the Antarctic Treaty. A continuing programme of scientific research has been carried out since 1958 under the New Zealand Antarctic Research Programme. Areas of study include zoology, botany, geology, meteorology, limnology and geo-chemistry. Monitoring of the hole in the ozone layer has recently been undertaken in the territory.

History

From the early 18th century European explorers ventured into the waters of the far south. In 1700 astronomer and explorer Edmond Halley, encountering icebergs, described them as 'great islands of ice of so incredible a height and magnitude'. Among subsequent explorers, James Cook reached the high latitude of 71°S in 1774. From the late 18th century commercial interests took off with the hunting of wildlife. In 1821–22 alone some 320,000 fur seals were killed; elephant and fur seals were slaughtered almost to extinction. Whales were similarly hunted and fell victim to the improving technology of harpooning.

James Ross, leading a British expedition in the mid-19th century, explored the embayment of what is now known as the Ross Sea. He saw the volcano of Mt Erebus and the ice barrier, collected numerous marine specimens (subsequently lost or damaged), and conducted experiments, advanced for their time, on ocean depths and temperatures.

In the 20th century, Antarctic expeditions, both for polar exploration and scientific purposes, were sponsored by various nations. In 1911, the Norwegian Roald Amundsen, camped on the eastern side of the Ross Sea, reached the South Pole. A month later, Captain Robert Scott's British team reached the Pole from their camp on the western side of the Ross Sea, but perished on the return journey, victims of atrocious weather and faulty planning. Later explorers include the American Richard Byrd, the first to fly over the Pole.

After the Second World War, the International Whaling Commission banned the hunting of certain species of whales, but the numbers of right, humpback, blue and fin whales remain vestigial in the Southern Ocean. Seals are protected under a convention of 1971.

In 1923 steps were taken to assent sovereignty over the Antarctic territory by vesting administration in the New Zealand Government by an order in council under the British Settlements Act of 1887. The New Zealand Antarctic Expedition established Scott Base on Ross Island in 1957; the following year, the Ross Dependency Research Committee was appointed to co-ordinate all New Zealand activity in the dependency.

In 1959, 12 nations, including New Zealand, signed the Antarctic Treaty, which reserves the Antarctic for peaceful purposes. The parties have agreed to freeze territorial claims, conduct scientific research according to accepted international standards, to share research and not to test nuclear or other weapons. By 2009, the treaty had been signed by 47 countries.

Administration

In 1995 the government concluded a year-long review of New Zealand's Antarctic structure. Key outcomes included the establishment of a New Zealand Antarctic Institute (Antarctica New Zealand), and the continuation of the Officials' Antarctic Committee (OAC) with enhanced terms of reference.

The OAC is an interdepartmental committee that contributes policy advice on Antarctic affairs to the government. Antarctica New Zealand is responsible for developing and managing New Zealand's national activities in the Ross Dependency and New Zealand's activities generally in Antarctica, and is a Crown entity managed by the Ministry of Foreign Affairs and Trade.

Tokelau

Status: New Zealand external territory, directly administered by New Zealand.

Geography

Tokelau consists of three atolls (Atafu, Nukunonu and Fakaofo) lying in the South Pacific 480km north of Apia, Samoa. The atolls are scattered: Atafu lies 64km north-west of Nukunonu, and Fakaofo 92km south-east of Nukunonu.

Area: Atafu (2.03 sq km), Nukunonu (5.46 sq km) and Fakaofo (2.63 sq km) – totalling 10.12 sq km.

Topography: Each atoll consists of a number of low-lying islets, surrounding a lagoon, nowhere higher than 5m. The projected rise in sea level as a result of the greenhouse effect of atmospheric pollution could put the territory at risk. The soil is thin and infertile.

Climate: Tropical with average annual temperature of 28°C and heavy rainfall.

Transport/Communications: There are no roads, no airstrip and no harbour. Vessels anchor offshore, and there is a regular sea link between the atolls and with Samoa.

Tokelau was the last country in the world without a telephone system. All government departments and most households are now connected to the telephone network. The international dialling code is 690. There are 264 main telephone lines per 1,000 people (2010).

Society

Population: 1,400 (2010), with about one-third of people on each of Atafu, Nukunonu and Fakaofo; population density for the territory as a whole is 138 per sq km.

Population has been declining, with emigration mainly to New Zealand and Samoa (about 6,800 Tokelauans live in New Zealand, 2006 New Zealand census). The people are of Polynesian origin.

Language: Tokelauan is the official language; English widely spoken. Local dialects are also spoken.

Religion: Mainly Christians (Congregationalists 67% and Roman Catholics 30%).

Health: Each of the three atolls has a 12-bed hospital manned by at least one doctor, several nurses and nurses' aides.

Education: Compulsory from age five to 15. There are three government schools, one on each atoll, providing education at all levels.

Additional secondary, tertiary and vocational education is provided in New Zealand and other Pacific countries, and there are links with the regional University of the South Pacific in Fiji.

Media: There is one newspaper (not daily) and a radio station on each atoll to broadcast shipping and weather reports.

Economy

Subsistence farming (coconuts, fruit), livestock production (pigs, ducks, poultry, goats) and fishing are the principal economic activities. There is a tuna-processing plant on Atafu and some handicraft production. Revenue is also raised through the sale of licences to fish in Tokelau's exclusive economic zone and through philatelic sales. Remittances from expatriate Tokelauans are an important source of income. The New Zealand Government allocated US$19 million to Tokelau in 2009/10.

History

The islands became a British protectorate in 1877. In 1916, the islands (known as the Union Islands until 1946) were annexed by the UK and included within the Gilbert and Ellice Islands Colony. In 1925, the Tokelau group was separated from the Colony and New Zealand assumed responsibility for administration. In 1948, it was included 'within the territorial boundaries' of New Zealand. The Tokelau Public Service, formerly based in Apia, Samoa, has now largely been relocated to the islands.

Administration

There is an administrator responsible to the minister of foreign affairs and trade in New Zealand. (The administrator may also be the Secretary of Foreign Affairs and Trade but at present the post is separate.) The Tokelau Apia Liaison Office (that is, the government office) is located in Samoa because of its better communications.

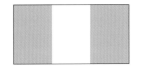

Nigeria

KEY FACTS

Joined Commonwealth:	1960 (suspended 1995–99)
Population:	158,423,000 (2010)
GDP p.c. growth:	1.9% p.a. 1990–2010
UN HDI 2011:	world ranking 156
Official language:	English
Time:	GMT plus 1hr
Currency:	Naira (N)

Geography

Area:	923,768 sq km
Coastline:	853km
Capital:	Abuja

The Federal Republic of Nigeria lies on the Gulf of Guinea and has borders with Benin (west), Niger (north), Chad (north-east across Lake Chad) and Cameroon (east). It comprises the Abuja Federal Capital Territory and 36 states.

Topography: Nigeria is a large country, 1,045km long and 1,126km wide. It has several important rivers, notably the Niger and its main tributary, the Benue, both of which are navigable. The Niger forms a delta some 100km wide, running into the sea west of Port Harcourt. In the north-east rivers drain into Lake Chad. The coastal region is low-lying, with lagoons, sandy beaches and mangrove swamps. Inland the country rises to the central Jos Plateau at 1,800m. The Adamawa Massif, bordering Cameroon, rises to 2,042m at Dimlang (Vogel Peak).

Climate: Tropical; hot and humid on the coast, with greater extremes of temperature inland and cold nights in the north during December and January. The rainy season is generally March–November in the south and May–September in the north. In the dry season the harmattan wind blows from the Sahara.

Environment: The most significant environmental issues are rapid deforestation, soil degradation, and desertification.

Did you know...

Chief Emeka Anyaoku of Nigeria was Commonwealth Secretary-General 1990–2000.

Wole Soyinka, born in Abeokuta in July 1934, was awarded the Nobel Prize in Literature in 1986; and Nigerians have won fourteen Commonwealth Writers' Prizes.

Nigeria is the most populous country in Africa with a population of over 150 million.

Vegetation: Mangrove and freshwater swamps in coastal areas, merging into an area of rainforest, containing hardwoods and oil palms. Moving north, the savannah and plateau regions have grasslands and hardy trees such as the baobab and tamarind. There is semi-desert vegetation in the north-east. In the north, forest depletion has been caused by overgrazing, bush fires and the use of wood as fuel, but there has been government-sponsored planting in an attempt to arrest the southward advance of the Sahara. Oil palms occur naturally and, being valuable, are often spared when forests are cleared. Forest covers 10% of the land area, having declined at 3.2% p.a. 1990–2010. Some 76% of forest is savannah woodland, 20% tropical rainforest and 4% swamp forest. Arable land comprises 37% and permanent cropland 3% of the total land area.

Wildlife: The Yankari National Park is an important stopover for migrating birds (some 600 species call there), and also has an elephant population. The Okomo Sanctuary is home to the endangered white-throated monkey. On the grasslands of the savannah are camels, antelope, hyenas and giraffes. An area of 30,100 sq km is protected (2003), or 3.3% of the land area.

Main towns: Abuja (federal capital since 1991, pop. 1.35m in 2010), Lagos (commercial centre and former capital, Lagos State, 9.97m), Ibadan (Oyo, 5.18m), Benin City (Edo, 2.41m), Kano (Kano, 2.38m), Port Harcourt (Rivers, 2.10m), Kaduna (Kaduna, 2.06m), Aba (Abia, 1.60m), Maiduguri (Borno, 1.13m), Ilorin (Kwara, 1.08m), Warri (Edo, 933,800), Onitsha (Anambra, 910,800), Akure (Ondo, 847,900), Abeokuta (Ogun, 801,300), Enugu (Enugu, 715,800), Oshogbo (Osun, 678,300), Zaria (Kaduna, 667,400), Ife (Osun, 635,200), Jos (Plateau, 622,800), Ondo (Ondo, 498,100), Gboko (Benue, 485,700), Owerri (Imo, 474,800), Jalingo (Taraba, 439,000), Asaba (Delta, 407,100), Oyo (Oyo, 383,700),

SPPU

ADAMAWA STATE GOVERNMENT

HE Gov.
Murtala Nyako

Empowering Adamawa State

" I appeal to the people of Adamawa to support Governor Murtala Nyako's administration for its tremendous achievements, especially in poverty eradication, through sustainable agricultural skills programmes across the state. "

Hon. Minister of Women's Affairs and Youth Development, Hajia Zainab Maina

The Nyako vision

> Economic development of Adamawa State within the context of Vision 20:2020

> Agriculture for food security and grassroot empowerment

> Economic empowerment of the people, with focus on the rural poor

> Business and vocational skills acquisition for the youth and women towards sustainable development and economic independence

> Local production of essential food items to citizens at affordable prices

The Special Projects and Programmes Unit (SPPU), an arm of the office of his Excellency Governor Murtala Nyako, is to oversee the implementation of the Grassroots Socio-Economic Empowerment Programme (GSEEP) by providing professional advice to the relevant implementing bodies such as ministries and parastatals.

In recent times, the SPPU has initiated GSEEP, the Special Assistants (SA) scheme for empowerment, the Laddo Dam (Cameroon) Hydro Electricity project, Adamawa Agricultural Development and Investment Limited (AADIL) and computer training for primary school pupils in conjunction with SUBEB, the trade enhancement programme for existing artisans in the state.

Contact
Mr Trevor Bullen
Managing Director
AADIL
Tel: +234 706 570 0957
trevorjbullen@gmail.com

aadilonline.com.ng

AGRICULTURE AS THE CENTREPIECE FOR DEVELOPMENT

An initiative of the State Government for sustainable agriculture

Grassroots Socio-Economic Empowerment Programme (GSEEP)

GSEEP is an initiative of his Excellency Governor Murtala Nyako. The programme is a holistic approach to providing a solution to the problem of poverty that is ravaging the indigenes of the state. His Excellency believes that poverty can only be reduced to the bare minimum if people are empowered with the right knowledge of modern farming methods, technical skills, trade enhancement and access to markets. The training includes an entrepreneurial component and support by microfinance institutions for microcredit.

Why GSEEP?

> Empowering people of Adamawa State by increasing access to business skills, marketable skills and household incomes

> Fostering linkages between skilled and unskilled people for mentorship in local agro based and non-agro based businesses for sustainable development

> Improving attitudes of youths towards promoting productivity, economic growth and sustainable agricultural development in Adamawa State

> Establishing a long term framework and structures that will bring about sustainable small, medium and mechanised agricultural production

> Establishing agricultural products processing and distribution opportunities

> Increasing internally generated revenue of Adamawa State

The GSEEP projects

TSAC – Technical Skill Acquisition Centre

FSAC – Farming Skills Acquisition Centre which carries out activities embracing every area of farming with particular adaptation to the Nigerian environment.

LASD – Local Apprenticeship Skills Development. GSEEP locates 'Master Trainers' and attaches trainees to them for thorough training in specified trades and vocations.

Human Resources Development – This section concentrates mainly on developing 'Special Assistants' (SA) who serve as training agents. There are currently about 15,000 SAs involved in the scheme.

GSEEP would not have achieved its much attributed objectives if **Adamawa Agricultural Development and Investment Limited (AADIL)** had not come into the limelight. AADIL has the status of a limited liability company and the State is 100% shareholder. Over 8,000 farmers have benefitted from AADIL's programmes so far.

The focus of AADIL is to: facilitate, encourage and provide necessary linkages, nationally and internationally for the development of the agricultural and agro-industrial complex of the State.

AADIL assists trained farmers with the processing and marketing of farm produce. In addition, individual farmers and farmers' unions/co-operative societies can sell their products through AADIL. In this way, farmers can cut down on the cost of storage, avoid waste and increase cash flow.

Nourishing and Building a Great Nation

For over 5 decades, Flour Mills of Nigeria Plc and its iconic Golden Penny brand have been a part of the lives of Nigerians at home and abroad. With annual turnover in the region of $3bn and a workforce of over 3,000, FMN has ambitious plans for the future. The Company's vision is to be a leading Food Group in Africa; providing an ever expanding portfolio of high quality and affordable products to consumers in the most convenient ways; delivered currently through a range of world class flour, semolina, pasta, noodles, and rice products, supported by the Golden Penny brand heritage and values.

In addition, FMN is increasing its focus on backward integration in the Agro Allied sector, which will be a vital support to the development of both its own Food Group interests and in the further development of the country's agricultural resources. Investments have been made and are ongoing in two farms in Nigeria and will extend further in order to support its sugar, rice, and edible oil interests. These plans will be supported by the fertilizer division which is the clear market leader in distribution of fertilizer within Nigeria.

FMN continues to have a significant presence in cement, where the focus is primarily on its shareholding in the Unicem business. It also has a number of support businesses providing critically important packaging, transport and logistics services to the whole Group.

www.fmnplc.com

FLOUR MILLS OF NIGERIA PLC
2, Old Dock Road, P.O.Box 341, Apapa, Lagos, NIGERIA.   RC 2343

24-7imc   aaan 0190

Ado (Ekiti, 378,500), Sokoto (Sokoto, 360,500), Minna (Niger, 322,200), Uyo (Akwa Ibom, 320,000), Calabar (Cross River, 318,400), Bauchi (Bauchi, 294,400), Ogbomosho (Oyo, 269,300), Katsina (Katsina, 213,600), Gombe (Gombe, 197,400), Makurdi (Benue, 171,000), Okene (Kogi, 122,100), Birnin Kebbi (Kebbi, 119,100), Yola (Adamawa, 111,800) and Nsukka (Enugu, 39,700).

Transport: 193,200km of roads, 15% paved, link all main centres. Some secondary roads are impassable during the rains.

There are around 3,530km of railway, the main routes running from Lagos to Kano, and from Port Harcourt to Maiduguri, with a branch line from Zaria to Gusau and Kaura Namoda. Much of the network is single-track, and the narrow gauge restricts speed and load-carrying capacity.

Main ports are at Apapa, Tin Can Island, Warri, Sapele, Port Harcourt and Calabar. Ferry services operate along the Niger and Benue rivers and along the coast.

Lagos international airport is 22km north of Lagos; other main international airports are at Abuja (35km from the city), Kano and Port Harcourt, and main domestic airports at Benin City, Calabar, Enugu, Jos, Kaduna, Lagos, Maiduguri, Sokoto and Yola.

Society

KEY FACTS 2010

Population per sq km:	171
Life expectancy:	51 years
Net primary enrolment:	63%

Population: 158,423,000 (2010); 50% lives in urban areas and 15% in urban agglomerations of more than 1 million people; growth 2.4% p.a. 1990–2010; birth rate 40 per 1,000 people (47 in 1970); life expectancy 51 years (40 in 1970).

Nigeria is one of the most ethnically diverse countries. There are some 250 ethnic groups, with the Hausa–Fulani, Yoruba and Igbo making up 70%.

Language: English (official language), Hausa, Yoruba, Igbo and more than 200 other languages and dialects.

Religion: Muslims (mainly in the north and west) 50%, Christians (mainly in the south) 40%, and the rest holding traditional beliefs.

Health: Public spending on health was 2% of GDP in 2009. 58% of the population uses an improved drinking water source and 32% have access to adequate sanitation facilities (2009). Infant mortality was 88 per 1,000 live births in 2010 (123 in 1960). In 2009, 3.6% of people aged 15–49 were HIV positive.

Education: There are nine years of compulsory education starting at age six. Primary school comprises six years and secondary two cycles each of three years. The school year starts in September.

By June 2011, the National Universities Commission had accredited 36 federal universities, 36 state universities, and 45 private universities, including 4 federal universities of technology, 3 federal universities of agriculture and the National Open University of Nigeria. The longest-established universities are University of Ibadan (1948); University of Nigeria, Nsukka (1960); Ahmadu Bello University, Zaria (1962); University of Lagos (1962); and Obafemi Awolowo University, Ile-Ife (1962). The first state university, Rivers State University of Science and Technology, was founded in 1979 and the first private universities, in 1999. Literacy among people aged 15–24 is 72% (2009).

Media: There are more than 100 national and regional newspapers, some state-owned, as well as Sunday papers, business weeklies and news magazines. Established titles with national distribution include *Daily Independent* (Lagos), *Daily Sun* (Lagos), *Daily Trust* (Abuja), *Leadership* (Abuja), *New Nigerian* (government-owned with Lagos and Kaduna editions), *Newswatch* (weekly), *Tell* (weekly), *The Champion* (Lagos), *The Daily Times* (Lagos), *The Guardian*, *The Punch*, *This Day* (Lagos) and *Vanguard* (Lagos).

The Federal Radio Corporation of Nigeria and Nigerian Television Authority provide national and regional public radio and TV services respectively. The state governments in all 36 states provide radio services and most, TV services, too. A number of private TV and radio stations are operating, mainly in the urban areas.

Some 39% of households have TV sets (2008). There are 9 personal computers (2005) and 284 internet users (2010) per 1,000 people.

Communications: Country code 234; internet domain '.ng'. Mobile phone coverage is expanding. There are internet cafes in Lagos.

There are 7 main telephone lines and 551 mobile phone subscriptions per 1,000 people (2010).

Public holidays: New Year's Day, Workers' Day (1 May), National Day (1 October), Christmas Day and Boxing Day.

Religious festivals whose dates vary from year to year include Mouloud (Prophet's Birthday), Good Friday, Easter Monday, Eid al-Fitr (End of Ramadan, three days) and Eid al-Kabir (Feast of the Sacrifice).

Economy

KEY FACTS 2010

GNI:	US$186.4bn
GNI p.c.:	US$1,180
GDP growth:	6.7% p.a. 2006–10
Inflation:	10.1% p.a. 2006–10

Nigeria is very vulnerable to fluctuations in international prices and demand for oil and gas, which accounts for more than 90% of export earnings and the greater part of federal revenue. During many years of military rule, economic management was generally weak. When oil prices were high, the revenues flowed into increased public spending and conspicuous consumption, and imports soared. GDP grew by 1.6% p.a. 1980–90.

Some public investment went into prestige industrial projects which were generally a burden on the economy, failing to generate profits, depending on imported components or materials and increasing external debt. But the development of non-oil industries that relied on local raw materials and would generate employment and exports was not encouraged and the consistently overvalued currency deterred exports.

By 1997–98 the economy was in a critical condition. Once self-sufficient in food, the country had become a major food importer. Development aid and foreign loans and investment had decreased dramatically. From May 1999, with the support of the IMF, the World Bank and the international community, the civilian government committed itself to reforming policies, including privatisation of state enterprises and modernisation of agriculture,

NATIONAL SPACE RESEARCH AND DEVELOPMENT AGENCY (NASRDA)
Building indigenous competence in space technology

Background

Nigeria's quest for space exploration started in 1976 when Nigeria declared its space ambition to members of the Economic Commission for Africa and Organization of African Unity (now the African Union) during an inter-governmental meeting in Addis-Ababa, Ethiopia.

It was not until 1999 that the National Space Research and Development Agency (NASRDA) was established to co-ordinate the development and applications of space technology in Nigeria. The establishment of NASRDA was followed by the approval of the National Space Policy in 2001. The policy established the National Space Council, chaired by the President and a Technical Advisory Committee. Finally, the National Space Research and Development Agency Bill was signed as an Act of Parliament on 27 August 2010 by the President. The Act founded the Centre for Space Science and Technology Education, Ile-Ife; Centre for Remote Sensing, Jos; Centre for Satellite Technology Development, Abuja; Centre for Geodesy and Geodynamics, Toro; Centre for Space Transport and Propulsion, Epe; and Centre for Basic Space Science and Astronomy, Nsukka.

Vision

To make Nigeria build indigenous competence in developing, designing and building appropriate hardware and software in space technology as an essential tool for its socio-economic development and enhancement of the quality of life of its people.

Mission

To use space technology capabilities as a tool for the:

- Development and management of agricultural and forestry resources.
- Assessment and management of national resources.
- Development of an effective and efficient communication system.
- Enhancement of transportation and tourism enterprises.
- Development of education and health care delivery systems (both rural and urban).
- Development and management of energy resources.
- Enhancement of human safety and mitigation of disasters.

The Nigerian Satellite Technology Development Programme

Nigeria currently has three earth observation satellites, as well as one communication satellite that were launched in the period between 2003 and 2011. The earth observation satellites include: NigeriaSat-1 (32m MS), NigeriaSat-2 (2.5m Pan, 5m MS, 32m MS) and NigeriaSat-X (22m MS). The communication satellite called NigcomSat-1R has 40 transponder payloads.

Nigeria plans to complement its optical satellite programme with the commencement of the development of a non-optical (Radar) satellite in 2012. This non-optical satellite will provide the much needed data for the southern parts of the country which are predominantly covered by clouds throughout the year.

Headquarters of NASRDA in Abuja

Satellite ground station in Abuja

Strategic Space Applications Building in Abuja

Contact

Dr S.O. Mohammed, Director General
Obasanjo Space Centre,
Opp. Pyakasa Junction,
Airport Road
P.M.B. 437, Garki, Abuja

Email: dg@nasrda.net
       dg@nasrda.gov.ng

www.nasrda.gov.ng

Nigeria has a long history, with its roots in early civilisations of distinguished artistry. The plateau area around Jos was a meeting point for cultural influences from the Upper Niger Valley (where agriculture developed independently as early as 5000 BC) and from Egypt. By 3000 BC, the plateau people – probably the Bantu people who later dominated Sub-Saharan Africa – were developing more complex societies and beginning to advance to the south. By 500 BC, the Nok culture was flourishing. Nok society produced elegant and technically accomplished terracotta heads and figures; they were agriculturalists making tools and weapons of iron.

In due course, in the north, strong state systems evolved, several based on divine kingship. The people kept cattle and horses, grew cotton and cereals, and worked in fabrics, leather and iron. They were in contact with Egypt and other north African societies. Two powerful empires arose – Hausa–Bokwoi (beginning as separate states from AD 100–1000) and Kanem–Bornu (from the 11th century). They converted to Islam, traded in gold, slaves, leather, salt and cloth across the Sahara, and by and large successfully kept their enemies at bay.

In the south-west, the Yoruba had, before AD 1000, founded Ife, still the spiritual centre of Yorubaland. The origins of Benin are connected with Ife; Benin culture produced bronze sculpture by the 'lost wax' technique. These are naturalistic but slightly idealised heads of great elegance, delicacy and beauty, regarded as a major contribution to the world's artistic heritage. Ife itself, however, fell victim to conquest by Oyo in the 14th century and later Ibadan and Abeokuta. The people of the south-east were heavily preyed upon by slave traders from the north and along the coast. Forced to abandon their settlements and move into the forests to evade their captors, the struggles of the Igbo peoples were preserved in long epics, memorised and passed down the generations.

Colonial period

In the 15th century, Benin began to trade with the Portuguese, selling slaves and acquiring spices, firearms, the art of writing and the Christian religion. By the 18th century, the British had displaced the Portuguese as leaders of the slave trade. A century later, in 1807, the missionaries' campaign against slavery had gained support, leading the British parliament to ban the slave trade. The navy began to patrol the coast, arresting slavers and settling captured slaves (most of them Nigerians) in the resettlement colony of Sierra Leone. Several missionaries in Nigeria were themselves freed Nigerian slaves who had converted to Christianity in Sierra Leone. The missionaries introduced quinine to control malaria, a new trade in palm oil also began, and the economies of southern Nigeria became increasingly powerful. Steamboats took this new culture up-river and into the forests.

In the early 19th century, there was upheaval in the north, as Fulani emirs declared a *jihad* (holy war) against the Hausa state of Gobir and created a new empire with city states, a common religious and judicial system and Qur'anic schools. The Muslim empire spread rapidly.

The Yoruba, under pressure, drew closer to Britain, which annexed Lagos in 1861. In 1884, British control expanded with the creation of the Oil Rivers Protectorate, set up under treaties with Yoruba rulers, and then the north, while the Igbo were conquered. By 1900, Britain had control of Nigeria.

The Colonial Office adopted the system of indirect rule, with traditional leaders continuing in power while owing allegiance to the colonial authority.

Many educated Nigerians objected to the system, since it entrenched traditional practices which, in a freer society, would have evolved into possibly more progressive forms. Nonetheless, the system prevented British settlers from dominating the economy, and Nigerian enterprise built a substantial export trade in cocoa, groundnuts, leather, cotton and vegetable oils.

Constitutional development

In 1914, six Africans were brought into the governor's advisory council. In 1922, a legislative council (ten Africans, four of them elected, and 36 Europeans) was empowered to legislate for the south. In 1947, the council's authority was extended to the whole country. It now had 28 African (four elected) and 17 European members. The 1947 constitution also set up regional houses of assembly in the east, west and north, with a House of Chiefs in the north. The 1951 constitution gave the balance of power to Nigerians. In 1954, Nigeria became a federation; in 1957 Eastern and Western regions gained internal self-government and Northern Nigeria two years later. Elections to the Federal House of Representatives in December 1959 brought in a new government. At its first meeting, the new House requested full sovereignty and Nigeria proceeded to independence on 1 October 1960.

Independence

Nigeria's independence government was led by the Northern People's Congress in alliance with the National Council of Nigerian Citizens (a largely Igbo party), with Sir Abubakar Tafawa Balewa as prime minister. In 1963, the country became a republic and Dr Nnamdi Azikiwe its first (non-executive) president.

The first of several coups occurred in January 1966 and Tafawa Balewa was among those killed. Army commander Major-General Aguiyi-Ironsi headed a new administration, which abolished the federation and instituted a unitary state. In July 1966, troops from the north retaliated with another coup in which Aguiyi-Ironsi was killed and Lt-Col Yakubu Gowon assumed the leadership. He restored the federal state and replaced the four regions with 12 states. He included civilians in government and promised to restore democratic rule as soon as possible.

In May 1967, Lt-Col Chukwuemeka Odumegwu Ojukwu declared eastern Nigeria an independent state named the Republic of Biafra. This led to civil war. Hostilities lasted until Biafra was defeated in January 1970 and Ojukwu went into exile; the war cost some one million lives.

In 1975, Gowon was deposed in a coup and replaced by Brigadier Murtala Muhammed, who introduced radical economic reforms, a new structure of 19 states and a programme for a return to civilian rule in four years. He was assassinated in an abortive coup in 1976. Lt-Gen Olusegun Obasanjo succeeded and continued Muhammed's policies: the ban on political activities was lifted (1978), multiparty elections were held (1979) and

➤

GOCHTECH
..ideas unlimited

Gochtech Nigeria Limited was incorporated in 1997 and commenced commercial services in 1998.

The Company is essentially a family business with Mr Godwin Chukwukere, Mrs Edith Chukwukere and Mr Collins O.C. Chukwukere as Shareholders/Directors.

Their fully equipped refrigeration workshop facilities have been upgraded recently, courtesy of the United Nations Industrial Development Organization which supplies the Company with environmentally friendly machines under a special United Nations grant.

Gochtech supplies goods, materials and services to different industries, ministries, government parastatals, multinationals, oil companies, telecommunications companies, private firms, hospitals and tertiary institutions.

MISSION

Gochtech Nigeria Limited is committed to high ethical standards in business with a strong desire to provide the best quality of services and products to our numerous customers.

Our seasoned staff, in the services and production shares a common and unifying spirit and goal to sustain the ideal purpose of providing efficient products and services delivery to all our clients.

SERVICES

Gochtech Nigeria Limited offers procurement, construction, electrochemical, industrial, marine, petroleum and general merchandise with special interests in:

- construction and rehabilitation of roads
- building construction
- procurement services
- sales and services of industrial refrigeration systems for bottling companies, breweries, cooling and plastic industries
- maintenance services for carbon dioxide production plant and production of carbon dioxide
- maintenance and repairs services of power generators
- polyurethane spray and rigid foam production
- supply of marine and petroleum products.

CONTACT

Mr Collins Chukwukere
Managing Director

Lagos Office
171, Borno Way
Ebute – Metta
Lagos
P.O. Box 1954
Tel: +234 1 724 8610
Email: cobicee@yahoo.com

www.gochgroup.com

➤ Shehu Shagari of the National Party of Nigeria became (executive) president, re-elected in 1983.

However, in 1983 a military coup put an end to this brief period of democracy. New head of state Major-General Muhammadu Buhari initiated a severe austerity programme with campaigns against idleness and self-enrichment. This provoked a further coup in 1985 bringing Major-General Ibrahim Babangida to power. He repealed the most unpopular decrees and, in 1987, promised a return to civilian rule by 1992. In 1989 two parties were formed (only two parties were permitted).

The transition to civilian rule went as far as elections to state assemblies in 1991 and presidential primary elections in 1992 (re-run 1993) before the whole process was halted. The newly created Social Democratic Party won the majority in both Houses, and its leader, Chief Moshood Abiola, was believed to be leading in the presidential elections. But before all the results had been announced, the elections were annulled by Babangida, who shortly after resigned. For a few months civilian Chief Ernest Shonekan was head of an interim government, and charged with holding yet further elections.

However, in November 1993, in Nigeria's seventh coup, General Sani Abacha assumed power and cancelled the scheduled return to civilian rule. He dissolved the interim national government, national and state assemblies, the state executive councils and the two political parties, and banned all political activity.

In June 1994 a constitutional conference was held to devise a programme for a return to civilian rule. The conference failed to reach consensus. Shortly before it opened, Chief Abiola, on the basis of the 1993 elections, proclaimed himself president. He was arrested and charged with treason; he was held in solitary confinement and was never brought to trial.

In March 1995, during a clamp-down after an alleged counter-coup, the military arrested prominent opponents of the regime and campaigners for a rapid return to democracy, including retired generals Olusegun Obasanjo and Shehu Musa Yar'Adua – whose political influence stemmed from the fact that they headed the military government which handed power to a civilian government in 1979. Obasanjo and Yar'Adua were tried for treason and sentenced to long terms of imprisonment. Shortly afterwards, in October, Abacha further postponed plans for a return to democracy, and announced a new three-year timetable for completing the transition by late 1998.

Amid the many political detentions of this period, one of Nigeria's most popular writers, Ken Saro-Wiwa, leader of the campaign against pollution of Ogoni lands and waters by the oil industry, and eight others were arrested and charged with the murder of local chiefs. They were tried by a military court and executed on 10 November 1995, hours after the Commonwealth Heads of Government Meeting had opened in New Zealand. In response, on 11 November, Commonwealth Heads of Government suspended Nigeria from membership of the Commonwealth for contravening the principles of the Harare Commonwealth Declaration, and called for the release of Abiola and 43 other political prisoners.

In 1996 five parties were registered and local elections took place in March 1997, when the United Nigeria Congress Party (UNCP)

and Democratic Party of Nigeria (DPN) won most seats. At the Commonwealth Heads of Government Meeting in Edinburgh, United Kingdom, in October 1997 Nigeria's suspension from Commonwealth membership was extended until 1 October 1998 by which time the Abacha government had said it would restore democracy and civilian government. If the transition programme failed, or was not credible, Nigeria would be expelled. In December 1997, UNCP gained a majority in 29 of the 36 state assemblies.

By April 1998 all five registered political parties had adopted Abacha as their candidate for the August presidential election, although he had not publicly agreed to stand. In the general election in the same month, a very low poll, UNCP took a majority of seats in both the House of Representatives and the Senate. Abacha died suddenly in June 1998 and was replaced as head of state by Chief of Defence Staff General Abdulsalami Abubakar, who promised to return the country to civilian rule and released nine political prisoners including Olusegun Obasanjo. Chief Abiola also died suddenly, in July 1998 while his release from detention was still being negotiated. He was 60 and, though some initially suspected foul play, an international team of pathologists who were called in to conduct an autopsy confirmed he died of natural causes. His health had however been adversely affected by the harsh detention conditions.

Abubakar dissolved the principal bodies associated with the Abacha regime's democracy programme, released detainees, allowed unfettered political activity and published a new election timetable. A new Independent National Electoral Commission was set up in August 1998. As a result of the local government elections in December 1998, the People's Democratic Party (PDP), All People's Party (APP) and Alliance for Democracy (AD) went forward to contest the state and federal elections. The PDP took 23 state governorships, APP eight and AD six. In the National Assembly elections, PDP won nearly 60% of the seats in the House of Representatives and the Senate. The presidential election gave PDP candidate Obasanjo a convincing victory with 62% of the votes against 38% for joint APP/AD candidate Chief Oluyemi Falae. These federal elections were closely monitored by international, including Commonwealth, observers. Although cases of serious irregularities were noted, especially in the presidential poll, when the turnout figures were often inflated, they were not deemed to have brought the overall result into question.

In the wake of the elections, the departing military rulers published a new constitution. When Obasanjo became president in May 1999, Nigeria's suspension from the Commonwealth was lifted. The 1999 constitution, which permitted the practice of Sharia law for consenting Muslims, opened the way for some northern states – led by Zamfara State in October 1999 – to seek to implement it. This plunged the country into a heated controversy and some violence as Christians in these states were not convinced by assurances that it would not adversely affect them. This continued as the northern states successively adopted Sharia law. Zamfara was first to carry out an amputation in March 2000 and Sokoto first to sentence a woman to death by stoning for adultery in October 2001 (later revoked).

Governor Patrick Yakowa:

Changing the face of Kaduna

Great signs of departure from the past in the general administration of Kaduna State, northwest Nigeria, may have manifested with Governor Patrick Ibrahim Yakowa's determination to change its fortunes through enhanced revenue generation and infrastructural development.

This departure signals a conscientious leap to embrace development strategies in the quest to lay a solid framework, not hitherto exploited, that could push the State to the forefront in the march towards the attainment of Millennium Development Goals (MDGs), as well as tackling other challenges that have restricted growth.

The agenda of the administration for growth is hinged on a number of carefully selected programmes that are a vital means of speedy development. These areas of focus include peace and security, qualitative education, agricultural development and poverty alleviation, improved healthcare delivery, infrastructural development, civil service reform, self-sufficiency, as well as job creation for youth and women development and empowerment.

Roads

Aware of a substantial gap in the state development process, from last year the administration began to ease city traffic and mobility by investing the sum of N13.8 billion (US$87.5 million) to build new bridges and access roads. These include the fourth bridge across Kaduna River, to link the northern and southern part of the city, roads at the state university's Kafanchan campus, Kofar Gayan-Jos Road, Soba-Ikara Road.

Health care

A 300-bed world-class, specialist hospital in the heart of the capital will provide, upon completion, up-to-date medical attention.

In reaction to the concern for infant and maternal mortality rates, huge sums have been expended on free medical care for women and children while the expansion and rehabilitation of hospitals and rural clinics and the supply of drugs are areas of focus.

Zaria water works under construction

20 km access road through Kamazou under construction

Building bridges and access roads

State

Contact: Mr Reuben Buhari, Special Adviser Media and Publicity, Government House Kaduna, Sir Kashim Ibrahim House
Tel: +234 802 358 485 4234 • Email: reubenhari@yahoo.com

www.kadunastate.gov.ng

As a policy drive, the government has committed itself in 2012 to revive and strengthen Primary Health Care Centres. Premium attention has been given to the State Primary Health Care Agency and Drugs and Medical Supplies Management Agency as a catalyst to ensure the quality of drugs and medical supplies in all secondary health facilities and primary health centres.

Education

The government executed projects worth about 2.2 billion naira (US$13.9 million) in 2011 to provide science equipment, furniture and the expansion or rehabilitation of libraries. Boreholes were drilled at schools to ensure provision of clean and safe water in line with MDG goals. School buildings found to be inadequate have been expanded and some rehabilitated in various schools in the three senatorial zones of Kaduna State.

Water schemes

Urban and rural water schemes are on-going in various towns and cities. Already, the sum of N292 million (US$1.85 million) has been invested on 36 solar-powered boreholes while 759 hand pumps and boreholes have also been constructed across the State. Currently, the construction of a multi-billion naira Zaria water project will benefit - upon completion of the 150 million litres per day water plant - seven local governments.

Agriculture

The main focus of Governor Yakowa's administration will be the transformation of the agricultural sector which holds huge potentials for growth in the State. His agricultural programmes include timely provision of fertilizer at a 50% subsidy to farmers and construction of dams and irrigation schemes to facilitate all-year farming in the central and northern senatorial zones. Farmers have also benefitted from a 'tractor programme' in which 186 units of tractors were sold at a 60% discount to promote mechanised, agricultural activities in the State.

Electricity

The Gurara Dam project generates 30 MW of electricity while a thermal plant, generating 84 MW, is in the pipeline which will be established at the Kudenda industrial layout in Kaduna metropolis, in addition to a Federal Government 215 MW plant in the vicinity. There is also a strong liaison between the State and Federal Government to establish two important hydro-power stations at Galma Dam in Kubau Local Government and Itisi in Kajuru Local Government, to generate and transmit sufficient energy in the rural areas.

His Excellency
Patrick Yakowa,
Executive Govenor

Classrooms under construction   The discounted tractor scheme   New housing scheme

Zenith Bank Plc

Zenith Bank was established in May 1990 and started operations in July same year as a commercial bank. It became a public liability company on June 17, 2004 and was listed on the Nigerian Stock Exchange on October 21, 2004 following a very successful Initial Public Offering (IPO). The bank is one of the biggest and most capitalized companies on the Nigerian Stock Exchange. It presently has a shareholder base of over 700,000, an indication of the strength and wide acceptance of the Zenith brand.

Zenith Bank Plc. has evolved through innovation, dynamism, rare business insight and excellent leadership to become a leading financial institution in Nigeria. Within the first decade of commencing operations, the bank made its mark in profitability and a number of other performance indices.

The bank has, over the years, redefined customer service standards and created diverse service delivery channels. The Zenith brand has become synonymous with the use of Information and Communication Technology (ICT) in banking and general innovation in the Nigerian banking industry. The bank continues to drive its competitive edge through the use of robust ICT platform in delivering exceptional customer services. Coupled with its strong brand recognition and strategically distributed branch network, the bank has maintained a good share of the Nigerian market. Zenith Bank also continues to reinvent its service excellence strategy to consolidate on its exceptional performance. Thus, its service channels, especially for the electronic solutions (e-products) are re-engineered and strengthened for greater efficiency and effectiveness.

Zenith Bank has become a brand prized for its tremendous success in e-banking, global credit guarantee status, niche marketing, cutting edge competitive advantage in a number of areas of financial services, provisioning and unwavering commitment to technological deployment in line with international best practices. The bank's competitive advantage as a financial powerhouse for value creation in Nigeria results from the combination of people, talent, proprietary knowledge, strong brand equity, leadership, integrity and excellent relationship management.

With over 315 branches, the bank has built on its successes in Nigeria to explore opportunities beyond the shores of Nigeria. Consequently, four foreign subsidiaries and one representative office have been established: Zenith Bank (Ghana) Limited, Zenith Bank (UK) Limited, Zenith Bank (Sierra Leone) Limited, Zenith Bank (Gambia) Limited and Zenith Bank (South Africa Rep Office).

The bank maintains sound corporate governance culture in line with global best practices. The bank's core values include service excellence, investment in human capital development, superior asset quality and strong credit culture. Zenith Bank has good and sustainable earnings, strong capital base, and is reputed for professionalism and excellent community development initiatives. The Bank has become synonymous with excellence. The impressive growth pattern and performance, over the years, have earned Zenith Bank excellent ratings from local and international agencies. Standard and Poors currently rates the bank B+/B. Also, Fitch Ratings currently rates Zenith Bank AA- (National) and B+ on Long-term foreign currency Issuer Default Rating (IDR).

The bank is confident it can sustain its superior performance and growth trajectory in the years ahead by accentuating the positive disposition that drives its determination to be a benchmark for the banking industry in Nigeria.

Godwin Emefiele
Group Managing Director / Chief Executive Officer

ZENITH
...in your best interest

- people

- technology

- service

www.zenithbank.com

Real Growth in GDP

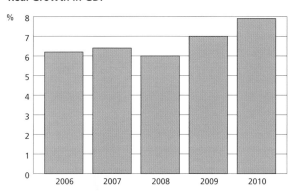

Inflation

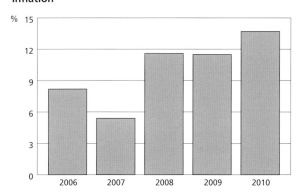

GDP by Sector (2010)

■ Agriculture	35%
□ Industry	37%
▨ Services	27%

with the public sector concentrating on infrastructure and education and the private sector leading economic growth.

But reversing the many years of weak and corrupt economic management was a daunting challenge and progress was slow. Nevertheless, in a climate of stronger international oil prices GDP growth picked up in 2000 and from 2003 was generally more than 6% p.a. for the rest of the decade, and at least 7% p.a. 2009–11, despite the world economic downturn of 2008–09.

Oil and gas

Nigerian oil has a low sulphur content and proven reserves of oil were estimated in January 2011 to be 37 billion barrels. Production in mid-2011 was at the rate of about 2.6 million barrels a day.

Proven reserves of gas were estimated in January 2011 to be 5.3 trillion cubic metres. Exports of liquefied natural gas began in 1999 and grew rapidly. The establishment of the West African Gas Pipeline is set to provide a secure basis for future gas exports.

OUR VISION

To become a world-class centre of excellence in Marine Science.

MISSION STATEMENT

To be a national Fisheries and Oceanography centre of excellence using dedicated, world-class scientists to collect, analyse and provide scientific data and information for the development of scientific products necessary for the sustainability, utilisation and management of Nigeria's aquatic marine resources, coastal and ocean environment for the benefit of our national and the global community at large.

GOAL

To assist the national development goals of food security, poverty reduction, marine environment cleanliness and sustainability.

MANDATE

- Genetic improvement of marine and brackish-water living resources in Nigeria
- Studies of abundance, distribution and biology of aquatic resources in Nigeria's brackish and marine waters
- Establishment of the physical and chemical characteristics of Nigeria's territorial waters
- Determination of the effects of pollution of Nigeria's coastal waters and its prevention
- Extension of research and liaison services in areas of its mandate
- The Institute also has a non-research function to provide vocational training in Fisheries, Oceanography and Aquaculture.

BACKGROUND

The Nigerian Institute for Oceanography and Marine Research (NIOMR) was established in November 1975 by the Research Institutes' Establishment Order. The Institute's headquarters on Victoria Island at Bar Beach, houses the Finance and Supply, Administration, Marine Geology/Geophysics Departments as well as the Economic and Statistics section of the Fisheries Resources Department.

NIOMR headquarters also hosts the Fishing Technology building, the 'Whitehouse', Library and the Engineering and Maintenance Department.

OUTSTATIONS

As the scope and magnitude of the Institute's activities broadened, it became necessary to establish outstations to cater for the growing demands of the Institute's services:

Buguma outstation was established for research and training in brackish-water aquaculture.

Aluu outstation houses the African Regional Aquaculture Centre (ARAC) located in Aluu, Port Harcourt, Rivers State. The Centre was established to provide training in Aquaculture Technology up to postgraduate level and is affiliated to the Rivers State University of Science and Technology for the award of a postgraduate diploma and a Masters of Technology degree in Aquaculture.

Sapele outstation is situated in Delta State to address both brackish and fresh water fishery issues.

Badore outstation is used as a demonstration centre for Aquaculture Research. It has a number of earthen ponds whose primary source of water is the Lagos Lagoon. Currently, a Fish Disease Laboratory, and fish feed and fish mill production facilities are being established at the centre.

Mariculture Centre, Badagry, Lagos State commenced construction in 2010 at Yovogan Beach. The first stage of the project involves the construction of a shrimp hatchery and accommodation of research scientists.

NIOMR Headquarters

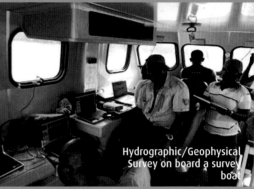
Hydrographic/Geophysical Survey on board a survey boat

Deploring Acoustic Doppler current profiler

NIOMR Tidal Gauge Station with Kalestro tide gaul

Water recirculatory flume tank for testing fishing nets

MARINE RESEARCH, LAGOS

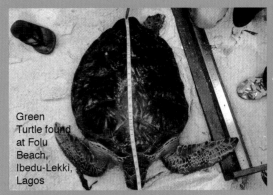

Green Turtle found at Folu Beach, Ibedu-Lekki, Lagos

Central Laboratory with Gas Chromatography equipment

R/V Sarkim Baka

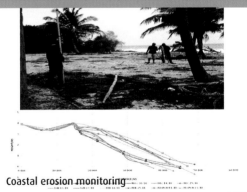

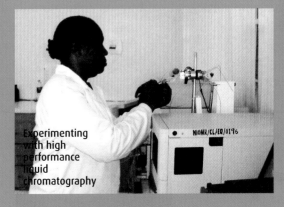

Coastal erosion monitoring

Experimenting with high performance liquid chromatography

DEPARTMENTS
- Fisheries Resources
- Fish Technology
- Aquaculture and Biotechnology
- Physical and Chemical Oceanography
- Biological Oceanography
- Marine Geology/Geophysics

There are also four service departments:
- Finance and Supply
- Administration
- Technical Services
- Information and Documentation

FACILITIES AND RESOURCES
In addition to the headquarters and outstations, NIOMR facilities include a Fish Technology/Oceanography annex, a marine shrimp hatchery, jetty and six laboratories: **Fisheries, Fish Technology, Fishing Technology, Physical/Chemical Oceanography, Marine Geology/Geophysics and a central laboratory.**

There are two tide gauges, a marine fabrication and maintenance workshop and a pilot plant for fish canning.

Research vessels
The Institute has a 7.5m fibre glass boat with a dismountable canopy for research work in the Lagos Lagoon, a 442m LOA and 272 GT pole-and-line tuna fishing/oceanographic research vessel named M.V. Sarkim Baka which is equipped with a standard hydrographic winch and modern position fixing gadgets.

The government awarded a contract for the building of a 36.3 LOA Demersal/Pelagic Deep Sea Oceanographic and Fisheries Research Vessel in 2010. It is currently under construction in Poland.

INTERNATIONAL COLLABORATION
- Participation in the ODINAFRICA Scientific Symposium: Contribution of Ocean Data Information to Sustainable Development Areas in Africa.
- A collaboration arrangement is in progress with the Second Institute of Oceanography (SIO), China and NIOMR for a joint sea cruise.

STAFF
The Institute has a staff of 357, comprising 117 research officers and supporting staff including 156 administrative personnel, 63 research technologists and 3 casual workers.

CONTACT

Dr Olajide Adeleke Ayinla, Executive Director

NIOMR Headquarters
3 Wilmot Point Road
Bar Beach
Victoria Island, Lagos
Lagos State
Nigeria
Tel: +234 813 216 2127
E-mail: info@niomr.org
and jideayinla@yahoo.com

www.niomr.org

AMCON

ASSET
MANAGEMENT
CORPORATION Of NIGERIA

Asset Management Corporation of Nigeria (AMCON) was established on 19th July 2010 as a tool for reviving and stabilising Nigeria's banking industry by purchasing the non-performing loans (NPLs) of the nation's banking industry.

Vision
To be a key stabilising tool in the Nigerian financial sector.

Mission
To positively assist the economy of Nigeria by:
- Spearheading the recapitalisation of affected Nigerian banks
- Providing a window for banks to sell off Non-Performing Loans (NPLs)
- Freeing up valuable resources and enabling banks focus on their core activities
- Getting banks lending again to the real sector to spur economic growth
- Increasing confidence in banks balance sheets
- Increasing access to restructuring/refinancing opportunities for borrowers

The purchase of Non-Performing Loans (NPLs) by AMCON helped restore confidence in the Nigerian banking industry. Before the formation of AMCON, NPLs ratio in the Nigerian banking industry was in excess of 35%. As of December 31 2011 the NPL ratio had fallen to less than 5%, enabling the banks to focus on lending.

AMCON has so far acquired over 10,000 NPLs worth N3.5 trillion (US$20 billion). In addition, AMCON injected fresh capital into eight Nigerian banks, five of which have entered into successful mergers. As a result of the recapitalisation of banks, AMCON currently owns Mainstreet Bank, Enterprise Bank and Keystone Bank. It intends to divest from these banks in the short to medium term with the help of a financial advisory firm that will be engaged subsequent to the adverts in local and foreign media publications.

The Corporation has also successfully restructured a number of key NPLs in critical sectors of the economy such as aviation, manufacturing, agriculture and oil and gas, securing their continued operations and future growth in line with the stated objectives of the Federal Government of Nigeria.

**Mr Mustafa Chike-Obi,
Managing Director**

Contact
Head Office
21 Danube Street
Maitama, P.M.B. 5358
Abuja, FCT
Tel: +234 9 876 1892 3
      +234 9 812 2820/22/24

Lagos Office
8th Floor
Mulliner Towers
39 Alfred Rewane Road
Ikoyi, Lagos
Tel: +234 1 277 3210

www.amcon.com.ng

... the spirit of enterprise

KEYSTONE BANK LIMITED

Constitution

Status:	Republic with executive president
Legislature:	National Assembly
Independence:	1 October 1960

The May 1999 constitution, like those of 1979 and 1989, and the draft constitution of 1995, provided for a federal republic with an executive president on the US model. Six new states were created in October 1996, bringing the total to 36. The president is elected every four years by universal adult suffrage and is required to include at least one representative of each of the 36 states in the cabinet. There is a bicameral National Assembly made up of a House of Representatives (with 360 seats) and a Senate (with 109 seats), each elected for four-year terms. The state governors and assemblies are also elected every four years.

The constitution also guarantees personal freedom and permits the exercise of Sharia law for consenting Muslims.

Politics

Last elections:	April 2011 (legislative and presidential)
Next elections:	April 2015
Head of state:	President Dr Goodluck Ebele Jonathan
Head of government:	the president
Ruling party:	People's Democratic Party

In the first elections to be held under a civilian government in twenty years, in April 2003 President Olusegun Obasanjo and the ruling People's Democratic Party (PDP) comfortably won presidential and National Assembly elections and did well in the governorship elections. Obasanjo was emphatically returned as president with 61.9% of the votes, his main rival, another former military leader, Muhammadu Buhari of the All Nigeria People's Party, polling 32.2%. Commonwealth observers concluded that in most states most electors were able to vote freely and the results of the elections reflected the wishes of the people. However, in certain places 'proper electoral processes appear to have broken down' and, in Rivers State in particular, 'there were widespread and serious irregularities and vote-rigging'.

The ruling PDP's candidate, Umaru Musa Yar'Adua, won the April 2007 presidential election with 70% of the votes, defeating Muhammadu Buhari of the All Nigeria People's Party (18%) and Atiku Abubakar of Action Congress (7%). Turnout was low and the many national and international observers reported serious and widespread deficiencies in the election process, including late opening of polls. Commonwealth observers concluded there were impediments to the full, free and fair expression of the will of voters and that an opportunity to build on the elections of 1999 and 2003 had been missed.

After a period of illness, three months of which he spent receiving medical treatment in Saudi Arabia, Yar'Adua died on 5 May 2010. Vice-President Goodluck Jonathan, who had been empowered by the National Assembly to act as president since February 2010, was sworn in as president on 6 May.

In April 2011 PDP candidate Jonathan won the presidential election in the first round, taking 59% of the votes cast and securing more than 25% of votes in at least 24 states. His main challenger, Buhari (now of the Congress for Progressive Change), took 32% of the

Knowledge through learning and research

UNIVERSITY OF LAGOS

The University of Lagos, founded in 1962, comprises nine Faculties and a College of Medicine. The Faculties offer a total of 121 programmes as well as Masters and Doctorate degrees in most of the programmes. There are two Centres, namely the Centre for Human Rights and the Centre for African, Regional Integration and Borderland Studies; and also a Distance Learning Institute.

Vice-Chancellor, Professor Adetokunbo B. Sofoluwe

Vision
To be a top-class institution for the pursuit of excellence in knowledge through learning and research, as well as in character and service to humanity.

Mission
To provide a conducive teaching, learning, research and development environment where staff and students can interact and compete effectively with their counterparts both nationally and internationally in terms of intellectual competence and zeal to add value to the world.

Research
The University holds annual research conferences and regular fairs; and rewards researchers for their outstanding research efforts. The University's research activities have attracted commendations from the National Universities Commission (NUC).

University of Lagos
Akoka, Yaba, Lagos, NIGERIA
Tel: +234 802 290 3999 • +234 805 507 3265 • +234 803 647 3219
Email: vc@unilag.edu.ng

www.unilag.edu.ng

votes cast. Voting was widely reported as peaceful and the Commonwealth observer group present, led by former President of Botswana, Festus Mogae, declared that the presidential and National Assembly elections were both credible and creditable, and reflected the will of the Nigerian people. However, as it became apparent that Jonathan had won the presidential contest, violent demonstrations erupted in northern Nigeria.

International relations

Nigeria is a member of the African, Caribbean and Pacific Group of States, African Union, Economic Community of West African States, Non-Aligned Movement, Organisation of Islamic Cooperation, United Nations and World Trade Organization.

Nigeria hosts the headquarters of the Economic Community of West African States in Abuja.

The country is also a member of the Organization of Petroleum Exporting Countries.

Traveller information

Local laws and conventions: Visitors should exercise discretion in behaviour and dress, especially in Muslim areas and when visiting religious sites.

Possession or use of, or trafficking in, illegal drugs is a serious offence and can result in lengthy prison sentences and heavy fines. Photography is not allowed in airports and may lead to arrest.

Shaking hands is customary on meeting and departing. Dress is casual for both men and women. It is common for business meetings to take place without a prior appointment. Business cards are expected. Office hours are Mon–Fri 0800–1700.

Immigration and customs: Visas are required by all travellers entering the country. Passports must be valid for at least six months beyond intended stay. Visitors should make a copy of the photopage of their passport and keep it on them at all times, and store their passports in a hotel safe.

A yellow fever vaccination certificate will be required by those arriving from infected areas.

Travellers are prohibited from bringing champagne, beer, mineral water, soft drinks, fruit, vegetables, cereal, eggs, jewellery, textile fabrics and mosquito netting into Nigeria.

Travel within the country: Traffic drives on the right and car hire is available in Lagos and Abuja, but it is advisable to book these through a hotel. An international driving permit is required, accompanied by two passport-size photos. Road travel is banned in Lagos between 0700–1000 on the last Saturday of every month for municipal road clean up, and this is strictly enforced.

Bus services and bush taxis connect all the main cities. Most hotels offer chauffeur-driven cars.

Trains are generally slow but are cheaper than buses. A daily service runs on the two main lines from Lagos to Kano and from Port Harcourt to Maiduguri. Sleeping cars are available but must be booked in advance. Domestic flights are very cheap, though visitors should be aware that they can be cancelled at short notice.

Travel health: Visitors should make sure they have comprehensive health insurance which includes medical evacuation. Vaccinations against meningococcal meningitis, tuberculosis and Hepatitis B are sometimes recommended, but current inoculation requirements should be checked well before travel.

Water used for drinking, brushing teeth or making ice should first have been boiled or otherwise sterilised. Powdered or tinned milk is available and is advised.

Money: The local currency is the naira. Currency must only be changed at approved facilities. Visitors should ensure that they bring enough money (sterling, US dollars or euros) to cover their costs. Acceptance of travellers cheques is limited to Abuja and larger towns. Credit cards are rarely accepted.

There were 2,778,365 tourist arrivals in 2005.

Further information

Federal Government of Nigeria: www.nigeria.gov.ng

National Assembly: www.nassnig.org

Central Bank of Nigeria: www.cenbank.org

Commonwealth Secretariat: www.thecommonwealth.org

Commonwealth of Nations: www.commonwealth-of-nations.org/Nigeria

Pakistan

KEY FACTS

Joined Commonwealth:	1947 (left in 1972, rejoined in 1989)
Population:	173,593,000 (2010)
GDP p.c. growth:	1.7% p.a. 1990–2010
UN HDI 2011:	world ranking 145
Official language:	Urdu
Time:	GMT plus 5hr
Currency:	Pakistan rupee (PRs)

Geography

Area:	796,095 sq km
Coastline:	1,050km
Capital:	Islamabad

Pakistan lies just north of the Tropic of Cancer, bordering (clockwise from west) Iran, Afghanistan, China and India. The Arabian Sea lies to the south. The country comprises four provinces: (from south to north) Sindh, Balochistan, Punjab and Khyber Pukhtoonkhwa (formerly North-West Frontier Province). The territory adjoining Khyber Pukhtoonkhwa is known as the Federally Administered Tribal Areas and the Pakistani-administered parts of Jammu and Kashmir in the north-east as Azad Kashmir and Northern Areas.

Area: 796,095 sq km, excluding territory in Jammu and Kashmir, whose status is in dispute.

Topography: Pakistan has great topographical variety. The high mountain region of the north includes part of the Himalayas, Karakoram and Hindukush. There are 35 peaks over 7,320m high, including K-2, the world's second-highest mountain. This region abounds in glaciers, lakes and green valleys. Southwards, the ranges gradually lose height. The western low mountain region covers much of Khyber Pukhtoonkhwa Province, with mountains cut by valleys and passes, including the Khyber Pass, 56km long, connecting Kabul in Afghanistan with Peshawar. The third region is

Did you know...

Dr Asma Jahangir of Pakistan was in 2010 appointed to the Commonwealth Eminent Persons Group, which presented its recommendations for reform in the Commonwealth to Commonwealth leaders at CHOGM in Australia in October 2011.

Cricketers Imran Khan and Wasim Akram, both born in Lahore, Punjab, achieved the 'all-rounder's double' and Wisden Leading Cricketer in the World.

Mohammed Hanif won the Commonwealth Writers' Prize Best First Book award, in 2009, with *A Case of Exploding Mangoes*.

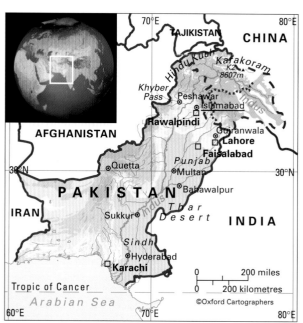

The designations and the presentation of material on this map, based on UN practice, do not imply the expression of any opinion whatsoever on the part of the Commonwealth Secretariat or the publishers concerning the legal status of any country, territory or area, or of its authorities, or concerning the delimitation of its frontiers or boundaries. There is no intention to define the status of Jammu and/or Kashmir, which has not yet been agreed upon by the parties.

the Balochistan plateau to the west. West of the Balochistan plateau is an area of desert with dry lakes, one 87km long. The Potohar upland lies between the Indus and Jhelum rivers in the Islamabad/Rawalpindi area. This is an arid region, with cultivation along the valleys. The fifth region is the Punjab plain watered by the River Indus and its eastern tributaries (Jhelum, Chenab, Ravi, Sutlej and Beas) and additionally irrigated by canals. The Sindh plain stretches between the Punjab plain and the Arabian Sea on both sides of the Indus river. The plain comprises a vast fertile tract with many lakes, and a desert spreading eastward into India.

In October 2005, a powerful earthquake, with its epicentre in the north of the country, close to Muzaffarabad in Pakistan-administered Kashmir, caused some 80,000 deaths and devastation of a large area which left millions homeless.

Climate: Extreme variations of temperature. The northern mountains are cold, with long and severe winters. Temperatures on the Balochistan plateau are high. Along the coastal strip, the climate is modified by sea breezes. In the rest of the country, the temperature rises steeply in summer. Seasons are: cold season (December to March), hot season (April to June), monsoon season (July to September) and post-monsoon season (October and November). Rainfall varies from 760–1,270mm in the Himalayan foothills to 210mm in Balochistan.

Environment: The most significant issues are soil erosion, deforestation, desertification, and water pollution with untreated sewage and industrial waste and by use of commercial pesticides.

Vegetation: Well-watered mountain slopes support forests of deodar, pine, poplar, shisham, willow and other species. Towering grasses and expanses of floating lotus flourish in the lake area of the Sindh plain. There are mangrove swamps to the south. Forest covers 2% of the land area, having declined at 2.0% p.a. 1990–2010. Arable land comprises 27% and permanent cropland 1% of the total land area.

Wildlife: Wildlife in the northern mountains includes brown bears, black Himalayan bears, musk deer, ibex, leopard and the rare snow-leopard. Chinkara gazelle have a wider distribution, while barking deer live closer to urban centres. In the delta, there are crocodiles, pythons and wild boar. Green turtles, an endangered species, regularly visit the Karachi coast during the egg-laying season. The haubara bustard is a winter visitor. Manchar Lake in Sindh is rich in water-birds. In 2003, there were 37,800 sq km of protected areas (4.9% of the land area).

Main towns: Islamabad (capital, pop. 689,200 in 2010), Karachi (Sindh Province, 13.21m), Lahore (Punjab, 7.13m), Faisalabad (Punjab, 2.88m), Rawalpindi (Punjab, 1.99m), Multan (Punjab, 1.61m), Hyderabad (Sindh, 1.58m), Gujranwala (Punjab, 1.57m), Peshawar (Khyber Pukhtoonkhwa, 1.44m), Quetta (Balochistan, 896,100), Sargodha (Punjab, 600,500), Bahawalpur (Punjab, 543,900), Sialkot (Punjab, 510,900), Sukkur (Sindh, 493,400), Larkana (Sindh, 456,500), Shekhupura (Punjab, 427,000), Jhang (Punjab, 372,600), Rahimyar Khan (Punjab, 353,100), Mardan (Khyber Pukhtoonkhwa, 352,100), Gujrat (Punjab, 336,700), Kasur (Punjab, 322,000), Mingaora (Khyber Pukhtoonkhwa, 279,900), Dera Ghazi Khan (Punjab, 273,300), Nawabshah (Sindh, 272,600), Wah (Punjab, 265,200), Sahiwal (Punjab, 251,600), Mirpur Khas (Sindh, 242,900), Okara (Punjab, 235,400), Kohat (Khyber Pukhtoonkhwa, 176,200), Abottabad (Khyber Pukhtoonkhwa, 148,600), Khuzdar (Balochistan, 148,100), Swabi (Khyber Pukhtoonkhwa, 115,000), Dera Ismail Khan (Khyber Pukhtoonkhwa, 111,900) and Zhob (Balochistan, 56,800).

Transport: There are 260,420km of roads, 65% paved, and 7,791km of railway, with 781 stations. Main lines run north–south, linking the main ports and industrial centre of Karachi with Islamabad, 1,600km to the north. All major cities and most industrial centres are linked by rail.

Karachi port handles the bulk of foreign trade. Port Qasim, south-east of Karachi, is also an important port. Major international airports are at Karachi, Islamabad and Lahore.

Society

KEY FACTS 2010

Population per sq km:	218
Life expectancy:	65 years
Net primary enrolment:	66%

Population: 173,593,000 (2010); density varies from more than 230 people per sq km in Punjab to 13 in Balochistan; 36% lives in urban areas and 18% in urban agglomerations of more than 1 million people; growth 2.2% p.a. 1990–2010; birth rate 27 per 1,000 people (43 in 1970); life expectancy 65 years (54 in 1970).

The population comprises Punjabis (44%), Pashtuns (15%), Sindhis (14%), Saraikis (11%), Muhajirs (7.6%), Balochis (3.6%), and other smaller groups including the tribal groups in the more remote northern areas.

Language: The official language is Urdu, but English is widely used. Regional languages are Punjabi, Pashtu, Sindhi and Saraiki. There are numerous local dialects.

Religion: Muslims 97%, the majority of whom are Sunni, with a minority (of about 20%) of Shia. There are small communities of Hindus, Christians, Qadianis and a few Parsis (Zoroastrians).

Health: Public spending on health was 1% of GDP in 2009. The main teaching hospitals are in Karachi, Lahore, Islamabad, Peshawar and Quetta. The network of medical services includes hospitals, dispensaries, rural health centres and basic health units. Family planning services are given at family welfare centres. 90% of the population uses an improved drinking water source and 45% have access to adequate sanitation facilities (2009). Malaria remains a serious problem. Infant mortality was 70 per 1,000 live births in 2010 (139 in 1960).

Education: Public spending on education was 2.4% of GDP in 2010. There are five years of primary education starting at age five, and seven years of secondary comprising cycles of three and four years. Some 60% of pupils complete primary school (2008). The school year starts in April.

In May 2011, the Higher Education Commission recognised 129 degree-awarding institutions, 73 in the public sector. Allama Iqbal Open University was established in 1974, the first open university in Asia. Fatima Jinnah Women's University, Rawalpindi, opened in 1998 and was Pakistan's first university exclusively for women. The female–male ratio for gross enrolment in tertiary education is 0.85:1 (2008). Literacy among people aged 15–24 is 71% (2008). There is an extensive literacy programme.

Media: The first Urdu journal appeared in 1836. By the 1990s there were more than 2,200 newspapers and periodicals, including some 270 dailies and 500 weeklies. Leading English-language papers include *Daily Times*, *Dawn*, *Pakistan Observer*, *The Frontier Post*, *The Nation*, *The News* and *Business Recorder* (financial daily); the main newspapers in Urdu *Ausaf*, *Jang* and *Nawa-i-Waqt*; and the principal weeklies *Pakistan and Gulf Economist*, and *The Friday Times*.

Pakistan Television Corporation provides national and regional public TV services. About 50 private TV channels broadcast by cable and satellite; some owned by newspaper groups, and one based in Dubai, United Arab Emirates. The Pakistan Broadcasting Corporation provides public radio services, operating some 25 stations, including an external service. More than 100 private FM stations are licensed to broadcast.

Some 56% of households have TV sets (2007). There are 168 internet users per 1,000 people (2010).

Communications: Country code 92; internet domain '.pk'. Mobile phone coverage is generally limited to main towns. Internet cafes can be found in most urban areas. There is a good postal service in the main towns.

There are 20 main telephone lines and 571 mobile phone subscriptions per 1,000 people (2010).

Public holidays: Pakistan Day (23 March), Independence Day (14 August), Defence Day (6 September), Allama Mohammad Iqbal Day (9 November) and Birthday of Quaid-i-Azam (25 December).

Religious festivals whose dates vary from year to year include Prophet's Birthday, Eid al-Fitr (End of Ramadan, two days), Eid al-Adha (Feast of the Sacrifice, two days) and Ashura. Christian holidays are taken by the Christian community only.

Economy

KEY FACTS 2010

GNI:	US$182.8bn
GNI p.c.:	US$1,050
GDP growth:	4.2% p.a. 2006–10
Inflation:	12.6% p.a. 2006–10

Pakistan has a predominantly agricultural economy, with agriculture (notably cotton), fisheries and forestry contributing about 20% of GDP, and it does have large deposits of natural gas; proven reserves of gas were estimated in January 2011 to be 800 billion cubic metres. From the 1950s, manufacturing took off rapidly.

The economy has been developed through a series of five-year plans. From the 1960s protectionist policies were adopted, followed by nationalisations in the 1970s and, from 1988,

Real Growth in GDP

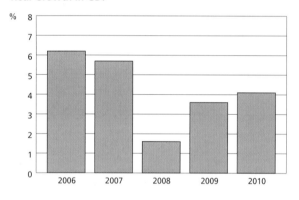

Inflation

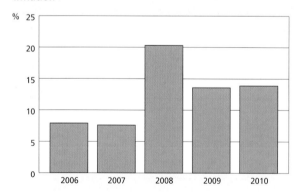

GDP by Sector (2010)

■	Agriculture	21%
□	Industry	25%
▨	Services	53%

encouragement of private enterprise and privatisation of state-owned banks and manufacturing enterprises.

After years of strong growth, the economy stalled in the latter 1990s, with a widening trade deficit and large external debt. In March 1997, the Sharif government embarked on an economic revitalisation programme to enhance exports, reduce inflation, generate employment and widen the tax base (there were then only one million income tax payers, mainly belonging to the urban middle class). An IMF structural adjustment programme was approved in October 1997, but suspended in May 1999, until progress on economic reform was accelerated.

After the October 1999 coup, the military government set a new agenda of reforms, opening the way for the renewal of IMF support in late 2000 and resulting in good growth in the 2000s. From November 2002, the civilian government continued with this agenda which included the resumption of privatisation, giving priority to agriculture, smaller enterprises and oil and gas exploration, as well as encouraging the development of a computer software industry. The economy grew by 6.6% p.a. over 2004–08, but then, in 2008, growth slowed (to an annual rate of 1.6%) in response to the global downturn and collapse of world demand, recovering in 2009 (3.6%) and 2010 (4.1%), despite the devastating floods which caused massive disruption to economic activity across the country from July 2010; it was 2.4% in 2011.

Constitution

Status:	Republic
Legislature:	Federal Legislature
Independence:	14 August 1947

The constitution in force at the time of the October 1999 coup was promulgated in 1973. The first amendment was introduced in 1974 and the fourteenth, in 1997. Much of it was suspended from 1977 and restored in December 1985. It was again suspended by the military government after the October 1999 coup, and was partially restored in November 2002, following the parliamentary elections.

The constitution proclaims Pakistan to be Islamic and democratic, with fundamental rights guaranteed, including the freedoms of thought, speech, religion and worship, assembly, association, and the press, as well as equality of status.

Under this constitution, the president is head of state and is elected for five years by an electoral college consisting of the members of both houses of parliament and of the four provincial assemblies. Until April 1997, the president had certain discretionary powers including the power to dissolve the National Assembly. These powers were restored by the military government immediately before the elections in October 2002 through the Legal Framework Order (LFO) together with other amendments. Under the eighteenth amendment of April 2010, however, the president's role once again became largely ceremonial.

There is a bicameral legislature. The lower house is the National Assembly. From 2002 the Assembly had 342 members, comprising 272 members directly elected by adult suffrage, plus 60 women and ten representatives of minorities (non-Muslims); these seats reserved for women and minorities' representatives are allocated proportionally to all parties gaining more than 5% of the directly elected seats. The prime minister is elected by the National Assembly. The upper house, the Senate, has 100 members (previously 87) elected for six years with about half of them retiring every three years. Each of the four provinces elects 22 senators, including four women and four technocrats; the remaining 12 are elected from the Federal Capital Territory and the tribal areas. Legal constitutional change requires the support of two-thirds of the total membership of the National Assembly and the Senate.

Politics

Last elections:	February 2008 (legislative), September 2008 (presidential)
Next elections:	2013 (legislative), 2013 (presidential)
Head of state:	President Asif Ali Zardari
Head of government:	Prime Minister Syed Yousaf Raza Gilani
Ruling party:	coalition led by Pakistan People's Party

In June 2001 Army Chief of Staff General Pervez Musharraf – who had led a military government since October 1999 – dissolved parliament and the four provincial legislatures; President Rafiq Tarar resigned; and Musharraf became president. A referendum held in April 2002 confirmed Musharraf's position as president for a period of five years.

National Assembly elections in October 2002 produced a hung parliament. The Pakistan Muslim League–Quaid-e-Azam (PML-Q), which supported Musharraf, took 77 seats, followed by Pakistan People's Party (PPP) with 63, Muttahida Majlis-e-Amal (MMA) with 45, Pakistan Muslim League (Nawaz) with 14 and Muttahida Qaumi Movement (MQM) with 13, leaving a large block of members of smaller parties and independents. The Commonwealth observer group present said that 'on election day this was a credible election', but that 'in the context of various measures taken by the government we are not persuaded of the overall fairness of the process as a whole'.

The National Assembly elected Chaudhry Amir Hussain (PML-Q) as speaker and Mir Zafarullah Khan Jamali (PML-Q) as prime minister. The continuing dispute between Musharraf and the opposition parties on the status of the Legal Framework Order (and especially his power to dismiss the prime minister and dissolve the Assembly) and Musharraf's own position as president and chief of army staff created political deadlock. Parliament was not functioning and the government ruled by decree. The MMA emerged as leader in the campaign against the Legal Framework Order as the Alliance for the Restoration of Democracy (ARD) – an alliance of PPP, Pakistan Muslim League (Nawaz), and several smaller parties – was weakened by the death of its leader and the absence of exiled leaders Benazir Bhutto and Nawaz Sharif.

In January 2004 Musharraf won confidence votes in the Assembly, the Senate and the four provincial assemblies. In May 2004, in view of the progress made towards democracy, CMAG readmitted Pakistan to the councils of the Commonwealth. In June 2004 the prime minister resigned and was succeeded by Chaudhry Shujaat Hussain until July when he made way for finance minister Shaukat Aziz on his winning a seat in the Assembly. In December 2004 Musharraf announced he would continue as president and chief of army staff until 2007 when elections were due.

In the presidential election held in October 2007 Musharraf was unofficially proclaimed winner pending a key ruling by the Supreme

Court regarding his eligibility to run for presidency while serving as chief of army staff.

Exiled Pakistan People's Party leader Benazir Bhutto returned to Pakistan in October 2007 after the presidential election. On the way from the airport to Karachi her convoy was hit by a suicide bomb attack. She survived, but hundreds were killed and injured.

In November 2007, ostensibly because of national security concerns, Musharraf declared a state of emergency effectively suspending the country's constitution by a provisional constitutional order (PCO). A news blackout was imposed on major private television stations. Several hundred protestors, journalists and political opponents of Musharraf were arrested and eight Supreme Court judges including the Chief Justice Iftikhar Muhammad Chaudary, who would not recognise the PCO, were dismissed and put under house arrest.

Musharraf came under increasing international pressure to restore the country's constitution and abide by the timetable for free and fair parliamentary elections. CMAG convened in Kampala on 22 November 2007 and suspended Pakistan from the councils of the Commonwealth, pending the restoration of democracy and the rule of law in that country.

Musharraf appointed a new chief justice and a caretaker prime minister, Muhammad Mian Soomro. He resigned as army chief and was sworn in as president for a five-year term. The state of emergency was lifted in December 2007.

Nawaz Sharif, exiled leader of Pakistan Muslim League (Nawaz), at his second attempt in the same year, was allowed to return. By end November 2007, both he and Bhutto had registered to participate in the following parliamentary elections. On 27 December 2007, as she was leaving an election rally in Rawalpindi, Bhutto was assassinated. Violence erupted throughout the country. Bilawal Bhutto Zardari, Benazir's son, was chosen as her eventual successor; her husband Asif Ali Zardari was to lead the PPP, as co-chair, until Bilawal had completed his education. The elections due for January were postponed.

The parliamentary elections were held in February 2008. Opposition parties won the most seats – PPP won 121 seats and Pakistan Muslim League (Nawaz) (PML-N) 91 – but no party had an absolute majority. The party supporting Musharraf, PML-Q, suffered huge losses, taking only 54 seats and many former ministers lost their seats. With no party securing a clear majority, PPP, PML-N, Awami National Party (ANP, ten seats) and Jamiat Ulema-e-Islam-Fazl (JUI-F, 6 seats) formed a coalition government headed by PPP's Syed Yousaf Raza Gilani, as prime minister.

On 12 May 2008, CMAG met in London and agreed that, since it last met in November 2007, the Government of Pakistan had taken positive steps to fulfil its obligations in accordance with Commonwealth fundamental values and principles. It accordingly restored Pakistan as a full member of the Commonwealth.

In the face of warnings by the PPP and PML-N leadership of impeachment by parliament, Musharraf announced his resignation as president in August 2008. In the ensuing presidential election, PPP co-chair Zardari was elected to replace Musharraf in September 2008. Zardari (securing 481 electoral college votes) defeated PML-N's candidate, Saeed-uz-zaman Siddiqui (153 votes), and PML-Q's Mushahid Hussain Syed (44). In the lead-up to the election PML-N left the governing coalition, which then comprised PPP, ANP, JUI-F and Muttahida Qaumi Movement.

Nine PML-N ministers resigned shortly after the presidential election, citing the apparent reluctance of the PPP to reinstate judges previously dismissed during the 2007 state of emergency. The move effectively ended the PPP- and PML-N-dominated coalition government and saw the beginning of a new one, consisting of the PPP, ANP, JUI-F and MQM.

In late February 2009 the Supreme Court confirmed the disqualification of Nawaz Sharif and his brother Shabhaz from holding elected office. Following the verdict, governor's rule was imposed in Punjab Province, where Shabhaz Sharif had held the post of chief minister, and Nawaz Sharif allied himself with the lawyers' movement which had been campaigning for the reinstatement of the chief justice, asserting that the Supreme Court verdict demonstrated the lack of an independent judiciary.

Confronted by the prospect of large-scale popular unrest, in March 2009 the government announced the reinstatement of deposed Chief Justice Iftikhar Chaudhry and requested a review of the Supreme Court judgment that had disqualified the Sharifs from holding elected office. In May 2009 the Supreme Court reversed the judgment and Shabhaz Sharif was reinstated as chief minister in Punjab Province. In July 2009 the Supreme Court quashed Nawaz Sharif's convictions of hijacking and terrorism (brought against him following the military coup of October 1999).

In November 2009 the Supreme Court revoked the National Reconciliation Ordinances of October 2007 which had granted immunity to those officials and politicians who had been charged with corruption and other offences. The revocation of the ordinances revived corruption charges against many of its beneficiaries.

On 19 April 2010 far-reaching constitutional reforms (the Eighteenth Amendment Bill) were signed into law, reducing key presidential powers and broadening the distribution of power within the government. The president no longer has the power to dismiss the prime minister or the parliament.

History

The region of Pakistan was one of the cradles of civilisation. Stone-age hunter-gatherers lived on the Potohar plateau and in the Soan Valley in northern Punjab 300,000 or more years ago. Excavations on the Balochistan plateau show a more advanced culture which flourished from 4000 to 2000 BC. At Kot Diji in the Khairpur district, an early bronze age culture developed in this period. These early civilisations reached their peak in the Indus valley cities, of which Harappa is the most notable. These societies had mastered town planning and pictographic writing.

In 327 BC Alexander the Great invaded with his Macedonian army. Later, Mauryans from India ruled the northern Punjab area, to be replaced by Bactrian Greeks from Afghanistan and central Asian tribes. Different religions prevailed in turn: Buddhism (under the Mauryans), Hinduism and, with Arab conquest in the eighth century, Islam.

Two main principalities emerged under Arab rule, that of al-Mansurah and that of Multan. The Ghaznarid sultans gained ascendancy in Punjab in the 11th century. The subsequent ascendancy of the Moghuls, who originated in Central Asia, lasted from 1536 to 1707; their rule lingered nominally until 1857. They established a sophisticated imperial administration and left a rich legacy of forts and walled cities, gardens and gateways, mosques and tombs.

In the early 17th century European traders arrived on the subcontinent. Through the East India Company, the British became the dominant force. After the unsuccessful uprising against Britain of 1857, the British took direct control. Slowly a national Muslim identity emerged, championed by Sir Syed Ahmed Khan (1817–89). The All India Muslim League was founded in 1907.

As the subcontinent moved towards independence, it became clear that Hindu and Muslim interests could not be reconciled. The campaign to establish an independent Muslim state came to prominence in the 1920s and 30s. It was led by the philosopher and poet Mohammad Iqbal and Mohammad Ali Jinnah.

Pakistan was created, as an Islamic state, out of the partition of the UK's Indian Empire, at independence in August 1947. It originally consisted of two parts, West Pakistan (now Pakistan) and East Pakistan (now Bangladesh), separated by 1,600km of Indian territory. Partition was followed by war with India over Kashmir and the mass migration of Muslims, Hindus and Sikhs to resettle within the new borders, an upheaval which led to violence, financial loss and death on a large scale. With the arrival of Indian Muslims and departure of Pakistan's Hindus and Sikhs, Pakistan became an almost entirely Muslim society. Jinnah, who is honoured as the Quaid-i-Azam, or great leader, died in 1948.

In 1956, Pakistan became a federal republic. It has been under military rule for long periods. Its first prime minister, Liaquat Ali Khan, was assassinated in 1951. In 1958, martial law was declared and political parties abolished. General (later Field Marshal) Ayub Khan became president in 1960 and allowed a form of guided 'basic democracy'. However, failure to win the 1965 war against India and accusations of nepotism and corruption undermined his position. In the east, the Awami League of Sheikh Mujibur Rahman voiced the grievances of the Bengali population. Ayub Khan resigned in 1969 and power was taken over by General Yahya Khan, who in December 1970 held the first national elections in independent Pakistan.

Mujib and the Awami League won an electoral majority in Pakistan's general election on a platform demanding greater autonomy for East Pakistan. At the same time Zulfikar Ali Bhutto's Pakistan People's Party (PPP) gained a majority in the West. Despite Mujib's victory, he was prevented by the Pakistan authorities from becoming prime minister of the combined state and the Awami League then issued their own plans for a new constitution for an independent state in the East. As a result of the military intervention that ensued, civil war broke out in the eastern region in 1971; the Indian army intervened in support of the Bengalis; Pakistan forces withdrew and Bangladesh became an independent state. In 1972 Pakistan withdrew from the Commonwealth but rejoined in 1989.

Under a new constitution introduced in 1973, Bhutto became prime minister. He undertook agrarian reform and the nationalisation of large sections of industry and the financial sector. In July 1977 the army, under General Zia ul-Haq,

➤

International relations

Pakistan is a member of the Non-Aligned Movement, Organisation of Islamic Cooperation, South Asian Association for Regional Cooperation, United Nations and World Trade Organization.

Traveller information

Local laws and conventions: Pakistan is a Muslim country, and local laws reflect this. Local customs and sensitivities should be respected at all times, especially during Ramadan and when visiting religious areas.

There are strict laws concerning alcohol, which is only available in major hotels to visitors who have been issued a liquor permit from the Excise and Taxation Office. During Ramadan, most restaurants close during the day, and there is a restriction on smoking and drinking in public places.

Photographs must not be taken at military establishments, airports, or any infrastructure, including bridges and dams, or from aircraft.

Importing alcohol is illegal. Possession of small quantities of illegal drugs can lead to imprisonment and drug smuggling can attract the death penalty.

Handshaking is the usual form of greeting and only the right hand should be used for the passing or receiving of objects.

Informal dress is acceptable for most occasions, but all visitors should dress modestly at all times. Appointments are necessary for business meetings and should be made well in advance. Business cards are customary. Office hours are Mon–Thur and Sat 0900–1700, Fri 0900–1230. (During Ramadan normal business hours may be interrupted.)

Immigration and customs: Most nationals require a visa to enter the country and passports must be valid for six months beyond the

➤ intervened in the urban unrest. Zia declared martial law and arrested Bhutto who was convicted, after a controversial trial, of conspiring to murder a political opponent. Despite international appeals, he was hanged in April 1979. Zia promised elections within 90 days, but ruled without them until his death. He assumed the presidency and embarked on a programme of Islamisation. Martial law and the ban on political parties were lifted in 1985, Bhutto's daughter Benazir returned from exile to lead the PPP and Zia died in a plane crash in August 1988.

Elections in November 1988 brought the PPP to power in coalition with the Mohajir Qaumi Movement (MQM). However, in October 1989 the MQM left the coalition and in August 1990 Bhutto was dismissed by the president Ghulam Ishaque Khan and charged with corruption. The National Assembly was dissolved and a caretaker leader installed until Islami Jamhoori Ittehad led by Nawaz Sharif won a decisive election victory in October 1990. Sharif pursued economic reforms and privatisation and instituted Sharia (Islamic) law until 1993 when president and prime minister resigned under pressure from the military, making way for fresh elections which brought Benazir Bhutto back to power by a small majority.

In November 1996, President Sardar Farooq Khan Leghari, prompted by the army high command and opposition leaders, used the eighth amendment to the constitution, and dissolved the National Assembly, bringing down the Bhutto government and alleging corruption, financial incompetence, and human rights violations. New elections were held in February 1997. The Pakistan Muslim League (Nawaz) – previously the main component of the Islami Jamhoori Ittehad – won 134 seats in the National Assembly and Sharif became prime minister. Bhutto's Pakistan People's Party retained only 18 seats. In April 1997, Sharif was able to gain the PPP's support to achieve the two-thirds majority necessary to repeal the eighth amendment, ending the president's ability to dissolve the National Assembly. He also took over from the president the power to appoint Supreme Court judges and military chiefs-of-staff.

In October 1999, Sharif ordered the dismissal of Army Chief of Staff General Pervez Musharraf, and refused permission to land

for the commercial aircraft in which he was returning to Karachi (from an official visit to Sri Lanka). The army countermanded the prime minister's orders and immediately seized power, dismissing the government and arresting Sharif. Musharraf justified his actions as necessary to restore both the economy and the deteriorating political situation. Pending the restoration of democracy the Commonwealth Ministerial Action Group (CMAG) suspended Pakistan from the councils of the Commonwealth.

Kashmir

The dispute with India over Kashmir escalated sharply in 1999, when militants with Pakistani military support crossed the Line of Control at Kargil and engaged in major battles with Indian forces. More than 1,000 people were killed in the fighting. In July 1999, Pakistan finally agreed to withdraw from Indian-controlled territory, but the state of tension, which had been heightened by the nuclear testing of 1998 (India had detonated five nuclear devices on 11 and 13 May 1998 and Pakistan responded with six on 28 and 30 May), persisted.

At the invitation of Indian Prime Minister Atal Bihari Vajpayee, in 2001 President General Pervez Musharraf attended a summit in India, focusing on their dispute over Kashmir. Although there was no substantive outcome, this first face-to-face meeting between leaders of the two countries since 1999 was characterised by a new interest on both sides in seeking a resolution to this long-standing problem. However, by May 2002 India had mobilised a vast army along the Line of Control and the two countries were again on the brink of war.

Tension eased considerably in October 2002 when India reduced its number of troops along the Line of Control; diplomatic relations were restored in August 2003 and a ceasefire along the Line of Control was agreed and took effect from 26 November 2003. Peace talks between India and Pakistan began in 2004, marking a historic advance in relations between the two countries. The talks led to the restoration of communication links and a range of confidence-building measures, including co-ordinated relief efforts in the aftermath of the October 2005 earthquake.

intended length of stay. Visitors should carry with them at all times a photocopy of their passport and Pakistani visa.

A yellow fever vaccination certificate is required by those travelling from an infected area.

The import of alcohol, matches, plants, fruit and vegetables is prohibited. The export of antiques is prohibited.

Travel within the country: Traffic drives on the left and car hire is available in major cities, as well as at Karachi, Lahore and Rawalpindi airports. An international driving permit is required. Tourists are advised to travel with local drivers or guides.

Pakistan Railways operates the rail network throughout the country; reservations are advised on long journeys. Regular bus services run between most towns and villages. Air-conditioned coaches are recommended for long distances and should be booked in advance.

Taxis are reasonably priced and widely available, and are by far the most efficient means of getting around urban areas. Autorickshaws are also available.

Most domestic flights are operated by Pakistan International Airlines.

Travel health: Comprehensive medical insurance is strongly recommended. Visitors will need protection against malaria, and should take insect repellent and suitable clothing to discourage bites. Mosquito-borne dengue fever also exists and similar precautions should be taken. Vaccinations against Japanese B encephalitis, tuberculosis and Hepatitis B are sometimes recommended, but visitors should check current inoculation requirements well before travel.

Water used for drinking, brushing teeth or making ice should have first been boiled or otherwise sterilised. Milk is unpasteurised and should be boiled. Powdered or tinned milk is available.

Money: American Express is the most widely accepted card, although Visa and Mastercard can also be used. Travellers cheques are generally accepted at most banks, the larger hotels and major shops, and should be taken in US dollars or pounds sterling to avoid additional charges. Banking hours are Mon–Sat 0900–1330, Fri 0900–1230.

There were 914,000 tourist arrivals in 2010.

Further information

Government of Pakistan: www.pakistan.gov.pk

National Assembly: www.na.gov.pk

Senate: www.senate.gov.pk

State Bank of Pakistan: www.sbp.org.pk

Commonwealth Secretariat: www.thecommonwealth.org

Commonwealth of Nations: www.commonwealth-of-nations.org/Pakistan

Papua New Guinea

KEY FACTS

Joined Commonwealth:	1975
Population:	6,858,000 (2010)
GDP p.c. growth:	–0.2% p.a. 1990–2010
UN HDI 2011:	world ranking 153
Official language:	English
Time:	GMT plus 10hr
Currency:	kina (K)

Geography

Area:	462,840 sq km
Coastline:	5,150km
Capital:	Port Moresby

The Independent State of Papua New Guinea in the South Pacific shares a land-border with Indonesia; its other near neighbours are Australia to the south and Solomon Islands to the east.

Papua New Guinea includes the eastern half of the world's second biggest island, New Guinea, bordering the Indonesian province of Irian Jaya to the west. The rest of the country is made up of about 600 small islands, the chief of which are the Bismarck Archipelago, the Trobriands, the Louisiade Archipelago, the D'Entrecasteaux Islands, and some of the islands in the Solomons group, including Bougainville. The country comprises the region of Port Moresby and 19 provinces (21 from 2012).

Topography: The centre of the main island is a rugged mountainous ridge, with several wide valleys, and foothills north and south. The rivers Sepik and Ramu drain the foothills to the north, and the rivers Fly, Kikori and Purari those in the south. Though fast-flowing, many rivers are navigable. There are active volcanoes along the north coast, and some volcanoes and warm pools in the south-east islands.

Climate: Tropical monsoon type, hot and humid all year, though somewhat cooler in the highlands. Rainfall is chiefly from December to March. High mountains receive occasional frost, even snow.

Did you know...

This country hosts a national chapter of the Commonwealth Human Ecology Council.

The country comprises about 600 small islands and has some 5,150km of coastline; only 13% of people live in urban areas, the lowest proportion in the Commonwealth.

Papua New Guinea has more than 800 indigenous languages, thought to be more than any other country in the world.

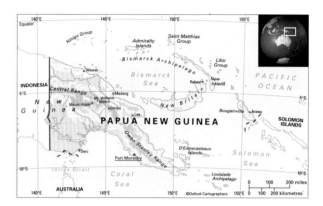

Environment: The most significant environmental issues are rainforest deforestation as a result of growing commercial demand for tropical timber; pollution from mining projects; and severe drought.

Vegetation: Rich and very varied: five kinds of lowland, and 13 kinds of mountain rainforest, five kinds of palm and swamp forests, three differing mangrove forests, and the world's greatest variety of orchid species. Forest covers 63% of the land area, having declined at 0.5% p.a. 1990–2010. Arable land comprises 1% and permanent cropland 1.3% of the total land area.

Wildlife: There are no large mammals but a rich variety of marsupials, reptiles and some 700 species of birds, including 38 species of the spectacular bird of paradise and related bower-birds. Papua New Guinea also has many thousands of unusual species of insect including the world's largest butterfly, the Queen Alexandra birdwing, and brilliant green scarab beetles which are used for jewellery. Indigenous marsupials include tree kangaroos, wallabies, bandicoots, cuscus and spiny anteaters. Dugong live in the waters near the coast. The creation of national parks was a slow process, the government being reluctant to interfere with traditional methods of land tenure, but there are now four national parks, and protection measures have been introduced, banning the export of birds of paradise.

Main towns: Port Moresby (capital, pop. 307,100 in 2010), Lae (Morobe, 96,200), Mendi (Southern Highlands, 43,100), Mount Hagen (Western Highlands, 41,500), Popondetta (Oro, 40,600), Arawa (on Bougainville, 38,600), Kokopo (on New Britain, 33,500), Madang (Madang, 29,100), Kimbe (on New Britain, 23,800), Wewak (East Sepik, 21,800), Bulolo (Morobe, 20,900), Goroka (Eastern Highlands, 20,900), Daru (Fly River, 18,300), Kavieng (on New Ireland, 18,200), Alotau (Milne Bay, 14,500), Vanimo (Sandaun, 11,500), Kundiawa (Simbu, 10,800), Wau (Morobe, 8,700) and Rabaul (on New Britain, 8,100).

Transport: Construction of roads is hampered by the rugged mountainous environment and the total national road network extends to 19,600km, 3.5% paved. Port Moresby is perhaps the only capital city that is not linked by road with the rest of the country. There is no railway.

Discover Papua New Guinea with Air Niugini

We believe our country is the most beautiful place in the world. And no airline is better placed to share our paradise with the world than Air Niugini.

We operate more flights in and out of Papua New Guinea than any other airline.

So make your connection to paradise with the airline that knows our beautiful country like no other.

Australia: Air Niugini operates up to 23 weekly flights to Australia including twice a week to Sydney. Daily flights to Cairns and Brisbane.

Pacific Region: Air Niugini operates twice weekly to Honiara in Solomon Islands and Nadi, Fiji.

Asia: Air Niugini operates four weekly services to

Singapore, three weekly services to Manila and once weekly services to Narita and Hong Kong.

For the right connections to popular or remote destinations throughout Papua New Guinea, contact your nearest Air Niugini office or preferred travel agent.

Air Niugini

Discover more! Visit www.airniugini.com.pg

Principal ports are Alotau (on the southern tip of New Guinea), Port Moresby (on the south coast), and Lae, Madang and Wewak (on the north coast), Rabaul (in New Britain), Kieta (Bougainville) and Momote (Manus Island). As there are relatively few roads, river transport is important, for both freight and passengers, and particularly on the River Sepik.

The international airport is Port Moresby at Jackson Field, 11km from the city. Domestic air services run to all centres of population and industry.

Society

KEY FACTS 2010

Population per sq km:	15
Life expectancy:	62 years

Population: 6,858,000 (2010); 13% lives in urban areas; growth 2.5% p.a. 1990–2010; birth rate 30 per 1,000 people (42 in 1970); life expectancy is 62 years (43 in 1970).

The people are of mixed (mostly Melanesian) race, with small communities of Polynesians on outlying atolls. There is a declining non-indigenous population (several thousand Australians and a small Chinese population).

Language: The official language is English, but Tok Pisin (an English-based Creole) is more widely used, and Hiri Motu is spoken around Port Moresby; there are over 800 indigenous languages.

Religion: Christians 90% (predominantly Protestants), though Christian beliefs often coexist with traditional beliefs.

Health: Public spending on health was 2% of GDP in 2009. State- and church-run hospitals, dispensaries and clinics, with charges low and related to ability to pay. 40% of the population uses an improved drinking water source and 45% have adequate sanitation facilities (2009). Infant mortality was 47 per 1,000 live births in 2010 (143 in 1960). In 2009, 0.9% of people aged 15–49 were HIV positive.

Education: There are eleven years of school education starting at age seven, comprising six years of primary, and five of secondary, with cycles of three and two years. The school year starts in January.

There are four public universities: University of Papua New Guinea (Port Moresby); Papua New Guinea University of Technology (Lae); University of Goroka (Goroka), which trains teachers; and University of Natural Resources and Environment (Kerevat, East New Britain), which trains people for agriculture and natural resource management. There are two private universities, one founded by the Roman Catholic Church and one by the Seventh Day Adventist Church. The seven tertiary institutions that offer courses in technical and vocational education include the National Polytechnic Institute at Lae. Literacy among people aged 15–24 is 68% (2009).

Media: Two daily papers, *The National* and *Post-Courier*, are published in English.

In such a large and sparsely populated country radio is the most important information source for most people. The National Broadcasting Corporation provides national and provincial radio stations; and there are several private radio stations.

The private TV service, EMTV, and public National Television Service are only received in and around Port Moresby and the provincial capitals.

Some 10% of households have TV sets (2006). There are 64 personal computers (2005) and 13 internet users (2010) per 1,000 people.

Communications: Country code 675; internet domain '.pg'. Mobile coverage is limited. Internet access is generally slow.

There are 18 main telephone lines and 278 mobile phone subscriptions per 1,000 people (2010).

Public holidays: New Year's Day, Queen's Official Birthday (Monday in June), Remembrance Day (23 July), Independence and Constitution Day (16 September), Christmas Day and Boxing Day. Regional festivals are held at various times during the year.

Religious festivals whose dates vary from year to year include Good Friday and Easter Monday.

Economy

KEY FACTS 2010

GNI:	US$8.9bn
GNI p.c.:	US$1,300
GDP growth:	6.0% p.a. 2006–10
Inflation:	5.3% p.a. 2006–10

Though the country is rich in mineral, agricultural, forestry and fisheries resources, development is still in the early stages, and has been hampered by volatile prices for agricultural and mineral exports. In addition, the main population centres are separated by

Real Growth in GDP

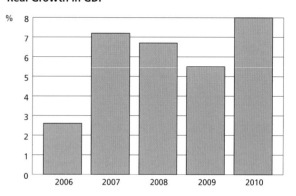

Inflation

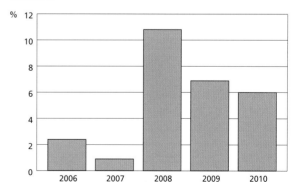

GDP by Sector (2010)

■ Agriculture	**32%**
□ Industry	**45%**
▨ Services	**23%**

ocean or inhospitable terrain. GDP grew by 1.9% p.a. 1980–90 and 3.8% p.a. 1990–2000.

Government policy has been to aim for steady, sustainable growth with an even sharing of the benefits throughout the country. To this end, it took minority shareholdings in most major industrial and mining developments (up to a maximum of 30% in mineral projects and 22.5% in petroleum projects).

GDP growth was uneven during the 1990s, registering 15% in 1993 as new mining investment came on stream, but falling to –3.6% in 1995, –3.9% in 1997 and –3.8% in 1998. By 1998 the country was in the most serious financial crisis since independence due to a prolonged drought, the continuing Bougainville crisis, the Asian economic downturn and the falling value of the kina. With the support of the World Bank and IMF, the government embarked on economic reforms including a programme of privatisation.

The economy recovered strongly during 1999 but then stalled, with good growth returning from 2003, as new mining and hydrocarbon projects came on stream, recording 4.9% p.a. over 2005–09. There was more vigorous growth of 7.2% in 2007 and 6.7% in 2008, moderating slightly to 5.5% in 2009, in response to the global downturn and collapse of world demand, before strengthening again to 8–9% p.a. in 2010–11.

Mining and energy

The country is richly endowed with mineral and hydrocarbon resources. Since commercial gold-mining began in 1989, mining and oil and gas production have made a significant contribution to

GDP. Oil production started in 1992. There are two oil refineries: one in Gulf of Papua; and one at Port Moresby. A liquefied natural gas project in the Southern Highlands and Western Province was expected to begin operating by 2014. Proven reserves of natural gas were estimated in January 2011 to be 400 billion cubic metres.

The principal copper mine at Ok Tedi in Western Province was developed and operated by an Australian company and then abandoned. Another important mine on the island of Bougainville closed in 1989 at the outbreak of political instability and, after political resolution in Bougainville, rehabilitation needed huge investment. There are substantial reserves of nickel/cobalt at Ramu in Madang Province. Nickel and cobalt exports – from the new plant at Ramu – were due to start in 2012.

Constitution

Status:	Monarchy under Queen Elizabeth II
Legislature:	National Parliament
Independence:	16 September 1975

Papua New Guinea is a constitutional monarchy recognising Queen Elizabeth II as head of state, represented by a governor-general who is nominated by parliament and serves for a term of six years.

Government is by parliamentary democracy, with a unicameral National Parliament of 109 members. Elections are held every five years, with universal adult suffrage.

After a general election parliament elects a prime minister who heads the national government. Parliament can only hold votes of no confidence in the prime minister when more than 18 months

INSTITUTE OF NATIONAL AFFAIRS OF PAPUA NEW GUINEA

P.O. Box 1530, Port Moresby, NCD, Papua New Guinea

Awareness, sound policies and commitment to PNG's future

Who we are

The Institute of National Affairs of Papua New Guinea (INA) is a privately funded, non-profit Papua New Guinea research institute established in 1977, which functions to provide independent policy advice and promote dialogue between the private sector, government and the wider community. Economic and social policy research is carried out by world-class academics to stimulate and facilitate dialogue on critical issues pertaining to PNG's future. The Institute is run by a Council that is drawn from leading figures from business, public life and academia in Papua New Guinea. It tries to encourage regional coverage so that research and activities are not only solely focused on the national capital.

Core values

PNG is currently experiencing a period of rapid economic growth, geared substantially to natural resource utilisation. This investment and growth brings a range of opportunities and challenges, which need to be addressed. INA's research and commentary is made on a non-partisan basis, in order to promote frank policy discussion with the government, private sector and wider society on socio-economic issues. INA plays an influential role in highlighting critical issues with government and other parties to encourage sound public policy geared to providing broad-based and sustainable economic and social development, employment and empowerment.

Port Moresby and harbour

Contact

Paul Barker
Executive Director

Tel: +675 321 1045
Fax: +675 321 7223
E-mail: paul.barker@cimcpng.org

www.inapng.com

has elapsed since an election and at least 12 months before a new election is due.

Government is structured at two levels: national and provincial. The 19 provincial governments can levy taxes and are responsible for local education, industry and business development, while national government is responsible for national finance, infrastructure, defence, foreign relations, trade, schools and hospitals.

Politics

Last elections:	June/July 2007
Next elections:	2012
Head of state:	Queen Elizabeth II, represented by governor-general, Sir Michael Ogio (2011–)
Head of government:	Prime Minister Peter O'Neill
Ruling party:	coalition led by People's National Congress

The political life of Papua New Guinea is one of diversity and is characterised by a tradition of fluid coalitions. A large number of candidates (more than 2,700 in 2007) contest the 109 seats at general elections, and the consequent low number of votes required to win seats means there is a high turnover of MPs. Allegiances are fragile and MPs often change parties more than once during the life of a parliament. Prime ministers have tended not to serve out a full term between elections, though they have often returned to power later.

The general election that commenced in mid-June 2002 was chaotic and violent, with the loss of at least 25 lives, and had to be extended for four weeks beyond the scheduled two-week voting period. Even then six Southern Highlands constituencies could not be declared because of missing ballot boxes. The National Alliance Party (NAP) won 19 of the declared seats, Sir Mekere Morauta's People's Democratic Movement 13, People's Progress Party eight, and Pangu Pati six, giving the National Alliance and its multiparty coalition a parliamentary majority and Alliance leader Sir Michael Somare once again became prime minister.

History

Melanesian people inhabited the area from 3000 or 2000 BC, living in groups isolated by dense forest. In consequence, no larger social order developed, and even today, more than 700 languages are spoken. Spanish and Portuguese sailors sighted the land in the early 16th century. There was some limited exploration in the 19th century, and a few settlements made. In 1884, Germany annexed the northern parts and Britain proclaimed a protectorate over the southern parts (which were formally annexed by Britain in 1888 and became British New Guinea). In 1906, Australia took over British New Guinea, renamed a year earlier as the Territory of Papua. The Australian army occupied German New Guinea in the First World War and in 1920 Australia received from the League of Nations a mandate for the government of New Guinea, as it was then called.

In 1942 the Japanese army occupied parts of New Guinea and Papua; the Australian military administered the rest. Under the Papua and New Guinea Act of 1949, the two parts were united for administration as the Territory of Papua and New Guinea and put under United Nations International Trusteeship.

The Act also set up a legislative council, under an administrator, with 28 members, of whom three were elected, nine appointed and 16 official. There had to be at least three Papua New Guineans among the appointed members. Under the Papua and New Guinea Act of 1963, the council became a house of assembly, with 64 members, ten of them nominated official members.

Consequently, at its opening in June 1964, the Assembly had a majority of elected Papua New Guineans. The following year, the House set up a Select Committee on Constitutional Development, whose recommendations were put into effect in 1967, when the number of elected seats in the House was increased to 84, and in 1968, when a new ministerial system was adopted and an administrator's executive council set up.

In 1970 an appointed spokesman for this council was recognised as the House's leader for government business. In 1971 the Select Committee recommended that the Territory prepare for self-government. Elections were held in April 1972. The House had 100 elected members, with an additional three appointed and

four official members, and Michael Somare became chief minister of a coalition government. Self-government was granted at the end of 1973 and in the spring of 1975 Australia gave up certain remaining powers over defence and foreign affairs.

In September 1975 Papua New Guinea proceeded to full independence, becoming an independent sovereign state as a constitutional monarchy with Queen Elizabeth II as head of state, represented by governor-general, Sir John Guise, a Papua New Guinean.

Sir Michael Somare, the prime minister at independence, was returned at the 1977 elections, but a parliamentary defeat in 1980 led to his replacement as prime minister by Sir Julius Chan, leader of the People's Progress Party, until 1982 when parliament re-elected Somare. The 1987 elections brought in another coalition government, headed by Paias Wingti. Somare resigned as leader of the Pangu Pati in May 1988 and a month later his successor, Sir Rabbie Namaliu, became prime minister, after Wingti had lost a vote of no confidence in the House. Paias Wingti was returned at the elections of 1992. Sir Julius Chan again became prime minister in 1994, following a leadership challenge and Supreme Court ruling. In early 1997 the government dispatched foreign mercenaries to Bougainville. The defence force rounded up and expelled the mercenaries and called for the prime minister's resignation. Chan dismissed the defence force chief, but the army refused to recognise his successor and Chan himself resigned in March 1997. The cabinet appointed a caretaker government headed by the minister for mining and petroleum, John Giheno.

In the elections held in June 1997, 16 ministers (including Chan) lost their seats and Bill Skate, the governor of Port Moresby, was elected prime minister by parliament after a month of negotiations. He headed a four-party coalition comprising his People's National Congress, the People's Democratic Congress and the two constituents of the previous ruling coalition, the People's Progress Party and the Pangu Pati. Beset by corruption scandals and an acute financial crisis, by mid-1999 Skate found his political support, which had at best been fragile, dwindling rapidly. In June 1999 he could no longer count on a majority in ➤

Following the parliamentary elections held in June–July 2007, in which NAP won 27 seats, Somare secured the agreement of a further 59 MPs to join his coalition, and in mid-August was duly re-elected prime minister by parliament.

In December 2010 the Supreme Court ruled Governor-General Sir Paulias Matane's re-election in June 2010 had been unconstitutional. At the National Parliament's next session in January 2011 Michael Ogio was elected governor-general, defeating the opposition candidate, Sir Pato Kakaraya, by 65 votes to 23.

In December 2010, Sir Michael Somare stepped aside in order to face a Leadership Tribunal hearing on allegations of financial mismanagement, and his newly appointed deputy, Samuel Abal, became acting prime minister. Following a two-week suspension from office by the Tribunal in April 2011, Somare began a long period of medical treatment in Singapore. In August 2011, amid increasing concerns that Somare would never be able to resume office, a parliamentary vote declared the office of prime minister vacant, and the People's National Congress leader and transport and works minister, Peter O'Neill, was elected prime minister, receiving 70 of the 94 votes cast, with support from both government and opposition members. Several parties filed a challenge against parliament's actions in the Supreme Court that month; these were joined by Somare following his return to Papua New Guinea in September.

O'Neill won another parliamentary vote of confidence in December 2011, after the Supreme Court had ruled that Somare be reinstated, and Parliament then passed retrospective legislation to legitimise O'Neill's position. In January 2012 there was a further move to enforce the Supreme Court ruling by some members of the Defence Force loyal to Somare. This was quickly halted by the majority of the Force.

International relations

Papua New Guinea is a member of the African, Caribbean and Pacific Group of States, Asia–Pacific Economic Cooperation, Non-Aligned Movement, Pacific Community, Pacific Islands Forum, United Nations and World Trade Organization.

Traveller information

Local laws and conventions: There are conservative standards of dress and behaviour in some regions. Permission should be sought before taking photographs of individuals and cultural sites (for example, spirit houses).

The country has very strict laws relating to the possession and sale of pornographic material and penalties include imprisonment. Penalties for possession, use or trafficking in illegal drugs are severe, and can result in long jail sentences and heavy fines.

Handshaking is the usual form of greeting. Dress is generally casual. Business meetings tend to be informal and are always conducted in English. Business cards are expected. Men should wear a lightweight suit and businesswomen are advised to dress conservatively. Office hours are Mon–Fri 0800–1630.

parliament, he resigned as prime minister in July shortly before parliament started its new session, and Sir Mekere Morauta emerged as his successor.

Bougainville

The greatest threat to stability since independence has been the attempted secession of the island of Bougainville, the site of the Panguna copper mine and one of the underpinnings of Papua New Guinea's economy in the 1980s. In 1990, a group calling itself the Bougainville Revolutionary Army (BRA) led a movement for secession by the island from Papua New Guinea. This act followed a period of violent political upheaval centred on the copper mine, and then spread through the island's society. Initially, the revolt was focused on the environmental damage caused by the mine and the lack of royalties being paid to the Bougainvilleans.

Numerous attempts were made to solve the problem, which damaged Papua New Guinea's economy and destroyed Bougainville's, and led to years of violence with many atrocities and the destruction of the mine and other infrastructure.

By 1994 some secessionist leaders were becoming dissatisfied with the hard-line stance of the BRA. At a meeting with the prime minister in November 1994, after which the Mirigina Charter was established, they agreed to the setting up of a transitional administration for the North Solomons Province (the Bougainville Transitional Government), which would have a council of chiefs nominating members of the provincial assembly. This administration was established in early 1995, with Theodore Miriung as its premier and talks on increased autonomy continued.

In October 1996 Premier Miriung was assassinated. Miriung was replaced by Gerard Sinato, who immediately called for tripartite talks between the BTG, the BRA and the Papua New Guinea Government. The government, however, had decided on a military solution and in early 1997 it contracted a group of foreign mercenaries to impose a permanent resolution of the Bougainville crisis. However, Papua New Guinea's defence force immediately

took to the streets and detained and then expelled the mercenaries.

In October 1997, following talks in Christchurch, New Zealand, a truce was signed between the new government and many of the Bougainville separatists, though not the BRA led by Francis Ona. After further negotiations, in January 1998 a permanent peace and amnesty were agreed with all the secessionists, taking effect after an official signing ceremony at the end of April 1998, and ending a nine-year conflict which had claimed the lives of some 20,000 people.

A process of negotiation on greater autonomy was initiated: a Bougainville assembly was established in January 1999; the Bougainville Reconciliation Government (BRG) was elected in May 1999 and Joseph Kabui voted president at its first sitting; and he then appointed a team to conduct the negotiations.

In March 2000, the 'Loloata Understanding' was concluded between the BRG and the Papua New Guinea Government, setting up the Bougainville Interim Provincial Government.

The Bougainville Peace Agreement was signed in Arawa in August 2001, providing for special autonomous status for Bougainville, with a gradual draw-down of substantial self-government powers from the Papua New Guinea Government, and the promise of a referendum on independence to be held between 2015 and 2020. These terms were enshrined in Bougainville's constitution which was approved by the Papua New Guinea Parliament in December 2004. The first Autonomous Bougainville Government was elected in May/June 2005, and a former leader of the pro-independence movement, Joseph Kabui, was elected president. James Tanis was elected president of Bougainville in a by-election held in December 2008, following the death of President Kabui in June that year.

The second Autonomous Bougainville Government elections were held in Bougainville in May 2010. Former provincial governor John Momis was elected president with 52.4% of the votes, while a large proportion of new members representing various political factions were elected to the House of Representatives.

Immigration and customs: All travellers need a visa to enter the country, and passports must be valid for at least six months beyond the intended length of stay. A return or onward ticket is also required.

There are strict quarantines controls on entering Papua New Guinea with fruit, vegetables and animal products.

A yellow fever vaccination certificate is required from travellers arriving from an infected area.

Travel within the country: Traffic drives on the left and car hire is available in the main towns. A national driving licence may be used for up to one month. Visitors should keep their driving licence on them at all times.

Taxis are available in the major centres and fares should be agreed in advance. There are also public buses, known locally as PMVs. There are no public transport operators on the rivers, but it is possible to hire motorised canoes in order to use these routes.

Travellers to Bougainville should be registered with the Provincial Administration on the island.

Travel health: Comprehensive health insurance is essential and should include evacuation facilities.

Visitors will need protection against malaria, together with insect repellent and suitable clothing to prevent bites. Dengue fever is common in coastal areas and is spread by day-biting mosquitoes.

All water should be boiled or sterilised before use.

Money: Local currency is the kina and the toea (1 kina = 100 toea). American Express is the most widely accepted credit card. Travellers cheques are accepted in most shops and hotels, and to avoid additional exchange rates should be taken in pounds sterling, US dollars or Australian dollars. Banking hours are Mon–Thur 0845–1500, Fri 0845–1600.

There were 126,000 tourist arrivals in 2009.

Further information

National Parliament: www.parliament.gov.pg

Bank of Papua New Guinea: www.bankpng.gov.pg

Commonwealth Secretariat: www.thecommonwealth.org

Commonwealth of Nations: www.commonwealth-of-nations.org/Papua_New_Guinea

NATIONAL INSTITUTE OF STATISTICS of RWANDA

The National Institute of Statistics of Rwanda (NISR) was created by Organic Law No.09/2005 as the primary data producer in different areas, and co-ordinating agency of all statistical activities in Rwanda. NISR provides statistics on a wide range of areas including the economy, society, population and the environment, covering government, business and communities.

Mission and Vision of NISR

The main mission of NISR is to provide relevant, reliable, coherent, timely and accessible statistical information and services to various sectors of the society in a co-ordinated and sustainable manner. The vision of NISR is to be an efficient information support to the realisation of Rwanda's Vision 2020 and to emerge as one of the leading National Statistical Systems in Africa.

Some results published by NISR in 2012

The GDP of Rwanda has grown substantially (8.29 per cent on average) over the past 10 years (2001-2010); with the agricultural and service sectors being the most dominant contributors to this growth along with a growing industry sector.

Integrated Household Living Condition Survey (EICV)

The EICV survey is conducted every five years and the recent EICV conducted in 2010/2011 has shown that poverty in Rwanda is 44.9 per cent, down from 77.8 per cent in 1994, with about a 12 per cent poverty reduction within the last five years.

Figure 1: Trend of Poverty in Rwanda

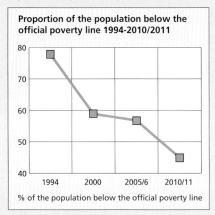

Proportion of the population below the official poverty line 1994-2010/2011

% of the population below the official poverty line

2010 Rwanda Demographic and Health Survey (RDHS)

The RDHS survey, conducted every five years, is designed to provide data for monitoring the population and health situation in Rwanda. The recent RDHS conducted in 2010/2011 has shown that child health in Rwanda was impressively improved.

Mr Yusuf Murangwa, Director General

Figure 2: Trends in child health

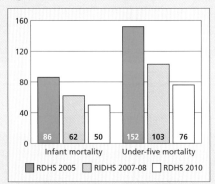

	Infant mortality			Under-five mortality		
RDHS 2005	86			152		
RIDHS 2007-08		62			103	
RDHS 2010			50			76

NISR is preparing the fourth Population and Housing Census (PHC) to update the total headcount in Rwanda, and this is expected to be conducted in August 2012.

Email: **info@statistics.gov.rw**
P.O. Box 6139, Kigali, Rwanda

Rwanda

KEY FACTS

Joined Commonwealth:	November 2009
Population:	10,624,000 (2010)
GDP p.c. growth:	2.3% p.a. 1990–2010
UN HDI 2011:	world ranking 166
Official languages:	Kinyarwanda, French, English
Time:	GMT plus 2hr
Currency:	Rwandan franc (Rwfr)

Geography

Area:	26,338 sq km
Coastline:	none
Capital:	Kigali

The Republic of Rwanda is a landlocked country with land borders with four countries: Uganda, United Republic of Tanzania, Burundi and Democratic Republic of Congo (clockwise from the north). Water covers 1,390 sq km of the country; the largest lakes include Bulera, Ihema, Kivu (straddling the border with the Democratic Republic of Congo), Mugesera and Muhazi, and there are many rivers. The country comprises five provinces.

Topography: The terrain is rugged with steep hills and deep valleys, rising in the north to the highest peak, Karisimbi (4,519m), which lies in a range of volcanoes. The country is popularly known as the 'land of a thousand hills'.

Climate: Though the country is close to the Equator, the climate is tempered by altitude; it is hot and humid in the valleys, and drier and cooler in the higher elevations. The rainy seasons are March–May and October–November; the hottest season August–September.

Environment: The most significant environmental issues are drought, limiting the potential for agriculture; overgrazing; soil erosion and degradation; and deforestation due to almost universal use of wood as a fuel.

Did you know...

Rwanda joined the Commonwealth in November 2009, becoming the association's 54th member.

In 2008 the Government of Rwanda decided to change the medium of education from French to English.

In September 2008 Rwanda became the first nation in the world to elect a majority of women MPs: 45 of the 80 members of the Chamber of Deputies.

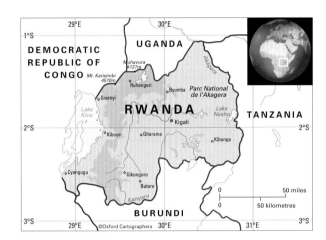

Vegetation: Thick equatorial rainforest is found in the north and west of the country – forest covering some 18% of the total land area – and savannah in the east. Forest cover has increased at 1.6% p.a. 1990–2010. Arable land comprises 53% and permanent cropland 11% of the total land area.

Wildlife: National parks and game reserves cover some 8% of the country and include the Volcanoes National Park (famous for its mountain gorillas) and Akagera National Park (elephants, buffaloes, giraffes and zebras).

Main towns: Kigali (capital, pop. 1.03m in 2010), Ruhengeri (117,500), Gisenyi (113,000), Butare (107,300), Gitarama (87,700), Ruhango (74,700), Byumba (74,700), Cyangugu (68,800), Kabuga (57,400), Nyanza (55,300), Rwamagana (53,000), Kibungo (48,900), Kibuye (47,900) and Gikongoro (34,800).

Transport: There are 14,000km of roads, 19% paved. There is no railway.

The main international airport is Kigali International.

Society

KEY FACTS 2010

Population per sq km:	403
Life expectancy:	55 years
Net primary enrolment:	96%

Population: 10,624,000 (2010); 19% lives in urban areas; growth 2.0% p.a. 1990–2010; birth rate 41 per 1,000 people (53 in 1970); life expectancy 55 years (44 in 1970).

The main ethnic groups are Hutus, comprising an estimated 85% of the population; Tutsis (14%); and Twa (less than 1%). Censuses carried out since the conflict of the 1990s have not included ethnicity.

Rwanda Revenue Authority

Road to Rwanda's self–reliance

Establishment

The Authority was established as part of the reform programme by the Government, designed to restore, strengthen and support its initiatives towards self-reliance. This will lead to the goal of providing the public with effective governance and public goods.

Vision

To become a world-class efficient and modern revenue agency fully financing national needs.

Mission

Mobilise revenue for economic development through efficient and equitable services that promote business growth.

Core strategic values

- Integrity
- Customer focus
- Transparency
- Professional service delivery
- Teamwork
- Leadership

Mandate and functions

- The Rwanda Revenue Authority (RRA) was established in 1998 as a quasi-autonomous body, mandated with the task of assessing, collecting, and accounting for tax, customs and other specified revenues.
- Advise government on fiscal policy.
- Implementation of fiscal policies as regulated by government.
- Effective administration and enforcement of the laws relating to those policies.
- Formulation of outreach programmes that improve compliance.
- Also collects non-tax revenues.

Performance trends

- Before 1994 the tax contribution to the national budget was approximately 10 billion Rwandan francs.
- Since 1998, the performance trends are as follows:

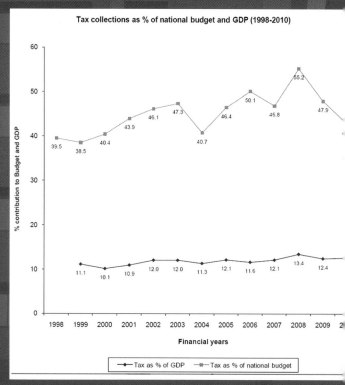

Enabling environment

- Strong support from Government and other partners
- One-stop-centre for all client needs
- Close collaboration with the private sector Federation through open discussion in tax issues forum
- Computer-based products e.g.:
  - SIGTAS for collection of domestic taxes
  - ASYCUDA++ for Customs Management
  - Online delivery of Tax Clearance Certificates
  - Online Tax Calculator for SMEs tax computation
  - E-registration
  - Call Centre

Other services

- One-stop-centre boarder post concept at major customs points.
- Block management (zoning business centre) for easier access to RRA services.
- Pre-clearance and pre-payment facilities at customs.

Short and medium-term priorities

- Increase tax base by facilitating growth of SMEs and reduction of informal sector.
- Implementation of projects in pipeline e.g. e-filing, e-payment, Electronic Single Window and Electronic Data Controller.

Contact

Ben Kagarama
Commissioner General
Tel: +250 252 595 520
Fax: +250 252 595 750
Mob: +250 788 301 099
Email: cg@rra@gov.rw
P.O. Box: 3987, Kigali, Rwanda
www.rra.gov.rw

Mr Ben Kagerama, Commissioner General

The RRA Headquarters in Kigali, Rwanda

Language: Kinyarwanda, French and English are the official languages, and Kiswahili is widely spoken.

Religion: Christians (mostly Roman Catholics) comprise about half the population and most of the rest hold traditional beliefs, often combined with Christianity. There is a small minority of Muslims, comprising about 2% of the population, according to the 2002 census.

Health: Public spending on health was 4% of GDP in 2009. 65% of the population uses an improved drinking water source and 54% of people have access to adequate sanitation facilities (2009). Infant mortality was 59 per 1,000 live births in 2010 (122 in 1960). In 2009, 2.9% of people aged 15–49 were HIV positive.

The King Faisal Hospital_, Kigali, is the country's principal referral centre and teaching hospital, Muhima Hospital is also located in Kigali, and there are health centres, health posts, clinics and dispensaries throughout the country.

Education: Public spending on education was 5.0% of GDP in 2010. There are six years of compulsory education starting at age seven, followed by six years of secondary education. In 2003 the government launched plans for a new school system with nine years of compulsory basic education. In October 2008 the government decided to change the medium of education from French to English.

The National University of Rwanda was established in 1963 with faculties of medicine and social sciences, and a teacher-training college. Faculties of law, sciences and technology, and the National Institute of Education followed, all now located at Butare in the south.

Media: *The New Times* (daily), *Rwanda Herald* and *Rwanda Newsline* are all published in English; *Umeseso* in Kinyarwanda.

Radio Rwanda provides public radio services in Kinyarwanda, French, English and Kiswahili, and there are several private commercial or faith radio stations. Télévision Rwandaise provides a public service in the urban areas.

Some 2% of households have TV sets (2007). There are 3 personal computers (2006) and 130 internet users (2010) per 1,000 people.

Communications: Country code 250 (no area codes); internet domain '.rw'.

There are 4 main telephone lines and 334 mobile phone subscriptions per 1,000 people (2010).

Public holidays: New Year's Day, Heroes' Day (1 February), Genocide Remembrance Day (7 April), Labour Day (1 May), Independence Day (1 July), Liberation Day (4 July), Assumption (15 August), Patriotism Day (1 October), All Saint's Day (1 November), Christmas Day and Boxing Day.

Religious festivals whose dates vary from year to year include Good Friday, Easter Monday and Eid al-Fitr (End of Ramadan, two days).

National Commission for Human Rights – Rwanda

The National Commission for Human Rights – Rwanda (NCHR) is a constitutional, independent and permanent national organ especially in charge of the promotion, protection and monitoring of the respect for human rights. The NCHR was established by law no 04/99 of March 12, 1999 and in accordance with the Paris Principles. Its mandate is set out in the Constitution of the Republic of Rwanda of June 4, 2003 as revised to date.

The NCHR shall submit its annual activity report and special reports on human rights violations comprising recommendations to Parliament and reserve a copy for the President of the Republic, the Cabinet and the Supreme Court. It encourages mediation, as deemed necessary, and can file complaints with competent courts.

The NCHR provides views on bills relating to human rights and sensitises relevant government institutions with regard to the ratification of International Human Rights Conventions and their integration into existing internal laws.

CONTACT

National Commission for Human Rights – Rwanda
PO Box 269 Kigali, Rwanda

Tel: +250 252 50 4273/4
Fax: +250 252 50 4270
E-mail: cndh@rwanda1.com

www.cndp.org.rw

Economy

KEY FACTS 2010

GNI:	US$5.5bn
GNI p.c.:	US$520
GDP growth:	7.5% p.a. 2006–10
Inflation:	9.1% p.a. 2006–10

Rwanda is landlocked and densely populated. It has relatively few exploitable resources and most people are engaged in subsistence agriculture which in the late 2000s contributed about 35% of GDP. Water resources are unevenly spread across the country and some areas experience periodic droughts. Commercial cultivation of coffee and tea was introduced by the colonial administration in the first half of the twentieth century.

History

By the 17th century Tutsis had established a kingdom in present-day Rwanda where Hutus, Tutsis and Twa were living. Rwanda became part of German East Africa in 1899. After the First World War, it came under Belgian administration under a League of Nations mandate, and, from 1920, as part of a UN trust territory, 'Ruanda–Urundi'.

After the Second World War, Rwanda continued to be administered by Belgium. In 1959, as the independence movement gathered pace, the ruling Tutsi elite formed a political party, Union Nationale Rwandaise. The Belgian authorities encouraged the Hutu majority also to aspire to political power and, in the same year, a rival party, Parti de l'émancipation du peuple Hutu (Parmehutu), was established.

As the 1960 local elections approached, Parmehutu initiated a Hutu uprising resulting in the death of many Tutsis and forcing King Kigeri V and tens of thousands of Tutsis to flee into exile in Uganda and Burundi. In 1961 the monarchy was abolished and Rwanda became a republic, gaining independence from Belgium in 1962, with Parmehutu leader Grégoire Kayibanda as president; many more Tutsis left the country and those who remained faced continuing state-sponsored violence and institutionalised discrimination. The most serious eruption of violence at this time was triggered in 1963 by an incursion from Burundi of exiled Rwandan Tutsis and resulted in the death of at least 15,000 Tutsis at the hands of Hutu gangs.

Kayibanda was overthrown in 1973 in a military coup led by army chief of staff Juvénal Habyarimana. There then ensued a period of military rule, until 1978, when a new constitution was promulgated and Habyarimana became president.

In 1990 forces of the Rwandan Patriotic Front (RPF) entered the country from Uganda and the civil war began. Though predominantly a Tutsi movement, the RPF did win the support of a significant element of moderate Hutus. A new constitution promoting multiparty democracy was introduced in 1991. Peace talks brokered by the UN in August 1993 resulted in a power-sharing agreement between Habyarimana and the RPF, the Arusha Accords.

In April 1994 an aircraft carrying Habyarimana and the Burundian president was shot down on its return from Arusha to Kigali, killing all the passengers. The president's violent death triggered the co-ordinated massacre of Tutsis – and some Hutus who opposed the government – by Hutu militia and elements of the Rwandan army. In response the RPF began a major offensive from the north. An estimated 800,000 Tutsis and moderate Hutus were killed in the months following the plane crash. In July 1994 the RPF took control of Kigali and formed an administration

based on the principles of power-sharing and national reconciliation which were the basis of the 1993 Arusha Accords. The administration comprised five political parties: the RPF, Christian Democratic Party, Liberal Party, Republican Democratic Movement and Social Democratic Party. Pasteur Bizimungu was inaugurated as president for a five-year term; the RPF military chief Paul Kagame became vice-president and defence minister. The government's priorities were security, rebuilding the economy and national reconciliation; it prohibited any official recognition of ethnicity. By February 2007 some 60,000 prisoners accused of genocide had been released.

Shortly after the new government took office, a 70-member Transitional National Assembly was formed, including representatives of the five governing parties and three other smaller parties, the Democratic Union for Rwandese People, Islamic Party and Socialist Party, as well as six representatives of the Rwandese Patriotic Army.

The UN Security Council created the International Criminal Tribunal for Rwanda (ICTR) in November 1994 to contribute to the process of national reconciliation and to the maintenance of peace in the region. The tribunal was established in Arusha, United Republic of Tanzania, in February 1995, for the prosecution of those responsible for genocide and other serious violations of international humanitarian law committed in Rwanda during 1994.

Some two million Hutus followed the Hutu militias into exile in Zaire, where they were accommodated in UN refugee camps. Many other Hutus fled to Tanzania. By 1995 the Hutu militias and Zairean government forces were initiating attacks on Zairean Banyamulenge Tutsis who lived in Eastern Zaire. In October 1996 Rwandan troops and Zairean Tutsis attacked the refugee camps where the Hutu militia were based with the aim of repatriating the refugees. In 1997 the Zairean regime was overthrown, Laurent Kabila became president and the country was renamed the Democratic Republic of Congo (DRC). However, in 1998, when it was clear that the new government of DRC was not going to return the Hutu militias to Rwanda, Rwanda began to lend its support to forces that opposed Kabila. However, in July 2002 Rwanda and the DRC agreed that Rwanda would withdraw its troops and DRC would work with Rwanda in disarming Hutu militia. By October 2002 Rwanda reported it had completed its withdrawal, and in March 2005 the main Hutu rebel group, Forces démocratiques pour la libération du Rwanda, announced the end of its armed struggle. In November 2007 Rwanda signed a peace agreement with the DRC, under which DRC was to hand over those implicated in the 1994 genocide to Rwanda or to the ICTR.

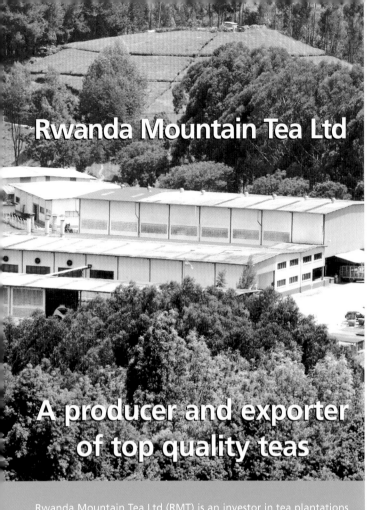

Rwanda Mountain Tea Ltd

A producer and exporter of top quality teas

Rwanda Mountain Tea Ltd (RMT) is an investor in tea plantations and processing facilities. Since its inception in 2006, RMT has grown to become one of the major players in the Rwandan tea industry, with shares in five tea estates, namely Rubaya, Nyabihu, Kitabi, Mata and Gisakura.

RMT's strategy is to mobilize resources towards producing the finest quality teas for export and local markets while expanding the Company through the acquisition of other tea factories to build strong and sustainable policies for growth. RMT offers for sale a mix of quality made tea products at competitive prices using knowledgeable, product-oriented personnel and strong marketing initiatives.

Vision
To be the regional leader in producing and exporting top quality teas to the world market.

Mission
Rwanda Mountain Tea strives to maintain consistent offering to the world market of some of the best quality teas while supporting the employees and tea farmers' community realize their fullest potential within a well protected natural environment.

RWANDA MOUNTAIN TEA LTD

Director General: Ephraim Turahirwa
Email: info@rwandamountaintea.com
        eturahirwa@gmail.com

Marketing Manager: Nyirahuku Bella
Email: rmtmarketing@yahoo.fr
Tel: +250 252 57 1935/6

www.rwandamountaintea.com

Real Growth in GDP

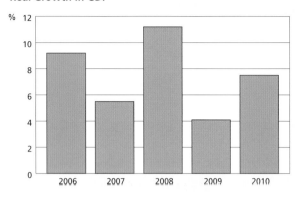

Inflation

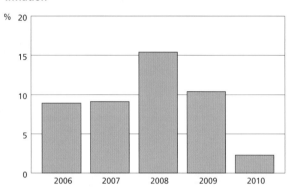

GDP by Sector (2010)

	Agriculture	34%
	Industry	16%
	Services	50%

During the long period of intercommunal conflict and massive displacement of people that lasted from independence in 1962 to the establishment in 1994 of the government of national unity led by the Rwandan Patriotic Front, development and diversification of economy and investment in infrastructure and education were on hold.

From 1994, with the strong support of the international donor community and a large injection of aid, the government embarked on a programme of economic reforms, which aimed to grow the private sector and develop a market economy and to promote investment in coffee, tea and minerals production. Foreign direct investment grew more slowly than aid.

The 2000s also saw large-scale privatisation in the utilities, transport and mining sectors and the emergence of new industries such as eco-tourism and electricity generation from methane gas at Lake Kivu. Growth in mining activity and of exports of minerals such as cassiterite (a tin ore), coltan (a metallic ore containing niobium and tantalum) and wolfram (tungsten) reduced the country's dependence on exports of coffee and tea.

With peace and stable democratic government, strong economic growth ensued, averaging more than 10% p.a. over 1996–2002, albeit much less on a per capita basis. It then slowed to 5.6% p.a. during 2003–07 and strengthened to 11.2% in 2008, moderating slightly to 4.1% in 2009, in response to the world economic downturn, before reverting to vigorous growth in 2010 (7.5%) and 2011 (7.2%).

Rwanda's external debt was substantially reduced when it reached completion point under the IMF/World Bank Heavily Indebted Poor Countries Initiative in March 2005 and qualified for the Multilateral Debt Relief Initiative in March 2006, bringing about a fall in external debt to 17% of GDP in 2006.

Constitution

Status:	Republic with executive president
Legislature:	Parliament
Independence:	1 July 1962

The present constitution came into force in June 2003, with the principal aim of promoting national unity and protecting personal liberties and human rights.

The executive president is the head of state and commander-in-chief of the armed forces, and is elected by universal adult suffrage for a seven-year term; he or she may serve a maximum of two terms. The president nominates the prime minister and appoints the council of ministers on the advice of the prime minister.

The bicameral legislature comprises the Chamber of Deputies and Senate. The Chamber of Deputies has 80 members, 53 directly elected every five years by universal adult suffrage and 27 representing: women (24 seats), youth (two) and disabled people (one). The Senate has 26 members, who serve for eight years; 12 represent the provincial government councils, and two represent academic institutions. The other members are nominated, eight by the president and four the Parties' Forum.

The constitution provides for an independent judiciary, comprising the Supreme Court, High Court, and provincial, district and municipal tribunals. There are also *gacaca* courts concerned only with crimes against humanity in 1990–94, and especially the genocide of 1994, in which ordinary Rwandans judge their peers.

Politics

Last elections:	August 2010 (presidential), September 2008 (parliamentary)
Next elections:	2017 (presidential), 2013 (parliamentary)
Head of state:	President Paul Kagame
Head of government:	the president
Ruling party:	Rwandan Patriotic Front

In April 2000 President Pasteur Bizimungu was succeeded by Rwandan Patriotic Front (RPF) leader Paul Kagame. Following endorsement of a new constitution by referendum in May 2003, Kagame won the presidential election in August 2003, with 95% of votes, and the RPF won the country's first multiparty parliamentary elections in September 2003, with 40 of the 53 directly elected seats and 74% of votes. The Social Democratic Party took seven seats and the Liberal Party six; turnout was nearly

100%. Former president Bizimungu received a 15-year jail sentence for embezzlement and inciting violence in June 2004; he was released in April 2007 when he received a presidential pardon.

When in November 2006 a French judge issued an international arrest warrant for Kagame, alleging that the RPF was responsible for shooting down the plane carrying former president Juvénal Habyarimana in April 1994, Rwanda broke off diplomatic relations with France. In October 2007 the Rwandan Government set up an inquiry into the plane crash that had sparked the genocide, which concluded in late 2009 that Habyarimana's own army had been responsible. In August 2008 Rwanda released a report naming more than 30 senior French officials alleged to have been involved in the 1994 genocide. Rwanda and France resumed diplomatic relations in November 2009.

In the parliamentary elections of September 2008 the RPF was returned taking 42 seats and 79% of votes; the Social Democratic Party won seven seats and the Liberal Party four. Turnout was again close to 100%.

In the presidential election of August 2010, when 98% of the electorate voted, Kagame won a resounding victory, receiving 93.1% of the votes cast. His main rival, Jean Damascene Ntawukuriryayo of the Social Democratic Party, secured 5.1%.

International relations

Rwanda is a member of the African, Caribbean and Pacific Group of States, African Union, Common Market for Eastern and Southern Africa, East African Community, Non-Aligned Movement, Organisation internationale de la Francophonie, United Nations and World Trade Organization.

Rwanda joined the East African Community in July 2007. Commonwealth leaders, holding their biennial CHOGM in Port of Spain, Trinidad and Tobago, admitted Rwanda as the association's 54th member on 28 November 2009.

Traveller information

Local laws and conventions: Taking photographs of government buildings is prohibited; plastic bags are also prohibited, and may be confiscated on arrival at the airport.

Appointments are generally necessary for business meetings and lightweight suits are appropriate. Business and government executives generally speak French, though the use of English is increasing. Office hours are Mon–Fri 0800–1230 and 1330–1700.

Immigration and customs: Visitors from most countries require a visa. Exceptions include Canada and the UK, whose nationals do not require visas for stays of up to three months. Passports must be valid for at least six months beyond the intended length of stay.

A yellow fever vaccination certificate may be required on arrival at Kigali International Airport, especially if coming from a country where yellow fever is present.

Travel within the country: Traffic drives on the right. There are some car hire companies in Kigali; an international driving licence is required. Fuel is relatively expensive.

Roads between Kigali and major towns are good, though landslides can occur in the rains.

Taxis are available in the larger towns. Fares should be agreed in advance and tipping is not usual.

Planes are available for charter.

Travel health: Comprehensive health insurance including emergency evacuation by air ambulance is essential. Vaccinations are recommended for diphtheria, Hepatitis A, tetanus, typhoid and yellow fever. All up-to-date vaccination requirements should be checked well in advance of travel.

Malaria is a problem in the country, and, as well as prophylaxis, visitors will need to take insect repellent and suitable clothing to protect against mosquito bites.

Regular outbreaks of cholera occur in rural areas, so visitors should make sure they boil water before use or only drink bottled water.

Money: The official currency is the Rwandan franc (Rwfr). Major credit cards are accepted at some hotels in Kigali; Mastercard is the most widely accepted. It might not be possible to cash travellers cheques outside Kigali. Banking hours are Mon–Fri 0800–1200 and 1400–1800 and Sat 0800–1300.

There were 699,000 tourist arrivals in 2009.

Further information

Government of Rwanda: www.gov.rw

Parliament: www.parliament.gov.rw

National Bank of Rwanda: www.bnr.rw

Commonwealth Secretariat: www.thecommonwealth.org

Commonwealth of Nations: www.commonwealth-of-nations.org/Rwanda

St Kitts and Nevis

KEY FACTS

Joined Commonwealth:	1983
Population:	52,000 (2010)
GDP p.c. growth:	2.2% p.a. 1990–2010
UN HDI 2011:	world ranking 72
Official language:	English
Time:	GMT minus 4hr
Currency:	Eastern Caribbean dollar (EC$)

Geography

Area:	261.6 sq km
Coastline:	135km
Capital:	Basseterre

The two-island country of St Kitts and Nevis lies in the northern part of the Leeward Islands group of the Lesser Antilles in the Eastern Caribbean. The two islands are separated by a channel some 3km in width.

Area: Total land area 261.6 sq km – St Kitts 168.4 sq km and Nevis 93.2 sq km.

Topography: The country consists of two mountainous islands of volcanic origin in the Eastern Caribbean. The larger island, St Kitts, is 37km long, with a central mountain range broken by ravines and a spacious fertile valley running down to the capital Basseterre. The highest point is Mount Liamuiga (1,156m). The beaches are mostly of black volcanic sand except for the south-eastern peninsula, which has beaches of golden sand. The almost circular island of Nevis to the south-east has beaches of silver sand and coconut groves, and rises to a central peak (Mt Nevis, 985m) which is usually capped with white clouds.

Climate: Tropical, cooled by the north-east trade winds. There is no distinct rainy season. The heat is not searing; the highest recorded temperature is 33°C. Hurricanes may occur between June and November.

Vegetation: The lower mountain slopes of St Kitts, particularly to the north, are arable and used for growing sugar cane.

Did you know...

The two mountainous islands of St Kitts and Nevis are of volcanic origin, with a highest point of 1,156m in St Kitts; many beaches in St Kitts are of black volcanic sand, while those in Nevis are silver.

Celebrated author Caryl Phillips, born in St Kitts in March 1958, won the Commonwealth Writers' Prize in 2004 with his book, *A Distant Shore*.

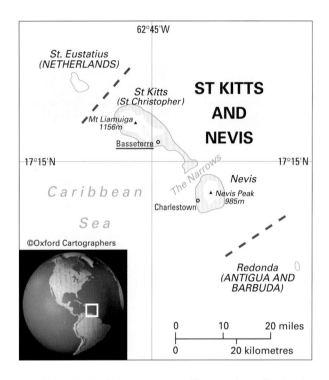

Uncultivated lowland slopes are covered in tropical woodland and exotic fruits. The higher slopes provide short grass for pasturage. Tropical rainforest or dense bushy cover occurs on the central range; unusually, the forested area is increasing in size. Nevis, where much of the land is cultivated by peasant farmers growing vegetables and coconuts, has a large coconut forest on the west side. Forest covers 42% of the total land area of St Kitts and Nevis and there was no significant loss of forest cover during 1990–2010.

Wildlife: Before the arrival of Europeans the only land-animal life was small rodents and reptiles. The French introduced the green vervet monkey to the islands, and mongooses and deer later followed. Birdlife includes pelicans and frigatebirds on the coast, hummingbirds in the forested areas and quail and pigeons in the mountains.

Main towns: Basseterre (capital, pop. 13,400 in 2010), St Paul's (1,300), Sadlers (1,000), Middle Island (900), Tabernacle (840), Mansion (830), Cayon (810) and Sandy Point (790) on St Kitts; Charlestown (2,200) on Nevis.

Transport: There are good road networks on St Kitts and Nevis, 43% paved. A regular passenger ferry service operates between Basseterre and Charlestown, taking 40 minutes. Basseterre has a deep-water port, with berthing facilities for cruiseships and cargo vessels. There is a smaller port at Sandy Point. Nevis has a 126m pier at Charlestown. There is also a smaller port at Newcastle.

The Robert Llewellyn Bradshaw International Airport at Golden Rock, St Kitts (3km from Basseterre), receives direct flights from the USA and Canada, while flights to other continents generally go via Antigua. The Nevis airfield is at Newcastle.

Society

KEY FACTS 2010

Population per sq km:	198
Life expectancy:	74 years (est.)
Net primary enrolment:	94%

Population: 52,000 (2010); some 12,000 on Nevis; 32% of the total population lives in urban areas; growth 1.3% p.a. 1990–2010; birth rate 14 per 1,000 people (est. 26 in 1970); life expectancy 74 years (est.)

The population is mainly of mixed African and European descent, with a UK-descended minority.

Language: English is the official language; an English-based Creole is widely spoken.

Religion: Mainly Christians (Anglicans, Methodists, Roman Catholics, Moravians and others).

Health: Public spending on health was 4% of GDP in 2009. There are general hospitals at Basseterre in St Kitts and Charlestown in Nevis, and many health clinics. 99% of the population uses an improved drinking water source and 96% adequate sanitation facilities (2009). Infant mortality was 7 per 1,000 live births in 2010.

Education: There are 12 years of compulsory education starting at age five, offered by state, private and church schools. Primary school comprises seven years and secondary six, with cycles of four and two years. Some 67% of pupils complete primary school (2007). The school year starts in September.

St Kitts and Nevis participates in the regional University of the West Indies, which has its main campuses in Barbados, Jamaica, and Trinidad and Tobago. The female–male ratio for gross enrolment in tertiary education is 2.10:1 (2008).

Media: The main political parties publish newspapers. Newspapers include *Sun St Kitts/Nevis* (daily, privately owned), *The Democrat* (weekly of People's Action Movement), *The Labour Spokesman* (bi-weekly of St Kitts-Nevis Trades and Labour Union), and *The St Kitts and Nevis Observer* (weekly).

The government provides national commercial radio and TV services, ZIZ Radio and ZIZ Television; and there are several private radio stations, and private TV channels are available via cable.

There are 760 internet users per 1,000 people (2010).

Communications: Country code 1 869; internet domain '.kn'. Mobile phone coverage extends over most of both islands. There are internet cafes in the main towns and a general post office on both St Kitts (located in Basseterre) and Nevis (in Charlestown).

There are 378 main telephone lines and 1,527 mobile phone subscriptions per 1,000 people (2010).

Public holidays: New Year/Carnival (two days), Labour Day (first Monday in May), Emancipation Day (first Monday in August), National Heroes' Day (16 September), Independence Day (19 September), Christmas Day and Boxing Day. Carnival begins on 24 December and ends on 2 January.

Religious festivals whose dates vary from year to year include Good Friday, Easter Monday and Whit Monday.

Economy

KEY FACTS 2010

GNI:	US$615m
GNI p.c.:	US$11,740
GDP growth:	1.3% p.a. 2006–10
Inflation:	4.1% p.a. 2006–10

St Kitts and Nevis was virtually a sugar monocrop economy until the late 1970s, when the government backed a drive into small-scale industrialisation. Tourism has become the largest source of foreign exchange. From 1984 a small offshore sector on Nevis grew rapidly, with around 18,000 companies registered by 1999, and in 2005 St Kitts initiated a registry of ships and yachts; by the end of the decade it had registered some 1,000 vessels. The Ross University School of Veterinary Medicine of the USA has an offshore campus on St Kitts, and Berne University – a US postgraduate distance-learning organisation, with administrative offices in Pennsylvania, USA – has had a campus on Nevis since 1992.

Real Growth in GDP

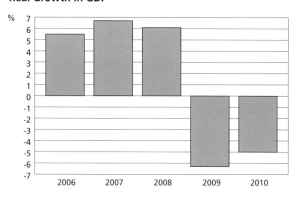

Inflation

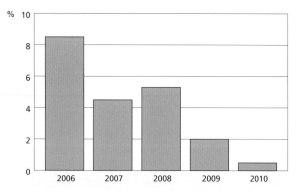

GDP by Sector (2010)

Despite the challenges of industrial diversification at such small scale, electronics assembly, food-processing, and beverages and clothing production have been developed, and by the 2000s sugar production only accounted for 20% of GDP, and finally ceased in 2005.

Foreign debt rose rapidly from the mid-1990s, in large measure due to the consequences of five hurricanes in five years. After strong growth in 2000 (6.5%), the economy hardly grew in 2001–03, reflecting the downturn in the USA and consequent fall in tourism, but there was investment in new tourist resorts and golf courses, and the economy picked up in 2004. It then maintained 5.0% p.a. over 2004–08, slowing from 2008 with the onset of the world economic downturn in that year, and shrinking by 6.3% in 2009 and 5.0% in 2010, before returning to modest growth in 2011.

Constitution

Status:	Monarchy under Queen Elizabeth II
Legislature:	National Assembly
Independence:	19 September 1983

St Kitts and Nevis is a constitutional monarchy, recognising Queen Elizabeth II as head of state. She is represented by a governor-general who takes advice from the prime minister and cabinet. The country is a sovereign democratic federal state, with a unicameral National Assembly of 14 members (plus the attorney-general if s/he is not an elected member). 11 Assembly members are elected for a term of no longer than five years by universal adult suffrage in eight constituencies in St Kitts and three in Nevis, and three are nominated 'senators', two on the advice of the prime minister and one on the advice of the leader of the opposition. The cabinet comprises the prime minister (who must be able to command the support of the majority of members of the National Assembly), five ministers and the attorney-general.

Nevis has its own legislature, premier and administration. The Nevis legislature, the Nevis Island Assembly, has five members elected by universal adult suffrage and three nominated members. The central government legislates for Nevis in matters concerning overall policy formation. Under the constitution, provision is made for the secession of Nevis at six months' notice, after a two-thirds majority in favour in the Nevis Assembly and a referendum, also with at least two-thirds in favour.

Politics

Last elections:	January 2010
Next elections:	2015
Head of state:	Queen Elizabeth II, represented by governor-general, Sir Cuthbert Montraville Sebastian (1996–)
Head of government:	Prime Minister Dr Denzil Llewellyn Douglas
Ruling party:	St Kitts–Nevis Labour Party

Dr Denzil Douglas and the St Kitts–Nevis Labour Party (SKNLP) were returned to power in the general election of October 2004, which was observed by a Commonwealth expert team. The ruling party took seven of the St Kitts seats, and the People's Action Movement (PAM) one. The Nevis seats were again divided between the Concerned Citizens' Movement (CCM; two seats) and the Nevis Reformation Party (NRP; one).

In January 2010 the SKNLP won its fourth consecutive general election, taking six seats in St Kitts and 47% of the national vote; and Douglas was returned as prime minister. The remaining seats were again divided between PAM (two in St Kitts; 32%), CCM (two in Nevis; 11%) and NRP (one in Nevis; 10%). The election was observed by a Commonwealth expert team.

Nevis

The CCM's long run of power was interrupted in the July 2006 Nevis Island Assembly elections, when NRP gained three seats and the CCM two. NRP leader Joseph Parry became premier.

In closely fought Nevis Island Assembly elections, in July 2011, the NRP (with three seats and 50.2% of the vote) defeated the CCM (two seats and 49.8%) and Parry continued as premier.

International relations

St Kitts and Nevis is a member of the African, Caribbean and Pacific Group of States, Association of Caribbean States, Caribbean Community, Non-Aligned Movement, Organisation of Eastern Caribbean States, Organization of American States, United Nations and World Trade Organization.

Traveller information

Local laws and conventions: It is an offence for anyone, including children, to dress in camouflage clothing. Visitors should always seek permission before photographing local people or their property. There are severe penalties for all drugs offences.

Dress is generally informal but conservative in the towns. Beachwear should be for beach only. Conference facilities are available in some hotels. Office hours are Mon–Fri 0800–1200 and 1300–1600.

Immigration and customs: Passports must be valid for at least six months beyond the intended length of stay. Visas are necessary for some nationals and all visa requirements should be checked well in advance of travel.

A yellow fever vaccination certificate will be requested from all those arriving from infected areas.

Travel within the country: Traffic drives on the left and a local driving licence must be purchased before visitors can drive on the islands. A local driving licence is available on production of a national driving licence at all car hire companies or police stations. Car hire is usually arranged before arriving on the islands.

There are regular passenger ferries between St Kitts and Nevis, and journey time is around 40 minutes. The bus network is privately run and provides a regular but unscheduled service. Taxis have set rates.

Travel health: Visitors should ensure they have comprehensive health insurance.

Vaccinations against tuberculosis and Hepatitis B are sometimes recommended, but all current inoculation requirements should be checked well in advance of travel. Dengue fever is found throughout St Kitts and Nevis, and visitors should ensure they take insect repellent and suitable clothing to protect themselves against mosquito bites.

Most of the drinking water comes from volcanic springs and is safe to drink; if there is any doubt, however, sterilisation is advisable. Bottled water is widely available. Milk is pasteurised.

Money: All major credit cards are accepted in most places and ATMs are widely available. The Eastern Caribbean dollar is closely linked to the US dollar, and it is advisable to take travellers cheques in US dollars to avoid additional exchange rate charges. Banking hours are Mon–Thur 0800–1400 and Fri 0800–1600.

There were 93,000 tourist arrivals in 2009.

Further information

Government of St Christopher and Nevis: www.gov.kn

Eastern Caribbean Central Bank: www.eccb-centralbank.org

Commonwealth Secretariat: www.thecommonwealth.org

Commonwealth of Nations: www.commonwealth-of-nations.org/St_Kitts_and_Nevis

History

The islands were originally settled from South America, and had Amerindian populations at the time of the first European landings. St Christopher (St Kitts) was sighted by Christopher Columbus on his second voyage in 1493. It was colonised by the English under Sir Thomas Warner in 1623 and during the following centuries sugar was grown on plantations worked by enslaved Africans. Already in 1624, however, another part of the island was colonised by the French (who also used slaves on their estates) and the two powers fought over the island during the 17th and 18th century until St Kitts was ceded to Britain by the Treaty of Versailles (1783). Nevis was settled by the English in 1628. It, too, was subject to attack, from the French and Spanish, in the 17th and 18th centuries, with less damage, however, to its economy. From 1816 the islands were administered, along with Anguilla and the British Virgin Islands, as a single colony and from 1871 as part of the Leeward Islands Federation.

The two islands, together with Anguilla, assumed the status of association with the UK in 1967, a situation which the Anguillans rejected from the outset, with rebellion beginning in 1967. In 1971, the UK and the other islands agreed that Anguilla would formally separate and remain a UK dependency when the country achieved its independence.

The country, as the Federation of St Christopher and Nevis, had internal self-government from 1976, and achieved independence on 19 September 1983, choosing to remain a constitutional monarchy with Queen Elizabeth II as head of state.

The St Kitts–Nevis Labour Party (SKNLP) held power from 1967 until defeat in 1980 by a coalition of the People's Action Movement (PAM) and Nevis Reformation Party (NRP), and PAM's Dr Kennedy Alphonse Simmonds became prime minister.

Simmonds was re-elected in 1984, 1989 and 1993, when the PAM and SKNLP each won four seats, and the PAM formed a governing alliance with the NRP, though the SKNLP had received 54% of the vote and NRP was itself losing support to the other main Nevis party, the Concerned Citizens' Movement (CCM).

In an early general election in 1995, after 15 years in opposition, the SKNLP was elected to office with an overwhelming majority of seven seats to the PAM's one. The CCM retained its two seats in Nevis and the NRP one. Labour Party leader Dr Denzil Douglas became prime minister.

In the elections in March 2000 the SKNLP won all eight St Kitts seats, while in Nevis the CCM retained two and the NRP one.

Nevis

On Nevis, discontent with the federation grew through the latter 1980s, with increasing calls for separation, and strikes among sugar and other agricultural workers. Elections in Nevis in 1992 then ousted the NRP, replacing it with the CCM.

At the Nevis Island Assembly elections in February 1997, three seats were won by the CCM and two by the NRP, CCM leader Vance Amory retaining the premiership. In October 1997, the five members of the Nevis Assembly voted to secede from the federation, triggering a referendum on Nevis which was held in August 1998. Only 62% of the voters of Nevis backed secession, which fell short of the required two-thirds majority. Prime Minister Denzil Douglas promised to work for greater autonomy for Nevis.

In the September 2001 Nevis Island Assembly elections, the CCM won four seats and the NRP one, and Amory was returned as premier. An unsuccessful attempt at triggering a referendum on Nevis was initiated in June 2003.

St Lucia

KEY FACTS

Joined Commonwealth:	1979
Population:	174,000 (2010)
GDP p.c. growth:	1.0% p.a. 1990–2010
UN HDI 2011:	world ranking 82
Official language:	English
Time:	GMT minus 4hr
Currency:	Eastern Caribbean dollar (EC$)

Geography

Area:	616 sq km
Coastline:	158km
Capital:	Castries

St Lucia is part of the Windward Islands group, which form an arc jutting out from the Eastern Caribbean into the Atlantic. It lies south of Dominica and north of Barbados.

Topography: St Lucia is a pear-shaped mountainous island of volcanic origin, 43km long. In the centre of the island, Mt Gimie rises to 950m, while Gros Piton (798m) and Petit Piton (750m) lie to the west, rising sheer out of the sea. Sulphurous springs, steam and gases bubble out of a volcanic crater a few kilometres from Petit Piton. The mountains are intersected by short rivers, debouching in places into broad fertile valleys.

Climate: The hot tropical climate is moderated all year round by the north-east trade winds. The dry season is January to April, the rainy season May to November.

Environment: The most significant environmental issues are deforestation and soil erosion, particularly in the north of the island.

Vegetation: With its economy traditionally based on agriculture, about 30% of the land area is under cultivation. Elsewhere there is rainforest with exotic and varied plant-life, many with brilliant flowers. Forest covers 77% of the land area.

Did you know...

The country has more Nobel laureates per capita than any other country: poet and playwright Derek Walcott, born in Castries, St Lucia, on 23 January 1930, was awarded the Nobel Prize in Literature in 1992; and Sir Arthur Lewis was Nobel economics laureate in 1979.

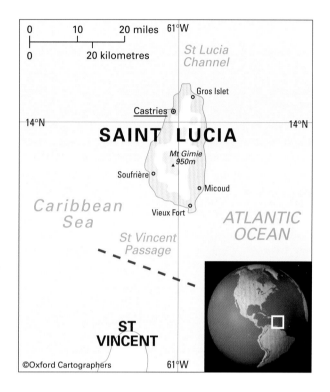

©Oxford Cartographers

Wildlife: This small island has rich birdlife including several unique species, for example the St Lucia oriole and the St Lucia black finch. The St Lucia parrot was the subject of a successful conservation programme established in 1978 which raised the population from some 150 birds to over 400. Native reptiles include the St Lucia tree lizard and the pygmy lizard.

Main towns: Castries (capital, pop. 67,700 in 2010, including Bexon, Babonneau, Ciceron and La Clery), Dennery (3,700), Laborie (3,500), Monchy (3,100), Vieux Fort (3,000), Grande Rivière (2,700), Augier (2,500), Micoud (2,200), Soufrière (1,500) and Anse La Raye (1,400).

Transport: There are 1,210km of roads, mainly unpaved. The main cross-island route runs from Castries in the north to Vieux Fort in the south.

The main ports are Castries and Vieux Fort. A fast catamaran service operates between St Lucia, Martinique and Dominica. Several cruise lines call at the island.

Hewanorra International Airport lies 67km south of Castries and George F L Charles, 3km to the north-east.

Society

KEY FACTS 2010

Population per sq km:	282
Life expectancy:	74 years
Net primary enrolment:	93%

Population: 174,000 (2010); 28% lives in urban areas; growth 1.2% p.a. 1990–2010; birth rate 18 per 1,000 people (41 in 1970); life expectancy 74 years (64 in 1970).

St Lucia's population is mostly of mixed African and European descent.

Language: English is the official language; a French-based Creole is widely spoken.

Religion: Mainly Christians (Roman Catholics 68%, Seventh Day Adventists 9%, Pentecostals 6%, Rastafarians, Anglicans; 2001 census).

Health: Public spending on health was 5% of GDP in 2009. The Victoria Hospital and the new Tapion Hospital provide a range of medical treatment, and the Golden Hope Hospital caters for psychiatric cases. There are cottage hospitals at Vieux Fort, Dennery and Soufrière, and more than 20 health centres. Nurses are trained in the nursing department of the Community College. 98% of the population uses an improved drinking water source (2009) and 89% adequate sanitation facilities (2006). Infant mortality was 14 per 1,000 live births in 2010.

Education: Public spending on education was 5.1% of GDP in 2010. There are ten years of compulsory education starting at age five. Primary school comprises seven years and secondary five, with cycles of three and two years. Some 93% of pupils complete primary school (2008). The school year starts in September.

The Sir Arthur Lewis Community College, at Castries, offers a diverse range of courses – including associate degree, diploma and certificate courses – and 89% of students are female (2011). St Lucia shares in the regional University of the West Indies, which has its main campuses in Barbados, Jamaica, and Trinidad and Tobago. The female–male ratio for gross enrolment in tertiary education is 2.58:1 (2009).

Media: There are no daily newspapers in St Lucia. The main newspapers are *The Star* and *The Voice* (both three times weekly); and *The Crusader*, *The Mirror* and *The Vanguard* (all weekly).

St Lucia's broadcast media are mostly privately owned; only the radio network, Radio Saint Lucia, is operated by the government.

There are 400 internet users per 1,000 people (2010).

Communications: Country code 1 758; internet domain '.lc'. Phonecard telephone booths, internet cafes and post offices are located throughout the island.

There are 215 main telephone lines and 1,142 mobile phone subscriptions per 1,000 people (2010).

Public holidays: New Year (two days), Independence Day (22 February), Labour Day (1 May), Carnival (two days in July), Emancipation Day (early August), Thanksgiving Day (early October), St Lucia Day (13 December), Christmas Day and Boxing Day.

Religious and other festivals whose dates vary from year to year include Good Friday, Easter Monday, Whit Monday and Corpus Christi.

Economy

KEY FACTS 2010

GNI:	US$1.1bn
GNI p.c.:	US$6,560
GDP growth:	2.9% p.a. 2006–10
Inflation:	3.1% p.a. 2006–10

Although St Lucia's per capita income is relatively high among developing countries, it has been disadvantaged by its economic dependence on bananas and by its small size, small population, limited physical and human resources, and the frequency of hurricanes.

It has nevertheless successfully exploited opportunities in tourism and small-scale industry, benefiting from trade preferences from the EU and USA, and creating a more diverse economy, with well developed manufacturing, and has substantially reduced its dependence on bananas, production and export prices of which have declined sharply. It has also encouraged development of an offshore financial services sector and a framework of sound regulation has been established.

Real Growth in GDP

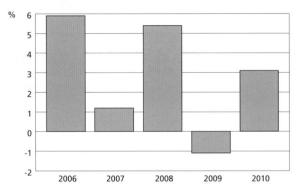

Inflation

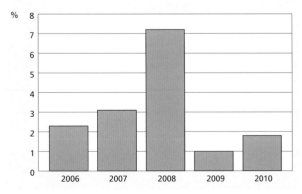

GDP by Sector (2010)

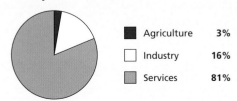

■	Agriculture	**3%**
☐	Industry	**16%**
▨	Services	**81%**

After steady growth in the late 1990s, the economy stalled in 2000, and was in recession during 2000–02, shrinking by over 4% in 2001, due to the downturn in the USA and consequent fall in tourism and weakening of international markets for manufactures and bananas. In 2003 tourism recovered strongly, with more air services to the island and construction of a new resort. Tourism income was then hit in 2007 by the impact of Hurricane Dean in August – GDP growth moderating that year to 1.2% – and again in 2008–09 by the world economic downturn, causing the economy to contract in 2009 (–1.1%), before recovering in 2010 (3.1%).

Constitution

Status:	Monarchy under Queen Elizabeth II
Legislature:	Parliament
Independence:	22 February 1979

St Lucia is a constitutional monarchy with Queen Elizabeth II as head of state, represented by a governor-general. The legislature is bicameral, with the House of Assembly of 17 directly elected members (plus the speaker) and a Senate of 11 appointed members, six by the prime minister (the leader of the largest party in the House of Assembly), three by the leader of the opposition and two by the governor-general. Parliament is elected for five years by universal adult suffrage.

Politics

Last elections:	November 2011
Next elections:	2016
Head of state:	Queen Elizabeth II, represented by governor-general, Dame Pearlette Louisy (1997–)
Head of government:	Prime Minister Dr Kenny Anthony
Ruling party:	St Lucia Labour Party

In September 1997 the country's first woman governor-general, Dr Pearlette Louisy, was appointed, following the resignation of Sir George Mallet.

Dr Kenny Anthony and the St Lucia Labour Party (SLP) were returned to government in the December 2001 general election, when his SLP won 14 Assembly seats and the United Workers Party (UWP) three.

Anthony stood for a third term in the December 2006 general election which was won by the opposition UWP with 11 seats while the SLP took six. UWP leader Sir John Compton, who had since 1964 served as head of government for a total of 29 years, became prime minister.

Following the death of Sir John Compton at the age of 82 in September 2007, Stephenson King, who had been acting for Compton during his illness, was sworn in as prime minister.

In the November 2011 election Kenny Anthony and the SLP ousted the UWP government, winning 11 seats (51% of the vote) to the UWP's six (47%), and Anthony began a third term as prime minister.

History

St Lucia was named by Christopher Columbus, who sighted the island on St Lucy's day 1502. The island has been much fought over. At some time before Columbus's arrival, the Caribs ousted the Arawaks; and European powers contended with the Caribs and one another for control between 1660 and 1814; in that period the flag of St Lucia changed 14 times.

After unsuccessful early attempts by the Spanish to take control, possession of the island was disputed, often bloodily, by the French and British. A small English group made a failed attempt to settle in 1605; another English colony, started in 1638, was annihilated by the Caribs three years later.

The Caribs resisted French settlement with equal vigour, until a peace treaty (1660) with them permitted settlement, and ensured the safety of some French settlers from Martinique who had arrived during the preceding decade. The British made further attempts to gain control, and the island changed hands again and again, and was a focus for Anglo-French hostilities during the Napoleonic Wars. The British ultimately took possession under the Treaty of Paris in 1814, and St Lucia became a Crown colony.

A prosperous plantation economy developed; it was based on sugar, and worked by enslaved Africans until Britain abolished slavery in 1834.

The island was a member of the Windward Islands Federation until 1959. In 1959, St Lucia joined the West Indies Federation, under which it was proposed that the British Caribbean countries should proceed to independence as a federation. Disagreements among the larger members led to dissolution of the federation in 1962, and the larger members proceeded alone to independence.

In 1967, St Lucia received a new constitution, giving full internal self-government under universal franchise, as one of the states of the Federated States of the Antilles. In February 1979, it became independent, as a constitutional monarchy and member of the Commonwealth, with John Compton of the United Workers Party (UWP) as its first prime minister.

The St Lucia Labour Party (SLP) won the election in 1979 and adopted a policy of close collaboration with Grenada, which had recently undergone a revolution led by Maurice Bishop, and was aligned with Cuba and North Korea. Allegations of corruption resulted in an early general election in 1982, when the UWP was returned with a large majority. It was re-elected in 1987 and 1992 (with an 11:6 majority). Prime Minister Compton adopted IMF adjustment measures and returned the country to operation of a market economy. He also pursued the integration of the Eastern Caribbean countries through the OECS.

In March 1996, at a UWP convention, Compton lost the leadership, after 30 years, and was replaced as prime minister by Dr Vaughan Lewis. An early general election in May 1997 resulted in victory for the SLP, winning 16 of the 17 seats, with 61% of the votes, and SLP leader Dr Kenny Anthony became prime minister. Lewis resigned as leader of the UWP, having lost his seat.

International relations

St Lucia is a member of the African, Caribbean and Pacific Group of States, Association of Caribbean States, Caribbean Community, Non-Aligned Movement, Organisation internationale de la Francophonie, Organisation of Eastern Caribbean States, Organization of American States, United Nations and World Trade Organization.

St Lucia hosts the headquarters of the Organisation of Eastern Caribbean States.

Traveller information

Local laws and conventions: It is an offence for anyone, including children, to dress in camouflage clothing. Visitors should ask before taking photographs of local people or their property. There are severe penalties for all drug-related crimes.

The Roman Catholic Church has a strong presence in St Lucia and the island has a fairly conservative culture. Visitors should dress modestly away from the beach. Casual clothing is generally acceptable.

Business visits and meetings may be conducted in English or French. Conference facilities are available in some of the island's hotels. Office hours are Mon–Fri 0800–1630, Sat 0830–1230.

Immigration and customs: A valid passport is required by all those arriving into the country. New arrivals must also present a return or onward ticket and show they have sufficient funds for their stay. Airport departure tax must be paid when leaving St Lucia.

A yellow fever vaccination certificate is required by all those arriving from infected countries.

Firearms, pornographic material and flowers and plants are prohibited imports.

Travel within the country: Traffic drives on the left and visitors will need to purchase a local driving permit, which can be obtained from car hire firms or police stations on presentation of a national driving licence. Some of the mountainous roads can be extremely steep with hairpin bends.

Boat charters are easily available at Castries, Marigot Bay and Rodney Bay, and several ferry lines connect St Lucia with Martinique.

There are regular minibus services that connect rural areas with the capital. Visitors may also catch one of the privately owned 14-seater minivans at marked bus stops or by flagging one down along the three major bus routes on the coastal road.

Taxis can be hailed in towns and have fixed fares for standard journeys, though all fares should be agreed on before starting out. Some taxi drivers offer a full-island tour for a little extra.

Travel health: Visitors must ensure they have comprehensive health insurance that includes medical evacuation. Health facilities are good but costs are high.

Dengue fever can occur, and visitors should protect themselves from mosquito bites by using insect repellent and wearing suitable clothing, especially in the evenings and during the rainy season when the dengue fever mosquito is most prevalent. Care should be taken when hiking near streams or ditches as the poisonous lancehead snake thrives along the island's coastline.

Tap water is generally considered safe to drink; bottled water is widely available.

Money: Major credit cards are widely accepted and ATMs are available in Castries, Rodney Bay, Soufrière and Vieux Fort. Travellers cheques in US dollars will ensure a better exchange rate. Banking hours are Mon–Fri 0800–1400 (some banks stay open until 1700 on Friday).

There were 278,000 tourist arrivals in 2009.

Further information

Government of St Lucia: www.stlucia.gov.lc

Parliament: www.stlucia.gov.lc/agencies/legislature.htm

Eastern Caribbean Central Bank: www.eccb-centralbank.org

Commonwealth Secretariat: www.thecommonwealth.org

Commonwealth of Nations: www.commonwealth-of-nations.org/St_Lucia

St Vincent and the Grenadines

KEY FACTS

Joined Commonwealth:	1979
Population:	109,000 (2010)
GDP p.c. growth:	3.6% p.a. 1990–2010
UN HDI 2011:	world ranking 85
Official language:	English
Time:	GMT minus 4hr
Currency:	Eastern Caribbean dollar (EC$)

Geography

Area:	389.3 sq km
Coastline:	84km
Capital:	Kingstown

St Vincent and the Grenadines, one of the Windward Island countries of the Eastern Caribbean, lies near the southern end of the Caribbean chain, about 97km north of Grenada. The country comprises six parishes, one of which being Grenadines.

Area: Total land area 389.3 sq km: St Vincent 344 sq km, and the Grenadines 45.3 sq km.

Topography: The country comprises the island of St Vincent and the northern Grenadines, a series of 32 islands and cays, stretching south-west towards Grenada. (The southern Grenadine islands are part of Grenada.) The larger northern Grenadines are Bequia (pronounced Beck-way), Canouan, Mayreau, Mustique, Isle D'Quatre and Union Island. St Vincent is volcanic in origin, and has an active volcano, La Soufrière, which erupted violently in 1812, and again in 1902. A mild eruption in 1971–72 created a volcanic dome in the crater lake, forming an island. This exploded in another eruption in 1979, blasting ash, steam and stones high into the air. A rugged mountain range runs from La Soufrière in the north to Mt St Andrew (750m) above the Kingstown Valley in the south. This mountainous backbone sends off lateral spurs which are intersected by wooded valleys and numerous streams. Many of the beaches of St Vincent are of black volcanic sand; there are some white-sand beaches. The Grenadines have been much celebrated for their beaches of fine white sand and clear waters.

Did you know...

Most of St Vincent is rugged and mountainous, volcanic in origin and with an active volcano, La Soufrière, which rises to 1,234m and is the island's highest point; it last erupted in April 1979, and last erupted violently in 1902.

Some 70% of the country's land area is forested.

Many of St Vincent's beaches are of black volcanic sand, while the Grenadine beaches are of fine white sand.

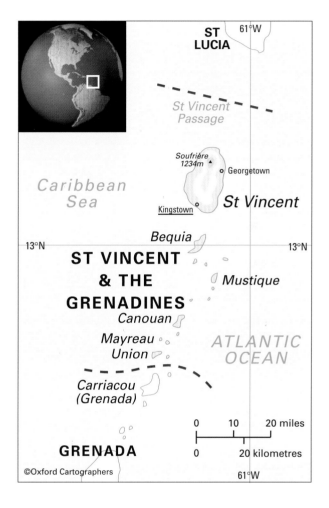

©Oxford Cartographers

Climate: Tropical, moderated by trade winds in June/July. The dry season is January to May, the rainy season May/June to September. There is significantly heavier rainfall in the mountainous interior. Tropical storms and hurricanes may occur June–November.

Environment: The most significant environmental issue is pollution of coasts and coastal waters by discharges from yachts and from industrial plants on shore.

Vegetation: The mountains of St Vincent support a luxuriant growth of tropical forest; coconuts and the more typical tropical coral island vegetation occur on the Grenadines and coastal fringes of St Vincent island. Forest covers 69% of the land area, having increased at 0.4% p.a. 1990–2010. The botanical gardens, founded in 1765, conserve rare species, including the mangosteen fruit tree, and a descendant from Captain Bligh's original breadfruit tree.

Wildlife: The Buccament Valley east of Layou is a tropical rainforest reserve, home to the endangered St Vincent parrot, as well as many other species such as the unique whistling warbler. Bequia's rich marine flora and fauna make it a popular resort for divers.

Main towns: Kingstown (capital, pop. 16,500 in 2010), Georgetown (1,400), Byera (1,200), Biabou (900) and Chateaubelair (630) on St Vincent; Port Elizabeth (770) on Bequia in the Grenadines.

Transport: There are 829km of roads, 70% paved. Cruiseships call at St Vincent. A mail boat runs several times a week through the Grenadines and ferries operate between the islands.

E T Joshua International Airport is at Arnos Vale, 3km south-east of Kingstown. There are small airports/airstrips on Bequia, Union Island, Canouan and Mustique. A new international airport was due to be opened at Argyle in the east of St Vincent in 2012.

Society

KEY FACTS 2010

Population per sq km:	280
Life expectancy:	72 years
Net primary enrolment:	98%

Population: 109,000 (2010); 49% lives in urban areas; growth 0.1% p.a. 1990–2010, depressed over this period by emigration; birth rate 17 per 1,000 people (40 in 1970); life expectancy is 72 years (63 in 1970).

The population is mostly of African or mixed descent, with Indian, European, and Carib minorities.

Language: English is the official language; an English-based Creole is widely spoken.

Religion: Mainly Christians (Anglicans 47%, Methodists 28%, Roman Catholics 13%); with a small community of Hindus.

Health: Public spending on health was 3% of GDP in 2009. As well as Kingstown General Hospital, there are district hospitals and health centres. Infant mortality was 19 per 1,000 live births in 2010.

Education: Public spending on education was 6.2% of GDP in 2010. There are 14 years of school education starting at age five. Primary school comprises seven years and secondary seven, with cycles of five and two years. The school year starts in September.

Tertiary education is provided at the regional University of the West Indies, which has its main campuses in Barbados, Jamaica, and Trinidad and Tobago.

Media: *The Herald* is a daily paper; weekly newspapers include *Searchlight*, *The News* and *The Vincentian*.

SVG Television and NBC Radio are the public service providers. There are several private radio stations.

There are 152 personal computers (2005) and 696 internet users (2009) per 1,000 people.

Communications: Country code 1 784; internet domain '.vc'. There are phonecard booths and internet cafes on most islands. The main post office is located in Kingstown, with branches throughout the country.

There are 199 main telephone lines and 1,205 mobile phone subscriptions per 1,000 people (2010).

Public holidays: New Year's Day, National Heroes' Day (14 March), Labour Day (first Monday in May), Carnival (Monday and Tuesday in July), Emancipation Day (first Monday in August), Independence Day (27 October), Christmas Day and Boxing Day. Carnival continues for ten days leading up to Carnival Tuesday.

Religious and other festivals whose dates vary from year to year include Good Friday, Easter Monday and Whit Monday.

Economy

KEY FACTS 2010

GNI:	US$688m
GNI p.c.:	US$6,300
GDP growth:	2.4% p.a. 2006–10
Inflation:	4.3% p.a. 2006–10

St Vincent and the Grenadines has a relatively undeveloped economy, nevertheless providing a relatively high quality of life. It is vulnerable as the economic base is very small, and is heavily dependent on agriculture and especially bananas.

Real Growth in GDP

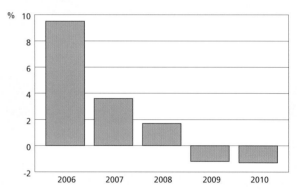

Inflation

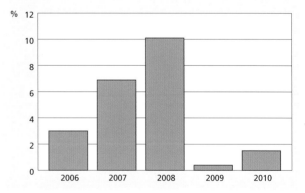

GDP by Sector (2010)

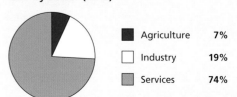

■	Agriculture	7%
□	Industry	19%
▩	Services	74%

The main export crop, bananas, was sold to the EU under its preferential arrangements, but since these ended in 2007, Caribbean banana producers have faced a tougher competitive environment, and small, less efficient producers have moved out of banana production. The government has encouraged diversification into tourism, manufacturing, offshore finance and call centres, and has promoted growth of the private sector.

Economic growth fluctuates with agricultural output and prices on world markets. The economy has, however, been prudently managed and inflation and debt have generally been relatively modest. By the mid-2000s, with new investment in tourism infrastructure, economic growth was strong – averaging 5.6% p.a. 2004–08 – but in the face of the world economic downturn of 2008–09, slowed sharply in 2008 (1.7%) and contracted in 2009 (–1.2%) and 2010 (–1.3%).

Constitution

Status:	Monarchy under Queen Elizabeth II
Legislature:	House of Assembly
Independence:	27 October 1979

St Vincent and the Grenadines is a constitutional monarchy and representative democracy, with Queen Elizabeth II as head of state, represented by a governor-general. The legislature is unicameral, with a House of Assembly of 23 members comprising 15 members elected at least every five years by universal adult suffrage (plus speaker and attorney-general) and six senators appointed by the governor-general (four on the advice of the prime minister and two on that of the leader of the opposition). The leader of the majority party in the House of Assembly becomes prime minister and selects and heads a cabinet.

History

The country's first known inhabitants were Arawaks, who were later driven out by Caribs; the latter put up a strong resistance to European colonisation. Christopher Columbus sighted the principal island on 22 January 1498, and named it after the saint whose feast falls on that day. No immediate European immigration followed this discovery. In 1627 Charles I of England granted the island to Lord Carlisle, but no settlers arrived. Charles II granted it to Lord Willoughby in 1672; possession was disputed by the British, French and Spanish. All these claims were resisted by the Caribs. The Caribs did not, however, oppose the settlement of a shipload of enslaved Africans who escaped after a shipwreck in 1673, and in due course seem to have merged with the Carib community through intermarriage. In 1773, under an Anglo/Carib treaty, the Caribs were allowed to continue to live independently in the north of the island. France took the island in 1779, but restored it to Britain in 1783, under the Treaty of Versailles. In 1795–96, the Caribs rebelled, aided by the French in Martinique; when this had been crushed, the rebels were deported to the island of Roatan in the Bay of Honduras. A plantation economy, based on slave labour, developed, producing sugar, cotton, coffee and cocoa. But in 1812 La Soufrière erupted and devastated much of the island. After the emancipation of slaves by Britain in 1834, indentured labour from the East Indies and Portugal was brought in to remedy the labour shortage.

In the second half of the 19th century sugar slumped and the economy remained very depressed for the rest of the century. In the early 20th century, a series of natural disasters further damaged the society: with a severe hurricane, and a further eruption of La Soufrière in 1902 which devastated the northern half of the island and killed 2,000 people.

St Vincent and the Grenadines was a member of the Federation of the West Indies. After its dissolution in 1962, and the move of larger Caribbean countries to independence individually, the transition towards independence began in St Vincent. At first, the smaller Eastern Caribbean countries attempted to set up a federation of their own, but negotiations among them were unsuccessful. Universal adult suffrage had already been

established (and the executive council became partly elective) in 1951. Internal self-government was achieved in 1969 and full independence in October 1979.

Elections held two months after independence in 1979 gave overwhelming victory to Milton Cato's St Vincent Labour Party (SVLP), the party which had campaigned most vigorously for independence.

The newly independent country faced a series of political difficulties with, first, an armed rebellion on Union Island by a Rastafarian minority led by Bumba Charles, and then protests early in the 1980s, which led to special 'public order' legislation. Cato called an early general election in mid-1984, but was defeated by James Fitz-Allen Mitchell's New Democratic Party (NDP), formed in 1975. Mitchell, then standing as an independent, had been premier between 1972–74.

Mitchell's NDP came to power in 1984 advocating policies of closer economic and ultimately political union with the neighbouring Eastern Caribbean countries. The country had played an active part in the establishment of the Organisation of Eastern Caribbean States in 1981, which achieved several of the aims the countries had failed to achieve through the aborted plan for an East Caribbean Federation.

The NDP was returned to power at the 1989 elections, and at the 1994 elections, when it took 12 seats, the remaining three seats going to the SVLP and Movement for National Unity coalition, which later merged to become the Unity Labour Party (ULP). In the general election in June 1998 the NDP narrowly won a fourth successive election taking eight of the House of Assembly's 15 seats, with only 45% of the votes cast.

Following public protests at the raising of MPs' remuneration and pensions, in May 2000, through the offices of OECS and CARICOM, the government agreed with the ULP that there would be a general election by end March 2001. In August 2000, Mitchell stepped down from the presidency of the ruling NDP and was replaced by Finance Minister Arnhim Eustace, who became prime minister in October.

Politics

Last elections:	December 2010
Next elections:	2015/2016
Head of state:	Queen Elizabeth II, represented by governor-general, Sir Frederick Ballantyne (2002–)
Head of government:	Prime Minister Dr Ralph Everard Gonsalves
Ruling party:	Unity Labour Party

The March 2001 general election was won by the Unity Labour Party (ULP) with 12 seats, ending almost 17 years of New Democratic Party (NDP) government and ULP leader Dr Ralph Gonsalves became prime minister.

In February 2005 the Constitutional Review Commission proposed far-reaching reforms including replacement of the British monarch as head of state by an indirectly elected president, establishment of a non-partisan 'council of elders' to advise on public appointments and issues of the day, and reconstituting the legislature to include representatives of civil society as well as directly elected and appointed members.

In the December 2005 general election the ULP was returned, again winning 12 seats, and Gonsalves continued as prime minister.

The ULP won a third consecutive general election in December 2010, with eight seats; Gonsalves was returned as prime minister. The NDP, led by Arnhim Eustace, secured the remaining seven seats.

International relations

St Vincent and the Grenadines is a member of the African, Caribbean and Pacific Group of States, Association of Caribbean States, Caribbean Community, Non-Aligned Movement, Organisation of Eastern Caribbean States, Organization of American States, United Nations and World Trade Organization.

Traveller information

Local laws and conventions: Illegal drugs are viewed seriously in St Vincent and the Grenadines, and there are severe penalties for possession of all drugs – including cannabis. It is an offence for anyone, including children, to wear camouflage clothing.

Casual clothing is widely acceptable; beachwear should be for beach only. English is spoken everywhere, often with a Vincentian patois. Office hours are Mon–Fri 0800–1615.

Immigration and customs: Passports must be valid for six months from the date of entry. Visitors must also be in possession of an onward ticket and have sufficient funds for their stay.

Firearms and ammunition and spear-fishing equipment are prohibited imports, and import licences are required for all foodstuffs. All prescription medications should be kept in their original container, clearly labelled to avoid misunderstandings.

A yellow fever vaccination certificate will be required from those arriving from an infected area.

Travel within the country: Traffic drives on the left-hand side and a local driving permit is required to drive on the islands. Visitors can obtain a local licence from car hire companies and police stations on presentation of a national driving licence. Some mountainous roads are extremely steep with hairpin bends.

Taxis are widely available and charge government-fixed rates. It is advisable to check the fare before setting off.

Small planes can be chartered for travel between islands and it is very easy to charter ships to sail between the islands – both privately and with a sea taxi.

Buses offer cheap, reliable transport between towns. A number of minibus/pick-up truck passenger services also operate throughout the islands and can be flagged down on bus routes.

Travel health: Medical services are generally good in St Vincent and the Grenadines, although full health insurance with emergency repatriation is recommended, as visitors are expected to pay full medical costs.

Mosquito-borne dengue fever is endemic to the Caribbean, and insect repellent and suitable clothing should be taken to protect against mosquito bites.

Mains water is normally chlorinated; bottled water is widely available.

Money: Major international credit and debit cards are widely accepted, and travellers cheques should be taken in US dollars to ensure a better exchange rate. ATMs can be found in all the towns. Banking hours are Mon–Thur 0800–1300 and Fri 0800–1700.

There were 73,000 tourist arrivals in 2009.

Further information

Government of St Vincent and the Grenadines: www.gov.vc

Eastern Caribbean Central Bank: www.eccb-centralbank.org

Commonwealth Secretariat: www.thecommonwealth.org

Commonwealth of Nations: www.commonwealth-of-nations.org/St_Vincent_and_the_Grenadines

Samoa

KEY FACTS

Joined Commonwealth:	1970
Population:	183,000 (2010)
GDP p.c. growth:	3.0% p.a. 1990–2010
UN HDI 2011:	world ranking 99
Official language:	Samoan
Time:	GMT plus 13–14hr
Currency:	tala or Samoan dollar (T)

Geography

Area:	2,831 sq km
Coastline:	403km
Capital:	Apia

The name Samoa, from *Sa* ('sacred') and *Moa* ('centre'), means 'Sacred Centre of the Universe'. Samoa (formerly Western Samoa) is an archipelago of nine islands at the centre of the south-west Pacific island groups, surrounded by (clockwise from north) Tokelau, American Samoa, Tonga, and Wallis and Futuna. The nine islands of Samoa are Apolima, Manono, Fanuatapu, Namu'a, Nuutele, Nuulua, Nuusafee, Savai'i (the largest, at 1,708 sq km including adjacent small islands) and Upolu (second largest, at 1,118 sq km including adjacent small islands). Five of the islands are uninhabited.

Topography: The islands are formed of volcanic rock, but none of the volcanoes has been active since 1911. The highest point, about 1,858m, is on Savai'i. Coral reefs surround much of the coastline and there is plentiful fresh water in the lakes and rivers. Much of the cultivated land is on Upolu.

In September 2009 a violent earthquake in the South Pacific, some 190km south of Samoa, caused a huge tsunami, which devastated coastal regions of the islands, killing at least 129 people and destroying hundreds of houses.

Did you know...

On 29 December 2011 Samoa advanced the clock by one day, moving to the west of the international date line, so as to be in the same time zone as trading partners such as Australia and New Zealand.

Samoans enjoy life expectancy of more than 70 years.

Two Samoans have been regional winners in the Commonwealth Writers' Prize: Albert Wendt, born in Apia in 1939, won with his novel, *Ola*, in 1992, and again with *The Adventures of Vela* in 2010; and Sia Figiel, born in Matautu Tai in 1967, won with her novel, *Where We Once Belonged*, in 1997.

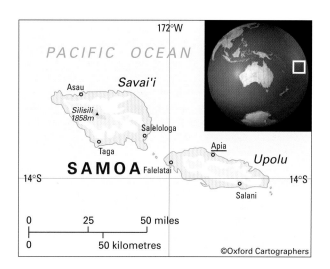

Climate: Tropical maritime. Hot and rainy from December to April and cooler, with trade winds, from May to November. Samoa is prone to hurricanes and cyclones which sometimes cause devastation. Cyclone Val, in December 1991 – the worst storm to hit the islands in over 100 years – destroyed over half the coconut palms. The country was again devastated in 1998.

Environment: The most significant environmental issue is soil erosion.

Vegetation: Dense tropical forest and woodlands cover 60% of the land area, having increased at 1.4% p.a. 1990–2010. Arable land comprises about 9% of the total land area.

Wildlife: Animal life is restricted to several species of bats and lizards and 53 species of birds. Birdlife includes the rare tooth-billed pigeon, thought to be a living link with prehistoric tooth-billed birds. Due to over-hunting, all species of native pigeons and doves are approaching extinction.

Main towns: Apia (capital, pop. 36,400 in 2010), Vaitele (7,300), Faleasiu (3,900), Vailele (3,200) and Leauvaa (3,200) on Upolu; Safotu (1,500), Sapulu (1,200) and Gataivai (1,100) on Savai'i.

Transport: There are 2,337km of roads, many being rural-access roads, 14% paved. Apia on Upolu is the international port. There is a ferry service between Upolu and Savai'i, and weekly services to Pago Pago in American Samoa.

The international airport, at Faleolo (34km west of Apia) can take Boeing 747s, but Samoa, like other Pacific island countries, is remote from world centres and too small for commercial airlines to run frequent flights. The national carriers, Polynesian Blue and Polynesian Airlines, fly to several regional and international destinations.

Society

KEY FACTS 2010

Population per sq km:	65
Life expectancy:	72 years
Net primary enrolment:	99%

Population: 183,000 (2010); 20% lives in urban areas; growth 0.6% p.a. 1990–2010, depressed over this period by emigration, mostly to New Zealand; birth rate 25 per 1,000 people (39 in 1970); life expectancy is 72 years (55 in 1970).

Predominantly Polynesian population, with small minorities of Chinese, European, or other Pacific descent. The people live mainly in extended family groups, known as *aiga*. These groups are headed by a leader, known as *matai*, who is elected for life. The population is largely concentrated in villages close to the shore. There are 131,103 Samoans living in New Zealand, more than half of whom were born there (2006 New Zealand census).

Language: Samoan is the official language; English is used in administration and commerce and is widely spoken.

Religion: Mainly Christians (Congregationalists 35%, Roman Catholics 20%, Methodists 15%, Latter-day Saints 13%; 2001 census).

Health: Public spending on health was 6% of GDP in 2009. Health provision includes the national hospital in Apia, the four district hospitals and the many health centres. Most medical training is undertaken at the Fiji School of Medicine. Patterns of illness and death are shifting to those of a developed country, with longer life expectancy and a rising incidence of lifestyle diseases. Infant mortality was 17 per 1,000 live births in 2010 (134 in 1960).

Education: Public spending on education was 5.7% of GDP in 2008. There are ten years of compulsory education starting at age five. The government began to introduce free education in 2009. As well as state schools, there are several faith schools. The school year starts in February.

The principal tertiary institution within the country is the National University of Samoa, which was established in Apia in 1984. Samoa was one of the founders of the regional University of the South Pacific, which has its main campus in Suva, Fiji, and the Alafua Campus in Apia, Samoa, where the university's School of Agriculture and Institute for Research, Extension and Training in Agriculture are located. There is virtually no illiteracy among people aged 15–24.

Media: *Samoa Observer* and *Samoa Times* are dailies. *Le Samoa* (weekly), *Savali* (fortnightly), and *Talamua Magazine* (monthly) are in both Samoan and English.

The Samoa Broadcasting Corporation provides public radio and TV services; there are several privately owned radio stations and TV channels.

There are 24 personal computers (2006) and 70 internet users (2010) per 1,000 people.

Communications: Country code 685; internet domain '.ws'. Samoa has its own analogue mobile phone system. Internet connections are available in Apia and a few other places across the islands.

There are 193 main telephone lines and 914 mobile phone subscriptions per 1,000 people (2010).

Public holidays: New Year (1–2 January), Mothers' Day (Monday in May), Independence Day (1 June), Fathers' Day (Monday in August), Lotu-a-Tamaiti (Monday after White Sunday, in October), Christmas Day and Boxing Day.

Religious festivals whose dates vary from year to year include Good Friday and Easter Monday.

Economy

KEY FACTS 2010

GNI:	US$549m
GNI p.c.:	US$3,000
GDP growth:	0.9% p.a. 2006–10
Inflation:	5.5% p.a. 2006–10

In addition to remittances from Samoans living overseas, mainly in New Zealand, the economy relies heavily on subsistence agriculture, with cash crops, notably coconut, grown for export. It is therefore vulnerable to natural hazards, such as cyclones and crop diseases, and to fluctuations in world prices for commodities. GDP grew by 0.4% p.a. 1979–89.

Real Growth in GDP

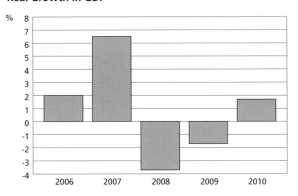

Inflation

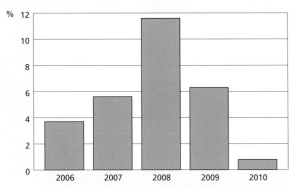

GDP by Sector (2010)

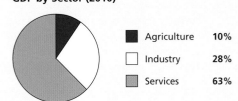

■	Agriculture	10%
□	Industry	28%
▨	Services	63%

There was serious cyclone damage in 1990, 1991 and 1998, when the coconut and banana crops were devastated. Compounding the problem was the taro leaf blight in 1993, which led to a further drop in agricultural output and exports. These setbacks resulted in fluctuating and often negative annual growth.

However, Samoa was early to embark on structural reforms and throughout the 1990s the government was controlling public-sector costs, encouraging diversification to reduce reliance on the agricultural sector and pursuing a programme of privatisation. These policies led to enhanced growth from the latter 1990s. Fisheries were developed, new manufacturing enterprises emerged and an offshore financial sector launched. Tourist numbers increased steadily.

Overall, the economy staged a remarkable recovery, showing generally good growth from 1995. But it remained vulnerable to natural disasters and international downturns, which have caused pauses in growth and rapid rises in inflation. In 2008–09 this generally good growth was interrupted both by the global economic downturn and then, in September 2009, by the devastating tsunami, causing the economy to contract by 3.7% in 2008 and by 1.7% in 2009, before recovering in 2010–11.

Fisheries

Since the mid-1990s there has been substantial growth in offshore fishing, using fish aggregating devices, and in fish farming. Fish and fish products is the major export.

Constitution

Status:	Republic
Legislature:	Parliament
Independence:	1 January 1962

Samoa is a democracy, with a unicameral legislature, the Fono; a prime minister who selects the cabinet; and a head of state, similar to a constitutional monarch. Under the constitution, the head of state is elected by the Fono for five years. However, by a special arrangement decided on in 1962 when the constitution came into force, Malietoa Tanumafili II (who died in 2007) and one other senior chief (who died in 1963) were to hold the office for life.

The prime minister, who must be a member of the Fono and be supported by a majority of its members, is appointed by the head of state. The prime minister chooses 12 members to form the cabinet, which has charge of executive government. The head of state must give their assent to new legislation before it becomes law.

The Fono has 49 members, 47 elected in 41 constituencies by universal adult suffrage, to be contested only by *matai* title holders (chiefs of *aiga*, or extended families, of whom there are around 25,000), and two elected from separate electoral rolls comprising those of foreign descent. The Fono sits for five-year terms.

Until 1991 only the *matai* were eligible to vote, but following a plebiscite universal adult suffrage was introduced in time for that year's elections. The *matai*, whose office is elective for life, still

History

Samoa seems, on archaeological evidence, to have been inhabited at least as far back as 1000 BC by Austronesian-speaking people. Evidence from legends and from genealogies shows that the country had frequent contact with Fiji and Tonga from the mid-13th century. There was some European contact in the first half of the 18th century, and settlement by refugees and beachcombers until the early 19th century. The Christian missionary John Williams came to Savai'i in 1830.

In 1889, Britain, the USA and Germany, all seeking influence in Samoa, held a conference in Berlin and signed a treaty giving the Samoan islands an independent government, with British, American and German supervision. Later in the same year, Britain relinquished its interest in the country, and the other two agreed that Germany should annex Western Samoa and the US Eastern Samoa. In 1914 the New Zealand army occupied Western Samoa, and in 1919 the League of Nations gave New Zealand a mandate to administer the country. An epidemic of influenza broke out in 1918; the Samoans at the time had no immunity to the disease and 20% of the population died in a few weeks.

Samoans resisted New Zealand's rule, with non-violent action (1926–36), culminating in the Mau uprisings. After the Second World War, the country was made a UN trust territory, with New Zealand's role now being to guide Western Samoa to independence.

A legislative assembly was set up in 1947. A constitution, which aimed at combining the traditional lifestyle with modern-style government, was adopted in August 1960. At a plebiscite organised by the UN and held in 1961, the nation voted for

independence. The country achieved independence on 1 January 1962, the first South Pacific island country to do so.

In 1970 Western Samoa joined the Commonwealth as a full member. Since 1962 it has had a Treaty of Friendship with New Zealand.

At elections in 1991, the Human Rights Protection Party (HRPP), led by Tofilau Eti Alesana, won 30 of the 49 seats in the Fono, defeating the other main political party, the Samoa National Development Party.

In April 1996, the HRPP was returned, Tofilau retaining his position as prime minister and minister for foreign affairs with the support of 34 members of the new Fono.

In July 1997, by act of parliament, the country changed its name from Western Samoa to Samoa. This change had been under discussion for some time, but was delayed by awareness of the sensitivities of American Samoa which, in the end, offered no opposition.

In November 1998 Tofilau resigned as prime minister; he became senior minister without portfolio and his deputy and finance minister, Tuilaepa Sailele Malielegaoi, succeeded him. Tofilau had been prime minister from 1982 to 1985 and from 1988 to 1998. He was 74 and had had problems with his health for several years. In March 1999 he died.

In January 2000, a memorandum of understanding was signed with American Samoa for mutual assistance on trade, health, education, agriculture and policing.

administer local government in the traditional manner. They are trustees for customary land held on behalf of the people, which makes up about 80% of all the land in the country.

Politics

Last elections:	March 2011
Next elections:	2016
Head of state:	Tuiatua Tupua Tamasese Efi (2007–)
Head of government:	Prime Minister Tuilaepa Lupesoliai Sailele Malielegaoi
Ruling party:	Human Rights Protection Party

In the general election in March 2001, the ruling Human Rights Protection Party (HRPP) – with 24 seats – won more seats than any other party, but was nonetheless challenged by the combined strength of the United Independents (11 seats) and Samoa National Development Party (SNDP; 13). On the resumption of parliament, however, HRPP leader Tuilaepa Sailele Malielegaoi was re-elected prime minister and enough independents joined the HRPP to give it an absolute majority.

The general election in March 2006 saw a return to power of the HRPP, increasing its number of seats to 33 with gains from both Samoa Democratic United Party (formerly SNDP, with ten seats) and independents (six).

Malietoa Tanumafili II, head of state since independence in January 1962, died in May 2007 aged 94. According to the constitution, in June 2007 the Fono elected Tuiatua Tupua Tamasese Efi as his successor for a five-year term.

In the March 2011 general election the HRPP and Prime Minister Tuilaepa Sailele Malielegaoi were returned with an increased majority. The HRPP and independents supporting the HRPP together secured 36 seats. The opposition Tautua Samoa Party won 13 seats.

International relations

Samoa is a member of the African, Caribbean and Pacific Group of States, Pacific Community, Pacific Islands Forum and United Nations.

At the Eighth World Trade Organization Ministerial Conference in Geneva in December 2011, Samoa's terms of entry were adopted. The country then had until 15 June 2012 to ratify its accession and would become a full member 30 days after ratification.

Traveller information

Local laws and conventions: Samoans adhere to traditional moral and religious codes of behaviour.

Permission should always be sought before taking photographs in villages. Alcohol may not be purchased on a Sunday, except by hotel guests and their visitors. Penalties for the possession and use of illegal drugs, including cannabis, are severe.

Sunday is a day of peace and quiet in Samoa, and visitors should behave quietly and travel slowly through villages, especially during evening prayer (usually between 1800 and 1900). Shoes must be removed when attending church or if entering a *fale* (Samoan house).

In business and commerce, English is the customary language. The best time to visit on business is from May to October. Office hours are Mon–Fri 0800–1200 and 1300–1630.

Immigration and customs: Passports must be valid for at least six months beyond the intended length of stay, and an onward or return ticket must be held.

A yellow fever vaccination certificate is required by those arriving from infected countries.

There are strict regulations regarding the import of firearms, fruits, pets and drugs.

Travel within the country: Traffic drives on the left (since September 2009) and car hire is available in most areas with an international driving permit. Speed limits are 40kph within the Apia area and 56kph outside the region.

Polynesian Airlines operates daily flights between the two main islands and there is also a ferry service.

Public buses cover most of the islands, though there are no timetables; travel information can be gained from the bus stand in Apia. Taxis are available, but are not metered, and fares should be agreed in advance of travel.

Travel health: Health care facilities are adequate for routine medical treatment. Travellers are advised to have a comprehensive travel and medical insurance policy.

Vaccinations against tuberculosis and Hepatitis B are sometimes recommended, but all current inoculation requirements should be checked well before travel.

Mains water is chlorinated; bottled water is also available.

Money: The local currency is the tala or Samoan dollar. Credit cards are accepted on a limited basis. Travellers cheques are accepted in major hotels, banks and tourist shops. Travellers cheques should be taken in either pounds sterling or US dollars in order to avoid additional exchange rate charges. The ANZ, National Bank, Samoa Commercial Bank and Westpac have branches at Salelologa on Savai'i. Banking hours are Mon–Fri 0900–1500; some banks open Sat 0900–1200.

There were 129,000 tourist arrivals in 2009.

Further information

Government of Samoa: www.govt.ws

Parliament: www.parliament.gov.ws

Central Bank of Samoa: www.cbs.gov.ws

Commonwealth Secretariat: www.thecommonwealth.org

Commonwealth of Nations: www.commonwealth-of-nations.org/Samoa

Seychelles

KEY FACTS

Joined Commonwealth:	1976
Population:	87,000 (2010)
GDP p.c. growth:	1.8% p.a. 1990–2010
UN HDI 2011:	world ranking 52
Official languages:	Creole, English and French
Time:	GMT plus 4hr
Currency:	Seychelles rupee (SRs)

Geography

Area:	455 sq km
Coastline:	491km
Capital:	Victoria

The Republic of Seychelles lies in the western part of the Indian Ocean, north of Madagascar and 1,593km east of Mombasa, Kenya. It is an isolated archipelago of outstanding natural beauty comprising about 115 islands, the largest and most economically important of which is Mahé.

Area: 455 sq km; maritime zone more than 1.3 million sq km.

Topography: There is a compact group of 41 mountainous granite islands, including Mahé (the largest), Praslin and La Digue. All three have high central granite ridges, the highest point being Morne Seychellois (905m) on Mahé. The other islands are built of coral, and are scattered, low-lying and sparsely populated.

Climate: Tropical. The south-east trade winds blow from May to October. The north-west monsoon winds bring heavy squalls of rain. January is the wettest month, July and August the driest. Temperature remains constant throughout the year, at 24–31°C, and humidity at around 80%. The country is outside the cyclone belt.

Did you know...

Seychelles is an archipelago of about 115 islands, spread across a maritime zone of more than 1.3 million sq km; 41 are mountainous granite islands, the highest point being Morne Seychellois (905m) on the largest island, Mahé; the other islands are built of coral, and are scattered, low-lying and sparsely populated.

Some 89% of Seychelles is covered by forest, more than any other country in the Commonwealth, and this figure has remained constant over 1990–2010.

Seychelles has one of the highest incomes per capita in Africa – US$9,760 in 2010 (a figure exceeded only by the oil-rich states of Equatorial Guinea and Libya).

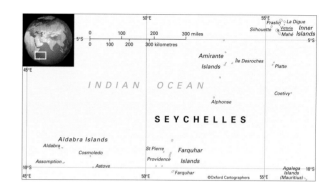

Environment: The most significant environmental issue is dependence on rainwater for supply of water.

Vegetation: The granite islands support luxuriant tropical forest on the mountain slopes. The coral islands are also densely covered with vegetation more characteristic of sandy coral soils. Generally, the most common trees are the coconut palm and casuarina. Others include banyans, screw pines and tortoise trees and the giant coco de mer palm, which is unique to the Seychelles and lives for up to 1,000 years. Of about 200 plant species, 80 are indigenous, including the bois rouge, the giant bois de fer and the capucin. Forest covers 89% of the land area and there was no significant loss of forest cover during 1990–2010.

Wildlife: Fruit bats, flying foxes, geckos and skinks are common, and there are more than 3,000 species of insects. The giant tortoise (which appears on the Seychelles coat of arms) survived near-extinction; there are now several thousand on Aldabra. There are many species of rare birds such as the bare-legged scops owl, Seychelles kestrel, black parrot, magpie robin and paradise flycatcher. Four islands are bird sanctuaries, including Bird Island, which is inhabited by millions of fairy terns.

Main towns: Victoria (capital, pop. 21,700 in 2010) and Anse Royale, both on Mahé.

Transport: There are 458km of roads, 96% paved; only Mahé, Praslin and La Digue have surfaced roads. Cruiseships and cargo ships call at Mahé.

Seychelles International Airport is at Point Larue, 10km from Victoria. There are airstrips on several outlying islands.

Society

KEY FACTS 2010

Population per sq km:	191
Life expectancy:	74 years (est.)
Net primary enrolment:	94%

Population: 87,000 (2010); 88% on Mahé, 7% on Praslin, 3% on La Digue and 2% on the other islands, with 55% living in urban areas; growth 1.0% p.a. 1990–2010; birth rate 15 per 1,000 people (est.); life expectancy 74 years (est.)

The population is of mixed African, French, Indian, Chinese and Arab descent. There are small minorities of Europeans, Indians and Chinese.

Language: The official languages are Creole, English and French. Seychellois Creole (Kreol Seselwa) is French-based and very widely used.

Religion: Mainly Christians (Roman Catholics 82%, Anglicans 6%, and small numbers of other Christians); Hindus 2% and Muslims 1% (2002 census). Belief in the supernatural and *gris-gris* (the old magic of spirits) often coexists with Christian and other beliefs. Sorcery was outlawed in 1958.

Health: Public spending on health was 3% of GDP in 2009. A network of polyclinics provides general medical care, dentistry and other services. There are also private general practitioners. The public health service depends heavily on medical personnel from overseas. There is no malaria, yellow fever or bilharzia. Infant mortality was 12 per 1,000 live births in 2010 (43 in 1978).

Education: There are ten years of compulsory education starting at age six. Primary school comprises six years and secondary five. Some 85% of pupils complete primary school (2008). The school year starts in January. Teaching is in Creole, French and English.

Providers of tertiary education under the Ministry of Education include National Institute of Education and Seychelles Institute of Technology (both located on Mahé). Providers under other ministries include the Farmers' Training Centre; Maritime Training Centre; National College of the Arts; National Institute for Health and Social Studies; and Seychelles Hospitality and Tourism Training College. Seychelles Institute of Technology offers courses to diploma level and has been providing first-year undergraduate degree courses in conjunction with the University of Manchester, UK, since 2001. Literacy among people aged 15–24 is 99% (2009).

Media: Seychelles Nation is the government-owned daily. Weeklies *Le Nouveau Seychelles* and *Regar* are owned by the Seychelles National Party; and weekly *The People* is owned by the People's Party.

The Seychelles Broadcasting Corporation provides public radio and TV services in Creole, French and English. Multichannel cable and satellite TV services are also available.

There are 216 personal computers (2007) and 410 internet users (2010) per 1,000 people.

Communications: Country code 248; internet domain '.sc'. Payphones are available in most districts on the inner islands. Internet connections are good in Seychelles. There are several internet cafes on Mahé, Praslin and La Digue. The main post office is in Victoria.

There are 255 main telephone lines and 1,359 mobile phone subscriptions per 1,000 people (2010).

Public holidays: New Year (two days), Labour Day (1 May), Liberation Day (anniversary of the 1977 coup, 5 June), National Day (18 June), Independence Day (29 June), Assumption (15 August), All Saints' Day (1 November), Immaculate Conception (8 December) and Christmas Day.

Religious festivals whose dates vary from year to year include Good Friday, Easter Monday and Corpus Christi.

Economy

KEY FACTS 2010

GNI:	US$845m
GNI p.c.:	US$9,760
GDP growth:	4.6% p.a. 2006–10
Inflation:	13.1% p.a. 2006–10

Seychelles is vulnerable, due to its small size, isolation, limited natural resources and dependence on tourism, which accounts for the bulk of foreign-exchange earnings. Though tourism worldwide grew strongly during the 1990s, and cheaper long-haul flights made destinations such as Seychelles more accessible, the industry became increasingly competitive. Imports needed for tourism were in large part responsible for the country's trade deficit. GDP grew by 1.4% p.a. 1979–89.

Consequently, the government made efforts to diversify the economy, encouraging farming, fishing and manufacturing, in the whole country including the outer islands. State-owned and parastatal enterprises accounted in the mid-1990s for more than half of GDP and some privatisation of state enterprises was under way during the 1990s. By the late 1990s, there was good growth for several years, and canned tuna became the major export.

Real Growth in GDP

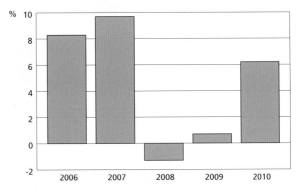

Inflation

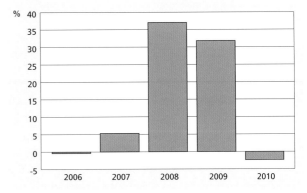

GDP by Sector (2010)

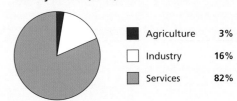

■ Agriculture	**3%**
□ Industry	**16%**
▨ Services	**82%**

But the economy underwent a small overall decline during 2001–04, before growth strengthened to 7.5% in 2005, 8.3% in 2006 and 9.7% in 2007, as a result of increased foreign direct investment and tourism receipts. Then, in 2008, in the teeth of the world economic downturn the economy stalled, and Seychelles turned to the IMF for emergency support. With a sharp fall in tourism income and cuts in public expenditure GDP declined by 1.3% in 2008. In response to economic reforms initiated in late November 2008, in 2010 the economy bounced back (growing by 6.2% in that year).

Constitution

Status:	Republic with executive president
Legislature:	National Assembly
Independence:	29 June 1976

The independence constitution provided for a multiparty state. The 1979 constitution made Seychelles a one-party state, the sole candidate for a presidential election to be nominated by the ruling party. This constitution was amended in 1992, when multiparty democracy was reintroduced and, after a process of consultation involving referendums, replaced by the 1993 constitution.

Under the 1993 constitution, Seychelles is a unitary republic, with a multiparty democracy. It has a unicameral parliament, the National Assembly, comprising up to 35 seats, 25 of which are elected by universal adult suffrage, on a first-past-the-post basis, and up to ten seats on the basis of proportional representation. Parliamentary

and presidential elections take place every five years, not necessarily at the same time. The president appoints a cabinet – not including members of parliament – and is empowered under the 1993 constitution to rule by decree.

In August 1996, the constitution was amended to create the office of vice-president.

Politics

Last elections:	May 2011 (presidential), September/October 2011 (legislative)
Next elections:	2016 (presidential and legislative)
Head of state:	President James Alix Michel
Head of government:	the president
Ruling party:	People's Party

Following the 1998 elections Wavel Ramkalawan formed a new party, the Seychelles National Party (SNP), to succeed his United Opposition party. In an early presidential election in September 2001, René was returned to office, securing 54% of the votes, defeating Ramkalawan (45%), in a much closer contest than in 1998. Though the SNP significantly strengthened its position in the parliamentary elections in December 2002, with 11 of the 34 elective seats and 42.6% of the votes, the ruling Seychelles People's Progressive Front (SPPF) remained in control of the National Assembly.

STRIVING FOR OUR SEYCHELLES

As it strives to develop the nation's global industry to its fullest potential, the SFA is taking the sensible line of fishing to safeguard stocks and ensure work, revenue and food security for generations to come.

RESPONSIBLE FISHING FOR SUSTAINABILITY

Seychelles Fishing Authority
P.O. Box 449, Fishing Port Victoria, Mahe, Seychelles
TEL: +248 467 0300, FAX: +248 422 4508,
EMAIL: management@sfa.sc, WEB: www.sfa.sc

Following the elections the SPPF chose vice-president and finance minister James Michel as their candidate for the presidential contest due in 2006, France Albert René being allowed only two terms under the constitution. In April 2004, after almost 27 years as head of state, René stood down and Michel became president.

Michel was endorsed by the electorate in the July 2006 presidential contest when, with 54% of the votes cast, he defeated the SNP's Wavel Ramkalawan.

In the parliamentary elections held in May 2007, the ruling SPPF, with 56% of the votes, again won 23 seats and the SNP, with 44%, took 11.

At its 24th National Congress in June 2009 the SPPF was renamed the People's Party.

In the May 2011 presidential election Michel was re-elected, winning 56% of the votes cast. His principal rival, Ramkalawan of the SNP, secured 41% of the votes. A Commonwealth expert team present declared the electoral process credible. Among its recommendations were that the government carry out a thorough review of electoral legislation, and establish an independent electoral commission, as recommended in the April 2010 report of the Constitutional Review Commission.

Following the presidential election in May 2011 the SNP boycotted parliament citing the slow pace of electoral reform. Some disaffected SNP members then formed a new party, the Popular

History

Although visited by Phoenicians, Malays and Arabs, and used in the 16th century by the Portuguese as a stopover point, the Seychelles remained largely uninhabited until the 17th century. Pirates and privateers set up bases on the islands and in 1741 the Governor of Mauritius (then called Île de France) sent Lazare Picault to explore them. The French claimed possession of the islands in 1756 and French settlers from Mauritius, with their African slaves, began to arrive from 1770.

British attempts to take possession in the late 18th century were confounded by the pacifying tactics of Governor Queau de Quinssy, who several times surrendered to British aggressors, then after their departure, raised the French flag again. After the Napoleonic Wars, by the Treaty of Paris (1814), the Seychelles was ceded to Britain, together with Mauritius. From then until 1903, it was administered from Mauritius.

The Seychelles had long provided a transit point for slaves from Africa. Britain abolished trade in slaves at the beginning of the 19th century (abolishing slavery itself in 1834) and British vessels were active in attacking Spanish, Arab and other slaving vessels. About 3,000 Africans rescued from Arab slave traders on the East African coast between 1861 and 1874 were removed to Seychelles, to become labourers on the plantations. The British also exiled some West African chiefs, who were continuing to resist British control, to Seychelles. There was also some Chinese and Indian settlement in the 19th century, most commonly by traders.

Poverty was widespread by 1918, due partly to a fall in vanilla prices (an artificial substitute having been discovered). New cash crops such as cinnamon and copra were then introduced. In the 1940s, the Association of Seychelles Taxpayers protested against the UK's management of the islands. In 1964 the Seychelles Democratic Party (SDP), led by James Mancham, and the Seychelles People's United Party (SPUP), led by France Albert René, were founded. The SDP favoured retaining close ties with the UK; the SPUP campaigned for autonomy.

Universal adult suffrage was introduced in 1967, for elections of members of the legislative council. The council became a 15-member legislative assembly in 1970 (later National Assembly) and general elections were held in which the SDP won six seats and the SPUP five. Mancham became chief minister. At the next elections in 1974, the SDP won 52% of the votes, the SPUP 47%; Seychelles achieved internal self-government in the following year.

Parliament then voted for independence, a new constitution was finalised in 1976, and Seychelles became an independent republic within the Commonwealth. Mancham became president and René prime minister.

At independence Mancham and the SDP's policies favoured development based on tourism and offshore financial services and alignment with the West, whereas René and the SPUP wanted a non-aligned policy and the development of a self-reliant economy centred on nationalised industry. The SPUP staged an armed coup in June 1977, while Mancham was in the UK attending a Commonwealth summit and Seychelles became a socialist state, with René as its president and the SPUP, renamed the Seychelles People's Progressive Front (SPPF), the sole political party. There was extensive nationalisation of enterprises, including hotels and industries.

There were a number of threatened coup plots against the René government, the most serious in 1981, when about 50 mercenaries, recruited in South Africa, attempted a landing in Mahé. When their weapons were discovered at the airport, the mercenaries escaped by hijacking an Air India jet, leaving five of their number behind.

However, opposition from exiled political supporters of the SDP and Mancham continued throughout the 1980s, and was reinforced by the turning of the international tide against centralised economic control and one-party rule towards the end of the decade. By 1990, opposition within the country also became vocal, and the government began to consider the need for change.

In December 1991, the government passed legislation to provide for multiparty democracy. Eight parties were registered by July 1992, and a constitutional commission elected to prepare a new constitution which paved the way for presidential and legislative elections in July 1993. René took 59% of votes in the presidential election and Sir James Mancham 36%; and the SPPF gained a large majority – 27 of the 33 seats – in the National Assembly.

In the March 1998 elections, President René (with 67% of the votes) was returned and his SPPF won 24 of the 25 Assembly seats (30 of 34 when seats allocated on a proportional basis were included). Mancham (14%) was overtaken by Wavel Ramkalawan of the United Opposition party (19%) as opposition leader.

Democratic Movement (PDM), to fight the parliamentary elections which were held from 29 September to 1 October 2011. The elections were again won by the People's Party led by President James Michel, taking all 25 elective seats in the National Assembly and receiving 89% of the votes cast. The PDM took 11% of the votes but failed to win any of the elective seats.

The Electoral Commission was appointed in August 2011 and the Forum for Electoral Reform – inaugurated in January 2012 with the support of all five registered political parties – embarked on a series of public hearings, with a view to making recommendations on reform of election law.

International relations

Seychelles is a member of the African, Caribbean and Pacific Group of States, African Union, Common Market for Eastern and Southern Africa, Non-Aligned Movement, Organisation internationale de la Francophonie, Southern African Development Community and United Nations.

Traveller information

Local laws and conventions: The possession or trafficking of drugs is illegal and can incur serious punishments.

It is an offence for anyone, including children, to wear camouflage clothing, and pornography in the form of obscene articles, publications, videotapes and software is prohibited. Collecting shells is strictly forbidden in nature reserves, marine parks and reserves in Seychelles. Permission must always be sought before taking photographs of local people.

Shaking hands is the customary form of greeting. Casual wear is the norm. Beachwear should be for the beach only. Businessmen are not expected to wear suits and ties, although a smart appearance is advised. Most executives speak English and/or French. Office hours are Mon–Fri 0800–1600.

Immigration and customs: Passports must be valid for six months from the date of entry. Visas may be needed for some nationals and visa requirements should be checked well in advance of travel.

The import of non-prescribed drugs, firearms, plants and plant products, animals and animal products, fireworks and explosives are prohibited. Videotapes must be declared on arrival and may be retained for security reasons. The importation of fruit, seeds, vegetables and meat products is strictly prohibited.

Any flora taken as souvenirs should have a certificate and an official export permit, which must be produced when checking in at the international airport.

A yellow fever vaccination certificate is required by all those arriving from infected areas.

Travel within the country: Traffic drives on the left and visitors can drive with a national driving licence. There are a limited number of cars available for hire on Mahé and Praslin, and reservations should be made well in advance.

Care should be taken when driving in mountainous areas, as roads are narrow and winding and there are few safety barriers. There is a 65kph speed limit on the open road and a 40kph speed limit in built-up areas and throughout Praslin.

Buses are the only means of public transport. Taxis can be found on Mahé and Praslin, and rates are government-controlled. Visitors should negotiate the fare before beginning their journey. Bicycles are a popular means of transport and are easily hired on the islands.

Privately owned schooners carry passengers between Mahé, Praslin and La Digue, and boats can be chartered privately to get to the other islands. Air Seychelles also provides scheduled and chartered flights between some of the islands.

Travel health: Comprehensive health insurance is essential.

Tap water is normally chlorinated; bottled water is widely available.

Money: Local currency is the Seychelles rupee. Visitors will find that most services on the islands, including hotel bills and care hire, require payment in hard currency. Using local currency is only allowed if an exchange receipt can be shown as proof of the conversion from foreign currency into local currency. Travellers cheques are widely accepted and should be in US dollars or pounds sterling to avoid additional charges. Most international credit cards can be used, and there are ATMs on Mahé and Praslin. Banking hours are Mon–Fri 0830–1430, Sat 0830–1100.

There were 158,000 tourist arrivals in 2009.

Further information

Office of the President of the Republic of Seychelles: www.statehouse.gov.sc

National Assembly: www.nationalassembly.sc

Central Bank of Seychelles: www.cbs.sc

Commonwealth Secretariat: www.thecommonwealth.org

Commonwealth of Nations: www.commonwealth-of-nations.org/Seychelles

Sierra Leone

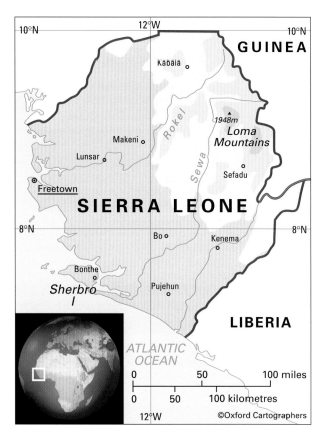

The Republic of Sierra Leone (Portuguese for 'Lion Mountain') in West Africa is bordered by Guinea to the north, Liberia to the south-east, and the Atlantic to the south and west.

Topography: Sierra Leone has some 402km of coast along the Atlantic Ocean, with magnificent beaches. Apart from the hilly Freetown peninsula (officially known as the Western Area), the coastal belt is flat, with a width of up to 110km. The land rises to the Guinea highlands in the east, with mountain peaks up to 1,917m. There are eight main rivers; the estuaries of two of them can be navigated by ocean-going vessels.

Climate: Tropical and humid all year, but cooler on the coast. The dry season is November to May, when the dusty harmattan wind blows from the Sahara; the rainy season lasts the rest of the year.

Environment: The most significant environmental issues are depletion of natural resources during the civil war; deforestation and soil exhaustion due to over-harvesting of timber, expansion of cattle grazing, and slash-and-burn agriculture; and overfishing.

Vegetation: Mangrove swamps occur along the coast, with thickly wooded hills on the Freetown peninsula, and grasslands, woods and savannah on the interior plains. The central inland area, formerly forested, has been cleared for agriculture. Forest – including mahogany and teak – covers 38% of the land area, having declined at 0.7% p.a. 1990–2010. Arable land comprises 15% and permanent cropland 1% of the total land area.

Did you know...

Aminatta Forna, who was raised in Sierra Leone and the UK, won the 2011 Commonwealth Writers' Prize with her novel *The Memory of Love*.

Sierra Leone hosts a national chapter of the Commonwealth Human Ecology Council.

Wildlife: Large game animals are now rare, but the Kilimi National Park in the north of the country has the largest concentration of chimpanzees in West Africa. The park is also home to 12 other primate species, including the colobus monkey, as well as the rare large bongo antelope and, in the river margins, pygmy hippopotami. After the civil war a chimpanzee sanctuary was established at Leicester in the Western Area.

Main towns: Freetown (capital, Western Province; pop. 836,600 in 2010), Bo (Southern, 215,400), Kenema (Eastern, 169,900), Makeni (Northern, 102,600), Koidu (Eastern, 91,600), Lunsar (Northern, 23,900), Port Loko (Northern, 22,700), Pandebu-Tokpombu (Eastern, 19,700), Kabala (Northern, 18,800), Waterloo (Western, 17,800), Kailahun (Eastern, 17,500), Segbwema (Eastern, 16,000), Magburaka (Northern, 16,000), Koindu (Eastern, 15,900) and Bonthe (Southern, 10,200).

Transport: There are 11,300km of roads, 8% paved, but in poor repair; secondary roads may be impassable in the rainy season. The railway system (nearly 600km in length) closed in 1974.

Freetown is the main port with a deep-water quay. There are smaller ports at Pepel, Bonthe, Niti and Sulima. Several rivers are navigable by small craft.

The international airport is at Lungi, 13km north of Freetown, and is separated from the capital by a river estuary.

Society

KEY FACTS 2010

Population per sq km:	82
Life expectancy:	47 years

Population: 5,868,000 (2010); 38% lives in urban areas; growth 1.9% p.a. 1990–2010; birth rate 39 per 1,000 people (46 in 1970); life expectancy 47 years (36 in 1970 and 40 in 1990); population figures are unreliable because during the civil war in the mid-1990s up to 50% of the population had to leave their homes – there was mass migration to towns and to neighbouring countries.

The vast majority of the people are of Bantu origin: Temne (35% in the 2008 census) and Limba (8%) people mostly in the Northern province; Mende people (31%) live in the Southern province and Eastern province. Additionally, there are nine other Bantu ethnic groups, including Kono (5%), Mandingo (2%) and Loko (2%). Krios (2%) are descendants of formerly enslaved 19th-century immigrants who live mostly in and around Freetown. The small Lebanese community, mostly of traders, decreased during the 1990s.

Language: English is the official language. Krio (an English-based Creole) is spoken in and around Freetown. Other major languages are Temne, Mende and Limba.

Religion: Muslims 60%, Christians 10%, with most of the remaining population holding traditional beliefs, which often coexist with other religions.

Health: Public spending on health was 1% of GDP in 2009. 49% of the population uses an improved drinking water source and 13% have access to adequate sanitation facilities (2009). Climatic conditions are conducive to the spread of tropical diseases (notably malaria and guinea worm), and civil war made the country vulnerable to cholera. There was a high incidence of maiming during the civil war. Infant mortality was 114 per 1,000 live births in 2010 (220 in 1960). In 2009, 1.6% of people aged 15–49 were HIV positive.

Education: Public spending on education was 4.3% of GDP in 2009. There are seven years of primary education starting at age five, and seven of secondary comprising cycles of five and two years. The school year starts in September.

The principal tertiary institutions are Fourah Bay College in Freetown and Njala University, with campuses in Bo and Njala. These universities, together with Milton Margai College of Education and Technology (Freetown), Eastern Polytechnic (main campus in Kenema) and other independent tertiary institutions, are all affiliated to the University of Sierra Leone. The country also has a number of teacher-training and technical/vocational institutions providing certificate and diploma courses. Literacy among people aged 15–24 is 58% (2009).

The government's education plan for 2007–15 aims to complete rehabilitation of the country's education system, after the years of civil war, in order to give all citizens access to quality education. The plan emphasises primary education, skills-training and tertiary education to meet development needs.

Media: There are many newspapers including *Awoko*, *Concord Times* and *Standard Times*.

Sierra Leone Broadcasting Corporation provides public radio and TV services. There are many private radio stations and ABC TV is a private TV channel.

There are 3 internet users per 1,000 people (2009).

Communications: Country code 232; internet domain '.sl'. Mobile phone coverage is limited to the Freetown area. The public telephone system does not extend beyond Western Area. The number of internet cafes is increasing, especially in Freetown. Post offices are found in the main towns.

There are 2 main telephone lines and 341 mobile phone subscriptions per 1,000 people (2010).

Public holidays: New Year's Day, Independence Day (27 April), Christmas Day and Boxing Day.

Religious and other festivals whose dates vary from year to year include Mouloud (Prophet's Birthday), Good Friday, Easter Monday, Eid al-Fitr (End of Ramadan) and Eid al-Adha (Feast of the Sacrifice).

Economy

KEY FACTS 2010

GNI:	US$2.0bn
GNI p.c.:	US$340
GDP growth:	5.5% p.a. 2006–10
Inflation:	10.3% p.a. 2006–10

With real GDP falling almost continuously from the 1980s to the start of the 2000s, the economy of Sierra Leone became very depressed, despite the country's rich resource base, notably diamonds, rutile (an oxide of titanium), bauxite and gold. Civil war in neighbouring Liberia and its spread within Sierra Leone, particularly

Real Growth in GDP

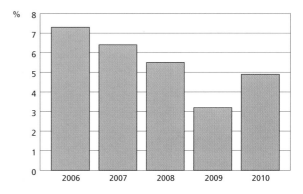

Inflation

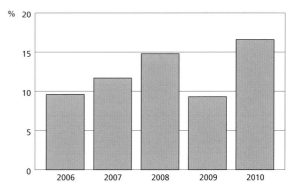

Ministry of Agriculture, Forestry and Food Security

FARMING FOR BUSINESS IN SIERRA LEONE

Agriculture is the backbone of Sierra Leone's economy, accounting for almost half its GDP and providing a living for over two thirds of the population.

SMALLHOLDER COMMERCIALISATION PROGRAMME (SCP)

Launched in 2010, SCP's goal is to empower the rural poor to chart their own course of attaining self-sufficiency as well as to increase their incomes on a sustainable basis with a view to boosting the general economy.

At the Smallholder Commercialisation Programme launch in Kenema City, His Excellency President Koroma stated that agricultural development is his government's 'top priority'

Found in every chiefdom, through the decentralised local government's extension services and in collaboration with FAO, WFP, UNIDO, UNDP and NGO development partners, Farmer Field and Life School (FFLS) training leads to the strengthening of Farmer Based Organisations (FBO) and the creation of a system of Agriculture Business Centres (ABCs) owned by FBOs. FFLS also covers production technology, processing, marketing and key life skills.

An ABC is not only a centre for agribusiness but a social cohesion point where farmers can meet to discuss pertinent issues and learn through agricultural extension messages

It is hoped that through the SCP, farmers' incomes would increase by 10 per cent through the rehabilitation of about 8000 hectares of tree crops; increased valued addition of produce through processing and marketing; improved extension services for farmers; and guaranteeing adequate farmers' representation at all levels to protect their interests in the value chain process and other areas.

CONTACT

Bakarr J. Bangura
Deputy Director of Agric. Extension
and Head of Field Operations
Tel: +232 76 72 4422
Email: bjbangura01@yahoo.co.uk

www.maffs.gov.sl

GDP by Sector (2010)

■	Agriculture	59%
□	Industry	5%
▨	Services	36%

from 1995, caused total collapse of the economy. The country was burdened by an economically counter-productive parallel economy, which increased in the lawless conditions of civil war. Around 90% of diamonds produced in Sierra Leone were estimated to leave the country illegally, and cash crops in the fertile south and east were being smuggled out. The cost of maintaining a large army and bringing in foreign troops put a further strain on the economy, and there were mass migrations of people to avoid the fighting.

Restoration of democracy in February 1998 and the peace agreement with the Revolutionary United Front of July 1999 opened the way for a very substantial commitment of aid by the international community, led by the UN, IMF and World Bank, to reintegrate the military into civilian life, to restore institutions, to rebuild the economy and alleviate poverty.

Delivery of this aid was impeded and delayed by the collapse of the peace agreement in May 2000 and during 2001 by the slow pace of demobilisation of rebel troops and of returning all areas of the country to peace and security, but during 2001 the rutile mines were rehabilitated and agricultural production was resumed in large areas of the country. In 2001, too, reserves of offshore oil and gas were discovered and the UN ban on the trade in uncut diamonds did begin to reduce smuggling.

The economy began to expand again in 2000, with a surge of growth in 2001 (18.2%) and 2002 (27.4%), moderating to 9.5% in 2003 and averaged 6.1% p.a. over 2005–09, while unemployment persisted at a high level, and inflation rose from practically nil in 2000–02 to more than 10% p.a. in the second half of the 2000s. As the world economic downturn depressed demand for Sierra Leone's exports, GDP growth again moderated to 3.2% in 2009, rising to 4.9% in 2010 and more than 5.0% in 2011.

In December 2006, Sierra Leone qualified for debt relief amounting to US$994 million under the IMF/World Bank Enhanced Heavily Indebted Poor Countries Initiative.

Constitution

Status:	Republic with executive president
Legislature:	Parliament
Independence:	27 April 1961

The independence constitution was abrogated during the series of military coups which followed. The 1971 constitution allowed for a ceremonial president; an amendment later that year created an executive presidency. A new constitution in 1978 established a one-party state, with the All People's Congress as the recognised party, and there was further constitutional amendment in 1985.

The 1991 constitution marked a return to a multiparty system, with many of the parliamentary features of the independence constitution, though the country was to remain a republic with an executive presidency. Implementation of this constitution was interrupted by an army coup. The National Provisional Ruling Council became the governing body, and rule was by decree.

These developments were in turn reversed by the implementation of the 1995 constitution, which (with amendments) restored the 1991 constitution, returning the country to a multiparty system with an executive presidency and a unicameral legislature. For the elections of May 2002, the legislature had a total of 124 members, comprising 112 directly elected – eight in each of 14 constituencies – and 12 paramount chiefs. Presidential and parliamentary elections are held at least every five years, under universal adult suffrage and proportional representation. The president forms a government and appoints a cabinet.

Politics

Last elections:	August/September 2007 (presidential and legislative)
Next elections:	2012 (presidential and legislative)
Head of state:	President Ernest Bai Koroma
Head of government:	the president
Ruling party:	All People's Congress

Following signature of the July 1999 peace agreement UN peacekeepers proceeded with disarming rebel troops and took control over a growing area of the country, and in May 2002 presidential and parliamentary elections were held with Commonwealth observers present. Ahmad Tejan Kabbah and the Sierra Leone People's Party (SLPP) won a landslide victory, receiving about 70% of the votes in the presidential election, defeating Ernest Bai Koroma, and in the parliamentary elections taking 83 of the 112 seats; Koroma's All People's Congress (APC) secured 22 seats and the Revolutionary United Front (RUF) none. The Commonwealth observers said that the conditions were such as to enable the will of the people to be expressed.

In the parliamentary elections in August 2007, the APC was the largest party with 59 seats, the SLPP won 43 seats and People's Movement for Democratic Change (PMDC) ten. The simultaneous first round of the presidential election was won by APC leader Ernest Bai Koroma with 44% of votes; the incumbent SLPP candidate, Solomon Berewa, came second with 38% and Charles Margai of PMDC third with 14%. Since no candidate received the 55% needed to secure the presidency, the leading two candidates, Koroma and Berewa, went into a second round. Koroma received 54.6% of second-round votes and was sworn in as president.

History

The Bulom are the earliest known inhabitants of the territory, with the Krim and Gola people arriving by AD 1400. The Mende and Temne settled in the 15th century, and the Fulani moved into the northern region.

Around that time the Portuguese were exploring the coast – Pedro de Cintra gave the country its present name in about 1462 – and built a fort on the site of Freetown. Europeans traded along the coast without formally establishing themselves. In 1787 Granville Sharp and other British abolitionists settled 400 people, formerly slaves, on a strip of land bought from Naimbana, a local chief. Over the following years more settlers arrived, many of them freed slaves from Jamaica and Nova Scotia. The British parliament declared the slave trade illegal in 1807, and a British naval station was established at Freetown to intercept slavers continuing to operate; people rescued from the slave-ships were also settled in Sierra Leone. Freetown became a British colony in 1808 and the coastal and inland area a protectorate in 1896. During the 19th century the colonial rulers forged administrative links with The Gambia, the Gold Coast (now Ghana) and Lagos in Nigeria.

In 1863 a legislative council was created. It was progressively enlarged and made more representative in 1924 and 1951, evolving in 1956 into the House of Representatives. By 1957 most men were eligible to vote; women who were taxpayers or owned property were also enfranchised. A new constitution came into force in 1961, establishing formally a unicameral parliament and Queen Elizabeth II as sovereign. On that basis Sierra Leone became independent on 27 April 1961.

At independence, two main parties shared the votes in a multiparty political system. First in office was the Sierra Leone People's Party (SLPP) during 1962–67 under Sir Milton Margai. The 1967 elections were won by the All People's Congress (APC) under Dr Siaka Stevens. Almost immediately, Stevens was arrested

in a coup, followed days later by another army coup which imposed military rule until the next year. Then, after a further coup, Stevens was reinstated as prime minister.

In 1971, the country became a republic with Stevens as executive president. The general election of 1973 was boycotted by the SLPP and easily won by the APC, which also won the following elections in 1977 after a campaign which sparked violence. In 1978 the country became a one-party state, led by the ruling APC. Single-party elections in 1982 were once again violent. In 1985 Major-General Joseph Momoh succeeded Stevens as president.

By the end of the 1980s, economic conditions were continuing to deteriorate and there was a growing demand for constitutional reform. The government responded by setting up a constitutional review commission. The commission's recommendation of a return to a multiparty democratic system was overwhelmingly endorsed in a referendum in August 1991. A new constitution was adopted, allowing for a transition towards multiparty elections. Political parties started to register in preparation for elections.

Civil war

The 1991 multiparty constitution was not, however, implemented. Fighting with a rebel movement, the Revolutionary United Front (RUF), which had started in March 1991, escalated, and there were incursions from neighbouring Liberia, the RUF in the south of the country being loosely in alliance with Liberian rebels.

In April 1992, Captain Valentine Strasser took control after a coup by junior army officers, and the constitution was suspended. The war escalated and, despite air and ground support from Nigeria, and troops provided by Guinea, by 1995 at one point the government was in secure control only of the ➤

Commonwealth observers reported that both parliamentary and presidential elections had been conducted in a democratic, credible and professional way in accordance with internationally accepted standards.

International relations

Sierra Leone is a member of the African, Caribbean and Pacific Group of States, African Union, Economic Community of West African States, Non-Aligned Movement, Organisation of Islamic Cooperation, United Nations and World Trade Organization.

Traveller information

Local laws and conventions: Visitors should ensure they respect local customs at all times – and particularly during Ramadan and when visiting religious sites.

All drug-related offences carry severe penalties, including steep fines and prison sentences. All precious stones need an export licence and the smuggling of stones is a grave offence.

It is advisable to carry some form of identification at all times. Visitors should always ask permission before taking pictures of local people or their property.

Generally, there are few social restrictions, though sensitivity is suggested in the rural areas, where the more traditional societies, with ruling chiefs, are still preserved.

Handshaking is the normal form of greeting. Casual wear is suitable everywhere and men are rarely expected to wear suits and ties.

Business meetings can be formal, and usually begin with an exchange of cards and introductory speeches. In Freetown, English is the most common language for business, though Krio and tribal languages are more prevalent in the countryside, where translators are available. Appointments and punctuality are expected, and September to June are the best months to visit on business. Office hours are Mon–Fri 0800–1200 and 1400–1630.

Immigration and customs: Passports must be valid for six months and visas are required by all except those from the member countries of the Economic Community of West African States. Business visitors should ensure they have an introductory letter and invitation from the local business outlining the purpose of the visit and providing contact details. There is an airport departure tax for all foreign visitors.

A vaccination certificate for yellow fever is required by those arriving from an infected area.

Narcotics and firearms without a licence from the Commissioner of Police in Freetown are prohibited.

Travel within the country: Traffic drives on the right and visitors will need an international driving permit. Cars can be hired through local companies and hotels. Visitors should carry their licence with them at all times. The main highways have tarred surfaces.

It is recommended that onward and return flights are confirmed 72 hours in advance.

capital. In January 1996, Strasser was overthrown by his deputy Brigadier Julius Maada Bio.

Multiparty elections and peace

Parliamentary and presidential elections under the 1991 multiparty constitution were finally held in February 1996. Of the 68 parliamentary seats, the SLPP won 27, the United National People's Party (UNPP) 17, People's Democratic Party 12, the APC five, the National Unity Party four, the Democratic Centre Party three. In a two-round presidential election the SLPP candidate, Ahmad Tejan Kabbah, defeated UNPP's Dr John Karefa-Smart and Kabbah was sworn in as president at the end of March 1996.

In talks between the government and RUF leader Corporal Foday Sankoh, agreement was reached in November 1996 to end the war that had caused the displacement of 2 million people and over 10,000 deaths. The agreement allowed the RUF to register as a political party and permitted it access to the media. In 1997 RUF leader Sankoh was arrested while on a visit to Nigeria.

In May 1997 the Kabbah government was overthrown in a military coup led by Major Johnny Paul Koroma, but in October 1997, in a deal brokered by ECOWAS in Conakry, Guinea, the rebel Armed Forces Revolutionary Council (AFRC) regime agreed to a six-month transition to restore the legitimate civilian government. Apart from a few skirmishes in the area of the diamond mines, the transitional period was reasonably peaceful until early February 1998 when renewed fighting broke out between Nigerian peacekeeping troops and Koroma's forces in Freetown and a few days later, on 12 February, the Nigerians captured Freetown and detained many members of the military regime, though not including Koroma himself. After nine months in exile in Conakry, President Kabbah returned to Freetown in March 1998. Parliament reconvened and about 50% of its members attended. Within a few days thousands of people had returned to their homes in Freetown.

In July 1998 the UN agreed to establish an observer mission to monitor the military and security situation in the country and to advise the government on the rebuilding of the police and security forces. Sankoh was returned to Freetown from detention in Lagos to face charges of treason and was sentenced to death in October 1998. On news of Sankoh's death sentence RUF and AFRC rebels launched a campaign of severe brutality in the towns and villages they took over as they advanced rapidly on Freetown and in January 1999 Nigerian troops halted their advance very close to the capital. A wider peace agreement was signed in July 1999, which included a power-sharing arrangement between Kabbah and the RUF (with four RUF leaders appointed to ministerial portfolios in November 1999), annulment of Sankoh's death sentence and the release of those sentenced for their role in the 1997 coup. UN Secretary-General Kofi Annan recommended the deployment of 6,000 troops to Sierra Leone to guarantee the peace agreement and this was increased to 11,000 on the departure of the Nigerians in 2000.

In May 2000, as the UN peacekeepers moved into the diamond-producing region and began to demobilise the rebels, the peace agreement collapsed when the rebels took 500 UN troops hostage and fighting resumed between the Sierra Leone Army and the rebels. Power-sharing ceased and Sankoh was arrested, though the hostages were released unharmed in due course. In July 2000 the UN resolved to ban trade in uncut diamonds from Sierra Leone until the government had established an authentication system but the illicit trade continued into 2001, when there were signs that the ban was beginning to be effective.

In June 2004 special courts with Sierra Leonean and UN-appointed judges began trying those both on government and rebel sides of the civil war accused of war crimes.

The national airline, Sierra National Airline LJ, does not operate internal flights; instead, private airlines can be chartered to fly to other towns and cities and even to neighbouring countries. The Sierra Leone Road Transport Corporation operates local and long distance bus services that are fast, cheap and connect all the major centres. Ferries connect all coastal ports.

There is a limited bus service in Freetown. Many people use minibuses (*poda-poda*), which operate within the city and surrounding towns, and charge a fixed rate. Taxis are available, but should only be used if they display a valid Tourist Board sticker on the windscreen.

Travel health: It is essential that visitors have comprehensive health insurance that includes medical repatriation.

Visitors will need protection against malaria as well as insect repellent and suitable clothing to discourage mosquito bites. There are infrequent outbreaks of cholera, which can be exacerbated during water shortages, and Lassa fever can be contracted in Kenema and in the east of the country. Vaccination against rabies and yellow fever is recommended, but all current vaccination requirements should be checked well in advance of travel.

Water should be boiled or bought in sealed bottles. Only powdered or tinned milk should be used.

Money: Credit cards are not accepted in Sierra Leone and all foreign exchange (preferably in US dollars or pounds sterling) must be through the banks and official exchange offices. However, visitors should be aware that exchange opportunities are limited. Banking hours are Mon–Thur 0800–1330 and Fri 0800–1400.

There were 40,000 tourist arrivals in 2005.

Further information

Office of the President of the Republic of Sierra Leone: www.statehouse.gov.sl

Parliament: www.sl-parliament.org

Bank of Sierra Leone: www.bsl.gov.sl

Commonwealth Secretariat: www.thecommonwealth.org

Commonwealth of Nations: www.commonwealth-of-nations.org/Sierra_Leone

Singapore

KEY FACTS

Joined Commonwealth:	1965
Population:	5,086,000 (2010)
GDP p.c. growth:	3.9% p.a. 1990–2010
UN HDI 2011:	world ranking 26
Official languages:	English, Chinese (Mandarin), Malay, Tamil
Time:	GMT plus 8hr
Currency:	Singapore dollar (S$)

Geography

Area:	699 sq km
Coastline:	193km
Capital:	Singapore

The name 'Singapore' derives from the Sanskrit *Singa Pura* ('City of the Lion'). Situated in South-East Asia and lying just north of the equator, the Republic of Singapore is separated from Peninsular Malaysia by the narrow Johor Straits (1km wide), crossed by a causeway. A number of smaller islands are included within its boundaries and a few kilometres to the south are islands belonging to Indonesia.

Area: Land area 699 sq km, including 63 small islands.

Topography: The land is flat apart from low hills (highest point is Bukit Timah at 163m). In the north-east large areas of swamp have been reclaimed. The island is drained by a number of small streams.

Climate: A hot and humid tropical climate, without defined seasons. Heavy showers November to January.

Environment: The most significant environmental issues are industrial pollution and seasonal smoke/haze resulting from forest fires in Indonesia; and the finite land and freshwater resources to support a very high population density.

Did you know...

Singapore has won the annual Commonwealth Essay Competition nine times since 1983 when it was launched; no other country has won more than three times.

Singapore is by far the most densely populated country in the Commonwealth.

Scholarships for postgraduate study in integrative science and engineering are awarded by Singapore to citizens of other Commonwealth countries under the Commonwealth Scholarship and Fellowship Plan.

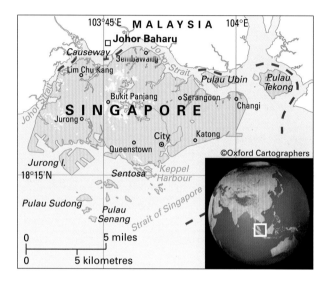

©Oxford Cartographers

Vegetation: Outside conservation areas, much of the natural dense forest and swamp flora have been cleared, although there is extensive planting on any spare ground in urban areas, and Singapore aims to be a 'garden city state'. To control the impact of industry and urban development, environmental regulations are strict. Forest covers 3% of the land area and there was no significant loss of forest cover during 1990–2010. Arable land comprises 1% of the total land area.

Wildlife: The last tiger was shot in 1932. Most of the animals found in Singapore are confined to the rainforest area of the nature reserves and include the flying lemur, squirrels and the long-tailed macaque. Despite the urbanisation of the country, there are over 300 species of birds.

Main towns: Singapore City, Jurong, Bukit Panjang, Serangoon, Katong and Changi.

Transport: There are 3,260km of roads, all paved, with 118 flyovers, the longest of which is the 2.1km Keppel Viaduct. The 42km Pan-Island Expressway is the longest road. Traffic congestion became a major problem and private traffic is rationed. A limited number of permits to put a vehicle on the public roads is auctioned every month, greatly increasing the cost of running a car. Traffic in the central business district is further discouraged by a system of tolls, policed electronically.

The Mass Rapid Transit System (MRT) connects the city with all residential areas and the international airport, serving more than 40 stations. A railway across the Straits of Johor causeway connects the island with the Peninsular Malaysian railway system and beyond to Thailand.

Singapore has an excellent harbour and is one of the world's busiest ports. It comprises six terminals, a container port and several deep-water wharves.

Changi International Airport, 20km east of Singapore City, has three terminals; the third terminal was opened in January 2008.

Society

KEY FACTS 2010

Population per sq km:	7,276
Life expectancy:	81 years

Population: 5,086,000 (2010); 100% lives in urban areas; growth 2.6% p.a. 1990–2010; birth rate 9 per 1,000 people (23 in 1970); life expectancy 81 years (69 in 1970).

The population is predominantly Chinese (77% in 2000 census), with Malays constituting 14% and Indians 8%, and small minorities of Europeans and Eurasians.

Language: English, Chinese (Mandarin), Malay and Tamil are the four official languages. Several other Chinese dialects are spoken, the most prevalent being Hokkien, Cantonese and Teochew. Singaporeans are mostly bilingual, in a mother tongue and English (the administrative language).

Religion: Buddhists 43%, Muslims 15%, Christians 15%, Taoists 9% and Hindus 4% (2000 census).

Health: Public spending on health was 2% of GDP in 2009. Private health care predominates in the primary sector; 80% of hospital care is through public provision. There are more than 20 hospitals, ten of which are government-run. Employees pay into a health insurance fund known as Medisave (which is part of the wider social welfare provision of the Central Provident Fund). The entire population uses an improved drinking water source and adequate sanitation facilities. Infant mortality was 2 per 1,000 live births in 2010, the lowest rate in the Commonwealth and among the lowest in the world (31 in 1960).

Education: Public spending on education was 3.3% of GDP in 2010. By the 1990s, primary education was virtually universal. There are six years of primary education starting at age six. Secondary education is streamed at three levels, according to measured ability, leading to junior college or vocational institutions. The school year starts in January.

The principal universities are National University of Singapore (founded in 1905); Nanyang Technological University (1981, as Nanyang Technological Institute); Singapore Management University (2000); Singapore Institute of Technology (2009); and Singapore University of Technology and Design (due to open in 2012). National University of Singapore has 36,000 students from 100 countries (2011); Nanyang Technological University has 33,000 from 90 countries; and Singapore Management University, some 7,000. SIM University, a private university founded in 2005, offers academic programmes aimed for working professionals. There are several other private universities, most of which in partnership with business schools or technology institutes in Europe or the USA.

Other tertiary institutions include National Institute of Education (founded 1950, as Teachers' Training College, becoming part of Nanyang Technological University in 1991); Singapore Polytechnic (1954); Ngee Ann Polytechnic (1963); Temasek Polytechnic (1990); Nanyang Polytechnic (1992); Institute of Technical Education (1992); and Republic Polytechnic (2002). Co-operation between industry and technological education is well developed, and retraining and education for older adults is an important goal. There is virtually no illiteracy among people aged 15–24.

Media: There are several daily newspapers, among which The *Straits Times* (founded in 1845), *Business Times* and *Today* are in English. Other dailies are in Chinese, Tamil or Malay.

MediaCorp, owned by a state investment agency, provides public TV and radio services.

Some 98% of households have TV sets (2006). There are 760 personal computers (2007) and 710 internet users (2010) per 1,000 people.

Communications: Country code 65; internet domain '.sg'. Mobile phone coverage is excellent. Internet cafes and post offices are located throughout the country.

There are 392 main telephone lines and 1,452 mobile phone subscriptions per 1,000 people (2010).

Public holidays: New Year's Day, Labour Day (1 May), National Day (9 August) and Christmas Day.

Religious and other festivals whose dates vary from year to year include Chinese New Year (three days), Good Friday, Wesak (Buddha Purnima, April/May), Hari Raya Puasa (End of Ramadan), Deepavali (Diwali, October/November) and Hari Raya Haji (Feast of the Sacrifice).

Economy

KEY FACTS 2010

GNI:	US$203.4bn
GNI p.c.:	US$40,070
GDP growth:	6.4% p.a. 2006–10
Inflation:	2.6% p.a. 2006–10

Singapore originally built its prosperity as an entrepot and as an importer of its neighbours' raw materials for processing. At independence in 1965, there was a basic electrical assembly industry and some oil refining. During the 1960s these two sectors took off rapidly. There was a huge expansion of oil refining, and in 1967, attracted by tax incentives, Texas Instruments set up a semiconductor plant. Other electronics companies soon followed, and Singapore swiftly became a world player in the electronics industry. Pharmaceuticals subsequently developed, then financial services and tourism stimulated the economy generally.

Singapore has a high level of government intervention, a strong currency, relatively low inflation, and a long track record of prudent macroeconomic management and outstanding growth. GDP grew by 6.7% p.a. 1980–90 and 7.6% p.a. 1990–2000. Substantial inward investment has stimulated rapid economic development and in the 1990s outward investment increased. Since the latter 1990s policy has aimed to increase the innovative, research and development aspects of electronics, biotechnology and other high-tech sectors, so that Singapore would become a centre where new ideas are born rather than one for executing them through skilled and efficient manufacturing.

In the wake of the Asian economic crisis investment and exports (but also imports) were depressed and growth fell sharply from 8.6% in 1997 to –0.9% in 1998, but recovered sharply in 1999–2000, when there was continued heavy investment in new infrastructure. The stock market was liberalised and banking restrictions were eased to allow more competition from foreign institutions.

Real Growth in GDP

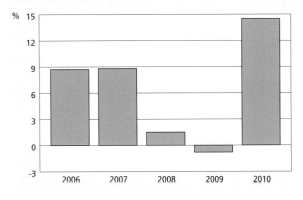

Inflation

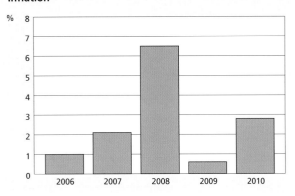

GDP by Sector (2010)

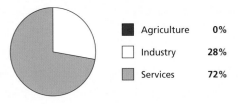

■ Agriculture	0%	
□ Industry	28%	
▨ Services	72%	

But the economy plunged into recession in 2001 – shrinking by 2.3% – as a result of the international downturn in information technology. It recovered quickly and returned to vigorous growth during 2004–07, averaging 8% p.a., before it again stalled in the world economic downturn of 2008–09, showing growth of only 1.5% in 2008 and a contraction of 0.8% in 2009. But the economy bounced back in 2010, when a surge of growth in the last quarter brought the annual growth rate to 14.5%, among the highest in the world for that year; it then grew more slowly in 2011 (about 5%).

Constitution

Status:	Republic
Legislature:	Parliament
Independence:	9 August 1965

Singapore is a republic and a parliamentary democracy, with an elective, non-executive presidency. The constitution came into force on 2 June 1959. It provides for a head of state, a prime minister and a cabinet, and a unicameral Parliament. Elections, under universal adult suffrage and compulsory voting, must be held at least every five years.

The prime minister is the leader of the majority party in parliament, who chooses a cabinet from among the members of parliament.

The Parliament is made up of three types of members: 87 elected members (75 elected in teams of between three and six to represent 14 group representation constituencies and nine in single-member constituencies); up to nine nominated members (NMPs); and up to three non-constituency members (NCMPs) from the opposition political parties. In early 2011 the Eleventh Parliament had 94 members, comprising 84 elected members, nine NMPs and one NCMP.

The president is directly elected by universal adult suffrage for a six-year term. In practice the president no longer has powers of veto over legislation or appointments. The position is largely ceremonial. The first presidential election was held in 1993 but, in 1999 and in 2005, when the election committee, under the very restrictive eligibility rules, found only one candidate to be eligible, there was no election.

Politics

Last elections:	May 2011
Next elections:	2016
Head of state:	President Dr Tony Tan Keng Yam (2011–)
Head of government:	Prime Minister Lee Hsien Loong
Ruling party:	People's Action Party

In an early general election in November 2001, the electorate gave the People's Action Party (PAP) a decisive endorsement, when it took 82 of the 84 elective seats with 75.3% of the votes. The Workers' Party (WP) and the four-party Singapore Democratic Alliance each won one seat.

In August 2004 Goh Chok Tong was succeeded by Lee Hsien Loong, son of Lee Kuan Yew and deputy prime minister since 1990.

The PAP was again returned with 82 seats in the May 2006 general election, receiving 66.6% of the votes. Opposition parties contested 47 seats, and it was the first time more than half the seats were contested.

In the May 2011 general election the PAP won 81 seats and received 60.1% of the votes. Opposition parties contested 82 seats. The WP (six seats and 12.8%) was the only other party to win seats, though the National Solidarity Party received a comparable number of the votes (12.0%).

In a hard-fought presidential contest, in August 2011, former deputy prime minister Tony Tan – with 35.2% of the votes cast – defeated his three rivals; Tan Cheng Bock secured 34.9% of the votes, Tan Jee Say 25.0% and Tan Kin Lian 4.9%. Dr Tan succeeded retiring President S R Nathan on 1 September 2011.

International relations

Singapore is a member of Asia–Pacific Economic Cooperation, Association of Southeast Asian Nations, Indian Ocean Rim Association for Regional Cooperation, Non-Aligned Movement, United Nations and World Trade Organization.

Singapore hosts the headquarters of Asia–Pacific Economic Cooperation.

Traveller information

Local laws and conventions: Possession of even small quantities of drugs can lead to imprisonment, and drug trafficking may result in the death penalty.

It is against the law to smoke in any public place or indoor restaurant or to drop a cigarette end in the street, and those caught will face an immediate fine. It is also prohibited to chew gum on the MRT system and failure to comply will attract an immediate fine.

Handshaking is the usual form of greeting. Visitors should remove their shoes if entering a private home or when visiting a temple or mosque. Dress is generally informal.

Business travellers should dress smartly for meetings and English is spoken in business circles. Appointments should be made and punctuality is important. Business cards are essential, although it is policy for government officials not to use them. Singapore is a popular destination for business conventions and has conference venues with state-of-the-art facilities. Office hours are Mon–Fri 0900–1300 and 1400–1700, Sat 0900–1300.

Immigration and customs: All visitors must have passports valid for six months from the date of arrival in Singapore. Visas are only required by some nationals. The length of stay permitted to foreign nationals also varies, depending on the country of origin, and must be checked well in advance of travel.

There are restrictions on entering Singapore with replica guns, radio communications equipment, weapons and ammunition, as well as fruit, vegetables and fish. Chewing gum and tobacco products must be declared on arrival, and all liquor or tobacco products with 'Singapore Duty Not Paid' on the packaging are prohibited.

A yellow fever vaccination certificate will be required from those arriving from infected areas.

History

Singapore was known to the Javanese as *Temasek* ('Sea Town') in the late 1300s, when Siam (Thailand) and the Majapahit Empire of Java were contending for control of the Malay Peninsula. In 1390 Prince Parameswara, in flight from Majapahit, briefly set himself up as prince of Temasek, but was driven out and fled to Malacca. In the early 1400s Temasek was ruled by Siam, but the Malacca sultanate soon took control of the island. The Portuguese took Malacca in 1511, and the Malaccan admiral established himself in Temasek, or Singapura, building a capital which he called Johor Lama.

In 1587 the Portuguese took and destroyed Johor Lama. They made another punitive expedition to Singapore in 1613, destroying a town at the river-mouth. The island, henceforth sparsely populated, remained partly the property of the Sultan of Johor, partly that of the Temenggong (the Malay ruler of the island). In 1819 these two rulers, for a financial inducement, permitted Sir Stamford Raffles, Lieutenant Governor of Bencoolen, to establish a British trading post on the island. Raffles was impressed by the magnificent harbour, and the island's suitable position for both Far East and local trade.

By 1824 Raffles's move was paying off so well that Britain bought the island from its two rulers. In 1826 it was united with Malacca and Penang as the Straits Settlements, which were made a Crown colony in 1867. In 1869 the Suez Canal was opened, increasing the amount of shipping calling at Singapore. Its prosperity increased further after the 1870s, when Malaysian rubber became one of its important exports.

From the mid-19th century, there was considerable immigration from all over the region. In the early 1920s Britain began constructing a great naval base, suitable for the biggest ships, in the Johor Straits. The base was finished in 1938. From February 1942 until August 1945 Singapore was occupied by the Japanese army. In 1946, separated from the Straits Settlements, Singapore became a colony with a provisional advisory council.

In 1955 Singapore became partially internally self-governing, with a legislative assembly with 25 elected members out of a total membership of 32, and a council of ministers. A speaker presided in the assembly. In 1959 it became a state with its own citizenship and complete internal self-government. The first prime minister was Lee Kuan Yew.

In September 1963 Singapore was incorporated into the Federation of Malaysia. But in August 1965 it left the Federation, by mutual agreement, after months of dispute between it and the federal government, over a variety of issues, including ethnic affairs. On 9 August 1965, Singapore became a separate independent state and joined the Commonwealth. In December 1965, it became a republic with a non-executive president.

The People's Action Party (PAP) was first elected in 1959 and was continuously in power for the rest of the century, in many elections winning every seat. In 1981 the Workers' Party (WP) won one seat in a by-election. Two opposition members were returned in the 1984 elections, one in 1988, and four in 1991.

During this period, Singapore developed a highly sophisticated economy with extensive social services and one of the world's highest rates of GNI per capita.

In 1990 Prime Minister Lee Kuan Yew of the PAP was succeeded by his former deputy Goh Chok Tong, who called elections in August 1991 and was returned to power, though with a reduced majority. In 1991 the presidency was made elective. Ong Teng Cheong won the first presidential election, held in 1993, and S R Nathan was the only candidate in the second presidential poll in August 1999.

The PAP won the general election of January 1997 taking 65% of the total vote, winning 81 seats (including all nine single-member constituencies). The prime minister, the two deputy prime ministers, the senior minister (former Prime Minister Lee) and many other ministers were returned unopposed. The Singapore Democratic Party took no seats, while the Singapore People's Party held its one seat with a decreased majority. The WP held its one seat with an increased majority, and its leader was offered a non-constituency seat.

Travel within the country: Traffic drives on the left hand side and visitors can use a national driving licence for stays of up to one month. For longer visits, an international driving permit is required. On entering Singapore, drivers are required to pay ERP (Electronic Road Pricing) – a system based on the principle of 'pay as you use'. Driving under the influence of alcohol can lead to imprisonment.

The MRT, one of the most advanced metro systems in the world, operates daily in and around Singapore offering inexpensive, fast and comfortable travel.

Taxis are widely available; they can be picked up from outside hotels and official ranks, or flagged down in the street. Fares are metered. Trishaws are also found in Singapore.

Travel health: Comprehensive medical insurance is recommended for all travellers, as health care is exceptionally good but can be very expensive. Visitors should also pack enough medication to last their stay, as some prescribed drugs are unavailable in Singapore. Dengue fever occurs in Singapore, so visitors should take insect repellent and suitable clothing to protect themselves from mosquito bites.

Money: Credit cards are widely accepted, and US dollars, Australian dollars, yen and sterling can be used at most major retail outlets. Travellers cheques can be cashed in most banks on presentation of a passport. Banking hours are Mon–Fri 1000–1500, Sat 0930–1300.

There were 9,161,000 tourist arrivals in 2010.

Further information

Government of Singapore: www.gov.sg

Parliament: www.parliament.gov.sg

Monetary Authority of Singapore: www.mas.gov.sg

Commonwealth Secretariat: www.thecommonwealth.org

Commonwealth of Nations: www.commonwealth-of-nations.org/Singapore

Solomon Islands

KEY FACTS

Joined Commonwealth:	1978
Population:	538,000 (2010)
GDP p.c. growth:	–1.0% p.a. 1990–2010
UN HDI 2011:	world ranking 142
Official language:	English
Time:	GMT plus 11hr
Currency:	Solomon Islands dollar (SI$)

Geography

Area:	28,370 sq km
Coastline:	5,310km
Capital:	Honiara

Solomon Islands, an archipelago in the south-west Pacific, consists of a double chain of rocky islands and some small coral islands. The major islands are Guadalcanal, Choiseul, Santa Isabel, New Georgia, Malaita and Makira (or San Cristobal). Vanuatu is the nearest neighbour to the south-east where the archipelago tapers off into a series of smaller islands. Its nearest neighbour to the west is Papua New Guinea. The country comprises the capital territory of Honiara and nine provinces, namely Central (provincial capital Tulagi), Choiseul (Taro Island), Guadalcanal (Honiara), Isabel (Buala), Makira and Ulawa (Kirakira), Malaita (Auki), Rennell and Bellona (Tigoa), Temotu (Lata), Western (Gizo).

Topography: The islands are remarkable for their steep rugged mountains, of which Makarakomburu (on Guadalcanal Island) is the highest at 2,293m. There are also several atolls and reef islands, plus several dormant and two active volcanoes. The rivers are fast-flowing and not navigable.

Climate: Equatorial; hot and humid. During the rainy season (November to April), there are fierce tropical storms – for example, Cyclone Zoë in December 2002, which devastated the isolated islands of Tikopia and Anuta.

Did you know...

The Commonwealth Youth Programme South Pacific Centre is based in Honiara.

The country is an archipelago consisting of a double chain of rocky islands and some small coral islands; the rocky islands are remarkable for their steep rugged mountains, of which the highest, Makarakomburu, on Guadalcanal Island, rises to 2,293m. Some 79% of Solomon Islands is covered by forest, though this area declined at 0.2% p.a. 1990–2010.

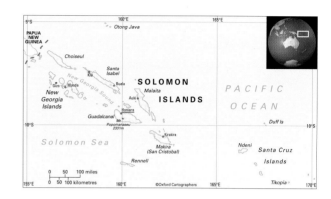

Environment: The most significant environmental issues are deforestation, soil erosion, and that much of the surrounding coral reef is dead or dying.

Vegetation: Forest covers 79% of the land, with dense tropical rainforest occurring on most islands, this percentage having declined at 0.2% p.a. 1990–2010. There are large tracts of rough grass on the northern side of Guadalcanal and Nggela Sule. Parts of the coast are swampy, supporting extensive mangrove forests. Elsewhere, the coast is dominated by coconut palms. Hardwoods now grown for timber include mahogany, acacia and teak.

Wildlife: Indigenous mammals are small and include opossums, bats and mice. There are crocodiles in the mangrove swamps and sea turtles nest on the shores from November to February. Birdlife (more than 150 species) includes many species of parrot and incubator bird.

Main towns: Honiara (capital, pop. 63,300 in 2010) on Guadalcanal, Auki (6,800) on Malaita, Munda (4,900) on New Georgia, Gizo (4,500) on Gizo in the New Georgia Islands, Uruuru (3,300) on Malaita, Buala (2,800) on Santa Isabel, Yandina (2,600) on Mbanika in the Russell Islands, Kirakira (2,000) on Makira, Tulagi (1,700) on Nggela Sule, Taro Island (1,200), Lata (630) on Ndeni in the Santa Cruz Islands and Tigoa (580) on Rennell and Bellona.

Transport: There are 1,390km of roads (mainly on Guadalcanal and Malaita), 2.4% paved, with some 470km of main roads, the rest private rural-access roads. The terrain is mountainous and there is heavy rainfall making road conditions unpredictable.

The international ports are Honiara (on Guadalcanal) and Yandina (on Rennell Island); other significant ports are Gizo and Noro (on New Georgia). Ferries ply between the islands. The international airport is at Henderson Field, 13km east of Honiara.

Society

KEY FACTS 2010

Population per sq km:	19
Life expectancy:	67 years
Net primary enrolment:	81%

MINISTRY OF COMMUNICATION AND AVIATION, SOLOMON ISLANDS

Solomon Islands Telecommunication and ICT
Connecting our people to each other and the world

'The telecommunications industry is important to the future economic growth and stability of Solomon Islands. The Telecommunications Commission has a challenging goal to ensure that Solomon Islanders have access to a wide array of affordable and high quality telecommunications service.'

Telecommunications Commission of the Solomon Islands (TCSI)
The role of TCSI is to regulate the telecommunications sector in the Solomon Islands.

Its main emphasis is to ensure that competition is allowed to flourish, which should result in the widespread availability of diverse and affordable services. It also manages key regulatory resources, such as access to radio frequencies needed by many telecommunications networks, the numbering plan by which telephone numbers are assigned, and the registry for the '.sb' internet domain; licensing telecommunications providers and providing advice to the government on telecoms policy, including how best to serve the geographically remote and the economically disadvantaged.

Solomon Islands Telecommunications and ICT Development Project – WORLD BANK
The Telecommunications Technical Assistance Project aims to facilitate increased access to a wide variety of reliable and affordable telecommunications services for the majority of the Solomon Islands population through efficient and well-regulated competition. There are four components to the project:

- **Sector policy support**
  This component comprises technical assistance for the Ministry of Communications and Aviation, in consultation with other ministries and agencies as appropriate, to develop a policy capability for telecommunications, and Information and Communication Technologies (ICT) in a broader sense.
- **Regulatory support**
  This component comprises operational support as well as advisory assistance and capacity-building for the telecommunications commission.
- **Technical assistance for universal access**
  This component will likely commence once the commercial rollout of telecommunications infrastructure and services is more clearly established. The programme will be sustained through the use of the two percent universal access levy established under the act which will be activated after 2014.
- **Project management**

AVIATION NEWS
Solomon Islands is likely to sign a new agreement with Airport Fiji to look after its upper air space by 2013 under a new partnership deal.

The Hon. Mr Walter Folatalu, Minister

Contact
Mr Francis Lomo
Permanent Secretary
Ministry of Communication and Aviation,
Solomon Islands
P.O. Box G8
Honiara
Solomon Islands
Tel: +677 3 6109
Fax: +677 2 8620/3 6108
fflomo@gmail.com

For more information about our operations, please visit www.tci.org.sb

Population: 538,000 (2010); 19% lives in urban areas; growth 2.8% p.a. 1990–2010; birth rate 32 per 1,000 people (46 in 1970); life expectancy 67 years (54 in 1970).

About 95% of the people are Melanesian, 3% Polynesian and 1% Micronesian (1999 census). There is a small expatriate population.

Language: The official language is English; an English-based Creole, Pidgin, is the most widely spoken language. There are more than 80 indigenous languages.

Religion: Mainly Christians (Church of Melanesia 33%, Roman Catholics 19%, South Seas Evangelicals 17%, Seventh Day Adventists 11%, United Church 10%; 1999 census).

Health: Public spending on health was 5% of GDP in 2009. The government runs six hospitals, as well as clinics and clinical aid posts. The churches run two hospitals as well as clinics. Infant mortality was 23 per 1,000 live births in 2010 (120 in 1960). Malaria remains the main health problem.

Education: There are six years of primary education and seven years of secondary. The school year starts in January.

Solomon Islands College of Higher Education offers teacher-training, finance, nursing and secretarial studies, and a range of technical subjects related to Solomon Islands' economy such as marine and fisheries studies, forestry and agriculture. The college also gives some first-year university courses. Solomon Islands is a partner in the regional University of the South Pacific, which has its main campus in Suva, Fiji, and a campus in Honiara, Solomon Islands.

The years of conflict during the early 2000s severely damaged and depleted the education system. In many parts of the country there was little or no access to educational facilities, as some schools were forced to contract or close. Following the restoration of order in 2003, the government set about rehabilitating and reforming the country's education system. With assistance from the governments of Australia and New Zealand, the government has been able to rehabilitate infrastructure, re-establish in-service training and provide teaching materials to primary schools.

Media: *Solomon Star* is a daily newspaper, and *Solomon Times* and *Solomons Voice* are weekly.

Radio is the main source of information for most people. Solomon Islands Broadcasting Corporation provides a national public radio service.

There are 46 personal computers (2005) and 50 internet users (2010) per 1,000 people.

Communications: Country code 677; internet domain '.sb'. Mobile phone coverage is limited to Honiara, Gizo and Munda. There are a few internet cafes in Honiara and Gizo.

There are 16 main telephone lines and 56 mobile phone subscriptions per 1,000 people (2010).

Public holidays: New Year's Day, Queen's Official Birthday (June), Independence Day (7 July), Christmas Day and National Day of Thanksgiving (26 December). Each province has its own holiday, some of which continue for several days.

Religious and other festivals whose dates vary from year to year include Good Friday, Easter Monday and Whit Monday.

Economy

KEY FACTS 2010

GNI:	US$552m
GNI p.c.:	US$1,030
GDP growth:	6.1% p.a. 2006–10
Inflation:	8.7% p.a. 2006–10

Solomon Islands' economy is based on agriculture, forestry and fisheries, which together account for around 40% of GDP and provide employment for the majority of the population. GDP grew by 6.4% p.a. 1979–89.

Agricultural resources are limited; only 35% of the land is suitable for cultivation and pressure on land is leading to soil impoverishment. Production can be affected by tropical storms.

During the 1990s fishing was a developing industry, encouraged by the declaration of a 320-km exclusive maritime zone. Forestry also contributed strongly, providing the dominant export product. The government was working with export partners and CDC Capital Partners to halt the depletion of forests.

Real Growth in GDP

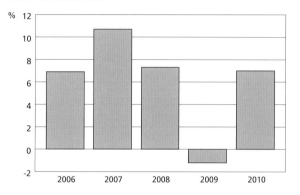

Inflation

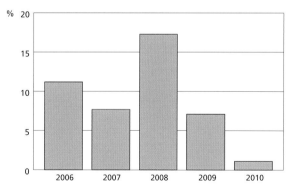

GDP by Sector (2010)

MINISTRY OF MINES, ENERGY and RURAL ELECTRIFICATION

Harnessing renewable energy resources of Solomon Islands

Solomon Islands' high dependency on imported diesel for its electricity sector has caused great difficulties, including a very high electricity tariff which impedes improvements in the welfare of its citizens and the expansion of manufacturing and services industries needed to broaden the economic base of the country.

The state-owned power utility, Solomon Islands Electricity Authority [SIEA], provides electricity to the urban centres of the country, which consists of around 20 per cent of the population. The rural-based population are not connected to the national network grid due to the uneconomical viability for such capital investment, especially the high cost of diesel.

The Government has committed itself to harness its renewable energy resources to substitute imported diesel.

Locally produced coconut oil as fuel for power generation

A biofuel pilot project in Auki, Malaita Province has been established with support from the Asian Development Bank under a regional initiative that aims at improving access to renewable energy in the Pacific. GHD Consultants of Australia have been contracted to assist SIEA with the design and implementation of the project.

Locally produced coconut oil (CNO) is being developed as a substitute for imported diesel. The project design is based on a thorough analysis of biofuel experiences in the Pacific region and elsewhere. It uses locally manufactured components and aims at transferring all required technological skills to SIEA. The lay-out of the biofuel facility includes a new 340 kW generator set. The unit is essentially a standard base load generator with some minor modifications such as a low load warning and additional fuel filter. The CNO is analysed in an on-site laboratory and then processed in a filtration unit that removes any residual water using a vacuum process. The CNO fuel is stored in a heated day tank to ensure that there is no solidification. Heating the fuel prior to combustion also helps to minimise the risk of incomplete combustion caused by the higher viscosity of the CNO.

The SIEA distribution system in Auki has expanded as part of the project to electrify more than 200 families who currently lack access to electricity. The connection to the grid has brought benefits to the community for accessing a safer, more reliable and higher quality energy source than compared to kerosene, which provides low quality luminosity and poses respiratory health risks.

left:

(top) CNO production by a local entrepreneur in Auki Town.
Picture by Gerhard Zieroth

(below) Biofuel unit at Auki Power Station.
Picture by Gerhard Zieroth

During a six-month trial period, the pilot project will systematically explore all options of using highly purified CNO as a substitute fuel. Intensive on-the-job operator training will be provided to ensure a full transfer of technology and understanding. Initially, the new fuel is introduced as in a mixture of diesel and CNO. Using blends with 20 per cent CNO allows operators to build confidence with the new fuel and it is planned to move to 100 per cent CNO use as soon as SIEA staff is familiarised with the technology. The design of the biofuel plant allows both the use of blends and of 100 per cent CNO in what is called 'dual fuel' mode. In this mode, the generator is started up on diesel oil and switched to 100 per cent CNO once the engine temperature stabilises and loads above 60 per cent of the engine's nominal rating are encountered. Switch over is manual but the plant can be converted to automatic switch over as required.

After the initial trial period, a comprehensive evaluation of the results and experiences will be performed. This evaluation will include a comparative analysis of all costs involved in the use of CNO. All technical parameters will also be monitored, and at the end of the trial period the engine will be stripped and evaluated for CNO induced problems such as carbon deposits at injector nozzles and combustion chambers. The evaluation will determine under which market conditions, CNO can be considered as a viable substitute fuel for SIEA.

Hydro-power for Honiara

Meanwhile, the Detailed Feasibility Study funded by the European Investment Bank (EIB) on the 14-15MW Tina River hydropower scheme will be completed in the near future.

The Tina River hydro-power project will be an IPP scheme and the Government hopes to see this project go through as the first ever CDM project in the country.

Contact

Mr John Korinihona
Director of Energy
Ministry of Mines, Energy and Rural Electrification
P.O. Box G37
Honiara
Solomon Islands
john.korinihona@yahoo.com

Tel: + 677 2 1522
Fax: +677 2 5811
www.parliament.gov.sb

right:
Mr Henry Pika,
Permanent Secretary

right:
(top) Biofuel generator
at Auki Power.
Picture by Gerhard Zieroth

(below) Operator training
provided by GHD Consultants
expert at Auki Power Station.
Picture by Gerhard Zieroth

Although public expenditure remained high, resulting in budget deficits and growth of public debt, economic growth was consistently good in the 1980s and 1990s until 1997 when the economy went into recession, due largely to the impact of the Asian economic downturn and consequent falls in export revenues. An economic reform programme was launched in early 1998 with the emphasis on public-spending cuts.

Recovery began in 1998–99, but was soon reversed as political unrest intensified: plant and equipment, along with infrastructure, were damaged; the gold mine at Gold Ridge was closed; and the economy collapsed, shrinking by 14% in 2000, 9% in 2001 and 2.4% in 2002, when the government was depending on aid to finance both the peace agreement (including economic development of the island of Malaita) and the budget.

After six years of recession the economy returned to vigorous growth in 2003. Strong growth continued in 2004–08, averaging 7.3% p.a. But the economy remains relatively small and undiversified and very dependent on exports of timber and logs. Aid constitutes some 44% of GNI (2009), and logging has reportedly been pursued at an unsustainable rate. The strong growth of the mid-2000s was halted in the world economic downturn of 2008–09, falling from 7.3% in 2008 to a contraction of 1.2% in 2009, and bouncing back with 7% in 2010.

Constitution

Status:	Monarchy under Queen Elizabeth II
Legislature:	National Parliament
Independence:	7 July 1978

Solomon Islands is a constitutional monarchy, with Queen Elizabeth II as head of state. The Queen is represented by a governor-general, who must be a citizen of the country and is elected by parliament. The National Parliament is unicameral, with 50 seats. Elections are held every four years on the basis of universal adult suffrage. The prime minister, who is chosen by parliament, must be an MP; the cabinet is chosen by the prime minister and holds executive power. Honiara has a town council for local government, and there are provincial administrations in the nine provinces.

Politics

Last elections:	August 2010
Next elections:	2014
Head of state:	Queen Elizabeth II, represented by governor-general, Sir Frank Ofagioro Kabui (2009–)
Head of government:	Prime Minister Gordon Darcy Lilo
Ruling party:	National Coalition for Reform and Advancement

History

Archaeological evidence suggests that the Solomon Islands have been inhabited since 1000 BC. European penetration began in 1568 when the Spaniard Alvaro de Mendana, exploring from South America, spent half a year in the islands. Believing that gold was present, he gave them the name of Solomon's Islands, after the legendary King Solomon's mines. During the 18th century a few European explorers visited the Islands, but made little impression on the inhabitants who lived in small isolated communities, often at war with one another.

In the next century, as Europe's penetration of the Pacific advanced, naval ships began to call, and missionaries and traders arrived. From 1870, the islands were subjected to 'blackbirding' (attacks little different from slave raids), when kidnappers from Queensland and Fiji abducted Solomon Islanders as labour for the sugar plantations. The Solomon Islanders fought back fiercely, leading to slaughter on both sides.

In 1893 Britain made the South Solomons (Guadalcanal, Savo, Malaita, San Cristobal, the New Georgia group) a Protectorate, to which the Santa Cruz group was added in 1898 and 1899. In 1900 Germany ceded to Britain the Shortlands group, Santa Isabel, Choiseul and Ontong Java. With the establishment of the copra industry in 1908, and the spread of Christianity throughout the islands, raiding and fighting as a way of life began to die out, and mission schools provided a basic educational system.

The Solomon Islands were occupied by the Japanese army during the Second World War, and counter-invaded by American and Allied troops. There was almost continuous fighting from 1941 to 1943, and Guadalcanal was the scene of a six-month battle which was crucial to the outcome of the war in the Pacific. The Solomon Islanders fought on the side of the Allies, achieving renown for their courage in battle, and several were subsequently decorated.

After the war, the movement for self-determination gathered strength. There was political unrest in Malaita and elsewhere, which was eased by the setting up, from 1952 onwards, of local government councils, elected by universal adult suffrage.

In 1974 the governing council approved a constitution that provided for a governor and a legislative assembly of 24 elected members. In 1975 the name 'British Solomon Islands Protectorate' was formally changed to the present name. On 2 January 1976 the country became internally self-governing, proceeding to full independence on 7 July 1978.

Solomon Islands came to independence under the leadership of Peter Kenilorea (later knighted), who had three periods in office, the first two consecutive. He was succeeded by his deputy Ezekiel Alebua in 1986. Other prime ministers since independence include Solomon Mamaloni, leading the Solomon Islands National Unity, Reconciliation and Progressive Party (1981–84, 1989–93 and 1994–97), and Francis Billy Hilly, leading the National Coalition Partners (1993–94).

At the general election in August 1997 Prime Minister Mamaloni's main challenger was Bartholomew Ulufa'alu, leading a new group, the Alliance for Change, comprising several small parties and independents. The new coalition won, and Ulufa'alu became prime minister.

In July 1998, while parliament was in recess, Ulufa'alu dismissed Finance Minister Manasseh Sogavare and brought two members of the opposition Group for National Security and Advancement into the cabinet. Sogavare then led a group of six MPs to join the opposition, and though he could barely command a majority in parliament, Ulufa'alu appeared determined to continue in government.

➤

Solomon Islands' politics has been characterised by fluid coalitions of parties and independents.

After conclusion of the peace agreement of February 2001 armed militia continued to be at large and many weapons remained in the hands of former militia members. A general election was nevertheless held in December 2001; Prime Minister Manasseh Sogavare and the ruling People's Progressive Party (PPP) were heavily defeated, retaining only three seats, and only 19 members of the previous parliament held their seats. The People's Alliance Party, led by former deputy prime minister Sir Allan Kemakeza, won 20 seats and the Solomon Islands Alliance for Change (SIAC) 12. Kemakeza formed a coalition with the Association of Independent Members (AIM) led by Snyder Rini (finance minister in the PPP government), and Kemakeza was elected prime minister by parliament.

In the April 2006 election – with Commonwealth observers present – 16 members of the government lost their seats. Kemakeza retained his seat but his People's Alliance Party was much reduced while Snyder Rini's AIM did well, with 13 newly elected members. Rini was subsequently elected prime minister by the new parliament. Rioting then broke out and a large portion of Chinatown in Honiara was destroyed by fire. In the same month Rini stood down when he no longer had the support of the majority of members of parliament and early in May 2006

parliament elected Manasseh Sogavare (leader of the Social Credit Party) prime minister.

Sogavare was ousted in December 2007 in a parliamentary vote of no confidence, which was precipitated by the defection in November of nine government ministers. The leader of the recently established Coalition for National Unity and Rural Advancement, and education minister in the Sogavare administration, Derek Sikua, became prime minister.

In the fourth round of voting, in June 2009, parliament elected Sir Frank Kabui to succeed Sir Nathaniel Waena as governor-general with effect from July.

In the election on 4 August 2010 the Solomon Islands Democratic Party, led by Steven Abana, secured 14 of the 50 seats in the National Parliament; the numerous other parties won 19 seats; and independents, the rest. The Commonwealth observer group present at the election reported that the people had freely exercised their democratic right.

In the parliamentary vote that followed the general election, Danny Philip, leader of the Solomon Islands Reform and Democratic Party (a coalition of parties and independent members), was chosen as prime minister, polling 26 votes; his only rival, Steven Abana, won the support of 23 members.

➤ Intercommunal conflict

In the latter part of 1998, growing intercommunal tensions in Guadalcanal Province erupted into violence. The indigenous people of Guadalcanal were concerned about continuing settlement on the island of large numbers of Solomon Islanders from other islands and especially from Malaita, who dominated the national public service and the private sector in the capital, Honiara, located in Guadalcanal.

During 1999 the violence intensified and many thousands of Malaitans (including many long-standing residents of Guadalcanal) were driven to take refuge in Honiara or return to Malaita. In June a state of emergency was declared and, at the government's request, the Commonwealth Secretary-General sent Sitiveni Rabuka, former prime minister of Fiji, to broker a peace deal. Agreement was reached on restoring peace and on the longer-term achievement of a more equitable ethnic balance in the national public service and the police force. A Commonwealth peace-monitoring group was to be provided.

Commonwealth-brokered peace

Following further unrest, in August 1999 Rabuka brokered a new peace agreement (known as the Panatina Agreement) which included a reduction in police presence in Guadalcanal Province with effect from mid-August. In September 1999 the state of emergency was ended and in October a Commonwealth peace-monitoring group began supervision of the handover of arms by the militants.

However, ethnic unrest continued into 2000, led by opposing militia – Malaita Eagle Force and Isatabu Freedom Movement. In

June 2000 the Malaita Eagle Force took the prime minister and governor-general captive and compelled the prime minister to resign. When it was able to convene a quorum of members on an Australian warship, parliament elected Manasseh Sogavare as prime minister and he formed a new government.

With the support of the Australian and New Zealand Governments, the warring militia and the national and provincial governments engaged in a peace process leading in October 2000 to the signing of a peace agreement in Townsville, Australia. This provided for a general amnesty for all members and former members of the militia on the condition that they hand in their arms within a given timeframe, and economic development of the island of Malaita. Former militia members were to be involved in the collection of arms and the return of law and order, and an international monitoring team was to supervise the handover of arms.

Sporadic outbreaks of violence continued. Another peace agreement was concluded in February 2001 but still there were armed militia at large and many weapons remained in the hands of former militia members.

In June 2003 Solomon Islands' then prime minister, Sir Allan Kemakeza, with the unanimous approval of parliament and the support of regional leaders, accepted Australia's offer to lead an international intervention force to restore law and order. The force of some 2,200 soldiers and police from Australia, New Zealand, Fiji, Kiribati, Papua New Guinea, Samoa, Tonga and Vanuatu, began operations in July 2003. Its first priority was to disarm the various militias and restore order. By 2005 the force had been reduced to a few hundred.

In November 2011, following defections from the ruling coalition, Prime Minister Philip resigned. In the parliamentary vote that followed former finance minister Gordon Darcy Lilo was chosen to be prime minister with the support of 29 of the 49 members who voted.

International relations

Solomon Islands is a member of the African, Caribbean and Pacific Group of States, Pacific Community, Pacific Islands Forum, United Nations and World Trade Organization.

Traveller information

Local laws and conventions: There is no tipping in Solomon Islands and visitors should honour this custom. Drug use or possession is illegal and can lead to imprisonment. Women visitors should not enter areas exclusively reserved for men. Swearing is a crime, and those caught may face a fine or jail sentence. Crossing private land may incur a fee to the landowner.

Dress is generally casual but modest, particularly for women. For business meetings ties are not required. English and French are widely spoken in business circles, and the best time to visit on business is from May to October. Office hours are Mon–Fri 0800–1200 and 1300–1630; Sat 0730–1200.

Immigration and customs: All passports must be valid for six months from date of entry. Visas are not needed by most nationals but visa requirements should be checked well in advance of travel.

It is prohibited to import weapons and offensive literature. Only fruit and vegetables from New Zealand can be brought into the country.

A yellow fever vaccination certificate is required by all those arriving from infected areas.

Travel within the country: Traffic drives on the left and visitors can use their national driving licence. Car hire is available through hotels in Honiara.

Travel to other islands is by domestic scheduled or charter flights and there are also ferry services. The more remote islands are serviced by small, motorised 'canoes'.

There is a limited bus network, and taxis are only available in Auki and Honiara. Fares should be agreed before travel.

Travel health: Visitors should ensure they have comprehensive medical insurance and should carry a basic medical kit when travelling to the more remote areas. Malaria is endemic, and insect repellent and suitable clothing should be taken to protect against mosquito bites.

All water for drinking or making ice should first be boiled or sterilised. Milk is unpasteurised and should be boiled before use.

Money: Automated foreign exchange machines are available in Honiara. Travellers cheques can be exchanged at most banks, and major credit cards are accepted in hotels and tourist resorts. Honiara has three ATMs. Banking hours are Mon–Fri 0830–1500.

There were 9,400 tourist arrivals in 2005.

Further information

Office of the Prime Minister and Cabinet of Solomon Islands: www.pmc.gov.sb

National Parliament: www.parliament.gov.sb

Central Bank of Solomon Islands: www.cbsi.com.sb

Commonwealth Secretariat: www.thecommonwealth.org

Commonwealth of Nations: www.commonwealth-of-nations.org/Solomon_Islands

South Africa

KEY FACTS

Joined Commonwealth:	1931 (Statute of Westminster; left in 1961, rejoined in 1994)
Population:	50,133,000 (2010)
GDP p.c. growth:	1.3% p.a. 1990–2010
UN HDI 2011:	world ranking 123
Official languages:	11 most widely spoken
Time:	GMT plus 2hr
Currency:	rand (R)

Geography

Area:	1,221,038 sq km
Coastline:	2,800km
Capital:	Tshwane (formerly Pretoria)

The Republic of South Africa has land borders with: Namibia, Botswana, Zimbabwe, Mozambique and Swaziland. Its sea borders are with the South Atlantic and Indian Oceans. Lesotho is enclosed within its land area. The country comprises nine provinces: Eastern Cape (provincial capital Bhisho), Free State (Bloemfontein), Gauteng (Johannesburg), KwaZulu–Natal (Pietermaritzburg), Limpopo (Polokwane), Mpumalanga (Nelspruit), Northern Cape (Kimberley), North-West (Mafikeng) and Western Cape (Cape Town).

Topography: The southern part of the ancient African plateau forms the centre of South Africa, falling through rolling hills and coastal plains to the coastal belt. The Great Escarpment, containing the Drakensberg and Cape mountain ranges, marks the high edge of the plateau. The plateau lies at an altitude of about 1,500m in the south and east, dipping towards the north and west. On the plateau, land is flat or undulating and dotted with round hills or 'koppies'. The Limpopo and Orange are the major river systems, although Natal and parts of the Cape are traversed by fast-flowing, seasonal rivers with coastal lagoons. Surface water is in short supply.

Did you know...

Of the many internationally acclaimed South African writers, two – Nadine Gordimer (in 1991) and John Maxwell Coetzee (in 2003) – have Nobel Prizes; and Coetzee (2000) and Manu Herbstein (Best First Book in 2002) have been overall winners in the Commonwealth Writers' Prize.

Scholarships for postgraduate study are awarded by South Africa to citizens of other Commonwealth countries under the Commonwealth Scholarship and Fellowship Plan.

Climate: Climate varies with altitude and continental position: Mediterranean climate in the Western Cape; humid subtropical climate on the northern KwaZulu-Natal coast; continental climate of the highveld; and arid Karoo and Kalahari fringes, with a great temperature range, giving very hot summer days and cold dry nights. The south-east trade winds, blowing first over KwaZulu-Natal, are the principal source of precipitation, falling in summer. Winter rains reach the Western Cape.

Environment: The most significant environmental issues are soil erosion, desertification, air pollution and resulting acid rain, and pollution of rivers from agricultural run-off and urban discharges. In a country with relatively few major rivers and lakes, extensive water conservation and control measures are necessary to keep pace with rapid growth in water usage.

Vegetation: Varies with climate, including temperate hardwood forest, dense coastal bush, Mediterranean scrub (including many varieties of aloes and proteas), vast grasslands of the veld dotted with flat-topped thorn trees, and bushveld scrub. South Africa's native flora have been developed as garden flowers all over the world. Forest covers 8% of the land area, having declined at 1.8% p.a. 1990–2010. Arable land comprises 12% and permanent cropland less than 1% of the total land area.

Wildlife: South Africa's wildlife, among which are the large mammals characteristic of the African grassland, includes species, such as the white rhino, that are endangered elsewhere. The game reserves such as the Kruger and Hluhluwe are considered among the world's best. The wide range of bird-species includes many migrants from the northern hemisphere. South Africa was a founder member of the International Union for the Conservation of Nature and Natural Resources (IUCN).

THE **GATEWAY** TO BUSINESS IN AFRICA AND SADC

If you're considering trading in Africa, you need the best access. Where speed-to-market is a priority. Where you have the competitive edge. Dube TradePort.

Between the southern hemisphere's largest container seaport (in Durban, South Africa) and largest bulk seaport (in Richard's Bay) and home to King Shaka International Airport, Dube TradePort is Africa's first purpose-built aerotropolis.

Transform your supply chain, access African and global markets. Fast!

Dube Cargo Terminal – The most secure, fully-automated cargo terminal in the Southern Hemisphere, with on-site customs and a single handler – Worldwide Freight Services.

TradeZone – A world first with integrated air-cargo services, where freight forwarders and shippers are located in a single facility with direct airside access – which means extremely fast processing and the certainty your cargo will arrive at its destination.

Dube AgriZone: Source the freshest perishables, offer produce with the longest shelf life from the most sophisticated agricultural growing, packing and distribution facility in Africa.

Dube City: The first green precinct in Africa, Dube City will offer a secure, world-class, cosmopolitan, 24-hour business, trade and retail experience.

iConnect: Access the most advanced IT with iConnect – Dube TradePort's dedicated IT and telecoms provider, delivering global connectivity.

For more information:
Tel: +27 32 8140000
www.dubetradeport.co.za

SOUTHERN AFRICA'S PREMIER
AIR LOGISTICS PLATFORM

Main towns: Tshwane (administrative capital, Gauteng, pop. 1.72m in 2010), Cape Town (legislative capital, Western Cape, 3.65m), Durban (KwaZulu–Natal, 3.51m), Johannesburg (Gauteng, 2.06m), Soweto (Gauteng, 1.80m), Nelson Mandela Metropole (Port Elizabeth, Eastern Cape, 1.18m), Pietermaritzburg (KwaZulu–Natal, 937,600), Benoni (Gauteng, 679,100), Welkom (Free State, 614,500), Bloemfontein (judicial capital, Free State, 609,000), Tembisa (Gauteng, 599,700), Boksburg (Gauteng, 488,600), Sihlangu (KwaZulu–Natal, 483,600), Vereeniging (Gauteng, 482,100), East London (Eastern Cape, 456,400), Krugersdorp (Gauteng, 422,900), Botshabelo (Free State, 416,800), Brakpan (Gauteng, 364,100), Richards Bay (KwaZulu–Natal, 335,900), Emalahleni (Mpumalanga, 320,700), Kimberley (Northern Cape, 184,800), Bhisho (Eastern Cape, 148,600), Polokwane (Limpopo, 140,200), Nelspruit (Mpumalanga, 118,600) and Mafikeng (North-West).

Transport: There are 364,130km of roads (17% paved) and 24,490km of railway (about half electrified). This substantial rail network serves not only South Africa with its mining and heavy industries, but also neighbouring countries.

Ports also serve South Africa and its landlocked neighbours: Botswana, Lesotho, Swaziland, Zambia and Zimbabwe. The main commercial ports are at Durban, Port Elizabeth, Cape Town and East London. Durban is the leading port, with capacity for deep-sea ro-ro vessels and a principal terminal of the 3,100km underground oil pipeline.

International airports are at Bloemfontein, Cape Town, Durban, Johannesburg and Port Elizabeth, while East London, Kimberley and Tshwane (Pretoria) are important domestic airports. There are also some 210 licensed aerodromes and 40 heliports.

Society

KEY FACTS 2010

Population per sq km:	41
Life expectancy:	52 years
Net primary enrolment:	90%

Population: 50,133,000 (2010); 62% lives in urban areas and 34% in urban agglomerations of more than 1 million people; growth 1.5% p.a. 1990–2010; birth rate 21 per 1,000 people (38 in 1970); life expectancy 52 years (53 in 1970 and 61 in 1990).

People of African origin constitute 79.0% of the population (2001 census), European origin 9.6%, mixed descent 8.9% ('coloureds') and Asian origin 2.5%. The African linguistic groups comprise Zulu (23.8% of the total population), Xhosa (17.6%), Pedi (9.4%), Tswana (8.2%), Sotho (7.9%), Tsonga (4.4%), Swati (2.7%), Venda (2.3%) and several smaller groups. The 'coloureds' include descendants of slaves brought from Malaya, Indonesia and Madagascar, and the Khoi-Khoi people of the Cape. There is also a substantial flow of inward migration of people seeking employment, most from neighbouring countries such as Lesotho, Mozambique and Zimbabwe.

Language: Official languages are Afrikaans, English, Ndebele, Sesotho sa Leboa (Northern Sotho), Sesotho, Setswana, siSwati, Tsonga, Venda, Xhosa and Zulu.

Religion: Christians 80% (2001 census), with a wide range of denominations; and minorities of Muslims, Hindus and Jews. Traditional and Christian forms of worship are often blended.

Health: Public spending on health was 3% of GDP in 2009. Durban Academic Hospital in KwaZulu-Natal, four new hospitals in Northern Province and many new health centres were built in the late 1990s. 91% of the population uses an improved drinking water source and 77% have access to adequate sanitation facilities (2009). Infant mortality was 41 per 1,000 live births in 2010 (89 in 1960).

AIDS is a dire problem. In 2009, 17.8% of people aged 15–49 were HIV positive. For many years the government appeared unable to accept the severity of the looming problem and failed to take measures to contain it. By 2000, when it became involved in controversy over its claim that AIDS was not caused by HIV, there were – by some international estimates – more HIV-positive cases in South Africa than any other country. By April 2002, however, the government had committed itself to lead the battle against HIV/AIDS, making antiretroviral drugs available through the health service.

Education: Public spending on education was 6.0% of GDP in 2010. There are nine years of compulsory education starting at age seven. The school year starts in January.

In February 2011, the Council on Higher Education recognised 23 public universities, including 2 concentrating on distance education and 6 universities of technology. It recognised 87 private higher education institutions and a further 27 were provisionally registered. There are some 840,000 students in public higher education institutions, some 130,000 of whom are postgraduate students (2009). Literacy among people aged 15–24 is 98% (2007).

Media: Among the many dailies in English are *Business Day*, *Cape Argus*, *Cape Times*, *The Citizen* and *The Star*. Leading Afrikaans-language dailies are *Beeld* (Johannesburg) and *Die Burger* (Cape Town). The most influential national weeklies are *Financial Mail*, *Mail & Guardian*, *The Sunday Independent* and *Sunday Times*.

State-owned South African Broadcasting Corporation (SABC) provides a comprehensive range of national and regional radio stations covering 11 languages and an external service for a pan-African audience, Channel Africa. There are very many private radio stations. SABC also operates three national TV networks and two pay-TV services. Many private TV channels are available nationally; and private TV network M-Net targets a pan-African audience.

Some 72% of households have TV sets (2009). There are 83 personal computers (2005) and 123 internet users (2010) per 1,000 people.

Communications: Country code 27; internet domain '.za'. Mobile phone coverage extends to most of the country. Internet cafes are located in most parts of the country.

There are 84 main telephone lines and 1,005 mobile phone subscriptions per 1,000 people (2010).

Public holidays: New Year's Day, Human Rights Day (21 March), Freedom Day (27 April), Workers' Day (1 May), Youth Day (16 June), National Women's Day (9 August), Heritage Day (24 September), Day of Reconciliation (16 December), Christmas Day and Day of Goodwill (26 December).

Religious festivals whose dates vary from year to year include Good Friday and Family Day/Easter Monday.

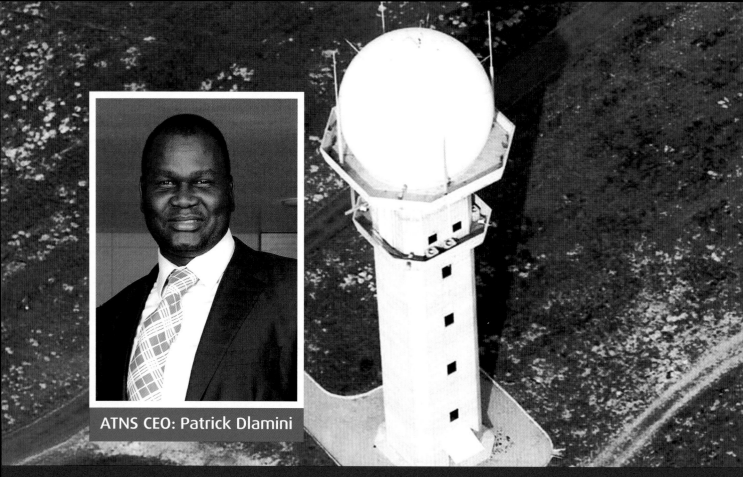

ATNS CEO: Patrick Dlamini

An overview of ATNS and its activities

The Air Traffic and Navigation Services Company Limited (ATNS) was incorporated in terms of the ATNS Act, Act 45 of 1993. Section 4 of the Act mandates ATNS to provide Air Traffic Management Solutions and Associated Services on behalf of the State in accordance with the International Civil Aviation Organisation (ICAO) Standards and Recommended Practices and the South African Civil Aviation (SACAA) Regulations and Technical Standards.

The business is anchored firmly in air traffic management and aviation safety; more specifically, safe, secure, efficient and cost-effective air transport for South Africa, and all people and materials travelling to, from, and within South Africa. In practice, this focus means that ATNS' sphere of influence increasingly extends over the country's borders, as the nation's reputation for high-quality, and very often innovative air traffic management spreads, both to neighboring

countries and across the continent, including the Indian Ocean region, and ultimately to selected global markets. In many of these regions highly productive partnerships have been formed, although our primary focus remains South Africa. **ATNS has played a major role in making South Africa a safe place to fly to and fly over.**

ATNS provides vital services within the region in which it operates, and its satellite communications coverage stretches from Cape to Cairo, including the Eastern part of Africa. ATNS also provides training for Africa, consultancy services and surveying. These services are provided in some 28 states with our partners who have opted to join us in making Africa a safe destination.

In terms of our mandate, ATNS routinely maintains a thorough understanding of development in the global air traffic management community, staying abreast of innovations in product and service offerings, technological developments

Please visit our website: www.atns.co.za
Email: marketing@atns.co.za
Contact: 0860 ATNS CO (0860 2867 26)
Address: Eastgate Office Park, South Boulevard Road, Block C, Bruma, 2198
 Follow us on Twitter Join us on Facebook

and customer expectations, in order to effectively respond to the needs of selected markets with relevant air traffic management solutions.

ATNS sources, develops, markets, distributes and supports a complete range of air traffic management and navigation services designed to meet the expectations of access, equity, safety, efficiency and affordability, and in this way supports its clients and the air traffic management community at large. **ATNS never takes its eyes off its objectives: to create safe capacity for the users; the need to be cost-efficient; and the need to consider the impact of what we are doing on the environment.**

The company believes it is imperative to stabilize and enhance air traffic management service provision in South Africa in order to create a platform from which ATNS can leverage strategic partnerships, using its global influence as well as harmonizing technologies and methods to become the leading air traffic management service provider in the AFI region. Through the pursuit of excellence it seeks to secure future growth, revenue, profits and influence as a provider of choice.

Key to all objectives is the question of attracting, developing, retaining and appropriately remunerating a diverse and motivated team that has the skills, experience, commitment and the drive to successfully implement this strategy. This success will in turn ensure a well-equipped resource base, benefiting from enhanced financial sustainability in support of increased business and tourism traffic to, from and within South Africa, and the further evolution of global air traffic and navigation and safety plans.

It is increasingly clear that ours is a business of partnerships. The ATNS vision is to create a seamless airspace throughout Africa, so that travelers enjoy the same safety standards wherever they go.

UNLOCKING WINNING PARTNERSHIPS

Desto
business solution provider

Growing competent people for Africa

Desto, established in 1994, is a South African based education and training company, with a related consulting and recruitment house with consultants placed at various local government departments and within the private sector. It is also a Private Further Education and Training (FET) College, registered in 2008.

Desto's core business areas are:

- Education and training services
- Consulting and recruitment services
- Education and training business management consultancy

The strategic direction of Desto is based on the principles of passion, vision, discipline and conscience. Desto's vision is to provide the South African marketplace with competent and skilled people, with hopes of implementing these principles in the rest of Africa.

Desto is focused on quality standards and excellence in service delivery and is ISO 9001/2008 certified. It has a number of accreditations with the South African Government Sector Education and Training Authorities (SETAs).

Desto's training product catalogue includes short courses and full qualifications in the following disciplines:

- Forestry
- Building and Construction
- Welding
- Air-conditioning
- Agriculture
- Adult Basic Educational Training (literacy and numeracy)
- New Venture Creation
- Project Management
- Business Administration
- End User Computing
- Information Technology Technical Support

Desto is accredited and certified to provide training to apprentices and Section 28 trade test candidates in specific designated trades. This includes accreditation and certification to conduct trade tests in accordance with the provisions of the Manpower Training Act of 1981 as amended and *The Conditions of Apprenticeship* as published for the South African Government.

Desto's designated trade offering:

- Air-conditioning and refrigeration
- Boilermaker/plater
- Bricklayer
- Carpenter
- Painter
- Plasterer
- Plumber
- Tiler
- Welder

Learnerships and apprenticeships result in a formal qualification recognised by the South African Government upon successful completion of the defined course modules and necessary tests.

Through its Education and Training Business Management competency, Desto also manages a number of campuses on behalf of public and private sector clients. Not only does it manage the campuses, but it also provides the instructors/facilitators, assessors and moderators.

Desto presents its courses from six campuses, mainly in the central and northern provinces of South Africa.

Desto is passionate about the development of a skilled Southern Africa, and focuses on the development of individuals with the aim to create employability and sustainable skills transfer.

Economy

KEY FACTS 2010

GNI:	US$304.6bn
GNI p.c.:	US$6,090
GDP growth:	3.1% p.a. 2006–10
Inflation:	6.9% p.a. 2006–10

Apartheid left South Africa with unequal distributions of income, distorted patterns of population settlement, imbalances in skills, low productivity and a large and inefficient bureaucracy. Furthermore, in the last decade of the old regime, prolonged recession (from low gold and other commodity prices, high expenditure on security forces, economic sanctions and disinvestment) led to weakening of the economic fabric. GDP grew by 1.0% p.a. 1980–90.

In August 2000, the government announced a programme of privatisation in telecoms, energy and transport, accounting for a substantial part of the state industrial sector. The large state companies would first be restructured and then privatised. But since this programme was opposed by many government supporters progress was slow.

Real Growth in GDP

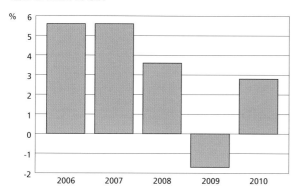

Inflation

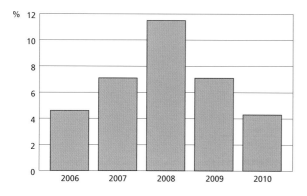

GDP by Sector (2010)

Agriculture	2%
Industry	31%
Services	67%

From the mid-1990s the economy picked up, led by manufacturing, tourism and financial services. It slowed in 1998, then continued to grow steadily from 1999; recording growth of 2.1% p.a. during 1990–2000. The government has promoted a programme of black economic empowerment, notably through the Broad Based Black Economic Empowerment Act (2003), which gives previously marginalised groups opportunities that were not available to them in the apartheid era. Strong domestic demand, as a result of rising disposable income and wealth, has driven the good steady growth during the 2000s, averaging 4.7% p.a. during 2004–08, with relatively low inflation. This long period of good growth was interrupted in the world economic downturn of 2008–09. GDP expanded by 3.6% in 2008 and contracted by 1.7% in 2009, but recovered in 2010 (2.8%) and 2011 (about 3%).

Mining

The country has the world's largest reserves of gold, manganese, platinum, chromium, andalusite, vanadium and alumino-silicates. It has substantial amounts of antimony, asbestos, coal, copper, diamonds, iron ore, lead, oil and gas, titanium, uranium, vermiculite, zinc and zirconium. Mining and minerals processing accounts for more than half of export revenue.

Offshore oil production from fields south-west of the Cape started in 1997, and substantial reserves of natural gas were discovered off the west coast in 2001.

Constitution

Status:	Republic with executive president
Legislature:	Parliament

The constitution came into effect in February 1997. It provides *inter alia* for the supremacy of the constitution, a federal state, a bill of rights, universal adult suffrage, regular multiparty elections, recognition of traditional leaders, 11 official languages, and democracy-buttressing institutions such as the Public Protector, and Commissions for Human Rights and Gender Equality. It also includes a Commission for the Promotion and Protection of the Rights of Cultural, Religious and Linguistic Communities.

The bicameral legislature comprises the 400-seat National Assembly – elected every five years by universal adult suffrage under proportional representation – and the 90-seat National Council of Provinces with direct representation of members of provincial governments. The president is elected by the National Assembly and can serve a maximum of two five-year terms. The deputy president and cabinet are appointed by the president.

Politics

Last elections:	April 2009
Next elections:	2014
Head of state:	President Jacob Gedleyihlekisa Zuma
Head of government:	the president
Ruling party:	African National Congress

In the third democratic general election, in April 2004, the African National Congress (ANC) won a decisive mandate, securing 70% of the votes, while the Democratic Alliance took 12% and the Inkatha Freedom Party 7%. The ANC achieved a majority in seven of the nine provinces and gained the two-thirds majority needed to

Metsimaholo Municipality

Putting our people at the centre of our efforts

Metsimaholo means "big water" in Sesotho and is situated in the Fezile Dabi District in the Free State. The three major towns that form part of Metsimaholo Local Municipality are Sasolburg (Municipal Head Office), Oranjeville and Deneysville.

Mission

Metsimaholo strives to be a leading municipality in delivering effective, affordable and sustainable quality services to its communities.

Vision

Having proper systems and processes; being accountable; ensuring sustainable, affordable and effective service delivery and communication; and capacity building of staff and communities.

Sasolburg

Sasolburg is a large industrial town on the southern banks of the Vaal River in the north of the Free State province. The town owes its existence to the petro-chemical industry that was established in 1954 in order to provide housing and facilities for Sasol (South African Coal, Oil and Gas) employees. Its refinery is one of the only two viable coal-derived oil refineries in the world.

Oranjeville

This town, situated on the banks of the Wilge River, was established during 1919 as a halfway stop for ox wagons between Heilbron, Frankfort and Vereeniging. The landowners eventually named it Oranjeville in honour of the 'Prince of Orange'.

Deneysville

Known as the Gateway to the Vaal Dam this small, rural village was established in 1939. It was named after Deneys Reitz, son of a former Free State President. Being a registered urban conservancy, Deneysville is a bird watcher's haven and it is also not unusual to catch a glimpse of hare, hedgehogs and porcupines in town.

Administration

The Municipal Manager, Mr X.W. Msweli, is the administrative head of the Metsimaholo Local Municipality. As the accounting officer, he has oversight responsibility for all managers. The Municipal Manager is accountable to the Executive Mayor and the Council on administrative matters.

The Metsimaholo Municipality has 36 seats. Following the 2006 local government elections, five political parties are represented in the municipality, namely the African National Congress, the Democratic Alliance, the United Democratic Movement, the Freedom Front Plus, Independent Democrats and the United Independent Front.

Tourism

SASOLBURG

Riemland Eco-Park is perfect for hiking and bird watching. The species of game to be found in the park include zebra, springbok, eland, gemsbok, impala, bontebok, duiker, steenbok, black wildebeest and tsesebe.

A bird sanctuary lies behind the Highveld Garden, where up to 70 different species of Highveld birds can be viewed. In the Vaal park wetland, beautiful and quite rare swallow-tailed bee-eaters have been spotted. Other places of interest:

Etienne Rousseau Theatre
Hiking trails
Botanical gardens
Art gallery
Arts and crafts
Water sports activities on the Vaal River

ORANJEVILLE

Oranjeville is renowned for its water sports activities. It is considered an angling mecca and hosts big national angling competitions. Oranjeville is also home to a large resort west of the town situated on the banks of the Vaal River.

DENEYSVILLE

Deneysville is a peaceful village with a host of restaurants, a crocodile ranch, gallery and art and craft centres. It remains the largest growing town in the Vaal complex. Various water sports and boating activities are on offer, such as *Around the Island Race* and *Sailsure Week*.

Alignment with other spheres of government

The strategic alignment between national, provincial and district service delivery priorities are a critical factor in ensuring that the municipal plans echoes integrated government priorities. Alignment between the Free State Growth and Development Strategy and the Municipality is also considered fundamental in ensuring that the Municipality continues to contribute to the economic development of the province.

Local Economic Development (LED)

- **Metsimaholo LED Strategy** The first draft is out for internal inputs and corrections.
- **LED Forum terms of references** are being compiled for the establishment of the business networking forum.

Social and Labour Projects (SLP) of MLM

Bricks and paving plant
Sasol mining
Poultry and piggery
Business incubator
Anglo Coal
Recycling plant

Contact

Mr Brutus Tshepo Mahlaku
Executive Mayor
Mobile: +27 79 095 5919
Office: +27 16 973 8316 • +27 16 973 8316
Fax: +27 16 976 2817
Email: brutus.mahlaku@metsimaholo.gov.za

Mr Xolela Msweli
Municipal Manager
Mobile: +27 83 447 3703
Office: +27 16 973 8314 • +27 16 973 8314
Fax: +27 16 976 5205
Email: xolela.msweli@metsimaholo.gov.za

DEPARTMENT OF HEALTH, SOUTH AFRICA
A long and healthy life for all South Africans

The focus of the health system's HIV, AIDS and TB programmes will be to provide health services by taking advantage of the re-engineered primary healthcare (PHC) approach that is centred around communities and households

Primary healthcare provides early and quality ante- and postnatal services as well as essential infant and child health services and nutritional advice

The Honourable Dr Pakishe Aaron Motsoaledi, Minister of Health

We commit to:
- Increase life expectancy
- Decrease maternal and child mortality
- Combat HIV/AIDS and decrease the burden of disease from TB
- Strengthen health system effectiveness

Mission

To improve health status through the prevention of illnesses and the promotion of healthy lifestyles and to consistently improve the healthcare delivery system by focusing on access, equity, efficiency, quality and sustainability.

The Department of Health's 10-Point Plan for the health sector includes the following priorities:
- providing strategic leadership and creating a social contract for better health outcomes
- implementing the National Health Insurance (NHI) system
- improving quality of health services
- overhauling the healthcare system and improving its management
- improving human resource management, planning and development
- revitalising infrastructure
- accelerating implementation of the HIV/AIDS and Sexually Transmitted Infections Strategic Plan 2007–2011 and increasing focus on tuberculosis (TB) and other communicable diseases
- reviewing the drug policy
- improving the effectiveness of the health system
- strengthening research and development

Statutory and Advisory Bodies

PUBLIC ENTITIES
- Medicines Control Council
- Compensation Commission for Occupational Diseases
- Council for Midical Schemes
- SA Medical Research Council

STATUTORY HEALTH PROFESSIONAL COUNCILS
- Allied Health Professions Council of South Africa
- South African Nursing Council
- South African Dental Technicians Council
- South African Pharmacy Council
- Health Professions Council of South Africa

Contact

Private Bag X828
Pretoria
0001

Tel: +27 12 395 8000/9000
Fax: +27 12 395 9019

www.doh.gov.za

Stone-age Khoisan hunter-gatherers inhabited the region for about 8,000 years. At some period before AD 300 iron-age communities of pastoralists (almost certainly people of the Bantu groups) were living in the interior. The San people (Bushmen) were pushed towards the hostile desert areas; the Khoi-Khoi (Hottentots) added pastoralism to their economy, possibly learned from the more advanced and powerful Bantu, and inhabited the South-West Cape.

People of the Bantu groups, constituting South Africa's majority, are related to the peoples of other east and southern African countries, and come from four main linguistic groups: the Nguni, Sotho-Tswana, Venda and Tsonga. The Nguni (including Zulu, Xhosa and Swazi peoples) are by far the largest.

The first European settlers – Dutch farmers sent to re-provision ships of the Dutch East India Company – arrived at the Cape in 1652. They were joined in 1688 by Huguenots (French Protestant refugees), followed by groups from Belgium, Britain, France and Germany, and augmented by often highly skilled slaves from Indonesia and Malaya.

Control of the Cape passed from the Dutch to the French and, after 1814, to the British. The European and racially mixed groups developed the language of Afrikaans, a sense of folk identity as Afrikaners, or Boers (farmers), and a religious identity as strict Calvinists. They developed a ranching-centred style of agriculture suitable to the terrain (and similar to that of the Bantu peoples) and, as their numbers grew and the distant administrative authority became more irksome and foreign, migrated towards the interior.

Continuing friction on the Eastern Cape frontier and the abolition of slavery by Britain triggered a significant migration, the Great Trek, which from 1836–38 onwards brought them into direct conflict with the African peoples. While the black societies welcomed the traders and missionaries, between them and the Boers was direct competition for land.

The Africans were themselves in upheaval in the 19th century. In Natal, a military genius, Shaka, had moulded the formerly insignificant Zulus into a powerful fighting force and developed an economy of war. The Xhosas had been weakened by 100 years of battle with the white settlers along the Eastern Cape frontier. The Boers trekked inland, defeating first the Ndebele and then other tribes, and establishing the Boer Republics of the Transvaal (South African Republic) and Orange Free State.

Meanwhile, Britain was also expanding, taking Natal in 1843 and then following the Boers inland. The first Indians came in 1860 to work as indentured labourers in the Natal sugar fields and, in 1867, diamonds were discovered, triggering adventurer immigrants from many countries. Gold was discovered in 1871 – in a Boer Republic. Britain went to war with the Boers and, with difficulty, defeated them. Having also finally defeated the Zulus, Britain gained control of all South Africa. The four provinces were united in 1910 into the dominion of the Union of South Africa, and the country's independence was formally recognised under the Statute of Westminster in 1931.

The country had come to independence with a constitution which effectively denied black rights. Most areas excluded black,

coloured and Indian people from the vote. Resistance to racial discrimination was begun by Mahatma Gandhi, who arrived in South Africa as a young lawyer in 1893. He led the first passive resistance to the pass laws in 1906. In 1912, the African National Congress (ANC) was founded, to fight for full constitutional rights for blacks.

However, South Africa steadily reduced black rights. In 1913, land acts severely limited the rights of blacks to own land or live in certain areas. In 1936, black voters were removed from the common voters' roll in the Cape.

The apartheid years

In 1948, the National Party (NP) came to power on an electoral platform of apartheid, and moved rapidly in enacting a policy of racial segregation into law. The ANC, in collaboration with the Indian Congress, Coloured People's Congress and Congress of Democrats (mainly white communists and anti-racists), launched the Freedom Charter and, in 1952, the Defiance Campaign in response. More apartheid laws, separating education and public amenities, followed. Then, in 1960, the police at Sharpeville shot and killed 69 peaceful demonstrators. The ANC, Pan-Africanist Congress (PAC), South African Communist Party (SACP) and other anti-apartheid movements were banned and went under ground or into exile. The ANC adopted a policy of armed struggle and Nelson Mandela, as head of its new military wing, launched a sabotage campaign. In 1963 Mandela, Walter Sisulu and other ANC leaders were sentenced to life imprisonment.

After the Sharpeville massacre the world woke up to apartheid. South Africa became a pariah nation, forced out of the Commonwealth and increasingly isolated internationally. The UN declared apartheid to be a danger to world peace in 1961 and a crime against humanity in 1966.

During the 1970s some 3 million people were forcibly resettled in 'homelands'. Further shockwaves ran through the international media when, in 1976, schoolchildren in Soweto protesting against school classes in the Afrikaans language were shot by police and this sparked a violent uprising throughout the country in which some 600 mainly young people were killed. Popular activist Steve Biko (a young leader of the Black Consciousness Movement) was beaten to death while in police custody in 1977, and his name became a rallying cry of resistance.

In 1983, the government introduced a new tricameral parliament, which gave representation (in separate chambers) to white, coloured and Indian people, but excluded blacks. Intended as an act of appeasement, this aroused new united opposition, led by a new umbrella body, the United Democratic Front, with strong representation from the churches and trade unions as well as political parties. In 1985, the Congress of South African Trade Unions was founded. Despite the powerful police and military apparatus, black resistance intensified.

From the mid-1980s, the Commonwealth, USA and EU introduced political, sporting, cultural and economic sanctions. The Commonwealth was consistently among the leaders in international action against apartheid, for example with its Gleneagles Agreement against sporting contacts with South Africa (1977). The ➤

SAFCOL is a state-owned forestry company best positioned to contribute to the socio-economic needs of the rural communities and to the sustainable development of commercial forestry in Southern Africa.

Maureen Manyama-Matome
Acting CEO of SAFCOL

Our vision is to be a world-class, global business engaged in multi-functional forestry, revolutionising the integration of forests and communities.

SAFCOL

South African Forestry Company Limited (SAFCOL) is a State Owned Company (SOC) which falls within the portfolio of the Department of Public Enterprises. The mandate of SAFCOL as determined by the Management of State Forests Act, No. 128 of 1992 is to ensure the sustainable management of forests and other assets within the SAFCOL Group so as to enhance the value of the Group and to play a catalytic role in the realisation of the State's afforestation, rural development and economic transformation goals.

SAFCOL's main South African operating subsidiary is Komatiland Forests (Pty) Ltd (KLF) which owns and manages the prime softwood saw log forestry assets in the Mpumalanga, Limpopo and KwaZulu-Natal provinces. KLF is one of the largest producers of high-quality saw logs in South Africa which boasts years of forestry certification with Forestry Stewardship Council™ (FSC™) (FSC-C013832). SAFCOL was the first forestry company in South Africa and in Africa to achieve the FSC certification in 1996 and to become a Level 2 BBBEE contributor in 2011, making us a leader in transformation in the forestry sector. The South African forestry sector comprises a total of 1 257 341 ha of plantation area. KLF consists of 18 plantations, covering a total area of 187 320 ha. Its main business is the conducting of forestry, timber-harvesting, timber-processing and related activities. KLF's forestry operations contribute towards the provision of jobs for many people through direct employment and in the forestry subsector through the use of contractors and service providers. SAFCOL's Mozambique operations, IFLOMA, total landholding area is 23 600 ha in extent of which 16 618 ha is plantable for commercial forestry. The operations are located in the Manica province, an ideal location from which to serve markets in Mozambique, Zimbabwe and South Africa.

Committed and motivated, the SAFCOL Group works tirelessly to make a difference in the lives of ordinary people living in rural communities close to its operations. Through KLF, the SAFCOL Group formulated specific goals with a focus on improving the lives of impoverished communities which lay adjacent to its plantations. To this effect, SAFCOL initiated a process in 2005 of signing "social compacts" which is a Memoranda of Understanding with its communities. A social compact is an agreement between the organisation and a community's representatives, binding both parties to mutually contributing to the well-being and sustainability of the other party. The purpose of the social compact is to formalise partnerships with the communities and to prioritise needs driven development projects for communities in and around SAFCOL's operations. As a State Owned Company, SAFCOL fully supports government's new growth path initiative which is evident in the projects which the Group undertakes.

SAFCOL believes that through partnerships with other role players more opportunities in community development can be achieved. SAFCOL has initiated green building by implementing timber frame structures within its socio-economic and enterprise development projects. Timber frame structures are favoured as a great alternative to traditional building as they are made of renewable resources, quick to erect and consist of very good insulation properties. These structures are environmentally friendly, easier to put up in challenging terrains and more cost effective than conventional building methods. This could contribute greatly in providing much needed infrastructure and alleviating the housing and infrastructural backlogs currently experienced in the country, while making contributions to reduction of carbon emissions.

For sustained and tangible community impact, SAFCOL would require partnerships with various stakeholders who are willing to assist in redressing the challenges of poverty faced by these communities and those that are dedicated towards their socio-economic development. The past, present and future of our social investment projects speaks volumes of the level of care and consideration that we afford our communities. To us, socio-economic development is not only about combating poverty, unemployment and offering skills development but also about ensuring sustainability of individuals, families and communities today, for a better life for the company and communities tomorrow.

Contact:
Pretoria Office: Tel +27 12 481 3500
Nelspruit Office: Tel +27 13 754 2700
e-mail: ceo@klf.co.za

www.safcol.co.za
GROWTH THROUGH PARTNERSHIP

A municipality of choice

V hembe District Municipality, known as the land of legends, is one of five district municipalities in Limpopo Province, South Africa. The District is ideally positioned for easy access to African markets, its proximity to Zimbabwe, Mozambique and Botswana provides investors with a powerful platform from which to access the South African region and to contribute to as well as benefit from the New Partnership for Africa's Development.

Established in 2000 with its headquarters in Thohoyandou, Vhembe District Municipality has experienced a transilient growth. As a predominantly rural district municipality it has achieved much in the promotion and management of local government, resulting in planning for sustainable development, economic growth and good governance.

Vhembe District municipality's potential is still to be fully realised,

but as service delivery and good governance underline its democratic and people-driven role, improving the lives of all will be possible. This is in line with its mission 'to be an accountable and community-driven municipality in addressing poverty and unemployment through sustainable socio-economic development and service delivery'.

The District Municipality has championed the cause of democratic governance and in preparation of sustainable development has, through participatory community processes, developed the most realistic Integrated Development Plan in the Limpopo Province. This has facilitated the implementation of prioritised services as reflected by the community's needs and priorities. Top priorities are water, sanitation and infrastructure to enable social and economic development.

The District Municipality is endowed with natural resources and untapped

potential. It has fertile soil with agro-industry potential, while mining and eco-tourism potential is also great.

Local Economic Analysis

Economic growth in the District Municipality takes precedence over all development strategies, as it ensures sustainability in realising the vision of the municipality to be 'the legendary cultural hub in the southern hemisphere and a catalyst for agro-industry and tourism development'.

Agriculture

Vhembe is a prolific fresh produce grower, with large-scale exports testifying to the quality of production and the efficiency of many farmers. Vhembe produces no less than 4,4 per cent of South Africa's total agricultural output, including 8,4 per cent of the country's sub-tropical fruit and 6,3 per cent of its citrus, according to Kayamandi Development Services which has

Nandoni Dam supplies water for domestic use

Phiphidi Waterfalls

Awelani Eco-Tourism Park at Tshikuyu Village creates employment opportunities

The Big Tree is the largest baobab tree in the country and has survived more than 3500 years

Mining

Vhembe's major investor, De Beers, is moving to ensure that the district will remain South Africa's biggest diamond producer and an increasingly important ecotourism destination.

Vhembe District Municipality is a beneficiary of the Commonwealth Local Governance Support Scheme. It has partnered in twinning with Gondal Municipality in India. The exchange of good governance practices, particularly around issues of economic and sustainable development, is facilitating remarkable, positive improvement. This will benefit all the people of the District.

'Agriculture plays a crucial role in economic development through employment creation, income generation, poverty eradication, food security, economic growth and equity.'

Executive Mayor
Cllr Dzhombere

Contact

Cllr. F.F. Dzhombere
Executive Mayor
Old Parliament
Government Complex
Tusk Venda Street
Private Bag X 5006
Thohoyandou
0950

Tel: +27 15 960 2008
Email: dzhomberef@vhembe.gov.za

Commonwealth also led the peaceful dismantling of apartheid, starting in 1985 with establishment of the Commonwealth Eminent Persons Group (led by Olusegun Obasanjo of Nigeria and former Australian Prime Minister Malcolm Fraser).

Within South Africa, political protest grew, and began to take an increasingly violent form, influenced by *Umkhonto we Sizwe* ('Spear of the Nation', the military wing of the ANC). The country was becoming ungovernable, and its economy disastrously weakened.

The ending of apartheid

In 1989, F W de Klerk succeeded P W Botha as president, and immediately began negotiations to unscramble apartheid. Within months Walter Sisulu and seven other imprisoned leaders were released and the bans on the ANC, PAC and SACP were lifted. In February 1990, Mandela was released. Apartheid laws were repealed. In August 1990, the ANC suspended the armed struggle, and began negotiations with the government.

Political violence intensified within South Africa, with fierce competition between the ANC and the Zulu traditionalist Inkatha Freedom Party. Nonetheless, all-party negotiations – the Convention for a Democratic South Africa – began in December 1991. An all-white referendum showed that the whites were in favour of abolishing apartheid and agreement was reached in June 1993. A multiparty transitional executive council was formed to partner the government until the elections for a new parliament could be held. As the reform process gathered momentum from 1989, international sanctions were lifted.

South Africa's first non-racial and democratic elections were held in April 1994, with Commonwealth, UN and other teams of observers present. The observers concluded that despite technical problems during the elections, the results were an overwhelming expression of the will of the people. The elections gave the ANC an overall majority with 252 seats, and 63% of the votes. The NP obtained 20% and the Inkatha Freedom Party (IFP) 11%.

Nelson Mandela, president of the ANC, was elected president of South Africa at the first sitting of the National Assembly in May 1994. Although the ANC had an overall majority, in the interests of achieving consensus, a Government of National Unity (GNU) was formed, with a cabinet comprising 18 ANC, six NP, three IFP MPs and one independent MP. Mandela appointed Thabo Mbeki (ANC) and F W de Klerk (NP) as deputy presidents. The then ANC Secretary-General Cyril Ramaphosa was elected Chairperson of the Constitutional Assembly. In June 1994 South Africa rejoined the Commonwealth and reclaimed its seat at the UN.

The Truth and Reconciliation Commission (TRC) was established with Archbishop Desmond Tutu as its chair in 1996 to provide a public forum for the personal accounts of human rights abuses during the apartheid years. It was attended by some 7,000 individuals (including ANC leaders, but not Buthelezi or de Klerk) and delivered its final report in October 1998. People attended hearings on a voluntary basis and were then entitled to apply to the TRC for amnesty from prosecution.

The NP withdrew from the GNU in 1996 to form the parliamentary opposition, but the IFP remained in the national government, although this collaboration was not reflected in the provincial government of KwaZulu-Natal. In October 1996 a new constitution was approved by the National Assembly and came into force in February 1997. At the 50th national conference of the ANC in December 1997, Mandela stood down as party president, making way for Thabo Mbeki.

In the second democratic general election in June 1999, the ANC received 66% of the votes, the Democratic Party (DP) 9%, the IFP just under 9%, the (renamed) New National Party (NNP) 7% and the newly formed United Democratic Movement (UDM) 4%. With 266 out of the National Assembly's 400 seats, the ANC was able to command a two-thirds majority (necessary for changes to the constitution) with the support of the Minority Front, which had one seat. Mbeki succeeded Mandela as president and IFP leader Mangosuthu Buthelezi was reappointed as home affairs minister, while the 22-member cabinet was partially reshuffled with Jacob Zuma becoming deputy president. The DP replaced the NNP as the official opposition, and in June 2000 the DP and the NNP merged to become the Democratic Alliance.

change the constitution, though they had not promised any changes in their manifesto.

In December 2007, Jacob Zuma defeated President Thabo Mbeki in the ANC leadership elections, paving the way for his candidacy in the 2009 presidential elections. In the same month, the ANC National Executive Committee 'recalled' Mbeki from the presidency, he resigned, and parliament elected ANC deputy leader Kgalema Motlanthe to succeed him.

A new political party, the Congress of the People (COPE), was launched in December 2008 under the leadership of Mosiuoa Lekota, former chairman of the ANC and a close ally of Mbeki.

Facing the challenge of COPE and the Democratic Alliance, the ANC nevertheless won 66% of votes in the parliamentary elections in April 2009. The Democratic Alliance, led by Helen Zille, received 17% of votes and COPE 7%. At the first sitting of the National Assembly in May 2009, Zuma was formally elected president; and he then appointed Motlanthe deputy president. COPE's candidate in the presidential contest was Bishop Mvume Dandala rather than its leader, Lekota.

International relations

South Africa is a member of the African, Caribbean and Pacific Group of States, African Union, Indian Ocean Rim Association for Regional Cooperation, Non-Aligned Movement, Southern African Customs Union, Southern African Development Community, United Nations and World Trade Organization.

Traveller information

Local laws and conventions: All drug-related offences carry severe penalties.

South Africa is one of the most multicultural countries in the world, and social etiquette and culture vary between the different ethnic groups. Handshaking is the most common greeting.

Dress is generally casual, though usually formal for business meetings. Appointments are necessary and punctuality is expected. Business cards are commonly exchanged. Mid-December to mid-January is the holiday period and is not a good time for scheduling business meetings. Office hours are Mon–Fri 0830–1630.

Immigration and customs: Passports must be valid for at least 30 days from the intended length of stay. Visitors from the UK, the USA, Canada, Australia and most European Union countries do not require visas. All other nationals should contact their local embassy for visa requirements. Passports must have at least one page left blank, or two pages if a visa is required.

Plant and plant materials – including margarine, honey and other vegetable oils – are restricted imports. Narcotics, flick knives, ammunition, explosives, meat, processed cheese and other dairy products, and obscene literature are all prohibited imports.

A yellow fever vaccination certificate will be required by those arriving from an infected area.

Travel within the country: Traffic drives on the left and visitors can drive on a national driving licence if it is in English. International car hire companies are available in most city centres and airports. The road network is well maintained and mostly tarred except for the very rural areas and some of the game parks.

The national roads are tolled but provide good facilities; visitors should note that credit cards cannot be used to buy petrol. Speed limits are 60kph in urban areas and 120kph on the main roads and are strictly enforced with steep fines. Seatbelts are obligatory and no additional petrol is allowed to be carried other than in the fuel tank.

A reliable national bus network connects much of the country and runs air-conditioned coaches which provide good facilities for passengers. The country is well served with domestic airlines that link the main towns, and intercity rail services, though slow, are a reliable way of travelling across the country. There are also luxury trains that run between Cape Town and Tshwane (Pretoria).

All towns have a good bus network. Taxis are widely available in the major cities, and fares are charged by distance and travel time; for longer routes fares should be negotiated.

Travel health: Medical facilities are good in towns and cities but limited in rural areas. Doctors and hospitals require cash payment, and treatment can be expensive. Visitors should ensure they have comprehensive health insurance.

Malaria is present in the eastern half of the country, and visitors should ensure they take insect repellent and suitable clothing to avoid mosquito bites. Diphtheria, Hepatitis A, tetanus, rabies and typhoid are also present. Visitors should avoid swimming or paddling in fresh water due to the risk of bilharzia.

Tap water is safe to drink and bottled water is available everywhere.

Money: Money can be changed at banks, bureaux de change and some hotels. Credit cards are widely accepted, though Visa and Mastercard are preferred. ATMs are located in all towns and cities. Travellers cheques are accepted at banks, restaurants, hotels and some shops, and should be taken in US dollars or pounds sterling to avoid additional exchange rate charges. Banking hours are Mon–Fri 0900–1530 and Sat 0830–1100.

There were 8,074,000 tourist arrivals in 2010.

Further information

South Africa Government Online: www.gov.za

Parliament: www.parliament.gov.za

South African Reserve Bank: www.reservebank.co.za

Commonwealth Secretariat: www.thecommonwealth.org

Commonwealth of Nations: www.commonwealth-of-nations.org/South_Africa

Sri Lanka

KEY FACTS

Joined Commonwealth:	1948
Population:	20,860,000 (2010)
GDP p.c. growth:	4.1% p.a. 1990–2010
UN HDI 2011:	world ranking 97
Official languages:	Sinhala, Tamil
Time:	GMT plus 5:30hr
Currency:	Sri Lanka rupee (SLRs)

Geography

Area:	65,610 sq km
Coastline:	1,340km
Capital:	Colombo

The Democratic Socialist Republic of Sri Lanka (formerly Ceylon) is an island in the Indian Ocean, separated from south-east India (Tamil Nadu state) by the Palk Strait. It is almost linked to the Indian mainland by Adam's Bridge, an atoll barrier, mostly submerged, lying between the offshore island of Mannar and India itself. The country comprises nine provinces (from south to north): Southern (provincial capital Galle), Sabaragamuwa (Ratnapura), Western (Colombo), Uva (Badulla), Eastern (Trincomalee), Central (Kandy), North-Western (Kurunegala), North-Central (Anuradhapura) and Northern (Jaffna).

Topography: Beyond the coastal plains, Sri Lanka's topography is dominated by an outstandingly beautiful central mountain massif of gneiss rock, with the highest point at Pidurutalagala (2,524m). The holy Adam's Peak (2,243m) is so called from a mark at the top in the likeness of a human footprint, variously attributed as the print of the Buddha, Vishnu or Adam, and is a place of pilgrimage. The coastal plains are broader in the north, tapering off in the long low-lying Jaffna peninsula. Several fast-flowing non-navigable rivers arise in the mountains. The Mahaweli Ganga, from which hydroelectric power is obtained, is the longest at 322km.

Did you know...

Sri Lanka was the first Commonwealth state to have a female prime minister. Sirimavo Bandaranaike served for three periods of office: 1960–65, 1970–77 and 1994–2000.

Scholarships are awarded by Sri Lanka to citizens of other Commonwealth countries under the Commonwealth Scholarship and Fellowship Plan.

Sanath Jayasuriya was Wisden Leading Cricketer in the World in 1996, and Muttiah Muralitharan in 2000 and 2006.

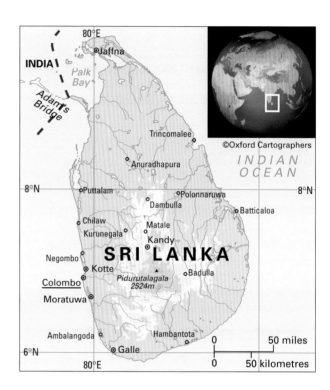

©Oxford Cartographers

One of the most violent earthquakes ever recorded occurred on 26 December 2004 in the Indian Ocean west of Sumatra generating a tsunami that swamped the east and south coasts of Sri Lanka causing approximately 31,000 deaths and devastation of the coastal area.

Climate: Tropical. The lowlands are always hot, particularly from March to May. The highlands are cooler. During December and January there is occasional frost on very high ground – for example, at Nuwara Eliya. The dry season is March to mid-May. The south-west monsoon season lasts from mid-May to September; the north-east monsoon season lasts from November to March.

Environment: The most significant environmental issues are: deforestation; soil erosion; coastal degradation as a result of mining activities and increased pollution; pollution of freshwater resources by industrial wastes and sewage; air pollution in Colombo; and the threat to wildlife populations of poaching and urbanisation.

Vegetation: Forest covers 29% of the land area, having declined at 1.2% p.a. 1990–2010. Vegetation is rich and luxuriant, with a great variety of flowers, trees, creepers and flowering shrubs. The flora of Sri Lanka were described by Linnaeus in 1747 from specimens collected by a fellow botanist. Among the many species of trees are the rubber tree, palm, acacia, margosa, satinwood, Ceylon oak, tamarind, ebony, coral tree and banyan. Flowers and shrubs include the orchid and rhododendron. There are about 3,300 species of plants, of which some 280 are threatened with extinction. Arable land comprises 19% and permanent cropland 15% of the total land area.

Wildlife: Nature reserves now cover 10% of the island. Wilpattu National Park in the north-west (813 sq km) is best known for leopards; Yala National Park in the south-east (112 sq km) is home to large elephant populations. However, reduction of the natural tropical hardwood forest is endangering several animal species.

Main towns: Colombo (commercial capital; Western Province; pop. 685,200 in 2010), Dehiwala–Mount Lavinia (greater Colombo, 234,600), Moratuwa (greater Colombo, 204,800), Negombo (145,000), Trincomalee (Eastern, 126,900), Sri Jayewardenepura–Kotte (administrative capital; greater Colombo, 126,900), Kandy (Central, 120,100), Vavuniya (108,800), Kalmunai (105,000), Galle (Southern, 97,800), Batticaloa (97,600), Katunayaka (92,500), Battaramulla (greater Colombo, 85,300), Jaffna (Northern, 84,400), Dambulla (77,100), Maharagama (greater Colombo, 75,100), Daluguma (74,400), Anuradhapura (North-Central, 68,200), Chavakachcheri (54,500), Ratnapura (Sabaragamuwa, 51,200), Badulla (Uva, 47,300), Point Pedro (40,000), Valvettithurai (34,700) and Kurunegala (North-Western, 29,100).

Transport: There are 97,290km of roads (81% paved) and 1,463km of railway. Rail links exist between the major towns. The lines run from Colombo north along the coast to Puttalam, north via Kurunegala and Anuradhapura to Mannar and to Jaffna; north-east to Trincomalee and Batticaloa; east to Kandy via Gampaha; and south along the coast to Galle and Matara.

The international ports are at Colombo, Galle, Talaimannar and Trincomalee. Bandaranaike international airport is 32km from Colombo.

The larger domestic airports are at Ratmalana (Colombo) in the south and Jaffna in the north.

Society

KEY FACTS 2010

Population per sq km:	318
Life expectancy:	75 years
Net primary enrolment:	95%

Population: 20,860,000 (2010); 14% lives in urban areas; growth 0.9% p.a. 1990–2010; birth rate 18 per 1,000 people (31 in 1970); life expectancy 75 years (43 in 1946 and 64 in 1970).

The largest ethnic group is Sinhalese (estimated at 74% of the population), followed by Sri Lankan Tamils (12%), Muslims (7%), Indian Tamils (5%), and small communities of Malays and Burghers (persons of Dutch or partly Dutch descent) and a small number of Veddhas, descended from the earliest inhabitants. Sinhalese settlers arrived in the 5th and 6th centuries BC.

Sri Lankan Tamils settled mainly from the 10th century onwards. Indian Tamils arrived later, brought in by the British in the 19th century as labour for the plantations. Some Indian Tamils were repatriated from 1964, and since 1988 all remaining Indian Tamils have attained Sri Lankan citizenship. The Muslims are mostly descendants of Arab traders, and the Burghers descendants of European settlers of the 17th century onwards.

Language: The official languages are Sinhala and Tamil. English is used in commerce and government and very widely understood.

Religion: Buddhists 69%, Muslims 8%, Hindus 7% and Christians 6% (2001 partial census; did not cover the predominantly Tamil north and north-east).

Health: Public spending on health was 2% of GDP in 2009. Both Western and Ayurvedic (traditional) medicine are practised, though most doctors practise Western medicine. A free health service is available, with hospitals and clinics countrywide, supplemented by several private hospitals and clinics in Colombo. 90% of the population uses an improved drinking water source and 91% of people have access to adequate sanitation facilities (2009). Infant mortality was 14 per 1,000 live births in 2010 (83 in 1960). Over 90% of children are born in hospital. Family planning is common, with about 68% of married women practising contraception. Polio has been eradicated, but malaria remains a problem.

Education: There are eleven years of compulsory education starting at age five. Some 99% of pupils complete primary school (2006). The school year starts in January.

The University Grants Commission recognises 15 universities and 17 institutes of higher education (2011), providing some 450 undergraduate courses. Leading universities include University of Colombo, which was established – as University of Ceylon – in 1942 when the Ceylon Medical College (founded 1870) and Ceylon University College (1921) were merged; University of Kelaniya; University of Peradeniya; and Open University of Sri Lanka, which provides courses through distance learning. Technical colleges offer courses up to diploma level in engineering and business. Literacy among people aged 15–24 is 98% (2008).

The tsunami of December 2004 and its aftermath affected over 350,000 children and around 650 schools, and rehabilitation and modernisation programmes were vigorously pursued. The Sri Lankan government, donor organisations and the international community have worked together to restore education facilities and to address the enduring psychological effects of the disaster.

Media: There are several daily newspapers in Sinhala, Tamil, and English including the state-owned *Daily News*, and the independent *Daily Mirror* and *The Island*, plus several weeklies including the state-owned *Sunday Observer* and independent *The Sunday Times*.

The public radio network of the Sri Lanka Broadcasting Corporation and many private stations broadcast in Sinhala, Tamil and English. The Independent Television Network and Sri Lanka Rupavahini Corporation both provide public TV services, and there are several private TV channels; public and private channels are also in Sinhala, Tamil and English.

Some 76% of households have TV sets (2007). There are 38 personal computers (2005) and 120 internet users (2010) per 1,000 people.

Communications: Country code 94; internet domain '.lk'. Mobile phone coverage is good in urban areas and the number of subscribers has grown rapidly. Internet cafes can be found in the main towns. Postal services are good.

There are 172 main telephone lines and 832 mobile phone subscriptions per 1,000 people (2010).

Public holidays: Independence Day (4 February), Sinhala and Tamil New Year (mid-April, two days), Labour Day (1 May) and Christmas Day.

Sri Lanka appears to have been inhabited from as early as 125,000 BC. Balangoda Man was the ancestor of the present-day Veddhas, a racial minority now inhabiting remote forests. The Great Dynasty (Mahavamsa) of the Sinhalese was established in 543 BC by King Vijaya, who came with his followers (the *Sinhala*, or 'Lion Race') from Bengal and settled in the north. Traces of the vast irrigation system they established still exist. About 300 years later, a royal prince from India named Mahinda, son of Asoka, introduced Buddhism. Tamil settlements began in the 10th century AD, and gave rise to a Tamil kingdom in Jaffna. There was a long struggle between Sinhalese and Tamil kings for the control of the north of the island.

By the end of the 13th century, the Sinhalese were forced to migrate to the south. Malaria set in when the irrigation and drainage systems were destroyed by continuing warfare. The Sinhalese population split into two separate kingdoms at the end of the 15th century, the up-country kingdom of Kandy and the low-country kingdom of Kotte.

In the 16th century the Kotte Kingdom sought protection from new arrivals, the Portuguese; and in 1597 Dharmapala, last of the Kotte kings, bequeathed his throne to the King of Portugal. The Portuguese soon subdued the north and so acquired most of the coastal belt of the country, leaving the central region to the Kingdom of Kandy.

From the mid-1630s, the King of Kandy helped the Dutch to dispossess the Portuguese; by 1656 the whole island had become a Dutch possession except for the Kingdom of Kandy. Later the Dutch also seized Kandy's coastal areas, cutting the Kandyans off from the outside world. British interests developed in the late 18th century when a British army invaded and forced the Dutch to accept its protection. In 1802 the Dutch colony became a British possession. The Kingdom of Kandy was invaded in 1815 and its monarchy was abolished. Thus the whole island came under British rule.

Plantations growing rubber, coconut and coffee were established in the 19th century. After the coffee plantations were destroyed by a fungus in the 1870s, planters successfully switched to tea. The country soon became the second largest producer (after India) of black tea. During this period, Indian Tamils were brought into the country as indentured labour for the tea estates.

Constitutional development of Ceylon (as the country was then called) began relatively early, with executive and legislative councils set up in 1833, and the first opening up of the colonial civil service to Ceylonese. Full self-government was achieved in 1946, under a new constitution, with a bicameral legislature (which became a single chamber in 1972), and Ceylon became fully independent and joined the Commonwealth in 1948.

The first prime minister of independent Ceylon was one of the leaders of the independence movement, D S Senanayake. He was the head of the United National Party (UNP, the former Ceylon National Congress supported by the Tamil Congress). After a split in the UNP in 1951, S W R D Bandaranaike formed the Sri Lanka Freedom Party (SLFP).

In 1956 the SLFP won a decisive electoral victory. The new government, nationalist and non-aligned, immediately began talks with the UK which ended in the return to Ceylon of the Katunayake airfield and the Trincomalee naval base.

In September 1959, Bandaranaike was assassinated. After elections the following year, his widow, Sirimavo Bandaranaike, led the SLFP to victory and became the first woman prime minister in the world. In March 1965, the UNP was voted back to power with Dudley Senanayake (son of Sri Lanka's first prime minister) as prime minister until 1970, when the elections returned the SLFP.

Sirimavo Bandaranaike's new government introduced a new constitution in 1972. Following the lead of India, Ceylon became a republic while remaining within the Commonwealth. Under the new constitution, the republic had a unicameral parliament, the National State Assembly, and a non-executive president. The first president was William Gopallawa, formerly governor-general, and Mrs Bandaranaike remained prime minister.

Throughout this period, Ceylon's government developed programmes of welfare and nationalisation. These led to marked improvements in health and literacy, but the economy began to decline. In 1971, there was a serious internal crisis with an uprising of Sinhalese youth, led by the Marxist Janatha Vimukti Peramuna (JVP), in protest about widespread unemployment. In 1972 the country's name was changed to Sri Lanka. In 1977 the Liberation Tigers of Tamil Eelam (LTTE or Tamil Tigers) was formed as the Sinhalese and Tamil communities polarised, and the civil war had begun by the early 1980s (see 'Communal conflict' in *History*).

The government lost popularity and, at the general election in 1977, the UNP under J R Jayewardene won a sweeping victory. The UNP government encouraged the private sector, and (under a new constitution in 1978) opted for a presidential form of government with proportional representation and renamed the country the Democratic Socialist Republic of Sri Lanka. The first presidential election, held in 1982, was won by Jayewardene. In December 1982, the life of the 1977 Parliament was extended, by a national referendum, for six more years.

In 1988 UNP's Ranasinghe Premadasa was elected to the presidency and in 1993 was killed by an LTTE suicide bomber. In 1994 UNP presidential candidate and opposition leader Gamini Dissanayake was killed, with more than 50 others, by a suicide bomber. After President Premadasa's assassination in 1993, D B Wijetunga took over as president and remained in office for about a year until the general election in August 1994.

The People's Alliance coalition, led by the SLFP, and consisting of seven mostly left-of-centre parties, came to power in the August 1994 general election. The leader of this coalition, Chandrika Bandaranaike Kumaratunga, became the prime minister, but relinquished her position to stand in the presidential election in November 1994, which she won. Her mother, Sirimavo Bandaranaike, became prime minister, her third term over a span of four decades.

In July 1999, the moderate Tamil politician Neelam Tiruchelvam, the architect of the government's devolution plans, was killed by a suicide bomber in Colombo. In an early presidential election of December 1999, having narrowly escaped assassination,

➤

➤ Kumaratunga won her second term with 51% of the votes while her main rival, UNP leader Ranil Wickremasinghe, received nearly 43%. The winning margin was less than in 1994.

In August 2000, the government failed to gain the two-thirds majority of parliament for its constitutional reform, designed to end the 17-year civil war (see 'Communal conflict' below). This entailed the devolution of substantial powers on elected councils in seven provinces and an interim appointed council in the two provinces (Northern and North-Eastern) with majority Tamil populations.

Communal conflict

After independence, the Sinhalese became the dominant social and political force and the Tamils felt that they were being marginalised, especially after 1956 when Sinhala was made the official language. Several different Tamil parties formed and demanded that the Northern and Eastern provinces become part of a federal state or, when this was refused, an independent homeland.

The Liberation Tigers of Tamil Eelam (LTTE or Tamil Tigers) was formed in 1977 and from around 1980 began attacks on politicians, the police and the army in the north. This brought a Sinhalese backlash in the south: in July 1983 there were riots against Tamils in Colombo and the south-west of the country, and Tamils fled to the north and Tamil Nadu in India. The army deployed in the north, the conflict escalated, and the Tamil Tigers gained effective control of Jaffna and the northern peninsula.

The Indian Government attempted to mediate and, in July 1987, President J R Jayewardene and Indian Prime Minister Rajiv Gandhi arranged a ceasefire, supervised by Indian troops. Under the Indo–Lanka Accord provincial councils were introduced as a solution to the conflict. The provincial councils for the Northern and Eastern provinces were to be temporarily merged into a single council.

Some Indian-supported Tamil groups accepted the arrangement, and elections for the new council proceeded. However, the Tamil Tigers refused to co-operate, and in 1988 Jayewardene asked the Indian Government to withdraw its troops. The Tigers took control of the vacated areas and fighting continued with few breaks into the 21st century and by 2001 it was estimated that more than 60,000 people had died in the conflict.

After it came to power in the August 1994 general election, the People's Alliance government engaged in peace talks with the LTTE, but after four rounds the Tigers unilaterally abrogated the ceasefire that had been in force and relaunched the war. Their leader, Velupillai Prabhakaran, appeared to remain committed to fighting for a separate state. In 1995, government forces recaptured the town of Jaffna, forcing the LTTE to withdraw into dense jungle, and the war continued.

From 1996 LTTE attacked substantial civilian and economic targets outside the operational area, and especially in Colombo. Ten days before the celebration to mark 50 years of independence, on 25 January 1998 a truck was exploded by LTTE suicide bombers as they drove it through the gates of the country's most sacred Buddhist site, the Temple of the Tooth at Kandy, killing 16 people. In mid-2001, the Tigers attacked the international airport near Colombo, destroying several civilian and military aeroplanes.

In February 2000 Norway agreed to provide a special envoy to act as intermediary in peace talks and he held several rounds of talks.

In March 2000, the LTTE began a new offensive on the Jaffna peninsula – held by government forces since 1995 – and the government declared a state of war for the first time and suspended all non-essential development projects. In April, the LTTE captured the strategic Elephant Pass base, denying government troops the only land route into the peninsula. By May, the Tigers had driven the government forces back to the suburbs of the city of Jaffna, proving themselves as a professional fighting force, deploying sophisticated weapons including heavy artillery captured at Elephant Pass.

Despite the declaration of a unilateral ceasefire from December 2000 to April 2001 by LTTE, and the continuing efforts of the Norwegian envoy, the warring parties could not agree to meet and deadlock continued until a UNP government was elected in December 2001. A ceasefire was agreed with the LTTE in February 2002, allowing Norwegian facilitators to organise peace talks between the government and the separatists. The first round of talks was held in Thailand in September 2002, when talks focused on reconstruction of the areas affected by the war and the return of displaced people, and dates for further talks were agreed.

As the peace talks proceeded, LTTE dropped its demand for a separate Tamil state and agreed to work towards a federal system and, for the first time, the government also agreed to share power with the LTTE. After the sixth round of talks, held in Japan in March 2003, progress slowed and LTTE failed to attend the international donor conferences focusing on Sri Lanka's development priorities in Tokyo in June 2003. However, with aid donors exerting increasing pressure, a seventh round of talks was eventually scheduled for November 2003 to discuss proposals for a power-sharing administration in the north and east of the country.

After the election in April 2004, there were efforts to get the stalled peace process under way again. The new government invited the Norwegian mediators to return to the country to arrange peace talks between LTTE and the government, but governing alliance partner JVP remained staunchly opposed to any solution that involved power-sharing.

In late 2006 there were two major set-backs to the peace process: in October peace talks with the Norwegian mediators in Geneva broke down without agreement; and in December, with hostilities already intensifying, the LTTE's senior negotiator, Anton Balasingham, died. For most of 2007 it was apparent that the ceasefire agreement signed in 2002 was no longer respected by the parties; the government officially withdrew from the agreement in January 2008.

By January 2009, after very intense fighting in the north-east of the country, government forces were reported to be in control of most of the country including the LTTE strongholds of the Jaffna Peninsula, Kilinochchi and Mullaitivu, and claimed they were very ➤

➤ close to defeating the LTTE. There were mounting concerns in the international community about the security of an estimated 250,000 civilians trapped in the conflict zone. In May 2009 LTTE leader and founder Velupillai Prabhakaran died in combat. The government proclaimed victory and the war that began in 1983 was declared over. At the conclusion of hostilities almost 300,000 displaced persons who had fled the conflict were housed in camps established by the government. At the beginning of 2010, the majority of internally displaced persons had been permitted to leave the camps.

Religious and other festivals whose dates vary from year to year include Tamil Thai Pongal Day (mid-January), Prophet's Birthday, Good Friday, Vesak Poya Days (two days generally in May) and Deepavali (Diwali, October/November). There is a Buddhist Poya holiday each month on the day of the full moon. With the exception of the Vesak Poya Days, when Poya Days fall at the weekend they are nonetheless observed on the full moon day. Eid al-Fitr (End of Ramadan) and Eid al-Adha (Feast of the Sacrifice) are observed only by Muslims, and Mahasivarathri only by Hindus.

Economy

KEY FACTS 2010

GNI:	US$46.7bn
GNI p.c.:	US$2,240
GDP growth:	6.4% p.a. 2006–10
Inflation:	11.3% p.a. 2006–10

While agriculture is central to Sri Lanka's economy – and tea, rubber and coconut continue to be important exports – manufacturing and services (including banking and financial services) are of increasing importance, especially textiles and

Real Growth in GDP

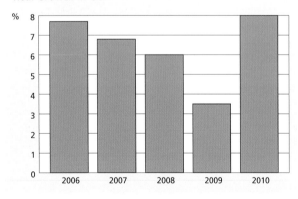

Inflation

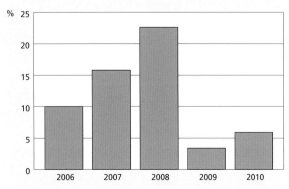

GDP by Sector (2010)

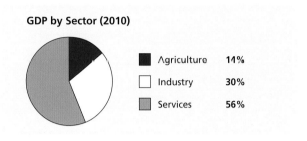

clothing which are major exports. Since 1989 the former policies of nationalisation have been superseded by extensive liberalisation, which has led to extensive privatisation of the formerly largely centralised economy, including agricultural enterprises, banking, transport services and utilities.

Sri Lanka had been aiming at achieving newly industrialised country status by the year 2000, but ethnic conflict adversely affected the economy, notably in the spheres of foreign investment and tourism, and particularly in the north and east of the country. Despite the conflict, tourism earnings generally held up in the 1990s and into the 2000s, though attacks on tourist areas such as the international airport in 2001 caused sharp falls. Foreign investment in manufacturing and infrastructure were maintained and manufacturing output grew by 6.3% p.a. 1980–90, 8.1% p.a. 1990–2000 and 4.5% p.a. 2000–10.

Thus, despite the disruption caused by the hostilities and relatively high spending on defence, the economy grew well throughout the 1990s, but plunged into recession in 2001 when it shrank by 1.5%, as export markets for clothing weakened sharply, recovering in 2002.

The massive tsunami of December 2004 that swamped the east and south coasts of Sri Lanka, causing approximately 31,000 deaths and devastation of the coastal area, displaced more than 400,000 people and destroyed property valued at an estimated US$1.5 billion. Despite this devastation of the economic infrastructure of the coastal areas in the south and east of the country, economic growth continued steadily, partly spurred by reconstruction, averaging 6.4% p.a. during 2004–08.

Then the economy slowed in 2008–09 as the world economic downturn depressed demand for Sri Lanka's exports, causing GDP growth to moderate to 3.5% in 2009, but in that year there was a compensatory surge of economic activity following the cessation of civil strife in May 2009, yielding growth of 8.0% in 2010 and about 8% in 2011.

Constitution

Status:	Republic with executive president
Legislature:	Parliament
Independence:	4 February 1948

Sri Lanka is a democratic republic with an executive presidency based on the French model. Under the 1978 constitution, the head of state and government is the president. There is universal adult suffrage with proportional representation; parliamentary and presidential elections are held every six years. Parliament has a single chamber with 225 members. Members are directly elected, but vacant seats occurring during the life of a parliament go to nominees of the party holding the seat.

Ministers are appointed by the president, who chairs the cabinet and appoints the independent judiciary. Amendments may be made to the constitution, subject to a two-thirds majority in parliament; however, to amend certain entrenched articles of the constitution approval in a national referendum is also required. The constitution provides for provincial councils.

The Eighteenth Amendment – enacted in September 2010 – removed the limit on the number of terms a president may serve, previously set at two.

Politics

Last elections:	January 2010 (presidential), April 2010 (parliamentary)
Next elections:	2016 (presidential and parliamentary)
Head of state:	President Mahinda Rajapaksa
Head of government:	the president
Ruling party:	United People's Freedom Alliance

After a violent campaign in which at least 70 people died, in the parliamentary elections of October 2000, the ruling People's Alliance (PA), led by President Chandrika Bandaranaike Kumaratunga, won 107 of the 225 parliamentary seats, the United National Party (UNP) 89 and the Marxist Janatha Vimukti Peramuna (JVP) ten. Sirimavo Bandaranaike was reappointed prime minister. However, short of a working majority, the new government was dependent on the support of the smaller parties, and this diverted its attention from new peace initiatives (see 'Communal conflict' in *History*) and its economic reform programme.

Parliamentary elections were held in December 2001 after the PA lost its majority in parliament. The UNP won 109 seats, the PA 77, JVP 16, Tamil National Alliance (TNA) 15 and Sri Lanka Muslim Congress (SLMC) five. With the support of the TNA and SLMC, the UNP commanded a majority in the National Assembly, and the president was obliged to appoint UNP leader Ranil Wickremasinghe prime minister and invite him to form a government.

Thus, in due course, President Kumaratunga found herself chairing a cabinet composed entirely of political opponents. The new government was nevertheless determined to pursue the peace process. But as the end of the government's first year in office approached (when the president had the power to dissolve parliament and call fresh elections), relations between the president and government became increasingly strained. However, both the president and prime minister remained committed to the peace process, and in 2002 the government signed a ceasefire agreement with the Liberation Tigers of Tamil Eelam (LTTE) and invited Scandinavian countries, led by Norway, to monitor the truce.

In November 2003, the week before the seventh round of peace talks was due to take place, the president sacked three ministers,

suspended parliament and first declared then lifted a state of emergency, calling for a government of national reconciliation, and plunging the country into political crisis. This endured until April 2004 when in a snap election the president's United People's Freedom Alliance (UPFA) – a new alliance with the JVP – took 105 seats and 46% of the votes, while the UNP won 82 seats and the Tamil National Alliance 22. President Kumaratunga formed a government and the UPFA's Mahinda Rajapaksa was sworn in as prime minister but, without an overall majority, they would be depending on the support of members of minority parties and any opposition members who crossed the floor.

In the presidential election in November 2005, UPFA leader Mahinda Rajapaksa, with just over 50% of the votes, defeated UNP leader Ranil Wickremasinghe. The overall turnout was 74%, even though many Tamils boycotted the election in the LTTE-controlled areas in the north and east of the country.

Almost two years before the expiry of his term of office, Rajapaksa called a presidential election in January 2010, when he faced a challenge from former head of the army General (Rtd) Sarath Fonseka, who had overseen the military victory against the LTTE that had been declared by the government in May 2009. In a poll with a 75% voter turnout, Rajapaksa was returned to office with 57.9% of the vote; Fonseka received 40.2% of the vote, but contested the election result in the courts. A Commonwealth expert team was present during the election period. At the release of the team's report, Commonwealth Secretary-General Kamalesh Sharma said that 'on the day of the election voters were free to express their will', but shortcomings primarily in the pre-election period meant that overall the election 'did not fully meet key benchmarks for democratic elections'.

Two weeks after the presidential election, Fonseka was arrested and detained by the military police. A government spokesperson alleged he had been plotting a coup. In August 2010 he was convicted by court martial of participating in political activities while on active service and stripped of his rank, medals and pension. In September the court martial convicted him of arms procurement offences and he was required to resign the parliamentary seat he won in the April 2010 election.

In the parliamentary elections of April 2010, the UPFA won 144 of 225 seats, securing 60.3% of votes cast; the UNP took 60 seats (29.3%); the Democratic National Alliance seven (5.5%); and the Tamil National Alliance 14 (2.9%).

International relations

Sri Lanka is a member of the Indian Ocean Rim Association for Regional Cooperation, Non-Aligned Movement, South Asian Association for Regional Cooperation, United Nations and World Trade Organization.

Traveller information

Local laws and conventions: Visitors should not enter a Buddhist temple wearing headgear or with bare legs or shoulders; footwear must also be removed.

Alcohol cannot be sold on *Poya* holidays. Visitors can be fined if they ignore instructions not to smoke or drink in public. Penalties for all drug offences are severe.

Photography and videotaping are not permitted near military bases and government buildings, and posing for photographs in front of a statue of Buddha is prohibited.

Shaking hands is the usual form of greeting. Informal dress is acceptable, except when visiting Buddhist temples, where modest clothing should be worn. Businesswear is generally casual, though women should dress conservatively. Appointments are necessary for meetings and punctuality is important. Business cards are usually exchanged on first introduction and English is widely used. Office hours are Mon–Fri 0900–1700.

Immigration and customs: Visas are required by all visitors, and passports must be valid for at least six months beyond the intended length of stay.

It is prohibited to import weapons, ivory, antiques, statues, old books, animals or birds, reptiles, tea, rubber and dangerous drugs.

A yellow fever vaccination certificate is required by all those arriving from infected areas.

Travel within the country: Traffic drives on the left and an international driving permit is required for foreign visitors. Car hire is inexpensive and is available from international agencies. There is a 56kph speed limit in built-up areas and 75kph outside towns. If another driver flashes their headlights, they are asserting their right of way.

Trains connect Colombo to most other cities, and first-class air-conditioned carriages are available on a few services. An intercity express service operates between Colombo and Kandy.

There is an extensive bus network that operates around the country. Taxis have yellow tops and red and white number plates. Most are metered but visitors should always agree the fare before travel. Motorised rickshaws are readily available for hire and chauffeur-driven cars are also available.

Visitors should seek advice from local authorities if they wish to travel to Anuradhapura.

Travel health: Comprehensive travel insurance is recommended. Emergency medical treatment is limited outside main cities, and treatment in private hospitals can be expensive.

Mosquito-borne diseases – dengue fever, chikungunya and malaria – are present in Sri Lanka, and visitors will need to bring insect repellent and suitable clothing to protect themselves against mosquito bites.

Water should be boiled or sterilised before used for drinking, brushing teeth or making ice. Many hotels provide bottled or mineral water for guests. Unpasteurised milk should be boiled before use.

Money: There are ATMs in major cities, but some do not accept international cards. Most major banks will change US dollar travellers cheques and accept Visa and Mastercard withdrawals. To avoid additional exchange rate charges, travellers are advised to take travellers cheques in US dollars or pounds sterling. Visitors should note that foreign currency can only be changed at authorised exchanges, banks and hotels, and that these establishments must endorse such exchanges on the visitor's Exchange Control D form, which is issued on arrival and must usually be returned at the time of departure. Banking hours are Mon–Sat 0900–1300.

There were 654,000 tourist arrivals in 2010.

Further information

Government of Sri Lanka: www.gov.lk

Parliament: www.parliament.lk

Central Bank of Sri Lanka: www.cbsl.gov.lk

Commonwealth Secretariat: www.thecommonwealth.org

Commonwealth of Nations: www.commonwealth-of-nations.org/Sri_Lanka

Swaziland

KEY FACTS

Joined Commonwealth:	1968
Population:	1,186,000 (2010)
GDP p.c. growth:	1.6% p.a. 1990–2010
UN HDI 2011:	world ranking 140
Official languages:	siSwati, English
Time:	GMT plus 2hr
Currency:	lilangeni, plural emalangeni (E)

Geography

Area:	17,364 sq km
Coastline:	none
Capital:	Mbabane

The Kingdom of Swaziland is a small landlocked country in the east of Southern Africa, bounded to the east by Mozambique and elsewhere by South Africa. The country comprises four regions: Hhohho (in the north), Manzini (west-central), Lubombo (east) and Shiselweni (south).

Topography: There are four regions, all running from north to south. The western Highveld, a continuation of the Drakensberg Mountains, rises to 1,862m. East of the Highveld is the grassy Middleveld, beside the Lowveld (also called the Bushveld) at around 150–300m with some higher ridges and knolls. The eastern region, the Lubombo, is a narrow escarpment. The four most important rivers, all flowing from the Highveld east towards the Indian Ocean, are the Komati, the Usutu, the Mbuluzi and the Ngwavuma. None is easily navigable. The Lowveld watercourses are wadis, except after heavy rain.

Climate: The Highveld is near-temperate and humid, the Middleveld and Lubombo subtropical, the Lowveld near-tropical. Swaziland is one of the best-watered countries in southern Africa although, in common with the region, rainfall may be unreliable and periods of drought occur in the Lowveld, for example in 2004–05. Summer (October–March) is the rainy season. There is

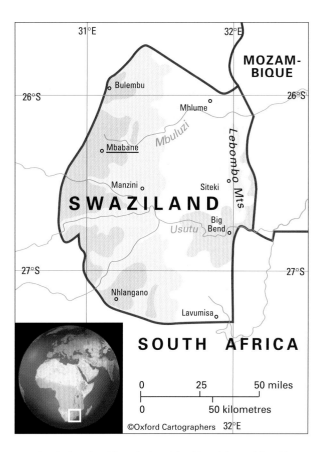

©Oxford Cartographers

occasional, short-lived frost in the Highveld and the Middleveld.

Environment: The most significant environmental issues are overgrazing, soil degradation, soil erosion, limited supplies of drinking water, and depletion of wildlife populations by excessive hunting.

Vegetation: Varies from the forested Highveld with its Usutu pines to the grassland and bush vegetation of the Lowveld. Forest covers 33% of the land area, having increased at 0.9% p.a. 1990–2010. Arable land comprises 10% and permanent cropland less than 1% of the total land area.

Wildlife: There are eight nature reserves inhabited by indigenous species, several of them under threat elsewhere, such as black and white rhinoceros, elephant, buffalo, hippopotamus, and a vast variety of bird species – including storks and vultures.

Main towns: Mbabane (capital, pop. 61,800 in 2010), Manzini (94,900), Malkerns (8,000), Nhlangano (7,000), Mhlume (6,800), Big Bend (6,700), Siteki (6,100), Simunye (5,500), Hluti (5,400), Pigg's Peak (4,600) and Lobamba (legislative capital, 3,800).

Transport: There are 3,590km of roads, at least 30% paved, linking with South Africa and Mozambique.

The others are already here.
When are **you** coming?

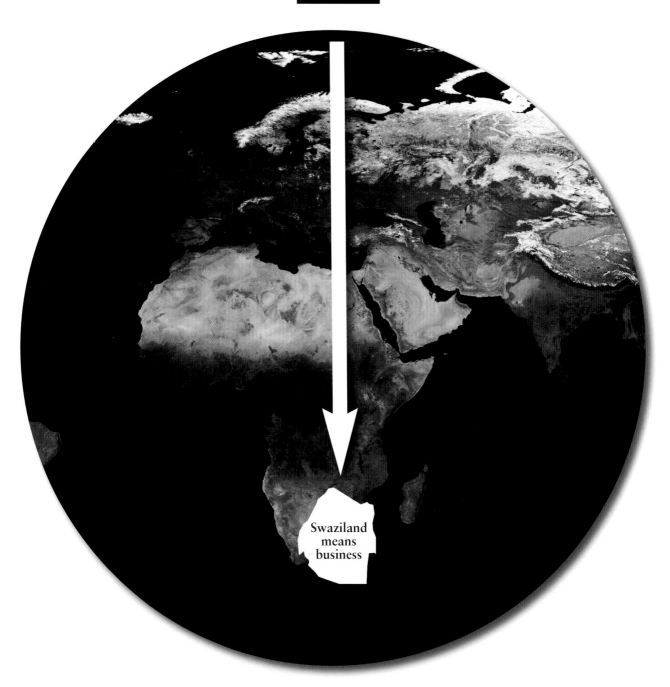

Swaziland
means
business

The Kingdom of Swaziland offers you:

One of Africa's most stable countries	A sound investment climate	Harmonious labour relations	Preferred international markets	Agreeable living conditions

... and SIDC – your investment partner.

Swaziland Industrial Development Company Limited
Tel: +268 2 404 4010 • Email: info@sidc.co.sz
www.sidc.co.sz

The 300km railway is used mainly for freight and continues in a north-easterly direction to Maputo in Mozambique, providing Swaziland with access to shipping. Since 1986, there has been a direct connection between Mpaka (35km east of Manzini) and the South African railway network. The passenger service from Durban to Maputo, Mozambique, passes through Swaziland, stopping at Mpaka.

A new international airport, Sikhuphe International Airport, sited to the east of Manzini, is due to replace Matsapha as the principal international airport in 2010.

Society

KEY FACTS 2010

Population per sq km:	68
Life expectancy:	48 years
Net primary enrolment:	83%

Population: 1,186,000 (2010); 21% lives in urban areas; growth 1.6% p.a. 1990–2010; birth rate 29 per 1,000 people (49 in 1970); life expectancy 48 years, having fallen sharply since the latter 1990s due to AIDS (48 in 1970, 61 in 1990 and 60 in 1997).

Swazis make up 90%; persons of other African, European or mixed descent 10%. Large numbers of Mozambicans fled to Swaziland to escape the civil war, but repatriation was completed in 1993.

Language: siSwati is the national language and English widely spoken.

Religion: Christians about 60% and most of the rest hold traditional beliefs. Traditional beliefs often coexist with Christian beliefs.

Health: Public spending on health was 4% of GDP in 2009. Services are provided by the state, missions and some industrial organisations. 69% of the population uses an improved drinking water source and 55% of people have access to adequate sanitation facilities (2009). Infant mortality was 55 per 1,000 live births in 2010 (150 in 1960). In 2009, 25.9% of people aged 15–49 were HIV positive.

Education: Public spending on education was 7.5% of GDP in 2010. There are seven years of primary education starting at age six and five of secondary comprising cycles of three and two years. Some 72% of pupils complete primary school (2006). The school year starts in January.

The University of Swaziland offers degrees in agriculture, commerce, education, humanities, law and sciences, as well as part-time courses in business. Swaziland College of Technology provides diploma and certificate courses in building, business, education and engineering. The Vocational and Commercial Training Institute offers business and technical training. Literacy among people aged 15–24 is 93% (2009). There is a national library and a mobile library service to remoter parts of the country.

Media: The English-language dailies are *The Times of Swaziland/Sunday Times* and *The Swazi Observer/The Weekend Observer*.

Three national radio stations and the sole national television channel, Swazi TV, are public services.

Some 35% of households have TV sets (2006). There are 37 personal computers (2006) and 80 internet users (2010) per 1,000 people.

Communications: Country code 268; internet domain '.sz'. Public telephones are widely available. Mobile phone coverage is good in urban areas. There are internet cafes in Mbabane and Manzini, and post offices in all the main towns.

There are 37 main telephone lines and 618 mobile phone subscriptions per 1,000 people (2010).

Public holidays: New Year's Day, King's Birthday (19 April), National Flag Day (25 April), Labour Day (1 May), Birthday of late King Sobhuza II (22 July), Independence Day (Somhlolo, 6 September), Christmas Day and Boxing Day.

Religious and other festivals whose dates vary from year to year include Good Friday, Easter Monday, Ascension Day, Umhlanga Reed Dance Day (August/September, date fixed at short notice) and Incwala ceremony (December/January, date fixed at short notice).

Economy

KEY FACTS 2010

GNI:	US$3.1bn
GNI p.c.:	US$2,630
GDP growth:	2.1% p.a. 2006–10
Inflation:	7.6% p.a. 2006–10

Despite subdued growth in the latter 1980s and early 1990s, a period much influenced by the economic problems and then political change in South Africa, Swaziland has, over the longer period, one of the best growth records in Africa, and has pursued liberal policies towards foreign and private investment – especially in mining and industry – since independence in 1968. GDP grew by 6.7% p.a. 1980–90 and 3.4% p.a. 1990–2000.

Real Growth in GDP

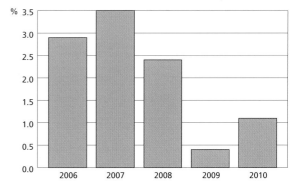

Inflation

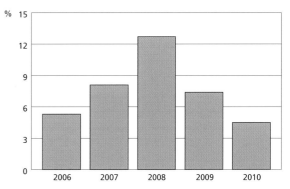

GDP by Sector (2010)

■ Agriculture	8%
□ Industry	45%
▨ Services	47%

Its vulnerability lies in heavy dependence on soft drink concentrate and sugar cane, and on South Africa, which provides imports, investment and employment. It does, however, have established wood pulp, fruit-canning, and clothing and textiles industries, and manufactures a variety of consumer goods, including refrigerators, footwear and plastic domestic goods.

There is dual administration of Swaziland's official financial assets. Those of the Swazi nation, comprising communal land resources (known as Swazi Nation Land) and minerals, are managed by Tibiyo TakaNgwane, an institution created by royal charter in 1968 and not responsible to parliament. The modern economy is managed by the government, but there is an increasing demand, backed by the unions, for far-reaching economic reform.

The economy grew well in the late 1990s but growth was generally slower in the 2000s, due to the deteriorating investment climate, erosion of trade preferences, declining competitiveness, weak institutional capacity and devastation of the workforce by HIV/AIDS (see 'Health' in Society above). Average GDP growth was 2.6% p.a. in 2000–08. In response to the world economic downturn of 2008–09 Swaziland's economy slowed; GDP growth was 0.4% in 2009, 1.1% in 2010 and dipped into recession in 2011.

Constitution

Status:	National Monarchy
Legislature:	Parliament
Independence:	6 September 1968

Under the 2006 constitution the Kingdom of Swaziland is an absolute monarchy. The monarch appoints the prime minister and approves the cabinet and can veto legislation and dissolve parliament, though since July 2005 he can no longer rule by decree.

Under the tinkhundla electoral system, which was introduced in 1978 and amended in 1993 and 2005, there is a bicameral parliament. The House of Assembly has up to 69 members, ten (including at least five women) appointed by the monarch, 55

History

The Nguni Swazi Kingdom rose to prominence early in the 19th century, under the leadership of King Sobhuza I, who enlarged the territory by conquering and absorbing numbers of non-Nguni people.

King Mswati II then moulded the young kingdom into a powerful military force. Through internal stability, military might and diplomacy, Swaziland remained an independent country until the 1890s, the King taking advantage of the rivalry between the British administration in Natal and the Boer republic of the Transvaal to avoid takeover by either.

From 1894 until 1902 the country was administered by the Boer republic, but not annexed. After the defeat of the Boers by Britain in 1902, Swaziland came under British control until independence.

King Sobhuza II reigned from 1921 to 1982 and is thought to have been the second-longest reigning monarch in world history – although he was only officially recognised as king in 1967 under the Swaziland Constitution Order of the British Government. Sobhuza II was a staunch conservative, determined to restore traditional customs and land rights, much of the land having been sold by the colonial authorities to individual European or African farmers. By the time of his death in 1982, almost 40% of the land of the Kingdom was back in the traditional communal system of land tenure.

Swaziland became independent on 6 September 1968 and joined the Commonwealth. In 1973, the King repealed the independence constitution, abolishing parliament and all political parties. The tinkhundla system of government was introduced in 1978 and overhauled in 1993 (see Constitution). When the King died in 1982, there was a four-year delay before Prince Makhosetive acceded to the throne as King Mswati III in 1986.

From the mid-1980s there was building pressure for a return to multiparty democracy. The reintroduction of universal adult suffrage in 1993 only served to increase this pressure. There was from the mid-1990s a succession of strikes organised by the Swaziland Federation of Trade Unions and increasingly public activity by opposition movements. A Constitutional Review Commission was set up in July 1996 to solicit the views of the Swazi nation on the type of constitution the people wanted, by visiting all the constituencies in the country and then submitting a report, including a draft new constitution by 1998.

Elections for pre-selected candidates were held in October 1998. About 60% of the registered voters cast their vote. The King confirmed Dr Sibusiso Barnabas Dlamini as prime minister. Most of the 16 ministers were royal appointees rather than elected members of parliament.

The Constitutional Review Commission finally presented its report to the King in November 2000, but it was not published. In 2001 the King attempted to give himself additional powers to contain the pressure for constitutional reform but climbed down in the face of national and international protests. In August 2001 he called a national gathering and the Commission's chairperson announced – to an audience of only about 10,000 people (the last national gathering was attended by 250,000) – that the King's powers were to be enlarged but gave no details of the fruits of the five-year review.

Subsequently the King set up a new commission to draft a new constitution and the draft was released in May 2003. However, under this constitution the country was to remain an absolute monarchy and, though freedom of assembly was to be allowed and the ban on political parties therefore technically lifted, under the continuing tinkhundla election system there is no role for parties.

elected by universal adult suffrage from a list provided by the tinkhundla (tribal or community committees) and four women elected by the two houses of parliament (one from each region). The Senate has up to 30 members, with ten chosen by the Assembly (including at least five women) and 20 by the monarch (at least eight women).

In each of the 55 tinkhundla, numerous candidates are nominated by show of hands; these are then reduced in secret ballots to three candidates per tinkhundla; the 55 Assembly members are elected in a general election.

The 2006 constitution made provision for an independent judiciary and for human rights, including freedom of assembly and association, but it made no reference to political parties.

Politics

Last elections:	September 2008
Next elections:	2013
Head of state:	King Mswati III
Head of government:	Prime Minister Dr Sibusiso Barnabas Dlamini
Ruling party:	no party system

Assembly and Senate elections for the pre-selected candidates were held in October 2003 and the turnout was low, especially in urban areas. A Commonwealth expert team was present. It said that while there were shortcomings 'the elections were well conducted', but that 'no elections can be credible when they are for a parliament which does not have power and when political parties are banned'. In November 2003 King Mswati III confirmed A T Dlamini as prime minister.

A new constitution – drafted by the Constitutional Review Commission, chaired by Prince David Dlamini – was approved by parliament and signed by the King in July 2005. It came into effect in February 2006.

In the first elections under the new constitution, a new parliament was elected in September 2008. The election was observed by a Commonwealth expert team. The King appointed Dr Sibusiso Barnabas Dlamini as prime minister; he had previously served in that position 1996–2003.

International relations

Swaziland is a member of the African, Caribbean and Pacific Group of States, African Union, Common Market for Eastern and Southern Africa, Non-Aligned Movement, Southern African Customs Union, Southern African Development Community, United Nations and World Trade Organization.

Traveller information

Local laws and conventions: Smuggling and drug taking are both illegal and can incur severe penalties. It is prohibited to photograph the Royal Palace, the Royal Family, uniformed police, army personnel, army vehicles or aircraft and bank buildings. Visitors should always ask permission before taking photographs of local residents.

Personal medications may be brought into the country, but a doctor's note is advisable in case of questioning by customs.

Traditional Swazi culture, in rural areas especially, plays an important role in daily life.

Dress is usually casual. English is widely used in business circles and appointments should always be made. Exchanging business cards is customary. Many hotels in the main cities can provide basic conference facilities. Office hours are Mon–Fri 0800–1300 and 1400–1645.

Immigration and customs: Passports must be valid for six months and visas are not necessary for visitors from South Africa, UK, the USA, Australia, Canada and many Commonwealth countries. Other nationals should consult their local consulate for current visa requirements.

A yellow fever vaccination certificate is required by all those arriving from infected areas.

Duty free allowances are counted as one for married couples travelling together.

Travel within the country: Traffic drives on the left and foreign drivers will require an international driving permit. Car hire is available through a number of international agencies. The maximum speed limit is 80kph.

A good bus network links many of the towns and cities, and there are minibus taxis that run shorter routes. Regular taxis are available in the larger towns.

Travel health: Medical facilities are generally limited outside of Mbabane but private services are available through some hotels. Visitors should ensure they have adequate health insurance that includes medical evacuation to South Africa.

Visitors will need protection against malaria together with insect repellent and suitable clothing to discourage mosquito bites. Hepatitis A, typhoid, tetanus and rabies are also present. Visitors should not swim or paddle in fresh water due to the risk of bilharzia, and should check for ticks after walking or hiking in rural areas, as tick bite fever can occur.

Mains water is generally safe to drink in urban areas, but elsewhere should be boiled or sterilised before use. Bottled water is also available. Milk is pasteurised.

Money: Local currency is the lilangeni (plural, emalangeni). The South African rand is accepted as legal tender, although coins cannot be used. Visitors are advised to exchange emalangeni back into their own currency before leaving Swaziland. American Express, Visa and Mastercard are widely accepted, and ATMs are available in most towns. Travellers cheques are easily changed but should be taken in US dollars, pounds sterling or euros to avoid additional charges. Banking hours are Mon–Fri 0830–1430 and Sat 0830–1100.

There were 754,000 tourist arrivals in 2008.

Further information

Government of Swaziland: www.gov.sz

Central Bank of Swaziland: www.centralbank.org.sz

Commonwealth Secretariat: www.thecommonwealth.org

Commonwealth of Nations: www.commonwealth-of-nations.org/Swaziland

Tonga

KEY FACTS

Joined Commonwealth:	1970
Population:	104,000 (2010)
GDP p.c. growth:	1.6% p.a. 1990–2010
UN HDI 2011:	world ranking 90
Official languages:	Tongan, English
Time:	GMT plus 13hr
Currency:	pa'anga or Tongan dollar (TOP; T$)

Geography

Area:	748 sq km
Coastline:	419km
Capital:	Nuku'alofa

The Kingdom of Tonga, known as 'The Friendly Islands', lies in the central south-west Pacific, surrounded (clockwise from the west) by Fiji, Tuvalu, Kiribati, Samoa, Cook Islands and, to the south, New Zealand. The islands, which straddle the international date line, lie to the east of the Tonga Trench, containing some of the deepest waters of the South Pacific. The main island sub-groups are Tongatapu, Vava'u and Ha'apai. The largest island is Tongatapu.

Area: 748 sq km; Tongatapu 256 sq km.

Topography: Of the 172 islands, only 36 are permanently inhabited. The islands to the east are of coral formation, the Lifuka and Nomuka groups with many small coral islands and reefs. The islands to the west are volcanic. There are active volcanoes on four of the islands, including Tofua Island whose crater is filled with hot water. Falcon, an active volcano under the sea, sends up lava and ash from time to time.

Climate: Hot and humid from January to March; cooler from April to December. Cyclones may occur November to April.

Environment: The most significant environmental issues are deforestation, damage to coral reefs by excessive coral and shell harvesting, and depletion of sea turtle populations by hunters.

Did you know...

Tonga is a monarchy.

Known as 'The Friendly Islands', it comprises 172 islands (36 inhabited; some coral and some volcanic, four with active volcanoes) and straddles the international date line.

Tongans enjoy life expectancy of more than 70 years.

On a per capita basis Tonga has one of the world's highest levels of remittances from nationals living abroad and certainly the highest among the small Pacific island states.

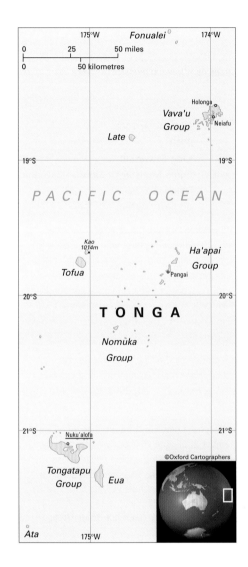

Vegetation: Tongatapu island is flat and covered in small agricultural plantations with coconut trees and other crops. Eua island is hilly and partly forested. The Vava'u Islands are densely wooded. Coconut palms grow along the coastline and cover some of the coral islands. Forest covers 13% of the total land area and there was no significant loss of forest cover during 1990–2010.

Wildlife: Tonga was the first South Pacific country to initiate a conservation programme, with a series of marine and forest reserves. The only land mammal indigenous to Tonga is the 'flying fox', actually a large fruit bat with a wingspan of up to 1 metre. It occurs in a large colony near the village of Kolovai on Tongatapu. Birds include the red-breasted musk parrot and the blue-crowned lory, said to be the most beautiful bird of the Pacific.

Main towns: Nuku'alofa (capital, pop. 24,300 in 2010), Mu'a (5,200), Haveloloto (3,500), Vaini (3,100) and Tofoa–Koloua (2,600) on Tongatapu; Neiafu (4,000) on Vava'u; Pangai (1,600) on Lifuka in the Ha'apai group of islands; and Ohonua (1,300) on Eua.

Transport: There are 680km of roads, 27% paved and the rest surfaced with impacted coral. The two main ports are at Nuku'alofa and Neiafu, and have shipping connections with Australia and Europe. Ferries run between the islands.

International airports are located at Fua'amotu (21km south-east of Nuku'alofa) and at Lupepau'u on Vava'u.

Society

KEY FACTS 2010

Population per sq km:	139
Life expectancy:	72 years

Population: 104,000 (2010); 23% lives in urban areas; growth 0.4% p.a. 1990–2010; birth rate 27 per 1,000 people (37 in 1970); life expectancy 72 years (65 in 1970).

The vast majority of the people are of Polynesian descent. Tonga suffers from heavy emigration, mostly to New Zealand, Australia and the USA. There are 50,478 Tongans living in New Zealand, more than half of whom were born there (2006 New Zealand census).

Language: Tongan and English are official languages.

Religion: Mainly Christians (Wesleyans, Roman Catholics, Anglicans, Church of Tonga, Free Church of Tonga).

Health: Public spending on health was 5% of GDP in 2009. There are public hospitals on the islands of Tongatapu, Ha'apai and Vava'u, and dispensaries throughout the islands. The entire population uses an improved drinking water source and 96% of people have access to adequate sanitation facilities (2009). Over time, the Tongan diet has moved away from traditional root crops to imported foods. Infant mortality was 13 per 1,000 live births in 2010.

Education: There are nine years of compulsory education starting at age five. More than 95% of primary students attend state schools, while about 90% of secondary students attend church schools. The school year starts in February.

Tonga is a partner in the regional University of the South Pacific, which has its main campus in Suva, Fiji, and a campus at 'Atele, about 7km from Nuku'alofa, where some 1,400 students are enrolled per semester for preliminary, foundation and degree courses, using the university's distance-learning facilities. Literacy among people aged 15–24 is 99% (2006).

Media: Newspapers include *Tonga Chronicle* (state-owned weekly), and *Times of Tonga* (published in New Zealand). *Matangi Tonga* is an online news service.

Tonga Broadcasting Commission provides public radio and TV services; there are several private radio stations and TV channels.

There are 59 personal computers (2005) and 120 internet users (2010) per 1,000 people.

Communications: Country code 676; internet domain '.to'. Mobile phone coverage is limited to Nuku'alofa. There are several internet cafes in Nuku'alofa and Neiafu. The main post office is in Nuku'alofa, with branches on Ha'apai and Vava'u.

There are 298 main telephone lines and 522 mobile phone subscriptions per 1,000 people (2010).

Public holidays: New Year's Day, ANZAC Day (25 April), Emancipation Day (4 June), Crown Prince's Birthday (12 July), King's Birthday (1 August), Constitution Day (4 November), Tupou I Day (4 December), Christmas Day and Boxing Day.

Religious festivals whose dates vary from year to year include Good Friday and Easter Monday.

Economy

KEY FACTS 2010

GNI:	US$342m
GNI p.c.:	US$3,280
GDP growth:	0.2% p.a. 2006–10
Inflation:	5.5% p.a. 2006–10

The economy is dominated by subsistence agriculture, and economic performance is heavily dependent on weather conditions and world commodity prices. However, the formal money economy has been growing as farmers have moved towards production of cash crops, some of which are exported, for example squash, which from the early 1990s was exported to Japan.

Real Growth in GDP

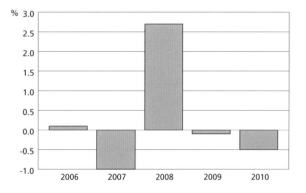

Inflation

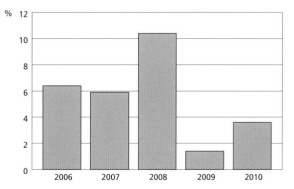

GDP by Sector (2010)

■ Agriculture	**20%**
□ Industry	**17%**
■ Services	**63%**

This very success, though, illustrates the vulnerability of small agricultural economies such as Tonga. In the early 1990s farmers rapidly switched to the new crop. By 1994, there was over-production, a collapse in local prices and unsold stocks. Drought in 1995 led to further falls in exports. Squash and, increasingly, fish products are, nonetheless, the most important exports, and squash remains more profitable than traditional crops such as copra and bananas.

The main source of foreign currency is the remittances of Tongans working abroad, followed by tourism. The government has recognised the need for economic reforms to expand the private sector and diversify the economy and has worked to gain public – and especially civil service – acceptance of the need.

From the late 1990s the economy continued to grow steadily (2.2% p.a., 1997–2006), but slowed from the mid-2000s, with no real growth over the rest of the decade. After the world economic downturn of 2008–09, when remittances fell and tourism was subdued, the economy went into reverse, contracting by 0.1% in 2009 and by 0.5% in 2010.

Constitution

Status:	National Monarchy
Legislature:	Parliament
Independence:	4 June 1970

Until 2010 the constitution was essentially King George Tupou I's constitution granted in 1875, under which executive power resided with the monarch.

Under the 2010 constitution, Tonga is a constitutional monarchy and a parliamentary democracy with a unicameral Legislative

Assembly consisting of 26 elected members, nine of whom are elected by and from among the country's 33 hereditary nobles, and 17 on the basis of universal adult suffrage (women received the vote in 1960) in a general election which must take place at intervals of no longer than 4 years.

The prime minister is chosen by the Legislative Assembly and appointed by the monarch. The prime minister selects his cabinet who are then appointed by the monarch. The prime minister may nominate up to four ministers from outside the Assembly and on appointment they become members of the Assembly.

All land belongs to the Crown. Large estates have been allotted to nobles. By law, every male Tongan at age 16 is entitled to a small piece of agricultural land and a small town plot. In practice, there is not enough land and the majority of men have not been allocated any land, and latterly there have been objections to the exclusion of women. Consequently, reform of the land tenure system has been under discussion.

Politics

Last elections:	November 2010
Next elections:	2014
Head of state:	King Tupou VI (2012–)
Head of government:	Prime Minister Lord Siale'ataonga Tu'ivakano

In the March 2002 elections the pro-democracy Human Rights and Democracy Movement (HRDM) increased its representation in parliament to seven of the nine people's seats and issued new proposals for constitutional reforms to strengthen democracy and reduce the powers of the King. The King reappointed Prime

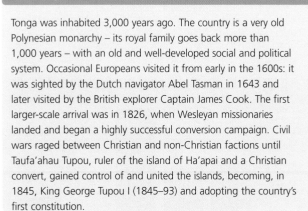

History

Tonga was inhabited 3,000 years ago. The country is a very old Polynesian monarchy – its royal family goes back more than 1,000 years – with an old and well-developed social and political system. Occasional Europeans visited it from early in the 1600s: it was sighted by the Dutch navigator Abel Tasman in 1643 and later visited by the British explorer Captain James Cook. The first larger-scale arrival was in 1826, when Wesleyan missionaries landed and began a highly successful conversion campaign. Civil wars raged between Christian and non-Christian factions until Taufa'ahau Tupou, ruler of the island of Ha'apai and a Christian convert, gained control of and united the islands, becoming, in 1845, King George Tupou I (1845–93) and adopting the country's first constitution.

Tonga was never a British colony. In 1900, the King agreed a treaty of friendship with Britain, which gave Britain control of foreign affairs, and kept Tonga free from other predatory powers. The treaty was frequently revised until May 1970, when Tonga became fully independent.

King Taufa'ahau Tupou IV succeeded his mother, Queen Salote Tupou III, on her death in 1965.

From 1990 a pro-democracy movement gathered strength, challenging Tonga's political system which endeavoured to combine its 1,000 year-old feudal system with democracy. Elections did not result in any changes in the executive and only a

small number of members of the Legislative Assembly were elected. The country did not, in consequence, have a developed party political system.

Tonga's first-ever political party, the People's Party, was formed in 1994 out of the pro-democracy movement. In the 1996 elections four of the nine people's seats were won by pro-democracy candidates and leading democracy campaigner Akilisi Pohiva had a convincing majority in his constituency.

In January 1999 the People's Party held a four-day convention on constitutional change and, with the new name of Human Rights and Democracy Movement (HRDM), it went into the elections of March 1999 with the hope of raising it numbers in the assembly from the six seats they by then controlled. In the event they won only five of the nine people's seats.

In April 1999 former prime minister (1965–91) and brother of King Taufa'ahau Tupou IV, Prince Fatafehi Tu'ipelehake, died. In January 2000, the King appointed his younger son, Prince 'Ulukalala Lavaka-Ata, to replace Baron Vaea as prime minister.

In October 2001, the country was rocked by financial scandal resulting in the resignation of two ministers, including the deputy prime minister. More than US$20 million – the proceeds of the sale of Tongan citizenship in the 1980s – had been placed in June 1999 with a company in the USA that had apparently disappeared.

Minister Prince 'Ulukalala Lavaka-Ata. Though such moves had been unsuccessful in the past, the frailty of the octogenarian King Taufa'ahau Tupou IV and uncertainty over the succession now gave them greater urgency. However, in October 2003, changes to the constitution gave greater power to the King, and increased state control over the media.

In the March 2005 election, the HRDM again won seven of the nine people's parliamentary seats, the remaining two taken by independents. In the same month two commoner and two noble representatives were appointed to cabinet.

In February 2006, Prime Minister Prince 'Ulukalala Lavaka-Ata resigned and Dr Feleti Vaka'uta Sevele became acting prime minister, the first popularly elected member of the Legislative Assembly to be appointed to the post. He was then confirmed as prime minister in March 2006.

In September 2006 King Taufa'ahau Tupou IV (1965–2006) died after a long illness and was succeeded as head of state by his eldest son who was sworn in as King George Tupou V. In November 2006, when it seemed that parliament would go into recess before enacting democratic reforms, pro-democracy demonstrations turned into riots and looting, at least six people died and many buildings in Nuku'alofa were destroyed. At the prime minister's invitation, 150 Australian and New Zealand troops and police came to Tonga to restore order, the King promised that by 2008 the majority of government posts would be filled by elected representatives rather than nobles and King's appointees, and parliament passed the reforms.

In the elections of April 2008, with a turnout reportedly less than 50%, HRDM and its ally, People's Democratic Party, together won six of the nine contested seats and independents took three.

In July 2008 the Constitutional and Electoral Commission was established, with the immediate task of making proposals for a more democratic system of government. In the same month the King's spokesperson announced that by 2010 the King would surrender his role in government to the prime minister and that most Assembly members would be elected. In November 2009 the final report of the Constitutional and Electoral Commission was delivered to the Legislative Assembly; the new constitution was approved by the Assembly in April 2010 and enacted in September 2010.

In the country's first democratic elections, held on 25 November 2010, the Friendly Islands Democratic Party, led by 'Akilisi Pohiva, won 12 of the 17 popularly elected seats, but remained short of a majority in the 26-seat Legislative Assembly. The remaining seats were taken by five independent people's representatives and nine nobles. The Assembly members initiated negotiations with a view to forming a new government. On 21 December 2010 a noble, Lord Tu'ivakano, was elected prime minister by the Assembly, defeating Pohiva by 14 votes to 12.

On 18 March 2012 King George Tupou V (2006–12) died and was succeeded as head of state by his brother, former prime minister (2000–06) and High Commissioner to Australia (2008–12) Crown Prince Tupouto'a Lavaka, who was sworn in as King Tupou VI.

International relations

Tonga is a member of the African, Caribbean and Pacific Group of States, Pacific Community, Pacific Islands Forum, United Nations and World Trade Organization.

Traveller information

Local laws and conventions: Visitors should note that Sunday is sacred in Tonga and it is unlawful to work or trade on this day; almost everything (except bakeries, a few restaurants and resorts) is closed. Drug taking is illegal and trafficking drugs attracts heavy penalties. Anyone appearing in public without a shirt will be fined.

Tonga is a conservative and religious society. Visitors should dress modestly; and beachwear should be for beach only. Shaking hands is the usual form of greeting.

English and French are the most common languages used in business circles. Contracts signed on a Sunday are void. Office hours are Mon–Fri 0830–1630.

Immigration and customs: Passports must be valid for six months, and visas are issued at the airport and are valid for one month. Visitors must also hold a return ticket and have sufficient funds for their stay.

The import of firearms, ammunition and pornography is prohibited, and the export of valuable artefacts and certain flora and fauna is restricted.

A yellow fever vaccination certificate is required by those arriving from an infected area.

Travel within the country: Traffic drives on the left. Visitors will need a local driving permit, which is obtained on presentation of a national driving licence and a small fee from the Police Traffic Department in Nuku'alofa. Car hire is only available in Nuku'alofa and Neiafu. Speed limits are low, but are strictly enforced.

There are regular ferry services between the islands, though timetables are subject to change, depending on the weather or demand.

Minibus services are available throughout Tongatapu. Taxis can be recognised by their 'T' licence plates. Visitors can also hire a chauffeur-driven car.

Travel health: Visitors should have comprehensive health insurance which includes air evacuation, as serious medical cases are flown to Australia or New Zealand.

Dengue fever is prevalent in Tonga, and visitors should ensure they take insect repellent and suitable clothing to protect against being bitten by dengue-carrying mosquitoes.

Tap water is chlorinated and is safe to drink in the main towns, and bottled water is widely available. Elsewhere, sterilisation of drinking water is sometimes advisable.

Money: The local currency is the pa'anga. Foreign currency exchange is available at banks and major hotels. There is limited use of credit cards but ATMs are available in Nuku'alofa and Neiafu. Banking hours are Mon–Fri 0900–1600, Sat 0830–1130.

There were 51,000 tourist arrivals in 2009.

Further information

Tonga Government Portal: www.pmo.gov.to

Parliament: www.parliament.gov.to

National Reserve Bank of Tonga: www.reservebank.to

Commonwealth Secretariat: www.thecommonwealth.org

Commonwealth of Nations: www.commonwealth-of-nations.org/Tonga

Ministry of Energy and Energy Affairs, Trinidad and Tobago

MINISTRY OF
ENERGY
AND ENERGY AFFAIRS
POWER. PROSPERITY. PROGRESS.

Commitment, Integrity, Innovation, Performance and Transparency

Responsibility

The Ministry of Energy and Energy Affairs (MEEA) is responsible for the overall management of the energy and minerals sectors in Trinidad and Tobago. These sectors continue to generate significant revenues which support the developmental objectives of the Government of the Republic of Trinidad and Tobago.

Vision

A global leader in the strategic development of the energy and minerals sectors.

Mission

The mission of the MEEA is to contribute to Trinidad and Tobago's prosperity through the sustainable development of the energy and mineral resources.

Divisions

The MEEA comprises the following eight technical divisions in addition to its administrative and support departments:

• Resource Management
• Contracts Management
• Commercial Evaluation
• Downstream and Retail Marketing
• Energy Research and Planning
• LNG and Gas Exports
• Minerals
• HSE and Measurement

State Agencies

The state agencies under the purview of the MEEA are:

• Lake Asphalt Trinidad and Tobago (LATT) 1978 Company Limited
• Petroleum Company of Trinidad and Tobago (Petrotrin)
• National Quarries Company Limited (NQCL)
• National Petroleum Marketing Company (NPMC) Limited
• National Gas Company (NGC) Limited
• National Energy Corporation (NEC)

Current Initiatives

• Exploration

  Analysts forecast a growing demand for natural gas to 2050. Trinidad and Tobago, as a gas producer, intends to respond prudently by increasing exploration and production capabilities and capitalizing on lead-time.

• Renewable Energy/Compressed Natural Gas/Natural Gas Vehicles (NGV)

  Renewable energy (RE), enhanced energy efficiency (EE) and utilization of compressed natural gas (CNG) in the transportation sector are important priorities in order to promote the sustainable development of the nation.

*Senator the Honourable
Kevin Ramnarine, Minister*

*Mr Richard Oliver,
Permanent Secretary (Acting)*

Contact

The Ministry of Energy and Energy Affairs
Level 26, Tower C,
International Waterfront Centre
1 Wrightson Road, Port-of-Spain
Republic of Trinidad and Tobago

Tel: +1 868 623 6542 • +1 868 627 8320
Fax: +1 868 625 0306 •+1 868 627 7922

www.energy.gov.tt

Trinidad and Tobago

KEY FACTS

Joined Commonwealth:	1962
Population:	1,341,000 (2010)
GDP p.c. growth:	5.0% p.a. 1990–2010
UN HDI 2011:	world ranking 62
Official language:	English
Time:	GMT minus 4hr
Currency:	Trinidad and Tobago dollar (TT$)

Geography

Area:	5,128 sq km
Coastline:	362km
Capital:	Port of Spain

The country, the most southerly of the West Indian island states, situated 11.2km off the Venezuelan coast, consists of two islands: Trinidad and Tobago.

Area: 5,128 sq km: Trinidad (4,828 sq km) and Tobago (300 sq km).

Topography: Trinidad and Tobago are unique among Caribbean islands in that only 10,000 years ago they were a part of the South American mainland; the geology and rich flora and fauna are closely akin to Venezuela. A mountain range runs along the north coast, rising to Trinidad's highest point, El Cirro del Aripo (940m); there are rolling hills in the south and the flat Caroni Plain lies in between. Trinidad is well supplied with rivers, some of which end in mangrove swamps on the coast. The Pitch Lake in the south-west is the world's largest natural reservoir of asphalt. A string of small islands off the north-west peninsula are the remnants of the land-link with the continent. There are sandy beaches in the north and east, and Trinidad has many excellent harbours. Tobago also

Did you know...

Kamla Persad-Bissessar became the first woman prime minister of Trinidad and Tobago in May 2010.

Sir Vidia Naipaul, born in Chaguanas, Trinidad, in August 1932, was awarded the Nobel Prize in Literature in 2001; and Earl Lovelace won the Commonwealth Writers' Prize in 1997.

Brian Lara, born in Santa Cruz, Trinidad, in May 1969, was Wisden Leading Cricketer in the World in 1994 and 1995.

Scholarships for postgraduate study are awarded by Trinidad and Tobago to citizens of other Commonwealth countries under the Commonwealth Scholarship and Fellowship Plan.

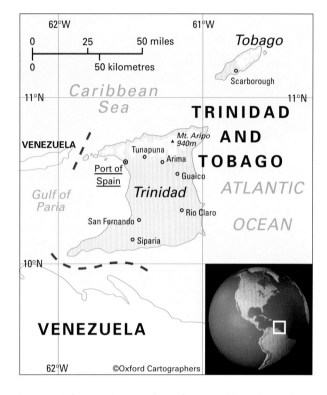

©Oxford Cartographers

has a central mountain range descending to a plain in the south-west and many fine beaches.

Climate: Tropical, tempered by north-east trade winds, with a temperature range of 22–31°C and an average annual rainfall of 1,631mm. The dry season is January to May and the wet season June to December, with a short dry sunny season called the *Petit Careme* during September and October.

Environment: The most significant environmental issues are water pollution from agricultural chemicals, industrial wastes and raw sewage; oil pollution of beaches; deforestation; and soil erosion.

Vegetation: Forest covers 44% of the land area, having declined at 0.3% p.a. 1990–2010. The forest is tropical evergreen: high in the mountains are mountain mangrove, tree-ferns and small palms; on the lower slopes, hog-plums and sand-box; and in the fresh and brackish swamps, mangrove and gable-palms. The most important agricultural areas are in the central plain of Trinidad. Arable land comprises 5% and permanent cropland 4% of the total land area.

Wildlife: There are many more species of birds and butterflies than on any other Caribbean island, including 15 varieties of hummingbird (131 species of birds and only one endangered, 2002). There is a wildlife sanctuary in the Northern Range on Trinidad at El Tucuche with agouti, golden tree-frogs and more than 400 species of birds, and the Caroni Swamp reserve is the home of thousands of scarlet ibis. The government has proposed a

Government of the Republic of Trinidad and Tobago
Ministry of Finance

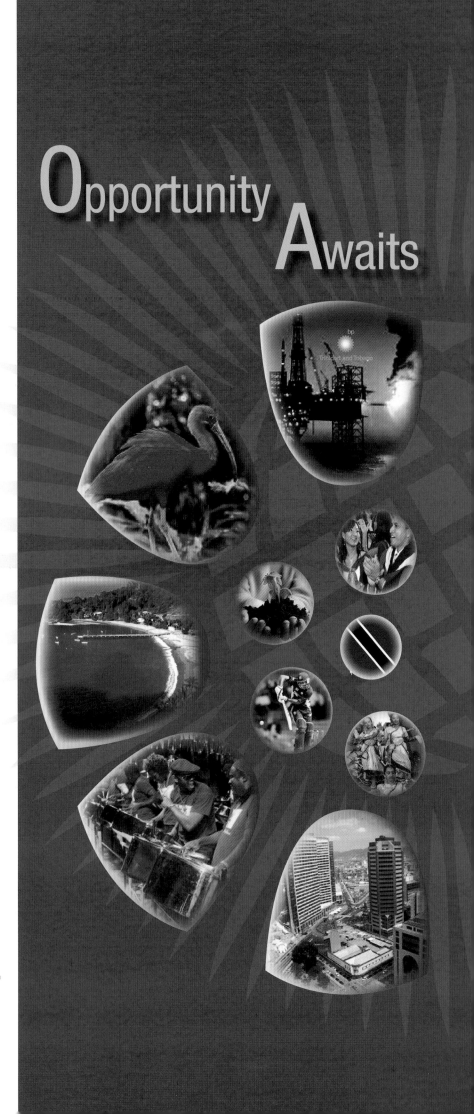

Opportunity Awaits

The resilience of our banking system in the face of the economic crisis has been commended (IMF Country Report, 2011). **Standard and Poor's** affirmed our long term foreign currency rating at 'A' in December 2010.

We have one of the highest per capita incomes and credit ratings in the region. Not only are we the number one destination for debt financing in the Caribbean but home to a number of multi–national companies in energy and other sectors.
Our well–educated citizenry stands ready to use their knowledge and skills.

We are **Trinidad and Tobago,** the gateway for Latin America, the Caribbean and the World.

www.finance.gov.tt

National Parks and Wildlife Bill, which aims to protect endangered species of which there are now relatively very few.

Main towns: Port of Spain (capital, pop. 50,300 in 2010), Chaguanas (77,400), San Fernando (57,300), San Juan (greater Port of Spain, 56,200), Arima (greater Port of Spain, 38,000), Marabella (greater San Fernando, 26,700), Tunapuna (greater Port of Spain, 19,100), Point Fortin (18,800), Sangre Grande (17,500) and Princes Town (11,000) on Trinidad; and Scarborough (4,800) on Tobago.

Transport: There are 8,320km of roads, 51% paved. There is no railway.

Port of Spain and Point Lisas are the main ports. Point Lisas deep-water port on the west coast serves the petro-chemical industries. Other terminals are at Pointe-à-Pierre, Point Fortin and Guayaguayare (petroleum); Claxton (cement); Tembladora (bauxite); Brighton (asphalt); Chaguaramas (dry-docks); and Scarborough on Tobago. Tourist cruiseships dock in Scarborough and Port of Spain.

Piarco International Airport, 25km east of Port of Spain, is a major regional centre for passenger and cargo traffic and aviation-related industries. Crown Point International Airport on Tobago can handle wide-bodied intercontinental aircraft.

Society

KEY FACTS 2010

Population per sq km:	262
Life expectancy:	70 years
Net primary enrolment:	96%

Population: 1,341,000 (2010); some 54,000 on Tobago; 14% of the whole population lives in urban areas; growth 0.5% p.a. 1990–2010; birth rate 15 per 1,000 people (27 in 1970); life expectancy 70 years (66 in 1970).

The population is of about 40% Indian, 38% African and 21% mixed descent, with smaller numbers of people of European, Latin American and Chinese descent (2000 census).

Language: English is the official and national language; English-, French- and Spanish-based Creoles, Indian languages including Hindi and Chinese dialects are also spoken.

Religion: Mainly Christians (Roman Catholics 26%, Anglicans 8%, Pentecostals 7%), Hindus 23% and Muslims 6% (2000 census).

Health: Public spending on health was 3% of GDP in 2009. Traditionally good services have suffered somewhat from reductions in public expenditure. 94% of the population uses an improved drinking water source and 92% have access to adequate sanitation facilities (2009). Infant mortality was 24 per 1,000 live births in 2010 (61 in 1960). In 2009, 1.5% of people aged 15–49 were HIV positive.

Education: There are seven years of compulsory education starting at age five. Primary school comprises seven years and secondary five, with cycles of three and two years. Some 93% of pupils complete primary school (2008). The school year starts in September.

Tertiary institutions include the St Augustine campus of the regional University of the West Indies (UWI), which also has main campuses in Barbados and Jamaica. At St Augustine UWI offers undergraduate and postgraduate courses in agriculture, education, engineering, humanities, law, medical sciences, sciences and social sciences. The University of Trinidad and Tobago was established in

2004 and includes the Eastern Caribbean Institute of Agriculture and Forestry. Other tertiary institutions include College of Science, Technology and Applied Arts; and Polytechnic Institute, which provides adult education in the evenings and shares premises with the Sixth Form Government School. There is virtually no illiteracy among people aged 15–24.

Media: English-language dailies include *Trinidad and Tobago Guardian*, *Daily Express* and *Newsday*; *The Bomb*, *The T'n'T Mirror* and *Sunday Punch* are weeklies.

The Caribbean News Media Group operates public radio and TV services; and there are a number of private radio stations and TV channels.

Some 88% of households have TV sets (2006). There are 132 personal computers (2007) and 485 internet users (2010) per 1,000 people.

Communications: Country code 1 868; internet domain '.tt'. Mobile phone coverage is good. There are numerous internet cafes and post office branches on the islands.

There are 219 main telephone lines and 1,412 mobile phone subscriptions per 1,000 people (2010).

Public holidays: New Year's Day, Spiritual Baptist Shouters' Liberation Day (30 March), Indian Arrival Day (30 May, 1845), Labour Day (19 June), Emancipation Day (1 August, 1834 and 1838), Independence Day (31 August), Republic Day (24 September), Christmas Day and Boxing Day.

Religious and other festivals whose dates vary from year to year include Carnival (Monday before Lent), Good Friday, Easter Monday, Corpus Christi, Eid al-Fitr (End of Ramadan) and Diwali (October/November). Carnival is celebrated during the month leading up to Carnival Day.

Economy

KEY FACTS 2010

GNI:	US$20.6bn
GNI p.c.:	US$15,380
GDP growth:	3.3% p.a. 2006–10
Inflation:	9.1% p.a. 2006–10

Trinidad and Tobago has a very sophisticated economy for a country of its size, embracing mineral extraction, agriculture, industry, tourism and services, but which is underpinned by a single commodity – oil – which was first discovered in 1866. The high

Real Growth in GDP

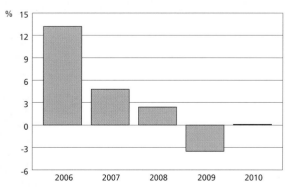

TRINIDAD AND TOBAGO

Preference for the poor and disadvantaged

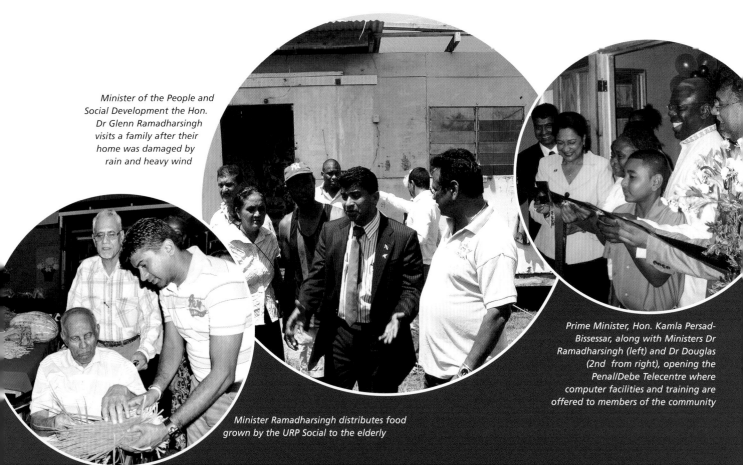

Minister of the People and Social Development the Hon. Dr Glenn Ramadharsingh visits a family after their home was damaged by rain and heavy wind

Minister Ramadharsingh distributes food grown by the URP Social to the elderly

Prime Minister, Hon. Kamla Persad-Bissessar, along with Ministers Dr Ramadharsingh (left) and Dr Douglas (2nd from right), opening the Penal/Debe Telecentre where computer facilities and training are offered to members of the community

The Ministry of the People and Social Development holds at its core a vision of People-centred Governance, Poverty Eradication and Social Justice. The Ministry serves to revolutionise Trinidad and Tobago's approach to core social problems by espousing two interconnected pillars for sustainable development.

These pillars – 'People-Centred Governance' and 'Poverty Eradication and Social Justice' - underpin the main thrust of the Ministry in addressing various forms of vulnerability through actively involving citizens in their own development. Using the analogy that 'a chain is only as strong as its weakest link', the Ministry maintains that to build a strong nation, the vulnerable must be protected and empowered. Accordingly, the Ministry implements programmes to target the multifaceted symptoms of poverty, while simultaneously focusing on its root causes.

The Ministry believes that the real concerns of people confronted with disaster, challenges and urgent issues must be tackled through outreach exercises, walkabouts, stakeholder sessions and rapid response times.

The Rights of Individuals to Social and Economic Security, Universal Prosperity (RISE UP) constitutes the Ministry's conditional component of the Targeted Conditional Cash Transfer Programme. Its framework encompasses four phases: Eligibility, Diagnostics, Work Phase and Autonomy.

Families eligible for social protection are identified via a means test. They then undergo Life Skills Development to evaluate their socio-economic position and establish practical goals to transcend poverty. Support is provided to enable clients to achieve these goals and their standard of living is reviewed over 15 months.

RISE UP's services seek to fulfil a range of needs, from income and food security to training and education, which will ultimately break the cycle of poverty.

RISE UP's phases are incorporated into other ministerial programmes including the Social Component of the Unemployment Relief Programme and the Poverty Reduction Programme, which offers skills-building and funding for micro-entrepreneurs.

The Ministry's 2011-2015 operational plans use applicable Millennium Development Goals as benchmarks, working with other government Ministries, the corporate sector and civil society to synergise resources for all citizens of Trinidad and Tobago.

www.ttconnect.gov.tt

Inflation

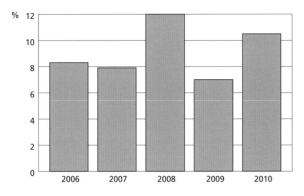

GDP by Sector (2010)

In the late 1980s, a programme of privatisation was under way and continued through the 1990s. At the same time industries based on natural gas, tourism and other service industries were developed. Tax receipts have been rising through more efficient collection, though many tax rates have been cut.

With the new industries on stream and oil prices strong, the economy was buoyant in the latter 1990s and 2000s, pausing briefly only in 2001–02, a period of political uncertainty, when the government was distracted from the structural reforms and investor confidence diminished. Then during 2002–06 the economy grew at 10% p.a., moderating to 4.6% in 2007. In the global economic downturn of

price of oil in the 1970s allowed considerable publicly financed development, but when the price fell in the 1980s the economy faltered badly. In the recession years (1985–89), GDP fell by 30% in real terms. Although the government had substantial reserves, these were exhausted by 1987, and the economy had to be supported by the IMF until 1993, when oil prices had recovered.

History

Until 1888, Trinidad and Tobago were separate territories. Both have a history of repeated invasion and conquest by competing European powers.

Trinidad, named *Iere* (probably meaning 'humming bird') by the Arawak inhabitants, was claimed for the Spanish Crown by Christopher Columbus in 1498. The embattled Spanish colony that developed was raided by the English, Dutch and French through the 17th century. Large-scale importation of African slaves enabled a plantation economy to develop. French Haitians (who were offered incentives by the Spanish Crown) swelled the settler population.

In 1797, the island surrendered to a British expedition and became a British Crown colony in 1802. Slaves were emancipated in 1834, free trade adopted in 1846, and more than 150,000 immigrants from India, China and Madeira brought in between 1845 and 1917. These indentured labourers came on short contracts, after which they were free to return home or buy plots of land. The Indians worked mainly on the sugar plantations of the Caroni and Naparima plains and introduced the cultivation of rice there.

Tobago's name derives from the Carib word *Tavaco*, the pipe in which the Amerindians smoked tobacco leaves, and was inhabited by Caribs at the time of Columbus's visit in 1498. These people had all been killed by 1632 when 300 Dutch settlers arrived. Further Dutch and French settlers followed. Tobago changed hands more frequently between 1650 and 1814 than any other Caribbean territory – ownership shifting from a settler (Cornelius Lampsius, declared owner and Baron of Tobago by Louis XIV of France) to the Duke of Courland, to a company of London merchants, to neutral status in 1748, to the English Crown by the Treaty of Paris of 1763.

Even then, Tobago was fought over. The French captured it in 1781; the British took it back in 1793; the French regained it

through the Treaty of Amiens (1802), but it was returned to the British in 1814. Despite these battles, Tobago was prosperous until its sugar industry was weakened by the abolition of slavery, a hurricane, the decline of West Indian sugar in general and the Belmanna riots. No longer viable as a separate colony, it was amalgamated with the larger island of Trinidad in 1888.

The Spanish constitution was retained after Trinidad became a British Crown colony in 1802. The governor was assisted by a council of advice and a cabildo elected by the taxpayers. The council of advice evolved into the nominated legislative council and the cabildo became Port of Spain's town council. When Tobago was amalgamated with Trinidad in 1888, the laws of Trinidad were extended to the smaller island and, after a period, the revenues of the two islands were merged and Tobago's debt to Trinidad cancelled. Tobago was administered by a commissioner (later a warden) appointed by the colony's governor.

In the 1920s, the labour movement organised trade unions, and pressure increased for greater local democracy and then independence. A new constitution brought a limited form of electoral representation to Trinidad for the first time (Tobago had had elections before). But only seven of the 25 members were elected, and high property and language qualifications limited the vote. This did not satisfy the growing demand for political expression, which led to the 1937 labour disturbances, an increase in the number of elected members in 1941 and, in 1945, universal adult suffrage.

In 1950, the constitution was redrawn, providing for a legislative council of 26 members, 18 of them elected; a policy-making executive council of nine (five elected by the legislative council), and a rudimentary ministerial system. Further constitutional changes followed, and by 1959, the legislative council had more elected members and an elected speaker, and the ministerial system had developed into a cabinet elected from the legislative council. The governor's powers were circumscribed: he did not ➤

Ancient canopies of verdant green, over 220 species of birds and a diverse wildlife, leather back turtles, stunning reefs, secluded waterfalls, these are just some of the natural wonders Tobago offers. Considered one of the world's best eco-destinations, Tobago is a haven for all nature enthusiasts.

Plan your next
Eco-Tobago Adventure

CONTACT:
Tobago Department of Tourism
Division of Tourism and Transportation
Tobago House of Assembly

Website: www.visittobago.gov.tt
Email: contact@visittobago.gov.tt

Contacts for overseas offices can be found on
www.visittobago.gov.tt

Eco-Tobago

An extraordinary journey into nature awaits you

www.visittobago.gov.tt

2008–09 demand for Trinidad and Tobago's manufactures weakened sharply and the economy shrank by 3.5% in 2009, and stood still in 2010 and 2011. Unemployment, which had fallen to an all-time low of 4.6% in 2008, rose rapidly in 2009–11.

Oil and gas

There are more than 30 producing oil and gas fields, many of them offshore. For a long time after the 1970s there were no very significant fields discovered but exploration in areas off the east coast led to discovery of the large Angostura field in 2001. In January 2011 proven oil reserves were estimated at 800 million barrels. Oil production increased from 113,500 barrels a day in 2001 to 144,500 in 2005, falling to 93,600 in the second quarter of 2011. Exploration has intensified following the Angostura find, but offshore fields are costly and slow to be brought on stream. There are two oil refineries: at Pointe-à-Pierre and at Point Fortin.

Trinidad and Tobago has estimated proven natural gas reserves of 400 billion cubic metres (January 2011). The Atlantic LNG Plant at Point Fortin started to export natural gas in 1999. It was then expanded in stages during the 2000s and the country is among the world's biggest exporters of LNG.

Manufacturing

Manufacturing and process industries are centred on the free-trade zone. The government established joint ventures with foreign companies to produce iron and steel, petrochemicals, cement, ammonia and other nitrogenous fertilisers, urea and methanol. Plans for construction of an aluminium smelter funded by China were announced in 2008. This followed rejection of US-based Alcoa's plans for a large smelter which were successfully challenged by environmentalists.

Trinidad and Tobago's natural gas has a high methane content with few impurities and is very suitable for methanol and ammonia production. The Point Lisas industrial estate has seven large, modern methanol plants, nine ammonia plants and a urea plant, with more under development, and the country is among the world's largest exporters of both methanol and ammonia.

It also assembles motor vehicles and produces consumer durables, such as television sets and gas cookers, and clothing, and there is a significant printing industry.

Constitution

Status:	Republic
Legislature:	Parliament
Independence:	31 August 1962

Trinidad and Tobago is a unitary republic with a representative government and a degree of regional autonomy. The head of state is a non-executive president elected by an electoral college comprising all the members of parliament. The executive is led by the prime minister who heads a cabinet chosen by him or her and responsible to parliament.

The legislature consists of the bicameral Parliament, with a directly elected 41-member House of Representatives and a 31-member Senate. Senators are appointed by the president, 16 on the advice of the prime minister, six on the advice of the leader of the opposition, and nine of the president's own choice. Elections are held every five years.

Tobago has a regional house of assembly, set up in 1980, with certain local powers over finances and other delegated responsibilities. It has 12 elected members and several members appointed by the political parties. Constitutional amendments have granted Tobago greater control over urban and rural development, health, education and housing, though its assembly has no legislative powers.

Politics

Last elections:	May 2010 (national)
Next elections:	2015 (national)
Head of state:	President Professor George Maxwell Richards (2003–)
Head of government:	Prime Minister Kamla Persad-Bissessar
Ruling party:	People's Partnership coalition

Following the tied December 2001 general election – when the People's National Movement (PNM) and the United National Congress (UNC) each secured 18 seats in the House of Representatives (and the National Alliance for Reconstruction none) – a fresh election was called in October 2002 when the PNM

secured a majority, with 20 seats with 50.7% of the votes, while the UNC took 16 with 46.5%. PNM leader Patrick Manning – whom the president had chosen to be prime minister and form a government after the tied election – resumed as prime minister.

In the elections in November 2007 (with the number of contested seats increased from 36 to 41), on a platform that highlighted its strong economic management and proposed introduction of an executive presidency, the ruling PNM won with 26 seats and 45.9% of votes. The main opposition UNC took 15 seats and 29.7% of votes and the newly established Congress of the People gained 22.6% of votes but no seats. PNM's majority was a few seats short of the two-thirds required to amend the constitution.

Following a threatened vote of no confidence against Prime Minister Manning in April 2010, he dissolved parliament. In the general election which followed in May 2010, a new five-party coalition, the People's Partnership, led by UNC leader Kamla Persad-Bissessar and including the Congress of the People, won 29 of the 41 seats in the lower house and 42.9% of the votes cast, soundly defeating the incumbent PNM (12 seats and 39.6%). Persad-Bissessar became prime minister, the first woman in the country's history to assume the role.

➤ normally chair cabinet meetings, and had to act in accordance with the cabinet's advice.

The 1956 elections gave the majority to the People's National Movement (PNM), led by Dr Eric Williams. Williams instituted further constitutional talks with the UK in 1959–60, resulting in full internal self-government and a bicameral legislature (nominated Senate and elected House of Representatives). The general election of 1961 was again won by the PNM, which implemented the new constitution.

In 1958 Trinidad and Tobago became a co-founder of the Federation of the West Indies, which aimed to become an independent country, but Jamaica withdrew in 1961, and Trinidad and Tobago also decided to seek its own independence. Further constitutional talks with the UK began, and a draft constitution was drawn up after much consultation. The country became independent in August 1962, and a republic in 1976.

The PNM under Williams (and after his death in 1981, George Chambers) had a long run of electoral successes. Economic conditions worsened in the early 1980s and the PNM was ousted in 1986 by a coalition of opposition parties, the National Alliance for Reconstruction (NAR) led by A N R Robinson. However, the coalition was troubled, and soon the United Labour Front (led by Basdeo Panday, Robinson's deputy) quit the alliance to form the United National Congress (UNC).

In July 1990, an attempted coup was staged by a militant Muslim faction, which stormed parliament and took Robinson and members of parliament hostage for five days and led to an outbreak of looting in poor areas of the capital. The hostages were released on the promise of an amnesty, but the NAR government was never able to recover and the PNM, under Patrick Manning, won an easy electoral victory in December 1991.

The PNM lost its substantial majority at the November 1995 elections: it won 17 seats, exactly the same number as Panday's

UNC, while the NAR won two and thus held the balance of power. The NAR chose to support the UNC, which was then able to form a government, headed by Panday. Following the retirement of President Noor Hassanali, A N R Robinson became the country's president in February 1997.

The UNC's position was strengthened by divisions within the PNM. Although its leader, Patrick Manning, won a leadership contest in October 1996, his challenger received 40% of the votes. Two PNM MPs subsequently left the party, becoming independents. Both later began to support the UNC and were appointed government ministers. Consequently, although the UNC–NAR coalition remained intact, the UNC had a parliamentary majority on its own from the middle of 1997.

In June–July 1999, ten convicted murderers were hanged. These executions – the first since 1994 – had been delayed for several years by appeals to the Privy Council in the UK, and had only been carried out when the Privy Council had ruled that hanging was not in itself inhumane. The Caribbean Court of Justice was subsequently established in Port of Spain as the final court of appeal for CARICOM countries.

In the December 2000 general election, the UNC was re-elected, winning 19 of the 36 elected seats, while PNM took 16 and NAR one; Panday continued as prime minister. However, the PNM immediately challenged the result on the grounds that two UNC candidates had had dual nationality. There was further controversy when the president was unwilling to appoint seven of Panday's nominations to cabinet posts who had all been defeated in the elections.

President Robinson finally gave way in February 2001 but the PNM's challenge to the legitimacy of the two UNC members took far longer to resolve and the new administration continued in 2001 amid considerable uncertainty, which was only dispelled when a fresh national election was called for December 2001.

Trinidad and Tobago Unified Teachers' Association

Striving for high-quality equitable education and teacher development

VISION

The Trinidad and Tobago Unified Teachers' Association (TTUTA) shall be the strong, proud, united voice of inspired education service professionals promoting education and social justice.

MISSION

To serve as a trade union which represents education service professionals and providing effective and efficient Industrial Relations and Professional Development services as well as social benefits, through the utilization of the most modern, appropriate technology and the constant mobilization of its human resources in an environment which promotes democracy, equality, equity and fraternity among its members.

TTUTA'S WORK

TTUTA was established in 1979 and is the official, legally recognized trade union for teachers at the primary and secondary level of the public Teaching Service in Trinidad and Tobago. It has some 11,000 members from some 600 schools across the country and also includes membership from school supervisors, curriculum officers, guidance personnel and teachers in the Early Childhood, Care and Education sector.

TTUTA works in partnership with the Ministry of Education and the Division of Education, Youth Affairs and Sport of the Tobago House of Assembly towards the development of education in Trinidad and Tobago.

TTUTA is an affiliate of the Caribbean Union of Teachers and Education International and is also part of the Joint Trade Union Movement in Trinidad and Tobago.

Corner Fowler Street and
Southern Main Road, Curepe,
Trinidad and Tobago

Email: gensec.ttuta@gmail.com
Tel: +1 868 645 2134
Fax: +1 868 662 1813

Mr Roustan Job, President

ttuta.org.tt / ttuta.org

International relations

Trinidad and Tobago is a member of the African, Caribbean and Pacific Group of States, Association of Caribbean States, Caribbean Community, Non-Aligned Movement, Organization of American States, United Nations and World Trade Organization.

Trinidad and Tobago hosts the secretariat of the Association of Caribbean States in Port of Spain.

Traveller information

Local laws and conventions: Drug traffickers face severe penalties in Trinidad and Tobago. The authorities are alert to the carriage of illicit drugs of any kind and checks are thorough.

It is against the law for anyone, including children, to dress in camouflage clothing. Visitors should ask before photographing local residents.

Handshaking is the usual form of greeting. Casual wear is usual, but beachwear must not be worn in towns.

Lightweight suits are the norm for business and business cards are usually exchanged. The best time to visit is from December to April, except during the Christmas festivities. Office hours are Mon–Fri 0800–1630.

Immigration and customs: Passports must be valid for six months beyond the intended length of stay. Visas are requested of some nationals and all visa requirements should be checked well in advance of travel. All visitors must be in possession of a return or onward ticket and have sufficient funds for their stay.

A yellow fever vaccination certificate will be needed by all those arriving from infected areas.

Travel within the country: Traffic drives on the left and visitors may use their national driving licence for up to 90 days. Car hire is available at both airports. Trinidad's highway system connects the east-west and the north-south corridors, and the speed limit is 80kph; in urban areas the speed limit is 50kph. There is a 50kph speed limit throughout Tobago.

Trinidad has a public bus service. Mini-vans, called Maxi Taxis, pick up and drop off passengers as they travel; they have no fixed timetable but are easy to flag down along most of the main roads near Port of Spain. In Tobago, there are regular bus services between Scarborough and Crown Point, Buccoo, Plymouth and Roxborough.

Taxis are available on both islands and official taxis are recognised by the 'H' on their licence plates. Taxis are not metered and fares should be agreed before travel.

Scheduled ferry services run daily between the two islands; high-speed CAT ferries take two hours 30 minutes.

A 30-minute flight is the most comfortable and convenient way of travelling between Trinidad and Tobago, and Caribbean Airlines operates hourly services.

Travel health: Visitors should have comprehensive health insurance. Dengue fever is endemic in the Caribbean, and visitors should protect themselves against mosquito bites by using insect repellent and wearing suitable clothing. Visitors should stay away from the poisonous manchineel trees. They are found on some beaches and are clearly marked; skin contact with any part of this tree or its fruit will result in severe blisters.

Drinking water outside of major cities in Trinidad should be boiled or sterilised before use; bottled water is widely available. The mains water in Tobago is safe to drink.

Money: The local currency is the Trinidad and Tobago dollar (TT$). Foreign currency can only be exchanged at banks and some hotels. Credit cards are widely accepted, but many traders may charge an additional 5% for their use. ATMs are common throughout Trinidad, but in Tobago are available only in Scarborough. Banking hours are Mon–Thur 0800–1400, Fri 0900–1200 and 1500–1700.

There were 436,000 tourist arrivals in 2008.

Further information

Government of the Republic of Trinidad and Tobago: www.gov.tt

Parliament: www.ttparliament.org

Central Bank of Trinidad and Tobago: www.central-bank.org.tt

Commonwealth Secretariat: www.thecommonwealth.org

Commonwealth of Nations: www.commonwealth-of-nations.org/Trinidad_and_Tobago

Tuvalu

KEY FACTS

Joined Commonwealth:	1978
Population:	10,000 (2010)
Official languages:	Tuvaluan, English
Time:	GMT plus 12hr
Currency:	Australian dollar; Tuvaluan dollar

Geography

Area:	26 sq km
Coastline:	24km
Capital:	Funafuti

Tuvalu, formerly the Ellice Islands, is a group of atolls lying south of the equator in the western Pacific Ocean, south of Kiribati and north of Fiji. Funafuti, the main island and capital, lies 1,046km north of Suva, Fiji. The other islands are Nanumanga, Nanumea, Niulakita, Niutao, Nui, Nukufetau, Nukulaelae and Vaitupu.

Area: 26 sq km, although the atolls extend in a chain 595km long.

Topography: The islands seldom rise higher than 4.5m above sea level. Five islands have large lagoons that are enclosed within the coral reef. The remaining four islands are pinnacles of land rising up solid from the seabed. Most people live on the island of Funafuti, on Funafuti Atoll.

Climate: The mean annual temperature is 30°C, with little seasonal variation, though March to October tends to be cooler. Humidity is high. Trade winds blow from the east for much of the year. Although the islands are north of the recognised hurricane belt, severe cyclones struck in 1894, 1972 and 1990. Rainfall is high, averaging 3,535mm p.a. The wettest season is November to February.

Environment: There are no streams or rivers in the country and ground water is not safe to drink; water needs are met by catchment of rainwater and, increasingly, by desalination. The Japanese Government has built one desalination plant and plans to

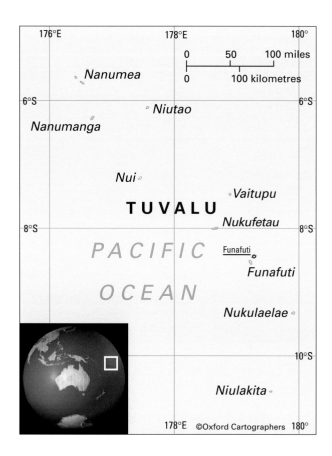

©Oxford Cartographers

build another. Some 40% of the island of Funafuti was severely damaged during the Second World War and is virtually uninhabitable. Other significant environmental issues are: beachhead erosion because of the removal of sand for building materials; excessive clearance of forest undergrowth for use as fuel; damage to coral reefs from the spread of the Crown of Thorns starfish; and rising sea level threatening the underground water table.

Vegetation: The heavy rainfall provides a more luxuriant vegetation than that on neighbouring Kiribati. Coconut palms cover most of the land. Forest covers 33% of the land area and there was no significant loss of forest cover during 1990–2010.

Wildlife: Lizards, turtles and several resident species of birds are the most notable forms of indigenous animal life. Birds include the reef heron, white-tailed tropic-bird, terns and noddies.

Main towns: Vaiaku (on Funafuti, 5,100 in 2010), Asau (on Vaitupu, 650), Lolua (on Nanumea, 570), Savave (on Nukufetau, 520) and Kua (on Niutao, 480).

Transport: Tuvalu has only a few roads (total extent 8km) and, before 2002 when tarring was completed, these were made from impacted coral and supplemented by dirt tracks.

Did you know...

With populations of about 10,000, Tuvalu and Nauru are the smallest Commonwealth member nations. They are also two of the world's smallest democracies.

Although Tuvalu had already fielded teams at the Commonwealth Games, the country only made its first appearance in an Olympic Games at Beijing in August 2008.

Tuvalu has been able to capitalise on its fortune in having rights to the highly marketable internet domain of '.tv'.

There is a deep-water lagoon at Funafuti, which ships are able to enter at Nukufetau. The islands are served by a passenger and cargo vessel, based at Funafuti, which occasionally calls at Suva, Fiji. Ships from Fiji, Australia and New Zealand call at Funafuti.

The only airfield is on Funafuti, at the eastern tip of the island. In 1992 a new runway was completed with Commonwealth technical assistance and international funding, replacing the old grass airstrip. There are scheduled flights from Majuro in the Marshall Islands, Tarawa in Kiribati, and Nadi and Suva in Fiji.

Society

KEY FACTS 2010

Population per sq km:	385
Life expectancy:	65 years (est.)
Net primary enrolment:	100%

Population: 10,000 (2010); population density on inhabited islands very high, especially on Funafuti; 50% lives in urban areas; growth 0.4% p.a. 1990–2010; birth rate 23 per 1,000 people (est.); life expectancy 65 years (est.)

In February 2000, a request was made to New Zealand for resettlement of about one-third of Tuvalu's population which was threatened by rising sea levels.

The Tuvaluans are a Polynesian people.

Language: Tuvaluan and English are official languages. The people of Nui Island speak the language of Kiribati, I-Kiribati.

Religion: Mainly Christians, mostly of the Church of Tuvalu (Ekalesia Tuvalu), autonomous since 1968 and derived from the Congregationalist foundation of the London Missionary Society. There are small Roman Catholic communities on Nanumea and Nui, and some Seventh Day Adventists and Baha'is.

Health: Public spending on health was 10% of GDP in 2009. There is a hospital on Funafuti and dispensaries on all the permanently inhabited islands. Health is generally good; there are occasional outbreaks of mosquito-borne dengue fever but no malaria. 97% of the population uses an improved drinking water source and 84% adequate sanitation facilities (2009). Infant mortality was 27 per 1,000 live births in 2010.

Education: There are nine years of compulsory education starting at age six. The school year starts in January.

The Maritime Training Institute on Funafuti (founded in 1979) provides vocational and technical training. Tuvalu is a partner in the regional University of the South Pacific, which has its main campus in Suva, Fiji, and a campus on Funafuti.

Media: The government publishes *Tuvalu Echoes* fortnightly in English, and a news sheet, *Sikuleo o Tuvalu*, in Tuvaluan.

Tuvalu Media Corporation provides a public radio service to all the islands; and access to TV broadcasts is via satellite.

There are 86 personal computers (2005) and some 250 internet users (2010) per 1,000 people.

Communications: Country code 688; internet domain '.tv'. There is internet access and a post office in Funafuti.

There are 165 main telephone lines and 254 mobile phone subscriptions per 1,000 people (2010).

Public holidays: New Year's Day, Commonwealth Day (second Monday in March), Gospel Day (11 May), Queen's Official Birthday (June), National Children's Day (early August), Independence (two days early in October), Heir to the Throne Day (9 November), Christmas Day and Boxing Day. Each island has its own exclusive holiday.

Religious and other festivals whose dates vary from year to year include Good Friday and Easter Monday.

Economy

KEY FACTS 2010

GNI: US$47m	
GNI p.c.:	US$4,760
GDP growth:	2.0% p.a. 2006–10
Inflation:	2.8% p.a. 2006–10

In terms of population, Tuvalu is among the smallest countries in the world. It has very few resources and few sources of revenue – fishing licences, remittances from overseas workers (especially seamen and those living in New Zealand), small-scale copra exports, sale of postage stamps and coins, sale of passports and

Real Growth in GDP

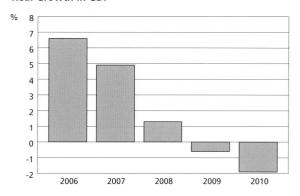

Inflation

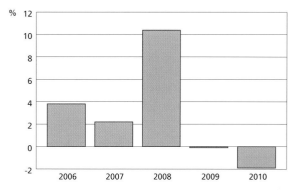

GDP by Sector (2010)

■ Agriculture	22%
□ Industry	9%
▨ Services	69%

resale of rights to international telephone codes (initially to the sex industry and subsequently for gambling) – and balance-of-payments deficits have to be made up by income from the Tuvalu Trust Fund and bilateral aid, especially from Australia and New Zealand. During 1988–98 GDP growth averaged 5.2% and was among the highest in Pacific Island economies.

In 1987, the governments of Australia, New Zealand, the UK, Japan and South Korea (and Tuvalu itself) acknowledged that the country would need financial support for the foreseeable future, and each government agreed to contribute money to set up a Tuvalu Trust Fund. The fund is invested by commercial fund managers and income is drawn by the government as required, so long as its current value is above its real value according to the Australian consumer price index. At its foundation, the fund totalled A$27.1 million; subsequent contributions – mainly by Tuvalu itself – added a further A$38.6 million; and the fund was valued in June 2007 at A$106.6 million.

In August 1998 a North American company agreed to lease Tuvalu's internet domain '.tv'. In December 2001 another company took over the lease agreeing to pay the Tuvalu Government US$2.2 million a year plus 5% of revenue exceeding US$20 million per year for the right to market '.tv' until December 2016.

People on Funafuti have a higher income than those living mainly at subsistence level on the outer islands. The country looks to regional co-operation, through the Pacific Community and in smaller groupings on matters of common interest such as fisheries, the marketing of copra and the expansion of regional air services.

After 1998 growth slowed, in the face of the international downturn. It then raced ahead in 2000–01, moderating but generally good in 2002–07, while inflation was no more than 5% p.a. Then, in response to the world economic downturn of 2008–09, the economy contracted – by 0.6% in 2009 and 1.9% in 2010.

Constitution

Status:	Monarchy under Queen Elizabeth II
Legislature:	Parliament
Independence:	1 October 1978

Tuvalu is a constitutional monarchy with a parliamentary democracy. The British sovereign is head of state and is represented by a governor-general, who must be a citizen of Tuvalu and is appointed by the head of state on the recommendation of the prime minister.

The prime minister is elected by parliament and is head of government. The cabinet consists of the prime minister, plus up to four other ministers, appointed by the governor-general from among the members of parliament, on the advice of the prime minister. The cabinet advises the governor-general who must accept its advice.

Parliament is composed of 15 members: two elected every four years by universal adult suffrage from seven electoral districts and one from the remainder. The speaker, elected by the members, presides over parliament.

The constitution provides for the operation of a judiciary and for an independent public service. It guarantees protection of all fundamental rights and freedoms, and provides for the determination of citizenship.

History

The population of Tuvalu, formerly known as the Ellice or Lagoon Islands, is thought to have dropped from 20,000 in 1850 to 3,000 in 1875, thanks to slave-traders and imported European diseases. The Gilbert and Ellice Islands Protectorate was established by Britain in 1892 (the Gilbert Islands are now called Kiribati) and the protectorate became a colony in 1916.

A referendum held in 1974 established that most Ellice islanders wanted separate status from the Gilbert Islands. The country was renamed Tuvalu, an old name meaning 'eight standing together' (Tuvalu has nine islands or island groups, but one has very little land above sea level). The Ellice Islands became a separate British dependency in October 1975, and gained independence as Tuvalu on 1 October 1978.

Toaripi Lauti, chief minister of the Tuvalu House of Assembly from October 1975, was independent Tuvalu's first prime minister (1978–81). He was succeeded by Dr Tomasi Puapua from 1981. Puapua was defeated in the September 1989 elections by Bikenibeu Paeniu.

In February 2000, the UN accepted Tuvalu as the organisation's 189th member and in September 2000 it became a full member of the Commonwealth, having been a special member since it joined in 1978.

The September 1993 elections resulted in a deadlock, Puapua and Paeniu both receiving equal support in the new parliament.

Puapua withdrew from the December 1993 elections and Paeniu was defeated by Kamuta Latasi, who became prime minister. In December 1996, the government was removed from power after an unexpected vote of no confidence gained the support of seven of the 12 members of parliament. In a subsequent secret parliamentary ballot, Paeniu was elected prime minister in preference to Latasi. In the general election of March 1998, seven assembly members were re-elected, the prime minister among them. Former Prime Minister Latasi was defeated in his Funafuti constituency. When parliament reconvened in April 1998 the members re-elected Paeniu as prime minister by ten votes to two.

In April 1999 Paeniu lost a no-confidence vote, and education and health minister Ionatana Ionatana was elected by parliament to succeed him. Ionatana died suddenly in December 2000 and Deputy Prime Minister Lagitupu Tuilimu acted as prime minister until parliament elected Faimalaga Luka to the post in February 2001. Koloa Talake was chosen to succeed Luka as prime minister when, in December 2001, four MPs changed their allegiance.

In 2001 New Zealand agreed to accept an annual quota of Tuvaluans wishing to emigrate as the sea level rises, starting from 2002 and continuing for at least 30 years. In 2003 discussions were under way about emigration of Tuvaluans to Niue, where the population had declined due to emigration to New Zealand.

Politics

Last elections:	September 2010
Next elections:	2014
Head of state:	Queen Elizabeth II, represented by governor-general, Sir Iakoba Italeli (2010–)
Head of government:	Prime Minister Willy Telavi
Ruling party:	no party system

There are no political parties in Tuvalu. Following the July 2002 general election, when Prime Minister Koloa Talake lost his seat, Saufatu Sopoanga was elected by parliament to be prime minister. However, after the by-elections in May 2003, he no longer commanded the support of the majority of MPs, but refused to recall parliament until after October 2003 when one opposition member was appointed to cabinet and, following another by-election, one more member joined the government benches. However, in August 2004 Sopoanga was unable to win a vote of confidence and in October 2004 Maatia Toafa was elected prime minister.

Eight new members were elected in the August 2006 general election, Prime Minister Toafa being the only member of his cabinet to retain their seat. Parliament subsequently elected Apisai Ielemia prime minister.

In the September 2010 general election, ten of the 15 members from the previous parliament were re-elected. Parliament then elected Maatia Toafa prime minister; he defeated Kausea Natano by eight votes to seven. On 21 December 2010, however, the new head of government was defeated in a no-confidence vote and on 24 December Willy Telavi was chosen by parliament to succeed him, defeating Enele Sopoaga by eight votes to seven.

International relations

Tuvalu is a member of the African, Caribbean and Pacific Group of States, Pacific Community, Pacific Islands Forum and United Nations.

Traveller information

Local laws and conventions: Drugs offences incur severe penalties in Tuvalu. Visitors may find that alcohol consumption is limited outside of licensed premises. Noisy or disruptive activities on a Sunday are not acceptable.

Tuvalu is a very traditional country and the Christian Church plays a fundamental role in the islanders' life; Sunday service is typically considered the most important weekly event. Casual dress is acceptable for visitors, casual but modest dress for women. Shoes must be removed before entering a church, a meeting house or a private home.

English is used for business; business ethics are very important among Tuvaluans. Office hours are Mon–Thur 0730–1615 and Fri 0730–1245.

Immigration and customs: Passports should be valid for at least six months beyond the intended length of stay. Airport departure tax is charged.

Pornographic material, pure alcohol, narcotics, weapons and ammunition are all prohibited imports. Plant and animal materials must be declared and quarantined. Some items are duty free but must be declared on arrival – including binoculars, cameras and unexposed film, portable radios, broadcasting equipment, portable tape recorders, portable typewriters and sports equipment.

Travel within the country: Traffic drives on the left. A limited number of taxis and minibuses operate in Tuvalu; most of these are found near the airport and in Funafuti. Many Tuvaluans travel on motorcycles and bicycles, both of which can be hired through hotels.

There are no domestic flights, but visitors can access the islands by passenger and cargo boats.

Travel health: Medical facilities are generally adequate for routine medical treatment. For more serious or complicated problems, medical evacuation to Fiji or Australia may be required, and all travellers should have comprehensive health insurance that includes this. Visitors will need insect repellent and suitable clothing to discourage mosquito bites.

Tuvalu's water supply comes from rainwater and desalination.

Money: Australian dollars and Tuvaluan dollars are used. Tuvalu's own national currency, the Tuvaluan dollar, is only available in coin form denomination up to and including one dollar, with Australian dollar notes solely being used thereafter. Credit cards are not accepted, though Mastercard may be used for cash advances at the National Bank of Tuvalu. Travellers cheques should be taken in Australian dollars. Banking hours are Mon–Thur 0930–1300, Fri 0830–1200.

There were 2,000 tourist arrivals in 2009.

Further information

Commonwealth Secretariat: www.thecommonwealth.org

Commonwealth of Nations: www.commonwealth-of-nations.org/Tuvalu

Forging Local Economic Safety Nets:
Uganda's Road from Independence

H.E. Gen. Yoweri Kaguta Museveni, President of the Republic of Uganda

Fifty years after independence in 1962, Uganda has braved many significant governance and economic challenges. With a young, fragile economy and democracy at the advent of independence, Uganda set out with a promise of hope to its citizens. The economy of Uganda had great potential, however previous political instability and erratic economic management produced a record of persistent economic decline that left Uganda among the world's poorest and least-developed countries.

The 1990s were characterised by strong economic growth, along with changes in the country's governance structures at sub-national level. In 1992, Uganda adopted decentralisation as the main mode of governance. This was later to be buttressed in the Constitution (1995) and the Local Governments Act (1997). The policy devolved powers and functional responsibilities over decision-making and service delivery to popularly elected local governments.

However, a Joint Review of Decentralisation held in 2004 revealed the serious limitations between economic policies and the benefits of the decentralisation policy. The major criticism at the time was the inability of the Government to exploit the comprehensive decentralised governance structures for more pro-poor economic development. As a result of this policy interrogation, a new and sixth objective on Decentralisation was

agreed: 'To Promote Local Economic Development (LED) in Order to Enhance People's Incomes'.

'The purpose of local economic development (LED) is to build up the economic capacity of a local area to improve its economic future and the quality of life for all. It is a process by which public, business and non-governmental sector partners work collectively to create better conditions for economic growth and employment generation.'
Source: World Bank

Local Governments in Uganda are continuously building networks with a variety of public and private agencies to plan, budget and implement custom-designed policies and projects geared at increasing the economic well-being of the respective communities.

Local Governments play an LED promotional role in terms of providing the right economic infrastructure, governance framework and through stimulating business development services. On the other hand, individual communities and areas within a given local government are also encouraged to adopt specific LED strategies to improve their economic competitiveness. As such, communities will continually improve their investment climate and business enabling environment and ultimately improve individual and taxable household incomes.

A number of best practices are merging and they include:
- Ensuring that the local investment climate is functional for local SMEs
- Encouraging the formation of new enterprises and attracting external investment
- Investing in hard and soft infrastructure
- Supporting the growth of particular clusters of businesses

- Engaging in conscious regeneration of conflict afflicted northern Uganda
- Targeting special interest and disadvantaged groups

The Decentralisation Policy, therefore, offers great opportunity not only to tackle poverty at household level but also to widen the tax base of the local governments. This enables them to finance service delivery and to be more accountable to their constituents.

The Hon. Adolf Mwesige, Minister of Local Government

Ministry of Local Government
Mr Patrick K Mutabwire
For Permanent Secretary
Workers' House, 2nd Floor, Southern Wing, Kampala, Uganda

Tel: +256 41 34 1224
Fax: +256 41 25 8127
Email: ps@molg.go.ug
www.molg.go.ug

Uganda

KEY FACTS

Joined Commonwealth:	1962
Population:	33,425,000 (2010)
GDP p.c. growth:	3.6% p.a. 1990–2010
UN HDI 2011:	world ranking 161
Official languages:	English, Kiswahili
Time:	GMT plus 3hr
Currency:	Uganda shilling (USh)

Geography

Area:	236,000 sq km
Coastline:	none
Capital:	Kampala

Uganda is a landlocked East African country lying astride the equator. It is bordered (clockwise from north) by Sudan, Kenya, United Republic of Tanzania, Rwanda and the Democratic Republic of Congo.

Area: 236,000 sq km including 36,330 sq km of inland water.

Topography: Water, with swampland, covers nearly 20% of the surface area. The largest lakes include Lake George, Lake Kyoga, and parts of Lakes Victoria, Albert and Edward. From its source in Lake Victoria, the White Nile flows northwards through the country. Mountains include the high Rwenzori range in the west (Margherita Peak on Mount Stanley is 5,110m) and Mount Elgon (4,253m) in the east.

Climate: Equatorial, tempered with breezes and showers. Cooler in the higher areas. Heavy rain from March to May, and in October and November. Little rainfall in the north-east; though north-east parts of the country experienced unusually heavy rainfall in the

©Oxford Cartographers

latter part of 2007 with heavy flooding displacing tens of thousands of people.

Environment: The most significant issues are: draining of wetlands for agricultural use; overgrazing, soil erosion and deforestation; water hyacinth infestation in Lake Victoria; and poaching.

Vegetation: Much of the country, being so well-watered, is richly fertile; there is arid semi-desert in the north-east. Most of the country's vegetation is savannah with tropical forests in areas of high rainfall. Drought-resistant bush, grasses and succulents grow in the north-east. Forest covers 15% of the land area, having declined at 2.3% p.a. 1990–2010. Arable land comprises 33% and permanent cropland 11% of the total land area.

Wildlife: Uganda has 7,200 sq km of national parks and game reserves, reflecting the extraordinary diversity of the country which comprises lakes, swamps, dense grassland, woodland, rolling plains, forests and mountains. There is a rich variety of wildlife, including elephants, Uganda kob, buffaloes, lions, rhinos, mountain gorillas and chimpanzees – 338 species of mammals and 830 species of birds.

Main towns: Kampala (capital, pop. 1.51m in 2010), Gulu (216,200), Lira (182,800), Jinja (97,300), Kasese (93,300), Mbarara (91,900), Kitgum (87,100), Mbale (80,700), Njeru (73,500), Arua (70,900), Entebbe (67,300), Masaka (66,900), Kabale (56,500), Iganga (55,500), Koboko (55,300), Tororo (53,800), Mukono (53,600), Hoima (53,300) and Mityana (49,500).

Did you know...

Samuel Kavuma of Uganda was in 2010 appointed to the Commonwealth Eminent Persons Group, which presented its recommendations for reform in the Commonwealth to Commonwealth leaders at CHOGM in Australia in October 2011.

Ugandans won the Commonwealth Essay Competition in 1989 and 2007.

Doreen Baingana was a regional winner in the Commonwealth Writers' Prize in 2006.

Dorcas Inzikuru took the Commonwealth Games Women's 3,000 Metres Steeplechase record in the Melbourne Games in 2006.

Transport: Some 70,750km of roads radiate from Kampala, 23% of which are paved. The railway network extends over 260km. At the end of 1993, passenger services between Kampala and Kenya were resumed after a break of 15 years. Entebbe International Airport is 35km south-west of Kampala.

Society

KEY FACTS 2010

Population per sq km:	142
Life expectancy:	54 years
Net primary enrolment:	92%

Population: 33,425,000 (2010); 13% lives in urban areas and 5% in urban agglomerations of more than 1 million people; growth 3.2% p.a. 1990–2010; birth rate 45 per 1,000 people (49 in 1970); life expectancy 54 years (50 in 1970 and 48 in 1990). The rural population predominates, with most settlement concentrated around Lake Victoria.

The majority of the population consists of Bantu peoples (Baganda 17%, Banyankore 10%, Basoga 8%, Bakiga 7%, Bagisu 5%, Bunyoro 3%) in the west, south and east; and most of the rest of Nilotic peoples (Iteso 7%, Langi 6%, Acholi 5%, Lugbara 4%, Alur, Karimojong and Kakwa) in the north and parts of the east; with minorities of Asians and refugees from neighbouring countries (2002 census).

Language: The official languages are English and Kiswahili; Kiswahili and Luganda are widely spoken and there are several other African languages.

Religion: Mainly Christians (Roman Catholics 42%, Anglicans 36%, Pentecostals 5%), Muslims 12%, and most of the rest holding traditional beliefs, which often coexist with other religions (2002 census).

Health: Public spending on health was 2% of GDP in 2009. Trained medical assistants (many of whom practise privately) make up (to some extent) for the lack of doctors. Formal health facilities, which are adequate everywhere except in the north of the country, are mostly provided by non-governmental organisations. 67% of the population uses an improved drinking water source and 48% of people have access to adequate sanitation facilities (2009). Infant mortality was 63 per 1,000 live births in 2010 (133 in 1960).

The chief causes of death among adults are AIDS-related illnesses, tuberculosis, malaria and illnesses related to maternity; among children, malaria, pneumonia, diarrhoea. Uganda was the first African country openly to confront the menace of AIDS; the government runs a comprehensive information campaign directed at the general public. In 2009, 6.5% of people aged 15–49 were HIV positive.

Education: Public spending on education was 3.2% of GDP in 2009. There are seven years of primary education starting at age six, followed by six years of secondary, with cycles of four and two years. The government phased in free primary schooling from 1997 and free secondary from 2007. Some 52% of pupils complete primary school (2008). The school year starts in February.

Makerere University (1922) and Mbarara University of Science and Technology (1989) are the longest-established public universities. Kyambogo University (2003), Gulu University (2004) and Busitema University (2007) were founded in the 2000s. The principal private universities include Busoga University (1999), Islamic University in Uganda (1988), Kampala International University (2001), Uganda

Christian University (1997) and Uganda Martyrs University (1993). The female–male ratio for gross enrolment in tertiary education is 0.80:1 (2009). Literacy among people aged 15–24 is 87% (2010).

Media: English-language dailies include *New Vision* (state-owned) and *Daily Monitor*; *The EastAfrican* and *The Observer* are published weekly.

Uganda Broadcasting Corporation operates public radio and TV services and, since liberalisation of the media in 1993, many private radio stations and TV channels have been launched.

Some 6% of households have TV sets (2007). There are 17 personal computers (2006) and 125 internet users (2010) per 1,000 people.

Communications: Country code 256; internet domain '.ug'. There are public phones in most towns and mobile phone coverage extends to all main towns; internet cafes are found in most large towns.

There are 10 main telephone lines and 384 mobile phone subscriptions per 1,000 people (2010).

Public holidays: New Year's Day, Liberation Day (26 January), International Women's Day (8 March), Labour Day (1 May), Uganda Martyrs' Day (3 June), National Heroes' Day (9 June), Independence Day (9 October), Christmas Day and Boxing Day.

Religious festivals whose dates vary from year to year include Good Friday, Easter Monday, Eid al-Fitr (End of Ramadan) and Eid al-Adha (Feast of the Sacrifice).

Economy

KEY FACTS 2010

GNI:	US$16.6bn
GNI p.c.:	US$500
GDP growth:	8.1% p.a. 2006–10
Inflation:	8.4% p.a. 2006–10

During the years of civil war and instability GDP declined dramatically, falling by 14.8% a year between 1978 and 1980, and the economy declined not only in size but also in sophistication. It grew by only 2.9% p.a. 1980–90, and by 1988 it had only recovered to close to 1972 levels.

When it came to power in 1986 the National Resistance Movement inherited a dreadful legacy. It embarked on a programme of structural adjustment and during the following decade the economy grew at an average 6.5% p.a. Tight fiscal and monetary discipline has been accompanied by trade liberalisation and a

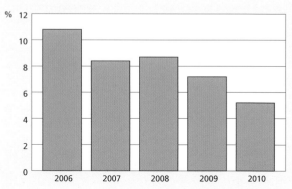

Real Growth in GDP

Inflation

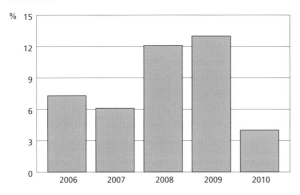

GDP by Sector (2010)

■ Agriculture	23%
□ Industry	25%
▨ Services	52%

programme of privatisation. By 2004 about two-thirds of some 140 public enterprises had been transferred into private hands. Strong growth was achieved with relatively low inflation (generally in single figures from the early 1990s), greatly reduced budget deficits and a relatively stable exchange rate. Manufacturing output grew by 14.1% p.a. 1990–2000. The main exports are coffee, fish and fish products (freshwater fish), gold, cotton, tobacco and tea.

However, this economic performance has not been sufficiently broad-based to raise living standards and quality of life for the majority of the people, and by 2000 the government had refocused its policy on poverty eradication.

Uganda was the first country to qualify for and benefit from the IMF/World Bank Heavily Indebted Poor Countries Initiative (in April 1998) with debt relief of US$700 million. In 2000, Uganda qualified for further debt relief under the Enhanced HIPC Initiative, ensuring a further US$1.3 billion reduction of its external debt.

The economy continued to grow at generally more than 5% p.a. in the 2000s, more strongly from 2005, remaining above 7%, even in the world economic downturn of 2008–09, in part due to strong agricultural production. Despite weakening demand for Uganda's exports, growth then moderated only slightly from 2010 (5.2%).

Oil

Oil has been discovered in the basin of Lake Albert in the west of the country. By 2011 estimated reserves of 2.5 billion barrels had been reported, confirming that Uganda was to become a significant oil-exporter in the 2010s.

Constitution

Status:	Republic with executive president
Legislature:	Parliament
Independence:	9 October 1962

The present constitution was promulgated in October 1995, completing a process begun in 1989. It provided that until 2000,

elections were to be held under the 'movement system' (introduced in 1986), whereby candidates stand as individuals to be elected on personal merit, and not as members of a political party. The 'movement system' ended in 2005 when the people voted in a constitutional referendum in favour of introduction of a multiparty political system.

The constitution provides for a unitary republic, an executive president directly elected every five years by universal adult suffrage and Parliament which comprises 375 elected members, 238 directly elected every five years by universal adult suffrage and the rest elected from special interest groups by electoral colleges: women (112 members), the defence forces (10 members), youth (5), disabled people (5) and workers (5). The president appoints the cabinet. Since 2005 there has been no limit on the number of terms a president may serve.

Politics

Last elections:	February 2011 (presidential and parliamentary)
Next elections:	2016 (presidential and parliamentary)
Head of state:	President Yoweri Kaguta Museveni
Head of government:	the president
Ruling party:	National Resistance Movement

Amid growing support for political pluralism, from within and without the ruling National Resistance Movement (NRM), a law enacted in June 2002 restricted party political activities to Kampala, barred civil servants and members of the security forces from joining parties other than NRM, and gave parties six months to register as a company, which the main parties immediately refused to do.

However, during 2003 President Yoweri Kaguta Museveni publicly committed himself to the reintroduction of multiparty politics before the elections due in 2006, subject to a referendum in July 2005, in which, with the opposition calling for a boycott, fewer than 50% of voters turned out to vote overwhelmingly in favour.

In 2004 Museveni announced that he had retired from the army, while remaining army commander-in-chief. This opened the way for him to participate in multiparty politics. During 2005 the government proposed substantial change to the constitution including lifting the limit of two presidential terms. In November 2005 Museveni said he would stand in the 2006 election, and his main rival Besigye was charged with treason and terrorism and taken into custody. Besigye was then released on bail in January 2006 and held some political rallies.

In the first multiparty elections for 25 years, held in February 2006, Museveni (with 59.3% of the votes) defeated Dr Kizza Besigye (37.4%) of the Forum for Democratic Change (FDC) in a turnout of 69%. The ruling NRM also won the parliamentary elections, securing 206 seats, while the FDC took 37, the Uganda People's Congress (UPC) nine, the Democratic Party (DP) eight and independents 37. The Commonwealth observer group present, led by former President of Botswana Sir Ketumile Masire, believed that the election had enabled the will of the people to be expressed and that the result reflected the wishes of those who were able to vote.

Museveni won the February 2011 presidential election with 68.4% of the votes cast and his main rival, Besigye, secured 26.0%. The concurrent parliamentary elections were won by the ruling NRM, with a total of 250 of the 375 seats in the enlarged Parliament. The

FDC took 34 seats, the DP 12, the UPC ten and independents 42. A Commonwealth observer group led by Dame Billie Miller, the former deputy prime minister of Barbados, was present at the elections.

International relations

Uganda is a member of the African, Caribbean and Pacific Group of States, African Union, Common Market for Eastern and Southern Africa, East African Community, Non-Aligned Movement, Organisation of Islamic Cooperation, United Nations and World Trade Organization.

Uganda was a member, with Kenya and United Republic of Tanzania, of the East African Community, which from 1967 had a common market and many shared services but collapsed in 1977. The three countries again embarked on developing regional co-operation in 1993, bringing about progressive harmonisation of standards and policies across a wide range of activities, and launching a new East African Community in January 2001 and East African Customs Union in January 2005. The Community was enlarged in July 2007 when Burundi and Rwanda became members.

Uganda is also a member of the Intergovernmental Authority on Development, which was established in 1986 by the six countries in the Horn of Africa to combat drought and desertification and promote food security in the region.

Traveller information

Local laws and conventions: Photographing airports or military installations is prohibited and commercial photographers should consult the Ministry of Information for a permit. Penalties for possession, use or trafficking of illegal drugs are severe, and convicted offenders can expect jail sentences and heavy fines.

Shaking hands is the usual form of greeting and casual dress is generally acceptable for most occasions. Ugandans operate a smart dress code for business. Business appointments must always be made, and English is widely used. Conference facilities are available in Kampala, which has an international conference centre. Office hours are Mon–Fri 0800–1300 and 1400–1700.

Immigration and customs: Passports must be valid for at least six months beyond the intended length of stay. Visas are required for visitors from all countries except Angola, Antigua and Barbuda, The Bahamas, Barbados, Belize, Burundi, Comoros, Cyprus, Eritrea, Fiji, The Gambia, Grenada, Ireland, Italy (diplomatic passport holders only), Jamaica, Kenya, Lesotho, Madagascar, Malawi, Malta,

History

Uganda has a long history, but few records of early settlement, although the country seems to have been inhabited very early. Bantu peoples were engaged in agriculture from 1000 BC and working in iron can be traced back to about AD 1000.

In the fertile south and west, powerful social and political orders developed, including the Bunyoro, Buganda, Busoga, Ankole and Toro kingdoms. In the 17th and 18th centuries, they formed profitable links with the Sudanese slave trade (which dominated the regional economy) and formed alliances among themselves. By the 19th century, the Buganda Kingdom, which was allied to the powerful Shirazis of Zanzibar, gained the ascendancy. Buganda was ruled by *Kabaka* (traditional kings) whose power was circumscribed by a council of nobles. Buganda's standing army and well-developed agriculture allowed the kingdom to survive the decline of the slave trade.

Various Europeans appeared during the 19th century. English Protestant and French Catholic missionaries came at the request of Kabaka Mutesa I, and Baganda loyalties split into 'Franza', 'Inglesa' and Muslim parties. In 1888 the Imperial British East Africa Company set up in Buganda with the Kabaka's permission, and in 1894 Buganda was declared a British Protectorate. In 1896, protectorate control was extended to Bunyoro, Ankole and Toro, and the British extended Buganda's administrative system to these societies. Cotton-growing for export, by smallholders, began in 1904.

Although control of the country passed to the British Colonial Office in 1905, Uganda was never fully colonised, as non-Africans were not allowed to acquire freeholds. By 1913, with the completion of the Busoga Railway the cotton industry was well established, though it suffered from the First World War and the Great Depression of 1932–33. In the 1920s, commercial production of coffee and sugar began. After the Second World War, high prices of coffee and cotton brought an economic boom.

The gradual transfer of power to the local people began in 1921, when a legislative and an executive council were set up. By 1955, half the membership of the legislative council were Africans, a party political system was developing and the executive council was developed into a ministerial system. In 1961 a general election returned Benedicto Kiwanuka's Democratic Party. In 1962 Uganda became internally self-governing, with Kiwanuka as first prime minister. However, the general election of April 1962 returned Milton Obote's Uganda People's Congress (UPC).

Uganda became fully independent in October 1962 and joined the Commonwealth. The Kabaka of Buganda, Sir Edward Mutesa (Kabaka Mutesa II), became the first (non-executive) president in 1963.

Milton Obote abrogated the 1962 constitution in 1966 and in 1967 the country became a unitary republic. The kingdoms were abolished and the president became head of the executive as well as head of state. (The kingdoms were restored in 1993, and the 1995 constitution has a provision on traditional leaders.)

Obote remained in power until January 1971, when a military coup was staged by former paratroop sergeant Idi Amin Dada. At first very popular, Amin moved quickly into a brutal authoritarianism. Under his orders, the authorities expelled Uganda's Asian community in 1972 and seized their property; they expropriated the property of the Jewish community, and terrorised intellectuals, destroying such symbols of 'intellectual' status as possession of books, spectacles and chess sets. Public order rapidly deteriorated, and murder, destruction of property, looting and rape became hallmarks of the regime. Amin declared himself president-for-life and, in 1978, invaded the United ➤

Mauritius, Rwanda, St Vincent and the Grenadines, Seychelles, Sierra Leone, Singapore, Solomon Islands, Swaziland, Tanzania, Tonga, Vanuatu, Zambia and Zimbabwe. Visitors should keep a copy of the relevant pages of their passport and visa on them at all times, while storing the originals in a safe place.

A yellow fever vaccination certificate is required by all those arriving from infected areas.

A special permit is needed to export game trophies.

Travel within the country: Traffic drives on the left and visitors will need an international driving permit. National speed limits are 100kph on highways and 80kph elsewhere. Car hire is available in Kampala, though those without experience of driving in the country are advised to organise a vehicle with a driver.

Bus services run throughout Uganda; visitors can also use the Post Bus, which is run by the Ugandan Post Office and is recommended when travelling between towns in Uganda.

In urban areas, there is an extensive network of *Matatas*, or minibuses, which are a quick and convenient method of transport. Taxis, identifiable by their black and white stripes, are widely available but are more expensive.

Travel health: Visitors should ensure they have comprehensive health insurance which includes air evacuation in case of serious accident or illness.

Water should be boiled or sterilised before use.

Money: The local currency is the Uganda shilling (USh). Foreign currency can be exchanged at banks and exchange bureaux. Credit cards and travellers cheques are not widely accepted outside of Kampala. The US dollar is traditionally the hard currency of preference, but euros and pounds sterling can also be used. Banking hours are Mon–Fri 0830–1400 and Sat 0900–1200.

There were 844,000 tourist arrivals in 2008.

Further information

Government of Uganda: www.government.ug

Parliament: www.parliament.go.ug

Bank of Uganda: www.bou.or.ug

Commonwealth Secretariat: www.thecommonwealth.org

Commonwealth of Nations: www.commonwealth-of-nations.org/Uganda

➤ Republic of Tanzania's northern territories. Tanzania, which had long opposed Amin's regime, took this for a declaration of war.

Supported by the Uganda National Liberation Front (UNLF, exiled Ugandans), the United Republic of Tanzania army marched into Uganda. Kampala was taken in April 1979, but Amin escaped and fled the country. Professor Yusuf Lule, a former Commonwealth Assistant Secretary-General and Chairman of UNLF, became president for two months, and was then replaced by Godfrey Binaisa who was himself replaced a year later in 1980 by a Military Commission led by Paulo Muwanga, which organised elections in December that year. Commonwealth and other observers were present.

The elections returned Dr Obote's UPC and were disputed. Obote was unable to restore economic and political stability to the devastated country, and the government became bogged down in fighting the National Resistance Army (NRA), led by Yoweri Museveni. The NRA had launched a protracted bush struggle in 1981 after accusing the government of rigging the 1980 elections. Obote was overthrown by his own Uganda National Liberation Army in a coup led by General Tito Lutwa Okello in July 1985, who then became president. However, this did not satisfy the NRA and its allies.

The NRA occupied Kampala in January 1986. Okello's government was ousted and Museveni became president, with Dr Samson Kisekka as prime minister and a broad-based cabinet of civilians. Civil war continued in the north, and the first three years of the new regime were dogged by continuing instability in the region. Museveni and the National Resistance Movement (NRM) took over a country in which conflict had resulted in 1 million deaths, 2 million refugees, more than 500,000 seriously injured people, and ruin of the economy and physical infrastructure. The NRM governed the country through a National Resistance Council

(NRC) which functioned as a parliament. After elections in 1989 based on universal adult suffrage, 8,096 village resistance councils were set up. Museveni sought democratic structures based on a non-party democracy, rather than a multiparty system, to avoid reviving the ethnic divisions which had so prolonged the civil war. Political party activities were suspended, though party structures were not made illegal.

Elections under the 'movement system' (see *Constitution*) were held in May and June 1996 (presidential and parliamentary) and June 1998 (local government). Museveni was returned as president with 75% of the votes. The national assembly of 276 members, sitting as individuals (although many of them with known political affiliations), was formed in July 1996.

In June 2000, as required by the constitution, a referendum was held on the movement system and 91% of voters supported its continuation; voter turnout was 47%. In the presidential election in March 2001, Museveni took 69% of the votes to win a further five-year term. Though the result was decisive, the election had been vigorously contested between Museveni and a former NRM colleague, Dr Kizza Besigye (28%). In the parliamentary elections in June 2001, more than 50 members were defeated – including ten cabinet ministers.

After 20 years of conflict along the country's northern border, abduction of more than 20,000 children and displacement of some two million people, a ceasefire between the Uganda Government and the Lord's Resistance Army (LRA) – a rebel group led by Joseph Kony – came into force on 29 August 2006. The truce opened the way for peace talks in Juba, mediated by the Government of Southern Sudan. With only intermittent minor skirmishes the ceasefire was maintained until June 2007, when the Uganda Government reached agreement with the LRA on a roadmap for long-term peace, reconciliation and accountability.

United Kingdom

KEY FACTS

Population:	62,036,000 (2010)
GDP p.c. growth:	2.1% p.a. 1990–2010
UN HDI 2011:	world ranking 28
Official language:	English
Time:	GMT plus 0–1hr
Currency:	pound sterling (£)

Geography

Area:	243,305 sq km
Coastline:	12,400km
Capital:	London

The United Kingdom of Great Britain and Northern Ireland (UK) is a union of four countries: England, Scotland, Wales and Northern Ireland. The Crown dependencies (the Channel Islands and the Isle of Man) are largely self-governing with the UK responsible for their defence and international relations and are not part of the United Kingdom. Profiles of the UK's overseas territories follow this profile. The UK consists of a group of islands off the western coast of Europe. The largest, Great Britain, comprises three countries: England, Scotland and Wales. Ireland, to the west, consists of the UK's province of Northern Ireland and the Irish Republic. There are several offshore islands and island groups, the largest lying off Scotland.

Time: GMT. The clock is advanced by one hour from the last Sunday in March to the last Sunday in October.

Area: 243,305 sq km – England 130,395; Scotland 78,313; Wales 20,754; Northern Ireland 13,843.

Did you know...

Queen Elizabeth II is Head of the Commonwealth and head of state of 16 Commonwealth countries.

The UK hosts in London the HQ of the Commonwealth Secretariat, Commonwealth Foundation, Association of Commonwealth Universities, Commonwealth Business Council, Commonwealth Games Federation, Commonwealth Local Government Forum and Commonwealth Parliamentary Association.

Scholarships and fellowships are awarded by the United Kingdom to citizens of other Commonwealth countries under the Commonwealth Scholarship and Fellowship Plan.

Three Britons have won the overall Commonwealth Writers' Prize and four the Best First Book award.

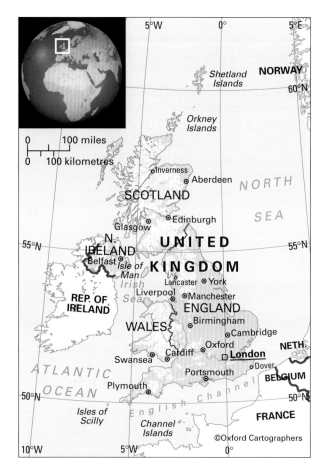

©Oxford Cartographers

Topography: The UK is just under 1,000km long and just under 500km across at the widest point. The country is low-lying in the east of England, with mountains in Wales, Scotland and Northern Ireland. The Pennine chain forms a ridge down northern England. The Cambrian Mountains stretch across Wales, with Snowdon in the north-west rising to 1,085m. Northern Ireland has the Sperrin, Antrim and Mourne Mountains. Scotland has almost 300 peaks over 913m and Ben Nevis in the Grampian range rises to 1,343m. The Scottish Orkney and Shetland islands in the north and Hebrides in the north-west are mountainous and fiorded island chains. The UK is well-watered, with navigable rivers including the Thames, Severn, Trent, Mersey and Tyne. There are many lakes, especially in the north-west (the Lake District) and in Scotland and Northern Ireland (known respectively as lochs or loughs).

Climate: The climate is mild, cool-temperate and oceanic. Rainfall is generally heaviest between September and January. Air currents across the Atlantic are warmed by the Gulf Stream and make the rainfall unpredictable but also give the country a warmer climate than usual for its latitude. The northerly latitude gives long days in summer and long nights in winter.

Environment: The most significant environmental issues are: continuing reduction of greenhouse gas emissions in line with Kyoto Protocol commitments; air pollution mainly by motor vehicles; and the need to recycle a progressively larger proportion of solid waste.

Vegetation: The original natural vegetation consisted largely of forest, but 76% of the land area is now cultivated farmland or pasture. There is moorland in Yorkshire (northern England), the south-west and Scotland. Forest areas have doubled since 1919 and represent 12% of the land area, having increased at 0.5% p.a. 1990–2010. Fourteen national parks in England, Wales and Scotland, regional parks and various designated areas help to protect the environment. Arable land comprises 25% of the total land area.

Wildlife: About 30,000 animal species are found in the UK. Indigenous wildlife originally included bears and wolves, but human settlement has long rendered these extinct. Surviving larger mammals include deer, otters, badgers and foxes; marshland areas support waders and other birds, and there are many migrants. Conservation schemes protect numerous species and important habitats. The Wildlife and Countryside Act 1981 extended the list of protected species, and three conservation agencies (English Nature, the Countryside Council for Wales and Scottish Natural Heritage) have schemes to recover and reintroduce threatened species.

Main towns: London (capital, England, pop. 7.74m in 2010), Birmingham (England, 942,800), Glasgow (Scotland, 578,800), Liverpool (England, 452,800), Edinburgh (Scotland, 451,900), Leeds (England, 441,000), Sheffield (England, 415,200), Manchester (England, 396,300), Bristol (England, 373,000), Cardiff (Wales, 316,800), Leicester (England, 296,600), Bradford (England, 279,000), Coventry (England, 267,800), Kingston upon Hull (England, 265,600), Belfast (Northern Ireland, 258,700), Plymouth (England, 253,200), Stoke-on-Trent (England, 249,100), Derby (England, 247,500), Wolverhampton (England, 246,100), Nottingham (England, 240,400), Southampton (England, 236,900), Portsmouth (England, 203,600), Swansea (Wales, 173,900), Norwich (England, 171,200), Newcastle-upon-Tyne (England, 168,100), Aberdeen (Scotland, 165,600), Oxford (England, 146,700) and Cambridge (England, 117,000).

Transport: There are 398,350km of roads, 100% paved; motorways account for some 3,500km. At least 70% of households own one or more cars, 27% owning two or more.

The world's first passenger steam railway (the Stockton and Darlington Railway) began operation in Britain in 1825. The system was nationalised in 1948 and privatisation was completed in 1997, though Railtrack, the company that managed the railway infrastructure, reverted to public ownership in 2001, as Network Rail. By the 2000s there were 16,321km of railway.

The Channel Tunnel was opened to traffic in 1994. It operates a fast undersea train shuttle between Folkestone in England and Calais in France, carrying cars, freight and passengers, linking London with Paris and Brussels. There are underground railway systems in London ('the tube') and Glasgow. Liverpool has a metro-like system. Several light rail systems were built during the 1990s, including the Docklands Light Railway, Tyne and Wear Metro, Manchester Metrolink, South Yorkshire Supertram, the Midland Metro and the Croydon Tramlink.

There are about 100 commercially significant ports and several hundred small harbours. The main ports are London, Dover, Tees and Hartlepool, Grimsby and Immingham, Southampton, Liverpool and Felixstowe. Forth, Sullom Voe (Shetland) and Milford Haven mostly handle oil.

London's international airports are Heathrow, Gatwick, Stansted and City Airport. Other major international airports are Manchester, Birmingham and Glasgow. There are more than 150 civil aerodromes.

Society

KEY FACTS 2010

Population per sq km:	255
Life expectancy:	80 years
Net primary enrolment:	100%

Population: 62,036,000 (2010); England 83.6%, Scotland 8.6%, Wales 4.9%, Northern Ireland 2.9% (2001 census); 80% lives in urban areas and 26% in urban agglomerations of more than 1 million people; growth 0.4% p.a. 1990–2010; birth rate 12 per 1,000 people (16 in 1970); life expectancy 80 years (72 in 1970 and around 50 in 1901).

According to the 2001 census, the ethnic origins of the population are 92.1% European; 4.0% Asian (1.8% Indian, 1.3% Pakistani, 0.5% Bangladeshi); 2% Caribbean or African; and 0.4% Chinese.

Language: English (official language); Welsh (an official language in Wales) is spoken by about 21% of people there (2001 census) and is the first language in much of rural north and west Wales; Scottish Gaelic is spoken in Scotland by some 70,000 people, many of whom live in the Hebrides. Many ethnic minorities speak the languages of their countries of origin.

Religion: The majority of adherents to a religion are Christians (71.8% in the 2001 census, of a wide variety of denominations); independent churches and new religious movements increased in the late 20th century. There are substantial communities of Muslims (2.8%), Hindus (1.0%), Sikhs (0.6%), Jews (0.5%) and Buddhists (0.3%). About one-quarter of the population does not profess any religion (22.9% in the 2001 census)

Health: Public spending on health was 8% of GDP in 2009. The National Health Service (NHS) provides free health care. It has a workforce of around 1 million people and is paid for mainly through general taxation. Cancer, heart disease and stroke are the major causes of death, while accidents are the commonest cause of death under 30. Up to the end of 2006, 73,000 people were estimated to be living with HIV. Cigarette smoking is the largest preventable cause of illness and death. About 27% of men and 13% of women drink alcohol to an extent that may put their health at risk. Infant mortality was 5 per 1,000 live births in 2010 (23 in 1960).

Education: Public spending on education was 5.4% of GDP in 2008. There are 11 years of compulsory education starting at age five. The school year starts in September.

After 16, when it is no longer compulsory, around 70% of young people stay in education, either at school or at further education colleges, and may then go on to higher education institutions. According to the higher education admissions service, UCAS, there are more than 300 institutions providing higher education courses, including universities, colleges of higher education and further

Stone circles like Avebury and Stonehenge are evidence of prehistoric cultures, especially notable in the milder south of England where ancient sites abound. Julius Caesar led token Roman expeditions into Britain in 55 and 54 BC. Roman colonisation began 80 years later, lasting from AD 43 to about 409. Scotland resisted occupation for most of the period.

After the departure of the Romans, Angles, Saxons and Jutes from northern Europe settled, the Angles giving their name to England. Several large kingdoms emerged: Northumbria in the north, Mercia in the midlands and Wessex in the south. Vikings from Scandinavia made incursions from the 8th century and settled widely in the north and east. Ireland was dominated by the Vikings during the 10th century. In 1066 England was invaded and conquered by the Norman duke William of Normandy (France).

In 1169 Henry II of England authorised an invasion of Ireland, following which a large part of the country came under the control of Anglo-Norman magnates. Wales came under English rule during the 13th century, during the reign of Edward I; but the continuing strength of Welsh national feeling was shown by a rising at the beginning of the 15th century.

Christianity spread in the 6th to 7th centuries. Much of Britain shifted from Roman Catholicism to Protestantism in the 16th century. England retained an Episcopalian church (governed by bishops), while Scotland embraced a Presbyterian system.

In 1603, King James VI of Scotland succeeded to the English throne, so uniting the two Crowns. However, England and Scotland remained separate political entities during that century, apart from an enforced period of unification under Oliver Cromwell in the 1650s. In 1707 both countries agreed on a single parliament for Great Britain.

Several campaigns were waged against Irish insurgents during the reign of Elizabeth I (1558–1603). The northern province of Ulster resisted English rule particularly strongly; following defeat of the rebels, Ulster was settled by immigrants from Scotland and England. Further risings were crushed by Oliver Cromwell. An uneasy peace prevailed throughout most of the 18th century. In 1782 the Irish Parliament was given legislative independence and in 1801 Ireland was joined to Great Britain by an Act of Union.

England has ousted its monarch on more than one occasion. During England's civil wars (1642–51), triggered by clashes between king and parliament, Charles I was executed and a republic briefly instated under Oliver and later Richard Cromwell (1649–60). In 1688 a bloodless 'revolution' took place, and James II was replaced by William and Mary.

Britain transformed itself from an agrarian to an industrial society from the 1760s to 1830s, the world's first industrial revolution. The country also developed a powerful navy and merchant fleet. It was the first nation to have a political anti-slavery movement; it led the government to ban the slave trade in 1807 and slavery in 1833–34.

In the 19th century, wealthy and industrialised, Britain became the major world power with an empire that included colonies on every continent. However, the 20th century reversed much of this. Two world wars, failure to keep pace with industrial advance, a severe brain drain and the independence of Commonwealth countries reduced Britain's position on the world stage. But it remains a leading liberal democracy, with art and literature, intellectual freedoms and parliamentary traditions of lasting influence.

Through the 1960s and 70s, the government switched between the Labour and Conservative parties. The general election of 1979, following the 'winter of discontent' of continual strikes and industrial unrest, gave a large majority for the then relatively unknown Conservative leader Margaret Thatcher and began a long period of Conservative government.

Thatcher implemented a radical programme of economic liberalisation, privatisation, trade union reform and reduction of public expenditure. She won the two succeeding elections until she resigned in 1990 following a Tory leadership contest. She was replaced by the then Chancellor of the Exchequer, John Major, who won the April 1992 elections, with a smaller but still substantial majority.

During this period, leadership of the opposition changed hands. Neil Kinnock, Labour Party leader since October 1983 who had driven through modernisation of the party, resigned after losing the 1992 elections, and was succeeded by John Smith, whose unexpected death in 1994 led to another leadership election, won by Tony Blair, who sought to modernise the party. Under the banner of 'New Labour', his reform of the party resulted in the jettisoning of traditional socialist policies.

Led by Blair, Labour won the May 1997 elections with the largest majority in its history – 418 seats, against 165 Conservatives, 46 Liberal Democrats and 30 others (mainly representing nationalist interests in Scotland, Wales and Northern Ireland). Blair became prime minister. John Major resigned as Conservative leader and was replaced by the former Welsh Secretary, William Hague.

In the general election in June 2001 – 11 months before the full five-year term – in a record low turnout, the Labour Party won a decisive victory with 413 seats and 41% of the votes; the Conservatives took 166 seats (32%) and the Liberal Democrats 52 (18%). Hague resigned as Conservative leader and was replaced by the former shadow defence secretary, Iain Duncan Smith. Then, in November 2003, following a no-confidence vote of Conservative MPs, he, in turn, was succeeded by shadow chancellor of the exchequer, Michael Howard.

Immediately after the terrorist attacks in the United States on 11 September 2001, the UK lent its total support to the US

➤ Government in building a broad coalition to fight international terrorism, then in military operations in Afghanistan from October 2001 and Iraq, from invasion in March 2003 to withdrawal of the last British troops in May 2011.

Constitutional development

England has had a single crown since the 10th century and a parliament since the 13th century. The constitution evolved through the struggle for power between them. Early parliaments – the term is first recorded in 1236 – were called to meet the king's expenses of government. Those who were summoned by name in due course formed the House of Lords; others who represented communities became the House of Commons. Individual freedoms, such as protection against unlawful imprisonment, were protected by the Habeas Corpus Act of 1679. By the early 18th century real power was passing from the monarch to parliament, and parliament developed a two-party system. From 1832, the vote, initially held by the land-owning classes only, was gradually extended until universal male suffrage was achieved in 1918. In 1928 the vote was extended to women and in 1969 the minimum voting age was reduced from 21 to 18.

The modern Conservative Party evolved out of the 18th-century Tory party and the Liberal Democrats out of the Whig party. The Labour Party, representing working people, emerged at the end of the 19th century.

Referendums over the introduction of a certain level of self-government were held in September 1997. The Scottish referendum produced a strong majority for a separate parliament (74%) with limited tax-raising powers (63% majority) on a turnout of over 60%. In Wales, the result was a narrow majority of 50.3%, on a turnout of 50%, for a Welsh Assembly.

The first elections to the new Scottish Parliament and Welsh Assembly were held on 6 May 1999. Labour emerged as the largest party in both legislatures, although without an overall majority in either. The elections were the first to be held in Great Britain under a system of proportional representation. In the 2007 elections the Scottish National Party (SNP) became the largest party in the Scottish Parliament. Then in 2011 it gained a majority and formed an SNP government, promising a referendum on Scottish independence from the United Kingdom during its term of office.

Northern Ireland

The deep divisions in Northern Irish society, dating from the time of the Irish independence struggle at the beginning of the 20th century, were exposed in an upsurge of violent conflict in the 1970s, which lasted into the 1990s. Most Protestants, who constitute the majority (50.6% in the 1991 census), are Unionists who want to remain British; many Roman Catholics (38.4%) are Nationalists or Republicans, who favour unity with the Irish

Republic. Thirty years of unrest led to some 3,500 killings and 36,000 injuries.

The Anglo–Irish Agreement of 1985 for the first time recognised Ireland's right to have a consultative role on Northern Ireland. When in August 1994 the Irish Republican Army (IRA) announced a ceasefire, its political wing, Sinn Fein, joined the multiparty talks. A continuing issue in all subsequent talks was that of IRA disarmament. Mediator US Senator George Mitchell broke the initial deadlock by recommending in January 1996 that disarmament should proceed by stages in parallel with the talks. However, in February the IRA resumed hostilities, and when talks formally began in June 1996, Sinn Fein was not included until the ceasefire was resumed and talks with all major parties were under way in October 1997. This resulted in the Good Friday Agreement of 10 April 1998, which constituted an elected assembly, a power-sharing executive of all major parties with devolved powers and cross-border institutions.

In return for a share of political powers for the Roman Catholic minority and for an involvement in Northern affairs for the Irish, Ireland was to relinquish the goal – enshrined in its constitution – of a united Ireland unless and until it is proved by vote to be the wish of the majority of the people of Northern Ireland. The Agreement was approved by the peoples of Ireland and Northern Ireland in May 1998 and the 108 members of the new assembly were elected in June 1998. However, formation of the cabinet was delayed by the IRA refusing to disarm; it was finally formed in December 1999 when the Ulster Unionists accepted a new deadline for the IRA to disarm in January 2000 after the government was formed.

A series of allegations of IRA paramilitary activity – culminating in the arrest of people accused of intelligence gathering inside the Northern Ireland Office – led in October 2002 to the resignation of Unionist ministers, and the suspension of the assembly and resumption of direct rule by the UK Government. Power-sharing under the Good Friday Agreement was resumed in May 2007, with Ian Paisley of the Democratic Unionist Party (DUP) as first minister and Martin McGuinness of Sinn Fein as deputy first minister, the Ulster Unionists having been overtaken by DUP in both UK elections of May 2005 and Northern Ireland elections of March 2007.

European relations

The UK joined the EU (then the European Economic Community) in January 1973. Some aspects of EU membership have been a source of contention within the country's economic, political and social spheres. Critical issues include possible adoption of the euro currency; the embracing of a policy enabling free movement of workers to the UK from EU member states, particularly those in the eastern parts of Europe; and the ratifying of EU treaties that bring about further economic and political integration – for instance, the Treaty of Lisbon of 2007.

education colleges. The female–male ratio for gross enrolment in tertiary education is 1.39:1 (2009). There is virtually no illiteracy among people aged 15–24.

Media: There are more than 100 daily and Sunday newspapers, of which some ten dailies and ten Sunday papers are national. 'Quality' newspapers include *Daily Telegraph* (established 1855), *Financial Times* (1888), *The Guardian* (1821), *The Independent* (1986), *The Scotsman* (1817 as a weekly, daily from 1855) and *The Times* (1785).

The BBC (British Broadcasting Corporation) provides national, regional and community public radio and TV services, and the international World Service radio and World News TV channel. The BBC is funded by an annual licence fee payable by all households with a TV set. The many other TV and radio broadcasters are funded by income from sales of advertising or by subscription, or by civil society organisations. All broadcasting is digital and the majority of stations and channels are exclusively digital; analogue broadcasts are due to be switched off in all regions of the UK by 2012. Terrestrial and satellite broadcasting reaches most households; in most urban areas cable transmission is also available; and many radio and TV programmes can be replayed via the internet.

Some 99% of households have TV sets (2007). There are 802 personal computers (2006) and 850 internet users (2010) per 1,000 people.

Communications: Country code 44; internet domain '.uk'. Coin- and card-operated phone booths are located throughout the country, and multimedia phone booths in larger cities. Mobile phone coverage is generally good. There are internet cafes in most urban areas, and growing numbers of coffee shops, bars and libraries offer wireless connections. Post offices are located in all towns and many villages.

There are 538 main telephone lines and 1,308 mobile phone subscriptions per 1,000 people (2010).

Public holidays: New Year's Day, May Day (first Monday in May), Spring Bank Holiday (last Monday in May), Summer Bank Holiday (last Monday in August, first Monday in August in Scotland only), Christmas Day and Boxing Day. Additionally in Scotland: Hogmanay (2 January); and in Northern Ireland: St Patrick's Day (17 March), and Battle of the Boyne Day (12 July). The Queen's Official Birthday (in June) is not a public holiday.

Religious and other festivals whose dates vary from year to year include Good Friday and Easter Monday.

Economy

KEY FACTS 2010

GNI:	US$2,387.1bn
GNI p.c.:	US$38,370
GDP growth:	0.3% p.a. 2006–10
Inflation:	2.7% p.a. 2006–10

The UK is among the largest economies in the world (ranking sixth in 2010, in terms of GNI – after the USA, China, Japan, Germany and France). For three decades after the Second World War, it was in decline relative to other industrialised democracies, especially in the 1970s when there was very high inflation, ending in the recession of the early 1980s.

Real Growth in GDP

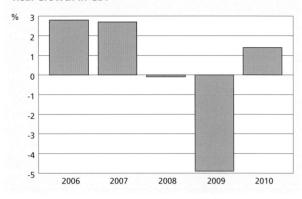

Inflation

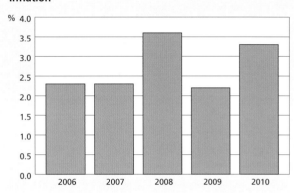

GDP by Sector (2010)

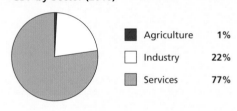

■	Agriculture	1%
□	Industry	22%
▨	Services	77%

However, during the 1980s the Conservative government managed to arrest this decline and GDP growth averaged 3.0% in that decade, one of the highest OECD rates, despite the slowdown at the end of the decade when the country was in recession again. During the 1990s growth averaged 2.5% p.a. and exports remained strong.

Interest rate policy was surrendered by the Treasury to the Bank of England in 1997 soon after Labour came to power.

Growth continued into the 2000s, despite the global slowdown in 2001–02, the very serious outbreak of foot and mouth disease in February 2001, and the impact of the terrorist attacks in the USA in September 2001 on air travel and tourism industries. GDP grew by 2.7% p.a. over 2003–07, while inflation remained at no more than 3% p.a.

From the second half of 2007 the country was increasingly affected by the global credit crunch, the resulting turmoil in financial markets throughout the world, high and volatile energy prices, and from 2008 the global economic downturn.

The then government and Bank of England moved during 2007–09 to prevent recession becoming depression. They initiated measures to stimulate the economy and to rescue financial institutions that were failing following the collapse of the sub-prime mortgage sector in the USA and consequent cessation of inter-bank lending.

The economy stalled during 2008, plunging into recession in the autumn, recording a contraction of 0.1% for that year and a further 4.9% in 2009. In 2010, when the new government launched its 5-year programme of public spending cuts aimed at eliminating the budget deficit, the economy grew by 1.4% and in 2011 by about 0.9%. Unemployment rose rapidly from 5.5% in 2008 to 8.4% in 2011.

Constitution

Status:	Monarchy under Queen Elizabeth II
Legislature:	UK Parliament

The UK does not have a written constitution. Acts of Union integrated England with Wales (1536–42), with Scotland (1707) and with Ireland (1801). In 1921 southern Ireland became the Irish Free State (later Republic of Ireland). The constitution is made up of common law, statute law and conventions, and may be changed by a simple act of parliament without any special procedure or majority.

The UK is a constitutional monarchy (with Queen Elizabeth II as head of state) and a parliamentary democracy (with parliament as the legislative organ). Parliament is bicameral, with an upper chamber, the House of Lords (comprising 89 hereditary peers, 678 life peers and 25 bishops in March 2011), and a lower chamber, the House of Commons (with 650 elected members). The prime minister and cabinet lead the executive. Parliamentary elections are held at least every five years, with universal adult suffrage.

A major constitutional process to change the membership of the House of Lords was begun in 1998. Of some 700 hereditary peers, only 92 were allowed to keep their seats after November 1999, whereon a second stage of reform was due to lead to the final removal of all hereditary peers and a wide-ranging debate about possible new methods to select members of the upper chamber.

Local government is conducted through local authorities, with specified powers in education, social services, etc. Councils are directly elected by voters in the relevant area.

The governments in Scotland, Wales and Northern Ireland are responsible for local government in their own regions. In England local government is devolved to two levels of authority: county/metropolitan area and district. In certain instances government is delivered by councils at both levels with responsibilities divided between the two, and in others, by the county/metropolitan area or district but not by both.

Politics

Last elections:	May 2010
Next elections:	2015
Head of state:	Queen Elizabeth II
Head of government:	Prime Minister David Cameron
Ruling party:	coalition of Conservatives and Liberal Democrats

In the hard-fought May 2005 general election, the ruling Labour Party, led by Tony Blair, won fewer seats (356) than in 2001, and received a reduced share of the votes (35.2%); while both the

Conservatives (with 197 seats and 32.3%) and the Liberal Democrats (with 62 seats and 22.0%) made gains. At 61.3%, voter turnout was only 2% higher than in 2001 and this was mainly due to an increase in postal voting. In December 2005 shadow education minister David Cameron became Conservative Party leader. In June 2007 Prime Minister Blair was succeeded as Labour Party leader and prime minister by Gordon Brown, who was the only candidate.

In the May 2010 election, the Conservative Party won 306 of the 649 seats contested (voting in one constituency was postponed following the death of a candidate) and 36.1% of votes, but failed to secure a parliamentary majority; the Labour Party took 258 seats (29.0%) and the Liberal Democrats 57 (23.0%). The Conservatives and Liberal Democrats formed a coalition with Cameron as prime minister and Liberal Democrat leader Nick Clegg as deputy prime minister; it was the country's first full coalition government for 65 years.

International relations

United Kingdom is a member of the Council of Europe, European Union, North Atlantic Treaty Organization, Organisation for Economic Co-operation and Development, Organization for Security and Co-operation in Europe, United Nations and World Trade Organization.

Traveller information

Local laws and conventions: Penalties for possession, use of, or trafficking in, illegal drugs are severe, and convicted offenders can expect long jail sentences and heavy fines.

Smoking is banned in all enclosed public places, including stations, pubs and restaurants.

Shaking hands is the usual form of greeting, for both men and women. Casual wear is widely acceptable in the UK.

Businesspeople are generally expected to dress smartly (suits are the norm). Appointments should be made and the exchange of business cards is customary. A knowledge of English is essential, though translators are available if needed. Office hours are Mon–Fri 0900–1730.

Immigration and customs: For all non-European Union nationals, passports must be valid for three months beyond the intended length of stay. EU citizens can enter the country on their national identity card. A visa is not required by those wishing to stay for up to six months.

Unlicensed drugs, offensive weapons, pornography, indecent and obscene material featuring children, counterfeit and pirated goods, and meat, dairy and other animal products are all prohibited imports.

Travellers are forbidden to take out of the country any meat, meat products, milk, and milk and dairy products from animals that are susceptible to foot and mouth disease; this includes sandwiches and packed lunches.

Travel within the country: Driving is on the left and a national driving licence is required. Car hire is available at all airports and in most towns and cities. Speed limits are 48kph in urban areas, 96kph on roads away from built-up areas and 112kph on motorways. Seatbelts are compulsory and drink-driving carries severe penalties. Many large towns and cities have a park-and-ride service, where drivers can park their cars outside the city and catch a bus into the centre.

Drivers of motor vehicles must pay a congestion charge on entering central London during normal weekday working hours.

Domestic flights serve the main cities, and scheduled ferry services link the mainland with the Isle of Wight, the Isle of Man, the Channel Islands, the Isles of Scilly, the Scottish islands and Ireland.

National bus services connect the country's main towns and cities, and a network of railways and intercity lines provide fast rail travel between London and the rest of the country.

Licensed taxis are widely available in all urban areas and are metered. Fares are usually higher after midnight. Many towns and cities also have unlicensed taxis, or minicabs, but they are not allowed to pick up customers in the street and must be booked by phone. London has an extensive underground railway system.

Travel health: Medical facilities are good around the country. The National Health Service (NHS) provides free health care for visitors from the EU and Commonwealth countries, as well as those from a country that has reciprocal health arrangements (Australia, New Zealand, Russia, Norway, Sweden, Finland and Iceland). All other visitors should ensure they have comprehensive health insurance. Immediate first aid or emergency treatment is free for all visitors.

Money: All major currencies can be exchanged in banks, exchange bureaux, some post offices and many hotels. Major credit cards are accepted in most places and ATMs are available across the country. Travellers cheques are widely accepted and should be in pounds sterling to avoid additional charges. Opening hours are decided by the individual banks and may differ considerably from branch to branch. Banks are usually open 0900–1730 weekdays (some banks open Saturday morning).

There were 28,133,000 tourist arrivals in 2010.

Further information

UK Government: www.direct.gov.uk

UK Parliament: www.parliament.uk

Bank of England: www.bankofengland.co.uk

Commonwealth Secretariat: www.thecommonwealth.org

Commonwealth of Nations: www.commonwealth-of-nations.org/United_Kingdom

United Kingdom: Overseas Territories

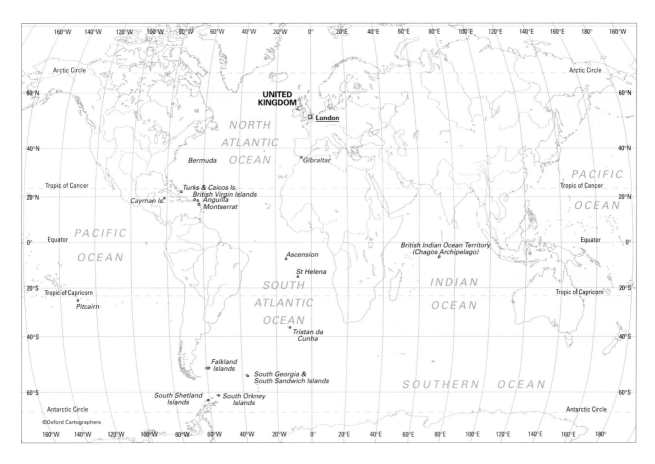

The UK's overseas territories are: Anguilla, Bermuda, British Antarctic Territory, British Indian Ocean Territory, British Virgin Islands, Cayman Islands, Falkland Islands, Gibraltar, Montserrat, Pitcairn (including Henderson, Ducie and Oeno Islands), St Helena and St Helena Dependencies (Ascension and Tristan da Cunha), South Georgia and the South Sandwich Islands, Turks and Caicos Islands.

The UK's overseas territories retain their connection with the UK by virtue of the wishes of their inhabitants and there is no intention either to delay independence for those territories that desire it or force it on those that do not. All the inhabited territories have assumed a very substantial measure of responsibility for the conduct of their own affairs.

Anguilla

Status: UK overseas territory

Geography

Anguilla is the most northerly of the Leeward Islands in the Eastern Caribbean. It includes the island of Sombrero to the north-west, on which there is a lighthouse, and several islets and cays (such as Scrub Island, Dog Island, Prickly Pear Cays and Sandy Island).

Time: GMT minus 4hr

Area: Anguilla island 96 sq km; Sombrero 5 sq km.

Topography. Anguilla island is long and relatively narrow (5km maximum), and mainly flat. The highest point, Crocus Hill, is 64m above sea level. There are about 30 white coral sand beaches. There are no rivers, but some salt ponds.

Climate: The tropical marine climate is generally pleasant and healthy; the hot season is July to October. Rainfall is erratic, averaging about 790mm p.a., September to January being the wettest months. During June to November, the hurricane season, squalls and thunderstorms occur, and hurricanes are always a possibility.

Environment: The most significant environmental issue is that supplies of drinking water are insufficient to meet the growing demand, largely because of the poor distribution system.

Vegetation: A thin layer of soil covers the rock, with pockets of fertile soil in places. Much of the island is covered in scrub. Forest covers 60% of the land area.

Main settlements: The Valley (capital, pop. 1,860 in 2010), North Side (2,270), The Quarter (1,580), Stoney Ground (1,470), George Hill (1,070), Island Harbour (1,070) and the Farrington.

Transport/Communications: A network of tarred, gravel and earth roads serve all parts of the island.

The main seaports are Sandy Ground at Road Bay on the north coast (cargo) and Blowing Point on the south coast for passenger services to Marigot in St Martin (25 minutes).

Wallblake Airport, the international airport, is situated in The Valley.

The international dialling code is 1 264. There are 410 main telephone lines (2010), 1,563 mobile phone subscriptions (2010) and 244 internet users (2009) per 1,000 people.

Society

Population: 15,960 (2010); 100% lives in urban areas; population density 158 per sq km; life expectancy 80 years.

Language: English

Religion: Mainly Christians (Anglicans 29%, Methodists 24%, Seventh Day Adventists, Baptists and Roman Catholics); Hindu, Jewish and Muslim minorities (2001 census).

Health: Princess Alexandra Hospital is at Sandy Ground. Infant mortality is about 3 per 1,000 live births (2009).

Education: There are 13 years of compulsory education starting at age five. Net enrolment ratios are 92% for primary (2006) and 81% for secondary (2005). The pupil–teacher ratio for primary is 16:1 and for secondary 10:1 (2007). The school year starts in September.

Tertiary education is provided at the regional University of the West Indies, which has campuses in Barbados, Jamaica, and Trinidad and Tobago.

Media: *The Light* (weekly) and *The Anguillian* (weekly). Radio Anguilla provides a public radio service.

Public holidays: New Year's Day, Labour Day (early May), Anguilla Day (last Friday in May), Queen's Official Birthday (Monday in June), August Monday (start of carnival week, the first week in August), August Thursday and Constitution Day (Thursday and Friday of the same week in early August), Separation Day (a Monday before Christmas), Christmas Day and Boxing Day.

Religious and other festivals whose dates vary from year to year include Good Friday, Easter Monday and Whit Monday.

Economy

Currency: Eastern Caribbean dollar

GDP: US$210m (2010)

Tourist arrivals: 57,890 (2009)

In the 1990s, the traditional industries of lobster fishing, farming, livestock rearing, salt production and boat building were overshadowed by high-class tourism, related construction and a developing offshore finance sector.

Thus, following the US economic slowdown of 2000, when there was a sharp fall in tourists coming to Anguilla, the economy hardly grew at all in 2000–02. There was a recovery in 2003, and a surge of growth from 2004, which was sustained until 2008, when the world economic downturn caused another substantial fall in income from tourism. The economy contracted by some 24% in 2009 and a very weak recovery was under way by 2011.

History

The island, formerly called by the Carib name *Malliouhana*, gained the Spanish name Anguilla because of its 'eel-like' shape. It was inhabited by Arawaks for several centuries before being colonised in 1650 by English settlers coming from St Kitts, after which it was administered by the English as part of the Leeward Islands colony. It has remained a British territory ever since.

In 1631 the Dutch built a fort on Anguilla, but they had to abandon it after a few years. In 1688 the island was invaded by a party of Irish, who settled and left their surnames to some of the modern inhabitants. There was an attempted French landing in 1745 near Crocus Bay (north coast). In 1796 French troops landed at Rendezvous Bay (south coast) and fought their way eastwards to Sandy Hill, where they were beaten back.

In 1825, against the wishes of the islanders, Anguilla became incorporated with St Kitts and Nevis. Politics on the island since then has been dominated by this issue. In 1872 an unsuccessful petition was sent to the British Colonial Office, asking for separate status and direct rule from Britain. In 1958 the islanders formally petitioned the governor, again unsuccessfully, requesting a dissolution of the political and administrative association with St Kitts. In 1958–62 Anguilla was, along with St Kitts and Nevis, a unit of the short-lived Federation of the West Indies.

Following the dissolution of the Federation in 1962, Anguilla became part of the Associated State of St Kitts-Nevis-Anguilla. In May 1967, Anguillans refused to recognise any longer the authority of the new state and evicted police from St Kitts. A referendum in June 1967 endorsed the decision to separate from St Kitts. A senior UK official resided on the island for a year from January 1968, monitoring the situation and discussing possible solutions with the Anguilla Council.

In March 1969, after the UK parliamentary Under-Secretary of State for Foreign and Commonwealth Affairs, William Whitlock, had been ejected, UK security forces occupied Anguilla, and the UK Government appointed a commissioner. Following negotiations, agreement was reached, and the UK Parliament's Anguilla Act (July 1971) provided for a formal separation of Anguilla when St Kitts and Nevis became independent. In December 1980, Anguilla was formally separated and reverted to the status of a UK dependent territory (subsequently UK Overseas Territory).

In the general election of March 1999, the Anguilla United Party (AUP) and the Anguilla Democratic Party (ADP) each won two seats and the opposition Anguilla National Alliance (ANA) three seats. However, the AUP/ADP government's majority was overturned in May 1999, when Finance Minister and ADP leader Victor Banks resigned. Then in January 2000, Chief Minister Hubert Hughes called another election for March 2000 – four years early. In the election the opposition United Front coalition (ANA plus Victor Banks) gained four seats, while the governing AUP took two, and ANA leader Osbourne Fleming became chief minister.

Constitution

The present constitution dates from April 1982, with an amendment in 1990. Under it, Anguilla is a self-governing dependency of the UK with a ministerial system of government. There is a governor appointed by the British monarch, an executive council and a unicameral house of assembly.

The governor is responsible for external affairs, offshore finance, defence, internal security (including the police force), the public service and administration of the courts. The executive council is presided over by the governor; it consists of the chief minister, three other elected ministers, deputy governor and attorney-general.

The house of assembly consists of seven elected members (directly elected for a five-year term), two *ex officio* members and two members whom the governor nominates, following consultation with the chief minister.

In January 2006 the government appointed a Constitutional and Electoral Reform Commission to take forward the constitutional reform process.

Politics

Last elections: February 2010

Next elections: 2015

Head of state: Queen Elizabeth II, represented by the governor

Chief minister: Hubert Hughes

Ruling party: Anguilla United Movement

In the February 2005 general election, the Anguilla United Front – AUF; now a separate party comprising the former Anguilla National Alliance (ANA) and Anguilla Democratic Party (ADP) – gained four seats, Anguilla Strategic Alliance took two seats and Anguilla United Movement (AUM) one. AUF leader Osbourne Fleming continued as chief minister.

In the election of February 2010 the AUM (with four seats and only 32.7% of votes) narrowly defeated the ruling AUF (two seats and 39.4%). The Anguilla Progressive Party received 14.7% of votes and took one seat. AUM leader Hubert Hughes became chief minister and finance minister.

Bermuda

Status: UK overseas territory

Geography

Bermuda lies in the North Atlantic, east of the USA, and roughly at the latitude of South Carolina. The islands and islets of The Bermudas lie along the southern rim of the summit of a submarine volcanic mountain.

Time: GMT minus 4hr. The clock is advanced by one hour from the first Sunday in April to the last Sunday in October.

Area: 53.3 sq km

Topography: Around 138 limestone islands and islets lie in the shape of a fishhook. The ten main islands form a close chain about 35km long, interconnected by bridges and causeways. The main island is about 23km by 1.6km. Coastlines have small bays, with beaches of fine pale sand, often of pink sand, surrounded by vivid blue-green waters. There are no rivers or lakes. The highest point of the main island is 79m above sea level.

Climate: Generally humid with average maximum (August) and minimum (February) temperatures of 32°C and 9°C. Average annual rainfall is 1,475mm. Hurricanes can occur in the summer; the country had severe hurricanes in August and September 1995.

Vegetation: Inland there is an abundance of subtropical plants including various palm trees, prickly pear and lantana shrubs; there are also many introduced flowering trees and bushes. Vegetables (cabbage, carrots, potatoes, beans), fruit (tomatoes, bananas, citrus) and flowers (especially lilies) on cultivated land. Forest covers 20% of the land area.

Wildlife: Lizards and green turtles; about ten species of bird; abundance of ants and mosquitoes. A Bermuda Act of 1620 'against the killing of sea turtles' is thought to be the world's earliest piece of conservation legislation. Further legislation followed in the 17th to 19th centuries to protect flora and fauna including cedar trees, bait fish and birds.

Main towns: Hamilton (capital), Tucker's Town and Flatts Village on Great Bermuda; St George on St George's Island; Freeport on Ireland Island.

Transport/Communications: There are 225km of public highways and 222km of private roads. Bermuda's first four-lane highway opened at Crow Lane in 1992.

There are three ports (Hamilton, St George and Freeport); Hamilton handles the main passenger and cargo traffic.

Bermuda International Airport (formerly called Kindley Field) is 15km from Hamilton. When the US air base was closed in 1995, the Bermuda Government took over management of the airport.

The international dialling code is 1 441. There are 890 main telephone lines, 1,358 mobile phone subscriptions and 842 internet users per 1,000 people (2010).

Society

Population: 64,600 (2010); 100% lives in urban areas; population density 1,212 per sq km; life expectancy 80 years.

About 55% of Bermudians are of African descent; most others are of European or mixed descent (2000 census).

Language: English. There is a small Portuguese-speaking community.

Religion: Predominantly Christians (Anglicans 23%, Roman Catholics 15%, Methodists 11%, and many other denominations; 2000 census).

Health: Facilities include King Edward VII Hospital (a general hospital), St Brendan's (for mental illnesses) and Agape House (for the terminally ill). Other services include child health clinics, school health services and clinics, a clinic for sexually transmitted diseases, family planning services, dental services for children, a physical abuse centre and a hostel for alcoholics. Infant mortality is about 2 per 1,000 live births (2009).

Education: There are 12 years of compulsory education starting at age five. The net enrolment rate at primary school level is 92% (2006). The pupil–teacher ratio for primary is 8:1 and for secondary 6:1 (2006). The school year starts in September.

Bermuda College provides post-secondary vocational courses and an associate degree programme. Adult literacy is more than 95%.

Media: *The Royal Gazette* (daily) and *Bermuda Sun* (bi-weekly).

Public holidays: New Year's Day, Bermuda Day (24 May), National Heroes' Day (a Monday in June), Emancipation Day and Somers Day (consecutive Thursday and Friday in July/August), Labour Day (first Monday in September), Remembrance Day (11 November), Christmas Day and Boxing Day.

Religious and other festivals whose dates vary from year to year include Good Friday.

Economy

Currency: Bermuda dollar (Bda$), at par with US$

GDP: US$5.8bn (2009)

Tourist arrivals: 235,860 (2009)

Bermuda's economy rested principally on tourism and earnings from the US and UK military bases. Closure of these bases coincided with a slowdown in tourism due to recession in the USA and the early 1990s were difficult years for the economy.

Since then, tourism, financial services and e-commerce have been successfully developed, and the country enjoys one of the world's highest per capita incomes. The Bermuda Land Development Company was established to plan, finance, market and develop the 324 hectares of land vacated by the US military.

In 2000 the economy slowed to a halt, as the impact of the US slowdown was felt on tourism. It then picked up in 2002 and was buoyant until 2008, when the collapse of international financial markets and the world economic downturn hit both financial services and tourism; GDP growth stalled, plunging from 3.0% in 2008 to a contraction of 4.8% in 2009 and a further 1.9% in 2010, before recovering weakly in 2011.

History

The Bermudas were visited about 1503 by a Spanish sailor, Juan de Bermudez, and had the name *La Bermuda* by 1510. Ferdinand d'Orviedo (also Spanish) sighted them in 1515. They remained uninhabited until 1609, when the *Sea Venture*, on its way to Virginia with British settlers, and commanded by Sir George Somers, was wrecked on one of the reefs. News spread of the beauty and fertility of the islands, and in 1612 King James I extended the charter of the Virginia Company to include them. The first emigrants went out in that year; others followed, and enslaved Africans were brought in with them. The islands, known as Somers Islands, were bought about 1615 by some entrepreneurs from the City of London. In 1684 the company's charter was annulled, and government passed to the Crown.

By the 19th century, the country had a valuable vegetable export industry, and, around the middle of the century, tourists began arriving (then, as now, mostly from North America).

During the Second World War, a US military base was established at Kindley Field; in 1948, under a treaty between the USA and the UK, its airport was opened to civilian aircraft. The base was closed down, and its personnel repatriated, in 1995.

The Parliamentary Franchise Act 1963 enfranchised everyone over the age of 25, and gave property owners the privilege of two votes. The Progressive Labour Party (PLP), Bermuda's first political party, was formed shortly before the 1963 elections, but the majority of seats went to independent candidates.

In the following year, most of the independent members formed the United Bermuda Party (UBP) with policies favouring strong professional and business development. A new constitution providing for self-government came into force in 1968, following a general election which was won by the UBP. The UBP was returned to power in seven subsequent elections.

A referendum on independence was held in August 1995, just after the country had suffered damage from Hurricane Felix. Voter turnout was low (59% of the 38,000 registered voters). The vote was decisive – 24% for independence and 73% against.

Premier Sir John Swan, who had campaigned for independence, and had said he would resign if the vote went against him, stood down within days of the referendum and was succeeded as leader of the UBP and premier by Dr David Saul, previously finance minister. In March 1997 Saul resigned from office and was replaced by Bermuda's first woman premier, Pamela Gordon.

In November 1998 the PLP, under the leadership of Jennifer Smith, achieved its first general election victory, winning 26 of the 40 seats and receiving 54% of the votes. The UBP, which had been in power for 30 years, won 14 seats; three cabinet ministers lost their seats. The National Liberal Party fought four seats and gained none, and together with the four independent candidates, took less than 2% of the votes.

Constitution

Bermuda is a UK overseas territory with a substantial measure of self-government. Its bicameral legislature is responsible for most internal affairs. There is an upper house of 11 members appointed by the governor (three at his/her discretion, five on the premier's advice, three on the advice of the leader of the opposition) and (following a constitutional change enacted in 2003) a 36-member house of assembly, elected in 36 constituencies by universal adult suffrage for a five-year term.

The governor is responsible for external affairs, defence and internal security. Appointed by and representing the UK monarch, the governor in turn appoints the majority leader in the house of assembly as premier. The premier appoints the cabinet, which must include at least six other members of the legislature.

Politics

Last elections: December 2007

Next elections: 2012/2013

Head of state: Queen Elizabeth II, represented by the governor

Head of government: Premier Paula Cox

Ruling party: Progressive Labour Party

In July 2003, the Progressive Labour Party (PLP), led by Jennifer Smith, defeated the United Bermuda Party (UBP) in a general election, winning 22 of the 36 seats, and was returned to power. The election was followed by a period of in-fighting within the PLP culminating on 28 July with Smith tendering her resignation as premier and party leader. William Alexander Scott became the new PLP leader and was sworn in as the new premier on 29 July.

In a leadership election at the PLP conference in October 2006, Dr Ewart Brown defeated Scott and was sworn in as premier a few days later. Brown was returned as premier in the December 2007 elections when the ruling PLP once again took 22 seats. UBP – led by Wayne Fubert – took the remaining 14.

In October 2010 Brown resigned as premier and leader of the PLP, and Deputy Premier and Finance Minister Paula Cox was elected by the party to succeed him. In her new cabinet she retained the finance portfolio.

British Antarctic Territory

Status: UK overseas territory

Geography

The British Antarctic Territory consists of that segment of the Antarctic continent lying south of latitude 60°S and between longitudes 20° and 80°W, comprising the Antarctic Peninsula with all adjacent islands, the South Orkney and South Shetland Islands and the Weddell Sea, as well as the landmass extending to the South Pole.

Area: 1,709,400 sq km

Topography: The Antarctic Peninsula and the islands are mountainous (Mt Jackson 3,184m). The mountains, the tail of the Andes chain, are connected to South America by a submarine ridge (the Scotia arc), which includes the active volcanoes of the South Sandwich Islands. The South Orkneys and South Georgia are also peaks of this chain. Of the 0.4% of the Antarctic continent which is ice-free, most is on the Antarctic Peninsula. No geological survey has been undertaken to establish whether commercially exploitable mineral resources exist in Antarctica. The Madrid Protocol (1991) bans all mineral resource activities on the continent. Scientists confirm that 180 million years ago, Antarctica was the centre of a southern supercontinent, 'Gondwana', which broke up to form Antarctica, South America, Africa, India and Australia. So it is

possible that minerals found in the other continents also exist in Antarctica. There may also be hydrocarbons (oil and gas) on the Antarctic continental shelf.

Climate: The centre of the landmass is cold with average annual temperatures of –50°C to –60°C. It is also theoretically a desert with annual snowfall equivalent to 7cm of rainfall. Nearer the coast, it is less cold (–10°C to –20°C) and receives more snow and some rain. Winds are moderate but are locally strong katabatic winds where cold air flowing from the interior is channelled by the local topography.

Vegetation: Sparse and primitive, with only lichens and mosses able to survive in the interior. Near the coast, where land is snow-free in summer, there are a few stands of flowering plants such as Antarctic hairgrass and Antarctic pearlwort. Antarctica has not always been a frozen continent. Seventy million years ago, some parts had a temperate climate, were forested and populated by the last dinosaurs. Scientists have found fossilised trees, ferns and other vegetation as well as the remains of ancient extinct animals.

Wildlife: The Antarctic Peninsula and islands are the most favoured breeding grounds for birds on the continent: seven species of penguin are resident in the area; petrels, cormorants, sheathbills, prions, skuas and terns breed there. Six species of seals live on and under the pack ice; they breed during the spring (September–November). The Weddell seal is the most southerly mammal, living under the sea ice on the coast all year round.

Settlements: Two British Antarctic Survey (BAS) research stations are manned the year round: Rothera on Adelaide Island, and Halley V on moving ice off the Caird Coast. There is a summer-only station at Signy in the South Orkney Islands.

Transport/Communications: Ships belonging to the British Antarctic Survey service the stations, and there is direct air support between the Falkland Islands and Rothera. The main stations are linked by satellite to the Survey headquarters in Cambridge, UK. Support is given to the British Antarctic Survey by the presence of the ice patrol vessel HMS *Endurance*, which is in Antarctic waters throughout the austral summer.

Society

Population: British Antarctic personnel number about 50 in winter, rising to more than 400 in summer. In addition to the British Antarctic Survey, the wintering bases of other Antarctic treaty parties are present in the British Antarctic Territory, with an estimated population varying from 450 in winter to 2,500 in summer. Cruiseships also bring tens of thousands of visitors each year to the British Antarctic Territory. The tourists stay three to five days on board ships in the area.

Economy

There is no economic activity. Scientific research and environmental monitoring are carried out. The Antarctic ozone hole was discovered by BAS scientists. Tourism is growing. The United Kingdom Antarctic Heritage Trust has a team at Port Lockroy each season. This historic site attracts tens of thousands of visitors a year.

History

The South Shetland Islands were discovered and taken possession of by Captain W Smith in 1819, the South Orkney Islands by Captain G Powell in 1821. The Antarctic Peninsula was discovered in 1820 by

Edward Bransfield and taken possession of for Britain in 1832 by John Biscoe. Thereafter, explorers penetrated the Weddell Sea and, finally, the great landmass of the continent. Ernest Shackleton's ship, *Endurance*, was trapped in pack ice in the Weddell Sea for a year during 1915–16. Britain registered the first claim to Antarctic Territory by Letters Patent in 1908, a claim that had to be adjusted in 1917 as it included part of Argentina and Chilean Patagonia. Britain's claim to the land between longitudes 20° and 80°W is contested by Argentina's claim to the region between 25° and 74°W, and Chile's claim to the region between 53° and 90°W.

In the 1950s, five-sixths of the Antarctic continent was claimed by seven countries. However, none of the claims was recognised by non-claimant states and the Antarctic Treaty (1959) was negotiated to put in place a mechanism to defuse disputes over sovereignty. It followed the unprecedented scientific co-operation in Antarctica demonstrated by 12 countries during the International Geophysical Year, 1957–58.

The Treaty came into force in 1961. Covering the area south of 60°S, its objectives are: to keep Antarctica demilitarised, nuclear-free and to ensure that it is used for peaceful purposes only; to promote international scientific co-operation in Antarctica; and to set aside disputes over territorial sovereignty.

An Environmental Protocol was added to the Antarctic Treaty in 1991, putting into abeyance indefinitely the exploration and exploitation of mineral resources in Antarctica. This prohibition may be reviewed after 50 years, or before if there is a consensus of treaty parties to do so.

There were 12 original signatories to the Treaty, including Australia, New Zealand, South Africa and the UK. The Treaty has been acceded to by 49 states (the 49th, Malaysia, became a member in October 2011), and 28 of these have Consultative Party status. The Consultative Parties meet annually.

Administration

Until 1989, the British Antarctic Territory was administered by a high commissioner, resident in the Falkland Islands. In 1989, the administration was moved to the Foreign and Commonwealth Office, London. The office of commissioner is held by the head of Overseas Territories Department and the administrator is the head of the Polar Regions Section.

Since 1967, the Department of Education and Science in the UK (later the Office of Science and Technology) has been financially responsible for the British Antarctic Survey through the Natural Environment Research Council. Station commanders are appointed magistrates and the courts of the territory are presided over by a senior magistrate or a judge of the Supreme Court. A Court of Appeal was set up in 1965 for hearing appeals from the territory.

British Indian Ocean Territory

Status: UK overseas territory

Geography

The British Indian Ocean Territory consists of a group of islands, the Chagos Archipelago, forming the southern extension of the Maldives Ridge off south-west India. It lies 1,770km east of Seychelles and 1,930km north-east of Mauritius.

Area: The territory covers approx. 54,400 sq km of ocean.

Topography/wildlife: The largest island, Diego Garcia, has an area of 44 sq km and is V-shaped, its two arms enclosing a large deep lagoon. The islands are home to a wide variety of flora and fauna, including several now-endangered species of crabs and turtles.

Society

Population: No permanent settled population. The only inhabitants are UK and US military personnel and civilian contract employees, all living on Diego Garcia. In September 2003, these numbered approximately 3,000 persons. The former population has been resettled (see *History* below).

Economy

There is no economic activity in the territory which is used for defence purposes, but there is a licensed fishery in the 370-km fisheries conservation and management zone.

History

The Chagos islands were first discovered by Portuguese mariners in the early 16th century. The French assumed sovereignty more than two centuries later and began to exploit the hitherto uninhabited islands for copra in the 1780s. The islands became British when ceded by France to Britain, together with Mauritius and Seychelles, in 1814. Following the French practice, they continued to be administered from Mauritius. Prior to Mauritius achieving independence and with the agreement of the Mauritius Council of Ministers, the islands were detached in 1965 to form part of the British Indian Ocean Territory (BIOT), together with some other small island groups that were detached from (but later reverted to) Seychelles.

The British Government entered into an agreement with the USA in 1966 whereby the Territory was to remain available for the defence needs of the two countries for an initial period of 50 years. Following this the copra plantations were run down and closed. In the late 1960s/early 1970s arrangements were made for the islanders to be relocated to Mauritius and Seychelles. The vast majority of them (some 1,200) were relocated to Mauritius. At that time, the UK made UK£650,000 available to the Mauritius Government for the express purpose of assisting resettlement.

In the mid-1970s a member of the Chagossian community in Mauritius started legal proceedings against the British Government in the English courts, claiming among other things that he had been wrongfully removed from the islands. Under an agreement reached in 1982 the legal proceedings were withdrawn and the UK made an ex gratia payment of UK£4 million for the benefit of the Chagossian community in Mauritius.

In 1998 another member of the Chagossian community instituted judicial review proceedings challenging the validity of BIOT's Immigration Ordinance 1971, which prohibited the entry of any person into any part of the Territory unless he obtained a permit to do so. The judgment in November 2000 held that the 1971 ordinance was indeed invalid and it was replaced by a new ordinance that allows the Chagossians to return and reside in any part of the Territory except (for defence reasons) Diego Garcia.

No Chagossians have returned to the islands to live since the new ordinance was enacted. The islands other than Diego Garcia are uninhabited and have no facilities on them to support a settled population. There are a few disintegrated remains of buildings from the copra plantation days, but these are unusable. There is no clean water supply, no power and no transport.

In February 2002, the Chagos Refugees Group, a Mauritius-based group of Chagos islanders, applied to the UK courts for further compensation and assisted resettlement on all of the islands including Diego Garcia. The court case started in October 2002 and, in October 2003, the courts found in favour of the UK Government but allowed the islanders to appeal on some of the issues.

In June 2004, the UK Government passed an order in council banning the islanders from the Chagos Islands and the islanders then applied for a judicial review of the order in council. In May 2006 the UK High Court overturned this order in council giving the islanders the right to return. In May 2007 the Court of Appeal upheld the High Court's decision ruling that the methods used in banning the islanders from returning to the islands was unlawful. In November 2007, the UK House of Lords gave the UK Government permission to challenge the Court of Appeal's ruling with the proviso that the government cover the cost of the appeal, whatever the outcome. In October 2008 the UK Law Lords upheld the UK Government's appeal, denying the islanders the right to return to the Islands.

Administration

The Chagos Archipelago is Crown property administered from London by a commissioner assisted by the officer in charge of the Royal Navy complement on Diego Garcia. The islands are also subject to a claim by Mauritius.

British Virgin Islands

Status: UK overseas territory

Geography

British Virgin Islands lies roughly midway between Puerto Rico and the northernmost of the Leeward Islands group in the Caribbean. It is an archipelago of more than 40 islands, 16 of which are inhabited. They are situated 96.5km east of Puerto Rico, with the US Virgin Islands between. To the east and south lie Anguilla, St Kitts and the other islands of the Lesser Antilles. Tortola is the largest island of the group.

Time: GMT minus 4hr

Area: 153 sq km. The largest of the islands are: Tortola (54 sq km), Anegada (39 sq km), Virgin Gorda (21 sq km) and Jost Van Dyke (9 sq km).

Topography: With the exception of Anegada (a flat reef-surrounded island of coral limestone at the northern tip of the group) the islands, which form a projection of the archipelago of Puerto Rico and the American Virgin Islands, are hilly.

Climate: Subtropical with annual rainfall averaging 1,250mm. Trade winds keep the air fresh.

Environment: The most significant environmental issue is the inadequacy of natural freshwater resources. Except for a few seasonal streams and springs on Tortola, most of the islands' water supply comes from wells and rainwater catchment.

Vegetation: The natural vegetation is mostly light bush and grass; there is some cultivated land, on which fruit and vegetables are grown. Forest covers 25% of the land area.

Wildlife: The islands are home to some rare birds (including the pearl-eyed thrasher) as well as flamingos and pelicans. There are two sea bird sanctuaries.

Main settlements: Road Town (capital, pop. 9,300 in 2010) and East End–Long Look on Tortola; The Valley on Virgin Gorda.

Transport/Communications: There are some 200km of roads, including a dual carriageway near Road Town.

Ferry services link main islands, including the United States Virgin Islands.

Beef Island Airport, although small, receives aircraft from Puerto Rico, the US Virgin Islands and the USA. It lies 14.5km from Road Town on Tortola, and Beef Island and Tortola are linked by road bridge. There are airports on Virgin Gorda and Anegada. Within the country, light aircraft ply between the islands.

The international dialling code is 1 284. There are 865 main telephone lines, 1,054 mobile phone subscriptions and 390 internet users per 1,000 people (2010).

Society

Population: 23,000 (2010); 40% lives in urban areas; population density 150 per sq km; life expectancy 77 years.

Some 82% of the people are of African descent; the balance is of European, Indian or mixed descent. About 30% are immigrants from St Kitts and Nevis or St Vincent and the Grenadines; 13% come from North America and Europe, and there is a growing section from the Dominican Republic.

Language: English

Religion: Predominantly Christians, including Methodists, Anglicans, Roman Catholics and Church of God.

Health: There are hospitals on Tortola and clinics on other islands. Infant mortality is about 14 per 1,000 live births (2009).

Education: There are 12 years of compulsory education starting at age five. Net enrolment rates are 93% for primary and 84% for secondary (2007). The pupil–teacher ratio for primary is 14:1 and for secondary 9:1 (2007). The school year starts in September.

Scholarships are available for students to go to the regional University of the West Indies, and to universities in the USA, Canada and the UK. The H Lavity Stoutt Community College opened in the late 1990s. There is virtually no adult illiteracy. Road Town has a public library, and there are library stations on the outer islands.

Media: *The Virgin Islands StandPoint* and *BVI Beacon* are weeklies.

Public holidays: New Year's Day, H Lavity Stoutt's Birthday (7 March), Commonwealth Day (second Monday in March), Queen's Official Birthday (one of the first three Saturdays in June, in line with the UK), Territory Day (1 July), Festival (Monday–Wednesday including the first Monday in August), St Ursula's Day (21 October), Christmas Day and Boxing Day.

Religious and other festivals whose dates vary from year to year include Good Friday, Easter Monday and Whit Monday.

Economy

Currency: US dollar

GDP: US$1.2bn (2009)

Tourist arrivals: 308,790 (2009)

Tourism and offshore financial services are the main economic activities, supplemented by agriculture and fishing. By mid-2009 some 405,870 international companies had been registered, generating substantial income for the government.

The economy grew steadily in the 2000s, mainly at more than 3% p.a. Then in 2008–09, when the global financial crisis and world economic downturn hit both financial services and tourism, GDP growth stalled, the economy contracting by 3.5% in 2009, recovering vigorously in 2010–11.

History

The Virgin Islands (*Las Virgenes*, or 'The Maidens') were discovered in 1493 by Christopher Columbus, who named them in honour of St Ursula and her company of 11,000 maidens. St Ursula's Day, 21 October, is a national holiday. As Europeans began moving into the Caribbean, the islands were often a shelter and meeting places for groups of pirates, who built a fort on Tortola, on which some of them settled down. The island was annexed by the Governor of the Leeward Islands in 1672, and such inhabitants as he found were moved to St Christopher (St Kitts). Between 1680 and 1717, European planters, with African slaves, moved into the islands; by 1717, there were 317 Europeans on Virgin Gorda and 159 on Tortola (plus an unrecorded population of slaves). In 1773 the planters were granted their own 12-member house of assembly and a legislative council.

The islands became part of the colony of the Leeward Islands in 1872. In 1956 the Leewards were de-federated, and the British Virgin Islands became a separate colony administered by the Governor of the Leeward Islands. The administrator of the islands became directly responsible to the Colonial Office in 1960; in 1971, the administrator's title was raised to governor.

At elections in February 1995, the Virgin Islands Party (VIP) won six of the 13 legislative council seats and formed a coalition with two independent members. Ralph O'Neal became chief minister.

In May 1999 O'Neal and the VIP were returned to office, with seven seats and 38% of the votes. The National Democratic Party took five seats and Concerned Citizens Movement one.

Constitution

The British Virgin Islands is a UK overseas territory. The 2007 constitution provides for a greater degree of internal self-government than previously and for fundamental rights and freedoms of the individual.

The legislature, the House of Assembly, comprises 13 elected and two appointed members. The UK monarch is represented by a governor responsible for external affairs, defence, internal security and the public service, and the administration of the courts. On all other matters, the executive has authority. The executive consists of the governor and the cabinet comprising the premier, the attorney-general and four other ministers appointed by the governor from the House of Assembly on the advice of the premier.

The High Court and Court of Appeal of the Eastern Caribbean Supreme Court have jurisdiction over the Islands.

Politics

Last elections: November 2011

Next elections: 2015

Head of state: Queen Elizabeth II, represented by the governor

Head of government: Premier Dr Orlando Smith

Ruling party: National Democratic Party

In the June 2003 elections the National Democratic Party (NDP) defeated the Virgin Islands Party (VIP), winning the majority of the seats and Dr Orlando Smith became chief minister.

The VIP won the August 2007 elections, securing ten of the 13 elective seats, and Ralph O'Neal began his third term as head of government and his first as premier, a post created in the new constitution of June 2007.

The NDP defeated the VIP in the November 2011 elections taking nine seats to the VIP's four. NDP leader Dr Orlando Smith was sworn in as premier.

Cayman Islands

Status: UK overseas territory

Geography

The Cayman Islands group lies between Cuba and Jamaica in the Caribbean. The territory is a group of three islands: Grand Cayman, Cayman Brac and Little Cayman.

Time: GMT minus 5hr

Area: 262 sq km

Topography: The Caymans are low-lying coral islands, nearly all less than 20m above sea level; the highest point is the eastern side of Cayman Brac, 43m above sea level. Grand Cayman, which is about 34km in length, has a big bay (the North Sound) on the north-west side; the bay is a good harbour for small boats. The west coast has the Seven Mile Beach, famous for its fine powdery sand. There are no rivers. Drinking water is obtained by desalination.

Climate: Tropical, tempered by cooling north-east trade winds from November to March; warm from May to October, with prevailing winds east-south-east. The hurricane season is from June to November. Hurricanes Allen (August 1980) and Paloma (November 2008) caused extensive damage on Cayman Brac, and Hurricanes Gilbert (September 1988) and Ivan (September 2004) very extensive damage and flooding on Grand Cayman.

Environment: The most significant environmental issue is the lack of natural freshwater resources.

Vegetation: Forest covers 50% of the land area.

Main towns: George Town (capital, pop. 29,100 in 2010), West Bay (12,700) and Bodden Town (7,700) on Grand Cayman. Cayman Brac has four small settlements: Stake Bay, West End, Creek and Spot Bay. Little Cayman has a permanent population of some 150.

Transport/Communications: Grand Cayman and Cayman Brac together have 785km of paved roads. A new road bypassing part of the busy West Bay Road on Grand Cayman was opened in 1998. Little Cayman also has some paved roads.

George Town is a port of registry for shipping, with a total of 1,400 vessels registered in 2000, and the port is an important calling centre for cargo carriers. Caymanian-owned ships, and ships with Caymanian registration, operate services with Florida and Jamaica.

The international airports are Owen Roberts Airport on Grand Cayman and Gerrard Smith Airport on Cayman Brac. Little Cayman has a private airstrip suitable for light aircraft.

The international dialling code is 1 345. There are 664 main telephone lines, 1,777 mobile phone subscriptions and 660 internet users per 1,000 people (2010).

Society

Population: 56,230 (2010); 100% lives in urban areas; population density 215 per sq km; the majority lives on Grand Cayman; life expectancy 81 years. The population increased by 52% between 1989 and 1999.

Cayman Islanders are partly of European, partly of African, mostly of mixed descent.

Language: English; there is a small Spanish-speaking community.

Religion: Mainly Christians, including followers of Church of God, and Roman Catholics, Presbyterians, Seventh Day Adventists, Baptists and Pentecostals.

Health: The government provides hospitals on Grand Cayman and Cayman Brac, and district clinics, an eye clinic and a dental clinic on Grand Cayman and a clinic on Little Cayman. A new hospital was opened in 1999 in George Town. A private hospital opened in 2000. Mosquitoes are controlled, to a great extent, by the Mosquito Research and Control Unit. Tropical diseases are uncommon. There is strong emphasis on anti-drug programmes, the islands being vulnerable because of their position on drug-smuggling routes. Infant mortality is about 7 per 1,000 live births (2009).

Education: There are 12 years of compulsory education starting at age five. There are some fee-paying church schools. Net enrolment ratios are 93% for primary and 79% for secondary (2007). The pupil–teacher ratio for primary is 11:1 (2007). The school year starts in September.

About 15% of school leavers go on to university. Tertiary education is provided in the Cayman Islands at the Community College (tertiary and adult), the Law School and the International College of the Cayman Islands. Adult literacy is more than 90%.

Media: *Caymanian Compass*, *Cayman Net News* and *Cayman News Service* (online) are published daily. Radio Cayman provides a public radio service.

Public holidays: New Year's Day, National Heroes' Day (Monday in late January), Discovery Day (third Monday in May), Queen's Official Birthday (Monday in June), Constitution Day (first Monday in July), Remembrance Day (11 November), Christmas Day and Boxing Day.

Religious festivals whose dates vary from year to year include Ash Wednesday, Good Friday and Easter Monday.

Economy

Currency: Cayman Islands dollar (CI$), fixed at CI$0.82:US$1

GDP: US$3.0bn (2009)

Tourist arrivals: 271,960 (2009)

In per capita terms, Cayman Islands is among the wealthiest economies in the world. The country has no direct taxation and a high percentage of home ownership. The economy is based on high-class tourism and offshore financial services, with a tiny proportion of the population engaged in agriculture and fishing.

In the absence of direct taxation, the sources of government revenue are import duty (on most goods), stamp duty on documents, and company and licence fees. The country provides a registry for international companies, banks and trust companies, insurance companies, investment funds, and ships and yachts. By May 2008 some 80,000 companies had been registered in Cayman Islands. A stock exchange was opened in 1997.

The economy grew slowly in the early 2000s, strengthening in 2005–07, due mainly to the increase in construction activity following Hurricane Ivan in September 2004, before stalling in 2008–10, when it was hit by a sharp contraction in both tourism and financial services, causing GDP to decline by 7% in 2009 and about 4% in 2010.

History

The islands were sighted by Christopher Columbus in 1503 on his last voyage to the West Indies. However, they appear on maps prior to that year, more or less correctly placed. The name 'Cayman', by which the group has been known since about 1530, is a Spanish corruption of the Carib word for 'crocodile'. The early history of European penetration is a record of environmental despoilation. The islands were once home to large numbers of crocodiles, which were exterminated in the sailors' search for fresh meat. The Spaniards first called the group *Las Tortugas* because the surrounding waters were full of turtles. These, too, were hunted to extermination by about 1800. From the early 16th century until the mid-17th century, English, Spanish and French ships called at the islands to hunt, but there was no settlement.

In 1670, the Treaty of Madrid recognised Britain's claim to the islands as part of the territory of Jamaica. Grand Cayman was subsequently colonised from Jamaica, the early population including many African slaves. Cayman Brac and Little Cayman were settled in the 1830s. Until the end of the days of sail, the islands were often called at by passing ships, and there was a thriving industry in building small schooners. When that prosperous period ended, they had little contact with the outside world; many people emigrated, settling in Nicaragua, the Bay Islands and Florida. From the 1940s, when air-travel was becoming common, they became accessible again.

In 1832 representative government was established with the formation of an elected legislative assembly, although the three islands had separate administrations until 1877. When Jamaica opted for independence in 1962, the Cayman Islands preferred to remain under the UK Crown, with their own administrator. In November 1971 the administrator's title was changed to that of governor.

In May 2002 the territory became an associate member of CARICOM.

Constitution

Under the November 2009 constitution, which provides for a greater degree of internal self-government than that of 1972, Cayman Islands is a UK overseas territory with representative government and the British monarch as head of state, represented by a governor. There are provisions for the rights and freedoms of the individual.

The legislative assembly has the speaker and 20 members (18 directly elected every four years plus the deputy governor and the attorney-general). The executive comprises the governor and the cabinet. The governor is responsible for external affairs, defence, internal security (including the police) and the overall organisation of the public service. The cabinet is responsible for all other matters. Together with the governor it includes the premier, deputy premier and at least five other ministers, who are all elected members of the legislative assembly; the deputy governor and attorney-general are *ex officio* members. The premier is eligible to serve for a maximum of two consecutive parliamentary terms.

Politics

Last elections: May 2009

Next elections: 2014

Head of state: Queen Elizabeth II, represented by the governor

Head of government: Premier McKeeva Bush

Ruling party: United Democratic Party

Until 2001, Cayman Islands had no political parties, and elections were fought by individuals in informal groupings. However, in November 2001 Minister of Tourism McKeeva Bush announced the formation of the United Democratic Party (UDP) and within a few days he became leader of government business, following an assembly vote of no confidence in Kurt Tibbetts (by nine votes to five).

The general election due in November 2004 was postponed until May 2005 after Hurricane Ivan devastated the islands in September 2004. The election was won by the People's Progressive Movement (PPM), with nine seats, and party leader Kurt Tibbetts then became leader of government business. The UDP took five seats and an independent one.

In the May 2009 elections, the UDP, led by McKeeva Bush, took nine seats, the PPM five, and independents one, and Bush was confirmed as leader of government business. Turnout was 73%.

Under the constitution that came into force in November 2009, Bush became the country's first premier.

Falkland Islands

Status: UK overseas territory

Geography

A group of islands consisting of East and West Falkland, and approximately 700 smaller islands, which lie about 480km north-east of the southern tip of South America.

Time: GMT minus 4hr. The clock is advanced by one hour from the first Sunday in September to the first Sunday in April.

Area: 12,173 sq km

Topography: The islands are deeply indented with many anchorages. The landscape is treeless moorland, with deep peat deposits, and hills ranging across the northern parts of both islands, rising to the highest points: Mt Usborne (705m) in East Falkland, and Mt Adam (700m) in West Falkland.

Climate: Temperate, cooled by the Antarctic current, lashed by gales in every month of the year, and with a moderate 625mm of rainfall per annum. There is little variation in temperature, which ranges 3–9°C.

Wildlife: There are no native mammals remaining. Around 65 species of bird breed on the islands, including the Falkland pipit and the striated caracara. Several million penguins breed there and sea mammals are abundant.

Main settlement: Stanley (pop. 2,230 in 2010), on East Falkland, is the only appreciable settlement.

Transport/Communications: There are some 50km of surfaced roads around Stanley and the airport, and 390km of unsurfaced gravel tracks. Most road travel outside Stanley is by Land Rover or motorcycle.

A commercial ship runs between the Falklands and the UK five times a year and the UK Ministry of Defence (MOD) operates a service about 11 times a year.

There are airports at Mt Pleasant and Stanley. Flights from the UK are provided by the MOD, refuelling at Ascension Island. There are scheduled weekly flights to and from mainland Chile. The government runs internal air services by light aircraft to some of the smaller islands.

The international dialling code is 500. There are 653 main telephone lines, 1,076 mobile phone subscriptions and 958 internet users per 1,000 people (2009).

Society

Population: 2,600 (2009); the majority population is of UK descent.

Language: English

Religion: Mainly Christians (67% in 2006 census); most of the rest did not profess any religion.

Health: Care is provided by the Falkland Islands Government. There are usually four doctors, two dentists and 20 qualified nurses present on the islands. The King Edward VII Memorial Hospital was completed in 1987. The hospital is run jointly by the Falkland Islands Government and the UK Ministry of Defence with some of the medical staff provided by the MOD.

Education: Education is free and compulsory from age five to 16 – seven years of primary and five years of secondary. There is one school in Stanley, comprising a junior school (for age five to 11 years) and a community school (11–16). Pupils unable to attend school in Stanley, where there is a hostel for up to 65 boarders, can be taught by peripatetic teachers and by radio/telephone.

Suitable students are funded to continue their studies at sixth-form level in the UK – for example, at Loughborough College or Peter Symonds College, or at other institutions at parental request. Some students go on to university.

Media: *Penguin News* is published weekly. The *Falkland Islands News Network* is published online (www.falklandnews.com) and incorporates Financial News and Information and Teaberry Express. Falkland Islands Radio Service provides public radio.

Public holidays: New Year's Day, Queen's Birthday (21 April), Liberation Day (14 June), Spring Holiday (Monday in October), Battle Day (8 December), Christmas Day and Boxing Day. Most government offices are closed for the Christmas period; the Stanley Races are held for two days after Boxing Day.

Religious and other festivals whose dates vary from year to year include Good Friday.

Economy

Currency: Falkland Islands pound, at par with pound sterling

In general terms, the Islands are self-supporting except for defence. The main economic activities are fishing (predominantly for squid and by licensed foreign trawlers) and sheep farming. Revenue is also generated by the sale of stamps and coins as collectors' items.

Tourism has grown rapidly and there are some 50,000 visitors a year, mainly from cruiseships in the austral summer months. Economic diversification is under way into industries such as meat production and agriculture.

Oil

In 2011 significant deposits of oil were found in the waters surrounding the Islands, with the prospect that Falklands could within a few years become a major oil production centre.

History

The first sighting of the Islands has been ascribed to various navigators, but the first known landing was by Captain John Strong in 1690, who named the Islands after the then Treasurer of the Navy, Viscount Falkland. The first occupation was by the French in 1764 under Antoine-Louis de Bougainville, who established a small colony on East Falkland. This was sold to Spain, who governed most of South America at that time, in 1767. In 1765, the British had taken possession of West Falkland and, in the next year, established a colony on Saunders Island to the north of West Falkland. The Spanish compelled the British settlers to leave in 1770, bringing the two nations to the brink of war, but were persuaded to hand back the colony in 1771. Both British and Spanish had left the Islands by the early 19th century.

In 1820, the Buenos Aires government, which had declared its independence of Spain in 1816, sent a ship to the Islands to claim sovereignty, and a colony was once more established on East Falkland under Luis Vernet as governor. In 1831, a US warship destroyed this settlement in reprisal for the arrest of three American sealing vessels. In 1832 the Argentinians again attempted to settle a garrison but were evicted when the HMS Clio arrived.

The British resumed occupation of the Islands, which has been continuous since. The Islands were given a governor in 1843. Grants-in-aid for the settlement were approved and continued until 1885, when the Islands became self-supporting.

Argentina did not abandon its claim to the Islands, and pursued this in UN talks from 1966 onwards, despite the islanders' overwhelming preference for retaining their association with the UK. During these years, links continued between the Falklands and Argentina, with air and sea communication, and facilities for education and medical care for the Falklanders. In April 1982, Argentine military forces invaded the Islands and overwhelmed the small UK garrison. A UK task force was dispatched and forced the Argentinians to surrender on 14 June 1982, after the loss of some 1,000 UK and Argentine lives.

After the election of the Menem government in Argentina in 1989, there was a rapprochement between the UK and Argentina. In 1990, diplomatic relations, broken off in 1982, were restored with Argentina, with both sides in effect agreeing to disagree on sovereignty over the Islands. In July 1999, the UK and Argentina agreed on some confidence-building measures between the

territory and Argentina, including co-operation in areas such as fisheries.

Constitution

Falkland Islands is a UK overseas territory by choice. Supreme authority is vested in the British monarch and exercised by a governor on the monarch's behalf, with the advice and assistance of the executive and legislative councils. The constitution includes the islanders' right to self-determination and provides for fundamental rights and freedoms of the individual.

The governor presides over an executive council of five, three elected and two *ex officio* members. The legislative council has eight elected members and the two *ex officio* members of the executive council.

After eight years of consultation and debate, a new constitution was adopted in November 2008, replacing that of October 1985 (with amendments in 1997 and 1998). It enhances democracy; provides for greater transparency and accountability; and clarifies the rights of individuals in line with the international agreements the UK is party to.

Gibraltar

Status: UK overseas territory

Geography

Gibraltar, at the mouth of the Mediterranean sea, is connected to Spain by a 1.6km-long sandy isthmus. To the west, across the Bay of Gibraltar, is the Spanish port of Algeciras; across the Strait of Gibraltar, 21km to the south, is Morocco.

Time: GMT plus 1hr. The clock is advanced by one hour from the last Sunday in March to the last Sunday in October.

Area: 6.5 sq km

Topography: Gibraltar is a narrow peninsula 4.8km long and 1.2km wide, aligned north/south, and rising to 426m on a limestone and shale ridge, known as 'the Rock' (hence Gibraltar's nickname). There is no natural fresh water, and drinking water is produced by desalination and stored in a reservoir on the Rock.

Climate: The climate is Mediterranean, with winter rainfall brought by westerly winds, and dry summers. Snow and frost are extremely rare. In summer the prevailing winds are easterly. Average annual rainfall (1997–2002) is 699mm.

Environment: The most significant environmental issue is the limited natural freshwater resources; rainwater is collected in large concrete or natural rock water catchments.

Vegetation: Gibraltar has more than 500 species of small flowering plants, including the unique candytuft. Olive and pine trees grow on the higher ground.

Wildlife: Various small mammals are found on the Rock, as well as the Barbary ape (the only wild monkey in Europe) and the only Barbary partridges in Europe.

Transport/Communications: There are 29km of roads, and a system of tunnels within the Rock; some 20,000 motor vehicles are registered.

Despite not being a natural haven, the harbour is extensive, and has been used for centuries as a refitting and revictualling centre for the navies of many nations. The port is able to take large ships and provides a base for transhipment, as well as being a UK naval base.

Gibraltar Airport is 1km north of the town centre on the North Front (the neck of the territory leading to Spain).

The international dialling code is 350. There are 821 main telephone lines, 1,026 mobile phone subscriptions and 650 internet users per 1,000 people (2010).

Society

Population: 29,440 (2010); 100% lives in urban areas; population density 4,529 per sq km; life expectancy 80 years.

Gibraltarians comprise 81% of the population (2001 census), other British nationals 12% and Moroccans 3%.

Language: English is the official language, and most people speak Spanish and English.

Religion: Predominantly Christians (Roman Catholics 78%, Anglicans 7%, others 3%), Muslims 4%, Jewish and Hindu minorities (2001 census).

Health: Infant mortality is about 6 per 1,000 live births (2009).

Social welfare: Benefit is provided for maternity, unemployment, illness, disability and death, and is funded through contributions.

Education: There are ten years of compulsory education starting at age five. The school year starts in September.

Media: *The Gibraltar Chronicle* (established 1801) and *Panorama* (online) are published daily; *The New People* and *Vox* weekly; and *The Gibraltar Magazine* and *Insight Magazine* monthly.

Radio Gibraltar and GBC Television provide public services operated by the Gibraltar Broadcasting Corporation.

Public holidays: New Year's Day, Commonwealth Day (second Monday in March), May Day (Monday in early May), Spring Bank Holiday (last Monday in May), Queen's Official Birthday (Monday in June), Summer Bank Holiday (Monday late in August), National Day (10 September), Christmas Day and Boxing Day.

Religious and other festivals whose dates vary from year to year include Good Friday and Easter Monday.

Economy

Currency: Gibraltar pound, at par with pound sterling

Gibraltar lacks natural resources and has to import fuels and foodstuffs. Hitherto dependent on a diminishing UK Ministry of Defence presence, financial services and tourism became increasingly important as Gibraltar sought to diversify its economy. There is considerable trade in re-export to Spain, including manufactured goods, fuels, beverages and tobacco and resale of fuel to shipping. From the 1990s structural reforms have brought about substantial growth in the private sector.

History

Gibraltar has a long and turbulent history owing to its unique position at a major crossroads of European commerce. It has been a stronghold of the Moors, but Spain held the Rock for 242 years of continuous occupation, during its period of greatest power and expansion in Europe and the Americas. However, when the Spanish King Charles II died in 1701, a disputed succession led to war, with Britain, Holland, Austria and the Holy Roman Empire joining forces to promote their candidate, the Archduke Charles of Austria. An English and Dutch fleet arrived in the Bay of Gibraltar in July 1704, and evicted the Spanish garrison on 4 August of that year. The Treaty of Utrecht (1713) ended the war and ceded Gibraltar to Britain.

Since then, British forces have withstood numerous sieges. The 'Great Siege' (1779–83), when the governor, General George Augustus Eliot, withstood a combined Spanish and French attack, was followed by the Treaty of Versailles, which confirmed Britain's title to Gibraltar. In 1805, after the Battle of Trafalgar, HMS *Victory* was towed into Gibraltar carrying the body of Admiral Nelson. It became of even more strategic importance to Britain with the opening of the Suez Canal in 1869, providing the main route to colonies in East Africa and Asia.

The Rock was of considerable significance in the two world wars of the 20th century as a centre for refitting ships, an air base and a key point in anti-submarine operations.

Successive Spanish governments have accepted the validity of the Treaty of Utrecht but argued that British sovereignty over the Rock is an anachronism. Spanish policy has been to recover sovereignty by peaceful means. During the 1960s, Franco's government imposed restrictions on communications between Spain and the Rock. But in a referendum in 1967, Gibraltarians voted 12,138 to 44 to stay British. A new constitution in 1969 emphasised Gibraltar's UK allegiance, while giving greater internal self-government. Spain responded by closing the border and severing telephone and transport links. Gibraltar joined the European Community in 1973 under the terms of the Act of Accession.

After the death of Franco in 1975 and the restoration of democracy in Spain, attitudes gradually softened and the border was reopened in 1985, in advance of Spain's entry into the European Community in January 1986.

Joe Bossano, leader of the Gibraltar Socialist Labour Party (GSLP) was chief minister from 1988 until the elections of May 1996. As chief minister he campaigned for Gibraltarian self-determination and opposed the Brussels Process (agreement between the British and Spanish Governments to start negotiations aimed at overcoming all the differences between them on Gibraltar). Bossano did not participate in meetings under the process, but did develop closer relations with the authorities of the Spanish Campo region adjacent to Gibraltar.

The 1996 elections were won by the Gibraltar Social Democrats (GSD), whose leader, Peter Caruana, became chief minister. The February 2000 elections were again won by the GSD, with eight of 15 elective seats in the parliament, and Caruana continued as chief minister. The GSD government favoured dialogue with Spain but was also committed to defending the Gibraltarians' right of self-determination and vigorously opposed any concessions on sovereignty without Gibraltar's consent.

The Brussels Process was restarted in the summer of 2001 with the aim of achieving a lasting resolution to the Gibraltar dispute. By July 2002, after several months of negotiations, the UK and Spain had reached broad agreement on many of the principles that could underpin a lasting settlement, but a number of issues remained unresolved. On 7 November 2002, the Gibraltar Government held a referendum to ask the people of Gibraltar whether they accepted the principle of joint sovereignty with Spain and 98.5% voted 'no'.

Constitution

The current constitution was promulgated in 2006 with the intention to provide for a modern relationship between Gibraltar and the UK – not one based on colonialism. It builds on the 1969 Gibraltar Constitution which formalised the devolution to local ministers of responsibility for a range of defined domestic matters.

The governor represents the British monarch who is head of state and retains direct responsibility for all matters not specifically allocated to local ministers: principally external affairs, defence and internal security.

The parliament comprises a speaker, at least 17 elected members and (since the 2007 elections) four *ex officio* members (the principal auditor, the ombudsman, the clerk to the parliament and any other officer prescribed by law). Elections to the parliament take place every four years. All British subjects over the age of 18 who fulfil residence requirements are entitled to vote. The territory comprises a single constituency and there is a block voting system under which each elector may vote for up to ten candidates.

The constitution provides for a police authority and commissions charged with appointing judicial and other public officials.

Politics

Last elections: December 2011

Next elections: 2015

Head of state: Queen Elizabeth II, represented by governor

Head of government: Chief Minister Fabian Picardo

Ruling party: coalition of Gibraltar Socialist Labour Party and Liberal Party

Peter Caruana and the Gibraltar Social Democrats (GSD) were returned with eight seats and 52% of votes in elections in November 2003, and the alliance led by Joe Bossano received 40% – the Gibraltar Socialist Labour Party (GSLP) five seats and the Liberal Party two seats.

In the elections of October 2007, the GSD won with a reduced vote (49%) but an increased majority (taking ten seats), and Caruana was returned as chief minister. The GSLP–Liberal alliance received 45% of votes and took seven seats.

The December 2011 elections were won by the alliance of the GSLP (seven seats) and Liberal Party (three seats); the remaining seven seats were taken by the GSD. GSLP leader Fabian Picardo became chief minister.

Montserrat

Status: UK overseas territory

Geography

Montserrat is one of the Leeward Islands in the Eastern Caribbean, lying 43km south-west of Antigua and 64km north-west of Guadeloupe.

Time: GMT minus 4hr

Area: 102 sq km

Topography: Entirely volcanic and very mountainous, with a rugged coastline. There are three mountain ranges: Silver Hills in the north; Centre Hills and the Soufrière Hills Volcano in the south. There are hot springs, ravines, black-sand beaches, and a white-sand beach at Rendezvous Bay in the north. The two waterfalls were destroyed by the volcano.

Climate: Tropical, usually tempered by sea breezes. Rainfall averages 1,475mm p.a.; most rain falls in the second half of the year. June to November is the hurricane season.

Environment: Environmental issues are mainly related to the presence of the active volcano on the island, but another significant issue is land erosion on slopes that have been cleared for cultivation.

Vegetation: Tropical; prior to the resumption of volcanic activity, mountain areas close to the volcano were thickly forested, with fruit and vegetables grown in the cultivated areas. But successive eruptions and pyroclastic flows reduced these areas to a scarred lunar-type landscape and it will be many years before they can be cultivated again. Forest covers 20% of the land area.

Main settlements: Plymouth, once a thriving capital, is now a ghost town, buried beneath more than 1 metre of volcanic ash; Brades (*de facto* capital, pop. 1,310 in 2010), St Peter's (790), St John's and Salem.

Transport/Communications: Many roads were damaged, destroyed or made inaccessible by volcanic activity. A new roads infrastructure has been built in the north of the island.

Plymouth, the only seaport with a harbour capable of handling cargo vessels, closed in June 1997. A new port facility has been constructed at Little Bay in the north and there is a ferry service to Antigua.

The nearest international airport is in Antigua, from where planes flew to W H Bramble Airport on the east side of the island. The airport was closed in June 1997 and helicopter services operate from Gerald's Heliport to Antigua (20 minutes' flying time). A new airport was opened in 2005.

The international dialling code is 1 664. There are 438 main telephone lines, 708 mobile phone subscriptions and 350 internet users per 1,000 people (2010).

Society

Population: 5,020 (2010); 14% lives in urban areas; population density 49 per sq km; population was 10,639 at the 1991 census; life expectancy 75 years.

Most of the people are of African descent, with some of European (mainly Irish) and some of mixed descent and, prior to the renewed volcanic activity, a number of retired North Americans.

Language: English is the official language.

Religion: Mainly Christians (Anglicans, Roman Catholics, Methodists, Pentecostals, Seventh Day Adventists).

Health: The Glendon Hospital has been relocated to the north of the island. Though very unpleasant, there is no evidence to suggest that ash falls have created any serious health problems other than those stemming from respiratory problems.

Education: There are ten years of compulsory education starting at age five. Net enrolment ratios are 92% for primary and 96% for secondary (2007). The pupil–teacher ratio for primary is 16:1 and for secondary 12:1 (2007). The school year starts in September.

Tertiary education is provided at the regional University of the West Indies, which has campuses in Barbados, Jamaica, and Trinidad and Tobago. Adult literacy is more than 90%.

Media: *The Montserrat Reporter* is published weekly. Radio Montserrat provides a public radio service.

Public holidays: New Year's Day, St Patrick's Day (17 March), Labour Day (first Monday in May), Queen's Official Birthday (Monday in June), August Monday (first Monday in August), Christmas Day, Boxing Day and Festival Day (31 December). St Patrick's Day is followed by a week of celebrations, and there are celebrations throughout 15 December–1 January.

Religious and other festivals whose dates vary from year to year include Good Friday, Easter Monday and Whit Monday.

Economy

Currency: Eastern Caribbean dollar

GDP: US$47m (2010)

Tourist arrivals: 6,310 (2009)

In the 1980s, the main economic activities were agriculture and tourism (especially luxury villa holidays) with some light engineering. Hurricane Hugo destroyed 90% of infrastructure in September 1989, severely damaging the tourism and agriculture sectors.

Since then the main economic activity has been reconstruction, which suffered a major setback when volcanic activity began in 1995. GDP fell from EC$163 million in 1995 to EC$91 million in 2000. Montserrat's economy and infrastructure have been rebuilt in the 2000s, including a new airport (opened in 2005) and ferry port.

Aid

The damage to the economy, first by Hurricane Hugo and then by the volcanic activity, has made Montserrat heavily dependent on aid. Main aid partners are the UK and Canada.

History

Montserrat was sighted by Christopher Columbus during his second voyage in November 1493. He named it Santa Maria de Montserrate after the Abbey of Montserrate near Barcelona. In 1632, the island became a British colony although the first settlers were largely Irish. More Irish settlers followed, driven out of Virginia in an anti-Catholic purge.

Enslaved Africans were brought to the island to work tobacco, indigo, cotton and sugar plantations. In 1678 the population consisted of 992 slaves and 2,682 mainly Irish-descended planters. By 1805 there were 9,500 slaves and about 1,000 settlers of European descent. Montserrat was captured by the French on three occasions for short periods but was finally restored to Britain in 1783.

The abolition of slavery in 1834 and falling sugar prices during the 19th century had an adverse effect on the island's economy. Moreover, the island has suffered frequent damage from hurricanes and earthquakes.

In 1869, the philanthropist Joseph Sturge of Birmingham formed the Montserrat Company. This company bought up the estates that were not economically viable, planted limes, started production of the island's famous lime juice, set up a school and sold smallholdings to the inhabitants, with the result that much of modern Montserrat is owned by smallholders.

From 1671 Montserrat and the other Leeward Islands were administered by a captain-general and commander-in-chief. In 1871 the Leeward Islands became a federal colony with a governor. The federation was abolished in July 1956, and Montserrat became a colony in its own right. In 1958 it joined the Federation of the West Indies; in 1962, when the Federation broke up, it gained separate administration; and in 1971 the administrator was promoted to governor.

From the time the People's Liberation Movement (PLM) took power from the Progressive Democratic Party in 1978, independence became a dominant issue of Montserrat politics. The PLM, under the leadership of John Osborne, retained its majority through the elections of 1983 and 1987.

However, the plans to push ahead to independence were frustrated by a series of misfortunes. In 1989, Hurricane Hugo devastated the island and made Montserrat dependent on aid for reconstruction. In 1990, there were irregularities in the offshore banking sector, which led to an investigation by police officers from the UK's Scotland Yard, followed by prosecutions and deregistration of many foreign banks. The government then thoroughly overhauled the sector and imposed more stringent controls.

In the 1991 elections the newly formed National Progressive Party, led by Reuben Meade, gained the majority. The Soufrière Hills Volcano reactivated in July 1995 after a lengthy period of dormancy. With the volcano increasing in vigour, the capital Plymouth and most of the population from the south of the island were evacuated to the safety of the north in April 1996. In due course an exclusion zone comprising roughly the southern two-thirds of the island was established.

The general election of November 1996 led to no overall majority for any party. The Movement for National Reconstruction (MNR) led by Bertrand Osborne formed a coalition government supported by former Chief Minister Meade and an independent. In August 1997 Bertrand Osborne resigned when three of his ministers withdrew their support. David Brandt, a lawyer and independent, formed a government.

The volcano erupted again with greater vigour on 25 June 1997. Pyroclastic flows swept down the north face of the volcano resulting in the deaths of 19 people. The deaths occurred in areas which had been declared out of bounds due to the threat of volcanic activity. The main part of the deserted capital, Plymouth, was destroyed in August 1997. There were, both in early August and late September, series of vigorous explosions, and then the largest pyroclastic flow to date occurred on Boxing Day 1997, destroying villages within the exclusion zone.

In April 1996 Montserratians resident on the island on 1 April 1996 had been offered resettlement in the UK provided they were able to travel at their own expense and 1,500 people took up this offer. By August 1997, with the situation worsening, the UK Government offered to pay airfares for those who wished to resettle in the UK or other parts of the Caribbean. By 1998 some 3,500 Montserratians had evacuated to the UK, 3,000 to neighbouring countries and 3,500 remained on the island.

In July 1998 scientists judged that the volcano had entered a period of repose, though in areas surrounding the volcano danger would remain for some years, but in November 1999 it became active again and there were further eruptions in March and June 2000 and July 2001. The largest eruption since 1997 occurred in July 2003. There were no human casualties, but agriculture was devastated and the entire island was covered in ash.

Constitution

In 1989, the constitution, formerly comprising various bills and acts, was consolidated into one document and came into force on 13 February 1990.

The constitution that came into force on 27 September 2011 introduced a greater degree of self government; stronger human rights provisions; and stronger measures to promote good governance.

Montserrat is an internally self-governing UK overseas territory. Government is executed through the governor appointed by the British monarch, the cabinet and the Legislative Assembly.

The governor appoints as premier the Legislative Assembly member who has the support of a majority of the elected members. The cabinet is presided over by the governor and includes the premier and three other ministers, appointed by the governor in accordance with the advice of the premier; and, *ex officio*, the financial secretary and attorney-general.

The Legislative Assembly has nine directly elected members and two *ex officio* members, the financial secretary and attorney-general. Elections are held at least every five years.

Politics

Last elections: September 2009

Next elections: 2014

Head of state: Queen Elizabeth II, represented by the governor

Head of government: Premier Reuben Meade

Ruling party: Movement for Change and Prosperity

In April 2001, the New People's Liberation Movement (NPLM) under the leadership of John Osborne won an early general election with seven seats; the remaining two seats were taken by the National Progressive Party led by Reuben Meade.

In the May 2006 general election the Movement for Change and Prosperity (MCP) took four seats, the governing NPLM three, Montserrat Democratic Party (MDP) one and independents one. Dr Lowell Lewis of the MDP received the support of the majority of the new legislative council and became chief minister.

The general election of September 2009 was won by the MCP, which took six seats; independents gained the other three, leaving the MDP without representation in parliament. MCP leader Reuben Meade was sworn in as chief minister. After the new constitution came into force, in October 2011 he was sworn in as premier.

John Osborne, who served as chief minister for 18 years (1978–91 and 2001–06), died on 2 January 2011.

Pitcairn Islands

Status: UK overseas territory

Geography

Pitcairn Island lies in the central South Pacific, approximately half-way between Panama and New Zealand. Henderson lies at 169km, Oeno at 121km and Ducie at 471km distance from Pitcairn.

Pitcairn is in the Western Hemisphere and on the American side of the International Date Line; so it and Cook Islands are almost one day behind their other Commonwealth Pacific neighbours.

Time: GMT minus 8hr

Area: 35.5 sq km; Pitcairn: 4.35 sq km; Henderson: 30.0 sq km.

Topography: Pitcairn, the only inhabited island in this territory, is a volcanic crater rising to 300m. It has precipitous coastal cliffs, with only one, moderately accessible, landing-place, Bounty Bay, near the main settlement of Adamstown. The soil on the islands is fertile.

Climate: Pitcairn has a subtropical climate, with mean monthly temperatures ranging from 19–24°C and an average annual rainfall of 2,000mm.

Wildlife: In 1989 Henderson Island was included on the UNESCO World Heritage List as a bird sanctuary. Four species of birds are unique to the island: Henderson fruit dove, Henderson rail, Henderson warbler and Henderson lorikeet.

Transport/Communications: The islanders use quad bikes as their main form of transport. There are also tractors and a bulldozer on Pitcairn, and two aluminium longboats. A supply ship makes scheduled calls approximately twice a year. Container ships, yachts and other vessels call on an ad hoc basis if they are passing; in 2000 there were 54 visits; in 2001, 58 visits; and in 2002, 56 visits. There is a basic telephone system on Pitcairn. Overseas telephone and fax communications are maintained via satellite only.

Society

Population: 50 (2010). Overpopulation on Pitcairn has been a problem in the past, leading to evacuations in 1831 and 1856, but the Pitcairners have always returned. The population reached a peak of 233 in 1937, and declined for many years, reaching 55 in 1993 and 40 in January 1998. It had risen to 66 by 1999 but declined again in the early 2000s.

Language: The official languages are English and (since 1997) Pitkern, a mixture of English and Tahitian, with English predominating.

Religion: The islanders have been Seventh Day Adventists since 1887 and do not therefore celebrate Easter.

Health: Medical care is provided by a trained nurse.

Education: Primary education is available on the island and secondary-level students participate in correspondence courses. There is one all-age school and education is compulsory from age five to 15 years. Scholarships are available for secondary and higher education in New Zealand.

Media: There is a monthly news sheet, *The Pitcairn Miscellany*, with worldwide circulation of about 1,400, and edited by the resident school teacher.

Public holidays: New Year's Day, Bounty Day (28 April), Queen's Official Birthday (one of the first three Saturdays in June, in line with the UK), Christmas Day and Boxing Day.

Religious and other festivals whose dates vary from year to year include Good Friday and Easter Monday.

Economy

Currency: New Zealand dollar

The annual budget for Pitcairn is around NZ$1 million. Despite prudent financial management, Pitcairn's annual expenditure consistently exceeds revenue. The main government revenue derives from the sale of postage stamps and of internet domain addresses. The islanders fish, and produce vegetables and fruit (including sweet potatoes, sugar cane, taro, oranges, bananas and coffee), for their own consumption, and for sale to the occasional passing ships. In the latter 1990s they developed beekeeping and honey production.

There is also a mail-order trade in carving and basketware; and island produce and curios are sold to passing cruiseships. Miro trees, which grow on the Henderson atoll, provide wood for handicrafts. A range of minerals, including manganese, iron, copper, gold, silver and zinc, has been discovered within the exclusive economic zone, which extends 370km offshore and comprises 880,000 sq km.

History

Although there are archaeological remains indicating habitation by Polynesian people 600 years ago, Pitcairn's modern population arises from its occupation in 1790 by Fletcher Christian and eight of the mutineers from HMS *Bounty*, 12 Tahitian women and six men. It became a British settlement in 1887, being placed under the jurisdiction of the British high commissioner for the Western Pacific in 1898, and the Governor of Fiji in 1952. The UK high commissioner in New Zealand has been the governor since 1970.

Administration

The island council has ten members – four councillors and the chairman of the internal committee are elected annually between 1 and 15 December, one is nominated by the council and two, including the island secretary, are appointed by the governor. It is presided over by the island mayor (elected every three years in December). A commissioner manages the day-to-day operations of the island and liaises with the Governor's Office in Wellington (New Zealand), the island council and the governor's representative on Pitcairn. A judicial system comprising a magistrate's court, supreme court and appeal court has been established. There is no taxation, nor any banking facilities.

St Helena and St Helena Dependencies

St Helena lies in the South Atlantic Ocean, with Ascension 1,131km to the north-west, and Tristan da Cunha 2,100km to the south.

St Helena

Status: UK overseas territory

Geography

St Helena lies 1,931km from the coast of Angola, Africa.

Time: GMT

Area: 122 sq km

Topography: St Helena is volcanic and mountainous, with perpendicular cliffs of 490 to 700m on the eastern, northern and western sides of the island, and mountains to 820m to the south. The only inland waters are small streams, few of them perennial, fed by springs in the central hills.

Climate: The climate is subtropical and mild, with annual rainfall varying from 200mm at sea level to 760mm in the centre, with continuous trade winds.

Vegetation: Indigenous vegetation includes cabbage trees, cedars, bamboo and banana plants. There are approximately 45 plants unique to St Helena. Arable land and pastures comprise some 15% of the land area and woods and forests some 7%.

Main settlements: Half Tree Hollow, Longwood, St Paul's and Jamestown.

Transport/Communications: There are 118km of paved roads and about 20km of earth roads, with 2,066 licensed vehicles at the end of 2000.

The only port is Jamestown. The RMS *St Helena* provides a passenger and freight service between St Helena and the UK, and more frequent services between St Helena, Ascension and Cape Town.

The international dialling code is 290. There are 525 main telephone lines and 191 internet users per 1,000 people (2009).

Society

Population: 4,000 (2009); population density 33 per sq km; life expectancy 79 years. The inhabitants are of diverse origins, and principally African, European and Chinese.

Language: English is the official language.

Religion: Mainly Christians (Anglicans at least 80%); St Helena forms a diocese of the Church of the Province of Southern Africa.

Health: Jamestown has a small hospital with several medical officers and a dentist.

Education: Education is free and compulsory for ten years from age five to 15. There are four years of primary and four years of secondary education; four first schools, three middle schools and one upper school. The school year starts in September.

Media: *St Helena Herald* and *The St Helena Independent* are weekly newspapers; and Radio St Helena is a radio station.

Economy

Currency: St Helena pound, at par with pound sterling

Fishing and agriculture are the main economic activities. Poultry, pigs, sheep, goats and cattle are produced for domestic consumption. A tourist office was established in 1998 with a view to developing tourism aimed at visitors sailing on the RMS St Helena.

Aid

Imports generally greatly exceed exports and the islanders rely on UK aid to make up the balance.

History

St Helena was discovered by the Portuguese navigator Joao da Nova in 1502 and named by him after the saint of that day. The

Dutch later annexed it, but it was finally taken over by the British East India Company in 1661, the charter being issued by King Charles II in 1673. It was brought under Crown government in April 1834. Napoleon was exiled on St Helena (in Longwood House, now a museum) from 1815 until his death in 1821. Jamestown was a busy port until 1870, when steam ships and the opening of the Suez Canal changed sea routes. It was of strategic importance during the Second World War.

Constitution

The present constitution came into force in 1989. It provides for a governor (of St Helena, Ascension and Tristan da Cunha), representing the British monarch who is head of state, and a legislative council (for St Helena), consisting of a speaker, three *ex officio* members and 12 elected members.

Administration

Five committees of the legislative council are responsible for general oversight of the activities of the five biggest spending government departments, and have in addition a range of statutory and administrative functions. The governor is also assisted by an executive council of the three *ex officio* members and the five chairpersons of the council committees. A process of constitutional modernisation began in 2003, with the aim of introducing a larger degree of self-government.

Ascension Island

Status: UK overseas territory

Geography

Time: GMT

Area: 88 sq km

Topography: Ascension Island is the peak of a 3,500m volcanic mountain range mostly submerged and rising 875m above sea level. There are on the island 44 dormant, but not extinct, volcanoes. There are no surface streams.

Climate: Tropical with strongly moderating and stabilising oceanic influence. Mean temperatures show very little seasonal variation (27–31°C) and rainfall is light (165mm at sea level and much higher on Green Mountain).

Vegetation: Though previously barren, with increasing precipitation, the island is becoming greener, with lush tropical vegetation on Green Mountain, where there is a farm, and increasingly in other parts of the island. An invasive thorn tree of Mexican origin has spread over half the island, transforming the bare volcanic scenery. Biological and mechanical measures have been adopted to limit further spread.

Wildlife: The island's 32 crescent-shaped beaches provide a critical breeding area for the endangered green turtles which visit each year from December to May. It is the most important seabird breeding site in the tropical Atlantic. Many thousands of sooty terns breed on the island while others including the endemic Ascension frigatebird, the red and yellow-billed tropic birds and the rare red-footed booby breed on Boatswain Bird Island and offshore rocks. The waters surrounding the island are rich in marine life, including tuna, sharks, marlin and sailfish.

Main settlement: Georgetown

Transport/Communications: There are 40km of roads. The RMS *St Helena* provides a regular service between the UK, Ascension, St Helena and Cape Town. A UK Ministry of Defence charter cargo ship calls monthly and a US supply ship calls six times a year. There are regular flights of the UK and US air forces. From October 2003, non-scheduled civilian charter flights were permitted to use the military Wideawake Airfield.

The international dialling code is 247.

Society

Population: 950 (2009); 1,123 (1998 census), 719 St Helenians, 192 Americans and the rest from the UK; population density 11 per sq km. There are no permanent residents; the population comprises employees and their families on contract to one of the organisations operating on the island or to the local government. Ascension is part of the Anglican diocese of St Helena and the Roman Catholic Apostolate of the South Atlantic and Antarctica.

Education: free and compulsory from age five to 16 years. There is one primary and one secondary school.

Media: *The Islander* is the weekly newspaper. The administrator's website, providing information on the territory, is at www.ascension-island.gov.ac.

Economy

Sales of postage stamps and raising of transit charges only provide limited revenue. A fiscal regime was introduced in April 2002, providing additional revenue through a combination of income tax, customs duties and a property tax.

The British Broadcasting Corporation established its Atlantic Relay Station in 1966 (for broadcasts to South America and West Africa). Since April 2001, the Ascension Island Government has provided and funded public services such as education, health care and infrastructure management. It also runs the savings bank, the post office and police force.

Ascension experienced rapid development in 1982 during the Falklands conflict between the UK and Argentina, and has continued to be utilised as a supply link to the South Atlantic. Agreement on use of Wideawake Airfield by civilian charter flights opened up opportunities for new economic activities.

History

Ascension was discovered by the Portuguese in 1501 and named on a subsequent visit on Ascension Day 1503. When Napoleon was exiled on St Helena in 1815, such was the respect he engendered that the British also placed garrisons on Ascension and Tristan da Cunha. After Napoleon died in 1821, the island was used as a base for ships engaged in the suppression of the slave trade on the West African coast and remained under the supervision of the British Admiralty until it was made a dependency of St Helena in 1922 and was then managed by the Eastern Telegraph Company (renamed Cable & Wireless in 1934), until the appointment of an administrator in 1964. The US first established a war-time air base there in 1942, which it then reoccupied in 1957 and later, for a period, used in connection with the tracking of the Apollo Space programme. In 1982 it was an important staging post for the UK in the Falklands conflict.

Administration

The Governor of St Helena is concurrently Governor of Ascension. There is a resident administrator, who administers the island on behalf of the governor and is also the chief magistrate (and is assisted by six justices of the peace), the coroner, registrar of births, marriages and deaths, immigration officer, harbour master and receiver of wrecks. Elections were held in November 2002 for the island's first advisory island council.

Tristan da Cunha

Status: UK overseas territory

Geography

Tristan da Cunha lies 2,400km west of Cape Town. The island group also includes Inaccessible Island, the three Nightingale Islands (all uninhabited) and Gough Island, which has a weather station.

Time: GMT

Area: 98 sq km

Topography: Tristan da Cunha is a small, almost circular, volcanic island, rising to 2,060m.

Climate: The climate is warm-temperate, with 1,675mm average annual rainfall in Edinburgh.

Wildlife: The group of islands provides breeding grounds for albatrosses, rock-hopper penguins and seals, and a number of unique species, including the flightless land rail. Gough Island is a world heritage site.

Main settlement: Edinburgh of the Seven Seas is the only permanent settlement.

Transport/Communications: Crawfish trawlers from Cape Town call about six times a year, and supplies are brought once a year both by RMS *St Helena* (from the UK) and *Agulhas* (from Cape Town). Several cruiseships also call each year. There is no airfield.

The international dialling code is 247. As of 2007, virtually all island homes had working telephones. There are permanent internet services.

Society

Population: 250 (2009), mainly of UK origin.

Religion: An Anglican chaplain is provided from South Africa and a Roman Catholic priest from the UK.

Health: The UK provides an optician and dentist (calling once each year), and a resident doctor.

Education: free and compulsory from age five to 15 years, provided at one all-age school.

Media: *The Tristan Times* is published weekly.

Economy

Tristan da Cunha supports itself through a substantial fishing industry based around the Tristan rock lobster, including a fish-freezing plant. Some income is also earned from the sale of stamps to philatelists, and handicrafts. Apart from capital projects, it has been financially independent from the UK since 1980.

History

The islands were discovered in 1506 by a Portuguese admiral, Tristão de Cunha. The first occupation of the island was the British garrison placed there in 1816, some of whom elected to stay on

after its withdrawal; by 1886 it had a population of 97. Missionaries provided services as priests, teachers, honorary commissioners and magistrates in the first half of the 20th century, but otherwise the islanders were virtually isolated until a meteorological and wireless station was built there during the Second World War. In 1948, a crawfish industry began, providing employment.

In 1961, a volcano erupted near the settlement of Edinburgh and the entire island had to be evacuated; a few have since settled in the UK but most islanders chose to return in 1963.

Administration

The Governor of St Helena is concurrently Governor of Tristan da Cunha. Locally, there is an administrator (also the magistrate), and an island council with three *ex officio* and eight elected members, one of whom must be a woman.

South Georgia and the South Sandwich Islands

Status: UK overseas territory

Geography

The island of South Georgia lies approximately 1,390km east-south-east of the Falkland Islands. It is some 170km long and varies in width from 2km to 40km.

The South Sandwich Islands are a further 640km to the south-east of South Georgia. The islands are volcanic, ice-bound in winter and difficult of approach. They are uninhabited and, like South Georgia, rich in wildlife.

Topography: South Georgia is extremely mountainous, and over half the island is permanently covered by snow or ice. The north-east, leeward side of the island offers a number of safe anchorages.

Vegetation and wildlife: The Territory is of great importance for sub-Antarctic flora and fauna. South Georgia is the breeding ground for some 95% of the world's Antarctic fur seal population as well as globally significant populations of elephant seals, albatrosses, petrels and penguins. Reindeer were introduced in about 1911 by Norwegian whaling companies. Only the coastal fringes of South Georgia support vegetation, mainly in the form of tussock grass. The Government of South Georgia and the South Sandwich Islands recognises the islands' significance for global conservation and is committed to providing a sustainable policy framework, which conserves, manages and protects the islands' rich natural environment while at the same time allowing for human activities and for the generation of revenue which allows this to be achieved. This framework was set out in the 2000 *South Georgia Environmental Management Plan*. The South Sandwich Islands represent a maritime ecosystem scarcely modified by human activities.

Society

Population: There is no permanent human population on South Georgia. However, there is a team of scientists from the British Antarctic Survey (BAS) based at the research station at the administrative centre of King Edward Point, replacing the small military detachment which had been there since British forces recaptured the island in 1982. This research station (built in 2001) provides valuable scientific advice to the South Georgia

Government on the sustainable management of the commercial fishery around South Georgia which represents the main source of income for the government. BAS also maintains an all-year research station on Bird Island off the north-west point of South Georgia. Other officials based at King Edward Point include a marine officer/harbour master and the curators of the South Georgia Museum.

Economy

Some 90% of government revenue is derived from the sale of fishing licences, with sales of stamps and commemorative coins, customs and harbour dues, and landing and transhipment fees contributing the rest.

History

In 1775 Captain James Cook made the first landing on South Georgia and claimed it in the name of King George III. In 1904, the first whaling station was established at Grytviken, and in 1909 Britain appointed a resident magistrate. The whaling industry collapsed in the mid-1960s and the whaling stations were abandoned. In 1982, the island was briefly occupied by Argentine forces. Until 1985, both South Georgia and the South Sandwich Islands were dependencies of the Falkland Islands, but from that date were constituted as a separate colony of the UK.

Concern over unregulated fishing led in 1993 to the establishment of a maritime zone of 370km around the islands and to the introduction in August 1993 of a regime for the conservation and management of the fisheries in the zone.

Administration

The Governor of the Falkland Islands is concurrently Commissioner for South Georgia and the South Sandwich Islands, and is responsible for the conduct of government business, including legislation. The commissioner is assisted by the first secretary at Government House in Stanley, who is concurrently assistant commissioner and director of fisheries, and by an operations manager. The attorney-general and financial secretary from the Falkland Islands fulfil parallel roles in South Georgia and the South Sandwich Islands.

South Georgia has a rich heritage stemming from its past prominence as a staging post for Antarctic discovery and a centre for sealing and whaling. Consequently it is attracting an increasing number of tourists and other visitors interested in research. The government welcomes such visits to the territory but all visitors, irrespective of their nationality and mode of transport, must apply in advance to the commissioner for permission to do so.

Turks and Caicos Islands

Status: UK overseas territory

Geography

Turks and Caicos Islands form the southern tip of the Bahamas chain in the north of the Caribbean region. Their nearest neighbour to the south is the Dominican Republic. They comprise two groups of about 40 islands. The Turks Islands take their name from the red flowers of a type of indigenous cactus which, to 17th-century Spanish sailors, resembled the headgear of Turkish men. Two of the eight Turks Islands are inhabited: Grand Turk and Salt Cay. Principal islands of the Caicos group (Spanish *cayos*: cays) are:

South Caicos, East Caicos, Middle (or Grand) Caicos, North Caicos, Providenciales and West Caicos.

Time: GMT minus 5hr. The clock is advanced by one hour from the first Sunday in April to the last Sunday in October.

Area: 500 sq km

Topography: The islands are all flat sandy cays, nowhere higher than 75m. The Turks Islands passage, a deep channel 35km across, separates the two island groups.

Climate: Constant south-east trade winds freshen the air in the otherwise tropical climate. Rainfall is variable: about 525mm on Grand Turk and generally higher in the Caicos Islands. Hurricanes are a danger.

Vegetation: Forest covers 80% of the land area.

Main settlements: Cockburn Town (capital) on Grand Turk; and Cockburn Harbour, straddling South and East Caicos. The most populous islands are Providenciales, Grand Turk, North Caicos, South Caicos and East Caicos.

Transport/Communications: There are surfaced and unsurfaced roads on all inhabited islands.

The main seaports are Grand Turk, Salt Cay, Providenciales and Cockburn Harbour. Regular cargo and postal services operate to/from Miami.

The country has three international airports, on Grand Turk, Providenciales and South Caicos. There are landing strips on Salt Cay, Pine Cay, Parrot Cay, Middle Caicos and North Caicos.

The international dialling code is 1 649. There are 113 main telephone lines per 1,000 people (2009).

Society

Population: 40,000 (2010); 92% lives in urban areas; population density 80 per sq km; population was 12,350 at the 1990 census. The population has grown rapidly due to immigration from other Caribbean countries, especially Haiti, including a substantial number of illegal immigrants, making it difficult to estimate the population; life expectancy 76 years.

Some 60% of the population are Turks and Caicos Islands nationals, around 20% from Haiti, 7% from The Bahamas and 4% from the USA. Most of the people are of African descent.

Language: The official and national language is English; Haitian immigrants speak a French-based Creole.

Religion: Mainly Christians (Baptists 40% in 1990, Anglicans 18%, Methodists 16%, Church of God 12%).

Health: The general hospital is on Grand Turk; it has a maternity ward and a geriatric block, an operating theatre and a laboratory with X-ray facilities. There are clinics, staffed by nurses and visited fortnightly by medical officers, on Salt Cay, South Caicos, Middle Caicos and North Caicos; there is a full-time medical officer on Providenciales and a health complex offering 24-hour secondary health care. Dental services are provided at a dental clinic and visits by dental professionals to the clinics. Further medical back-up is available in The Bahamas, Jamaica and the USA. Infant mortality is about 13 per 1,000 live births (2009).

Education: There are 13 years of compulsory education starting at age four. Net enrolment ratios are 78% for primary and 70% for secondary (2005). The pupil–teacher ratio for primary is 15:1 and for secondary 9:1 (2005). The school year starts in September.

At tertiary level, the Community College on Grand Turk offers vocational and professional education, and the new Windsor University at Cockburn Town on Grand Turk provides medical training. There are three public libraries.

Media: The newspapers are *Turks and Caicos Free Press* (weekly), *Turks and Caicos Sun* and *Turks and Caicos Weekly News*. Radio Turks and Caicos on Grand Turk provides a public service to all islands.

Public holidays: New Year's Day, Commonwealth Day (second Monday in March), National Heroes' Day (last Monday in May), Queen's Official Birthday (Monday in June), Emancipation Day (first Monday in August), National Youth Day (last Friday in September), Columbus Day (Monday in October), International Human Rights Day (24 October), Christmas Day and Boxing Day.

Religious and other festivals whose dates vary from year to year include Good Friday and Easter Monday.

Economy

Currency: US dollar

GDP: US$830m (2009)

Tourist arrivals: 231,900 (2009)

Tourism and financial services have become the main economic activities in Turks and Caicos Islands. Reflecting the openness of the economy, its close links with the USA and use of the US dollar as domestic currency, domestic prices tend to follow US prices. The main export is seafood products, including lobster and conch.

The economy was sluggish in 2001–02, owing to the slowdown in the US, but expanded strongly in 2003–07. Then in 2008, when the global financial crisis and world economic downturn hit both tourism and financial services, GDP growth stalled, plunging to 2.2% in 2008, and going sharply into reverse in 2009 (–5.0%) and 2010 (–1.2%); it was still negative in 2011.

History

The islands, then uninhabited, were discovered by Juan Ponce de Leon in 1512, but there was no settlement. After about 1678 Bermudians came and went; they raked sea salt between March and November. Driven away by the Spaniards in 1710, they returned soon afterwards, despite harassment. After the American War of Independence (1775–81) loyalist planters from the southern part of what is now the United States settled on the islands, bringing African-descended slaves with them.

After the abolition of slavery (1834), many of the planters left, but their former slaves remained, and the islands were administered from The Bahamas until 1848, when the inhabitants petitioned for, and were granted, separate colonial status, with an elected Legislative Board and an administrative president. In 1873, following another petition from the inhabitants, the islands were annexed to Jamaica, but kept their own legislative board and had their own commissioner.

In the period of the Cold War, Turks and Caicos was used for deployment of various Western armaments. The USA retained an air base on South Caicos from 1944 to 1947, and in 1952 a guided missile base was set up on Grand Turk.

In 1959 moves towards representative government were put into effect. The Governor of Jamaica also became Governor of the Turks and Caicos Islands. An assembly and executive council were established. In 1962, when Jamaica chose to become independent, the country became a Crown colony without a governor, but with an administrator. In November 1965 the Governor of The Bahamas also became the Governor of the Turks and Caicos Islands. In 1973, when The Bahamas became independent, the islands got their own governor, responsible for defence, internal security and foreign affairs, and their own legal jurisdiction. Under the constitution of August 1976, provision was made for a chief minister and up to three ministers empowered to govern the country in accordance with decisions of the executive council.

The general election in January 1995 was won by the People's Democratic Movement (PDM), with eight seats in the legislative council; the Progressive National Party (PNP) took four and one seat was won by an independent. PDM leader Derek Taylor became chief minister and minister of finance, economic development and planning.

In March 1999 the PDM again won with nine of the 13 elective seats and 52% of the votes; the PNP took four seats.

Constitution

The constitution of August 2006 provides for a governor (representing the British monarch, who is head of state); a cabinet of two *ex officio* members (the financial secretary and the attorney-general), the premier and other ministers; and (replacing the legislative council) a unicameral house of assembly of 21 members, 15 of whom are directly elected for a four-year term, four nominated from the cabinet, one *ex officio* (the attorney-general) and the speaker.

In August 2009 the UK Government suspended ministerial government and the House of Assembly and imposed direct rule for a period of up to two years, when elections would be held. In September 2010 the UK Government announced the indefinite postponement of elections until certain requirements were met; these included conclusion of the investigation into allegations of corruption against some former members of the PNP government, and far-reaching constitutional and public administration reforms.

Politics

Last elections: February 2007

Next elections: 2012

Head of state: Queen Elizabeth II, represented by the governor

***de facto* Head of government:** Governor Damian Roderic Todd

Ruling party: none while constitution partially suspended

In the April 2003 election, when the ruling People's Democratic Movement (PDM) was returned for a third consecutive term, the opposition Progressive National Party (PNP) filed election petitions against the results in two constituencies. The chief justice declared the results in both districts void and the PDM no longer had a majority in the legislative council. The governor, acting in accordance with the constitution, issued writs for by-elections in the two constituencies to be held on 7 August. The PNP won both seats in the by-elections giving them a majority of 8:5 in the legislative council, and Michael Misick was sworn in as chief minister on 15 August 2003. Under the new constitution in August 2006 Misick's title was changed to Premier.

In the February 2007 general election, the ruling PNP received 60% of the votes and was returned with 13 seats, the PDM taking the remaining two elective seats.

In February 2009, an investigation led by a British judge found a 'high probability of systemic corruption' in Misick's administration. The resignation of Misick and several of his ministers followed and Galmo Williams became premier until August 2009 when the UK Government dissolved the cabinet and legislature and Governor Gordon Wetherell assumed executive powers.

Damian Roderic Todd was sworn in as governor in September 2011. He affirmed the UK Government's commitment to holding elections in 2012.

TANZANIA MINERALS AUDIT AGENCY
THE UNITED REPUBLIC OF TANZANIA
MINISTRY OF ENERGY AND MINERALS

Tanzania is renowned for its mineral wealth, including Tanzanite, which is uniquely found in Tanzania

About TMAA

Tanzania Minerals Audit Agency (TMAA) is a semi-autonomous institution established in 2009 to facilitate maximisation of government revenue from the mining industry through effective monitoring and auditing of mining operations and ensuring sound environmental management in mining areas.

Vision

To be a centre of excellence in monitoring and auditing of mining operations.

Mission

To conduct financial and environmental audits, as well as auditing of quality and quantity of minerals produced and exported by miners, in order to maximise benefits to the government from the mining industry for the sustainable development of the country.

TMAA conducts mineral sample analysis

Roles and functions

- Monitoring and auditing large, medium and small scale miners to determine the revenue generated and facilitate collection of payable royalties;
- Gathering taxable information and providing the same to the Tanzania Revenue Authority (TRA) and other relevant authorities;
- Monitoring and auditing of environmental management, environmental budgets and expenditure for progressive rehabilitation and mine closures;
- Collecting, analysing, interpreting and disseminating minerals production and exports data for projecting government revenue, planning purposes and decision-making in the administration of the mining industry;
- Counteracting minerals smuggling and minerals royalty evasion in collaboration with relevant government authorities;
- Assessing value of minerals produced by large, medium and small scale miners to facilitate collection of payable royalties;
- Advising the government on all matters relating to the administration of the mineral sector;
- Promoting and conducting research and development in the mineral sector that will lead to increased government revenue; and
- Examining and monitoring implementation of feasibility reports, mining programmes and plans, annual mining performance reports, environmental management plans and reports of mining companies.

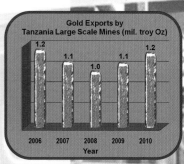

Gold Exports by
Tanzania Large Scale Mines (mil. troy Oz)

1.2	1.1	1.0	1.1	1.2
2006	2007	2008	2009	2010

Year

TMAA audits mineral production and exports

Contact

Eng. Paul M. Masanja
CEO

Headquarters

Plot 1129 Chole Road
Masaki, Kinondoni
P.O. Box 23400,
Dar es Salaam,
Tanzania
Tel: +255 22 260 1819/2109
Fax: +255 22 260 1326

Mwanza office

5th Floor,
PPF Plaza,
Plot #17/2 & 18,
Kenyatta Drive
P.O. Box 362,
Mwanza,
Tanzania
Tel: +255 28 250 6052
Fax: +255 28 250 6051
Email: info@tmaa.go.tz
www.tmaa.go.tz

TMAA audits quality and quantity of minerals produced and exported

TMAA monitors and audits environmental management activities in mining areas

United Republic of Tanzania

KEY FACTS

Joined Commonwealth:	1961
Population:	44,841,000 (2010)
GDP p.c. growth:	2.4% p.a. 1990–2010
UN HDI 2011:	world ranking 152
Official languages:	Kiswahili, English
Time:	GMT plus 3hr
Currency:	Tanzanian shilling (TSh)

Geography

Area:	945,090 sq km
Coastline:	1,420km
Capital:	Dodoma

The United Republic of Tanzania borders the Indian Ocean to the east, and has land borders with eight countries: (anti-clockwise from the north) Kenya, Uganda, Rwanda, Burundi, the Democratic Republic of Congo (across Lake Tanganyika), Zambia, Malawi and Mozambique. The country includes Zanzibar (consisting of the main island Unguja, plus Pemba and other smaller islands).

Topography: The country comprises several distinct zones: a fertile coastal belt; the Masai Steppe and mountain ranges to the north (with Mt Kilimanjaro rising to 5,895m); and a high plateau in the central and southern regions. There are over 61,000 sq km of inland water. Unguja Island (36km from the mainland) is fertile, hilly and densely populated on the west side, low and thinly peopled in the east.

Climate: Varies with geographical zones: tropical on the coast, where it is hot and humid (rainy season March–May); semi-temperate in the mountains (with the Short Rains in November–December and the Long Rains in February–May); and

Did you know...

Filbert Bayi took the Commonwealth Games Men's 1,500 Metres record at the Christchurch Games (New Zealand) in 1974.

The country includes the highest and lowest points in Africa – the summit of Mt Kilimanjaro (5,895m above sea level) and the floor of Lake Tanganyika (358m below sea level).

Tanzanian national Dr William Shija was appointed Secretary-General of the Commonwealth Parliamentary Association, and Dr Asha-Rose Migiro, UN Deputy Secretary-General, in 2007.

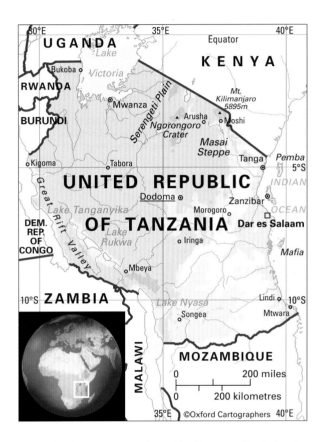

drier in the plateau region with considerable seasonal variations in temperature.

Environment: The most significant environmental issues are drought, soil degradation, deforestation, desertification and destruction of coral reefs.

Vegetation: Lush tropical at the coast; the rest of the country, apart from urban areas, is savannah and bush. Forest and woodland cover 38% of the land area, having declined at 1.1% p.a. 1990–2010. Arable land comprises 11% and permanent cropland 1% of the total land area.

Wildlife: The national parks and game reserves cover 16% of the country and include Serengeti National Park (famous for its vast migratory herds of plains animals, notably wildebeest, zebra, eland and kudu). Small bands of chimpanzees are found in the Gombe National Park along Lake Tanganyika. The steep mountain walls of Ngorogoro Park's volcanic crater have provided protection and a natural enclosure for animals in an environment of great natural beauty. Rhino and elephant populations are still being depleted by poaching despite government protective measures.

Main towns: Dodoma (capital, pop. 179,800 in 2010), Dar es Salaam (commercial and administrative centre, 3.21m), Mwanza

TANZANIA COMMUNICATIONS REGULATORY AUTHORITY

The Tanzania Communications Regulatory Authority (TCRA), established in 2003, is a quasi-independent government body, regulating the electronic communications (telecommunication, broadcasting and internet), postal services and management of the national frequency spectrum in the country.

Strategic objectives

- To encourage private participation in network development.
- To provide reliable information and communication services based on international standards.
- To protect consumer interests through rigorous enforcement of established standards and licence conditions.
- To establish a level playing field to promote effective competition.
- To conduct research through collaboration with institutions of higher education and other stakeholders.
- To collaborate with other regulators and international organisations.
- To encourage sharing of infrastructure facilities.
- To exercise efficient management of the radio frequency spectrum and telecommunication numbers.

Accomplishments and ongoing activities of the Authority

- Implementation of a converged licensing framework
- Introduction of internet exchange points
- Introduction of .tzcc TLD domain name registration
- Telecentres opened in a number across the country
- Introduction of consumer complaints guidelines
- Sensitisation of operators on consumer issues
- Initiation and co-ordination of postal code new physical addressing project
- Co-ordination of central equipment identification and SIM registration
- Implementation of a new and comprehensive numbering plan
- Content monitoring in broadcasting
- Introduction of child helpline
- Introduction of zonal office
- Awarded as best regulator in Africa in 2006 and in 2009

(581,200), Zanzibar Town (495,100), Arusha (448,400), Mbeya (317,700), Morogoro (279,400), Tanga (245,200), Kigoma (182,800), Tabora (161,200), Moshi (157,900), Kasulo (142,700), Musoma (139,100), Songea (138,000), Iringa (111,000), Shinyanga (97,300), Sumbawanga (96,200) and Mtwara (79,500).

Transport: There are 78,890km of roads, 8.6% paved. There are also two railway systems, extending to a total of 4,460km, and running on two different gauges. One links Dar es Salaam with central, western and northern Tanzania and Kenya (Tanzania Railways Corporation, gauge 1m, extending to 2,600km); the other links Dar es Salaam to Zambia (Tanzania–Zambia Railways Authority, or Tazara).

The main ports are at Dar es Salaam, Mtwara, Tanga and Zanzibar. Regular boat services carry passengers and freight between Dar es Salaam and Zanzibar. Ferries provide freight and passenger transport on Lake Victoria.

There are three international airports (Dar es Salaam, Kilimanjaro and Zanzibar) and more than 50 local airports and airstrips. Because of the size of the country and scattered population, air services have become the most significant form of internal transport for official and business travel.

Society

KEY FACTS 2010

Population per sq km:	47
Life expectancy:	57 years
Net primary enrolment:	97%

Population: 44,841,000 (2010); 26% lives in urban areas and 7% in urban agglomerations of more than 1 million people; growth 2.8% p.a. 1990–2010; birth rate 41 per 1,000 people (48 in 1970); life expectancy 57 years (47 in 1970 and 51 in 1990).

Most of the people are of Bantu origin, with some 120 ethnic groups on the mainland, none of which exceeds 10% of the population. The biggest group is the Sukuma; others include Nyamwezi, Masai, Haya Gogo, Chagga, Nyaliyusa and Hehe. The population also includes Asian and expatriate minorities. The people of Zanzibar are of Bantu, Persian and Arab origin.

Language: The official language is Kiswahili (which is universally spoken in addition to various other African languages), and is the medium of instruction in primary schools. English is the second official language, the country's commercial language, and also the teaching language in secondary schools and higher education.

Religion: (on mainland) Muslims 35%, Christians 30%, and a small number of Hindus, with most of the rest holding traditional beliefs; (in Zanzibar) Muslims virtually 100%.

Health: Public spending on health was 4% of GDP in 2009. Muhimbili Medical Centre, Dar es Salaam, is the country's principal referral centre and teaching hospital. Other referral hospitals are at Moshi, Mwanza and Mbeya. 54% of the population uses an improved drinking water source and 24% of people have access to adequate sanitation facilities (2009). Infant mortality was 50 per 1,000 live births in 2010 (142 in 1960). In 2009, 5.6% of people aged 15–49 were HIV positive.

Education: Public spending on education was 6.8% of GDP in 2008. There are seven years of compulsory education starting at age seven. Primary school comprises seven years and secondary six, with cycles of four and two years. Some 74% of pupils complete primary school (2008). The school year starts in January.

The principal public universities are University of Dar es Salaam, Sokoine University of Agriculture (at Morogoro) and Open University of Tanzania, which was established for distance education in 1995. There are a number of private universities including Hubert Kairuki Memorial University (with faculties of medicine and nursing, in Dar es Salaam, established 1997) and International Medical and Technological University (Dar es Salaam, 1995). Literacy among people aged 15–24 is 77% (2009).

Media: The government-owned *Daily News* is published in English. *Uhuru* is owned by the ruling party (CCM) and is in Kiswahili. There are several independent newspapers including *The Guardian* and *Daily Mail*, plus the weeklies *The Arusha Times*, *Business Times* and *The Express*.

The Tanzania Broadcasting Corporation provides public radio and TV services in Kiswahili and English; there are several private TV channels, and many private radio stations, especially in the urban areas.

The first private television channel was launched in mainland Tanzania in 1994, following the introduction of multiparty democracy, and public-service TV followed in 2001.

There are no private broadcasters or newspapers in Zanzibar, though many people on the islands receive mainland broadcasts and read the mainland press. TV Zanzibar and Voice of Tanzania–Zanzibar are both state-operated.

Some 8% of households have TV sets (2007). There are 9 personal computers (2005) and 110 internet users (2010) per 1,000 people.

Communications: Country code 255; internet domain '.tz'. There are many public phones throughout the country. Mobile phone coverage is limited to urban areas. Internet cafes are found in main towns; those in more remote places rely on satellite access. Postal services are good.

There are 4 main telephone lines and 468 mobile phone subscriptions per 1,000 people (2010).

Public holidays: New Year's Day, Zanzibar Revolution Day (12 January, 1964), Sheikh Abeid Amani Karume Day (7 April, Zanzibar only), Union Day (26 April), Labour Day (1 May), Saba Saba (Industry Day, 7 July), Nane Nane (Farmers' Day, 8 August), Nyerere Day (14 October), Republic Day (9 December), Christmas Day and Boxing Day.

Religious festivals whose dates vary from year to year include Prophet's Birthday, Good Friday, Easter Monday, Eid al-Fitr (End of Ramadan, two days) and Eid al-Adha (Feast of the Sacrifice).

Economy

KEY FACTS 2010

GNI:	US$23.4bn
GNI p.c.:	US$530
GDP growth:	6.9% p.a. 2006–10
Inflation:	8.6% p.a. 2006–10

Tanzania came to independence in 1961 with a severely underdeveloped economy and extremely limited infrastructure. In an effort to bring about rapid yet socially equitable development, it became an early proponent of African socialism, launched in 1967

Real Growth in GDP

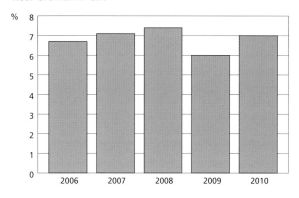

Inflation

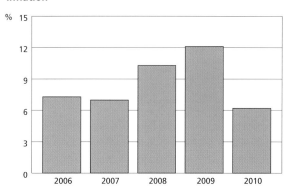

GDP by Sector (2010)

■ Agriculture	**29%**
□ Industry	**23%**
▨ Services	**48%**

with nationalisation of banking, finance, industry and marketing boards; and the resettlement of peasants in communal *ujamaa* villages, created out of large estates.

However, after an initial boom, the formal economic base shrank, production fell and the parallel economy became a way of life. The Ugandan war, falls in commodity prices and failures of the policy itself brought the country to the verge of bankruptcy by the mid-1980s.

Since 1986 new policy directions and IMF-backed structural adjustment programmes have, at considerable cost to social programmes, helped integrate the parallel economy and stimulate growth, which for the most part has been ahead of population growth since the policy change. From the mid-1990s the government embarked on a programme of economic liberalisation and diversification.

The Dar es Salaam Stock Exchange was opened in March 1998. The government has encouraged foreign investment in industry, and especially mining where investments have been made in gold, nickel and cobalt mining. Hundreds of public enterprises were privatised during the 1990s and the programme was continuing in the 2000s, with privatisation of Air Tanzania and Tanzania Railways Corporation. The principal exports are gold, diamonds and other gemstones, coffee, fish and seafood, tobacco, cotton, cashew nuts and tea.

In July 2001, an immense new gold mine was commissioned near Mwanza, with the potential to make the country one of the world's largest producers of gold. In 2004, natural gas began to flow from the island of Songo Songo, in southern Tanzania, via pipeline to a power station and cement plant at Dar es Salaam. Following new discoveries of offshore gas in 2011, the government has estimated proven gas reserves to be 280 billion cubic metres. Good indications of substantive oil deposits have also been found.

After averaging 2.9% p.a. in the 1990s, GDP growth strengthened in the 2000s; it was sustained at 6% p.a. or more during 2001–08, continuing in 2009 (6.0%), 2010 (7.0%) and 2011 (about 6.5%), despite the adverse international economic climate.

Constitution

Status:	Republic with executive president
Legislature:	Parliament
Independence:	9 December 1961 (mainland), 10 December 1963 (Zanzibar)

The unicameral legislature, the National Assembly, includes some members directly elected by universal adult suffrage (in 239 constituencies in 2010), some women members nominated by the parties in proportion to the number of seats they hold in the Assembly (102 following the October 2010 election), up to ten presidential appointees, five delegates from the Zanzibar parliament and, *ex officio*, the attorney-general. General elections are held every five years.

The executive president is elected in separate presidential elections held simultaneously with general elections. He or she must represent a registered political party and have a running mate for the position of vice-president of the Union. The president may serve a maximum of two five-year terms.

The Zanzibar administration has its own president and a House of Representatives of 50 directly elected members, 15 female nominees (by the parties in proportion to the number of seats they hold in the House), ten presidential nominees, and five *ex officio* members; one seat is reserved for the attorney-general. The House is responsible for legislation on domestic matters and, in practice, external trade.

From October 2000, use of the full official name of United Republic of Tanzania was adopted.

Politics

Last elections:	October 2010 (presidential and legislative)
Next elections:	2015 (presidential and legislative)
Head of state:	President Jakaya Mrisho Kikwete
Head of government:	the president
Ruling party:	Chama Cha Mapinduzi

According to evidence at Olduvai Gorge and in the Manonga Valley, Tanzania may be humanity's place of origin. Around AD 500 Bantu peoples, the ancestors of the majority of the modern population, began entering the area. Arab coastal settlement and the introduction of Islam took place between AD 800 and 900. Around AD 1200 the Omanis settled in Zanzibar; in collaboration with some of the coastal peoples of the mainland, they set up a slave trade, with parties of slavers raiding communities in the interior and driving people to local markets at such inland centres as Tabora. From there, they would be sold on to major centres at the ports. The sultanate of Kilwe enjoyed a period of prosperity in the 14th and 15th centuries but the coastal towns suffered a decline thereafter, with the arrival of Portuguese adventurers (though there was little Portuguese settlement).

In 1884 Dr Karl Peters journeyed into the interior to acquire territory, through treaties with chiefs, on behalf of the German emperor. In the late 1880s Germany took over the area from the coast to (and including) Ruanda and Urundi, calling it the Protectorate of German East Africa. There was rather sparse German settlement: the people objected to being 'protected'. In 1905–06 there was an all-out rebellion, which was put down by a strategically engineered famine, leading to about 200,000 deaths.

At the time, Britain was concerned with the islands of Zanzibar and Pemba, which were declared a British Protectorate in 1890. In 1919, the League of Nations gave Britain a mandate to administer part of German East Africa, now known as Tanganyika. (Belgium, with a similar mandate, took over the administration of Rwanda and Burundi.) In 1946 Tanganyika became a UN trust territory.

A legislative council was set up in 1926. It was enlarged in 1945 and restructured in 1955 to give equal representation to Africans, Asians and Europeans, sitting as 30 'unofficials' with the 31 'officials'. In 1954, a schoolteacher, Julius Nyerere, founded the Tanganyikan African National Union (TANU), which promoted African nationalism and won a large public following. The colonial authorities responded with constitutional changes increasing the voice of the African population while reserving seats for minority communities. Elections were held in 1958–59 and again in 1960. The result was overwhelming victory for TANU, which by this period was campaigning for independence as well as majority rule. The new government and the UK agreed at a constitutional conference to full independence for Tanganyika in December 1961. Zanzibar achieved independence in 1963 as a separate country.

Tanganyika became a republic in December 1962, one year after achieving independence, and the first presidential election brought the TANU leader, Julius Nyerere, to the presidency. In 1965 the constitution was changed to establish a one-party system. Meanwhile, in Zanzibar, the Sultan was overthrown in a revolution in January 1964, the constitution was abrogated and the country became a one-party state under the Afro-Shirazi Party. In April 1964 Tanganyika and Zanzibar united as the United Republic of Tanzania. In 1967 Nyerere made the Arusha Declaration, unveiling his political philosophy of egalitarianism, socialism and self-reliance. In 1977, TANU and the Afro-Shirazi

Party merged to form the Chama Cha Mapinduzi (CCM). Ali Hassan Mwinyi succeeded Nyerere in 1985.

Presidential elections were held every five years from 1965 with, under the one-party system, the electorate voting 'yes' or 'no' to a single presidential candidate. In general elections (held at the same time as the presidential elections) the choice was between two candidates put forward by the CCM. Pressure for reform grew within the United Republic, and among international donors. The government responded with constitutional changes that permitted opposition parties from 1992 and so brought in a multiparty system, under which parliamentary and presidential elections were held in October 1995 and contested by 13 political parties.

The October 1995 elections were not completed on schedule, as the National Electoral Commission found irregularities at certain polling stations. The vote in seven Dar es Salaam constituencies was annulled and re-run on 17 November. Ten opposition parties announced that they would boycott the repeat elections, and all the opposition presidential candidates withdrew. The CCM emerged with a substantial majority (approximately 75% of the vote) in the parliamentary elections. The presidential election held at the same time brought to power CCM leader Benjamin Mkapa. (Ali Hassan Mwinyi, who had served two terms as president, was not eligible to stand again and had retired before the election.)

Former President Julius Nyerere died in October 1999 after a long illness. As one of Africa's foremost international statesmen he was widely mourned and many world leaders attended his funeral in Dar es Salaam.

Zanzibar

The October 1995 presidential and legislative elections in Zanzibar, the first to be held since the restoration of multiparty democracy, were fiercely contested by CCM and the Zanzibar-based Civic United Front (CUF) and the results – which gave the CCM a very small majority in both elections – were strongly disputed by the CUF, whose members began to boycott the Zanzibar parliament. This impasse was finally resolved when an agreement was reached through the good offices of the Commonwealth Secretary-General.

At the October 2000 elections in Zanzibar Abeid Amani Karume, the CCM's presidential candidate, and the CCM were officially declared the winners but a high level of tension persisted. Then, through the good offices of the Commonwealth Secretary-General and with continuing pressure from the national government and the international community, talks got under way, and in October 2001 the parties reached agreement on a peace accord. The main planks of the accord were the holding of by-elections in those seats of the Zanzibar parliament which had been declared vacant when CUF members refused to take them up; reform of Zanzibar's election law and setting up of a permanent election register; and giving statutory force to the impartiality of Zanzibar's state-owned press. Progress in implementing the accord was slow, but the by-elections in Pemba were held peacefully in May 2003, the results were readily accepted by CCM and CUF, and efforts to foster political reconciliation continued.

In October 2000, in the United Republic's second multiparty elections, Chama Cha Mapinduzi (CCM) leader Benjamin Mkapa won more than 70% of the votes in the national presidential election, and the ruling CCM took 244 seats in the National Assembly, with the balance of 31 seats won by the Zanzibar-based Civic United Front (CUF; 15) and smaller parties.

Presidential and legislative elections were held in Zanzibar in October 2005 ahead of the national elections. The CCM's candidate, Abeid Amani Karume, won the presidential poll with 53% of the votes, while the CUF's Seif Sharif Hamad took 46%. The ruling CCM also won the parliamentary elections with 30 of the 50 elective seats. The CUF did not accept the result of these fiercely contested, and in places violent elections but the Commonwealth observer group present said that the conditions overall were such as to enable the people to express their will.

In December 2005 the CCM was also successful in the national presidential and legislative elections. Having served two full terms Mkapa was not eligible to stand again for the presidency and, in a 72% turnout, CCM candidate Jakaya Kikwete was elected president. CCM took 206 seats in the National Assembly, with Zanzibar-based CUF (19 seats) accounting for most of the rest.

In the October 2010 national presidential election, with a turnout of 42%, Kikwete was returned with 61.2% of the votes cast, while Willbrod Slaa of Chama Cha Demokrasia na Maendeleo (CHADEMA) secured 26.3% and Ibrahim Lipumba (CUF) 8.1%. In the concurrent parliamentary elections the CCM won 186 seats, the CUF 23 and CHADEMA 22. In Zanzibar, CCM's Ali Mohamed Shein narrowly won the presidency with 50.1% of the votes cast; his main challenger Seif Sharif Hamad of the CUF received 49.1%.

International relations

United Republic of Tanzania is a member of the African, Caribbean and Pacific Group of States, African Union, East African Community, Indian Ocean Rim Association for Regional Cooperation, Non-Aligned Movement, Southern African Development Community, United Nations and World Trade Organization.

United Republic of Tanzania was a member (with Kenya and Uganda) of the East African Community, which from 1967 had a common market and many shared services, but collapsed in 1977. The three countries again embarked on developing regional co-operation in 1993, bringing about progressive harmonisation of standards and policies across a wide range of activities, and launching a new East African Community in January 2001 and East African Customs Union in January 2005. The Community was enlarged in July 2007 when Burundi and Rwanda became members. United Republic of Tanzania hosts the headquarters of the East African Community in Arusha.

Traveller information

Local laws and conventions: All drugs are illegal in the United Republic of Tanzania, and anyone found in possession will be fined. There are severe penalties (including long prison sentences) for those caught drug trafficking.

Visitors should carry some form of identification on them at all times. It is customary always to ask permission before taking photographs of people – especially the Masai.

Visitors should dress modestly and cover their legs and shoulders when away from tourist resorts. When meeting and parting, hands are always shaken. It is the convention to use the right hand, not the left, to shake hands, or to pass or receive items.

For business, dress is smart and a good appearance is highly regarded. There are conference facilities in the larger hotels in Dar es Salaam and Arusha. Office hours are Mon–Fri 0800–1200 and 1400–1630; Sat 0800–1230. During the Muslim fasting month of Ramadan, normal business hours may be disrupted.

Immigration and customs: All visitors to United Republic of Tanzania require a visa, and passports must be valid for at least six months beyond the intended length of stay.

A yellow fever vaccination certificate will be required by all those arriving from infected areas.

Travel within the country: Traffic drives on the left and car hire is available in major cities. Those with an English-language driving licence do not need an international driving permit to drive in the country.

There is a good public bus service connecting most areas, and buses are modern, with air-conditioning, toilets and refreshments.

Taxis are widely available but do not have meters, so fares must be agreed before starting out. It is also possible to hire a chauffeur-driven car.

Travel health: Medical facilities are limited, especially outside Dar es Salaam, and all treatment must be paid for. Visitors should make sure they have comprehensive health insurance. Vaccinations are recommended for Hepatitis B and (occasionally) meningococcal meningitis. All up-to-date vaccination requirements should be checked well in advance of travel.

Malaria is a problem in the country, and visitors will need to take insect repellent and suitable clothing to protect against mosquito bites.

Regular outbreaks of cholera occur in rural areas, so visitors should make sure they boil water before use or only drink bottled water.

Money: The official currency is the Tanzanian shilling (TSh). Money can be exchanged at banks and authorised dealers, and visitors must keep their receipts when changing money as they may be asked to present them at departure. Cash can be withdrawn from ATMs using Visa or Mastercard, and any sizeable town now has at least one bank with an ATM. Major credit cards are accepted in most hotels. Travellers cheques may be cashed with authorised dealers or bureaux de change. Banking hours are Mon–Fri 0830–1230 (though some places are open until 1600) and Sat 0830–1300.

There were 794,000 tourist arrivals in 2010.

Further information

Government of the United Republic of Tanzania: www.tanzania.go.tz

Parliament: www.parliament.go.tz

Bank of Tanzania: www.bot-tz.org

Commonwealth Secretariat: www.thecommonwealth.org

Commonwealth of Nations: www.commonwealth-of-nations.org/United_Republic_of_Tanzania

Vanuatu

KEY FACTS

Joined Commonwealth:	1980
Population:	240,000 (2010)
GDP p.c. growth:	6.8% p.a. 1990–2008
UN HDI 2011:	world ranking 125
Official languages:	Bislama, English, French
Time:	GMT plus 11hr
Currency:	vatu (Vt)

Geography

Area:	12,190 sq km
Coastline:	2,530km
Capital:	Port Vila

The Republic of Vanuatu's land area is made up of a group of islands in the south-west Pacific, lying south of Solomon Islands and east of the state of Queensland in Australia. The country comprises six provinces: Malampa, Penama, Sanma, Shefa, Tafea and Torba.

Topography: Vanuatu is a Y-shaped archipelago, some 900km long. It forms a double chain of about 40 mountainous islands and 40 islets and rocks of volcanic and coral origin; about 65 of these are inhabited. Some islands (including Tanna, Lopévi and Ambrym) have active volcanoes. Many of the rocky islands are steeply mountainous, the highest peaks (on Espíritu Santo) rising to over 1,800m. Fresh water is plentiful.

Climate: Oceanic tropical, with south-east trade winds from May to October. The period from November to April is humid, with moderate rainfall. Cyclones may occur between November and April.

Environment: The most significant environmental issues are that a majority of the population does not have access to a safe and reliable supply of water (although it is improving), and deforestation.

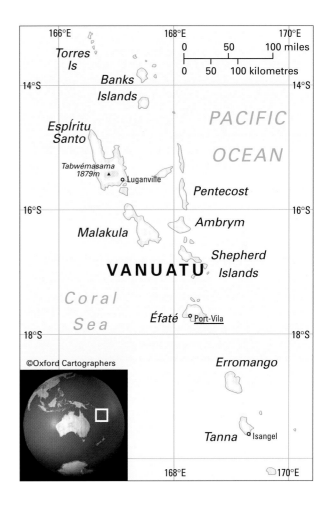

Did you know...

Vanuatu is an archipelago comprising a double chain of about 40 islands and 40 islets and rocks of volcanic and coral origin (about 65 inhabited), some islands having active volcanoes and many are steeply mountainous, rising on Espíritu Santo to over 1,800m; fresh water is plentiful. The country has more than 2,500km of coastline.

Vanuatuans enjoy life expectancy of more than 70 years.

Vegetation: The rocky islands are thickly forested, with narrow coastal plains where cultivation is possible. Forest covers 36% of the land area and there was no significant loss of forest cover during 1990–2010.

Wildlife: Vanuatu is home to 11 species of bat, including the white flying-fox. It is also the easternmost habitation of the dugong, or sea-cow. Espíritu Santo has the richest bird population, with 55 species including the incubator bird which leaves its eggs to incubate in hot volcanic sand from which the young birds emerge fully fledged.

Main towns: Port Vila (capital, pop. 47,500 in 2010) and Mele (2,500) on Efaté; Luganville (13,800) and Port Olry (2,900) on Espíritu Santo; Norsup (2,400) on Malakula; and Isangel (1,700) on Tanna.

Transport: There are 1,070km of roads, 24% paved, most of which are on Efaté.

Ferries link the islands. Additionally, there are shipping services, run by a number of operators, to Australia, New Zealand and New Caledonia. The main ports are Port Vila and Luganville.

The chief airports are at Bauerfield, near Port Vila, and Pekoa on Espíritu Santo Island; there are some 30 smaller airfields.

Society

KEY FACTS 2010

Population per sq km:	20
Life expectancy:	71 years

Population: 240,000 (2010); concentrated near the coast on the four main islands, 26% living in urban areas – Efaté has the fastest-growing population, as people migrate to the capital; growth 2.5% p.a. 1990–2010; birth rate 30 per 1,000 people (43 in 1970); life expectancy 71 years (53 in 1970).

Most of the population is Melanesian, known as ni-Vanuatu (98.5% in the 1999 census), the rest of mixed Micronesian, Polynesian and European descent.

Language: The national language is Bislama; English and French are widely spoken and also official languages. There are more than 100 Melanesian languages and dialects.

Religion: Mainly Christians (Presbyterians 31%, Anglicans 13%, Roman Catholics 13% and Seventh Day Adventists 11%; 1999 census).

Health: Public spending on health was 3% of GDP in 2009. The major hospitals are in Port Vila and Luganville, with health centres and dispensaries throughout the country. 83% of the population uses an improved drinking water source and 52% of people have access to adequate sanitation facilities (2009). Malaria is widespread. Infant mortality was 12 per 1,000 live births in 2010 (141 in 1960).

Education: Public spending on education was 5.0% of GDP in 2009. Primary education, in French or English, starts at age six and is provided free of charge (with effect from 2010). Some 71% of pupils complete primary school (2008). The school year starts in February.

Vanuatu is a partner in the regional University of the South Pacific, which has its main campus in Suva, Fiji, and a campus, the Emalus Campus, in Port Vila, Vanuatu, where 700–1,000 students per semester are enrolled for certificate, diploma, degree and postgraduate courses, using the university's distance-learning facilities. The university's law school and teaching programmes in Pacific languages and early childhood education are based at the Emalus Campus.

Institutions offering tertiary education include the Institute of Technology, which offers courses in business and technical education; Institute of Teacher Education; and College of Nursing Education, all of which are located in Port Vila. Literacy among people aged 15–24 is 94% (2009).

Media: *Vanuatu Weekly* is published by the government in Bislama, French and English. Independent newspapers include *Vanuatu Daily Post*, and the weeklies *The Vanuatu Independent*, *Nasara* and *Ni-Vanuatu*.

The Vanuatu Broadcasting and Television Corporation provides public TV and radio services, broadcasting in Bislama, French and English, and there are some private commercial and faith radio stations.

There are 14 personal computers (2005) and 80 internet users (2010) per 1,000 people.

Communications: Country code 678; internet domain '.vu'. There are public phones in post offices. Mobile coverage is generally good. Port Vila and Luganville have several internet cafes, and internet access is provided by some post offices.

There are 21 main telephone lines and 1,191 mobile phone subscriptions per 1,000 people (2010).

Public holidays: New Year's Day, Father Walter Lini Day (21 February), Custom Chief's Day (5 March), Labour Day (1 May), Children's Day (24 July), Independence Day (30 July), Assumption (15 August), Constitution Day (5 October), Unity Day (29 November), Christmas Day and Family Day (26 December).

Religious festivals whose dates vary from year to year include Good Friday, Easter Monday and Ascension Day.

Economy

KEY FACTS 2010

GNI:	US$633m
GNI p.c.:	US$2,640
GDP growth:	5.3% p.a. 2006–10
Inflation:	3.6% p.a. 2006–10

The Vanuatu economy is based on agriculture, fishing, tourism and offshore financial services. Much of the agriculture is subsistence farming. As most exports are agricultural – for example, copra, coconut oil, kava, beef, timber, cocoa and coffee, Vanuatu is

Real Growth in GDP

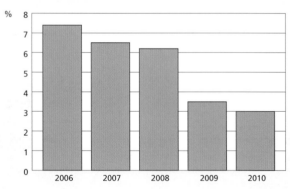

Inflation

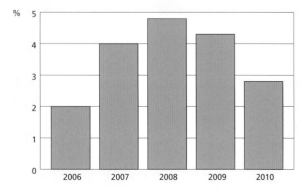

GDP by Sector (2010)

■ Agriculture	19%
□ Industry	10%
▨ Services	70%

vulnerable to fluctuations in world commodity prices. The country has inherent economic difficulties (it is remote and isolated, so faces heavy transport costs, and it is prone to cyclone damage) and is therefore dependent on aid for development projects.

Vanuatu created an offshore tax haven in 1971, with a very liberal financial regime. Many banks set up in the country and by the late 1980s the offshore financial sector contributed 12% of GDP. However, from the late 1990s this tax-haven came under growing pressure from the OECD's campaign to counter money laundering and many of the more than 100 banks closed. By 2003 only seven banks were able to comply with the tighter regulations the government introduced to meet the OECD's requirements.

A long strike by public-sector workers in 1993–94 and subsequent dismissal of all those involved plunged the country into crisis, which was only resolved when the Asian Development Bank agreed (in 1997) to financial support to lift the economy, but its support was tied to a Comprehensive Reform Programme. At the core of this were structural reforms, including reducing the public sector, tighter fiscal control and boosting exports.

The government continued in the 2000s to be committed to encouraging the private sector and foreign investment, improving living standards and reducing economic inequalities. In 2001–02 the economy shrank by more than 2% p.a. It then recovered and the growth rate strengthened, averaging more than 5% p.a. over 2003–08, a recovery that has been attributed to sound fiscal and monetary management, increased private capital inflows and better donor relations. Vanuatu maintained a good growth rate in 2008 (6.2%), 2009 (3.5%) and 2010 (3.0%), despite the adverse international economic climate.

Constitution

Status:	Republic
Legislature:	Parliament
Independence:	30 July 1980

Vanuatu is a republic with a non-executive presidency. The president is elected by parliament together with the presidents of the regional councils and serves a five-year term. The single-chamber Parliament has 52 members, directly elected every four years by universal adult suffrage with an element of proportional representation. Parliament appoints the prime minister from among its members, and the prime minister appoints a council of ministers from among the MPs.

The constitution provides for a certain amount of decentralisation, intended to promote regional autonomy and local participation. In 1994, the 11 local councils were replaced by six provincial governments. The district councils of chiefs elect the National Council of Chiefs, which is consulted, and makes representations, on customary law and traditional factors affecting government.

In October 2004, parliament passed constitutional amendments designed to reduce political instability. These amendments included banning no-confidence votes in the first and last 12-month periods of a parliamentary term and, after the first 12 months of a term, required a by-election in any constituency where the member crossed the floor. Before taking effect these amendments were to be put to the electorate in a national referendum.

Politics

Last elections:	September 2008
Next elections:	2012
Head of state:	President Iolu Johnson Abbil
Head of government:	Prime Minister Sato Kilman
Ruling party:	coalition led by People's Progress Party

From 1991 political life in Vanuatu has been characterised by coalition governments with fluctuating support and the splitting off of political parties.

The May 2002 general election saw coalition partners Union of Moderate Parties (UMP) and Vanua'aku Pati (VP) comfortably returned to power, the UMP with 15 seats and the VP with 14, while Willie Jimmy's National United Party (NUP) took eight. The victorious partners put VP leader Edward Natapei forward to be prime minister, with Serge Vohor – whose UMP had won the most seats – his deputy. During 2003, relations between the NUP and the government improved, but despite some discussion on its joining the coalition, the NUP continued in opposition.

During 2004 the presidency changed hands several times before an early general election in July 2004. Though the UMP (15 seats) emerged from the election with the most parliamentary seats, it appeared that the ruling VP (14 seats) – in coalition with NUP (eight seats) – would be able to form a new government. However, when the parliament convened, some VP members crossed the floor and Serge Vohor of the UMP was elected prime minister. In the fourth round of the subsequent presidential election, Kalkot Mataskelekele emerged as president. In December 2004 a no-confidence vote went against Vohor, and Ham Lini, NUP leader and brother of former Prime Minister Father Walter Lini, was elected prime minister.

In the general election of September 2008 the VP won 11 of 52 seats and NUP eight. These two parties agreed to work together and VP leader Edward Natapei was elected prime minister – with the support of 28 MPs. He was opposed by Maxime Carlot Korman (the candidate of the Vanuatu Republican Party) who received 24 votes.

At the end of President Mataskelekele's term, in August 2009, Korman, the speaker of parliament, became acting president. Presidential elections were held by parliament in September 2009 and Iolu Johnson Abbil was elected in the third round.

In December 2010, while he was travelling to the UN Climate Change Conference in Mexico, Prime Minister Natapei lost a parliamentary no-confidence vote (15–30), and the leader of the People's Progress Party and of the opposition Alliance bloc in parliament, Sato Kilman, was sworn in as prime minister.

On 24 April 2011, following a parliamentary no-confidence vote against Kilman and his cabinet, Serge Vohor of the UMP was elected prime minister by parliament. Then on 13 May 2011, when

The islands of Vanuatu have been inhabited since 500 BC, and the region was part of the Tongan Empire into the 14th century. European sailors visited it briefly and at long intervals from early in the 17th century. The name 'New Hebrides' was given to the islands by Captain James Cook on his visit in 1774. In 1789 the islands were called at by rescuers seeking Captain Bligh and his officers, who had been turned loose with provisions in an open boat after the mutiny on the *Bounty*.

During the 19th century French and English Christian missionaries and some traders and planters settled on some of the islands which became an Anglo–French condominium by 1906. The New Hebrides, as it was then called, was ruled by separate British and French administrations, laying the foundations for some of the problems that have erupted since independence.

After the Second World War, a power struggle developed between the dual colonial interests and the indigenous islanders, initially over the alienation of land by the Europeans. The first major change was agreement, at a meeting between France and the UK in 1974, to setting up a representative assembly (with a majority elected by universal franchise) to replace the colonial advisory council. The first national elections followed in November 1975, but disagreements among the four chiefs representing traditional interests delayed elections to the seats reserved for chiefs.

Just a few months after the assembly had come into full operation in early 1977, a second boycott brought its operations to a halt. The largest party, the Vanua'aku Pati (VP), led by an Anglican priest, Father Walter Lini, objected to the reservation of six seats for members of the Chamber of Commerce. Reluctant to make any compromise agreement, the VP went on to boycott the ensuing conference in Paris in July 1977 and the subsequent general election. A government of national unity was formed in 1978 and, with advisory help from France and the UK, a new constitution providing for independence in 1980 was adopted in October 1979. Elections in November 1979 gave victory to the VP, and Lini became prime minister. The archipelago gained independence on 30 July 1980 as Vanuatu and joined the Commonwealth.

After independence, the VP remained in power for 11 years, under the leadership of Lini. During this period an attempt at secession, supported by the Na-Griamel movement and some francophone inhabitants, was suppressed. Lini was twice re-elected prime minister (1983 and 1987). After the 1987 elections, Lini was challenged for the party leadership by Barak Sope, who subsequently formed a new party – the Melanesian Progressive Party (MPP) – and for a brief period became prime minister of an interim government, pending elections. However, before these elections could be held, Lini resumed as prime minister. Sope and several members of the interim government were arrested on charges of treason. They were convicted but their prison sentences were subsequently quashed following appeals from the

international community. In September 1991, Donald Kalpokas succeeded Lini as leader of the VP and prime minister.

The general election of December 1991 brought in a new government, a coalition led by Maxime Carlot Korman, leader of the francophone Union of Moderate Parties (UMP). The coalition surprisingly included members of the National United Party (NUP), a party formed by former Prime Minister Lini who had broken away from the VP. The NUP itself split in mid-1993, with Lini's group joining the opposition, alongside the VP, the MPP and the Fren Melanesia Party (FMP). Korman maintained his majority, governing until the general election of 1995. The immediate result of the 1995 elections was a coalition government led by Serge Vohor (UMP). After two months, he was replaced by Korman. Less than eight months later, in September 1996, Korman lost a vote of no confidence and resigned after members of his coalition government were criticised by the national ombudsman in her report on the uncovering of a massive bank fraud. Vohor once again became prime minister.

Divisions within the government over implementation of the Asian Development Bank-funded economic reforms led to its defeat in November 1997 and to the dissolution of parliament. On 12 January 1998 a state of emergency was declared following rioting in Port Vila, which broke out as 500 people attempted to withdraw their investments in the National Provident Fund, following allegations that politicians had misused the Fund. There was an early general election in March 1998, when a record 220 candidates contested 52 seats (increased from 50 since the previous elections in 1995). The VP won 18 seats, the UMP 12, the NUP 11 and other parties 11; no party had an overall majority. However, after 12 days of negotiations Donald Kalpokas (VP) and Lini (NUP) formed a coalition government. Kalpokas was elected prime minister, with the support of 35 members of parliament; he appointed Lini as deputy prime minister. In October 1998, Kalpokas dismissed Lini, excluding the NUP from the coalition, and formed new alliances with the UMP and the John Frum Movement (JFM). Vanuatu's leader at independence and first prime minister (1980–91), Father Walter Lini, died at the age of 57 in February 1999.

During August 1999 opposition parties won three of the four by-elections to be held, giving them control of 26 of the 52 parliamentary seats, and putting them in a strong position to defeat the government, which finally occurred in November 1999 after two government members defected to the opposition and Barak Sope (MPP) was elected prime minister by 28 votes to 24. However, the new government was soon involved in political controversy and its authority was undermined by leaks of cabinet documents to the press. In April 2001, after nine members of the ruling coalition defected to the opposition, Sope lost a no-confidence vote, and VP leader Edward Natapei became prime minister and immediately announced there would be an inquiry into the previous government's controversial deal with a Thai businessman.

the Court of Appeal ruled that Vohor's election was unconstitutional, Kilman was restored to office. On 16 June 2011, after the Supreme Court had ruled that Kilman's election in December 2010 had also been unlawful, Natapei was appointed to lead a caretaker administration until a fresh parliamentary vote was held on 26 June 2011, when Kilman defeated Vohor (29:23) and resumed as prime minister.

International relations

Vanuatu is a member of the African, Caribbean and Pacific Group of States, Non-Aligned Movement, Organisation internationale de la Francophonie, Pacific Community, Pacific Islands Forum and United Nations.

The World Trade Organization (WTO) approved Vanuatu's accession in October 2011 and the Vanuatu Parliament passed enabling legislation in December 2011, but in the face of strong opposition to WTO membership by the major national civil society organisations, in early 2012 the president was yet to approve the legislation.

Traveller information

Local laws and conventions: Drinking kava, a locally produced non-alcoholic drink, is an ancient tradition in Vanuatu, but it should be drunk in moderation. Visitors wishing to explore the islands must be aware that Vanuatu has strict land-ownership regulations. Most local residents will allow visitors to take their photograph but permission must always be sought first.

Visitors to Vanuatu should show respect at all times for the country's traditional values and its people's strong Christian beliefs; and should also avoid wearing revealing clothing in public.

Informal wear is suitable for most occasions. Business is normally conducted in English or French. Office hours are Mon–Fri 0730–1130 and 1330–1630.

Immigration and customs: Passports must be valid for at least six months beyond the intended length of stay and visitors must hold a valid onward or return ticket. All food, fruits, animal products and plants must be declared on entry into Vanuatu.

Travel within the country: Traffic drives on the right and visitors can drive on their national driving licence. Cars can be hired from international agencies located in Port Vila. There is no public transport on Vanuatu. Private buses and minibuses run but there are no timetables. The most common way of catching a bus is to flag one down and tell the driver where to go. Taxis are also available and are metered.

Inter-island travel is by boat from Port Vila and Espíritu Santo, or by Vanair, the domestic airline. However, both services can be infrequent, so should be confirmed before travel. Visitors should exercise caution when considering visiting active volcanoes on any of the islands in Vanuatu, and should check with the Vanuatu Tourist Office for latest reports on volcanic activity before travelling.

Travel health: Medical facilities in Vanuatu are adequate for routine treatments. Visitors should ensure they have comprehensive medical insurance, as serious cases will require air evacuation to Australia or New Zealand for treatment.

Malaria and dengue fever are common, and visitors should ensure they have insect repellent and suitable clothing to protect against mosquito bites.

Mains water is chlorinated and safe to drink; bottled water is widely available.

Money: Local currency is the vatu, though Australian dollars are accepted in major cities. There are ATMs at the ANZ and Westpac banks, and the use of credit cards is mainly restricted to Port Vila and Luganville. Travellers cheques are widely accepted. Banking hours are Mon–Fri 0800–1500.

There were 101,000 tourist arrivals in 2009.

Further information

Government of Vanuatu: www.governmentofvanuatu.gov.vu

Parliament: www.parliament.gov.vu

Reserve Bank of Vanuatu: www.rbv.gov.vu

Commonwealth Secretariat: www.thecommonwealth.org

Commonwealth of Nations: www.commonwealth-of-nations.org/Vanuatu

MINISTRY OF COMMUNITY DEVELOPMENT, MOTHER AND CHILD HEALTH

Deputy Minister Hon. Jean Kapata, MP talking to beneficiaries of Food Security Pack programme in Mfuwe

Facilitating the provision of socio-economic empowerment to the vulnerable

The Ministry of Community Development, Mother and Child Health (MCDMCH) is one of Zambia's key social sector ministries contributing significantly to reduction in poverty, improvement in the living standards of vulnerable individuals and promotion of the health of mothers and children. In pursuing this role, MCDMCH operates within the overall government policy framework which provides an enabling environment for active participation of individuals and the private sector in the provision of community development, social welfare and maternal and child health services. MCDMCH plays an essential facilitative role spanning the provision of community development, social welfare services, registration and co-ordination of Non-Governmental Organisations and the promotion of mother and child health. MCDMCH's interventions reach people at the grassroot level, countrywide.

Mission
To effectively and efficiently facilitate the provision of socio-economic empowerment and social assistance support to the poor and vulnerable, and the promotion of Maternal and Child Health.

Vision
To have a Zambian Society where every poor and vulnerable person is empowered to live a productive and meaningful life by 2030.

Goal
To ensure availability and accessibility of policy guidelines, resources and infrastructure at points of service delivery in order to contribute to the reduction in poverty and improve the quality of life.

Leadership
The Ministry is headed by Cabinet Minister Honourable Dr Joseph Katema, MP and assisted by Deputy Minister Honourable Jean Kapata, MP. The Chief Executive Officer is the Permanent Secretary Professor Elwyn Chomba.

Mandate
The specific mandate of the Ministry includes the following subjects:
- Community Development Policy
- Disabilities Affairs Policy
- NGO Policy
- Social Welfare Policy
- Non-Formal Education and Skills Training
- Community Development Training
- Women's Development
- Supporting Self-Help Initiatives
- Juvenile Correctional Services
- Probational Services
- Rehabilitation of Persons with Disabilities
- Social Safety-Nets
- Child Welfare Services
- Welfare Service and Counselling Organisations
- Adoption Services
- Food Programme Management
- Group Housing
- Maternal and Child Health

Contact
Professor Elwyn Chomba
Permanent Secretary
Ministry of Community Development, Mother and Child Health
Community House
Sadzu Road
P/Bag W252
LUSAKA, ZAMBIA

Tel: +260 1 22 5327
Fax: +260 1 23 5342
Email: echomba@zamnet.zm

Zambia

KEY FACTS

Joined Commonwealth:	1964
Population:	13,089,000 (2010)
GDP p.c. growth:	0.6% p.a. 1990–2010
UN HDI 2011:	world ranking 164
Official language:	English
Time:	GMT plus 2hr
Currency:	kwacha (ZK)

Geography

Area:	752,614 sq km
Coastline:	none
Capital:	Lusaka

Zambia is a landlocked, fertile and mineral-rich country on the Southern African plateau. It is bordered by: (clockwise from the north) the United Republic of Tanzania, Malawi, Mozambique, Zimbabwe, Botswana, Namibia (via the Caprivi Strip), Angola and the Democratic Republic of Congo. The country comprises ten provinces (from south to north): Southern, Western, Lusaka, Central, Eastern, North-Western, Copperbelt, Northern, Muchinga (whose creation was announced in October 2011) and Luapula.

Topography: Most of Zambia is high plateau, deeply entrenched by the Zambezi river (and its tributaries, the Kafue and Luangwa) and the Luapula river. The Zambezi flows to the south, turning eastwards to make the border with Zimbabwe. In the north are three great lakes: the Tanganyika, Mweru and Bangweulu. The man-made Lake Kariba stretches along the southern border. The Mafinga Mountains form part of a great escarpment running down the east side of the Luangwa river valley. The country rises to a higher plateau in the east.

Climate: Tropical, but seldom unpleasantly hot, except in the valleys. There are three seasons: a cool dry season April–August; a hot dry season August–November; and a wet season, which is even hotter, November–April. Frost occurs in some areas in the cool season. Rainfall is 508–1,270mm p.a.

Did you know...

The Commonwealth Youth Programme Africa Centre is based in Lusaka.

Kalusha Bwalya, born in Mufulira in 1963, was African Footballer of the Year in 1988.

Zambia is one of seven landlocked Commonwealth countries, all of which are in Africa.

Environment: The most significant environmental issues are: deforestation, soil erosion, and desertification; health risk posed by inadequate water treatment facilities; threat to big game populations by poaching; and air pollution and resulting acid rain in the areas surrounding mining and refining operations in Copperbelt Province.

Vegetation: Forest – mostly savannah bushveld – covers 67% of the land area, having declined at 0.3% p.a. 1990–2010. The high eastern plateau consists of open grassy plains with small trees and some marshland. Arable land comprises 5% of the total land area.

Wildlife: Zambia has a wealth of wildlife, including big mammals and numerous species of antelopes. There are 19 national parks and 34 game management areas, about one-third of the country's area. South Luangwa has one of Africa's largest elephant populations. Kafue National Park has the largest number of antelope species of any African park, including the rare red lechwe, an aquatic antelope. It is also a home of the fish eagle, Zambia's national emblem. Decline in animal numbers has been slowed by the government's commitment to wildlife conservation, and the enforcement of measures against poaching and weapon-carrying in the conservation areas. There are 233 mammal species, of which 12 are thought to be endangered.

Main towns: Lusaka (capital, pop. 1.45m in 2010), Kitwe (Copperbelt Province, 527,800), Ndola (Copperbelt, 495,800), Kabwe (Central, 214,700), Chingola (Copperbelt, 178,400), Mufulira (Copperbelt, 141,300), Livingstone (Southern, 133,800), Luanshya (Copperbelt, 132,300), Kasama (Northern, 111,500), Chipata (Eastern, 109,500), Kalulushi (Copperbelt, 100,900), Mazabuka (Southern, 95,600), Chililabombwe (Copperbelt,

CHONGWE DISTRICT COUNCIL

Development and progress

Chongwe District, one of four districts in Lusaka Province, is situated about 45 km east of Lusaka on Great East Road.

Strengths

- The District has abundant land resources that can sustain crops, livestock and fish farming.
- Land that could be irrigated, is abundant. In some areas, rivers like Chongwe, Lusemfwa and Mwapula have pools or ponds that do not dry out even during the drought years. These could be used as a source of irrigation. In addition, there are.

Agriculture

Agriculture is the main economic activity of the District. Major crops include maize, cotton, groundnuts and sunflowers.

FARMING SYSTEMS

CATEGORY	DEFINITION	FARMING SYSTEMS
Small scale	< 5 ha	Mixed (crop and livestock) and traditional
Medium scale	5 ha – 20 ha	Mixed (crop and livestock) and improved traditional management
Large scale	20 ha >	Mixed, mechanised and commercial in management and production

The majority of trade originating from the District is by large-scale farmers who supply livestock products to Lusaka and, in recent years, provided horticultural products to international markets.

The District has potential for development in mining, tourism and other industrial activities.

Identifiable mining activities in the District are sand mining and quarrying. The District supplies huge quantities of building and river sand to neighbouring Lusaka District. Sand mining is largely done by small-scale miners and thus has not been utilised effectively to benefit the District in terms of employment, income and levies to the Council.

Tourist attractions

- Chinyunyu Hot Spring: Planning is under way for the development of a health resort and construction of a geothermal power plant to provide electric power to the local community located 50 kilometres east of Lusaka on the Great East Road.
- Ancient paintings in the caves in Lukoshi area and surrounding hills, such as Leopard Hills.
- Safari hunting and game viewing in the Game Management Areas of Shikabeta.
- Lodges, camping and motel facilities such as Chaminuka Lodge with game farming and lodging facilities.
- Cultural ceremonies: *Chakwela Makumbi, Nkomba Lyanga* and *Chibwela Kumunshi*

Support programmes

- Through the Food Reserve Agency (FRA), the government has so far paid K14.5 billion to farmers in Chongwe District towards the purchase of maize grown in the 2010/2011 farming season. The agricultural sector in the area has seen an improvement with the deployment of agricultural extension officers assisting with crop diversification. In addition, the District's Fertiliser Input Support Programme (FISP) is doing well, with over 600,000 50kg bags of white maize expected to be bought, exporting much of it to Mozambique and Kenya while some of the staple food will be ferried to hunger-stricken Somalia. From this venture, Zambia is expected to earn over K2 billion.
- A programme to distribute relief food in Chongwe District began six years ago with the aim of benefiting the aged, sick

and disabled. This programme continues under the administration of the Disaster Management and Mitigation Unit (DMMU), within the office of the Vice-President.

- Several major roads have been upgraded in the district at a total cost of K13 billion. Inaccessible areas have since received a facelift through the government's Rural Roads Unit (RRU) programme, opening feeder roads that had not been graded for years.

- Four new schools have been built in the District, namely Matipula Basic School, Twikatane Basic School in Lukoshi ward near Mikango barracks, Lwangwa Bridge Basic School and Sinjela Secondary School for Girls.

- Several health facilities have been built and others are currently under construction to enable local people improved access to health services.

- With the new US$2 million water processing plant at Chongwe River, the Chongwe community has not only seen an improvement in water supply but also a decrease in waterborne diseases caused by untreated water.

- Zambia Electricity Supply Company (ZESCO) is constructing a 33/11 kV sub-station in the district which will also supply power to Luangwa district.

Seeds for Africa Project is a teaching tool for educating land owners of Chongwe District on how to plant and grow commercial crops of Leucaena trees, used for a variety of purposes including firewood, fibre, livestock fodder and charcoal

Below: *Since the launch of the Bicycles for Educational Empowerment Program (BEEP) in June 2009, World Bicycle Relief has successfully delivered 2,574 bicycles to Chongwe and Mumbwa Districts' students, teachers and community supporters at 19 schools*

Ministry of Chiefs and Traditional Affairs

Traditional leaders have welcomed the announcement of the new Ministry of Chiefs and Traditional Affairs and the appointment of the Honourable Emerine Kabanshi, MP as the Minister.

Paramount Chief Chitimukulu

Chief Monze

Chief Mumena

Chief Nzamane

Paramount Chief Mpezeni

Senior Chief Ishindi

Senior Chief Kanongesha

Senior Chief Mwata Kazembe

Senior Chief Ndungu

Chief Musele

Senior Chief Puta

Senior Chieftainess Nkomeshya Mukamambo II

Strength in diversity

The strength of culture in our chiefdoms lies in its diversity whose features include national heritage sites, museums and arts in their various forms, traditions, beliefs and ceremonies.

Vision

A Zambia that conserves heritage and preserves cultural diversity for sustainable national development.

Mission

Administration and promotion of chiefs' affairs, traditional governance systems, conservation and preservation of Zambia's heritage, culture and arts for sustainable development and national identity.

The Ministry of Chiefs and Traditional Affairs is responsible for the administration of chiefs and their affairs in chiefdoms, provision of governance systems in these chiefdoms, conservation and preservation of both movable and immovable items of culture and national heritage. The whole complex of distinctive spiritual, material, intellectual and emotional features that characterises a society or social group is in the hands of people living in various chiefdoms spread all over Zambia. The culture of these different chiefdoms includes arts, modes of life, the fundamental rights of the human being, value systems, traditions and beliefs. It represents a unique and irreplaceable body of values and its presence is demonstrated through traditions and forms of expression.

During the next three-year period, the Ministry of Chiefs and Traditional Affairs will focus on infrastructure development in five priority public sector institutions, namely the House of Chiefs, Cultural Affairs, National Museums Board, National Arts Council of Zambia and National Heritage Conservation Commission. The other focus areas include the harmonisation of political and legal policies and frameworks, improvement in the traditional governance systems, culture and arts promotion and marketing, research in culture and arts and human skills development. Furthermore, the Ministry will focus on the provision of requisite infrastructure and skills for the promotion of creative industries for socio-economic development and preservation of Zambia's national heritage.

Contact: Mr Coillard C. Chibbonta, Permanent Secretary, Ministry of Chiefs and Traditional Affairs, Lusaka
tel: +260 211 254 158

72,000), Mongu (Western, 71,800), Choma (Southern, 58,500), Kapiri Mposhi (Central, 56,800), Kansanshi (North-Western, 51,900), Kafue (Lusaka, 46,500), Mansa (Luapula, 45,100), Monze (Southern, 40,800), Sesheke (Western, 33,400) and Mpika (Northern, 31,100).

Transport: There are 91,440km of roads, 22% paved, and 1,273km of railway (not including the Tazara Railway). Roads can be hazardous during the rainy season. There is access to the Mozambican port of Beira (also to Maputo) via Livingstone and the Zimbabwe railway system; to the Tanzanian port of Dar es Salaam,

History

Archaeological findings at Kabwe indicate that Zambia was inhabited around 10,000 BC. More complete records date from the arrival of the Luba and Lunda peoples during the 14th to 15th century, from what are now the Democratic Republic of Congo and Angola. The Bemba are descendants of the Luba and the Lozi of the Lunda. The Ngoni peoples came north from South Africa to eastern Zambia. David Livingstone, the British missionary and explorer, travelled through Zambia in the mid-19th century. He was followed by British settlers in the 1880s and 1890s. Arab slave-trading flourished in the territory throughout the 19th century, until it was ended by the British in 1893.

In 1889, the British South Africa Company received a Royal Charter to explore, develop and administer the territory. In 1924 the company ceded administrative control of Zambia, called Northern Rhodesia, to the British Crown and serious exploitation of the country's main resource, copper, began. The capital moved from Livingstone to Lusaka in 1935. The Federation of Northern and Southern Rhodesia and Nyasaland, with its own constitution, existed from 1953 to 1963.

In the mid-1950s Kenneth Kaunda founded the Zambia African National Congress (ZANC), a breakaway from the more conservative African National Congress (ANC), to fight for civil and voting rights for the African population. ZANC was quickly banned by the colonial authorities, and Kaunda arrested. During his internment, his followers evaded the ban by remoulding the ZANC as the United National Independence Party (UNIP), taking the name from the main platform of its programme. Kaunda became chairman of the UNIP on his release in 1960. In turn, the UNIP was outlawed but it had caught the popular imagination and political demonstrations spread across the country. The UK accepted the demands and, in January 1964, introduced a new constitution giving the country internal self-government, and organising elections. UNIP emerged as the majority party and proceeded towards independence; the Republic of Zambia became independent and a member of the Commonwealth on 24 October 1964.

United National Independence Party

Within a decade of independence, economic conditions worsened. Demand for copper was already beginning to fall and there was tumult in Southern Africa. Landlocked Zambia was badly affected by all the major conflicts of the period. The closure of the border with Zimbabwe, then Rhodesia (under the sanctions programme aimed at Ian Smith's illegal regime), disrupted exports. Civil war broke out in Angola and, in 1975, the Benguela railway was closed. Mozambique's long battle against the Renamo dissidents began shortly after its independence in 1975; rail and oil lines were targets for attack. Sanctions against South Africa also affected Zambia's trade and transport. Refugees from these troubled countries and Namibia

(engaged in the independence war with South Africa) were given sanctuary in Zambia.

The UNIP government of Kenneth Kaunda created a one-party state (lasting from 1973 until 1991) in an unsuccessful attempt to strengthen national unity. A coup plot in 1980 involved local business leaders and the governor of the Bank of Zambia. Several trade union leaders, including Frederick Chiluba, were detained during a wave of strikes in 1981, unions now having become the main focus of opposition to UNIP. Popular discontent was fuelled by the effects of IMF-backed recovery programmes. From 1986, demonstrations (sometimes violent) against food price increases began to take a more political form, leading to demands for a more democratic system of government.

Restoration of multiparty democracy

In July 1990, the 17-year ban on organised opposition groups was lifted. Three days later, the Movement for Multiparty Democracy (MMD) was founded. The elections in October 1991 gave a substantial majority to the MMD and its presidential candidate, Frederick Chiluba. However, continuing discontent with economic conditions and the effects of severe drought led to a new wave of strikes within a year. A breakaway group of nine MMD MPs formed the National Party in August 1993.

In March 1994 the government appointed a commission to rewrite the constitution and a draft new constitution was submitted to the president in June 1995, the commission recommending that it should be approved by a national referendum. The government argued that it should instead be adopted by the National Assembly before the elections that were due in November 1996. The Assembly did so in June 1996, despite international criticism and the suspension of some aid. Among controversial government amendments to the constitution were clauses that specified that a president could serve a maximum of two five-year terms, thus disallowing the candidacy of Kenneth Kaunda, former president for 27 years and presidential candidate of the opposition UNIP. UNIP also objected to clauses debarring any person from candidacy whose parents are not or were not Zambian citizens (Kaunda's parents came from Malawi).

Most of the opposition parties boycotted the November 1996 elections (UNIP because its leader was debarred under the new constitution). There was a landslide victory for the MMD. But because of the boycott, many leading opposition parties did not have any seats in the National Assembly. Turnout was 56% of those registered to vote, although it is estimated that only 50% of those eligible were registered. The MMD won 131 of the 150 Assembly seats, and Chiluba won 73% of the presidential vote. The largest opposition party was then the National Party, with five seats.

LUNDAZI DISTRICT COUNCIL
Nature's gift to

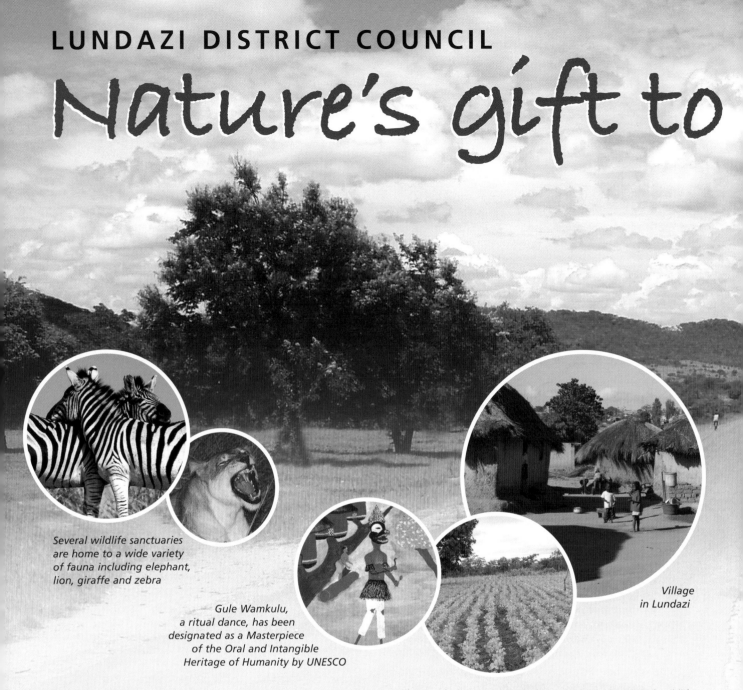

Several wildlife sanctuaries are home to a wide variety of fauna including elephant, lion, giraffe and zebra

Gule Wamkulu, a ritual dance, has been designated as a Masterpiece of the Oral and Intangible Heritage of Humanity by UNESCO

Village in Lundazi

Background

Lundazi District covers 8741 square miles in the Eastern Province of Zambia, sharing an international border with the Republic of Malawi. Magnificent plateaus and beautiful valleys make up the major ecological zones along the district's latitude and longitude. Lundazi District Council is responsible for preserving the cultural richness and natural beauty of the district and promoting tourism and sustainable investment and development.

Attractions

- Be immersed in the mellow languages of Chewa, Nyanja and Timbuka.
- Witness the Chiwa male initiation rite.
- Taste the renowned Chama rice.
- Experience the culture of the Timbuka people through *Gule Wamkulu*, a ritual dance performed at initiation ceremonies, funerals and other important occasions. Together with the *Vimbuza* healing dance, the *Gule Wamkulu* has been designated as Masterpieces of the Oral and Intangible Heritage of Humanity by UNESCO.
- Enjoy the dry, soothing heat of the Luangwa River Valley and the contrasting scenery of rolling green mountains.

- The Lundazi community invites visitors to its several wildlife sanctuaries such as Lukusuzi, Luambe and North Luangwa National Parks, home to a wide variety of fauna including elephants, buffalos, lions, giraffes and monkeys.

Facilities

- Lundazi is a growing district with modern structures. New buildings are being built for government departments, such as the Ministry of Education's offices.
- Upgraded water and sanitation systems.
- In addition to its current fully equipped hospital, Lundazi District is proud to announce the construction of a new and larger District Hospital which will offer specialised services.
- Lundazi District has recently been selected by the 30-30-30 project initiative for the construction of two elementary schools and two health clinics over the next five years.
- Electricity and fresh running water are available under Lundazi's Clean and Healthy Campaign.

Business opportunities

The district includes fertile valleys with potential to be further cultivated for maize, cotton, tobacco, groundnuts, soy bean and sunflower production. Investment opportunities exist in mining

Zambia

Lundazi District
Council Buildings

Small-scale
businesses are
encouraged to
improve household incomes

Investment
opportunities exist in
mining for a number of
plentiful mineral deposits of
semi-precious and precious stones

for a number of plentiful mineral deposits of semi-precious and precious stones including aquamarine, coal and alluvial gold, mica, beryl uranium and beautiful multi-coloured bismuth-bearing tourmaline stones.

- Lodge construction and tourism development is being considered in the vicinity of the Lukusuzi, Luambe and North Luangwa National Parks.
- Road construction and expansion are planned in order to enhance vehicular access to and within the Lundazi District.
- The Lundazi airport is also being considered for expansion and development.
- Although Lundazi's existing telecommunication system is sufficient, upgrade offers are welcomed in order to ensure maximum efficiency and quality.
- Agricultural processing, flora culture and mining are all open for potential partnership, investment and sponsorship.

Key investment opportunities

- Agriculture processing
- Gemstone mining
- Airstrip expansion
- Road construction

Organisational partners

- **Women for Change** is a project funded by the Canadian International Development Agency and the Lundin Foundation. Focused on the district of Lundazi, Women for Change aims at improving gender and human rights knowledge amongst rural villagers, promoting social empowerment and starting a range of rurally sustainable small-scale businesses to improve household-level incomes, alleviating poverty.
- **Zambia Land Alliance** promotes secured access, ownership and control over land through lobbying and advocacy, research and community participation.
- **Justice for Women and Orphans Project** provides assistance for orphans and vulnerable children in the Lundazi, Senanga and Kaoma districts of Zambia to access primary education and to transition on to higher education or sustainable livelihoods.

Contact

Godfrey Mabili, Executive Mayor
Mr Sidney Muwowo, Council Secretary
Lundazi District Council

Tel: +260 216 48 0475 (dir) • +260 216 48 0205
Email: gainbuo@yahoo.com

COPPERBELT PROVINCE

Situated in Northern Zambia, the region encompasses the mineral-rich Copperbelt. This is one of the great mining districts of the world containing very high grade deposits including two of the world's ten biggest copper deposits. Many of the deposits contain high cobalt concentrations and some deposits also hold significant uranium resources.

Districts

Copperbelt Province is divided into 10 districts:

1 Chililabombwe **2** Chingola **3** Mufulira **4** Kalulushi **5** Kitwe
6 Ndola – capital city **7** Luanshya **8** Lufwanyama **9** Mpongwe **10** Masaiti

Vision

To have a diversified and self sustaining economy that meets the aspirations of the Copperbelt Province community by 2030.

Mission

To effectively and efficiently promote and coordinate sustainable development in the province in order to ensure quality and timely service delivery to the community in a transparent, accountable and equitable manner.

Functions

- To ensure effective management and efficient utilisation of financial, human and material resources.
- To interpret and disseminate government policies.
- To facilitate the preparation and implementation of District and Provincial Strategic Plans.
- To ensure effective implementation of the National Decentralisation Policy.
- To co-ordinate, monitor and evaluate development programmes.
- To establish and maintain an effective management information system.
- To provide effective logistical and administrative support services.
- To ensure implementation of the National Gender Policy.

Investment potentials

Mining and quarrying

In addition to copper, the Province is also well-endowed with semi-precious and precious stones, notably the world's much sought after emeralds. The Province has one limestone producer and two cement producing companies.

Beryl quartz

Bornite

Manufacturing

There is investment potential in the processing of agricultural products, textile, wood and non-wood products, cement, copper products, gemstone cutting and polishing and handicrafts.

Agriculture

The Province has a vast network of rivers and streams that makes it possible for cultivation of crops throughout the year.

Forestry

About 14% of the total provincial land is protected forest and plantations. Copperbelt is a major supplier of both soft and hard wood, exported in its raw form.

Tourism

There is potential for water sports in dams and rivers; spas at the hot springs; and leisure resorts and safari lodges in the various districts along the Kafue and Kafubu Rivers.

What makes the province a good destination for investment?

The Province is a viable place for investment not only because of the peaceful environment and efficient public administration, but also because of the existing infrastructure, ready market for goods and services and the availability of both skilled and unskilled labour.

Contact

Mr John Kufuna, Minister
Mr Christopher Mutembo, Permanent Secretary
Mr Clifford Banda, Chief Planning Officer
PO Box 70153
Ndola
Copperbelt Province
Zambia
Tel: +260 21 261 3434
Fax: +260 21 261 3997
Email: mwakayeye@gmail.com

via the Tazara Railway; and to Durban in South Africa, also via Livingstone and the Zimbabwe railway system. In 2003 a South African consortium was granted a 20-year licence to manage Zambia Railways.

The western route to the sea, the Benguela Railway (through the Democratic Republic of Congo to the Angolan port of Benguela) was closed in 1975 due to upheavals in the Democratic Republic of Congo (then Zaire) and Angola. However, by 2007 restoration of the route was in progress following a grant, of up to US$300m, received by Angola from China. Since 2000, plans have been under way for a new rail route from Lusaka to Blantyre in Malawi, giving access to the port of Nacala in Mozambique.

There are international airports at Lusaka (26km east of the city) and Mfuwe (in the South Luangwa National Park), and more than 100 other airports and airstrips throughout the country.

Society

KEY FACTS 2010

Population per sq km:	17
Life expectancy:	49 years
Net primary enrolment:	92%

Population: 13,089,000 (2010); 36% lives in urban areas and 11% in urban agglomerations of more than 1 million people; growth 2.5% p.a. 1990–2010; birth rate 46 per 1,000 people (49 in 1970); life expectancy 49 years; it fell from a peak of about 52 years in the latter 1980s, due to AIDS, but began to rise again in the early 2000s.

There are 73 indigenous ethnic groups of Bantu origin. The largest, representing about 18% of the population, is the Bemba of the north-east and Copperbelt. Others include the Tonga of Southern Province, the Nyanja of Eastern Province and Lusaka, and the Lozi of the west. There are small minorities of Europeans and Asians.

Language: English is the official language and is widely spoken. There are seven main African languages: Bemba, Kaonde, Lozi, Lunda, Luvale, Nyanja and Tonga.

Religion: Mainly Christians (denominations include Roman Catholics, Anglicans, Pentecostals, New Apostolic Church, Lutherans, Seventh Day Adventists); Christian beliefs are often blended with traditional beliefs; plus minorities of Muslims and Hindus.

Health: Public spending on health was 3% of GDP in 2009. The health service has suffered under cutbacks required by economic adjustment programmes. 60% of the population uses an improved drinking water source and 49% have access to adequate sanitation facilities (2009). Infant mortality was 69 per 1,000 live births in 2010. Infant mortality rates fell from 141 per 1,000 live births in 1965 to 90 in 1980, then, due to AIDS, rose to 112 in 1999 and only began to fall again in 2002. Malaria is prevalent. There are regular outbreaks of cholera. Zambia was one of the first countries to admit the severity of the AIDS pandemic. AIDS prevention, control and management programmes are given prominence in all health programmes. In 2009, 13.5% of people aged 15–49 were HIV positive.

Education: Public spending on education was 1.3% of GDP in 2008. There are seven years of compulsory primary education starting at age seven, and five years of secondary, with cycles of two and three years. Some 53% of pupils complete primary school (2008). The school year starts in January.

The University of Zambia was established in Lusaka in 1965; Copperbelt University, Kitwe, in 1986; and Mulungushi University, Kabwe, in 2008. There are a number of private universities, including Zambia Open University, which enrolled its first students in 2005 (established 2004), and Cavendish University, Lusaka (established 2004). Literacy among people aged 15–24 is 75% (2009).

Media: The daily newspapers are the state-owned *Zambia Daily Mail* and *Times of Zambia*, and independent *The Post*; all are published in English. Weeklies include the state-owned *Sunday Times of Zambia*.

Zambia National Broadcasting Corporation provides public radio and TV services in the main national languages and English; there are several private commercial and faith radio stations, mainly reaching the urban areas.

There are 11 personal computers (2005) and 100 internet users (2010) per 1,000 people.

Communications: Country code 260; internet domain '.zm'. Most public buildings provide public phones. Mobile phone coverage is limited to urban areas, where there are also some internet cafes.

There are 7 main telephone lines and 416 mobile phone subscriptions per 1,000 people (2010).

Public holidays: New Year's Day, Women's Day (8 March), Youth Day (12 March), Labour Day (1 May), Africa Day (25 May), Heroes' Day (first Monday in July), Unity Day (Tuesday following Heroes' Day), Farmers' Day (first Monday in August), Independence Day (24 October) and Christmas Day.

Religious festivals whose dates vary from year to year include Good Friday and Easter Monday.

Economy

KEY FACTS 2010

GNI:	US$13.8bn
GNI p.c.:	US$1,070
GDP growth:	6.4% p.a. 2006–10
Inflation:	10.8% p.a. 2006–10

With very large reserves of copper and cobalt, Zambia was one of the most prosperous countries in Sub-Saharan Africa until its economy foundered with the slump in world copper prices in the mid-1970s. This landlocked country's transport network was also crucially disrupted by civil unrest or liberation wars in the surrounding countries of Angola, Congo, Mozambique, Namibia, South Africa and Zimbabwe. The economy remains vulnerable to fluctuations in copper prices, and to drought.

The early 1990s was a difficult period, with the impact of a two-year drought being exacerbated by weak copper prices. In 1992, the government launched an economic reform programme with substantial divestment of state enterprises. By 2004, 259 state enterprises had been sold off. In 2006 75% of the shares in Zambia National Commercial Bank (one of the few remaining major state-owned enterprises) was sold to Rabobank (of the Netherlands) and to the Zambian public. The reform programme encouraged a more diversified economy and development of exports such as flowers, fruit and vegetables, gemstones, cotton lint and sugar. It was continued, with the support of the IMF, into the 2000s, when the emphasis was on poverty reduction.

Office of the Auditor General, Zambia

Accountability and transparency

∙∙

Mandate

The Office of the Auditor General (OAG) is a public institution charged with the responsibility of providing external auditing services to the government in order to enhance accountability and transparency in the utilisation of public resources.

The Office is established under Article 121(1) of the Constitution. The head of the institution is the Auditor General, appointed by the President and subject to ratification by the National Assembly.

The duties and responsibilities of the Auditor General are enshrined in:

- Article 121(2) of the Constitution
- The Public Audit Act No. 8 of 1980
- The Public Finance Act No. 15 of 2004

Anna O. Chifungula, Auditor General

Vision

Our vision is to be a professional supreme auditing institution that enhances accountability in the management of public resources in Zambia

Mission

To provide quality auditing and related consultancy services to the government and other institutions in order to enhance accountability and value for money in the management of public resources for the benefit of society.

Goal

To increase the scope and coverage, and improve the quality of audit services in order to contribute to the enhancement of accountability in the management of resources.

Values

Integrity
Confidentiality
Impartiality
Trust

Auditor General Ms Anna O. Chifungula was awarded an achievement award by ACCA for her professionalism and contribution to society through her work as Auditor General of Zambia

21st Commonwealth Auditors-General Conference

Performance

Achievements from 2003 to date

- The Auditor General has offices in all nine provinces of Zambia.
- Following the restructuring that was approved in July 2004, the Office has succeeded in training and recruiting qualified professional staff.
- Under the Public Expenditure Management and Financial Accountability (PEMFA), five new provincial offices and an extension to the head office were constructed.
- Transport logistics for the Office improved with the procurement of 24 additional motor vehicles for the nine provincial offices under PEMFA; 45 vehicles have been procured under government funding between 2006 and 2010.

Staff editing the Auditor General's report

- The Office has improved its communication through Information Technology. Through its website the Office has managed to disseminate information to its various stakeholders.
- Audit timing has improved due to the advancements in data extraction through Computer Aided Audit Techniques (CAAT) software.
- Audit quality issues have been improved by developing the Code of Ethics, standardising working papers, audit manuals and guidelines.

Focus is now on Performance Audits (value for money) to ensure the three E's are achieved: Economy, Efficiency and Effectiveness in resource utilisation.

The outcome has been:

- Increased number of audit staff from 90 in 2003 to 356 in 2010. Increase in chartered accountants (CIMA and ACCA) holders from five in 2003 to 80 in 2010.
- Increase in MBA and degree holders from nil in 2003 to 56 in 2010. Audit coverage increased from 30 per cent in 2003 to 80 per cent in 2010.
- Now able to audit local councils where major misapplication and misappropriation of government resources have occurred.
- Now able to audit 36 of the 72 districts in Zambia.

Impact of our quality audit report has been:

- The Executive through the Ministry of Finance has ensured that to date 93 per cent of the audit recommendations by Public Accounts Committee (PAC) are executed.
- There has been increased commitment by PAC to the Auditor General's report.
- Media coverage on our report has increased as all the private media and pubic media cover PAC hearings.
- Government support has increased through increased funding to our office from US$420,924 in 2003 to US$9,064,964.34 in 2010.
- Increased co-operating partners' confidence in accountability and transparency of expenditures in government finances; Institutional Capacity Building support to our office has increased from US$1,027,607 in 2003 to US$10,833,123.50 in 2010.

International relations and audit activities

The Office is a member of international organisations such as:

- The International Organization of Supreme Audit Institutions (INTOSAI), and an active member and participant in the activities of its sub-groupings such as:
  - Working Group on Environmental Auditing
  - Public Debt Work Group
  - Economic Regulation and Private, Public Partnership
- The African Organization of Supreme Audit Institutions (AFROSAI) and one of its language sub-groups, the African Organization for Supreme Audit Institutions – English speaking (AFROSAI-E)
- Conference of Commonwealth Auditors General

Awards

The OAG is recognised as a **platinum employer** by the Association of Certified Chartered Accountants (ACCA).

Contact

Office of the Auditor General
Plot 7951
Haile Selassie Avenue
P.O. Box 50071, Lusaka, Zambia

Tel: +260 211 25 5760-2
Fax: +260 211 25 0349
Email: auditorg@ago.gov.zm
www.ago.gov.zm

Real Growth in GDP

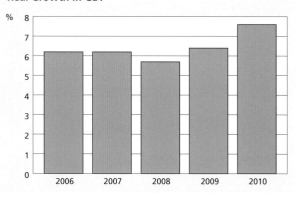

Inflation

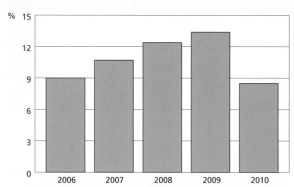

GDP by Sector (2010)

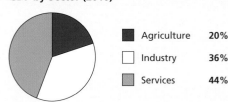

■ Agriculture	**20%**
□ Industry	**36%**
▩ Services	**44%**

Tight fiscal policy brought inflation down from the very high levels of the mid-1990s (183% in 1993) to be generally in single figures from the mid-2000s. Privatisation of the copper mines by 2000 resulted in new investment and better management, and by 2004 world copper prices were rising. However, the decision in 2002 of Anglo-American to pull out of mining in Zambia for a time put in peril the higher levels of growth needed to reduce poverty.

Zambia qualified in 2005 for debt relief under the IMF/World Bank Heavily Indebted Poor Countries Initiative, deriving US$224 million in debt relief, which released it from 80% of its annual debt-service commitments.

This development reflected macroeconomic stability and sound fiscal policies, which had resulted in good growth in the 2000s, strengthening to an average 5.9% p.a. over 2005–09. Zambia maintained a good growth rate in 2008 (5.7%) and in 2009–11 (6.8% p.a.), despite the adverse international economic climate.

Constitution

Status:	Republic with executive president
Legislature:	Parliament
Independence:	24 October 1964

The 1996 constitution provides for an executive president, who is head of state and commander-in-chief of the armed forces. The president is limited to a maximum of two five-year terms. The vice-president and the cabinet are appointed by the president from the National Assembly. The cabinet is responsible for formulating policy and for advising the president on policy. It is accountable to the National Assembly.

The legislative powers of the republic are vested in parliament, which consists of the president and the National Assembly, whose 150 members are elected every five years from single-member constituencies. The president has the power to nominate eight special members of the National Assembly, five of whom can serve in the cabinet.

Both the president and the National Assembly are elected by universal adult suffrage. The election regulations are drawn up by an Electoral Commission, which may also prescribe and review the limits of constituency boundaries. The constitution contains a bill of rights, setting out the fundamental rights and freedoms of the individual, and providing protection from discrimination on the grounds of race, tribe, gender, place of origin, marital status, political opinions, colour or creed.

The most controversial of the recommendations of the draft report of the National Constitutional Conference, published in July 2009, concerned limiting the powers of the president and changing the basis of presidential elections so that presidents are elected by at least 50% of the electorate, rather than the simple majority required by the 1996 constitution, thus introducing the potential for multiple rounds of voting. Supporters of this change believed that this would strengthen the prospects of a fragmented opposition, while detractors argued it would increase the cost of elections.

Politics

Last elections:	September 2011 (presidential and legislative)
Next elections:	2016 (presidential and legislative)
Head of state:	President Michael Sata
Head of government:	the president
Ruling party:	Patriotic Front

In May 2001 Vice-President Christon Tembo and more than 80 senior members of the Movement for Multiparty Democracy (MMD) left the party to form the Forum for Democracy and Development (FDD). Since, under the 1996 constitution, Frederick Chiluba could not stand for a third term of office and he was unable to muster enough support for constitutional change, Levy Patrick Mwanawasa was chosen in August as MMD's candidate for the 2001 presidential election, the third since the restoration of multiparty politics in July 1990.

In a very close contest and with only 29% of the votes Mwanawasa won the December 2001 presidential election, Anderson Mazoka of the United Party for National Development (UPND) came second with 27%, Tembo (FDD) secured 13%, Tilyeni Kaunda (United National Independence Party – UNIP) 10% and Ben

---

Private and faith-based training institutions have taken the lead in Zambia to provide quality health professional education and training. Lusaka Apex Medical University (LAMU) and Churches Health Association of Zambia (CHAZ) are effectively contributing towards resolving the critical skilled human resource shortage in Zambia and the southern Africa sub-region, and provide new options for domestic capacity building that are more cost efficient than studying abroad.

Churches Health Association of Zambia

CHAZ with its 144 hospitals and other health facilities, operated by various Christian denominations on a not-for-profit basis, is a major partner to government in the health service delivery in rural areas. Eleven of the health facilities are training schools for nurses and laboratory technicians.

CHAZ provides a package of integrated curative and preventive health services:

- Public health education concerning diseases such as Malaria, Tuberculosis, HIV/AIDS, maternal and child health.
- Procurement, storage and distribution of health and non-health products, and support to church health facility supply systems.
- Focus on disease interventions such as Antiretroviral Therapy and Malaria case management.

Training information can be obtained from: **jcti@chaz.org.zm**

P.O. Box 34511, Lusaka, Zambia
Tel: +260 211 23 7328/22 9702
Fax: +260 211 22 3297
E-mail: ed@chaz.org.zm
www.chazhealth.org.zm

Lamu Apex Medical University

LAMU is Zambia's first privately-owned medical university and offers training in most medical and health related disciplines in an endeavour to supplement government efforts to develop professional human resources in the health sector.

LAMU provides:

- training opportunities to high school leavers wishing to pursue a career in medicine and other health-related professions.
- options for qualified health professionals to upgrade and improve their academic qualifications through various postgraduate programmes.
- targeted training, in-service and short course programmes, in selected areas of health services.

LUSAKA APEX MEDICAL UNIVERSITY

P.O. BOX 31909, LUSAKA, ZAMBIA
Tel: +260 211 29 3800
E-mail: lamu@coppernet.zm
www.lamuniversity.org

Mwila (Republican Party) 5%. In the simultaneous general election the MMD won 69 seats, the UPND 49, UNIP 13 and the FDD 12, but, even with its eight nominated members, the MMD was short of an absolute majority. The opposition was, however, fragmented and during 2003 Mwanawasa encouraged further fragmentation by bringing several individual opposition members into positions in his government.

In a fiercely contested presidential election in September 2006, Mwanawasa won a second term substantially increasing his share of the votes to 43%. Michael Sata of the Patriotic Front came second with 29% of the votes; Hakainde Hichilema of United Democratic Alliance came third with 25%. In the simultaneous parliamentary elections Mwanawasa's MMD gained 72 seats and with the eight nominated members a narrow overall majority over the Patriotic Front (46 seats) and the United Democratic Alliance (27).

President Levy Mwanawasa suffered a stroke in June 2008 and died in August of that year. Vice-President Rupiah Banda became acting president in June 2008 and was sworn in as president in November, shortly after he won the October 2008 presidential by-election with 40.6% of votes. He defeated Sata of the Patriotic Front (38.6%) and Hichilema of the UPND (20%). Turnout was 45%.

Presidential, parliamentary and local elections were held on the same day in September 2011. Michael Sata (Patriotic Front) won the presidential election, securing about 43% of the votes cast; the incumbent Banda (MMD) took about 36% and Hichilema (UPND) about 18%. In the parliamentary elections the Patriotic Front won 60 seats, MMD 55 and UPND 28. A Commonwealth observer group led by former Nigerian president General Yakubu Gowon affirmed that the elections represented further progress for Zambia in strengthening its democratic processes and that voters were able to express their will freely.

International relations

Zambia is a member of the African, Caribbean and Pacific Group of States, African Union, Common Market for Eastern and Southern Africa, Non-Aligned Movement, Southern African Development Community, United Nations and World Trade Organization.

Zambia hosts the headquarters of the Common Market for Eastern and Southern Africa in Lusaka.

Traveller information

Local laws and conventions: Possession or use of illegal drugs is prohibited and punishments can be severe.

Visitors are able to take photographs in most places but are advised to avoid military installations. Permission must be sought before taking photographs of local residents. Tipping in hotels has been abolished by law, and a 10% sales tax is usually added to bills.

Customs and traditional beliefs vary between the different regions of Zambia. Shaking hands is the normal form of greeting.

Formal dress is expected for business meetings and English is widely used. Office hours are Mon–Fri 0800–1300 and 1400–1700.

Immigration and customs: Passports must be valid for at least six months beyond the intended length of stay, and should also contain at least two blank pages. Nationals of Commonwealth countries do not require visas to enter Zambia except for the

following countries that have a reciprocal visa regime with Zambia: Australia, Canada, The Gambia, Ghana, India, New Zealand, Nigeria, Pakistan, Papua New Guinea, Sri Lanka, Sierra Leone, and the UK. More often than not, nationals of non-Commonwealth countries require visas.

A yellow fever vaccination certificate will be required by all those arriving from infected areas.

Customs may ask to see prescriptions for any medication bought into Zambia. Souvenirs may be exported without restriction but game trophies, such as teeth, bones, horns, shells, claws, skin, hair, feathers or other durable items are subject to export permits.

Travel within the country: Traffic drives on the left and visitors will need an international driving permit to drive. Car hire is available in several main cities. The general speed limit on national highways is 100kph and is reduced to 65kph in built-up areas. It is illegal to drink-drive or to use a mobile phone while driving.

There are three main train lines which operate frequent services from Livingstone to Lusaka, from Lusaka to the Copperbelt, and from Kapiri Mposhi to the northern border with United Republic of Tanzania. Chartered flights also run services between the main centres.

There is a network of buses connecting the major towns; buses are generally frequent, clean and inexpensive. Urban bus services are provided by private minibuses. Taxis are widely available but are not metered and fares should be agreed in advance. Chauffeur-driven cars are also available to hire.

Travel health: Comprehensive medical insurance that includes emergency air evacuation is recommended.

Visitors will need protection against malaria as well as insect repellent and suitable clothing to prevent mosquito bites. Tuberculosis is present in some parts of the country and it may be advisable to be vaccinated against this, although all up-to-date vaccination requirements must be checked well in advance of travel. Outbreaks of cholera and dysentery are frequent, especially in the rainy season.

All water should be filtered and boiled or bought in sealed bottles.

Money: The local currency is the kwacha. Only reputable banks and bureaux should be used for changing foreign currency, as there are counterfeit notes in circulation. Major credit cards are increasingly being accepted, though paper transactions rather than electronic are the norm. Travellers cheques are widely accepted and should be taken in US dollars, pounds sterling or euros to avoid additional exchange rate charges. ATMs are available that accept Visa. Banking hours are Mon–Fri 0815–1430. (Some banks open 0815–1030 on the first and last Saturday of the month.)

There were 812,000 tourist arrivals in 2008.

Further information

Office of the President, Republic of Zambia: www.statehouse.gov.zm

Parliament: www.parliament.gov.zm

Bank of Zambia: www.boz.zm

Commonwealth Secretariat: www.thecommonwealth.org

Commonwealth of Nations: www.commonwealth-of-nations.org/Zambia

Reference

Directory of Commonwealth Organisations

The Commonwealth is often described as a 'family' of nations and peoples. The sense of family is most apparent in the wide network of societies, institutions, associations, organisations, funds and charities that support the Commonwealth. This network links people of different nations, ethnicities, cultures and trajectories of economic development, enabling diverse professions, businesses (public and private) and civil society initiatives to learn from one another.

The directory lists intergovernmental and non-governmental associations of different types. The intergovernmental organisations are those set up by Commonwealth governments to organise co-operation (e.g. Commonwealth of Learning). Non-governmental or civil society organisations listed here are those that serve the Commonwealth by facilitating co-operation in some professional, cultural or welfare area, foster Commonwealth friendship, or in other ways advance the aims of the Harare Commonwealth Declaration.

Wider international bodies – even those that are very important to Commonwealth countries – are not included in this list, with the exception of those that had their roots in the Commonwealth and have since spread more widely, but still have a largely Commonwealth constituency (e.g. Sightsavers).

This directory is intended to be a comprehensive listing of Commonwealth organisations and each year, as new organisations come to our attention, they are included. Please write to the editor if you know of an organisation that should be included, but is not.

Association for Commonwealth Literature and Language Studies (ACLALS)*

c/o Department of Literatures in English, University of the West Indies, Mona Campus, Kingston 7, Jamaica

Tel: +876 927 2217
Fax: +876 927 4232
Contact: Tanya Shirley (Secretary/Treasurer)

An association of academics, practitioners and writers, ACLALS assists and promotes the study and research of Commonwealth literatures and languages.

Foundation: 1964

Accredited to the Commonwealth: 2005

Affiliated to the International Federation for Modern Languages and Literature (FILLM) and the Commonwealth Consortium for Education (CCfE).

Officers: Dr Michael A Bucknor (Department of Literatures in English, University of the West Indies, Mona Campus, Kingston 7, Jamaica); Vice-Chairs: Professor Evelyn O'Callaghan (Barbados), Dr Patricia Saunders (Trinidad and Tobago/USA); Secretary/Treasurer: Tanya Shirley (Jamaica).

There are regional chairs for the different chapters of the association which are in Canada, the Caribbean, Europe, India, Malaysia, South Africa, South Pacific, Sri Lanka, East Africa and the USA. These branches hold an annual or a triennial conference in their regions, while ACLALS holds its major conference triennially. The next conference is scheduled to be held in St Lucia, in 2013.

Note

* indicates that this organisation is accredited to the Commonwealth. Accreditation provides formal recognition for Commonwealth organisations and establishes their membership in the Commonwealth Association. It indicates to other organisations and to the public that the organisation meets the Commonwealth's eligibility criteria, and is committed to the purposes and goals of the Commonwealth.

(The) Association of Commonwealth Universities (ACU)*

Woburn House, 20–24 Tavistock Square, London WC1H 9HF, UK

Tel: +44 20 7380 6700
Fax: +44 20 7387 2655
Email: info@acu.ac.uk
www.acu.ac.uk

The ACU is the oldest international inter-university network in the world, with over 500 member institutions spread across six continents. Its mission is to strengthen the higher education institutions within its membership through international co-operation and understanding.

Foundation: 1913

Officers: Chair of Council: Professor E Nigel Harris, Vice-Chancellor of the University of the West Indies, Jamaica; Secretary-General: Professor John Wood CBE FREng

Activities: The ACU's portfolio of services includes: an annual Conference of Executive Heads; professional networks in key functional areas (Research Management, Human Resource Management, Public Relations, Marketing and Communications, Libraries and Information, University Extension, Graduate Employment); a benchmarking programme enabling participating universities to compare key management processes; research and policy analysis; negotiated discounts on recruitment advertising and academic journals. The ACU also leads and supports a range of programmes in the field of international higher education, contributing its expertise in generating partnerships and networking opportunities. The ACU provides the secretariat for the Commonwealth Scholarship Commission in the UK, the Marshall Aid Commemoration Commission, the Commonwealth Universities Study Abroad Consortium, and the Staff and Educational Development Association.

Publications: *Bulletin* (4 issues a year), *ACU Insights* (monthly), *Research Global* (3 issues a year), *Capacity* (2 issues a year), *Impact* (3 issues a year), *LINK* (3 issues a year), *Genius* (2 issues a year), *Annual Report*; and various reports and papers on key issues in international higher education.

Commonwealth Advisory Bureau (CA/B)

Institute of Commonwealth Studies, University of London, Senate House, London WC1E 7HU, UK

Tel: +44 20 7862 8865
Fax: +44 20 7862 8813
Email: CAB@sas.ac.uk
www.commonwealthadvisorybureau.org

The Commonwealth Advisory Bureau is the independent think-tank and advisory service for the modern Commonwealth of 54 nations and some two billion citizens. Part of the Institute of Commonwealth Studies, University of London, it specialises in issues of Commonwealth policy including globalisation, democracy, civil society and human rights.

Foundation: 1999 (established as the Commonwealth Policy Studies Unit)

Officers: Director: Daisy Cooper; Assistant Director: Dr Leo Zeilig

Activities: CA/B runs projects in numerous countries across the Commonwealth. It produces quality research-based reports and briefings to inform and influence policy-makers in over one-quarter of the world's countries. It seeks to put the policy choices before the Commonwealth into sharper focus, exploring options and suggesting new directions. CA/B projects are changing the way people think on issues such as making elections fairer, recognising the needs of indigenous peoples and assisting development in small island states. It is committed to continuing its work to inform and improve policy- and decision-making across the Commonwealth.

The CA/B's Policy Briefing Series provides expert independent analysis and policy advice to decision-makers around the Commonwealth. The series includes an in-depth Policy Briefing ahead of every Commonwealth Heads of Government Meeting as well as various Commonwealth ministerial meetings, including Education, Finance, Health, Law and Youth.

CA/B also offers confidential and impartial advice to countries interested in applying to join the Commonwealth, and can help existing member countries make the most of Commonwealth membership for maximum impact at home and abroad.

(The) Commonwealth Association*

c/o 19 Rosebery Gardens, London W13 0HD, UK

Tel: +44 7710 842886
Email: info@comassoc.org
General information and enquiries: Cheryl Dorall (tel: +44 7710 842886)
www.comassoc.org

The association's membership is drawn from former staff members of the Commonwealth Secretariat, Commonwealth Foundation, Commonwealth of Learning, and salaried staff from Commonwealth organisations and associations which are accredited to the Commonwealth by the Commonwealth Secretariat. Former staff of Commonwealth Youth Programme (CYP) Centres, and experts and volunteers who have served the Commonwealth Fund for Technical Co-operation (CFTC) or the Commonwealth Service Abroad Programme (CSAP) are also eligible to be members.

The association offers active support for the values of the Commonwealth and the programmes of the Commonwealth Secretariat, Commonwealth Foundation, Commonwealth of Learning and other Commonwealth organisations.

Foundation: 2001

Officers: Chairperson: Patsy Robertson; Vice-Chair: Stuart Mole; Secretary: Cheryl Dorall

Activities: In general, networking with other Commonwealth organisations in support of common objectives; organising public talks on current affairs issues. Since 2007, organising oral history of major programmes and projects of the Commonwealth Secretariat; joint campaign in support of the people of Zimbabwe; fundraising for young albinos in Tanzania to get better education and healthcare. In 2011, organised major briefing on the theme of reform of the Commonwealth ahead of CHOGM 2011 summit.

Commonwealth Association of Architects (CAA)*

PO Box 1166 Stamford PE2 2HL, UK

Tel: +44 1780 238091
Fax: +44 1780 238091
Email: admin@comarchitect.org
www.comarchitect.org

CAA is a membership organisation for institutes representing architects in Commonwealth countries. Formed in 1965 to promote co-operation for advancement of architecture in the Commonwealth, it currently has 33 members.

Officers: President: Mubasshar Hussain (Bangladesh); Senior Vice-President: Rukshan Widyalankara (Sri Lanka); Immediate past president: Gordon Holden (Australia); Honorary Secretary/Treasurer: Nick Willson (UK); Chair of Education: Mansur Ahmadu (Nigeria); Chair of Validation Panel: Clare Newton (UK); Chair of Practice: Christos Panayiotides (Cyprus); Chair of Communication: Jayantha Perera (Sri Lanka); Vice-President Africa (West): Jimoh Farowaja (Nigeria); Vice-President Americas: William Harris (Guyana); Vice-President Asia: Chandana Edirisuriya (Sri Lanka); Vice-President Europe: Vincent Cassar (Malta); Vice-President Oceania: John Sinclair (New Zealand); Executive Director: Tony Godwin (UK)

Activities: CAA runs a multinational validation system for inter-recognition of courses in architecture enhancing standards in architectural

education and facilitating mobility of students and practising architects between courses and countries. CAA promotes the exchange of architectural knowledge and runs a triennial General Assembly and conference hosted by a member institute together with an international student competition. CAA has developed 'An architect's guide to designing for sustainability' and works at CHOGM together with the other Commonwealth built environment professions as BEPIC to raise awareness of, and to promote solution to, the challenges of rapid urbanisation.

Commonwealth Association of Museums*

PO Box 30192, Chinook Postal Outlet, Calgary, Alberta T2H 2V9, Canada

Tel: +1 403 938 3190
Fax: +1 403 938 3190
Email: irvinel@fclc.com
www.maltwood.uvic.ca/cam

The Commonwealth Association of Museums is a professional association supported by the Commonwealth Foundation, London. Its focus is on the role of cultural institutions in strengthening civil society. In order to work towards the betterment of museums and their societies, its aims are to: promote professional training and development of Commonwealth museum workers; promote links between museums and among museum workers and between museums and their communities; and collaborate with international organisations and individuals to promote museums. Membership is open to institutions, associations and individuals from the Commonwealth and associates from outside the Commonwealth. There are members in 40 countries.

Foundation: 1974

Officers: President of the Executive Council: Rooksana Omar (South Africa); Past president: Martin Segger (Canada); International Treasurer and London Representative: Timothy Mason (UK); Secretary-General: Lois Irvine (Canada)

Commonwealth Association of Paediatric Gastroenterology and Nutrition (CAPGAN)*

c/o Professor B Sandhu, Bristol Royal Hospital for Children, Upper Maudlin Street, Bristol BS2 8BJ, UK

Tel: +44 117 342 8828; +44 7977 411429
Fax: +44 117 342 8831
Email: bhupinder.sandhu@uhbristol.nhs.uk
bsandhu@blackberry.orange.co.uk
www.capgan.org

CAPGAN promotes the knowledge of and training in paediatric gastroenterology, hepatology and nutrition (PGHAN) throughout the Commonwealth, but especially among developing countries. It also fosters collaborative research in these fields; is a source of authoritative advice to both national and international agencies within the Commonwealth on the problems of paediatric gastroenterology and hepatology, and in particular the problems of childhood diarrhoea and malnutrition; and advocates for the needs of children particularly in relation to nutritional and diarrhoeal diseases and for an even distribution of resources. It is affiliated to 22 paediatric societies/associations within the Commonwealth. A recent biennial scientific meeting was held at the Institute of Child Health in London on 21–23 July 2011 with a reception at

Marlborough House (capgan2011@gmail.com; visit www.capgan.org/Meeting2011/CAPGANmeeting 2011.pdf), and before that in Blantyre, Malawi, in August 2009. The next meeting will be as part of World Congress of PGHAN in Taipei, Taiwan, 14–18 November 2012, and then Sri Lanka in 2013.

Foundation: 1984

Officers: President: Professor Tahmeed Ahmed; Immediate past president: Professor Bhupinder Sandhu; President-elect: Professor David Brewster; Secretary: Dr Barbara Golden; Treasurer: Dr Susan Hill

Commonwealth Association of Planners (CAP)*

c/o The Royal Town Planning Institute in Scotland, 18 Atholl Crescent, Edinburgh EH3 8HQ, UK

Tel: +44 131 229 9628
Fax: +44 131 229 9332
Email: annette.odonnell@rtpi.org.uk
www.commonwealth-planners.org

CAP seeks to focus and develop the skills of urban and regional planners across the Commonwealth to meet the challenges of urbanisation and the sustainable development of human settlements. There are two classes of membership. Full membership is open to national organisations of professional planners in Commonwealth countries and international organisations of individual professional planners in Commonwealth countries where no national organisation of professional planners exists. Affiliate membership is open to organisations in Commonwealth countries involved in professional activities in national, regional and local planning, and organisations in Commonwealth countries involved in planning education and research.

Officers: President and Chief Executive: Christine Platt MRTPI (South Africa); Secretary-General: Clive Harridge MRTPI (UK)

Commonwealth Association of Polytechnics in Africa (CAPA)

c/o Kenya Polytechnic University College, Haile Selasse Avenue, Nairobi, Kenya; PO Box 52428-00200, Nairobi, Kenya

Tel: +254 20 2249 974
Email: capa@kenpoly.ac.ke
www.capa-online.org

The Association was formed on the recommendation of the 7th Commonwealth Education Conference held in Accra, Ghana, in March 1977. It was envisaged that CAPA would play a role similar to that of the Association of Commonwealth Universities, but with a focus on Africa. CAPA groups together about 150 institutions in 17 African countries. Its main objective is the promotion of technical and vocational education and training, technology transfer and skills development in Africa. It does this through policy advocacy and dialogue with governments, development partners and educational institutions, as well as networking and information sharing among member institutions.

Foundation: 1978

Officers: Secretary-General: Dr Olubunmi Owoso

The mission of CAPA is to provide a dynamic forum for:

- gathering, testing and sharing innovative ideas in technical and vocational education and training (TVET)

- promotion of capacity-building initiatives, and
- policy analysis and advocacy in favour of skills development for wealth creation.

The motto for CAPA is 'Championing Excellence in Skills Development'.

Commonwealth Association for Public Administration and Management (CAPAM)*

L'Esplanade Laurier, 300 Laurier Avenue West, West Tower, Room A-1245, Ottawa, Ontario K1N 6Z2, Canada

Tel: +1 613 996 5026
Fax: +1 613 947 9223
Email: capam@capam.org
www.capam.org

CAPAM is a membership organisation dedicated to strengthening public management and consolidating democracy and good governance throughout the Commonwealth. It achieves this by building networks across the Commonwealth, through which it exchanges experiences on new developments, innovations and the reform of public administration.

Foundation: 1994

Officers: President: Paul Zahra (Malta); Vice-President: Ramesh Misra (India); Honorary Treasurer: Lim Soo Hoon (Singapore); Executive Director: David Waung

Activities: Conferences and seminars designed to promote networking and to advance innovation in public management, including: the annual Senior Public Executive Seminar; the annual Integrated Service Delivery Seminar; customised in-country executive seminars; and thematic regional seminars. The International Innovations Awards Programme (since 1997), with gold, silver and bronze winners, is announced at the biennial conferences. CAPAM has established a repository of materials on good practice in public administration housed online in the CAPAM e-library.

Publications: *Commonwealth Innovations* (quarterly); *International Review of Administrative Science* (quarterly); CAPAM Featured Reports (conferences).

Commonwealth Association of Public Sector Lawyers

PO Box 403, Mosman, New South Wales 2088, Australia

Tel: +61 2 9969 3298
Fax: +61 2 9969 3298
Email: capsl@bigpond.com
www.capsl.org

An association of lawyers with a professional concern to promote interest in public sector law and its practice in the Commonwealth, and to provide a focus and forum for the exchange of information and ideas.

Foundation: 1996

Officers: Acting Chair: Greg Ross (Australia); Secretary: Greg Ross (Australia); Assistant Secretary: Nigel Roberts (UK); Treasurer: Michael Antrum (Australia)

Activities: The organisation provides opportunities for contact, and facilitating and promoting exchange and secondment arrangements, between Commonwealth countries. It holds seminars on public sector legal issues.

Commonwealth Association of Science, Technology and Mathematics Educators (CASTME)*

c/o Scholarships Department, University of Westminster, 101 New Cavendish Street, London W1W 6XH, UK

UK Secretary, Chris McLaren
Email: Chris.McLaren@winchester.ac.uk
www.castme.org.uk

CASTME works to advance the social relevance of the teaching of science, technology and mathematics through networking of educators in these subjects in the Commonwealth and promote this through delivering the relevant Millennium Development Goals (MDGs).

Foundation: 1974

Officers: Chair: Colin Matheson, University of Westminster (email: mathesc@westminster.ac.uk); Administrator: Chris McLaren

Activities: The association promotes networking between science, technology and mathematics educators to promote good practice in the teaching of science, technology and mathematics, and in the development of curricula and learning materials and activities for learners with an emphasis on the MDGs. CASTME publishes a journal focusing on socially relevant aspects of the subjects and the links between them. An electronic newsletter was established in the Commonwealth Year of Science and Technology (2010) to update members and interested educators. To promote innovations, CASTME runs an annual award scheme in which teachers and teacher educators are invited to submit completed innovative projects. Professionals from some 35 Commonwealth countries have received such awards. At the present time CASTME has branches in Europe, Mauritius, Asia and Africa. CASTME has also developed a number of capacity-building scholarships with the University of Westminster (UK), for suitably qualified applicants to take Masters programmes and who will return to their home countries to develop CASTME's aims and in particular the MDGs. It established a number of new initiatives in 2010 for the Commonwealth Year of Science and Technology.

Commonwealth Association of Surveying and Land Economy (CASLE)*

c/o Faculty of Environment and Technology, School of the Built and Natural Environment, University of the West of England, Bristol BS16 1QY, UK

Tel: +44 117 328 3036
Fax: +44 117 328 3036
Email: susan.spedding@uwe.ac.uk
eborrill@btinternet.com
chitra.weddikkara@gmail.com
www.casle.org

CASLE helps to form and develop professional bodies in its field, and to set standards for all specialisms in surveying including land and marine surveying, quantity surveying, estate management and land economy. It helps Commonwealth countries to acquire the quantity and quality of indigenous skills in surveying and land economy required to carry out their social and economic development programmes.

Foundation: 1969

Officers: President: Professor Chitra Weddikkara (Sri Lanka); Secretary-General: Edward Borrill; Assistant Secretary-General: Susan Spedding; Honorary Treasurer: Barry Woodman

Commonwealth Association of Tax Administrators (CATA)*

c/o Commonwealth Secretariat, Marlborough House, Pall Mall, London SW1Y 5HX, UK

Tel: +44 20 7747 6473/4
Fax: +44 20 7747 6225
Email: cata@commonwealth.int
www.cata-tax.org

CATA is an intergovernmental organisation established by Commonwealth finance ministers to promote the improvement of tax administration in all its aspects within the Commonwealth with particular emphasis on developing countries. The long-term objective is to provide training to tax officials in technical and administrative skills, adopt best practices and to build capacity in tax administrations enabling member governments to evolve well-designed, equitable and revenue-optimising tax systems backed by efficient, modern and effective tax administrations.

Foundation: 1978

Officers: President: M Sudhamo Lal (Mauritius); Chairman: Lloyd Muhara (Malawi); Acting Vice-Chairman: Peter Steeds (UK); Executive Director: Tutu Bakwena (Botswana)

Commonwealth Broadcasting Association (CBA)*

17 Fleet Street, London EC4Y 1AA, UK

Tel: +44 20 7583 5550
Fax: +44 20 7583 5549
Email: cba@cba.org.uk
www.cba.org.uk

The CBA has been supporting and working with public service broadcasters (PSBs) across the Commonwealth since 1945. It has more than 100 members in over 50 countries and currently focuses on supporting PSBs through digital transition.

Foundation: 1945

Secretariat: Secretary-General: Sally-Ann Wilson (sally-ann@cba.org.uk); Finance Manager: Mervyn Warner; Project Manager: Jasmine Dhariwal (jas@cba.org.uk); Project Manager: Adam Weatherhead (adam@cba.org.uk); Researcher: Mandy Turner (mandy@cba.org.uk)

Activities: The CBA holds a biennial pan-Commonwealth broadcasting conference. The next conference, on the theme of Media Leadership in Crisis, Emergency and Disaster, takes place in Brisbane, Australia, in April 2012. The CBA offers members high quality training courses in all areas of broadcasting. It produces a number of specialist publications on subjects such as broadcasting regulation and editorial guidelines. Additionally, it runs a News Exchange, facilitating the exchange of news stories between participating members, and WorldView, which provides funding and assistance for producers to improve UK media coverage – of the wider world. Your WorldView is an online platform for new and emerging film-makers to showcase their work to broadcasters and debate development issues.

Publications: *CBA Annual Directory and Handbook*. A new professional media journal is to be launched in spring 2012.

Commonwealth Business Council (CBC)*

18 Pall Mall, London SW1Y 5LU, UK

Tel: +44 20 7024 8200
Fax: +44 20 7024 8201
Email: info@cbcglobal.org
www.cbcglobal.org

CBC promotes economic empowerment for shared prosperity within the Commonwealth and beyond. To this end, CBC works to promote and facilitate trade and investment across the Commonwealth and between emerging and developed markets, improve corporate citizenship, national and international economic governance, and further the spread of e-commerce and the use of ICTs for development. CBC is a membership organisation, bringing together 120 major companies from the Commonwealth, including many industry leaders and some of the world's largest companies. CBC also works very closely with its public sector constituency, bringing together the private sector and governments on a range of issues important to the economic development of all member countries.

Foundation: 1997

Officers: CBC is managed by a Board of Management, chosen from among its Council membership, co-chaired by Dr Mohan Kaul (UK) and John Denton (Australia); Director-General and CEO: Sir Alan Collins KCVO CMG

Activities: Policy papers and programmes; investment and trade conferences and workshops, including the Commonwealth Business Forum and national and regional investment forums; topical working groups and allied activities; and advisory services to individual governments on economic and commercial matters. All these activities aim at improved collaboration by Commonwealth governments and business on trade and investment for shared prosperity. CBC also offers a range of commercial services to both public and private constituents, including education and training services, publication services, technology services and business support, and business introduction services.

Publications: Policy reports and submissions to Commonwealth Heads of Government and ministerial meetings; investment surveys, business environment surveys, specially commissioned studies and conference reports; and newsletter.

Commonwealth Centre for Electronic Governance (CCEG)

c/o Rajkumar Prasad (CEO), B 5/2, IIND Floor, Model Town-I, Delhi 110009, India

Tel: +91 981 006 3137
Email: rajkumar@electronicgovindia.net
www.electronicgovindia.net

The mission of CCEG is to promote electronic governance by providing a knowledge base of best practices and policies for information technology implementation in public-sector organisations. CCEG also advises and provides expertise to governments around the world on e-governance, e-government and e-democracy. It delivers courses on the implementation of e-governance. Membership comprises representatives of government agencies and non-profit organisations from all regions of the Commonwealth. CCEG has a board of directors, a patron's committee and an advisory council.

The Centre works with the Commonwealth Secretariat's programmes on e-governance and e-government, while drawing expertise and financial resources from the developed countries of the Commonwealth. It is a designated think-tank of the Commonwealth Secretariat.

Officers: Chair, Advisory Council: Michael Turner (Canada); Vice-Chair, Advisory Council: Rogers W'O Okot-Uma; Chief Executive and Chair of Board of Directors: Professor Thomas B Riley

Commonwealth Consortium for Education (CCfE)*

Commonwealth House, 7 Lion Yard, Tremadoc Road, London SW4 7NQ, UK

Tel: +44 1306 501788 (Honorary Secretary)
Fax: +44 1306 501788 (Honorary Secretary)
Email: peterrcwilliams@onetel.com
www.commonwealtheducation.org

The objectives of the Consortium are to promote the development of education throughout the Commonwealth by mobilising the contribution of education-based NGOs, and to constitute a forum to promote co-operation among member organisations. Membership is open to any pan-Commonwealth organisation in the fields of education, youth and culture, with associate membership available to other international or national Commonwealth organisations sharing the Consortium's objectives. In 2011 there were 17 full members and five associate members.

Foundation: 2001

Officers: Chair: Professor Colin Power (CASTME); Alternate Chair: Mark Robinson (CHEC); Communications Secretary: Stephen Blunden (Link Community Development); Honorary Secretary: Peter Williams (Council for Education in the Commonwealth); Treasurer: John Wood (ACU)

Activities

- A major conference every three years to coincide with the Conferences of Commonwealth Education Ministers

  – in 2003 (15CCEM in Edinburgh) on 'the recruitment, retention and mobility of teachers'

  – in 2006 (16CCEM in Cape Town) on 'promoting school and college partnerships in the Commonwealth'

  – in 2009 (17CCEM in Kuala Lumpur) on 'learning to live together: education for social cohesion'. Next in series – under consideration – August 2012 at 18CCEM in Mauritius.

- Biennial workshops on the occasion of the Commonwealth People's Forum at CHOGM

  – Valletta 2005: Networking Commonwealth people for implementing the MDGs in education.

  – Kampala 2007: Education for transformation: joined-up policies for Commonwealth education development.

  – Port of Spain 2009: Education for peace-building.

- Projects

  – Summer 2010: with Link Community Development and Zimbabwe Ministry of Education. Two workshops, *Education in Zimbabwe: Working Together for a Better Future*

  – Spring 2011: with Link Community Development and Royal Commonwealth Society. *Using Commonwealth School Partnerships to Promote Commonwealth Citizenship and Awareness*

  – Spring 2012 (planned): in partnership with Link Community Development and others: Workshop in East Africa on *Achievable Education for All*.

- Submissions and representations to Commonwealth bodies and governments on issues concerning Commonwealth education.

- Participation in Commonwealth working groups and consultative meetings.

Publications

- *Implementing the Edinburgh Commonwealth Action Plan for Education* – major report undertaken for the Commonwealth Secretariat in 2005.

- *Working together in Education: A Commonwealth Update* – containing 13 briefing notes on different aspects of Commonwealth education co-operation, 2009.

- *Commonwealth Education Directory* 2009 (being updated for new edition in 2012)

- A quarterly *Commonwealth Education Calendar* of forward meetings and events.

- Annual Report on activities (latest for 2011).

Commonwealth Countries League (CCL)*

c/o Executive Chair and Commonwealth Fair Co-ordinator, 37 Priory Avenue, Sudbury, Middlesex HA0 2SB, UK

Tel: +44 20 8248 3275
Email: rennie158@btinternet.com
www.ccl-int.org

Officers: Hon Secretary: Tricia George (zenisageorge@yahoo.co.uk);

Chairman: Majorie Rennie

Foundation: In 1925, as the British Commonwealth League by a group of women drawn from many of the countries that make up today's Commonwealth, now known as the Commonwealth Countries League.

Objectives: 'To secure equality of liberties, status and opportunities between men and women and to promote mutual understanding and friendship throughout the Commonwealth Countries.'

Structure: The League is administered by an executive committee elected annually by and from the membership. In addition representatives from affiliated organisations can attend the executive meetings on a non-voting basis. A president is appointed at the AGM every three years.

The League is recognised by both the Commonwealth Secretariat and the Commonwealth Foundation for observer status at the triennial meetings of the Commonwealth ministers responsible for women's affairs, the triennial meetings of Commonwealth education ministers and the Commonwealth Heads of Government Meetings.

The CCL works with civil society to promote the education and advancement of women throughout the Commonwealth as a contributory factor in the alleviation of world poverty.

Activities: The CCL has a programme of informative talks and social functions. In 2011 and 2012 it held two conferences on health issues. The CCL organises the annual Commonwealth Fair in association with the high commissioners, the spouses of the high commissioners and affiliated organisations to raise funds for the CCL Education Fund, and administers the CCL Alumnae Association. In 1967 the CCL president while visiting an orphanage in Sierra Leone met a very bright girl needing funds to continue her education. It was then realised that there must be many girls in the Commonwealth with potential who, for a variety of reasons, were unable to fulfil them. This led to the formation of the Commonwealth Countries' League Education Fund, a Secondary Education Sponsorship Scheme for Girls, which became a registered charity in 1982 (see below).

Finance: Members' dues; fund-raising.

NGO relations: Member of:

* Commonwealth Consortium for Education
* Federation of International Women's Associations in London.

Links with:

* International Alliance of Women
* Council of Commonwealth Societies
* Corona Worldwide.

Publications: *News Update* (3 times a year); Annual Report; brochures.

Members: Affiliated societies constituted on national, state or district basis; individuals, open to men and women from all Commonwealth countries.

Commonwealth Countries League Education Fund (CCLEF)

29 Tennyson Street, Swindon SN1 5DT, UK

Tel: +44 1793 616 693; +44 7760 201452 (mobile)
Fax: +44 0870 123 1813
Email: ccl.edfund@googlemail.com
www.ccl-int.org

The Commonwealth Countries League Education Fund – established in 1967 (Registered Charity No. 1048908) – is a secondary/high school sponsorship scheme for girls of academic potential but lacking financial support. They are monitored throughout their sponsorship and the success stories are considerable with these girls. More than 3,000 girls have been supported, becoming teachers, doctors, lawyers, scientists, accountants and agricultural officers. Educated girls, with a highly developed sense of responsibility, provide a better future for themselves, their communities and families.

Officers: Board of Trustees: Jenny Groves (Chairman), Judith Fisher (Hon Treasurer), Ann Chivers, Leolynn Jones, Sheila Kennard, Parveen Yusuf; Anne Munt-Davies, Andrew Fox, Judith Hardy; Fundraiser: Ladi Dariya; Administrative Secretary: Casmir Chanda

Commonwealth Dental Association (CDA)*

c/o Ulrike Matthesius, CDA Administrator, 64 Wimpole Street, London W1G 8YS, UK

Tel: +44 20 7563 4133
Fax: +44 20 7563 4556
Email: administrator@cdauk.com
www.cdauk.com

The CDA aims to improve dental and oral health in Commonwealth countries, by raising the skills of practitioners and increasing the community's awareness of the importance of oral health. CDA's membership comprises the national dental associations in the countries of the Commonwealth, and 'friends' of CDA.

Foundation: 1991

Officers: President: Dr Hilary Cooray (Sri Lanka); President-elect: Dr William O'Reilly (Australia); Executive Secretary: Dr Sam Thorpe OOR (Sierra Leone); Treasurer: Dr Anthony S Kravitz OBE (UK)

Commonwealth Education Trust/Commonwealth Institute*

6th Floor, New Zealand House, 80 Haymarket, London SW1Y 4TE, UK

Tel: +44 20 7024 9822
Fax: +44 20 7024 9833
Email: info@cet1886.org
www.cet1886.org

The CET invests in primary and secondary education and the training and professional development of teachers, thereby enhancing the opportunities for children in the Commonwealth to develop the skills necessary to contribute to the economic and social development of their communities.

Officers: Chair: Judith Hanratty CVO OBE; Vice-Chair: The Lord Fellowes GCB GCVO QSO; Finance Director and Secretary: Judy Curry

Activities: CET works with accredited educationalists and educational centres of excellence to use its financial and business knowledge to structure sustainable, scalable and transferable projects based on applied research.

To this end CET has financed the University of Cambridge to establish a Centre for Commonwealth Education within the Faculty of Education. The activities of the Centre reflect the Faculty's long-standing commitment to, and reputation in, the field of high quality teaching and research in initial and continuing education, in leadership for learning, and in pedagogy and practice within schools and classrooms (www.educ.cam.ac.uk/centres/cce).

CET has financed a five-year longitudinal control and intervention study to evaluate the ways in which lessons in physical activity can affect children's health and educational attainment. Medical practitioners and educationalists from across the Commonwealth contributed to the research and an independent report on the results of the study by the Australian National University is available on application to the Trust.

CET has published an illustrated collection of stories and poems from across the Commonwealth to celebrate the 125th anniversary of the Trust (www.ariverofstories.com).

CET has invested in a wholly owned subsidiary, 1886 Investments Limited, in order to develop the commercial potential of some of its activities and ensure their sustainability.

Commonwealth Engineers Council (CEC)*

One Great George Street, London SW1P 3AA, UK

Tel: +44 20 7665 2005
Fax: +44 20 7223 1806
Email: neil.bailey@ice.org.uk
www.ice.org.uk/cec

The CEC links professional engineering institutions of the Commonwealth to foster co-operation and exchange of information, support the development of indigenous engineering institutions, and foster the education, training and professional development of engineers. The CEC also encourages development of young engineers throughout the Commonwealth, in particular through their engagement in sustainable development and poverty alleviation.

Foundation: 1946

Officers: President: Tom Foulkes; Secretary: Neil Bailey

Commonwealth Forestry Association (CFA)*

The Crib, Dinchope, Craven Arms, Shropshire SY7 9JJ, UK

Tel: +44 1588 672 868
Fax: +44 870 011 6645
Email: cfa@cfa-international.org
www.cfa-international.org

The mission of the CFA is to promote good management, use and conservation of forests and forest lands. Its vision is to promote the well-being of the world's forests and those who benefit from them. Membership is open to nationals of all countries, not just Commonwealth countries.

Foundation: 1921 (as Empire Forestry Association)

Officers: Patron: Queen Elizabeth II; President: Jim Ball; Chair: John Innes; Vice-Chair: Reem Hajjar; Technical Director and Editor: Alan Pottinger

Commonwealth Foundation

Marlborough House, Pall Mall, London SW1Y 5HY, UK

Tel: +44 20 7930 3783
Fax: +44 20 7839 8157
Email: geninfo@commonwealth.int
www.commonwealthfoundation.com

See profile of the Commonwealth Foundation in the 'Official Commonwealth Organisations' section of this publication.

Commonwealth Games Federation (CGF)*

2nd Floor, 138 Piccadilly, London W1J 7NR, UK

Tel: +44 20 7491 8801
Fax: +44 20 7409 7803
Email: info@thecgf.com
www.thecgf.com

First held in 1930 in Hamilton, Canada, today the Commonwealth Games is the world's second-largest multi-sports event, and the fourth most-watched global broadcast sports event. Featuring athletes from 71 nations and territories the Commonwealth Games has provided some of the most memorable moments in world sport; from England's Roger Bannister and Australia's John Landy duelling it out over the 'Miracle Mile' at the 1954 Vancouver Games, to Northern Irish boxer Barry McGuigan winning the Gold at the 1978 Edmonton games – instantly becoming a figure of unity to a then divided nation. The achievements of athletes such as Australia's Dawn Fraser and Ian Thorpe at the Commonwealth Games are the stuff of legend, but who can forget the amazing 4ft 9in weightlifter Precious McKenzie? Barred from competing for South Africa due to apartheid, McKenzie competed for England and New Zealand, and won four consecutive gold medals. It's the inspiring athletes such as McKenzie as much as their diversity and world-class action that make 'the friendly games' such an indispensable, and enjoyable, part of the global sports calendar. It's a chance for smaller nations to shine, and for sports popular among Commonwealth nations – such as netball, rugby 7s and Lawn Bowls – to play on a unique stage.

Officers: President: HRH Prince Imran (Malaysia); Chief Executive: Michael Hooper

Activities: The Federation promotes the Commonwealth Games, held every four years. It also encourages and supports the holding of single sport championships in Commonwealth countries and promotes and develops sport throughout the Commonwealth. The next Commonwealth Games will be held in Glasgow in Scotland in 2014 and the Gold Coast, Australia, in 2018. The next Commonwealth Youth Games will be in Samoa in 2015 followed by St Lucia in 2017.

The CGF is represented on CABOS (Commonwealth Advisory Body on Sport), and provides direction and advice to governments across the Commonwealth on how sport can be used as a means of social and educational development.

Commonwealth Geographical Bureau (CGB)*

c/o Department of Geography, University of Otago, PO Box 56, Dunedin, New Zealand

Tel: +64 3 479 8773
Fax: +64 3 479 9037
Email: j.a.binns@geography.otago.ac.nz
www.commonwealthgeography.org

The CGB promotes interaction among geographers in universities and other institutions in Commonwealth countries by providing information about important activities, and supporting the participation of geographers at Commonwealth workshops and meetings. The CGB is particularly interested in providing technical knowledge and technology transfers from more developed Commonwealth countries to geographers and geography departments in the less developed countries of the Commonwealth.

Foundation: 1968

Officers: President: Professor Tony Binns (New Zealand); Honorary Secretary: Professor Elizabeth Thomas-Hope (Jamaica); Honorary Treasurer: Professor Nigel Walford (UK)

Activities: The Bureau sponsors meetings of Commonwealth geographers, especially from developing countries, either in the form of training workshops or academic conferences.

Commonwealth Hansard Editors Association

House of Commons, London SW1A 0AA, UK

Tel: +44 20 7219 3388
Fax: +44 20 7219 0290
Email: sutherlandl@parliament.uk
www.commonwealth-hansard.org

The Commonwealth organisation of the editors of *Hansard*, the official reports and records of the proceedings of Commonwealth parliaments.

Foundation: 1984

Officers: Secretary: Lorraine Sutherland

Activities: A triennial conference for the discussion of reporting techniques and procedures, in particular the management of the latest developments in information, printing and publishing technology. Particular emphasis is placed on assistance to smaller and newly emerging Commonwealth states.

Commonwealth Human Ecology Council (CHEC)*

The Diary House, Rickett Street, London SW6 1RU, UK

Tel: +44 20 7386 6135/6136
Email: chec@btopenworld.com
www.checinternational.org

Registered Charity No.: 272018

Founded in 1969 by Zena Daysh CNZM and Hon Doctorate University of Waikato (New Zealand), CHEC is accredited to the Commonwealth, has been an NGO in Special Consultative Status with the UN Economic and Social Council (ECOSOC) and is a Member, IUCN Commission on Education and Communication. Zena Daysh died on 23 March 2011; CHEC's Governing Board has rededicated itself to continuing the charity's work and moved into new premises in December 2011.

Officers: Honorary President: The Hon Levi Oguike (CHEC – Nigeria); Hon Patron: Emeritus Professor N R E Fendall (Liverpool School of Tropical Medicine); Vice-Chairman: Professor T K N Unnithan (Honorary President of CHEC – India); Hon Treasurer: John Bonham (CHEC – UK); Hon Secretary: Eva Ekehorn (CHEC – UK)

Members of the Governing Board are drawn from a wide variety of Commonwealth countries, including the UK.

Mission: CHEC adopts an integrated and holistic approach to thinking, understanding and decision-making, which is one of the keys to dealing with the complexities that are associated with human ecology. The opening paragraph of CHEC's mission statement reads: 'Human Ecology embraces the principles of natural and moral philosophy. It draws on knowledge and understanding from the sciences and humanities, to promote holistic, integrative, sustainable initiatives, ideas and developmental projects to enhance and strengthen people's relationships with each other and the natural and built environment on which they depend.' CHEC aims to continue to build and improve harmonious relationships between humans and nature through education, health, practical projects and advocacy among individuals, communities, organisations and governments throughout the Commonwealth and the wider world.

Activities

- CHEC commenced work in 2008 on the Commonwealth Fisheries Programme (CFP) (www.commonwealthfisheries.org). In 2010 CHEC reported on its research into governance of inshore fisheries and the sustainability of livelihoods in fisher-folk communities around the Commonwealth. In 2011, CHEC and its partner in this project, the Commonwealth Policy Studies Unit (since renamed Commonwealth Advisory Bureau), arranged an international meeting to consult on priorities for follow-up work. This concentrated on consolidating and applying the findings of the

first phase of the CFP and worked to build partnerships for further work, including dissemination of the lessons that had been identified. Presentations were made to the Commonwealth People's Forum Workshop on Climate Change, Environment and Disaster Management in Perth, Australia. A pamphlet was also circulated at CHOGM 2011 titled 'A Commonwealth Fisheries Policy: A Call to Action to Secure Sustainability for Livelihood, Food and Biodiversity'. The recommendations seem to have been reflected in both the CHOGM Communiqué and the Perth Declaration on Food Security Principles.

- Projects in Uganda and Tanzania, with the support of the Commonwealth Foundation, have been developed from discussions at the 2007 Kampala CHOGM with the Community Based Impact Assessment Network for Eastern Africa (CIANEA). These concerned training in gender mainstreaming in integrated water resources management and has led to the development of training manuals for Gender and Water Ambassadors, who are working on issues affecting poorer men and women within the Lake Victoria region. To follow up on this, CHEC has received a Commonwealth Foundation Special Grant for Women as Agents for Change for a workshop on 'Capacity Building in Gender Mainstreaming in Water Resource Management' to evaluate trainers and trainees working hand in hand in training sessions. This week-long workshop in January 2012 comprised 36 participants from various bodies drawn from Burundi, Kenya, Rwanda, Tanzania and Uganda.

- The year 2011 saw the conclusion of the European Union's Intelligent Energy Europe three-year project 'SAUCE – Schools at University for Climate Energy' with the publication of the *SAUCE Handbook and SAUCE Resources Guide* (www.schools-at-university.eu). This project brings primary school children into universities to experience the higher education environment, and to see how they as children and through their later studies in the arts, social and natural sciences and technology can make a contribution to renewable energy provision and climate change adaptation and mitigation. CHEC, having supported the UK programme, is now seeking to support dissemination of the project to other Commonwealth countries, first through Cyprus and Malta as EU Commonwealth partners and then beyond through local and regional partner universities.

- With the Society for Human Ecology (SHE), based in the USA and Germany, and the School of Environment and Development at the University of Manchester (UK), CHEC is building follow-up work from its 2009 International Conference on 'Human Ecology for an Urbanising World' held in Manchester. Issue No. 23 of CHEC's *Human Ecology Journal*, published in 2011, set out papers and outcomes emanating from this meeting and plans are in progress to take further activity forward.

Country Chapters: CHEC works through its Country Chapters and local contacts. These together cover all regions of the Commonwealth, and Chapters, all set up independently under CHEC's umbrella, include Australia, Canada, The Gambia, India, Kenya, Malta, New Zealand, Nigeria, Pakistan, Sierra Leone, Sri Lanka and Uganda.

Other links: CHEC is a partner within ComHabitat and has partnership status with Habitat, the UN Centre for Human Settlements, and works actively to promote human settlements and rural development projects. It has been represented at the World Urban Forum in Rio de Janeiro (WUF 5). It publishes *Human Ecology Journal* and communicates its activities through *CHEC Points* and its *Annual Report* published each autumn.

Commonwealth Human Rights Initiative (CHRI)*

B-117 2nd floor, Sarvodaya Enclave,
New Delhi – 110017, India

Tel: +91 11 4318 0200/11 4318 0225–299
Fax: +91 11 2686 4688
Email: info@humanrightsinitiative.org
www.humanrightsinitiative.org

CHRI Africa Office

House No. 9, Samora Machel Street, Asylum Down, opposite Beverly Hills Hotel, Near Trust Towers, Accra, Ghana

Tel/fax: +233 302 971 170
Email: chriafrica@humanrightsinitiative.org
chri_info@yahoo.com.au

CHRI London Office

School of Advanced Study, University of London, 2nd Floor, South Block, Senate House, Malet Street, London WC1E 7HU, UK

Tel: +44 20 7862 8857
Fax: +44 20 7862 8820
Email: chri@sas.ac.uk

CHRI is an international NGO that works for the practical realisation of human rights throughout the Commonwealth. It has been headquartered in India since 1993. CHRI also has offices in Ghana and the UK.

CHRI advocates for better respect for, protection and promotion of international human rights standards and ensuring greater adherence to Commonwealth Harare principles. Issues relating to accountability and participation in governance – access to justice and access to information – are at the heart of CHRI's work. It also overviews the human rights situation in countries of the Commonwealth, looking especially at human rights defenders, compliance with international treaty obligations and monitoring the performance of Commonwealth members of the United Nations Human Rights Council.

Foundation: 1987. CHRI's founding organisations are Commonwealth Journalists Association, Commonwealth Lawyers Association, Commonwealth Legal Education Association, Commonwealth Parliamentary Association, Commonwealth Press Union and Commonwealth Broadcasting Association.

Chief Functionaries: Chair, Advisory Commission and Executive Committee, Africa Office: Samuel Awuku Okudzeto (Ghana); Chair, Executive Committee (Headquarters): B G Verghese (India); Chair, Executive Committee (UK): Neville Linton (UK); Director: Maja Daruwala

Activities: Within the access to justice programme, CHRI's main focus is on police reform and prison reforms. The programme also includes judicial education.

CHRI's right to information (RTI) programme works to promote and protect the right to access information, and to catalyse the development and implementation of RTI regimes in all regions of the Commonwealth focusing on Africa, the Caribbean, the Pacific Islands and South Asia. For each Commonwealth Heads of Government Meeting, CHRI produces a report on an issue of human rights concern within the Commonwealth (these can be downloaded at CHRI's website) and organises the Commonwealth Human Rights Forum to coincide with the meeting to ensure the active engagement of civil society.

The Commonwealth Jewish Council and Trust

BCM Box 6871, London WC1N 3XX, UK

Tel: +44 20 7222 2120
Fax: +44 20 7222 1781
Email: info@cjc.org.uk
www.cjc.org.uk

The Commonwealth Jewish Council is the roof body of 37 Commonwealth Jewish communities. It provides links between them and with Commonwealth governments. The Commonwealth Jewish Council is a registered charity, and provides assistance for affiliated communities, in connection with educational, religious and other charitable needs.

Foundation: 1982

Charity no.: 287564

Officers: President: Gideon Wittenberg; Vice-Presidents: Paul Secher, Rev. Malcolm Weisman OBE; Chairman: Flo Kaufmann; Trustees: Marlene Bethlehem, Mitchell Coen, Jason Holt, Lord Janner of Braunstone, Flo Kaufmann (Chair), Samuel Marshall, Dorothy Reitman; Director: Maureen Gold; Co-ordinator: Alanna Cawston

The Commonwealth Journalists Association (CJA)

c/o Lower Suite, 1099 Ambercroft Lane, Oakville, Ontario L6M 1Z6, Canada

Tel: +1 416 575 5377
Fax: +1 416 923 7206
Email: bcantley@nna-ccj.ca
www.commonwealthjournalists.com

The CJA works to improve journalistic standards and skills in Commonwealth countries, promotes the role of the media in good governance and development, and fosters interest in Commonwealth affairs. The CJA's Executive Director is based in a Toronto (Canada) suburban community and works with an Executive Committee made up of representatives from all regions of the Commonwealth.

Foundation: 1978

Officers: President Emeritus: Derek Ingram (UK); Past President and President Emeritus: Hassan Shahriar (Bangladesh); President: Rita Payne (UK); Vice-Presidents: Chris Cobb (Canada), Mahendra Ved (India), Joshua Kyalimpa (Uganda), Farid Hossain (Bangladesh); Honorary Secretary-Treasurer: Murray Burt (Canada); other international executive committee members: Syed Nahas Pasha (UK), Drito Alice (Uganda), Caroline Jackson (Malaysia), Newton Sibanda (Zambia), Fauzia Shaheen (Pakistan), Jayanta Roy Chowdhury (India), Shyamal Dutta (Bangladesh), Will Henley (UK); Executive Director: Bryan Cantley (in Toronto)

Activities: Training courses and workshops are organised for journalists in developing Commonwealth countries. The CJA also works closely with journalists in developed countries to improve journalists' skills, standards and ethics, and to promote the Commonwealth. The CJA intervenes in defence of journalists' personal and professional rights where these are threatened, sometimes in concert with other Commonwealth organisations.

Commonwealth Judicial Education Institute (CJEI)*

Room 306, 6061 University Avenue, Halifax, Nova Scotia B3H 4H9, Canada

Tel: +1 902 494 1002
Fax: +1 902 494 1031
Email: cjei@dal.ca
www.cjei.org

The CJEI is incorporated as a charity under the laws of Nova Scotia, Canada. It was established to provide support for the creation and strengthening of national judicial education bodies; to encourage regional and pan-Commonwealth networking and exchange of human and material resources; to train core judicial education faculty; to develop programme modules for the use of all Commonwealth countries; and to design judicial education programmes to support judicial reform. There are three levels of oversight:

- the Patrons – a panel made up of Commonwealth chief justices and other distinguished jurists

- an Advisory Board made up of executive heads of judicial education bodies in Commonwealth countries

- a corporate Board of Directors drawn from all regions of the Commonwealth and representative of different levels of court and court administration.

Officers: President: The Rt Hon Sir Dennis Byron; Chair: Judge (R) Sandra E Oxner; Treasurer/Secretary: Larry Smith CA

Commonwealth Lawyers Association (CLA)*

Institute of Commonwealth Studies,
17 Russell Square, London WC1B 5DR, UK

Tel: +44 20 7862 8824
Fax: +44 20 7862 8816
Email: cla@sas.ac.uk
www.commonwealthlawyers.com

The CLA's objectives, as enshrined in its constitution, are to maintain and promote the rule of law throughout the Commonwealth by:

- ensuring that the people of the Commonwealth are served by an independent and efficient legal profession

- preserving and fostering a common bond of Commonwealth

- strengthening professional links among lawyers

- maintaining the honour and integrity of the profession and promoting uniform standards of professional ethics, and

- supporting improved standards of education and exchanges of lawyers and students.

Foundation: 1983

Officers: President: Mohamed Husain (South Africa); Secretary-General: Claire Martin

Activities: The CLA holds biennial (previously triennial) Commonwealth Law Conferences that are normally organised by the law society/bar council of the host country. The next CLC will be held in April 2013 in Cape Town, South Africa. The association is developing a programme of capacity-building projects in Commonwealth jurisdictions, in partnership with local law societies and bar associations. Among the areas to be covered are constitutionalism and rule of law, corruption, terrorism and continuing legal education.

Commonwealth of Learning (COL)

1055 West Hastings Street, Suite 1200, Vancouver, British Columbia V6E 2E9, Canada

Tel: +1 604 775 8200
Fax: +1 604 775 8210
Email: info@col.org
www.col.org

See profile of the Commonwealth of Learning in the 'Official Commonwealth Organisations' section of this publication.

Commonwealth Legal Advisory Service (CLAS)

Charles Clore House, 17 Russell Square, London WC1B 5JP, UK

Tel: +44 20 7862 5151
Fax: +44 20 7862 5152
Email: info@biicl.org
www.biicl.org

CLAS provides legal research services on request to attorneys-general, other government agencies and official law reform agencies in the Commonwealth in respect of laws and legal developments in Commonwealth jurisdictions.

Foundation: 1962

Commonwealth Legal Education Association (CLEA)*

c/o Legal and Constitutional Affairs Division, Commonwealth Secretariat, Marlborough House, Pall Mall, London SW1Y 5HX, UK

Tel: +44 20 7747 6415
Fax: +44 20 7004 3649
Email: clea@commonwealth.int
www.clea-web.org

CLEA fosters and promotes high standards of legal education in the Commonwealth. Its programme of action is designed to make legal education socially relevant and professionally useful.

Foundation: 1971

Officers: President: David McQuoid-Mason (South Africa); Vice-Presidents: John Hatchard (UK), Ronnie Bodoo Singh, Peter Slinn (UK), Joe Silva (Sri Lanka); General Secretary: Dr Clare Chambers-Jones (UK)

Activities: CLEA holds conferences on legal education and related topics. It developed model courses for Commonwealth law schools on human rights in the Commonwealth, and tackling transnational crime, tackling corruption and the misuse of public office, and teaching Islamic law. It organises the Commonwealth Law Moot competition, the Commonwealth law students' essay competition and the Commonwealth Law Lecture series. It publishes a newsletter (3 p.a.), *Commonwealth Legal Education*, and the *Journal of Commonwealth Law and Legal Education* (twice yearly).

Commonwealth Library Association (COMLA)

PO Box 144, Mona, Kingston 7, Jamaica

Tel: +1 876 978 2274
Fax: +1 876 927 1926
Email: norma.amenukpodo@uwimona.edu.jm

COMLA supports library associations in the Commonwealth by promoting the interests of libraries and librarians and facilitating networks for information delivery and exchange. Its membership comprises national library associations and major library institutions in countries that do not yet have an association. From 2002 librarians have been eligible to become individual members.

Foundation: 1972

Officers: Interim President: Elizabeth Watson (University of the West Indies, Cave Hill Campus, Barbados); Honorary Executive Secretary: Norma Y Amenu-Kpodo (Jamaica)

Activities: Activities focus on the mutual recognition of educational qualifications, professional development, improvement of rural library services and on the development of library services for distance learners, information literacy and access to information; developing digital resources; seminars and workshops; and assisting in improving management practices of member associations. It publishes *COMLA Bulletin*.

Commonwealth Local Government Forum (CLGF)*

CLGF headquarters, 16a Northumberland Avenue, London WC2N 5AP, UK

Tel: +44 20 7389 1490
Fax: +44 20 7389 1499
Email: info@clgf.org.uk
www.clgf.org.uk

Pacific Regional Office, GPO Box 159, Suva, Fiji

Tel: +679 330 0257
Fax: +679 330 2729
Email: clgfsuva@connect.com.fj

The CLGF works to promote and strengthen democratic local government throughout the Commonwealth and to encourage the exchange of good practice in local government structures and services.

CLGF is based in London with regional project offices in the Pacific, India and South Africa. It works through its 170 members in 40 Commonwealth countries, particularly the national local government associations, ministries dealing with local government, individual local authorities, and regional and international partners. It brings together practitioners from all spheres of government who are involved in local government to pool experiences and share good practice.

Its members include local councils and municipalities, local government associations and ministries of local government. Trade unions, training and research institutions and professional or employers' associations are welcome as associate members.

Foundation: 1995

Officers: Chair: Mayor Zenaida Moya-Flowers (Mayor, Belize City Council – stepping down in May 2012); Vice-Chairpersons: Mayor Amos Masondo (President, South African Local Government Association), the Hon Adolf

Mwesige (Minister of Local Government, Uganda); Secretary-General: Carl Wright; Deputy Secretary-General: Lucy Slack; Director of Communications: Sue Rhodes; Regional Project Manager (Pacific): Karibaiti Taoaba; Project Officer (India): Anuya Kuwar; Project Officer (Southern Africa): Nyasha Simbanegavi

Activities: CLGF encourages local democracy through local election support and monitoring, exchange of experience and good practice, technical projects and partnerships to strengthen local government capacity and implement the Commonwealth principles on good practice for local democracy and good governance, and knowledge sharing on innovations and good practice in local government. It organises symposiums and workshops on democracy and local government issues in all regions of the Commonwealth. The Commonwealth Local Government Good Practice Scheme funds technical co-operation partnerships between local authorities.

CLGF is the voice for local government in the Commonwealth, advocating decentralisation and good local governance and the role of local government in tackling poverty, delivering the MDGs and other global issues at key Commonwealth and international forums. The Forum holds the biennial Commonwealth Local Government Conference. The sixth conference was held in Cardiff, UK, in March 2011. The next conference will be held in Kampala, Uganda, in May 2013 (visit www.clgc2013.org).

Publications: *CLGF Bulletin* (2/3 p.a.); *CLGF enews* – a regular update on what's happening in local government throughout the Commonwealth; *Commonwealth Local Government Handbook* (a complete guide to local government systems in Commonwealth countries with case studies of innovative reforms in local government structures and services, published bi-annually); *E-journal of Commonwealth Local Governance and Democracy* (from early 2008); *Aberdeen Agenda: Commonwealth Principles on Good Practice for Local Democracy and Good Governance*; research, workshop and conference reports.

Commonwealth Magistrates' and Judges' Association (CMJA)*

Uganda House, 58–59 Trafalgar Square, London WC2N 5DX, UK

Tel: +44 20 7976 1007
Fax: +44 20 7976 2394
Email: info@cmja.org
www.cmja.org

The CMJA provides a unique network for judicial officers in Commonwealth countries in order to assist them to advance the administration of justice. Thus its aims are to promote the independence of the judiciary; and to advance education in the law, the administration of justice, the treatment of offenders and the prevention of crime.

Foundation: 1970

Officers: President: Her Hon Mrs Justice Norma Wade-Miller; Executive Vice-President: Judge Timothy Workman; Secretary-General: Dr Karen Brewer

Activities: Promoting and protecting judicial independence and the implementation of the Commonwealth (Latimer House) Principles and the highest of standards within the judiciary.

Running educational conferences and undertaking training for judicial officers at all levels around the Commonwealth at the request of the local or regional judicial organisation, and undertaking projects to improve the administration of justice in the Commonwealth.

Commonwealth Medical Association (CMA)*

British Medical Association Building, International Department, Tavistock Square, London WC1H 9JP, UK

Tel: +44 207 383 6069
Fax: +44 207 383 6644
Email: cmaliaison@cma.bma.org.uk

The main aim of the CMA is to assist and strengthen the capacities of National Medical Associations of countries within the Commonwealth to improve the health and well-being of their communities and countries.

Foundation: 1962

Officers: President: Dr Gordon Caruana Dingli (Malta); Immediate Past President: Dr Sundaram Arulrhaj (India); Secretary: Dr Oheneba Owusu-Danso (Ghana); Treasurer: Dr Margaret Mungherera (Uganda); Vice-Presidents – European region: Professor Vivienne Nathanson (UK); Canadian/Caribbean region: Dr Solaiman Juman (Trinidad and Tobago); South-East Asian and Australian region: Dr David Quek Kwang Leng (Malaysia); Central Asian region: Dr Lalitha Neelangani Mendis (Sri Lanka); West African region: Dr Kwabena Opoku-Adusei (Ghana); Central, Eastern and Southern African region: Dr Mphata Norman Mabasa (South Africa)

Activities: Regional and international workshops on health issues; medical and health research; advocacy on health issues; capacity-building for member national medical associations; and collaborations with other international bodies, civil society and governance institutions, with similar objectives.

Commonwealth Medical Trust (Commat)*

BMA House, Tavistock Square, London WC1H 9JP, UK

Tel: +44 1689 878 372
Email: office@commat.org
www.commat.org

Commat's work is focused on the promotion of health and prevention of disease and disability (especially in the area of reproductive health) and the advancement of human rights and medical ethics – particularly for the poor and other marginalised groups in Commonwealth and other developing countries, and with special reference to the role that can be played by medical practitioners and their professional associations. National Commat organisations have been established in Pakistan and Uganda.

Foundation: 1995

Officers: Director: Marianne Haslegrave

COMNET Foundation for ICT Development (COMNET)

'Alfir' Reggie Miller Street, Gzira GZR 1541, Malta

Tel: +356 2132 3393
Fax: +356 2132 3390
Email: info@comnet.org.mt
www.comnet.org.mt

COMNET Foundation for ICT Development (COMNET) is an independent foundation whose mission is to help realise the transformational potential of information and communication technologies (ICTs) for development among Commonwealth and other developing countries. Established in the mid-1990s, COMNET is a joint initiative of the Maltese Government and the Commonwealth Secretariat. The Foundation's major thrust is to facilitate the sharing of experience and capacity-building. Activities in the recent past have included assistance in the development of national ICT strategies, telecommunications regulation and e-government services, through training and consultancy projects.

Foundation: 1995

Officers: Chair: Joseph V Tabone (joseph.v.tabone@mca.org.mt); Executive Manager: Sandra Hyzler (sandra.hyzler@comnet.org.mt); Communications Officer: Lara Pace (lara.pace@comnet.org.mt)

Activities: Today, the Foundation's principal focus is the Commonwealth Connects Programme (www.commonwealthconnects.net). COMNET is also the Commonwealth Secretariat's lead partner agency tasked with building a contact network, developing a repository of Commonwealth ICT assets, nurturing links with donor agencies, and co-ordinating projects under the aegis of this programme.

The Connects Programme is a vehicle for technology and knowledge transfer in areas such as e-government services, telecommunications regulation and related activities having a bearing on national, social and economic development.

COMNET has also been entrusted the lead of the Commonwealth Internet Governance Forum (CIGF; www.commonwealthigf.org). The purpose of this initiative is to inform and engage stakeholders on public policy issues relating to internet governance. Recent CIGF initiatives reflecting the priorities of participants have been the compilation of resources on child protection online.

Online resources and publications: Commonwealth Connects (www.commonwealthconnects.net); Commonwealth Connects ICT Assets Database (www.connectsdatabase.org); Commonwealth IGF Blog (www.commonwealthigf.org)

Commonwealth Nurses Federation*

c/o Royal College of Nursing, 20 Cavendish Square, London W1G 0RN, UK

Tel: +44 20 7647 3593
Fax: +44 20 7647 3413
Email: jill@commonwealthnurses.org
www.commonwealthnurses.org

The purpose of the CNF is to contribute to the improved health of citizens of the Commonwealth by fostering access to nursing education, influencing health policy, developing nursing networks and strengthening nursing leadership.

Foundation: 1973

Officers: President: Susie Kong (Singapore); Vice-President: Satish Chawla (India); Executive Secretary: Jill Iliffe; Treasurer: Angela Neuhaus

Activities: The Federation's work programme includes regional and in-country workshops and

training aimed at raising the profile and standards of nursing and midwifery in Commonwealth countries; participating in and influencing health policy development at a Commonwealth level; and research and other initiatives on key areas of concern to nurses and midwives such as workforce planning, migration and HIV and AIDS.

Commonwealth Organisation for Social Work (COSW)*

Representative to Commonwealth Institutions (UK): Terry Bamford

Tel: +44 20 7229 6993
Email: terrybamford@aol.com
www.commonwealthsw.org

COSW is an organisation for citizens of the Commonwealth who are interested in promoting and supporting social work and social development. It contributes the social work perspective to Commonwealth activities. It is supported by social work associations in the Commonwealth and has formal links with the International Federation of Social Workers (IFSW). COSW upholds the code of ethics of IFSW and promotes its professional principles.

Foundation: Established in 1994 at a meeting of social workers from Commonwealth countries during the biennial conference of the IFSW in Colombo, Sri Lanka. COSW was formally accredited in 2007.

Officers: Chairs: Ngoh-Tiong Tan (Singapore), Charles Mbugua (Kenya); Honorary Secretary-General: Monique Auffrey (Canada); Treasurer: Fiona Robertson (New Zealand); Board members: Terry Bamford (UK), Nigel Hall (UK/Zimbabwe), David Jones (UK), K S Ramesh (India)

The Commonwealth Parliamentary Association (CPA)*

Secretariat: Suite 700, Westminster House, 7 Millbank, London SW1P 3JA, UK

Tel: +44 20 7779 1460/20 7219 4666
Fax: +44 20 7222 6073
Email: hq.sec@cpahq.org
andrew@cpahq.org
www.cpahq.org

The Commonwealth Parliamentary Association links members of national, state, provincial and territorial parliaments and legislatures across the Commonwealth. Its mission is to promote the advancement of parliamentary democracy by enhancing knowledge and understanding of democratic governance. It seeks to build an informed parliamentary community able to deepen the Commonwealth's democratic commitment and to further co-operation among its parliaments and legislatures.

Foundation: 1911 (as the Empire Parliamentary Association)

Officers: President: Hon Chamal Rajapakse MP (Speaker of Parliament, Sri Lanka); Chair of the Executive Committee: Rt Hon Sir Alan Haselhurst MP (Member of the House of Commons, United Kingdom); Secretary-General: Dr William F Shija

Activities: The CPA pursues its objectives by means of: annual Commonwealth Parliamentary Conferences, regional conferences and other symposiums; interparliamentary visits; parliamentary seminars and workshops; publications, notably *The Parliamentarian* and newsletters on CPA activities and parliamentary and political events; and Parliamentary

Information and Reference Centre communications. Active CPA Branches now exist in more than 180 national, state, provincial and territorial parliaments and legislatures, with a total membership in excess of 17,000 parliamentarians.

Commonwealth Partnership for Technology Management (CPTM)

CPTM Smart Partners' Hub, 63 Catherine Place, London SW1E 6DY, UK

Tel: +44 20 7798 2500
Fax: +44 20 7798 2525
Email: smart.partnership@cptm.org
www.cptm.org

CPTM is an independent government/private sector partnership created to provide advisory services to Commonwealth countries, institutions and organisations on technology management as a tool for socio-economic development. Its mission is 'to enhance national capabilities for the creation and participation in wealth through sound management of technology, using public/private sector partnerships'. Members comprise Commonwealth governments, public and private sector organisations, and individual networkers (academics, civil servants, business and trade union professionals).

Foundation: 1995

Officers: Chair: Tan Sri Datuk Dr Omar bin Abdul Rahman; Chief Executive: Dr Mihaela Y Smith PJN KMN

Activities: Each year CPTM develops a portfolio of projects to be implemented in Commonwealth countries. This includes tasks as diverse as enhancing National Visions for strategic development, Quality Standards management for improved productivity and trade, as well as both Financial Inclusion and Innovation and Technology initiatives. The national, regional and international Smart Partnership Dialogue Programme brings government leaders, private sector, media, labour and civil society together in an informal and inclusive environment to co-operate in studying social and business issues and developing improved means for the management of the socio-economic environment throughout the Commonwealth and beyond. This has emerged as the flagship programme of CPTM, enjoying unprecedented support from Heads of Government, the private sector and labour organisations.

Commonwealth Pharmacists Association (CPA)*

1 Lambeth High Street, London SE1 7JN, UK

Tel: +44 20 7572 2364
Fax: +44 20 7572 2504
Email: admin@commonwealthpharmacy.org
www.commonwealthpharmacy.org

The Commonwealth Pharmacists Association is an organisation of Commonwealth professional pharmaceutical bodies and individual members, dedicated to promoting and disseminating the pharmaceutical sciences throughout the Commonwealth and to improving the quality and range of services offered by pharmacists in particular by:

- promoting high standards of professional conduct among pharmacists, having due regard for the honour and traditions of the profession

- effecting close links between members of the profession in Commonwealth countries and

facilitating personal contacts between pharmacists and students

- encouraging the creation of a national professional pharmaceutical association in any Commonwealth country where none exists, fostering high standards of pharmaceutical education at all levels and of practice in all branches of the profession, and holding CPA conferences (the 11th CPA Conference was held in Durban, South Africa, from 29 May to 1 June 2011, on the theme 'pharmacy – versatile, responsive, aware')

- facilitating the dissemination of knowledge and information about the pharmaceutical sciences and the professional practice of pharmacy

- advocating high standards of control over the quality and distribution of drugs, wherever appropriate by professional means, and to that end encouraging suitable legislation and its implementation, and

- liaising with similar associations or allied health professional groups within and outside of the Commonwealth to assist in attaining these objectives.

Foundation: 1970, as the Commonwealth Pharmaceutical Association

Officers: President: Ivan Kotzé (South Africa); Vice-Presidents: Raymond Anderson (United Kingdom), Cecil Jacques (Guyana); Honorary Secretary: Roger Odd (UK); Treasurer: John Farwell (UK)

Commonwealth Policy Studies Unit (CPSU)*

See Commonwealth Advisory Bureau (CA/B).

Commonwealth Scholarship Commission in the United Kingdom (CSC)

c/o The Association of Commonwealth Universities, Woburn House, 20–24 Tavistock Square, London WC1H 9HF, UK

Tel: +44 20 7380 6700
Fax: +44 20 7387 2655
Email: info@cscuk.org.uk
www.dfid.gov.uk

The Commonwealth Scholarship Commission in the United Kingdom (CSC) is responsible for managing Britain's contribution to the Commonwealth Scholarship and Fellowship Plan (CSFP). The CSC supports around 700 awards annually. Awards are funded by the Department for International Development (for developing Commonwealth countries), and the Foreign and Commonwealth Office, the Department for Business, Innovation and Skills and the Scottish Government (for developed Commonwealth countries), in conjunction with UK universities. The CSC's secretariat is provided by the Association of Commonwealth Universities; financial administration services for award holders are provided by the British Council.

Foundation: 1959

Activities: The CSC makes available seven types of award:

- scholarships for PhD research

- scholarships for master's study

- shared scholarships for developing country students who would not otherwise be able to undertake master's level study in the UK, jointly supported by UK universities

- academic fellowships aimed at mid-career staff in developing country universities

- split-site scholarships to support PhD candidates to spend up to one year in the UK as part of their doctoral studies

- professional fellowships for mid-career professionals in developing countries, and

- distance learning scholarships enabling developing country students to study UK master's degree courses while living in their home countries.

The CSC also nominates UK citizens for scholarships to study in other Commonwealth countries under the CSFP.

Commonwealth Scholarship and Fellowship Plan (CSFP)

c/o Commonwealth Scholarship Commission in the United Kingdom, The Association of Commonwealth Universities, Woburn House, 20–24 Tavistock Square, London WC1H 9HF, UK

Tel: +44 20 7380 6700
Fax: +44 20 7387 2655
www.csfp-online.org

The CSFP is an international programme under which Commonwealth governments offer scholarships and fellowships to citizens of other Commonwealth countries. The Plan was established at the first Conference of Commonwealth Education Ministers in 1959 and it is reviewed by ministers at their triennial meetings – the only scholarship scheme in the world to receive such high-level recognition. Since then, over 29,000 individuals have held awards, hosted by more than 20 countries. The CSFP is one of the primary mechanisms of pan-Commonwealth exchange.

Foundation: 1959

Activities: There is no central body that manages the CSFP. Instead, participation is based on a series of bilateral arrangements between home and host countries. The participation of each country is organised by a national nominating agency, which is responsible for advertising awards applicable to their own country and making nominations to host countries. In the UK, which is the biggest contributor to the Plan, this process is managed by the Commonwealth Scholarship Commission in the United Kingdom.

Commonwealth Secretariat

Marlborough House, Pall Mall, London SW1Y 5HX, UK

Tel: +44 20 7747 6385
Fax: +44 20 7930 0827
www.thecommonwealth.org
www.csdrms.org
www.commonwealthconnects.net
www.genderandtrade.org

See profile of the Commonwealth Secretariat in the 'Official Commonwealth Organisations' section of this publication.

The Commonwealth Society for the Deaf (Sound Seekers)

34 Buckingham Palace Road, London SW1W 0RE, UK

Tel: +44 20 7233 5700
Fax: +44 20 7233 5800
Email: admin@sound-seekers.org.uk
www.sound-seekers.org.uk

Charity Registration No. 1013870

Sound Seekers' aim is to work towards alleviating deafness and hearing loss in developing Commonwealth countries.

Foundation: 1959

Officers: Chair: Malcolm Harper; Vice-Chair: Ivan Tucker OBE; Treasurer: W T Fraser-Allen; Chief Executive: Gary Williams

Activities: Works in partnership with host governments and key NGOs to develop hospital-based audiology services and community outreach services via a mobile HARK! (hearing assessment, treatment and research clinic). Targets children who live in areas where access to screening of hearing is difficult or non-existent. Trains key personnel in-country to conduct hearing assessments, fit hearing aids, advise on ear care and to look after and maintain equipment, and send recycled hearing aids and audiology equipment where it is needed.

Commonwealth Telecommunications Organisation (CTO)*

64–66 Glenthorne Road, Hammersmith, London W6 0LR, UK

Tel: +44 208 600 3800
Fax: +44 208 600 3819
Email: info@cto.int
l.dealwis@cto.int
www.cto.int

The CTO is an international development partnership between Commonwealth governments, non-Commonwealth countries, businesses and civil society organisations. It provides the international community with effective means to help bridge the digital divide and achieve social and economic development, by delivering to member organisations unique knowledge-sharing programmes in the use of information and communication technologies (ICTs) in the specific areas of telecommunications, IT, broadcasting and the internet.

Foundation: 1901

Officers: Chief Executive Officer: Professor Tim Unwin; Chief Operating Officer: Bashir Patel; Corporate Secretary/Senior Manager Programmes: Lasantha De Alwis

A chairperson and two vice-chairpersons elected by the Full Member countries along with two other members appointed by the Sector members and the CEO constitute the Executive Committee.

Activities: Since its creation in 1901, the CTO and its predecessor organisations have been at the centre of continuous and extensive ICT development programmes, providing funding, co-operation and assistance. Over the last two decades alone, the organisation has delivered more than 3,500 bilateral and multilateral ICT capacity-building projects together with policy, regulatory and operational expert assistance. The CTO actively promotes partnerships between governments, businesses and other stakeholders to accelerate poverty reduction and fulfil the global development agenda for ICT in education, agriculture, health, governance and commerce. In the last two decades, the CTO has offered training and expert assistance to some 35,000 ICT professionals. Every day around the world, CTO delivers more than 120 hours' worth of expertise and training to its members and partners involved in developing, deploying, using or promoting ICT

in some form. Every year, the CTO holds around 10 international conferences across the Commonwealth on topical ICT themes such as Rural Connectivity, e-Governance, Digital Switchover and Cybersecurity. The CTO also provides consultancy services on a wide range of areas from strategic planning to universal access and carries out research on topical subjects such as local content, applications and value added services.

Publications: *Annual Report*; research reports

Commonwealth Universities Study Abroad Consortium (CUSAC)

Association of Commonwealth Universities, Woburn House, 20–24 Tavistock Square, London WC1H 9HF, UK

Tel: +44 20 7380 6700
Fax: +44 20 7387 2655
Email: cusac@acu.ac.uk
www.cusac.org.uk

The Consortium aims to bring together like-minded universities to find ways of increasing mobility across Commonwealth countries at minimal cost in a spirit of reciprocity and mutual exchange. There are currently about 65 members from 21 Commonwealth countries and five regions.

Foundation: 1993

Officers: The Executive Committee has representatives elected from Africa, the Americas, Asia, Australasia and Europe. The ACU provides the secretariat for CUSAC. Contact persons at the ACU are Deborah Bennett, Executive Secretary CUSAC; and Kathleen Williams, Administrator CUSAC.

Activities: Student and staff exchange. Through the bilateral linkages of its members, CUSAC extends the benefits of studying abroad to a wider group of students across the Commonwealth. As an umbrella organisation, it enables its members to share and access information through networking and benchmarking events as well as electronically. It also administers a bursary programme aimed at assisting student exchanges between member universities.

Commonwealth Veterinary Association (CVA)

123, 7th B Main Road, 4th Block (West), Jayangar, Bangalore 560 011, India

Tel/Fax: +91 80 663 5210
Email: shireen@blr.vsnl.net.in
www.commonwealthvetassoc.org

The CVA promotes the veterinary profession within the Commonwealth by encouraging the highest professional standards of education, ethics and service. It promotes the creation of national veterinary associations and statutory bodies to regulate veterinary science in any Commonwealth member country where they do not exist. Its membership now includes the national associations of 54 countries and five associate members and one corporate member.

Foundation: 1967

Officers: President: Dr S Abdul Rahman (India); Secretary: Dr Karen Reed (UK); Treasurer: Dr Peter Thornber (Australia); Past President: Dr Richard Suu-Ire (Ghana); Programme Director: Dr Bob McCracken (UK)

Commonwealth War Graves Commission

2 Marlow Road, Maidenhead, Berkshire SL6 7DX, UK

Tel: +44 1628 634221
Fax: +44 1628 771208
Email: casualty.enq@cwgc.org
www.cwgc.org

The Commission marks and maintains graves, builds memorials and keeps records of Commonwealth service men and women who died in the First and Second World Wars.

Foundation: 1917 (as the Imperial War Graves Commission)

Officers: President: The Duke of Kent; Chair: The Secretary of State for Defence in the UK; Vice-Chair: Admiral Sir Ian Garnett KCB; Director-General and Secretary to the Commission: Alan Pateman-Jones

Commonwealth Youth Exchange Council (CYEC)*

7 Lion Yard, Tremadoc Road, Clapham, London SW4 7NQ, UK

Tel: +44 20 7498 6151
Fax: +44 20 7622 4365
Email: mail@cyec.org.uk
www.cyec.org.uk

Foundation: 1970

Officers: Chair: Lord Hameed CBE; Chief Executive: Vic Craggs OBE

CYEC is an education and youth development charity working to promote and advance educational exchange between people and institutions in different Commonwealth countries.

CYEC's main objectives are the development of young people, educators and their institutions through promotion of Commonwealth and international understanding. CYEC works to further these objectives through a range of partnerships across the Commonwealth. CYEC has three main programme areas, as below.

1 **Youth programmes:** demographics dictate that young people are recognised as key stakeholders in the future of the Commonwealth and, of course, are crucial partners in development. All CYEC's youth programmes are informed by the key principle of youth participation. Activities are designed 'by and with' young adults as opposed to 'for' young people:

- high quality two-way group exchanges linking UK young people in local communities with their peers across the Commonwealth

- the development of pan-Commonwealth initiatives supporting young adults as active citizens contributing to development in their communities and across the Commonwealth network, including the biennial Commonwealth Youth Forum held in the wings of CHOGM

- youth leadership events and programmes.

2 **Interchange Programme for Professional Educators:** this includes an established bilateral post-to-post teacher exchange programme between the UK and Australia and Canada.

3 **Raising awareness of the Commonwealth and its values:** publications, resources, training workshops and events for young people, educationalists and organisations.

Conference of Commonwealth Meteorologists (CCM)*

c/o International Relations, Met Office,
FitzRoy Road, Exeter, Devon EX1 3PB, UK

Tel: +44 1392 886 784
Fax: +44 1392 885 681
Email: commonwealth@metoffice.gov.uk
www.commonwealthmet.org

The Conference of Commonwealth Meteorologists is both a convening and an informal network of the heads of Commonwealth national meteorological and hydrological services (NMHSs). The CCM, which was first established in 1929, gives directors the opportunity to discuss and resolve issues of mutual concern. The aim of the CCM is to enhance the benefits of meteorology to society through increased co-operation between NMHSs, governments and other organisations including the private sector. Through their expertise in various fields related to weather, water and climate and their capabilities (including round-the-clock operations) CCM members play a significant role in the safety of life and properties and in providing expert information on the science of climate change and its impacts. The CCM was formally accredited as an Associated Organisation of the Commonwealth in September 2005.

Conference of Commonwealth Speakers and Presiding Officers

5th Floor, 131 Queen Street, House of Commons, Ottawa, Ontario K1A 0A6, Canada

Tel: +1 613 996 1102
Fax: +1 613 992 3674
Email: cspoc@parl.gc.ca
www.cspoc.org/contact-e.asp

The Conference provides speakers and presiding officers of national parliaments in the Commonwealth with a unique opportunity to gather together in a forum of their own to exchange information and express views on matters of common concern. (*Note:* speakers, or presiding officers, are the members of parliament who chair parliamentary proceedings; they must be above party concerns in their duties as chairs, and expert interpreters of the rules of procedure by which their parliaments operate.)

Foundation: 1969

Contact: Eric Janse, Secretary to the Standing Committee

The Council of Commonwealth Societies (CCS)

c/o The Royal Commonwealth Society, 25 Northumberland Avenue, London WC2N 5AP, UK

Tel: +44 20 7766 9200
Fax: +44 20 7930 9705
Email: observance@thercs.org
www.commonwealthday.org

The CCS (formerly the Joint Commonwealth Societies' Council), through the Royal Commonwealth Society, promotes the celebration of the annual Commonwealth theme, particularly during Commonwealth Week and on Commonwealth Day. A particular focus of its work is the multifaith Commonwealth Day Observance in Westminster Abbey, London. The CCS has a membership that comprises UK-based Commonwealth organisations and additional partner members including the UK Foreign and

Commonwealth Office and Commonwealth high commissions.

Foundation: 1947

Officers: Chair: Lord Watson of Richmond; Secretary: Jessica Smith

Council for Education in the Commonwealth (CEC)*

Commonwealth House, 7 Lion Yard, Tremadoc Road, London SW4 7NQ, UK

Tel: +44 1277 212357
Fax: +44 1277 212357
Email: secretariat@cecomm.org.uk
www.cecomm.org.uk

The Council is a UK Parliament-based non-governmental organisation in London, and provides a forum for activating interest in and support for education in the Commonwealth. It seeks to mobilise opinion and action in the UK and elsewhere on behalf of Commonwealth education co-operation. Membership is open to individuals and organisations. All Commonwealth high commissioners accredited to London are honorary members.

Foundation: 1959

Officers: Executive Chair: Alan Evans; Deputy Executive Chair: Rosemary Preston; Secretary: Vacant; Honorary Treasurer: Sonny Leong; Advocacy and Activities: Kabir Shaikh

The Council also has three parliamentary chairs (Gavin Williamson MP, Simon Hughes MP, David Lammy MP) and four patrons (Lord Judd, Lord Luce, Lord McNally and Lord Boswell).

Activities: An annual Gladwyn lecture by an eminent expert on an educational topic of relevance to the Commonwealth. Three or four other meetings on educational issues are held each year. The Council lobbies both the British Government and the Commonwealth regarding the importance of education for the children and people of the Commonwealth. It issues two to three *Commonwealth Education News* per year. These and other documents are made available through the Council's website, which is regularly updated.

CPU Media Trust

The Trust is a 'virtual' organisation with no physical office. Initial contact is via:

Email: office@cpu.org.uk
www.cpu.org.uk

Foundation: June 2009

Officers: Lord Black of Brentwood, Executive Director of The Telegraph Media Group, chairs the Board of Trustees. The other seven trustees are all key media figures with wide-reaching and long-standing involvement in the Commonwealth media. A consultant, Lindsay Ross, who was formerly the Executive Director of the Commonwealth Press Union, assists them. The Board meets quarterly.

Aims: The CPU Media Trust is pledged to uphold and defend the freedom, interests and welfare of the media in Commonwealth countries and is committed to a professional, ethical and effective media across the Commonwealth. It actively promotes the highest professional and ethical standards, and monitors and opposes any measures designed to affect the freedom of the media and of journalists in any member state of the Commonwealth. Its primary concerns are

supporting media freedom and media rights, the training of journalists in the skills necessary for them to enable their work, and a thorough understanding of media law and the establishment and support of self-regulatory bodies throughout the Commonwealth. 2010 saw the reinstatement of online training courses for journalists throughout the Commonwealth.

History: The CPU Media Trust was established in June 2009, following the closure of the Commonwealth Press Union in December 2008.

The origins of the CPU go back to the early part of the twentieth century when Sir Harry Brittain – an eminent journalist and politician – working with the great press barons of the time, organised the first Imperial Press Conference, a week-long countrywide event that began in London on 9 June 1909. At the end of the Conference, it was unanimously agreed to create the Empire Press Union, which would act as a networking organisation for the press of the British Empire and Dominions. Over the next 41 years, the organisation organised regular conferences across the empire with delegates drawn from the proprietors and senior editors of the various newspaper houses. These conferences enabled key newspaper figures to plan and enact key media strategy across the ever-growing empire.

In 1950, in tune with the changing times and the formation of the new Commonwealth from the ashes of empire, the organisation's name was changed to the Commonwealth Press Union and a new charter was devised. The mission of this new organisation was to safeguard the interests of the Commonwealth press, train journalists and provide a networking opportunity every three or four years in the form of an international conference. The membership of this new organisation was institutional rather than individual with, at its height, more than 1,500 newspaper houses or individual newspapers across the new Commonwealth.

Over the years the CPU trained thousands of journalists in almost every country or region of the Commonwealth, and established a solid reputation for defending the freedom of the Commonwealth press and organising successful and high profile conferences every two or four years. As funding became increasingly difficult to secure for training and related projects, it became apparent that the organisation could no longer continue in its past form.

Sadly, the decision was taken to close down in December 2008 after 99 years. However, it is intended that the new CPU Media Trust will provide a 'virtual' successor to the old organisation, taking forward its aims and aspirations to support the twenty-first century's media.

The English-Speaking Union (ESU)

Dartmouth House, 37 Charles St, London W1J 5ED, UK

Tel: +44 20 7529 1550
Fax: +44 20 7495 6108
Email: library@esu.org
www.esu.org

ESU promotes international understanding and human achievement through the widening use of the English language throughout the world. It has active groups in over 50 countries.

Foundation: 1918

Officers: Chair: Dame Mary Richardson DBE; Director-General: Peter Kyle OBE CCMI

Institute of Commonwealth Studies*

School of Advanced Study, University of London, 2nd Floor, South Block, Senate House, Malet Street, London WC1E 7HU, UK

Tel: +44 20 7862 8844
Fax: +44 20 7862 8813
Email: ics@sas.ac.uk
http://commonwealth.sas.ac.uk

The Institute of Commonwealth Studies is the only postgraduate academic institution in the UK devoted to the study of the history and politics of the Commonwealth and of Commonwealth countries.

Foundation: 1949

Officers: Director: Professor Philip Murphy; Administrative Manager: Paul Sullivan

Activities: The Institute provides a forum for teachers, researchers and graduate students with Commonwealth research interests, providing seminars, conferences and symposiums (see website for details), library facilities and academic advice. It registers students for doctoral research, and for the MA in Understanding and Securing Human Rights. An important part of the Institute is the Commonwealth Advisory Bureau (CA/B, formerly the Commonwealth Policy Studies Unit), the think-tank for the modern Commonwealth. It also provides a base for the Commonwealth Human Rights Initiative (CHRI) and for a variety of externally funded research projects, and it hosts every year a number of visiting research fellows from other universities and institutions.

The Round Table: Commonwealth Journal of International Affairs

School of Law, University of Ulster at Jordanstown, Shore Road, Newtownabbey, Co Antrim BT37 0QB, UK

Tel: +44 28 9036 8876
Fax: +44 28 9036 6847
Email: theroundtable@hotmail.co.uk

(Secretary) 4 Gerard Place,
Oxford OX4 3HD, UK

Tel: +44 1865 774 362
Fax: +44 1865 355 035
Email: alex.may@oup.com
www.tandf.co.uk/journals
www.moot.org.uk

The Round Table provides analysis and commentary on all aspects of international affairs. The journal is a major source for coverage of the policy issues concerning the contemporary Commonwealth, with occasional articles on themes of historical interest. As part of its centenary celebrations, it organised a number of commemorative events, including seminars, book launches and conferences around the Commonwealth during 2010.

Foundation: 1910

Officers: Chair: Stuart Mole; Editor: Venkat Iyer; Book Reviews Editor: Terry Barringer; Commonwealth Update Editor: Oren Gruenbaum; Secretary: Alex May; Treasurer: Mark Robinson

Activities: As well as producing the journal, the editorial board organises occasional seminars, conferences and meetings on themes of Commonwealth interest.

Royal Commonwealth Ex-Services League (RCEL)*

Haig House, 199 Borough High Street, London SE1 1AA, UK

Tel: +44 20 3207 2413
Email: mgordon-roe@commonwealthveterans.org.uk
www.commonwealthveterans.org.uk

RCEL provides financial assistance to Commonwealth veterans in need who served the Crown and who are resident outside the UK. In 2003 it became the Royal Commonwealth Ex-Services League by order of Queen Elizabeth II.

Foundation: 1921 (as the Empire Service League)

Officers: Grand President: Prince Philip, Duke of Edinburgh KG KT; Deputy Grand President: General Sir Sam Cowan KCB CBE; Secretary-General: Colonel Paul Davis CBE

The Royal Commonwealth Society (RCS)*

25 Northumberland Avenue,
London WC2N 5AP, UK

Tel: +44 20 7766 9200
Fax: +44 20 7766 9200
Email: info@thercs.org
www.thercs.org
Library:
www.lib.cam.ac.uk/deptserv/rcs

The RCS is an education charity working to promote international understanding, particularly among young people, through the vehicle of the modern Commonwealth. It runs a range of events, youth projects and research activities. Founded in 1868, its home is the Commonwealth Club, a contemporary members' club and events venue in the heart of London. The RCS has some 4,000 members in the UK and a presence in over 40 Commonwealth countries through a network of branches and societies. Incorporated under Royal Charter, the Patron of the RCS is Queen Elizabeth II.

Foundation: 1868

Officers: President: Baroness Prashar CBE; Chair: Peter Kellner; Director: Dr Danny Sriskandarajah

Activities: With a remit to promote international understanding across the Commonwealth, especially among young people, the RCS boasts an impressive portfolio of charitable activities. The *Young Commonwealth Competitions* encourage thousands of young people to respond to global challenges through annual creative writing, film and photographic awards. The Nkabom Commonwealth Youth Leadership Programme unites 18 to 25 year-olds from across the globe in a different Commonwealth location every two years and alumni join an international, proactive network of emerging leaders. Commonwealth Youth Summits give school children across the UK a chance to learn about international issues in an interactive and meaningful forum. The Jubilee Time Capsule (JTC) is another innovative RCS project set to become the most complete digital legacy of the Diamond Jubilee. A crowd-sourced People's History of the last 60 years, tens of thousands of memories from across the Commonwealth have been submitted to the JTC. The 60 very best entries will be 'sealed' in a capsule and given to Her Majesty in 2012.

The RCS hosts regular art exhibitions, highlighting the work of emerging artists from around the

world. It runs public engagement projects, including most recently the UK civil society consultation on the draft Charter of the Commonwealth. The RCS also runs series of public debates on topics of Commonwealth and international interest with high-profile speakers. In March of each year, the RCS organises the Commonwealth Day Observance held at Westminster Abbey in London and attended by HM the Queen and, in December, hosts the Commonwealth Carol Service in St Martin-in-the-Fields, Trafalgar Square.

The home of the RCS, the Commonwealth Club, acts as a centre for the exchange of ideas and a leading London venue for discussing subjects of Commonwealth interest. Members range from long-serving diplomats interested in international affairs to young professionals looking for a stylish central London location to work, relax and meet like-minded people. The Club's versatile facilities can also be hired by non-members and all profits go towards funding the Society's charitable activities.

Publications: The RCS publishes a magazine, *RCS Exchange*, three times a year. This contains details of upcoming events, membership information, news about the Society's charitable projects, interviews and comment pieces on topics of Commonwealth interest. A monthly e-newsletter is also sent to members and a wider network of people interested in RCS events. An engaging website features sections on the Commonwealth Club, the Membership, the Society and its Youth work. An *Annual Review* is published in March and offers an overview of the year's activities. Occasional one-off publications are produced, including most recently a book to mark HM The Queen's Diamond Jubilee: *Queen and Commonwealth: Celebrating Her Majesty's Diamond Jubilee 1952–2012*.

In 2011, the RCS also published research reports and briefing papers to support its campaign with global children's charity Plan to end early and forced marriage in the Commonwealth. Individual projects, including the Young Commonwealth Competitions and Commonwealth Youth Summits, produce their own publications and resources.

Royal Over-Seas League*

Over-Seas House, Park Place, St James's Street, London SW1A 1LR, UK

Tel: +44 20 7408 0214 ext 206
Fax: +44 20 7499 6738
www.rosl.org.uk

The Royal Over-Seas League is a self-funded Commonwealth organisation incorporated by Royal Charter which offers residential clubhouse, conference and private dining facilities in London and Edinburgh, organises Commonwealth art exhibitions, an annual music competition, and develops joint welfare projects with specific countries. Full membership is open to men and women who are citizens of Commonwealth countries; affiliated membership is open to citizens of other countries.

Foundation: 1910

Officers: Patron: Queen Elizabeth II; Vice-Patron: Princess Alexandra; President: Lord Luce KG GCVO DL; Chairman: Sir Anthony Figgis KCVO CMG; Honorary Treasurer: Simon Ward FCA; Director-General: Major General Roddy Porter MBE

Sightsavers (The Royal Commonwealth Society for the Blind)*

Grosvenor Hall, Bolnore Road, Haywards Heath, West Sussex RH16 4BX, UK

Tel: +44 1444 446 600
Fax: +44 1444 446 688
Email: info@sightsavers.org
www.sightsavers.org

Sightsavers is the UK's leading charity working in the developing world to prevent and cure blindness, and to promote and support the social inclusion of blind children and adults.

Foundation: 1950

Officers: Chair of the Trustees: Lord Crisp of Eaglescliffe; Chief Executive: Dr Caroline Harper OBE

Activities: Since its foundation, Sightsavers has treated over 212.5 million people for blinding and potentially blinding conditions and restored sight to more than 7.2 million people. It works with local partner organisations, and places emphasis on developing sustainable programmes. It currently operates in more than 30 developing countries in Africa, Asia and the Caribbean.

Soroptimist International Commonwealth Group*

Headquarters Office, 87 Glisson Road, Cambridge CB1 2HG, UK

Tel: +44 1223 311 833
Fax: +44 1223 467 951
Email: hq@soroptimistinternational.org
www.soroptimistinternational.org

Soroptimist International (SI) is the umbrella organisation of the four individual Federations of Soroptimist Clubs, spanning 125 countries/territories, including 33 Commonwealth countries. It is a worldwide organisation for women in management and professions working through service projects to advance human rights and the status of women. SI established a Commonwealth Group in 1998.

Officers: International President 2011–2013: Alice Wells; Treasurer 2011–2013: Patricia Carruthers; Immediate Past International President 2011–2013: Hanne Jensbo; Executive Director: Rosie Coutts

Victoria League for Commonwealth Friendship

Victoria League House, 55 Leinster Square, London W2 4PW, UK

Tel: +44 20 7243 2633
Fax: +44 20 7229 2994
Email: membership@victorialeague.co.uk
www.victorialeague.co.uk

The Victoria League promotes friendship and understanding among the people of the Commonwealth.

Foundation: 1901

Officers: Chair: Lyn Hopkins BSc MBA FCA ASIP; General Manager: Doreen Henry

Activities: The League aims to welcome and assist all members and visitors from every part of the Commonwealth, giving hospitality, organising events and issuing a diary of events. It also provides hostel accommodation for Commonwealth students.

Membership of international and regional organisations

	UN	WTO	ACP	NAM	OIF	OIC	OECD	NATO	AU	COMESA	EAC	ECOWAS	IGAD
Antigua and Barbuda	✓	✓	✓	✓									
Australia	✓	✓					✓						
The Bahamas	✓		✓	✓									
Bangladesh	✓	✓		✓		✓							
Barbados	✓	✓	✓	✓									
Belize	✓	✓	✓	✓									
Botswana	✓	✓	✓	✓					✓				
Brunei Darussalam	✓	✓		✓		✓							
Cameroon	✓	✓	✓	✓	✓	✓			✓				
Canada	✓	✓			✓		✓	✓					
Cyprus	✓	✓			✓								
Dominica	✓	✓	✓	✓	✓								
Fiji	✓	✓	✓										
The Gambia	✓	✓	✓	✓		✓			✓			✓	
Ghana	✓	✓	✓	✓	✓				✓			✓	
Grenada	✓	✓	✓	✓									
Guyana	✓	✓	✓	✓		✓							
India	✓	✓		✓									
Jamaica	✓	✓	✓	✓									
Kenya	✓	✓	✓	✓					✓	✓	✓		✓
Kiribati	✓		✓										
Lesotho	✓	✓	✓	✓					✓				
Malawi	✓	✓	✓	✓					✓	✓			
Malaysia	✓	✓		✓		✓							
Maldives	✓	✓		✓		✓							
Malta	✓	✓											
Mauritius	✓	✓	✓	✓	✓				✓	✓			
Mozambique	✓	✓	✓	✓		✓			✓				
Namibia	✓	✓	✓	✓					✓				
Nauru	✓		✓										
New Zealand	✓	✓					✓						
Nigeria	✓	✓	✓	✓		✓			✓			✓	
Pakistan	✓	✓		✓		✓							
Papua New Guinea	✓	✓	✓	✓									
Rwanda	✓	✓	✓	✓	✓				✓	✓	✓		
St Kitts and Nevis	✓	✓	✓	✓									
St Lucia	✓	✓	✓	✓	✓								
St Vincent and the Grenadines	✓	✓	✓	✓									
Samoa	✓		✓										
Seychelles	✓		✓	✓	✓				✓	✓			
Sierra Leone	✓	✓	✓	✓		✓			✓			✓	
Singapore	✓	✓		✓									
Solomon Islands	✓	✓	✓										
South Africa	✓	✓	✓	✓					✓				
Sri Lanka	✓	✓		✓									
Swaziland	✓	✓	✓	✓					✓	✓			
Tonga	✓	✓	✓										
Trinidad and Tobago	✓	✓	✓	✓									
Tuvalu	✓		✓										
Uganda	✓	✓	✓	✓		✓			✓	✓	✓		✓
United Kingdom	✓	✓					✓	✓					
United Republic of Tanzania	✓	✓	✓	✓					✓		✓		
Vanuatu	✓		✓	✓	✓								
Zambia	✓	✓	✓	✓					✓	✓			
Totals	**54**	**47**	**40**	**41**	**10**	**12**	**4**	**2**	**19**	**8**	**4**	**4**	**2**

UN	United Nations	OECD	Organisation for Economic Co-operation and Development
WTO	World Trade Organization	NATO	North Atlantic Treaty Organization
ACP	African, Caribbean and Pacific Group of States	AU	African Union
NAM	Non-Aligned Movement	COMESA	Common Market for Eastern and Southern Africa
OIF	L'Organisation internationale de la Francophonie	EAC	East African Community
OIC	Organisation of Islamic Cooperation (formerly Organisation of the Islamic Conference)	ECOWAS	Economic Community of West African States
		IGAD	Intergovernmental Authority on Development

Membership of international and regional organisations

	SACU	SADC	APEC	ASEAN	IOR-ARC	PC	PIF	SAARC	ACS	CARICOM	OAS	OECS	EU
Antigua and Barbuda									✓	✓	✓	✓	
Australia			✓		✓	✓	✓						
The Bahamas									✓	✓	✓		
Bangladesh					✓			✓					
Barbados									✓	✓	✓		
Belize									✓	✓	✓		
Botswana	✓	✓											
Brunei Darussalam			✓	✓									
Cameroon													
Canada			✓								✓		
Cyprus													✓
Dominica									✓	✓	✓	✓	
Fiji						✓							
The Gambia													
Ghana													
Grenada									✓	✓	✓	✓	
Guyana									✓	✓	✓		
India					✓			✓					
Jamaica									✓	✓	✓		
Kenya					✓								
Kiribati						✓	✓						
Lesotho	✓	✓											
Malawi		✓											
Malaysia			✓	✓	✓								
Maldives								✓					
Malta													✓
Mauritius		✓			✓								
Mozambique		✓			✓								
Namibia	✓	✓											
Nauru						✓	✓						
New Zealand			✓			✓	✓						
Nigeria													
Pakistan								✓					
Papua New Guinea			✓			✓	✓						
Rwanda													
St Kitts and Nevis									✓	✓	✓	✓	
St Lucia									✓	✓	✓	✓	
St Vincent and the Grenadines									✓	✓	✓	✓	
Samoa						✓	✓						
Seychelles		✓											
Sierra Leone													
Singapore			✓	✓	✓								
Solomon Islands						✓	✓						
South Africa	✓	✓			✓								
Sri Lanka					✓			✓					
Swaziland	✓	✓											
Tonga						✓	✓						
Trinidad and Tobago									✓	✓	✓		
Tuvalu						✓	✓						
Uganda													
United Kingdom													✓
United Republic of Tanzania		✓			✓								
Vanuatu						✓	✓						
Zambia		✓											
Totals	**5**	**11**	**7**	**3**	**11**	**11**	**10**	**5**	**12**	**12**	**13**	**6**	**3**

SACU	Southern African Customs Union	SAARC	South Asian Association for Regional Cooperation
SADC	Southern African Development Community	ACS	Association of Caribbean States
APEC	Asia–Pacific Economic Cooperation	CARICOM	Caribbean Community
ASEAN	Association of Southeast Asian Nations	OAS	Organization of American States
IOR-ARC	Indian Ocean Rim Association for Regional Cooperation	OECS	Organisation of Eastern Caribbean States
PC	Pacific Community	EU	European Union
PIF	Pacific Islands Forum		

Fiji was suspended from participation in the Pacific Islands Forum in May 2009

Commonwealth Declarations and Statements

London Declaration

The London Declaration formed the substance of the Final Communiqué of the 1949 Commonwealth Prime Ministers' Meeting.

The Governments of the United Kingdom, Canada, Australia, New Zealand, South Africa, India, Pakistan and Ceylon, whose countries are united as Members of the British Commonwealth of Nations and owe a common allegiance to the Crown, which is also the symbol of their free association, have considered the impending constitutional changes in India.

The Government of India have informed the other Governments of the Commonwealth of the intention of the Indian people that under the new constitution which is about to be adopted India shall become a sovereign independent republic. The Government of India have however declared and affirmed India's desire to continue her full membership of the Commonwealth of Nations and her acceptance of The King as the symbol of the free association of its independent member nations and as such the Head of the Commonwealth.

The Governments of the other countries of the Commonwealth, the basis of whose membership of the Commonwealth is not hereby changed, accept and recognise India's continuing membership in accordance with the terms of this declaration.

Accordingly the United Kingdom, Canada, Australia, New Zealand, South Africa, India, Pakistan and Ceylon hereby declare that they remain united as free and equal members of the Commonwealth of Nations, freely co-operating in the pursuit of peace, liberty and progress.

London, UK, 26 April 1949

Lusaka Declaration

The Lusaka Declaration of the Commonwealth on Racism and Racial Prejudice, issued at the Commonwealth Heads of Government Meeting in Lusaka, Zambia, in 1979, ensured that the battle against all forms of racism, within the Commonwealth's own societies and anywhere in the world, became and would remain one of the association's core concerns.

We, the Commonwealth Heads of Government, recalling the Declaration of Commonwealth Principles made at Singapore on 22 January 1971 and the statement on Apartheid in Sport, issued in London on 15 June 1977, have decided to proclaim our desire to work jointly as well as severally for the eradication of all forms of racism and racial prejudice.

The Commonwealth is an institution devoted to the promotion of international understanding and world peace, and to the achievement of equal rights for all citizens regardless of race, colour, sex, creed or political belief, and is committed to the eradication of the dangerous evils of racism and racial prejudice.

We now, therefore, proclaim this Lusaka Declaration of the Commonwealth on Racism and Racial Prejudice.

United in our desire to rid the world of the evils of racism and racial prejudice, we proclaim our faith in the inherent dignity and worth of the human person and declare that:

- the peoples of the Commonwealth have the right to live freely in dignity and equality, without any distinction or exclusion based on race, colour, sex, descent, or national or ethnic origin

- while everyone is free to retain diversity in his or her culture and lifestyle, this diversity does not justify the perpetuation of racial prejudice or racially discriminatory practices

- everyone has the right to equality before the law and equal justice under the law

- everyone has the right to effective remedies and protection against any form of discrimination based on the grounds of race, colour, sex, descent, or national or ethnic origin.

We reject as inhuman and intolerable all policies designed to perpetuate apartheid, racial segregation or other policies based on theories that racial groups are or may be inherently superior or inferior.

We reaffirm that it is the duty of all the peoples of the Commonwealth to work together for the total eradication of the infamous policy of apartheid which is internationally recognised as a crime against the conscience and dignity of mankind and the very existence of which is an affront to humanity.

We agree that everyone has the right to protection against acts of incitement to racial hatred and discrimination, whether committed by individuals, groups or other organisations.

We affirm that there should be no discrimination based on race, colour, sex, descent or national or ethnic origin in the acquisition or exercise of the right to vote; in the field of civil rights or access to citizenship; or in the economic, social or cultural fields, particularly education, health, employment, occupation, housing, social security and cultural life.

We attach particular importance to ensuring that children shall be protected from practices which may foster racism or racial prejudice. Children have the right to be brought up and educated in a spirit of tolerance and understanding so as to be able to contribute fully to the building of future societies based on justice and friendship.

We believe that those groups in societies who may be especially disadvantaged because of residual racist attitudes are entitled to the fullest protection of the law.

We recognise that the history of the Commonwealth and its diversity require that special attention should be paid to the problems of indigenous minorities. We recognise that the same special attention should be paid to the problems of immigrants, immigrant workers and refugees.

We agree that special measures may in particular circumstances be required to advance the development of disadvantaged groups in society. We recognise that the effects of colonialism or racism in the past may make desirable special provisions for the social and economic enhancement of indigenous populations.

Inspired by the principles of freedom and equality which characterise our association, we accept the solemn duty of working together to eliminate racism and racial prejudice. This duty involves the acceptance of the principle that positive measures may be required to advance the elimination of racism, including assistance to those struggling to rid themselves and their environment of the practice.

Being aware that legislation alone cannot eliminate racism and racial prejudice, we endorse the need to initiate public information and education policies designed to promote understanding, tolerance, respect and friendship among peoples and racial groups.

We are particularly conscious of the importance of the contribution the media can make to human rights and the eradication of racism and racial prejudice by helping to eliminate ignorance and misunderstanding between people and by drawing attention to the evils which afflict humanity. We affirm the importance of truthful presentation of facts in order to ensure that the public are fully informed of the dangers presented by racism and racial prejudice.

In accordance with established principles of International Law and, in particular, the provisions of the International Convention on the Elimination of All Forms of Racial Discrimination, we affirm that everyone is, at all times and in all places, entitled to be protected in the enjoyment of the right to be free of racism and racial prejudice.

We believe that the existence in the world of apartheid and racial discrimination is a matter of concern to all human beings. We recognise that we share an international responsibility to work together for the total eradication of apartheid and racial discrimination.

We note that racism and racial prejudice, wherever they occur, are significant factors contributing to tension between nations and thus inhibit peaceful progress and development. We believe that the goal of the eradication of racism stands as a critical priority for governments of the Commonwealth, committed as they are to the promotion of the ideals of peaceful and happy lives for their people.

We intend that the Commonwealth, as an international organisation with a fundamental and deep-rooted attachment to principles of freedom and equality, should co-operate with other organisations in the fulfilment of these principles. In particular the Commonwealth should seek to enhance the co-ordination of its activities with those of other organisations similarly committed to the promotion and protection of human rights and fundamental freedoms.

Lusaka, Zambia, 7 August 1979

Edinburgh Declaration

The Edinburgh Commonwealth Economic Declaration (Promoting Shared Prosperity) recognises that the Commonwealth, with its shared traditions and global reach, is uniquely placed to play a key role in promoting trade and investment, eradicating poverty and protecting the environment, to the mutual benefit of its members.

Today's globalised world poses both opportunities and challenges. Expanding trade and investment flows, driven by new technologies and the spread of market forces, have emerged as engines of growth. At the same time, not all countries have benefited equally from the globalisation of the world economy, and a significant number are threatened with marginalisation. Globalisation therefore needs to be carefully managed to meet the risks inherent in the process.

We believe that world peace, security and social stability cannot be achieved in conditions of deep poverty and growing inequality. Special measures are needed to correct this, and in particular to help the integration of countries, especially small states and the Least Developed Countries, in the global economy and address the uneven development that threatens many countries. To redress these problems, we believe the following broad principled approaches should be pursued:

- the world economy should be geared towards promoting universal growth and prosperity for all

- there must be effective participation by all countries in economic decision-making in key international fora

- the removal of obstacles that prevent developing countries playing their full part in shaping the evolution of the global economy, and

- international regimes affecting economic relations among nations should provide symmetrical benefits for all.

We also believe that commitment to market principles, openness to international trade and investment, the development of human and physical resources, gender equality, and good governance and political stability remain major components of economic and social progress; and that wealth creation requires partnerships between governments and the private sector. The Commonwealth, with its shared traditions and global reach, is uniquely placed to play a key role in promoting shared prosperity amongst its members.

Trade

We welcome the progress made in recent years in dismantling trade barriers and establishing a rule-based international trading system. However, significant barriers to trade in goods and services remain, and the benefits of the expansion of world trade are still unevenly shared. We have therefore resolved to:

- support expansion of duty-free market access with flexible rules of origin for the exports of the Least Developed Countries; work for a successor arrangement to the Lomé Convention which, without prejudice to the outcome, gives the ACP countries, particularly small states, adequate transitional arrangements; and in particular, encourage the EU and WTO members to accommodate the legitimate interests of the ACP banana producers and facilitate the diversification of their economies

- strengthen the multilateral trading system within the framework of the WTO, in order to prevent regional arrangements from becoming exclusive

trading blocs and provide for the greatest flow of international trade on the basis of agreed rules which are fair and equitable; and support the full implementation of the Uruguay Round Agreements

- oppose the introduction of new non-tariff barriers and the use of unilateral actions and bilateral pressures which run counter to the spirit of the WTO

- maintain the momentum towards freer trade through multilateral negotiations, as outlined in the built-in agenda and other issues under discussion in the WTO, including progress on agriculture and financial and other services, taking into account the interests of all countries at different stages of development, and

- continue to support regional arrangements, consistent with multilateral liberalisation under the WTO, which promote the economic growth of their members.

Specifically we have decided to:

- establish a Trade and Investment Access Facility under the Commonwealth umbrella to assist developing countries with the process of adjusting to, and taking advantage of, the opportunities of globalisation. The new Facility will provide technical assistance to help countries identify and manage the potential economic and social impacts of trade in goods and services and investment liberalisation; identify new sources of revenue and market opportunities; and help countries fulfil WTO requirements. The Facility will be co-ordinated with the proposed WTO/UNCTAD/ITC integrated framework for trade-related technical assistance

- explore the scope for deepening trade relationships among Commonwealth members, and therefore request the Secretariat to report to us, before the 1999 CHOGM, on the scope and possible systems and mechanisms for improving trade among members of the Commonwealth, in ways which are consistent with the provisions of the WTO and regional trading arrangements

- launch a Commonwealth action programme to remove administrative obstacles to trade by simplifying and harmonising customs procedures, disseminating information, and eliminating bureaucratic and technical hurdles

- examine the growing importance of 'electronic commerce' in trade and the developmental implications of the use of cyberspace for commercial and financial transactions, and

- promote Commonwealth Export Training Centres for management training in exporting and other trade-related skills.

We welcome the recommendations of the first ever Commonwealth Business Forum held in London on 22–23 October 1997. We believe that the Forum can be an important link between the private and public sectors and foster vibrant private sector business links. It should continue to meet every two years. We are also arranging to set up a Business Council, under Lord Cairns and Mr Cyril Ramaphosa, made up of a small group of major private sector leaders from different regions of the Commonwealth, as well as other mechanisms, in consultation with the Commonwealth Secretary-General, to encourage greater private sector involvement in the promotion of trade and investment. In this context, we also agree to support and strengthen the work of the Commonwealth Partnership for Technology Management (CPTM).

Investment

We believe that investment flows can bring substantial benefits, and that sound macroeconomic policies and financial systems, strong regulatory and supervisory frameworks and political stability are essential in encouraging inward flows. At the same time, we recognise that volatility in such flows can greatly complicate economic management. They also remain concentrated in a few regions and countries. We agree to:

- encourage investment flows by establishing open and transparent investment regimes for business activity, and by simplifying bureaucratic procedures and regulations

- encourage capital exporting countries, where it is prudent, to consider relaxing restrictions on institutional investors to enable them to take advantage of portfolio diversification opportunities in emerging and new markets

- support the development of regional and multilateral arrangements and infrastructure that take into account the realities of developing countries, and that can help to facilitate private capital flows

study the lessons to be learned from recent developments in currency markets and in particular on how countries can be protected from the destabilising effects of market volatility, including those resulting from speculative activities, and how the effectiveness of existing early warning systems can be improved, and

support strengthening of global and regional mechanisms to help countries handle capital market volatility.

Specifically we have decided to:

endorse the recommendations of the Commonwealth working group on the role of national and international policies in promoting private capital flows, and call for the rapid finalisation of a Commonwealth Code of Good Practice for national policies that attract and sustain private capital flows

welcome the launch of the Africa Fund, the Kula Fund for the Pacific, and the South Asia Regional Fund under the aegis of the Commonwealth Private Investment Initiative (CPII); and call for the extension of CPII to embrace additional regions and sectors

launch a Commonwealth investment promotion programme which will: help establish enabling environments for attracting private investment flows; encourage the creation of new mechanisms for risk insurance and guarantees; provide assistance for strengthening supervisory and regulatory frameworks; and improve the flow of information on investment opportunities, and

encourage 'smart partnerships' involving the private and public sectors.

Development

We welcome the improving growth prospects in many parts of the developing world, including evidence of recovery in Sub-Saharan Africa. At the same time, we remain concerned at the persistence of extreme poverty in many countries and the lack of capacity to reduce it. We have therefore agreed to:

work to halve the proportion of people living in extreme poverty by the year 2015

seek to reverse the decline in Official Development Assistance (ODA) flows, recognising the role of ODA as an essential instrument of partnership for development and poverty reduction in developing countries, particularly the Least Developed Countries and small states, and for helping to create the conditions for increased trade and investment, including skills and infrastructure development

work towards a comprehensive solution of the debt problem, and pursue vigorously the rapid implementation of the Highly Indebted Poor Countries (HIPC) Initiative, in line with the Mauritius Mandate, which has the aim of enabling HIPC countries to have embarked by the year 2000 on securing a sustainable exit from their debt burden; as well as consider extending such relief to other developing countries, including small states, in similar circumstances, and

promote the role of micro-credit schemes in reducing poverty through increased assistance from the international community.

We welcome the report of the Chairperson of the Commonwealth Ministerial Group on Small States and its recommendations for action based on the Commonwealth report, *A Future for Small States: Overcoming Vulnerability*. In particular, we encourage international financial institutions to review their graduation policies, consider broader criteria covering the special vulnerabilities of their smaller members, and establish a task force to address the concerns of small states. We endorse the recommendation to set up a small ministerial group to discuss small states' concerns with major multilateral agencies and to report to governments on the outcome as soon as possible.

We underscore the importance of good governance including increased openness in economic decision-making and the elimination of corruption through greater transparency, accountability and the application of the rule of law in economic, financial and other spheres of activity. We endorse the request by our Finance Ministers to the Commonwealth Secretary-General to establish an expert group to work on these issues.

Environment

We have a shared interest in protecting our environment, a global resource in which all countries have a stake. The costs of protecting it should be borne in accordance with shared and differentiated responsibilities. It is therefore incumbent on the global community to strengthen co-operation to achieve sustainable development, so that we can protect our planet for future generations. In particular, we look to a successful outcome at the

Kyoto Conference of Parties to the UN Convention on Climate Change, involving realistic and achievable goals, significant reductions in greenhouse gas emissions and recognition that we all need to play a role.

We have therefore agreed to:

endorse the Programme for the Further Implementation of Agenda 21 as agreed by this year's UN General Assembly Special Session, particularly in respect of freshwater, forest resources and the transfer of environmentally sound technologies to developing countries. We recognise that new and additional resources will be needed to implement the programmes and will use our best endeavours to provide these

underline the importance of a successful outcome at Kyoto, with all countries playing their part within the Berlin Mandate, and with developed countries pursuing vigorously an outcome that would produce significant reductions in their greenhouse gas emissions through the adoption of a protocol or other legal instrument

call on the Kyoto Conference to recognise that, after Kyoto, all countries will need to play their part by pursuing policies that would result in significant reductions of greenhouse gas emissions if we are to solve a global problem that affects us all

call for agreement at Kyoto to arrangements to monitor the reduction of emissions regularly

initiate action in the international community to strengthen disaster relief response and mechanisms for the provision of urgent and adequate assistance to small states that suffer the effects of natural disasters which are increasing in frequency and magnitude, and

welcome the contribution of the Iwokrama International Rain Forest Programme in Guyana to the implementation of the Rio agreements on forests, biodiversity and climate change, and agree to use our best endeavours to increase resources to sustain the Programme and catalyse further international funding.

Conclusion

In pursuance of these commitments, we agree to enhance the Commonwealth's role in building consensus on global economic issues and on an equitable structuring of international economic relations.

We also agree to sustain and where possible increase bilateral assistance among our members; and to ensure the flow of resources to the Secretariat and its various Funds, especially the Commonwealth Fund for Technical Co-operation (CFTC); and to the Commonwealth Foundation, Commonwealth of Learning (COL) and the CPTM.

We believe the Commonwealth can play a dynamic role in promoting trade and investment so as to enhance prosperity, accelerate economic growth and development and advance the eradication of poverty in the 21st century. We plan to pursue this with vigour.

Edinburgh, UK, 25 October 1997

Fancourt Declaration

The Fancourt Commonwealth Declaration on Globalisation and People-Centred Development expresses the concern of Commonwealth leaders at the 1999 summit in South Africa that, while globalisation offers unprecedented opportunities for wealth creation and for the improvement of the human condition, its benefits are not shared equitably.

In today's world, no country is untouched by the forces of globalisation. Our destinies are linked together as never before. The challenge is to seize the opportunities opened up by globalisation while minimising its risks.

On the positive side, globalisation is creating unprecedented opportunities for wealth creation and for the betterment of the human condition. Reduced barriers to trade and enhanced capital flows are fuelling economic growth.

The revolution in communications technologies is shrinking the distance between nations, providing new opportunities for the transfer of knowledge and the development of skills-based industries. And technological advance globally offers great potential for the eradication of poverty.

But the benefits of globalisation are not shared equitably. Prosperity remains the preserve of the few. Despite the progress of the past 50 years, half the world's population lives on less than US$2 per day. Many millions live in conditions of extreme deprivation. The poor are being marginalised. Expanded capital flows have also brought with them the risk of greater financial instability, undermining the hope that a commitment to open markets can lift the developing world, especially the least developed countries, out of poverty and debt.

The persistence of poverty and human deprivation diminishes us all. It also makes global peace and security fragile, limits the growth of markets, and forces millions to migrate in search of a better life. It constitutes a deep and fundamental structural flaw in the world economy.

The greatest challenge therefore facing us today is how to channel the forces of globalisation for the elimination of poverty and the empowerment of human beings to lead fulfilling lives.

The solution does not lie in abandoning a commitment to market principles or in wishing away the powerful forces of technological change. Globalisation is a reality and can only increase in its impact. But if the benefits of globalisation are to be shared more widely, there must be greater equity for countries in global markets.

We call on all nations fully to implement the Uruguay Round commitments to dismantle barriers to trade for the mutual benefit of all. Moreover, recognising in particular the significant contribution that enhanced export opportunities can make for reducing poverty, we call for improved market access for the exports of all countries, particularly developing countries, and the removal of all barriers to the exports of the least developed countries.

Strong export growth remains a key element in the ability of developing countries to improve their living standards to the levels enjoyed in the industrialised world. We support efforts that would enable developing countries to build up their skills and manufacturing capacities, including the production and export of value-added goods, so as to enhance growth and achieve prosperity.

Likewise, we urge that the forthcoming Ministerial Meeting of WTO to launch the next round of global negotiations on trade be one with a pronounced developmental dimension, with the aim of achieving better market access in agriculture, industrial products and services in a way that provides benefits to all members, particularly developing countries. The Round should be balanced in process, content and outcome.

We fully believe in the importance of upholding labour standards and protecting the environment. But these must be addressed in an appropriate way that does not, by linking them to trade liberalisation, end up effectively impeding free trade and causing injustice to developing countries.

We also call on the global community to establish innovative mechanisms to promote capital flows to a wider number of countries; and to urgently initiate reform of the international financial architecture to minimise financial instability and its impact on the poor.

We believe that the elimination of poverty is achievable, but only if we take determined and concerted action at national and international levels. We reiterate our commitment to work for a reversal of the decline in official development assistance flows. Urgent action is also required to tackle the unsustainable debt burden of developing countries, particularly the poorest, building on the recent initiatives agreed internationally. We believe such development assistance must be focused on human development, poverty reduction and on the development of capacities for participating in expanding world markets for goods and capital. Above all, we recognise the responsibilities of national governments to promote pro-poor policies and human development.

If the poor and the vulnerable are to be at the centre of development, the process must be participatory, in which they have a voice. We believe that the spread of democratic freedoms and good governance, and access to education, training and health care are key to the expansion of human capabilities, and to the banishment of ignorance and prejudice. Recognising that good governance and economic progress are directly linked, we affirm our commitment to the pursuit of greater transparency, accountability, the rule of law and the elimination of corruption in all spheres of public life and in the private sector.

We are concerned at the vast gap between rich and poor in the ability to access the new technologies, at the concentration of the world's research resources in market-driven products and processes, the increasing tendency to claim proprietary rights on traditional knowledge, and at bio-piracy. We call on the world community to use the opportunities offered by globalisation for adopting practical measures for overcoming these challenges; for example, by extending the benefits of global medical research through the provision of drugs at affordable prices to the poor in developing countries.

We welcome the spread of ideas, information and knowledge in building civil support for social equality, and in opposing all forms of discrimination and other injustices based on ethnicity, gender, race and religion. But, while better communications have increased human contact, there is for some a growing sense of social exclusion and a general failure of moral purpose. Persistence of inequalities faced by women, continued high levels of youth

unemployment, lack of adequate support systems for the aged, children and the disabled in many parts of the world and increased threats to the diversity of cultures and beliefs all contribute to the undermining of just and stable society. We therefore call for a renewed commitment to eliminate all forms of discrimination and to take measures that promote respect for the diverse languages, cultures and beliefs, and traditions of the world, which enrich all our lives.

Recognising that the full exploitation of the opportunities for development created by globalisation is not possible without security, political stability and peace, we commit ourselves, in partnership with civil society, to promote processes that help to prevent or resolve conflicts in a peaceful manner, support measures that help to stabilise post-conflict situations, and combat terrorism of all kinds.

Good governance requires inclusive and participatory processes at both national and international levels. We call on the global community to search for inclusive processes of multilateralism which give a more effective voice in the operations of international institutions to developing countries, and which recognise the particular vulnerabilities of small states.

We believe that the Commonwealth, an association of diverse sovereign nations reflecting different stages of development and united by common values, has a vital role to play in promoting consensus at national and international levels and in providing practical assistance for the creation of capacities needed to promote people-centred development. At the threshold of a new millennium, we look to the Commonwealth, and its family of organisations, to contribute significantly to making the above aspirations a reality.

Fancourt, George, South Africa, 14 November 1999

Coolum Declaration

The Coolum Declaration (The Commonwealth in the 21st Century: Continuity and Renewal) addresses the role of the association, and renews the enduring commitment of Heads of Government to shared values and principles.

At the outset of this new millennium we, the Heads of Government of the Commonwealth of Nations, meeting at Coolum, Australia, renew our enduring commitment to the values and principles which we share.

We stand united in:

- our commitment to democracy, the rule of law, good governance, freedom of expression and the protection of human rights

- our respect for diversity and human dignity; our celebration of the pluralistic nature of our societies and the tolerance it promotes; and our implacable opposition to all forms of discrimination, whether rooted in gender, race, colour, creed or political belief

- our determination to work to eliminate poverty, to promote people-centred and sustainable development, and thus progressively to remove the wide disparities in living standards among us and overcome the special challenges facing our small state and less developed country members, and

- our collective striving after international peace and security, the rule of international law, and the elimination of people-smuggling and the scourge of terrorism.

We reiterate in the strongest terms our condemnation of all forms and manifestations of terrorism. In the aftermath of the events of 11 September 2001 and following our statement of 25 October 2001, we solemnly reaffirm our resolve as a diverse community of nations individually and collectively to take concerted and resolute action to eradicate terrorism. We pledge to work together in fulfilling our international obligations to deny any safe haven for terrorists.

We cannot accept that nearly half the world's population should live in poverty, nor that disease, illiteracy and environmental degradation should continue to blight the lives of many of our people, nor the fact that in too many societies women continue to face discrimination. The benefits of globalisation must be shared more widely and its focus channelled for the elimination of poverty and human deprivation. We stress the importance of equality of access to economic opportunities and the need to apply new international standards such as the OECD Harmful Tax Initiative evenly, equitably and without exception.

The Fancourt Declaration and the UN Millennium Declaration have laid a firm base for us to push back the frontiers of poverty and underdevelopment. In pursuit of the Millennium Development Goals, we call on governments to seize the opportunities presented by the Financing for Development Conference (Monterrey, Mexico, 18–22 March 2002) and the World Summit on Sustainable Development (Johannesburg, South Africa, August/September 2002) to chart a more sustainable and equitable growth path for the world. We also welcome the ground-breaking proposal from Africa to tackle poverty through the New Partnership for Africa's Development, and will use our best efforts to support similar partnerships in other regions of the Commonwealth. More broadly, we call on all nations to work to reduce the growing gap between rich and poor, and to enhance international support to democracies fighting poverty.

Recognising the links between democracy and good governance on the one hand, and poverty, development and conflict on the other, we call on the Commonwealth Secretary-General to constitute a high-level expert group to recommend ways in which we could carry forward the Fancourt Declaration. This group should focus on how democracies might best be supported in combating poverty, and should report to the next CHOGM.

We are deeply conscious of the threat HIV/AIDS poses to hard-won social and economic progress in much of Africa and elsewhere. As leaders committed to each one of our citizens developing their human potential to the full, we pledge ourselves to combating this pandemic and the spread of other communicable diseases. We urge both the public and private sector, and international organisations, to join with us in a renewed effort to tackle the challenge HIV/AIDS presents to our countries and their people, and to humanity itself.

We recognise the particular vulnerabilities of small states, as well as the need for concerted action by the international community to address their special needs. We further appreciate the importance of systemic changes to respond to these needs, and we commit the Commonwealth to pursue innovative and practical support mechanisms for small states.

Many other challenges confront us daily. As leaders guiding our nations into the 21st century, we need a Commonwealth that both builds on our enduring values and adapts to our evolving needs. We seek a Commonwealth in tune with the future: an organisation which draws on its history, plays to its strengths, vigorously pursues its members' common interests and seizes the opportunities open to it to shape a better world for our children.

We envisage a modern and vibrant Commonwealth working to serve its peoples, with a simplified structure and a clear focus on what it does best. We want the Commonwealth to be an effective defender of democratic freedoms and a peace-maker in conflict, and to work tirelessly in promoting people-centred economic development.

We have adopted the High Level Review Group (HLRG) Report which charts a clear future course for the Commonwealth in line with this vision. The HLRG Report sets out concrete steps to build a Commonwealth for the 21st century:

- We determine materially to strengthen the Commonwealth's capacity to support its members' pursuit of democratic values and the rule of law. We have clarified the conditions under which the Commonwealth Ministerial Action Group will in future address serious or persistent violations of the Harare Principles, which go beyond the unconstitutional overthrow of member governments. A clear set of procedures – in which the Secretary-General and the Chairperson in Office will have an important part to play – will help ensure transparent and effective dealing with any member state concerned. We are committed to strengthening the Good Offices role of the Commonwealth Secretary-General and have agreed to strengthen the Commonwealth's work in supporting democratic practice, in resolving tensions, in conflict prevention and resolution, and in post-conflict rebuilding, working in consultation with regional organisations as appropriate.

- In pursuit of a more equitable distribution of the benefits of globalisation and in pursuit of the Millennium Development Goals, we are committed to forging new opportunities for our members in trade, in investment and in private sector development. We have agreed steps which will help our organisation better identify and promote its members' economic and development needs in an increasingly competitive international environment. We recognise the importance of enhancing market access in the global trading system, particularly for the poorest and smallest countries. To this end, we welcome and give our strong support to the agreement reached in Doha on the World Trade Organization's new multilateral trade negotiations. Through an enhanced facilitation role, we want our organisation to help member states get better access to international assistance, and to focus the Commonwealth's own related programmes more effectively on the assistance it is best-equipped to provide. We support the HLRG's strategy to bridge the information and communications technology gap between rich and poor.

- Recognising that the Commonwealth's future lies in the hands of its youth, we have agreed to create a pan-Commonwealth 'Youth for the Future' initiative composed of four related components for technology and skills transfer, and for fostering youth enterprise. We seek to engage youth, young professionals and youth volunteers more closely, harnessing their skills and enthusiasm to make a major practical contribution to the work of the Commonwealth.

- We seek to rationalise and streamline the Commonwealth's governance and organisation to provide a simplified structure capable of responding more quickly and effectively to members' needs.

- We call on the many intergovernmental, professional and civil society bodies which help to implement our Commonwealth values, to join with us in building closer Commonwealth 'family' links, and strengthening consultation and collaboration. We are convinced of the need for stronger links and better two-way communication and co-ordination between the official and non-governmental Commonwealth, and among Commonwealth NGOs. This will give Commonwealth activities greater impact, ensuring that every programme produces lasting benefit.

We cherish our shared history and are proud of what we have achieved together over the years. We are convinced that acting on the recommendations of the HLRG Report will better equip the Commonwealth to meet the challenges of the future. Our common values and unique ways of working together provide a special strength in this, which we treasure. We call on our Secretary-General to work assiduously with the Chairman in Office, the new governing mechanisms and the wider Commonwealth family to translate the outcomes of the review into a practical reality which benefits all our people.

As we plan for our future, we congratulate Her Majesty Queen Elizabeth II on her completion of 50 years as the Head of the Commonwealth. We are grateful for her dedication in the service of the Commonwealth and her strong commitment to the association for over half a century.

Coolum, Australia, 5 March 2002

Aso Rock Declaration

Building on the landmark declarations – the Declaration of Commonwealth Principles, Harare Commonwealth Declaration, and Fancourt Commonwealth Declaration on Globalisation and People-Centred Development – Heads of Government committed themselves to strengthen development and democracy, through partnership for peace and prosperity.

We, the Heads of Government of the Commonwealth of Nations, meeting at Abuja, Nigeria, from 5 to 8 December 2003, commit ourselves to strengthen development and democracy, through partnership for peace and prosperity. Building on the landmark declarations in Singapore, Harare and Fancourt, we are committed to democracy, good governance, human rights, gender equality and a more equitable sharing of the benefits of globalisation.

We recognise that the governments of the Commonwealth are partners sharing a fundamental responsibility for the development, security and well-being of their people. We acknowledge their central role in guaranteeing stability, good economic management and governance, and in promoting sustainable growth and development.

We welcome the Report of the Commonwealth Expert Group on Development and Democracy which was constituted following the 2002 Coolum CHOGM. We have noted its key recommendations for Commonwealth actions, focusing on how democracies can best be supported in combating poverty.

We believe that efforts aimed at eradicating poverty and improving governance are essential for greater international equity and global peace and security. We recognise that the Millennium Development Goals (MDGs) have mobilised governments, international institutions and civil society to reduce poverty with renewed vigour and commitment.

We recognise that globalisation has significant potential benefits for all. However, the world is characterised by uneven development, and we therefore stress that globalisation must provide real opportunities for developing countries to transform their economies and societies through diversification for the benefit of their people. It is the strategic goal of the Commonwealth to help their pre-industrial members to transition into skilled working- and middle-class societies, recognising that their domestic policies must be conducive to such transitions.

We further recognise that while development and democracy are goals each in its own right, they must be mutually reinforcing, with a clear 'democratic dividend', in terms of delivering tangible benefits to people. We are convinced that broad-based prosperity creates the stability conducive to the promotion of democracy; and that strong democratic institutions better promote development.

Accordingly, we commit ourselves to make democracy work better for pro-poor development by implementing sustainable development programmes and enhancing democratic institutions and processes in all human endeavours. We recognise that building democracy is a constantly evolving process. It must also be uncomplicated and take into account national circumstances. Among the objectives we seek to promote are the following:

- a participatory democracy characterised by free and fair elections and representative legislatures
- an independent judiciary
- a well-trained public service
- a transparent and accountable public accounts system
- machinery to protect human rights
- the right to information
- active participation of civil society, including women and youth
- substantially increased and more effective financial resources
- adherence to the internationally agreed targets of 0.7 per cent of GNP for development assistance
- financing and realisation of the MDGs, and
- increased democracy at the global level, including enhanced participation and transparency in international institutions.

Promoting free and fair trade

We fully commit ourselves to an effective, equitable, rules-based multilateral trading system, developed under the auspices of the World Trade Organization (WTO), to support pro-poor development and democracy. To this end, we have issued a separate Statement on Multilateral Trade, which is annexed to this declaration.

Poverty eradication and the MDGs

We reiterate our collective commitment and determination to attain the MDGs, especially in regard to health and education. We welcome the efforts of the Commonwealth to attain the MDGs, in particular for poverty eradication, through technical assistance programmes in developing member countries. We affirm our enthusiasm and resolve to increase aid levels to support the MDGs. We welcome the initiative of the United Kingdom for an international finance facility, and call upon other developed countries to consider this and similar options to alleviate poverty in developing countries. We commit ourselves to support appropriate private-sector initiatives to promote foreign direct investment and capital flows to developing member countries.

Role of women

We recognise the critical role which women play in development and resolve to ensure that development processes empower women to play that full role.

Action against corruption and recovery of assets

We recognise that corruption erodes economic development and corporate governance. We welcome the successful conclusion of the United Nations Convention Against Corruption and urge the early signature, ratification and implementation of the convention by member states. We pledge maximum co-operation and assistance amongst our governments to recover assets of illicit origin and repatriate them to their countries of origin. This will make more resources available for development purposes. To this end, we request the Secretary-General to establish a Commonwealth working group to help advance effective action in this area.

Debt management

We recognise that the debt burden constitutes a major obstacle to allocating resources to key socio-economic sectors in developing member countries. We also acknowledge the need for a deeper, broader and more flexible approach to debt relief and debt cancellation for developing member countries, to achieve long-term debt sustainability and release resources, particularly for health and education. We welcome the advisory and consensus-building work of the Commonwealth Heavily Indebted Poor Countries (HIPC) Ministerial Forum and encourage its efforts to achieve HIPCs' sustainable exit from debt. We support the provision of additional resources through

topping-up at the completion point under HIPC and a more comprehensive approach to address unsustainable debt.

Financing for development

We believe the Commonwealth should lead the international community in ensuring that the official development assistance target is achieved. Recognising that poor member countries urgently need increased resources for pro-poor development, we call on the international community to respond positively through the following measures:

- improve aid effectiveness through reductions in tied aid, increased direct budgetary support and implementation of the Rome Declaration on Harmonisation
- support social safety nets to reduce the impact of poverty on the most vulnerable groups and to mitigate the transition costs of reforms designed to enhance the efficiency and competitiveness of economies
- strengthen the capacity of the international financial architecture to assist poor countries to address the impact of exogenous shocks such as a sharp deterioration in their terms of trade and natural disasters
- encourage the private sector to play a major role in the promotion of trade and investment, and
- encourage greater participation of poor and vulnerable groups in the preparation of poverty reduction strategy papers for the IMF, World Bank and wider donor community.

Commonwealth Fund for Technical Co-operation

We note the commendable assistance provided by the CFTC to the development efforts of our member countries and commit ourselves to continued support for the Fund. We agree that the resources available to the Fund should be enhanced and on no account be permitted to decline below their current levels in real terms.

Health

We are committed to combating HIV/AIDS, malaria, tuberculosis and other infectious diseases which remain a threat to sustainable development. We recognise that diseases such as HIV/AIDS, malaria and tuberculosis are not only health problems but are also development issues. The high incidence of such diseases can also reverse the development process. We continue to believe that strong political leadership and education remain crucial components of the multisectoral response to combating HIV/AIDS. The threat from HIV/AIDS is especially great in Sub-Saharan Africa, which has two-thirds of the world's 40 million persons living with HIV/AIDS, and in the Caribbean. We call for reforms at the national level to create effective health delivery systems, as well as adequate external support to achieve this. We welcome the recent WTO agreement on affordable drugs and call for its interpretation and implementation in a manner that makes appropriate drugs available at low cost to poor countries.

Education

We affirm that education, whether formal or informal, is central to development in any society and is of the highest priority to the Commonwealth. In an increasingly divided and insecure world, education must play a crucial role for people, both young and old, for them to optimise their opportunities and to bridge divides.

We commend all efforts by Commonwealth organisations and agencies to develop greater education resources and to create an enabling environment to foster an enterprise culture. We encourage all governments, noting the value of distance education and the benefits of technology, to draw upon best practices throughout the Commonwealth and welcome the increased support for education in the Commonwealth through the new Centre for Commonwealth Education at Cambridge University.

Youth

We recognise that more than 50 per cent of the population of the Commonwealth is below 30 years of age. All Commonwealth efforts to achieve the MDGs must reflect this demographic reality by including young people in development and democracy.

Combating illicit trafficking in human beings

We recognise the growing problem of human trafficking, especially in women and children. We are committed to combating this scourge through international co-operation and we call on member countries which have not yet done so to ratify the UN Convention Against Transnational Organised Crime and Protocols.

Partnership for peace and prosperity

We strongly reaffirm our commitment to multilateralism, international co-operation, partnership, and productive working relationships between government and civil society organisations. We also reaffirm our commitment to enhance global democracy, by ensuring that international institutions reflect the voice of their developing country members and are themselves models of good practice in democratic accountability, participation and transparency. We recognise that the Commonwealth as an association has distinctive strengths and comparative advantages that could be effectively utilised for the mutual benefit of member states. We therefore urge greater partnership within our community.

Furthermore we urge all countries to implement their commitments under the Monterrey Consensus and the Plan of Implementation of the World Summit on Sustainable Development.

We commend the African Union for taking the bold step to address development and good governance through the New Partnership for Africa's Development. In this regard, we support the Commonwealth Secretariat's activities in developing a comprehensive programme of assistance to support the efforts of Commonwealth countries in Africa.

We recognise that conflict and instability erode the prospects of development. We are therefore committed to help mobilise international support and resources for conflict prevention, resolution and management. We also commit ourselves to efforts to curb illicit trade in small arms and light weapons and to support prompt response in providing international assistance to conflict areas.

Conclusion

We urge the Commonwealth Secretary-General to direct resources to support the priorities identified in this declaration. We also urge relevant Commonwealth ministerial meetings to give additional momentum to these priorities, and request the Secretary-General to provide a report on progress made to the next Commonwealth Heads of Government Meeting.

Aso Rock Statement on Multilateral Trade

We, the Heads of Government of the Commonwealth, representing countries at all levels of development, reaffirm our commitment to a transparent, rules-based multilateral trading system. We recognise that such a system is in the interests of all countries, especially poor and vulnerable ones. We firmly believe that all countries have a right to full development. We are convinced that increasing trading opportunities is the most potent weapon to combat poverty. A multilateral trading system that is more responsive to the needs of developing countries is particularly important for the Commonwealth, a third of whose nearly 2 billion people live on less than $1 a day and nearly two-thirds on less than $2 a day. We, in the Commonwealth, therefore, attach the highest priority to delivering the Doha Development Agenda.

We regret the breakdown of negotiations in Cancún. We support immediate re-engagement by all concerned and urge that all show the flexibility and political courage necessary to deliver a balanced Round.

Positive outcomes are essential in the areas of agriculture, non-agricultural market access, services, implementation issues and special and differential treatment. On agriculture, we call for the early phasing out of all forms of export subsidies, substantial reductions in trade-distorting domestic support and significant improvements in market access. In the area of industrial products, tariff escalation and tariff peaks must be addressed, as they are a major impediment to development. Finally special and differential treatment must be made precise, effective and operational in all WTO agreements.

The time that remains for a successful conclusion of the Round is now very short. We are, therefore, dispatching a ministerial mission to key capitals to call on major players and to urge them to negotiate positively and flexibly to reinvigorate the Doha Round and to move expeditiously to a final agreement.

We stress that multilateral trade liberalisation can offer significant benefits for all. We also recognise that poor and vulnerable countries should undertake trade liberalisation in ways that minimise transition costs and any negative impact on the poor. We recognise the special difficulties of developing economies, particularly of vulnerable small states that have lost trade preferences, and call for concerted action to assist them diversify their economies.

We call upon the Commonwealth Secretariat to strengthen its technical capacity-building programmes for developing Commonwealth countries to negotiate and implement their obligations within the WTO system, and of Commonwealth ACP countries in their negotiations with the EU on Economic Partnership Agreements, in ways consistent with their development interests. Where there is significant Commonwealth consensus on particular trade issues, we pledge to bring the full weight of the association to bear on them.

Aso Rock, Abuja, Nigeria, 8 December 2003

Malta Declaration on Networking the Commonwealth for Development

The Malta Declaration affirms the importance of harnessing new technologies and strengthening networks to bridge the digital divide and accelerate economic development in the Commonwealth.

We, the Heads of Government of the Commonwealth, meeting in Malta from 25 to 27 November 2005, firmly believe that our Commonwealth is a rich, globally representative, relevant and dynamic network of nations and peoples, well equipped to respond to the pressing challenges of our time.

Ours is a network of governments and peoples, nurtured by shared values, institutions and conventions, as well as a common working language and history of collaboration. These attributes provide a platform on which to build and consolidate the foundations of democracy in our societies as well as to redress social and economic disparities in a co-ordinated and effective manner.

We reaffirm that democracy and development are organically interlinked and mutually reinforcing. Democratic governance facilitates sustainable development. At the same time, poverty and inequity can place democracy in peril. We therefore reiterate our firm commitment to the achievement of the Millennium Development Goals and are deeply concerned by the uneven progress attained so far.

We are determined to intensify our efforts to meet the Millennium Development Goals and their associated targets, and to help one another to do so. We are mindful in particular of the Goal to develop a global partnership for development. In this regard, we are committed to making available the benefits of new technologies, especially information and communication technologies (ICTs), in partnership between the public and private sectors.

We view ICTs as powerful instruments of development rather than ends in themselves, delivering savings, efficiencies and growth in our economies. We also recognise the ability of ICTs to act as catalysts in creating new economic synergies, offering opportunities to overcome the constraints of remoteness, small size, and other factors which have traditionally acted as a brake on development.

We firmly believe that the Commonwealth can contribute meaningfully to measures aimed at bridging and closing the digital divide, and are resolved to do so. ICTs provide an opportunity for individuals to learn, to grow, to participate more actively in society and to compete more effectively in markets.

We support the Digital Solidarity Fund as endorsed by the World Summit on the Information Society. Our goal is to see information technology made accessible to all. We recognise that this requires, in particular, investment in infrastructure, effective telecommunications, education, and co-ordinated public policy. We also recognise that the wealth of human and technical capital within the Commonwealth can be shared for the benefit of our developing member states. We will therefore use and seek to strengthen existing mechanisms and resources toward that end, collaborating with partners in other organisations within and beyond the Commonwealth, as well as with the corporate sector and civil society. We will also seek to use ICT networks to enhance the effectiveness of existing Commonwealth networks.

We endorse the *Commonwealth Action Programme for the Digital Divide* as our roadmap. We view the Commonwealth's priorities, in particular, as being the development of policy and regulatory capacity, the modernisation of education and skills development, the promotion of entrepreneurship for poverty elimination, the promotion of local access and connectivity, and the strengthening of local and regional networks. We request the Secretary-General to establish the Steering Committee of relevant existing Commonwealth agencies, including member states, to work with the Commonwealth Secretariat in implementing the Action Programme.

We welcome the launch of an Indian initiative on a Pan-African E-Network project that will link all the 53 member states of the African Union and assist in the achievement of the Millennium Development Goals, especially in respect of education and health.

We also endorse the establishment of a Special Fund to enable implementation of the specific activities and to achieve the performance targets envisaged in the Action Programme, and call for contributions to the Fund so that it can become operational without delay. In this context, we note with appreciation the substantial contributions to the Fund announced by India and Malta.

Malta, 27 November 2005

Kampala Declaration on Transforming Societies to Achieve Political, Economic and Human Development

The Kampala Declaration calls for the inclusiveness of transformation, to involve citizens at every level, and to be as much a democratic transformation as an economic one.

We, the Heads of Government of the Commonwealth, recall that our Declaration of Commonwealth Principles unequivocally decries the wide disparities in wealth between different sections of humanity and reaffirms the Commonwealth's commitment to raise standards and achieve a more equitable international society free of poverty, ignorance and disease.

Those Principles have been further elaborated and strengthened over the years to underline that development rests on the foundations of democratic governance, the rule of law, respect for human rights, gender equality and peace and security. The Commonwealth has also pledged and continued to pursue a stable international economic framework within which growth can be achieved, together with sound economic management at the national level that recognises the central role of the market economy.

We note that the membership of the Commonwealth comprises countries at different levels of political, economic and human development, and that historical factors and circumstances have been a significant contributory factor. We also recognise that many of our members are endowed with natural advantages upon which they have the potential to achieve positive economic and social transformation, while many members also have natural handicaps that constrain such transformation.

The experience of newly industrialised members of the Commonwealth shows the way forward for developing countries, and demonstrates that qualitative economic transformation occurs where the following conditions exist:

- Economies are open and their natural competitiveness is enabled.

- The rule of law prevails.

- A rules-based and fair multilateral trading system exists and is respected by all.

- National development strategies with a long-term perspective following consultation with all stakeholders including women and youth.

- Investment based on confidence and certainty that improves productivity.

- Cost-efficient and effective growth of the primary, secondary and tertiary sectors of economies that is promoted in a comprehensive and coherent fashion, including addition of value to primary products and reductions in transaction and other business costs.

- Modernisation and renewal of national infrastructure, including through partnerships between the public and private sectors.

- Policies which nurture a strong private sector.

- Efficient and effective public services that are delivered on the premise of providing services to all.

- Modernisation and innovation policies in the areas of science and technology.

- Education and technical training are accorded high priority in public expenditure, with the objective of speeding up the transition from rural-based towards skilled, middle class-based, industrialised and diversified societies.

- Strengthened public health systems to address in particular infectious illnesses as well as non-communicable and lifestyle diseases to create healthy and productive societies.

We must allow all our member countries to benefit from these foundations of economic transformation. We therefore attach importance and priority to efforts aimed at sharing experiences and best practice, as well as technology and assistance between Commonwealth countries.

We recognise that human and political transformation cannot be successful or enduring unless people themselves have a strong sense of ownership of the institutions put in place to govern and support their lives and welfare. Nor will human transformation occur sustainably unless people have a growing sense of achievement, benefit, and self-worth.

We note that the Millennium Development Goals (MDGs) are designed to achieve the most significant fundamental transformation of humanity, and are largely linked to poverty reduction, health, education and gender equality targets. We also note with satisfaction the achievement of a number of MDGs by some member countries. We, however, express our deep concern that many Commonwealth countries are falling behind the MDG targets at this half-way point to the 2015 end year. Goals related to maternal and child deaths, HIV/AIDS, and elimination of gender disparities require urgent action in many countries.

We reaffirm our commitment to intensify our efforts to meet the MDGs and their associated targets, and to help one another to do so. We note in particular, the recognition that countries in Africa are proving that large scale progress in achieving the MDGs is possible under conditions of adequate financing, much of which should flow from a strengthened global partnership for development.

We recall the Goal committing all nations to develop a global partnership for development and acknowledge the developed countries that have increased resources for development by 30 per cent since Monterrey. Despite this, however, we note with concern the overall decline in official development assistance (ODA) in 2006. We call on the international community as a whole, and in particular the donor community, to honour pledges and make concrete efforts to meet commitments made with regard to financing for development.

We urge the United Nations Secretary-General to convene a meeting in 2008 that brings together Heads of Government with leaders from the private sector, and other interested parties to review progress and to consider ways to assist those lagging behind to accelerate the action that is needed to attain the MDGs.

We recognise that strongly development-oriented outcomes to the Doha Round of multilateral trade negotiations as well as the Economic Partnership Agreement negotiations between the European Union and the African-Caribbean-Pacific (ACP) group of countries would make the most significant contributions to the attainment of the MDGs.

We also recognise that neither economic nor human development is possible in a sustainable way without democracy and good governance. We therefore affirm the importance of leadership that embraces the Commonwealth's fundamental values, and that is tolerant and encouraging of innovation, creativity and diversity.

We recognise that the challenge of transformation requires international collaboration and co-operation. The Commonwealth's common values and norms place us in a strong position of comparative advantage to learn and benefit from each other. We commit ourselves to explore ways in which each of us can share and strengthen our relations with each other in order to support transformation for us all. We call on the Commonwealth Secretariat to assist in developing an action plan to facilitate transformation in member countries.

Kampala, Uganda, 25 November 2007

Port of Spain Climate Change Consensus: The Commonwealth Climate Change Declaration

This declaration, issued by Commonwealth leaders at their November 2009 summit in Trinidad and Tobago, called for continued implementation of all six elements of the 2007 Lake Victoria Commonwealth Climate Change Action Plan, and stressed that a global climate change solution was central to the survival of peoples, the promotion of development and facilitation of a global transition to a low emission development path.

The challenge of our time

Climate change is the predominant global challenge. We convened a Special Session on Climate Change in Port of Spain to discuss our profound concern about the undisputed threat that climate change poses to the security, prosperity, economic and social development of our people. For many it is deepening poverty and affecting the attainment of the Millennium Development Goals. For some of us, it is an existential threat.

We reaffirm our commitment to the Lake Victoria Commonwealth Climate Change Action Plan and its further implementation, in particular by contributing to the efforts of member states in transforming their economies and strengthening the capacity and voice of vulnerable groups.

We recognise the unprecedented opportunity of our meeting just ahead of the 15th Conference of the Parties to the UN Framework Convention on Climate Change in Copenhagen. We approach Copenhagen with ambition, optimism and determination. We welcome the attendance of leaders at the Copenhagen conference. The needs of the most vulnerable must be addressed. Their voice must be heard and capacity to engage strengthened. Many of us from small island states, low-lying coastal states and least developed countries face the greatest challenges, yet have contributed least to the problem of climate change.

In keeping with the spirit of the theme of CHOGM 2009, *Partnering for a More Equitable and Sustainable Future*, we warmly welcomed the United Nations Secretary-General, the Prime Minister of Denmark and the President of France.

We represent a third of the world's population in all continents and oceans, and more than one quarter of the Parties to the United Nations Framework Convention on Climate Change. We have the global reach and diversity to help forge the inclusive global solutions needed to combat climate change.

Science, and our own experience, tells us that we only have a few short years to address this threat. The average global temperature has risen because of the increase in carbon and other greenhouse gas emissions. The latest scientific evidence indicates that in order to avoid dangerous climate change that is likely to have catastrophic impacts we must find solutions using all available avenues. We must act now.

We believe an internationally legally binding agreement is essential. We pledge our continued support to the leaders-driven process guided by the Danish Prime Minister and his efforts to deliver a comprehensive, substantial and operationally binding agreement in Copenhagen leading towards a full legally binding outcome no later than 2010. In Copenhagen we commit to focus our efforts on achieving the strongest possible outcome.

Copenhagen and beyond

A global climate change solution is central to the survival of peoples, the promotion of development and facilitation of a global transition to a low emission development path. The agreement in Copenhagen must address the urgent needs of developing countries by providing financing, support for adaptation, technology transfer, capacity-building, approaches and incentives for reducing emissions from deforestation and forest degradation, and for afforestation and sustainable management of forests.

In addition, we will strive to significantly increase technological and technology support to developing countries to facilitate the deployment and diffusion of clean technologies through a range of mechanisms. We will work to facilitate and enable the transition to low-emission economies, climate resilience, and in particular, support, including through capacity-building, for increasing the climate resilience of vulnerable economies. We will also aim to develop cleaner, more affordable and renewable energy sources.

We must explore global mechanisms through which those identified technologies can be disseminated as rapidly as possible.

Ensuring the viability of states should underpin a shared vision for long-term co-operative action and a long-term global goal for emission reductions. In building towards an international agreement, all countries will need to play their part, in accordance with the principle of common but differentiated responsibilities and respective capabilities.

We need an ambitious mitigation outcome at Copenhagen to reduce the risks of dangerous climate change without compromising the legitimate development aspirations of developing countries. We stress our common conviction that urgent and substantial action to reduce global emissions is needed and have a range of views as to whether average global temperature increase should be constrained to below 1.5 degrees or to no more than 2 degrees Celsius above pre-industrial levels. We also recognise the need for an early peaking year for global emissions. Developed countries should continue to lead on cutting their emissions, and developing countries, in line with their national circumstances, should also take action to achieve a substantial deviation from business-as-usual emissions including with financial and technical support, and also supported by technology and capacity-building.

Progress towards predictable and adequate finance for adaptation and mitigation measures must be achieved in any new multilateral approach. Public and private financial resources for developing countries will need to be scaled up urgently and substantially by 2020. We recognise that adaptation finance in particular should be targeted towards the poorest and most vulnerable countries. The provision of finance should be additional to existing official development assistance commitments. In this respect, we acknowledge the potential role of the private sector and carbon markets.

In addition, we recognise the need for an early start to the provision for financial resources. Fast start funding, constituting grant funding, should provide substantial support for adaptation, REDD plus[1] and clean technology. We welcomed the initiative to establish, as part of a comprehensive agreement, a Copenhagen Launch Fund starting in 2010 and building to a level of resources of $10 billion annually by 2012. Fast start funding for adaptation should be focused on the most vulnerable countries. We also welcomed a proposal to provide immediate, fast disbursing assistance with a dedicated stream for small island states, and associated low-lying coastal states of AOSIS[2] of at least 10 per cent of the fund. We also recognise the need for further, specified and comparable funding streams, to assist the poorest and most vulnerable countries, to cope with, and adapt to the adverse impacts of climate change. We recognise that funding will be scaled up beyond 2012.

We agree that an equitable governance structure to manage the financial and technological support must be put in place. We agree that a future governance structure should provide for states to monitor and comply with arrangements entered under a new Copenhagen agreement.

Port of Spain, Trinidad and Tobago, 28 November 2009

Notes

1. Reducing emissions from deforestation and forest degradation in developing countries; and the role of conservation, sustainable management of forests and enhancement of forest carbon stocks in developing countries.

2. Alliance of Small Island States.

Trinidad and Tobago Affirmation of Commonwealth Values and Principles

In the 60th anniversary year of the modern Commonwealth, Heads of Government reiterated their strong and abiding commitment to the association's fundamental values and principles. Heads also agreed that consideration be given to strengthening the role of CMAG.

We, the Heads of Government of the Commonwealth, meeting in Port of Spain in this the 60th anniversary year of the modern Commonwealth, take pride in our collective achievements over the past six decades and, as we look to the future, reaffirm our strong and abiding commitment to the Commonwealth's fundamental values and principles.

We reaffirm that the special strength of the Commonwealth lies in the diversity of its membership, bound together not only by shared history and tradition but also by an ethos of respect for all states and peoples, of shared values and principles, and of concern for the vulnerable.

We reaffirm our belief in the Commonwealth as a voluntary association of sovereign independent states whose pursuit of common principles continues to influence international society to the benefit of all. We are resolved to make the Commonwealth an even stronger and more effective international organisation as we look ahead to the rest of the 21st century.

We recall earlier statements through which the Commonwealth's values and principles have been defined and strengthened over the years, including the Singapore Declaration, the Harare Declaration, the Millbrook Action Programme, the Latimer House Principles and the Aberdeen Principles.

Our values and principles

We solemnly reiterate our commitment to the Commonwealth's core values:

International peace and security: believing firmly that international peace and security, economic growth and development and the rule of law are essential to the progress and prosperity of all; and expressing our commitment to an effective multilateral system based on inclusiveness, equity and international law as the best foundation for achieving consensus and progress on major global challenges;

Democracy: reaffirming our belief in the inalienable right of the individual to participate by means of free and democratic political processes in shaping the society in which they live; underlining that not only governments but all political parties and civil society also have responsibilities in upholding and promoting democratic culture and practices as well as accountability to the public in this regard; and recognising that parliaments and representative local government and other forms of local governance are essential elements in the exercise of democratic governance;

Human rights: reaffirming our commitment to the Universal Declaration of Human Rights and human rights covenants and instruments; and recalling our belief that equality and respect for protection and promotion of civil, political, economic, social and cultural rights for all without discrimination on any grounds, including the right to development, are foundations of peaceful, just and stable societies, and that these rights are universal, indivisible, interdependent and interrelated and cannot be implemented selectively;

Tolerance, respect and understanding: recognising that tolerance, respect and understanding strengthen democracy and development; recognising also that respect for the dignity of all human beings is critical to promoting peace and prosperity;

Separation of powers: recognising the importance of maintaining the integrity of the roles of the Executive, Legislature and Judiciary;

Rule of law: reiterating that each country's Legislature, Executive and Judiciary are the guarantors of the rule of law and emphasising that access to justice and an independent judiciary are fundamental to the rule of law, enhanced by effective, transparent, ethical and accountable governance;

Freedom of expression: emphasising that peaceful, open dialogue and the free flow of information, including through a free, vibrant and professional media, enhance democratic traditions and strengthen democratic processes;

Development: stressing the importance of economic and social transformation to, *inter alia*, eliminate poverty and meet the basic needs of the vast majority of the people of the world; seeking the removal of wide disparities and unequal living standards, guided by the Millennium Development Goals (MDGs); reiterating that economic and social progress enhances the sustainability of democracy;

Gender equality: reaffirming gender equality and empowerment as an essential component of human development and basic human rights, and acknowledging the advancement of women's rights as a critical precondition for effective and sustainable development;

Access to health and education: reaffirming our commitment to health and education for all citizens, both as human rights and as instruments for poverty alleviation and sustainable development;

Good governance: reiterating our commitment to promote the rule of law, ensure transparency and accountability and root out, both at national and international levels, systemic and systematic corruption; and

Civil society: acknowledging the important role that civil society plays in our communities and nations as partners in promoting and supporting Commonwealth values and the interests of the people.

We reiterate our commitment to the core principles of consensus and common action, mutual respect, inclusiveness, transparency, accountability, legitimacy, and responsiveness.

Working together to strengthen our values and principles: looking to the future

We reaffirm our full support for the Good Offices role of the Secretary-General in supporting adherence to Commonwealth principles; in conflict prevention and resolution; and as an instrument to protect and promote the Commonwealth's fundamental values.

We recognise the vital role of the Commonwealth Ministerial Action Group (CMAG) as the custodian of the Commonwealth's fundamental political values. We call on CMAG to explore ways in which it could more effectively deal with the full range of serious or persistent violations of such values by member states and to pronounce upon them as appropriate.

We also express our continuing support for the Commonwealth Secretariat's work on strengthening democratic institutions, processes and culture. In this context, we welcome the Secretariat's collaboration with the Commonwealth Parliamentary Association (CPA), the Commonwealth Local Government Forum (CLGF) and other relevant organisations to promote best practice and democratic culture.

We underscore the importance of coherence in order to protect the Commonwealth's image and credibility. We urge all Commonwealth organisations to subscribe and adhere to Commonwealth values and principles in every possible way, including by acting in conformity with the letter and spirit of the decisions of CMAG.

Acknowledging the key role of elections in furthering and entrenching democratic processes and accountability, and affirming our commitment to the Commonwealth Secretariat's work in strengthening democratic institutions, processes and culture through election observation, we endorse the proposed Commonwealth Network of National Election Management Bodies. This Network would facilitate experience-sharing and serve to create support mechanisms, promote good practices and facilitate opportunities for peer support across the Commonwealth, thus enhancing member countries' capacity to hold credible elections which enjoy the confidence of the people. Through this Network, we envisage the Commonwealth advancing the norm of the highest electoral standards.

We welcome forward-looking, contemporary and innovative initiatives that generate and strengthen creative networking and partnerships within the Commonwealth community, and that underpin adherence to the Commonwealth's fundamental values and principles, mindful especially of the theme of the 2009 CHOGM, *Partnering for a More Equitable and Sustainable Future*. In that regard, we endorse the proposed Commonwealth Partnership Platform Portal (CP3), and encourage support for it.

We note the need to strengthen Commonwealth processes, institutional frameworks and capacities for delivering collective action and global public goods as highlighted by the Report of the High Level Group in 2002 and the 'Commonwealth Conversation'. We call for the creation of an Eminent Persons Group to undertake an examination of options for reform in order to bring the Commonwealth's many institutions into a stronger and more effective framework of co-operation and partnership. We are committed to securing a greater level of co-ordination and collaboration between all Commonwealth contributors and stakeholders, particularly including governments, civil society, business, the diversity of Commonwealth professional and other associations that bring together our citizens, academia and others.

We call for the Commonwealth Secretary-General to consolidate and further strengthen ongoing efforts to improve the Secretariat's governance, its responsiveness to changing priorities and needs, and its ability to enhance the public profile of the organisation. We commit ourselves to supporting the Secretariat in this endeavour. We also underline the importance we attach to intensifying the Secretariat's commitment to strategic partnerships with other international organisations and partners in order to promote the Commonwealth's values and principles.

We call for the Eminent Persons Group to examine, *inter alia*, the format, frequency, and content of ministerial meetings in order to ensure that these continue to support the Commonwealth's values and principles, and provide the greatest possible addition of value and cost-effectiveness. We affirm that such meetings should also continue to have mandates that are focused; time-bound; affordable; of the highest possible relevance at the national level and in international exchanges; and are delivered.

By these and other practical measures, we believe that the Commonwealth will build a stronger and more resilient and progressive family of nations founded on enduring values and principles. By such measures, we also believe that the Commonwealth will remain relevant to its times and people in future.

Port of Spain, Trinidad and Tobago, 29 November 2009

The Declaration of Port of Spain: Partnering for a More Equitable and Sustainable Future

The Declaration of Port of Spain affirmed the key role of partnerships in forging a more sustainable and equitable future for all people, recognising that to effectively address the unprecedented combination of social, economic and environmental challenges facing the world would require international co-operation, sustained commitment and collective action.

We, the Heads of Government of the Commonwealth, meeting in Port of Spain, Trinidad and Tobago, from 27 to 29 November 2009, affirm the key role of partnerships in forging a more sustainable and equitable future for all people.

Our meeting takes place at a time when the world faces an unprecedented combination of social, economic and environmental challenges. These include a profound and debilitating global economic and financial crisis, volatility in key commodity prices, and the alarming impacts of climate change, which threaten the safety and livelihoods of millions. We also note with grave concern that many of the world's poorest communities are most vulnerable to these challenges.

We recognise that challenges of this magnitude cannot be resolved by any one country alone and that effectively addressing them will require international co-operation, sustained commitment and collective action. This calls for the strengthening of multilateral co-operation, based on mutual respect, openness and partnership. We therefore commit ourselves to deepening the Commonwealth's existing networks of co-operation and call for a fresh impetus to foster new and more effective political and economic partnerships. We will also capitalise on the Commonwealth's unique abilities to advocate for partnerships with other members of the international community and to promote, within each country, partnerships among the different levels of government, civil society, youth and the private sector.

This renewed emphasis on Commonwealth partnerships and collaboration should focus on areas which offer clear practical opportunities to improve lives, build more resilient communities and strengthen the bonds and ties between nations.

Protecting the poorest and most vulnerable

At our meeting in Kampala in 2007, we recognised that the Millennium Development Goals (MDGs) are designed to achieve the most fundamental transformation of humanity, including in the areas of poverty reduction, health, education and gender equality. While significant progress is being made in many countries, we remain deeply concerned that many Commonwealth countries are falling behind the MDG targets.

Noting that the global economic and financial crisis has profoundly affected both developed and developing countries and that the process of recovery is still slow and uncertain in many countries, we will collaborate to find ways to provide immediate help to the poorest and most vulnerable, and to develop responses to protect the people that are most at risk, particularly those in poor developing countries.

We therefore commit ourselves to the strengthening and creation of partnerships and networks to increase development effectiveness, emphasising high-impact initiatives with clearly measurable outcomes. To this end we pledge to take measures to improve the quality of the data used to inform policies in key areas such as health, poverty and education, strengthen the linkages between research and policy-making, and mainstream issues of gender and gender equality into policies and programmes. We will share our ideas and best practices, and deliver practical support through Commonwealth networks, including a new Commonwealth Partnership Platform Portal (CP3). We urge a stronger role for the Commonwealth Secretariat in assisting the developing country members to access and utilise the resources available to cope with the economic crisis. We will also strive to implement the recommendations of the High Level Report on Democracy and Pro-Poor Growth as well as those of the Report of the Commission on Growth and Development.

Debt

At our meeting in Kampala in 2007 we expressed concern that many countries were still weighed down by large and unsustainable debt burdens, and we reiterated the need to address the debt problems of middle-income countries, given the increasing share of government revenue taken by debt servicing and the implications for social spending.

In this regard, we commend the World Bank Debt Management initiative, which was developed in partnership with the Commonwealth Secretariat, and which was designed to help the governments of low-income and highly indebted middle-income countries to manage their national debts. We call on the international financial institutions to provide new and enhanced funding windows for concessionary financing for middle-income countries with serious debt burdens.

In keeping with the calls made by Finance Ministers at the Commonwealth Ministerial Debt Sustainability Forum, we also call on donor countries to honour their bilateral commitments with respect to the promised aid levels and cancellation of debt.

Economic governance

We will restore business confidence, the basis for investment and growth, by promoting the implementation of sound macroeconomic policies, including open, competitive markets with efficient and transparent regulation, good governance and prudent and accountable management of public and private funds.

We also give our full support to the process of reform of international financial institutions and call for the urgent and comprehensive implementation of reform that responds to the needs of all countries. We should also seek to create mechanisms within established institutions that can assist small and vulnerable states.

Science, technology and innovation

We recognise that many Commonwealth countries already collaborate in innovation, particularly in key areas such as information and communication technologies. We believe that there must now be a far stronger emphasis on science, technology and innovation (STI) as key drivers of the type of economic transformation, employment generation and growth that will be

required to emerge from the present economic crisis, attain our development objectives and realise our collective vision of sustainable development.

We therefore commit to promote increased investment in STI, as well as the rapid dissemination of technologies and ideas. In this regard, we request the Commonwealth Secretariat to identify, in collaboration with the Commonwealth Business Council, mechanisms for financing research to advance the development and adoption of new technologies and to assist member states to access the environmental development funds managed by the World Bank and the United Nations.

In addition, we will encourage new public–private sector partnerships, foster the expansion of the small and medium size enterprise (SME) sector, and promote new knowledge-based and creative industries.

Strengthening synergy and co-ordination

As we seek to strengthen the CHOGM process, we recognise that a more co-ordinated, integrated and coherent approach to implementation of the decisions reached at Meetings of Heads of Government is needed, alongside strategies to ensure the sustainability of collective Commonwealth planning and action.

We will therefore take all necessary steps to increase co-ordination among Commonwealth institutions, and to ensure that Commonwealth ministerial meetings are more integrated with the CHOGM process. We will also strongly encourage co-operation and co-ordination among Commonwealth institutions, international financial institutions, regional development banks and other international bodies.

The global role of the Commonwealth

The Commonwealth is a platform for its membership to communicate, share ideas and co-ordinate action across large geographical and cultural distances. It can therefore generate and sustain effective international action on global challenges. As a result of its diversity and representativeness, the Commonwealth can strengthen old partnerships and forge new ones in order to play a leadership role in the international arena for the promotion of a more equitable and sustainable future for all, and particularly to work as an advocate for small and vulnerable states. Together, we pledge to act as a catalyst for positive change in the international community in these challenging times.

Port of Spain, Trinidad and Tobago, 29 November 2009

A Declaration on Young People: 'Investing in Young People'

In this declaration Heads of Government acknowledge the role and active contributions of young people in promoting development, peace and democracy, and recognise that the future successes of the Commonwealth rest with young people.

We, the Heads of Government of the Commonwealth, welcome the emphasis on young people in this, the 60th year since the foundation of the modern Commonwealth, with its theme of *thecommonwealth@60: serving a new generation*. We acknowledge with gratitude the role and active contributions of young people in promoting development, peace, democracy, and in protecting and promoting other Commonwealth values such as tolerance and understanding, including respect for other cultures. We recognise that the future successes of the Commonwealth rest with the continued commitments and contributions in these ways of our young people.

We appreciate the views and outcomes of young people that have been conveyed to us from the Commonwealth Youth Forum. We note young people's calls to be involved as agents of peace-building, and as agents for awareness of – and response to – climate change. We also hear young people's call to be facilitated as drivers of economic development, as young entrepreneurs.

We note the principles of youth development endorsed by Commonwealth Youth Ministers, and affirm our own support for the Commonwealth Plan of Action for Youth Empowerment.

We endorse coherence in the national, regional and global dimensions of advancing supportive policies towards youth. We also recognise the benefits of engaging youth at all levels of policy dialogue and curriculum development.

In this respect, we reaffirm our support for promoting 'youth mainstreaming', and recognise in particular the benefits of sharing best practice and knowledge of mainstreaming, to assist ministries and stakeholders in building comprehensive and coherent youth-related policies for national needs.

We endorse the project by the Commonwealth Secretariat to develop a comprehensive and replenished resource bank on youth affairs, consisting of data, best practices and thinking in this field, as a reference tool for the development of ambitious and coherent national policies by member states.

We commend the Commonwealth Secretariat on its work to date in supporting the establishment of national youth plans and national youth councils in member countries.

We note with concern that unemployment affects young people more than any other social group. We acknowledge the work of the pilot Commonwealth Youth Credit Initiative (CYCI), and encourage initiatives to expand the scheme, and to support comprehensive skills development for youth in partnership with civil society and business.

We seek to enhance the CYCI, by turning it into an integrated and holistic enterprise development programme, which is built around comprehensive and mutually reinforcing skills development, funding, and mentorship. We pledge to support the new initiative, which should engage a considerably wider range of funders and partners, including our own Ministries of Youth, international finance institutions, regional organisations, banks, and businesses. We welcome initial and generous donations that have been made by Asian and African Banks to support further growth in this area.

We also appeal for voluntary contributions for special youth initiatives including the Commonwealth Young Professionals Programme, and the network of Centres of Excellence based in the four Commonwealth Youth Programme (CYP) Regional Centres.

We recommend that greater partnerships with national and international actors, including inter-generational alliances, be engendered towards the fulfilment of the youth development vision of the Commonwealth.

We recognise the opportunities for young people provided by the Commonwealth Scholarship and Fellowship Plan (CSFP), celebrating its 50th anniversary in 2009. We express our appreciation for initial commitments of £1.6 million to date made towards the CSFP Anniversary Endowment Fund, and anticipate the Fund receiving further political and financial support.

Port of Spain, Trinidad and Tobago, 29 November 2009

Commonwealth Statement on Action to Combat Non-Communicable Diseases

Here, concerned that non-communicable diseases account for over half of all deaths worldwide and noting international co-operation is critical in addressing this emerging health crisis, Commonwealth leaders call for a UN summit to be held in 2011 in order to develop strategic responses to these diseases and their repercussions.

We, the Heads of Government of the Commonwealth, representing one-third of the world's population, affirm our commitment to addressing the burgeoning incidence of non-communicable diseases (NCDs), and to increasing the ability of our countries to respond to this emerging health crisis.

We recognise that NCDs presently account for over half of all deaths worldwide and that they significantly reduce life expectancy, quality of life and productivity. They place growing pressures on our health systems and our economies, thereby posing a serious threat to sustainable development.

We further note that poverty and NCDs are linked and that it is the poorest people who are most vulnerable to the impacts of these diseases. In many instances the costs associated with treating NCDs and related complications can push entire households into poverty, severely limiting family members' prospects for the future, especially those of women and girls, on whose shoulders traditionally rests the burden of caring for the sick.

Noting the Action Plan on Non-Communicable Diseases adopted by the Caribbean Community (CARICOM) during their 2007 Summit on Non-Communicable Diseases, we will work towards reducing the incidence of NCDs by fostering multi-sectoral policies and community-based initiatives to discourage tobacco use and unhealthy diets and to promote physical activity.

We will also work to fully integrate NCD prevention and control into our national health systems. In this regard, we will strengthen primary care to address the needs of people who are already facing NCDs, and support the universal access of essential medicines for people living with NCDs.

We firmly believe that the incidence and burdens of NCDs can be reduced through comprehensive and integrated preventive and control strategies at the individual, family, community, national and regional levels and through collaborative programmes, partnerships and policies supported by governments, the private sector, NGOs and our other social, regional and international partners. We therefore call for global engagement of the private sector, civil society and governments in efforts to combat these diseases.

Aware that surveillance is key to effectively combating NCDs, we commit to supporting initiatives to include the monitoring of NCDs and their risk factors in existing national health information systems.

Noting that international co-operation is critical in addressing the phenomenon of NCDs, we call for their inclusion in global discussions on development, such as those which will occur within the framework of the UN Economic and Social Council (ECOSOC) 2010 Co-ordination Segment. We similarly declare our support for the call to integrate indicators to monitor the magnitude, trend and socio-economic impact of NCDs into the core Millennium Development Goals (MDGs) monitoring and evaluation system during the MDG Review Summit in 2010.

We further call for a Summit on NCDs to be held in September 2011, under the auspices of the United Nations General Assembly, in order to develop strategic responses to these diseases and their repercussions.

Port of Spain, Trinidad and Tobago, 29 November 2009

Commonwealth Secretariat publications

A list of 2011 books and almanacs, working papers and expert reports, plus downloadable e-books, derived from experience around the Commonwealth.

Commonwealth books and almanacs

Commonwealth Education Partnerships 2011/12
Commonwealth Secretariat
(published by Nexus Strategic Partnerships)
Paperback
£55.00
ISBN 978-0-9563060-6-7
(published October 2011)

Commonwealth Education Partnerships is the essential overview of education in the Commonwealth. As Commonwealth ministries of education and higher education prepare for the 18th Conference of Commonwealth Education Ministers (Mauritius, 2012), the 2011/12 edition of *Commonwealth Education Partnerships* looks at progress towards Education for All and the Millennium Development Goals. The publication also contains:

* case studies from around the Commonwealth on widening access to quality education
* education for employment and health
* education in difficult circumstances
* trends in financing for education
* innovations in e-learning and m-learning
* approaches to inclusive education, and
* education profiles of all member countries.

Commonwealth Finance Ministers Reference Report 2011
Commonwealth Secretariat
(published by Henley Media Group)
Paperback
£35.00
ISBN 978-0-9563722-7-7
(published September 2011)

The *Commonwealth Finance Ministers Reference Report* is an annual publication providing Commonwealth finance ministers with a central source of information regarding macro and microfinancial issues and trade relations that affect Commonwealth nations. It includes case studies of successful projects with transferable solutions, articles on the key issues discussed at the Finance Ministers Meeting and in-depth analyses from economic experts within the financial community. This edition of the

publication was produced for the Commonwealth Finance Ministers Meeting and the parallel Commonwealth Central Bank Governors Meeting in Washington DC, USA, September 2011.

Commonwealth Heads of Government Meeting 2011
Commonwealth Secretariat
(published by Henley Media Group)
Paperback
£35.00
ISBN 978-0-9563722-8-4
(published November 2011)

This biennial publication is written by Commonwealth experts and presents current thought and pertinent analysis on Commonwealth issues and challenges. In-depth articles and case studies focus on topical issues, including the theme of the 2011 meeting: 'Building National Resilience, Building Global Resilience'. It is published with the ultimate goal of strengthening co-operation between government and business and facilitating the efforts to achieve the Millennium Development Goals. This official CHOGM publication is produced for the Commonwealth Secretariat and is distributed by the host nation to all delegates attending the summit. As with the meetings themselves, the publication discusses a wide range of issues ranging from education to inward investment. Following the summit, the publication is distributed to a wider government, multilateral and business audience to encourage collaboration and investment across the Commonwealth.

Commonwealth Health Ministers' Update 2011
Commonwealth Secretariat
(published by Pro-Brook Publishing)
Paperback
£35.00
ISBN 978-1-8492905-9-3
(published May 2011)

Produced for the annual Commonwealth Health Ministers Meeting, the *Commonwealth Health Ministers' Update 2011* is a resource for ministers on topical health priorities. The theme for the 2011 meeting was 'Non-communicable diseases – A priority for the Commonwealth'. This accompanying update provides comprehensive and essential information on the non-communicable disease epidemic, including:

* an overview of non-communicable diseases in the Commonwealth
* prevalence reports from Commonwealth regions
* how Commonwealth countries are responding to non-communicable diseases
* how to protect vulnerable groups within country populations

* case studies of key initiatives to control non-communicable diseases, and
* the economic impact of non-communicable diseases.

A special reference section summarises the latest information on non-communicable diseases in the Commonwealth and the responses by member countries.

Commonwealth Local Government Handbook 2011/12
Commonwealth Local Government Forum
(published by Publications UK Ltd)
Paperback
£50.00
ISBN 978-0-9555447-4-3
(published April 2011)

The *Commonwealth Local Government Handbook* is a complete reference book to local government in the Commonwealth. Updated and revised annually, it details the systems of local government in the 54 countries of the Commonwealth, looking at how local government is structured, how elections take place, what services local government is responsible for, how local government is financed and what reforms are envisaged. The profiles in the 2011 edition have been extended to include more information on the legislative framework, relations with central government, community involvement, monitoring and scrutiny systems, and finances. The profiles are in a format that allows easy country-to-country comparison.

Commonwealth Ministers Reference Book 2011
Commonwealth Secretariat
(published by Henley Media Group)
Paperback
£35.00
ISBN 978-0-9563722-6-0
(published August 2011)

The *Commonwealth Ministers Reference Book* is an essential source of information on key aspects of policy issues for all Commonwealth ministers, from trade to transport. It includes over 40 articles covering a range of topics with opinion pieces, case studies and transferable solutions written by multisectoral authors from across the globe. A set of ministerial briefings at the front of the book provides short updates on key issues of concern to all ministers, whatever their particular portfolio. They include a variety of papers from promoting good governance in the Commonwealth to advice on peace-building and conflict resolution. The book also includes a directory of all Commonwealth ministers, with over 1,000 minister and relevant ministry contact details listed. This is an essential publication for ministries, government officials and organisations wishing to do business with Commonwealth governments. Regularly updated ministerial directories as well as news and articles from across the Commonwealth can be found on www.commonwealthministers.com

The Commonwealth Yearbook 2011
Commonwealth Secretariat
(published by Nexus Strategic Partnerships)
Paperback
£69.99
ISBN 978-0-9563060-4-3
(published June 2011)

The *Commonwealth Yearbook* is the flagship annual publication of the Commonwealth Secretariat. It is the essential reference guide to the countries, organisations, activities and values of the modern Commonwealth. The 2011 edition has been fully updated and includes:

- the history, structure and activities of the Commonwealth Secretariat and other leading organisations

- a guide to Commonwealth Heads of Government Meetings and other key events

- full texts of essential communiqués and declarations

- The Commonwealth at the Crossroads – essays from influential thinkers on the future of the association

- comprehensive profiles of 54 member states including overseas territories

- a directory of around 80 Commonwealth intergovernmental, cultural and professional organisations

- an extensive statistics and reference section.

Economic affairs/trade

Catching Up: What LDCs Can Do, and How Others Can Help
Paul Collier
Paperback
£15.00
ISBN 978-1-8492905-1-7
(published February 2011)

Despite solid gains made during the last decade, the Least Developed Countries (LDCs) are not keeping pace with other countries, and the gap between them and the rest of the developing world has in fact widened. This means that LDCs will have to progress even faster to avoid being left further behind. In this publication, economist and award-winning author of *The Bottom Billion*, Paul Collier, suggests a menu of strategic policies around which governments might rally that could help LDCs to reduce this differentiation. He argues that the only actors who can lead this process are the governments of LDCs themselves working together towards clear and well-founded goals. He emphasises the need for effective change and highlights potential future problems associated with the management of natural resources and the threat of climate change. Implementing the right policies, he argues, is essential if LDCs are to catch up and not become detached from the rest of mankind.

Effectiveness of Aid for Trade in Small and Vulnerable Economies: An Empirical Assessment
Economic Paper Series 91
Dirk Willem te Velde, Massimiliano Cali and Mohammad Razzaque

Paperback
£15.00
ISBN 978-1-8492904-8-7
(published March 2011)

This Economic Paper presents the first analyses of the use and effectiveness of Aid for Trade (AfT), the initiative to help developing countries boost their involvement in the global economy, for small and vulnerable economies (SVEs). It examines in detail the extent to which SVEs have been able to access AfT funds and to what extent this assistance has helped them to improve their trade performance. Well-designed trade-related assistance will help SVEs face the challenges posed by their characteristics, particularly when the prospects for small states have been deteriorating further due to preference erosion and the emergence of new and large competitors.

The Impact of China and India on Sub-Saharan Africa: Opportunities, Challenges and Policies
Oliver Morrissey and Evious Zgovu
Paperback
£15.00
ISBN 978-1-8492905-5-5
(published May 2011)

China and India's demand for oil and other raw materials to fuel their recent economic development has led to significant trading partnerships with Africa, especially Sub-Saharan Africa (SSA). China in particular is becoming a major player on the continent, not only in exports but also in terms of investment and aid flows to SSA countries. Through detailed country-level analysis, this study offers unique contributions to the understanding of the relationship between China, India and SSA. The authors review and assess the economic impacts, identify the challenges involved and provide recommendations to assist policy-makers enhance the ability of SSA countries, individually and regionally, to derive benefits and to take advantage of new opportunities. This book is for academics, policy-makers and anyone interested in understanding the detailed dynamics that underpin the promises and challenges associated with South–South development.

Making Trade in Services Supportive of Development in Commonwealth Small and Low-income Countries
Economic Paper Series 93
Patrick Macrory and Dr Sherry Stephenson
Paperback
£15.00
ISBN 978-1-8492907-0-8
(published November 2011)

This Economic Paper assesses new innovative measures in trade in service negotiations that reflect the vulnerabilities and challenges faced by developing countries. It outlines the approaches that can help small and low-income countries employ the Special and Differential Treatment Arrangements provided under the WTO GATS in a manner that is practical and supportive of their economic development.

Negotiating at the World Trade Organization
Lessons from the Commonwealth Series 2
Vinod Rege
Paperback
£20.00

ISBN 978-1-8492902-2-7
(published February 2011)

Negotiating at the World Trade Organization provides a unique insider's guide to the issues that have concerned developing country negotiators at that body since its establishment in 1995. Published in the 'Lessons from the Commonwealth' series, it highlights the continuing issues that all delegations are grappling with, from a developing country perspective. It will be invaluable to those arriving in Geneva who need to brief themselves on the continuing story of the WTO negotiations, and those in national capitals in daily touch with their negotiating teams. The author, Vinod Rege, is a former director at GATT (General Agreement on Tariffs and Trade), and was engaged as a consultant to Commonwealth developing countries at the WTO over a ten-year period until 2008.

Potential Supply Chains in the Textiles and Clothing Sector in South Asia: An Exploratory Study
Paperback
£15.00
ISBN 978-1-8492907-6-0
(published November 2011)

Even though individual nations in South Asia are among the world's fastest-growing economies it is, as a region, the least integrated. This pioneering study from UNCTAD, the Commonwealth Secretariat and the Centre for WTO Studies at the Indian Institute of Foreign Trade examines one of the leading manufacturing sectors in South Asia – textiles and clothing – to assess the prospects for developing production linkages through regional co-operation. The findings show there is significant unexploited scope for intra-regional trade which would enhance the competitiveness of the region overall. The insights gleaned from the study will also benefit other sectors and regions of the developing world, where regional integration and South–South co-operation might be important routes to trade-led development.

Promoting IT Enabled Services
Lessons from the Commonwealth Series 3
Edited by Nikhil Treebhoohun
Paperback
£20.00
ISBN 978-1-8492905-4-8
(published December 2011)

Trade in services enabled by information and communication technologies could be an engine of growth for many developing countries looking to diversify from commodities-based economies. For this trade policy to be successful governments must establish effective policies and develop the correct regulatory framework, infrastructure and human capital. This handbook explains the key issues from the viewpoints of the regulator, the investor, the policy-maker and the donor. It provides detailed analysis of the Mauritian experience, which holds useful lessons for small states in particular. It will help policy-makers to learn directly from other countries' experience of developing IT enabled services and will assist private sector organisations to understand how governments frame their policies.

Trade Effects of Rules on Procurement for Commonwealth ACP Members
Economic Paper Series 92
Paperback

£20.00
ISBN 978-1-8492906-9-2
(published November 2011)

This Economic Paper assesses the potential trade effects of rules on procurement policies in Commonwealth ACP (African, Caribbean and Pacific) countries. It provides a practical guide for policy-makers and negotiators to determine the impact of government procurement rules and policies taken at the national level or negotiated in trade agreements.

Education

Education in Small States: Policies and Priorities
Michael Crossley, Mark Bray and Steve Packer
Paperback
£15.00
ISBN 978-1-8492903-6-4
(published June 2011)

This publication argues for work by the Commonwealth and others on the particular and distinct challenges of education in small states, and for the need to examine the impact of changing global contexts, to document the changing nature and significance of recent and contemporary education policy priorities, and to advance the case for new and strengthened initiatives for education in small states. The study will be of direct interest to a wide range of stakeholders involved in educational and social development in small states, to policy-makers, administrators, researchers, students, comparative educationalists, international agency personnel and practitioners at all levels in small states, throughout the Commonwealth and beyond.

Enhancing Teacher Professionalism and Status: Promoting Recognition, Registration and Standards
Kimberly Ochs
Edited by Roli Degazon-Johnson and James Keevy
Paperback
£10.00
ISBN 978-1-8492903-8-8
(published January 2011)

Ensuring that teachers' professionalism is appropriately recognised and rewarded is a challenge, especially at a time when that professional status itself is often under threat. The Fifth Commonwealth Teachers' Research Symposium brought together teachers, researchers and education policy-makers to share experiences from developed and developing countries both within and outside the Commonwealth. This research event was a further contribution to ensuring that teachers with professional qualifications of good standard are able to move freely between countries of the Commonwealth and the wider world, having those qualifications and skills recognised and valued.

Women and the Teaching Profession: Exploring the Feminisation Debate
(co-published with UNESCO)
Fatimah Kelleher, with Francis O Severin, Matselane B Khaahloe, Meera Samson, Anuradha De, Tepora Afamasaga-Wright and Upali M Sedere
Paperback
£20.00
ISBN 978-1-8492907-2-2
(published November 2011)

The debates on women and teaching have been wide ranging and, in some cases, contentious. They have included reviews of why the profession can become gender imbalanced in favour of women, the impacts of this on learning processes and student education, and the implications on women's overall empowerment within society and the economy. Most of the research to date has concentrated on developed countries such as the UK, Australia and Canada, where women have been a significant majority in the teaching workforce for decades. This study looks at how the teacher feminisation debate applies in developing countries. Drawing on the experiences of Dominica, Lesotho, Samoa, Sri Lanka and India, it provides a strong analytical understanding of the role of female teachers in the expansion of education systems, and the surrounding gender equality issues.

Elections

Nigeria National Assembly and Presidential Elections, 9 and 16 April 2011
Commonwealth Observer Group reports
Paperback
£10.00
ISBN 978-1-8492906-0-9
(published August 2011)

This is the Report of the Commonwealth Observer Group for the Nigerian Parliamentary and Presidential elections. The Group was led by Festus Mogae, former President of Botswana, and comprised 13 eminent persons in total.

Seychelles Presidential Election, 19–21 May 2011
Commonwealth Observer Group reports
Paperback
£10.00
ISBN 978-1-8492906-7-8
(published September 2011)

This is the Report of the Commonwealth Observer Group for the Seychelles Presidential Election. The Group was led by Dr Julian R Hunte, the former Foreign Minister of St Lucia, and comprised five eminent persons in total.

Tanzania General Elections, 31 October 2010
Commonwealth Observer Group reports
Paperback
£10.00
ISBN 978-1-8492904-9-4
(published January 2011)

This is the Report of the Commonwealth Observer Group for the Tanzania General Elections. The Group was led by the Rt Hon Paul East QC, a former Attorney-General of New Zealand, and comprised 15 eminent persons in total.

Uganda Presidential and Parliamentary Elections, 18 February 2011
Commonwealth Observer Group reports
Paperback
£10.00
ISBN 978-1-8492905-6-2
(published April 2011)

This is the Report of the Commonwealth Observer Group for the Uganda Parliamentary and Presidential elections. The Group was led by Dame Billie Miller, former Deputy Prime Minister and former Minister of Foreign Affairs and

Foreign Trade of Barbados, and comprised 13 eminent persons in total.

Gender

Who Cares?: The Economics of Dignity
Marilyn Waring, Robert Carr, Anit Mukherjee and Meena Shivdas
Paperback
£15.00
ISBN 978-1-8492901-9-7
(published October 2011)

At the centre of the HIV/AIDS response are the 12 million people who need care and treatment. Those who are ill require support from carers who provide physical, social and psychological support. Yet these carers – essential actors in the response – are often invisible to the system that relies on them. The writers argue that focusing on the carer, at the household level, directs assistance where it is most effective and most needed, will respect human rights, and will help achieve the Millennium Development Goals in health.

Health

Developing an E-Health Strategy: Commonwealth Workbook of Methodologies, Content and Models
Tom Jones
Paperback
£25.00
ISBN 978-1-8492903-2-6
(published February 2011)

Because e-health is a core resource for healthcare systems, every country needs good policies, strategies and plans, both for information and communication technology (ICT), and for the associated organisational changes that support improved health and healthcare. E-health is this combination of ICT and organisational change. This book will help health system decision-makers identify key policy issues in developing an e-health strategy and make the right decisions about the way forward. It is designed to be used in workshops with a team comprising people from many different backgrounds, such as senior civil servants responsible for health, ICT and finance, doctors, nurses, healthcare managers, ICT managers and suppliers. A team like this often has different views and ideas and using the workbook can help to put these together. Readers can use the workbook in many different ways: as a checklist for the agenda and topics for the team. They can use the parts that are most important to them and their work, and can add to the templates so they fit their precise needs better. Because e-health is not a single project with a fixed timescale and permanent solution, the effort and investment needed has many parts. It is complex, it changes constantly, and it is continuous. The workbook covers all the topics that will need to be addressed.

Human rights

Agricultural Trade and Human Rights
Commonwealth Secretariat Discussion Paper Series 12
José Maurel, Sujeevan Perera, Purna Sen and Christina Hajdu
Pamphlet
ISBN 978-0-8509291-7-1
(published November 2011)

This Discussion Paper examines the human rights impacts of international agricultural trade in developing countries. Businesses in importing countries make decisions that affect the incentives for producers to meet human rights standards; yet these businesses are far removed from the communities who depend on trade for their livelihoods. This is especially relevant in the highly vulnerable agricultural sector, where producers lack alternative livelihoods and where international supply chains are long and complicated. The Paper looks at the commercial challenges that undermine human rights and the policy initiatives that are being developed to address these challenges. It identifies a number of areas of concern and provides recommendations for future action.

Universal Periodic Review: Lessons, Hopes and Expectations
Dr Purna Sen, Research by Monica Vincent and Jade Cochran
Paperback
£10.00
ISBN 978-1-8492904-3-2
(published July 2011)

The UN Human Rights Universal Periodic Review (UPR) mechanism has been in place for over two years. 2008 and 2009 saw this mechanism succeed in promoting dialogues on human rights in countries from all continents and all regions, including 25 Commonwealth states. Since the inception of the UPR, the Commonwealth Secretariat has engaged with Commonwealth countries on UPR. It has offered training and helped share information and good practices, research and observations. Governments have held consultations, prepared national reports, responded to questions and recommendations during the review in Geneva, and are now beginning to implement those recommendations. National human rights institutions and civil society organisations have engaged with the process through stakeholder reports and advocacy. This publication presents the experiences of key UPR actors, as shared at the Commonwealth Mid-Term Review of UPR held in 2010. It then provides timely analysis and evaluation of the UPR mechanism at all three stages of the process: preparation of the UPR report; the review in Geneva; and UPR follow up and implementation, including country by country analysis of recommendations received by each Commonwealth country. *Universal Periodic Review: Lessons, Hopes and Expectations* draws together the lessons of Commonwealth countries' experiences in 2008 and 2009, and hopes and expectations for the future of UPR.

Public administration

Alternative Service Delivery Revisited
Commonwealth Secretariat Discussion Paper Series 10
John Wilkins
Pamphlet
ISBN 978-0-8509291-8-8
(published March 2011)

Alternative Service Delivery (ASD) is a process of government reform that reviews public programmes and services to choose the most appropriate organisational forms and delivery mechanisms to achieve government objectives. It has regained currency in Commonwealth public sector development recently, as governments deal with the fiscal and budgetary effects of the global economic crisis. This Discussion Paper first explains the concept and methodology behind ASD. It then profiles two contrasting country

cases of Commonwealth ASD experience, and summarises the lessons learned about good practice. Finally, it considers the prospects for ASD and raises questions for further exploration.

Decentralisation in Commonwealth Africa: Experiences from Botswana, Cameroon, Ghana, Mozambique and Tanzania
Edited by Janet Kathyola and Oluwatoyin Job
Paperback
£25.00
ISBN 978-1-8492904-4-9
(published July 2011)

The aim of a well-designed decentralisation programme is to deliver effective services to all citizens and to deepen democracy through active popular participation in local governance. Through detailed case studies of decentralisation policies in five Sub-Saharan African countries – Botswana, Cameroon, Ghana, Mozambique and Tanzania – this book examines the challenges presented, lessons learned, and recommends ways to improve policy implementation. It is clear from the analysis that there is no 'one size fits all' design of decentralisation policy. Policy-makers worldwide can use the lessons learned and good practices presented here to better inform and advance their own decentralisation agenda.

Innovations in Public Expenditure Management: Country Cases from the Commonwealth
Edited by Andrew Graham
Paperback
£25.00
ISBN 978-1-8492906-8-5
(published September 2011)

A key feature of a professional and credible public service is transparent and accountable financial management. In a rapidly changing and often challenging public sector environment, public servants are seeking new and creative approaches to enhance the efficiency and effectiveness of their work. This collection of case studies, broadly drawn from Commonwealth developed and developing countries, examines innovations in public financial management and provides practical information on best practices and recommendations for new initiatives. It will be valuable for public sector leaders and policy-makers as they work to improve their public financial management systems.

Resource Guide on Decentralisation and Local Government
Commonwealth Secretariat Local Government Reform Series 3
Compiled by Zoë Scott and Munawwar Alam
Paperback
£20.00
ISBN 978-1-8492902-9-6
(published July 2011)

Estimates suggest that decentralisation is currently being pursued in over 80 per cent of developing countries worldwide. For many people, local government is the part of government that most directly impacts on their lives, particularly via the provision of local services like water, sanitation, primary education and primary healthcare. This resource guide provides practical guidance for designing, implementing and evaluating decentralisation reforms and local government practices to ensure they are as effective as possible. It also

synthesises and presents current debates on the impact of decentralisation and local government on
poverty reduction, service delivery and conflict as well as providing links to cutting-edge research and recent case studies. The guide includes summaries of key texts. Each short summary provides a link to an extended summary, which can be found in the alphabetised appendix.

Tax, Governance and Development
Commonwealth Secretariat Discussion Paper Series 11
Max Everest-Phillips
Pamphlet
ISBN 978-0-8509291-6-4
(published July 2011)

This Discussion Paper outlines why taxation matters to Commonwealth developing countries not simply for raising revenues to pay for development, but as a means of shaping the governance context that influences that development. In seeking to reduce poverty, promote growth and improve governance, the Commonwealth must pay more attention not just to how much revenue is raised through taxation or how it is spent, but how taxes are raised. The Paper concludes with ideas on how to promote tax reforms that improve governance.

The Contract System of Employment for Senior Government Officials: Experiences from the Caribbean
Managing the Public Service: Strategies for Improvement Series 17
Edited by Philip Osei and Joan Nwasike
Paperback
£20.00
ISBN 978-1-8492904-6-3
(published May 2011)

This publication reviews the effects of the reforms implemented under the 'new public management' programme on the roles and conditions of service of permanent secretaries and directors in Belize, Guyana, Jamaica and St Lucia. These countries introduced the contract system of employment, and their experiences highlight the importance of acknowledging context in considering the implications of the contract system, and the challenges of implementation.

The Contract System of Employment for Senior Government Officials: Experiences from the Pacific
Managing the Public Service: Strategies for Improvement Series 18
Faamausili Dr Matagialofi Lua'iufi and S Omar Z Mowlana
Paperback
£20.00
ISBN 978-1-8492905-3-1
(published July 2011)

This publication reviews the effects of the reforms implemented under the 'new public management' programme on the roles and conditions of service of permanent secretaries in the Cook Islands, Papua New Guinea, Samoa, Tonga and Vanuatu. These countries introduced the contract system of employment, and their experiences highlight the importance of acknowledging context in considering the implications of the contract system, and the challenges of implementation.

Small states

Assessing the Structure of Small Welfare States
Social Policies in Small States Series 4
Geoff Bertram
Paperback
£10.00
ISBN 978-1-8492905-0-0
(published March 2011)

The country case studies and thematic papers in this series examine social policy issues facing small states and the implications for economic development. They show how, despite their inherent vulnerability, some small states have been successful in improving their social indicators because of the complementary social and economic policies they have implemented. Historically, the welfare state evolved as the most efficient policy response to caring for a large, homogeneous population. This traditional model, however, loses importance as population size falls below three to four million, especially for states where a significant number of the population migrate and send remittances home, and where the country is the recipient of overseas aid. Facilitating the international mobility of people therefore becomes central to social policy and insofar as the welfare state occurs, it tends to be focused on the labour market. This paper examines how the characteristics of small states influence their pursuit of a welfare state. Many of the small states discussed have not previously featured in mainstream thinking about the relationship between country size and the extent of the welfare state.

Development Challenges of HIV/AIDS in Small States: Experiences from the Pacific, Southern Africa and the Caribbean
Karl Theodore, Mahendra Reddy and Happy Siphambe
Paperback
£20.00
ISBN 978-1-8492905-8-6
(published October 2011)

Development Challenges of HIV/AIDS in Small States provides an up-to-date and comprehensive analysis of the economic impacts of the epidemic in the Pacific, Southern Africa and the Caribbean. The authors examine specific features of these three regions that contribute towards the spread of HIV/AIDS and identify the responses by various local and external stakeholders. What is clear from the research is that small states must see in the epidemic opportunities for modernisation and, with external support, put emphasis on strengthening policy design and implementation in key areas to strengthen the development effort so urgently needed by their populations.

Integrating Sustainable Development into National Frameworks: Policy Approaches for Key Sectors in Small States
Edited by Janet Strachan and Constance Vigilance
Paperback
£20.00
ISBN 978-1-8492903-4-0
(published May 2011)

This book brings policy-making for sustainable development into the mainstream of decision-making at all levels of governance and in all sectors. It builds on the 2005 internationally agreed 'Mauritius Strategy', which aims to implement the integration of sustainable development by small island developing states (SIDS). Designed as a handbook for policy-makers and planners in government, as well as business and civil society leaders, it covers seven of the twenty issues that have been outlined in the Mauritius Strategy as being important for the sustainable development of SIDS – disaster management; marine resources; freshwater resources; land resources; energy resources; tourism resources; and trade. It brings together best practices, policy options and development prospects that small states can pursue in order to achieve real progress in these fields. It covers the progress and experiences of countries in the Caribbean region, the Pacific region, and the Atlantic, Indian Ocean and Mediterranean region in their implementation of sustainable development in these areas. It also provides a useful point of reference and stimulus to policy-makers and their supporting colleagues from all sectors. This book brings policy-making for sustainable development into the mainstream of decision-making at all levels of governance and in all sectors.

Issues in Monetary and Fiscal Policy in Small Developing States: A Case Study of the Caribbean
Anthony Birchwood and Dr Marielle Goto
Paperback
£15.00
ISBN 978-1-8492906-1-6
(published September 2011)

This study examines how monetary and fiscal policies are implemented in Caribbean small states, tracing the differences and similarities in tax structure, current expenditure and current revenues. It shows the impact of monetary policy on inflation and the importance of exchange rate regimes to the effectiveness of monetary policy in the region. The authors show that fiscal stabilisation in the region is very low and as such countries within the region would benefit from insurance mechanisms and stabilisation funds.

Issues in Monetary and Fiscal Policy in Small Developing States: A Case Study of the Pacific
T K Jayaraman and Professor Paresh Narayan
Paperback
£15.00
ISBN 978-1-8492906-2-3
(published October 2011)

This study examines how monetary and fiscal policies are implemented in Pacific small states and the impact on growth and development in these countries. It carefully sets out both the policy and institutional constraints in monetary and fiscal policy management, provides case study examples of policy implementation in practice, and suggests policy options that can be used by these countries.

Macroeconomic Policy Frameworks of Small States: A Case Study of Malta
Dr Gérard Adonis
Paperback
£15.00
ISBN 978-1-8492906-3-0
(published September 2011)

Malta's socio-economic successes have been remarkable. Key policy decisions have enabled this small island state to cope with its inherent vulnerabilities. This book reviews the implementation of macroeconomic policies in Malta, identifying the key issues, lessons learned and best practices which could be adapted by other small states. It also sets out the country's challenges for the future, which include managing a huge fiscal deficit, a high unemployment rate and attending to the conflicting demands of environmental conservation and economic development.

Partnerships for Sustainable Development in Small States
Cletus I Springer and John L Roberts
Paperback
£15.00
ISBN 978-1-8492906-4-7
(published October 2011)

Partnerships for Sustainable Development in Small States examines measures through which small states can work together with the international community to strengthen their ability to pursue economic and social development. Due to their size and vulnerability, national practices alone would leave these countries unable to cope with the pressing challenges they face in areas such as climate change, sustainable manufacturing and renewable energy technologies. In Chapter 1, development-planning specialist Cletus I Springer examines the scope for effective partnerships and reviews the progress that has been made nationally, regionally and internationally. In Chapter 2, John L Roberts, Associate Professor at the University of Mauritius, highlights the need for new partnerships and notes new trends, such as the greater use of technology, that can be developed to address challenges more effectively.

Small States: Economic Review and Basic Statistics, Volume 15
Paperback
£25.00
ISBN 978-1-8492903-7-1
(published July 2011)

This unique annual collection of key economic and statistical data on states with fewer than five million inhabitants is an essential reference for economists, planners and policy-makers. The Commonwealth's definition of small states is those with a population of 1.5 million or lower. For comparison purposes this volume presents, where available, data on states with a population of up to five million. The book contains 68 tables covering selected economic, social, demographic and Millennium Development Goal indicators culled from international and national sources and presents information unavailable elsewhere. A detailed parallel commentary on trends in Commonwealth small states, looking at growth, employment, inflation, human development, and economic policy, permits a deeper understanding of developments behind the figures. The book also includes three articles focusing on public private partnerships: 'Public–Private Partnerships in Mauritius' by Vishwanaden Soondram' 'Public–Private Partnerships: Mobilising Private Sector Funding' and 'Public–Private Partnerships: Frequently Asked Questions' by Hee Kong Yong. Soondram works as a lead analyst at the Mauritius Ministry of Finance and Economic Development and Yong works as an adviser (Public Private Partnerships) in the Governance and Institutional Development Division of the Commonwealth Secretariat.

Social Policies in Malta
Social Policies in Small States Series 3
Rose Marie Azzopardi
Paperback
£15.00
ISBN 978-1-8492902-4-1
(published March 2011)

Malta is a high-income developed small state, with an impressive level of economic growth and a multitude of social services, which have helped to provide free health and education to all its citizens and benefits to low-income earners. However, various national and global factors are now threatening the sustainability of this extensive social security model. This paper examines the economic, political and social development of the island, particularly since independence, highlighting the successes and failures of the social development strategies adopted and suggesting how these lessons can inform future policy decisions.

Social Policies in Seychelles
Social Policies in Small States Series 5
Liam Campling, Hansel Confiance and Marie-Therese Purvis
Paperback
£15.00
ISBN 978-1-8492906-5-4
(published December 2011)

Seychelles has one of the most extensive social policy programmes in the developing world, and has been identified as a model for the rest of Africa. As a small state, however, it remains economically vulnerable and in 2008 had to accept a financial rescue package from the IMF. This book provides comprehensive analysis of social policy development in the country from the colonial era onwards, focusing on the political and economic developments that have led to the current situation. The challenge now is to maintain current levels of social policy interventions in the face of severe indebtedness and the stagnation of economic growth.

Tools for Mainstreaming Sustainable Development in Small States
Edited by John L Roberts and Constance Vigilance
Paperback
£30.00
ISBN 978-1-8492905-2-4
(published June 2011)

Tools for Mainstreaming Sustainable Development in Small States provides a thorough grounding in bringing sustainable development to the forefront of policy-making. By taking a cross-departmental approach to national planning, more human and financial resources would be available for policy implementation. This is of particular relevance to small states, as they have limited access to resources and are by nature inherently vulnerable. The book is divided into four parts. Part 1 explores how small states can move from the Mauritius Strategy of Implementation (MSI) to devising practical national strategies; Part 2 addresses the need for legislative change; Part 3 tackles the social and environmental aspects of progress with MSI; and finally, Part 4 examines methods for monitoring progress. Contributors to the chapters range from international academics to economists, providing both a theoretical and practical approach. Through case study examples from small states, this book offers invaluable insights into the complexities of implementing sustainable development.

Taxation

Interactive Tutorial of Tax Audit Techniques in Cash Based Economies
(published by the Commonwealth Association of Tax Administrators)
CD-ROM
£24.00
ISBN 978-0-9553540-3-8
(published April 2011)

This interactive guide will help users learn and understand the topics covered in the CATA publication *Tax Audit Techniques in Cash Based Economies*, although it can be used on its own. Each topic covered includes a self-assessment to help users review their learning. The guide was designed and developed by Pakistan Revenue Automation (Pvt) Ltd, a company owned by the Federal Board of Revenue of Pakistan.

Commonwealth bibliography

This brief guide includes a range of books, reports and journal articles on the history and development of the modern Commonwealth. It also gives details of libraries with good holdings on the Commonwealth.

Selected primary sources

A Commonwealth of the People: Time for Urgent Reform (London: Commonwealth Secretariat, 2011)
The report of the Commonwealth Eminent Persons Group, containing proposals for Commonwealth and Secretariat reform, presented to Commonwealth Heads of Government at CHOGM 2011 in Perth, Australia.

British Documents on the End of Empire
A massive project based at the Institute of Commonwealth Studies. It comes in three series: Series A represents the general volumes and contains documents for successive British governments relating to the empire as a whole; Series B represents the country volumes and provides territorial studies of how, from a British government perspective, former colonies achieved their independence, and countries within an empire regained their autonomy; Series C, a support series, provides archival guides to official sources in the form of handbooks to the records of the former colonial empire, which are deposited at the National Archives.

The Commonwealth at the Summit: Communiqués of Commonwealth Heads of Government Meetings (London: Commonwealth Secretariat)
Three volumes, the first covering 1944–1986, the second 1987–1995, the third 1997–2005.

Bennett, J, Sriskandarajah, D and Ware, Z, *Common What? Emerging Findings of the Commonwealth Conversation* (London: Royal Commonwealth Society, 2009)
A summary of the findings of the Commonwealth Conversation, a global public consultation on the future of the Commonwealth launched in July 2009.

Keith, A B, *Speeches and Documents on the British Dominions from Self Government to National Sovereignty, 1918–1931* (Oxford: Oxford University Press, 1948)
Documents on British colonial policy, including the Statute of Westminster.

Madden, F and Fieldhouse, D (eds), *Select Documents on the Constitutional History of the*

British Empire and Commonwealth (New York: Greenwood Press, 1987–94). Vol. 4 *Settler Government 1840–1900*; Vol. 5 *The Dependent Empire and Ireland, 1840–1900*; Vol. 6 *The Dominions and India Since 1900*; Vol. 7 *Dependent Empire, 1900–1948: Colonies, Protectorates and Mandates* (eds F Madden and J Darwin)

Mansergh, N, *Documents and Speeches on British Commonwealth Affairs* – Vol. 1 1931–52; Vol. 2 1952–62 (Oxford 1953 and 1963)

Selected secondary sources

General history

Falconer, J, *Commonwealth in Focus: 130 Years of Photographic History* (Brisbane: International Cultural Corporation of Australia, 1982)
A catalogue of historical photographs shown at the 1982 Commonwealth Games in Brisbane.

Hall, H D, *Commonwealth: A History of the British Commonwealth of Nations* (New York: Van Nostrand Rheinold, 1971)
Covers the first half of the 20th century.

Hancock, W K, *Survey of British Commonwealth Affairs*. Two volumes by Hancock titled *Problems of Nationality, 1918–1936* and *Problems of Economic Policy, 1918–1939* (OUP, 1937–1942)
For other volumes, see Mansergh and Miller.

Judd, D and Slinn, P, *The Evolution of the Modern Commonwealth, 1902–1980* (London: Macmillan, 1982)

Mansergh, N, *The Commonwealth Experience* (London: Macmillan, 1982). Vol. 1 *The Durham Report to the Anglo-Irish Treaty*; Vol. 2 *From British to Multiracial Commonwealth*

Mansergh, N, *Survey of British Commonwealth Affairs: Problems of War-Time Co-operation and Postwar Change, 1939–1952* (OUP, 1958)

McIntyre, W D, *British Decolonization, 1946–1997: When, Why and How Did the British Empire Fall?* (London: Macmillan, 1998)
A good introduction to the subject, with a final chapter titled 'The Commonwealth: disillusionment, detachment and rediscovery'.

Miller, J D B, *Survey of Commonwealth Affairs: Problems of Expansion and Attrition, 1953–1969* (OUP, 1974)
Extensive treatment of some of the major international questions affecting the Commonwealth.

Miller, J D B, *The Commonwealth in the World* (London: Duckworth, 1965, 3rd edn)
Traces the Commonwealth to the mid-1960s.

Palmer, A, *Dictionary of the British Empire and Commonwealth* (London: Murray, 1996)
A useful reference companion to the events and personalities that have shaped the Commonwealth.

Walker, P G, *The Commonwealth* (London: Secker & Warburg, 1962)
The author was Britain's Under-Secretary, then Secretary of State for Commonwealth Relations from 1947 to 1951.

Dominion status

Eddy, J (ed.), *The Rise of Colonial Nationalism: Australia, New Zealand, Canada and South Africa First Assert Their Nationalities* (Sydney: Allen & Unwin, 1988)

MacGregor Dawson, R, *The Development of Dominion Status, 1900–1936* (London: Cass, 1965; first published in 1937)

Wheare, K, *The Statute of Westminster and Dominion Status* (OUP, 1953, 5th edn)
The standard work on the Statute of Westminster, covering its text, scope and implications.

The modern Commonwealth

Ball, M, *The 'Open' Commonwealth* (Durham, North Carolina: Duke University Press, 1971)
An analysis of how the Commonwealth functions at both official and unofficial levels.

Banerji, A, 'The 1949 London declaration: birth of the modern Commonwealth', *Commonwealth Law Bulletin*, Vol. 25, 1999, pp1–7

Bogdanor, V, *The Monarchy and the Constitution* (Oxford: Clarendon Press, 1995)
Final chapter explores the post-war constitutional relationship of Commonwealth countries and the role of Queen Elizabeth II, Head of the Commonwealth.

Bourne, R (ed.), *Shridath Ramphal: The Commonwealth and The World – Essays in honour of his 80th birthday* (London: Hansib, 2008)
Twelve essays spanning his career.

Brown, J M and Louis, W R (eds), *Oxford History of the British Empire*: Vol. 4 The Twentieth Century (OUP, 1999)
A major work with a host of well-known contributors.

Groom, A J R and Taylor, P, *The Commonwealth in the 1980s: Challenges and Opportunities* (London: Macmillan, 1984)

Ingram, D, *The Imperfect Commonwealth* (London: Rex Collings, 1977)
A seasoned Commonwealth observer comments on personalities and events from 1969 to 1977.

Lloyd, L, *Diplomacy with a difference: the Commonwealth Office of High Commissioner* (Leiden: Nijhoff, 2007)
An important work on one of the peculiarities of the Commonwealth.

May, A (ed.), *The Commonwealth and International Affairs* (Routledge 2010)
A selection of the best articles published in *The*

Round Table: The Commonwealth Journal of International Affairs over the past century.

Mayall, J (ed.), *The Contemporary Commonwealth: An assessment 1965–2009* (Routledge 2010)
A collection of essays to mark the centenary of the journal The Round Table. The book gives an analysis of the modern Commonwealth since 1965, when the Commonwealth Secretariat was established.

McDonald, T, *The Queen and Commonwealth* (London: Methuen, 1986)
A general work on the Queen's ceremonial role.

McIntyre, W D, *A Guide to the Contemporary Commonwealth* (Basingstoke: Palgrave, 2001)
An authoritative guide to the Commonwealth by a prolific writer.

McIntyre, W D, *The Significance of the Commonwealth* (London: Macmillan, 1991)

Ramphal, S, 'Ours and the world's advantage: the constructive Commonwealth', *International Affairs*, Vol. 60, No. 3, Summer 1984, pp371–389
A former Secretary-General's assessment of the Commonwealth in the 1980s.

Sharma, K, *Imagining Tomorrow: Rethinking the Global Challenge* (New York: UN, 2000)
Essays looking at globalisation, the Millennium Development Goals, human rights and poverty.

Shaw, T M, *Commonwealth: Inter- and Non-State Contributions to Global Governance* (London: Routledge, 2007)
A recent general book on the Commonwealth by the former Director of the Institute of Commonwealth Studies. Looks at the role of governments and NGOs.

Srinivasan, K, *The Rise, Decline and Future of the British Commonwealth* (Basingstoke: Palgrave Macmillan, 2005)
A controversial and rather pessimistic view of the Commonwealth by a former Deputy Secretary-General. For responses to it, see 'Whose Commonwealth? Responses to Krishnan Srinivasan's The Rise, Decline and Future of the British Commonwealth', *The Round Table*, Vol. 96, Issue 308, 2007, pp57–70.

Commonwealth Secretariat

Anyaoku, E, *The Inside Story of the Modern Commonwealth* (London and Ibadan: Evans Brothers, 2004)
The autobiography of the third Commonwealth Secretary-General.

Anyaoku, E, *The Missing Headlines* (Liverpool: Liverpool University Press, 1997)
Selected speeches, mainly from Chief Anyaoku's first five years in office.

Chan, S, *The Commonwealth in World Politics: A Study in International Action, 1965–1985* (London: Lester Crook, 1988)

Chan, S and Alner, J, *Twelve Years of Commonwealth Diplomatic History* (New York: Edwin Mellen Press, 1992)
A look at Commonwealth summit meetings from 1979 to 1991.

Doxey, M, *The Commonwealth Secretariat and the Contemporary Commonwealth* (London: Macmillan, 1989)
The standard work on the establishment and development of the Secretariat, now in need of updating.

McIntyre, W D, 'Canada and the Creation of the Commonwealth Secretariat, 1965', *International Journal*, Vol. 53, No. 4, Autumn 1998, pp753–777
Contains a good deal of information on the background to the establishment of the Secretariat and Arnold Smith's contribution to its development.

Ramphal, S, *One World to Share* (London: Hutchinson Benham, 1979)
Selected speeches of the second Commonwealth Secretary-General.

Smith, A, *Stitches in Time: The Commonwealth in World Politics* (London: Deutsch, 1981)
Reflections of the first Commonwealth Secretary-General, written with Clyde Sanger.

Journals

A number of journals on Commonwealth affairs are published, some of which have book review sections and listings of new materials. These include, with current publishers, the following.

Commonwealth and Comparative Politics (Abingdon: Taylor and Francis)
Published four times a year. Previously titled *Journal of Commonwealth Political Studies* (1961–1973) and *Journal of Commonwealth and Comparative Politics* (1974–1997).

The Parliamentarian
The journal of the Commonwealth Parliamentary Association.

The Round Table: The Commonwealth Journal of International Affairs (Abingdon, United Kingdom: Taylor and Francis)
Founded in 1910. Published six times a year. Includes *Commonwealth Bookshelf*, an annotated list of new books, and *Commonwealth Update*, a guide to mainly political developments throughout the Commonwealth.

Further study

Larby, P and Hannam, H, *The Commonwealth* (Oxford: Clio Press, 1993)
A substantial bibliography on various aspects of the history, development and nature of the Commonwealth. In need of updating.

Libraries

While many national and local libraries will have resource material on the Commonwealth, the principal collections are located in the United Kingdom.

Commonwealth Secretariat Library
Marlborough House, Pall Mall,
London SW1Y 5HX, UK
Tel: +44 20 7747 6164
Email: library@commonwealth.int
(Library website:) **www.thecommonwealth.org**

Extensive collection of books, pamphlets and report literature, including many of the materials mentioned in this bibliography. Has an emphasis on recent and current materials. Since 1997 the Secretariat has been releasing its records into the public domain under a 30-year rule. Requests for access to the papers should be made to the Archivist, Hilary McEwan.

Institute of Commonwealth Studies: library services
University of London, Library Office, 4th Floor, Senate House, Malet Street,
London WC1E 7HU, UK
Tel: +44 20 7862 8500
Fax: +44 20 7862 8480
(Website:) **http://commonwealth.sas.ac.uk**
(Library catalogue website:)
http://catalogue.ulrls.lon.ac.uk

Part of the School of Advanced Study of the University of London. Extensive collections on Commonwealth history and the social sciences. Includes archives.

Royal Commonwealth Society Collection, Cambridge University Library
West Road, Cambridge, CB3 9DR, UK
Tel: +44 1223 333 000
Email: rcs@lib.cam.ac.uk
www.lib.cam.ac.uk/deptserv/rcs

Very large collection, including a wealth of historical material. Transferred from the Royal Commonwealth Society to Cambridge University Library in 1993.

The National Archives
Ruskin Avenue, Kew, Richmond-upon-Thames, Surrey TW9 4DU, UK
Tel: +44 20 8876 3444
www.nationalarchives.gov.uk (includes a guide to its holdings in the area of imperial and Commonwealth history)

The national archives of the United Kingdom, with a wealth of material of interest to the Commonwealth historian.

This list was compiled by David Blake, Librarian, Commonwealth Secretariat 1999–2008. The listings here are by no means comprehensive. The Commonwealth Secretariat produces a wide range of materials on current Commonwealth activities and concerns. A catalogue can be downloaded at **www.thecommonwealth.org/publications**.

The Commonwealth Advisory Bureau based at the Institute of Commonwealth Studies in London produces a range of publications on policy issues. Further details can be found at **http://www.commonwealthadvisorybureau.org/publications**

Event	Athlete/Team	Country	Record	Year	Venue
Men's 100m	Ato Boldon	Trinidad and Tobago	9.88 (seconds)	1998	Kuala Lumpur, Malaysia
Women's 100m	Debbie Ferguson	The Bahamas	10.91 (seconds)	2002	Manchester, England
Men's 200m	Frank 'Frankie' Fredericks	Namibia	19.97 (seconds)	1994	Victoria, Canada
Women's 200m	Merlene Joyce Ottey	Jamaica	22.19 (seconds)	1982	Brisbane, Australia
Men's 400m	Iwan Gwyn Thomas	Wales	44.52 (seconds)	1998	Kuala Lumpur, Malaysia
Women's 400m	Amantle Montsho	Botswana	50.10 (seconds)	2010	Delhi, India
Men's 800m	Stephen 'Steve' Cram	England	1:43.22 (mins)	1986	Edinburgh, Scotland
Women's 800m	Maria Lurdes Mutola	Mozambique	1:57.35 (mins)	2002	Manchester, England
Men's 1500m	Filbert Bayi	Tanzania	3:32.16(mins)	1974	Christchurch, New Zealand
Women's 1500m	Nancy Jebet Lan'gat	Kenya	4:05.26 (mins)	2010	Delhi, India
Women's 3,000m	Angela Chalmers	Canada	8:32.17 (mins)	1994	Victoria, Canada
Men's 5,000m	Augustine Choge	Kenya	12:56.41 (mins)	2006	Melbourne, Australia
Women's 5,000m	Paula Radcliffe	England	14:31.42 (mins)	2002	Manchester, England
Men's 10,000m	Wilberforce Talel	Kenya	27:45.39 (mins)	2002	Manchester, England
Women's 10,000m	Selina Kosgei	Kenya	31:27.83 (mins)	2002	Manchester, England
Men's 110m Hurdles	Colin Ray Jackson	Wales	13.08 (seconds)	1994	Victoria, Canada
Women's 100m Hurdles	Gillian Russell	Jamaica	12.70 (seconds)	1998	Kuala Lumpur, Malaysia
Men's 400m Hurdles	Louis van Zyl	South Africa	48.05 (seconds)	2006	Melbourne, Australia
Women's 400m Hurdles	Jana Pittman	Australia	53.82 (seconds)	2006	Melbourne, Australia
Men's 3,000m Steeplechase	Johnstone Kipkoech	Kenya	8:14.72 (mins)	1994	Victoria, Canada
Women's 3,000m Steeplechase	Dorcas Inzikuru	Uganda	9:19.51 (mins)	2006	Melbourne, Australia
Men's High Jump	Clarence Nicholas Saunders	Bermuda	2.36 metres	1990	Auckland, New Zealand
Women's High Jump	Hestrie Cloete	South Africa	1.96 metres	2002	Manchester, England
Men's Long Jump	Yusuf Alli	Nigeria	8.39 metres	1990	Auckland, New Zealand
Women's Long Jump	Bronwyn Thompson	Australia	6.97 metres	2006	Melbourne, Australia
Men's Triple Jump	Jonathan David Edwards	England	17.86 metres	2002	Manchester, England
Women's Triple Jump	Ashia Nana Hansen	England	14.86 metres	2002	Manchester, England
Men's Pole Vault	Steve Hooker	Australia	5.80 metres	2006	Melbourne, Australia
Women's Pole Vault	Kym Howe	Australia	4.62 metres	2006	Melbourne, Australia
Men's Javelin	Mike O'Rourke	New Zealand	89.48 metres	1982	Brisbane, Australia
Women's Javelin	Theresa 'Tessa' Sanderson	England	69.80 metres	1986	Edinburgh, Scotland
Men's Shot Put	Dylan Armstrong	Canada	21.02 metres	2010	Delhi, India
Women's Shot Put	Valerie Vili	New Zealand	20.47 metres	2010	Delhi, India
Men's Discus Throw	Frantz Kruger	South Africa	66.39 metres	2002	Manchester, England
Women's Discus Throw	Beatrice Roini Faumuina	New Zealand	65.92 metres	1998	Kuala Lumpur, Malaysia
Men's Hammer Throw	Stuart Rendell	Australia	77.53 metres	2006	Melbourne, Australia
Women's Hammer Throw	Sultana Frizell	Canada	68.57 metres	2010	Delhi, India
Men's 4x100m Relay	England	England	38.20 (seconds)	1998	Kuala Lumpur, Malaysia
Women's 4x100m Relay	The Bahamas	The Bahamas	42.44 (seconds)	2002	Manchester, England
Men's 4x400m Relay	Jamaica	Jamaica	2:59.03 (mins)	1998	Kuala Lumpur, Malaysia
Women's 4x400m Relay	Australia	Australia	3:25.63 (mins)	2002	Manchester, England
Women's 10km Road Walk	Jane Kara Saville	Australia	43.57 (seconds)	1998	Kuala Lumpur, Malaysia
Men's 20km Walk	Nathan Deakes	Australia	1:25:35 (hours)	2002	Manchester, England
Women's 20km Walk	Jane Kara Saville	Australia	1:36:34 (hours)	2002	Manchester, England
Men's 30km Road Walk	Simon Francis Baker	Australia	2:07:47 (hours)	1986	Edinburgh, Scotland
Men's 50km Walk	Nathan Deakes	Australia	3:52:40 (hours)	2002	Manchester, England
Men's Marathon	Ian Reginald Thompson	England	2:09:12.0 (hours)	1974	Christchurch, New Zealand
Women's Marathon	Kerryn Ann McCann	Australia	2:30:05 (hours)	2002	Manchester, England
Men's Decathlon	Francis 'Daley' Thompson	England	8,663 points	1986	Edinburgh, Scotland
Women's Heptathlon	Jane Christina Flemming	Australia	6,695 points	1990	Auckland, New Zealand
Women's Pentathlon	Mary Elizabeth Peters	Northern Ireland	5,148 points	1970	Edinburgh, Scotland
Men's 100 Yard Dash	Henry 'Harry' Jerome	Canada	9.4 (seconds)	1966	Kingston, Jamaica
Women's 100 Yard Dash	Dianne Marie Burge	Australia	10.6 (seconds)	1966	Kingston, Jamaica
Men's 220 Yard Dash	Stanley Fabian Allotey	Ghana	20.7 (seconds)	1966	Kingston, Jamaica
Women's 220 Yard Dash	Marlene Mathews-Willard	Australia	23.6 (seconds)	1958	Cardiff, Wales
Men's 440 Yard Run	Wendell Adrian Mottley	Trinidad and Tobago	45.2 (seconds)	1966	Kingston, Jamaica
Men's 880 Yard Run	Noel Stanley Clough	Australia	1:46.9 (mins)	1966	Kingston, Jamaica
Women's 880 Yard Run	Dixie Isabel Willis	Australia	2:03.7 (mins)	1962	Perth, Australia
Men's 1 Mile Run	Kipchoge 'Kip' Keino	Kenya	3:55.3 (mins)	1966	Kingston, Jamaica
Men's 3 Mile Run	Kipchoge 'Kip' Keino	Kenya	12:57.4 (mins)	1966	Kingston, Jamaica
Men's 6 Mile Run	Nabiba 'Naftali' Temu	Kenya	27:14.6 (mins)	1966	Kingston, Jamaica
Men's 120 Yard Hurdles	Keith Alvin Gardner	Jamaica	14.0 (seconds)	1958	Cardiff, Wales

Commonwealth Games athletics records

Event	Athlete/Team	Country	Record	Year	Venue
Women's 80m Hurdles	Norma Claire Thrower	Australia	10.7 (seconds)	1958	Cardiff, Wales
Men's 440 Yard Hurdles	Gerhardus 'Gert' Potgieter	South Africa	49.7 (seconds)	1958	Cardiff, Wales
Men's 2 Mile Steeplechase	George William Bailey	England	9.52.0 (seconds)	1930	Hamilton, Canada
Men's 4x110 Yard Relay	Ghana	Ghana	39.8 (seconds)	1966	Kingston, Jamaica
Women's 4x110 Yard Relay	Australia	Australia	45.3 (seconds)	1966	Kingston, Jamaica
Men's 4x440 Yard Relay/ 1 Mile Relay	Trinidad and Tobago	Trinidad and Tobago	3:02.8 (mins)	1966	Kingston, Jamaica
Women's 440 Yard relay	Australia	Australia	47.9 (seconds)	1950	Auckland, New Zealand
Women's 660 Yard Relay	Australia	Australia	1:13.4 (mins)	1950	Auckland, New Zealand
Men's 20 Mile Walk	Noel Frederick Freeman	Australia	2:33:33 (hours)	1970	Edinburgh, Scotland

World records held by Commonwealth athletes

Event	Athlete/Team	Country	Record	Year	Venue
Men's 100m	Usain Bolt	Jamaica	9.58 (seconds)	2009	Berlin, Germany
Men's 200m	Usain Bolt	Jamaica	19.19 (seconds)	2009	Berlin, Germany
Men's 800m	David Lekuta Rudisha	Kenya	1:41.01 (mins)	2010	Rieti, Italy
Men's 1,000m	Noah Ngeny	Kenya	2:11.96 (mins)	1999	Rieti, Italy
Men's 3,000m	Daniel Komen	Kenya	7:20.67 (mins)	1996	Rieti, Italy
Men's 10km	Leonard Patrick Komon	Kenya	26.44 (mins)	2010	Utrecht, Netherlands
Men's 15km	Leonard Patrick Komon	Kenya	41:13 (mins)	2010	Nijmegen, Netherlands
Men's 25,000m	Moses Cheruiyot Mosop	Kenya	1:12:25.4 (hours)	2011	Eugene, Oregon, USA
Men's 25km	Samuel Kiplimo Kosgei	Kenya	1:11:50 (hours)	2010	Berlin, Germany
Men's 30,000m	Moses Cheruiyot Mosop	Kenya	1:26:47.4 (hours)	2011	Eugene, Oregon, USA
Men's 30 km	Peter Cheruiyot Kirui	Kenya	1:27:37* (hours)	2011	Berlin, Germany
Men's Marathon	Patrick Makau Musyoki	Kenya	2:03:38* (hours)	2011	Berlin, Germany
Men's Triple Jump	Jonathan David Edwards	UK	18.29 metres	1995	Göteborg, Sweden
Men's 4x100m Relay	Jamaica	Jamaica	37.04* (seconds)	2011	Daegu, Korea
Men's 4x800m Relay	Kenya	Kenya	7:02.43 (mins)	2006	Brussels, Belgium
Men's 4x1,500m Relay	Kenya	Kenya	14:36.23 (mins)	2009	Brussels, Belgium
Men's Road Relay	Kenya	Kenya	1:57:06 (hours)	2005	Chiba, Japan
Women's 10km	Paula Radcliffe	UK	30:21 (mins)	2003	San Juan, Puerto Rico
Women's 20,000m	Tegla Loroupe	Kenya	1:05:26.6 (hours)	2000	Borgholzhausen, Germany
Women's 20km	Mary Jepkosgei Keitany	Kenya	1:02:36 (hours)	2011	Ras al-Khaimah, UAE
Women's Half Marathon	Mary Jepkosgei Keitany	Kenya	1:05:50 (hours)	2011	Ras al-Khaimah, UAE
Women's 25,000m	Tegla Loroupe	Kenya	1:27:05.9 (hours)	2002	Mengerskirchen, Germany
Women's 25km	Mary Jepkosgei Keitany	Kenya	1:19:53 (hours)	2010	Berlin, Germany
Women's 30,000m	Tegla Loroupe	Kenya	1:45:50.0 (hours)	2003	Warstein, Germany
Women's Marathon	Paula Radcliffe	UK	2:15:25 (hours)	2003	London, UK

awaiting ratification

Literary prize-winners: The Nobel Prize in Literature

Year	Author	Country of origin	Category
1907	Rudyard Kipling	UK	Fiction and poetry
1913	Rabindranath Tagore	India	Poetry
1932	John Galsworthy	UK	Fiction and drama
1950	Bertrand Russell	UK	Philosophy
1953	Winston Churchill	UK	History
1973	Patrick White	Australia	Fiction
1983	William Golding	UK	Fiction
1986	Wole Soyinka	Nigeria	Fiction and drama
1991	Nadine Gordimer	South Africa	Fiction
1992	Derek Walcott	St Lucia	Poetry and drama
1995	Seamus Heaney	UK	Poetry
2001	V S Naipaul	Trinidad and Tobago	Fiction and non-fiction
2003	James Maxwell Coetzee	South Africa	Fiction
2005	Harold Pinter	UK	Drama
2007	Doris Lessing	UK	Fiction

Year	Category	Author	Country of origin	Title
1987	Best Book	Olive Senior	Jamaica	Summer Lightning
1987	Best First Book	Witi Ihimaera	New Zealand	The Matriarch
1988	Best Book	Festus Iyayi	Nigeria	Heroes
1988	Best First Book	George Turner	Australia	The Sea and the Summer
1989	Best Book	Janet Frame	New Zealand	The Carpathians
1989	Best First Book	Bonnie Burnard	Canada	Women of Influence
1990	Best Book	Mordecai Richler	Canada	Solomon Gursky Was Here
1990	Best First Book	John Cranna	New Zealand	Visitors
1991	Best Book	David Malouf	Australia	The Great World
1991	Best First Book	Pauline Melville	Guyana	Shape-Shifter
1992	Best Book	Rohinton Mistry	Canada	Such a Long Journey
1992	Best First Book	Robert Antoni	The Bahamas	Divina Trace
1993	Best Book	Alex Miller	Australia	The Ancestor Game
1993	Best First Book	Gita Hariharan	India	The Thousand Faces of Night
1994	Best Book	Vikram Seth	India	A Suitable Boy
1994	Best First Book	Keith Oatley	UK	The Case of Emily V
1995	Best Book	Louis de Bernieres	UK	Captain Corelli's Mandolin
1995	Best First Book	Adib Khan	Australia	Seasonal Adjustments
1996	Best Book	Rohinton Mistry	Canada	A Fine Balance
1996	Best First Book	Vikram Chandra	India	Red Earth, Pouring Rain
1997	Best Book	Earl Lovelace	Trinidad and Tobago	Salt
1997	Best First Book	Ann-Marie MacDonald	Canada	Fall on Your Knees
1998	Best Book	Peter Carey	Australia	Jack Maggs
1998	Best First Book	Tim Wynveen	Canada	Angel Falls
1999	Best Book	Murray Bail	Australia	Eucalyptus
1999	Best First Book	Kerri Sakamoto	Canada	The Electrical Field
2000	Best Book	John Maxwell Coetzee	South Africa	Disgrace
2000	Best First Book	Jeffrey Moore	Canada	Prisoner in a Red-Rose Chain
2001	Best Book	Peter Carey	Australia	True History of the Kelly Gang
2001	Best First Book	Zadie Smith	UK	White Teeth
2002	Best Book	Richard Flanagan	Australia	Gould's Book of Fish
2002	Best First Book	Manu Herbstein	South Africa	Ama, a Story of the Atlantic Slave Trade
2003	Best Book	Austin Clarke	Barbados	The Polished Hoe
2003	Best First Book	Sarah Hall	UK	Haweswater
2004	Best Book	Caryl Phillips	St Kitts and Nevis	A Distant Shore
2004	Best First Book	Mark Haddon	UK	The Curious Incident of the Dog In the Night-time
2005	Best Book	Andrea Levy	UK	Small Island
2005	Best First Book	Chimamanda Ngozi Adichie	Nigeria	Purple Hibiscus
2006	Best Book	Kate Grenvllle	Australia	The Secret River
2006	Best First Book	Mark McWatt	Guyana	Suspended Sentences: Fictions of Atonement
2007	Best Book	Lloyd Jones	New Zealand	Mister Pip
2007	Best First Book	D Y Béchard	Canada	Vandal Love
2008	Best Book	Lawrence Hill	Canada	The Book of Negroes
2008	Best First Book	Tahmima Anam	Bangladesh	A Golden Age
2009	Best Book	Christos Tsiolkas	Australia	The Slap
2009	Best First Book	Mohammed Hanif	Pakistan	A Case of Exploding Mangoes
2010	Best Book	Rana Dasgupta	UK	Solo
2010	Best First Book	Glenda Guest	Australia	Siddon Rock
2011	Best Book	Aminatta Forna	Sierra Leone	The Memory of Love
2011	Best First Book	Craig Cliff	New Zealand	A Man Melting

Year	Author	Country of origin	Category
1969	Percy Howard Newby	UK	Something to Answer For
1970	Bernice Rubens	UK	The Elected Member
1971	V S Naipaul	Trinidad and Tobago	In a Free State
1972	John Berger	UK	G
1973	J G Farrell	UK	The Siege of Krishnapur
1974†	Nadine Gordimer	South Africa	The Conservationist
1974†	Stanley Middleton	UK	Holiday
1975	Ruth Prawer Jhabvala	India	Heat and Dust
1976	David Storey	UK	Saville
1977	Paul Scott	UK	Staying On
1978	Iris Murdoch	UK	The Sea
1979	Penelope Fitzgerald	UK	Offshore
1980	William Golding	UK	Rites of Passage
1981	Salman Rushdie	India	Midnight's Children
1982	Thomas Keneally	Australia	Schindler's Ark
1983	James Maxwell Coetzee	South Africa	Life & Times of Michael K
1984	Anita Brookner	UK	Hotel du Lac
1985	Keri Hulme	New Zealand	The Bone People
1986	Kingsley Amis	UK	The Old Devils
1987	Penelope Lively	UK	Moon Tiger
1988	Peter Carey	Australia	Oscar and Lucinda
1989	Kazuo Ishiguro	UK	The Remains of the Day
1990	A S Byatt	UK	Possession
1991	Ben Okri	Nigeria	The Famished Road
1992†	Michael Ondaatje	Sri Lanka	The English Patient
1992†	Barry Unsworth	UK	Sacred Hunger
1994	James Kelman	UK	How Late it Was, How Late
1995	Pat Barker	UK	The Ghost Road
1996	Graham Swift	UK	Last Orders
1997	Arundhati Roy	India	The God of Small Things
1998	Ian McEwan	UK	Amsterdam
1999	James Maxwell Coetzee	South Africa	Disgrace
2000	Margaret Atwood	Canada	The Blind Assassin
2001	Peter Carey	Australia	True History of the Kelly Gang
2002	Yann Martel	Canada	Life of Pi
2003	D B C Pierre	Australia	Vernon God Little
2004	Alan Hollinghurst	UK	The Line of Beauty
2006	Kiran Desai	India	The Inheritance of Loss
2008	Aravind Adiga	India	The White Tiger
2009	Hilary Mantel	UK	Wolf Hall
2010	Howard Jacobson	UK	The Finkler Question
2011	Julian Barnes	UK	The Sense of an Ending

* Also commonly known as the Booker Prize; open to citizens of the Commonwealth and Irish nationals
† Year of joint award

Definitions, acronyms and abbreviations

Definitions

Adult literacy: generally, the percentage of people aged 15 and over who can, with understanding, read and write a short, simple statement about their everyday life.

Annual percentage change: during a period (for example, GDP growth p.a. 1990–2003 or inflation p.a. 1990–2003) is always the annual average compound change.

Arable land: as defined by the FAO, land on which temporary crops are growing or are to be grown, including meadows, pastures and land which is temporarily lying fallow.

GDP (gross domestic product): as defined by the World Bank, total value added at purchasers' prices by all resident and non-resident producers in the economy, plus taxes (less subsidies) not included in the calculation of value added.

GNI (gross national income): as defined by the World Bank, sum of gross value added by resident producers (plus taxes less subsidies) and net primary income from non-resident sources (previously referred to as GNP).

Growth: in national income or domestic product this is always real growth unless stated to be otherwise. Thus, GDP growth is at constant prices and growth in output is in volume rather than value terms.

Infant mortality: as defined by the UN, the probability of dying between birth and exactly one year of age expressed per 1,000 live births.

Inflation and CPI: in use by all the major collators of raw economic data, e.g. the UN, IMF and World Bank. The consumer price index (CPI) forms the basis on which inflation rates are calculated. CPI is an index number measuring the average price of consumer goods and services purchased by households. It is a key statistic for economic and social policy-making and has substantial and wide-ranging implications for governments, businesses and households.

Life expectancy: as defined by the UN, the number of years newborn children would live if subject to the mortality risks prevailing for the cross-section of population at the time of their birth.

Net primary/secondary enrolment ratio: the number of students enrolled in primary/secondary school who belong to the age group that officially corresponds to primary/secondary schooling, divided by the total population of the same age group.

Permanent cropland: land occupied by crops for long periods where crops do not need to be replanted each year, for example cocoa, coffee, rubber, fruit trees and vines but not trees grown for timber or wood.

Public holidays: in most Commonwealth countries when a fixed-date holiday falls on a Sunday or, in many countries, a Saturday, the holiday is observed on the following Monday, and, increasingly, fixed-date holidays are celebrated on the closest Monday or Friday.

Purchasing Power Parity (PPP): for the purpose of comparing levels of poverty across countries, the World Bank uses estimates of consumption converted to US dollars using purchasing power parity (PPP) rates rather than exchange rates. PPP conversion allows national accounts aggregates in national currencies to be compared on the basis of their purchasing powers of the currencies in their respective domestic markets free from differences in price levels across countries, much the same way as constant price estimates do in a time series comparison of real values free from differences in prices over time.

Acronyms and abbreviations

This list includes short forms used in this book, plus forms commonly used in discussion of the areas covered by *The Commonwealth Yearbook*. It does not, however, include acronyms for national political parties unless these are mentioned outside the profile of the particular country.

°C	temperature in degrees Celsius
ACAIS	Association of Commonwealth Amnesty International Sections
ACARM	Association of Commonwealth Archivists and Records Managers
ACDA	Arms Control and Disarmament Agency
ACEAB	Association of Commonwealth Examination and Accreditation Bodies
ACLALS	Association for Commonwealth Literature and Language Studies
ACP	African, Caribbean and Pacific Group of States
ACS	Association of Caribbean States
ACU	Association of Commonwealth Universities
ADB	Asian Development Bank
ADEA	Association for the Development of Education in Africa
ADF	Asian Development Fund
AfDB	African Development Bank
AfDF	African Development Fund
AIDAB	Australian International Development Assistance Bureau
AIDS	acquired immune deficiency syndrome
AIPPA	Access to Information and Protection of Privacy Act
AMREF	African Medical and Research Foundation
ANC	African National Congress (South Africa)
APEC	Asia-Pacific Economic Cooperation
ASAS	Association of Southern African States (a SADC body)
ASEAN	Association of Southeast Asian Nations
AU	African Union
BBC	British Broadcasting Corporation
BCEL	British Commonwealth Ex-Services League
bn	billion (1,000 million)
BSA	Broadcasting Services Act
CAA	Commonwealth Association of Architects
CAB	Commonwealth Advisory Bureau
CABI	CAB International (formerly Commonwealth Agricultural Bureaux)
CABOS	Commonwealth Advisory Body on Sport
CACG	Commonwealth Association for Corporate Governance
CAETA	Commonwealth Association for the Education and Training of Adults
CAIP	Commonwealth Association of Indigenous Peoples
CALRAs	Commonwealth Association of Law Reform Agencies
CAP	Commonwealth Association of Planners
CAPA	Commonwealth Association of Polytechnics in Africa
CAPAM	Commonwealth Association for Public Administration and Management
CAPGAN	Commonwealth Association of Paediatric Gastroenterology and Nutrition

CARDI	Caribbean Agricultural Research and Development Institute		**CMA**	Commonwealth Monetary Area
CARICAD	Caribbean Centre for Development Administration		**CMAG**	Commonwealth Ministerial Action Group on the Harare Declaration
CARICOM	Caribbean Community		**CMDF**	Commonwealth Media Development Fund
CASLE	Commonwealth Association of Surveying and Land Economy		**CMJA**	Commonwealth Magistrates' and Judges' Association
CASTME	Commonwealth Association of Science, Technology and Mathematics Educators		**CODESA**	Convention for a Democratic South Africa
CATA	Commonwealth Association of Tax Administrators		**COL**	Commonwealth of Learning
CATC	Commonwealth Air Transport Council		**COMBINET**	Commonwealth Business Network: IT network of Commonwealth Chambers of Commerce
CBA	Commonwealth Broadcasting Association		**COMESA**	Common Market for Eastern and Southern Africa
CBC	Commonwealth Business Council		**COMLA**	Commonwealth Library Association
CBD	Convention on Biological Diversity		**COMMACT**	Common Wealth Network for People Centred Development International
CCCA	Co-ordination Committee for Commonwealth Agencies		**Commat**	Commonwealth Medical Trust
CCEA	Commonwealth Council for Educational Administration		**COMNET-IT**	Commonwealth Network of Information Technology for Development
CCEAM	Commonwealth Council for Educational Administration and Management		**ComSec**	Commonwealth Secretariat
CCEG	Commonwealth Centre for Electronic Governance		**COSW**	Commonwealth Organisation for Social Work
CCGE	Commonwealth Consultative Group on Environment		**CPA**	Commonwealth Parliamentary Association
CCL	Commonwealth Countries League		**CPA**	Commonwealth Pharmacists Association
CCPA	Conference of Commonwealth Postal Administrations		**CPAD**	Communications and Public Affairs Division, Commonwealth Secretariat
CCS	Council of Commonwealth Societies		**CPAG**	Commonwealth Peacekeeping Assistance Group (South Africa)
CCT	Commonwealth Committee on Terrorism		**CPAT**	Commonwealth Plan of Action on Terrorism
CDA	Commonwealth Dental Association		**CPF**	Commonwealth People's Forum
CDB	Caribbean Development Bank		**CPI**	consumer price index
CDC	Commonwealth Development Corporation		**CPII**	Commonwealth Private Investment Initiative
CEAC	Commission for East African Cooperation		**CPTM**	Commonwealth Partnership for Technology Management
CEC	Commonwealth Engineers Council		**CRHCS-ECSA**	Commonwealth Regional Health Community Secretariat for East, Central and Southern Africa
CEC	Council for Education in the Commonwealth		**CSAP**	Commonwealth Service Abroad Programme
CEDAW	Convention on the Elimination of All Forms of Discrimination against Women		**CSD**	Corporate Services Division, Commonwealth Secretariat
CEF	Commonwealth Equity Fund		**CS-DRMS**	Commonwealth Secretariat Debt Recording and Management System
CEMAC	Communauté économique et monétaire de l'Afrique centrale		**CSFP**	Commonwealth Scholarship and Fellowship Plan
CER	Closer Economic Relations (agreement between New Zealand and Australia)		**CSIRO**	Commonwealth Scientific and Industrial Research Organisation (Australia)
CERD	Committee on the Elimination of Racial Discrimination (UN)		**CSO**	Civil Society Organisations
CET	Common External Tariff		**CTB**	Commonwealth Telecommunications Bureau
CFA	Commonwealth Forestry Association		**CTO**	Caribbean Tourism Organization
CFA franc	currency of the African francophone countries		**CTO**	Commonwealth Telecommunications Organisation
CFPM	Commonwealth Forum for Project Management		**CTUC**	Commonwealth Trade Union Council
CFTC	Commonwealth Fund for Technical Co-operation		**cu m**	cubic metres
CGB	Commonwealth Geographical Bureau		**CUSAC**	Commonwealth Universities Study Abroad Consortium
CHDP	Commonwealth Health Development Programme		**CVA**	Commonwealth Veterinary Association
CHEC	Commonwealth Human Ecology Council		**CWGC**	Commonwealth War Graves Commission
CHEMS	Commonwealth Higher Education Management Service		**CXC**	Caribbean Examinations Council
CHESS	Commonwealth Higher Education Support Scheme		**CYCI**	Commonwealth Youth Credit Initiative
CHOGM	Commonwealth Heads of Government Meeting		**CYEC**	Commonwealth Youth Exchange Council
CHR	Commission on Human Rights (UN)		**CYP**	Commonwealth Youth Programme
CHRI	Commonwealth Human Rights Initiative		**D8**	Group of Eight Islamic Developing Countries
CIDA	Canadian International Development Agency		**DAC**	Development Assistance Committee of the OECD countries
CITEP	Commonwealth Industrial Training and Experience Programme		**DFID**	Department for International Development (UK)
CITES	Convention on International Trade in Endangered Species of Wild Fauna and Flora		**DSG**	deputy secretary-general
CJA	Commonwealth Journalists Association		**EAC**	East African Community
CJEI	Commonwealth Judicial Education Institute		**EAD**	Economic Affairs Division, Commonwealth Secretariat
CLA	Commonwealth Lawyers Association		**EAGA**	East Asian Growth Area
CLAS	Commonwealth Legal Advisory Service		**EC**	European Community (formerly often referred to as EEC, now EU)
CLEA	Commonwealth Legal Education Association			
CLGF	Commonwealth Local Government Forum			
CLU	Commonwealth Liaison Unit			

ECA	Economic Commission for Africa	IBRD	International Bank for Reconstruction and Development (World Bank)
ECCB	Eastern Caribbean Central Bank	ICAO	International Civil Aviation Organization
ECDB	Eastern Caribbean Development Bank	ICC	International Chamber of Commerce
ECE	Economic Commission for Europe	ICCO	International Cocoa Organization
ECLAC	Economic Commission for Latin America and the Caribbean	ICJ	International Court of Justice
ECO	Economic Cooperation Organization (Central Asian Islamic states)	ICO	International Coffee Organization
ECOSOC	Economic and Social Council of the UN	ICT	information and communication technology
ECOWAS	Economic Community of West African States	IDA	International Development Association
ECPF	Emerging Commonwealth Privatisation Fund	IDB	Inter-American Development Bank
EEZ	exclusive economic zone (maritime zones)	IDD	international direct dialling (telecoms)
email	electronic mail	IDRC	International Development Research Centre, Canada
EPA	Economic Partnership Agreement	IEA	International Energy Authority
EPG	Eminent Persons Group	IEC	independent electoral commission
EPI	expanded programme on immunisation (against childhood diseases)	IFAD	International Fund for Agricultural Development
EPZ	export processing zone	IFC	International Finance Corporation
ERP	economic reconstruction programme, or economic reform programme	IFRC	International Federation of Red Cross and Red Crescent Societies
ESAF	enhanced structural adjustment facility	IGAD	Intergovernmental Authority on Development
ESAMI	Eastern and Southern African Management Institute	IGC	Inter-Governmental Conference (of the EU)
ESCAP	Economic and Social Commission for Asia and the Pacific	IHO	International Health Organization
est.	estimate (or estimated)	ILO	International Labour Organization
ESU	English-Speaking Union	IMF	International Monetary Fund
EU	European Union	IMO	International Maritime Organization
FAO	Food and Agriculture Organization	IOR-ARC	Indian Ocean Rim Association for Regional Cooperation
FATF	Financial Action Task Force	IORI	Indian Ocean Rim Initiative
FDI	foreign direct investment	IPZ	international processing zone
FFA	South Pacific Forum Fisheries Agency (now the Pacific Islands Forum Fisheries Agency)	IRF	International Road Federation
Frelimo	Front for the Liberation of Mozambique	IT	information technology
FTZ	free trade zone	ITC	International Trade Centre
G7	Group of Seven Industrialised Countries	ITU	International Telecommunication Union
G8	Group of Eight Industrialised Countries	km	kilometre(s)
G15	Group of Fifteen Developing Countries	kph	kilometres per hour
GATS	General Agreement on Trade in Services	£	unless otherwise indicated, the UK pound sterling
GATT	General Agreement on Tariffs and Trade	LCAD	Legal and Constitutional Affairs Division, Commonwealth Secretariat
GCE	General Certificate of Education	LDC	least developed country
GDP	gross domestic product	LECT	League for the Exchange of Commonwealth Teachers
GEF	global environment facility	LIAT	Leeward Islands Air Transport Service
GIDD	Governance and Institutional Development Division, Commonwealth Secretariat	LoS	Law of the Sea
GMT	Greenwich Mean Time	m	million, or metre(s)
GNI	gross national income	MEN	multilateral environmental agreements
GNP	gross national product	MDG	Millennium Development Goal
GSP	generalised system of preferences	mm	millimetre(s)
GST	goods and services tax	MP	member of parliament
GSTP	global system of trade preferences	mph	miles per hour
ha	Hectare	MRU	Mano River Union
Habitat	UN Centre for Human Settlements	MSG	Melanesian Spearhead Group
HIPC	heavily indebted poor country	MSME	micro, small and medium enterprises
HIV	human immuno-deficiency virus	NAFTA	North American Free Trade Agreement
HLRG	High Level Review Group	NAM	Non-Aligned Movement
hr	hours (as in 0800hr)	NATO	North Atlantic Treaty Organization
HRU	Human Rights Unit, Commonwealth Secretariat	NEPAD	New Partnership for Africa's Development
Hz	hertz (unit of frequency; referring here to electricity)	NGO	non-governmental organisation
IAEA	International Atomic Energy Agency	NP	National (Nationalist) Party (several countries)
IBCC	International Bureau of the Chambers of Commerce of the ICC	NPT	Nuclear Non-Proliferation Treaty
		NWM	national women's machinery
		OAS	Organization of American States

OAU	Organization of African Unity (now the African Union)	**SPARTECA**	South Pacific Regional Trade and Economic Cooperation Agreement
OCUNA	Organisation of Commonwealth United Nations Associations	**SPBEA**	South Pacific Board for Educational Assessment
ODA	official development assistance	**SPC**	Secretariat of the Pacific Community
ODI	Overseas Development Institute	**SPED**	Strategic Planning and Evaluation Division, Commonwealth Secretariat
OECD	Organisation for Economic Co-operation and Development	**SPF**	South Pacific Forum (now the Pacific Islands Forum)
OECS	Organisation of Eastern Caribbean States	**sq km**	square kilometre(s)
OIC	Organisation of the Islamic Conference	**STPD**	Social Transformation Programmes Division, Commonwealth Secretariat
OIF	L'Organisation internationale de la Francophonie	**TCDC**	technical co-operation among (or between) developing countries
OPEC	Organization of Petroleum Exporting Countries	**TEC**	Transitional Executive Council (interim government in South Africa)
OSCE	Organization for Security and Co-operation in Europe	**Teu**	twenty-foot equivalent (measurement of cargo)
p.a.	per annum	**TV**	Television
PAD	Political Affairs Division, Commonwealth Secretariat	**UAE**	United Arab Emirates
PARTA	Pacific Regional Trade Agreement	**UI**	unemployment insurance
PAYE	(Commonwealth) Plan of Action for Youth Empowerment	**UK**	United Kingdom of Great Britain and Northern Ireland
p.c.	per capita	**UN**	United Nations
PC	Pacific Community	**UNAIDS**	Joint United Nations Programme on HIV/AIDS
PICTA	Pacific Island Countries Trade Agreement	**UNCAC**	United Nations Convention against Corruption
PIF	Pacific Islands Forum	**UNCED**	UN Conference on Environment and Development
PIFFA	Pacific Islands Forum Fisheries Agency	**UNCHS**	UN Centre for Human Settlements
PIFS	Pacific Islands Forum Secretariat	**UNCIP**	UN Commission for India and Pakistan
PIIDS	Pacific Islands Industrial Development Scheme	**UNCLoS**	UN Convention on the Law of the Sea
PMRU	Project Management and Referrals Unit, Commonwealth Secretariat	**UNCSTD**	UN Commission on Science and Technology for Development
PoA	plan of action	**UNCTAD**	UN Conference on Trade and Development
pop.	Population	**UNDP**	UN Development Programme
PPP	purchasing power parity	**UNEP**	UN Environment Programme
PQLI	physical quality of life index	**UNESCO**	UN Educational, Scientific and Cultural Organization
PRE	economic rehabilitation programme	**UNETPSA**	UN Educational and Training Programme for Southern Africa
PTA	Preferential Trade Area (Eastern and Southern Africa)	**UNFICYP**	UN Force in Cyprus
PV	Present Value	**UNFPA**	UN Fund for Population Activities
RADO	Regional Anti-Doping Organization	**UNHCR**	Office of the UN High Commissioner for Refugees
RAMSI	Regional Assistance Mission to Solomon Islands	**UNICEF**	UN Children's Fund
RASC	Royal Agricultural Society of the Commonwealth	**UNIDO**	UN Industrial Development Organization
RCS	Royal Commonwealth Society	**UNIPOM**	UN India-Pakistan Observer Mission
RDP	Reconstruction and Development Programme, South Africa	**UNMOGIP**	UN Military Observer Group in India and Pakistan
REDD	Reducing Emissions from Deforestation and Forest Degradation	**UPU**	Universal Postal Union
Renamo	Mozambique National Resistance Movement	**US/USA**	United States of America
Rs	rupees; unless otherwise indicated, the Indian rupee	**USP**	University of the South Pacific
SAARC	South Asian Association for Regional Cooperation	**UWI**	University of the West Indies
SACU	Southern African Customs Union	**VAT**	value added tax
SADC	Southern African Development Community	**VSO**	Voluntary Service Overseas
SAP	structural adjustment programme	**WADA**	World Anti-Doping Agency
SASD	Special Advisory Services Division, Commonwealth Secretariat	**WFC**	World Food Council
SATCC	Southern African Transport and Communications Commission	**WFP**	World Food Programme
SCF	Save the Children Fund (now known as Save the Children)	**WHO**	World Health Organization
SCFM	Special Commonwealth Fund for Mozambique	**WIPO**	World Intellectual Property Organization
SDP	Sport for Development and Peace	**WMO**	World Meteorological Organization
SDRs	special drawing rights	**WTO**	World Trade Organization
SGO	Secretary-General's Office, Commonwealth Secretariat	**WWF**	World Wide Fund for Nature
SIDS	Small island developing states	**www**	World Wide Web (internet)
SME	single market economy	**YAD**	Youth Affairs Division, Commonwealth Secretariat
SMEs	small and medium-sized enterprises (in business)	**YDI**	Youth Development Index
SNL	Swazi National Land	**YFF**	Youth for the Future
SOA	Summit of the Americas process		
SOPAC	South Pacific Applied Geoscience Commission		

	Total population	GNI per capita	GDP per capita growth	Net primary enrolment ratio	Adult literacy rate	Life expectancy	Infant mortality per 1,000 live births	HIV/AIDS prevalence among those aged 15–49	Personal computers per 1,000 people	Human Development Index ranking out of 187 countries
	('000) 2010	(US$) 2010	(% p.a.) 1990–2010	(%) 2007–09	(%) 2005–2010	(years) 2010	2010	(%) 2009	2005–08	2011
Antigua and Barbuda	89	13,170	1.7	90	99	75*	7		207	60
Australia	22,268	43,770*	2.3	97		82	4	0.1		2
The Bahamas	343	21,984**	1.0	92		75	14	3.1	123	53
Bangladesh	148,692	700	3.5	89	56	69	38	<0.1	23	146
Barbados	273	15,034**	0.8			77	17	1.4	158	47
Belize	312	3,810	1.9	100		76	14	2.3	153	93
Botswana	2,007	6,790	3.5	87	84	53	36	24.8	63	118
Brunei Darussalam	399	26,750†	-0.4	97	95	78	6		89	33
Cameroon	19,599	1,180	0.6	92	71	51	84	5.3	11	150
Canada	34,017	43,270	1.9			81	5	0.3	944	6
Cyprus	1,104	29,430	2.1	99	98	79	3		383	31
Dominica	68	6,760	1.7	98		76*	11			81
Fiji	861	3,630	1.2	92		69	15	0.1	60	100
The Gambia	1,728	450	0.1	76	47	58	57	2	35	168
Ghana	24,392	1,230	2.4	76	67	64	50	1.8	11	135
Grenada	104	6,930	2.9	98		76	9			67
Guyana	754	2,870	2.5	99		70	25	1.2	38	117
India	1,224,614	1,330	4.9	97	63	65	48	0.3	32	134
Jamaica	2,741	4,800	0.7	81	86	73	20	1.7	67	79
Kenya	40,513	790	0.3	83	87	57	55	6.3	14	143
Kiribati	100	2,010	1.2				39			122
Lesotho	2,171	1,040	2.2	73	90	48	65	23.6	3	160
Malawi	14,901	330	1.0	91	74	54	58	11	2	171
Malaysia	28,401	7,760	3.2	94	93	74	5	0.5	232	61
Maldives	316	5,750	4.9	96	98	77	14	<0.1	202	109
Malta	417	19,270	2.6	91	92	79	5	0.1		36
Mauritius	1,299	7,750	3.5	94	88	73	13	1	174	77
Mozambique	23,391	440	4.3	91	55	50	92	11.5	14	184
Namibia	2,283	4,500	2.1	90	89	62	29	13.1	239	120
Nauru	10	2,802**				65*	32			
New Zealand	4,368	29,695†	1.9	99		81	5	0.1	530	5
Nigeria	158,423	1,180	1.9	63	61	51	88	3.6	9	156
Pakistan	173,593	1,050	1.7	66	56	65	70	0.1		145
Papua New Guinea	6,858	1,300	-0.2		60	62	47	0.9	64	153
Rwanda	10,624	520	2.3	96		55	59	2.9	3	166
St Kitts and Nevis	52	11,740	2.2	94		74*	7			72
St Lucia	174	6,560	1.0	93		74	14			82
St Vincent and the Grenadines	109	6,300	3.6	98		72	19		152	85
Samoa	183	3,000	3.0	99	99	72	17		24	99
Seychelles	87	9,760	1.8	94	92	73*	12		216	52
Sierra Leone	5,868	340	1.1		41	47	114	1.6		180
Singapore	5,086	40,070	3.9		95	81	2	0.1	760	26
Solomon Islands	538	1,030	-1.0	81		67	23		46	142
South Africa	50,133	6,090	1.3	90	89	52	41	17.8	83	123
Sri Lanka	20,860	2,240	4.1	95	91	75	14	<0.1	38	97
Swaziland	1,186	2,630	1.6	83	87	48	55	25.9	37	140
Tonga	104	3,280	1.6		99	72	13		59	90
Trinidad and Tobago	1,341	15,380	5.0	96	99	70	24	1.5	132	62
Tuvalu	10	4,760				64*	27		86	
Uganda	33,425	500	3.6	92	73	54	63	6.5	17	161
United Kingdom	62,036	38,370	2.1	100		80	5	0.2	802	28
United Republic of Tanzania	44,841	530	2.4	97	73	57	50	5.6	9	152
Vanuatu	240	2,640	6.8		82	71	12		14	125
Zambia	13,089	1,070	0.6	92	71	49	69	13.5	11	164

*2009 figure ** GDP per capita 2010 † GDP per capita 2009 < denotes less than here and following

Data reproduced with permission from: UNICEF, The State of the World's Children Report 2012, UNICEF, New York, 2012

Geography and population

	Total area (sq km) 2010	Total population ('000) 2010	Population under 18 (%) 2010	Population over 60 (%) 2010	Population per square km 2010–15	Projected population growth (% p.a.) 2010	Birth rate (per '000)
Antigua and Barbuda	443	89	31	10	201	1.0	
Australia	7,682,395	22,268	23	20	3	1.3	14
The Bahamas	13,939	343	28	10	25	1.1	15
Bangladesh	143,998	148,692	38	6	1,033	1.3	20
Barbados	431	273	22	16	633	0.2	11
Belize	22,965	312	42	6	14	2.0	25
Botswana	582,000	2,007	39	6	3	1.1	24
Brunei Darussalam	5,765	399	31	6	69	1.7	19
Cameroon	475,442	19,599	47	6	41	2.1	36
Canada	9,976,000	34,017	20	20	3	0.9	11
Cyprus	9,251	1,104	22	18	119	1.1	12
Dominica	750	68	32	14	91	0.0	
Fiji	18,333	861	35	8	47	0.8	22
The Gambia	11,295	1,728	51	5	153	2.7	38
Ghana	238,537	24,392	45	6	102	2.3	32
Grenada	345	104	34	10	301	0.4	19
Guyana	214,970	754	40	10	4	0.2	18
India	3,287,263	1,224,614	37	8	373	1.3	22
Jamaica	10,991	2,741	35	11	249	0.4	18
Kenya	582,646	40,513	49	4	70	2.7	38
Kiribati	811	100	36	6	123	1.5	
Lesotho	30,355	2,171	45	7	72	1.0	28
Malawi	118,484	14,901	53	5	126	3.2	44
Malaysia	329,758	28,401	36	8	86	1.6	20
Maldives	298	316	34	6	1,060	1.3	17
Malta	316	417	19	22	1,320	0.3	9
Mauritius	2,040	1,299	27	12	637	0.5	13
Mozambique	799,380	23,391	51	6	29	2.2	38
Namibia	824,269	2,283	43	6	3	1.7	26
Nauru	21	10	40	3	476	0.6	
New Zealand	270,500	4,368	25	18	16	1.0	15
Nigeria	923,768	158,423	49	5	171	2.5	40
Pakistan	796,095	173,593	42	6	218	1.8	27
Papua New Guinea	462,840	6,858	45	4	15	2.2	30
Rwanda	26,338	10,624	49	4	403	2.9	41
St Kitts and Nevis	262	52	33	11	198	1.2	
St Lucia	616	174	32	10	282	1.0	18
St Vincent and the Grenadines	389	109	32	10	280	0.0	17
Samoa	2,831	183	45	7	65	0.5	25
Seychelles	455	87	49	11	191	0.3	
Sierra Leone	71,740	5,868	49	4	82	2.1	39
Singapore	699	5,086	22	16	7,276	1.1	9
Solomon Islands	28,370	538	46	5	19	2.5	32
South Africa	1,221,038	50,133	36	8	41	0.5	21
Sri Lanka	65,610	20,860	30	12	318	0.8	18
Swaziland	17,364	1,186	46	6	68	1.4	29
Tonga	748	104	44	8	139	0.4	27
Trinidad and Tobago	5,128	1,341	25	11	262	0.3	15
Tuvalu	26	10	40	9	385	0.2	
Uganda	236,000	33,425	55	4	142	3.1	45
United Kingdom	243,305	62,036	21	23	255	0.6	12
United Republic of Tanzania	945,090	44,841	51	5	47	3.1	41
Vanuatu	12,190	240	45	5	20	2.4	30
Zambia	752,614	13,089	53	5	17	3.0	46

Data reproduced with permission from: UNICEF, The State of the World's Children Report 2012, UNICEF, New York, 2012

Largest countries

	Total area (sq km)
Canada	9,976,000
Australia	7,682,395
India	3,287,263
South Africa	1,221,038
United Republic of Tanzania	945,090
Nigeria	923,768
Namibia	824,269
Mozambique	799,380
Pakistan	796,095
Zambia	752,614
Kenya	582,646
Botswana	582,000
Cameroon	475,442
Papua New Guinea	462,840
Malaysia	329,758
New Zealand	270,500
United Kingdom	243,305
Ghana	238,537
Uganda	236,000
Guyana	214,970
Bangladesh	143,998
Malawi	118,484
Sierra Leone	71,740
Sri Lanka	65,610
Lesotho	30,355
Solomon Islands	28,370
Rwanda	26,338
Belize	22,965
Fiji	18,333
Swaziland	17,364
The Bahamas	13,939
Vanuatu	12,190
The Gambia	11,295
Jamaica	10,991
Cyprus	9,251
Brunei Darussalam	5,765
Trinidad and Tobago	5,128
Samoa	2,831
Mauritius	2,040
Kiribati	811
Dominica	750
Tonga	748
Singapore	699
St Lucia	616
Seychelles	455
Antigua and Barbuda	443
Barbados	431
St Vincent and the Grenadines	389
Grenada	345
Malta	316
Maldives	298
St Kitts and Nevis	262
Tuvalu	26
Nauru	21

Most populous countries

	Total population ('000) 2010	Percentage of total Commonwealth
India	1,224,614	55.883
Pakistan	173,593	7.922
Nigeria	158,423	7.229
Bangladesh	148,692	6.785
United Kingdom	62,036	2.831
South Africa	50,133	2.288
United Republic of Tanzania	44,841	2.046
Kenya	40,513	1.849
Canada	34,017	1.552
Uganda	33,425	1.525
Malaysia	28,401	1.296
Ghana	24,392	1.113
Mozambique	23,391	1.067
Australia	22,268	1.016
Sri Lanka	20,860	0.952
Cameroon	19,599	0.894
Malawi	14,901	0.680
Zambia	13,089	0.597
Rwanda	10,624	0.485
Papua New Guinea	6,858	0.313
Sierra Leone	5,868	0.268
Singapore	5,086	0.232
New Zealand	4,368	0.199
Jamaica	2,741	0.125
Namibia	2,283	0.104
Lesotho	2,171	0.099
Botswana	2,007	0.092
The Gambia	1,728	0.079
Trinidad and Tobago	1,341	0.061
Mauritius	1,299	0.059
Swaziland	1,186	0.054
Cyprus	1,104	0.050
Fiji	861	0.039
Guyana	754	0.034
Solomon Islands	538	0.025
Malta	417	0.019
Brunei Darussalam	399	0.018
The Bahamas	343	0.016
Maldives	316	0.014
Belize	312	0.014
Barbados	273	0.012
Vanuatu	240	0.011
Samoa	183	0.008
St Lucia	174	0.008
St Vincent and the Grenadines	109	0.005
Grenada	104	0.005
Tonga	104	0.005
Kiribati	100	0.005
Antigua and Barbuda	89	0.004
Seychelles	87	0.004
Dominica	68	0.003
St Kitts and Nevis	52	0.002
Nauru	10	<0.001
Tuvalu	10	<0.001
	2,191,395	

Greatest proportion of youth

Population under 18 (%)
2010

Uganda	55.3
Zambia	53.0
Malawi	52.8
United Republic of Tanzania	51.2
The Gambia	50.8
Mozambique	50.7
Sierra Leone	49.5
Seychelles	49.4
Nigeria	49.2
Kenya	48.9
Rwanda	48.7
Cameroon	47.3
Swaziland	46.2
Solomon Islands	46.1
Papua New Guinea	45.4
Ghana	45.0
Samoa	44.8
Lesotho	44.7
Vanuatu	44.6
Tonga	44.2
Namibia	43.3
Pakistan	42.2
Belize	42.0
Guyana	40.2
Nauru	40.0
Tuvalu	40.0
Botswana	39.1
Bangladesh	37.6
India	36.5
South Africa	36.1
Kiribati	36.0
Malaysia	35.9
Jamaica	35.1
Fiji	34.7
Grenada	33.7
Maldives	33.5
St Kitts and Nevis	32.7
Dominica	32.4
St Vincent and the Grenadines	32.1
St Lucia	31.6
Antigua and Barbuda	31.5
Brunei Darussalam	31.1
Sri Lanka	29.5
The Bahamas	28.0
Mauritius	27.0
Trinidad and Tobago	25.1
New Zealand	24.9
Australia	23.0
Cyprus	22.2
Barbados	22.0
Singapore	21.8
United Kingdom	21.1
Canada	20.3
Malta	18.9

Greatest proportion of population aged 60 and over

(%)
2010

United Kingdom	23.2
Malta	22.2
Canada	20.2
Australia	19.6
Cyprus	18.1
New Zealand	18.1
Singapore	16.1
Barbados	16.0
Dominica	13.7
Sri Lanka	12.1
Mauritius	11.7
St Kitts and Nevis	11.1
Seychelles	11.0
Trinidad and Tobago	10.8
Jamaica	10.5
The Bahamas	10.1
Grenada	9.7
Antigua and Barbuda	9.6
St Lucia	9.5
St Vincent and the Grenadines	9.5
Guyana	9.5
Tuvalu	8.8
Fiji	8.1
Tonga	8.1
South Africa	7.8
India	7.5
Malaysia	7.5
Lesotho	7.2
Samoa	7.1
Botswana	6.1
Bangladesh	6.0
Maldives	6.0
Pakistan	6.0
Kiribati	5.6
Brunei Darussalam	5.6
Namibia	5.6
Swaziland	5.6
Mozambique	5.6
Cameroon	5.5
Belize	5.5
Ghana	5.5
The Gambia	5.0
Malawi	5.0
Nigeria	5.0
Solomon Islands	5.0
Vanuatu	5.0
United Republic of Tanzania	4.5
Zambia	4.5
Kenya	4.0
Papua New Guinea	4.0
Rwanda	3.6
Uganda	3.6
Sierra Leone	3.5
Nauru	3.0

Greatest urbanisation

People living in urban areas (%)
2010

Nauru	100
Singapore	100
Malta	95
Australia	89
New Zealand	86
Bahamas	84
Canada	81
United Kingdom	80
Brunei Darussalam	76
Malaysia	72
Cyprus	70
Dominica	67
South Africa	62
Botswana	61
Cameroon	58
Gambia	58
Seychelles	55
Belize	52
Fiji	52
Jamaica	52
Ghana	51
Nigeria	50
Tuvalu	50
Saint Vincent and the Grenadines	49
Barbados	44
Kiribati	44
Mauritius	42
Maldives	40
Grenada	39
Mozambique	38
Namibia	38
Sierra Leone	38
Pakistan	36
Zambia	36
Saint Kitts and Nevis	32
Antigua and Barbuda	30
India	30
Guyana	29
Bangladesh	28
Saint Lucia	28
Lesotho	27
United Republic of Tanzania	26
Vanuatu	26
Tonga	23
Kenya	22
Swaziland	21
Malawi	20
Samoa	20
Rwanda	19
Solomon Islands	19
Sri Lanka	14
Trinidad and Tobago	14
Papua New Guinea	13
Uganda	13

Greatest population density

Population per square km
2010

Singapore	7,276
Malta	1,320
Maldives	1,060
Bangladesh	1,033
Mauritius	637
Barbados	633
Nauru	476
Rwanda	403
Tuvalu	385
India	373
Sri Lanka	318
Grenada	301
St Lucia	282
St Vincent and the Grenadines	280
Trinidad and Tobago	262
United Kingdom	255
Jamaica	249
Pakistan	218
Antigua and Barbuda	201
St Kitts and Nevis	198
Seychelles	191
Nigeria	171
The Gambia	153
Uganda	142
Tonga	139
Malawi	126
Kiribati	123
Cyprus	119
Ghana	102
Dominica	91
Malaysia	86
Sierra Leone	82
Lesotho	72
Kenya	70
Brunei Darussalam	69
Swaziland	68
Samoa	65
United Republic of Tanzania	47
Fiji	47
Cameroon	41
South Africa	41
Mozambique	29
The Bahamas	25
Vanuatu	20
Solomon Islands	19
Zambia	17
New Zealand	16
Papua New Guinea	15
Belize	14
Guyana	4
Botswana	3
Canada	3
Australia	3
Namibia	3

Economy

	GNI (US$'000) 2010	GNI per capita (US$) 2010	Average GDP growth (% p.a.) 2006-10	Inflation (% p.a.) 2006-10	Public spending: General government total expenditure (% of GDP) 2010	Public debt: General government gross debt (% of GDP) 2010	Foreign direct investment, net inflows (% of GDP) 2010	Net exports of goods and services§ (% of GDP) 2010
Antigua and Barbuda	1,168,629	13,170	1.2	2.3	21	70	12.6	-10
Australia	957,529,000*	43,770 *	2.8	3.0	37	21	4.5	-2.00
The Bahamas	7,538,000**	21,984**	-1.5	2.6	21	45	11.8	-12*
Bangladesh	104,680,897	700	6.2	7.7	15		1.3	-7
Barbados	4,109,500**	15,034**	0.7	5.8	43	118	7.8	-5
Belize	1,313,459	3,810	2.5	2.5	29	81	12.5	-8‡
Botswana	13,632,837	6,790	2.9	9.2	39	13	6.6	-3
Brunei Darussalam	10,732,435†	26,750†	0.7	0.9	40		1.5	-51‡
Cameroon	23,169,403	1,180	2.8	3.1	19	12	-0.1	-5
Canada	1,475,864,609	43,270	1.2	1.7	44	84	3.9	-2
Cyprus	23,654,583	29,430	2.4	2.4	47	61	15.4	-6
Dominica	458,226	6,760	3.2	3.1	34	54	12.2	-23
Fiji	3,122,845	3,630	0.2	4.8	29	56	8.6	-12
The Gambia	769,958	450	4.6	4.3	22	58	9.6	-19
Ghana	30,080,473	1,230	6.5	13.6	24	37	4.3	-13
Grenada	723,862	6,930	-0.9	3.8	27	99	17.1	-29
Guyana	2,163,562	2,870	4.2	6.3	31	60	8.7	
India	1,553,937,385	1,330	8.4	8.7	26	64	3.6	-3
Jamaica	12,966,651	4,800	-0.0	12.3	33	143	10.1	-18
Kenya	31,810,201	790	4.5	12.5	32	52	0.3	-13
Kiribati	199,852	2,010	0.5	4.8	90		2.0	0
Lesotho	2,247,822	1,040	4.0	7.1	56	34	6.9	-65
Malawi	4,885,956	330	7.4	9.3	38	37	4.2	-10
Malaysia	220,362,357	7,760	4.5	2.7	31	54	3.3	18
Maldives	1,817,841	5,750	9.4	6.3	39	59	7.5	-18
Malta	7,957,770	19,270	2.3	2.4	43	67	9.6	2
Mauritius	9,924,679	7,750	4.5	6.5	25	50	3.9	-12
Mozambique	10,344,420	440	7.3	9.5	32	38	6.0	-18
Namibia	10,286,037	4,500	4.1	7.1	33	19	4.6	1
Nauru	28,020**	2,802**	-4.8	2.4				
New Zealand	126,679,321†	29,695†	1.4	2.9	35	32	4.3	2
Nigeria	186,405,944	1,180	6.7	10.1	33	17	4.0	13
Pakistan	182,788,124	1,050	4.2	12.6	20	57	3.3	-5
Papua New Guinea	8,934,585	1,300	6.0	5.3	33		-0.4	3
Rwanda	5,536,951	520	7.5	9.1	26	23	2.2	-17*
St Kitts and Nevis	615,165	11,740	1.3	4.1	38	156	25.3	-18
St Lucia	1,141,764	6,560	2.9	3.1	32	65	14.3	-13
St Vincent and the Grenadines	88,361	6,300	2.4	4.3	33	67	22.7	-30
Samoa	548,988	3,000	0.9	5.5	51		8.1	-27
Seychelles	844,857	9,760	4.6	13.1	37	83	26.2	-8*
Sierra Leone	2,008,894	340	5.5	12.4	27	65	2.9	-12
Singapore	203,441,331	40,070	6.4	2.6	18	96	4.8	28
Solomon Islands	552,364	1,030	6.1	8.7	53	26	14.7	-30
South Africa	304,590,826	6,090	3.1	6.9	32	34	3.5	-2
Sri Lanka	46,738,286	2,240	6.4	11.3	23		1.8	-9
Swaziland	3,119,466	2,630	2.1	7.6	40	18	3.7	-19
Tonga	341,659	3,280	0.2	5.5	33		1.2	-47
Trinidad and Tobago	20,625,045	15,380	3.3	9.1	41	40	10.3	28‡
Tuvalu	46,745	4,760	2.0	2.8			5.6	
Uganda	16,552,792	500	8.1	8.4	20	24	5.0	-10
United Kingdom	2,387,064,419	38,370	0.3	2.7	47	76	3.5	-3
United Republic of Tanzania	23,366,171	530	6.9	8.6	28	40	1.9	-14
Vanuatu	633,434	2,640	5.3	3.6	28		7.4	-6
Zambia	13,815,688	1,070	6.4	10.8	23	25	6.4	9

*2009 figure   ** GDP per capita 2010   † GDP per capita 2009   < denotes less than here and following
Data reproduced with permission from: UNICEF, The State of the World's Children Report 2012, UNICEF, New York, 2012

Largest economies

	GNI (US$'000) 2010
United Kingdom	2,387,064,419
India	1,553,937,385
Canada	1,475,864,609
Australia	957,529,000*
South Africa	304,590,826
Malaysia	220,362,357
Singapore	203,441,331
Nigeria	186,405,944
Pakistan	182,788,124
New Zealand	126,679,321†
Bangladesh	104,680,897
Sri Lanka	46,738,286
Kenya	31,810,201
Ghana	30,080,473
Cyprus	23,654,583
United Republic of Tanzania	23,366,171
Cameroon	23,169,403
Trinidad and Tobago	20,625,045
Uganda	16,552,792
Zambia	13,815,688
Botswana	13,632,837
Jamaica	12,966,651
Brunei Darussalam	10,732,435†
Mozambique	10,344,420
Namibia	10,286,037
Mauritius	9,924,679
Papua New Guinea	8,934,585
Malta	7,957,770
The Bahamas	7,538,000**
Rwanda	5,536,951
Malawi	4,885,956
Barbados	4,109,500**
Fiji	3,122,845
Swaziland	3,119,466
Lesotho	2,247,822
Guyana	2,163,562
Sierra Leone	2,008,894
Maldives	1,817,841
Belize	1,313,459
Antigua and Barbuda	1,168,629
St Lucia	1,141,764
Seychelles	844,857
The Gambia	769,958
Grenada	723,862
St Vincent and the Grenadines	688,361
Vanuatu	633,434
St Kitts and Nevis	615,165
Solomon Islands	552,364
Samoa	548,988
Dominica	458,226
Tonga	341,659
Kiribati	199,852
Tuvalu	46,745
Nauru	28,020**

Highest income per capita

	GNI per capita (US$) 2010
Australia	43,770*
Canada	43,270
Singapore	40,070
United Kingdom	38,370
New Zealand	29,695†
Cyprus	29,430
Brunei Darussalam	26,750†
The Bahamas	21,984**
Malta	19,270
Trinidad and Tobago	15,380
Barbados	15,034**
Antigua and Barbuda	13,170
St Kitts and Nevis	11,740
Seychelles	9,760
Malaysia	7,760
Mauritius	7,750
Grenada	6,930
Botswana	6,790
Dominica	6,760
St Lucia	6,560
St Vincent and the Grenadines	6,300
South Africa	6,090
Maldives	5,750
Jamaica	4,800
Tuvalu	4,760
Namibia	4,500
Belize	3,810
Fiji	3,630
Tonga	3,280
Samoa	3,000
Guyana	2,870
Nauru	2,802**
Vanuatu	2,640
Swaziland	2,630
Sri Lanka	2,240
Kiribati	2,010
India	1,330
Papua New Guinea	1,300
Ghana	1,230
Cameroon	1,180
Nigeria	1,180
Zambia	1,070
Pakistan	1,050
Lesotho	1,040
Solomon Islands	1,030
Kenya	790
Bangladesh	700
United Republic of Tanzania	530
Rwanda	520
Uganda	500
The Gambia	450
Mozambique	440
Sierra Leone	340
Malawi	330

*2009 figure   ** GDP/GDP per capita 2010   † GDP/GDP per capita 2009*

Fastest growth

	Average GDP growth (% p.a.) 2006-10
Maldives	9.4
India	8.4
Uganda	8.1
Rwanda	7.5
Malawi	7.4
Mozambique	7.3
United Republic of Tanzania	6.9
Nigeria	6.7
Ghana	6.5
Zambia	6.4
Singapore	6.4
Sri Lanka	6.4
Bangladesh	6.2
Solomon Islands	6.1
Papua New Guinea	6.0
Sierra Leone	5.5
Vanuatu	5.3
The Gambia	4.6
Seychelles	4.6
Kenya	4.5
Malaysia	4.5
Mauritius	4.5
Pakistan	4.2
Guyana	4.2
Namibia	4.1
Lesotho	4.0
Trinidad and Tobago	3.3
Dominica	3.2
South Africa	3.1
Botswana	2.9
St Lucia	2.9
Cameroon	2.8
Australia	2.8
Belize	2.5
Cyprus	2.4
St Vincent and the Grenadines	2.4
Malta	2.3
Swaziland	2.1
Tuvalu	2.0
New Zealand	1.4
St Kitts and Nevis	1.3
Antigua and Barbuda	1.2
Canada	1.2
Samoa	0.9
Barbados	0.7
Brunei Darussalam	0.7
Kiribati	0.5
United Kingdom	0.3
Tonga	0.2
Fiji	0.2
Jamaica	-0.0
Grenada	-0.9
The Bahamas	-1.5
Nauru	-4.8

Lowest inflation

	Inflation (% p.a.) 2006-10
Brunei Darussalam	0.9
Canada	1.7
Antigua and Barbuda	2.3
Malta	2.4
Nauru	2.4
Cyprus	2.4
Belize	2.5
The Bahamas	2.6
Singapore	2.6
Malaysia	2.7
United Kingdom	2.7
Tuvalu	2.8
New Zealand	2.9
Australia	3.0
St Lucia	3.1
Dominica	3.1
Cameroon	3.1
Vanuatu	3.6
Grenada	3.8
St Kitts and Nevis	4.1
The Gambia	4.3
St Vincent and the Grenadines	4.3
Kiribati	4.8
Fiji	4.8
Papua New Guinea	5.3
Tonga	5.5
Samoa	5.5
Barbados	5.8
Maldives	6.3
Guyana	6.3
Mauritius	6.5
South Africa	6.9
Namibia	7.1
Lesotho	7.1
Swaziland	7.6
Bangladesh	7.7
Uganda	8.4
United Republic of Tanzania	8.6
India	8.7
Solomon Islands	8.7
Rwanda	9.1
Trinidad and Tobago	9.1
Botswana	9.2
Malawi	9.3
Mozambique	9.5
Nigeria	10.1
Zambia	10.8
Sri Lanka	11.3
Jamaica	12.3
Sierra Leone	12.4
Kenya	12.5
Pakistan	12.6
Seychelles	13.1
Ghana	13.6

Greatest public spending

	General government total expenditure (% of GDP) 2010
Kiribati	90.3
Lesotho	56.3
Solomon Islands	53.5
Samoa	50.9
United Kingdom	46.8
Cyprus	46.6
Canada	43.8
Barbados	43.3
Malta	42.8
Trinidad and Tobago	40.5
Swaziland	40.2
Brunei Darussalam	40.1
Maldives	39.1
Botswana	38.6
St Kitts and Nevis	38.3
Malawi	37.6
Australia	37.2
Seychelles	37.2
New Zealand	35.1
Dominica	34.3
Namibia	33.1
Nigeria	33.1
Papua New Guinea	32.8
Tonga	32.8
St Vincent and the Grenadines	32.6
Jamaica	32.5
Mozambique	32.5
Kenya	32.4
South Africa	32.0
St Lucia	32.0
Malaysia	31.1
Guyana	30.9
Belize	28.9
Fiji	28.5
Vanuatu	27.7
United Republic of Tanzania	27.6
Sierra Leone	27.3
Grenada	27.1
Rwanda	26.4
India	26.0
Mauritius	25.4
Ghana	24.1
Sri Lanka	22.9
Zambia	22.7
The Gambia	22.1
The Bahamas	21.2
Antigua and Barbuda	20.8
Pakistan	20.3
Uganda	19.9
Cameroon	18.6
Singapore	17.8
Bangladesh	14.6

Greatest public debt

	General government gross debt (% of GDP) 2010
St Kitts and Nevis	156
Jamaica	143
Barbados	118
Grenada	99
Singapore	96
Canada	84
Seychelles	83
Belize	81
United Kingdom	76
Antigua and Barbuda	70
Malta	67
St Vincent and the Grenadines	67
St Lucia	65
Sierra Leone	65
India	64
Cyprus	61
Guyana	60
Maldives	59
The Gambia	58
Pakistan	57
Fiji	56
Dominica	54
Malaysia	54
Kenya	52
Mauritius	50
The Bahamas	45
Trinidad and Tobago	40
United Republic of Tanzania	40
Mozambique	38
Malawi	37
Ghana	37
Lesotho	34
South Africa	34
New Zealand	32
Solomon Islands	26
Zambia	25
Uganda	24
Rwanda	23
Australia	21
Namibia	19
Swaziland	18
Nigeria	17
Botswana	13
Cameroon	12

Greatest foreign investment

Foreign direct investment, net inflows
(US$m)
2010

Seychelles	26.2
St Kitts and Nevis	25.3
St Vincent and the Grenadines	22.7
Grenada	17.1
Cyprus	15.4
Solomon Islands	14.7
St Lucia	14.3
Antigua and Barbuda	12.6
Belize	12.5
Dominica	12.2
The Bahamas	11.8
Trinidad and Tobago	10.3
Jamaica	10.1
Malta	9.6
The Gambia	9.6
Guyana	8.7
Fiji	8.6
Samoa	8.1
Barbados	7.8
Maldives	7.5
Vanuatu	7.4
Lesotho	6.9
Botswana	6.6
Zambia	6.4
Mozambique	6.0
Tuvalu	5.6
Uganda	5.0
Singapore	4.8
Namibia	4.6
Australia	4.5
New Zealand	4.3
Ghana	4.3
Malawi	4.2
Nigeria	4.0
Mauritius	3.9
Canada	3.9
Swaziland	3.7
India	3.6
United Kingdom	3.5
South Africa	3.5
Pakistan	3.3
Malaysia	3.3
Sierra Leone	2.9
Rwanda	2.2
Kiribati	2.0
United Republic of Tanzania	1.9
Sri Lanka	1.8
Brunei Darussalam	1.5
Bangladesh	1.3
Tonga	1.2
Kenya	0.3
Cameroon	-0.1
Papua New Guinea	-0.4

Greatest trade balance

Net exports of goods and services*
(% of GNI)
2010

Singapore	28
Trinidad and Tobago	28**
Malaysia	18
Nigeria	13
Zambia	9
Papua New Guinea	3
Malta	2
New Zealand	2
Namibia	1
Kiribati	0
Australia	-2
Canada	-2
South Africa	-2
Botswana	-3
India	-3
United Kingdom	-3
Barbados	-5
Cameroon	-5
Pakistan	-5
Cyprus	-6
Vanuatu	-6
Bangladesh	-7
Belize	-8**
Seychelles	-8†
Sri Lanka	-9
Antigua and Barbuda	-10
Malawi	-10
Uganda	-10
The Bahamas	-12†
Fiji	-12
Mauritius	-12
Sierra Leone	-12
Ghana	-13
Kenya	-13
St Lucia	-13
United Republic of Tanzania	-14
Rwanda	-17†
Jamaica	-18
Maldives	-18
Mozambique	-18
St Kitts and Nevis	-18
The Gambia	-19
Swaziland	-19
Dominica	-23
Samoa	-27
Grenada	-29
St Vincent and the Grenadines	-30
Solomon Islands	-30
Tonga	-47
Brunei Darussalam	-51**
Lesotho	-65

* Net exports are the difference between the monetary value of exports and imports (i.e. exports minus imports)
** 2008 figure   † 2009 figure

Education

	Net primary enrolment rate (%) 2007–09	Net secondary enrolment rate (%) 2007–09	Primary pupil-teacher ratio 2007–09	Secondary pupil-teacher ratio 2007–09	Gross tertiary enrolment ratio (%) 2007–09	Gross enrolment ratio for all levels combined (%) 2007–10	Adult literacy rate (%) 2005–08	Public spending on education (% of GDP) 2007–10
Antigua and Barbuda	90	88	16	13	15	80	99	2.8
Australia	97	88			77	108		4.4
The Bahamas	92	86	15	13		76		
Bangladesh	89	42	46	25	8	55	56	2.4
Barbados			14	15		101		6.7
Belize	100	65	23	17	11	77		6.1
Botswana	87		25	14		70	84	7.8
Brunei Darussalam	97	89	12	10	17	84	95	2.0
Cameroon	92		46		9	62	71	3.5
Canada								4.8
Cyprus	99	96	14	10	43	85	98	7.4
Dominica	98	89	16	14	3	73		4.5
Fiji	92		26	19				4.6
The Gambia	76	42	37	24	5	54	47	5.0
Ghana	76	46	33	18	6	64	67	5.7
Grenada	99	85	17	18	59	91		
Guyana	99		26	22	11	69		3.7
India	97				13	62	63	
Jamaica	81	77		20	24	85	86	6.0
Kenya	83	50	47	30	4	67	87	6.9
Kiribati			25	17		73		
Lesotho	73	29	34	17		58	90	13.1
Malawi	91	25				63	74	4.6
Malaysia	94	68	15		32		93	4.1
Maldives	96	69	13				98	11.5
Malta	91	82	11	9	32	79	92	5.9
Mauritius	94		22	16	26	76	88	3.1
Mozambique	91	15	61	38		59	55	
Namibia	90	54	30	25	9	70	89	8.1
Nauru	72		20	21		56		
New Zealand	99	96	15	14	78	111		6.4
Nigeria	63	26	46	28			61	
Pakistan	66	33	40		6	44	56	2.4
Papua New Guinea							60	
Rwanda	96		68	23	5	66		5.0
St Kitts and Nevis	94	88	14	10		75		5.6
St Lucia	93	80	20	16	16	73		5.1
St Vincent and the Grenadines	98	90	17	13				6.2
Samoa	99	71	32	21			99	5.7
Seychelles	94	97	14	13		87	92	
Sierra Leone		25		24			41	4.3
Singapore			17	15			95	3.3
Solomon Islands	81	30				55		
South Africa	90	72	31	25			89	6.0
Sri Lanka	95		23				91	
Swaziland	83	29	32	19		65	87	7.5
Tonga	99						99	
Trinidad and Tobago	96	74	18	14			99	
Tuvalu								
Uganda	92	21	49	18	4	69	73	3.2
United Kingdom	100	91	17		57	90		5.4
United Republic of Tanzania	97		54	35	1		73	6.8
Vanuatu			24				82	5.0
Zambia	92	43	63	22			71	1.3

Greatest overall participation in education

New Zealand	111
Australia	108
Barbados	101
Grenada	91
United Kingdom	90
Seychelles	87
Jamaica	85
Cyprus	85
Brunei Darussalam	84
Antigua and Barbuda	80
Malta	79
Belize	77
The Bahamas	76
Mauritius	76
St Kitts and Nevis	75
Kiribati	73
Dominica	73
St Lucia	73
Botswana	70
Namibia	70
Guyana	69
Uganda	69
Kenya	67
Rwanda	66
Swaziland	65
Ghana	64
Malawi	63
India	62
Cameroon	62
Mozambique	59
Lesotho	58
Nauru	56
Solomon Islands	55
Bangladesh	55
The Gambia	54
Pakistan	44

Highest public spending on education

Lesotho	13.1
Maldives	11.5
Namibia	8.1
Botswana	7.8
Swaziland	7.5
Cyprus	7.4
Kenya	6.9
United Republic of Tanzania	6.8
Barbados	6.7
New Zealand	6.4
St Vincent and the Grenadines	6.2
Belize	6.1
Jamaica	6.0
South Africa	6.0
Malta	5.9
Samoa	5.7
Ghana	5.7
St Kitts and Nevis	5.6
United Kingdom	5.4
St Lucia	5.1
Rwanda	5.0
The Gambia	5.0
Vanuatu	5.0
Canada	4.8
Malawi	4.6
Fiji	4.6
Dominica	4.5
Australia	4.4
Sierra Leone	4.3
Malaysia	4.1
Guyana	3.7
Cameroon	3.5
Singapore	3.3
Uganda	3.2
Mauritius	3.1
Antigua and Barbuda	2.8
Bangladesh	2.4
Pakistan	2.4
Brunei Darussalam	2.0
Zambia	1.3

Highest enrolment at primary level

	Net primary enrolment ratio (%) 2007–09
United Kingdom	100
Belize	100
New Zealand	99
Samoa	99
Tonga	99
Cyprus	99
Guyana	99
Grenada	99
St Vincent and the Grenadines	98
Dominica	98
Australia	97
Brunei Darussalam	97
India	97
United Republic of Tanzania	97
Maldives	96
Rwanda	96
Trinidad and Tobago	96
Sri Lanka	95
Seychelles	94
Malaysia	94
Mauritius	94
St Kitts and Nevis	94
St Lucia	93
Zambia	92
Uganda	92
Fiji	92
The Bahamas	92
Cameroon	92
Malawi	91
Malta	91
Mozambique	91
Namibia	90
Antigua and Barbuda	90
South Africa	90
Bangladesh	89
Botswana	87
Kenya	83
Swaziland	83
Solomon Islands	81
Jamaica	81
Ghana	76
The Gambia	76
Lesotho	73
Nauru	72
Pakistan	66
Nigeria	63

Highest enrolment at secondary level

	Net secondary enrolment ratio (%) 2007–09
Seychelles	97
New Zealand	96
Cyprus	96
United Kingdom	91
St Vincent and the Grenadines	90
Dominica	89
Brunei Darussalam	89
St Kitts and Nevis	88
Antigua and Barbuda	88
Australia	88
The Bahamas	86
Grenada	85
Malta	82
St Lucia	80
Jamaica	77
Trinidad and Tobago	74
South Africa	72
Samoa	71
Maldives	69
Malaysia	68
Belize	65
Namibia	54
Kenya	50
Ghana	46
Zambia	43
The Gambia	42
Bangladesh	42
Pakistan	33
Solomon Islands	30
Lesotho	29
Swaziland	29
Nigeria	26
Malawi	25
Sierra Leone	25
Uganda	21
Mozambique	15

Best class sizes at primary school level

	Primary pupil-teacher ratio 2007–09
Malta	11
Brunei Darussalam	12
Maldives	13
Barbados	14
Cyprus	14
St Kitts and Nevis	14
Seychelles	14
The Bahamas	15
Malaysia	15
New Zealand	15
Antigua and Barbuda	16
Dominica	16
Grenada	17
St Vincent and the Grenadines	17
Singapore	17
United Kingdom	17
Trinidad and Tobago	18
Nauru	20
St Lucia	20
Mauritius	22
Belize	23
Sri Lanka	23
Vanuatu	24
Botswana	25
Kiribati	25
Fiji	26
Guyana	26
Namibia	30
South Africa	31
Samoa	32
Swaziland	32
Ghana	33
Lesotho	34
The Gambia	37
Pakistan	40
Bangladesh	46
Cameroon	46
Nigeria	46
Kenya	47
Uganda	49
United Republic of Tanzania	54
Mozambique	61
Zambia	63
Rwanda	68

Best class sizes at secondary school level

	Secondary pupil-teacher ratio 2007–09
Malta	9
Brunei Darussalam	10
Cyprus	10
St Kitts and Nevis	10
Antigua and Barbuda	13
The Bahamas	13
St Vincent and the Grenadines	13
Seychelles	13
Botswana	14
Dominica	14
New Zealand	14
Trinidad and Tobago	14
Barbados	15
Singapore	15
Mauritius	16
St Lucia	16
Belize	17
Kiribati	17
Lesotho	17
Ghana	18
Grenada	18
Uganda	18
Fiji	19
Swaziland	19
Jamaica	20
Nauru	21
Samoa	21
Guyana	22
Zambia	22
Rwanda	23
The Gambia	24
Sierra Leone	24
Bangladesh	25
Namibia	25
South Africa	25
Nigeria	28
Kenya	30
United Republic of Tanzania	35
Mozambique	38

	Life expectancy (years) 2010	Infant mortality per 1,000 live births 2010	One-year-olds immunised with one dose of measles (%) 2010	HIV/AIDS prevalence among those aged 15–49 (%) 2009	HIV/AIDS deaths 2009	Access to an improved water source (% of population) 2008	Access to adequate sanitation facilities (% of population) 2008	Medical doctors (per 100,000 population) 1997–2009	Government expenditure on health (% of GDP) 2009
Antigua and Barbuda		7	98					17	4.0
Australia	82	4	94	0.1	<100	100	100	299	6.0
The Bahamas	75	14	94	3.1			100	105	3.0
Bangladesh	69	38	94	<0.1	<200	80	53	30	1.0
Barbados	77	17	85	1.4	<100	100	100	181	4.0
Belize	76	14	98	2.3	<500	99	90	83	4.0
Botswana	53	36	94	24.8	5,000	95	60	34	8.0
Brunei Darussalam	78	6	94					142	3.0
Cameroon	51	84	79	5.3	37000	74	47	19	2.0
Canada	81	5	93	0.3	<500	100	100	191	7.0
Cyprus	79	3	87			100	100	230	2.0
Dominica		11	99					50	4.0
Fiji	69	15	94	0.1	<100			45	3.0
The Gambia	58	57	97	2		92	67	4	3.0
Ghana	64	50	93	1.8	18000	82	13	9	3.0
Grenada	76	9	95				97	98	4.0
Guyana	70	25	95	1.2	<500	94	81	48	7.0
India	65	48	74	0.3	170000	88	31	60	1.0
Jamaica	73	20	88	1.7	1200	94	83	85	3.0
Kenya	57	55	86	6.3	80000	59	31	14	1.0
Kiribati		39	89					30	10.0
Lesotho	48	65	85	23.6	14,000	85	29	5	6.0
Malawi	54	58	93	11	51000	80	56	2	4.0
Malaysia	74	5	96	0.5	5800	100	96	94	2.0
Maldives	77	14	97	<0.1	<100	91	98	160	5.0
Malta	79	5	73	0.1	<100	100	100	307	6.0
Mauritius	73	13	99	1	<500	99	91	106	2.0
Mozambique	50	92	70	11.5	74000	47	17	3	4.0
Namibia	62	29	75	13.1	6700	92	33	37	4.0
Nauru		32				90	50		
New Zealand	81	5	91	0.1	<100	100	-	238	8.0
Nigeria	51	88	71	3.6	220000	58	32	40	2.0
Pakistan	65	70	86	0.1	5800	90	45	81	1.0
Papua New Guinea	62	47	55	0.9	1300	40	45	5	2.0
Rwanda	55	59	82	2.9	4100	65	54	2	4.0
St Kitts and Nevis		7	99			99	96	110	4.0
St Lucia	74	14	95			98		47	5.0
St Vincent and the Grenadines	72	19	99					75	3.0
Samoa	72	17	61				100	27	6.0
Seychelles		12	99					151	3.0
Sierra Leone	47	114	82	1.6	2800	49	13	2	1.0
Singapore	81	2	95	0.1	<100	100	100	183	2.0
Solomon Islands	67	23	68					19	5.0
South Africa	52	41	65	17.8	310000	91	77	77	3.0
Sri Lanka	75	14	99	<0.1	<200	90	91	49	2.0
Swaziland	48	55	94	25.9	7,000	69	55	16	4.0
Tonga	72	13	99			100	96	29	5.0
Trinidad and Tobago	70	24	92	1.5	<1000	94	92	118	3.0
Tuvalu		27	85			97	84	64	10.0
Uganda	54	63	55	6.5	64000	67	48	12	2.0
United Kingdom	80	5	93	0.2	<1000	100	100	274	8.0
United Republic of Tanzania	57	50	92	5.6	86000	54	24	1	4.0
Vanuatu	71	12	52			83	52	12	3.0
Zambia	49	69	91	13.5	45000	60	49	6	3.0

Lowest infant mortality

Infant mortality per 1,000 live births
2010

Singapore	2
Cyprus	3
Australia	4
Canada	5
Malaysia	5
Malta	5
New Zealand	5
United Kingdom	5
Brunei Darussalam	6
Antigua and Barbuda	7
St Kitts and Nevis	7
Grenada	9
Dominica	11
Seychelles	12
Vanuatu	12
Mauritius	13
Tonga	13
The Bahamas	14
Belize	14
Maldives	14
St Lucia	14
Sri Lanka	14
Fiji	15
Barbados	17
Samoa	17
St Vincent and the Grenadines	19
Jamaica	20
Solomon Islands	23
Trinidad and Tobago	24
Guyana	25
Tuvalu	27
Namibia	29
Nauru	32
Botswana	36
Bangladesh	38
Kiribati	39
South Africa	41
Papua New Guinea	47
India	48
Ghana	50
United Republic of Tanzania	50
Kenya	55
Swaziland	55
The Gambia	57
Malawi	58
Rwanda	59
Uganda	63
Lesotho	65
Zambia	69
Pakistan	70
Cameroon	84
Nigeria	88
Mozambique	92
Sierra Leone	114

Best life expectancy

Life expectancy (years)
2010

Australia	82
Canada	81
New Zealand	81
Singapore	81
United Kingdom	80
Cyprus	79
Malta	79
Brunei Darussalam	78
Barbados	77
Maldives	77
Belize	76
Grenada	76
The Bahamas	75
Sri Lanka	75
Malaysia	74
St Lucia	74
Jamaica	73
Mauritius	73
St Vincent and the Grenadines	72
Samoa	72
Tonga	72
Vanuatu	71
Guyana	70
Trinidad and Tobago	70
Bangladesh	69
Fiji	69
Solomon Islands	67
India	65
Pakistan	65
Ghana	64
Namibia	62
Papua New Guinea	62
The Gambia	58
Kenya	57
United Republic of Tanzania	57
Rwanda	55
Malawi	54
Uganda	54
Botswana	53
South Africa	52
Cameroon	51
Nigeria	51
Mozambique	50
Zambia	49
Lesotho	48
Swaziland	48
Sierra Leone	47

Highest prevalence of HIV/AIDS

HIV/AIDS prevalence among those aged 15–49 (%)
2009

Swaziland	25.9
Botswana	24.8
Lesotho	23.6
South Africa	17.8
Zambia	13.5
Namibia	13.1
Mozambique	11.5
Malawi	11.0
Uganda	6.5
Kenya	6.3
United Republic of Tanzania	5.6
Cameroon	5.3
Nigeria	3.6
The Bahamas	3.1
Rwanda	2.9
Belize	2.3
The Gambia	2.0
Ghana	1.8
Jamaica	1.7
Sierra Leone	1.6
Trinidad and Tobago	1.5
Barbados	1.4
Guyana	1.2
Mauritius	1.0
Papua New Guinea	0.9
Malaysia	0.5
Canada	0.3
India	0.3
United Kingdom	0.2
Australia	0.1
Fiji	0.1
Malta	0.1
New Zealand	0.1
Pakistan	0.1
Singapore	0.1
Bangladesh	<0.1
Sri Lanka	<0.1
Maldives	<0.1

Most deaths due to HIV/AIDS

HIV/AIDS deaths
2009

South Africa	310,000
Nigeria	220,000
India	170,000
United Republic of Tanzania	86,000
Kenya	80,000
Mozambique	74,000
Uganda	64,000
Malawi	51,000
Zambia	45,000
Cameroon	37,000
Ghana	18,000
Lesotho	14,000
Swaziland	7,000
Namibia	6,700
Botswana	5,800
Malaysia	5,800
Pakistan	5,800
Rwanda	4,100
Sierra Leone	2,800
Papua New Guinea	1,300
Jamaica	1,200
Trinidad and Tobago	<1,000
United Kingdom	<1,000
Belize	<500
Canada	<500
Guyana	<500
Mauritius	<500
Bangladesh	<200
Sri Lanka	<200
Barbados	<100
Australia	<100
Fiji	<100
Maldives	<100
Malta	<100
New Zealand	<100
Singapore	<100

Highest public spending on health per capita

	(US$) 2009
Canada	4,380
Australia	3,867
United Kingdom	3,285
New Zealand	2,634
The Bahamas	1,558
Singapore	1,501
Malta	1,446
Trinidad and Tobago	1,069
Barbados	1,041
Brunei Darussalam	791
Antigua and Barbuda	653
St Kitts and Nevis	634
Botswana	612
South Africa	485
Grenada	447
St Lucia	443
Mauritius	383
Seychelles	366
Dominica	361
Malaysia	336
Maldives	331
St Vincent and the Grenadines	301
Tuvalu	290
Namibia	258
Jamaica	231
Belize	217
Samoa	205
Tonga	161
Kiribati	159
Swaziland	156
Guyana	133
Fiji	130
Vanuatu	106
Sri Lanka	84
Solomon Islands	72
Lesotho	70
Nigeria	69
Cameroon	61
Rwanda	48
Zambia	47
Ghana	45
India	45
Sierra Leone	44
Uganda	43
Papua New Guinea	37
Kenya	33
The Gambia	26
United Republic of Tanzania	25
Mozambique	25
Pakistan	23
Malawi	19
Bangladesh	18

Highest public expenditure on health as proportion of GDP

	(%) 2009
Kiribati	10.0
Tuvalu	10.0
Botswana	8.0
New Zealand	8.0
United Kingdom	8.0
Canada	7.0
Guyana	7.0
Australia	6.0
Lesotho	6.0
Malta	6.0
Samoa	6.0
Maldives	5.0
St Lucia	5.0
Solomon Islands	5.0
Tonga	5.0
Antigua and Barbuda	4.0
Barbados	4.0
Belize	4.0
Dominica	4.0
Grenada	4.0
Malawi	4.0
Mozambique	4.0
Namibia	4.0
Rwanda	4.0
St Kitts and Nevis	4.0
Swaziland	4.0
United Republic of Tanzania	4.0
The Bahamas	3.0
Brunei Darussalam	3.0
Fiji	3.0
The Gambia	3.0
Ghana	3.0
Jamaica	3.0
St Vincent and the Grenadines	3.0
Seychelles	3.0
South Africa	3.0
Trinidad and Tobago	3.0
Vanuatu	3.0
Zambia	3.0
Cameroon	2.0
Cyprus	2.0
Malaysia	2.0
Mauritius	2.0
Nigeria	2.0
Papua New Guinea	2.0
Singapore	2.0
Sri Lanka	2.0
Uganda	2.0
Bangladesh	1.0
India	1.0
Kenya	1.0
Pakistan	1.0
Sierra Leone	1.0

Most medical doctors per capita

	Number of doctors per 100,000 people	Source year
Malta	307	2009
Australia	299	2009
United Kingdom	274	2009
New Zealand	238	2007
Cyprus	230	2006
Canada	191	2006
Singapore	183	2009
Barbados	181	2005
Maldives	160	2007
Seychelles	151	2004
Brunei Darussalam	142	2008
Trinidad and Tobago	118	2007
St Kitts and Nevis	110	2000
Mauritius	106	2004
The Bahamas	105	1998
Grenada	98	1998
Malaysia	94	2008
Jamaica	85	2003
Belize	83	2009
Pakistan	81	2009
South Africa	77	2004
St Vincent and the Grenadines	75	2000
Tuvalu	64	2008
India	60	2005
Dominica	50	1997
Sri Lanka	49	2006
Guyana	48	2000
St Lucia	47	2002
Fiji	45	2003
Nigeria	40	2008
Namibia	37	2007
Botswana	34	2006
Kiribati	30	2006
Bangladesh	30	2007
Tonga	29	2002
Samoa	27	2005
Cameroon	19	2003
Solomon Islands	19	2005
Antigua and Barbuda	17	1999
Swaziland	16	2004
Kenya	14	2004
Uganda	12	2005
Vanuatu	12	2008
Ghana	9	2009
Zambia	6	2006
Papua New Guinea	5	2008
Lesotho	5	2003
The Gambia	4	2008
Mozambique	3	2006
Rwanda	2	2005
Malawi	2	2008
Sierra Leone	2	2008
United Republic of Tanzania	1	2006

Most nurses and midwives per capita

	Number of nurses and midwives per 100,000 people	Source year
New Zealand	1,087	2007
United Kingdom	1,030	2009
Canada	1,005	2006
Australia	959	2009
Seychelles	793	2004
Malta	663	2009
Swaziland	630	2004
Singapore	590	2009
Tuvalu	582	2008
Brunei Darussalam	488	2008
Barbados	486	2005
St Kitts and Nevis	471	2000
The Bahamas	447	1998
Maldives	445	2007
Dominica	417	1997
South Africa	408	2004
Cyprus	398	2006
Grenada	398	1998
St Vincent and the Grenadines	379	2000
Mauritius	373	2004
Trinidad and Tobago	356	2007
Antigua and Barbuda	328	1999
Kiribati	302	2004
Tonga	293	2007
Botswana	284	2006
Namibia	278	2007
Malaysia	273	2008
Guyana	229	2000
St Lucia	216	2002
Fiji	198	2003
Belize	196	2009
Sri Lanka	193	2007
Vanuatu	170	2008
Jamaica	165	2003
Nigeria	161	2008
Cameroon	160	2004
Solomon Islands	145	2005
Uganda	131	2005
India	130	2005
Kenya	118	2002
Ghana	105	2009
Samoa	94	2005
Zambia	71	2006
Lesotho	62	2003
The Gambia	57	2008
Pakistan	56	2009
Papua New Guinea	51	2008
Rwanda	45	2005
Mozambique	31	2006
Malawi	28	2008
Bangladesh	27	2007
United Republic of Tanzania	24	2006
Sierra Leone	17	2008

	CO2 emissions per capita (tonnes)	CO2 emissions, average annual change (%)	CO2 emissions overall increase/decrease from 1990 to 2008* (%)	Forest area (% of total land area)	Forest area, average annual change (%)	Forest area, overall increase/decline from 1990 to 2010 (%)	Energy use (kg of oil equivalent per capita)	Electric power consumption (kilowatt-hour per capita)
	2008	1990–2008	1990–2008	2010	1990–2010	1990–2010	2007–09	2009
Antigua and Barbuda	5.2	2.2	+49	22	0.00	0	1,699	
Australia	18.9	1.8	+39	19	-0.17	-3	5,971	11,113
The Bahamas	6.4	0.6	+11	51	0.00	0	2,156	
Bangladesh	0.3	6.3	+200	11	-0.18	-3	201	252
Barbados	5.3	1.3	+26	19	0.00	0	1,476	
Belize	1.4	1.7	+36	61	-0.65	-12	571	
Botswana	2.5	4.5	+122	20	-0.94	-17	1,034	1,503
Brunei Darussalam	27.0	2.8	+65	72	-0.42	-8	7,971	8,662
Cameroon	0.3	6.4	+205	42	-0.99	-18	361	271
Canada	16.4	1.1	+21	34	0.00	0	7,532	15,467
Cyprus	9.9	3.4	+84	19	0.36	+7	2,298	4,620
Dominica	1.9	4.4	+117	60	-0.53	-10	628	
Fiji	1.5	2.4	+53	56	0.31	+6	627	
The Gambia	0.2	4.3	+115	48	0.41	+9	84	
Ghana	0.4	4.4	+119	22	-2.03	-34	388	265
Grenada	2.4	4.0	+103	50	0.00	0	784	
Guyana	2.0	1.6	+34	77	0.00	0	667	
India	1.5	5.3	+152	23	0.34	+7	585	597
Jamaica	4.5	2.4	+53	31	-0.12	-2	1,208	1,902
Kenya	0.3	3.3	+78	6	-0.34	-6	474	147
Kiribati	0.3	1.5	+32	15	0.00	0	116	
Lesotho				1	0.48	+10	9	
Malawi	0.1	3.9	+101	34	-0.92	-17		
Malaysia	7.7	7.5	+268	62	-0.45	-9	2,391	3,614
Maldives	3.0	10.4	+497	3	0.00	0	985	
Malta	6.3	0.9	+18	0			1,935	4,423
Mauritius	3.1	5.7	+170	17	-0.54	-10	947	
Mozambique	0.1	4.8	+131	50	-0.53	-10	427	453
Namibia	1.9	42.2	+56,586	9	-0.92	-17	764	1,576
Nauru	14.1	0.4	+8	0				
New Zealand	7.8	1.8	+38	31	0.34	+7	4,032	9,346
Nigeria	0.6	4.2	+111	10	-3.17	-48	701	121
Pakistan	0.9	4.9	+138	2	-2.00	-33	502	449
Papua New Guinea	0.3	-0.1	-2	63	-0.46	-9		
Rwanda	0.1	0.2	+3	18	1.58	+37		
St Kitts and Nevis	4.9	7.7	+277	42	0.00	0	1,645	
St Lucia	2.3	5.0	+140	77	0.33	+7	760	
St Vincent and the Grenadines	1.9	5.2	+149	69	0.39	+8	642	
Samoa	0.9	1.4	+29	60	1.38	+32	320	
Seychelles	8.1	10.4	+498	89	0.00	0	2,411	
Sierra Leone	0.2	7.1	+243	38	-0.67	-13		
Singapore	7.0	-2.1	-31	3	0.00	0	3,704	7,949
Solomon Islands	0.4	1.2	+23	79	-0.24	-5	129	
South Africa	8.8	1.5	+31	8	-1.83	-31	2,921	4,532
Sri Lanka	0.6	6.5	+212	29	-1.16	-21	449	408
Swaziland	0.9	5.4	+157	33	0.89	+19	373	
Tonga	1.7	4.7	+129	13	0.00	0	567	
Trinidad and Tobago	37.3	6.2	+193	44	-0.32	-6	15,158	5,662
Tuvalu				33	0.00	0		
Uganda	0.1	8.8	+358	15	-2.29	-37		
United Kingdom	8.5	-0.5	-8	12	0.49	+10	3,184	5,692
United Republic of Tanzania	0.2	5.7	+172	38	-1.08	-19	451	86
Vanuatu	0.4	1.5	+31	36	0.00	0	157	
Zambia	0.1	-1.4	-23	67	-0.33	-6	617	635

Highest consumption of oil per capita

	Energy use (kg of oil equivalent per capita) 2007–09
Trinidad and Tobago	15,158
Brunei Darussalam	7,971
Canada	7,532
Australia	5,971
New Zealand	4,032
Singapore	3,704
United Kingdom	3,184
South Africa	2,921
Seychelles	2,411
Malaysia	2,391
Cyprus	2,298
The Bahamas	2,156
Malta	1,935
Antigua and Barbuda	1,699
St Kitts and Nevis	1,645
Barbados	1476
Jamaica	1,208
Botswana	1,034
Maldives	985
Mauritius	947
Grenada	784
Namibia	764
St Lucia	760
Nigeria	701
Guyana	667
St Vincent and the Grenadines	642
Dominica	628
Fiji	627
Zambia	617
India	585
Belize	571
Tonga	567
Pakistan	502
Kenya	474
United Republic of Tanzania	451
Sri Lanka	449
Mozambique	427
Ghana	388
Swaziland	373
Cameroon	361
Samoa	320
Bangladesh	201
Vanuatu	157
Solomon Islands	129
Kiribati	116
The Gambia	84
Lesotho	9

Highest electricity consumption per capita

	Electric power consumption (kilowatt-hour per capita) 2009
Canada	15,467
Australia	11,113
New Zealand	9,346
Brunei Darussalam	8,662
Singapore	7,949
United Kingdom	5,692
Trinidad and Tobago	5,662
Cyprus	4,620
South Africa	4,532
Malta	4,423
Malaysia	3,614
Jamaica	1,902
Namibia	1,576
Botswana	1,503
Zambia	635
India	597
Mozambique	453
Pakistan	449
Sri Lanka	408
Cameroon	271
Ghana	265
Bangladesh	252
Kenya	147
Nigeria	121
United Republic of Tanzania	86

Most CO₂ emissions per capita

	CO₂ emissions (tonnes per capita) 2008
Trinidad and Tobago	37.3
Brunei Darussalam	27.0
Australia	18.9
Canada	16.4
Nauru	14.1
Cyprus	9.9
South Africa	8.8
United Kingdom	8.5
Seychelles	8.1
New Zealand	7.8
Malaysia	7.7
Singapore	7.0
The Bahamas	6.4
Malta	6.3
Barbados	5.3
Antigua and Barbuda	5.2
St Kitts and Nevis	4.9
Jamaica	4.5
Mauritius	3.1
Maldives	3.0
Botswana	2.5
Grenada	2.4
St Lucia	2.3
Guyana	2.0
Dominica	1.9
Namibia	1.9
St Vincent and the Grenadines	1.9
Tonga	1.7
Fiji	1.5
India	1.5
Belize	1.4
Swaziland	0.9
Pakistan	0.9
Samoa	0.9
Nigeria	0.6
Sri Lanka	0.6
Vanuatu	0.4
Solomon Islands	0.4
Ghana	0.4
Papua New Guinea	0.3
Kiribati	0.3
Bangladesh	0.3
Cameroon	0.3
Kenya	0.3
The Gambia	0.2
Sierra Leone	0.2
United Republic of Tanzania	0.2
Zambia	0.1
Uganda	0.1
Mozambique	0.1
Malawi	0.1
Rwanda	0.1

Fastest rise in CO₂ emissions

	CO₂ emissions overall increase/decrease from 1990 to 2008* (%) 1990–2008
Namibia	+56,586
Seychelles	+498
Maldives	+497
Uganda	+358
St Kitts and Nevis	+277
Malaysia	+268
Sierra Leone	+243
Sri Lanka	+212
Cameroon	+205
Bangladesh	+200
Trinidad and Tobago	+193
United Republic of Tanzania	+172
Mauritius	+170
Swaziland	+157
India	+152
St Vincent and the Grenadines	+149
St Lucia	+140
Pakistan	+138
Mozambique	+131
Tonga	+129
Botswana	+122
Ghana	+119
Dominica	+117
The Gambia	+115
Nigeria	+111
Grenada	+103
Malawi	+101
Cyprus	+84
Kenya	+78
Brunei Darussalam	+65
Fiji	+53
Jamaica	+53
Antigua and Barbuda	+49
Australia	+39
New Zealand	+38
Belize	+36
Guyana	+34
Kiribati	+32
South Africa	+31
Vanuatu	+31
Samoa	+29
Barbados	+26
Solomon Islands	+23
Canada	+21
Malta	+18
The Bahamas	+11
Nauru	+8
Rwanda	+3
Papua New Guinea	-2
United Kingdom	-8
Zambia	-23
Singapore	-31

*A 100% increase means that CO₂ emissions increased one time on top of the original figure. For example if there were 200,000 tonnes of CO₂ emissions in 1990, there are now 400,000 tonnes in 2008

A 10,000% increase means that CO₂ emissions increased 100 times on top of the original figure. For example if there were 200,000 tonnes of CO₂ emissions in 1990, there are now 20,200,000 tonnes in 2008

Smallest forest area relative to total land area

	Forest area (% of total land area) 2010
Malta	0
Nauru	0
Lesotho	1
Pakistan	2
Singapore	3
Maldives	3
Kenya	6
South Africa	8
Namibia	9
Nigeria	10
Bangladesh	11
United Kingdom	12
Tonga	13
Kiribati	15
Uganda	15
Mauritius	17
Rwanda	18
Barbados	19
Cyprus	19
Australia	19
Botswana	20
Ghana	22
Antigua and Barbuda	22
India	23
Sri Lanka	29
New Zealand	31
Jamaica	31
Swaziland	33
Tuvalu	33
Canada	34
Malawi	34
Vanuatu	36
United Republic of Tanzania	38
Sierra Leone	38
Cameroon	42
St Kitts and Nevis	42
Trinidad and Tobago	44
The Gambia	48
Mozambique	50
Grenada	50
The Bahamas	51
Fiji	56
Dominica	60
Samoa	60
Belize	61
Malaysia	62
Papua New Guinea	63
Zambia	67
St Vincent and the Grenadines	69
Brunei Darussalam	72
St Lucia	77
Guyana	77
Solomon Islands	79
Seychelles	89

Most rapid deforestation

	Forest area, overall increase/decline from 1990 to 2010 (%) 1990–2010
Nigeria	-48
Uganda	-37
Ghana	-34
Pakistan	-33
South Africa	-31
Sri Lanka	-21
United Republic of Tanzania	-19
Cameroon	-18
Botswana	-17
Malawi	-17
Namibia	-17
Sierra Leone	-13
Belize	-12
Mauritius	-10
Mozambique	-10
Dominica	-10
Papua New Guinea	-9
Malaysia	-9
Brunei Darussalam	-8
Kenya	-6
Zambia	-6
Trinidad and Tobago	-6
Solomon Islands	-5
Bangladesh	-3
Australia	-3
Jamaica	-2
Antigua and Barbuda	0
The Bahamas	0
Barbados	0
Canada	0
Grenada	0
Guyana	0
Kiribati	0
Maldives	0
St Kitts and Nevis	0
Seychelles	0
Singapore	0
Tonga	0
Tuvalu	0
Vanuatu	0
Fiji	+6
Cyprus	+7
India	+7
New Zealand	+7
St Lucia	+7
St Vincent and the Grenadines	+8
The Gambia	+9
Lesotho	+10
United Kingdom	+10
Swaziland	+19
Samoa	+32
Rwanda	+37

Information and Communication Technology

	Main telephone lines (per 1,000 people) 2010	Compound average annual growth in lines (%) 2004–09	Main telephone lines, overall increase/decrease from 2005 to 2010* (%) 2005–10	Mobile cellular subscribers (per 1,000 people) 2010	Compound average annual growth in mobile cellular subscribers (%) 2005–10	Mobile cellular subscribers, overall increase from 2005 to 2010** (%) 2005–10	Internet users (per 1,000 people) 2010	Personal computers (per 1,000 people) 2005–2008
Antigua and Barbuda	409	-0.1	-0.5	1,894	14.3	95	800	207
Australia	389	-3.1	-14.4	1,010	4.1	22	760	
The Bahamas	377	-0.6	-2.9	1,249	13.5	88	430	123
Bangladesh	6	-3.4	-15.9	462	50.1	663	37	23
Barbados	503	0.4	+1.9	1,281	11.2	70	702	158
Belize	97	-2.2	-10.4	623	15.1	102	140	153
Botswana	69	0.1	+0.7	1,178	33.2	319	60	63
Brunei Darussalam	200	-1.0	-4.8	1,091	13.3	87	500	89
Cameroon	28	40.0	+437.9	441	30.8	283	40	11
Canada	500	-1.3	-6.2	707	7.2	41	816	944
Cyprus	374	-0.3	-1.6	937	5.7	32	530	383
Dominica	229	-4.0	-18.4	1,558	15.2	103	475	
Fiji	151	2.9	+15.4	811	27.8	240	148	60
The Gambia	28	2.1	+10.9	855	43	497	92	35
Ghana	11	-2.9	-13.6	715	43.4	507	96	11
Grenada	272	0.7	+3.6	1,167	21.1	160	335	
Guyana	199	6.4	+36.1	736	14.6	97	299	38
India	29	-6.9	-30.1	614	52.9	734	75	32
Jamaica	96	-3.8	-17.5	1,161	9.9	61	261	67
Kenya	9	5.8	+32.8	616	40.2	441	259	14
Kiribati	41	-0.5	-2.4	101	72.7	1,567	90	
Lesotho	18	-4.2	-19.6	455	31.6	295	39	3
Malawi	11	9.3	+55.9	204	48.5	621	23	2
Malaysia	161	0.9	+4.8	1,192	11.6	73	563	232
Maldives	152	8.3	+48.6	1,565	19.4	143	283	202
Malta	596	4.2	+22.9	1,093	7	41	630	
Mauritius	298	1.6	+8.4	917	12.6	81	283	174
Mozambique	4	5.9	+33.5	309	36.9	380	42	14
Namibia	67	1.8	+9.4	672	27.9	242	65	239
Nauru	0		-100.0	605			60	
New Zealand	428	1.6	+8.2	1,149	7.3	42	830	530
Nigeria	7	-3.0	-14.2	551	36.3	370	284	9
Pakistan	20	-8.1	-34.6	571	50.7	677	168	
Papua New Guinea	18	13.7	+90.3	278	91.1	2,445	13	64
Rwanda	4	10.9	+68.2	334	73.9	1,491	130	3
St Kitts and Nevis	378	-0.5	-2.5	1,527	9.4	57	760	
St Lucia	215	-0.8	-4.1	1,142	13.5	88	400	
St Vincent and the Grenadines	199	-0.7	-3.6	1,205	13.3	87		152
Samoa	193	12.6	+81	914	47.5	598	70	24
Seychelles	255	0.6	+2.8	1,359	14.9	100	410	216
Sierra Leone	2	-12.8	-49.6	341				
Singapore	392	1.6	+8.2	1,452	11	68	710	760
Solomon Islands	16	2.5	+13.5	56	38	400	50	46
South Africa	84	-2.2	-10.7	1,005	8.2	48	123	83
Sri Lanka	172	23.5	+187.7	832	38.9	416	120	38
Swaziland	37	4.7	+25.7	618	29.7	266	80	37
Tonga	298	17.7	+126.3	522	12.7	82	120	59
Trinidad and Tobago	219	-1.9	-9.0	1,412	15.4	105	485	132
Tuvalu	165	12.7	+77.8	254	14	92	250	86
Uganda	10	30.2	+273.8	384	57.7	875	125	17
United Kingdom	538	-0.4	-2.0	1,308	4.4	24	850	802
United Republic of Tanzania	4	2.5	+13	468	47.9	608	110	9
Vanuatu	21	-6.4	-28.6	1190.5	86.4	2,146	80	14
Zambia	7	-1.0	-4.9	416.2	41.8	474	100	11

Most landlines per capita

Main telephone lines per 1,000 people

	2010
Malta	596
United Kingdom	538
Barbados	503
Canada	500
New Zealand	428
Antigua and Barbuda	409
Singapore	392
Australia	389
St Kitts and Nevis	378
The Bahamas	377
Cyprus	374
Mauritius	298
Tonga	298
Grenada	272
Seychelles	255
Dominica	229
Trinidad and Tobago	219
St Lucia	215
Brunei Darussalam	200
Guyana	199
St Vincent and the Grenadines	199
Samoa	193
Sri Lanka	172
Tuvalu	165
Malaysia	161
Maldives	152
Fiji	151
Belize	97
Jamaica	96
South Africa	84
Botswana	69
Namibia	67
Kiribati	41
Swaziland	37
India	29
The Gambia	28
Cameroon	28
Vanuatu	21
Pakistan	20
Lesotho	18
Papua New Guinea	18
Solomon Islands	16
Ghana	11
Malawi	11
Uganda	10
Kenya	9
Zambia	7
Nigeria	7
Bangladesh	6
United Republic of Tanzania	4
Mozambique	4
Rwanda	4
Sierra Leone	2
Nauru	0

Fastest growth in telephones

Main telephone lines, overall increase/decrease from 2005 to 2010*
(%)

Cameroon	+437.9
Uganda	+273.8
Sri Lanka	+187.7
Tonga	+126.3
Papua New Guinea	+90.3
Samoa	+81.0
Tuvalu	+77.8
Rwanda	+68.2
Malawi	+55.9
Maldives	+48.6
Guyana	+36.1
Mozambique	+33.5
Kenya	+32.8
Swaziland	+25.7
Malta	+22.9
Fiji	+15.4
Solomon Islands	+13.5
United Republic of Tanzania	+13.0
The Gambia	+10.9
Namibia	+9.4
Mauritius	+8.4
New Zealand	+8.2
Singapore	+8.2
Malaysia	+4.8
Grenada	+3.6
Seychelles	+2.8
Barbados	+1.9
Botswana	+0.7
Antigua and Barbuda	-0.5
Cyprus	-1.6
United Kingdom	-2.0
Kiribati	-2.4
St Kitts and Nevis	-2.5
The Bahamas	-2.9
St Vincent and the Grenadines	-3.6
St Lucia	-4.1
Brunei Darussalam	-4.8
Zambia	-4.9
Canada	-6.2
Trinidad and Tobago	-9.0
Belize	-10.4
South Africa	-10.7
Ghana	-13.6
Nigeria	-14.2
Australia	-14.4
Bangladesh	-15.9
Jamaica	-17.5
Dominica	-18.4
Lesotho	-19.6
Vanuatu	-28.6
India	-30.1
Pakistan	-34.6
Sierra Leone	-49.6
Nauru	-100.0

* A 100% increase means that main telephone lines increased one time on top of the original figure. For example if there were 200,000 main telephones in 2005, there are now 400,000 lines in 2010

Most mobile cellular subscribers per capita

	Mobile cellular subscribers (per 1,000 people) 2010
Antigua and Barbuda	1,894
Maldives	1,565
Dominica	1,558
St Kitts and Nevis	1,527
Singapore	1,452
Trinidad and Tobago	1,412
Seychelles	1,359
United Kingdom	1,308
Barbados	1,281
The Bahamas	1,249
St Vincent and the Grenadines	1,205
Malaysia	1,192
Vanuatu	1,191
Botswana	1,178
Grenada	1,167
Jamaica	1,161
New Zealand	1,149
St Lucia	1,142
Malta	1,093
Brunei Darussalam	1,091
Australia	1,010
South Africa	1,005
Cyprus	937
Mauritius	917
Samoa	914
The Gambia	855
Sri Lanka	832
Fiji	811
Guyana	736
Ghana	715
Canada	707
Namibia	672
Belize	623
Swaziland	618
Kenya	616
India	614
Nauru	605
Pakistan	571
Nigeria	551
Tonga	522
United Republic of Tanzania	468
Bangladesh	462
Lesotho	455
Cameroon	441
Zambia	416
Uganda	384
Sierra Leone	341
Rwanda	334
Mozambique	309
Papua New Guinea	278
Tuvalu	254
Malawi	204
Kiribati	101
Solomon Islands	56

Fastest growth in mobile cellular subscribers

	Mobile cellular subscribers, overall increase from 2005 to 2010* (%) 2010
Papua New Guinea	2,445
Vanuatu	2,146
Kiribati	1,567
Rwanda	1,491
Uganda	875
India	734
Pakistan	677
Bangladesh	663
Malawi	621
United Republic of Tanzania	608
Samoa	598
Ghana	507
The Gambia	497
Zambia	474
Kenya	441
Sri Lanka	416
Solomon Islands	400
Mozambique	380
Nigeria	370
Botswana	319
Lesotho	295
Cameroon	283
Swaziland	266
Namibia	242
Fiji	240
Grenada	160
Maldives	143
Trinidad and Tobago	105
Dominica	103
Belize	102
Seychelles	100
Guyana	97
Antigua and Barbuda	95
Tuvalu	92
The Bahamas	88
St Lucia	88
Brunei Darussalam	87
St Vincent and the Grenadines	87
Tonga	82
Mauritius	81
Malaysia	73
Barbados	70
Singapore	68
Jamaica	61
St Kitts and Nevis	57
South Africa	48
New Zealand	42
Canada	41
Malta	41
Cyprus	32
United Kingdom	24
Australia	22

* A 100% increase means that mobile cellular subscribers increased one time on top of the original figure. For example if there were 200,000 mobile subscribers in 2005, there are now 400,000 subscribers in 2010

A 1,000% increase means that mobile cellular subscribers increased 10 times on top of the original figure. For example if there were 200,000 mobile subscribers in 2005, there are now 2,200,000 subscribers in 2010

Most PCs per capita

	PCs per 1,000 people 2005–2008
Canada	944
United Kingdom	802
Singapore	760
New Zealand	530
Cyprus	383
Namibia	239
Malaysia	232
Seychelles	216
Antigua and Barbuda	207
Maldives	202
Mauritius	174
Barbados	158
Belize	153
St Vincent and the Grenadines	152
Trinidad and Tobago	132
The Bahamas	123
Brunei Darussalam	89
Tuvalu	86
South Africa	83
Jamaica	67
Papua New Guinea	64
Botswana	63
Fiji	60
Tonga	59
Solomon Islands	46
Guyana	38
Sri Lanka	38
Swaziland	37
The Gambia	35
India	32
Samoa	24
Bangladesh	23
Uganda	17
Vanuatu	14
Kenya	14
Mozambique	14
Cameroon	11
Zambia	11
Ghana	11
United Republic of Tanzania	9
Nigeria	9
Rwanda	3
Lesotho	3
Malawi	2

Most internet users per capita

	Internet users per 1,000 people 2010
United Kingdom	850
New Zealand	830
Canada	816
Antigua and Barbuda	800
Australia	760
St Kitts and Nevis	760
Singapore	710
Barbados	702
Malta	630
Malaysia	563
Cyprus	530
Brunei Darussalam	500
Trinidad and Tobago	485
Dominica	475
The Bahamas	430
Seychelles	410
St Lucia	400
Grenada	335
Guyana	299
Nigeria	284
Mauritius	283
Maldives	283
Jamaica	261
Kenya	259
Tuvalu	250
Pakistan	168
Fiji	148
Belize	140
Rwanda	130
Uganda	125
South Africa	123
Sri Lanka	120
Tonga	120
United Republic of Tanzania	110
Zambia	100
Ghana	96
The Gambia	92
Kiribati	90
Swaziland	80
Vanuatu	80
India	75
Samoa	70
Namibia	65
Botswana	60
Nauru	60
Solomon Islands	50
Mozambique	42
Cameroon	40
Lesotho	39
Bangladesh	37
Malawi	23
Papua New Guinea	13

	Total population	GNI per capita	GDP per capita growth	Net primary enrolment ratio	Adult literacy rate	Life expectancy	Infant mortality per 1,000 live births	HIV/AIDS prevalence among those aged 15–49	Personal computers per 1,000 people	Human Development Index ranking
	('000)	(US$)	(% p.a.)	(%)	(%)	(years)		(%)		out of 187 countries
	2010	2010	1990–2010	2007–09	2005–2010	2010	2010	2009	2005–08	2011
Antigua and Barbuda	89	13,170	1.7	90	99	75‡	7		206.8	60
The Bahamas	343	21,984**	1.0	92		75	14	3	123	53
Barbados	273	15,034**	0.8			77	17	1	158	47
Belize	312	3,810	1.9	100		76	14	2	153	93
Botswana	2,007	6,790	3.5	87	84	53	36	25	63	118
Brunei Darussalam	399	26,750†	-0.4	97	95	78	6		89	33
Cyprus	1,104	29,430	2.1	99	98	79	3		383	31
Dominica	68	6,760	1.7	98		76‡	11			81
Fiji	861	3,630	1.2	92		69	15	0	60	100
The Gambia	1,728	450	0.1	76	47	58	57	2	35	168
Grenada	104	6,930	2.9	98		76	9			67
Guyana	754	2,870	2.5	99		70	25	1	38	117
Jamaica	2,741	4,800	0.7	81	86	73	20	2	67	79
Kiribati	100	2,010	1.2				39			122
Lesotho	2,171	1,040	2.2	73	90	48	65	24	3	160
Maldives	316	5,750	4.9	96	98	77	14	<0.1	202	109
Malta	417	19,270	2.6	91	92	79	5	0		36
Mauritius	1,299	7,750	3.5	94	88	73	13	1	174	77
Namibia	2,283	4,500	2.1	90	89	62	29	13	239	120
Nauru	10	2,802**				65‡	32			
Papua New Guinea	6,858	1,300	-0.2		60	62	47	1	64	153
St Kitts and Nevis	52	11,740	2.2	94		74‡	7			72
St Lucia	174	6,560	1.0	93		74	14			82
St Vincent and the Grenadines	109	6,300	3.6	98		72	19		152	85
Samoa	183	3,000	3.0	99	99	72	17		24	99
Seychelles	87	9,760	1.8	94	92	73‡	12		216	52
Solomon Islands	538	1,030	-1.0	81		67	23		46	142
Swaziland	1,186	2,630	1.6	83	87	48	55	26	37	140
Tonga	104	3,280	1.6		99	72	13		59	90
Trinidad and Tobago	1,341	15,380	5.0	96	99	70	24	2	132	62
Tuvalu	10	4,760				64‡	27		86	
Vanuatu	240	2,640	6.8		82	71	12		14	125
Total	28,261									
Commonwealth	**2,191,395**									

Total population of small states as a percentage of the Commonwealth: 1.3%

In this and following tables 32 countries that are designated as small states by the Commonwealth are featured.

** *GDP per capita 2010*   †*GDP per capita 2009*   ‡*2009 figure*   < *denotes less than here and following*

Greatest population density

	Population per square km 2010
Malta	1,320
Maldives	1,060
Mauritius	637
Barbados	633
Nauru	476
Tuvalu	385
Grenada	301
St Lucia	282
St Vincent and the Grenadines	280
Trinidad and Tobago	262
Jamaica	249
Antigua and Barbuda	201
St Kitts and Nevis	198
Seychelles	191
The Gambia	153
Tonga	139
Kiribati	123
Cyprus	119
Dominica	91
Lesotho	72
Brunei Darussalam	69
Swaziland	68
Samoa	65
Fiji	47
The Bahamas	25
Vanuatu	20
Solomon Islands	19
Papua New Guinea	15
Belize	14
Guyana	4
Botswana	3
Namibia	3

Fastest population growth

	Projected population growth (% p.a.) 2010–15
The Gambia	2.7
Solomon Islands	2.5
Vanuatu	2.4
Papua New Guinea	2.2
Belize	2.0
Namibia	1.7
Brunei Darussalam	1.7
Kiribati	1.5
Swaziland	1.4
Maldives	1.3
St Kitts and Nevis	1.2
The Bahamas	1.1
Cyprus	1.1
Botswana	1.1
Lesotho	1.0
Antigua and Barbuda	1.0
St Lucia	1.0
Fiji	0.8
Nauru	0.6
Mauritius	0.5
Samoa	0.5
Tonga	0.4
Grenada	0.4
Jamaica	0.4
Seychelles	0.3
Trinidad and Tobago	0.3
Malta	0.3
Tuvalu	0.2
Barbados	0.2
Guyana	0.2
Dominica	0.0
St Vincent and the Grenadines	0.0

Lowest income per capita

	GNI per capita (US$) 2010
The Gambia	450
Solomon Islands	1,030
Lesotho	1,040
Papua New Guinea	1,300
Kiribati	2,010
Swaziland	2,630
Vanuatu	2,640
Nauru	2,802*
Guyana	2,870
Samoa	3,000
Tonga	3,280
Fiji	3,630
Belize	3,810
Namibia	4,500
Tuvalu	4,760
Jamaica	4,800
Maldives	5,750
St Vincent and the Grenadines	6,300
St Lucia	6,560
Dominica	6,760
Botswana	6,790
Grenada	6,930
Mauritius	7,750
Seychelles	9,760
St Kitts and Nevis	11,740
Antigua and Barbuda	13,170
Barbados	15,034*
Trinidad and Tobago	15,380
Malta	19,270
The Bahamas	21,984*
Brunei Darussalam	26,750**
Cyprus	29,430

* GDP per capita 2010
** GDP per capita 2009

Slowest growth

	GDP per capita growth (% p.a.) 1990–2010
Solomon Islands	-1.0
Brunei Darussalam	-0.4
Papua New Guinea	-0.2
The Gambia	0.1
Jamaica	0.7
Barbados	0.8
The Bahamas	1.0
St Lucia	1.0
Fiji	1.2
Kiribati	1.2
Swaziland	1.6
Tonga	1.6
Antigua and Barbuda	1.7
Dominica	1.7
Seychelles	1.8
Belize	1.9
Cyprus	2.1
Namibia	2.1
Lesotho	2.2
St Kitts and Nevis	2.2
Guyana	2.5
Malta	2.6
Grenada	2.9
Samoa	3.0
Botswana	3.5
Mauritius	3.5
St Vincent and the Grenadines	3.6
Maldives	4.9
Trinidad and Tobago	5.0
Vanuatu	6.8

Most personal computers per capita

	PCs per 1,000 people 2005–08
Cyprus	383
Namibia	239
Seychelles	216
Antigua and Barbuda	207
Maldives	202
Mauritius	174
Barbados	158
Belize	153
St Vincent and the Grenadines	152
Trinidad and Tobago	132
The Bahamas	123
Brunei Darussalam	89
Tuvalu	86
Jamaica	67
Papua New Guinea	64
Botswana	63
Fiji	60
Tonga	59
Solomon Islands	46
Guyana	38
Swaziland	37
The Gambia	35
Samoa	24
Vanuatu	14
Lesotho	3

Most internet users per capita

	Internet users per 1,000 people 2010
Antigua and Barbuda	800
St Kitts and Nevis	760
Barbados	702
Malta	630
Cyprus	530
Brunei Darussalam	500
Trinidad and Tobago	485
Dominica	475
The Bahamas	430
Seychelles	410
St Lucia	400
Grenada	335
Guyana	299
Mauritius	283
Maldives	283
Jamaica	261
Tuvalu	250
Fiji	148
Belize	140
Tonga	120
The Gambia	92
Kiribati	90
Swaziland	80
Vanuatu	80
Samoa	70
Namibia	65
Botswana	60
Nauru	60
Solomon Islands	50
Lesotho	39
Papua New Guinea	13

Acknowledgements

The publishers hereby acknowledge the assistance of all the contributors who have helped in the production of the *Commonwealth Yearbook*.

Nicola Perou, Sherry Dixon, Commonwealth Secretariat
Rupert Jones-Parry with Andrew Robertson, Commissioning Editor
Andrew Robertson, Commissioning and Research
Richard Green, Country Profiles Editor
Mushtaq Zaman, Commonwealth Secretariat
Kate Collins, Commonwealth Secretariat

Nexus

Production

Chrissie Eaves-Walton, Manager
Samantha Masters, Design
Sandra Stafford, Sub-editor
David James Lawton, Design
Mark Mniszko, Design
Marvin Kuzamba, Data Research
Esme Chapman, Editorial
Jessica Murphy, Editorial
Abbie Sharman, Editorial

Sales and marketing

Nigel Blake
Michele Brewer
Daniel Carpenter
Rowan Frost
Yvonne Gertenbach
Simon Goodlad
Alan Grant
Andrew Henry
Alex Holland
Mark Layzell
Dulce Lewcock
Becky Lyons
Julia Schmidt
Tom Scott
Jon Thorne

Project partners

Abuka & Partners 421
Adamawa State Government 404
African Center for Economic Transformation....................18
Agriculture and Allied Employees Union of Nigeria 420
Ahmed Zakari & Co. 114
Air Energi Pacifica Ltd...434
Air Niugini 430
Air Traffic and Navigation Services Co...........................488
Alexander Hotels Limited 342
Asset Management Corporation of Nigeria 418
Attorney General, Mozambique 368
AUDI AG 7
Barbados Olympic Association, Inc. 224
Botswana Couriers 232
Botswana Institute for Development Policy Analysis 241
Botswana Sectors of Educators Trade Union 234
Cameroon Customs 246
Cavmont Bank 592
Centum Investment Co. Ltd..330
Chaguaramas Development Authority.............................526
Chimoio City Professional School...................................372
Chongwe District Council 582
Churches Health Association of Zambia 593
City of Windhoek...384
Co-operative Bank of Kenya Limited 326
Copperbelt Province...588
Department of Health, South Africa 494
Desto...490
Dube Tradeport 486
Ebonyi State University 82
EMOSE 370
Flour Mills of Nigeria Plc..406
Ghana Free Zones Board...292
Ghana Mine Workers Union 282
Ghana National Association of Teachers.........................283
Gochtech Nigeria Ltd 410
Government of Gibraltar...90
Governor-General's Residence of Grenada 88
Guyana Elections Commission 304
Homefoods Processing and Cannery Ltd 286
InnoLead Consulting 240
Institute of National Affairs of Papua New Guinea..........432
Jamaica Olympic Association 316
Jorisma Investments (Pty) Ltd 238
Kaduna State Government 412
Kenya Pipeline Company Ltd..322
Lamu Apex Medical University 593
Lundazi District Council..586
Maldives Inland Revenue Authority 254
Manet Group 290
Marlin Maritime Ltd 10
Matola City Council 374
Metsimaholo Local Municipality.....................................492
Ministry of Agriculture, Forestry and Food Security, Sierra Leone 468

Ministry of Chiefs and Traditional Affairs, Zambia 584
Ministry of Communications and Aviation, Solomon Islands........478
Ministry of Community Development, Mother and Child Health, Zambia 580
Ministry of Defence, Namibia...380
Ministry of Employment and Social Welfare, Ghana 280
Ministry of Energy and Energy Affairs, Trinidad and Tobago 518
Ministry of Energy, Ghana..288
Ministry of Finance and Economic Planning, Ghana.......284
Ministry of Finance, Trinidad and Tobago 520
Ministry of Forestry, Solomon Islands 134
Ministry of Gender, Children and Social Development, Kenya 328
Ministry of Health, Ghana..287
Ministry of Local Government, Uganda 534
Ministry of Mines, Energy and Rural Electrification, Solomon Islands............480
Ministry of Safety and Security, Namibia........................278
Ministry of the People and Social Development, Trinidad and Tobago..........522
Ministry of Women and Social Action, Mozambique 375
MTC Consultancy Holdings...128
Namibian Directorate of Civil Aviation 382
National Commission for Human Rights – Rwanda..........440
National Institute of Statistics of Rwanda 436
National Space Research and Development Agency, Nigeria........408
National Sports Authority, Ghana 278
Ndeya Manufacturing 386
Nigeria Union of Teachers 415
Nigerian Civil Aviation Authority 186
Nigerian Institute for Oceanography and Marine Resources........416
Office of the Auditor General, Zambia 590
Olam Mozambique Ltd 373
Pamoja Women Development Programme 324
Progreen Plc 251
Rwanda Mountain Tea Ltd 442
Rwanda Revenue Authority 438
Seychelles Fishing Authority 464
Sierra Leone Roads Authority 470
Small Business Association, Barbados 226
South African Forestry Company Limited 496
Standard Bank (Mauritius) Limited 362
Swaziland Industrial Development Company Ltd..............510
Tanzania Communications Regulatory Authority 570
Tanzania Minerals Audit Agency 568
Tax Administration Jamaica 318
Tobago House of Assembly...524
Trinidad and Tobago Unified Teachers Association..........528
Tshimologo Business Services 236
Union of Industry, Commerce and Finance Workers 294
University of Lagos 419
Urban Development Corporation 314
Vesper Tanzania...572
Vhembe District Municipality 498
World Trade Center Africa Initiative 124
Zambia Congress of Trade Unions 14
Zambia Union of Financial Institutions and Allied Workers............110
Zenith Bank of Nigeria (Plc)..414